2007

PRACTICE UNDER THE CALIFORNIA FAMILY CODE

Dissolution
Legal Separation
Nullity

CONTRIBUTING EDITORS:
M. Dee Samuels, Esq.
Hon. Frederick A. Mandabach

Project Manager
JON E. HEYWOOD
CEB Publications Attorney

CONTINUING EDUCATION OF THE BAR ▪ CALIFORNIA
Oakland, California
For update information call 1-800-232-3444
Website: ceb.com

Library of Congress Catalog No. 92-70751

ISBN 978-0-7626-1233-8

FA-31957

CONTINUING EDUCATION OF THE BAR ▪ CALIFORNIA

By agreement between the Board of Governors of the State Bar of California and The Regents of the University of California, Continuing Education of the Bar—California (CEB) offers an educational program for the benefit of practicing lawyers. This program is administered by a Governing Committee whose members include representatives of the State Bar and the University of California.

Practice books are published as part of this program. Authors are given full opportunity to express their individual legal interpretations and opinions; these opinions are not intended to reflect the position of the State Bar of California or of the University of California. Materials written by employees of state or federal agencies are not to be considered statements of governmental policies.

CEB is self-supporting. CEB receives no subsidy from State Bar dues or from any other source. CEB's only financial support comes from the sale of CEB publications, programs, and other products. CEB's publications and programs are intended to provide current and accurate information and are designed to help attorneys maintain their professional competence. Publications are distributed and oral programs presented with the understanding that CEB does not render any legal, accounting, or other professional service. Attorneys using CEB publications or orally conveyed information in dealing with a specific legal matter should also research original sources of authority. CEB's publications and programs are not intended to describe the standard of care for attorneys in any community, but rather to be of assistance to attorneys in providing high quality service to their clients and in protecting their own interests.

CEB considers the publication of any CEB practice book the beginning of a dialogue with our readers. The periodic updates to this book will give us the opportunity to make corrections or additions you suggest. If you are aware of an omission or error in this book, please share your knowledge with other California lawyers. Send your comments to:

Update Editor
Continuing Education of the Bar—California
300 Frank H. Ogawa Plaza, Suite 410
Oakland, CA 94612-2001
customer_service@ceb.ucop.edu

Contents

Preface

Practice Under the California Family Code (formerly Practice Under the California Family Law Act) offers a combination of valuable features available in no other book:

- A practical, comprehensive treatment of the handling of marital actions, *i.e.,* dissolution, legal separation, and nullity actions;

- The combined perspectives of the contributing editors, a Northern California attorney (M. Dee Samuels) and a Southern California judge (Hon. Frederick A. Mandabach, retired);

- A single-volume softcover format that permits easy transportation between office, courtroom, conference room, and home;

- Annual replacement volumes that eliminate the need for both separate supplement volumes and interleafed supplement pages; and

- A companion pamphlet that summarizes key recent cases and legislation in family law, conveniently sized for both courtroom and office use. See Practice Under the California Family Code: Case and Legislation Highlights 2007 (Cal CEB Annual).

Part I provides personal reflections on family law practice by the contributing editors. Part II covers the substantive law underlying any marital action. Part III offers a step-by-step guide to the procedures in any such action.

Practice Under the California Family Code is a core part of a broad family law practice library that now includes California Child Custody Litigation and Practice (Cal CEB 2006), California Marital Settlement and Other Family Law Agreements (3d ed Cal CEB 2005), Dissolution Strategies: From Intake to Judgment (Cal CEB 2005), Dividing Pensions and Other Employee Benefits in California Divorces (Cal CEB 2006), California Domestic Partnerships (Cal CEB 2005), California Juvenile Dependency Practice (Cal CEB 2002), and Planning and Conducting Family Law Discovery (Cal CEB Action Guide September 2004).

M. Dee Samuels is a Certified Specialist in Family Law. She has written and lectured extensively in the area of family law and has been an Adjunct Professor of Community Property. She has served on the Council of the Family Law Section of the American Bar Association and has chaired Family Law Committees of the ABA Family Law Section, and served as Executive Editor of the *Family Advocate*. She has written for the *Family Advocate, The Compleat Lawyer, Trial,* and the Matthew Bender Trial Advocacy Series, and previously for CEB.

Frederick (Fred) Mandabach is a recently retired Superior Court Judge. He was first assigned to Family Law as a superior court commissioner in 1982, spent several years in that position and, after serving as a municipal court judge, returned to superior court as presiding family law judge in 1989. He served in a variety of judicial assignments before returning to the family law court in 1999. He has handled hundreds of contested family law matters from the simplest to the most complex. He was the co-recipient for 1993 of the Judicial Officer of the Year Award from the California State Bar Family Law Section. Judge Mandabach has also spent years in the Juvenile and Dependency assignments, as well as serving on a Child Abuse Prevention Committee. He has masters degrees in both tax law and business, and thus enjoys complex family law cases. In the past he has served on California State Bar Family Law Subcommittees. He also served on the Family Law Subcommittee of the Judicial Council Joint Committee, and on the Judicial Council Joint Committee on Legal Forms, by appointment of the Chief Justice. His SupportMaster computer program was used in superior courts before the current popular programs were available. He is a coauthor of the *Deductor* series, published by California Family Law Report, Inc. He has lectured at judicial and attorney continuing education programs. He is a former assistant professor with the Claremont Colleges and former adjunct professor at two other educational institutions. Judge Mandabach retired from the bench during 2006 and is currently working with faculty and students of the Claremont Colleges on a study of the economics underlying child support. He is also a current member of the Judicial Nominees Evaluation Commission.

Practicing family law attorneys served as consultants on the original edition by reviewing the chapter manuscripts. Their names are listed on the Acknowledgments page.

The late Bob Pickus, a CEB Attorney, served as project supervisor on the original edition and was responsible for chaps 1–11, 13, 15–16, and 20 in that edition. Former CEB Attorney Susan Ellenbogen was responsible for chaps 12, 14, 17–19, and 21 in that edition.

The contributing reviewer of the 2007 update was Mary T. Muse. Ms. Muse served as Commissioner in El Dorado County from 1987 to 1996, with a family and probate law assignment. During that time, she was on the Family Law Committee of the California Judges' Association and on the California Judicial Studies Planning Board. She has taught and written on family law and has been a member of the Executive Committee of the Family Law Section of the State Bar (FLEXCOM); she served as advisor to FLEXCOM until 2003. Ms. Muse maintains a law practice in El Dorado County with an emphasis on mediation and continues to sit on assignment in family law matters.

CEB legal staff who worked on this update were Publications Attorney Jon E. Heywood and Legal Editors Bonnie Riley and Tamarah Haet. Dorie Riepe handled copyediting and production. The index was updated by Kathryn Te Selle. Composition was performed by CEB's Electronic Publishing staff.

Robin D. Kojima
Practice Group Manager
Family Law

Pamela J. Jester
Director

Acknowledgments

The following attorneys served as original consultants on this book by reviewing and commenting on one or more chapter manuscripts. Their valuable suggestions have made the book more accurate, more practical, and more reflective of actual practice:

Sandra I. Blair, San Francisco
Lisa E. Brandon, Beverly Hills
Nancy Bennett Bunn, Orange
Harold J. Cohn, Los Angeles
Jill A. Demmel, Sacramento
Robert P. Des Jardins, Santa Ana
Jan C. Gabrielson, Los Angeles
Beverly Jean Gassner, Ontario
Lawrence M. Gassner, Ontario
Max A. Goodman, Los Angeles
Gordon W. Hackett, San Bruno
Wendy A. Herzog, Los Angeles
Edward B. Huntington, San Diego
Paul E. Jacobs, San Jose
S. Michael Love, El Cajon
Pamela E. Pierson, San Francisco
Richard I. Sherman, Berkeley
John R. Schilling, Newport Beach
Madeleine Simborg, Corte Madera
Kristi Cotton Spence, Burlingame
Sorrell Trope, Los Angeles
Bernard N. Wolf, San Francisco

Selected Developments

Cite as: Practice Under the California Family Code: Dissolution, Legal Separation, Nullity (Cal CEB Annual)

Summarized below are some of the more important developments included in this update since publication of the 2006 edition:

Attorney Fees

A court retains jurisdiction to make an award of attorney fees pursuant to a *Borson* motion, even if a substitution of attorney form has been filed, when the motion was submitted while the attorney was still of record. *Marriage of Erickson & Simpson* (2006) 141 CA4th 707, 46 CR3d 253. See §9.9.

Child Custody and Visitation

A stipulated agreement to terminate one parent's rights is void as against public policy, absent contemplation of a second- or stepparent adoption. *Marriage of Jackson* (2006) 136 CA4th 980, 39 CR3d 365. See §7.38.

A trial court need not grant a full evidentiary hearing on a noncustodial parent's request to modify physical custody of a child in the face of a proposed relocation by the parent who has sole legal and physical custody; it may, instead, deny that request in a motion hearing if the moving party fails to establish a prima facie showing that the proposed relocation will cause detriment to the child. *Marriage of Brown & Yana* (2006) 37 C4th 947, 38 CR3d 610. See §§7.30, 7.60.

To be enforceable by contempt, a court order must be in writing and either signed by the judge and filed with the court or set forth in a detailed minute order. *In re Marcus* (2006) 138 CA4th 1009, 41 CR3d 861. See §14.39.

Legislation clarifies that in custody or visitation proceedings, a child may not be placed in a home in which a registered sex offender or child abuser resides, and may not be permitted to have unsupervised visitation with that person, unless the court states its reasons in writing or on the record. Fam C §3030. See §7.28.

Legislation provides that a petition for visitation by a grandparent may be filed when a child has been adopted by a *stepparent*. Fam C §3104. See §7.58A.

Child and Spousal Support

A lump-sum personal injury award that is not differentiated among the various elements of damages is not gross income for purposes of child support calculation. *Marriage of Heiner* (2006) 136 CA4th 1514, 39 CR3d 730. See §8.10.

Unliquidated but marketable stock received by a business owner in connection with the sale of a business is not gross income for purposes of child support calculation. *Marriage of Perlstein* (2006) 137 CA4th 1361, 40 CR3d 910. See §8.10.

Rent received by a parent who subleased a portion of his principal residence is properly included when calculating his income for purposes of child support. *County of Orange v Smith* (2005) 132 CA4th 1434, 34 CR3d 383. See §8.21.

Before spousal support may be terminated or reduced, the supported spouse must be given a *"Gavron* warning" and reasonable advance notice of such change. *Marriage of Schmir* (2005) 134 CA4th 43, 35 CR3d 716. See §6.10.

Under Fam C §4230(n), the court may consider monetary gifts given to the supported spouse from a third party when setting spousal support. *Marriage of Shaughnessy* (2006) 139 CA4th 1225, 43 CR3d 642. See §§6.10, 6.24.

As used in Fam C §4337, the term "remarriage" does not include a supported spouse's attempt to remarry prior to the dissolution of the existing marriage, and such void marriage may not be the basis for termination of spousal support. *Marriage of Campbell* (2006) 136 CA 4th 502, 38 CR 3d 908. See §6.27.

Legislation imposes civil liability on a person or business entity that knowingly assists a child support obligor who has an unpaid child support obligation to escape, evade, or avoid current payment of those unpaid child support obligations. CC §§1714.4., 1714.41. See §20.94.

Legislation adds a new chapter to the Family Code to regulate the practice of private child support collection, and requires that court orders (and court-approved agreements) for child support issued on or after January 1, 2010, include a separate money judgment for fees that may be incurred to collect support. Fam C §§5610–5616. See §20.98.

Community Property

The presumption of undue influence when one spouse obtains an advantage over the other does not apply to a marital settlement agreement achieved through mediation. *Marriage of Kieturakis* (2006) 138 CA4th 56, 41 CR3d 119. See §18.49.

Under *Marriage of McTiernan & Dubrow* (2005) 133 CA 4th 1090, 35 CR 3d 287, Bus & Prof C §§14100 and 14102's definitions of transferable goodwill do not encompass a business that is a natural person, and a movie director's expected future job assignments are not assets of the community. The court further held that payment of community obligations after separation does not "ipso facto" constitute payment of the necessities of life, and financial transactions effected by a spouse are not within "usual course of business" even if that spouse managed the community property during the marriage. See §§5.2, 5.61, 11.11.

If one party's deliberate or reckless failure to keep proper records prevents parties from valuing that party's business at the time of trial, good cause exists to value the business as of the parties' separation date. *Marriage of Nelson* (2006) 139 CA4th 1546, 44 CR3d 52. See §5.43.

Judgments

Legislation recasts provisions regarding the enforcement of family law judgments, providing that such judgments are enforceable until paid in full or otherwise satisfied. It also provides that the enforcement of an order under the Family Code may be granted in a limited civil case. CCP §580, Fam C §§290–291, 4502. See §20.97.

Parentage

Application of the conclusive presumption of paternity pursuant to Fam C §7611 is proper even when a mother's marriage to a presumed father ends shortly after birth of child, when the child's relationship to the biological father is absent. *Lisa I. v Superior Court* (2006) 133 CA4th 605, 34 CR3d 927. See §8.4.

Procedure in General

CCP §410.30 permits any party, not just the respondent, to bring a forum non conveniens motion; thus a wife could bring a forum non conveniens motion in spite of having initially filed a dissolution action in Los Angeles, when parties were German nationals who regularly spent time in both the United States and Germany. *Marriage of Taschen* (2005) 134 CA4th 681, 36 CR3d 286. See §4.7.

A trial court retains the equitable power to set a judgment aside when it is based on a fraud perpetrated on the court. *Marriage of Deffner* (2006) 143 CA4th 662, 49 CR3d 424. **Caution:** This case was recently depublished. It appears in §18.49 and on page 18 of the companion pamphlet.

Fam C §2024.6(a), which provides for a court to order sealed, on request by a party, a pleading that lists the parties' financial assets and liabilities and provides the location or identifying information about those assets and liabilities sealed, has been held unconstitutional. The court found it was "not narrowly tailored to serve the privacy interests it is intended to protect, and less restrictive means of protecting the privacy interests are available." *Burkle v Burkle* (2006) 135 CA4th 1045, 37 CR3d 805. See §10.72.

Restraining and Protective Orders

Legislation amends provisions for the relinquishment of firearms by persons subject to a protective order, by mandating relinquishment on a law enforcement officer's request, by clarifying the time period and method of relinquishment, and making the failure to timely file a receipt showing relinquishment a violation of the order. Fam C §6389. See §11.6.

Judicial Council Forms and Court Rules

New and revised Judicial Council forms have been inserted in the text. For questions about a particular form, see the California Courts website at http://www.courtinfo.ca.gov/forms. In addition, effective January 1, 2007, an extensive reorganization of the California Rules of Court took effect. California Rules of Court citations in this publication have been updated with the new rule number. Concordance tables of old and new rule numbers and a link to any amendments to the Rules are available on http://www.ceb.com.

Cutoff Dates

We completed legal editing of this book at the end of November 2006.

We reviewed case citations through these cutoffs:

- Shepard's California Citations at 39 C4th 179, 143 CA4th 1538, 162 L Ed 2d 883, 419 F3d 1026, 980 F Supp 2d 684;

- Shepard's United States Citations at 162 L Ed 2d 883, 419 F3d 1026, 980 F Supp 2d 684;

- Shepard's Federal Citations at 162 L Ed 2d 883, 419 F3d 1026, 980 F Supp 2d 684.

We reviewed California and federal statute citations for amendments and repeals through these cutoffs:

- Stats 2006, ch 910;

- 119 Stat 2036.

We try to add significant statutory and judicial developments, subsequent histories of cases, and other matters such as new forms and regulations after legal editing is completed, but readers should not assume that all developments after the listed cutoff dates have been included.

1

Achieving Professional Camaraderie in Family Law Practice

M. Dee Samuels, Esq.

The Stresses of Family Law Practice. This is a reflection on some of the stresses of family law practice and how one group of attorneys discovered a wonderful way to deal with those stresses and in doing so, reaped more benefits than they dreamed could come out of their experiment.

Family law is a fascinating blend of drama, high emotion, and complex legal issues ranging from heart-wrenching custody cases to challenging financial and business matters. Anger, distrust, and hostility spill over from clients to attorneys who at times find themselves as stressed and as polarized as their clients. Throw in a few difficult opposing counsel and cantankerous judges, and the attorneys representing the unhappy clients also experience feelings of anger and frustration. The family law bar is a small, specialized group of attorneys who are likely to have repeated interactions with each other. Especially in high conflict cases, rough spots can develop between counsel and easily turn into jagged edges. These kinds of dynamics between attorneys never make the case better for their clients and are harmful to both as human beings.

Where to Turn? Additionally, without very careful work and personal life boundaries, family law practice is all-consuming and balance in the attorney's life flies out the door. No one else but another family law attorney would really understand our life and its stresses. Seeing colleagues at professional meetings presents a tempting opportunity to commiserate, but keeping a distance is safer, because after all, they are "opposing counsel"—if not in today's case, the next one through your door. The very people who could understand us and our stress, better than anyone else, are not available to us. Absent being in a firm in which there are other friendly attorneys to talk to, the family law attorney can feel isolated. Even in a firm, it is not likely the attorneys take time to really talk unless they are using each other as a sounding board on a specific issue in a case.

An Experiment in Camaraderie. Seven years ago, a colleague proposed that a number of women family law attorneys form a kind of study group. More accurately, it would be a group that would explore how we as women practiced law, including litigation, and how we interacted with each other primarily as opposing counsel. We all enthusiastically agreed to meet and willingly stepped into the project. We all knew each other from working opposite sides of cases and from various professional groups. While we respected each other, there were definitely rough edges between some of us that had developed from the friction of two people zealously advocating for the opposing result in the courtroom and representing clients who were very angry with each other.

The colleague who convened us proposed that we have a psychologist facilitate our meetings and that, in addition to looking at our litigation styles and interactions with opposing counsel, we should explore what kind of models existed in litigating and which we had chosen, whether consciously or not, to follow as lawyers and litigators. We wondered if we were following a specifically male model in our work because that was probably what existed at the time we started our careers. Most of us had had male mentors who were older partners in our firms when we first went to work. Certainly male attorneys far outnumbered female attorneys in our early years, and therefore were our primary role models. That is not to say it was not a good model, but we wanted to make conscious decisions about how we practiced and to find out if we could relate to each other in a kinder, more humane way.

One of our first sessions involved looking at the language often used in litigation, and that we ourselves used. Sure enough, we discovered that the language we and others used to describe litigation frequently was couched in sports and war metaphors: "Take no prisoners," "full court press," "scorched earth litigation," "going into battle," "control the territory," "all's fair in love and war." We looked at whether these terms fit our styles, whether they were necessary for us to use, and what sort of effect they had on the attitudes of all involved, both counsel and clients. We felt energized and excited by our start.

Our early meetings were set to last a half day, led by the facilitator and followed by a convivial lunch together. We continued to explore the nature of our practices, including interactions with clients, staff, and ways to reduce stress in our lives. We looked at our problem-solving styles and specific problems common to the practice of family law, what made us enjoy the practice and what did not. We began to uncover the reasons for the rough edges between us. We discovered we were developing a strong sense of trust and camaraderie among ourselves. We went from "going to the group" to being "our group."

A big step occurred when we had our first meeting at a place other than an office. We met at someone's home to bid farewell to one of our members at her retirement (she has since returned to the group). Unanimously, we decided our future meetings should be in member's homes rather than in an office. Soon thereafter, we realized we were ready to graduate to running our own meetings and thanked our facilitator for her wisdom and expertise in guiding us though our early years giving us such a solid start. Without a trained leader, we might not have been successful in our venture.

We had learned some new ways of relating to each other as well as other opposing counsel and of dealing with some of the pressures of the practice. One of the valuable lessons was to make clear to a new opposing counsel in a case our expectations for the professional interaction. For example, agreeing to discuss the inevitable accusations that came up in family law cases before writing "the lawyer letter" could be extremely helpful in keeping a case floating in calmer waters.

We began to realize we had birthed something very valuable to us professionally and personally. We had a group with whom we could discuss significant issues and our confidence would be respected. Importantly, we began to understand how the pressure of our profession in general, and specifically in family law, affected us as individuals—thereby affecting our professional relationships and our family lives. We found delight in sharing in each other's professional successes and comfort in sharing the difficulties.

Our next developmental step was a weekend stay at a member's country home, exploring a single topic during that time. One of our members acted as a facilitator and we devoted both formal and informal discussion to that topic, as well as sharing meals we prepared together. By now, we were several years into our group process, finding it incredibly valuable and were exploring significant aspects of our professional lives—such as what it would mean to take a sabbatical, different models of practice, or even to consider retirement. Having each other now as role models and sounding boards allowed us to share a great deal of collective wisdom—garnered over years of practice, professional growth, and developing leading personal reputations.

We were ready for yet another group step: we traveled to Washington, D.C. to participate in the March for Women's Lives, bringing our daughters and sisters with us. We even had T-shirts made to identify us as a group!

We have come a long way together. Our group still meets and our meeting situations vary from dinners, full day sessions, and weekends spent locally, to weekend meetings out of the area. Our meetings still focus on a topic that is important to the group. In sharing practice-related problems and successes, as well as personal joys and tragedies, we have come to recognize the comfort of an unprecedented kind of professional group. This gathering of attorneys has transcended its original professional boundaries to provide us with a collective sense of joy and of belonging to "our group"—with its unique understanding and support.

It has helped us immeasurably deal with the pressures of being women family law attorneys. We have learned the value of friendship in our profession. As leaders in our field, we think we have developed a model for younger lawyers. Indeed, we were honored recently to have a dinner meeting with a new group of younger women lawyers who have formed their own group. They remind us very much of ourselves 15 to 20 years ago. Their group is not exactly like ours, but unique to and for them, yet dealing with many of the same issues as we have dealt with—professional pressures and balance in their lives as they rise to the top of their field. We are proud to be an example to them and somewhat envious that they started so much sooner than we! We hope our example will inspire others to explore how professional relationships can be a source of positive growth and support. We feel incredibly enriched by our group, both professional and personally.

2

A View From the Family Law Bench

Hon. Frederick A. Mandabach

If you are an attorney trying to hone your approach to handling family law hearings and trials, you might start by imagining that you have agreed to sit as a judge pro tem for a day of family law. Envision the lawyers you would prefer to see assigned to appear in your department. Then envision those you hope will never be assigned to your department. Think about how they differ.

You probably hope:

- To make it through the day without looking incompetent by being forced to tackle thorny issues with no warning and no help from the lawyers;

- To see clearly organized, well-written trial briefs and motion papers that outline the issues, provide clear statements of the law, and, when appropriate, provide references to commonly used treatises;

- That the lawyers will present their cases in a way that allows you to keep the facts organized and to be able to decide the cases shortly after they have been submitted;

- That counsel will have their exhibits well organized and available to you so that you can follow along as they try their cases;

- That you won't get "shoe box" cases, which sprinkle and interweave the evidence of 25 to 30 discrete issues of varying importance throughout the record;

- That the lawyers will be on time and will finish within the time limits;

- That the lawyers will maintain their equanimity even when your rulings go against them; and

- That the proceedings will not become acrimonious, with everyone simultaneously making angry statements while the court reporter "waves the white flag."

These are the basic rules for being the type of attorney that judges like to see in court. Because it is a judge, not a jury, deciding your case, why not make the judge want to see you arrive to try the case?

Self-Represented Persons Also May Benefit from This Publication

When this publication was introduced more than 10 years ago, the premise was that it would serve to meet the need of family law attorneys who wanted a small, up-to-date volume that could be used to refresh memory on a topic, to find case names and citations, to look for concepts or theories by locating a remembered case, and generally to provide the security of ready access to this very wide area of law. And, we were addressing attorneys.

It became clear to me, however, that others had begun using this work when a self-represented party cited this volume during his or her hearing. The opening paragraph of this chapter addresses attorneys. If you are not an attorney, you will probably not be able to visualize a circumstance in which you were called upon to be a judge. You can, however, get some idea of the judicial mindset by thinking of a time that you were asked to referee a dispute. You probably would have been assisted if the persons involved had given you the facts in a reasonable period of time, had made you aware of any special rules that might have affected the decision, and had kept their composure when presented with the result. That is what the judge hopes to see.

Be Prepared

If you were to ask family law judges for one piece of advice, you would probably hear the same thing repeatedly: be prepared. Judges appreciate lawyers and litigants who are prepared because the proceedings tend to flow smoothly and fit within time estimates. Time is very precious to everyone in family law. With so much to do and so little time in which to do it, anyone who conserves time is a hero to the overworked family law judge. The attorneys and litigants will benefit directly as well. Any attorney who has gone into a hearing or a trial with everything in place knows the feeling of confidence this inspires and what assets self-confidence and the feeling of control can be in the courtroom.

The unprepared attorney is known to us all. We have all encountered attorneys who attempt both to prepare and to present the case
during the proceedings. The result is usually an excessive expenditure
of time and effort, a loss of focus, a blurring of issues, and further
delays when this approach pushes the hearing or trial beyond the
time allotted.

Develop an Appropriate Style

In the courtroom, life quite often imitates art, with the techniques
of the latest television series working their way into the hearing.
Although these techniques bring sure-fire success on the tiny screen,
that is only because the script was written that way. By all means,
try new techniques, but be sure they are helpful before you use
them on an important issue. Likewise, adopting other attorneys' techniques can be hazardous.

Family law can be very stressful work for the judge as well as
for the lawyers and litigants. Judges appreciate attorneys who seek
to minimize the stress level in the courtroom. Most judges prefer,
for example, to see witnesses treated with courtesy rather than to
see them savaged on the stand. Some very successful attorneys show
unfailing courtesy. Instead of dispensing pain and suffering, they
use less offensive methods to dismantle witnesses. A lie can be
unmasked with humor as well as by tirade. A courteous and calm
attorney can often transfer some of these positive feelings to the
case as a whole.

Maintain a Helpful Attitude

We all know that in dealing with others we achieve more success
if we approach them with a helpful attitude. Unfortunately, by the
time the average person reaches the courtroom, he or she may have
gone through a great deal of stress and frustration. The attorneys
and litigants may have endured traffic delays, difficult parking, the
metal detector experience, long lines, and even unpleasant exchanges
with opponents. Many people give way to their feelings and vent
their frustrations in the courtroom. This is not beneficial in personal
life and it is not helpful in the courtroom. What is helpful is to
remind oneself at the outset to approach the court with a positive
and helpful attitude. This is more likely to set the stage for positive
results.

A helpful attitude toward the opposition can also be beneficial.
Anyone involved with the dissolution process knows that it represents

for most people the pinnacle of pain. The feelings of hurt and betrayal permeate the proceedings. Some litigants seem to see their time in court as a last opportunity to transfer some of the pain to the other party. However, this is not an effective method to either alleviate pain or advance their case. Instead, it has a very negative effect in the courtroom. A better approach is for the litigant to keep in mind that the judge is the one making the decision. Make the judge, not the other party, your intended audience.

Who Is the Judge?

This chapter began by referring to the person on the bench as the "judge." To a person who might drop into the courtroom to observe the case, the person on the bench is the "judge." However, the person on the bench in a family law court may be a judge, a commissioner, or a judge pro tempore (an attorney authorized for that day to serve as a judge). Because this chapter will be referring to that person from time to time, it would be distracting to say "judge, commissioner, or judge pro tempore" at each occurrence. For the sake of brevity and ease of reading, this chapter will use the term "judge" to refer to all three types of bench officers unless the text indicates otherwise.

Because the reader may be self-represented, he or she may wonder whether it makes a difference if the bench officer is a commissioner or judge pro tempore rather than a judge. What every attorney knows is that the qualities of the bench officer, rather than the title, are what matter. The challenge to the courts is to provide an adequate number of bench officers to properly take care of the cases before the court. However, as the population of California has grown, and family law caseloads along with it, the number of judges has lagged behind this growth. Courts have responded to the need by appointing qualified attorneys to serve as commissioners and judges pro tempore.

Know Your Judge

It is always important to know your audience. In family law, the audience is, of course, the judge. If you know in advance who the judge will be, it will be helpful to learn his or her preferences. Since the judge is the person you must convince, it is a good idea to spend some time ascertaining what will help you do that. In one case, an attorney went on at length about what he deemed the glaring inadequacies of a particular family law form. He made this presentation, however, before a judge who was a member of the advisory committee that drafted it.

There are numerous ways in which knowing the judge becomes important. Some judges, for example, appreciate introductory statements. Others, who may have carefully reviewed the moving and responding papers or trial briefs, will probably find an opening statement annoying. If you do not know the judge's preference, why not ask? You should routinely ascertain whether the judge is irritated by certain styles, *e.g.,* bullying or demeaning litigants.

Attorneys quickly learn judicial preferences by observation, speaking with other lawyers, or, sometimes, by reading profiles available in law libraries. Failure to do this can be embarrassing. Self-represented litigants may, if they have the time, sit in the courtroom (if there is space) to get some impression of the bench officer and his or her expectation of litigants at a hearing.

A major focus in family law is on saving time in the courtroom. However, lack of courtroom time is just part of the problem. The average judge is required to read and process small mountains of paper before and after courtroom time and during breaks. Most judges expect litigants to notify the court in advance if a matter will not go forward on the hearing date so that the judge can focus his or her attention on the cases that will proceed. It is very disheartening to have an attorney on a complex case announce only at the hearing itself that the case was resolved at an earlier time. Often the judge worked late into the night to be prepared for the case. So let the court know in advance that the judge does not need to read your file.

Know Your Opponent

It is also important to know the approach of opposing counsel. Family law attorneys seem to be either those who work well with other attorneys and adopt the principle of "give a little, take a little" or those who believe in taking no prisoners. It helps, for example, to know whether the other side will be playing total hardball before getting deeply into the proceedings.

In one case, the petitioner's attorney called the respondent under Evid C §776. The questioning proceeded entirely without objection. When it was time for the respondent's attorney to present his case, however, the petitioner's attorney had nothing but objections. "Sir, what is your name?" The objections flew: hearsay (the naming parent was an out-of-court declarant), best evidence (calling for the contents of the birth certificate), improper lay opinion, no foundation, *etc.* Finally, the respondent's attorney asked for something a bit unusual in a court trial: a side-bar conference. He wanted to argue, out of his client's hearing, that the opposing counsel's approach was unfair. After all, the complaining attorney had made no objections during his opponent's examination and now the opponent's objections were everywhere. Sadly, "it's not fair" is not a proper evidentiary objection.

So, if you are unfamiliar with your opponent's style but believe he or she follows a relaxed style regarding evidence objections, be sure to have a discussion of this matter with your opponent and the judge. Set out the ground rules so that there are no surprises. If you get an agreement on the ground rules, put that on the record. Then if your opponent fails to follow the agreement, bring it to the attention of the judge. The Evidence Code is still the Evidence Code and the judge cannot ignore it. However, that same judge will be exercising discretion in ruling on many other motions and objections. The point is, do not start off by granting your opponent great latitude on evidentiary matters unless there is a record that your opponent will follow the same approach. You can be civil while insisting on fairness.

If your opponent is going to be a total hardball player, you may have to adopt that posture yourself at the beginning. Sometimes the hardball player will call a truce, but at other times, unfortunately, he or she will deliver total misery during the entire proceeding.

Presenting Your Evidence

Many practitioners act as if the Evidence Code does not apply to family law. However, a well-considered objection by an opponent will quickly stop the flow of your evidence. There is no special body of evidence for family law. However, the family law practitioner will have a level of comfort with evidence only if he or she has thought through the proper manner in which to introduce it. Some of the evidentiary problems frequently encountered in family law are those dealing with documents of title and the presumptions relating to them, proof of payment of obligations, and the introduction of records of banks and other institutions. Family law matters often turn on statements made in the past, so one needs to be clear on what is and is not hearsay and the exceptions that apply if it is hearsay.

A careful litigator should be prepared to respond to evidentiary objections and to raise them if appropriate. It can be very helpful to chart out the possible evidentiary objections well in advance of the trial and put the notes into a folder. There are excellent evidence treatises that address most every question the practitioner will see but the best time to use them is before trial. This can prevent the diversion of critical time during trial.

Some practitioners engage in objectionable conduct that cannot be discerned by an appellate court by simply reading the testimony. An example is a lawyer rushing the witness stand while clenching his fists and raising his voice. A more subtle example is the attorney who finds an excuse to stand over or behind the witness and then remains there after the reason for approaching the witness has passed. If there is conduct that seems to have as its only purpose the intimidation or harassment of the witness, an objection should be considered. This may just be the beginning. If a record is made of offensive conduct when it first occurs, it provides part of a basis for action a court may wish to take in regard to later conduct.

Protecting the record is the task of the litigator as well as the judge. Little things do matter. For example, if the judge inquires of the parties whether they have reached a stipulated agreement on certain matters, be sure there is an unequivocal response. An equivocal or unclear response could later be used to argue that there was a misunderstanding about the basis of a party's claim. If the basis was in error, the trial may have to be repeated. So do not be shy. Make a litigant clarify equivocal responses.

Protect Your Credibility and Reputation

If a lawyer has a significant volume of family law practice, he or she soon gets to know the bench officers handling family law cases in the area. If a judge is consistent, the practitioner should be able to predict the outcome on any common issue before that judge with a fair degree of certainty. The bench officers have a similar opportunity. Attorneys tend to handle issues in a certain way or in a limited number of ways. Some family law bench officers could probably provide you with an outline of your usual ways of trying specific types of cases.

If you plan to return to a particular court, by all means maintain your credibility. From time to time, a lawyer will cite cases for principles of law not to be found in the text or will vigorously argue "well-known rules" that appear nowhere in print. Anyone can on occasion make such a mistake. If a lawyer does so too often, however, judges tend to look askance at his or her work and pass the word to other bench officers. An expression one hears from time to time is, "That is an attorney you want to keep in front of you."

It pays to be kind to court staffs. They are prone to tell their judges about certain lawyers who are unctuous to the judge but dreadful to the staff. Recall how you reacted the last time you were told that a client was outrageous with your staff.

Conserving Your Time and Energy

On the subject of conserving time, some attorneys are better than others. Judges appreciate attorneys and litigants who save the court time. If the judge has read and considered your points and authorities or documents, you do not need to repeat them to the judge. If for some reason the judge has not read your papers, then by all means repeat what is in your papers. If you have learned to "read" the judge, and you believe he or she is persuaded to adopt your view of the case, you could ask if he or she would like further argument or a question answered. If the other side dissuades the judge from your position, you could then present counter-arguments. If the judge still agrees with you after hearing the other side, there is certainly no reason to argue.

What to Do About "Gaming"

Newspaper reports and appellate cases are often critical of judges and attorneys for continuing cases over and over. While many conscientious lawyers and litigants struggle to conserve court time, there are others who do the opposite. Instead, they "game" the system. This is seen most frequently with the litigator who obtains a temporary order and converts it to a quasi-permanent order through endless delays.

Examples are temporary orders for child custody or for the temporary use of an important asset. The time for trial arrives, but the attorney does not. Someone will appear for the absent attorney on the date of the hearing, with no advance notice to the other side, and request a continuance. Sometimes, there is a legitimate reason; sometimes there is not. The court also has an interest in setting requirements to obtain such a continuance so that only legitimate reasons are allowed.

A careful litigator should make sure a continuance is truly needed. There is a good reason to make a record. Courts and attorneys are subjected to considerable criticism for needless delays. In the absence of a record, you may not be able to show what you did to prevent unnecessary delays.

Litigation Strategies and Alternatives to Consider

With courtroom time in such short supply, people throughout the state are looking for ways to maximize the use of the time that is available. One approach that has proved to be helpful is to select a single significant issue for a separate trial. Many litigants feel a strong need for a judge to consider their evidence. Sometimes, a hearing and decision on a single issue seems to satisfy this need. Often after such a hearing the remaining issues can be resolved.

Another great time saver is mediation. Once again, having someone listen to the facts and give feedback seems to meet the need some people have for a hearing. Some courts have set up robust court-sponsored mediation programs. There are also many private mediation programs. Whether the program is public or private, it appears that having a knowledgeable mediator listen to both sides can often help resolve the case.

Although experienced lawyers are familiar with and largely favorable to the settlement of cases, the litigants and the public often have a negative view of settlement. So why should a person consider settling a case? In a perfect world, the result of litigation should be that each party receives his or her fair share, no more and no less. Sometimes, even though most people might agree about what would be a reasonable outcome of a case before a trial, the actual outcome is different. There are many reasons. Evidence that seemed strong before trial may appear weak in the crucible of a trial. Witnesses who appeared strong before trial may be shown to be biased, unreliable, or even liars. Evidence may become unavailable. Unexpected events may occur. Whatever the reason, the outcome may be less than hoped for. Extremely few cases have a 100 percent probability of success. The problems that can reduce the value of the case are "hazards of litigation." The value of a case before trial is the maximum result multiplied by the reasonable percentage of winning at trial. You can only learn the true percentage of success by having the trial. This is why people settle cases.

Even if mediation does not totally resolve the case, it may move the case in that direction. Litigants often have unrealistic expectations of the trial outcome. Mediation can expose the litigants to a neutral person's view of the case without going through a trial. This can help the litigant adjust his or her expectations. Usually mediation is worth a try.

Assistance for the Self-Represented Litigant

The law requires a judge to treat a self-represented litigant no differently than an attorney. Self-represented litigants are rightfully insistent that no special or preferential treatment be accorded to attorneys. However, the rule against special treatment runs both ways. If an attorney fails to file necessary hearing papers and arrives unprepared, he or she can expect adverse consequences. If a self-represented litigant likewise arrives without having made the necessary preparation, he or she cannot reasonably expect special treatment to overcome this lack of preparation. It also will be difficult to convince a court to grant an unexpected continuance without the imposition of financial consequences.

The self-represented party has several solutions. To attempt to acquire the necessary knowledge and skills before the hearing to act as his or her own attorney is a possibility, not a probability. It is often like watching an amateur competing against a professional. However, what can the person with limited funds do? In some counties, there are panels of lawyers who offer reduced rates to people of limited means. Another possibility is "unbundling." With greater and greater numbers of litigants representing themselves, some attorneys have adapted their practices to assist people desiring limited professional assistance. Those attorneys will assist with a particular part of the case but will not be responsible for any other matters unless they reach a contrary agreement.

A particular danger lurks for the self-represented litigant who plans to try handling the case without assistance and to seek help only if and when it appears needed. Self-represented parties who do their own initial paperwork will be making sworn statements. These sworn statements cannot simply be disowned at a later time. Sometimes, savings on doing the initial paperwork can lead to major problems later. For example, an ill-considered choice of the date of the parties' separation can cause tremendous problems. Further, if a self-represented person wants to have an attorney appear in court, he or she needs to remember that few attorneys are available on short notice.

Every resident of California knows that population growth has put increasing demands on resources. The courts share in the pressure on services. The Judicial Council and the Administrative Office of the Court have responded by introducing technology to assist the self-represented. One of their efforts is the very helpful website at http://www.courtinfo.ca.gov/selfhelp/family/.

At the local level, resources to assist the self-represented vary from county to county. In general, the litigant has a number of places to start. The court clerk's office, the county bar association, and the county law library will be helpful in locating programs to assist self-represented litigants. The most important point to keep in mind is to look for help as early as possible and to be aware that appointments are required for services. This means that it will probably take more than one time away from work to be ready for the hearing. If you wait until the date of the court appearance, it will be too late to get help for the day's hearing. If you use these resources to be prepared for a scheduled matter, it will greatly reduce your stress. At the same time it will greatly help stretch the limited court resources.

Conclusion

Family law judges recognize that the tasks facing family law attorneys and litigants are terribly demanding. Nevertheless, they maintain expectations of how attorneys *and litigants* ideally should prepare and present their cases. These expectations are not hard to ascertain, and striving to meet them can make family law practice a more positive experience for everyone concerned.

3
Dissolution, Legal Separation, and Nullity

§3.1   I. SCOPE OF CHAPTER

This chapter introduces and compares the three types of marital actions: dissolution (whether regular or summary), legal separation, and nullity. Specifically, the chapter compares standard dissolution, legal separation, and nullity with respect to grounds, statutory residency requirements, whether the respondent's consent or default is required, the effect of the judgment on the parties' marital status, and the availability of other orders. It also provides a complete discussion of summary dissolution and indicates important considerations in choosing among the available alternatives in a given case.

NOTE➤ Registered domestic partners. As of January 1, 2005, provisions for dissolution, legal separation, and nullity of registered domestic partnerships became operative. The rights and obligations of these partners under California law are generally the same as those of spouses, but federal law does not generally recognize the domestic partnership. See generally Fam C §297.5. The statutory scheme for registered domestic partnership includes a method of terminating a domestic partnership without court action that largely parallels procedures for summary dissolution of marriage, except that the termination is handled through the office of the Secretary of State. See Fam C §299(a)–(b). However, if the parties do not meet requirements for this administrative termination, they must utilize the judicial procedures established for married couples in dissolving or nullifying their partnership, or in obtaining a legal separation. See Fam C §299(d). Couples who are registered as domestic partners only with a city (or city and county) and not with the State of California, however, are not subject to this statutory scheme, and therefore cannot dissolve their domestic partnerships in family court. *Velez v Smith* (2006) 142 CA4th 1154, 1169, 48 CR3d 642. On related forms and discussion, see chap 10. For a full discussion of domestic partnership matters, see California Domestic Partnerships (Cal CEB 2005).

II. DISSOLUTION AND LEGAL SEPARATION

§3.2   A. Grounds

A judgment of dissolution of marriage or of legal separation may be granted only on the grounds of (1) irreconcilable differences that have caused the irremediable breakdown of the marriage or (2) incurable insanity. Fam C §2310. The "irreconcilable differences" alleged as the grounds in virtually every petition for dissolution or legal separation are defined by statute as those grounds that are determined by the court to be substantial reasons for not continuing the marriage and that make it appear that the marriage should be dissolved. Fam C §2311 (former CC §4507). What is required to meet the statutory requirements is "the existence of substantial marital problems which have so impaired the marriage relationship that the legitimate objects of matrimony have been destroyed and as to which there is no reasonable possibility of elimination, correction or resolution." *Marriage of Walton* (1972) 28 CA3d 108, 118, 104 CR 472.

As a practical matter, courts have been quite liberal in finding the requisite irreconcilable differences and, consequently, their existence is rarely an issue in dissolution or legal separation proceedings. On rare occasions, at a hearing with both spouses present, one will state that there is a possibility of reconciliation. Usually the other spouse will make it clear that this is a false hope. If it appears to the court, however, that there is a reasonable possibility of reconciliation, the court must continue the proceeding for no more than 30 days. Fam C §2334.

Note that the Family Code speaks of irreconcilable differences that have led to the "*irremediable*" breakdown of the marriage. Courts hear many variations of the word "irremediable" (*e.g.*, "irremedial"). Counsel should be sure to pronounce the word correctly.

§3.3   B. Dissolution Residency Requirement; Legal Separation Petition to Avoid Delay

A judgment of dissolution of marriage may not be entered unless at least one of the parties was a resident of California for 6 months, and of the county in which the petition was filed for three months, immediately before the filing of the petition. Fam C §2320. This residency requirement is mandatory and may not be circumvented by stipulation or consent. There is no statutory residency requirement, however, for a judgment of legal separation.

It is not uncommon for a new arrival in California to seek a dissolution. There is a minimum 6-month waiting period between the service of the summons and petition (or the appearance of the respondent) and the termination of the marriage. Fam C §2339. A new arrival may be concerned that the 6-month residency requirement for a dissolution and the 6-month waiting period may result in a wait approaching a year before the marriage may be terminated. This delay can be shortened by the party's filing a petition for legal separation and then amending the petition to one for dissolution when the residency requirement is met. The filing date of the amended petition or pleading is deemed to be the date of commencement of the proceeding for the dissolution of the marriage for the purposes only of the residence requirements of Section 2320. Fam C §2321(a). Therefore, a judgment of dissolution may theoretically be final within 6 months after original jurisdiction over respondent is obtained by service of the summons and petition for legal separation. See Fam C §2339(a). Another reason for proceeding in this manner is to enable the petitioner to seek pendente lite orders (*e.g.*, for support) while waiting to meet the residency requirement for a judgment of dissolution. On temporary orders generally, see chap 11. Additionally, because automatic restraining orders (*e.g.*, against disposing of property and changing insurance beneficiaries) are effective against the respondent when he or she is served, an early filing of a petition for legal separation may provide the petitioner with some timely protection against the respondent's dissipation of assets. See Fam C §§233(a), 2040; §11.11. On the special jurisdictional requirements for child custody orders, see §§7.5–7.13.

Notice requirements for the amended petition depend on whether the respondent has appeared in the action. It had generally been assumed that, when the respondent had appeared, either a stipulation or the granting of a noticed motion would be required before the court could allow the filing of the amended petition. CCP §473. In *Marriage of Dick* (1993) 15 CA4th 144, 157, 18 CR2d 743, however, the court held, without mentioning §473, that a noticed motion was not required to amend a pleading to change a request for a legal separation to one for a dissolution. Rather, only notice of the amendment was required. See also CCP §576 (court may allow amendment of any pleading at any time before or after commencement of trial). With or without a stipulation or noticed motion, notice of the amendment must be given in the manner provided by Judicial Council rules (Fam C §2321(b)). Mailing a copy of the amended petition to the respondent's attorney will suffice. CCP §1012.

If the respondent has not appeared in the action, the petition may be amended once without any application to the court. CCP §472.

Under Fam C §2321(b), notice may be given by mail to the respondent's last known address, or by personal service, as long as the intent to amend when the residency requirement is satisfied was set forth in the initial petition. Such a statement should always be included in the petition for legal separation when the petitioner plans to amend it later to request a dissolution, because it is always possible that the respondent will not appear. The petitioner may simply place the notation "10. See attached" immediately above the declaration under penalty of perjury on the petition for legal separation (for petition form, see §10.12) and attach a sheet containing the following statement: "On satisfaction of the residency requirement of Family Code §2320, Petitioner intends to amend this petition to seek a judgment of dissolution of marriage." Although Fam C §2321(b) specifically authorizes service of notice of the amendment by mail when the statement of intent to amend was included in the original petition, it is unclear whether the statement will eliminate the need to serve the amended petition in the manner provided for service of summons. See *Marriage of Rhoades* (1984) 157 CA3d 169, 172, 211 CR 531. Consequently, the safest course is to serve the amended petition by personal service (see §10.31) or by mail and acknowledgment of receipt (see §§10.33–10.34).

When the respondent has been served with the summons and the original petition, the amended petition does not require either a new summons or a new service of summons. Comment to CCP §412.10; see CCP §410.50. When the respondent has not been served, however, a new summons should be requested (CCP §412.10) and a copy served with the amended petition. Comment to CCP §412.10.

§3.4 C. Legal Separation Judgment Requires Consent or Default

A judgment of legal separation may be granted only if (1) both parties consent or (2) the respondent does not appear and the petition requested a legal separation. Fam C §2345. The practical effect of this requirement is to give the respondent the power to prevent the petitioner from obtaining a judgment of legal separation by filing a response that indicates that he or she does not consent to the judgment. The respondent may simply place the following statement immediately above the declaration under penalty of perjury on the response to the petition for legal separation: "10. Respondent does not consent to a judgment decreeing the legal separation of the parties. (Family Code section 2345.)" For response form, see §10.52.

§3.5 D. Effect of Judgment on Parties' Marital Status

A judgment of dissolution of marriage terminates the parties' marital status, and they are free to remarry, as of the date indicated in the judgment. Fam C §2340. A judgment of legal separation, on the other hand, does not terminate the parties' marital status; but either party may file a subsequent action to dissolve the marriage (Fam C §2347).

In a dissolution action, the earliest the parties' marital status may be terminated is 6 months after the court acquires jurisdiction over the respondent. Fam C §2339. When the judgment terminating the marital status is obtained after the 6-month date, the earliest the status may be terminated is the date the judgment is granted. The court has authority to postpone termination of the parties' marital status to a time later than the earliest date at which the marriage could be terminated, *e.g.*, to enable them to file joint tax returns for the current tax year or preserve health insurance coverage for one spouse as a dependent of the other. Fam C §2339(b). Likewise, as long as 6 months after acquisition of jurisdiction over the respondent have passed, the court may terminate the parties' marital status before granting a judgment on the other issues in the action, *e.g.*, to enable a party to remarry. Fam C §2337.

The matter of the termination date of the parties' marital status requires the attorney's care and diligence. Clients should be informed early on that (1) there is no way to obtain termination of the marital status in less than 6 months after the court obtains jurisdiction over the respondent and (2) marital status does not terminate automatically by the mere passage of the 6 months. Some clients mistakenly assume that it is the passage of the requisite time that terminates their marriage, without understanding the necessity for a judgment, and take subsequent actions, from filing tax returns as a single person to remarrying, based on that assumption. In such instances, it may be possible to obtain an earlier marital status termination date nunc pro tunc under Fam C §2346. But the ability to cure such problems by a nunc pro tunc judgment was substantially limited by the 1989 amendment to former CC §4513, predecessor of Fam C §2346. A nunc pro tunc order may not result in a marital status termination date earlier than the trial, uncontested hearing, or submission of a default affidavit under Fam C §2336. Fam C §2346(d). On nunc pro tunc entry of judgments, see §§17.59–17.64.

Counsel should also take care in explaining the consequences of a termination of marital status prior to division of all property (*e.g.*, automatic severance of joint tenancy, failure of nonprobate transfers under Prob C §5600, and danger of loss of survivor benefits relating to employer-provided retirement or life insurance if former spouse dies before a judgment dividing the property is entered) and ensure that appropriate orders to protect the client are in place before status is bifurcated.

§3.6 E. Availability of Other Orders

In either an action for dissolution or one for legal separation, the court may make a wide range of orders in addition to decreeing the dissolution or legal separation itself, including, as applicable, adjudicating the property rights of the parties of property (see chap 5), spousal support (see chap 6), child custody and visitation (see chap 7), child support (see chap 8), attorney fees and costs (see chap 9), restraining orders (see Fam C §§2045, 6360; chap 11), and restoration of a former name (see Fam C §2080). See Fam C §§2010, 2550. Except for the restoration of a former name, however, any requirements for the exercise of personal jurisdiction (see §§4.4–4.5) and child custody jurisdiction (see §§7.2–7.15) must be met before the orders may be made. Unlike parties to nullity actions, who must establish putative-spouse status to seek certain types of orders (see §§3.20–3.22), parties to dissolution and legal separation actions may obtain orders on division of property, spousal support, and attorney fees and costs without meeting any such threshold requirements, as long as theirs is a valid marriage.

III. NULLITY

A. Grounds

§3.7 1. Marriage Must Be Void or Voidable

A judgment of nullity may be granted only when a marriage is adjudged void or voidable under conditions provided by statute. Fam C §§2200–2201 (void marriages), 2210 (voidable marriages). In brief, a marriage is void in cases of incest and bigamy, and is voidable in cases of minority, a current spouse mistakenly believed to be deceased, unsound mind, fraud, force, and physical incapacity. For discussion of particular grounds, see §§3.8–3.15. A judgment of nullity may not be granted on any other ground. See *Price v Price* (1938) 24 CA2d 462, 466, 75 P2d 655. Further, the statutory grounds must have existed at the time of the marriage. Fam C §§2200–2201, 2210; *McDonald v McDonald* (1936) 6 C2d 457, 460, 58 P2d 163.

A void marriage is void from the beginning. Fam C §§2200 (incestuous marriages), 2201 (bigamous marriages). Technically, no marriage has occurred, regardless of whether a judgment of nullity is obtained. Nevertheless, it is sound practice to obtain a judgment of nullity in a void marriage because it provides a judicial determination, as a matter of public record, that eliminates any doubt about the parties' marital status. Also, depending on the circumstances, a party to a void marriage may be entitled to assert property and support rights as though the marriage had been valid. See §§3.20–3.21. Finally, when the parties have children, issues of custody, visitation, and child support can be addressed in a nullity action. See §3.23.

A voidable marriage, on the other hand, is valid unless and until it is judicially declared a nullity. *McDonald v McDonald* (1936) 6 C2d 457, 461, 58 P2d 163.

2. Particular Grounds: Void Marriage

§3.8   a. Incest

Marriages between parents and children, ancestors and descendants of every degree, brothers and sisters, half brothers and half sisters, uncles and nieces, and aunts and nephews are incestuous and void from the beginning. Fam C §2200.

§3.9   b. Bigamy

A marriage entered into while either party is married to another person is usually bigamous and void from the beginning. Fam C §2201. See *Marriage of Campbell* (2006) 136 CA4th 502, 509, 38 CR3d 894 (purported remarriage by person involved in dissolution litigation who lacks judgment dissolving current marriage is void). There are, however, two specified exceptions under which such a marriage is merely voidable. Fam C §2201; see §3.11.

3. Particular Grounds: Voidable Marriage

§3.10   a. Minority

A marriage is voidable if, at the time of the marriage, the petitioner was under age 18 and the requisite parental and court consents were not obtained, unless the petitioner freely cohabited with the respondent as husband or wife after attaining age 18. Fam C §2210(a). The required consents are set forth in Fam C §§302–303.

A nullity action filed by a party who was underage at the time of the marriage must be filed within 4 years after the party attains age 18. Fam C §2211(a)(1). The action may be filed by the party's parent or guardian if it is filed before the party attains age 18. Fam C §2211(a)(2).

A minor who intentionally misrepresents his or her age in order to get a marriage license is not thereby barred from petitioning to have the marriage annulled. *Ruiz v Ruiz* (1970) 6 CA3d 58, 85 CR 674.

§3.11   b. Bigamy

A marriage is voidable if, at the time of the marriage, either party was married to another person and (1) for 5 successive years immediately preceding the marriage, the party's spouse had been absent and not known to the party to be living or (2) at the time the marriage was entered into, the party's spouse was generally reputed or believed by the party to be dead. Fam C §2210(b).

An action to obtain a judgment of nullity of a voidable bigamous marriage may be filed by either party during the life of the other, or by the party's prior spouse at any time. Fam C §2211(b).

§3.12   c. Unsound Mind

A marriage is voidable if, at the time of the marriage, either party was of unsound mind, unless that party, after coming to reason, freely cohabited with the other as husband or wife. Fam C §2210(c). A party is "of unsound mind" when he or she is incapable of understanding the nature of the marriage contract and the duties and responsibilities it creates. *Dunphy v Dunphy* (1911) 161 C 380, 383, 119 P 512. The degree of mental capacity at the time of the marriage ceremony determines its validity. Thus, a marriage entered into during a lucid interval is valid. *Briggs v Briggs* (1958) 160 CA2d 312, 320, 325 P2d 219.

An action for a judgment of nullity on the ground of unsound mind may be filed by the spouse, or by a relative or conservator of a party of unsound mind, at any time before the death of either party. Fam C §2211(c).

§3.13   d. Fraud

A marriage is voidable if either party's consent was obtained by fraud, unless that party afterwards, with full knowledge of the facts constituting the fraud, freely cohabited with the other as husband or wife. Fam C §2210(d). The false representations or concealment constituting the fraud must relate to a matter of substance and directly affect the purpose of the party deceived in entering the marriage. *Handley v Handley* (1960) 179 CA2d 742, 746, 3 CR 910. "[F]raud must go to the *very essence* of the marital relation before it is sufficient for an annulment." *Marriage of Johnston* (1993) 18 CA4th 499, 502, 22 CR2d 253. In *Johnston,* allegations that, in the words of the appellate court, "the husband turned out to be, in the eyes of his wife, a lazy, unshaven disappointment with a drinking problem" were found insufficient to justify a judgment of nullity. 18 CA4th at 502. Similarly, a spouse's premarital misrepresentation of his or her financial status is insufficient to grant an annulment based on fraud. *Marriage of Meagher and Maleki* (2005) 131 CA4th 1, 9, 31 CR3d 663 (reversing annulment granted to wife whose husband misrepresented financial status before marriage in alleged attempt to gain control of her assets). For a client who has married based on representations that, although false, may not meet the standard for a nullity based on fraud, the requirement can be a difficult one to understand and accept. The attorney must exercise considerable care in explaining the applicable law and in advising the client about the likelihood of the court's granting a judgment of nullity based on fraud.

An action for a judgment of nullity on the ground of fraud may be filed only by the injured party and must be filed within 4 years after discovery of the facts constituting the fraud. Fam C §2211(d). Such statutes of limitations usually commence to run in advance of actual knowledge, however, and begin when the injured party becomes aware of facts that would make a reasonably prudent person suspicious. *Hobart v Hobart Estate Co.* (1945) 26 C2d 412, 438,

159 P2d 958. But when there is a fiduciary relationship between the parties, *e.g.,* husband and wife, it is recognized that facts that would ordinarily require investigation may not excite suspicion and, consequently, the same degree of diligence is not required. 26 C2d at 440.

§3.14   e. Force

A marriage is voidable if either party's consent was obtained by force, unless that party afterwards freely cohabited with the other as husband or wife. Fam C §2210(e). Threats alone may be sufficient for a judgment of nullity only if they were the inducing cause of the coerced party's consent to the marriage and if his or her free exercise of will was overcome by the threats to such an extent as to render the consent apparent rather than real. *Nicholson v Nicholson* (1917) 174 C 391, 393, 163 P 219.

An action for a judgment of nullity on the ground of force may be filed only by the injured party and must be filed within 4 years after the date of the marriage. Fam C §2211(e).

§3.15   f. Physical Incapacity

A marriage is voidable if either party was, at the time of the marriage, physically incapable of entering into the marriage state and the incapacity continues and appears to be incurable. Fam C §2210(f). The physical incapacity required is the inability to engage in normal copulation. *Stepanek v Stepanek* (1961) 193 CA2d 760, 762, 14 CR 793.

An action for a judgment of nullity on the ground of physical incapacity may be filed only by the nonincapacitated party and must be filed within 4 years after the date of the marriage. Fam C §2211(f).

§3.16   B. No Statutory Residency Requirement

For a judgment of nullity, unlike a judgment of dissolution (see §3.3), there is no statutory residency requirement.

§3.17   C. No Requirement of Consent or Default

For a judgment of nullity, unlike a judgment of legal separation (see §3.4), there is no requirement that either the respondent consent or his or her default be entered.

§3.18 D. Effect of Judgment on Parties' Marital Status

A judgment of nullity restores the parties to the status of unmarried persons. Fam C §2212(a). Technically, this is true only of voidable marriages, because parties to void marriages were never validly married. See §3.7. Unlike a dissolution judgment, which may specify a future date on which the marital status ends (see Fam C §2340), a judgment of nullity always results in the parties being free to remarry immediately. Whereas a dissolution judgment merely dissolves the existing marriage, and leaves intact the marriage relationship between the date of marriage and the date of termination of the marital status, a judgment of nullity is said to "relate back" and erase the marriage and all its implications from the outset. *Sefton v Sefton* (1955) 45 C2d 872, 874, 291 P2d 439. Legally, it is as though the parties had never married. It should be noted, however, that a party to a nullity action who qualifies as a "putative spouse" may be treated much as a true spouse would be treated for purposes of property division, support, and attorney fees and costs. See §§3.20–3.22. Also, the doctrine of "relation back" has been deemed not to apply when its application would unjustly affect the rights of an innocent third party. In *Sefton v Sefton, supra,* for example, the court held that the granting of an annulment of a voidable marriage on the grounds of fraud did not entitle a party to revive an alimony obligation that had terminated on her remarriage. 45 C2d at 876. Later courts extended *Sefton* to apply when the annulment was of a void marriage on the grounds of bigamy. *Fry v Fry* (1970) 5 CA3d 169, 85 CR 126; *Berkely v Berkely* (1969) 269 CA2d 872, 75 CR 294. One court has held, however, that if a party who obtained an annulment on the grounds of force could establish that the remarriage was not due to any voluntary act on her part, the trial court would have the authority to reinstate spousal support based on equity. *Marriage of Weintraub* (1985) 167 CA3d 420, 426, 213 CR 159.

E. Availability of Other Orders

§3.19 1. Putative Marriage Doctrine

When a marriage is invalid due to some legal infirmity, an innocent party may nevertheless be entitled, under the putative marriage doctrine, to orders in addition to the decree of nullity. *Marriage of*

Vryonis (1988) 202 CA3d 712, 717, 248 CR 807. To be deemed a "putative spouse," and thereby entitled to such relief, a party must have had a good faith and objectively reasonable belief that the marriage was legally valid. 202 CA3d at 720. A marriage need not be a void or voidable one (see §3.7) to be deemed putative, as long as the party or parties had the requisite reasonable good faith belief in its validity. 202 CA3d at 718. See also *Estate of DePasse* (2002) 97 CA4th 92, 108, 118 CR2d 143 (knowing lack of validly issued marriage license does not allow finding of objectively reasonable belief); *Welch v State* (2000) 83 CA4th 1374, 100 CR2d 430 (subjective but not objectively reasonable belief is insufficient). Thus, for example, a marriage that is not legally valid because of the lack of a proper marriage ceremony may, depending on the circumstances, give rise to putative-spouse status even though it is neither void nor voidable.

Even when the marriage is deemed putative, however, any requirements for the exercise of personal jurisdiction (see §§4.4–4.5) and child custody jurisdiction (see §§7.2–7.15) must be met before the court may grant any additional orders other than restoration of a former name.

It may be that in limited circumstances a party who does not qualify as a putative spouse because he or she knew that the marriage was invalid can, nevertheless, be awarded, on the basis of estoppel, relief normally available only to a putative spouse. See *Marriage of Recknor* (1982) 138 CA3d 539, 542, 187 CR 887. But see *Marriage of Vryonis* (1988) 202 CA3d 712, 722 n5, 248 CR 807 (estoppel not available when party asserting it knew true facts).

2. Particular Issues

§3.20 **a. Division of Property**

When division of property is in issue and the court finds that either or both parties are entitled to the status of a putative spouse, the court must divide the property acquired during the union that would have been community or quasi-community property had the union been valid. Fam C §2251. Termed "quasi-marital property," the property must be divided in accordance with Fam C §§2500–2660. Fam C §2251(a)(2). Thus, the property will be divided in the same way that community and quasi-community property are divided in a proceeding for dissolution of a valid marriage.

It is unclear whether a nonputative spouse may demand an equal division of the quasi-marital property under Fam C §2251 when the other party is a putative spouse who does not consent to the division. See *Marvin v Marvin* (1976) 18 C3d 660, 680 n18, 134 CR 815 (noting dispute concerning interpretation of former CC §4452, predecessor of Fam C §2251, but finding resolution unnecessary to decision).

§3.21   b. Support for Putative Spouse

A party found to be a putative spouse may be awarded support from the other party, both during the pendency of a nullity proceeding and in a judgment of nullity, as if the marriage had not been void or voidable. Fam C §2254.

§3.22   c. Attorney Fees and Costs

Awards of attorney fees and costs in nullity proceedings are governed by Fam C §2255. Under that section, the court may award attorney fees and costs, in accordance with Fam C §§2030-2034:

- In an action based on a void marriage (see Fam C §§2200-2201), to either party; and

- In an action based on a voidable marriage (see Fam C §2210), to a party found to be innocent of fraud or wrongdoing in inducing or entering into the marriage and free from knowledge of the existence of any prior marriage or other impediment to the contracting of the present marriage.

§3.23   d. Child Custody, Child Support, Restraining Orders, and Restoration of Former Name

Matters on which orders may be requested in a nullity action without any requirement of putative-spouse status include child custody, child support, restraining orders, and restoration of a former name. See Fam C §§2045, 2080, 2253, 6323, 6360.

IV. SUMMARY DISSOLUTION

§3.24   A. Statutory Prerequisites

California's summary dissolution procedure is set forth in Fam

C §§2400–2406. This procedure is available only if, at the time the joint petition is filed, all the conditions set forth in Fam C §2400(a) exist. In ascertaining whether summary dissolution is an available option, counsel should consider particularly the following requirements:

- There are no children of the relationship, and the wife, to her knowledge, is not pregnant (Fam C §2400(a)(3));

- The marriage is of no more than 5 years' duration (Fam C §2400(a)(4));

- Neither party has any interest in real property (an exception is made for a lease of a residence occupied by either party if it does not include an option to purchase and will terminate within one year) (Fam C §2400(a)(5));

- Amounts owed on debts incurred by either or both of the parties after the date of marriage, excluding debts relating to automobiles, do not exceed $5000 (Fam C §2400(a)(6) (indexed for inflation; see below));

- The total net fair market value of community property assets (excluding automobiles and specifically including any deferred compensation or retirement plan) is less than $33,000 and neither party has separate property assets (excluding automobiles) with a net value of more than $33,000 (Fam C §2400(a)(7) (indexed for inflation; see below));

- The parties have executed an agreement setting forth the division of community assets and the assumption of community liabilities and have executed all documents necessary to effect the agreement (Fam C §2400(a)(8)); and

- The parties waive any of their rights to spousal support (Fam C §2400(a)(9)).

Family Code §2400 is indexed for inflation. It provides that on the first day of each odd-numbered year, beginning on January 1, 1985, the statutory limitation on the value of obligations set forth in Fam C §2400(a)(6) must be adjusted in accordance with changes in the California Consumer Price Index. The same adjustment must be made on the limitations on the value of assets set forth in Fam C §2400(a)(7) on the first day of each odd-numbered year, beginning on January 1, 1993. Fam C §2400(b). The Judicial Council is required to compute and publish the amounts. Fam C §2400(b). The joint petition form (Judicial Council Form FL-800; see §3.27) is scheduled to be revised every 2 years to reflect the current figures. For the most recent figures, counsel should thus consult Judicial Council Form FL-800.

§3.25 B. Standard Dissolution Contrasted

There are many differences between a summary dissolution and a standard dissolution. Among the most significant are the following:

- Summary dissolution has a much more limited availability than standard dissolution. The many requirements that must be met to file a joint petition in a summary proceeding are set forth in Fam C §2400(a), and the most significant of these are enumerated in §3.24. Only two of the many requirements (i.e., residence and irreconcilable differences) apply in a standard dissolution proceeding.

- In addition to a judgment terminating the parties' marital status, summary dissolution provides only orders for division of property (assets and obligations) at the time of the judgment and for restoration of a former name. See Fam C §2404. Most significant is that the parties must, in the joint petition, waive the right to receive spousal support from each other at any time. Fam C §2400(a)(9). A standard dissolution, however, offers a wide range of orders, both pendente lite and at the time of the judgment.

- Either party to a summary dissolution proceeding may terminate the proceeding unilaterally at any time before entry of the final judgment. Fam C §2402. Thus, a party seeking a summary dissolution, unlike one seeking a standard dissolution, requires the consent, or at least the acquiescence, of the other party throughout the proceedings in order to obtain the judgment.

C. Procedures

§3.26 1. Discussion

The summary dissolution procedures are quite simple. There are only two steps:

- The parties file a Joint Petition for Summary Dissolution of Marriage (Judicial Council Form FL-800) (see §3.27), signed by both of them under penalty of perjury. Fam C §2401. The parties must attach three forms (see §§3.28–3.30) that the Judicial Council has determined will be required in summary dissolutions in order to implement the provisions for preliminary declarations of disclosure under Fam C §§2100–2113, applicable to proceedings commenced on or after January 1, 1993 (Fam C §2113). See Fam C §2109; Items 9 and 10 on the joint petition form. For a complete discussion of declarations of disclosure, see §§13.44–13.49. Also, unless the parties have no community assets or liabilities, they must attach a marital property agreement (see §3.31). See Fam C §2400(a)(8); Item 11 on the joint petition form.

- After 6 months have elapsed from the filing of the joint petition, either party may file a single form containing a Request for Judgment, a Judgment of Dissolution of Marriage, and a Notice of Entry of Judgment (Judicial Council Form FL-820) (see §3.32). The court issues and signs the final judgment, and the clerk mails the notice of entry. Fam C §2403.

At any time before the filing of the Request for Final Judgment, however, either party may revoke the joint petition and terminate the proceedings by filing a Notice of Revocation of Petition for Summary Dissolution (Judicial Council Form FL-830) (see §3.33). Fam C §2402(a)–(b). Although Fam C §2402(c) states that the revoking party must mail a copy of the notice of revocation to the other party, that task is performed by the clerk.

§3.27   2. Form: Joint Petition for Summary Dissolution of Marriage (Judicial Council Form FL-800)

FL-800

ATTORNEY OR PARTY WITHOUT ATTORNEY *(Name, State Bar number and address)*:	*FOR COURT USE ONLY*
TELEPHONE NO.: FAX NO. *(Optional)*:	
E-MAIL ADDRESS *(Optional)*:	
ATTORNEY FOR *(Name)*:	

SUPERIOR COURT OF CALIFORNIA, COUNTY OF
STREET ADDRESS:
MAILING ADDRESS:
CITY AND ZIP CODE:
BRANCH NAME:

MARRIAGE OF
HUSBAND:

WIFE:

JOINT PETITION FOR SUMMARY DISSOLUTION OF MARRIAGE	CASE NUMBER:

We petition for a summary dissolution of marriage and declare that all the following conditions exist on the date this petition is filed with the court:

1. We have read and understand the *Summary Dissolution Information* booklet (form FL-810).

2. We were married on *(date)*:
   (A summary dissolution of your marriage will not be granted if you file this petition more than five years after the date of your marriage.)

3. One of us has lived in California for at least six months and in the county of filing for at least three months preceding the date of filing.

4. There are no minor children who were born of our relationship before or during our marriage or adopted by us during our marriage. The wife, to her knowledge, is not pregnant.

5. Neither of us has an interest in any real property anywhere. **(You may have a lease for a residence in which one of you lives. It must terminate within a year from the date of filing this petition. The lease must not include an option to purchase.)**

6. Except for obligations with respect to automobiles, on obligations incurred by either or both of us during our marriage, we owe no more than $5,000.

7. The total fair market value of community property assets, not including what we owe on those assets and not including automobiles, is less than $33,000.

8. Neither of us has separate property assets, not including what we owe on those assets and not including automobiles, in excess of $33,000.

9. We have each filled out and given the other an *Income and Expense Declaration* (form FL-150).

10. We have each filled out and given the other copies of the worksheets on pages 8, 10, and 12 of the *Summary Dissolution Information* booklet (form FL-810) used in determining the value and division of our property. We have told each other in writing about any investment, business, or other income-producing opportunities that came up after we were separated based on investments made or work done during the marriage and before our separation. This meets the requirements of preliminary declaration of disclosure.

11. *(Check whichever statement is true.)*
    a. ☐ We have no community assets or liabilities.
    b. ☐ We have signed an agreement listing and dividing all our community assets and liabilities and have signed all the papers necessary to carry out our agreement. A copy of our agreement is attached to this petition.

12. Irreconcilable differences have caused the irremediable breakdown of our marriage, and each of us wishes to have the court dissolve our marriage without our appearing before a judge.

13. ☐ The wife desires to have her former name restored. Her former name is *(specify name)*:

    ☐ The husband desires to have his former name restored. His former name is *(specify name)*:

Page 1 of 2

Form Adopted for Mandatory Use Judicial Council of California FL-800 [Rev. January 1, 2006]	**JOINT PETITION FOR SUMMARY DISSOLUTION OF MARRIAGE** (Family Law—Summary Dissolution)	Family Code, §§ 2109, 2400–2406 www.courtinfo.ca.gov

FL-800

HUSBAND:	CASE NUMBER:
WIFE:	

14. Upon entry of judgment of summary dissolution of marriage, we each give up our rights to appeal and to move for a new trial.

15. **Each of us forever gives up any right to spousal support from the other.**

16. We agree that this matter may be determined by a commissioner sitting as a temporary judge.

17. **Mailing address of husband**
   Name:
   Address:

   City:
   State:
   Zip Code:

18. **Mailing address of wife**
   Name:
   Address:

   City:
   State:
   Zip Code:

I declare under penalty of perjury under the laws of the State of California that the foregoing and all attached documents are true and correct.

Date:

▶ _____
            (SIGNATURE OF HUSBAND)

I declare under penalty of perjury under the laws of the State of California that the foregoing and all attached documents are true and correct.

Date:

▶ _____
            (SIGNATURE OF WIFE)

You have a right to revoke this petition any time before a request for judgment is filed. You will remain married until one of you files for and obtains a judgment of dissolution. You may not request a judgment of dissolution sooner than six months from the date this petition is filed.

NOTICE: Dissolution may automatically cancel the rights of a spouse under the other spouse's will, trust, retirement benefit plan, power of attorney, pay on death bank account, transfer on death vehicle registration, survivorship rights to any property owned in joint tenancy, and any other similar thing. It does not automatically cancel the rights of a spouse as beneficiary of the other spouse's life insurance policy. You should review these matters, as well as any credit cards, other credit accounts, insurance polices, and credit reports to determine whether they should be changed or whether you should take any other actions. However, some changes may require agreement of your spouse or a court order. (See Family Code sections 231–235.)

FL-800 [Rev. January 1, 2006]

**JOINT PETITION FOR SUMMARY
DISSOLUTION OF MARRIAGE
(Family Law—Summary Dissolution)**

Page 2 of 2

Copies: Original (file with court clerk); one copy for each party; office copies.

§3.28 3. Form: Worksheet for Determining Value and Division of Community Property

HUSBAND:	CASE NUMBER:
WIFE:	

VII. (SAMPLE) WORKSHEET FOR DETERMINING VALUE AND DIVISION OF COMMUNITY PROPERTY

(This side of the sheet will help you determine whether you are **eligible** to use the summary dissolution. The grand total value* of your community property cannot be more than $33,000.)

(This side of the sheet will help you decide on a fair division of your property. It will help you prepare your property settlement agreement.)

A. Bank accounts, credit union accounts, retirement funds, cash value of insurance policies, etc.

Item	Amount	Wife Receives	Husband Receives
Savings account	150	150	
Life insurance (cash value)	250	250	
Pension plan—wife	600	600	
Pension plan—husband	500		500
Checking account	180		180
Subtotal A	1680	1000	680

B. Items you own outright (for example, stocks and bonds, sports gear, furniture, household items, tools, interests in businesses, jewelry, etc.; do not include cars or trucks).

Item	Fair Market Value	Wife Receives	Husband Receives
Furniture & furnishings— wife's apartment	775	775	
Furniture & furnishings—husband's apartment	300		300
Terriers season tickets	285		285
Savings bonds	200	200	
Jewelry—wife	200	200	
Pet parrot and cage	40		40
Subtotal B	1800	1175	625

C. Items you are buying on credit (for example, stereo equipment, appliances, furniture, tools, etc.; do not include cars or trucks).

Item	Fair Mkt Value	Minus Amount Owed	=	Net Fair Market Value	Wife Receives	Husband Receives
Stereo set	305	150	=	155		155
Color television	400	100	=	300		300
Golf clubs	350	50	=	300		300
			=			
Subtotal C				755	0	755
Subtotals A + B + C = grand total value of community property				4235	2175	2060

Copies: Original (attach to original of joint petition and file with court clerk); one copy for each party; office copies.

Comment: This form is included within the Summary Dissolution Information booklet (Judicial Council Form FL-810), available in California Judicial Council Forms Manual §3 (Cal CEB 1981).

§3.29   4. Form: Worksheet for Determining Value of Separate Property

HUSBAND:	CASE NUMBER:
WIFE:	

VII. (SAMPLE) WORKSHEET FOR DETERMINING COMMUNITY OBLIGATIONS AND THEIR DIVISION

(This side of the worksheet will help you to determine whether you are **eligible** to use the summary dissolution. The total amount of your community obligations (debts) cannot be more than $5,000. Do not include car or truck loans. Be sure you include any other debts you took on while you were living together as husband and wife. List the amount you owe on the items from your **Worksheet for Determining Value and Division of Community Property.** Then add all other debts and bills including loans, charge accounts, medical bills, and taxes you owe.)

(This side of the worksheet will help you decide on a fair way to divide up your community obligations. You will use this information in preparing a **property settlement agreement.**)

Item	Amount Owed	Wife Will Pay	Husband Will Pay
Stereo set	150		150
Color TV	100		100
Golf clubs	50		50
Dr. R. C. Himple	74		74
Sam's Drugs	32		32
College loan	500		500
Cogwell's charge account	275	275	
Mister Charge account	68		68
Green's Furniture	123	123	
Dr. Irving Roberts	37	37	
Wife's parents	150	150	
TOTAL	1559	585	974
		Wife's Share of Community Obligations	Husband's Share of Community Obligations

Copies: Original (attach to original of joint petition and file with court clerk); one copy for each party; office copies.

Comment: This form is included within the Summary Dissolution Information booklet (Judicial Council Form FL-810), available in California Judicial Council Forms Manual §3 (Cal CEB 1981).

§3.30 5. Form: Worksheet for Determining Community Obligations

VIII. WHAT SHOULD BE INCLUDED IN THE PROPERTY SETTLEMENT AGREEMENT?

A property settlement agreement should contain at least five parts:

I. Preliminary Statement
This part identifies the husband and wife, states that the marriage is being ended, and states that both husband and wife agree on the details of the agreement.

II. Division of Community Property
This part has two sections:
What the wife receives.
What the husband receives.

III. Division of Community Obligations
This part has two sections:
The amount the wife must pay and whom she must pay it to.
The amount the husband must pay and whom he must pay it to.

IV. Waiver of Spousal Support
This part states that each spouse gives up all rights of financial support from the other.

V. Date and Signature
Both husband and wife must write the date and sign the agreement.

An example of a property settlement agreement is found on pages 14–16.

Copies: Original (attach to original of joint petition and file with court clerk); one copy for each party; office copies.

Comment: This form is included within the Summary Dissolution

Information booklet (Judicial Council Form FL-810), available in California Judicial Council Forms Manual §3 (Cal CEB 1981).

§3.31   6. Form: Marital Property Agreement

MARITAL PROPERTY AGREEMENT

This agreement is made between _ _ _ _ _ _, hereafter referred to as "Husband," and _ _ _ _ _ _, hereafter referred to as "Wife." Its purpose is to make a final and complete settlement of all property rights between the parties.

Husband will be awarded the following community assets. Wife transfers to Husband as his separate property all her rights and interests in each asset:

[List each asset]

Wife will be awarded the following community assets. Husband transfers to Wife as her separate property all his rights and interests in each asset:

[List each asset]

Husband will be assigned the following community liabilities. Husband will pay and hold Wife harmless from each liability:

[List each liability]

Wife will be assigned the following community liabilities. Wife will pay and hold Husband harmless from each liability:

[List each liability]

The community assets and liabilities divided above constitute all the community assets and liabilities of the parties.

The foregoing is agreed to by:

Date: _____   _____
                     Husband

Date: _____   _____
                     Wife

Copies: Original (attach to original of joint petition and file with court clerk); one copy for each party; office copies.

§3.32 7. Form: Request for Judgment, Judgment of Dissolution of Marriage, and Notice of Entry of Judgment (Judicial Council Form FL-820)

FL-820

ATTORNEY OR PARTY WITHOUT ATTORNEY (Name and address):	FOR COURT USE ONLY
TELEPHONE NO. : FAX NO. (Optional): ATTORNEY FOR (Name):	
SUPERIOR COURT OF CALIFORNIA, COUNTY OF STREET ADDRESS: MAILING ADDRESS: CITY AND ZIP CODE: BRANCH NAME:	
MARRIAGE OF PETITIONERS HUSBAND: WIFE:	

REQUEST FOR JUDGMENT, JUDGMENT OF DISSOLUTION OF MARRIAGE, AND NOTICE OF ENTRY OF JUDGMENT	CASE NUMBER:

1. The *Joint Petition for Summary Dissolution of Marriage* (form FL-800) was filed on *(date):*
2. No notice of revocation has been filed and the parties have not become reconciled.
3. I request that judgment of dissolution of marriage be
   a. ☐ entered to be effective now.
   b. ☐ entered to be effective (nunc pro tunc) as of *(date):*
      for the following reason:

I declare under penalty of perjury under the laws of the State of California that the foregoing is true and correct.
Date:

_____ ▶ _____
(TYPE OR PRINT NAME)   (SIGNATURE OF HUSBAND OR WIFE)

4. ☐ Husband, ☐ Wife, who did **not** request his or her own former name be restored when he or she signed the joint petition, now requests that it be restored. The applicant's former name is:

Date:

_____ ▶ _____
(TYPE OR PRINT NAME)   (SIGNATURE OF PARTY WISHING TO HAVE HIS OR HER NAME RESTORED)

(For Court Use Only)
JUDGMENT OF DISSOLUTION OF MARRIAGE

5. THE COURT ORDERS
   a. A judgment of dissolution of marriage will be entered, and the parties are restored to the status of unmarried persons.
   b. ☐ The judgment of dissolution of marriage will be entered nunc pro tunc as of *(date):*
   c. ☐ Wife's former name is restored *(specify):*
   d. ☐ Husband's former name is restored *(specify):*

   e. Husband and wife must comply with any agreement attached to the petition.

Date:

_____
JUDGE OF THE SUPERIOR COURT

NOTICE: Dissolution may automatically cancel the rights of a spouse under the other spouse's will, trust, retirement benefit plan, power of attorney, pay on death bank account, transfer on death vehicle registration, survivorship rights to any property owned in joint tenancy, and any other similar thing. It does not automatically cancel the rights of a spouse as beneficiary of the other spouse's life insurance policy. You should review these matters, as well as any credit cards, other credit accounts, insurance policies, retirement benefit plans, and credit reports to determine whether they should be changed or whether you should take any other actions.

Page 1 of 2

Form Adopted for Mandatory Use Judicial Council of California FL-820 [Rev. January 1, 2003]	**REQUEST FOR JUDGMENT, JUDGMENT OF DISSOLUTION OF MARRIAGE, AND NOTICE OF ENTRY OF JUDGMENT** (Family Law—Summary Dissolution)	Family Code, § 2403 www.courtinfo.ca.gov.

HUSBAND:	CASE NUMBER:
WIFE:	

NOTICE OF ENTRY OF JUDGMENT

6. You are notified that a judgment of dissolution of marriage was entered on *(date)*:

Date: Clerk, by _____ , Deputy

CLERK'S CERTIFICATE OF MAILING

I certify that I am not a party to this cause and that a true copy of the *Notice of Entry of Judgment* was mailed first class, postage fully prepaid, in a sealed envelope addressed as shown below, and that the notice was mailed
at *(place):*   California,
on *(date):*

Date: Clerk, by _____ , Deputy

HUSBAND'S ADDRESS   WIFE'S ADDRESS

Copies: Original and two copies (submit to court clerk); office copies.

§3.33 **8. Form: Notice of Revocation of Petition for Summary Dissolution (Judicial Council Form FL-830)**

FL-830

ATTORNEY OR PARTY WITHOUT ATTORNEY *(Name and Address)*:	TELEPHONE NO.:	FOR COURT USE ONLY

ATTORNEY FOR *(Name)*:

SUPERIOR COURT OF CALIFORNIA, COUNTY OF

STREET ADDRESS:

MAILING ADDRESS:

CITY AND ZIP CODE:

BRANCH NAME:

MARRIAGE OF

PETITIONER:

RESPONDENT:

NOTICE OF REVOCATION OF PETITION FOR SUMMARY DISSOLUTION

CASE NUMBER:

Notice is given that the undersigned terminates the summary dissolution proceedings and revokes the *Joint Petition for Summary Dissolution of Marriage* (form FL-800) filed on *(date)*:

I declare under penalty of perjury under the laws of the State of California that the foregoing is true and correct.

Date:

▶

(TYPE OR PRINT NAME)   (SIGNATURE OF DECLARANT)

COMPLETE THIS NOTICE, EXCEPT FOR THE PLACE AND DATE OF MAILING AND CLERK'S NAME. SUBMIT THE ORIGINAL AND TWO COPIES TO THE COUNTY CLERK'S OFFICE. IF NO REQUEST FOR JUDGMENT HAS BEEN FILED, THE CLERK WILL NOTIFY YOU THAT THIS NOTICE OF REVOCATION HAS BEEN FILED BY COMPLETING THE CERTIFICATE BELOW.

CLERK'S CERTIFICATE OF MAILING

I certify that I am not a party to this cause and that a copy of the foregoing was mailed first class postage prepaid, in a sealed envelope as shown below, and that the mailing of the foregoing and execution of this certificate occurred at *(place)*:   California, on

(Date):

Clerk, by _____, Deputy

Name and address of husband   Name and address of wife

NOTICE

IF THE CLERK'S CERTIFICATE OF MAILING ABOVE HAS BEEN DATED AND SIGNED BY THE CLERK, THIS SUMMARY DISSOLUTION PROCEEDING IS ENDED. YOU ARE STILL MARRIED.

Form Adopted for Mandatory Use Judicial Council of California FL-830 [Rev. January 1, 2003]	**NOTICE OF REVOCATION OF PETITION FOR SUMMARY DISSOLUTION** (Family Law—Summary Dissolution)	Page 1 of 1 Family Code, § 2402 www.courtinfo.ca.gov.

Copies: Original and two copies (submit to court clerk); office copies.

§3.34   D. Attorney's Role

It is clear that attorneys play a smaller role in summary dissolution proceedings than they do in standard dissolution proceedings. Indeed, it is likely that many of the parties who proceed by summary dissolution do so without consulting attorneys at all. Nevertheless the Judicial Council summary dissolution brochure is required to state that it is in the parties' best interests to consult an attorney on the dissolution of their marriage (Fam C §2406(b)(1)), and attorneys may certainly provide advice and even appear of record in such proceedings.

When the attorney is consulted for advice but will not be the client's attorney of record, the attorney should seek to ensure that the client understands the limited scope of the attorney's responsibilities and that the understanding is confirmed in writing, *e.g.,* in the fee agreement. Whether or not the attorney will be the attorney of record, the attorney should make clear to both parties which of them the attorney is representing, and that he or she is not representing both, and should confirm that advice in writing, *e.g.,* by letter to the unrepresented party.

V. CHOOSING FORM OF ACTION

§3.35   A. Dissolution Versus Legal Separation

For most parties initiating marital actions in California (*i.e.,* those whose marriage is neither void (see §§3.8–3.9) nor voidable (see §§3.10–3.15)), the choice in the form of action is either a dissolution or a legal separation. A party to a voidable marriage who either chooses not to seek a judgment of nullity or is ineligible for such a judgment (*e.g.,* the statute of limitations (see §§3.10, 3.13–3.15) has run) has the same two options.

Most parties choose dissolution rather than legal separation because a judgment of dissolution terminates the marriage and restores the parties to the status of unmarried persons. Fam C §2300. Legal separation is an appropriate choice, however, for parties who wish to separate their lives just as formally and fully as parties to a dissolution do, but who want to remain legally married, whether for religious or other personal reasons (*e.g.,* maintenance of medical insurance coverage, assuming such coverage will continue to be available after judgment of legal separation is entered, qualification for derivative social security benefits). A judgment of legal separation basically determines the same issues that a judgment of dissolution does except that it does not set a date for termination of the marital status. *Faught v Faught* (1973) 30 CA3d 875, 106 CR 751. It should be noted that, at any time after a judgment of legal separation is granted, either party may file a separate dissolution action to terminate the marriage. Fam C §2347. However, issues adjudicated in a legal separation proceeding are res judicata and may not be reopened in a subsequent dissolution proceeding. *Faught v Faught, supra* (duration of spousal support).

When a judgment of dissolution is desired but the parties have not met the residency requirement of Fam C §2320, a petition for legal separation may be filed and then, when the residency requirement is met, amended to request a judgment of dissolution. Fam C §2321. This procedure enables the parties to seek pendente lite relief or to start the minimum 6-month period before their marital status may be terminated, without waiting until the residency requirement is met. For further discussion, see §3.3.

A judgment of legal separation may be granted only if (1) both parties consent or (2) the respondent does not appear and the petition requested a legal separation. Fam C §2345. Consequently, unless it is being filed with the intent to amend it to one for dissolution when the residency requirement is met, a petition for legal separation should not be filed if opposition from the respondent is anticipated. For further discussion, see §3.4.

§3.36   B. Dissolution Versus Nullity

A party who is eligible to file a petition for a judgment of nullity based on a voidable marriage (see §§3.10–3.15) will have a choice between an action for a judgment of dissolution (or legal separation) and one for a judgment of nullity.

Among the reasons for choosing to seek a judgment of dissolution are the following:

- In some instances, it may be difficult to establish grounds for a judgment of nullity based on a voidable marriage (see §§3.10–3.15). Even when proof is difficult, however, the petition may request a judgment of nullity and a judgment of dissolution in the alternative. See Cal Rules of Ct 5.114. Then, if grounds for a judgment of nullity are not established, the petitioner may seek a judgment of dissolution.

- The parties may not wish to acknowledge in a public court proceeding the underlying facts establishing that their marriage is voidable.

- A party who is not a putative spouse (see §3.19) may be entitled to orders (*e.g.,* division of property, support, attorney fees and costs) in a dissolution action that he or she could not obtain in a nullity action.

Among the reasons for choosing to seek a judgment of nullity are the following:

- A judgment of nullity is effective immediately without the 6-month waiting period from service of process (or the respondent's appearance) to termination of the marriage that applies in a dissolution proceeding.

- A party may prefer, as a matter of legal status, never to have been married to the other party, rather than to have been married and then divorced.

- A judgment of nullity may allow application of the "relation-back" doctrine, thereby restoring rights that were lost as a result of the marriage. See §3.18.

When the responding party is not a putative spouse (see §3.19), it may be possible to prevent that party from obtaining orders (*e.g.,* division of property, support, attorney fees and costs) in a nullity action that he or she could obtain in a dissolution action.

§3.37   C. Standard Dissolution Versus Summary Dissolution

When the parties meet the statutory requirements for the summary dissolution procedure (see Fam C §2400(a)), they will be able to choose between a summary dissolution and a standard dissolution.

The primary advantage of the summary procedure, particularly when parties will proceed in pro per, is its simplicity. Although they may still benefit from legal advice on whether the summary procedure is appropriate and in preparing their property settlement agreement, many parties will be able to process their own summary dissolution.

The primary disadvantage of the summary procedure is that either party may unilaterally terminate the proceeding by filing a notice

of revocation at any time before entry of the final judgment. Fam
C §2402. If either party then initiates a standard dissolution proceeding within 90 days after the filing of the notice of revocation, however, the period of time between the filing of the joint petition and
the filing of the notice of revocation may be applied to satisfying
the 6-month requirement of Fam C §2339 for termination of the
marriage in the standard dissolution proceeding. Fam C §2342.

§3.38   VI. LIMITED SCOPE REPRESENTATION

The Judicial Council has adopted rules to help attorneys provide
limited scope representation (sometimes called "unbundling") to family law litigants who would like the assistance of an attorney for
parts of their cases, even if they cannot afford full representation.
See Cal Rules of Ct 5.70–5.71. On limiting the scope of representation in fee agreements, see Fee Agreement Forms Manual §§1.6–1.7
(Cal CEB 1989).

A. Nature of Limited Representation

§3.39   1. Drafting Documents

An attorney who contracts with a family law client to draft or
help draft legal documents, but does not make or contract to make
an appearance in the case, is not required to disclose in the documents
that he or she was involved in their preparation. Cal Rules of Ct
5.70(a). If the litigant seeks a court order for attorney fees to pay
for those services, however, the information necessary to determine
fees, including the attorney's name, basis for billing, tasks performed,
and amount billed, must be disclosed to the court. Cal Rules of
Ct 5.70(b). Rule 5.70 does not apply to an attorney who has made
a general appearance or has contracted with the client to make an
appearance on any issue that is the subject of the pleadings. Cal
Rules of Ct 5.70(c).

§3.40   2. Appearance

An attorney making an appearance for a limited issue or for only
one hearing must provide notice to the court using mandatory Notice
of Limited Scope Representation (Judicial Council Form FL-950).
For form, see §3.41.

§3.41   3. Form: Notice of Limited Scope Representation (Judicial Council Form FL-950)

FL-950

ATTORNEY OR PARTY WITHOUT ATTORNEY *(Name, state bar number, and address):*	FOR COURT USE ONLY

TELEPHONE NO.:   FAX NO. *(Optional):*

E-MAIL ADDRESS *(Optional):*

ATTORNEY FOR *(Name):*

SUPERIOR COURT OF CALIFORNIA, COUNTY OF

STREET ADDRESS:

MAILING ADDRESS:

CITY AND ZIP CODE:

BRANCH NAME:

PETITIONER/PLAINTIFF:

RESPONDENT/DEFENDANT:

OTHER PARENT/CLAIMANT:

NOTICE OF LIMITED SCOPE REPRESENTATION	CASE NUMBER:

[ ] Amended

1. Attorney *(name):*
   and party *(name):*
   have a written agreement that attorney will provide limited scope representation to the party.

2. Attorney will represent the party
   [ ] at the hearing on: [ ] and for any continuance of that hearing
   [ ] until submission of the order after hearing
   [ ] until resolution of the issues checked on page 1 by trial or settlement
   [ ] other *(specify duration of representation):*

3. Attorney will serve as "attorney of record" for the party **only** for the following issues in this case:
   a. [ ] Child support: (1) [ ] Establish   (2) [ ] Enforce   (3) [ ] Modify *(describe in detail):*

   b. [ ] Spousal support: (1) [ ] Establish   (2) [ ] Enforce   (3) [ ] Modify *(describe in detail):*

   c. [ ] Restraining order: (1) [ ] Establish   (2) [ ] Enforce   (3) [ ] Modify *(describe in detail):*

   d. [ ] Child custody and visitation: (1) [ ] Establish   (2) [ ] Enforce   (3) [ ] Modify *(describe in detail):*

   e. [ ] Division of property *(describe in detail):*

   f. [ ] Pension issues *(describe in detail):*

www.courtinfo.ca.gov

Form Adopted for Mandatory Use
Judicial Council of California
FL-950 [New July 1, 2003]   **NOTICE OF LIMITED SCOPE REPRESENTATION**

PETITIONER/PLAINTIFF:	CASE NUMBER:
RESPONDENT/DEFENDANT:	
OTHER PARENT/CLAIMANT:	

g. ☐ Contempt *(describe in detail):*

h. ☐ Other *(describe in detail):*

i. ☐ See attachment 3i.

4. By signing this form, the party agrees to sign form MC-050, *Substitution of Attorney–Civil* at the completion of the representation as set forth above.

5. The attorney named above is "attorney of record" and available for service of documents only for those issues specifically checked on pages 1 and 2. For all other matters, the party must be served directly. The party's name, address, and phone number are listed below for that purpose.

Name:

Address *(for the purpose of service):*

Phone: Fax:

This notice accurately sets forth all current matters on which the attorney has agreed to serve as "attorney of record" for the party in this case. The information provided herein is not intended to set forth all of the terms and conditions of the agreement between the party and the attorney for limited scope representation.

Date:

▶ _____

    (TYPE OR PRINT NAME)   (SIGNATURE OF PARTY)

Date:

▶ _____

    (TYPE OR PRINT NAME)   (SIGNATURE OF ATTORNEY)

PETITIONER/PLAINTIFF:	CASE NUMBER:
RESPONDENT/DEFENDANT:	
OTHER PARENT/CLAIMANT:	

PROOF OF SERVICE BY ☐ **PERSONAL SERVICE** ☐ **MAIL**

1. At the time of service I was at least 18 years of age and **not a party to this legal action.**

2. I served a copy of the *Notice of Limited Scope Representation* as follows *(check either a. or b. below):*
   a. ☐ **Personal service.** The *Notice of Limited Scope Representation* was given to:
       (1) Name of person served:
       (2) Address where served:

       (3) Date served:
       (4) Time served:

   b. ☐ **Mail.** I placed a copy of the *Notice of Limited Scope Representation* in the United States mail, in a sealed envelope with postage fully prepaid. The envelope was addressed and mailed as follows:
       (1) Name of person served:
       (2) Address:

       (3) Date of mailing:
       (4) Place of mailing *(city and state):*
       (5) I live in or work in the county where the *Notice* was mailed.

3. Server's information:
   a. Name:
   b. Home or work address:

   c. Telephone number:

I declare under penalty of perjury under the laws of the State of California that the information above is true and correct.

Date:

_____
(TYPE OR PRINT NAME)

▶

_____
(SIGNATURE OF PERSON SERVING NOTICE)

§3.42   B. On Completion of Limited Representation

When the attorney has completed the tasks specified in the Notice of Limited Scope Representation (Judicial Council Form FL-950) and the client has not signed a Substitution of Attorney (Judicial Council Form MC-050), the attorney may be relieved as counsel by (Cal Rules of Ct 5.71):

- Filing optional Application to Be Relieved as Counsel Upon Completion of Limited Scope Representation (Judicial Council Form FL-955) with the court;

- Serving optional Form FL-955 and optional Objection to Application to Be Relieved as Counsel Upon Completion of Limited Scope Representation (Judicial Council Form FL-956) on the client;

- Serving optional Form FL-955 on all other parties and counsel of record in the case; and

- If no objection is filed within 15 days from the date the Form FL-955 was served on the client, filing with the court:

  - An updated Form FL-955 indicating the lack of objection, and

  - A proposed optional Order on Application to Be Relieved as Counsel Upon Completion of Limited Scope Representation (Judicial Council Form FL-958).

If an objection is filed within 15 days after the attorney serves the Form FL-955 on the client, the clerk sets a hearing to take place no later than 25 days from the date the objection is filed and sends notice of the hearing to the parties and counsel. Cal Rules of Ct 5.71(e).

If no objection is filed, the clerk forwards the file with the proposed order for the judge to sign. The attorney serves a copy of the signed order on the client and on all parties who have appeared in the case. Cal Rules of Ct 5.71(f). The court may delay the effective date of the order relieving counsel until proof of service of a copy of the signed order on the client has been filed with the court. Cal Rules of Ct 5.71(f).

The Judicial Council forms relating to the attorney's withdrawal from a limited scope of representation case are optional, not mandatory.

On withdrawing as attorney after judgment in a full representation case, see §§17.87–17.88.

§3.43   VII. USE OF COLLABORATIVE LAW PROCESS

During the past decade, a growing number of attorneys have made use of collaborative negotiation techniques in resolving their family law cases. This approach to handling cases has come to be known as "collaborative practice" or a "collaborative law process." As of January 1, 2007, this process is recognized by statute. Fam C §2013.

Section 2013 defines "collaborative law process" as one in which the parties and any professionals they engage to assist them agree in writing to use their best efforts and to make a good-faith attempt to resolve disputes related to the family law matters on an agreed basis without resorting to adversary judicial intervention. Fam C §2013(b). Section 2013 specifically authorizes the use of a collaborative process in reaching a written agreement between the parties. Fam C §2013(a).

An uncodified portion of the legislation that enacted §2013 states that it is the legislature's intent that further legislation be enacted to provide a procedural framework for the practice of collaborative law. Stats 2006, ch 496, §5. For related discussion, see Dissolution Strategies: From Intake to Judgment, chap 4 (Cal CEB Annual).

4

Jurisdiction and Venue

§4.1   I. SCOPE OF CHAPTER

Jurisdiction is a court's power to hear and make a decision in an action and to make rulings that will be recognized and enforced. This chapter covers jurisdiction in marital actions, including the exclusive subject matter jurisdiction of the superior court, the requirement that at least one party be domiciled in the state for the court to have jurisdiction over the parties' marital status, and the requirement of personal jurisdiction over a nonresident respondent for the court to make orders affecting him or her on financial and property issues. On proper service of process, which is also a jurisdictional requirement unless the respondent files a response or otherwise makes a general appearance, see §§10.26–10.42. On requirements for jurisdiction over child custody and visitation issues, see §§7.2–7.15.

The chapter also covers venue, *i.e.,* the county where an action takes place.

II. JURISDICTION

§4.2   A. Subject Matter Jurisdiction

The superior court has exclusive subject matter jurisdiction in marital actions, including exclusive authority to adjudicate issues of marital status (*i.e.,* judgments of dissolution, legal separation, and nullity), child custody, child support, spousal support, division of property, and attorney fees and costs. Fam C §§200, 2010; *Marriage of Lackey* (1983) 143 CA3d 698, 702, 191 CR 309. When another court makes an order on such issues, its error is jurisdictional and, consequently, may be attacked at any time (*e.g.,* as a defense to enforcement). 143 CA3d at 701.

§4.3   B. Marital Status

Provided that the respondent appears or is properly served, California has jurisdiction to grant a judgment of dissolution, a judgment of nullity, and probably a judgment of legal separation if either party is domiciled in this state. *Williams v North Carolina* (1942) 317 US 287, 87 L Ed 279, 63 S Ct 207 (dissolution); *Whealton v Whealton* (1967) 67 C2d 656, 662, 63 CR 291 (nullity); *Aldabe v Aldabe* (1962) 209 CA2d 453, 464, 26 CR 208 (dissolution); see Restatement (Second) of Conflict of Laws §75 (1971) (legal separation). This is true even when the respondent is a nonresident over whom California does not have personal jurisdiction. See *Hudson v Hudson* (1959) 52 C2d 735, 742, 344 P2d 295. On the bases for personal jurisdiction, see §4.4. A judgment of nullity and probably a judgment of legal separation may be granted even when *neither* party is a domiciliary, as long as both parties have appeared in the action. *Whealton v Whealton* (1967) 67 C2d 656, 664, 63 CR 291 (nullity); see Restatement (Second) of Conflict of Laws §75 (1971) (legal separation).

Although it is sufficient for a judgment of nullity or legal separation that one party be domiciled in California at the time the petition is filed, it is *not* sufficient for a judgment of dissolution. Family Code §2320 implements the domicile requirement in dissolution cases by providing that a judgment of dissolution may not be entered unless at least one party was a "resident" of California for six months immediately before the filing of the petition.

Strictly speaking, a person's "domicile" is where he or she lives and intends to remain, and it is thus a more comprehensive term than "residence," which is simply any place a person lives for any period of time. *Smith v Smith* (1955) 45 C2d 235, 239, 288 P2d 497. For purposes of Fam C §2320, however, "resident" means "domiciliary." *Whealton v Whealton* (1967) 67 C2d 656, 660, 63 CR 291 (discussing former CC §128 (one-year residency requirement for divorce)). Thus, for California to grant a dissolution judgment, at least one party must have lived in California, *with the intent to remain here,* for at least six months immediately before the filing of the petition. See *Marriage of Dick* (1993) 15 CA4th 144, 156, 18 CR2d 743. But see *Marriage of Thornton* (1982) 135 CA3d 500, 512, 185 CR 388 (court declined to hold mere "residence," as distinguished from "domicile," sufficient for dissolution jurisdiction in all circumstances, but held it sufficient in this case because no more proper forum was available). Domicile issues commonly arise in cases in which a party, as in *Thornton,* is a member of the military who maintains a residence in California but claims domicile elsewhere. For a discussion of "residence" versus "domicile" in the context of the so-called "Deadbeat Parents Punishment Act of 1998" (18 USC §228), see §20.94.

When the domicile requirement is not met, the respondent may raise the issue either in the pending proceeding (*e.g.,* by a motion to quash the proceeding (see 135 CA3d at 503)) or at some later time (*e.g.,* as a defense to enforcement (*Crouch v Crouch* (1946) 28 C2d 243, 249, 169 P2d 897)). For discussion of motions to quash the proceeding, see §10.62.

Under the concept of "divisible divorce," California may have jurisdiction to grant a dissolution of marriage (or a judgment of nullity or of legal separation) against a nonresident respondent but not have jurisdiction to make orders affecting that party with respect to child custody, child support, spousal support, division of property, or attorney fees and costs. See *Estin v Estin* (1948) 334 US 541, 549, 92 L Ed 1561, 1569, 68 S Ct 1213; *Marriage of Gray* (1988) 204 CA3d 1239, 1248, 251 CR 846. Consequently, before filing a marital action against a nonresident respondent, an attorney must consider not only whether California has jurisdiction to grant the relief requested with respect to the parties' marital status, but also, as a separate matter, whether California has or can acquire jurisdiction to grant any other forms of relief the petitioner seeks.

C. Financial and Property Issues

§4.4   1. Child Support, Spousal Support, and Attorney Fees and Costs

To make orders in a marital action that affect the respondent with respect to financial issues, a court must have personal jurisdiction over the respondent. *Kulko v Superior Court* (1978) 436 US 84, 91, 56 L Ed 2d 132, 140, 98 S Ct 1690; *Titus v Superior Court* (1972) 23 CA3d 792, 799, 100 CR 477. Personal jurisdiction over the respondent is required even to permit the court to order the petitioner to fulfill obligations (*e.g.,* to pay spousal support) to the respondent. See *Vanderbilt v Vanderbilt* (1957) 354 US 416, 418, 1 L Ed 2d 1456, 1459, 77 S Ct 1360. In most California marital actions, the respondent is a California resident, and the court has personal jurisdiction over him or her on that basis (see California Civil Procedure Before Trial §6.68 (4th ed Cal CEB 2004)).

A nonresident respondent may challenge the assertion of personal jurisdiction by filing a timely motion to quash service of summons. CCP §418.10. See, *e.g., Judd v Superior Court* (1976) 60 CA3d 38, 41, 131 CR 246. For discussion of motions to quash service of summons, see §10.61. Alternatively, the respondent may allow his or her default to be taken and then (1) appeal the judgment on jurisdictional grounds, (2) file a separate proceeding to set the judgment aside (see, *e.g., Marriage of Van Sickle* (1977) 68 CA3d 728, 732, 137 CR 568), or (3) assert the judgment's invalidity as a defense to enforcement (see, *e.g., Marriage of Merideth* (1982) 129 CA3d 356, 360, 180 CR 909). Consequently, when a prospective respondent is not a California resident and the prospective petitioner desires orders on financial issues, the latter's attorney must evaluate whether personal jurisdiction over the respondent can be established. A respondent can move to quash and simultaneously answer, demur, or move to strike and will not be considered to have made an appearance unless the court denies the motion. CCP §418.10(e). If the court denies the CCP §418.10 motion, the respondent is not deemed to have generally appeared until entry of the order denying the motion. If the motion is denied and the respondent petitions for a writ of mandate, the respondent is not deemed to have generally appeared until final conclusion of the proceedings on the writ petition. Failure to make a §418.10 motion at the time of filing a demurrer or motion to strike is a waiver of the issues of lack of personal jurisdiction, inadequacy of process, inadequacy of service, inconvenient forum, or delay in prosecution. CCP §418.10(e)(3). See Civ Proc Before Trial §19.6.

Personal jurisdiction in California courts is governed by CCP §410.10, which provides that a court may exercise jurisdiction "on any basis not inconsistent with the Constitution of this state or of the United States." Personal jurisdiction should be distinguished from proper service of process (see §§10.26–10.42). Each of these, along with subject matter jurisdiction (see §4.2), is one of the three requirements that must be met in order for a court to make orders that bind the respondent with respect to financial issues.

The basic requirement for a court's exercise of personal jurisdiction over a nonresident is that he or she have minimum contacts with the forum state such that the maintenance of the action there does not offend traditional notions of fair play and substantial justice. *International Shoe Co. v Washington* (1945) 326 US 310, 316, 90 L Ed 95, 102, 66 S Ct 154. When a nonresident is personally served with process in the forum state, however, the minimum contacts requirement does not apply. *Burnham v Superior Court* (1990) 495 US 604, 109 L Ed 2d 631, 110 S Ct 2105. Consequently, when an attorney anticipates efforts to subject his or her client to personal jurisdiction in a state where the client does not want to litigate and where personal jurisdiction is questionable, it might be appropriate to caution the client about being present in that state. But see *Marriage of Fitzgerald & King* (1995) 39 CA4th 1419, 1426, 46 CR2d 558 (service of OSC or notice of motion, as distinguished from service of process, insufficient to confer personal jurisdiction).

The California Judicial Council has recognized the following bases that may be sufficient to give a court personal jurisdiction over an individual: (1) presence in the state; (2) domicile; (3) residence; (4) citizenship; (5) consent; (6) appearance in the action; (7) doing business in the state; (8) doing an act in the state; (9) doing an act elsewhere that causes an effect in the state; (10) ownership, use, or possession of a thing in the state; or (11) other relationships to the state that make the exercise of jurisdiction reasonable. Comment to CCP §410.10. For a complete discussion of the bases for asserting personal jurisdiction over individuals, see Civ Proc Before Trial §§6.66–6.88.

An attorney faced with a personal jurisdiction issue in a marital action must become familiar not only with the "minimum contacts" test of *International Shoe Co. v Washington, supra*, and the recognized bases for asserting personal jurisdiction, but also with the relevant case law. Broadly speaking, courts have approved assertions of personal jurisdiction over nonresidents whose own contacts with California were significant and over nonresidents who had abandoned their families, forcing them to come to California and rely on public assistance. See, *e.g., Khan v Superior Court* (1988) 204 CA3d 1168, 251 CR 815 (although respondent allegedly had not resided in California for preceding 21 years, parties had lived here together before then for six years, during which time two of their children were born, they owned real property here, and respondent maintained bank account and driver's license here); *McGlothen v Superior Court* (1981) 121 CA3d 106, 175 CR 129 (nonresident respondent abandoned family, forcing them to move to wife's parents' home in California and rely on public assistance); *Marriage of Lontos* (1979) 89 CA3d 61, 152 CR 271 (nonresident respondent had continuous and extensive contacts with California, including home ownership, driver's license, vehicle registration, and bank account, and abandoned his family, forcing them to return to the family home in California and rely on public assistance). But see *Muckle v Superior Court* (2002) 102 CA4th 218, 227, 125 CR2d 303 (even though husband had prior contacts with California, no personal jurisdiction over him when he had no contact with state at time dissolution filed).

As long as the nonresidents have not abandoned their families and forced them to rely on California's welfare, the courts have generally rejected assertions of personal jurisdiction over nonresidents whose own contacts with California were insignificant. See, *e.g., Kulko v Superior Court, supra* (father who remained in New York while wife and, eventually, parties' two children moved to California not subject to personal jurisdiction here simply because he consented to one child's living here during school year and sent her here for that purpose); *Titus v Superior Court, supra* (father not subject to personal jurisdiction in California based solely on his having sent children here to visit and having sent agreement to their mother here concerning children's temporary custody).

An attorney planning to file a marital action in California but anticipating that the respondent may challenge jurisdiction should begin immediately to compile evidence of the other party's contacts with California, *e.g.,* voter registration, driver's license, automobile registration, homestead declaration, applications showing residence, property ownership records, tax records, and tax returns. If it is anticipated that the respondent may file an action in another jurisdiction, the California action should be filed, and service effected, as soon as possible. See *Marriage of Hanley* (1988) 199 CA3d 1109, 1116, 245 CR 441, overruled on other grounds in *Leadford v Leadford* (1992) 6 CA4th 571, 575, 8 CR2d 9 (as between actions in California and another state, that in which service is first effected has the exclusive right to proceed, even if the other action is the one in which a petition was first filed).

§4.5   2. Division of Property

Historically, the presence of property in a state gave that state jurisdiction to determine rights in the property regardless of the relationship of the property owner to the state, a proposition derived from *Pennoyer v Neff* (1878) 95 US 714, 24 L Ed 565, overruled in *Shaffer v Heitner* (1977) 433 US 186, 212, 53 L Ed 2d 683, 703, 97 S Ct 2569. In *Shaffer v Heitner* (1977) 433 US 186, 212, 53 L Ed 2d 683, 703, 97 S Ct 2569, however, the United States Supreme Court, finding that the continued acceptance of that proposition would allow state court jurisdiction that is fundamentally unfair to the defendant, held that all assertions of state court jurisdiction, whether over persons or property, must be evaluated according to the "minimum contacts" standard of *International Shoe Co. v Washington* (1945) 326 US 310, 316, 90 L Ed 95, 102, 66 S Ct 154, *i.e.,* minimum contacts with the forum state such that the maintenance of the action there does not offend traditional notions of fair play and substantial justice. Of course, the presence of property in a state, even though no longer in itself sufficient to establish personal jurisdiction over an owner, may still bear on the issue of personal jurisdiction by providing contacts between the owner and the state. *Shaffer v Heitner* (1977) 433 US 186, 207, 53 L Ed 2d 683, 700, 97 S Ct 2569. The impact of *Shaffer,* for purposes of marital actions, is to make the test of a court's jurisdiction over property issues, with respect to property located in California as well as that located elsewhere, the same as the test for jurisdiction over financial issues (see §4.4). On a court's jurisdiction over issues with respect to property located outside California, see *Rozan v Rozan* (1957) 49 C2d 322, 330, 317 P2d 11; *Muckle v Superior Court* (2002) 102 CA4th

218, 226, 125 CR2d 303; *Marriage of Ben-Yehoshua* (1979) 91 CA3d 259, 269, 154 CR 80.

Shaffer v Heitner, supra, does, however, expressly leave open one question that pertains to jurisdiction over property issues in a marital action, *i.e.*, whether the presence of property in a state is a sufficient basis for jurisdiction to determine the parties' interests in it when no other forum is available to the petitioner. 433 US at 211 n37, 53 L Ed 2d at 702 n37. Thus it may be that California could assert jurisdiction with respect to property present in this state, even absent personal jurisdiction over the respondent, when, *e.g.*, the respondent's whereabouts are unknown.

Satisfying the minimum contacts standard is insufficient to establish jurisdiction to divide a military pension because Congress has expressly dictated a more restrictive standard under the Federal Uniformed Services Former Spouses' Protection Act (FUSFSPA) (10 USC §1408). 10 USC §1408(c)(4); *Marriage of Hattis* (1987) 196 CA3d 1162, 1167, 242 CR 410. Under §1408, personal jurisdiction may be based only on (1) residence (if other than because of military assignment), (2) domicile, or (3) consent. In this context, "domicile" means "present domicile." *Marriage of Hattis, supra*. In *Hattis*, the court found that California could exercise personal jurisdiction over the respondent with respect to child support because the minimum contacts standard was met, but it could not exercise jurisdiction with respect to division of his military pension because the more restrictive standard of 10 USC §1408(c)(4) was not met. 196 CA3d at 1170.

Satisfying the minimum contacts standard is also insufficient to establish jurisdiction to divide quasi-community property because the federal Constitution requires a more restrictive standard. "Quasi-community property" is real or personal property acquired by either spouse while domiciled elsewhere that would have been community property if acquired while domiciled in California, or property acquired in exchange for such property. Fam C §125. The quasi-community property statute may constitutionally be applied only when both parties have changed their domicile to California and thereafter either spouse files a marital action. *Marriage of Roesch* (1978) 83 CA3d 96, 106, 147 CR 586; *Marriage of Fransen* (1983) 142 CA3d 419, 431, 190 CR 885. But see *Marriage of Jacobson* (1984) 161 CA3d 465, 472, 207 CR 512 (quasi-community property statute may be applied to military retirement benefits when one spouse domiciled here and other spouse consents to have California law apply).

§4.6 D. Child Custody and Visitation Issues

Jurisdiction over child custody and visitation issues is subject to the provisions of the Uniform Child Custody Jurisdiction and Enforcement Act (Fam C §§3400–3465) and the Parental Kidnapping Prevention Act of 1980 (Pub L 96–611, §§6–10, 94 Stat 3568; see in particular 28 USC §1738A). For discussion, see §§7.4–7.15.

The fact that a court in a marital action does not have jurisdiction over child custody and visitation issues will not prevent it from exercising whatever jurisdiction it may have over the parties' marital status and financial and property issues. Fam C §3427(d).

§4.7 E. Inconvenient Forum Distinguished

The question of whether a court may exercise jurisdiction over an action must be distinguished from that of whether the court is an inconvenient forum (also called forum non conveniens). Rather than challenging a court's personal jurisdiction, a motion under CCP §410.30 to stay or dismiss on the grounds of inconvenient forum concedes jurisdiction and asks the court to use discretion in declining to exercise jurisdiction because it is more convenient to litigate the action in a forum outside California. For discussion and illustration of the application of the doctrine of inconvenient forum in a marital action, see *Jagger v Superior Court* (1979) 96 CA3d 579, 158 CR 163. In *Jagger*, the court of appeal concluded that:

- The respondent was subject to personal jurisdiction in California (96 CA3d at 582 n1);

- The trial court had nonetheless abused its discretion in failing to apply the doctrine of inconvenient forum (96 CA3d at 585); and

- A stay, which is the usual remedy (so that if obstacles develop to litigation in the convenient forum the parties may resume litigation in California), was more appropriate than dismissal (96 CA3d at 589).

Note that CCP §410.30 permits any party, not just the respondent, to bring a forum non conveniens motion. *Marriage of Taschen* (2005) 134 CA4th 681, 688, 36 CR3d 286 (party who initially petitioned for dissolution could bring forum non conveniens motion).

For a complete discussion of motions to dismiss or to stay on grounds of inconvenient forum, see California Civil Procedure Before Trial, chap 21 (4th ed Cal CEB 2004). It should be noted that Fam C §3427, part of the Uniform Child Custody Jurisdiction and Enforcement Act (Fam C §§3400–3465), governs inconvenient forum motions in child custody matters. See §§7.12, 7.15.

§4.8   III. VENUE

A petition for dissolution of marriage may be filed in a county in which either party has been a resident for three months immediately before the filing, as long as the party was also a California resident for six months immediately before the filing. Fam C §2320; see CCP §395. A petition for legal separation or for a judgment of nullity may be filed in a county in which either party resides at the time of the filing. CCP §395.

A respondent in a dissolution action who contends that the petition was filed in an improper county may raise that issue by filing a timely motion (1) to quash the proceeding (see, *e.g.*, *Marriage of Thornton* (1982) 135 CA3d 500, 503, 185 CR 388); or (2) to change venue (CCP §397(a)); see, *e.g.*, *Forster v Superior Court* (1992) 11 CA4th 782, 787, 14 CR2d 258). For discussion, see §§10.62 (motion to quash proceeding), 10.63 (motion for change of venue). Lack of proper venue is not, however, a jurisdictional defect and, consequently, a judgment is valid despite improper venue unless it is challenged by an appeal, a motion, or a writ. Improper venue, unlike lack of jurisdiction, may *not* be raised as a defense to enforcement. 3 Witkin, California Procedure, *Actions* §702 (4th ed 1997).

In ruling on a motion to change venue on the basis of filing in an improper county, a court has discretion to assess reasonable expenses and attorney fees as sanctions against an attorney who files an action in the wrong county or an attorney who files a motion to change venue that is found to be without merit. Such a liability may *not* be made chargeable to the party the attorney represents. CCP §396b(b); *Metzger v Silverman* (1976) 62 CA3d Supp 30, 40, 133 CR 355.

A respondent who concedes that the petitioner has properly filed in the county where the petitioner resides may nonetheless file a motion to change venue to the county where the respondent resides on the grounds that the ends of justice would be promoted by the change. CCP §397(e). For discussion and illustration of such a motion to change venue, see *Silva v Superior Court* (1981) 119 CA3d 301, 173 CR 832.

When marital actions between the same parties are filed in two different venues, only the action in which the respondent is *served* first is entitled to proceed, even if the other action was *filed* first. *Mungia v Superior Court* (1964) 225 CA2d 280, 37 CR 285.

5

Property

§5.1   I. SCOPE OF CHAPTER

This chapter covers the subject of property in the context of marital actions. Emphasis is placed on the three major components of resolving property issues: characterization, valuation, and division. For each component there are discussions of (1) general principles and (2) specific assets requiring special treatment. The discussion of property division includes an introduction to the tax aspects most commonly of importance in marital actions.

At the request of either party, a court has jurisdiction to divide the separate property interests of the parties held by them as joint tenants or as tenants in common, including any interests in property held jointly with third parties. Fam C §2650. In such instances, valuation of separate property assets may be required. Nevertheless, to simplify their presentation, valuation and division issues are discussed in this chapter as though only community property items were being divided.

§5.2   II. WHAT "PROPERTY" ENCOMPASSES

Most assets in which interests are asserted in marital actions are clearly "property" subject to the California statutes relating to community property. Nevertheless, the term "property" as used in such statutes does not encompass every property right the parties might acquire. *Marriage of Aufmuth* (1979) 89 CA3d 446, 461, 152 CR 668, 677, disapproved on other grounds in 27 C3d at 815. *Aufmuth* held that a professional education is not property subject to division by the court in a marital action. 89 CA3d at 461. Likewise, the right to practice a profession is not property subject to division. 89 CA3d at 461. Family Code §2641 now provides for reimbursement to the community as the exclusive remedy for contributions to a party's education or training that substantially enhances his or her earning capacity. See §5.96.

Term insurance is an asset that has generated substantial controversy over whether it is to be treated as "property" for purposes of marital actions. See *Marriage of Gonzalez* (1985) 168 CA3d 1021, 214 CR 634 (policy is property subject to division); *Marriage of Lorenz* (1983) 146 CA3d 464, 468, 194 CR 237 (policy is not subject to division); *Estate of Logan* (1987) 191 CA3d 319, 325, 236 CR 368 (term life insurance is not property subject to division unless insured dies or becomes uninsurable during period for which community funds used to pay premiums).

Accrued vacation time that cannot be taken in the form of cash is not property subject to division in marital actions. *Marriage of Lorenz, supra*. Accrued vacation pay, however, is probably divisible. See *Suastez v Plastic Dress-Up Co.* (1982) 31 C3d 774, 779, 183 CR 846 (vacation pay is deferred compensation); *Marriage of Gonzalez* (1985) 168 CA3d 1021, 1024, 214 CR 634 (vacation pay, like pension rights, may be commuted to present value and divided).

Although most marital actions do not generate issues concerning whether particular assets are divisible as "property," attorneys should be alert to that possibility. See, *e.g., Marriage of McTiernan & Dubrow* (2005) 133 CA4th 1090, 1112, 35 CR 3d 287 (statutory definitions of transferable goodwill do not encompass "business" that is natural person; thus movie director's elite professional status did not generate goodwill and expected future job assignments could not be considered divisible community assets). An attorney who succeeds, without the benefit of clear legal authority, in having an asset of the other party deemed "property" may greatly increase what his or her client is awarded. See, *e.g., Marriage of Brown* (1976) 15 C3d 838, 126 CR 633 (nonvested pension rights). And an attorney who succeeds in having such status denied to an asset of his or her client preserves the asset in its entirety for the client. See, *e.g., Marriage of Aufmuth* (1979) 89 CA3d 446, 461, 152 CR 668, disapproved on other grounds in 27 C3d at 815 (professional education).

"Property" in the Family Code includes real and personal property and any interest therein. Fam C §113.

III. TYPES OF PROPERTY

§5.3　　　A. Community and Separate

All property acquired during marriage by a married person domiciled in California (whether acquired by the husband, the wife, or both) is either community property or separate property. California's statutory scheme defines community property negatively, *i.e.,* all property acquired by a California domiciliary during marriage that is not specified by statute to be separate property. Fam C §760. Separate property includes all property owned before marriage (Fam C §770(a)(1)) and all property acquired during marriage that is:

- Acquired by gift or inheritance (Fam C §770(a)(2));

- Produced by separate property (*i.e.,* "rents, issues, and profits") (Fam C §770(a)(3)); or

- Acquired after the date of separation (Fam C §771(a)).

§5.4   B. Quasi-Community

Quasi-community property is real or personal property acquired by either spouse while domiciled outside of California that would have been community property if acquired while domiciled in California, or property acquired in exchange for such property. Fam C §125.

§5.5   C. Quasi-Marital

Quasi-marital property is property acquired by parties to an invalid marriage that would have been community or quasi-community property had the marriage been valid, as long as either party qualifies as a putative spouse. Fam C §2251; *Marriage of Vryonis* (1988) 202 CA3d 712, 717, 248 CR 807. To be deemed a "putative spouse," a party must have had a good-faith and objectively reasonable belief that the marriage was legally valid. Fam C §2251; 202 CA3d at 720. See §3.19.

§5.6   D. Joint Tenancy

Joint tenancy property is property owned by two or more persons in equal shares and created by a document that expressly declares that title is held as joint tenants. CC §683. A husband and wife may own property as joint tenants. Fam C §750.

The characteristic of joint tenancy property that distinguishes it from other forms of co-ownership is the right of survivorship, *i.e.,* on the death of one joint tenant, his or her share is automatically acquired by the other joint tenant (or tenants). Until July 1, 2001, when CC §682.1 became operative and authorized an estate of community property with a right of survivorship, this characteristic was incompatible with other forms of co-ownership, because such interests are subject to testamentary disposition or intestate succession. See *Siberell v Siberell* (1932) 214 C 767, 773, 7 P2d 1003. See §5.8A, discussing community property with right of survivorship under CC §682.1.

§5.7   E. Tenancy in Common

Tenancy-in-common property is property owned by two or more persons that is not a partnership interest, joint tenancy property, or community property. CC §686. A husband and wife may own property as tenants in common. Fam C §750.

§5.8   F. Partnership

A partnership is an association of two or more persons to conduct a business for profit as co-owners. Corp C §16101(7). See also CC §684. A husband and wife may enter into a partnership. See *McCall v McCall* (1934) 2 CA2d 92, 94, 37 P2d 496.

§5.8A   G. Community Property With Right of Survivorship

A husband and wife may hold property as "community property with a right of survivorship." CC §682.1(a); Fam C §750. On the death of one spouse, such community property passes to the survivor without administration, just as does joint tenancy property. Before either spouse's death, the right of survivorship may be terminated in the same way as a joint tenancy may be severed. CC §682.1(a). Section 682.1 does not apply to certain financial institution joint accounts. CC §682.1(b).

IV. CHARACTERIZATION

§5.9   A. Context and Approach

The initial step in addressing property issues in a marital action is to characterize the individual property items held by the parties as community property or separate property. The court has authority to make that determination even though it may not have authority to dispose of an asset it determines to be separate property. *Marriage of Buford* (1984) 155 CA3d 74, 78, 202 CR 20, disapproved on other grounds in 41 C3d at 451 n13. The court may also apportion community and separate interests in particular assets. 154 CA3d at 78 n2, 202 CR at 23 n2. It is only after characterization (and often valuation) of property that the court may apply the law applicable to property division. *Lehman v Superior Court* (1986) 179 CA3d 558, 562, 224 CR 572.

The law regarding characterization of property has developed piecemeal, by both statutes and case law, and has produced a wide variety of factors that courts consider. See §§5.10–5.40. It is essential that these factors not be considered in isolation. In many instances, different factors may suggest different results. It is thus imperative to consider the overall characterization scheme in order to properly characterize a particular item.

Assume, for example, that spouses purchase an automobile during marriage but before separation, pay for it with funds from earnings during marriage, and register the automobile in the name of one spouse alone. Under the general community property presumption of Fam C §760, the automobile is presumed to be community property because of the time of its acquisition. See §5.11. But the general community property presumption may be overcome in several ways, one of which is by the common-law presumption from the form of title, under which the automobile will be the separate property of the spouse in whose name title is taken unless the other spouse can establish an agreement or understanding to the contrary. It is not sufficient to trace the funds used to purchase the automobile. See §5.19.

The status of property as community or separate is ordinarily determined as of the time of its acquisition (*Giacomazzi v Rowe* (1952) 109 CA2d 498, 500, 240 P2d 1020) and also by the law in effect at the time of its acquisition (*Marriage of Bouquet* (1976) 16 C3d 583, 587, 128 CR 427). Statutory enactments and amendments affecting characterization of property may be applied retroactively, however, when retroactive application (1) was intended by the legislature and (2) does not constitute an unconstitutional deprivation of property. See 16 C3d at 586. In *Bouquet,* the supreme court gave retroactive application to an amendment to former CC §5118, predecessor of Fam C §771(a), that made the husband's postseparation earnings and acquisitions his separate property. For a contrary result, see *Marriage of Buol* (1985) 39 C3d 751, 218 CR 31, which denied retroactive application of former CC §4800.1, predecessor of Fam C §2581 (property acquired by parties in joint form during marriage is community property absent writing to the contrary) to cases pending before the statute's effective date. For further discussion of the retroactivity issue with respect to Fam C §2581, see §5.20. In some instances, the legislature specifies that a statute is not to be applied retroactively, thereby eliminating any potential litigation over the issue. See, *e.g.,* Fam C §852(e) (requirement that transmutation be in writing not applicable to transmutation made before effective date of statute), discussed in §5.28.

B. Factors Considered

1. Time of Acquisition

§5.10   a. Before Marriage

Property acquired by either spouse before marriage, and any "rents, issues, and profits" from such property, are ordinarily the separate property of the acquiring spouse. Fam C §770. On the meaning of "acquired," see §5.13.

§5.11   b. During Marriage and Before Separation

Except as provided in Fam C §§770 and 781, property acquired by a California domiciliary during marriage and before separation is presumed to be community property. See Fam C §§760, 771(a). On the meaning of "acquired," see §5.13; on the meaning of "separation," see §5.12. Under Fam C §770, property that (1) is acquired by gift or inheritance (see §5.14) or (2) consists of "rents, issues, and profits" from separate property (see §5.15) is separate property, even when acquired during marriage and before separation. Family Code §781 addresses characterization of personal injury damages. See §5.29.

The presumption of Fam C §760 (former CC §5110) regarding property acquired during marriage and before separation is often characterized as the general community property presumption. See, *e.g., Marriage of Lucas* (1980) 27 C3d 808, 814, 166 CR 853. Unlike the "common-law" presumption from the form of title (see §5.19), the general community property presumption may be overcome simply by tracing the acquisition to separate property. 27 C3d at 814. On tracing, see §5.23.

§5.12   c. During Marriage but After Separation

Property acquired by either spouse during marriage but after separation (*i.e.,* "while living separate and apart") is ordinarily the acquiring spouse's separate property. Fam C §771(a). On the meaning of "acquired," see §5.13. The phrase "living separate and apart" in Fam C §771(a) requires both a parting of the ways with no present intention of resuming marital relations and, more important, conduct evidencing a complete and final break in the marital relationship. *Marriage of von der Nuell* (1994) 23 CA4th 730, 736, 28 CR2d 447; *Marriage of Baragry* (1977) 73 CA3d 444, 448, 140 CR 779. Analysis of each party's living situation can be particularly important in determining whether "separation" has actually taken place. In the seminal *Baragry* case, for example, the date of separation was found *not* to be the date a husband moved out and began living with his girlfriend, but rather 4 years later when he finally petitioned for dissolution. Among other facts seen as evidence of a continued marriage were that he frequently ate dinner at the family home, maintained his mailing address there, took his family on vacations and sporting events, and his wife to social events, continued to file joint income tax returns with his wife, and regularly brought his laundry home for her to wash and iron. 73 CA3d at 448.

The date of separation occurs when either party does not intend to resume the marriage and his or her actions bespeak the finality of the marital relationship. There must be problems that have so impaired the marital relationship that the legitimate objects of matrimony have been destroyed and there is no reasonable possibility of eliminating, correcting, or resolving the problems. *Marriage of Hardin* (1995) 38 CA4th 448, 451, 45 CR2d 308. Thus even spouses who live in separate residences may not be "living separate and apart" for purposes of the statute. *Marriage of Baragry, supra.* Nor does the filing of a petition for dissolution necessarily compel a finding that spouses who live in separate residences are separated under Fam C §771(a) when the legal action is not pursued. *Marriage of Marsden* (1982) 130 CA3d 426, 435, 181 CR 910. In *Marriage of Peters* (1997) 52 CA4th 1487, 61 CR2d 493, the court of appeal held that the standard of proof for the date-of-separation issue is preponderance of the evidence, rejecting a contention that the higher standard of clear and convincing evidence should apply. Although in most cases involving the "living separate and apart" standard the appellate courts found that the parties' conduct did not evidence a complete and final break in the relationship, these cases did not consider whether the parties must live in separate residences to be living "separate and apart." In *Marriage of Norviel* (2002) 102 CA4th 1152, 1162, 126 CR2d 148, the court expressly held that "living apart physically is an indispensable threshold requirement to separation, whether or not it is sufficient, by itself, to establish separation."

Thus, unless there is evidence of "unambiguous, objectively ascertainable conduct amounting to a physical separation under the same roof" (192 CA4th at 1164), an essential component of separation is that the parties maintain separate residences at different addresses.

Spouses who separate and then reconcile may have more than one period during their marriage for which the property acquired is separate property by virtue of Fam C §771(a). See *Patillo v Norris* (1976) 65 CA3d 209, 135 CR 210.

For discussion of the separation requirements for "alimony tax treatment" under income tax laws, see §6.33.

§5.13   d. When Property Is "Acquired"

Property may be "acquired" either at a discrete time (*e.g.,* purchase of a residence, automobile, or household furnishings) or over a period of time (*e.g.,* work performed to earn retirement benefits or other deferred compensation). Either way, it is not always clear when the property was acquired. Further, when property is acquired over a period of time, it may have to be apportioned between community and separate interests.

Cases involving real property have been a major source of confusion over time of acquisition. In this area, courts have applied an "inception-of-title" approach. Under this approach, property is deemed to have been acquired at the time that the right that subsequently results in full title begins to come into existence. *Giacomazzi v Rowe* (1952) 109 CA2d 498, 500, 240 P2d 1020. For discussion and application of the inception-of-title approach, see *Marriage of Joaquin* (1987) 193 CA3d 1529, 239 CR 175 (leasehold interest did not become community property by virtue of renewal during marriage because interest was "acquired" before marriage when option to renew was given).

Cases involving payments for services rendered have been another major source of discussion over time of acquisition. Courts have generally focused on when the services were performed rather than when payment is received. Thus, retirement benefits are community property to the extent that the work performed to earn them was done during marriage and before separation, regardless of when the payments are actually received. *Marriage of Brown* (1976) 15 C3d 838, 126 CR 633. This characterization also extends to survivor and death benefits. Fam C §2610. For discussion of apportionment of retirement benefits between community and separate estates, see §5.30. Likewise, payments for services rendered during marriage and before separation are community property, even when received after separation (*Marriage of House* (1975) 50 CA3d 578, 123 CR 451), and payments for services rendered before marriage are separate property, even when received during marriage (*Thomasset v Thomasset* (1953) 122 CA2d 116, 123, 264 P2d 626, disapproved on other grounds in *See v See* (1966) 64 C2d 778, 786, 51 CR 888).

2. Method of Acquisition

§5.14   a. Gift or Inheritance

Property acquired by a spouse by gift or inheritance is separate property, regardless of when it is acquired. Fam C §770. In approaching characterization issues involving such transfers, the attorney should be aware that superficial appearances are not always controlling. See, *e.g., Downer v Bramet* (1984) 152 CA3d 837, 843, 199 CR 830 (although deed of interest in ranch by employer to husband was without obligation and therefore a gift, it was community property to extent it was remuneratory in recognition of services rendered between marriage and separation).

Either spouse can, by making a gift to the other, convert his or her separate property or interest in community property into the other spouse's separate property. An interspousal gift made on or after January 1, 1985, may be deemed a transmutation of property if a writing sufficient to satisfy Fam C §852 accompanies the gift. See §5.28. For interspousal gifts made on or after January 1, 1985, that are not deemed to constitute transmutations because they are insubstantial in value in light of the marriage circumstances and are primarily intended for the recipient's use (Fam C §852(c)), and for all such gifts made before 1985, a writing is not required.

NOTE➤ A valid transmutation under Fam C §852(a) and *Estate of MacDonald* (1990) 51 C3d 262, 272 CR 153 requires a writing in which the adversely affected spouse expresses a clear understanding that the document changes the character or ownership of specific property. Thus, for example, merely signing a consent form to change an Individual Retirement Account beneficiary without an express declaration that there is a change in character or ownership is insufficient for a transmutation.

51 C3d at 273. Further, partial performance of an oral agreement to transmute will not suffice, and common-law quasi-contractual concepts do not apply. *Marriage of Benson* (2005) 36 C4th 1096, 1107, 32 CR3d 471.

To establish a gift, there must be not only delivery and acceptance, but also an intention by the donor to make an unconditional gift. The alleged donee bears the burden of establishing that a gift was intended. *Marriage of Frick* (1986) 181 CA3d 997, 1015, 226 CR 766. In some instances, however, there is a presumption of a gift, which shifts the burden of proof to the alleged donor. When, for example, one spouse uses separate or community funds to purchase property in the name of the other spouse alone, the common-law presumption from the form of title applies, and the alleged donor may rebut the presumption that the property is the other spouse's separate property only by evidence of a contrary agreement or understanding. *Marriage of Frapwell* (1975) 49 CA3d 597, 601, 122 CR 718; see §5.19. For the exception to the writing requirement in the case of gifts of items of a personal nature (Fam C §852(c)), see §5.28.

b. Rents, Issues, and Profits

§5.15   (1) General Rule

"Rents, issues, and profits" (see Fam C §770) generally take on the character of the assets from which they derive. Thus, rents, issues, and profits from community property are generally community property, and those from separate property are generally separate property. Fam C §770; *Boyd v Oser* (1944) 23 C2d 613, 621, 145 P2d 312. Examples of property that generally takes on the character of the property from which it is derived include business profits, income from investments (*e.g.*, stock dividends), and proceeds from the sale of property. See *Beam v Bank of America* (1971) 6 C3d 12, 17, 98 CR 137; *Hicks v Hicks* (1962) 211 CA2d 144, 152, 27 CR 307.

(2) Exception: Spouse's Efforts Devoted to Property

§5.16   (a) Before Separation

Because income arising from a spouse's skill and efforts between marriage and separation is community property, the community should receive a fair share of the economic benefit that derives from a spouse's significant devotion of time and effort during that period to the handling of his or her separate property, *e.g.*, businesses, real estate, stocks. In such cases, the court must apportion the total economic benefit between community property and separate property. *Beam v Bank of America* (1971) 6 C3d 12, 17, 98 CR 137. Unless such efforts are deemed a gift, the same rule should apply when one spouse's time and effort are devoted to the *other* spouse's separate property.

California courts have developed two basic approaches to apportioning separate property's profits or increased value when time and effort have been devoted to the separate property between marriage and separation. The "*Pereira* approach" allocates to separate property a fair return on its investment and allocates the balance of the profits or increased value to community property as arising from the spouse's efforts. *Beam v Bank of America* (1971) 6 C3d 12, 18, 98 CR 137; *Pereira v Pereira* (1909) 156 C 1, 7, 103 P 488. The "*Van Camp* approach" allocates the reasonable value of the spouse's efforts to community property and allocates the balance of the profits or increased value to separate property as attributable to the normal earnings of the separate property investment. *Beam v Bank of America, supra*; *Van Camp v Van Camp* (1921) 53 CA 17, 29, 199 P 885.

In *Beam,* the supreme court went on to state that after a court determines the community income, whether through the *Pereira* or the *Van Camp* approach, it deducts the community's living expenses from that income to determine the balance of the community property interest. *Beam v Bank of America* (1971) 6 C3d 12, 21, 98 CR 137. But see *Marriage of Frick* (1986) 181 CA3d 997, 1018, 226 CR 766 (reversal of trial court's deduction of community expenses from community income in applying *Pereira* approach).

The court is free to choose the approach that is most appropriate and equitable in a particular situation, depending on whether the separate property investment or the community property efforts of the spouse are the chief contributing factor in producing the profits or increased value. *Beam v Bank of America* (1971) 6 C3d 12, 18, 98 CR 137. Thus, the approach to be applied should be the one that produces the better result for the party who prevails on the issue of the chief contributing factor. Consequently, an attorney faced with a *Pereira/Van Camp* issue should (1) prepare to argue that the investment was the chief contributing factor if the client is the one with the separate property interest and, if not, that the efforts were the chief factor and (2) ascertain whether *Pereira* or *Van Camp* will produce the better result for the client. For a helpful discussion of the *Pereira/Van Camp* approach generally, see *Marriage of Dekker* (1993) 17 CA4th 842, 21 CR2d 642.

The court is not bound to adopt any particular percentage as the fair return on the investment in applying the *Pereira* approach or to adopt the spouse's fixed salary as the reasonable value of his or her efforts in applying the *Van Camp* approach. *Beam v Bank of America, supra.* But, lacking any evidence to support a more realistic figure, the court will adopt the legal rate of interest as the fair return on the investment in applying *Pereira. Weinberg v Weinberg* (1967) 67 C2d 557, 565, 63 CR 13. Thus, counsel must also be prepared to argue for a percentage return or for a value for the spouse's efforts, or both, that will serve the client's interests.

When the separate property's profits or increased value is attributable entirely or almost entirely to the return on the investment, and not in any significant degree to the efforts of either spouse, the property remains separate property, and no allocation between separate property and community property need be made. *Estate of Ney* (1963) 212 CA2d 891, 895, 28 CR 442. Conversely, when personal efforts are entirely or almost entirely responsible and the contribution of the investment is negligible, the property is entirely community property, and no allocation need be made. *Austin v Austin* (1961) 190 CA2d 45, 51, 11 CR 593.

§5.17   (b) After Separation

Because income arising from a spouse's skill and efforts after separation is separate property (Fam C §771(a)), the spouse should receive a fair share of the economic benefit that derives from his or her significant devotion of time and effort during that period to the handling of community property. This situation is, of course, the reverse of that found in *Pereira/Van Camp* (see §5.16) and, consequently, the appropriate apportionment formula will be applied in reverse. The *Pereira* approach allocates a fair return to the community property and the balance of the profits or increased value to the spouse's separate property. The *Van Camp* approach allocates the reasonable value of the spouse's services to his or her separate property and the balance of the profits or increased value to the community property. *Marriage of Imperato* (1975) 45 CA3d 432, 438, 119 CR 590.

When the community property's profits or increased value after separation is not due in any significant degree to the efforts of either spouse, it is entirely community property, and no allocation between separate property and community property need be made. See *Marriage of Shelton* (1981) 118 CA3d 811, 815, 173 CR 629, 631.

§5.18 c. Loan or Extension of Credit

The character of property acquired by loan or extension of credit is determined according to the intent of the lender or seller to rely, for satisfaction of the obligation, on community property (*e.g.,* earnings of the spouses) or separate property (*e.g.,* real property owned by one spouse and pledged as security). *Gudelj v Gudelj* (1953) 41 C2d 202, 210, 259 P2d 656. Consequently, proceeds of an unsecured loan obtained during marriage and before separation are usually community property because the lender is usually deemed to have been relying for payment on the spouses' earnings, which are community property. See *Bank of Cal. v Connolly* (1973) 36 CA3d 350, 375, 111 CR 468. Proceeds, on the other hand, of a loan obtained during marriage and before separation and secured by a deed of trust are usually characterized in accordance with the character of the hypothecated property because the lender is usually deemed to have relied for payment on the security. Thus, loans secured by a spouse's separate property are usually that spouse's separate property (see, *e.g., Marriage of Neal* (1984) 153 CA3d 117, 125, 200 CR 341, disapproved on other grounds in 39 C3d at 763 n10), and loans secured by community property, *e.g.,* by the purchased property itself, are usually community property (see, *e.g., Bank of Cal. v Connolly, supra*). But these are only general rules, and counsel must be prepared to evaluate and litigate each case on the basis of its particular facts. See, *e.g., Bank of Cal. v Connolly, supra* (loan proceeds were community property, despite separate property security, when loan officer testified that bank relied primarily on borrowers' general credit and not on additional security of hypothecated property).

It is unclear whether a spouse asserting a separate property interest based on the lender's intent to rely on the spouse's separate property security for payment must show that the lender intended to rely solely on the security (*Marriage of Grinius* (1985) 166 CA3d 1179, 1187, 212 CR 803) or whether it is sufficient to show that the lender intended to rely primarily on the security (*Gudelj v Gudelj, supra*).

Without evidence of the lender's intent to rely on separate property, loan proceeds acquired during marriage and before separation will be community property, in accordance with the general presumption of Fam C §760 (see §5.11). *Marriage of Aufmuth* (1979) 89 CA3d 446, 455, 152 CR 668, disapproved on other grounds in 27 C3d at 815.

Loan proceeds acquired during marriage but after separation will be the separate property of the borrowing spouse if the transaction is unrelated to community property. *Marriage of Stephenson* (1984) 162 CA3d 1057, 1085, 209 CR 383.

3. Title

§5.19   a. "Common Law" Presumption From Form of Title

The form in which title is taken creates a presumption that title is held as shown in the instrument. *Marriage of Lucas* (1980) 27 C3d 808, 166 CR 853. This presumption is a "common law" presumption, unlike the general community property presumption (see §5.11) and the presumptions regarding property acquired (1) in joint form during marriage (see §5.20), (2) as "husband and wife" (see §5.21), and (3) by a married woman by a written instrument before 1975 (see §5.22), all of which are statutory. The common law presumption may be rebutted only by evidence of a contrary agreement or understanding, not by tracing the funds used to purchase the property or by evidence of a party's undisclosed intention at the time of execution. *Marriage of Lucas, supra*. Under Evid C §662, the party seeking to rebut the presumption carries the burden of proving his or her claim by "clear and convincing" evidence. *Marriage of Weaver* (1990) 224 CA3d 478, 486, 273 CR 696.

When, however, Evid C §662 conflicts with the presumption of undue influence, under Fam C §721(b), that arises when an interspousal transfer favors one spouse, Evid C §662 cannot be applied. *Marriage of Delaney* (2003) 111 CA4th 991, 4 CR3d 378; *Marriage of Haines* (1995) 33 CA4th 277, 39 CR2d 673. The burden of rebutting the presumption of undue influence is on the spouse who acquired an advantage or benefit from the transaction. *Marriage of Delaney,* at 297. *Marriage of Balcof* (2006) 141 CA4th 1509, 1520, 47 CR3d 183 (presumption not rebutted regarding writing transferring husband's community assets to wife, when tainted by undue influence—after threat of divorce and of obstructing his relationship with children, and other extreme conduct). For example, when a couple agreed that a wife would sign a quitclaim deed in order to obtain a lower interest rate on their mortgage and the evidence showed that she acknowledged that title to the residence would be taken in the husband's name alone, an appellate court found that the husband had rebutted the presumption of undue influence by a preponderance of the evidence. *Marriage of Mathews* (2005) 133 CA4th 624, 632, 35 CR3d 1.

Property in joint title. When property is acquired by married persons in joint tenancy form on or after January 1, 1984, or in any joint form (*e.g.,* tenancy in common, joint tenancy, community property) on or after January 1, 1987, the common law presumption is supplanted, for purposes of property division, by the community property presumption of Fam C §2581 (see §5.20), which may be rebutted only by a writing. On retroactive application of Fam C §2581 to property acquired before the dates stated above, see §5.20. When the community property presumption applies and cannot be rebutted, a spouse who made separate property contributions to acquire the jointly held property may nevertheless be entitled to reimbursement. Fam C §2640. See *Marriage of Weaver* (2005) 127 CA4th 858, 865, 26 CR3d 121. See also §5.95.

With respect to an account held by spouses in joint form with a financial institution, the common law presumption is supplanted, at least in some proceedings, by the community property presumption of Prob C §5305. This presumption may be rebutted by (1) a written agreement that the funds were not to be community property or (2) tracing to a separate property source (unless the spouses agreed in writing that the funds were to be community property). It is not entirely clear, however, to what extent this presumption applies in marital actions.

Property in sole title. It should be noted that the common-law presumption applies not only when title is acquired in joint form, but also when it is acquired in the name of one spouse alone (see, *e.g., Marriage of Broderick* (1989) 209 CA3d 489, 496, 257 CR 397), and it continues to be significant in the latter case no matter when the property is acquired because Fam C §2581 (and Prob C §5305) applies only when title is acquired in joint form. Further, when one spouse obtains sole title to property as part of a transaction involving the other spouse's execution of a quitclaim deed to the property, a presumption of undue influence arises regarding the advantaged spouse that he or she must rebut. See *Marriage of Mathews* (2005) 133 CA4th 624, 632, 35 CR3d 1.

§5.20   b. Property Acquired in Joint Form During Marriage

General community presumption. For purposes of property division on dissolution or legal separation, any property acquired by the parties in joint form during marriage including tenancy in common, joint tenancy, community property, or tenancy by the entirety (the latter being available in some states, but not in California) is presumed to be community property. Fam C §2581. The presumption may be rebutted only by (1) a clear statement in the deed or other documentary evidence of title by which the property is acquired that the property is separate property or (2) proof of a written agreement between the parties that the property is separate property. Fam C §2581; see *Marriage of Neal* (1984) 153 CA3d 117, 124, 200 CR 341, disapproved on other grounds in 39 C3d at 763 n10. Not every such writing will be sufficient to overcome the presumption. *Marriage of Cairo* (1988) 204 CA3d 1255, 1261, 251 CR 731 (quitclaim deed resulting from fraudulent misrepresentations not effective to rebut presumption). When the community property presumption is rebutted, the property is separate property, subject to any applicable community property interest under *Marriage of Lucas* (1980) 27 C3d 808, 816, 166 CR 853 (see §5.26). When the community property presumption cannot be rebutted, a spouse who made separate property contributions to the acquisition of the property may nevertheless be entitled to reimbursement. Fam C §2640. See *Marriage of Walrath* (1998) 17 C4th 907, 918, 72 CR2d 856 (discussed in §5.95); *Marriage of Weaver* (2005) 127 CA4th 858, 26 CR3d 121.

Multiple-party accounts. Under Prob C §5305, the community property presumption of Fam C §2581 is made expressly inapplicable to an account held in joint form by spouses with a financial institution. Although the account is presumed to be community property, the presumption may be rebutted not only by a written agreement that the funds were not to be community property, but also by tracing to a separate property source (unless the spouses agreed in writing that the funds were to be community property). Prob C §5305. It is not entirely clear, however, to what extent the presumption of §5305 applies in marital actions.

Determining when property is "acquired." Property owned as separate property before marriage is "acquired" for purposes of Fam C §2581 when title is transferred to joint form during marriage, even when the transfer is required by a lender refinancing the property. *Marriage of Neal, supra*. When the community property presumption is rebutted, the property remains separate property, subject to any applicable community property interest under *Marriage of Moore* (1980) 28 C3d 366, 371, 168 CR 662 (see §5.25). On reimbursement when the community property presumption cannot be rebutted, see §5.95.

Property owned as separate property before marriage and that is transmuted to joint title during the marriage is subject not only to the community property presumption of Fam C §2581 but also to the fiduciary duty provisions of Fam C §721. See *Marriage of Delaney* (2003) 111 CA4th 991, 4 CR3d 378. When evidence is offered that one spouse has been disadvantaged by the other in any interspousal property transaction, under the rationale of *Marriage of Haines* (1995) 33 CA4th 277, 39 CR2d 673, the Evid C §662 presumption from form of title (see §5.19) cannot be applied. *Marriage of Delaney* (2003) 111 CA4th 991, 997, 4 CR3d 378. Thus, if the spouse who had owned the property before marriage alleges undue influence, the burden shifts to the spouse who was put on title to establish that the transfer was freely and voluntarily made with full knowledge of the transaction's effect on the separate property. 111 CA4th at 1000. *Marriage of Balcof* (2006) 141 CA4th 1509, 1520, 47 CR3d 183; *Marriage of Mathews* (2005) 133 CA4th 624, 632, 35 CR3d 1.

Retroactivity issues. There has been an ongoing controversy over retroactive application of former CC §4800.1, predecessor of Fam C §2581. The law in effect before the enactment of former CC §4800.1 also established a presumption that property acquired in joint form during marriage is community property, but the presumption could be overcome by proof of an agreement or understanding to the contrary, and the proof was not required to be written. *Marriage* *of Lucas* (1980) 27 C3d 808, 815, 166 CR 853. In *Marriage of Buol* (1985) 39 C3d 751, 754, 218 CR 31, the California Supreme Court held that former CC §4800.1 could not constitutionally be applied to cases pending before its effective date to require a writing to rebut the community property presumption. Subsequently, in *Marriage of Hilke* (1992) 4 C4th 215, 14 CR2d 371, the supreme court upheld retroactive application of former CC §4800.1 in a case in which the interest impaired, a joint tenancy survivorship interest, was an expectancy interest, not a present vested one. Absent a vested interest, the court noted, retroactive legislation does not violate due process. See also *Marriage of Heikes* (1995) 10 C4th 1211, 44 CR2d 155 (supreme court held that former CC §4800.2, companion provision of former CC §4800.1, cannot be applied to property acquired before its effective date); *Marriage of Griffis* (1986) 187 CA3d 156, 231 CR 510 (court of appeal held that former CC §4800.1 cannot be applied to property acquired before its effective date).

Former joint tenancy-community property presumption. It should be noted that the initial version of former CC §4800.1, which became effective January 1, 1984, applied only to property acquired "in joint tenancy form." The subsequent version, which applies to all property acquired "in joint form" and is carried forward in Fam C §2581, became effective January 1, 1987. Thus, to the extent that Fam C §2581 cannot be applied to property acquired before January 1, 1984, to require a writing to rebut the presumption that property taken during marriage in joint tenancy form is community property, it probably cannot be applied to property acquired before January 1, 1987, that is taken during marriage in any joint form other than joint tenancy.

Effect of party's death. As a general rule, the death of one of the spouses abates a cause of action for dissolution, but does not deprive the court of jurisdiction it has retained to determine collateral property rights if the court has previously rendered a judgment dissolving the marriage. *Marriage of Hilke* (1992) 4 C4th 215, 220, 14 CR2d 371. Accordingly, Fam C §2581 presumptively applies to the division of property held by the parties in joint form if a former spouse dies after entry of a bifurcated judgment dissolving the parties' marital status and reserving property issues for later adjudication. See *Marriage of Hilke* (1992) 4 C4th 215, 221, 14 CR2d 371; *Marriage of Allen* (1992) 8 CA4th 1225, 10 CR2d 916. However, under the nonprobate transfer rules, a joint tenancy in property will be severed if, at the time of the transferor's death, the former spouse is not the surviving spouse as a result of a dissolution. Prob C §5601(a). Therefore, it appears that a party's death after a judgment that dissolves a marriage and reserves property issues for later adjudication would sever a joint tenancy between the parties and preclude the application of §2581—but this result would not necessarily follow with respect to property held in *other* joint forms. See Fam C §2581, Prob C §5601(a).

PRACTICE TIP➤ This possibly undesirable result can be avoided if the parties stipulate to, or the nonmoving spouse can obtain, an order before bifurcating the issue of marital status providing that the joint tenancy is not intended to be severed pending a judgment on reserved issues. See Prob C §§5600(b)(3), 5601(b)(2).

In contrast, when a spouse dies during the pendency of a dissolution action but before a judgment of dissolution is entered, Fam C §2581 does not apply, and the property will pass, by operation of law, to the survivor. *Marriage of Hilke, supra*; *Estate of Blair* (1988) 199 CA3d 161, 166, 244 CR 627. See Fam C §2040(c) (warning required on summons form).

§5.21   c. Property Acquired as "Husband and Wife"

Property acquired by spouses by an instrument in which they are described as husband and wife is presumed to be community property unless a different intention is expressed in the instrument. Fam C §803(c). This presumption overrides the presumption that property acquired by a married woman by a written instrument before 1975 is her separate property (see §5.22). Fam C §803. Because it is a presumption from the form of title (see §5.19), the husband-and-wife presumption may be overcome only by evidence of a written or oral agreement to the contrary; tracing to a separate property source is not sufficient. *Marriage of Fabian* (1986) 41 C3d 440, 446, 224 CR 333; *Marriage of Cademartori* (1981) 119 CA3d 970, 174 CR 292. The agreement must be established by a preponderance of the evidence. *Marriage of Fabian, supra*.

When property is acquired by married persons in joint tenancy form on or after January 1, 1984, or in any joint form (*e.g.*, tenancy in common, joint tenancy, community property) on or after January

1, 1987, any presumption otherwise created by description of the acquiring parties as husband and wife is supplanted, for purposes of property division, by the community property presumption of Fam C §2581 (see §5.20), which may be rebutted only by a writing. On retroactive application of Fam C §2581 to property acquired before the dates stated above, see §5.20. When the community property presumption of Fam C §2581 applies and cannot be rebutted, a spouse who made separate property contributions to acquire the property may nevertheless be entitled to reimbursement. *Marriage of Walrath* (1998) 17 C4th 907, 913, 72 CR2d 856; *Marriage of Weaver* (2005) 127 CA4th 858, 865, 26 CR3d 121; Fam C §2640. See §5.95. To the extent that Fam C §2581 cannot be applied retroactively, the husband-and-wife presumption of Fam C §803(c) still applies. See *Marriage of Cairo* (1988) 204 CA3d 1255, 1260, 251 CR 731.

On community property with right of survivorship, see §5.8A.

§5.22   d. Property Acquired by Married Woman by Written Instrument Before 1975

Property acquired by a married woman by a written instrument before 1975 is presumed to be her separate property unless a different intention is expressed in the instrument. Fam C §803. When the separate property presumption in favor of a married woman is raised, the general community property presumption of Fam C §760 (see §5.11) does not apply. *Marriage of Ashodian* (1979) 96 CA3d 43, 48, 157 CR 555. This separate property presumption is superseded, however, by the presumption that property acquired by spouses by an instrument in which they are described as husband and wife is community property unless a different intention is expressed in the instrument (see §5.21). Fam C §803(c).

The separate property presumption in favor of a married woman requires clear and convincing evidence for rebuttal. 96 CA3d at 47. Unlike the common-law presumption (see §5.19) and the husband-and-wife presumption (see §5.21), it does not require evidence of a written or oral agreement for rebuttal. When the husband is ignorant of the form of title and does not consent to it, it is sufficient to trace the purchase to community funds. *Marriage of Rives* (1982) 130 CA3d 138, 162, 181 CR 572. When the husband consents to the form of title, however, an additional presumption arises that he intended a gift to the wife, requiring rebuttal of that presumption in addition to tracing to community funds. The husband's testimony that he did not intend a gift has been held sufficient for this purpose. 130 CA3d at 162.

4. Source of Funds

§5.23   a. Commingling and Tracing

"Commingling" refers to the mixing of community property funds and separate property funds. It commonly occurs when one spouse deposits his or her separate funds in a bank account in which community funds have been or are later deposited. When commingled funds are the source of an acquisition, a question may arise regarding whether the separate and community contributions can be traced and identified. Tracing cannot overcome a presumption arising from the form of title (see §5.19), but it can overcome the general presumption in Fam C §760 that property acquired during marriage is community property (see §5.11). *Marriage of Lucas* (1980) 27 C3d 808, 814, 166 CR 853. Consequently, the importance of commingling and tracing in characterizing property acquired with commingled funds is limited to situations in which there is no written indication of ownership interests as between the spouses with respect to the property acquired. 27 C3d at 815. Tracing might, for example, enable a spouse to overcome the general community property presumption and show that furniture purchased during the marriage is wholly or partially separate property. But if separate and community funds are commingled in such a manner that it is impossible to trace the source of the acquisition, the acquisition will be deemed to be entirely community property. *Marriage of Mix* (1975) 14 C3d 604, 611, 122 CR 79.

Two methods by which commingled funds used to acquire property might be traced to a separate property source are set forth in *Mix* (14 C3d at 612). The first method involves direct tracing, which requires that (1) the amount of separate funds on deposit be ascertainable, (2) the separate funds continue to be on deposit when a withdrawal is made for the purpose of purchasing the specific property in dispute, and (3) the drawer's intention be to withdraw the separate funds. The second method involves a consideration of family expenses and is based on the presumption that family expenses are paid from community funds. If it can be shown that, at the time of the acquisition of the property in dispute, all community income in the commingled account has been exhausted by family expenses, the remaining funds are necessarily separate funds.

Whether the direct tracing method or the family expense method is used, it is necessary to show that the particular requirements were met *at each specific time* that an item of property was acquired or a payment was made. Thus, with the direct tracing method, it must be shown that, *at the time of each acquisition or payment,* sufficient separate funds were available in the particular account from which payment was made to cover the payment and that the drawer's intent was to use separate funds. *Marriage of Higinbotham* (1988) 203 CA3d 322, 329, 249 CR 798. Making this showing will require records establishing, respectively, each item of community and separate income deposited into the account and each community and separate payment made from the account. It will not be sufficient to merely show that the difference between the total of separate deposits and the total of separate withdrawals over the entire relevant period was sufficient to cover the acquisitions or payments at issue. Likewise, with the family expense method, the records must establish that community income in the account had been exhausted by family expenses *at the time of each particular acquisition or payment. See v See* (1966) 64 C2d 778, 784, 51 CR 888. This proof will also require records establishing each item of community and separate income deposited and each community and separate withdrawal made.

Tracing may also be important in establishing entitlement to reimbursement, under Fam C §2640, for separate property contributions to the acquisition of community property (see §5.95), for separate property contributions to the acquisition of property of the other spouse's separate property (see §5.95A), or in characterizing, under Prob C §5305, an account held in joint form by spouses with a financial institution.

§5.24   b. Payments on Separate Property From Community Funds

When community funds are used to make mortgage payments on separate property, it has long been the law that the community acquires an interest in the property by virtue of the principal payments. See, *e.g., Marriage of Moore* (1980) 28 C3d 366, 371, 168 CR 662 (property acquired before marriage); *Marriage of Broderick*

(1989) 209 CA3d 489, 503, 257 CR 397 (property acquired during marriage). See also §§5.25–5.26.

The effect of using community funds to pay for improvements to separate property has been unclear, however, regarding both the community's right to reimbursement (*Marriage of Camire* (1980) 105 CA3d 859, 866, 164 CR 667) and the extent of any interest the community acquired in the property. See *Marriage of Wolfe* (2001) 91 CA4th 962, 966, 110 CR2d 921 (court allowed reimbursement of dollars invested but did not address whether community had right to pro tanto interest in separate property's enhanced value). In *Marriage of Allen* (2002) 96 CA4th 497, 116 CR2d 887, the court held that there is no presumption of a gift when a spouse consents to the use of community funds to make capital improvements to the other spouse's separate property, reasoning that *Marriage of Camire, supra,* predated the *Moore-Marsden* rule. In *Bono v Clark* (2002) 103 CA4th 1409, 128 CR2d 31, a probate matter that followed an unconcluded marital dissolution, the court agreed with *Allen* and held that if the improvements contributed to an increase in the separate property's value as measured by a formula set out in the case, then the community is entitled to a pro tanto interest in the separate property. If the improvements did not increase the separate property's value, then the community is entitled to reimbursement for its expenditures toward the improvements. 103 CA4th at 1425. A spouse who uses separate property to improve the other spouse's separate property cannot seek relief by requesting that the community be reimbursed for his or her contributions. See *Marriage of Cross* (2001) 94 CA4th 1143, 114 CR2d 839.

§5.25 (1) Property Acquired Before Marriage

It is not uncommon for community funds to be used for mortgage payments on property purchased by one or both of the spouses before marriage. When this occurs, the community acquires a pro tanto interest in the ratio that the payments on the purchase price made with community funds bear to the total payments on the purchase price, and any appreciation must be apportioned accordingly. *Marriage of Moore* (1980) 28 C3d 366, 371, 373, 168 CR 662, 664. In calculating the respective separate and community interests, amounts paid for interest, taxes, and insurance are excluded because they do not increase the owner's equity in the property. 28 C3d at 373. In addressing the respective contributions of the separate and community property to the purchase price, the value of the loan taken to purchase the property must be recognized. The proceeds will be treated as a separate property contribution when the loan is based on separate assets and treated as a community property contribution when the loan is based on community assets. 28 C3d at 373.

The proper approach to apportioning between separate and community interests when one party purchases property, by making a down payment and securing a loan, before marriage and the community makes payments on the loan during marriage, is set forth in *Marriage of Marsden* (1982) 130 CA3d 426, 181 CR 910. In *Marsden,* the husband purchased a leasehold and house before marriage for $38,300. He made down payments of $8300 and secured a loan for the remaining $30,000. By the time of the marriage, the husband had reduced the principal due on the loan by $7000. The trial court found the fair market value of the house and leasehold interest at the time of the marriage to be $65,000. Thus, the appreciation before marriage was $26,700 ($65,000 minus $38,300). Between the date of marriage and the date of separation, payments from community funds further reduced the principal due on the loan by $9200. Between the date of separation and the time of trial, the husband reduced the principal due by an additional $655. The trial court found the fair market value at the time of trial to be $182,500. Thus, the appreciation during marriage was $117,500 ($182,500 minus $65,000). 130 CA3d at 436, 181 CR at 915. The balance on the loan at the time of trial was $13,145. 130 CA3d at 440.

The *Marsden* court (130 CA3d at 439) determined the community property interest to be 24.02 percent, *i.e.,* the ratio that the payments on the purchase price made with community funds ($9200) bore to the total payments on the purchase price ($38,300). Note that the loan proceeds, to the extent that they have not been offset by community loan payments, are recognized as a separate property contribution toward the purchase price. The separate property interest was the remaining 75.98 percent, *i.e.,* the ratio that the payments on the purchase price made with separate funds ($8300 down payments, plus $30,000 loan proceeds less $9200 community payments, equals $29,100) bore to the total payments on the purchase price. The separate property was credited with:

Down payments	$8,300.00
Loan payments	
Before marriage	7,000.00
During marriage	655.00
100% of appreciation before marriage	26,700.00
75.98% of appreciation during marriage	+89,276.50
	$131,931.50

The community property was credited with:

Loan payments	$9,200.00
24.02% of appreciation during marriage	+28,223.50
	$37,423.50

The separate property interest of $131,931.50 was confirmed to the husband and, in addition, he was awarded half of the community interest of $37,423.50, or $18,711.75, for a total of $150,643.25. The wife was awarded half of the community interest, or $18,711.75. The husband was assigned the balance due on the loan. Thus:

Husband's share of equity	$150,643.25
Wife's share of equity	18,711.75
Loan balance	0 + 13,145.00
Fair market value	$182,500.00

The following is a worksheet that might be used to make the *Marsden* calculations in other *Moore/Marsden* situations:

1. Enter purchase price. _____

2. Enter amount of down payment. _____

3. Enter amount of payments on loan principal made with separate funds. _____

4. Enter fair market value at date of marriage.   _____

5. Enter amount of payments on loan principal   _____
   made with community funds.

6. Enter fair market value at time of division.   _____

7. Subtract line 1 from line 4.   _____

8. Subtract line 4 from line 6.   _____

9. Divide line 5 by line 1.   _____

10. Multiply line 8 by line 9.   _____

11. Subtract line 10 from line 8.   _____

12. Add lines 2, 3, 7, and 11. This is the separate   _____
    property interest.

13. Add lines 5 and 10. This is the community   _____
    property interest.

When both parties have made separate property contributions to the purchase price of the property, each party acquires a separate property interest to be ascertained by making the *Marsden* calculations. *Marriage of Rico* (1992) 10 CA4th 706, 12 CR2d 659. Following the principle set forth in Fam C §2552, requiring the court to value assets and liabilities as near as practicable to the time of trial, the proper valuation date for a community property residence for purposes of a dissolution proceeding is the date of trial unless there is some reason that renders this result inequitable. *Marriage of Sherman* (2005) 133 CA4th 795, 800, 35 CR3d 137.

In one case, the *Moore/Marsden* approach was applied when a community property home was converted by a quitclaim deed during the marriage to the husband's separate property, and community funds were thereafter used to make loan payments. *Marriage of Broderick* (1989) 209 CA3d 489, 501, 257 CR 397. The only community contributions to be included in determining the community interest in the home, however, were those made after the execution of the quitclaim deed. 209 CA3d at 503.

Although it is usually applied to family residences, the approach set forth here is equally applicable to other real property. See, *e.g.,* *Marriage of Frick* (1986) 181 CA3d 997, 1007, 226 CR 766 (real property used to operate hotel and restaurant).

Likewise, although it is usually applied to the use of community funds to make payments on one spouse's preexisting loan, this approach is equally applicable to the use of proceeds from a community loan to pay off the preexisting separate loan. *Marriage of Branco* (1996) 47 CA4th 1621, 1627, 55 CR2d 493.

Marriage of Moore, supra, although it did not expressly consider the issue, appears to foreclose the spouse who owns the separate property from seeking to avoid the community interest by arguing that the community payments were a gift to him or her. One court allowed such an argument, however, and held, on that basis, that a residence was entirely separate property despite community payments on two mortgages. *Marriage of Stoner* (1983) 147 CA3d 858, 864, 195 CR 351. But in another case, although noting that the conflict has never been directly addressed in any California published decision, the court concluded that *Moore* is binding precedent, which provides the community with a proportional interest even when the payment of community funds was made with the knowledge and apparent consent of the spouse asserting the community interest. *Marriage of Gowdy* (1986) 178 CA3d 1228, 1230, 1234, 224 CR 400.

It is interesting to note the distinction between community funds applied to separate property and separate funds applied to community property or the other spouse's separate property estate. In the former situation, the rule is of judicial origin (*Marriage of Moore, supra*) and apportionment is the remedy. In the latter situations, the rule is statutory (Fam C §2640; see §5.95 and §5.95A) and reimbursement is the remedy.

On use of community funds to make improvements to separate property, see §5.24.

§5.26   (2) Property Acquired During Marriage

In most instances, property acquired during marriage is community property, usually because it is acquired in joint form and the resulting presumption of community property status cannot be rebutted (see §5.20). In some instances, however, property acquired during marriage will be separate property (*e.g.,* title acquired in joint form but community property presumption rebutted, title acquired in name of one spouse alone and resulting separate property presumption not rebutted (see §5.19)).

When separate property is acquired during marriage with a down payment from separate funds and a loan based on community assets, apportionment of separate and community interests in the property is required. The separate property acquires an interest in the ratio that the down payment bears to the purchase price, the community property acquires an interest in the ratio that the community loan bears to the purchase price, and any appreciation must be apportioned accordingly. *Marriage of Lucas* (1980) 27 C3d 808, 816, 166 CR 853. The calculations are illustrated in *Lucas* (27 C3d at 816 n3):

Assume that property is purchased for $100,000, with one spouse paying the entire down payment of $20,000 from separate funds and the remaining $80,000 coming from a loan based on community credit. The result is a separate property interest of 20 percent (the ratio of the down payment to the purchase price) and a community property interest of 80 percent (the ratio of the loan to the purchase price). At the time of trial, the fair market value is $175,000 (thus the appreciation is $75,000) and the community has reduced the loan by $2000. The separate property's share of the equity is:

Down payment	$20,000
20% of appreciation	+ 15,000
	$ 35,000

The community property's share of the equity is:

80% of appreciation	$60,000
Loan payments	+ 2,000
	$62,000

5. Agreements Between the Parties

§5.27   a. Before Marriage

The property rights of spouses prescribed by law in the event of a marital action may be altered by a premarital agreement. Fam C §§1500, 1612(a)(3). Such agreements are also called "antenuptial" or "prenuptial" agreements. Premarital agreements executed on or after January 1, 1986, are governed by the Uniform Premarital Agreement Act (Fam C §§1600–1617); those executed before that date are governed by prior law. Fam C §§1503, 1601.

Under the Uniform Premarital Agreement Act, a premarital agreement must be in writing and signed by both parties. Fam C §1611. Exceptions to the writing requirement under prior law (*e.g.,* performance constituting detrimental reliance on other party's promise) are equally applicable to the Act. *Hall v Hall* (1990) 222 CA3d 578, 587, 271 CR 773. The agreement is enforceable without consideration. Fam C §1611. It becomes effective on marriage and thereafter may be amended or revoked only by a written agreement signed by the parties. Fam C §§1613–1614. Possible defenses against enforcement specifically provided by the statute are involuntary execution, unconscionability, laches, and estoppel. Fam C §§1615, 1617.

A number of factors are relevant to the issue of whether the premarital agreement was entered into voluntarily. Family Code §1615(c) (as amended by Stats 2001, ch 286) overrules to a large extent *Bonds v Bonds* (2000) 24 C4th 1, 99 CR2d 252 (one party's lack of independent counsel is only one factor in determining whether premarital agreement was entered into voluntarily) by providing that a premarital agreement is *involuntary* unless, among other things, the party against whom the agreement is asserted:

- Was represented by independent legal counsel or, after being advised in writing to seek such counsel, in a separate writing expressly waived such representation;

- Had the opportunity to review the document for at least seven calendar days before it was signed; and

- If unrepresented, was fully informed in writing, in a language in which that party was proficient, of the terms and basic effects of the agreement and made written acknowledgment of the receipt of this information.

None of the writings can be executed under duress, fraud, or undue influence. Fam C §1615(c)(4).

Under prior law, which governs premarital agreements executed before January 1, 1986, such agreements were required to be in writing, and to be executed and acknowledged or proved in the same manner as a grant of land is required to be executed and acknowledged or proved. Former CC §5134. These requirements have sometimes been judicially construed, however, to uphold otherwise valid premarital agreements in cases in which technical compliance was lacking. See, *e.g., Marriage of Garrity & Bishton* (1986) 181 CA3d 675, 685, 226 CR 485 (oral agreement effective if executed by conduct after marriage); *Marriage of Cleveland* (1977) 76 CA3d 357, 360, 142 CR 783 (unacknowledged agreement effective when parties swore, one in deposition and the other in oral testimony, that agreement had been executed by them). Prior law also provided that the agreements were to be recorded in every county where real property affected by the agreement is located. Former CC §5135. However, this requirement was designed to protect third-party creditors without knowledge of the agreement and does not bar enforcement of an unrecorded agreement by one party against the other. *Estate of Cutting* (1916) 174 C 104, 109, 161 P 1137. Although, under prior law, premarital agreements were required to be supported by consideration, a promise of marriage subsequently performed will be deemed sufficient. *Estate of Womack* (1955) 137 CA2d 112, 115, 289 P2d 871. But when the consideration to one party was completely inadequate, that fact may tend to support an attempt to set aside the agreement on grounds of fraud. *Estate of Nelson* (1964) 224 CA2d 138, 142, 36 CR 352.

Public policy generally supports premarital agreements about property. Most such agreements by which the parties address property owned before the date of marriage and that acquired afterward are valid. *Marriage of Noghrey* (1985) 169 CA3d 326, 330, 215 CR 153. But, at least for agreements executed before January 1, 1986, premarital agreements that promote dissolution are unenforceable on public-policy grounds. *Marriage of Dawley* (1976) 17 C3d 342, 346, 131 CR 3. For examples of agreements held unenforceable because they were held to be promotive of dissolution, see *Marriage of Dajani* (1988) 204 CA3d 1387, 1389, 251 CR 871 (dowry payable to wife on dissolution); *Marriage of Noghrey* (1985) 169 CA3d 326, 331, 215 CR 153 (money and property provided for wife only on dissolution). In *Marriage of Bellio* (2003) 105 CA4th 630, 129 CR2d 556 (agreeing with *Marriage of Noghrey, supra,* and disagreeing with *Marriage of Dajani, supra*), the court stressed that the test is whether the payment provision threatens a marriage relationship that might otherwise endure. 105 CA4th at 633. In *Bellio*, a provision for a $100,000 payment to the wife in event of dissolution or her husband's death was found to make the marriage "economically feasible" for the wife and thus was "realistic planning that takes account of the possibility of dissolution." 105 CA4th at 635, quoting *Marriage of Dawley* (1976) 17 C3d 342, 358, 131 CR 3.

Public policy does not prohibit premarital spousal support waivers that are entered into voluntarily by intelligent, self-sufficient, well-educated people who have the advice of counsel. *Marriage of Pendleton & Fireman* (2000) 24 C4th 39, 99 CR2d 278 (waiver of spousal support in premarital agreement not per se unenforceable). According to Fam C §1612(c), such waivers are enforceable only when the party against whom enforcement is being sought was represented by independent counsel at the time of the waiver. The enforceability of a spousal support waiver may also depend on whether it is unconscionable at the time enforcement is sought. See Fam C §1612(c).

An otherwise unenforceable provision does not become enforceable simply because the party against whom enforcement is sought was represented by counsel when the agreement was made. Fam C §1612(c).

It is unclear whether agreements about property executed on or after January 1, 1986, and therefore subject to the Uniform Premarital Agreement Act, may be invalidated on the grounds that they promote dissolution. The Act specifically provides that premarital agreements may address six enumerated subjects (Fam C §1612(a)(1)-(6)), including the parties' respective rights in the property of either or both of them (Fam C §1612(a)(1)) and the disposition of property in the event of a marital action (Fam C §1612(a)(3)); the Act then provides, in a separate subsection, that such agreements may address "[a]ny other matter ... not in violation of public policy" (Fam C §1612(a)(7)). It is unclear whether the public-policy limitation applies only to "any other matter" (*e.g.*, spousal support, attorney fees) or to the six enumerated subjects as well.

For a comprehensive discussion of premarital agreements, including sample clauses and a complete sample agreement, see California Marital Settlement and Other Family Law Agreements, chap 17 (3d ed Cal CEB 2005).

§5.28 b. During Marriage

Postnuptial transmutations of property. The property rights of spouses prescribed by law in the event of a marital action may be altered by a marital agreement, *i.e.*, an agreement during marriage. Fam C §§850, 1500. Such agreements are also called "postnuptial" agreements and, because they may potentially transmute the form of property, *e.g.,* from community to separate, "transmutation" agreements. The term "transmutation" is also sometimes used, however, in reference to premarital agreements. See, *e.g., Marriage of Garrity & Bishton* (1986) 181 CA3d 675, 685, 226 CR 485.

Written express declaration required for transmutation. Marital agreements may transmute community property to separate property, separate property to community property, or separate property of one spouse to separate property of the other spouse. Fam C §850. Under Fam C §852, marital agreements executed on or after January 1, 1985, must be in writing. The writing must be an "express declaration" that is made, joined in, consented to, or accepted by the spouse whose interest in the property is adversely affected. Fam C §852(a). To be an "express declaration" for purposes of Fam C §852(a), the writing must contain language expressly stating that the characterization or ownership of the property is being changed. *Estate of MacDonald* (1990) 51 C3d 262, 272, 272 CR 153. The writing need not use the term "transmutation" or any other particular word or expression. 51 C3d at 273. But the transmutation must be established by the writing alone, without reliance on extrinsic evidence of an intent to transmute. 51 C3d at 273. See also *Marriage of Starkman* (2005) 129 CA4th 659, 664, 28 CR3d 639 (couple's transfer of property into revocable trust, with general assignment, and trust agreement having language indicating that transferred property was community unless identified as separate—which husband failed to do—was insufficient to constitute transmutation of husband's separate property to community); *Marriage of Campbell* (1999) 74 CA4th 1058, 1065, 88 CR2d 580 (no error for trial court to refuse to consider extrinsic evidence that property had been orally transmuted to community property); *Marriage of Barneson* (1999) 69 CA4th 583, 593, 81 CR2d 726 (no valid transmutation because documents transferring stock lacked specific language directing change in ownership or characterization of stock).

Transactions that are not transmutations. Family Code §852 does not apply to (1) gifts of tangible articles of a personal nature that are used principally by the recipient and are not substantial in light of the circumstances of the marriage (Fam C §852(c); on substantial value, see *Marriage of Steinberger* (2001) 91 CA4th 1449, 1465, 111 CR2d 521) or (2) property in which separate property and community property are commingled or otherwise combined

(Fam C §852(d)). When one spouse uses separate property to improve the other's separate property residence, a transmutation generally *has not* occurred, but the circumstances surrounding the transaction must be examined to determine if the requirements of Fam C §852 have been met. See *Marriage of Cross* (2001) 94 CA4th 1143, 114 CR2d 839, superseded by statute on another point. Further, the improvements are potentially subject to reimbursement on marital dissolution, as discussed in §5.94A. Fam C §2640(c). Likewise, §852 does not apply to marital agreements executed before January 1, 1985, which are governed by prior law. Fam C §852(e). Prior law permitted oral marital agreements and even implied agreements. *Marriage of Schoettgen* (1986) 183 CA3d 1, 9, 227 CR 758.

Note that a waiver of a right to a joint and survivor annuity or survivor's benefits under the federal Retirement Equity Act of 1984 (Pub L 98–397, 98 Stat 1426) is not a transmutation of the community property rights of the person executing the waiver. Fam C §853(b).

After a petition is filed to initiate a marital action, Fam C §852 no longer applies, and Fam C §2550 (parties may divide community estate by written agreement or by oral agreement in open court) governs. *Marriage of Maricle* (1990) 220 CA3d 55, 269 CR 204; see §5.71.

Unenforceable provisions. Marital agreements are unenforceable as being against public policy to the extent that they contain liquidated damages clauses that are invoked by a spouse's misconduct during the marriage. *Marriage of Mehren & Dargan* (2004) 118 CA4th 1167, 13 CR3d 522 (postmarital agreement whereby husband promised wife certain community property if he used illegal drugs is unenforceable because it violates public policy favoring no-fault divorce); *Diosdado v Diosdado* (2002) 97 CA4th 470, 118 CR2d 494 (one spouse's extramarital sexual relationship cannot result in damages claim by other spouse).

Premarital agreements contrasted. Neither Fam C §1615, enacted in response to *Bonds v Bonds* (2000) 24 C4th 1, 99 CR2d 252 (see §5.27) nor *Bonds* applies to marital agreements. *Marriage of Friedman* (2002) 100 CA4th 65, 122 CR2d 412.

In addition, unlike a premarital agreement (Fam C §1615(a)(2)(A)) or an agreement made in contemplation of dissolution (Fam C §§2104–2105), a postnuptial agreement is not subject to statutory disclosure requirements. *Marriage of Burkle* (2006) 139 CA4th 712, 746, 43 CR3d 181.

For a comprehensive discussion of marital agreements, including sample clauses and a complete sample agreement, see California Marital Settlement and Other Family Law Agreements, chap 18 (3d ed Cal CEB 2005).

6. Special Rules for Specific Types of Property

§5.29   a. Personal Injury Damages

General characterization rules. Characterization of money or other property received or to be received as personal injury damages depends on when the cause of action arose, and it is not affected by when the proceeds are received. When the cause of action arose during marriage and before separation, the proceeds are community property. Otherwise, they are the separate property of the injured spouse. Fam C §§781(a), 2603(a). See *Marriage of Klug* (2005) 130 CA4th 1389, 31 CR3d 327 (malpractice suit against attorney who represented both spouses and colluded with husband to transfer significant community funds to offshore accounts). Proceeds received by one spouse under a cause of action for personal injury against the other spouse are separate property, regardless of when the cause of action arose. Fam C §781(c).

Proceeds of an uninsured motorist claim constitute personal injury damages under Fam C §§781(a) and 2603(a). *Marriage of Jackson* (1989) 212 CA3d 479, 486, 260 CR 508 (addressing former CC §4800(b)(4), predecessor of Fam C §2603).

Division rules. Community property personal injury damages are subject to special rules with respect to division in marital actions. Equal division of personal injury damages may not be required even when they are community property. Fam C §2603(b). For discussion, see §5.74.

b. Employment-Related Assets

§5.30   (1) Retirement Benefits

As indicated in §5.13, retirement benefits (and other deferred compensation) are property that is "acquired," for purposes of characterization, over a period of time, rather than at a discrete time. To the extent, then, that the work done to earn them is performed between the date of marriage and the date of separation, the benefits are community property. *Marriage of Brown* (1976) 15 C3d 838, 126 CR 633. See *Marriage of Drapeau* (2001) 93 CA4th 1086, 114 CR2d 6 ("early retirement benefit" was contractual right earned during marriage and thus community property). Conversely, to the extent that the work is performed before the date of marriage or after the date of separation, the benefits are the employee-spouse's separate property. The community interest is unaffected by whether or not the rights are "vested" or "matured." *Marriage of Brown, supra.* A "vested" right is one that survives the employee's discharge or voluntary termination and a "matured" right is an unconditional right to retire and obtain an immediate payment of benefits. 15 C3d at 842.

The apportionment of retirement benefits between the community and separate property estates must be reasonable and fairly representative of the relative contributions of the respective estates. *Marriage of Poppe* (1979) 97 CA3d 1, 11, 158 CR 500.

Defined benefit plans. A defined benefit plan is one in which an employee will be entitled on retirement to a fixed monthly benefit during the remainder of his or her life, with the amount of the benefit usually calculated based on a formula multiplying years of service times the employee's salary over a certain period of time. The most common approach in apportioning such retirement benefits between the community and separate property estates is the "time rule." 97 CA3d at 8. Under this rule, the benefits are community property in the ratio that the time worked between the date of marriage and the date of separation bears to the entire time of employment. *Marriage of Judd* (1977) 68 CA3d 515, 522, 137 CR 318. The remaining portion of the benefits (*i.e.,* in the ratio that the time worked before the date of marriage or after the date of separation bears to the entire time of employment) is the employee's separate property. See *Marriage of Gowan* (1997) 54 CA4th 80, 62 CR2d 453 (application of time rule to entire period of employment affirmed even though employment was split and, at time of judgment, parties did not anticipate future return to same employer).

Assume, for example, that a spouse's retirement benefits are the result of 24 years of employment: 3 years before marriage, 20 years between the date of marriage and the date of separation, and 1 year after separation. Applying the time rule, the community property component of the benefits is that fraction whose numerator is 20 (the time worked between the date of marriage and the date of separation) and whose denominator is 24 (the entire time of employment). The community component is thus 20/24, or 5/6. The nonemployee's share of the benefits is half of the community component, or 5/12. The employee's share is the remainder, or 7/12.

Although the time rule is the most frequently used method for apportioning retirement benefits between the community and separate estates, the basis for apportionment is a matter for the trial court's discretion. *Marriage of Poppe, supra.* Apportionment on the basis of the time rule is appropriate only when the amount of the retirement benefits is substantially related to the number of years of service. 97 CA3d at 8. In *Poppe,* the amount of the Naval Reserve pension was largely a function of the number of "points" earned (essentially one point for each drill attended) and was not a function of the number of years served. 97 CA3d at 5. Consequently, the court of appeal reversed the trial court's application of the time rule and strongly suggested that, on remand, the trial court should apportion on the basis of points. 97 CA3d at 11. On that basis, the community share of the retirement benefits would be the fraction whose numerator is the number of points earned between the date of marriage and the date of separation and whose denominator is the total number of points earned. 97 CA3d at 5.

Even when the time rule is appropriate, its application may require tailoring to the specific facts presented. See *Marriage of Henkle* (1987) 189 CA3d 97, 234 CR 351. In *Henkle,* one of the parties was an Air Force colonel with 26 years of service at the time of the marriage. The parties separated and the colonel retired 6 years later. The spouse, arguing for the usual approach in applying the time rule, urged that the community share in the retirement benefits should be the fraction whose numerator was the years of service between the date of marriage and the date of separation (*i.e.,* 6) and whose denominator was the total years of service (*i.e.,* 32). The court of appeal noted, however, that the maximum amount of benefits was earned after 30 years' service, and the additional 2 years' service did not increase the benefits to which the colonel was entitled. Consequently, the correct community share was the fraction whose numerator was the years of service between the date of marriage and the date of separation *during which benefits were being earned* (*i.e.,* 4) and whose denominator was the total years of service *during which benefits were being earned* (*i.e.,* 30). See also *Marriage of Bowen* (2001) 91 CA4th 1291, 1300, 111 CR2d

431 (proper application of time rule depends on date benefit is earned, not when plan is funded).

See also *Marriage of Lehman* (1998) 18 C4th 169, 74 CR2d 825. In *Lehman*, the employee spouse received an enhanced early retirement benefit, several years after the marriage ended, including several additional, putative years of service credit. The supreme court held that the nonemployee spouse had a community property interest in the retirement benefits as enhanced by the early retirement program. In applying the time rule to apportion the benefits, the supreme court declined to follow the suggestion in *Marriage of Gram* (1994) 25 CA4th 859, 867, 30 CR2d 792, disapproved on other grounds in 18 C4th at 187, that additional, putative years of service offered to an employee spouse as an enhanced early retirement benefit should be added to the denominator (*i.e.,* the total years of service). In *Lehman*, the supreme court said that no putative years should be added to either the denominator or the numerator (*i.e.,* years of service during marriage and before separation) because "such years are *fictive*—they have no independent existence, but are merely a means by which the employer effects the enhancement." 18 C4th at 188. See also *Marriage of Drapeau* (2001) 93 CA4th 1086, 114 CR2d 6.

The lesson of the *Lehman, Poppe,* and *Henkle* cases is that counsel should not blindly assume that all retirement benefits are to be allocated between the community and separate estates by a rote application of the time rule. It is important to examine the particular plan at issue to ascertain the precise relationship between the time of service and the amount of the benefits.

Defined contribution plans. A defined contribution plan is one in which contributions are paid into an account by the employer, the employee, or both. For these plans, application of the time rule is not required; rather, the characterization as community or separate property is analyzed similarly to a bank account, stock portfolio, or other investment account.

On valuation of retirement benefits, see §§5.57–5.58. On division of defined benefit retirement plans, see §§5.92–5.93. On tax aspects of disposition of retirement benefits, see §5.108.

§5.31 (2) Stock Options

When stock options are granted to an employee before the date of separation but do not become exercisable until after separation, the court has broad discretion in allocating the community- and separate-property interests. *Marriage of Hug* (1984) 154 CA3d 780, 782, 201 CR 676. Such options have been referred to as "intermediate" options. *Marriage of Nelson* (1986) 177 CA3d 150, 153, 222 CR 790. Like retirement benefits (see §5.30), stock options are community property to the extent that the work done to earn them is performed between the date of marriage and the date of separation. Thus, it becomes necessary to ascertain the periods of employment to which the options may properly be allocated. This in turn requires an examination of the circumstances of the grants to determine whether the options should be characterized as deferred compensation, incentives for future performance, or both. *Marriage of Hug* (1984) 154 CA3d 780, 786, 201 CR 676.

In *Hug*, the appellate court affirmed the trial court's implied finding that the intermediate options at issue were primarily deferred compensation earned from the commencement of employment and its use, accordingly, of a time rule under which the community interest in an option is the ratio that the time worked between the commencement of employment and the date of separation bears to the time worked between the commencement of employment and the date the option is first exercisable. Multiplying the community interest in an option by the total number of shares that can be purchased on the date the option is first exercisable yields the number of shares with respect to which the option is community property. With respect to the remaining shares, the option is the employee's separate property. 154 CA3d at 782, 789.

A different time rule was upheld in *Marriage of Nelson, supra*. Under *Nelson*, the community interest in an intermediate option is the ratio that the time worked between the date of the grant and the date of separation bears to the time worked between the date of the grant and the date the option is first exercisable. 177 CA3d at 155. Whereas the *Hug* court viewed the stock options at issue as primarily deferred compensation, and accordingly adopted a formula that recognizes work performed from the commencement of employment, the *Nelson* court viewed the options as primarily future incentives and, accordingly, adopted a formula that recognizes only work performed from the granting of the options. See 177 CA3d at 155 n3 (noting that emphasis on period following each grant was appropriate because only prospective increases in value of stock could result in profit to option holders).

In a third case, intermediate stock options were found to be "golden handcuffs," designed to ensure that the employee would remain with the employer. *Marriage of Harrison* (1986) 179 CA3d 1216, 1227, 225 CR 234. Thus they were primarily future incentives (as in *Nelson*) rather than deferred compensation (as in *Hug*). Accordingly, the court followed *Nelson* in attributing the options to work performed from the date the options were granted, rather than from the date employment commenced. *Marriage of Harrison, supra.* The community interest in an option under *Harrison* is the ratio that the time worked between the granting of the option and the date of separation bears to the time worked between the granting of the option and the date on which the stock is vested and not subject to divestment. 179 CA3d at 1223 n1, 1225. Note that the latter period (*i.e.,* the "denominator") runs to the date the stock is vested, rather than to the date the option is exercisable, as in *Nelson*. The distinction occurs because, under the "nonqualified" options in *Harrison*, the stock could be purchased on the day the option was granted, but it would be subject to divestment if the employee were terminated for cause, or were to leave voluntarily without the employer's consent, before specified dates. For a case reversing the trial court for following *Nelson* rather than *Harrison,* and for a review of these three approaches, see *Marriage of Walker* (1989) 216 CA3d 644, 265 CR 32.

It should be recalled that the discussion here addresses "intermediate" stock options, *i.e.,* options that are granted before separation but that do not become exercisable until after separation. One case that addressed options granted *after* separation affirmed a ruling that they were entirely the separate property of the employee spouse, noting that the employee had no expectation of the grant and could profit only if the stock value rose after the date of the grant. *Marriage of Nelson* (1986) 177 CA3d 150, 157, 222 CR 790. Presumably, a stock option granted after separation that is found to be in part deferred compensation for work performed before separation will be apportioned between community and separate property interests. A claim of a community interest in a stock option granted after *dissolution,* however, would appear to be too speculative for exercise of jurisdiction over it. *Marriage of Hug* (1984) 154 CA3d 780, 793 n4, 201 CR 676.

In addressing stock options, tax aspects should not be overlooked. When tax liability has already been incurred, clearly what is to be divided is the net *after-tax* value of the community interest. See

Marriage of Walker (1989) 216 CA3d 644, 651, 265 CR 32; *Marriage of Harrison* (1986) 179 CA3d 1216, 1227, 225 CR 234. In *Marriage of Nelson, supra,* however, the court of appeal affirmed consideration of tax liability even though neither the time at which it might arise nor its extent was yet determinable. 177 CA3d at 156. For further discussion, see §5.103 and Dividing Pensions and Other Employee Benefits in California Divorces, chap 10 (Cal CEB 2006).

(3) Disability Pay

§5.32   (a) Pensions

Because they are received on account of disability and not as deferred compensation, disability payments received after the date of separation are generally the separate property of the disabled spouse. *Marriage of Flockhart* (1981) 119 CA3d 240, 243, 173 CR 818.

Often, however, disability payments are elected in lieu of retirement benefits, which, to the extent they are earned by virtue of employment during marriage and before separation, are community property (see §5.30). In this situation, the payments are compensation for disability (and are thus entirely the employee-spouse's separate property) only to the extent that they exceed what would have been received as retirement benefits. The balance remains community property to the extent it would have been community property if received as retirement benefits. *Marriage of Stenquist* (1978) 21 C3d 779, 787, 148 CR 9. The result is the same even if the employee-spouse has not been employed long enough to enable him or her to choose between retirement benefits and disability benefits. *Marriage of Justice* (1984) 157 CA3d 82, 88, 204 CR 6. Any tax savings resulting from the tax-exempt nature of the disability pension is the employee-spouse's separate property. The comparison is to be made between the net after-tax disability benefits and what the net after-tax retirement benefits would have been. *Marriage of Higinbotham* (1988) 203 CA3d 322, 334, 249 CR 798.

When a disabled employee receives disability benefits before reaching the age at which he or she is eligible to retire, a redetermination of the respective community and separate interests may be required when the age of retirement eligibility is subsequently reached. Although the payments received before the employee reaches the age of retirement eligibility are his or her separate property, the primary purpose of the payments may shift when the age is reached to retirement support rather than disability compensation resulting from premature retirement. If so, the payments received thereafter are community property to the extent that they are attributable to employment during marriage and before separation. *Marriage of Samuels* (1979) 96 CA3d 122, 128, 158 CR 38. See also *Marriage of Pace* (1982) 132 CA3d 548, 183 CR 314; *Marriage of Webb* (1979) 94 CA3d 335, 339, 156 CR 334.

The community interest in retirement benefits is also protected with respect to military benefits under Title 10, Chapter 61 of the United States Code (10 USC §§1201–1221). Chapter 61 retirement benefits are based on both longevity of service and a rating of disability. The Federal Uniformed Services Former Spouses' Protection Act (FUSFSPA) (10 USC §1408) originally excluded Chapter 61 retired pay entirely from the "disposable retired pay" subject to division by state courts in marital actions. Congress amended FUSFSPA, however, so that it now excludes from disposable retired pay only the disability component of Chapter 61 retired pay. 10 USC §1408(a)(4)(C). See generally *Adkins v Rumsfeld* (4th Cir 2006) 464 F3d 456, 473 (upholding FUSFSPA against various constitutional challenges). Thus, like nonmilitary benefits, the retirement component of Chapter 61 retired pay remains community property to the extent that it is attributable to service performed during the marriage and before separation.

The community interest is not protected, however, with respect to military retirement benefits waived in order to receive disability benefits under Title 38 of the United States Code. A retiree who becomes disabled as a result of military service may receive Title 38 disability benefits, but only to the extent that he or she waives a corresponding amount of retirement pay. Because military disability benefits are tax-exempt, such a waiver increases the retiree's after-tax income. Retirement benefits waived to receive Title 38 disability benefits are excluded from the disposable pay subject to division in state-court marital actions. 10 USC §1408(a)(4)(B); *Mansell v Mansell* (1989) 490 US 581, 583, 104 L Ed 2d 675, 681, 109 S Ct 2023, 2025. The result is that the entire disability benefit, including any portion corresponding to the retirement benefits that were waived, is the member's separate property. But see *Marriage of Krempin* (1999) 70 CA4th 1008, 1021, 83 CR2d 134 (trial court may fashion equitable remedy so that nonmilitary spouse may still receive designated portion of military retirement benefits after retired spouse opts to receive disability in lieu of retirement benefits). For further discussion of the problems *Mansell* creates for the nonmember spouse, see §5.38 and Dividing Pensions and Other Employee Benefits in California Divorces, chap 17 (Cal CEB 2006).

§5.33   (b) Private Insurance

When disability insurance is purchased during marriage with community funds, benefits received after separation are separate property insofar as they were intended by the parties to replace the insured spouse's lost earnings in the event of disability and are community property insofar as they were intended to provide retirement income. *Marriage of Saslow* (1985) 40 C3d 848, 860, 221 CR 546. The court may consider the parties' intent both at the time the insurance was originally purchased and at times that decisions were made to continue the insurance in force rather than to let it lapse. Without evidence of actual intent, the court may determine a normal retirement age at which the disabled spouse would have been most likely to retire had no disability occurred. 40 C3d at 861.

When disability insurance premiums are paid, whether partially or entirely, after separation, benefits received after separation are entirely separate property. *Marriage of Elfmont* (1995) 9 C4th 1026, 39 CR2d 590.

§5.34   (4) Termination Pay

In characterizing termination (or severance) benefits as community or separate property, as in characterizing disability pay (see §§5.32–5.33), courts have traditionally looked to the purpose of the particular payments. *Marriage of Lawson* (1989) 208 CA3d 446, 451, 256 CR 283. Thus, vested "termination benefits" in an insurance sales agent's employment agreement with an insurer were community property to the extent they were attributable to the period during marriage and before separation because they, like retirement benefits, represented a form of deferred compensation. *Marriage of Skaden* (1977) 19 C3d 679, 139 CR 615. Likewise, "severance pay" received by a retired professional football player under his union's collective bargaining agreement with the National Football League was deemed to be a form of deferred compensation and thus subject to division in a marital action. *Marriage of Horn* (1986) 181 CA3d 540, 548,

226 CR 666. Similarly, an "enhanced early retirement" benefit merely compressed the normal retirement plan process by immediately granting additional age and service credits and was, therefore, a form of deferred compensation. *Marriage of Gram* (1994) 25 CA4th 859, 866, 30 CR2d 792, disapproved on other grounds in 18 C4th at 187. See discussion at §5.3.

Several cases reached the opposite conclusion, however, finding that particular types of termination pay are present compensation for loss of future earnings, rather than compensation for past services, and are thus the employee's separate property when received after separation. See *Marriage of Lawson* (1989) 208 CA3d 446, 453, 256 CR 283 (severance pay intended as future compensation during transition period); *Marriage of DeShurley* (1989) 207 CA3d 992, 995, 255 CR 150 (severance pay characterized as compensation for forgoing future employment with airline); *Marriage of Wright* (1983) 140 CA3d 342, 345, 189 CR 336 (termination payment made in recognition of prospective loss of earnings); *Marriage of Flockhart* (1981) 119 CA3d 240, 243, 173 CR 818 ("weekly layoff benefit" received because decline of industry results in loss of earnings).

In *Marriage of Frahm* (1996) 45 CA4th 536, 543, 53 CR2d 31, however, the court did not look to the purpose of the payments, or to whether they were payment for past services. Rather, it said that employment benefits are community property to the extent that they derive from employment during marriage and before separation. 45 CA4th at 544. In *Frahm*, the employer, wishing to reduce its work force, offered incentives to employees who agreed to terminate their employment or take early retirement. Because the severance payment derived from the employer's beneficence, and not the employee's employment, it was the employee's separate property.

In *Marriage of Lehman* (1998) 18 C4th 169, 74 CR2d 825, the California Supreme Court provided further illumination of termination pay issues. In *Lehman*, the husband's pension was enhanced by a retirement benefit offered by his employer in order to encourage early retirement. Finding *Gram* and *Frahm* "each correct in its result as to characterization" on its respective facts, the court stated that the employee spouse's right to retirement benefits that accrued, in part, during marriage before separation, underlies the right to the enhancement. 18 C4th at 183. Thus, the enhancement was not a separate property retirement benefit, but rather a modification of an asset in existence during the marriage, and thus community property. The court dismissed the argument that the enhancement was a severance payment because it "called itself, and was, in fact, an increase *in retirement benefits*," distinguishing *Marriage of Lawson* (1989) 208 CA3d 446, 256 CR 283, in which the employee spouse had not previously accrued any right to severance payment offered by that employer. 18 C4th at 186. For a case relying on *Lehman* to reach a similar result regarding a military voluntary separation program to reduce active duty forces, see *Marriage of Babauta* (1998) 66 CA4th 784, 788, 78 CR2d 281. For a case distinguishing *Lehman*, see *Marriage of Steinberger* (2001) 91 CA4th 1449, 1461, 111 CR2d 521, in which post-severance employment credits were used in the denominator of the time rule calculation because they were not putative years as in *Lehman*, but a new right created after separation. *Steinberger* also discusses severance pay as separate property because derived from a post-termination noncompetition agreement negotiated after separation. See §5.30 for a discussion of the use of the time rule to apportion the employee spouse's enhanced retirement benefits between community property and the separate property interest of the employee spouse alone.

§5.35   (5) Retiree Health Insurance

The continuing right to employer-subsidized retiree health insurance without evidence of good health is a property right that has some value. When the employee or retiree continues to pay for the health insurance with his or her separate funds, however, the right is not subject to valuation or division on dissolution. Rather, it is the employee or retiree's separate property, and there is no community asset to divide. *Marriage of Havins* (1996) 43 CA4th 414, 50 CR2d 763. This rule applies even when the plan is 100 percent subsidized by the employer and the employee's obligation is merely to "renew" the policy. *Marriage of Ellis* (2002) 101 CA4th 400, 408, 124 CR2d 719.

In contrast to the rules governing community property, some federal plans provide for continued health insurance for former spouses. See, *e.g.*, Civil Service Retirement Spouse Equity Act of 1984 (Pub L 98–615). An attorney whose client is married to a current or former federal employee should investigate whether such an entitlement exists. See generally *Stanley v Richmond* (1995) 35 CA4th 1070, 1094, 41 CR2d 768 (involving malpractice action in which attorney failed to advise client that she could continue to receive free health care had she been awarded only one dollar of husband's VA pension).

§5.36   (6) Workers' Compensation Benefits

Workers' compensation benefits received after separation are the separate property of the injured spouse. *Marriage of Fisk* (1992) 2 CA4th 1698, 4 CR2d 95; *Marriage of McDonald* (1975) 52 CA3d 509, 125 CR 160. Before *Fisk*, there was some question about whether *McDonald* remained valid in light of subsequent legislative action (see Fam C §§781(a) and 2603) on personal injury damages. Personal injury damages are separate property only when the cause of action arises before marriage or after separation, regardless of when the damages are received. See §5.29. But *Fisk* rejects treating workers' compensation benefits like personal injury awards. *Marriage of Fisk* (1992) 2 CA4th 1698, 1706, 4 CR2d 95.

A lump sum permanent disability award that an injured spouse receives before separation is that spouse's separate property to the extent that the award is compensation for the diminished earning capacity the injured spouse will suffer after the date of separation. *Raphael v Bloomfield* (2003) 113 CA4th 617, 6 CR3d 583.

§5.36A   (7) Other Miscellaneous Employee Benefits

As the types of employment benefits increase, attorneys must be aware that a community property interest may exist in them. See, *e.g.*, *Marriage of Doherty* (2002) 103 CA4th 895, 126 CR2d 919 (wife's employment-related mortgage subsidy was not community property because, although negotiated during the marriage, it was not vested and required her continued employment).

§5.37   7. Federal Preemption

California courts may not apply community property law when to do so would violate the federal supremacy clause (US Const art VI, cl 2). *Hisquierdo v Hisquierdo* (1979) 439 US 572, 59 L Ed 2d 1, 99 S Ct 802. For application of community property law to violate the supremacy clause, Congress must have "positively required by direct enactment" that state law be preempted and the community property law must do "major damage" to "clear and substantial" federal interests. 439 US at 581.

Hisquierdo dealt with retirement benefits received under the Railroad Retirement Act of 1974 (45 USC §§231–231v), and the Court held that treating the benefits as community property violated the supremacy clause. Congress responded by amending the Act to expressly provide for community property characterization and treatment of most benefits under the Act (including, most notably, the "Tier II" annuity component, *i.e.,* benefits based on railroad retirement earnings alone) in accordance with a judgment of dissolution, legal separation, or nullity or with the terms of any court-approved property settlement incident to any such judgment. 45 USC §231m(b)(2). The amendment exempted the "Tier I" annuity component, *i.e.,* benefits based on earnings in the railroad industry and in employment covered by the Social Security Act, however, and thus federal law, under *Hisquierdo,* continues to preempt state community property law with respect to Tier I benefits.

§5.38   a. Military Retirement Benefits

The issue of characterization of military retirement benefits has been heatedly contested for many years, with each side having had periods in which its view prevailed. In 1974, the California Supreme Court held that military retirement benefits were community property subject to division. *Marriage of Fithian* (1974) 10 C3d 592, 111 CR 369. After ruling, in *Hisquierdo v Hisquierdo* (1979) 439 US 572, 59 L Ed 2d 1, 99 S Ct 802 (see §5.37), that treating retirement benefits received under the Railroad Retirement Act of 1974 (45 USC §§231–231v) as community property violated the supremacy clause, the United States Supreme Court took up the issue of military retirement benefits and held that federal law likewise precluded California courts from dividing military retirement pay in accordance with community property laws. *McCarty v McCarty* (1981) 453 US 210, 69 L Ed 2d 589, 101 S Ct 2728. Congress subsequently enacted the Federal Uniformed Services Former Spouses' Protection Act (FUSFSPA) (10 USC §1408), which allows state courts to divide "disposable retired pay" as property of the military member and his or her spouse in accordance with state law (10 USC §1408(c)(1)). Moreover, FUSFSPA was made retroactive to June 25, 1981, the day before the decision in *McCarty. Marriage of Curtis* (1992) 7 CA4th 1, 8, 9 CR2d 145. Thus, *McCarty* no longer had any prospective effect whatever. Note that a state court's authority is subject to the following limitation: "The total amount of the disposable retired pay of a member payable under all court orders ... may not exceed 50 percent of such disposable retired pay." 10 USC §1408(e)(1).

The question remained, however, whether *McCarty* had any retroactive effect. California courts have uniformly held that it did not. See, *e.g., Casas v Thompson* (1986) 42 C3d 131, 140, 228 CR 33, 38. Consequently, pre-*McCarty* cases continued to be governed by pre-*McCarty* California case law, which provided for division of military retirement benefits as community property. *Marriage of Curtis* (1992) 7 CA4th 1, 12, 9 CR2d 145. But a 1990 amendment to FUSFSPA provides that courts may not make a postjudgment division of military retirement pay as community property if the judgment of dissolution, legal separation, or nullity (including a court-ordered, -ratified, or -approved property settlement incident to such a judgment) was issued before June 25, 1981, and neither treated the retirement pay as community property nor reserved jurisdiction to do so. 10 USC §1408(c)(1). If, however, such a postjudgment division of retirement benefits was issued before November 5, 1990, and the division would be valid except for this amendment, the amendment does not affect the obligation to make any payment due before November 5, 1992, of future benefits as they become payable to the military member, or any payment of past benefits due at any time. 7 CA4th at 16; see Pub L 101-510, §555(e)(1), 104 Stat 1570 (1990).

Even assuming that a court has jurisdiction to divide military retirement benefits, some controversy has arisen over the scope of that jurisdiction. The California Supreme Court has held that the limitation to disposable retired pay limits only the scope of direct enforcement against a retiree's pay and not a court's ability to divide gross, rather than "disposable," military retirement pay. *Casas v Thompson* (1986) 42 C3d 131, 151, 228 CR 33. In *Mansell v Mansell* (1989) 490 US 581, 104 L Ed 2d 675, 109 S Ct 2023, however, the Court rejected this interpretation with respect to amounts waived in order to receive disability benefits, which is one of the deductions from gross retirement pay required by the Act in determining "disposable" pay. See §5.32. As a result, it appears that California courts may divide, to the extent deemed community property, only the net payment amounts remaining after deducting from gross retirement pay the amounts:

• Owed by the member to the United States for previous overpayments of retired pay and for recoupments required by law result-ing from entitlement to retired pay (10 USC §1408(a)(4)(A));

- Deducted from retired pay as a result of forfeitures of retired pay ordered by a court-martial or as a result of a waiver of retired pay required by law in order to receive disability benefits under Title 5 or Title 38 of the United States Code (10 USC §1408(a)(4)(B));

- That represent the disability component of a member's retire-ment pay under Title 10, Chapter 61 of the United States Code (10 USC §1408(a)(4)(C)); or

- Deducted under Title 10, Chapter 73 of the United States Code to provide an annuity to a spouse or former spouse (10 USC §1408(a)(4)(D)).

It should be noted that additional deductions from gross retirement pay, including amounts properly withheld for federal income taxes, were previously allowed and that current law applies only to dissolu-tions, legal separations, and nullities that became effective after the end of the 90-day period beginning on November 5, 1990, which appears to mean after February 2, 1991. Former 10 USC §1408(a)(4)(A)-(F); see Pub L 101–510, §555(e)(2), 104 Stat 1570 (1990). Note that one court of appeal has held that the trial court may fashion an equitable remedy so that a nonmilitary spouse can receive her designated portion of military benefits even though the retired spouse opted to receive disability in lieu of retirement benefits. *Marriage of Krempin* (1999) 70 CA4th 1008, 1021, 83 CR2d 134. The *Krempin* court hinted that the wife's claim could have been even stronger if the parties had included an indemnity provision in their marital settlement agreement, specifying their intentions should the military spouse choose to waive pension benefits in favor of disability benefits. For more detailed and specific information about differing forms of military retirement benefits, see Dividing Pensions and Other Employee Benefits in California Divorces, chap 17 (Cal CEB 2006).

§5.39   b. Social Security Benefits

Federal preemption precludes treatment of social security benefits as community property. They must be treated as the employee's separate property. *Marriage of Hillerman* (1980) 109 CA3d 334, 345, 167 CR 240.

Despite the characterization of social security "primary" benefits (*i.e.,* benefits earned through one's own employment) as separate property, a party may qualify for "derivative" benefits (*i.e.,* benefits earned through the former spouse's employment), as long as the length of the marriage, measured to the date the parties' marital status is terminated, is at least ten years. 42 USC §402(b)-(c). An attorney representing a client whose marriage is approaching ten years' duration and for whom social security derivative benefits may be available must take every reasonable precaution to avoid a marital status termination date that results in loss of the benefits. The safest approach, if practicable, is to delay filing the petition until the duration of the marriage is at least nine years and six months, so that the marital status cannot be terminated before the ten-year requirement is met. See Fam C §2339.

§5.40   c. Military Life Insurance Policies

Federal preemption precludes treatment of military insurance policies or their proceeds as community property. *Ridgway v Ridgway* (1981) 454 US 46, 61, 70 L Ed 2d 39, 52, 102 S Ct 49.

V. VALUATION

§5.41   A. "Value" Defined

For purposes of property division in marital actions, the "value" of a marketable asset is the highest price on the date of valuation that would be agreed to by a seller who is willing to sell but under no obligation or urgent necessity to do so and a buyer who is ready, willing, and able to buy but under no particular necessity to do so. *Marriage of Cream* (1993) 13 CA4th 81, 89, 16 CR2d 575. See also CCP §1263.320 (definition of "fair market value" for eminent domain cases).

§5.42   B. When Required

Whether valuation of a specific community property asset is required depends on the treatment given that asset as part of the overall equal division of the community estate required by Fam C §2550. To assign community assets to the respective parties as part of an overall equal division of community assets and liabilities, the court must value all such assets, except for those equally divided in kind (*e.g.,* disposition of 100 shares of stock by award of 50 shares to each party). *Marriage of Micalizio* (1988) 199 CA3d 662, 672, 245 CR 673. Likewise, valuation is required when one party will purchase the other's interest in community property. *Hong v Hong* (1965) 237 CA2d 239, 241, 46 CR 710. On the other hand, valuation is not required for community assets that will be sold, with the proceeds divided equally between the parties, or for community assets that will continue to be jointly owned by the parties in equal shares.

C. Time

§5.43 1. General Rule

In making an equal division of the community estate, the court must ordinarily value the community assets and liabilities "as near as practicable to the time of trial." Fam C §2552(a). *Marriage of Sherman* (2005) 133 CA4th 795, 800, 35 CR3d 137. On the court's discretion under Fam C §2552(b) to grant a motion for an alternate valuation date, see §5.44.

As used in Fam C §2552(a), "time of trial" means the trial at which the property is actually divided. *Marriage of Walters* (1979) 91 CA3d 535, 539, 154 CR 180. Thus, for example, in a bifurcated proceeding in which the court terminates the marriage but reserves jurisdiction to divide the community property at a later date, the trial referred to in Fam C §2552(a) is the latter hearing, not the former. On remand from an appeal, the court should consider equitable factors in determining whether to value community assets as of the original trial or the retrial. *Marriage of Bergman* (1985) 168 CA3d 742, 761 n17, 214 CR 661; *Marriage of Hayden* (1981) 124 CA3d 72, 79, 177 CR 183.

The requirement of Fam C §2552(a) that valuation take place "as near as practicable" to the time of trial reflects the legislature's recognition that there may be situations in which the value of community property cannot be determined at the precise time of trial. In this situation, trial courts have a reasonable degree of flexibility in achieving substantial justice. *Marriage of Olson* (1980) 27 C3d 414, 422, 165 CR 820. In *Olson,* the family residence was lost to foreclosure after trial and issuance of an intended decision, but before issuance of the judgment. The supreme court reversed the denial of a motion to reopen for the purpose of revaluing the community property. Thus, the words "as near as practicable to the time of trial" can mean after trial but before issuance of a judgment. See also *Marriage of Johnson* (1983) 143 CA3d 57, 61, 191 CR 545 (revaluation required when court found value of boat at time of trial to be $90,000 and it was sold before judgment for $140,000). When there is no intervening sale or forfeiture, however, a mere change in value between the trial and issuance of the judgment does not require the court to reopen for the purpose of revaluing. *Marriage of Hahn* (1990) 224 CA3d 1236, 1240, 273 CR 516. Although the *Hahn* court emphasized that the valuation the husband sought to overturn was established by stipulation, it appears that the lack of a sale or forfeiture would have been sufficient to deny a reopening even without the stipulation on value. After judgment is entered, the risk of sudden appreciation or depreciation in value of the property awarded is borne by the parties. See Fam C §2552; *Marriage of Connolly* (1979) 23 C3d 590, 600, 153 CR 423 (court's valuation of stock was reasonable at time of trial, even though shares were selling for nearly four times that amount less than four weeks after judgment was entered).

When a community asset cannot be accurately valued at the time of trial, the court should reserve jurisdiction over the asset. Fam C §§2550, 2552; *Marriage of Munguia* (1983) 146 CA3d 853, 859, 195 CR 199. However, it can be hazardous to reserve jurisdiction over a pension plan or other retirement vehicle without at least apportioning the parties' community and separate interests in such an asset. See *Marriage of Bergman* (1985) 168 CA3d 742, 748, 214 CR 661.

§5.44 2. Alternate Valuation Date

Family Code §2552(b) provides for an exception to its general rule, discussed in §5.43, that the court must value the community assets and liabilities "as near as practicable to the time of trial." On 30 days' notice by the moving party and a showing of good cause, the court may value some or all of the assets and liabilities as of any date after separation and before trial to make an equal division in an equitable manner. When an alternate valuation date is allowed, the date of separation is the date that is typically selected.

The required notice is provided on the Judicial Council form of Application for Separate Trial (Judicial Council Form FL-315; see form in §14.67). See Cal Rules of Ct 5.126. The notice must be accompanied by a declaration that sets forth:

- The proposed alternate valuation date (Cal Rules of Ct 5.126(b)(1));

- Whether the proposed alternate valuation date will apply to all or only a portion of the assets and, if only a portion, each such asset separately identified (Cal Rules of Ct 5.126(b)(2)); and

- The reasons supporting the alternate valuation date (Cal Rules of Ct 5.126(b)(3)).

The court's authority to select an alternate valuation date is designed to remedy certain inequities that might otherwise arise because of the requirement of valuation as near as practicable to the time of trial, *e.g.,* when the community estate is either dissipated or greatly increased by the actions of one spouse after the date of separation. *Marriage of Barnert* (1978) 85 CA3d 413, 423, 149 CR 616. Similarly, an alternate date is appropriate if one party's deliberate or reckless failure to keep proper records prevents the parties from valuing a business at the time of trial. *Marriage of Nelson* (2006) 139 CA4th 1546, 1552, 44 CR3d 52 (good cause existed to value business as of separation date). Selection of an alternate valuation date is also consistent with the rule (Fam C §771(a); see §5.12) that earnings and accumulations of a spouse after separation are his or her separate property. *Marriage of Stevenson* (1993) 20 CA4th 250, 254, 24 CR2d 411. The *Stevenson* court took the position that the value of a small business that depends largely on the operating spouse's personal skill, industry, and guidance should generally be determined as of the date of separation. 20 CA4th at 254. See also *Marriage of Duncan* (2001) 90 CA4th 617, 625, 108 CR2d 833. It may be that the same rule will apply to large businesses as well. When an asset is valued as of the date of separation, the community shares in the value as of that date, and the increase or decrease between the date of separation and the time of trial is allocated entirely to the spouse whose actions were responsible for it.

When the increase or decrease in value between the date of separation and the date of trial is attributable in significant measure both to the actions of one spouse and to nonpersonal factors (*e.g.,* market conditions, return on investment), the proper approach is to value the asset as of the time of trial and apportion the increase or decrease since separation between the community and separate interests. *Marriage of Imperato* (1975) 45 CA3d 432, 436, 119 CR 590. For discussion, see §5.17. Such an apportionment does not require notice under Fam C §2552(b). *Marriage of Hargrave* (1985) 163 CA3d 346, 355, 209 CR 764. Finally, when the increase or decrease is attributable entirely to nonpersonal factors, the valuation should be made as of the time of trial. *Marriage of Priddis* (1982) 132 CA3d 349, 357, 183 CR 37.

For another basis for granting an alternate valuation date, see *Marriage of Stallcup* (1979) 97 CA3d 294, 301, 158 CR 679, 682 (alternate valuation date soon after separation upheld when party claiming postseparation business reverses failed to provide discovery on that issue).

§5.45   D. Determination of Value

Valuation of community property items in marital actions is a question of fact for the trial court. *Marriage of Asbury* (1983) 144 CA3d 918, 923, 193 CR 562. Evidence on valuation is typically presented by the respective attorneys, relying heavily on expert witnesses, *e.g.,* appraisers, actuaries. But the court may, on its own motion, appoint experts to investigate, report, and testify whenever expert evidence is or may be required in determining the value of property. Evid C §730; *Marriage of Drivon* (1972) 28 CA3d 896, 105 CR 124.

1. Methods of Proof Generally

§5.46   a. Special Evidence Code Rules

Except when another rule is provided by statute, proof in marital actions of the value of real property (including real and personal property valued as a unit) is governed by Evid C §§810–823. Evid C §§810–811. Under §§810–823, the value of real property may be shown only by opinion testimony, either by an expert witness or by an owner or owner's spouse. Evid C §813(a). Whether offered by an expert witness or by an owner or owner's spouse, the opinion must be based on matters that can reasonably be relied on by an expert in forming an opinion about value. Evid C §814. In forming an opinion about the value of real property, a witness may rely on, *e.g.,* the terms and circumstances of any reasonably recent bona fide sale or contract for sale pertaining to the property or to comparable property, or the terms and circumstances of any lease in effect within a reasonable time before the valuation and pertaining to the property. Evid C §§815–817. The witness may not, however, rely on, *e.g.,* an offer or listing with respect to any property (see Evid C §822(a)(2), (b)), the value of any property as assessed for taxation purposes (see Evid C §822(a)(3), (b)), or the amount of taxes due (see Evid C §822(a)(3), (b)).

Proof of the value of personal property, unlike that of real property (or of real and personal property valued as a unit), is not governed by Evid C §§810–823 (Evid C §811) and, consequently, is not limited to opinion testimony. Rather, independent proof (*e.g.,* comparable sales) may be offered.

§5.47 b. Expert Testimony

The opinion testimony of an expert witness is frequently offered in valuing property in marital actions. Such a witness must have special knowledge, skill, experience, training, or education sufficient to qualify him or her as an expert on valuation of the particular asset. Evid C §720(a).

The trial court is not required to accept the opinion of an expert regarding the value of an asset but may exercise its broad discretion to make an independent determination based on the evidence presented. *Marriage of Bergman* (1985) 168 CA3d 742, 753, 214 CR 661. When, however, the evidence presented is insufficient to enable the court to properly determine the value of an asset, the court must require the parties to furnish additional evidence or appoint its own expert to testify on the issue (see Evid C §730). *Marriage of Hargrave* (1985) 163 CA3d 346, 355, 209 CR 764.

§5.48 c. Owner Testimony

In a marital action, either spouse may offer opinion testimony on the value of community real property (including real and personal property valued as a unit) (Evid C §813(a)(2)) or personal property (see *Mears v Mears* (1960) 180 CA2d 484, 505, 4 CR 618, disapproved on other grounds in 64 C2d at 785 (business)). With respect to real property, but not personal property, the opinion must be based on matters that may reasonably be relied on by an expert in forming an opinion about value. Evid C §§811, 814.

§5.49   d. Sales Price

An expert or owner offering opinion testimony about the value of community property may rely on the terms and circumstances of any reasonably recent bona fide sale or contract for sale pertaining to the property. Evid C §815. Such evidence is admissible as independent proof, however, only with respect to personal property. Evid C §§811, 813; *Mears v Mears* (1960) 180 CA2d 484, 504, 4 CR 618, disapproved on other grounds in 64 C2d at 785 (dogs).

§5.50   e. Comparable Sales

An expert or owner offering opinion testimony about the value of community property may rely on the terms and circumstances of any reasonably recent bona fide sale or contract for sale pertaining to comparable property. Evid C §816. With respect to real property (including real and personal property valued as a unit), but not personal property, such evidence is not admissible as independent proof (Evid C §§811, 813) and may be relied on for opinion testimony only when the sale was made sufficiently near the date of valuation, and the property was sufficiently near and like the property being valued, to make the sales terms of one a reasonable indicator of the value of the other (Evid C §816).

§5.51   f. Agreements Between Co-Owners

Co-owners of businesses often enter into corporate stock purchase agreements or partnership agreements fixing the value of their interests, *e.g.,* in the event of withdrawal or death. Such agreements have sometimes been relied on in marital actions to fix the value of the interests covered for purposes of property division. See, *e.g., Marriage of Fonstein* (1976) 17 C3d 738, 746, 131 CR 873 (partnership agreement); *Marriage of Nichols* (1994) 27 CA4th 661, 33 CR2d 13 (law firm stock purchase agreement); *Marriage of Rosan* (1972) 24 CA3d 885, 890, 101 CR 295 (same).

Although agreements between co-owners are usually relevant to determining value, they are not necessarily the deciding factor. Even when signed by both spouses, these agreements are not entered into for purposes of marital actions. See, *e.g., Marriage of Fenton* (1982) 134 CA3d 451, 461, 184 CR 597 (what shareholder in professional corporation is entitled to receive on withdrawal or termination is not controlling for purposes of marital actions); *Marriage of Slater* (1979) 100 CA3d 241, 245, 160 CR 686 (asset being divided was partner's interest in ongoing business, not his contractual withdrawal rights).

It might be said that agreements between co-owners set a floor, but not a ceiling, for valuation purposes. One cannot very well argue for a value for continuing a business that is less than the amount that can be received on withdrawal or termination. But the value for continuing may well be greater than the value on withdrawal. See, *e.g., Marriage of Fenton* (1982) 134 CA3d 451, 463, 184 CR 597 (value of goodwill cannot be eliminated by recital in stock purchase agreement).

§5.52   g. Offers to Buy or Sell

Offers to buy or sell property are not admissible as independent proof of the value of either real or personal property and may not be relied on for opinion testimony on the issue. *Mears v Mears* (1960) 180 CA2d 484, 505, 4 CR 618, disapproved on other grounds in 64 C2d at 785 (business); see Evid C §822(a)(2), (b) (real property).

§5.53   h. Tax Valuations

The valuation of property as assessed for tax purposes is not admissible as independent proof of its value and may not be relied on for opinion testimony on the issue. See Evid C §822(a)(3), (b).

2. Specific Assets

§5.54   a. Real Property

Real property is one of the types of asset on which valuation issues most commonly arise in marital actions. Except when another rule is provided by statute, proof of the value of real property (or of real and personal property valued as a unit) is governed by Evid C §§810–823 (for discussion, see §5.46).

§5.55   (1) Valuation Methods

As noted in *Marriage of Folb* (1975) 53 CA3d 862, 868, 126 CR 306, overruled on other grounds in *Marriage of Fonstein* (1976)

17 C3d 738, 749, 131 CR 873, three methods of valuing real property, all to be presented through expert testimony, are generally recognized:

Market approach. Based on sales terms for comparable properties, this approach is used primarily for family residences. Adjustments for differences between the properties sold and the property to be valued are usually required. See Evid C §816.

Income approach. Used for income-producing properties, for which sales of comparable properties are harder to find than for family residences, this approach is based on a capitalized value of the reasonable net rental value attributable to the property. The expert estimates the net income the property is likely to produce during its probable remaining economic life and then selects a capitalization rate to translate that income into an indication of market value. See Evid C §819.

Cost approach. This approach is used for unique properties. The expert estimates the current cost to reproduce or replace the improvements on a parcel of property. The cost is then reduced by an estimate of the amount the improvements have depreciated and increased by the value of the land (estimated from comparable sales). See Evid C §820.

Note, however, that a witness is not limited to these three approaches. Evid C §814.

§5.56 (2) Costs of Sale

In valuing real property, costs of sale (*i.e.,* real estate commissions and closing costs) are deducted when a sale appears likely, regardless of whether the sale is specifically ordered in the judgment. When a sale is speculative, however, costs are not deducted. Compare *Marriage of Denney* (1981) 115 CA3d 543, 552, 171 CR 440, and *Marriage of Drivon* (1972) 28 CA3d 896, 105 CR 124 (deductions affirmed), with *Marriage of Stratton* (1975) 46 CA3d 173, 119 CR 924 (deduction reversed).

b. Retirement and Other Deferred Compensation

§5.57 (1) Defined Benefit Plans

A defined benefit plan is one in which the benefits may be ascertained by reference to factors such as the employee's age at retirement, years of service at retirement, and highest income level achieved. *Marriage of Bergman* (1985) 168 CA3d 742, 748 n4, 214 CR 661. The last of these factors is often calculated by reference to the average compensation over a specified period (*e.g.,* three years) immediately before retirement. Benefits from defined benefit plans, unlike those from defined contribution plans (see §5.58), do not depend on amounts contributed or the performance of investments made by the plan trustee.

The goal in valuing a defined benefit plan is to ascertain the present value of pension benefits to be received in the future, for which the actuarial method has traditionally been employed. 168 CA3d at 752. Expert testimony on the issue usually depends on the expert's assumptions about interest, mortality, and vesting. See *Marriage of Stephenson* (1984) 162 CA3d 1057, 1082, 209 CR 383. Other assumptions may also be important. For example, some dissolution retirement experts consider future salary increases in valuing pension benefits, but others do not. Compare Denner, *Projected Average Salary in Pension Valuation: To Use or Not to Use?* 4 Cal Fam L Monthly, No. 12 (July 1988) with Parkyn, *Actuarial Present Value of What Pension Benefits?* 10 Fam L News 134 (1987).

On apportionment of retirement benefits between community and separate estates, see §5.30. On division of defined benefit retirement plans, see §§5.92–5.93.

§5.58   (2) Defined Contribution Plans

A defined contribution plan is one in which a specified amount is contributed annually (*e.g.,* in equal contributions by employer and employee) into an individual account and invested on the employee's behalf. See *Marriage of Bergman* (1985) 168 CA3d 742, 748 n4, 214 CR 661. Profit-sharing plans, stock bonus plans, and savings plans are common examples of defined contribution plans.

Expert testimony is not required to value a defined contribution plan. The value of the community interest as of the time of trial is the amount of the contributions between the date of marriage and the date of separation, together with the changes in value through the time of trial that resulted from investments of those contributions. See 168 CA3d at 748 n4.

On apportionment of retirement benefits between community and separate estates, see §5.30.

§5.59   c. Small Businesses and Professional Practices

Small businesses and professional practices are probably the most difficult assets to value for purposes of property division in marital actions and routinely require expert testimony. The market value of a going concern is determined by valuing several components, *e.g.,* accounts receivable (see §5.60), goodwill (see §5.61), fixed assets, liabilities. See, *e.g., Marriage of Lopez* (1974) 38 CA3d 93, 110, 113 CR 58, disapproved on other grounds in 20 C3d at 453 (law practice). On valuing closely held corporations, see §5.62.

§5.60   (1) Accounts Receivable

Accounts receivable are a major asset of most small businesses and professional practices. But in valuing a business or practice, this asset is rarely included at face value. Rather, a reduction for bad debts is appropriate. See *Marriage of Lopez* (1974) 38 CA3d 93, 110, 113 CR 58, disapproved on other grounds in 20 C3d at 453 (court should value "*properly aged* accounts receivable"). See also *Marriage of Garrity & Bishton* (1986) 181 CA3d 675, 689 n15, 226 CR 485 (expert reduced accounts receivable by percentage "allowance for uncollectible accounts"). Because the percentage of uncollectible receivables varies from one business or practice to another, expert testimony on bad debts may be essential to establish the percentage write-off appropriate for the business or practice at issue. See *Burton v Burton* (1958) 161 CA2d 572, 578, 326 P2d 855 (disallowance of deduction for bad debts upheld when no evidence of such losses). Reductions may also be appropriate for future collection costs, taxes to be paid on the amounts collected, or both, but there is no clear case law on these issues.

PRACTICE TIP➤ One possible approach would be to require the spouse with access to the business to provide periodic accounts receivable reports (including documentation of attempts at collection) to the other spouse and divide any aged receivables pro rata as they are received.

§5.61   (2) Goodwill

Goodwill is a common and difficult valuation issue in cases involving community interests in small businesses or professional practices.

"Goodwill" is the expectation of continued public patronage. Bus & P C §14100. It is the competitive advantage that a business acquires over time that is expected to bring it customers in the future. See *Marriage of Foster* (1974) 42 CA3d 577, 581, 117 CR 49.

No rigid rule for determining the existence or value of goodwill has been established. Each case must be determined on its own facts. *Marriage of Lopez* (1974) 38 CA3d 93, 109, 113 CR 58, disapproved on other grounds in 20 C3d at 453. Courts have listed a number of factors to be considered in valuing goodwill. See *Marriage of Webb* (1979) 94 CA3d 335, 344, 156 CR 334 (business); *Marriage of Lopez*, supra (practice). Goodwill may not be valued, however, by any method that includes the operating spouse's postseparation efforts. *Marriage of King* (1983) 150 CA3d 304, 310, 197 CR 716. Furthermore, California courts have rejected the concept that a natural person can create or generate goodwill apart from a business he or she may operate; and it is improper to find goodwill in the career of a self-employed individual, despite his or her unique talents or elite professional standing. See *Marriage of McTiernan & Dubrow* (2005) 133 CA4th 1090, 1098, 1102, 35 CR3d 287 (self-employed motion picture director with "unique and idiosyncratic talents" does not have goodwill that can be transferred; therefore, trial court erred in finding goodwill in his career using excess earnings method).

Two popular methods that experts use in valuing goodwill are the gross receipts multiplier method and the capitalized excess earnings method. See *Mueller v Mueller* (1956) 144 CA2d 245, 252, 301 P2d 90. See also *Marriage of Foster* (1974) 42 CA3d 577, 581, 117 CR 49 (expert used latest three months' gross receipts, *i.e.,* annual gross income multiplied by 0.25, to value goodwill); *Marriage of Watts* (1985) 171 CA3d 366, 371, 217 CR 301 (finding of no goodwill reversed when trial court by implication intended to employ capitalized excess earnings method but did not do so).

The approach under the gross receipts multiplier method is to ascertain the annual gross income of the business or practice and then multiply by a numerical factor (*e.g.,* 0.25). The annual gross income might be derived from reference to the current year, the year immediately past, or an average over past years. The multiplier selected often reflects a rule of thumb that has developed over time and is customarily accepted for the particular type of business at issue, sometimes adjusted for its particular circumstances (*e.g.,* low overhead compared with the type of business generally).

With the capitalized excess earnings approach, the starting point is to determine the annual net pretax earnings, by reference to any period reasonably illustrative of the current rate of earnings, and to deduct a fair return on the net tangible assets used by the business, calculated using the percentage prevailing in the particular type of business at the time of valuation. In determining the annual net pretax earnings, the court should use a range of years to determine average earnings; using only one year is reversible error. *Marriage of Rosen* (2002) 105 CA4th 808, 130 CR2d 1, citing *Marriage of Garrity & Bishton* (1986) 181 CA3d 675, 226 CR 485. The excess earnings are then determined by deducting the annual salary of a typical salaried employee with experience commensurate with that of the spouse who is the proprietor or professional. Finally, the excess earnings are capitalized by dividing them by the selected capitalization rate (*e.g.,* 0.20) to yield the value of the goodwill. Factors that influence the capitalization rate include (1) the nature of the business, (2) the risk involved, and (3) the stability or irregularity of earnings. Rev Rul 68-609, 1967-1 Cum Bull 576.

A careful reading of the cases demonstrates that goodwill is clearly not subject to anything resembling precise calculation. Although there are some limitations on its discretion (*e.g.,* goodwill may not be valued by any method that includes the operating spouse's postseparation efforts), a court has, as a practical matter, substantial ability to choose a figure for goodwill that will result in what it regards as an appropriate overall property division.

NOTE▶ For an example of how one appellate court determined a husband's community property interest in a law firm in which his wife was a partner but was not entitled to claim a portion of the goodwill, accounts receivable, or works in progress of the firm, see *Marriage of Iredale & Cates* (2004) 121 CA4th 321, 16 CR3d 505 (no abuse of discretion to use value of wife's capital account to determine husband's community property interest in wife's law firm, since she could claim no interest in goodwill, accounts receivable, or works in progress of firm as going concern).

§5.62   (3) Closely Held Corporations

A closely held corporation is one that has few shareholders and whose shares are not generally traded in the securities market. *Mar-*

riage of Hewitson (1983) 142 CA3d 874, 881 n2, 191 CR 392. Valuing closely held stock can be difficult because of the lack of an established market. 142 CA3d at 882.

There is no required appraisal method for the valuation of interests in closely held corporations. Because of the differences between publicly traded and closely held corporations, however, the court may not rely solely on an expert opinion based on the price-earnings ratio of publicly traded companies (*i.e.,* the "comparable company method"). 142 CA3d at 885.

Depending on the circumstances, the court may set the corporation's value at either its market value or its investment value. 142 CA3d at 887. In *Hewitson,* the court listed and discussed a variety of approaches that may be used to decide the investment value and the market value of closely held shares. 142 CA3d at 881.

Additionally, the Internal Revenue Service has listed eight factors for use in valuing closely held stock. Rev Rul 59-60, 1959-1 Cum Bull 237. Courts are urged to use the factors, unless there is some statutory or decisional proscription against their use, in valuing closely held stock for purposes of marital actions. *Marriage of Micalizio* (1988) 199 CA3d 662, 673, 245 CR 673 (factors listed at 199 CA3d 674 n4). For a novel approach to dividing an interest in a closely held business, see Vanita Spaulding and Mark Bowers, *New Uses for an Old Tool: ESOPs in Divorce Court,* Family Law News, vol 28, no 2 (2006).

§5.63   d. Stock

The market value of publicly held stock that is actively traded on an exchange may be determined by reference to the price at which it was traded on the valuation date. *Marriage of Hewitson* (1983) 142 CA3d 874, 882, 191 CR 392. Judicial notice of a publication such as The Wall Street Journal will suffice. Evid C §452(h); see *Marriage of Brigden* (1978) 80 CA3d 380, 385 n3, 145 CR 716. See also *Marriage of Carter* (1971) 19 CA3d 479, 491, 97 CR 274.

On valuation of stock in closely held corporations, see §5.62.

§5.64   e. Promissory Notes

The value of a promissory note is its "market value," *i.e.,* the value as established by sales in the course of ordinary business.

Marriage of Tammen (1976) 63 CA3d 927, 930, 134 CR 161. The value of an interest-bearing promissory note is normally set at the amount due on the principal.

In some instances, however, circumstances relating to a note may make its value substantially lower than that suggested by its face value. See, *e.g., Marriage of Hopkins* (1977) 74 CA3d 591, 598, 141 CR 597 (rate of interest below prevailing rate, failure to provide for acceleration, *e.g.,* on borrower's death or on sale or refinancing of home); *Marriage of Tammen* (1976) 63 CA3d 927, 931, 134 CR 161 (long-deferred payments, inferiority of security (*i.e.,* second deed of trust), probable effects of inflation, concerns about protecting against foreclosure of first deed of trust).

f. Life Insurance

§5.65 (1) Term Insurance

A term life insurance policy covers a specified period, after which it expires without cash value. Term insurance has been a subject of conflicting authority, both on methods of valuation and, indeed, on whether there is any property interest to be valued at all. On the issue of whether term insurance is to be treated as "property" for purposes of marital actions, the courts have adopted four different views. One view holds that term insurance is simply not property subject to division. *Marriage of Lorenz* (1983) 146 CA3d 464, 468, 194 CR 237 (Second Dist., Div. Four). A second view holds that term insurance *is* property subject to division. *Marriage of Gonzalez* (1985) 168 CA3d 1021, 214 CR 634 (Fourth Dist., Div. Three). A third view holds that term insurance is property subject to division only when the insured dies or becomes uninsurable during the period for which community funds were used to pay premiums. *Estate of Logan* (1987) 191 CA3d 319, 325, 236 CR 368 (First Dist., Div. Five). The fourth view agrees with *Logan,* except regarding cases in which the insured becomes uninsurable during the period for which community funds were used to pay premiums, in which event the policy is not subject to division, because the insured had no enforceable right to renew. *Marriage of Spengler* (1992) 5 CA4th 288, 6 CR2d 764 (Third Dist.).

When a term insurance policy is considered divisible property, valuation will be required. *Marriage of Gonzalez, supra,* suggests several factors a court might examine to properly determine the value of a term life insurance policy. These factors include the face value, the amount of the premium, the insured's life expectancy, whether the policy is convertible to whole life insurance, the replacement cost, and when, if ever, the policy "vests" and is deemed fully paid. 168 CA3d at 1026. *Estate of Logan, supra,* on the other hand, finds the factors listed in *Gonzalez* to be of questionable relevance and suggests that a better measure might be the actuarial present value of the proceeds payable under the policy, considering the shortened life expectancy resulting from whatever has caused the uninsurability. 191 CA3d at 326 n8. Bear in mind that, under *Logan,* the valuation issue arises only when the insured has become uninsurable.

§5.66 (2) Whole Life Insurance

A whole life insurance policy, unlike a term policy, builds up cash reserves. For purposes of property division, the policy is usually valued at its cash surrender value, which is usually stated in the policy itself. See, *e.g., Marriage of Holmgren* (1976) 60 CA3d 869, 871, 130 CR 440. But although cash surrender value provides a convenient means of valuing a policy, it may not always be an accurate one. *Marriage of Gonzalez* (1985) 168 CA3d 1021, 1026, 214 CR 634. If, *e.g.,* the insured has become uninsurable, the cash surrender value is probably a poor measure of the policy's actual value.

§5.67 g. Automobiles

Automobiles are often valued at the mid-point between the high and low retail values shown in Kelly's Blue Book (http://www.kbb.com). See *Marriage of Carter* (1971) 19 CA3d 479, 492, 97 CR 274. When circumstances show that a different valuation method should be used, expert testimony by a qualified appraiser may be appropriate.

§5.68 h. Furniture, Furnishings, and Tools

In valuing furniture, furnishings, and tools, the age of an item is normally much more important than its purchase price or replacement cost. Used furniture has a low value on the open market. When the value will justify it, use of an appraiser is appropriate. Although no case has expressly so held, a court *may* be willing to consider evidence of completed sales of similar items on online auction houses such as www.ebay.com. Counsel should observe the rules for laying a foundation for judicial notice if this approach is attempted. See Evid C §453.

VI. DIVISION

§5.69   A. Extent of Court's Authority

The court in marital actions must divide all community, quasi-community, and quasi-marital property of the parties, unless the parties divide it themselves by agreement. Fam C §§63, 2251, 2550. On the other hand, the court normally has no authority to dispose of either spouse's separate property (*Marriage of Buford* (1984) 155 CA3d 74, 78, 202 CR 20, disapproved on other grounds in 41 C3d at 451 n13), although it may apportion community and separate interests in particular assets (155 CA3d at 78 n2). On the request of either party, the court must also divide separate property interests of the parties held by them as joint tenants or as tenants in common, including any interests in property held jointly with third parties. Fam C §2650; *Marriage of Weaver* (2005) 127 CA4th 858, 871, 26 CR3d 121. The court may also *confirm* separate property to the owner spouse. *Marriage of Hebbring* (1989) 207 CA3d 1260, 1275, 255 CR 488.

Although the court has limited authority over separate property, it may require a party who has destroyed or withheld the other's separate property to reimburse that party for the loss. *Marriage of Hebbring, supra*; *Marriage of McNeill* (1984) 160 CA3d 548, 568, 206 CR 641, overruled on other grounds in *Marriage of Fabian* (1986) 41 C3d 440, 451 n13, 715 P2d 253.

Judgments of dissolution and settlements that result in transfers of property between spouses are subject to the Uniform Fraudulent Transfer Act (CC §§3439–3439.12). *Mejia v Reed* (2003) 31 C4th 657, 669, 3 CR3d 390; *Filip v Bucurenciu* (2005) 129 CA4th 825, 838, 28 CR3d 884. Spouses drafting settlement agreements must be aware that they do not have "a one-time-only opportunity to defraud creditors by including the fraudulent transfer in an MSA." 31 C4th at 668. On when a third party might attack a judgment or settlement agreement as a fraudulent transfer, see §18.61.

B. Equal-Division Requirement

§5.70   1. Basic Rule

Under Fam C §2550, the court must divide the "community estate" (*i.e.,* the community and quasi-community (see Fam C §63) assets and liabilities of the parties) equally, except as the parties agree (see §5.71) or as otherwise provided in Fam C §§2500–2660 (see §§5.72–5.74, 5.79, 5.83–5.84). Thus, except to the extent that the exceptions apply, the court must divide the community and quasi-community assets and liabilities so that the "net" values (*i.e.,* assets less liabilities) received by the respective parties are equal. *Marriage of Olson* (1980) 27 C3d 414, 421, 165 CR 820. Family Code §2550 also applies to quasi-marital property. Fam C §2251. On methods of division, see §§5.86–5.89.

2. Exceptions to Basic Rule

§5.71   a. Agreement of Parties

Family Code §2550 (former CC §4800(a)) expressly provides that the parties to a marital action may divide their community estate by agreement, in which event they are not limited by the equal-division requirement. The agreement must, however, be written or, if oral, made in open court. See *Marriage of Maricle* (1990) 220 CA3d 55, 269 CR 204 (out-of-court oral agreement unenforceable even though performed).

Before the petition is filed, however, agreements between spouses regarding property are governed by Fam C §852 (former CC §5110.730). *Marriage of Maricle, supra;* see §5.28.

§5.72   b. Deliberate Misappropriation

When one party has deliberately misappropriated community assets to the exclusion of the other party's interest in them, the court may make an unequal division of the community estate to the extent necessary to reimburse the other party for his or her loss. Fam C §2602; *Marriage of Economou* (1990) 224 CA3d 1466, 1483, 274 CR 473. An act of "deliberate misappropriation" under this section has been described as "calculated thievery." *Marriage of Schultz* (1980) 105 CA3d 846, 855, 164 CR 653.

As a practical matter, however, few cases address misappropriation by reference to this section. More common are cases decided by reference to the management and control statutes (Fam C §§1100–1102 (former CC §§5125–5125.1, 5127)). There are two types of situations in which reimbursement has most often been required:

- Unilateral transfer of community property (see, *e.g., Marriage of Stephenson* (1984) 162 CA3d 1057, 1070, 209 CR 383); and

- Use of community property for a separate property purpose (see, *e.g., Marriage of Lister* (1984) 152 CA3d 411, 199 CR 321).

§5.73   c. Low-Asset Case in Which One Party Cannot Be Located

When the net value of the community estate is less than $5000 and one party cannot be located with reasonable diligence, the court may award the entire community estate to the other party on such conditions as it deems proper. Fam C §2604. Clearly, the requirements of the statute will be met when the respondent cannot be located with reasonable diligence from the time of service of summons through the time of judgment. But it appears that the requirements would also be met when either party cannot be located at the time of judgment, regardless of whether the respondent could be located at the time of service.

§5.74   d. Personal Injury Damages

"Community estate personal injury damages" (*i.e.,* all community property personal injury damages except those commingled with other assets of the community estate) are divided in accordance with special rules. Fam C §2603. On whether personal injury damages are community property or the separate property of the injured spouse, see §5.29.

Community estate personal injury damages must be assigned to the injured party unless the court determines that the interests of justice require another disposition, after taking into account (1) the economic condition and needs of each party, (2) the time that has elapsed since recovery of the damages or accrual of the cause of action, and (3) all other facts of the case. When the court determines that another disposition is required, the noninjured party must be assigned the proportion, to a maximum of half the damages, that the court decides is just. Fam C §2603(b). For example, when the community has incurred costs in caring for the injured party, courts will often award a portion of the damages to the noninjured party to offset his or her share of those costs.

Property purchased with community estate personal injury damages remains subject to Fam C §2603 unless commingling with other community property makes it impossible to trace the source of the property. *Marriage of Devlin* (1982) 138 CA3d 804, 810, 189 CR 1 (land and mobile home purchased with personal injury proceeds retained character of proceeds).

Family Code §2603 provides an exception to the equal-division mandate of Fam C §2550. When more than half of the personal injury damages are awarded to the injured party, the other party is *not* entitled to an offsetting award of other community property to equalize the overall division. *Marriage of Morris* (1983) 139 CA3d 823, 189 CR 80.

§5.75   e. Particular Debts

The Family Code provisions on division of property (Fam C §§2500–2660) provide for exceptions to the equal-division requirement in the assignment of particular debts. See §§5.79 (excess of community debts over community assets), 5.83 (education loans), 5.84 (tort liability incurred while acting other than for benefit of community).

§5.76   f. Award of Retirement Benefits to Victim of Attempted Murder by Spouse; Related Law

When a spouse is convicted of attempting to murder the other spouse as punishable under Pen C §664(a), the victim spouse will be entitled to receive an award of all of the community property interest in his or her own retirement benefits. Fam C §782.5. The Probate Code also prevents any person "who feloniously and intentionally caused the decedent's death" from receiving any property, interest, or benefit under the will or other testamentary instrument or process. Prob C §250.

In addition, there is a line of federal cases holding that insurance proceeds that are subject to federal law may not pass to a beneficiary who caused the death of the decedent. See, *e.g., Shoemaker v Shoe-*

maker (6th Cir 1959) 263 F2d 931, 932 (public policy founded on principle that no one permitted to profit from own wrong to take proceeds of insurance, "unless the beneficiary was insane at the time, or the killing was accidental, or was committed in self-defense").

§5.76A   g. Judgment for Civil Damages for Domestic Violence by One Spouse Against Other

Effective January 1, 2005, the court may enforce a judgment for civil damages for an act of domestic violence perpetrated by one spouse upon the other against the abusive spouse's share of community property if a proceeding for dissolution or legal separation is pending (before the entry of final judgment). Fam C §2603.5. On restrictions on the payment of spousal support to an abusive spouse, see §6.10. *Marriage of Cauley* (2006) 138 CA4th 1100, 1106, 41 CR3d 902.

§5.77   3. Statutory Scheme for Assignment of Debts

The Family Code provisions on division of property (Fam C §§2500–2660) provide a detailed scheme for assignment of debts in a marital action. Although the starting point for division of property is the requirement that the court divide the community estate (*i.e.*, assets and liabilities) equally (see Fam C §2550; §5.70), the only debts that are included in that division are those incurred between the date of marriage and the date of separation that are not separate debts incurred for other than the benefit of the community (Fam C §§2620–2625; see §5.79). All other debts are assigned in other ways. See §§5.78, 5.80–5.81.

§5.78   a. Incurred Before Marriage

A debt incurred by either spouse before the date of marriage must be confirmed to the spouse who incurred it, without offset. Fam C §2621.

§5.79   b. Incurred During Marriage and Before Separation

Debts incurred by either spouse after the date of marriage but before the date of separation must be divided as part of the overall division of the community estate as set forth in Fam C §§2550–2552 and 2601–2604 (*i.e.,* community estate to be divided equally, subject to specified exceptions). Fam C §2622(a). A separate debt incurred during this period for other than the benefit of the community, however, must be confirmed to the spouse who incurred it, without offset. Fam C §2625; *Marriage of Cairo* (1988) 204 CA3d 1255, 1267, 251 CR 731. Also, to the extent that community debts exceed community (and quasi-community) assets, the *excess* of debt is not assigned as part of the overall division, but rather as the court deems just and equitable, taking into account the parties' relative abilities to pay. Fam C §2622(b). On other debts that are not divided as part of the overall division of the community estate, see §§5.83 (educational loans), 5.84 (tort liability incurred while acting other than for benefit of community).

NOTE➤ Community income tax debts that arise from jointly filed tax returns are subject to the above general provisions. A potential avenue to relief from joint liability for such debts is found in the so-called "innocent spouse" rules of federal law. IRC §6015. In addition, a taxpayer who is granted relief under IRC §6015 also may be eligible for similar California relief if the facts and circumstances are the same. See Rev & TC §18533(i), (m) (repealing existing version of statute as of January 1, 2009).

§5.80   c. Incurred After Separation but Before Entry of Judgment

Under Fam C §2623, assignment of a debt incurred after the date of separation but before entry of judgment depends on the purpose for which the debt was incurred:

- If incurred for the "common necessaries of life" of either spouse or for the "necessaries of life" of children of the marriage for whom support may be ordered, the debt must be confirmed to either spouse according to their respective needs and abilities to pay when the debt was incurred, unless there was a court order or written agreement for support or for the payment of such debts (Fam C §2623(a)); and

- If not incurred for necessaries, the debt must be confirmed to the spouse who incurred it, without offset (Fam C §2623(b)).

When the current scheme for assignment of debts in a marital action was enacted, all debts incurred during marriage, including those incurred after separation, were debts for which the parties' community property (except for the earnings of a spouse who did not incur the debt) was liable under former CC §5120.110, predecessor of Fam C §§910–911. Former CC §5120.110 was subsequently amended to exclude debts incurred after separation. As a result, it may be that a debt incurred after separation but before entry of judgment must be confirmed, as a "separate debt" under Fam C §2625 (all separate debts must be confirmed to spouse who incurs them), to the spouse who incurred it, even if it was incurred for necessaries.

§5.81 d. Incurred After Entry of Judgment but Before Termination of Marital Status

A debt incurred by either spouse after entry of judgment but before termination of the parties' marital status must be confirmed to the spouse who incurred it, without offset. Fam C §2624.

§5.82 e. Reimbursement for Debts Paid After Separation but Before Trial

The court may order reimbursement when appropriate for debts paid after separation but before trial. Fam C §2626. See §5.99. See, e.g., Marriage of Williams (1989) 213 CA3d 1239, 262 CR 317 (community entitled to reimbursement under former CC §4800(e) for payment, after separation but before trial, of husband's child support arrearage incurred before marriage). But see Marriage of Sherman (2005) 133 CA4th 795, 804, 35 CR3d 137 (addressing 3-year statute of limitations provided by Fam C § 920(c)(1) for such claims arising during marriage and need to prove spouse paying separate support debts had nonexempt separate income when debts were paid with community property).

§5.83 f. Special Rule: Education Loans

Regardless of Fam C §§2550–2552 and 2620–2624 (equal-division requirement and debt allocation scheme), education loans must be assigned in accordance with Fam C §2641. Fam C §2627. Under Fam C §2641(b)(2), a loan incurred during marriage for the education or training of a party that has substantially enhanced that party's earning capacity must be assigned to the party, without offset. The required assignment must be reduced or modified, however, to the extent circumstances render it unjust (*e.g.,* community has substantially benefited from loan). Fam C §2641(c). For discussion of assignment under Fam C §2641, see §5.96.

§5.84   g. Special Rule: Tort Liability Incurred While Acting Other Than for Benefit of Community

Regardless of Fam C §§2550–2552 and 2620–2624 (equal-division requirement and debt allocation scheme), a tort liability subject to Fam C §1000(b)(2) (liability incurred while acting other than for benefit of community) must be assigned to the party who incurred it, without offset. Fam C §2627. See *Marriage of Bell* (1996) 49 CA4th 300, 56 CR2d 623 (allocation to wife of entire obligation to pay settlement arising out of her embezzlement reversed because community shared in benefit from embezzlement; allocation to wife of attorney fees for her defense and tax liability arising out of embezzlement affirmed).

§5.85   C. Methods

As long as the resulting division is equal, the trial court is vested with considerable discretion in dividing community property to ensure that an equitable division is reached. *Marriage of Fink* (1979) 25 C3d 877, 885, 160 CR 516. Although in-kind division is the judicially preferred method of division (*Marriage of Brigden* (1978) 80 CA3d 380, 390, 145 CR 716), other methods are appropriate when economic circumstances warrant (Fam C §2601); *Marriage of Fink, supra*). It should be noted that courts will often use more than one method in fashioning an overall division, *e.g.,* divide some assets in kind and award others by the asset distribution method. The available methods (see *Marriage of Cream* (1993) 13 CA4th 81, 88, 16 CR2d 575) are discussed in §§5.86–5.89.

Note the requirement that the method chosen provide for an equal division. For an example of a method that failed to do that, see *Marriage of Cream, supra* (absent stipulation, court has no authority to order interspousal auction of community asset as substitute for court valuation and award of asset).

§5.86   1. In-Kind Division

Under an in-kind division, each party is awarded a portion (usually half) of a particular asset. See, *e.g., Marriage of Behrens* (1982) 137 CA3d 562, 572, 187 CR 200 (in-kind division of closely held shares).

§5.87   2. Asset Distribution (or "Cash Out")

Under the asset distribution method, the court assigns one or more community assets to one party and one or more community assets to the other. See, *e.g., Marriage of Fink* (1979) 25 C3d 877, 886, 160 CR 516 (court awarded assets to respective parties with attention to personal and practical considerations). Often, however, it is not possible to assign community assets and liabilities to the respective parties in a way that produces an equal division of the community estate. In that event, to equalize what would otherwise be an unequal division, the court may order a payment by one party, from his or her separate property, to the other party. For this reason, the asset distribution method is commonly known as the "cash-out" method (see, *e.g., Marriage of Bergman* (1985) 168 CA3d 742, 749, 214 CR 661). The payment is usually made in accordance with the terms of a promissory note. See, *e.g., Marriage of Slater* (1979) 100 CA3d 241, 248, 160 CR 686. When, however, a promissory note's actual value is substantially less than its face amount, the result may be an unequal division. See §5.64. See also *Marriage of Hopkins* (1977) 74 CA3d 591, 597, 141 CR 597 (promissory note not justified when payor able to pay cash). For possible tax consequences of a "cash out" division, see §5.103.

§5.88   3. Sale and Division of Proceeds

The court may order an asset sold and the proceeds divided (usually equally) between the parties. See, *e.g., Marriage of Holmgren* (1976) 60 CA3d 869, 873, 130 CR 440 (family residence).

§5.89   4. Continued Co-Ownership as Tenants in Common

The court may order an asset held by the parties as tenants in common and retain jurisdiction to partition the undivided interests at a later date. See, *e.g., Marriage of Duke* (1980) 101 CA3d 152,

155, 161 CR 444 (family residence). The court may *not,* however, order the property to be held in joint tenancy. *Marriage of Stallworth* (1987) 192 CA3d 742, 747 n2, 237 CR 829. A deferred-partition order usually concerns a family residence, in which case it is termed a "deferred sale of home order" and is governed by Fam C §§3800–3810. See §5.90.

D. Specific Assets

§5.90   1. Family Residence: Deferred Sale

Family Code §§3800–3810 provide for a "deferred sale of home order." Such an order temporarily delays the sale of the family home and awards temporary but exclusive use and possession to one of the parties. The party must have sole or joint physical custody of one or more minor children or of one or more adult children for whom support is authorized under Fam C §§3900–3901 (adult unmarried children under age 19 who are full-time high school students and are not self-supporting) or Fam C §3910 (incapacitated and needy adult children). The purpose of the order is to minimize adverse effects of the marital action on the children's welfare. Fam C §3800(b). Provided that the requirements of Fam C §§3800–3810 are met, a deferred sale of home order may be made even when the nonresident parent has a substantial separate property interest in the home. *Marriage of Braud* (1996) 45 CA4th 797, 813, 53 CR2d 179.

When a party requests a deferred sale of home order, the court must first determine whether it is economically feasible to maintain mortgage, property tax, and insurance payments during the period of deferred sale and to maintain the home in a condition comparable to that at the time of trial. Fam C §3801(a). In making the determination, designed to prevent any circumstance that would jeopardize the parties' equity in the home, the court must consider the resident parent's income, the availability of spousal support and child support, and any other source of funds available to make the payments. Fam C §3801(b)–(c).

If the court decides that it is not economically feasible to defer sale of the home, it must deny the order. But if it decides that a deferred sale is economically feasible, the court must consider all of the following in exercising its discretion to grant or deny the order:

- The length of time the children have lived in the home (Fam C §3802(b)(1));

- The children's placements or grades in school (Fam C §3802(b)(2));

- The accessibility from the home of the children's schools and other services or facilities used by them, including child care (Fam C §3802(b)(3));

- Whether the home has been adapted to accommodate any physical disabilities of the children or the resident parent and, if so, whether a change of residence may adversely affect the resident parent's ability to meet the children's needs (Fam C §3802(b)(4));

- The emotional detriment to the children associated with a change of residence (Fam C §3802(b)(5));

- The extent to which the home's location permits the resident parent to continue his or her employment (Fam C §3802(b)(6));

- The financial ability of each parent to obtain suitable housing (Fam C §3802(b)(7));

- The tax consequences to the parents (Fam C §3802(b)(8));

- The economic detriment to the nonresident parent if the order is granted (Fam C §3802(b)(9)); and

- Any other factors the court deems just and equitable (Fam C §3802(b)(10)).

If the court determines, after considering the required items, that a deferred sale of home order is necessary to minimize the adverse impact of the marital action on the children's welfare, it may make such an order, specifying its duration. Fam C §§3802(a), 3803. Title should be held by the parties as tenants in common and not as joint tenants. *Marriage of Stallworth* (1987) 192 CA3d 742, 747 n2, 237 CR 829. Normally, the resident parent is responsible for all mortgage payments, property taxes, homeowner's insurance, and reasonable maintenance. *Marriage of Horowitz* (1984) 159 CA3d 368, 373 n5, 205 CR 874 (predating codification but still descriptive of normal practice on responsibility for payments). The court may make an order specifying the parties' respective responsibilities for payment of costs of improvements. Fam C §3806.

Unless the parties agree otherwise in writing:

- The order may be modified or terminated at any time at the discretion of the court (Fam C §3807); and

- If the resident parent remarries, or if there is otherwise a change of circumstances affecting the determinations required by Fam C §3801 or §3802 or the economic status of the parties or children on which the award is based, there is a rebuttable presumption that further deferral of the sale is no longer appropriate (Fam C §3808).

In making a deferred sale of home order, the court must reserve jurisdiction to determine any issues that arise with respect to the order, *e.g.,* home maintenance, tax consequences. Fam C §3809.

NOTE➤ In the event of a deferred sale of the home order, the order should specifically exclude the "out" spouse from the home in order to preserve the ability to exclude gain when the home is ultimately sold. IRC §121(e)(3)(B). See §5.105.

On adjustments to child support amounts payable by the nonresident parent, see §8.18.

On the effect of a supporting spouse filing a bankruptcy petition after a marital dissolution, see Personal and Small Business Bankruptcy Practice in California, chap 16 (Cal CEB 2003).

§5.91   2. Out-of-State Real Property

When the community estate includes interests in out-of-state real property, Fam C §2660 establishes a preference that the property be divided without changing the manner in which record title is held, but does not remove the court's discretion to order otherwise. *Marriage of Fink* (1979) 25 C3d 877, 885, 160 CR 516 (trial court within its discretion in concluding that practical and equal division of community property required affecting record title to Florida property).

Family Code §2660 recognizes that a California judgment cannot directly affect real property in another state unless the judgment is allowed that effect by the other state's laws. Consequently, it establishes a preference for a division accomplished without changing the interests in the out-of-state real property. But in some instances this approach may be impractical, *e.g.,* when the value of the out-of-state real property exceeds the value of the remaining community property. In that event, the court may order the parties to take such actions (*e.g.,* execute conveyances, and sell property and divide proceeds) as may be necessary to effect an equal division and, if one party does not comply, may award the other party the money value of the interest he or she would have received or hold the noncomplying party in contempt. 25 C3d at 884 n5, quoting Comment to former CC §4800.5 (predecessor of Fam C §2660).

3. Defined Benefit Retirement Plan

§5.92   a. Methods of Division

Defined benefit retirement plans present a challenging property-division issue in many marital actions. A defined benefit plan is one in which the benefits may be ascertained by reference to factors such as the employee's age at retirement, years of service at retirement, and highest income level achieved. *Marriage of Bergman* (1985) 168 CA3d 742, 748 n4, 214 CR 661.

In marital actions, defined benefit plans may be divided by either: (1) a present in-kind division (see §5.86) or (2) the asset distribution method (or "cash-out" method) (see §5.87). The court has broad discretion in determining which approach to use and neither method is judicially preferred. 168 CA3d at 749. *Bergman* contains a good discussion of considerations in weighing the advantages and disadvantages of each approach in a given situation.

Some cases and commentators refer to a third method of disposition, *i.e.,* a reservation of jurisdiction to divide retirement benefits at a later date. This approach should be distinguished from a present in-kind division, in which the court divides the benefits at the time of judgment and reserves jurisdiction only to make orders necessary to implement that division. Some courts have approved reservations of jurisdiction to divide benefits in the future. See *Marriage of Ramer* (1986) 187 CA3d 263, 275, 231 CR 647 (Fourth Dist., Div. Two); *Marriage of Carl* (1977) 67 CA3d 542, 546, 136 CR 703 (Second Dist., Div. Five). But *Marriage of Bergman, supra* (First Dist., Div. Five), held that a court does not have authority to postpone division in this way. 168 CA3d at 756. Acknowledging that former CC §4800(a) (predecessor of Fam C §2550) allows the court to make the property division in its judgment "or at a later time if it expressly reserves jurisdiction to make such a property division," *Bergman* characterizes the latter approach as providing only for bifurcation of issues and not as allowing a court to reserve jurisdiction indefinitely to divide a community asset. 168 CA3d at 755. *Bergman* also offers the policy argument that there is no good reason to perpetuate the litigation indefinitely when retirement benefits can be divided at the same time as the parties' other property. 168 CA3d at 757.

Although the validity of reserving jurisdiction to divide retirement benefits in the future remains unsettled, it is not a recommended approach. Not only is it possibly invalid, but it presents a number of potential problems, including the risk that one of the parties might die prior to entry of an order dividing the benefits or the possibility that, when the time comes to divide the benefits, one of the parties might be reluctant or even unavailable to reopen negotiations or litigation. The nonemployee spouse also risks complete divestment of his or her survivor benefit if the employee spouse remarries before entry of an order designating the former spouse as "surviving spouse." *Rivers v Central & S.W. Corp.* (5th Cir 1999) 186 F3d 681 (former spouse who failed to obtain QDRO before employee's retirement was "forever barred" from interest in his pension plan); *Samaroo v Samaroo* (3d Cir 1999) 193 F3d 185; *Hopkins v AT&T Global Info. Solutions Co.* (4th Cir 1997) 105 F3d 153 (order that former spouse be designated as surviving spouse rejected because surviving spouse benefit had vested in subsequent spouse on employee's retirement). While case law in this area is unsettled and no 9th Circuit opinion regarding posthumous or nunc pro tunc QDROs pertaining to survivor benefits has been published, it would appear most prudent to obtain orders dividing the benefit and designating any survivor rights prior to or simultaneously with the dissolution judgment. For further discussion, see Dividing Pensions and Other Employee Benefits in California Divorces (Cal CEB 2006).

NOTE➤ In a case concerning federal retirement benefits, the Federal Circuit Court of Appeals has explicitly stated that an order purporting to reserve jurisdiction over the division of retirement and other employee benefits is ineffective. The court cited regulations of the Office of Personnel Management (which administers federal retirement benefits) that specifically exclude from the "definition of 'first order dividing marital property' any court order 'issued under reserved jurisdiction or any other court orders issued subsequent to the original written order that divide any marital property regardless of the effective date of the court order.' 5 CFR. §838.1004(e)(4)(ii)(B)." *Rafferty v Office of Personnel Management* (5th Cir 2005) 407 F3d 1317. While *Rafferty* was decided by the Federal Circuit and therefore does not create binding precedent for California courts, the cautious practitioner would be wise to consult with an attorney experienced in federal employee benefits procedures before signing off on a judgment for dissolution.

Retirement benefits are subject to division in marital actions, regardless of whether they are (1) benefits being received, (2) benefits that are matured (*i.e.,* employee has unconditional right to retire and obtain immediate payment of benefits) but are not being received, or (3) benefits that are not matured. In any of these three instances, the benefits may be divided by the asset distribution method or by an in-kind division. Under the asset distribution method, the court values the community interest in the benefits, typically relying on expert testimony by actuaries, awards it to the employee spouse, and equalizes the division of community property by awarding to the other spouse other community property, an equalizing payment, or both. Under an in-kind division, the court determines the community portion of the benefits and then orders that half of the community portion of each payment is the nonemployee-spouse's share.

The court is also required to make whatever orders are necessary or appropriate to ensure that each party receives his or her full community share in all survivor and death benefits available through the plan. Fam C §2610. Such benefits may consist of any or all of a survivor annuity, lump-sum death benefit, or refund of an employee's contributions to the plan. Failure to explicitly provide for the allocation of such benefits can be fatal to the nonemployee spouse's claim once the employee spouse dies. *Rafferty v Office of Personnel Management* (Fed Cir 2005) 407 F3d 1317. The court might order, *e.g.,* that the community interest in death benefits be divided equally between the parties (Fam C §2610(a)(1)) or that the employee spouse make a particular election with respect to death benefits (Fam C §2610(a)(2)). Note, however, that, depending on the nature of the benefit, the court may not have authority to order that the nonemployee spouse be permitted to designate a successor-in-interest to his or her community interest in the retirement benefits. *Marriage of Shelstead* (1998) 66 CA4th 893, 78 CR2d 365; see *Boggs v Boggs* (1997) 520 US 833, 138 L Ed 2d 45, 117 S Ct

1754; *Marriage of Schofield* (1998) 62 CA4th 131, 139, 73 CR2d 1 (trial court could make postjudgment order that increased wife's share of husband's federal civil service pension to include payment of arrearages after husband tried to prevent wife from receiving benefits from the account allocated to her by combining two retirement accounts that the dissolution judgment had divided).

Family Code §2610 also authorizes the court, on the agreement of the nonemployee spouse, to order the division of accumulated community property contributions and service credit as provided in the following or similar enactments (Fam C §2610(a)(3)):

- Government Code §§21290–21298 (Public Employees' Retirement System);

- Education Code §§22650–22666 (State Teachers' Retirement System Defined Benefit Program);

- Government Code §§31685–31685.96 (County Employees' Retirement System);

- Government Code §§75050–75059.1 (Judges' Retirement System); and

- Education Code §§27400–27413 (State Teachers' Retirement System Cash Balance Benefit Program).

Note that, by its own terms, Fam C §2610(a)(3) is applicable only with the consent of the nonemployee spouse. When a plan subject to Fam C §2610(a)(3) is involved, counsel should ascertain, probably with an actuary's assistance, whether the client will fare better under the code sections whose use is authorized by Fam C §2610(a)(3) or under another approach. Division of the benefits into separate accounts in accordance with §2610(a)(3) may work to the disadvantage of the nonemployee spouse.

Family Code §2610, in language similar to that used in ERISA (see 29 USC §1056(d)(3)(D)), expressly prohibits court orders that require a retirement plan to provide increased benefits determined on the basis of actuarial value (Fam C §2610(a)(2)) or to make payments in any manner that increases the benefits provided by the plan (Fam C §2610(b)(1)).

Note that a prospective alternate payee's community share of retirement benefits may be lost if he or she dies before the dissolution judgment is entered. *Regents of University of California v Benford*

(2005) 128 CA4th 867, 874, 27 CR3d 441. In addition, even when a judgment dividing a plan has been entered, a deceased former spouse is not an alternate payee for ERISA purposes. *Branco v UFCW-N. Cal. Employers Joint Pension Plan* (9th Cir 2002) 279 F3d 1154 (after nonemployee former wife died, her QDRO-ordered share reverted to surviving former husband; deceased wife cannot be "qualifying recipient" and her estate and heirs cannot be "beneficiary" or "alternate payee").

On implementation of orders requiring payment by the plan to the nonemployee, see §§12.7–12.25 (joinder of plan), 17.68–17.79 (qualified domestic relations orders (QDROs)), 17.80–17.83 (orders dividing public pension benefits).

On apportionment of retirement benefits between community and separate estates, see §5.30. On valuation of retirement benefits, see §§5.57–5.58.

§5.93   b. *Gillmore* Election

When benefits in a defined benefit retirement plan (see §5.92) are matured but the employee chooses to continue working, the nonemployee spouse is entitled to demand payment of his or her share without waiting for the employee to retire. *Marriage of Gillmore* (1981) 29 C3d 418, 428, 174 CR 493. It appears that division of the community interest may be accomplished by either the asset distribution (or "cash-out") method (*i.e.,* the employee buys out the nonemployee's share of the benefits by paying the present value of the nonemployee's share), or by an in-kind division (*i.e.,* payment of the nonemployee's share on a monthly basis). 29 C3d at 429. Although *Gillmore* does not specify how the monthly amount to be paid under an in-kind division is to be determined, it appears that the payments should be the amounts the nonemployee would have received if the employee had retired at the time of the election. *Marriage of Jacobson* (1984) 161 CA3d 465, 475, 207 CR 512.

It should be noted, however, that one case held that a *Gillmore* election requires a "cash out" and that only after the present value of the nonemployee's share is determined actuarially does the court have discretion to determine whether the employee will pay that discounted value in a lump sum or in installments. *Marriage of Shattuck* (1982) 134 CA3d 683, 687, 184 CR 698. But see *Marriage of Jacobson* (1984) 161 CA3d 465, 468, 475, 207 CR 512, 513 (court of appeal, purporting to distinguish *Shattuck,* affirmed monthly payments to nonemployee of amounts she would have received had employee retired at time of election).

The nonemployee spouse who makes a *Gillmore* election gives up any increased payments in the future that might have otherwise resulted from increases in the employee's age, period of service, or salary. *Marriage of Gillmore* (1981) 29 C3d 418, 428 n9, 174 CR 493. On the other hand, the nonemployee retains the right to share in any increase in benefits (*e.g.,* cost-of-living adjustments) that would have been received if the employee had actually retired at the time of the election. *Marriage of Scott* (1984) 156 CA3d 251, 254, 202 CR 716.

When the benefits are matured at the time of trial, the nonemployee may either make a *Gillmore* election then or postpone receipt of the benefits until the employee retires. The nonemployee may not elect to receive the benefits beginning at some point between the time of trial and the time of retirement. *Marriage of Castle* (1986) 180 CA3d 206, 216, 225 CR 382. When, on the other hand, the benefits are not matured at the time of trial and the court reserves jurisdiction, the nonemployee may make the election at any time after they mature. See, *e.g., Marriage of Gillmore* (1981) 29 C3d 418, 421, 174 CR 493. If the employee spouse continues to work and the nonemployee spouse chooses immediate payment, the nonemployee is entitled to receive such payment as of the date on which he or she files a motion seeking immediate payment. *Marriage of Cornejo* (1996) 13 C4th 381, 385, 53 CR2d 81.

An attorney whose client is a nonemployee spouse considering whether to assert his or her *Gillmore* rights should consider not only the availability of an order, but also its potential enforceability against the plan itself. The nonemployee's *Gillmore* rights are specifically recognized under the Retirement Equity Act of 1984 (Pub L 98-397, 98 Stat 1426). 29 USC §1056(d)(3)(E)(i). The Act covers all private plans. In addition, California law requires the State Teachers' Retirement System (with respect to its Defined Benefit Program), the Public Employees' Retirement System, the Judges' Retirement System, and the County Employees' Retirement System to recognize *Gillmore* rights. Ed C §22664(a)(1)-(3) (STRS); Govt C §21295 (PERS), §75050 (JRS), §31685 (CERS). Such statutes ensure that a *Gillmore* order will be implemented by the retirement plan through direct payments to the nonemployee spouse. On implementation of orders requiring payment by the plan to the nonemployee, see §§12.7–12.25 (joinder of plan), 17.68–17.79 (qualified domestic relations orders (QDROs)). In some instances, however, the plan may be required to pay only a part, but not all, of the court-ordered amounts directly to the nonemployee spouse. See 29 USC §1056(d)(3)(E)(i)(II). In that event, the nonemployee will have to seek the remainder from the employee. On enforcement of orders generally, see chap 20.

The nonemployee is entitled to a *Gillmore* order even when the employee is a member of a plan that is not subject to legislation requiring that it implement such orders. Unless the plan itself has chosen to provide for direct payment, however, the payments will have to come from the employee spouse, rather than the plan, and enforcement will have to be sought against that spouse if he or she does not make the required payments voluntarily. See Fam C §2610(b)(2); *Marriage of Nice* (1991) 230 CA3d 444, 281 CR 415 (public plan may not be ordered to pay nonemployee spouse before employee retires when not otherwise obligated to do so); *Marriage of Jacobson* (1984) 161 CA3d 465, 472, 207 CR 512 (military service member may not be ordered to retire to effect direct payments from plan to nonmember spouse but may be ordered to reimburse nonmember for his or her pension share while member remains on active duty).

Like any other property right in a marital action, a party's right to make a *Gillmore* election may be waived in a marital settlement agreement. The intention to do so, however, must be express and unequivocal. The agreement on its face must manifest the parties' clear intention that the employee spouse have full control over the date on which payments to the nonemployee spouse will commence. *Marriage of Crook* (1992) 2 CA4th 1606, 1611, 3 CR2d 905.

If electing to receive benefits under *Gillmore*, it is important to understand the tax consequences to the payor and payee. Historically, the Internal Revenue Service has applied the "assignment of income" doctrine to direct, out-of-pocket payments made by the employee spouse to the alternate payee, taxing the amount paid as income to the payor. However, in a 2005 anomalous ruling that remained on appeal when this publication went to press, the tax court held that an employee spouse who chose not to retire when eligible but whose former wife made a *Gillmore* election to begin receiving benefits could exclude the payments he made to the wife from his gross income, choosing not to apply the assignment-of-income doctrine. *John Michael Dunkin* (2005) 124 TC No 10.

§5.94   4. Business or Professional Practice

Although in-kind division (see §5.86) is the judicially preferred method of dividing community property (*Marriage of Brigden* (1978) 80 CA3d 380, 390, 145 CR 716), that method is ordinarily not used when a family business is at issue. Marital actions usually involve such interpersonal hostility that continuing the business partnership is impracticable. *Marriage of Lotz* (1981) 120 CA3d 379, 385, 174 CR 618. When both parties have been operating the business, want it, and can purchase it, the court will usually have to value the business and award it to one of them; a sale should not be ordered. *Marriage of Cream* (1993) 13 CA4th 81, 89, 16 CR2d 575.

A business should be awarded to the operator spouse when he or she has qualities (*e.g.,* knowledge, experience, relationships with customers) that are essential to its success and the other spouse does not. See, *e.g., Marriage of Burlini* (1983) 143 CA3d 65, 70, 191 CR 541 (coin-laundry business); *Marriage of Smith* (1978) 79 CA3d 725, 751, 145 CR 205 (sign-making business). But when the nonoperator spouse does not lack qualities crucial to continued operation of a business, it may be awarded to him or her. *Marriage of Kozen* (1986) 185 CA3d 1258, 1262, 230 CR 304 (award of one Burger King franchise to each spouse upheld when nonoperator spouse would be able to run franchise after attending training program).

As a practical matter, when a spouse is engaged in a business or professional practice that requires a license (*e.g.,* building contractor, cosmetologist, attorney, physician), the business or professional practice will certainly be awarded to the licensed spouse.

E. Reimbursement

§5.95   1. Separate Property Contributions to Acquisition of Community Property

A party is entitled to reimbursement for contributions to the acquisition of community property to the extent that he or she traces the contributions to a separate property source, unless the party has waived the right to reimbursement in writing. Fam C §2640; *Mar-*

riage of Fabian (1986) 41 C3d 440, 444, 224 CR 333. In *Marriage of Walrath* (1998) 17 C4th 907, 918, 72 CR2d 856, the definition of "property" in Fam C §2640 was found to include not only the original community property to which separate property had been contributed, but also any subsequent property acquired with the proceeds from refinancing the original community property. On tracing, see *Marriage of Braud* (1996) 45 CA4th 797, 822, 53 CR2d 179 (reimbursement under Fam C §2640 reversed for insufficient evidence to trace payments to separate property source). Note that §2640 does not apply to assets that have not been transmuted from separate to community property status. *Marriage of Koester* (1999) 73 CA4th 1032, 1037, 87 CR2d 76 (incorporation of husband's separate property business was not acquisition of community property; trial court should have applied *Pereira* formula instead of §2640). See §5.16 for discussion of *Pereira* formula for allocating to the community a share of benefits derived from one spouse's efforts devoted to separate property. Section 2640 applies to contributions to the acquisition of *any* community property, not merely property whose characterization is governed by its companion statute, Fam C §2581 (former CC §4800.1) (see §5.20). *Marriage of Witt* (1987) 197 CA3d 103, 108, 242 CR 646. Family Code §2640 does not, however, govern reimbursement when separate property is used *after separation* to pay community obligations existing at separation or to make improvements on community property. See §§5.99–5.100.

Without the requisite written waiver, the contributor is entitled to reimbursement even if he or she intended a gift to the community. 197 CA3d at 108. The specific statutory requirement to avoid the reimbursement is that the contributor "has made a written waiver of the right to reimbursement or signed a writing that has the effect of a waiver." Fam C §2640(b). Although the meaning of these words is not entirely clear, it appears that they will be narrowly construed. The deed itself that creates the presumption, under Fam C §2581, that the property is community property (see §5.20) is not sufficient to constitute a waiver of reimbursement. *Marriage of Kahan* (1985) 174 CA3d 63, 71, 219 CR 700. For a writing to constitute a waiver of the right to reimbursement, there must be either an actual intention to relinquish the right or conduct so inconsistent with the intent to enforce the right as to induce a reasonable belief that it has been relinquished. *Marriage of Perkal* (1988) 203 CA3d 1198, 1203, 250 CR 296. In *Perkal*, it was held that the fact that the contributing party wrote "For A Gift" on the deed did not satisfy the requirements for a waiver of the right to reimbursement when the party testified that his purpose was to avoid payment of a documentary transfer tax and a possible reassessment for property tax purposes and that he had no reason to know about former CC §4800.2, which had taken effect less than a month before. See also *Marriage of Lange* (2002) 102 CA4th 360, 125 CR2d 379 (wife's preparation and husband's acceptance of promissory note and deed of trust on family residence did not waive her §2640 reimbursement rights); *Marriage of Carpenter* (2002) 100 CA4th 424, 122 CR2d 526 (premarital agreement silent on right of reimbursement did not constitute waiver under §2640).

Reimbursable contributions include downpayments (earnest money if for actual improvements); payments for improvements, including school fees associated with a building permit; and payments that reduce the principal of a loan used to finance a purchase or improvements, but they do not include payments for loan interest or for property maintenance, insurance, or taxes. See *Marriage of Cochran* (2001) 87 CA4th 1050, 1062, 104 CR2d 920. Reimbursable contributions do *not* include separate property payments of community credit card debts during the marriage, even when the lender required the payment so that the couple could qualify for a loan to purchase real property. *Marriage of Nicholson & Sparks* (2002) 104 CA4th 289, 127 CR2d 882. Reimbursement is without interest or adjustment for any change in monetary values and must not exceed the net value of the property at the time of the property division. Fam C §2640(a). Reimbursement is limited to the actual amount of the contribution, even when the contribution reduces the debt by a greater amount. *Marriage of Tallman* (1994) 22 CA4th 1697, 28 CR2d 323 (sellers accepted $40,000 in full satisfaction of $53,000 loan balance; paying party entitled only to reimbursement of $40,000). The contributor is entitled to receive the reimbursement "off the top." The balance of the equity in the property is then divided equally between the parties. 203 CA3d at 1202 n4.

When community property was initially the separate property of one spouse, that spouse is deemed to have a made a contribution to the acquisition of community property under Fam C §2640. The measure of the value of the contribution is the value of the separate property equity in the property as of the date of its conversion, *i.e.,* fair market value less outstanding encumbrances and any community property share in the equity resulting from community contributions to payments on the purchase price before the conversion. Documentation of the exact value of the separate property asset is not required if it is real property. *Marriage of Stoll* (1998) 63 CA4th 837, 842, 74 CR2d 506 (husband could testify as to his opinion about the value of the house). The community share in the equity, if any, is calculated according to the formula in *Marriage of Moore* (1980) 28 C3d 366, 168 CR 662, as modified by *Marriage of Marsden* (1982) 130 CA3d 426, 181 CR 910 (see §5.25). *Marriage of Neal* (1984) 153 CA3d 117, 124 n11, 125, 200 CR 341, disapproved on other grounds in 39 C3d at 763 n10. *Neal* states that the community gets credit for its contributions only if they are found not to be gifts to the separate property. But it appears that, under *Marriage of Moore, supra,* the community is entitled to the credit even if the contributions were intended as gifts. See §5.25. *Marriage of Walrath* (1998) 17 C4th 907, 918, 72 CR2d 856, provides the tracing method for reimbursement when the community asset purchased with separate property funds is refinanced and used to purchase additional community property.

Family Code §2640 (former CC §4800.2) cannot be applied to property acquired before its effective date of January 1, 1984. *Marriage of Heikes* (1995) 10 C4th 1211, 44 CR2d 155. The law in effect before passage of former CC §4800.2 allowed no reimbursement to the separate property contributor without an agreement or understanding providing for it. *Marriage of Lucas* (1980) 27 C3d 808, 815, 166 CR 853.

Note that application of Fam C §2640 is not appropriate in the context of a deferred sale of home award (see §5.90). Rather, the court should reapportion the parties' shares in the family home in unequal percentages that reflect their respective ownership interests and order that they be paid in proportion to those interests at the time of sale. *Marriage of Braud* (1996) 45 CA4th 797, 819, 53 CR2d 179.

§5.95A   2. Separate Property Contributions to Acquisition of Other Spouse's Separate Property Estate

Effective January 1, 2005, in the division of the community estate on marital dissolution or legal separation, a party must be reimbursed for separate property contributions to the acquisition of property of the *other* spouse's *separate* property estate made during the marriage, absent a written transmutation or waiver of right to reimbursement. The amount to be reimbursed must be without interest or adjustment for change in value and may not exceed the net value of the property at the time of division. Fam C §2640(c).

§5.96 3. Community Property Contributions to Education or Training

Under Fam C §2641, the community is entitled to reimbursement for contributions to the education or training of a party that substantially enhances the party's earning capacity. Fam C §2641(b)(1). The education for which reimbursement is sought must have substantially or demonstrably enhanced a spouse's earning capacity. *Marriage of Graham* (2003) 109 CA4th 1321, 135 CR2d 685 (law school education for police officer spouse does not presumptively enhance earning capacity). It is not necessary, however, that the party actually work in an occupation in which the benefits of the enhanced earning capacity are realized. Rather, it is sufficient that he or she retains the potential to realize the benefits in the future. Comment to Fam C §2641.

Reimbursable contributions may be either (1) direct payments for education or training or (2) payments on a loan incurred for education or training. Fam C §2641(a). Community payments on loans for education or training are reimbursable even if the debts were incurred before marriage. *Marriage of Weiner* (2003) 105 CA4th 235, 129 CR2d 288. Reimbursable contributions must, however, be related to the education experience itself, *e.g.,* tuition, books, fees, supplies, transportation. They do not include ordinary living expenses, which the parties would incur regardless of the education or training. *Marriage of Watt* (1989) 214 CA3d 340, 354, 262 CR 783. For the contributions made in any particular calendar year, the amount reimbursed must include interest at the legal rate accruing from the end of the calendar year. Fam C §2641(b)(1). The legal rate contemplated is that provided by CCP §685.010 for money judgments. Comment to Fam C §2641. The reimbursement required under Fam C §2641 must be reduced or modified to the extent circumstances render the reimbursement unjust. Fam C §2641(c). Illustrations of such circumstances provided by the statute include:

- The community has substantially benefited from the education or training. It is rebuttably presumed that the community has substantially benefited with respect to contributions made more than ten years before commencement of the action and that it has not substantially benefited with respect to contributions made less than ten years before commencement of the action. Fam C §2641(c)(1).

- The education or training at issue is offset by the education or training received by the other party for which community contributions were also made. Fam C §2641(c)(2).

- The education or training enables the recipient party to engage in gainful employment that substantially reduces his or her need for support. Fam C §2641(c)(3).

Reimbursement to the community for its contributions, and assignment to a party of any loans incurred for his or her education or training (Fam C §2641(b)(2); see §5.83), as provided under Fam C §2641 constitute the exclusive remedy for a party's education or training and any resulting enhancement of earning capacity. The contributing party may, however, also seek recognition, under Fam C §4320(b) (former CC §4801(a)(2)), of his or her contributions to the other party's attainment of an education, training, a career position, or a license in determining long-term spousal support (see §6.10). Fam C §2641(d). In considering contributions under Fam C §4320(b), unlike those under Fam C §2641, contributions for ordinary living expenses are recognized. *Marriage of Watt* (1989) 214 CA3d 340, 350, 262 CR 783.

The provisions of Fam C §2641 are subject to an express written agreement of the parties to the contrary. Fam C §2641(e).

§5.97   4. "Liability of Marital Property" Statutes

In some instances, a party to a marital action will be entitled to exercise reimbursement rights under Fam C §§900–1000, a portion of the Family Code titled "Liability of Marital Property," when property has been applied to satisfy liabilities. Such rights may usually be exercised only within three years after the party claiming reimbursement acquires actual knowledge of the facts giving rise to the rights. Assuming that the three-year period has not expired, the reimbursement rights must be exercised in the marital action or they will, in effect, be waived. Fam C §920(c). Presumably, timely exercise of the rights in a marital action could be achieved by a party's raising the issue in a petition or response filed within three years after he or she acquires actual knowledge of the underlying facts.

With respect to reimbursement rights arising from satisfaction of tort liabilities, the limitations period is seven years. Fam C §1000(c).

Insofar as they apply to marital actions, the statutes provide for reimbursement as follows:

- If a party's separate property is applied to satisfy a debt incurred by the party's spouse for "necessaries" or "common necessaries" of life at a time when nonexempt property in the community estate or the spouse's separate property is available, the party is entitled to reimbursement to the extent the property was available. Fam C §914(b).

- If property in the community estate is applied to satisfy a child or spousal support obligation of a party from another relationship at a time when nonexempt separate income of the party is available, the community estate is entitled to reimbursement from the party to the extent the income was available. Fam C §915(b). *Marriage of Sherman* (2005) 133 CA4th 795, 804, 35 CR3d 137.

- If a party's separate property is applied, at a time when community property is available, to satisfy a tort liability incurred by the party while acting for the benefit of the community, the party is entitled to reimbursement to the extent that community property was available. Conversely, if community property is applied, at a time when a party's separate property is available, to satisfy a tort liability incurred by the party while acting other than for the benefit of the community, the community is entitled to reimbursement to the extent that the separate property was available. Fam C §1000(b)–(c).

The reimbursement rights arise whether the property is applied to the satisfaction of the debt voluntarily or involuntarily and whether the debt is thereby satisfied entirely or partially, but these rights are subject to express written waivers. Fam C §920(a). The measure of reimbursement is the value of the property at the time the right to reimbursement arises. Fam C §920(b). Thus, rights of reimbursement enforceable in marital actions do not include interest.

5. Separate Property Used for Community Purposes

§5.98   a. Before Separation

A party who uses his or her separate property for community purposes during marriage and before separation is deemed to have made a gift to the community and, accordingly, is not entitled to reimbursement absent an agreement by the parties to the contrary. *Marriage of Lucas* (1980) 27 C3d 808, 816, 166 CR 853. When the use of the separate property constitutes a contribution to the acquisition of community property under Fam C §2640, however, the party will be entitled to reimbursement to the extent that he or she traces the contribution to a separate property source, unless the party has waived the right to reimbursement in writing. See §5.95. On reimbursement for separate property contributions to the acquisition of the other spouse's separate property estate (see Fam C §2460(c); see §5.95A).

b. After Separation

§5.99   (1) To Pay Community Debts

When a party uses his or her separate property for community purposes after separation, the party is, as a general rule, entitled to reimbursement. *Marriage of Epstein* (1979) 24 C3d 76, 84, 154 CR 413. Reimbursement for separate property mortgage payments on community property after separation, unlike that for preseparation payments (see §5.98), is not governed by Fam C §2640 (former CC §4800.2). Thus reimbursement is not limited to principal reduction payments. *Marriage of Hebbring* (1989) 207 CA3d 1260, 1272, 255 CR 488.

The *Epstein* court, however, indicated that reimbursement should not be ordered when payment was made under circumstances in which it would have been unreasonable to expect reimbursement, and it listed the following examples (24 C3d at 84):

- There was an agreement between the parties that the payment would not be reimbursed;
- The paying party truly intended the payment to constitute a gift;
- The payment was made on a debt for the acquisition or preserva-

tion of an asset the paying party was using, and the amount paid was not substantially in excess of the value of the use; and

- The payment constituted a discharge of the paying party's spousal or child support duty.

See, *e.g., Marriage of Stallworth* (1987) 192 CA3d 742, 750, 237 CR 829 (no reimbursement for payments on residence that paying party was occupying); *Marriage of Tucker* (1983) 141 CA3d 128, 136, 190 CR 127 (no reimbursement for payments on refrigerator in paying party's possession when payments not substantially in excess of value of use); *Marriage of Green* (1989) 213 CA3d 14, 22, 261 CR 294 (no reimbursement when house and car payments made in partial satisfaction of support obligations).

The family law court may exercise its traditional equity powers to decide whether it is reasonable to order reimbursement to a spouse who uses separate property to pay more support than otherwise required and to prevent the supported spouse's unjust enrichment. See *Marriage of Peet* (1978) 84 CA3d 974, 149 CR 108. See also *Marriage of Weiner* (2003) 105 CA4th 235, 129 CR2d 288; *Marriage of Dandona & Araluce* (2001) 91 CA4th 1120, 1125, 111 CR2d 390. On reimbursement under Fam C §3653 (modifying or terminating support order) see §§6.20, 8.31, 21.2.

Effective January 1, 1987, former CC §4800(e), predecessor of Fam C §2626, provided specific statutory authority for the court to order reimbursement for debts paid after separation when it deems it appropriate. Family Code §2626 presumably supplements, rather than alters, the court's authority under *Marriage of Epstein, supra*. See *Marriage of Hebbring, supra* (referring to broad discretion under *Epstein* and former CC §4800(e) to order reimbursement for postseparation payments from separate property).

§5.100 (2) To Improve Community Property

The applicability of Fam C §2640 seems to be the same for improvements as for mortgage payments (see §5.99), *i.e.,* Fam C §2640 governs reimbursement for separate property payments for improvements on community property before separation but not after. See *Marriage of Reilley* (1987) 196 CA3d 1119, 1124 n3, 242 CR 302 (in discussing "payments for improvements" under former CC

§4800.2, court found "every indication" that legislature intended section to govern reimbursement only for contributions *before* separation). But in the case of improvements, the proper amount of reimbursement is not necessarily the amount paid. When any increase in value is slight compared with the amount paid for the improvements, it may be appropriate to limit reimbursement to the resulting increase in the property's value, particularly when the result would otherwise be substantial elimination of the community equity. But, even then, other factors (*e.g.,* parties' agreement to make improvements, improvements necessary to preserve asset) may justify reimbursement in the amount paid. 196 CA3d at 1123.

§5.101   6. Community Property Used for Separate Purposes

The trial court may order reimbursement to the community when a party unilaterally uses community property to pay his or her separate obligations. See, *e.g., Marriage of Frick* (1986) 181 CA3d 997, 1014, 226 CR 766 (preseparation); *Marriage of Epstein* (1979) 24 C3d 76, 89, 154 CR 413 (postseparation). See also §5.72 and cases cited there.

A party may, however, be allowed to use a reasonable amount of community funds for required postseparation support, without the requirement of reimbursement, when no support order has been made. *Marriage of Stallworth* (1987) 192 CA3d 742, 752, 237 CR 829.

In appropriate cases, the community may be entitled to reimbursement for the reasonable value of a party's exclusive use of community property after separation. *Marriage of Jeffries* (1991) 228 CA3d 548, 552, 278 CR 830; *Marriage of Watts* (1985) 171 CA3d 366, 374, 217 CR 301. In *Jeffries,* the wife had exclusive use of the family residence and the husband made the mortgage payments. The court of appeal affirmed a decision that, in effect, required the wife to reimburse the community for the reasonable rental value of her exclusive use of the residence after separation and required the community to reimburse the husband for the postseparation mortgage payments.

When the mortgage payments are made by the party *occupying* the residence, a claim by the other party for reimbursement for the value of the use may serve only to offset a claim by the occupying party for reimbursement for the payments. A net gain for the party claiming reimbursement for the value of the use in such circumstances will be likely only when the value of the use is substantially greater than the amount of the payments.

On reimbursement for postseparation payment of community debts from separate property, see §5.99.

§5.102 7. Community Property Payments in Connection With Separate Property Personal Injury Claim

When personal injury damages are the separate property of the injured party under Fam C §781(a) (see §5.29), and expenses connected with the injuries have been paid from the other party's separate property or from community property, the other party is entitled to reimbursement for such expenses from the damages received. Fam C §781(b). The reimbursement requirement of Fam C §781(b) (former CC §5126(b)) does not apply to workers' compensation awards. *Marriage of Fisk* (1992) 2 CA4th 1698, 1706, 4 CR2d 95.

F. Tax Aspects

§5.103 1. Consideration by Court

The general rule under California law is that a court need not consider potential tax consequences that may arise after the property division. *Marriage of Fonstein* (1976) 17 C3d 738, 748, 131 CR 873. In *Fonstein,* the trial court erred in reducing the value assigned to a law partnership interest by the estimated tax consequences the attorney-spouse might incur if he withdrew at some future time. But when the tax consequences at issue are "immediate and specific," the court must consider them in dividing the property. The distinction is between (1) a tax liability, no matter how certain, to arise in the future if an asset is sold, liquidated, or otherwise reduced to cash and (2) a taxable event that has occurred during the marriage or will occur in connection with the property division. 17 C3d at 749 n5.

In *Marriage of Epstein* (1979) 24 C3d 76, 87, 154 CR 413, the supreme court held that a property division must take account of any taxes actually paid as a result of a court-ordered sale of the family residence. The *Epstein* court distinguished *Fonstein* as involving a speculative future tax liability arising on the hypothetical sale of an asset, whereas the taxable event in *Epstein* occurred as a result of enforcement of the court's property division order. 24 C3d at 87. *Epstein* suggested that the trial court can take account of tax liability when required to do so by providing that the liability be borne equally by the parties and, in unusual cases, by retaining jurisdiction to supervise the payment of taxes and adjust the property division. 24 C3d at 88.

In *Marriage of Davies* (1983) 143 CA3d 851, 857, 192 CR 212, the court of appeal narrowly construed *Epstein* to reject the contention that the court should retain jurisdiction to allocate the tax liability arising from a court-ordered sale of the family residence for two years to take into consideration any tax deferral under former IRC §1034 (see §5.106). Rather, it was held, the court should merely order that the parties bear equally any tax liability that is not deferred. 143 CA3d at 858. In *Marriage of Harrington* (1992) 6 CA4th 1847, 8 CR2d 631, the parties, in accordance with their marital settlement agreement, sold the family residence and divided the proceeds equally, but the agreement did not address liability for capital gains taxes. The court of appeal held that each party alone was liable for capital gains taxes due on his or her share of the profits.

Note that in *Marriage of Nelson* (1986) 177 CA3d 150, 156, 222 CR 790, the court of appeal affirmed a credit against potential tax liability resulting from the exercise of stock options awarded as part of the property division. The *Nelson* court recognized that the credit did not meet the "immediate and specific" test, but affirmed it based on former CC §4800(b)(1) (predecessor of Fam C §2601) (when economic circumstances warrant, court may award asset to one party on such conditions as it deems proper to effect substantially equal property division). The economic circumstance cited was that, because the options were nonassignable and therefore had to be awarded to the employee spouse, the more equitable distribution, *i.e.*, to divide in kind and leave each party at the mercy of his or her own tax circumstances, was not available. *Nelson* appears to give some support to creative efforts to achieve court consideration of tax consequences even when the "immediate and specific" test is not met.

It is important to bear in mind the "immediate and specific" limitation when negotiating a settlement regarding two assets having different tax consequences. For instance, offsetting the value of a spouse's retirement benefits against the family home could have the result that the spouse who is awarded the family home receives that asset tax-free (as long its appreciation at the time of a future sale is not greater than $250,00; see §5.105), but the spouse who is awarded the community retirement benefits will have to pay ordinary income tax on the money received. This imbalance can be adjusted in settlement negotiations, while the trial court may not feel it has the power to take these factors into account, though perhaps *Nelson* could provide an effective argument.

Note that tax consequences *must* be considered by the court in determining whether to grant or deny a deferred sale of home order. Fam C §3802(b)(8); see §5.90.

§5.104 2. Nonrecognition of Gain or Loss on Transfers Between Parties "Incident to Divorce"

Internal Revenue Code §1041 generally provides that transfers between spouses and those transfers between former spouses that are incident to divorce are not treated as taxable events and thus do not result in the recognition of gain or loss. Rather, for capital gains purposes, the transfers are treated as though they were gifts. Therefore, the transferee spouse holds the property at the transferor spouse's basis. IRC §1041(b). Note, however, that any interest portion of payments received will be taxable income to the recipient. *Linda Gibbs*, TC Memo 1997-196. California has adopted the nonrecognition rules of IRC §1041. Rev & T C §18031. See also *John L. Seymour* (1997) 109 TC 279, in which the court found that interest paid as part of a marital settlement agreement equalizing payment with a promissory note secured by a mortgage deed on the former family home may be deductible to the payor as qualified residence interest or home equity indebtedness.

As a practical matter, transfers that are "incident to" *any* marital action, not only to dissolutions, will be subject to IRC §1041's nonrecognition provisions. Transfers incident to legal separations qualify because §1041 governs all transfers between spouses (IRC §1041(a)(1)) and the marital status of the parties is unaffected by a judgment of legal separation. Transfers incident to nullity actions are specifically included under §1041 by temporary regulations. Temp Reg §1.1041-1T(b) Q&A-8.

A transfer is "incident to the divorce" if the transfer (1) occurs within one year after the marriage ceases or (2) is "related to the cessation of the marriage." IRC §1041(c). A transfer is "related to the cessation of the marriage" if it is made under a judgment or marital settlement agreement and occurs within six years after the marriage ceases. Temp Reg §1.1041–1T(b) Q&A-7; IRS Letter Ruling 9348020 (transfer of real property to former spouse, under marital settlement agreement, three years after divorce deemed related to cessation of marriage). Any other transfer is presumed not related. This presumption may be rebutted only by a showing that the transfer was made to effect the division of property owned by the spouses at the time the marriage ceased, *e.g.,* when a transfer was not made earlier because of factors such as legal or business impediments to transfer or disputes about valuation, but was made promptly after the impediment was removed. Temp Reg §1.1041–1T(b) Q&A-7. See IRS Letter Rulings 9644053 (annuity payments to be made more than six years after divorce related to cessation of marriage when stock awarded to payor would not generate enough income to permit annuity to be paid off within six years), 9306015 (transfer of interest in residence to former spouse not related to cessation of marriage when it occurred more than eight years after divorce and was not contemplated by divorce judgment).

WARNING➤ Although private letter rulings can provide a useful indication of the position the IRS may take on a particular issue, they may not be used or cited as precedent. IRC § 6110(j)(3).

In certain cases, a transfer of property to a third party "on behalf of" a spouse or former spouse will be treated as a transfer to the spouse or former spouse, allowing the transferor to avoid recognition of gain. See Temp Reg §1.1041–1T(c) Q&A-9. See also *Carol M. Read* (2000) 114 TC 14. In *Read,* the Tax Court found that one spouse's transfer of stock to the parties' corporation, as required by dissolution judgment, was a transfer "on behalf of" the other spouse within the meaning of Q&A-9 and, accordingly, entitled to IRC §1041 relief. The Tax Court rejected the petitioner's proposed standard of "primary and unconditional obligation" as inappropriate in the context of corporate redemption in a dissolution setting. See also *Arnes v U.S.* (9th Cir 1992) 981 F2d 456 (IRC §1041 relieves wife of having to recognize gain on family corporation's redemption, under spouses' marital settlement agreement, of her half of stock because redemption was "on behalf" of husband). Compare *Arnes* with *Ingham v U.S.* (9th Cir 1999) 167 F3d 1240 (wife not entitled to refund of tax paid on proceeds of sale of property awarded to her in dissolution because sale not made "on behalf" of husband). The *Ingham* court noted that, in *Arnes,* the dissolution judgment required the husband to purchase the wife's stock, whereas the Ingham dissolution required the wife to make an equalizing payment, not necessarily to sell the property. See also *Gloria T. Blatt* (1994) 102 TC 77 (IRC §1041 does not shield wife from tax liability, because corporate redemption *not* "on behalf of" husband).

Although the transfer of property has no immediate tax consequences under IRC §1041, an attorney should always consider future tax consequences to the client of receiving a particular asset in the property division. Because the basis follows each asset, obtaining high-basis assets is clearly preferable to obtaining low-basis assets. The attorney may be able to negotiate a more advantageous marital settlement agreement for the client by considering future tax consequences. The attorney will probably not have much success, however, in persuading the court to consider such future tax consequences if the case is tried. On court consideration of tax aspects generally, see §5.103.

3. Exclusion or Deferral of Gain on Sale of Family Home to Third Party

§5.105   **a. Current Law**

Internal Revenue Code §121 provides for exclusion of gain on the sale of a principal residence. To qualify, a taxpayer must have owned and used the home as his or her principal residence for periods aggregating at least two years during the 5-year period immediately preceding the sale. IRC §121(a).

The amount of gain excluded generally may not exceed $250,000. IRC §121(b)(1). There are exceptions, however, for married taxpayers who file a joint return for the taxable year of the sale. They may exclude up to $500,000, provided that either spouse has owned the home, and both spouses have used the home as their principal residence, for periods aggregating at least two years during the 5-year period immediately preceding the sale, and the exclusion is not being applied to a second sale within any two-year period occurring entirely on or after May 7, 1997. IRC §§121(b)(2)(A), 121(b)(3)(A), 121(b)(3)(B). For married taxpayers who file a joint return for the taxable year of the sale but do not meet these requirements, the limitation on gain excluded will be the sum of the limitations to which the respective spouses would be entitled if unmarried, with each treated as owning the property during the period that either of them owned the property. IRC §121(b)(2)(B).

Prorated exclusions are available to taxpayers who fail to meet the requirements regarding ownership, use, or time elapsed since the most recent prior sale to which the exclusion applied, provided that the sale is by reason of a change in place of employment, health, or, to the extent regulations provide, unforeseen circumstances. See IRC §121(c).

For purposes of IRC §121, the period of the transferee's ownership of property transferred in a transaction described in IRC §1041(a) will include the period the transferor owned the property. IRC §121(d)(3)(A). Transactions described in IRC §1041(a) include (1) transfers between spouses, and (2) transfers between former spouses that are incident to divorce. For discussion of IRC §1041, see §5.104.

Also for purposes of IRC §121, an individual will be treated as using property as his or her principal residence during any period of ownership in which the individual's spouse or former spouse is granted use of the property under a decree of divorce or separate maintenance (or a written instrument incident to such a decree), another form of decree requiring a spouse to make payments for the support or maintenance of the other spouse, or a written separation agreement. IRC §121(d)(3)(B); see IRC §71(b)(2). This provision is important because, with proper planning, it should enable a spouse who is excluded from the family residence in connection with dissolution proceedings to avoid losing the benefits of IRC §121 if the residence is subsequently sold to a third party.

Note that the taxpayer may elect that IRC §121 not apply to any particular sale to which it otherwise would apply. IRC §121(f).

The provisions of IRC §121 described here apply generally to sales on or after May 7, 1997. Pub L 105-34, §312(d)(1), 111 Stat 788. At the taxpayer's election, however, these provisions will not apply to sales on or before August 5, 1997. See Pub L 105-34, §312(d)(2), 111 Stat 788. The taxpayer may also elect not to have these provisions apply to a sale on or after August 5, 1997, if:

- The sale is under a contract binding on August 5, 1997 (Pub L 105-34, §312(d)(4)(A), 111 Stat 788); or

- Under former IRC §1034, gain would have been deferred because of a new residence that was acquired either on or before August 5, 1997, or under a binding contract in effect on August 5, 1997 (Pub L 105–34, §312(d)(4)(B), 111 Stat 788).

Note also that former IRC §1034 (deferral of gain on sale of family home to third party) was repealed effective May 7, 1997. On former law, see §5.106.

§5.106 b. Former Law

Former law still applies to sales of principal residences to which amended IRC §121, as discussed in §5.105, does not apply.

Former IRC §121 provided a once-in-a-lifetime exclusion of $125,000 in gain on the sale of a principal residence by an individual age 55 or over who elected the exclusion. To qualify, a taxpayer had to have owned and used the home as his or her principal residence for periods aggregating at least three years during the 5-year period immediately preceding the sale. Former IRC §121(a)(2). The election was not available if an earlier election under former §121 had been made by either the taxpayer or his or her spouse. Former IRC §121(b)(2).

§5.107 4. Exemptions From Property Tax Reassessment and Documentary Transfer Tax

When a real property interest previously held by both spouses is awarded by a dissolution or legal separation judgment to one of them, or will continue to be held by both spouses but in a different form (*e.g.,* when joint tenancy changes to tenancy in common), the transfer does not constitute a "change of ownership" triggering a reassessment under Proposition 13 (Cal Const art XIIIA). Rev & T C §63. To ensure that no reassessment occurs, however, it will be advisable to include on the deed a written recital of the fact that the transaction does not constitute a "change of ownership," citing Rev & T C §63. It appears that the exemption would not be available with respect to transfers under a judgment of nullity because Rev & T C §63 expressly addresses itself to "any *interspousal* transfer" and limits its references to "spouses" and judgments of dissolution and legal separation.

Recordation of a deed transferring real property under a judgment of dissolution, legal separation, or nullity is exempt from imposition of the documentary transfer tax, as long as the deed includes a written recital, signed by either party, stating that the deed is entitled to the exemption. Rev & T C §11927.

NOTE➤ Beginning with "the lien date for the 2006–2007 fiscal year," any real property transfer between registered domestic partners (see Fam C §297) is *not* a "change of ownership," and therefore does not subject the affected property to reassessment. Rev & T C §62(p). For related discussion, see California Domestic Partnerships, chap 7 (Cal CEB 2005).

§5.108   5. Disposition of Retirement Benefits

When, incident to a marital action (see §5.104), community property retirement benefits are awarded entirely to the employee spouse by the asset distribution (or "cash-out") method (see §5.87), the transfer of other community property to the nonemployee spouse to achieve an equal division is not treated as a taxable event and thus does not result in the recognition of gain or loss. Rather, for capital gains purposes, the transfer is treated as though it were a gift. IRC §1041; *Hazel Eileen Balding* (1992) 98 TC 368. Nevertheless, the possibility exists that the nonemployee spouse might incur tax liability, under the "assignment of income" doctrine, when the benefits are ultimately paid by the employer to the employee spouse. In *Helvering v Horst* (1940) 311 US 112, 118, 85 L Ed 75, 79, 61 S Ct 144, the Supreme Court explained that the power to dispose of income is equivalent to its ownership and, consequently, the exercise of that power to procure payment of income to another is deemed to be the realization of the income by the party who exercises the power. For tax purposes, then, the income is treated as received by the party who assigns it, rather than by the party who actually receives it. The assignment of income doctrine has been described as holding that the fruit may not be attributed to a different tree from that on which it grew. See *Lucas v Earl* (1930) 281 US 111, 115, 74 L Ed 731, 733, 50 S Ct 241. In *Johnson v U.S.* (9th Cir 1943) 135 F2d 125, 130, the court held that the wife's half of community receivables remained taxable to her even though it had been transferred to the husband in a property settlement between the parties and subsequently collected by him.

There is no definitive authority on whether the assignment of income doctrine will apply when the employee spouse is ultimately paid community property retirement benefits awarded entirely to him or her incident to a marital action. See *Hazel Eileen Balding* (1992) 98 TC 368, 373 n8. Two cases have found no assignment of income problem when assets were distributed in connection with marital actions. See *Kenfield v U.S.* (10th Cir 1986) 783 F2d 966, 970 (partnership interest); *Richard P. Schulze,* TC Memo 1983–263 (claim for damages). But see IRS Letter Ruling 8813023, obtained by the parties in *Hazel Eileen Balding, supra.* In that letter ruling, the divorce judgment had awarded a military pension to the member spouse as his separate property under *McCarty v McCarty* (1981) 453 US 210, 69 L Ed 2d 589, 101 S Ct 2728.

NOTE➤ IRS Letter Rulings specifically rule on the cases addressed therein. The IRS does not express or imply an opinion on the federal tax consequences of transactions other than those of the taxpayer requesting the ruling. IRS Letter Rulings may not be used or cited as precedent.

After enactment of the Federal Uniformed Services Former Spouses' Protection Act (10 USC §1408) (see §5.38), the parties modified their judgment to provide the nonmember spouse with large lump-sum cash payments in exchange for her community interest in the pension benefits. The IRS took the position that the cash payments were taxable to the nonmember under the assignment of income doctrine, rather than nontaxable under IRC §1041 (see §5.104), because they represented the "right to future income rather than gain."

As indicated above, the court in *Balding* rejected the IRS position with respect to the transfers to the nonmember spouse, but it did not decide whether the assignment of income doctrine would apply when the pension payments are ultimately made to the member. The IRS position seems inconsistent with §1041, but it must be taken into consideration, at least in the absence of any case authority directly to the contrary. In a 2005 case that remained on appeal when this publication went to press, the court in *John Michael Dunkin* (2005) 124 TC No 10 held that an employee spouse who chose not to retire when eligible but whose former wife made a *Gillmore* election to begin receiving benefits could exclude the payments he made to the nonemployee wife from his gross income, choosing not to apply the assignment-of-income doctrine.

Given the uncertainty about the applicability of the assignment of income doctrine, whenever the employee spouse will receive the nonemployee spouse's share in retirement benefits, counsel for the nonemployee must consider the possibility of assignment of income problems. Counsel should seek a provision indemnifying his or her client for any tax liability on payments received by the other party. For a sample provision, see California Marital Settlement and Other Family Law Agreements §20.60 (3d ed Cal CEB 2005), covering tax liability arising from distribution of benefits by the retirement plan.

When community property retirement benefits from a qualified plan are divided in kind (see §5.86) and the plan makes direct payments of their respective shares to both spouses, each will be taxed on the payments he or she receives. See IRC §402(e)(1)(A) (spouse or former spouse of employee treated as distributee of payments received from private plan under "qualified domestic relations order" (QDRO) (see §§17.68–17.79)). See also *Kay A. Clawson*, TC Memo 1996–446 (each party taxable on share received under QDRO despite QDRO language providing that employee alone would be liable for tax on amount distributed); IRS Letter Ruling 8629030 (husband's share of military retirement benefits includable in his gross income and wife's share includable in hers); *Robert L. Karem* (1993) 100 TC 521 (when nonemployee received her community share of pension benefits from employee, rather than directly from plan under a QDRO, employee was liable for tax on entire distribution); IRS Letter Ruling 9340032 (employee liable for tax on entire distribution from *nonqualified* plan, even though nonemployee received her community share directly from plan). Internal Revenue Code §402(e)(1)(A) was formerly IRC §402(a)(9), enacted as part of the Retirement Equity Act of 1984 (REA) (Pub L 98–397, 98 Stat 1426). Some commentators have suggested that the REA made all payments received by either party from a private plan taxable to that party even when the benefits are awarded entirely to the employee spouse. If correct, that would eliminate, in a private plan, the potential assignment of income problem discussed above. But the statute did not do that expressly and, in the absence of clear authority, it must be assumed that potential assignment of income problems will continue to exist.

NOTE➤ A 2005 Tax Court decision that remained on appeal as this publication went to press may lend support to that view. In that case, payments made by a former husband to his former

wife pursuant to a family court's dissolution judgment—which
ordered him to pay his former wife her community share of
his retirement benefits directly until he retired—were determined to be nontaxable to the former husband. In that instance,
the husband had been eligible to retire but deferred retirement
and the family court had ordered him to make payments, citing
Marriage of Gillmore (1981) 29 C3d 418, 174 CR 493. *John
Michael Dunkin* (2005) 124 TC No 10.

§5.109   6. Whether Court May Order Parties to File Joint Returns

It has traditionally been assumed that a court may not order parties
to a marital action to file joint tax returns. In *Marriage of Partridge*
(1990) 226 CA3d 120, 128, 276 CR 8, however, the court of appeal
directed the trial court to enter a judgment directing the parties to
file joint returns. Perhaps sensing that such an order might be prob-
lematic, the appellate court added the phrase "insofar as federal law
permits" to its order and further directed the trial court to reserve
jurisdiction to take further action if the parties were unable to file
a return as ordered. Note that federal law makes joint returns permissive, not required, for married taxpayers. IRC §6013.

6

Spousal Support

§6.1   I. SCOPE OF CHAPTER

This chapter covers spousal support, both temporary (*i.e.,* pendente lite) and long-term (*i.e.,* so-called permanent) support. In each case, consideration is given to determination, modification, and duration of spousal support. An introduction to the tax aspects of spousal support is also provided.

On family support, see §6.35. See also California Marital Settlement and Other Family Law Agreements §8.31 (3d ed Cal CEB 2005).

II. TEMPORARY SUPPORT

§6.2   A. When Available

While a dissolution or legal separation action is pending, the court may order either spouse to pay any amount necessary for the support of the other spouse, consistent with Fam C §§4320(i), (m), and 4325. Fam C §3600. The same is true in a nullity action, if the party for whose benefit the order is made is found to be a putative spouse. Fam C §2254. On qualifying as a putative spouse, see §3.19.

An action is "pending" from the time the petition is filed until its final adjudication on appeal or until the time for appeal has passed. CCP §1049; Fam C §§2250(a), 2330(a). Thus, although an appeal may suspend implementation of the court's spousal support order contained in the judgment, the supported party may seek an order for temporary support during the pendency of the appeal. See *Bain v Superior Court* (1974) 36 CA3d 804, 807, 111 CR 848.

It had long been assumed that the earliest date to which an order for temporary spousal support may be retroactive is the date of filing of the notice of motion or order to show cause. See, *e.g., Marriage of Economou* (1990) 224 CA3d 1466, 1476, 274 CR 473. In *Marriage of Dick* (1993) 15 CA4th 144, 165, 18 CR2d 743, however, the court held that a temporary spousal support order could be made retroactive to the date of filing of a petition requesting spousal support. Those assuming that the filing date of the notice of motion or order to show cause is the operative date have typically cited as authority, as did the support payor in *Dick,* language in former CC §4801(a), the substance of which is now found in Fam C §4333: "Any order for spousal support may be made retroactive to the date of filing of the notice of motion or order to show cause therefor, or to any subsequent date." The *Dick* court found this citation unpersuasive because, it stated, former CC §4801(a) governed only long-term spousal support, not temporary spousal support. *Marriage of Dick, supra.* It is true that former CC §4801(a) opened with a reference to "any judgment decreeing the dissolution of a marriage or a legal separation of the parties," and that most of the subsection was clearly directed only to long-term orders, but the language quoted above, with its reference to "the notice of motion or order to show cause," seemed to contemplate temporary, rather than long-term (*i.e.,* judgment) orders. Until this issue is definitively resolved, counsel should be prepared to argue the position that benefits his or her client.

When a spouse is convicted of attempting to murder the other spouse as punishable under Pen C §664(a), whether or not physical injury occurred, the victim spouse will be entitled to a prohibition of any temporary or long-term spousal support award, or medical, life, or other insurance benefits or payments, from the victim spouse to the other spouse. Fam C §4324.

B. Determining Amount

§6.3 ## 1. Approach Generally

Temporary support may be ordered in any amount based upon the party's need and the payor's ability to pay, and findings of the trial court on need and ability are reviewed under the abuse of discretion standard. Although the factors listed in Fam C §4320 (see §6.10) are mandatory considerations only in determining long-term spousal support, they are at least suggestive of the circumstances courts will consider in setting temporary support. See *Marriage of Wittgrove* (2004) 120 CA4th 1317, 16 CR3d 489. As in the case of making a permanent order, a court making a temporary support award must not base it on income information that is manifestly unrepresentative of a party's true income. See, *e.g., Riddle v Riddle* (2005) 125 CA4th 1075, 1083, 23 CR3d 273 (trial court abused discretion by calculating income for pendente lite child and spousal support based on only latest two months of salesperson's earnings instead of properly representative sample).

It has been suggested that the purpose of temporary spousal support is to enable the recipient to live in his or her accustomed manner pending disposition of the action. See, *e.g., Estate of Fawcett* (1965) 232 CA2d 770, 784, 43 CR 160. See also *Marriage of Wittgrove, supra; Marriage of Winter* (1992) 7 CA4th 1926, 1932, 10 CR2d 225 (when parties live very modestly in comparison to their means, using substantial funds for savings and investments, temporary support may be set at amount that allows for that level of savings and investments).

Courts recognize, however, that incomes that provide a certain standard of living while the parties are living together are usually insufficient to provide the same standard of living when the parties are maintaining separate households. As a result, a court is often unable to provide fully for the financial needs of both parties. All the court can do, and all it is required to do, is to equitably allocate the family income, considering the parties' individual incomes and expenses, to maintain the parties in as close to their preseparation condition as possible, pending the trial. See *Marriage of Burlini* (1983) 143 CA3d 65, 68, 191 CR 541. Counsel should communicate this reality to the client at the outset if the client is to develop realistic expectations about the case and the results that may be attained.

§6.4 2. Use of Guideline Formula

Many courts consult the statutory guideline amount displayed by the support calculation software they use in setting temporary spousal support. Counsel should always ascertain whether and what guideline is used in the county in which the action is pending. For instance, Santa Clara Ct R 3.C provides that a recipient not receiving child support will be entitled to 40 percent of the net income of the payor less 50 percent of the net income of the payee. If child support has been calculated, the above percentages are calculated on the net incomes of the parties after child support payments have been factored in. The so-called Santa Clara formula is followed by some other counties (*e.g.*, Sacramento and San Francisco counties). Other counties, including Yolo and Contra Costa, use the formula provided in Alameda Ct R 11.2, which is identical to the Santa Clara formula in the situation in which no child support obligation exists, but provides a specific calculation based on Fam C §§4055–4069 if child support is also being paid. See *Marriage of Winter* (1992) 7 CA4th 1926, 1933, 10 CR2d 225 (trial court's use of guideline based solely on income affirmed, even though parties were unusually frugal, using substantial funds for savings and investments). Note that the guideline formula may not be the basis for setting *long-term* support. *Marriage of Zywiciel* (2000) 83 CA4th 1078, 1082, 100 CR2d 242 (trial court erred in calculating spousal support using computer program designed to calculate temporary spousal support); *Marriage of Schulze* (1997) 60 CA4th 519, 527, 70 CR2d 488 (same); *Marriage of Burlini* (1983) 143 CA3d 65, 69, 191 CR 541.

When special circumstances are present (*e.g.,* tax consequences other than as contemplated by guideline formula, support obligations arising from prior relationship, unusually high monthly payments, special expenses), the formula should be modified in light of those circumstances. 143 CA3d at 70. Thus, counsel must be prepared to advance any special circumstances whose consideration may benefit the client, including proposals for the specific adjustments to be made, and to anticipate and address countervailing circumstances likely to be raised by the other party. When special circumstances are present, counsel should inquire about any applicable local rules and the particular judge's approach. Note, however, that the income of a supporting party's subsequent spouse or nonmarital partner may not be considered when determining or modifying spousal support. Fam C §4323(b).

If the parties have children together, the amounts to be allocated for the children from the parents' respective incomes under the statewide uniform child support guidelines (see Fam C §§4050–4076) will generally be deducted before the spousal support figure is calculated based on the remaining amounts. See former CC §4722(b) (mandatory minimum child support amount allocated to each parent under the Agnos Child Support Standards Act of 1984 (former CC §§4720–4732 and local rules as discussed above) must be determined before any spousal support amount is set).

§6.5　　　C. Duration

An order for temporary spousal support is terminated by (1) issuance of a judgment (*Wilson v Superior Court* (1948) 31 C2d 458, 462, 189 P2d 266), (2) dismissal (*Moore v Superior Court* (1970) 8 CA3d 804, 810, 87 CR 620), or (3) expiration under its own terms. Without such termination, however, temporary support payments continue to become due, even when the action is not actively prosecuted, and obligations that accrue before termination remain enforceable after termination. *Moore v Superior Court, supra.*

§6.6　　　D. Modification, Termination, or Set Aside

An order for temporary spousal support may be modified or terminated by the court at any time. Modification or termination may not, however, affect the payor's liability for payments that became due before the notice of motion or order to show cause to modify or terminate was filed. Fam C §3603. Any attempt by a trial court to allow a future retroactive modification of its temporary support order is in excess of its jurisdiction, and the order is voidable. *Marriage of Murray* (2002) 101 CA4th 581, 124 CR2d 342.

Case law holds that a temporary spousal support order may be modified without a showing of a change of circumstances. See, *e.g., Sande v Sande* (1969) 276 CA2d 324, 329, 80 CR 826. As a practical matter, however, many trial courts will deny modification of temporary spousal support when no change of circumstances is shown. Otherwise, a motion for modification might serve, in effect, as a substitute for an appeal, enabling a party who is unhappy with an order to return to the trial court and seek a more favorable one. Because it is always possible that a showing of a change in circumstances will be required, counsel should make sure that findings are part of the record so that a change of circumstances can subsequently be shown, if necessary.

Under the set-aside provisions of Fam C §§3690-3693, a court may, on any terms that may be just, relieve a party from all or any parts of a support order after the six-month time limit of CCP §473 (see §§18.24-18.35) has run. Fam C §3690(a). For discussion of these provisions, which apply to both spousal and child support orders, see §§8.33A-8.33E and the forms in §§8.33F-8.33H.

III. LONG-TERM SUPPORT

§6.7　　A. Statutory Authority

Family Code §4330 provides that in a judgment of dissolution or legal separation the court may order a party to pay spousal support to the other in any amount, and for any period of time, that the court deems just and reasonable. The same is true for a judgment of nullity, as long as the party for whose benefit the order is made is found to be a putative spouse. Fam C §2254. On qualifying as a putative spouse, see §3.19.

The court may also order a party who is required to pay spousal support to furnish reasonable security for payment. Fam C §4339. Note, however, that the court's authority to order security is limited by the requirement that the security be "reasonable." See *Marriage of Johnson* (1982) 134 CA3d 148, 161, 184 CR 444 (lien on party's entire community property share for uncertain duration rejected as "clearly unreasonable").

Even though the support obligation terminates on either party's death, a trial court has jurisdiction to provide funds for the supported party, in the event of the supporting party's death, by (1) including, as a component of the support award, an amount sufficient to purchase an annuity for the supported party or to maintain insurance for his or her benefit on the life of the supporting party, or (2) requiring the supporting party to establish a trust for the supported party. Fam C §4360 (former CC §4801.4); *Marriage of Ziegler* (1989) 207 CA3d 788, 255 CR 100. Under Fam C §4360, the court may order the supporting party to maintain life insurance for the benefit of the supported party; such an order carries the obligation not to do anything that would interfere with benefits being paid under the policy. *Tintocalis v Tintocalis* (1993) 20 CA4th 1590, 25 CR2d 655.

When a spouse is convicted of attempting to murder the other spouse as punishable under Pen C §664(a), whether or not physical injury occurred, the victim spouse will be entitled to a prohibition of any temporary or long-term spousal support award, or medical, life, or other insurance benefits or payments, from the victim spouse to the other spouse. Fam C §4324.

§6.8 B. Considerations in Making Award

Wide discretion is vested in the trial court in setting the amount and duration of long-term spousal support. *Marriage of Wilson* (1988) 201 CA3d 913, 916, 247 CR 522. The court must *apply,* however, not merely recognize, the criteria listed in Fam C §4320 (former CC §4801(a)). *Marriage of Fransen* (1983) 142 CA3d 419, 425, 190 CR 885. Consequently, in setting long-term support, unlike temporary support (see §6.4), the court may not simply use support guideline formulas. *Marriage of Zywiciel* (2000) 83 CA4th 1078, 1081, 100 CR2d 242 (record must reflect that court weighed §4320 factors in setting permanent support); *Marriage of Schulze* (1997) 60 CA4th 519, 527, 70 CR2d 488 (trial court erred in calculating spousal support using a computer program designed to calculate temporary spousal support). *Marriage of Burlini* (1983) 143 CA3d 65, 69, 191 CR 541, 543. The criteria in Fam C §4320 apply both in setting spousal support at the time of the judgment and also in any subsequent proceedings for modification or termination. *Marriage of Prietsch & Calhoun* (1987) 190 CA3d 645, 655, 235 CR 587. For discussion of the criteria, see §§6.9–6.10.

§6.9 1. Must Be Based on Marital Standard of Living

In awarding long-term spousal support, the court must base its decision on the standard of living established during the marriage. Fam C §4330(a). The marital standard of living is meant to be weighed, under the circumstances of the case, along with all other applicable factors in Fam C §4320 (see §6.10) in reaching a fair and reasonable result. Thus, the court may fix support at an amount greater than, equal to, or less than the amount the supported spouse may require to maintain the marital standard of living. See *Marriage of De Guigne* (2002) 97 CA4th 1353, 1362, 119 CR2d 430 (when parties lived beyond their income based on husband's decision to liquidate capital assets, inappropriate to base his support obligations on investment income alone and permit him to shelter and benefit from substantial non-income-producing assets); *Marriage of Zywiciel* (2000) 83 CA4th 1078, 1081, 100 CR2d 242 (marital standard not measure of support, but rather reference point against which to measure statutory guideline); *Marriage of Kerr* (1999) 77 CA4th 87, 95, 91 CR2d 374 (proper to use unexercised stock options as basis for spousal and child support proper, but error to award percentage amounts beyond marital standard of living or children's needs); *Marriage of Smith* (1990) 225 CA3d 469, 475, 274 CR 911. The weight given to the marital standard of living will necessarily be substantially less after a brief marriage in which the standard was determined by the supporting spouse's separate property assets than after a long-term marriage in which the couple developed a standard of living together. *Marriage of Huntington* (1992) 10 CA4th 1513, 1521, 14 CR2d 1.

The "marital standard of living" is intended to be a general description of the station in life the parties had achieved by the date of separation. Although more specific findings are encouraged, particularly when the parties are represented by counsel, it will be sufficient to use the everyday understanding of the term, *i.e.,* upper, middle, or lower income. *Marriage of Smith* (1990) 225 CA3d 469, 491, 274 CR 911.

In determining the marital standard of living, the actual standard (*i.e.,* actual expenditures) will normally control. 225 CA3d at 484. In some cases, however, focusing on expenditures may not be appropriate. *Marriage of Weinstein* (1991) 4 CA4th 555, 565, 5 CR2d 558. In some instances, this focus may produce an unreasonably high measure of the marital standard of living. For example, if the parties live beyond their means, the trial court may base its spousal support award on the parties' income rather than on their expenditures. 4 CA4th at 566. Similarly, when the parties' standard of living during the marriage is unreasonably high, not only because they lived beyond their means, but also because one party worked excessive hours, the marital standard of living should be set at what would have been a reasonable standard given what the earning party would have earned had he or she worked at a reasonably human pace. *Marriage of Smith* (1990) 225 CA3d 469, 493, 274 CR 911.

In other cases, focusing on expenditures may produce an unreasonably low measure of the marital standard of living. When, for instance, the marital standard of living is deliberately maintained at a low level to enable one spouse to undertake a professional education that is expected to yield a higher standard for the parties in the future, the court should consider the impact on the marital standard of living of the spouse's absence from the full-time work force. *Marriage of Watt* (1989) 214 CA3d 340, 351, 262 CR 783. Likewise, when the parties live very modestly in comparison to their means, using substantial funds for savings and investments, the marital standard of living may be set at a standard that allows for that level of savings and investments. See *Marriage of Winter* (1992) 7 CA4th 1926, 1932, 10 CR2d 225. In *Winter,* the court of appeal affirmed the trial court's use of the guideline formula for temporary support that was based solely on income. 7 CA4th at 1933.

The court is required to make specific factual findings regarding the marital standard of living whether or not it is requested to do so. Fam C §4332.

§6.10   2. Circumstances Court Must Consider

In addition to considering the marital standard of living when ordering long-term spousal support, the court must consider all of the following 14 circumstances (also called "4320 factors") that apply to the respective parties. A court's failure to consider and apply each of the relevant factors may be deemed an abuse of discretion. *McTiernan v Dubrow* (2005) 133 CA4th 1090, 1105, 35 CR3d 287 (order limiting spousal support to 2 years reversed because trial court omitted analysis of husband's ability to pay and wife's needs); *Marriage of Cheriton* (2001) 92 CA4th 269, 305, 111 CR2d 755 (abuse of discretion for trial court not to consider husband's wealth). The factors are as follows (Fam C §4320(a)–(n)):

(1) The extent to which each party's earning capacity will maintain the standard of living established during the marriage. The court must take into account (a) what might be required for the supported party to develop or acquire marketable skills and (b) the extent to which his or her earning capacity is or will be impaired by any periods of unemployment during the marriage to devote time to domestic duties. Fam C §4320(a).

A party who interrupted employment during a relatively brief marriage may be entitled to spousal support for only a short period, in order to bring his or her skills to a level that will allow reentry into the job market. A party who was out of the job market throughout a lengthy marriage, however, may be entitled to support for a long period, possibly even for life. *Marriage of Brantner* (1977) 67 CA3d 416, 420, 136 CR 635. But when a party requesting support has failed to exercise due diligence in seeking employment, the court may consider that fact, even to the extent, in appropriate circumstances, of denying support entirely. *Marriage of Mason* (1979) 93 CA3d 215, 221, 155 CR 350.

When spousal support is at issue, the court may order a party (ordinarily the party seeking support) to submit to an examination by a vocational training consultant. The order requires a noticed motion and a finding of good cause. Failure to comply with the order could result in sanctions. Fam C §4331(a)–(c).

(2) The extent to which the supported party contributed to the supporting party's attainment of an education, training, a career position, or a license. Fam C §4320(b).

Family Code §4320 should be interpreted broadly to require consideration of *all* of the supported spouse's contributions to assist the supporting spouse in acquiring an education and enhanced earning capacity, including contributions for ordinary living expenses. The employed spouse's contributions should be weighed heavily in ordering long-term support. *Marriage of Watt* (1989) 214 CA3d 340, 350, 262 CR 783. An unpaid homemaker who was the primary caretaker for the children of the marriage while the other spouse's career was fostered is entitled to the same consideration for his or her contributions that an employed spouse receives. *Marriage of Ostler & Smith* (1990) 223 CA3d 33, 49, 272 CR 560.

The contributing party may seek the court's recognition of the contributions under Fam C §4320(b) in its decision on long-term support, reimbursement for contributions to education or training under Fam C §2641 (see §5.98), or both. Fam C §2641(d). In measuring contributions under Fam C §2641, however, contributions for ordinary living expenses are *not* recognized. *Marriage of Watt* (1989) 214 CA3d 340, 354, 262 CR 783.

(3) The supporting party's ability to pay, taking into account his or her earning capacity, earned and unearned income, assets, and standard of living. Fam C §4320(c).

Normally, the supporting party's ability to pay will be measured by his or her actual income. See *Marriage of Rosen* (2002) 105 CA4th 808, 130 CR2d 1. When, however, the supporting party has the ability and the opportunity to earn more than he or she is earning, but is unwilling to do so, the court may apply an earning-capacity standard to deter that party's shirking of family obligations. *Marriage of Regnery* (1989) 214 CA3d 1367, 263 CR 243. Compare *Regnery* with *Marriage of Everett* (1990) 220 CA3d 846, 269 CR 917, which affirmed a refusal to impute additional income to the support payor, despite evidence of his substantially higher income years before in the same profession, based on the payor's sincere efforts to make a success of his business and pay child support and on concern that a higher order might not be in the children's best interests. See also *Marriage of Eggers* (2005) 131 CA4th 695, 700–701, 32 CR3d 292 (error for court to impute income based on earnings from father's lost job without reaching issues of his ability and opportunity to work); *Marriage of Cohn* (1998) 65 CA4th 923, 76 CR2d 866 (income may be imputed to self-employed party with substantial likelihood of producing income with reasonable effort, but amount imputed must have some tangible evidentiary foundation); *Marriage of Reynolds* (1998) 63 CA4th 1373, 74 CR2d 636 (68-year-old payor could not be compelled to work after usual retirement age of 65 in order to maintain level of spousal support he paid while working); *Marriage of LaBass & Munsee* (1997) 56 CA4th 1331, 66 CR2d 393 (parent who shows other parent had ability and opportunity to work full-time but was unwilling to do so need not show that other parent would actually secure work if he or she sought it); *Marriage of Hinman* (1997) 55 CA4th 988, 64 CR2d 383 (payor's motive for reducing income irrelevant; decision must be based on whether payor has ability and opportunity to work and whether considering earning capacity would be in best interests of children for whom support is sought); *Marriage of Stephenson* (1995) 39 CA4th 71, 80, 46 CR2d 8 (when spousal support payor elects to retire early and does not seek available employment reasonably remunerative under the circumstances, court may properly impute income to him or her); *Marriage of Padilla* (1995) 38 CA4th 1212, 1218, 45 CR2d 555 (payor's motivation for reducing available income irrelevant when ability and opportunity to adequately and reasonably provide for child are present); *Marriage of Ilas* (1993) 12 CA4th 1630, 16 CR2d 345 (affirmed refusal to reduce spousal and child support when payor quit job as pharmacist to become full-time medical student and payee was unemployed); *Marriage of Meegan* (1992) 11 CA4th 156, 13 CR2d 799 (affirmed reduction of spousal support to zero when payor who quit job to take residence at monastery and prepare for priesthood acted in good faith and payee would suffer only minimal reduction in living standard).

A determination of the supporting party's earning capacity should not be based on an extraordinary work regimen, even if engaged in by the supporting spouse during the marriage. Rather, the determination should be based on an "objectively reasonable work regimen" as it would exist at the time the support determination is made. *Marriage of Simpson* (1992) 4 C4th 225, 234, 14 CR2d 411. To base a spousal support award on earning capacity, the trial court must make a finding of earning capacity; it is reversible error to base the support award on an erroneous finding of actual income. *Marriage of Rosen* (2002) 105 CA4th 808, 130 CR2d 1.

(4) Each party's needs, based on the standard of living established during the marriage. Fam C §4320(d) (former CC §4801(a)(4)).

The needs to be considered must be reasonable ones, commensurate with a spouse's station in life, and not merely bare necessities. *Marriage of Siegel* (1972) 26 CA3d 88, 92, 102 CR 613. On the rebuttable presumption of decreased need for support under Fam C §4323 when the supported party is cohabiting with someone of the opposite sex, see §6.26. On the standard of living established during the marriage, see §6.9.

In ascertaining a supported party's needs, the trial court may provide funds for him or her in the event of the supporting party's death. See §6.7.

(5) Each party's assets (including separate property) and obligations. Fam C §4320(e) (former CC §4801(a)(5)).

All assets of a prospective supporting party, whether separate property or the community property to be divided in the marital action, are available as sources of long-term spousal support. *Marriage of Epstein* (1979) 24 C3d 76, 91 n14, 154 CR 413; *Marriage of Cheriton* (2001) 92 CA4th 269, 305, 111 CR2d 755 (abuse of discretion for trial court not to take husband's wealth into account when analyzing ability to pay). The assets need not be in the party's name as long as they are under his or her control. *Marriage of Dick* (1993) 15

CA4th 144, 161, 18 CR2d 743. Similarly, at least when there are no children, a prospective supported party who has or acquires separate property, including employment income, sufficient for his or her proper support may not receive spousal support. Fam C §4322; see also *Marriage of Terry* (2000) 80 CA4th 921, 930, 95 CR2d 760 (current income is not sole measure of sufficiency for Fam C §4322; court must also consider actual and potential income); *Marriage of McNaughton* (1983) 145 CA3d 845, 850, 194 CR 176 (former CC §4806, predecessor of Fam C §4322, applicable only when supported party's income sufficient to meet his or her needs). Obligations, too, may have an effect on long-term spousal support. See, *e.g.,* former CC §4722(b) (mandatory minimum child support amount allocated to each parent under the Agnos Child Support Standards Act of 1984 (former CC §§4720–4732) must be determined before any spousal support amount is set).

(6) The duration of the marriage. Fam C §4320(f).

When long-term spousal support is ordered, the duration of the marriage is often the primary factor considered in addressing the duration and a termination date of the support. The court should not base its decision solely on duration, however, but must consider each of the factors listed in Fam C §4320 (former CC §4801(a)) that applies to the case. *Marriage of Prietsch & Calhoun* (1987) 190 CA3d 645, 663, 235 CR 587. There are no rules for which universal application may be claimed, and the oft-cited rule of thumb that the duration of support equals half the duration of the marriage has been strongly criticized, particularly when applied to long-term marriages. *Marriage of Brantner* (1977) 67 CA3d 416, 423, 136 CR 635. Nevertheless, certain guidelines may be fashioned on how the duration of the marriage should be considered in awarding spousal support. *Marriage of Prietsch & Calhoun, supra.*

In short-term marriages, duration will usually work against anything but short-term support with a fixed termination date, and spousal support will usually be ordered when the needs of minor children or the employment circumstances of the supported party require it until the supported party can readjust to single status. When spousal support is ordered following medium-term marriages, the duration of the marriage more strongly supports open-ended jurisdiction, but it does not by itself preclude the fixing of a termination date. The longer the marriage, the more likely it is that it would constitute an abuse of discretion for the court to fix a date for termination of jurisdiction over spousal support without a clear showing that it is reasonably probable that the supported party will be self-sufficient by that date. *Marriage of Prietsch & Calhoun, supra.* On retention of jurisdiction generally, see §6.11.

(7) The supported party's ability to be gainfully employed without interfering with the interests of dependent children in his or her custody. Fam C §4320(g).

Family Code §4320(g) seeks to balance two potentially conflicting policy goals: (a) encouraging the supported party to find suitable employment and (b) ensuring that dependent children can receive needed attention from the custodial parent. In *Marriage of Rosan* (1972) 24 CA3d 885, 893, 101 CR 295, the court of appeal noted that the trial court may consider whether a supported party has made adequate efforts to find suitable employment, but it also concluded in that particular case that it was not unreasonable for the supported party to defer seeking employment or preparation for employment for one year after separation because she had custody of the parties' two children, including one whose behavioral or emotional problems had required her to terminate her schooling and employment during the marriage.

(8) Each party's age and health. Fam C §4320(h).

Other things being equal, an older, less healthy party is obviously more likely to receive a favorable long-term spousal support order than is a younger, more healthy party. Regardless of the facts of the particular case, however, support may not be ordered on the basis of the age and health of the respective parties alone. In *Marriage of Wilson* (1988) 201 CA3d 913, 247 CR 522, the court of appeal upheld termination of spousal support after 58 months, following a marriage of 70 months, even though the 46-year-old supporting party had the earning capacity to continue making support payments and the 48-year-old supported party was permanently disabled. The trial court relied primarily on the duration of the marriage, but properly weighed all the factors required by former CC §4801(a), predecessor of Fam C §4320.

(9) Documented evidence of any history of domestic violence (see Fam C §6211) between the parties, including emotional dis-

tress resulting from the violence. Fam C §4320(i) (formerly included in Fam C §4320(h)).

To give it the same weight as the other §4320 circumstances that the court considers when ordering long-term spousal support, documented evidence of domestic violence was made a separate subsection of §4320, effective January 1, 2002. See Stats 2001, ch 293, §2.

(10) The immediate and specific tax consequences to each party. Fam C §4320(j) (former Fam C §4320(i).

Income tax consequences of spousal support to both the paying and the receiving party have always been a factor the court may consider in awarding long-term spousal support. See, *e.g., Marriage of Lopez* (1974) 38 CA3d 93, 116, 113 CR 58. Effective January 1, 1989, former CC §4801(a)(9) made their consideration mandatory. On tax aspects of spousal support, see §§6.28–6.37.

(11) The balance of the hardships to each party. Fam C §4320(k) (former Fam C §4320(j)).

This circumstance was added effective January 1, 1997, and relettered effective January 1, 2002.

(12) The goal that the supported party be self-supporting within a reasonable period of time. Fam C §4320(l) (former Fam C §4320(k)).

This circumstance was added effective January 1, 1997, and relettered effective January 1, 2002. Except in the case of a marriage of long duration as described in Fam C §4336 (see §6.11), for purposes of Fam C §4320, a "reasonable period of time" will generally be one half the length of the marriage, but nothing in §4320 is intended to limit the court's discretion to order support for a greater or lesser period of time, based on any of the other factors listed in that section and the circumstances of the parties. Fam C §4320(l). In 1997 through 1999, former §4320(k) (now Fam C §4320(l)) applied regardless of the length of the marriage.

When making a spousal support order, the court may advise the supported party that he or she should make reasonable efforts to assist in providing for his or her support needs, taking into account the particular circumstances considered by the court under Fam C §4320 (outlined in this section), unless, in the case of a marriage of long duration as provided for in Fam C §4336 (see §6.11), the court decides this warning is inadvisable. Fam C §4330(b). Such notice is often referred to as a *"Gavron* warning," after the case of the same name. See *Marriage of Schmir* (2005) 134 CA4th 43, 55, 35 CR3d 716 (former wife should have been given reasonable advance notice of termination of spousal support and opportunity to obtain employment, because present ability to earn income did not mean she could earn instantly); *Marriage of Gavron* (1988) 203 CA3d 705, 712, 250 CR 148.

In *Marriage of Schaffer* (1999) 69 CA4th 801, 81 CR2d 797, the court applied former Fam C §4320(k) to affirm a trial court decision denying spousal support to a wife who had unsuccessfully pursued an apparently unsuitable career in social work. The wife did not seek other employment but, through a series of postjudgment hearings for modification, managed to extend an initial two years of support into 15. The appellate court found no error in terminating spousal support based on examination of the wife's course of conduct over the 15-year period, holding that the former §4320(k) guideline, applied retroactively to consider events predating its inception, took priority over the "change of circumstances rule": "The statutory guideline flies in the face of a reading of the material change of circumstance rule that would prevent a trial judge from looking at long-term patterns of job training and employability." 69 CA4th at 810.

(13) The criminal conviction of an abusive spouse when the court is reducing or eliminating a spousal support award under Fam C §4325. Fam C §4320(m).

This circumstance was added effective January 1, 2002. Family Code §4325, also effective January 1, 2002, raises the rebuttable presumption that when there has been a criminal conviction for an act of domestic violence by one spouse against the other within 5 years before, or any time after, filing of the dissolution petition, a court should not make a spousal support award to the abusive spouse. To rebut the presumption, the court may consider, among other things, documented evidence of a convicted spouse's history as a domestic violence victim. See *Marriage of Cauley* (2006) 138 CA4th 1100, 41 CR3d 902 (former wife's conviction for domestic violence against former husband rendered agreement for nonmodifiable and nonterminable spousal support to her unenforceable on public policy grounds; §4325 presumption not rebutted).

(14) Any other factors the court deems just and equitable. Fam C §4320(n) (former Fam C §4320(m)).

This circumstance was relettered effective January 1, 2002.

In addressing long-term spousal support, a court should consider almost everything that bears on present and prospective matters relating to the lives of the parties. *Marriage of Cosgrove* (1972) 27 CA3d 424, 434, 103 CR 733. Note, however, that the income of a supporting party's subsequent spouse or nonmarital partner may not be considered when determining or modifying spousal support. Fam C §4323(b). Factors that the courts have considered in addition to those specified in Fam C §4320(a)–(m) include:

- Support responsibilities to third parties (see, *e.g., Marriage of Epstein* (1979) 24 C3d 76, 90, 154 CR 413 (supporting party's education expenditures for adult child); *Marriage of Paul* (1985) 173 CA3d 913, 919, 219 CR 318 (supported party's education expenditures for adult child); *Marriage of Siegel* (1972) 26 CA3d 88, 93, 102 CR 613 (supported party's expenditures for disabled adult daughter and her child); but see *Marriage of Serna* (2000) 85 CA4th 482, 489, 102 CR2d 188, criticizing *Paul* and *Siegel* for improperly allowing supported spouse's subsidy to adult children to be consideration in spousal support, and *Marriage of McElwee* (1988) 197 CA3d 902, 911, 243 CR 179, in which court refused to order indirect adult child support through an increase in spousal support);

- Suppression of the standard of living during marriage in anticipation of an increased standard on completion of a spouse's education (*Marriage of Watt* (1989) 214 CA3d 340, 351, 262 CR 783);

- The need for household help and child care expenses while obtaining an education and during employment in order to become self-supporting (*Marriage of Ostler & Smith* (1990) 223 CA3d 33, 47, 272 CR 560); and

- Monetary gifts to the supported spouse from a third party (*Marriage of Shaughnessy* (2006) 139 CA4th 1225, 1240, 43 CR3d 642 (court may consider annual gift to supported spouse from her parents)).

§6.11 C. Retention of Jurisdiction

An important issue whenever a court makes an order regarding long-term spousal support is whether the court may properly limit the order to a specified period and not reserve jurisdiction to extend it. In *Marriage of Morrison* (1978) 20 C3d 437, 453, 143 CR 139, the supreme court held that a trial court should not terminate jurisdiction to extend a support order after a lengthy marriage unless the record clearly indicates that the supported party will be able to adequately meet his or her financial needs at the time selected for termination of jurisdiction. Beyond finding that the 28-year marriage in *Morrison* qualified, however, the court did not provide any guidance on what duration constitutes a "lengthy" marriage.

Additional guidance was subsequently provided by amended former CC §4801(d), predecessor of Fam C §4336, which established a rebuttable presumption affecting the burden of providing evidence that a marriage of ten years or more, measured from the date of marriage to the date of separation, is a marriage "of long duration." In determining whether a marriage is of long duration, the court may consider periods of separation during the marriage. In some circumstances, a court may find that a marriage of less than ten years is one of long duration. Fam C §4336(b); *Marriage of Baker* (1992) 3 CA4th 491, 499, 4 CR2d 553.

Other than providing guidance on whether a marriage is of long duration, however, amended former CC §4801(d) does not seem to have altered preexisting law under *Marriage of Morrison, supra*. Family Code §4336(a) provides that, when a marriage has been of long duration, the court retains jurisdiction indefinitely unless the parties agree to the contrary in writing or the court terminates support. Further, Fam C §4336(c) expressly provides that a court may terminate spousal support in subsequent proceedings on a showing of changed circumstances. *Marriage of Christie* (1994) 28 CA4th 849, 858, 34 CR2d 135. There is nothing in Fam C §4336 to suggest that courts are not still limited, in marriages of long duration, by the *Morrison* standard (*i.e.*, for termination of jurisdiction to extend a support order, the record must clearly indicate the supported party's ability to meet his or her financial needs at the time selected for termination). See 28 CA4th at 859.

Note that the application of *Marriage of Morrison, supra*, is limited to lengthy marriages. *Marriage of Bukaty* (1986) 180 CA3d 143, 148, 225 CR 492. On considering duration generally in awarding long-term spousal support, see discussion of Fam C §4320(f) in §6.10. See also *Marriage of Hebbring* (1989) 207 CA3d 1260, 1265, 255 CR 488.

§6.12   D. Forms of Orders

Court orders for long-term spousal support take a variety of forms. Without a proper agreement of the parties to the contrary, however, support payments must terminate on either party's death or on the supported party's remarriage. Fam C §4337. On what is necessary to waive the Fam C §4337 support termination provisions, see §6.27. The order must contain provisions for its termination and it must be subject to subsequent modification or termination by the court under Fam C §3591. For samples and discussion of common forms of long-term support orders a court may make in the absence of an agreement of the parties, see §§6.13–6.19.

When the parties are reaching an agreement on long-term spousal support, they are not bound by statutory limitations. Possible variations are limited only by the creativity and willingness of the negotiators. The parties might agree, for example, that support will be non-modifiable or that it will continue beyond the supporting party's death (*i.e.,* be payable by his or her estate). For samples and discussion of long-term support provisions parties may agree on, see California Marital Settlement and Other Family Law Agreements, chap 8 (3d ed Cal CEB 2005). For complying with IRS definition of "alimony or spousal maintenance," including requirement that support terminate on death of payee, under IRC §71, see §§6.28–6.37.

§6.13   1. Modifiable Amount for Indefinite Term

A common form of long-term spousal support order is one that provides for a modifiable amount of support for an indefinite term, *e.g.*:

Petitioner will pay to respondent for spousal support the sum of $500 per month, payable in advance, one half on or before the first day of each month and one half on or before the 15th day of each month, commencing July 1, 2005, and continuing until either party's death, respondent's remarriage, or modification or termination by further Court order, whichever occurs first.

The absence of a specified termination date may not always be appropriate, particularly in short-term marriages. On considering duration of marriage in addressing long-term spousal support, see §§6.10 (discussion of Fam C §4320(f)), 6.11. The provisions in the sample order for termination on either party's death or the supported party's remarriage and for subsequent modification or termination by the court are mandatory (and will be deemed to apply if the order is silent on the issue of termination) in the absence of the parties' agreement to the contrary. Fam C §§3591, 4337. On termination, see §6.27.

When the court makes an open-ended long-term spousal support order, a change of circumstances will be required to terminate support. *Marriage of Heistermann* (1991) 234 CA3d 1195, 1201, 286 CR 127.

§6.14   2. Modifiable Amount for Definite Term

Long-term spousal support orders sometimes provide for a modifiable amount of support for a definite term, *e.g.*:

Petitioner will pay to respondent for spousal support the sum of $500 per month, payable in advance, one half on or before the first day of each month and one half on or before the 15th day of each month, commencing July 1, 2005, and continuing until either party's death, respondent's remarriage, or June 30, 2007, whichever occurs first. Spousal support may be modified as to amount, but not as to duration. If not terminated earlier, spousal support will terminate absolutely on June 30, 2007.

Having a specified termination date is not always appropriate, particularly in long-term marriages. On considering duration of marriage in addressing long-term support, see §§6.10 (discussion of Fam C §4320(f)), 6.11. Even when the court sets a specified termination date, the support must remain modifiable *as to amount* during the support payment period (*Marriage of Morrison* (1978) 20 C3d 437, 454 n11, 143 CR 139), unless the parties agree to the contrary (Fam C §3591(c)).

§6.15   3. Modifiable Amount for Specified Period; Reservation of Jurisdiction

In some instances, a court will order spousal support in a modifiable amount for a specified period, with a reservation of jurisdiction thereafter, *e.g.*:

Petitioner will pay to respondent for spousal support the sum of $500 per month, payable in advance, one half on or before the first day of each month and one half on or before the 15th day of each month, commencing July 1, 2005, and continuing until either party's death, respondent's remarriage, modification or termination by further Court order, or June 30, 2007, whichever occurs first. If June 30, 2007, occurs first, then effective on that date spousal support will be reduced to zero, with the Court reserving jurisdiction, continuing until either party's death, respondent's remarriage, or further Court order, to order spousal support payable by petitioner to respondent.

Under this form of order, a motion would have to be filed by the supported party before payments could be ordered for any period beyond the specified date or by the supporting party before jurisdiction could be terminated. Jurisdiction can also be retained by reducing support to $1 per year (*Marriage of Forcum* (1983) 145 CA3d 599, 605, 193 CR 596), sometimes referred to as a "jurisdictional amount" (see, *e.g., Marriage of Foreman* (1986) 183 CA3d 129, 131, 228 CR 4).

An order that reduces support at a particular future date to a nominal amount cannot be based on mere supposition about the supported party's future circumstances. Rather, evidence in the record must support a reasonable inference that the supported party can be self-supporting at that time. *Marriage of Prietsch & Calhoun* (1987) 190 CA3d 645, 656, 235 CR 587.

§6.16 4. Modifiable Amount for Specified Period; Burden on Supported Party to Avoid Termination

In some instances, a court will order spousal support in a modifiable amount until a specified termination date and require the supported spouse, in order to avoid termination, to show good cause for extension on a motion filed before the termination date, *e.g.*:

Petitioner will pay to respondent for spousal support the sum of $500 per month, payable in advance, one half on or before the first day of each month and one half on or before the 15th day of each month, commencing July 1, 2005, and continuing

until either party's death, respondent's remarriage, modification or termination by further Court order, or June 30, 2007, whichever occurs first. If not terminated earlier, spousal support will terminate absolutely on June 30, 2007, unless extended by Court order, on a showing by respondent of good cause, on a motion filed before or on June 30, 2007.

This form of order is commonly referred to as a *"Richmond* order" (see *Marriage of Richmond* (1980) 105 CA3d 352, 164 CR 381). Such an order cannot be based on mere speculation about the supported party's future employment qualifications or opportunities. 105 CA3d at 356. Rather, like any order that reduces support at a particular future date, evidence in the record must support a reasonable inference that the supported party can be self-supporting at the time conditionally set for termination. See *Marriage of Prietsch & Calhoun* (1987) 190 CA3d 645, 656, 235 CR 587.

§6.17   5. Decreasing Amounts

Courts sometimes make orders for long-term spousal support payable in decreasing amounts. Commonly known as "step-down orders," they may take any of the approaches toward duration presented by orders with single, modifiable amounts (see §§6.13–6.16), *e.g.*:

Petitioner will pay to respondent for spousal support, payable in advance, one half on or before the first day of each month and one half on or before the 15th day of each month, unless terminated earlier as set forth below, the following sums:

$500 per month for the period from July 1, 2005, through June 30, 2007;

$300 per month for the period from July 1, 2007, through June 30, 2009; and

$100 per month for the period from July 1, 2009, through June 30, 2011.

Spousal support will be payable until either party's death, respondent's remarriage, modification or termination by further Court order, or June 30, 2011, whichever occurs first. If not terminated earlier, spousal support will terminate absolutely on June 30, 2011, unless extended by Court order, on a showing

by respondent of good cause, on a motion filed before or on June 30, 2011.

When the step-down order is an initial order automatically decreasing support amounts at specified intervals, there must be evidence in the record to support a reasonable inference that the supported party's needs will decrease with each step-down. *Marriage of Prietsch & Calhoun* (1987) 190 CA3d 645, 656, 235 CR 587. But in a case reviewing earlier support orders in which the trial court found reason to order an immediate reduction in support but used a step-down to "ease the impact of the decrease," the appellate court found no need to show decreased need at each step-down level. *Marriage of Rising* (1999) 76 CA4th 472, 478, 90 CR2d 380.

§6.18   6. No Amount Payable Now; Reservation of Jurisdiction

When circumstances do not presently support an award of long-term spousal support but also do not justify termination, a court may simply reserve jurisdiction, *e.g.*:

Neither party will pay spousal support to the other. The Court reserves jurisdiction, however, until either party's death, respondent's remarriage, or modification or termination by further Court order, whichever occurs first, to order such support payable by petitioner to respondent on a proper showing of a change of circumstances.

Under this form of order, a motion would have to be filed by the supported party before payments could be ordered or by the supporting party before jurisdiction could be terminated.

§6.19   7. Jurisdiction Terminated

Under appropriate circumstances, the court may simply terminate jurisdiction over spousal support, *e.g.*:

Jurisdiction over spousal support is terminated. No Court will have jurisdiction to order spousal support payable by either party to the other at any time, regardless of any circumstances that may arise.

Termination of jurisdiction over spousal support is not always appropriate, particularly in long-term marriages. On considering duration of marriage in determining long-term spousal support, see §§6.10 (discussion of Fam C §4320(f)), 6.11.

E. Modification

§6.20   1. Statutory Authority

Long-term spousal support orders may generally be modified or terminated as the court deems necessary. Fam C §3651. There are, nevertheless, circumstances under which a support order may limit, or even eliminate, the court's authority to modify or terminate. See §§6.21–6.23. Without such circumstances, however, the court's statutory authority to modify or terminate is retained, even though not expressly stated. See *Verdier v Verdier* (1950) 36 C2d 241, 247, 223 P2d 214.

An order may not be modified or terminated with respect to any amount that accrues before the date of filing of the notice of motion or order to show cause to modify or terminate. Fam C §3651(c). When the modification is entered due to the unemployment of either party, it must be made retroactive to the later of the date of service or the date of unemployment, unless the court finds good cause not to make the order retroactive and states its reasons on the record. Fam C §3653(b). If the order is entered retroactively, the support obligor may be entitled to, and the support obligee may be ordered to repay, according to the terms specified in the order, any amounts previously paid under the prior order that are in excess of the amounts due under the retroactive order. Fam C §3653(c). See *Marriage of Dandona & Araluce* (2001) 91 CA4th 1120, 1124, 111 CR2d 390 (reimbursement under Fam C §3653 retroactive; court has discretion to order repayment).

The court may order that the repayment by the support obligee be made over any period of time and in any manner (including, but not limited to, an offset against future support payments or a future wage assignment) that the court deems just and reasonable. Fam C §3653(c). In determining whether to order a repayment, and in establishing the terms of repayment, the court must consider all the following factors (Fam C §3653(c)):

- The amount to be repaid;

- The duration of the support order before modification or termination;

- The financial impact on the support obligee of any particular method of repayment, e.g., an offset against future support payments or a future wage assignment; and

- Any other facts or circumstances that the court deems relevant.

A court has authority to modify a spousal support agreement, whether entered into before or after judgment, that has not been approved by a court or merged into a judgment or order. Fam C §3591; *Marriage of Maytag* (1994) 26 CA4th 1711, 32 CR2d 334.

2. Limitations on Court's Authority

§6.21 a. Judgment in Short-Term Marriage That Neither Awards Support Nor Reserves Jurisdiction

In *Marriage of Ostrander* (1997) 53 CA4th 63, 61 CR2d 348, the court of appeal held that, after a marriage of long duration, a judgment that neither awards spousal support nor reserves jurisdiction to do so does not preclude later jurisdiction to award such support unless it contains specific language of termination. The *Ostrander* court relied on Fam C §4336 (absent written agreement to contrary or court order terminating support, court retains jurisdiction to award spousal support indefinitely when marriage is "of long duration") (see §6.23). It would appear, however, that a judgment that neither awards spousal support nor reserves jurisdiction to do so *would* preclude later spousal support jurisdiction when the marriage was *not* of long duration. See Fam C §4335; *McClure v McClure* (1935) 4 C2d 356, 359, 49 P2d 584; §6.23. On determining whether marriage is "of long duration," see §6.11.

§6.22 b. Parties' Agreement Precluding Modification

The court's authority to modify or terminate a spousal support order is expressly made subject to the parties' written agreement, or in-court oral agreement, to the contrary. Fam C §3591(c). Such agreements may provide that the support provisions are nonmodifiable without exception, *i.e.,* that they may not be modified under any circumstances as to either amount or duration. See, *e.g., Marriage of Sasson* (1982) 129 CA3d 140, 180 CR 815. In *Sasson,* the agreement provided that the wife would receive $350 per month for six years, then $250 per month for two years, after which spousal support would terminate, unless it terminated earlier by virtue of the wife's remarriage or either party's death. The provision was made unequivocally nonmodifiable. 129 CA3d at 142. When the supported party entered into a relationship that was very much like a marriage, and even represented to family and friends that she was remarried, but in reality did not remarry, the supporting party requested that spousal support be terminated. The court of appeal upheld the trial court's denial of the request, finding that the supported party was entitled to rely on the agreement and receive the support it provided as long as she did not remarry.

Parties may also agree to restrict modifiability without precluding it entirely. See, *e.g., Marriage of Rabkin* (1986) 179 CA3d 1071, 225 CR 219. In *Rabkin,* the agreement provided for spousal support amounts established in contemplation of a prompt sale of the family residence. Accordingly, it specifically precluded the sale, and the purchase or rental of other housing, from constituting a change of circumstances on which a motion to modify the support might be based. The agreement provided, however, that the supported party could seek increased support if the residence was not sold by a specified date, but it limited the amount she could seek. 179 CA3d at 1076. After the supporting party requested and received a support reduction based, at least in part, on the sale of the residence, the supported party appealed, claiming that an agreement that modification cannot be based on certain specified events is just as valid as one that makes support unconditionally nonmodifiable. 179 CA3d at 1078. The court of appeal agreed. 179 CA3d at 1081.

Considerable litigation has been generated over whether particular agreements preclude modification of spousal support. There is a general rule in favor of the modifiability of support. *Marriage of Hufford* (1984) 152 CA3d 825, 828, 199 CR 726. Nevertheless, earlier cases stressed the fact that no "magic words" were necessary to make spousal support nonmodifiable and appeared willing to infer that intent from general language. 152 CA3d at 834. See, *e.g., Marriage of Smiley* (1975) 53 CA3d 228, 125 CR 717 (general provision that "agreement is entire, indivisible, and shall constitute an integrated agreement, which is not subject to modification"); *Marriage of Forgy* (1976) 63 CA3d 767, 134 CR 75 (general provision that "agreement is absolute, unconditional, and irrevocable"); *Marriage of Kilkenny* (1979) 96 CA3d 617, 158 CR 158 (same); *Marriage of Nielsen*

(1980) 100 CA3d 874, 878, 161 CR 272 (general provision that "Agreement shall not depend for its effectiveness on [court] approval, nor be affected thereby").

More recent cases have emphasized the need for specific unequivocal language to preclude judicial modification. *Marriage of Hufford* (1984) 152 CA3d 825, 834, 199 CR 726. See, *e.g., Fukuzaki v Superior Court* (1981) 120 CA3d 454, 174 CR 536 (general provisions, including that agreement's purpose is to make final and complete settlement of all rights and obligations concerning wife's support and that agreement is entire, insufficient to avoid court's power to modify when support paragraph itself was silent on modification issue); *Marriage of Forcum* (1983) 145 CA3d 599, 605, 193 CR 596 (specific spousal support provision for $1 per year, purpose of which is to reserve jurisdiction to modify amount of payments, prevails over general language, which would otherwise be sufficient to preclude modification; that agreement was effective on execution and did not depend for its effectiveness on court approval); *Marriage of Hufford, supra* (provision that agreement is entire and may not be modified except by written agreement of parties insufficient to avoid modifiability).

For attorneys negotiating spousal support agreements, the lesson of these cases is clear. When the support provisions are to be nonmodifiable, whether fully or partially, that fact should be indicated expressly and unambiguously in the provisions. See *Marriage of Forcum* (1983) 145 CA3d 599, 604, 193 CR 596. For a full set of sample spousal support agreement forms and discussion, see California Marital Settlement and Other Family Law Agreements, chap 8 (3d ed Cal CEB 2005).

Note that Fam C §3591(c) and the discussion in this section do not apply to agreements entered into before January 1, 1970. Fam C §3593. For such agreements, modifiability depends on whether the agreement was "integrated" (*i.e.,* whether property and support provisions constituted reciprocal consideration) and on the law in effect at the time of execution. On the law governing such agreements, see former CC §139 (Stats 1967, ch 1308). As with other contractual terms, an agreement that precludes modifiability of spousal support will not be upheld if it violates public policy. In one case, for example, the parties' marital settlement agreement provided for nonmodifiable spousal support to the wife, who later harassed and threatened her then-former husband. The wife did not rebut the

Fam C §4325 presumption that a party convicted of interspousal domestic violence may not be awarded spousal support, and the court properly granted the former husband's motion to terminate the support payments. *Marriage of Cauley* (2006) 138 CA4th 1100, 1106, 41 CR3d 902.

§6.23 c. Order for Definite Term

When the most recent long-term spousal support order specifies a period during which support is to be paid, whether the support may subsequently be extended beyond the end of the period depends initially on whether the marriage was "of long duration," as that term is used in Fam C §4336 (see §6.11). If the marriage was of long duration, the court may extend the support term unless the parties specifically agree to the contrary in writing. *Marriage of Jones* (1990) 222 CA3d 505, 513, 271 CR 761. When the marriage was *not* of long duration, however, support may not be extended unless the court expressly retained jurisdiction to do so in the most recent order. Fam C §4335; *Marriage of Segel* (1986) 177 CA3d 1030, 1038, 223 CR 430. But in no event can there be jurisdiction to grant a motion for modification filed *after* the spousal support expiration date. 177 CA3d at 1040.

The rule for lengthy marriages was added to former CC §4801(d) effective January 1, 1988, and was subsequently interpreted in *Marriage of Jones, supra.* In *Jones,* the parties' agreement provided for specified support amounts until October 1, 1989, and stated that payments would terminate on either party's death, the recipient's remarriage, or October 1, 1989. 222 CA3d at 508. If the marriage had not been "of long duration," the court could not have extended support beyond October 1, 1989, because there was no language in the order that could reasonably have been interpreted as reserving jurisdiction. 222 CA3d at 513. Given that the marriage was of long duration, however, extension was permitted because there was, likewise, no language specifically prohibiting it. 222 CA3d at 514. The same result was reached in *Marriage of Brown* (1995) 35 CA4th 785, 41 CR2d 506. In *Brown,* the parties' agreement provided for monthly spousal support payments by the husband of $2000 for 60 months, beginning after sale of the family residence and the wife's relocation to a new home. It further provided that after payment of the 60th installment the husband's spousal support obligation would terminate and "no Court shall have any jurisdiction to extend the within award of spousal support either as to amount or duration after said date" (35 CA4th at 787). The court of appeal, noting the absence of any specific language to the contrary, held that the trial court retained jurisdiction, before the termination date, to extend the duration of support beyond the termination date. 35 CA4th at 788. See also *Marriage of Ousterman* (1996) 46 CA4th 1090, 54 CR2d 403 (agreement that precluded modification by supported party until certain date held to allow such modification after that date). Note that the rule for lengthy marriages applies only to proceedings filed on or after January 1, 1988, and to proceedings pending on January 1, 1988, in which the court has not entered a permanent spousal support order or in which the court order is subject to modification. Fam C §4336(d); *Marriage of Beck* (1997) 57 CA4th 341, 67 CR2d 79.

Several cases have interpreted the other rule in former CC §4801(d) (see Fam C §4335), limited effective January 1, 1988, to marriages that are not of long duration, which permits an extension beyond a specified date only when jurisdiction to extend is expressly retained in the most recent order. Note that cases decided before former CC §4801(d) was amended do not concern themselves with the duration of the particular marriage. In *Marriage of Vomacka* (1984) 36 C3d 459, 462, 204 CR 568, the stipulated judgment provided for retention of jurisdiction over spousal support until September 1, 1984, at which time the supported party's "right to request" such support would terminate. If the parties intended that no payments could be ordered for any period after September 1, 1984, they neglected to say so unambiguously. The trial court modified the order in 1982 to provide for a specified monthly payment until either party's death, the supported party's remarriage, or further court order. 36 C3d at 462. The supporting party appealed, contending that the modification would impermissibly allow support to continue beyond September 1, 1984, but the California Supreme Court affirmed, holding that the supported party's "right to request" support until a specified date necessarily included retention of jurisdiction to extend support beyond that date. 36 C3d at 474.

In *Marriage of Benson* (1985) 171 CA3d 907, 910, 217 CR 589, the support provision at issue provided for a specified amount "until the death of either party, [the supported party's] remarriage, until modified by a court of competent jurisdiction or until the expiration of eight (8) years, whichever occurs first." Before the expiration of eight years, the trial court modified the order to provide for support beyond the eight-year date. 171 CA3d at 910. The court of appeal affirmed, holding that, as in *Marriage of Vomacka, supra,* the reserved jurisdiction to modify was sufficient to permit the trial court to extend the duration of the order. 171 CA3d at 913.

Supporting parties fared better in three later cases. In *Marriage of Foreman* (1986) 183 CA3d 129, 131, 228 CR 4, the order provided that support would be a specified amount for ten years, be reduced to $1 per year for one year, "and then terminate." It further provided that the payments would be nonmodifiable for a specified period, after which "said support payments" would be modifiable. When the supported party sought modification to provide support beyond the date set for termination, the trial court held that it had no jurisdiction to grant the request. The court of appeal affirmed, holding that the order the supported party sought to modify, unlike those in *Vomacka* and *Benson,* contained no language from which reservation of jurisdiction might be inferred, and noting that the only modification language referred to modifying *payments.* 183 CA3d at 133. Thus, the provision for modification was expressly limited to payment amounts and did not imply a reservation of power to extend their duration. 183 CA3d at 134. It should be remembered, however, that *Foreman* was decided before the amendment to former CC §4801(d), discussed above. It is unclear whether the provision in *Foreman* would be sufficient to preclude extension under the test set forth in *Marriage of Jones, supra,* for marriages "of long duration."

Subsequently, in *Marriage of Zlatnik* (1988) 197 CA3d 1284, 243 CR 454, the court of appeal found express termination language in the words "in no event shall husband be obligated to pay spousal support to wife after April 30, 1986." *Zlatnik* provides a good example of language designed to indicate that jurisdiction is not to be retained to order spousal support payments beyond a specified date. This language should preclude extension even under the *Jones* standard for marriages of long duration.

Finally, in *Marriage of Iberti* (1997) 55 CA4th 1434, 64 CR2d 766, the marital settlement agreement incorporated in the judgment provided that "spousal support shall irrevocably terminate no later than July 15, 1996 and shall terminate prior thereto upon the first occurrence of any of the following events: ... [¶] (3) After July 15, 1993, if [wife] is not a full time student at an accredited college or university successfully completing 10 units each semester or quarter and is actively pursuing a Bachelors degree." The wife dropped out of college as of May 1995. The court of appeal found the provision unambiguous and the wife's reasons for leaving school (she claimed she did so because of her mother's mental illness and subsequent suicide) therefore irrelevant, and affirmed the trial court's termination of support. This language should preclude extension even under the *Jones* standard for marriages of long duration.

Former CC §4801(d), predecessor of Fam C §§4335–4336, governing whether support may be extended beyond a specified term, has a history of legislative changes and litigation over more than two decades. Experienced practitioners are mindful of the pitfalls in this area. In particular, when the parties intend to deprive the court of jurisdiction to extend the duration of a spousal support order after a long-term marriage, great care must be taken to make that intention clear and to meet the requirements of Fam C §§4335–4336 and case law.

For a full set of sample spousal support agreement forms and discussion, see California Marital Settlement and Other Family Law Agreements, chap 8 (3d ed Cal CEB 2005).

§6.24　　3. Change of Circumstances Requirement

To obtain modification of a spousal support order, the moving party must show a material change of circumstances since the order was made. *Marriage of Gavron* (1988) 203 CA3d 705, 710, 250 CR 148. The "circumstances" referred to are the same ones the court is required, under Fam C §4320, to consider in making the initial long-term order at the time of the judgment. See *Marriage of Sammut* (1980) 103 CA3d 557, 563, 163 CR 193. On the specific circumstances the court must consider, see §6.10. The change of circumstances requirement applies whether the order to be modified was litigated or based on an agreement of the parties. *Marriage of Hentz* (1976) 57 CA3d 899, 901, 129 CR 678.

Even when a showing of changed circumstances is made, however, it does not necessarily mandate a modification. *Marriage of Poppe* (1979) 97 CA3d 1, 10, 158 CR 500. Rather, in ruling on a motion for modification, as in ruling on an initial long-term spousal support order, the court must consider the factors set forth in Fam C §4320 (see §6.10), especially the reasonable needs and financial abilities of the parties. *Marriage of Prietsch & Calhoun* (1987) 190 CA3d 645, 655, 235 CR 587. Thus, although a showing of changed circumstances is necessary to obtain the court's consideration of a modification of spousal support, it does not ensure that a modification will be granted.

Like other aspects of spousal support, the change of circumstances requirement is subject to agreement of the parties. For example, when the parties agree to a modification, no finding of changed circumstances is required. *Marriage of Maxfield* (1983) 142 CA3d 755, 759, 191 CR 267. The parties may also agree, as part of a support provision, that specified occurrences will or will not constitute the requisite change of circumstances to allow subsequent modification of that provision. See, *e.g., Marriage of Rabkin* (1986) 179 CA3d 1071, 1081, 225 CR 219. In *Rabkin,* the parties agreed that the sale of the family residence and two other specified events could not be considered changes in circumstances justifying modification. They also provided, on the other hand, that an upward modification of support *could* be sought if the residence was not sold by a specified date, but set a maximum amount for the potential increase.

The requisite change of circumstances cannot be an event that was delineated by a previous court order. Thus, the termination of child support will not justify an increase in spousal support, because it occurred as expected by the parties. *Marriage of Lautsbaugh* (1999) 72 CA4th 1131, 85 CR2d 688.

The failure of an assumption on which a spousal support order is based can constitute the change of circumstances required to justify a subsequent modification. *Marriage of Jacobs* (1980) 102 CA3d 990, 993, 162 CR 649. In *Jacobs,* the long-term support award in the judgment was based on the assumption that, by the time specified for reduction in support to $1 per year, the supported party's psychiatric problems would be alleviated to the extent that she could become self-supporting. The court of appeal held that the failure of that assumption to materialize constituted the requisite change of circumstances for modification of the support order. See also *Marriage of Shaughnessy* (2006) 139 CA4th 1225, 43 CA3d 642 (supported spouse's failure to comply with court order to make good-faith efforts to become self-supporting may constitute change in circumstances warranting spousal support modification); *Marriage of Beust* (1994) 23 CA4th 24, 29, 28 CR2d 201 (as long as the supported party has made reasonable efforts to become self-supporting, a change of circumstances may be established by unrealized expectations of his or her ability to become self-supporting within a specified period of time). When it may be relevant in subsequent proceedings whether the assumptions on which particular orders are based have material-ized, it may simplify the resolution of future disputes if the underlying assumptions are set out in the orders themselves.

4. Effect of Particular Changes

§6.25   a. Supporting Party's Increased Ability to Pay

A supported party may justify an increase in spousal support based on the supporting party's increased ability to pay, as long as (1) the amount of support in the order being modified was inadequate to meet the supported party's reasonable needs, according to the marital standard of living, at the time the order was made or (2) the amount required to meet the supported party's needs has increased since that time due to a change of circumstances, *e.g.,* inflation or a change in health that precludes employment. When the additional require-ment is not met, the supporting party's increased ability to pay will not alone justify an increase in support. *Marriage of Zywiciel* (2000) 83 CA4th 1078, 1081, 100 CR2d 242; *Marriage of Smith* (1990) 225 CA3d 469, 495, 274 CR 911; *Marriage of Hoffmeister* (1987) 191 CA3d 351, 364, 236 CR 543. In a support modification proceed-ing, the trial court is precluded from considering, whether directly or indirectly, the income of the supporting spouse's subsequent spouse or nonmarital partner. *Marriage of Romero* (2002) 99 CA4th 1436, 122 CR2d 220 (abuse of discretion to consider income of payor's new spouse or partner in relation to payor's standard of living or increased ability to pay).

§6.26   b. Supported Party's Nonmarital Cohabitation

When a supported party is cohabiting with a person of the opposite sex, there is a rebuttable presumption, affecting the burden of proof, of a decreased need for support, unless the parties agree otherwise in writing. It is not required that the supported party and the other person hold themselves out to be husband and wife. Fam C §4323. Cohabitation under the statute cannot be established, however, merely by something akin to a boarding house arrangement. *Marriage of Thweatt* (1979) 96 CA3d 530, 534, 157 CR 826. Rather, there must be a sexual relationship, a romantic involvement, or at least a home-maker-companion relationship. 96 CA3d at 535. When cohabitation is found to exist, the burden is on the supported party to show that, despite the relationship, his or her need for support has not diminished. *Marriage of Schroeder* (1987) 192 CA3d 1154, 1161, 238 CR 12.

Proving a romantic relationship in a courtroom setting is often interesting, sometimes even humorous, *e.g.,* inferring such a relationship from the alleged boyfriend's coming out for the newspaper in his bathrobe. Sometimes a party attempts to prove a romantic relationship when it is not disputed. It might be helpful to ask whether cohabitation under Fam C §4323 may be established by stipulation before wading into the proof.

§6.27   F. Termination

A party's spousal support obligation must terminate on either party's death or on the supported party's remarriage unless the parties agree to the contrary in writing. Fam C §4337 (former CC §4801(b)); *Marriage of Cesnalis* (2003) 106 CA4th 1267, 131 CR2d 436; *Marriage of Thornton* (2002) 95 CA4th 251, 115 CR2d 380; *Lucas v Elliott* (1992) 3 CA4th 888, 4 CR2d 746; *Marriage of Glasser* (1986) 181 CA3d 149, 151, 226 CR 229. Thus, when spousal support is to continue, for example, beyond the supported party's remarriage, that intention should be indicated expressly and unambiguously in the support provision. See *Marriage of Thornton, supra.* No particular words are required to waive the termination provisions of Fam C §4337, however. *Marriage of Cesnalis* (2003) 106 CA4th 1267, 1272, 131 CR2d 436. Thus, if a written agreement mentions termination at all, and is reasonably susceptible to interpretation, then extrinsic evidence may be admitted to resolve whether the agreement waives §4337. 106 CA4th at 1272. In *Cesnalis*, the parties' agreement mentioned that death would terminate support but did not refer to termination on remarriage; the court permitted the wife to introduce extrinsic evidence that their intention in omitting any reference to remarriage was to waive the §4337 requirement that support would terminate on her remarriage.

Likewise, when the most recent long-term spousal support order specifies a period during which support is to be paid, and the marriage was not "of long duration," as that term is used in Fam C §4336 (former CC §4801(d)), the support must terminate at the end of that period unless the court expressly retained jurisdiction in the order to extend support beyond that date. Fam C §4335 (former CC §4801(d)); *Marriage of Segel* (1986) 177 CA3d 1030, 1038, 223 CR 430; see §6.23. When, on the other hand, the most recent long-term spousal support order specifies a period during which support is to be paid, but the marriage was of long duration, the court may extend the support term unless the parties specifically agree to the contrary in writing. Fam C §4336; *Marriage of Jones* (1990) 222 CA3d 505, 513, 271 CR 761; see §6.23.

When a court orders spousal support payments made for a contingent period, the liability terminates on the happening of the contingency. Fam C §4334.

On a proper showing, spousal support may be terminated by the court at any time, unless the parties agree in writing, or orally in open court, to the contrary. A termination may not apply, however, to any amount that accrues before the date of filing of the notice of motion or order to show cause to terminate. Fam C §3651(c).

As used in Fam C §4337, the term "remarriage" does not include a supported spouse's *attempt* to remarry prior to the dissolution of an existing marriage. *Marriage of Campbell* (2006) 136 CA 4th 502, 510, 38 CR 3d 908 (husband may not terminate temporary spousal support obligation based on wife's void marriage).

IV. TAX ASPECTS

§6.28　　A. Requirements for Payments to Be Includable in Payee's Gross Income and Deductible by Payor

The principal statutory authority on the taxability of spousal support payments is IRC §71 (which refers to such payments as alimony or spousal maintenance). If the requirements of this section are met, support payments will be includable in the payee's gross income and, under IRC §215, the payments will also be deductible by the payor. California law conforms to federal law in this regard. Rev & T C §§17081, 17201.

The requirements for qualification for treatment of payments as spousal support under IRC §71 were substantially revised by the portion of the Tax Reform Act of 1984 (Pub L 98–369, 98 Stat 494), originally labeled the Domestic Relations Tax Reform Act and commonly referred to as DRTRA, and further amended by the Tax Reform Act of 1986 (Pub L 99-514, 100 Stat 2085). Consequently, this discussion of requirements for qualification under IRC §71 applies only to (1) judgments, agreements, and orders executed after December 31, 1984, and (2) modifications after that date of such documents executed before January 1, 1985, if the modification expressly makes the current provisions applicable. Temp Reg §1.71-1T(e) Q&A-26. See also *Johnson v Commissioner* (9th Cir 2006) 441 F3d 845. California law was brought into conformity with these federal amendments only for tax years beginning on or after January 1, 1987 (Stats 1987, ch 1138, §§53-54, 66, 189; Rev & T C §§17081, 17201), and, consequently, for California tax purposes, the discussion applies only to those tax years. On the specific requirements for spousal support to be includable under IRC §71 (and, therefore, deductible under IRC §215), see §§6.29-6.36.

§6.29 1. Payments in Cash

To be includable in the support payee's gross income and deductible by the support payor, the payments must be made in cash. IRC §§71(b)(1), 215(a)-(b). Checks and money orders payable on demand qualify as "cash" payments. Transfers of services, property, or debt instruments, execution of a note by the payor, and use of the payor's property do not qualify. Temp Reg §1.71-1T(b) Q&A-5.

§6.30 2. Received by or on Behalf of Spouse or Former Spouse

To be includable and deductible, the payments must be received by (or on behalf of) a spouse or former spouse. IRC §§71(b)(1)(A), (d), 215(a)-(b). Payments to a third party on behalf of the support payee (*e.g.,* rent, mortgage, tax, or tuition payments) will qualify if made under the terms of the applicable judgment, agreement, or order. See, *e.g., Deborah Lynn Israel,* TC Memo 1995-500 (when obligation to pay ex-wife's rent would be reduced to one-third of rent if parties' child resided with support payor more than half the year, only one-third of rental amount was "on behalf of" ex-wife and, therefore, deductible spousal support; remainder was nondeductible child support). Premium payments for life insurance on the payor's life under the terms of the judgment, order, or agreement (see Fam C §4360) will qualify to the extent that the support payee is the owner of the policy. Payments, on the other hand, to maintain property owned by the payor will not qualify, even when the property is used by the support payee. Temp Reg §1.71–1T(b) Q&A-6.

Payments to a third party on behalf of the support payee will qualify if made at the support payee's written request, even though not made under the terms of the applicable judgment, agreement, or order, provided that certain other requirements are met. Temp Reg §1.71–1T(b) Q&A-7.

§6.31   3. Received Under Judgment, Written Agreement, or Order

To be includable and deductible, the payments must be received under a judgment, written agreement, or order. IRC §§71(b)(1)(A), (b)(2), 215(a)-(b). Each payment must be made under a qualifying instrument that was in effect when the payment was due. Counsel for the payor must ensure that this requirement is met. Otherwise, the payments will not be includable in the payee's gross income or deductible by the client. See, *e.g., Mumtaz A. Ali,* TC Memo 2004-284 (voluntary payments before existence of written divorce or separation agreement were not received under "divorce or separation instrument," and not deductible by payor despite court order retroactively deeming them unallocated family support); *Dorothy Herrmann,* TC Memo 1964-61 (voluntary payments). Clearly, oral agreements (*Mack R. Herring* (1976) 66 TC 308, 310) and unilateral written offers (*Kirk A. Keegan, Jr.,* TC Memo 1997-359; *Leonard F. Auerbach,* TC Memo 1975-219) are insufficient. Counsel should obtain a written agreement signed by the parties. Likewise, oral modifications of written agreements will not alter the amount of support to be included and deducted. *William Ellis,* TC Memo 1990-456. However, payments made pursuant to a minute order and tentative decision will qualify. *Norman D. Peterson,* TC Memo 1998-27 (spousal support paid in accordance with minute order and tentative decision is made "under divorce or separation instrument").

§6.32   4. Not Designated as Nonincludable in Gross Income and Nondeductible

For the payments to be includable and deductible, the judgment, agreement, or order must not designate them as not includable in gross income under IRC §71 and not deductible under IRC §215.

IRC §§71(b)(1)(B), 215(a)-(b). Thus, parties who wish to *avoid* includability and deductibility may do so by clearly stating that intention in their agreement or stipulated judgment or order. Depending on the details of the parties' respective tax situations, this procedure might be practical when the parties are in the same tax bracket or when the payee's bracket is higher than the payor's, *e.g.*, payor's income derived largely from tax-exempt municipal bonds.

§6.33   5. If Judgment Entered, Parties Must Not Be Members of Same Household

If a judgment has been entered, for the payments to be includable and deductible, the parties must not be members of the same household when the payments are made. IRC §§71(b)(1)(C), 215(a)-(b).

If judgment has not been entered, this restriction does not apply. Temp Reg §1.71-1T(b) Q&A-9. Thus, payments made before judgment under a written agreement or temporary order will qualify for inclusion in the payee's gross income even if the parties are members of the same household. After entry of judgment, however, at least one party will have to vacate the residence for the payments to qualify. Parties who physically separate themselves within a dwelling formerly shared by both of them will still be considered to be members of the same household. The parties will not be treated as members of the same household with respect to a particular payment when one of them is preparing to depart from the household when the payment is made and does so within one month thereafter. Temp Reg §1.71-1T(b) Q&A-9.

§6.34   6. No Liability for Payments or Substitute for Payments After Payee's Death

For the payments to be includable and deductible, there must be no liability to make them for any period after the payee's death or to make any payment (in cash or property) as a substitute for such payments after the payee's death. IRC §§71(b)(1)(D), 215(a)-(b); *Rosalie J. Webb*, TC Memo 1990-540. This provision is designed to avoid inclusion of what is in reality child support or part of a property division in the payee's gross income by labeling it spousal support. Consequently, if the payor is required to continue to make payments after the payee's death, none of the payments before or after the payee's death will qualify for inclusion in the payee's gross income. Temp Reg §1.71-1T(b) Q&A-10. See *John R. Okerson* (2004) 123 TC 258 (when divorce agreement terms require payor spouse, on payee spouse's death, to make substitute payments for alimony paid during payee's life, payments do not qualify as alimony for federal income tax purposes, despite intent of parties and court); *Gordon B. Cologne,* TC Memo 1999-102 (payor cannot deduct as alimony his payment of wife's share of joint federal income tax liability, allocated to him by settlement agreement; his liability for full amount of joint return would survive her death); *R. Lawrence Smith III,* TC Memo 1998-166 (payor ordered to pay former wife's attorney fees may not deduct payments as spousal support because obligation to pay did not terminate on wife's death). See also *Helen C. Hopkinson,* TC Memo 1999-154 (tuition expenses and attorney fees paid on wife's behalf were includable in her gross income as alimony; tuition would necessarily terminate on wife's death and settlement agreement specifically included attorney fees as spousal support that would terminate on death). Likewise, if the payor is required to make any payments (in cash or in property) after the payee's death as a *substitute* for continuation of part or all of the predeath payments, only the remaining portion of the predeath payments (*i.e.,* the portion for which there is no substitute payment after death) will receive spousal support treatment under IRC §71. Temp Reg §1.71-1T(b) Q&A-14.

The Tax Reform Act of 1984 (Pub L 98-369, 98 Stat 494) required, for the payments to be includable and deductible, that the judgment, agreement, or order *expressly state* that the payor would have no liability to make payments for any period after the payee's death. Former IRC §71(b)(1)(D). The Tax Reform Act of 1986 (Pub L 99-514, §§1843(b), 1881, 100 Stat 2085), however, *eliminated* that requirement retroactively. *Lawrence H. Heller,* TC Memo 1994-463. Thus, in *Heller,* the court looked to former CC §4801(b) (predecessor of Fam C §4337 (support obligation under court order terminates on either party's death or on payee's remarriage unless otherwise agreed to in writing)) to determine that the payor would have no liability for payments for any period after the payee's death. But see *William J. Wells,* TC Memo 1998-2. Although petitioner argued that family support payments to be paid until the children married, died, or finished high school, among other conditions, would terminate on the death of the recipient under Fam C §4337, the Tax Court thought that the payments were child support that would continue after the death of the payee. The Tax Court stated further that Fam C §4337 only applied to spousal support orders and did not address "family support payments" as used in the *Wells* marital termination agreement. See also §8.27 for further discussion of family support. It is advisable to include an express statement about the effect of payee's death so that the payor can establish terminability by reference to the instrument itself and not have to rely on Fam C §4337. See *Carol A. Johanson,* TC Memo 2006-105 (because marital settlement agreement failed to provide for termination of spousal support upon payee's death, Fam C §4337 controlled). Note that, when support is paid under an agreement and there is no court order, terminability may be established only by an express statement in the agreement because Fam C §4337 will not apply.

§6.35   7. Not Fixed as Payable for Child Support

That part of any payment that the terms of the judgment, agreement, or order designate (in terms of an amount of money or a part of the payment) as payable for child support will not be includable or deductible. If any amount specified in the judgment, agreement, or order will be reduced (a) on the happening of a contingency relating to a child of the support payor (*e.g.,* attaining a specified age, marrying, dying, leaving school) or (b) at a time that can clearly be associated with such a contingency, payments made before the reduction takes effect will be treated, to the extent of the reduction, as fixed for child support and, therefore, neither includable nor deductible. IRC §§71(c)(1)-(2), 215(a)-(b). See, *e.g., William J. Wells,* TC Memo 1998-2 (termination conditions referred to events in children's lives including marriage, death, and graduation from high school); *Donald Warren Fosberg,* TC Memo 1992-713 (support reduced to zero when youngest child reached age 18); IRS Letter Ruling 9251033 (support reduced on specified dates that, although not identified as such, were 18th birthdays of couple's three children). For a case, on the other hand, in which the event that would result in a reduction was found not to be a contingency relating to a child, see *Madeline Davis Heller,* TC Memo 1994-423 (any child support increase offset by corresponding spousal support decrease).

There are two situations in which payments will be presumed to be reduced at a time clearly associated with the happening of a contingency relating to a child of the payor. In all other situations, reductions will not be treated as being reduced at such a time. The first situation is when the payments are to be reduced within six months before or after the date a child is to attain age 18, 21, or the local age of majority. The second situation is when the payments are to be reduced on two or more occasions that occur within one year before or after a different child of the support payor attains a certain age between 18 and 24, inclusive. The certain age must be the same for each such child, but need not be a whole number of years. The presumption may be rebutted in either situation by showing that the time at which the payments are to be reduced was determined independently of any contingencies relating to the payor's children. Temp Reg §1.71–1T(c) Q&A-18.

Obviously, this provision is designed to avoid inclusion and deductibility of what is in reality child support by labeling it spousal support. While a practical result may be that the practitioner is dissuaded from proposing family support, if it offers both parties more net spendable income than the spousal-support/child-support combination, all options should be explored. Careful drafting of the resulting order should protect the parties from adverse tax consequences. For further discussion of family support, see California Marital Settlement and Other Family Law Agreements §8.31 (3d ed Cal CEB 2005).

§6.36 8. No Joint Return

For the payments to be includable and deductible, the parties must not file a joint return. IRC §§71(e), 215(a)–(b). The parties may not file joint returns for the year during which the termination of their marital status becomes effective or for any year thereafter. IRC §6013(d)(1)(A), (d)(2). Thus, for such tax years, this requirement has no effect. When, however, the parties' marital status will not be terminated by the end of a given year, spousal support paid during that year will be includable in the payee's gross income and deductible by the payor only if the parties file separate returns. Depending on how income is split between the parties, filing separate returns could result in the parties' being taxed at higher rates. Consequently, when support payments will be made during a tax year for which the parties will be eligible to file joint returns, consideration must be given to the likely liabilities under both joint and separate returns before determining whether spousal support treatment under IRC §§71 and 215 is desirable.

§6.37   B. Recapture of Front-Loaded Spousal Support

Provisions for recapture of front-loaded spousal support under IRC §71(f) are designed to prevent property-division provisions from being disguised as spousal support in order to be includable in the payee's gross income and deductible by the payor. Recapture determinations involve comparisons of the payment amounts for each of three years. For purposes of the comparisons, the three years are the first taxable year for which payments qualify as spousal support under IRC §71 and the two years immediately following. IRC §71(f)(6). The determinations are made as follows:

- If the spousal support payments in the second year exceed those in the third year by more than $15,000, the excess over $15,000 is recaptured in the third year. IRC §71(f)(4).

- Calculate the average of (1) the spousal support payments (less any excess payments recaptured under IRC §71(f)(4); see the immediately preceding paragraph) in the second year and (2) the payments in the third year. If the payments in the first year exceed that average by more than $15,000, the excess over $15,000 is recaptured in the third year. IRC §71(f)(3).

The payor must report any recaptured amounts as ordinary income in the third year. The payee deducts a corresponding amount from gross income in the third year. IRC §71(f)(1).

The recapture rules do not apply:

- To spousal support payments that cease as a result of either party's death or the payee's remarriage before the end of the third year (IRC §71(f)(5)(A));

- To payments under temporary support orders (IRC §71(f)(5)(B)); or

- To payments, over a period of at least three years, of a fixed percentage or percentages of the payor's income from a business or property or from compensation for employment or self-employment (IRC §71(f)(5)(C)).

The discussion above addresses IRC §71(f), as amended by the Tax Reform Act of 1986 (Pub L 99–514, 100 Stat 2085). It applies to (1) judgments, written agreements, and orders executed after December 31, 1986, and (2) modifications after that date of such documents executed before January 1, 1987, if the modification expressly makes the current provisions applicable. Tax Reform Act of 1986, §1843(c)(1), (c)(2)(B).

7

Child Custody and Visitation

§7.1   I. SCOPE OF CHAPTER

This chapter addresses the subjects of child custody and visitation. It focuses on mandated mediation and on the considerations involved in awarding custody and visitation.

Specific attention is given to the matter of jurisdiction, which is governed by the Uniform Child Custody Jurisdiction and Enforcement Act (Fam C §§3400–3465) and the Parental Kidnapping Prevention Act of 1980 (PKPA) (Pub L 96–611, §§6–10, 94 Stat 3568; the relevant provisions of the PKPA are codified in 28 USC §1738A). Judicial determination of children's surnames is also discussed, and an introduction to tax aspects of custody issues is provided. On special rules concerning Indian (Native American) children in "custody proceedings" concerning those children, see Fam C §§170–185, 3041.

§7.2   II. JURISDICTION

In most instances in which custody or visitation issues arise in a marital action, no existing custody or visitation order has been made by any other state or country, and the child and the contesting parties have all been in California for a substantial period of time. In such instances, it is unlikely that any interstate jurisdictional issue will arise. The basic jurisdictional question will, therefore, be whether the court has authority under the Family Code (see Fam C §§200, 2010(b), 3101(a), 3103(a)) (see §7.3) to make the requested orders. When interstate jurisdictional conflicts arise, however, jurisdiction is controlled by California's Uniform Child Custody Jurisdiction and Enforcement Act (Fam C §§3400-3465) and the federal Parental Kidnapping Prevention Act of 1980 (PKPA) (Pub L 96-611, §§6-10, 94 Stat 3568; the relevant provisions of the PKPA are codified in 28 USC §1738A). See §§7.4-7.15.

In international conflicts, parties should be aware of the possible applicability of the Hague Convention on the Civil Aspects of International Child Abduction, adopted on October 25, 1980, and the International Parental Kidnapping Crime Act (IPKCA) 18 USCS §1204. See §7.4.

§7.3 A. Marital Actions Generally

In marital actions, the court has jurisdiction over the custody of "minor children of the marriage." Fam C §2010(b). This jurisdiction is subordinate, however, to California and federal statutes governing interstate conflicts (see §§7.4-7.15). The phrase "children of the marriage" includes only those children who are natural or adopted children of *both* parties. *Perry v Superior Court* (1980) 108 CA3d 480, 481, 166 CR 583. But when a parent's initial pleading lists his or her children as children of the marriage and the parties stipulate to orders that award custody rights to the other party, the parent cannot later attack the orders on the ground that the other party is merely a stepparent. *Marriage of Hinman* (1992) 6 CA4th 711, 8 CR2d 245. Although Fam C §2010(b) mentions only "custody," it authorizes jurisdiction over visitation issues as well. See *Perry v Superior Court, supra*.

The court may also award reasonable visitation rights to one party with respect to a minor child of the other party, or to a grandparent with respect to a minor child of a party, if the visitation is found to be in the child's best interest. Fam C §§3101(a) (stepparent), 3103(a) (grandparent). See §7.58A.

When a minor child is adjudged a dependent of the juvenile court, that court acquires exclusive jurisdiction over all custody issues. Welf & I C §§302(c), 304. Thus, the court in a marital action may make no orders regarding custody or visitation with respect to a child who is a dependent of the juvenile court. A juvenile court's exit order terminating its jurisdiction over such a child is a final judgment that cannot be modified by the family court unless it finds that there has been a significant change of circumstances and that modification is in the best interest of the child. Welf & I C §302(d). *Marriage of M.* (2006) 140 CA4th 96, 102, 44 CR3d 388.

On the other hand, several courts have held that a juvenile court may properly assume jurisdiction with respect to a child who was the subject of custody or visitation issues previously litigated in a marital action, regardless of the degree to which the same issues will be heard in the dependency action. *In re Desiree B.* (1992) 8 CA4th 286, 10 CR2d 254 (rejecting dicta in *In re Brendan P.* (1986) 184 CA3d 910, 230 CR 720, in which same court stated that juvenile court could not assume jurisdiction simply to relitigate issues resolved in another forum); *In re Travis C.* (1991) 233 CA3d 492, 503, 284 CR 469 (despite continued hearing pending in family law court, juvenile court has jurisdiction over petition containing same factual allegations). The California Supreme Court has not ruled directly on this issue. As noted in *In re Travis C.* (1991) 233 CA3d 492, 503 n8, 284 CR 469, however, the supreme court did order depublication of a case that held that a juvenile court should have deferred to a family law court's jurisdiction when the family law court had assumed jurisdiction first.

B. Interstate and International Conflicts

§7.4   1. Governing Statutes

Interstate. The issue of whether California may exercise jurisdiction over child custody and visitation issues is governed by California's Uniform Child Custody Jurisdiction and Enforcement Act (Fam C §§3400–3465) and the federal Parental Kidnapping Prevention Act of 1980 (PKPA) (Pub L 96–611, §§6–10, 94 Stat 3568; the relevant provisions of the PKPA are codified in 28 USC §1738A). The California Act became effective on January 1, 2000, replacing the former Uniform Child Custody Jurisdiction Act (former Fam C §§3400–3425). The California Act applies to any motion or other request for relief made on or after January 1, 2000, in a child custody proceeding or to enforce a child custody determination, regardless of when the proceeding was commenced or the determination made. See Fam C §3465.

Because the new Act completely replaced the former Act, case law under the former Act is likely to be of limited, if any, value in interpreting the new Act. Nevertheless, faced with issues under the new Act, prudent counsel will consult the prior case law and consider its possible application, with particular reference to the degree of similarity between the specific provisions of the prior and current versions that apply to the client's situation. When the similarity of the respective applicable provisions is substantial, a court might be persuaded to consider the prior case law.

The California Act speaks only of "custody" issues and, accordingly, the same will be true of the discussion in this text. Nevertheless, note that for the California Act "custody" includes "visitation." See Fam C §3402(c)–(d). Similarly, although the California Act and, accordingly, this text speak only in terms of "states," note that the California Act governs cases involving international as well as interstate conflicts. See Fam C §3405. The PKPA, on the other hand, governs only interstate conflicts. 28 USC §1738A(a), (b)(8).

In applying and construing the California Act, consideration must be given to the need to promote uniformity of the law with respect to its subject matter among states that enact it. Fam C §3461.

The two acts have similar purposes. *Marriage of Pedowitz* (1986) 179 CA3d 992, 999, 225 CR 186 (interpreting prior California Act). Should the two acts conflict, the federal PKPA takes precedence. 179 CA3d at 999. Conflicts between them, however, should be rare.

California's ability to exercise jurisdiction will differ, under either Act, depending on whether the issue before the court is an initial determination (see §§7.5–7.13) or a modification of a prior custody or visitation order (see §§7.14–7.15).

International. In international conflicts, parties should be aware of the possible applicability of the Hague Convention on the Civil Aspects of International Child Abduction, adopted on October 25, 1980, and the International Parental Kidnapping Crime Act (IPKCA) 18 USCS §1204. The Hague Convention became operative in the United States effective July 1, 1988, through the International Child Abduction Remedies Act (ICARA) (42 USC §§11601–11611). The Convention establishes legal rights and procedures for the prompt return of children who have been wrongfully removed or retained. 42 USC §11601(a)(4). The Convention applies only to children under age 16 who are removed from and taken to ratifying countries. There are more than 50 ratifying countries, which include Argentina, Australia, Austria, Belize, Burkina Faso, Canada, Denmark, Ecuador,

France, Germany, Greece, Hungary, Ireland, Israel, Luxembourg, Mexico, Monaco, the Netherlands, New Zealand, Norway, Poland, Portugal, Romania, Spain, Sweden, Switzerland, the United Kingdom, and the United States. (For a chart showing status of ratification for member and nonmember countries, see http://hcch.e-vision.nl/index_en.php?act=conventions.status&cid=24.)

Ninth Circuit Hague cases. For recent Ninth Circuit cases applying the Hague Convention through ICARA, see, *e.g.*:

- *Von Kennel Gaudin v Remis* (9th Cir 2005) 415 F3d 1028 (district court should have considered alternative options for transferring children back to Canada, the home jurisdiction, rather than transfer custody to father in Hawaii);

- *Holder v Holder* (9th Cir 2004) 392 F3d 1009 (when mother traveled with children to California and refused to return them to former family residence in Germany, no Hague Convention relief available to father when 4-year residence in Germany resulted from father's deployment there and family had not intended that Germany become children's new habitual residence);

- *Gonzalez v Gutierrez* (9th Cir 2002) 311 F3d 942 (discussing Hague Convention right of access to child versus right to custody);

- *Holder v Holder* (9th Cir 2002) 305 F3d 854 (father did not waive Hague Convention remedy by litigating custody dispute in California state court).

Hague cases in other circuits. For construction of the Hague Convention as applied through ICARA in other federal circuits, see, *e.g.*:

- *Croll v Croll* (2d Cir 2000) 229 F3d 133 (Hague Convention history and drafters' intent indicate that custody rights are not created by *ne exeat* clauses);

- *Bader v Kramer* (4th Cir 2006) 445 F3d 346, 350 (district court mistakenly concluded that German court order setting forth visitation schedule altered German law presumption of joint custody);

- *Kijowska v Haines* (7th Cir 2006) 463 F3d 583, 587 (child's "habitual residence" is not domicile, not only "because a small child lacks the state of mind required for a determination of domicile so defined" but because domicile defined differently in different jurisdictions and "equating habitual residence to domicile would reraise the spectre of forum shopping"); *Koch v Koch* (7th Cir 2006) 450 F3d 703 (following 9th Circuit's approach in *Mozes v Mozes* (9th Cir 2001) 239 F3d 1067 to find that parents' intent under facts was to reside in Germany indefinitely); *Van De Sande v Van De Sande* (7th Cir 2005) 431 F3d 567, 571 (no mitigation of "grave risk of harm" to child created by existence of legal remedies or deterrents for child or spousal abuse in country of habitual residence);

- *Furnes v Reeves* (11th Cir 2004) 362 F3d 702 (discussing Hague Convention right of access to child versus right to custody, and finding that custody rights are created by *ne exeat* clauses and criticizing conclusion in *Croll*).

Criminal sanctions. For criminal sanctions under IPKCA, see *U.S. v Fazal-Ur-Raheman-Fazal* (1st Cir 2004) 355 F3d 40; *People v Lazarevich* (2004) 124 CA4th 140, 21 CR3d 1.

2. Initial Custody Determination

§7.5 a. Bases for Jurisdiction

The bases on which California may assume jurisdiction to make an initial child custody or visitation order under the Uniform Child Custody Jurisdiction and Enforcement Act (Fam C §§3400-3465 (former CC §§5150-5174)) are set forth in Fam C §§3421 and 3424. As long as jurisdiction is established under the California Act and its notice requirements are met, neither the physical presence of nor personal jurisdiction over a party or child is required to make a custody determination. See Fam C §3421(c). On notice requirements under the California Act, see Fam C §3425. Notice is not required for the exercise of jurisdiction with respect to a person who submits to the court's jurisdiction. Fam C §3408(c).

The bases on which California may assume jurisdiction under the Parental Kidnapping Prevention Act of 1980 (PKPA) (Pub L 96-611, §§6-10, 94 Stat 3568) are set forth in 28 USC §1738A(c)(2)(A)-(D). On notice requirements under the PKPA, see 28 USC §1738A(e).

For discussion of the individual bases for jurisdiction, see §§7.6–7.9A.

§7.6   (1) California Is Child's Home State

Under the Uniform Child Custody Jurisdiction and Enforcement Act (Fam C §§3400–3465), California may assume jurisdiction if it is the child's home state at the time the action is commenced. Fam C §3421(a)(1). California may also assume jurisdiction if (Fam C §3421(a)(1)):

- California had been the child's home state within 6 months before the action is commenced;

- The child is absent from California; and

- A parent or a person acting as a parent continues to live in California.

A child's "home state" is the state in which the child has lived with a parent, or a person acting as a parent, for at least the 6 months immediately preceding or, if the child is less than 6 months old, from birth. Periods of temporary absence of any of the specified persons count as part of the required period. Fam C §3402(g). See, e.g., *In re Baby Boy M.* (2006) 141 CA4th 588, 46 CR3d 196 (despite child's birth in California it could not be child's home state, given lack of evidence child ever lived in California and mother's testimony she gave child to alleged biological father who expressed intent to raise him in Georgia). A "person acting as a parent" is a nonparent who (1) has physical custody of the child, or has had physical custody for a period of 6 consecutive months, including any temporary absence, within 1 year immediately before commencement of a child custody proceeding, and (2) has been awarded custody by a court or claims a right to custody under California law. Fam C §3402(m).

The corresponding provision under the Parental Kidnapping Prevention Act of 1980 (PKPA) (Pub L 96–611, §§6–10, 94 Stat 3568) is substantially the same. 28 USC §1738A(c)(2)(A).

§7.7   (2) No Other State Exercising Jurisdiction; California Has Significant Connection and Substantial Evidence

Under the Uniform Child Custody Jurisdiction and Enforcement

Act (Fam C §§3400–3465), California may assume jurisdiction if no other state is the child's home state under the criteria specified in Fam C §3421(a)(1) (see §7.6) or a court of the child's home state has declined to exercise jurisdiction on the grounds that California is the more appropriate forum under the criteria specified in Fam C §§3427–3428, and (Fam C §3421(a)(2)):

- The child and the child's parents, or the child and at least one parent or a "person acting as a parent" (for definition, see §7.6), have a significant connection with California other than mere physical presence; and

- Substantial evidence is available in California concerning the child's care, protection, training, and personal relationships.

The corresponding provision under the Parental Kidnapping Prevention Act of 1980 (Pub L 96–611, §§6–10, 94 Stat 3568) is substantially the same. 28 USC §1738A(c)(2)(B).

§7.8 (3) All Courts of Other States With Jurisdiction Have Deferred to California

Under the Uniform Child Custody Jurisdiction and Enforcement Act (Fam C §§3400–3465), California may assume jurisdiction if all courts having jurisdiction under the criteria specified in Fam C §3421(a)(1) (see §7.6) or §3421(a)(2) (see §7.7) have declined to exercise jurisdiction on the ground that a California court is the more appropriate forum to determine the child's custody under the criteria specified in Fam C §3427 or §3428. Fam C §3421(a)(3).

§7.9 (4) Jurisdiction in No Other State

Under the Uniform Child Custody Jurisdiction and Enforcement Act (Fam C §§3400–3465), California may assume jurisdiction if no court of any other state would have jurisdiction under the criteria specified in Fam C §3421(a)(1) (see §7.6), §3421(a)(2) (see §7.7), or §3421(a)(3) (see §7.8). Fam C §3421(a)(4).

§7.9A (5) Emergency Custody Determination

A California court has temporary emergency jurisdiction if a child is present in California and (1) the child has been abandoned or (2) it is necessary in an emergency to protect the child because the child, or the child's sibling or parent, is subjected to, or threatened with, mistreatment or abuse. Fam C §3424(a). Family Code §3424 is part of the Uniform Child Custody Jurisdiction and Enforcement Act (Fam C §§3400-3465). The legislature has expressly provided that, in enacting Fam C §3424(a), it intended to expand the grounds on which a court may exercise temporary emergency jurisdiction and further intended that these grounds include those that existed under former Fam C §3403 as that section read on December 31, 1999, particularly including cases involving domestic violence. Fam C §3424(e).

If no previous child custody determination is entitled to be enforced under the Uniform Child Custody Jurisdiction and Enforcement Act (Fam C §§3400-3465) and a child custody proceeding has not been commenced in a court of a state having jurisdiction under the criteria specified in Fam C §§3421-3423, a child custody determination made under Fam C §3424 remains in effect until an order is obtained from a court of a state having such jurisdiction. If such a proceeding has not been or is not commenced, a child custody determination made under §3424 becomes a final determination if it so provides, in which event California becomes the child's home state. Fam C §3424(b).

If a previous child custody determination is entitled to be enforced under the California Act, or a child custody proceeding has been commenced in a court of a state having jurisdiction under the criteria specified in Fam C §§3421-3423, any order issued by a California court under Fam C §3424 must specify a period that the court considers adequate to allow the person seeking an order to obtain one from the other state. The California order remains in effect until an order is obtained from the other state within the period specified or the period expires. Fam C §3424(c).

A California court that has been asked to make a child custody determination under Fam C §3424 and that becomes informed that a child custody proceeding has been commenced in, or a child custody determination has been made by, a court of another state having jurisdiction under the criteria specified in Fam C §§3421-3423 must immediately communicate with the other court. A California court exercising jurisdiction under §§3421-3423 that becomes informed that a child custody proceeding has been commenced in, or a child custody determination has been made by, a court of another state under a statute similar to Fam C §3424 must immediately communicate with the other court to resolve the emergency, protect the parties' and child's safety, and determine a period for the duration of the temporary order. Fam C §3424(d). Under Fam C §3424, a court has jurisdiction to determine the existence of an emergency and make a temporary custody order, but not to conduct a dependency proceeding under Welf & I C §300. See *In re A.C.* (2005) 130 CA4th 854, 30 CR3d 431 (juvenile court lacked jurisdiction over child whose parents, both Mexican nationals, had placed her in California hospital for medical treatment but there was no basis for California's exercise of emergency jurisdiction); *In re C.T.* (2002) 100 CA4th 101, 121 CR2d 897 (although court did not have jurisdiction under the act to find that father abused child, that finding was sufficient to invoke the act's emergency jurisdiction).

§7.10   b. Declining Exercise of Jurisdiction

Even when California has jurisdiction under one of the bases set forth in Fam C §3421(a)(1)-(4) (see §§7.6-7.9), it may decline to exercise its jurisdiction on any one of three specified bases. See §§7.11-7.13.

§7.11   (1) Proceeding Pending in Another State

Except as otherwise provided in Fam C §3424 (emergency custody determination; see §7.9A), California may not exercise its jurisdiction under Fam C §§3421-3430 if, at the time the petition was filed, a child custody proceeding was pending in a court of another state exercising jurisdiction substantially in conformity with the Uniform Child Custody Jurisdiction and Enforcement Act (Fam C §§3400-3465), unless the other state has terminated or stayed its proceeding because a California court is a more convenient forum under the criteria specified in Fam C §3427. Fam C §3426(a). The Parental Kidnapping Prevention Act of 1980 (Pub L 96-611, §§6-10, 94 Stat 3568) has a similar provision. 28 USC §1738A(g).

Also except as provided in Fam C §3424, a California court, before hearing a child custody proceeding, must examine the court documents and other information supplied by the parties under Fam C §3429 (see §§10.17-10.18, 10.54). Fam C §3426(b). If the court determines that a custody proceeding has been commenced in a court in another state having jurisdiction substantially in accordance with the California Act, it must stay its proceeding and communicate with the court of the other state. If the other court does not determine that the California court is a more appropriate forum, the California court must dismiss its proceeding. Fam C §3426(b).

§7.12 (2) Inconvenient Forum

A California court that has jurisdiction under the Uniform Child Custody Jurisdiction and Enforcement Act (Fam C §§3400–3465) to make a custody determination may decline to exercise jurisdiction at any time if it determines that it is an inconvenient forum under the circumstances and that a court of another state is a more appropriate forum. The issue of inconvenient forum may be raised on the motion of a party, the court's own motion, or the request of another court. Fam C §3427(a).

Before determining whether it is an inconvenient forum, a California court must consider whether it is appropriate for a court of another state to exercise jurisdiction. For this purpose, the court must allow the parties to submit information and must consider all relevant factors, including (Fam C §3427(b)):

- Whether domestic violence has occurred and is likely to continue in the future and which state could best protect the parties and the child;

- The length of time the child has resided outside California;

- The distance between the California court and the court in the state that would assume jurisdiction;

- The degree of financial hardship to the parties in litigating in one forum over the other;

- Any agreement of the parties regarding which state should assume jurisdiction;

- The nature and location of the evidence, including the child's testimony, required to resolve the pending litigation;

- The ability of each court to decide the issue expeditiously and the procedures necessary to present the evidence; and

- The familiarity of each court with the facts and issues.

If the California court determines that it is an inconvenient forum and the court of another state is a more appropriate one, the California court must stay the proceedings on the condition that a child custody proceeding be promptly commenced in the other state and may impose any other condition it considers just and proper. Fam C §3427(c).

If a child custody determination is incidental to an action for dissolution of marriage or another proceeding, a California court may decline to exercise its custody jurisdiction under the California Act while retaining jurisdiction over the other action. Fam C §3427(d).

If it appears to the California court that it is clearly an inappropriate forum, it may require the party who commenced the proceeding to pay, in addition to the costs of the local proceeding, necessary travel and other expenses, including attorney fees, incurred by the other parties or their witnesses, with payment made to the court clerk for remittance to the proper party. Fam C §3427(e).

§7.13   (3) Petitioner's Unjustifiable Conduct

Except as otherwise provided in Fam C §3424 (emergency custody determination; see §7.9A), or by any other California law, if a California court has jurisdiction under the Uniform Child Custody Jurisdiction and Enforcement Act (Fam C §§3400–3465) because a person seeking to invoke its jurisdiction has engaged in unjustifiable conduct, the court must decline to exercise its jurisdiction unless (Fam C §3428(a)):

- The parents, and all persons acting as parents (for definition, see §7.6), have acquiesced in the exercise of jurisdiction;

- A court of the state otherwise having jurisdiction under the criteria specified in Fam C §§3421–3423 determines that California is a more appropriate forum under the criteria specified in Fam C §3427; or

- No court of any other state would have jurisdiction under the criteria specified in Fam C §§3421–3423.

If a California court declines to exercise jurisdiction because of a party's unjustifiable conduct, it may fashion an appropriate remedy to ensure the child's safety and prevent a repetition of the conduct, including staying the proceeding until a child custody proceeding is commenced in a court having jurisdiction under the criteria specified in Fam C §§3421–3423. Fam C §3428(b).

If a California court dismisses a petition or stays a proceeding because of a party's unjustifiable conduct, it must assess against that party necessary and reasonable expenses including costs, communication expenses, attorney fees, investigative fees, witness expenses, travel expenses, and child care during the course of the proceedings, unless the party from whom expenses are sought establishes that the assessment would be clearly inappropriate. Fam C §3428(c).

In making a determination under Fam C §3428, a court may not consider as a factor weighing against the petitioner any taking of the child, or retention of the child after a visit or other temporary relinquishment of physical custody, from the person who had legal custody if there is evidence that the taking or retention of the child was a result of domestic violence, as defined in Fam C §6211, against the petitioner. Fam C §3428(d).

3. Modification of Custody Determination

§7.14   a. Bases for Jurisdiction

Under the Uniform Child Custody Jurisdiction and Enforcement Act (Fam C §§3400–3465), except as otherwise provided under Fam C §3424 (emergency custody determination; see §7.9A), a California court that has made a child custody determination consistent with Fam C §3421 or §3423 has exclusive, continuing jurisdiction over the determination until either (Fam C §3422(a)):

- A California court determines that the child, the child and one parent, or the child and a person acting as a parent (for definition, see §7.6) do not have a significant connection with California and that substantial evidence is no longer available in California concerning the child's care, protection, training, and personal relationships; or

- A California court or a court of another state determines that the child, the child's parents, and any person acting as a parent do not presently reside in California.

As long as parent who is exercising visitation rights continues to live in California, if a California court issued the original order it maintains jurisdiction over child custody determinations. *Grahm v Superior Court* (2005) 132 CA4th 1193, 34 CR3d 270. A California court that has made a child custody determination but does not have exclusive, continuing jurisdiction under Fam C §3422 may modify that determination only if it has jurisdiction to make an initial determination under Fam C §3421. Fam C §3422(b).

Except as otherwise provided under Fam C §3424, a California court may not modify a child custody determination by a court of another state unless a California court has jurisdiction to make an initial determination under Fam C §3421(a)(1) or (2) and either (Fam C §3423):

- The court of the other state determines that it no longer has exclusive, continuing jurisdiction under the criteria specified in Fam C §3422 or that a California court would be a more convenient forum under a provision substantially in accordance with Fam C §34272; or

- A California court or a court of the other state determines that the child, the child's parents, and any person acting as a parent do not presently reside in the other state.

In a proceeding to modify a child custody determination, a California court must determine whether a proceeding to enforce the determination has been commenced in another state. If so, the California court may (Fam C §3426(c)):

- Stay the proceeding for modification pending entry of an order of a court of the other state enforcing, staying, denying, or dismissing the enforcement proceeding;

- Enjoin the parties from continuing with the enforcement proceeding; or

- Proceed with the modification under conditions it considers appropriate.

The corresponding provisions under the Parental Kidnapping Prevention Act of 1980 (PKPA) (Pub L 96–611, §§6–10, 94 Stat 3568) conform generally with Fam C §§3422–3423. Under the PKPA, a court that has made a custody order consistent with 28 USC §1738A (see §§7.5–7.9) has continuing jurisdiction to modify that order as long as it continues to have jurisdiction under its own state law and remains the residence of the child or any custody contestant. 28 USC §1738A(d). A court may modify another state's court order only when it has jurisdiction to do so and the other state no longer has jurisdiction or has declined to exercise jurisdiction to modify its order. 28 USC §1738A(f). On notice requirements under the PKPA, see 28 USC §1738A(e).

§7.15   b. Declining Exercise of Jurisdiction

A California court that has jurisdiction under the Uniform Child Custody Jurisdiction and Enforcement Act (Fam C §§3400–3465) to make a custody determination may decline to exercise jurisdiction at any time if it determines that it is an inconvenient forum under the circumstances and that a court of another state is a more appropriate forum. Fam C §3427(a). For further discussion of Fam C §3427, which applies to both initial custody determinations and modification of custody determinations, see §7.12.

III. CUSTODY

§7.16   A. Types of Orders

Under California law, child custody has two parts: physical custody (see §7.17) and legal custody (see §7.18). Either type of custody may be awarded to one parent ("sole custody") or to both parents ("joint custody"). Fam C §§3003–3007. Technically, an order simply for "joint custody" means that the parties will have joint physical custody and joint legal custody. Fam C §3002. A court may award joint legal custody, however, without awarding joint physical custody. Fam C §3085.

In ordering joint physical custody or joint legal custody, the court may specify one parent as the child's primary caretaker, and one home as the child's primary home, for purposes of public assistance eligibility. Fam C §3086. The term "primary physical custody" has no legal meaning. *Marriage of Rose & Richardson* (2002) 102 CA4th 941, 946 n2, 126 CR2d 45.

In making a custody order after the trial of a question of fact in a custody proceeding, a court must, on the request of either party, issue a statement of the decision explaining the factual and legal basis for its decision pursuant to CCP §632. Fam C §3022.3. For discussion of statements of decision, see chap 17.

§7.17   1. Physical Custody

"Sole physical custody" means that the child will reside with, and under the supervision of, one parent, subject to the court's power to order visitation. Fam C §3007. "Joint physical custody" means that each parent will have significant periods of physical custody. Joint physical custody must be shared by the parents in a manner that ensures the child frequent and continuing contact with both parents, subject to Fam C §§3011 (see §§7.22–7.25) and 3020 (see §§7.19, 7.22). Fam C §3004 (former CC §4600.5(d)(3)). Joint physical custody does *not* require, however, that exactly half of the child's time be spent with each parent. *Marriage of Birnbaum* (1989) 211 CA3d 1508, 1515, 260 CR 210.

An order for joint physical custody must address the respective periods of time the child will be with, and under the supervision of, each parent. Specifically, the order must state the rights of each parent to the physical control of the child in sufficient detail to enable a parent deprived of that control to implement laws for relief of child snatching and kidnapping. Fam C §3084.

NOTE➤ Child custody mediators, whether court-employed or private, sometimes use boilerplate provisions that may not always be specific enough to comply with Fam C §3084. Counsel should exercise judgment and attempt, either by stipulation or request to the court, to modify vague terms and make them more specific.

Custody orders sometimes use terms for physical custody (*e.g.,* "primary" physical custody, "shared" physical custody) that are different from those defined by Fam C §§3004 and 3007. Such terms generally reflect an effort to provide for physical custody that will achieve greater acceptance by the parties of the custody provisions. In formulating such provisions, however, the drafter must take care to avoid subsequent problems in understanding or enforcing the provisions or problems regarding such related matters as income tax exemptions for dependents (see §7.63) and entitlement to public assistance.

The existing de facto arrangement, rather than the words used in the judgment, is scrutinized by the court in determining whether a parent has primary physical custody and the other visitation or whether a shared parenting arrangement exists. This is a distinction that, under *Marriage of Burgess* (1996) 13 C4th 25, 40 n12, 51 CR2d 444, affects whether the court must make a *de novo* determination of the best interest of the child or recognize the presumptive right of a primary custodian move. *Marriage of Lasich* (2002) 99

CA4th 702, 717, 121 CR2d 356 (parties' arrangement was sole physical custody for mother with liberal visitation for father, despite language in judgment stating they had "joint physical custody," disapproved on other grounds in *In re Marriage of LaMusga* (2004) 32 C4 1072, 1091, 12 CR3d 356). See §7.30.

§7.18   2. Legal Custody

"Sole legal custody" means that one parent will have the right and responsibility to make decisions regarding the health, education, and welfare of the child. Fam C §3006. "Joint legal custody" means that the parents will share that right and responsibility. Fam C §3003.

Under an order for joint legal custody, either parent acting alone may make decisions regarding the health, education, and welfare of the child unless the order specifies circumstances requiring the consent of both parents. An order specifying such circumstances must also indicate the consequences of failure to obtain mutual consent. A joint legal custody order may not be construed to permit an action that is inconsistent with the physical custody order for the child unless the court expressly authorizes the action. Fam C §3083.

B. Considerations in Making Awards

1. Statutory Guidelines

§7.19   a. Frequent and Continuing Contact With Both Parents

The legislature has declared that it is the public policy of the state to ensure minor children frequent and continuing contact with both parents after their separation or dissolution, and to encourage parents to share the rights and responsibilities of child rearing in order to effect this policy, except when that contact would not be in the child's best interest as set forth in Fam C §3011. Fam C §3020(b). On the factors a court is required, under Fam C §3011, to consider, among any others it finds relevant, in determining the child's best interest, see §§7.22–7.25. In ordering sole custody, the court must consider, among other factors, which parent as custodial parent is more likely to allow the child frequent and continuing contact with the noncustodial parent, consistent with Fam C §§3011 and 3020. Fam C §3040(a)(1).

Note, however, that when the public policy in favor of frequent and continuing contact with both parents conflicts with the public policy in favor of ensuring each child's health, safety, and welfare, expressly including freedom from child abuse and domestic violence in the child's residence (see Fam C §3020(a); §7.22), any physical or legal custody or visitation order must be made in a manner that ensures the child's health, safety, and welfare and the safety of all family members. Fam C §3020(c).

The policy of frequent and continuing contact must also be viewed in light of other policies, such as that which allows the custodial parent the freedom to relocate, codified in Fam C §7501. See also *Marriage of LaMusga* (2004) 32 C4th 1072, 1088, 12 CR3d 356; *Marriage of Burgess* (1996) 13 C4th 25, 38, 51 CR2d 444. A custodial parent's presumptive right to relocate with a child is subject to "the power of the court to restrain a removal that would prejudice the rights or welfare of the child." Fam C §7501(a). The trial court has broad discretion to determine, in light of all of the circumstances, what custody arrangement serves the best interest of a minor child. Fam C §3040(b). This discretion is not limited by Fam C §3020. *Marriage of LaMusga*, 32 C4th at 1088. For a full discussion of "move-away" cases decided after *LaMusga*, see §7.30.

§7.20 b. Child's Best Interest

Custody must be awarded according to the child's best interest. Fam C §3040(a). It may not be awarded by reference to the parents' interests or to achieve equity between the parents. *Marriage of Stoker* (1977) 65 CA3d 878, 881, 135 CR 616 (error to award custody to punish parent rather than on basis of what is best for child).

The legislature has declared that it is the public policy of the state to ensure minor children frequent and continuing contact with both parents after their separation or dissolution and to encourage parents to share the rights and responsibilities of child rearing in order to effect this policy, except when that contact would not be in the child's best interest as set forth in Fam C §3011. Fam C §3020(b). The legislature has further declared that it is the public policy of the state to ensure that each child's health, safety, and welfare, expressly including freedom from child abuse and domestic violence in the child's residence, be the court's primary concern in determining the child's best interest when making physical or legal custody and visitation orders. Fam C §3020(a). When these two policies conflict, any physical or legal custody or visitation order must be made in a manner that ensures the child's health, safety, and welfare and the safety of all family members. Fam C §3020(c).

On the factors a court is required, under Fam C §3011, to consider, among any others it finds relevant, in determining the child's best interest, see §§7.22–7.25. In ordering sole custody, the court must consider, among other factors, which parent as custodial parent is more likely to allow the child frequent and continuing contact with the noncustodial parent, consistent with Fam C §§3011 and 3020. Fam C §3040(a)(1). See *Marriage of LaMusga* (2004) 32 C4th 1072, 1100, 88 P3d 81 (based on custody evaluator's findings that mother was partly motivated to move out of state by desire to take children away from day-to-day interactions with father, court ordered custody to change to father in event of mother's move).

§7.21 c. No Preference for Sole or Joint Custody in Contested Proceedings

California law establishes no preference or presumption in contested proceedings for either sole or joint custody. Fam C §3040. When the parents *agree* to joint custody, however, there is a presumption affecting the burden of proof that joint custody is in the child's best interest. Fam C §3080.

§7.22 d. Child's Health, Safety, and Welfare

The legislature has declared that it is the public policy of the state to ensure that each child's health, safety, and welfare, expressly including freedom from child abuse and domestic violence in the child's residence, be the court's primary concern in determining the child's best interest when making physical or legal custody and visitation orders. Fam C §3020(a). See also Fam C §3011(a) (in determining child's best interest, court must consider child's health, safety, and welfare). When this policy conflicts with the public policy in favor of frequent and continuing contact with both parents (see Fam C §3020(b); §7.19), any physical or legal custody or visitation order must be made in a manner that ensures the child's health, safety, and welfare and the safety of all family members. Fam C §3020(c).

§7.23   e. Abuse; Domestic Violence

In determining the child's best interest, the court must consider any history of abuse by one parent (or any other person seeking custody) against (Fam C §3011(b)(1)–(3)):

- Any child to whom he or she is related by blood or affinity or with whom he or she has had a caretaking relationship, no matter how temporary;

- The other parent; or

- A parent, current spouse, or cohabitant of the parent or other person, or a person with whom the parent or other person has a dating or engagement relationship.

As a prerequisite to consideration of allegations of abuse, however, the court may require substantial independent corroboration, *e.g.,* written reports by law enforcement or social welfare agencies, courts, or medical facilities. Fam C §3011(b).

When allegations about a parent under Fam C §3011(b) have been brought to the court's attention in the proceeding, and the court awards sole or joint custody to that parent, the court must state its reasons in writing or on the record, and must ensure that any order regarding custody or visitation is specific as to time, day, place, and manner of transfer of the child, as set forth in Fam C §6323(b). Fam C §3011(e)(1). These requirements do not apply if the parties stipulate in writing or on the record regarding custody or visitation. Fam C §3011(e)(2).

On a court finding that a party seeking custody of a child has perpetrated domestic violence (for definition, see Fam C §3044(c)) against the other party seeking custody of the child or against the child or the child's siblings within the previous 5 years, there is a rebuttable presumption that an award of sole or joint physical or legal custody of the child to the perpetrator is detrimental to the child's best interest, under Fam C §3011. Fam C §3044(a). On what satisfies the requirement of a finding by the court, see Fam C §3011(d). The presumption may be rebutted only by a preponderance of the evidence. Fam C §3044(a). In determining whether the presumption has been overcome, the court must consider a number of specified factors addressing the child's best interest and whether the perpetrator has successfully completed any of a variety of programs, complied with any protective order if on probation or parole, and committed any further acts of domestic violence. See Fam C §3044(c). The preference for frequent and continuing contact with both parents or with the noncustodial parent in Fam C §§3020(b) and 3040(a)(1) may not be used to rebut the presumption in whole or in part. Fam C §3044(b)(1), as amended by Stats 2003, ch 243, effective January 1, 2004.

§7.24 f. Contact With Parents

In determining the child's best interest, the court must consider the nature and amount of the child's contact with both parents, except as provided in Fam C §3046. Fam C §3011(c).

Family Code §3046 provides that if a party is absent or relocates from the family residence, the court must not consider the absence or relocation as a factor in determining custody or visitation when either:

- The absence or relocation is of short duration and the court finds that during that period (1) the party has demonstrated an interest in maintaining custody or visitation, (2) the party has maintained or made reasonable efforts to maintain regular contact with the child, and (3) the party's behavior has demonstrated no intent to abandon the child; or

- The absence or relocation was because of an act or acts of actual or threatened domestic or family violence by the other party.

Family Code §3046 does not apply (and thus the court must consider a party's absence or relocation) in cases involving:

- A party against whom a protective or restraining order has been issued excluding the party from the dwelling of the other party or the child, or otherwise enjoining the party from assault or harassment against the other party or the child; or

- A party who abandons a child as provided in Fam C §7822 (abandoned child as grounds for action to have child declared free from parental custody and control).

NOTE➤ For special considerations concerning children of American Indian parents, see Fam C §7822(e)(1)-(2).

§7.24A   g. Contact With Siblings

In *Marriage of Williams* (2001) 88 CA4th 808, 105 CR2d 923, the court addressed a trial court order awarding custody of two of the couple's four children to one parent and two to the other. After commenting that "At a minimum the children have a right to the society and companionship of their siblings," the appellate court reversed and directed the trial court to order separation of the siblings only on a showing of compelling circumstances, articulated "in a manner which permits meaningful appellate review." In reaching its conclusion, the court referred, in part, to a provision of the Welfare and Institutions Code as an expression of public policy that siblings should be kept together whenever possible, absent extraordinary medical, emotional, or educational needs. 88 CA4th at 814, 815 (citing, in part, Welf & I C §16002, concerning children placed in foster care). See also *Marriage of Heath* (2004) 122 CA4th 444, 452, 18 CR3d 760 (addressing need for separate counsel for each sibling if there is potential conflict).

§7.25   h. Use of Controlled Substances or Alcohol

In determining the child's best interest, the court must consider the habitual or continual illegal use of controlled substances, or the habitual or continual abuse of alcohol, by either parent. Before considering such allegations, however, the court may require independent corroboration, *e.g.,* written reports from law enforcement agencies, courts, social welfare agencies, or medical facilities. Fam C §3011(d).

In response to concerns expressed in *Wainwright v Superior Court* (2000) 84 CA4th 262, 269, 100 CR2d 749 about lack of statutory authority to compel drug testing in custody cases and related constitutional issues, the legislature enacted Fam C §3041.5. Under that section, a court may order any parent who is seeking custody of, or visitation with, a child who is the subject of the proceeding to undergo testing for the illegal use of controlled substances and the use of alcohol if there is a judicial determination based on a preponderance of evidence that there is the habitual, frequent, or continual illegal use of controlled substances or the habitual or continual abuse of alcohol by the parent or legal custodian. This evidence may include, but is not limited to, a conviction within the last 5 years for the illegal use or possession of a controlled substance. The court must order the least intrusive method of testing for the illegal use of controlled substances or the habitual or continual abuse of alcohol by either or both parents or the legal custodian. A parent or legal custodian who has undergone drug testing has the right to a hearing, if requested, to challenge a positive test result. But a positive test result, even if challenged and upheld, does not, by itself, constitute grounds for an adverse custody decision. Fam C §3041.5(a). The statute applies not only in family court proceedings, but also in guardianship proceedings. Fam C §3041.5(a).

Since Fam C §3041.5 was enacted, one court of appeal held that a trial court could not order a mother in a child custody dispute to submit to a hair follicle drug test. It stated that because Fam C §3041.5(a) requires that tests use the "least intensive method" and to be "in conformance with" federal employment procedures and standards (allowing only urine tests), only urine tests were allowed. *Deborah M. v Superior Court* (2005) 128 CA4th 1181, 1193, 27 CR3d 757.

NOTE➤ Family Code §3041.5 is repealed as of January 1, 2008, unless a later enacted statute (enacted before January 1, 2008) deletes or extends that date. Fam C §3041.5(b).

When allegations about a parent under Fam C §3011(d) have been brought to the court's attention in the proceeding, and the court awards sole or joint custody to that parent, the court must state its reasons in writing or on the record, and must ensure that any order regarding custody or visitation is specific as to time, day, place, and manner of transfer of the child, as set forth in Fam C §6323(b). Fam C §3011(e)(1). These requirements do not apply if the parties stipulate in writing or on the record regarding custody or visitation. Fam C §3011(e)(2).

§7.26 i. Parent's Gender

The court may not prefer a parent as custodial parent because of that parent's gender. Fam C §3040(a)(1). In addition to a court not utilizing a preference as between male and female parents, it is clear that two parents of the same gender can be accorded parental rights (and therefore custody) rights. See *Kristine H. v. Lisa R.* (2005) 37 C4th 156, 162, 33 CR3d 81; *K.M. v. E.G.* (2005) 37 C4th 130, 144, 33 CR3d 61; *Elisa B. v Superior Court* (2005) 37 C4th 108, 122, 33 CR3d 46; *Sharon S. v Superior Court* (2003) 31 C4th 417, 422, 2 CR3d 699 (second-parent adoption).

For comprehensive treatment of the California Domestic Partner Rights and Responsibilities Act of 2003 (Stats 2003, ch 421), effective January 1, 2005, and the implications of domestic partnerships on parental rights and obligations, see California Domestic Partnerships (Cal CEB 2005).

§7.27 j. Child's Preference

If a child is of sufficient age and capacity to form an intelligent preference regarding custody, the court must consider and give due weight to the child's wishes in making a custody determination. Fam C §3042(a). The child's age alone is not determinative of whether the child's wishes must be considered and weighed. Rather, such qualities as the child's sincerity, bearing, and degree of maturity should be judged. *Marriage of Rosson* (1986) 178 CA3d 1094, 1103, 224 CR 250, disapproved on other grounds in *Marriage of Whealon* (1997) 53 CA4th 132, 139, 61 CR2d 559, and overruled on other grounds in *Marriage of Burgess* (1996) 13 C4th 25, 39, 51 CR2d 444. In *Rosson,* the wishes of children 10 and 13 years old whom the mediator found to be "very mature" were properly considered and given some weight. In *Marriage of Mehlmauer* (1976) 60 CA3d 104, 110, 131 CR 325, on the other hand, the trial court did not err in finding that the wishes of a child 14 years old were not supported by mature reasoning.

A child's wishes are entitled to greater consideration in modification proceedings than in the initial custody determination, because in the former situation the child will have lived with the arrangement and will have a more informed basis for his or her preference. *Marriage of Rosson* (1986) 178 CA3d 1094, 1103, 224 CR 250, disapproved on other grounds in *Marriage of Whealon* (1997) 53 CA4th 132, 139, 61 CR2d 559, and overruled on other grounds in *Marriage of Burgess* (1996) 13 C4th 25, 39, 51 CR2d 444.

The court must control the examination of the child witness to protect the child's best interest. When the child's best interest so dictate, the court may preclude calling the child as a witness and provide alternative means of obtaining information about the child's preferences. Fam C §3042(b). See also Evid C §765(b) (control of questioning of witness under age 14).

PRACTICE TIP➤ Local rules and practices vary on whether a child should attend a custody mediation with his or her parents, and if this is permitted, how old the child must be to attend. It is important to be familiar with the local court rules and Family Court Services practices in this regard. See, *e.g.*, Orange Ct. R 704.E. (mediation arising from ex parte requests for modification of custody may include children if they are of sufficient age to communicate); Sacramento Ct. R 14.08 (requiring parties to bring children age five and older to mediation).

§7.28 k. Person Required to Register as Sex Offender or Convicted of Child Abuse Crime

A person who (1) is required to register as a sex offender under Pen C §290 as a result of conduct toward a victim who was a minor, or (2) has been convicted of child abuse under Pen C §273a, §273d, or §647.6 may not be awarded physical or legal custody of, or unsupervised visitation with, any child unless the court finds that there is no significant risk to the child and states its reasons in writing or on the record. The child may not be placed in a home in which that person resides, nor permitted to have unsupervised visitation with that person, unless the court states the reasons for its findings in writing or on the record. Fam C §3030(a)(1). The court may not disclose or cause to be disclosed the custodial parent's place of residence or employment or the child's school, unless the court finds that the disclosure would be in the child's best interest. Fam C §3030(e).

No person shall be granted physical or legal custody of, or unsupervised visitation with, a child if anyone residing in the person's household is required, as a result of a felony conviction in which the victim was a minor, to register as a sex offender under Pen C §290, unless the court finds there is no significant risk to the child and states its reasons in writing or on the record. The child may not be placed in a home in which that person resides, nor permitted to have unsupervised visitation with that person, unless the court states the reasons for its findings in writing or on the record. Fam C §3030(a)(2).

The fact that a child is permitted unsupervised contact with a person who is required, as a result of a felony conviction in which the victim was a minor, to be registered as a sex offender under Pen C §290, shall be prima facie evidence that the child is at significant risk. When making a determination regarding significant risk to the child, the prima facie evidence constitutes a presumption affecting the burden of producing evidence. However, this presumption does not apply if there are factors mitigating against its application, including whether the party seeking custody or visitation is also required, as the result of a felony conviction in which the victim was a minor, to register as a sex offender under Pen C §290. Fam C §3030(a)(3).

NOTE➤ On grounds for *modification* of custody or visitation based on a child (1) being in the legal or physical custody of, or subject to unsupervised visitation with, a person who is required to register as a sex offender for committing a felony against a minor, or (2) having a legal or physical custodian or person who visits the child without supervision who lives with such a registered sex offender, see Fam C §3030.5.

§7.28A   l. Person Convicted of Rape

A person who has been convicted under Pen C §261 (rape) may not be awarded custody of, or visitation with, a child conceived as a result of that violation. Fam C §3030(b). The court may not disclose, or cause to be disclosed, the custodial parent's place of residence or employment or the child's school unless the court finds that the disclosure would be in the child's best interest. Fam C §3030(e).

§7.28B   m. Person Convicted of First-Degree Murder

A person who has been convicted of first-degree murder under Pen C §189 may not be awarded custody of, or unsupervised visitation with, a child whose other parent was the victim of the murder, unless the court finds that there is no risk to the child's health, safety, and welfare and states its reasons in writing or on the record. Fam C §3030(c).

In making its finding, the court may consider, among other things (Fam C §3030(c)):

- The child's wishes, if the child is of sufficient age and capacity to reason so as to form an intelligent preference;

- Credible evidence that the convicted parent was a victim of abuse (see Fam C §6203) committed by the deceased parent, including, *e.g.*, written reports from law enforcement, child protective services, and other social welfare agencies, courts, medical facilities or other public or private nonprofit organizations that provide services to domestic violence abuse victims; and

• Testimony of an expert witness (see Evid C §1107), that the convicted parent experiences intimate partner battering.

Unless and until a custody or visitation order is issued under Fam C §3030(c), no person may permit or cause the child to visit or remain in the convicted parent's custody without the consent of the child's custodian or legal guardian. Fam C §3030(c).

§7.29   n. Existing Restraining Orders

The court is encouraged to make a reasonable effort to ascertain whether any emergency protective order, protective order, or other restraining order is in effect that concerns the parents or the child. If so, the court is encouraged not to make a custody order that is inconsistent with the restraining order unless the court finds that (1) the custody order cannot be made consistent with the restraining order and (2) the custody order is in the child's best interest. Fam C §3031(a).

When custody or visitation is granted to a parent in a case in which domestic violence is alleged and a restraining order has been issued, the custody or visitation order must specify the time, day, place, and manner of transfer of the child in order to limit the child's exposure to potential domestic conflict or violence and to ensure the safety of all family members. When the court finds that a party is staying in a shelter or other confidential location, the order must be designed to prevent disclosure of the location. Fam C §3031(b). Further, the court must consider whether the child's best interest, based on the circumstances of the case, require that any custody or visitation arrangement be limited to situations in which a third party specified by the court is present or that custody or visitation be suspended or denied. Fam C §3031(c).

Under appropriate circumstances (*e.g.*, when the client is a protected party whose protection may be compromised by a conflicting custody order), counsel should bring any restraining orders to the court's attention.

2. Other Factors

§7.30   a. Child's Need for Stability and Continuity; "Move-Away" Cases

Although the child's need for stability and continuity is always a major factor in awarding custody, it becomes increasingly important when the child has lived with one parent for a significant period. In such instances, that need will often, but not always, dictate that maintenance of the existing custody arrangement is in the child's best interest. *Burchard v Garay* (1986) 42 C3d 531, 538, 229 CR 800. This emphasis has been of particular importance in so-called "move-away" cases, *i.e.,* when one parent seeks to move a substantial distance and to take the child with him or her.

When a parent who has sole physical custody under an existing order seeks to relocate, the noncustodial parent who seeks a change of custody to prevent the child's relocation bears the initial burden of showing that relocation would cause detriment to the child. On such a showing, the trial court must reevaluate the child's custody and determine whether a change in custody to the noncustodial parent is in the best interest of the child. *Marriage of LaMusga* (2004) 32 C4th 1072, 1078, 12 CR3d 356. See also *Marriage of Burgess* (1996) 13 C4th 25, 38, 51 CR2d 444; *Osgood v Landon* (2005) 127 CA4th 425, 434, 25 CR3d 379. While the custodial parent's proposed move does not automatically constitute a change in circumstances requiring reevaluation of a custody order, the likely impact of the proposed move on the noncustodial parent's relationship with the child is a relevant factor in determining whether the move would cause detriment to the child. *Marriage of LaMusga,* 32 C4th at 1097. A trial court is not required to grant a full evidentiary hearing on a noncustodial parent's request to modify physical custody of a child in the face of a proposed relocation by the parent who has sole legal and physical custody of the child. Instead, it may deny that request in a motion hearing after mediation has been completed if the moving party fails to establish a prima facie showing that he proposed relocation will cause detriment to the child. See *Marriage of Brown & Yana* (2006) 37 C4th 947, 962, 38 CR3d 610 (offer of proof regarding characteristics of city custodial parent planned to move to, such as high student-to-teacher ratio, high dropout rate, amount of crime, transience of inhabitants, was insufficient to justify full evidentiary hearing on detrimental effect of move).

In any "move-away" case, the court must consider what custodial arrangement is in the best interest of the child. The supreme court in *LaMusga* identified several factors that trial courts should ordinarily consider when deciding move-away cases. In addressing the significance of one such factor, the motivation of the custodial parent to move away, the court quoted *Burgess,* stating that a change of custody "is not justified simply because the custodial parent has chosen, for any sound good faith reason, to reside in a different location, but only if, as a result of relocation with that parent, the child will suffer detriment rendering it 'essential or expedient for the welfare of the child that there be a change.'" *Marriage of LaMusga,* 32 C4th at 1099 (indicating that appellate court in *Marriage of Bryant* (2001) 91 CA4th 789, 110 CR2d 791 overstated absence of bad faith in holding that once trial court found that mother was not acting in bad faith, "no further inquiry into the reasons for the proposed move" was necessary or appropriate). The trial court should exercise broadest discretion in ruling on the move by considering a wide range of relevant factors. 32 C4th at 1101. If the existing custody order requires the custodial parent to obtain the other parent's consent or a court order before relocating, the custodial parent bears the burden of obtaining judicial review and making the requisite good faith showing, but the noncustodial parent retains the burden of establishing that relocation would be detrimental to the child. *Marriage of Abrams* (2003) 105 CA4th 979, 130 CR2d 16.

If the custodial parent seeks to move to a foreign county, he or she must show that the other's parenting rights can be preserved in light of the cultural, transportation, and financial problems posed by an international move. *Marriage of Condon* (1998) 62 CA4th 533, 73 CR2d 33. Under *Condon,* at a minimum, the child must have continuing contact with the parent remaining in the United States and the California custody order must be guaranteed enforceable in the foreign country. *Marriage of Abargil* (2003) 106 CA4th 1294, 131 CR2d 429. To protect the child's relationship with the noncustodial parent, however, the custodial parent may be (1) ordered to post a substantial financial bond to ensure compliance with the court's orders, (2) prohibited from applying for modification of the judgment in any but a California court; and (3) required to register the California judgment with the foreign authorities before leaving the state. *Marriage of Abargil* (2003) 106 CA4th 1294, 131 CR2d 429.

When the parents share joint physical custody under an existing order and in fact, and one parent seeks to relocate with the child, the nonmoving parent who seeks a change of custody to prevent the child's relocation need only establish that the change of custody will be in the child's best interest. The trial court must determine de novo what primary custody arrangement is in the child's best interest. *Marriage of Burgess* (1996) 13 C4th 25, 40 n12, 51 CR2d 444; *Marriage of Seagondollar* (2006) 139 CA4th 1116, 1127, 43 CR3d 575 (cumulative procedural errors of trial court deprived father of due process); *Brody v Kroll* (1996) 45 CA4th 1732, 53 CR2d 280.

In determining whether the parents' arrangement fits under the sole physical custody or joint physical custody rules, courts focus on the actual arrangement rather than on the terms of the order. See *Marriage of Lasich* (2002) 99 CA4th 702, 121 CR2d 356 (mother who had children 80 percent or more of the time was their primary physical custodian, despite judgment's "joint physical custody" label); *Marriage of Biallas* (1998) 65 CA4th 755, 76 CR2d 717 (joint physical custody requires significant time with both parents; alternate weekends, one night per week, and occasional hour in evening not sufficient); *Marriage of Whealon* (1997) 53 CA4th 132, 61 CR2d 559 (when, although father had generous visitation rights, child spent vast majority of time with mother, father carried burden assigned to noncustodial parent who seeks change of custody).

In making an initial custody order, when no final determination had ever been made, the court was authorized to use the "best interest" standard rather than deferring to the custodial parent's presumptive right to move established in *Marriage of Burgess* (1996) 13 C4th 25, 34, 51 CR2d 444, in deciding to transfer custody to the father, even though the mother had had primary custody for the first 6 years of the child's life, when the mother decided to move away. *Ragghanti v Reyes* (2004) 123 CA4th 989, 997, 20 CR3d 522. There is no requirement that the amount of the noncustodial parent's visitation be increased when a move-away order is issued. *Marriage of Edlund & Hales* (1998) 66 CA4th 1454, 1474, 78 CR2d 671.

§7.31   b. Emotional Bonds

A custody determination must be based on a true assessment of the emotional bonds between parent and child, on an inquiry into "the heart of the parent-child relationship. . . the ethical, emotional, and intellectual guidance the parent gives to the child throughout his formative years, and often beyond." It must also reflect a factual determination of how best to provide continuity of attention, nurturing, and care. *Burchard v Garay* (1986) 42 C3d 531, 540, 229 CR 800, quoting *Marriage of Carney* (1979) 24 C3d 725, 739, 157 CR 383.

§7.32   c. Race

Custody determinations may not be made on the basis of race, despite any concern for the effects that racial prejudice in the society at large may have on the child. *Palmore v Sidoti* (1984) 466 US 429, 80 L Ed 2d 421, 104 S Ct 1879. In *Palmore,* the Supreme Court held that custody could not be changed from the mother to the father on the basis of possible injury to the child from prejudice against the mother's interracial marriage.

§7.33   d. Sexual Conduct

A party's sexual conduct is not relevant in awarding custody unless there is compelling evidence that it has a significant bearing on the child's welfare. *Marriage of Wellman* (1980) 104 CA3d 992, 999, 164 CR 148 (abuse of discretion to require that mother with custody have no nonmarital overnight visitation with member of opposite sex in children's presence).

§7.34   e. Sexual Orientation

Prior to the enactment of legislation establishing the rights of couples to register with the Secretary of State as domestic partners (Fam C §§297–299.6), courts had held that a party's sexual orientation could not in itself be determinative in awarding custody. Rather, it was a factor to be considered, insofar as the court found it relevant, in determining what award would be in the child's best interest. *Nadler v Superior Court* (1967) 255 CA2d 523, 63 CR 352; see *Marriage of Birdsall* (1988) 197 CA3d 1024, 243 CR 287 (provision restricting homosexual father from exercising overnight visitation with son in presence of anyone known to be homosexual reversed for lack of showing of detriment to child). See also *Chaffin v Frye* (1975) 45 CA3d 39, 45, 47, 119 CR 22 (court of appeal noted that mother's homosexuality was only one of multiple factors justifying custody award to mother's parents, but stated that trial court could properly conclude that permanent residence with homosexual couple would be detrimental to children and contrary to their best interest).

Whether a contemporary California court would consider a parent's sexual orientation as a custody factor is unclear, but this seems increasingly unlikely. Indications that courts will not do so include the following, for example:

- Same-sex couples can now register as domestic partners and become entitled to the same rights and obligations with respect to a child of either of them as spouses (see Fam C §297.5(d));

- Even nonregistered same-sex partners can be considered parents to children of their relationship (*Elisa B. v Superior Court* (2005) 37 C4th 108, 122, 33 CR3d 46); and

- The Supreme Court has expressly sanctioned adoption by a second parent of the same sex as the natural parent (*Sharon S. v Superior Court* (2003) 31 C4th 417, 2 CR3d 699).

§7.35 f. Religious Practices

Custody may not be denied to a party on the basis of his or her religious beliefs or practices without compelling evidence that the beliefs or practices will be harmful to the child. *Marriage of Weiss* (1996) 42 CA4th 106, 109, 49 CR2d 339 (premarital agreement concerning future religious upbringing of children not enforceable; parent's religious activity with child cannot be enjoined absent showing of harm to child); *Marriage of Urband* (1977) 68 CA3d 796, 137 CR 433 (mother was Jehovah's Witness). See *Marriage of Murga* (1980) 103 CA3d 498, 505, 163 CR 79 (court may not enjoin noncustodial parent from discussing religion with child or involving child in religious activities absent showing of harm to child); *Marriage of Mentry* (1983) 142 CA3d 260, 190 CR 843 (order prohibiting noncustodial father from engaging children in any religious activity or discussion and from providing them with religious materials reversed).

The basis for this prohibition is found in the US Const amend I, as is perhaps best explained in *Wisconsin v Yoder* (1972) 406 US 205, 213, 32 LEd2d 15, 92 SCt 1526. In that case, the United States Supreme Court explained that

[a] State's interest in universal education, however highly we rank it, is not totally free from a balancing process when it impinges on fundamental rights and interests, such as those specifically protected by the Free Exercise Clause of the First Amendment, and the traditional interest of parents with respect to the religious upbringing of their children so long as they, in the words of *Pierce* [*v Society of Sisters* (1925) 268 US 510, 534, 69 LEd 1070, 45 SCt 571], 'prepare (them) for additional obligations.'

§7.36   g. Physical Handicap

A court may not determine custody solely on the basis of a party's physical handicap. Rather, it is but one factor to be considered in viewing the handicapped person and the family as a whole. *Marriage of Carney* (1979) 24 C3d 725, 736, 157 CR 383. See also *Marriage of Levin* (1980) 102 CA3d 981, 162 CR 757. Similarly, the fact of one sibling's disability does not permit a court to presume detriment to the other sibling that would warrant a custody order separating them. See *Marriage of Heath* (2004) 122 CA4th 444, 18 CR3d 760.

§7.37   h. Disparity of Incomes

In awarding custody, the court may not rely on the parties' relative economic positions. *Burchard v Garay* (1986) 42 C3d 531, 539, 229 CR 800; *Marriage of Fingert* (1990) 221 CA3d 1575, 1580, 271 CR 389. If the income of the party otherwise best qualified to have custody is insufficient to provide proper care for the child, the remedy is to award an appropriate amount of child support, not to award custody to the other party. *Burchard v Garay, supra*. Likewise, the court may not base its decision on an assumption that the care provided by a single, working parent who will be dependent on day care is inferior to that provided by a remarried parent whose new spouse can care for the child at home. *Burchard v Garay* (1986) 42 C3d 531, 540, 229 CR 800. Nor may the court rely on the assumption that because a child's biological parent has remarried and can stay home to care for the child, the remarried parent should have custody. *Marriage of Loyd* (2003) 106 CA4th 754, 131 CR2d 80 (custody modification).

§7.38   i. Parents' Agreement

The court need not accept an agreement of the parties on child custody. See *Puckett v Puckett* (1943) 21 C2d 833, 839, 136 P2d 1; *Van der Vliet v Van der Vliet* (1927) 200 C 721, 254 P 945. Further, the parties cannot divest the court of jurisdiction over custody issues by stipulation. *Marriage of Goodarzirad* (1986) 185 CA3d 1020, 1026, 230 CR 203. See also *Marriage of Weiss* (1996) 42 CA4th 106, 117, 49 CR2d 339 (premarital agreement to raise children in spouse's faith unenforceable). A stipulated agreement to terminate one parent's rights is likewise void as against public policy, absent contemplation of a second-parent or stepparent adoption. *Marriage of Jackson* (2006) 136 CA4th 980, 991, 39 CR3d 365; *Kristine M. v David P.* (2006) 135 CA4th 783, 792, 37 CR3d 748. An agreement between the parties for joint legal and joint physical custody, however, creates a presumption that such an arrangement is in the child's best interest. Fam C §§3080, 3002.

The court's authority to override an agreement of the parties on custody has not gone entirely unquestioned, however. See *Marriage of Wellman* (1980) 104 CA3d 992, 996, 164 CR 148 (suggesting in dicta that court may not have authority to raise and decide custody issue absent dispute between parties). See also *Marriage of Schwartz* (1980) 104 CA3d 92, 163 CR 408 (accepting trial court's authority to reject parties' agreement, but reversing for ruling on basis of "unshakable prejudice" against parties' agreement).

When the parties have an agreement or understanding regarding custody or temporary custody, a copy of the agreement or a declaration regarding the understanding must be attached to a petition or motion. As promptly as possible after the filing, the court must, except in exceptional circumstances, enter an order granting temporary custody in accordance with the agreement or understanding. Fam C §3061.

C. Mediation

§7.39   1. When Required

Mediation is required whenever it appears that an issue of custody or visitation regarding a minor child is contested, whether the order sought is an initial order or a modification. Fam C §3170(a). The mediation must be set before, or concurrent with, the setting of the matter for hearing. Fam C §3175. A party's failure to mediate may estop him or her from being heard on a custody or visitation request. *Marriage of Economou* (1990) 224 CA3d 1466, 1487, 274 CR 473.

The duration of the mediation is within the court's discretion. When mediation is unsuccessful in resolving the custody or visitation dispute, the trial court has met the statutory requirement and has considerable discretion in determining whether the facts and circumstances justify an order for additional mediation. *Marriage of Green* (1989) 213 CA3d 14, 25, 261 CR 294.

§7.40   2. Purposes

Mediation of a custody dispute has several purposes: to reduce any acrimony between the parties; develop an agreement ensuring the child's close and continuing contact with both parents that is in the child's best interest, consistent with Fam C §§3011 and 3020; and effect a settlement regarding visitation rights of all parties that is in the child's best interest. Fam C §3161. The mediator must seek a settlement that is in the child's best interest, as provided in Fam C §3011. Fam C §3180(b). Considerations specified by Fam C §3011 in determining the child's best interest are the child's health, safety, and welfare; any history of abuse by one parent against specified persons; the nature and amount of the child's contact with both parents; and use of controlled substances or alcohol. Fam C §3011.

§7.41   3. Mediator

By statute, a court must make a mediator available for mandatory custody mediation. See Fam C §3160. The mediator may be a member of the professional staff of a family conciliation court, probation department, or mental health services agency, or any other person or agency designated by the court. Fam C §3164(a). Mediators are required (1) to meet educational requirements in a behavioral science that is substantially related to marriage and family relationships; (2) to meet requirements of experience in counseling, psychotherapy, or both; and (3) to possess specified knowledge relevant to their work. Fam C §§3164(b), 1815. Courts are required to develop local rules addressing requests for a change of mediators. Fam C §3163.

In some counties mental health professionals in private practice who are under contract to the court may be assigned to court-ordered mediation or parties may request private mediation as an alternative to utilizing the court's Office of Family Court Services. See, *e.g.*, Sacramento Ct R 14.08(C)(3)(b).

PRACTICE TIP➤ Many counties have developed special local rules and forms concerning mediation; thus, when taking a case in an unfamiliar county, it is advisable to consult with a colleague who practices there, or with a cooperative court clerk, regarding how that court handles custody mediation.

Counsel for a party is not permitted to communicate ex parte with any court-appointed or court-connected evaluator or mediator, except to schedule appointments, unless the parties stipulate otherwise, with certain exceptions involving cases of domestic violence. Fam C §216.

§7.42   4. Confidentiality

Family Code §3177 provides that mediation proceedings must be private and confidential and that all communications from the parties to the mediator made in the proceedings, whether verbal or written, will be deemed to be official information within the meaning of Evid C §1040 (public entity's privilege to refuse and prevent disclosure of official information). Because the privilege is held by court personnel and not the parties, however, Fam C §3177 does not give either party a right to raise confidentiality of the mediation process to bar a mediator's testimony if local rules permit it. Although court personnel must not disclose confidential information to the public, they may disclose the information to the court if local rules provide for such disclosure. *Marriage of Rosson* (1986) 178 CA3d 1094, 1105, 224 CR 250, disapproved on other grounds in *Marriage of Whealon* (1997) 53 CA4th 132, 139, 61 CR2d 559, and overruled on other grounds in *Marriage of Burgess* (1996) 13 C4th 25, 39, 51 CR2d 444. Even if local rules do not specifically so provide, counsel should always request that information submitted to the court that contains psychological evaluations of a child or recommendations regarding custody of, or visitation with, a child be placed in the confidential portion of the court file of the proceeding. Fam C §3025.5.

A crucial distinction has arisen between counties in which the mediation is kept confidential from the public but not from the court and counties in which confidentiality is total. It is good practice for an attorney to inform the client of the extent to which local rules ensure the confidentiality of communications made in mediation.

§7.43   5. Exclusion of Counsel

The mediator has authority to exclude attorneys from participation in the mediation proceedings when the mediator deems it appropriate or necessary. Fam C §3182(a). In fact, attorneys rarely participate in the sessions, but they often meet or confer with the mediator at some time before or after the sessions, bearing in mind the prohibition on ex parte communications. Fam C §216.

§7.44   6. Interview of Child

The mediator may interview the child who is the subject of the proceedings when the mediator deems it appropriate or necessary. Fam C §3180(a). Local rules and practices vary on the age at which a child is deemed mature enough to be interviewed.

§7.45   7. Special Provisions for Parties With History of Domestic Violence

When there has been a history of domestic violence between the parties or a protective order is in effect, the mediator must meet with the parties separately and at separate times if a party alleging domestic violence in a written declaration under penalty of perjury or protected by the order requests separate meetings. Fam C §3181(a). For definitions, see Fam C §§6211 ("domestic violence") and 6218 ("protective order").

Similarly, when a protective order is in effect, a "support person" must be permitted to accompany the party protected by the order during any orientation or mediation session, including separate mediation sessions. The mediator may exclude the support person, however, if he or she participates in the session or acts as an advocate, or if his or her presence is disruptive. Fam C §6303(c).

Domestic violence cases are to be handled by Family Court Services in accordance with a separate written protocol to be approved by the Judicial Council. Fam C §3170(b).

§7.46   8. Mediator's Recommendations

The mediator may, consistent with local rules, make a recommendation to the court on custody or visitation. Fam C §3183(a) (former CC §4607(e)). Unless permitted by a local rule duly adopted in writing, however, no recommendation may be made. *Marriage of*

Rosson (1986) 178 CA3d 1094, 1104, 224 CR 250, disapproved on other grounds in *Marriage of Whealon* (1997) 53 CA4th 132, 139, 61 CR2d 559, and overruled on other grounds in *Marriage of Burgess* (1996) 13 C4th 25, 39, 51 CR2d 444. Further, the mediator may not make a recommendation to the court unless both parties are given the right to examine the mediator at a hearing on the matters covered by the recommendation. 178 CA3d at 1105; *McLaughlin v Superior Court* (1983) 140 CA3d 473, 482, 189 CR 479.

Note that, absent a stipulation to the contrary between the parties, a mediator may not communicate ex parte with the court, unless the mediator determines such communication is needed to inform the court of his or her belief that a restraining order is necessary to prevent an imminent risk to the physical safety of the child or the party. Fam C §§216(a), 216(c)(3).

A crucial distinction has arisen between counties in which the mediator may make a recommendation to the court, subject to the parties' right to examine the mediator at a hearing, and counties in which no recommendation may be made. It is good practice for an attorney to inform the client of whether local rules permit the mediator to make a recommendation to the court.

When the parties have still not reached an agreement after the mediation proceedings, the mediator may recommend that an investigation be conducted under Fam C §§3110–3116 (see §7.49) or that other services be offered to assist the parties to resolve the controversy before any hearing. Fam C §3183(b). In appropriate cases, the mediator may recommend that restraining orders be issued, pending a decision, to protect the child's well-being. Fam C §3183(c). When it would be in the child's best interest, the mediator may recommend appointment, under Fam C §§3150–3153, of counsel to represent the child (see §7.51). Fam C §3184.

§7.47   9. Agreements

Mediation agreements must be limited to the resolution of issues relating to parenting plans, custody, and visitation. Fam C §3178(a). If an agreement is reached, the mediator must report it to the parties' attorneys on the day of the mediation or as soon thereafter as practicable and, in any event, before it is reported to the court. Fam C §3186(a). No agreement may be confirmed or otherwise incorporated into a court order unless each party has (1) assented, either in person or through counsel of record, in open court or by written stipulation or (2) failed to appear at a noticed hearing on the issues involved in the agreement. Fam C §3186(b)-(c).

§7.48   10. Uniform Standards of Practice

The Judicial Council has adopted uniform standards of practice for court-connected mediation of child custody and visitation disputes. See Cal Rules of Ct 5.210.

§7.49   D. Evaluation and Report

In any contested proceeding involving child custody or visitation rights, the court may appoint a child custody evaluator to conduct a child custody evaluation if the court determines the appointment would be in the child's best interest. The evaluation must be conducted in accordance with standards adopted by the Judicial Council, under Fam C §3117 and otherwise, regarding child custody evaluations. When directed to do so by the court, the child custody evaluator must file a written confidential report on his or her evaluation that may be considered by the court. The report must be filed with the court clerk and served on the parties or their attorneys and any other counsel appointed for the child under Fam C §3150 at least 10 days before any custody hearing. Fam C §3111(a). The report may be received in evidence on stipulation of all interested parties and is competent evidence regarding all matters contained in it. Fam C §3111(c). See also *Marriage of deRoque* (1999) 74 CA4th 1090, 1096, 88 CR2d 618 (no error for trial court to fashion own modification of custody schedule rather than following evaluator's recommendation; trial court "fine-tuned" the recommendation to better address family's timeshare problems).

The evaluator must have completed the domestic violence and child abuse training program described in Fam C §1816 and have complied with Cal Rules of Ct 5.220 (uniform standards of practice) and 5.230 (domestic violence training standards). Fam C §3110.5(a).

Except with regard to scheduling appointments, attorneys may not communicate ex parte with court-appointed or court-connected evaluators. Similarly, a court-appointed or court-connected evaluator may not communicate ex parte with the court, unless the parties stipulate otherwise, or in limited circumstances in the case of domestic violence. An ex parte communication may be permitted when the evaluator determines that it is needed to inform the court of his or her belief that a restraining order is necessary to prevent an imminent risk to the physical safety of the child or the party. Fam C §§218(a), (c)(3).When there has been a history of domestic violence between the parties or a protective order is in effect, the evaluator must meet with the parties separately and at separate times if a party alleging domestic violence in a written declaration under penalty of perjury or the party protected by the order requests separate meetings. Fam C §3113. For definitions, see Fam C §§6211 ("domestic violence") and 6218 ("protective order").

No party may be deemed by any statement or conduct to have waived the right to cross-examine the child custody evaluator unless the statement or conduct occurs after the evaluator's report has been received by the party or his or her attorney. Fam C §3115.

The court must inquire into the financial circumstances of the child's parents or guardians and may require them to repay the court for part or all of the expense incurred for the evaluation, report, and recommendation. Fam C §3112(a).

Counsel should check local policy regarding how often evaluations occur, the circumstances under which they occur, and the applicable procedures.

§7.50   E. Court-Ordered Mental Health Examinations

On its own motion or that of any party, the court may appoint a psychiatrist or other mental health professional to examine the parents and children, report to the court, and testify on custody or visitation issues. Evid C §730; *Kim v Kim* (1989) 208 CA3d 364, 372, 256 CR 217.

On mental health examinations as part of the discovery process, see §13.34.

§7.51   F. Appointment of Attorney for Child

In a custody or visitation proceeding, the court may appoint private counsel to represent the child's interest if the court determines that such an appointment would be in the child's best interest. Fam C §3150(a). Guidelines for the court to follow in making the determination are in Cal Rules of Ct Appendix Div I §20.5. The appointed attorney will continue to represent the child unless relieved by the court on substitution of other counsel or for cause. Fam C §3150(b).

The appointed attorney's duties, prerogatives, and rights are set forth in Fam C §§3151 and 3152. The court may require that the attorney prepare a written statement of issues and contentions setting forth the facts that bear on the child's best interest. Fam C §3151(b); see Fam C §3151.5. The attorney will receive a reasonable sum for compensation and expenses, the amount to be set by the court and paid by the parties in the proportions the court deems just. If the court finds that the parties together cannot pay part or all of the cost of appointed counsel, the county must pay the portion the court finds the parties unable to pay. Fam C §3153. Public funding is only available if all the parties together are financially unable to pay all or part of the attorney fees. *Marriage of Perry* (1998) 61 CA4th 295, 71 CR2d 499 (grandmother who successfully moved to be joined as party to custody action regarding her grandson can be ordered to pay expenses of father's attorney and child's attorney that were attributable to her claims).

Note that a court has no authority to appoint a guardian ad litem, as distinguished from an attorney, for a child in a family law case. *Marriage of Lloyd* (1997) 55 CA4th 216, 64 CR2d 37.

PRACTICE TIP➤ As a practical matter, an attorney appointed to represent a child can exert great influence in the case because his or her recommendations or observations often may carry disproportionate weight with the court. Counsel should advise any parent who has "fallen out of favor" with the court or has serious parenting issues to address to pay careful attention to minor's counsel's observations or suggestions.

§7.52   G. Court-Ordered Counseling

Whenever custody or visitation issues are contested, the court may require the parents or any other party and the child to participate in outpatient counseling with a licensed mental health professional or other community counseling services, including mental health or substance abuse services, for up to one year. Fam C §3190(a). The counseling must be designed to facilitate communication between the parties regarding the child's best interest, reduce conflict over custody or visitation, and improve the quality of each party's parenting skills. Fam C §3191. Before making such an order, the court must find that the dispute poses a substantial danger to the child's best interest and that counseling is in the child's best interest, and it must set forth the reasons for the findings. Fam C §3190(a), (d)(1).

In determining whether a custody or visitation dispute poses a substantial danger to the child's best interest, the court must consider, in addition to any other factors it judges relevant, any history of domestic violence within the past 5 years between the parents, between one or both parents and the child, between one or both parents and another party seeking custody or visitation rights with the child, or between such a party and the child. Fam C §3190(b).

When there has been a history of abuse by either parent against the child, or by one parent against the other, and a protective order is in effect, the court may order the parents to participate in counseling separately and at separate times. Fam C §3192.

Each party is to bear the costs of his or her own counseling separately, unless good cause is shown for a different apportionment. Fam C §3192. If the court finds that the financial burden created by the order for counseling does not jeopardize a party's other financial obligations, it must fix the cost and order the entire cost of the services to be borne by the parties in the proportion the court deems reasonable. Fam C §3190(c). Costs associated with a minor's participation in counseling are to be apportioned in accordance with rules for apportioning responsibility for specified expenses relating to child support (see §§8.23–8.24). Fam C §3192. The court, in its finding, must explain why it has found that the financial burden created by the order does not jeopardize a party's other financial obligations. Fam C §3190(d)(2).

Although the court may not order the parents to return to court when the counseling is completed, any party may, at that time, file an order to show cause or notice of motion requesting that counseling continue, in which event the court may order it. Fam C §3190(d).

§7.53 H. Calendar Preference

When custody is the only contested issue in a case, the case must be given preference over other civil cases (except those entitled by law to special precedence) for assigning a trial date, and it must be given an early hearing. Fam C §3023(a). When there is more than one contested issue, the custody issue must receive a separate trial and be given the same preference for assigning a trial date that it would receive if custody were the only contested issue. Fam C §3023(b). If a child support issue has also been bifurcated, the two must be tried together. Fam C §4003.

§7.54 I. Notice of Change of Residence

The court may require a parent to notify the other parent if, without a prior written agreement, he or she plans to change the child's residence for more than 30 days. The notice must be given by mail, return receipt requested, postage prepaid, to the other parent's last known address, with a copy sent to the other parent's counsel of record. The notice must be given before the contemplated change of residence and, to the extent feasible, it must be given at least 45 days in advance to allow time for mediation of a new custody agreement. Fam C §3024.

§7.55 J. Accusations of Abuse or Neglect

If allegations of child sexual abuse are made during a child custody proceeding and the court has concerns about the child's safety, the court may take any reasonable, temporary steps it deems appropriate to protect the child's safety until an investigation can be completed. Fam C §3027.

No parent may be placed on supervised visitation, be denied custody of or visitation with his or her child, or have his or her custody or visitation rights limited, solely because the parent (Fam C §3027.5(a)):

- Lawfully reported suspected sexual abuse of the child;

- Otherwise acted lawfully, based on a reasonable belief, to determine whether his or her child was the victim of sexual abuse; or

- Sought treatment for the child from a licensed mental health professional for suspected sexual abuse.

The court may, however, order supervised visitation or limit a parent's custody or visitation if it finds substantial evidence that the parent, with the intent to interfere with the other parent's lawful contact with the child, made a report of child sexual abuse, during a child custody proceeding or at any other time, that he or she knew was false at the time it was made. Any such order, under Fam C

§3027.5(b) or any statute regarding the making of a false child abuse report, may be imposed only after the court has determined that the limitation is necessary to protect the child's health, safety, and welfare and the court has considered the state's policy of ensuring that children have frequent and continuing contact with both parents as declared in Fam C §3020(b) (see §7.19). Fam C §3027.5(b).

If the court finds that a party, a party's attorney, or a witness knowingly made a false accusation of child abuse or neglect during a child custody proceeding, it may impose reasonable sanctions, not to exceed all costs incurred by the party accused as a direct result of defending the accusation, and award reasonable attorney fees incurred in recovering the sanctions, against the person who made the accusation. Fam C §3027.1(a). The person requesting the sanctions proceeds by serving an order to show cause on the person against whom sanctions are sought at least 15 days before the hearing. Fam C §3027.1(b). A sanctions award under this section does not require that the falsity of the accusation be established during the underlying custody hearing. *Marriage of Dupre* (2005) 127 CA4th 1517, 26 CR3d 328.

A motion by a parent for reconsideration of an existing child custody order must be granted if the motion is based on the fact that the other parent was convicted of a crime in connection with falsely accusing the moving parent of child abuse. Fam C §3022.5.

§7.56   K. Financial Compensation for Noncompliance With Order

When a parent fails to assume the caretaker responsibility contemplated by a custody or visitation order or by a written or oral agreement between the parents, or when a parent has been thwarted by the other parent when attempting to exercise custody or visitation rights under such an order or agreement, the court may order financial compensation. Fam C §3028(a). The compensation is limited to the reasonable expenses incurred by the parent who is seeking the compensation. The expenses may include the value of caretaker services but are not limited to the cost of services provided by a third party. Fam C §3028(b).

The compensation may be requested by an order to show cause or notice of motion. The application must allege, within the 6 months preceding the filing of the order to show cause or notice of motion, at least $100 of expenses incurred, three occurrences of failure to assume the caretaker responsibility, or three instances of the thwarting of efforts to exercise custody or visitation rights. Fam C §3028(c).

Attorney fees must be awarded to the prevailing party on a showing of the other party's ability to pay. Fam C §3028(d).

§7.57 L. Birth Certificate May Be Required

In a marital dissolution action in which the respondent has neither appeared (personally or by counsel) nor been personally served, the court may not grant or modify any custody order unless the petitioner submits a certified copy of the child's birth certificate to the court. In a legal separation or nullity action, the petitioner must submit the certified copy if the respondent has not appeared, regardless of whether the respondent has been personally served. Fam C §3140(a)-(b). Regardless of the form of the action, the court may waive the requirement for good cause shown. Fam C §3140(c).

IV. VISITATION

§7.58 A. Noncustodial Parent

When one parent is awarded sole physical custody (see §7.17), reasonable visitation rights must be awarded to the other parent unless it is shown that the visitation would be detrimental to the child's best interest. See Fam C §3100(a) (former CC §4601); *Camacho v Camacho* (1985) 173 CA3d 214, 219, 218 CR 810. Thus, without a showing of such detriment, the court may not deny or restrict visitation solely on the basis of, *e.g.*, a party's sexual preference (see *Marriage of Birdsall* (1988) 197 CA3d 1024, 243 CR 287) or religious practices (see *Marriage of Murga* (1980) 103 CA3d 498, 505, 163 CR 79).

Beyond the requirement that visitation be awarded to a noncustodial parent absent a showing of detriment to the child, specific guidelines regarding visitation determinations include the following:

- Clearly, visitation awards are subject to the public policies declared in Fam C §3020. The first is to ensure that each child's health, safety, and welfare, expressly including freedom from child abuse and domestic violence in the child's residence, be the court's primary concern in determining the child's best interest when making physical or legal custody and visitation orders.

Fam C §3020(a). The second is to ensure frequent and continuing contact between a child and both parents after separation or dissolution except when that contact would not be in the child's best interest, as provided in Fam C §3011. Fam C §3020(b). When these two policies conflict, any physical or legal custody or visitation order must be made in a manner that ensures the child's health, safety, and welfare and the safety of all family members. Fam C §3020(c).

• The court is encouraged to make a reasonable effort to ascertain whether any emergency protective order, protective order, or other restraining order is in effect that concerns the parents or the child. If so, the court is encouraged not to make a visitation order that is inconsistent with the restraining order unless the court finds that (1) the visitation order cannot be made consistent with the restraining order and (2) the visitation order is in the child's best interest. Fam C §3031(a). Under appropriate circumstances (*e.g.,* when the client is a protected party whose protection may be compromised by a conflicting custody order), counsel should bring any restraining orders to the court's attention.

• When visitation is granted to a parent in a case in which domestic violence is alleged and a restraining order has been issued, the visitation order must specify the time, day, place, and manner of transfer of the child in order to limit the child's exposure to potential domestic conflict or violence and to ensure the safety of all family members. If a criminal protective order has been issued under Pen C §136.2, the visitation order must make reference to and acknowledge the precedence of enforcement of any appropriate criminal protective order. Fam C §3031(c). When the court finds that a party is staying in a shelter or other confidential location, the order must be designed to prevent disclosure of the location. Fam C §3031(b). Further, the court must consider whether the child's best interest, based on the circumstances of the case, require that any visitation arrangement be limited to situations in which a third party specified by the court is present or that visitation be suspended or denied. Fam C §3031(c). Counsel should note the availability of supervised visitation and exchange services, whether under the administration of the family law division of the local superior court (see Fam C §§3200–3204) or otherwise, and become familiar with local resources.

- No person required to register as a sex offender under Pen C §290 as a result of conduct toward a victim who was a minor, or convicted of child abuse under Pen C §273a, §273d, or §647.6, may be awarded unsupervised visitation unless the court finds that there is no significant risk to the child and states its reasons in writing or on the record. The child may not be placed in a home in which that person resides, nor permitted to have unsupervised visitation with that person, unless the court states the reasons for its findings in writing or on the record. Fam C §3030(a)(1).

- No person may be granted physical or legal custody of, or unsupervised visitation with, a child if anyone residing in the person's household is required, as a result of a felony conviction in which the victim was a minor, to register as a sex offender under Pen C §290, unless the court finds there is no significant risk to the child and states its reasons in writing or on the record. The child may not be placed in a home in which that person resides, nor permitted to have unsupervised visitation with that person, unless the court states the reasons for its findings in writing or on the record. Fam C §3030(a)(2).

- The fact that a child is permitted unsupervised contact with a person who is required, as a result of a felony conviction in which the victim was a minor, to be registered as a sex offender under Pen C §290, is prima facie evidence that the child is at significant risk. When making a determination regarding significant risk to the child, the prima facie evidence constitutes a presumption affecting the burden of producing evidence. However, this presumption does not apply if there are factors mitigating against its application, including whether the party seeking custody or visitation is also required, as the result of a felony conviction in which the victim was a minor, to register as a sex offender under Pen C §290. Fam C §3030(a)(3).

- No person who has been convicted under Pen C §261 (rape) may be awarded custody of, or visitation with, a child conceived as a result of that violation. Fam C §3030(b).

- No person who has been convicted of first-degree murder under

Pen C §189 may be awarded custody of, or unsupervised visitation with, a child whose other parent was the victim of the murder unless the court finds that there is no risk to the child's health, safety, and welfare and states its reasons in writing or on the record. Fam C §3030(c). Unless and until a custody or visitation order is issued under Fam C §3030(c), no person may permit or cause the child to visit or remain in the convicted parent's custody without the consent of the child's custodian or legal guardian. Fam C §3030(c).

- An incarcerated parent is entitled to a hearing to determine his or her visitation rights, and the court is encouraged to devise alternative means to provide meaningful access to prisoners who cannot personally appear in court. *Hoversten v Superior Court* (1999) 74 CA4th 636, 642, 88 CR2d 197.

- Visitation rights may not be conditioned on timely payment of child support. *Camacho v Camacho* (1985) 173 CA3d 214, 219, 218 CR 810. On the relationship between child support and visitation, including circumstances involving estoppel after parental concealment of a supported child, see §8.35.

- A noncustodial parent may not be compelled to visit his or her child. *Louden v Olpin* (1981) 118 CA3d 565, 173 CR 447. On filing a petition to declare a minor free from a natural parent's custody and control based on abandonment, see Fam C §7822.

- When reasonably necessary to prevent the child's removal from the court's jurisdiction, visitation may be conditioned on the visiting parent's relinquishment of passports. *Marriage of Economou* (1990) 224 CA3d 1466, 1486, 274 CR 473. See Fam C §3048 (listing required elements of custody orders, factors that may indicate child may be at risk of abduction by parent, and measures court may order to prevent this, including passport relinquishment).

§7.58A   B. Stepparent, Grandparent, and Sibling

The court in a marital action may award reasonable visitation rights to any other person having an interest in the child's welfare. Fam C §3100(a).

Stepparents. The court may grant reasonable visitation to a stepparent if visitation by the stepparent is determined to be in the best interest of the minor child. Fam C §3101(a). That authority may be limited by the preferences of the natural parents. When the natural parents are unified against such visitation, stepparent visitation may be ordered only if it is in the best interest of the child and denial of visitation would be detrimental to the child. *Marriage of James and Claudine W.* (2003) 114 CA4th 68, 7 CR3d 461 (Fam C §3101 was unconstitutionally applied under circumstances). For cases holding a stepparent to be a parent by estoppel, see §8.2.

Grandparents. Grandparents may also petition for visitation with their grandchildren in the following situations:

- A parent is deceased (Fam C §3102);

- A dissolution or other family law proceeding is pending in which child custody is already at issue (Fam C §3103);

- The parents are not married to one another, including after a marital dissolution (see Fam C §3104(b); *Marriage of Harris* (2004) 34 C4th 210, 211–222, 17 CR3d 842); or

- The parents are married but are living separate and apart on a permanent or indefinite basis and meet numerous other statutory criteria. Fam C §3104(b).

Grandparents can petition for visitation under Fam C §3102 when a child whose biological parent is deceased has been adopted by a stepparent or grandparent. Unlike §3104, discussed below, parental unfitness is not an issue in a §3102 petition. *Fenn v Sherriff* (2003) 109 CA4th 1466, 1 CR3d 185. The contrary holding in *Lopez v Martinez* (2000) 85 CA4th 279, 102 CR2d 71 (adoption by stepparent precludes grandparent visitation) is limited to its findings, which were based on §3104, not §3102. 109 CA4th at 1476.

Section 3103 permits a grandparent to petition for visitation if a dissolution or other family law proceeding is pending in which child custody is already at issue. Fam C §3103. In marital dissolution proceedings, grandparents may petition for visitation under Fam C §3103 only until entry of a judgment dissolving the marriage and awarding custody of the child. Thereafter, Fam C §3104 governs grandparent visitation. *Marriage of Harris* (2004) 34 C4th 210, 222, 17 CR3d 842.

A court may order visitation under Fam C §3104 only if it (1) finds that there is a preexisting bond between grandparent and child such that visitation is in the child's best interest and (2) balances the child's interest in visitation against the parents' right to exercise parental authority. Fam C §3104(a). Section 3104 applies if the parents are not married, including after a marital dissolution. It also can apply, however, to married parents if any of the following circumstances exist (Fam C §3104(b)):

- They are living separately and apart on a permanent or indefinite basis;

- One parent has been absent for over a month without the other knowing the whereabouts of the absent parent;

- One parent joins in the petition with the grandparents;

- The child *is not* residing with either parent; or

- The child has been adopted by a stepparent.

If a change of circumstances occurs such that none of the above circumstances exists, one or both parents may move to terminate grandparent visitation, and the court must grant the termination. Fam C §3104(b). See *Marriage of Harris* (2004) 34 C4th 210, 222, 17 CR3d 842.

In *Marriage of Harris,* the California Supreme Court upheld Fam C §3104 as constitutional, both on its face and as applied. *Marriage of Harris* (2004) 34 C4th 210, 226–227, 230, 17 CR3d 842 (construing *Troxel v Granville* (2000) 530 US 57, 147 L Ed 2d 49, 120 S Ct 2054; *Lopez v Martinez* (2000) 85 CA4th 279, 102 CR2d 71). The court construed two specific presumptions found in §3104. One of these, also found in §3103(d), rebuttably presumes that grandparent visitation is not in a child's best interest if the parents agree that the grandparents should not be granted visitation. Fam C §3104(e). The *Harris* majority concluded that this presumption does not apply when one of the parents supports the grandparent's petition for visitation, even if the other opposes it. *Marriage of Harris,* 34 C4th at 221. The other provision, found only in Fam C §3104(f), applies the same rebuttable presumption against grandparent visitation if a parent who has been awarded *sole legal and physical custody* in another proceeding objects to that visitation—the situation that existed in *Harris.* The supreme court held that the trial court erroneously failed to apply this §3104(f) presumption and therefore remanded for reconsideration of the visitation order in light of that presumption. *Marriage of Harris,* 34 C4th at 230. For additional cases on grandparent visitation, see *Marriage of Ross and Kelley* (2003) 114 CA4th 130, 7 CR3d 287; *Zasueta v Zasueta* (2002) 102 CA4th 1242, 126 CR2d 245; *Punsley v Ho* (2001) 87 CA4th 1099, 105 CR2d 139.

Siblings. Under Fam C §3102, sibling visitation may be ordered in certain circumstances. See *Herbst v Swan* (2002) 102 CA4th 813, 125 CR2d 836 (visitation order properly denied).

V. MODIFICATION

§7.59 A. Authority

Child custody and visitation awards are subject to modification for as long as the child is a minor. See Fam C §§3022, 3087–3088. Parents cannot divest the court of its jurisdiction by stipulation. *Marriage of Goodarzirad* (1986) 185 CA3d 1020, 1026, 230 CR 203. Likewise, parents cannot confer jurisdiction on the court by agreement, particularly after a child reaches the age of majority. In general, subject matter jurisdiction cannot be conferred on a court by consent, waiver, or estoppel. *Marriage of Jensen* (2003) 114 CA4th 587, 598, 7 CR3d 701 (court lacked subject matter jurisdiction to order visitation pursuant to parents' marital settlement agreement regarding disabled child who was no longer minor).

NOTE➤ On grounds for *modification* of custody or visitation based on a child (1) being in the legal or physical custody of, or subject to unsupervised visitation with, a person who is required to register as a sex offender for committing a felony against a minor, or (2) having a legal or physical custodian or person who visits the child without supervision who lives with such a registered sex offender, see Fam C §3030.5.

§7.60 B. Change of Circumstances

A substantial change of circumstances since the order was made must generally be shown for the court to modify either a legal or physical custody order. See *Marriage of Carney* (1979) 24 C3d 725, 730, 157 CR 383; *Marriage of McLoren* (1988) 202 CA3d 108, 111, 247 CR 897. A change of circumstances need not be shown, however, when there has been no prior court order, *i.e.,* when the order being made is an initial order rather than a modification of a prior order. *Burchard v Garay* (1986) 42 C3d 531, 535, 229 CR 800. When one parent has had custody for a significant period by agreement without a court order, the noncustodial parent who seeks a change in custody by court order bears the burden of persuading the court that the change is in the child's best interest, but need not first establish a substantial change of circumstances. 42 C3d at 536. See *Ragghanti v Reyes* (2004) 123 CA4th 989, 997, 20 CR3d 522 (court authorized to use "best interest" standard rather than deferring to current custodial parent's presumptive right to move in deciding to transfer custody to father). Similarly, a substantial change in circumstances need not be shown to modify a stipulated custody order that does not clearly indicate that it is final, *i.e.,* when the stipulated custody is temporary in nature, custody may be modified based on the best interest of the child rather than on changed circumstances *and* the child's best interest. *Montenegro v Diaz* (2001) 26 C4th 249, 109 CR2d 575 (changed circumstances test is adjunct to best interest test, applicable whenever final custody was established by judicial decree). See also *Marriage of Rose & Richardson* (2002) 102 CA4th 941, 126 CR2d 45 (when judgment recited that parties would meet with therapist or counselor to resolve custody and visitation issues and would return to Conciliation Court before filing hearing request, order was not intended to be final custody determination). On the best interest standard, see §7.20.

There are two situations in which the change of circumstances requirement does not apply, even when the moving party seeks to modify a court order. First, the rule does not apply when the order being modified is a pendente lite order. *Marriage of Lewin* (1986) 186 CA3d 1482, 1487, 231 CR 433. Second, no change of circumstances is required when there is no change in the "label" given the arrangement (*e.g.,* one party retains sole custody, parties retain joint custody), but merely in the specific times the child spends with each parent. *Marriage of Birnbaum* (1989) 211 CA3d 1508, 1513, 260 CR 210 (parties continued to have joint legal and joint physical custody but schedule of times with respective parents was changed); *Enrique M. v Angelina V.* (2004) 121 CA4th 1371, 18 CR3d 306. In a now-vacated opinion, the Fifth District Court of Appeal declined to follow *Birnbaum,* holding instead that the "change of circumstances" requirement should be preserved in cases involving modification of timeshare arrangements to prevent "never-ending litigation" for parents of a litigious nature who are inclined to "tinker" with their custody schedules. *Marriage of Congdon* (review dismissed Jan. 13, 2000, and remanded to court of appeal; CAVEAT: Cal Rules of Ct 977 restricts citing superseded opinion at 70 CA4th 358 (advance reports), 82 CR2d 686).

Assuming that the change of circumstances requirement either is met or does not apply, the court then has authority to entertain the motion to modify custody, which it evaluates with reference to the same criteria (see §§7.19–7.38) that apply in an initial custody determination. See *Marriage of Rosson* (1986) 178 CA3d 1094, 1102, 1102 n6, 224 CR 250, disapproved on other grounds in *Marriage of Whealon* (1997) 53 CA4th 132, 139, 61 CR2d 559, and overruled on other grounds in *Marriage of Burgess* (1996) 13 C4th 25, 39, 51 CR2d 444. A party is entitled to a court hearing on the facts relating to the alleged change of circumstances, not merely an in-chambers review. *Marriage of Dunn* (2002) 103 CA4th 345, 126 CR2d 636.

In "move-away" cases in which a noncustodial parent seeks to obtain sole physical custody of a child if the custodial parent moves, the "likely consequences of a proposed change in the residence of a child, when considered in the light of all the relevant factors, may constitute a change of circumstances" that would warrant a change in custody. *Marriage of LaMusga* (2004) 32 C4th 1072, 1097, 12 CR3d 356 (clarifying that statement in *Marriage of Edlund & Hales* (1998) 66 CA4th 1454, 1469, 78 CR2d 671, that "changed circumstance" must consist of "more than the proposed move" does not mean that relocation alone cannot constitute detriment). A court may deny a modification request in a law-and-motion hearing that occurs after mediation if the moving party fails to make a prima facie showing that the proposed relocation of the child's residence will cause detriment to the child. *Marriage of Brown & Yana* (2006) 37 C4th 947, 962, 38 CR3d 610.

§7.61 VI. TERMINATION

A custody order terminates when the child reaches age 18 (see Fam C §3022), dies, or becomes emancipated (see Fam C §7050(b)). Under statutory law, a child becomes emancipated when he or she enters into a valid marriage, is on active duty with any of the United

States armed forces, or receives a declaration of emancipation from a California court. Fam C §7002. Additionally, under case law, a court may find that a minor has become emancipated when he or she leaves home and becomes self-supporting. *Marriage of Lehrer* (1976) 63 CA3d 276, 279, 133 CR 709; see Fam C §7001 (Emancipation of Minors Law).

When a custodial parent dies, any custody order made in a marital action terminates. *Guardianship of Donaldson* (1986) 178 CA3d 477, 485, 223 CR 707. The other parent is then immediately entitled to custody. Fam C §3010(b); 178 CA3d at 486.

§7.62　　VII.　CHILDREN'S SURNAMES

On occasion, the court in a marital action may be called on to decide the surname to be given to a minor child. The specific issue may be either (1) the name to be used by the child initially (and the name to be listed on the child's birth certificate) (see *Marriage of Douglass* (1988) 205 CA3d 1046, 252 CR 839) or (2) whether to change a previously given name (see *Marriage of Schiffman* (1980) 28 C3d 640, 169 CR 918).

Whether the issue arises at birth or at some subsequent time, the question is to be decided according to the child's best interest. *Marriage of Douglass* (1988) 205 CA3d 1046, 1054, 252 CR 839. Among the factors the court might consider in determining what surname is in the child's best interest are (1) the length of time the child has used a particular name, (2) the nature of the child's relationships with his or her respective parents, (3) the effect of any proposed name on those relationships, and (4) the child's need to identify with a particular family unit through the use of a common name. *Marriage of Schiffman* (1980) 28 C3d 640, 647, 169 CR 918. See also *Marriage of McManamy & Templeton* (1993) 14 CA4th 607, 18 CR2d 216 (name change reversed for lack of substantial evidence that it would be in child's best interest).

§7.63　　VIII.　TAX ASPECTS

The parent with physical custody (see §7.17) of a child for the greater portion of a tax year is normally entitled to claim the child as a dependent for purposes of the federal tax exemption. IRC §152(e)(1). See *Daniel Aaron Baker*, TC Memo 2006-60 (taxpayer (father) not entitled to claim dependency exemption, child tax credit, or "one qualifying child" earned income tax credit when no custody order was in place, child apparently lived with mother, and no evidence offered that he provided support to child).

The other parent may claim the child as a dependent, however, if, by agreement, the parent with physical custody signs a declaration that he or she will not claim the child as a dependent for the particular year and the other parent attaches copies of the declaration to his or her tax returns. IRC §152(e)(2). The declaration is contained in Internal Revenue Service Form 8332, available from the IRS.

Internal Revenue Code §152(e)(2) provides that a parent may claim a dependency exemption if "a decree of divorce or separate maintenance or written separation agreement between the parents applicable to the taxable year beginning in such calendar year provides that the noncustodial parent shall be entitled to any deduction allowable under IRC §151 for such child, **or** the custodial parent will sign a written declaration (in such manner and form as the Secretary may prescribe) that such parent will not claim such child as a dependent for such taxable year" (emphasis added). IRC §152(e)(2)(A)(i)–(ii). Although not mandatory under that section, IRS Form 8332 *should* be used because it clearly will comply with IRS rules and regulations. See *William C. White,* TC Memo 1996-438 (noncustodial parent's deductions for dependency exemptions disallowed when custodial parent's letter, acknowledging decree awarding exemptions to noncustodial parent and directing custodial parent to execute required documents, deemed not to conform to substance of Form 8332). See also *Miller v Commissioner* (2000) 114 TC 184 (noncustodial father cannot claim dependency exemption awarded to him in dissolution because mother had not executed Form 8332 and dissolution orders attached to his tax return did not conform to substance of Form 8332). But see *Michael K. Boltinghouse,* TC Memo 2003-134 (requirements of IRC §152(e)(2) met when noncustodial father attached separation agreement that granted him dependency exemption to his tax return, although agreement was not incorporated into final divorce decree). It should be noted that the noncustodial parent may continue to claim a dependency exemption for federal tax purposes, in accordance with prior law, under the terms of a decree or agreement executed before January 1, 1985, that awards the exemption to him or her, unless the decree or agreement is modified on or after that date to expressly provide that the new rules apply. IRC §152(e)(4).

California law generally conforms with federal law in this area, with one exception. California has a joint custody head of household credit for parents who have joint physical custody arrangements and do not qualify for the standard head of household status. Rev & T C §17054.5. Internal Revenue Service Form 8332 may be used for California tax purposes.

When parents have joint physical custody (see §7.17) of a child, it is advisable, if possible, for them to agree on which parent will be entitled to claim the child as a dependent for each year and to sign releases accordingly, to avoid future problems with the tax authorities and each other. Depending on the particular circumstances, parents without joint physical custody provisions may also gain from negotiating dependency exemptions and credits. Counsel should consider whether the noncustodial parent would benefit more than the custodial parent from claiming the exemption and credit and, if so, whether any release by the custodial parent should be accompanied by an increase in the amount of child support in order to fairly distribute the resulting benefit between the parents. Note, however, that dependency exemptions are phased out for high-income taxpayers (IRC §151(d)(3)), with the result that in some cases it may not make sense to allocate the exemptions to a higher-income noncustodial parent.

It should also be noted that the court may allocate the dependency exemption and credit to the noncustodial parent, even without an agreement, and order the custodial parent to execute a release. *Monterey County v Cornejo* (1991) 53 C3d 1271, 1280, 283 CR 405, 411. But see *Nancy L. Cafarelli,* TC Memo 1994–265 (when custodial parent executed release for all future years, but not for current year, noncustodial parent could not claim exemption for current year even though court had ordered custodial parent to execute release for that year).

Note that the federal child tax credit under IRC §24 may be claimed only by a parent who is entitled to take a dependency exemption for the child for the same tax year. See IRC §24(c)(1).

For a sample marital settlement agreement form allocating dependency exemptions and credits, and discussion, see California Marital Settlement and Other Family Law Agreements §6.16 (3d ed Cal CEB 2005).

For income tax topics concerning custody of children of registered domestic partners, see California Domestic Partnerships, chap 15 (Cal CEB 2005).

8
Child Support

§8.1 I. SCOPE OF CHAPTER

This chapter covers the subject of child support, with emphasis on the statewide uniform guideline found in Fam C §§4050–4076. A number of related topics are also addressed, including parentage issues, modification and termination of child support orders, and tax aspects of child support. On "expedited support orders," see §11.3.

§8.2 II. AUTHORITY

Whenever the support of a minor child, or an adult child for whom support is authorized under Fam C §3901 or §3910, is at issue, the court may order either or both parents to pay any amount necessary for the child's support. Fam C §4001. A minor child is one under 18 years of age. Fam C §6500.

An adult child for whom support is authorized under Fam C §3901 is one who is an unmarried full-time high school student who is not self-supporting. Support continues until the child completes the 12th grade or attains age 19, whichever occurs first. Fam C §3901(a) (former CC §196.5); *Marriage of Everett* (1990) 220 CA3d 846, 852, 269 CR 917. There is no requirement that a supported child demonstrate a good-faith effort to graduate from high school as soon as possible, nor is a parent's duty of support conditioned on "the child's participation only in those classes that propel her or him toward graduation at the earliest possible date." *Marriage of Hubner* (2001) 94 CA4th 175, 189, 114 CR2d 646.

An adult child for whom support is authorized under Fam C §3910 is one who "is incapacitated from earning a living and without sufficient means." Fam C §3910(a). See *Marriage of Drake* (1997) 53 CA4th 1139, 1154, 62 CR2d 466 (issue of whether child is "without sufficient means" should be resolved in terms of likelihood child will become public charge). See *Jones v Jones* (1986) 179 CA3d 1011, 1013, 225 CR 95 (adult child who is not physically or mentally disabled may not bring action against parent to compel payment for college education).

Support may also be ordered for an adult child by agreement of the parties. Fam C §3587. For further discussion and sample agreements, see California Marital Settlement and Other Family Law Agreements §§7.18–7.20 (3d ed Cal CEB 2005). Note that the Family Code does not include a corollary to Fam C §3587 for child custody of or visitation with an adult child. *Marriage of Jensen* (2003) 114 CA4th 587, 596, 7 CR3d 701.

The parties may not by agreement divest the court of jurisdiction to order child support. *Marriage of Ayo* (1987) 190 CA3d 442, 235 CR 458 (minor child); *Marriage of Lambe & Meehan* (1995) 37 CA4th 388, 44 CR2d 641 (disabled adult child). The parties also may not stipulate to a binding form of alternative dispute resolution that would have the effect of divesting the court of its jurisdiction over child support. *Marriage of Bereznak & Heminger* (2003) 110 CA4th 1062, 2 CR3d 351 (binding arbitration). In addition, public policy prohibits a parent from agreeing to waive or limit a child's right to support. *Kristine M. v David P.* (2006) 135 CA4th 783, 789, 37 CR3d 748. However, parents may stipulate to a support amount that is below the uniform statewide support guideline if certain conditions are met and the court approves the stipulation (see §8.17). Fam C §4065. The court is expressly authorized, on a showing of good cause, to order a parent required to pay child support to provide reasonable security for payment. Fam C §4012. See *Marriage of Drake* (1997) 53 CA4th 1139, 1154, 62 CR2d 466 (concerns about ability of parent's estate to pay child support following parent's death may constitute requisite "good cause"). Note, however, that the court's authority in ordering that security be provided is limited by the requirement that the security be "reasonable." See *Marriage of Johnson* (1982) 134 CA3d 148, 161, 184 CR 444 (lien on party's entire community property share for uncertain duration rejected as "clearly unreasonable"). On the court's authority to order a "child support security deposit" under Fam C §§4550–4573, see §20.58.

In the past, a court normally had no authority to make a child support order against a stepparent in a marital action. In rare instances, however, a stepparent has been estopped to deny child support liability. Estoppel requires that (1) the person represented to the child that he or she was the child's true parent, with the intent that the child rely on the representation; and (2) the child, ignorant of the truth, relied on the representation and treated the person as a parent, giving love and affection to the person. *Clevenger v Clevenger* (1961) 189 CA2d 658, 671, 11 CR 707. See also *Marriage of Pedregon* (2003) 107 CA4th 1284, 132 CR2d 861; *Marriage of Johnson* (1979) 88 CA3d 848, 152 CR 121; *Marriage of Valle* (1975) 53 CA3d 837, 126 CR 38. When estoppel applies, the steppar-ent is deemed a "putative parent" and the court may order the stepparent to pay child support as if he or she were the child's natural parent. See 53 CA3d at 842. On case law regarding parentage and nonmarital partners, see §§8.3–8.5.

Cal Rules of Ct 5.365 establishes procedures for determining primary and subordinate court files in consolidated cases involving child support orders and provides that all filings in these cases after consolidation must be in the primary file.

Child support arrearages are subject to simple interest at the prevailing rate, to be calculated in accordance with CCP §695.221. *Marriage of McClellan* (2005) 130 CA4th 247, 251, 30 CR3d 5; *Marriage of Hubner* (2004) 124 CA4th 1082, 1089, 22 CR3d 549 ("[s]tatutory interest on unpaid child support payments accrues as a matter of law as to each installment when each installment becomes due... whether the judgment clearly states when or if interest will accrue on unpaid child support obligations, and whether or not the payer parent was personally notified unpaid child support would be subject to accruing interest"). For issues concerning child support enforcement and related penalties, see chap 20.

§8.3   III. PARENTAGE ISSUES AND SUPPORT

Although parentage issues more commonly arise in other types of cases, particularly in actions under the Uniform Parentage Act (Fam C §§7600–7730) and in public assistance reimbursement proceedings under Fam C §17402, they do sometimes arise in marital actions. See, *e.g., Groner v Groner* (1972) 23 CA3d 115, 99 CR 765. Historically, as in *Groner,* the issue has arisen when the wife sought a child support order and the husband opposed it by denying paternity. The issue may also arise when the husband seeks a custody or visitation order and the wife opposes it on the basis that the husband is not the child's father.

In the case of sperm donation, pursuant to Fam C §7613, the donor will be excluded as a presumed father even if he had had a prior sexual relationship with the mother and played an ongoing role in the child's life. *Steven S. v Deborah D.* (2005) 127 CA4th 319, 326, 25 CR3d 482.

NOTE▸ The passage of the California Domestic Partner Rights and Responsibilities Act of 2003 (Fam C §§297–299.6), which became operative January 1, 2005, provides at §297.5(d) that "the rights and obligations of registered domestic partners with respect to a child of either of them shall be the same as those of spouses," thereby bringing same-sex couples into the family court arena. Further, during 2005, in a child support case involving a lesbian couple **not** registered as domestic partners under those statutes, the Supreme Court found a woman to be a presumed mother (under Fam C §7611(d)) of twins whose birth mother was her partner. The court found that both women had intended to become parents (using artificial insemination from the same anonymous sperm donor) and held that the woman not biologically related to the children met the criteria of Fam C §7611(d) by receiving the children into her home and openly holding them out as her natural children, and thus was obligated to pay child support to her former partner. *Elisa B. v Superior Court* (2005) 37 C4th 108, 122, 33 CR3d 46. In companion cases, the Supreme Court also issued its opinion in *K.M. v. E.G.* (2005) 37 C4th 130, 144, 33 CR3d 61 and *Kristine H. v Lisa R.* (2005) 37 C4th 156, 162, 33 CR3d 81. While in these cases child custody rather than support was in dispute, the court's finding that the "second mom" was a parent in each of these two cases (involving lesbian couples who became parents by using reproductive technology) is also binding for child support purposes. For further discussion of the "lesbian parentage" cases, see §§7.26, 7.34. On rights of persons under a written "assisted reproduction agreement," see Fam C §§7606, 7620, 7630, 7633.

For comprehensive treatment of the California Domestic Partner Rights and Responsibilities Act of 2003 (Stats 2003, ch 421), effective January 1, 2005, and the implications of domestic partnerships on parental rights and obligations, see California Domestic Partnerships (Cal CEB 2005).

§8.4   A. Conclusive Presumption

When the mother is living with her husband at the time a child is conceived, and the husband is not impotent or sterile, the child is "conclusively presumed" to be the husband's child. Fam C §7540 (former Evid C §621(a)); *City & County of San Francisco v Strahlendorf* (1992) 7 CA4th 1911, 9 CR2d 817. Sterility is defined in the strictest sense, *i.e.,* the exception applies only when the presumed father could not produce live sperm count at the time of conception.

Marriage of Freeman (1996) 45 CA4th 1437, 1449, 53 CR2d 439. Under Fam C §§7550-7557, there is an exception to the conclusive presumption of Fam C §7540. The court can consider blood tests performed under Fam C §7555, along with other credible evidence, to make a finding of nonpaternity. *City & County of San Francisco v Givens* (2000) 85 CA4th 51, 101 CR2d 859. A notice of motion for blood tests must be filed within 2 years after the child's birth. Fam C §7541(b)-(c).

The United States Supreme Court upheld the constitutionality of former Evid C §621 in *Michael H. v Gerald D.* (1989) 491 US 110, 105 L Ed 2d 91, 109 S Ct 2333. The court was extremely divided, however, upholding the conclusive presumption in a five-to-four decision that contained five separate opinions and left open the possibility that the presumption might still be unconstitutional as applied to substantially different facts. The plurality opinion itself expressly left open the possibility that the decision might be different when the husband and wife did not wish to raise the wife's child jointly. 491 US at 129 n7, 105 L Ed 2d at 110 n7. A California court of appeal subsequently distinguished *Michael H.* on that basis, and found the conclusive presumption unconstitutional as applied, in a case in which the marital relationship ended 8 days after the child's birth. *In re Melissa G.* (1989) 213 CA3d 1082, 1088, 261 CR 894.

Later cases challenging the constitutionality of the conclusive presumption have turned on the relationship between the biological father and the child. In *Dawn D.,* the California Supreme Court relied on *Michael H.,* and held that a biological father's "mere desire to establish a personal relationship with the child is not a fundamental liberty interest" protected by due process. *Dawn D. v Superior Court* (1998) 17 C4th 932, 942, 72 CR2d 871. Focusing on the absence of an existing relationship between the biological father and the child, the court held that the biological father did not have a constitutionally protected interest in establishing paternity or in creating a relationship with the child when none existed, and that application of Fam C §§7611 and 7630 did not deprive him of due process. See also *Lisa I.* (2006) 133 CA4th 605, 614, 34 CR3d 927 (application of conclusive presumption proper even when mother's marriage to presumed father ended shortly after birth of child, when relationship to biological father is absent). For another case in which application of the conclusive presumption was upheld, see *Rodney F. v Karen M.* (1998) 61 CA4th 233, 238, 71 CR2d 399. In *Rodney,* a married woman conceived a baby just as she ended an extramarital affair. The man with whom she had the affair brought an action to establish paternity. Blood tests, granted by order of the trial court, showed a 99.5 percent probability of paternity. The trial court's decision to apply the conclusive presumption of paternity for the mother's husband was upheld by the court of appeal, which further held that it was error to grant the purported father's motion for blood tests because he was not a presumed father as defined in Fam C §7611. (The blood tests were not authorized by Fam C §7541 and thus could not overcome the conclusive presumption of paternity.) The court in *Rodney* acknowledged that, in essence, it was creating a "fictional family" but saw itself constrained by precedent and assigned responsibility for change of this policy to the legislature. 61 CA4th at 242. See also *Susan H. v Jack S.* (1994) 30 CA4th 1435, 37 CR2d 120 (conclusively presumed father lived with child and mother as family unit until child was over three years old, and maintained paternal relationship and shared custody after separation). See also *Craig L. v Sandy S.* (2004) 125 CA4th 36, 53, 22 CR3d 606 (biological father had standing to attempt to rebut the presumption that mother's husband was presumed father after he paid child support to mother and agreed with her on a visitation schedule with the child); *Brian C. v Ginger K.* (2000) 77 CA4th 1198, 92 CR2d 294 (unconstitutional to apply conclusive presumption when alleged biological father established parent-child relationship and child not born into "extant marital union"); *Alicia R. v Timothy M.* (1994) 29 CA4th 1232, 1237, 34 CR2d 868 (refusal to apply conclusive presumption proper when "marriage" had been annulled, blood tests established that "husband" was not child's father, and there was no longer a parent-child relationship between "husband" and child); *Comino v Kelley* (1994) 25 CA4th 678, 30 CR2d 728 (affirmed refusal to apply conclusive presumption when marriage was for sake of mutual convenience or economic advantages and child never lived in family unit with mother and her husband); *County of Orange v Leslie B.* (1993) 14 CA4th 976, 17 CR2d 797 (conclusive presumption cannot be applied to protect biological father from child support obligation when mother's marriage ended before child was born and child knows identity of biological father).

Paternity set-asides. In 2004, the legislature amended Fam C

§§7557 and 7634, and added Fam C §§7635.5 and 7645–7649.5. Fam C §§7645–7649.5 empower a court to grant a motion to set aside or vacate a judgment establishing paternity if all of the enumerated conditions are met. Among other things, the moving party must include in the motion information regarding the child, the previously established father and mother, and the biological mother and father of the child; a declaration that the person filing the motion believes that the previously established father is not the biological father of the child, the specific reasons for this belief, and a declaration that the person desires that the motion be granted; and a declaration that the marital presumption set forth in Fam C §7540 does not apply. The time for bringing the motion is described in Fam C §7646(a)(1)–(3).

This legislation was enacted to provide relief for child support payers who were precluded from presenting evidence of nonpaternity to the court once the 2-year statute of limitations provided by Fam C §7541 or the 6-month deadline for rescinding a voluntary declaration of paternity had expired.

Family Code §7658 provides that, even if the moving party can prove the previously established father is not the biological father, the court may deny the motion to vacate the paternity judgment if it determines that denial of the motion is in the best interest of the child, after considering: the age of the child; the length of time since the entry of the judgment establishing paternity; the nature, duration, and quality of any relationship between the previously established father and the child, including the duration and frequency of any time periods during which the child and the previously established father resided in the same household or enjoyed a parent-child relationship; the request of the previously established father that the parent-child relationship continue; notice by the biological father of the child that he does not oppose preservation of the relationship between the previously established father and the child; the benefit or detriment to the child in establishing the biological parentage of the child; whether the conduct of the previously established father has impaired the ability to ascertain the identity of, or get support from, the biological father; and additional factors deemed by the court to be relevant to its determination of the best interest of the child.

The Judicial Council has produced a series of forms for such set-aside actions:

- FL-272: Notice of Motion to Set Aside Judgment of Paternity;

- FL-273: Declaration in Support of Motion to Set Aside Judgment of Paternity;

- FL-274: Information Sheet for Completing Notice of Motion to Set Aside Judgment of Paternity;

- FL-276: Response to Notice of Motion to Set Aside Judgment of Paternity;

- FL-278: Order After Hearing on Motion to Set Aside Judgment of Paternity.

All of these forms are available in California Judicial Council Forms Manual §3 (Cal CEB 1981).

Family Code §7648.3 prohibits the court from setting aside or vacating a paternity judgment that was issued by a tribunal of another state or that was entered in California, and genetic tests were conducted prior to entry of the judgment that did not exclude the previously established father as the child's biological father. Family Code §7648.8 makes it clear that the procedure described here does not apply to adoptions, nor can it be used for setting aside or vacating a paternity judgment relating to a child conceived by artificial insemination pursuant to Fam C §7613 or pursuant to a surrogacy agreement. (Fam C §7648.9).

NOTE➤ The passage of this legislation effectively provided a window of amnesty for child support obligors who were previously unable to contest paternity judgments because too much time had passed since the birth of the child. While the legislation will prospectively aid victims of paternity fraud or mistaken identification, existing "previously established" fathers were required to act on or before December 31, 2006. Fam C §7646(a)(3).

Note that all hospitals must participate in the establishment of paternity by providing voluntary declarations of paternity to unmarried parents before the mother leaves the hospital after giving birth. Fam C §§7570–7577. On procedures for setting aside voluntary declarations of paternity when no previous action has been filed, see Cal Rules of Ct 5.350.

§8.5   B. Rebuttable Presumption

There is a rebuttable presumption of paternity whenever an alleged father meets the requirements of Fam C §7611, which may be met in any one of the following six ways:

- He and the child's natural mother are or have been married to each other and the child is born during the marriage or within 300 days after the marriage is terminated (Fam C §7611(a));

- He and the child's natural mother have attempted to marry each other before the child's birth by a marriage solemnized in apparent compliance with law but that is or could be declared invalid and either (1) if the marriage is voidable (see §§3.10–3.15), the child is born during the marriage or within 300 days after its termination or (2) if the marriage is void (see §§3.8–3.9), the child is born within 300 days after cohabitation terminates (Fam C §7611(b));

- He and the child's natural mother have, after the child's birth, married each other, or attempted to marry each other by a marriage solemnized in apparent compliance with law but that is or could be declared invalid, and either (1) the alleged father, with his consent, is named as the father on the child's birth certificate; or (2) the alleged father is obligated to support the child under a written voluntary promise or by court order (Fam C §7611(c));

- He receives the child into his home and openly holds out the child as his natural child (Fam C §7611(d)) (for a case applying this subsection, see *In re Spencer W.* (1996) 48 CA4th 1647, 56 CR2d 524), *Librers v Black* (2005) 129 CA4th 114, 126, 28 CR3d 188 for cases applying this subsection to a presumption of maternity, see *In re Salvador M.* (2003) 111 CA4th 1353, 1359, 4 CR3d 705; *Elisa B. v Superior Court* (2005) 37 C4th 108, 122, 33 CR3d 46.

- The child was born and resides in a nation with which the United States engages in an Orderly Departure Program or successor program and the alleged father acknowledges that he is the child's father in a declaration under penalty of perjury (Fam C §7611(e)); or

- The child was conceived after the death of a parent (other than by human cloning), and the conditions set forth in Prob C §249.5 are satisfied (Fam C §7611(f)).

A presumption under Fam C §7611 is a rebuttable presumption affecting the burden of proof and may be rebutted only by clear and convincing evidence. Fam C §7612(a).

Until recently, the California Supreme Court did not have to consider whether, under Fam C §7612, biological paternity by a competing presumptive father necessarily defeated a nonbiological father's presumption of paternity. *In re Nicholas H.* (2002) 28 C4th 56, 70, 120 CR2d 146 (when no other man claims fatherhood, man does not lose status of presumed father by admitting he is not biological father). In *In re Jesusa V.* (2004) 32 C4th 588, 10 CR3d 205, the court determined that when two men qualify as presumptive father, biological paternity will not necessarily trump a competing claim of paternity. The court's analysis of legislative intent and its articulation that the Fam C §7611 presumption may be rebutted in an "appropriate" action indicated that the legislature did not intend to create an automatic preference for biological fathers. This analysis was clarified in *Elisa B. v Superior Court* (2005) 37 C4th 108, 122, 33 CR3d 46. The Supreme Court cited the Uniform Parentage Act ("UPA"), which provides that "provisions applicable to determine a father and child relationship shall be used to determine a mother and child relationship '[I]nsofar as practicable.'" Fam C §7650. It had earlier decided that "a child can have two parents, both of whom are women," citing its decision in *Sharon S. v Superior Court* (2003) 31 C4th 417, 2 CR3d 699.

§8.6 C. Order for Genetic Tests

A court is authorized to order genetic tests in any civil action in which paternity is a relevant fact. Uniform Act on Blood Tests To Determine Paternity (Fam C §§7550–7557; Fam C §7551). Only the mother, child, and alleged father can be compelled to submit to the genetic tests in a civil action involving paternity. Fam C §7551; CCP §2032.010(a). See *William M. v Superior Court* (1990) 225 CA3d 447, 275 CR 103 (parents of deceased putative father held not to be proper parties to paternity action and, thus, could not be compelled to submit to blood tests).

§8.6A   1. Paternity Must Be Relevant Fact

Whenever paternity is at issue, the court *may*, on its own motion or on a suggestion made by or on behalf of any person who is involved, order a mother, child, and alleged father to submit to genetic tests. When a party files a motion for genetic tests at a time when the proceedings will not be unduly delayed, the court *must* make the order. However, see *Rodney F. v Karen M.* (1998) 61 CA4th 233, 71 CR2d 399 (error to grant purported father's motion for blood tests in his paternity action because he was not the presumed father as defined in Fam C §7611; although blood tests showed high probability that married woman's boyfriend was the father, blood tests were not authorized by Fam C §7541 and thus could not overcome conclusive presumption of paternity).

The requirement that paternity is a relevant fact does not apply to cases in which paternity has previously been established and that prior finding is entitled to res judicata of fact. *Brown v Superior Court* (1979) 98 CA3d 633, 159 CR 604. Courts have specifically refused to reopen earlier paternity determinations to permit retesting by newer and more accurate methods. See, *e.g.*, *De Weese v Unick* (1980) 102 CA3d 100, 162 CR 259.

If the results of a genetic test meet the requirements of Fam C §7555, there is a rebuttable presumption of paternity. Fam C §7555. Even if the test results do not create a presumption of paternity, the results may still be admissible to prove paternity affirmatively. See *Cramer v Morrison* (1979) 88 CA3d 873, 153 CR 865 (interpreting former Evid C §985; now Fam C §7554).

On sanctions for noncompliance, see §8.6E.

§8.6B   2. Tests Not Required in Certain Cases

The statute does not apply to *probate* proceedings when a child alleged to be born out of wedlock is seeking genetic tests of the surviving mother, who is not a party to the action. See *Estate of Sanders* (1992) 2 CA4th 462, 468, 3 CR2d 536. The court in *Sanders* also rejected the argument that Prob C §1000 requires application of CCP §§2032.010–2032.650. Thus, DNA testing will not be required of the children of the deceased in a probate proceeding to determine parentage of a child who claims that the deceased was the natural father. 2 CA4th at 474.

Parents, as representatives of their son's estate, cannot be compelled to submit to a blood test to determine whether their deceased son was the father of the child in a paternity suit. *William M. v Superior Court* (1990) 225 CA3d 447, 275 CR 103 (discovery properly denied because decedent's parents were not proper defendants in paternity action).

NOTE➤ Probate Code §1000 states that the rules of practice applicable to civil actions, including discovery proceedings, also apply to proceedings under the Probate Code, unless the code specifies otherwise.

§8.6C   3. Testimony of Examiners

The party or person at whose suggestion the tests have been ordered may demand that additional qualified experts perform independent tests under order of court. Fam C §7552 (former Evid C §893). In addition, any party may produce other expert evidence on paternity. Experts called by a party must be compensated by the party, and only ordinary witness fees may be taxed as costs for their services. Fam C §7557 (former Evid C §897).

Experts appointed to conduct genetic tests must be called by the court as witnesses to testify to their findings and are subject to cross-examination by the parties. Fam C §7552 (former Evid C §893). It is unclear whether this requirement also applies to additional experts appointed at the demand of a party or other affected person. The test results of these additional experts may, however, be offered in evidence. Fam C §7552 (former Evid C §893).

§8.6D   4. Appointment of Examiners

The court ordering the tests will name the examiners, determine the number and qualifications of any additional examiners demanded by a party or other affected person, and set the rate of compensation. Fam C §§7552-7553 (former Evid C §§893-894). The court must perform these functions; it cannot simply rely on a party to arrange the examination. See *Michael B. v Superior Court* (1978) 86 CA3d 1006, 150 CR 586.

NOTE➤ The qualifications for examiners set forth in CCP §2032.020(b) do *not* apply to tests performed under Fam C §§7550-7557.

The compensation of each expert ordered by the court must be fixed at a reasonable amount and paid as the court orders. The court may apportion compensation between the parties or between the parties and the county and may order any portion or all of the compensation taxed as costs in the action. Fam C §7553 (former Evid C §894). Because the test results may be key to the defense in a paternity action, the court cannot condition the examination on an indigent's advance payment of examination expenses. *Michael B. v Superior Court, supra.*

Experts who have not conducted a genetic examination under order of the court but who have been called by a party to the proceedings must be compensated by the party calling them. Fam C §7557 (former Evid C §897).

§8.6E   5. Sanctions for Noncompliance

The Uniform Act on Blood Tests To Determine Paternity (Fam C §§7550–7557) contains its own sanctions for noncompliance. If a party refuses to submit to a test, the court may either resolve the issue of paternity against the person who refuses or "enforce its order if the rights of others and interests of justice so require." A party's refusal is itself admissible in evidence in a proceeding to determine paternity. Fam C §7551. See, *e.g., County of El Dorado v Schneider* (1987) 191 CA3d 1263, 1266, 237 CR 51 (constitutional rights of alleged father who refused to submit to blood tests not violated when court invoked former Evid C §892 and resolved paternity issue against him).

§8.7   IV. STATEWIDE UNIFORM GUIDELINES

Family Code §§4050–4076 provide a statewide uniform guideline for making child support awards. The steps to be carried out by the court in each case in implementing the guideline are as follows:

- Calculating a formula amount that is rebuttably presumed to be the correct amount. See §§8.8–8.15.

- Considering specified factors on which rebuttal of the presumption may be based and, when the presumption is rebutted, adjustment of the child support amount accordingly. See §§8.16–8.21.

- Considering specified expenses related to child support and, when appropriate, increasing the child support amount in light of such expenses. See §§8.23–8.25.

- Making appropriate adjustments, if any, to accommodate seasonal or fluctuating income of either parent. See §8.26.

In most cases, the child support order must allocate the support amount so that the amount for the youngest child is the amount of support for one child, the amount for the next youngest child is the difference between the amount for one child and the amount for two children, and so forth. Such an allocation is not required, however, when there are different time-sharing arrangements for different children or when the court determines that it would be inappropriate. Fam C §4055(b)(8).

In some instances in which the court modifies a child support order issued before July 1, 1992, the effective date of the statewide uniform guidelines, it may order a two-step phase-in of the new support amount. Fam C §4076; see §8.32.

Note that the statewide uniform guideline applies to support for an adult child for whom support is authorized under Fam C §3910 (adult child who is incapacitated from earning living and without sufficient means) (see §8.2). *Marriage of Drake* (1997) 53 CA4th 1139, 1155, 62 CR2d 466.

§8.8 A. Calculation of Guideline Formula Amount

The statewide guideline provides a formula for a tentative child support amount in each case. That amount depends on (1) the parents' respective net monthly disposable incomes (see §§8.9–8.11), (2) the number of children for whom support is being determined, and (3) the parents' respective periods of primary physical responsibility for the children (see §8.12). Once these factors are known, the formula amount is determined by applying the formula to them. See §8.13.

1. Preliminary Determinations

§8.9 a. Net Monthly Disposable Income

The statewide guideline directs the court to calculate net monthly disposable income by ascertaining annual gross income, applying specified deductions to arrive at net annual disposable income, and dividing by 12 to obtain the monthly figure. Fam C §§4059–4060.

If the monthly figure does not accurately reflect the actual or prospective earnings of a party at the time the support determination is made, the court may adjust the amount appropriately. Fam C §4060.

§8.10   (1) Gross Income

Items included in gross income. Under the statewide guideline, gross income includes income from any source except income derived from (1) child support payments actually received or (2) any public assistance program for which eligibility is based on need. Fam C §4058(a), (c). One court of appeal decided the exception listed in (c) includes Supplemental Security Income (SSI) benefits, resolving "[t]he apparent conflict between subdivisions (a)(1) and (c) of Fam C §4058. . . by construing subdivision (c) to include SSI benefits within the exception precluding courts from considering 'income derived from any public assistance program, eligibility for which is based on a determination of need.'" *Elsenheimer v Elsenheimer* (2004) 124 CA4th 1532, 1541, 22 CR3d 447. In addition, at least one court has held that spousal support payments received from a party to the child support proceeding are implicitly excluded. *Marriage of Corman* (1997) 59 CA4th 1492, 69 CR2d 880. Gross income includes, but is not limited to, the following:

- Income such as commissions, salaries, royalties, wages, bonuses, rents, dividends, pensions, interest, trust income, annuities, workers' compensation benefits, unemployment insurance benefits, disability insurance benefits, social security benefits, and spousal support actually received from a person not a party to the order at issue (Fam C §4058(a)(1));

- Income from the proprietorship of a business, *i.e.,* gross receipts less required expenditures (Fam C §4058(a)(2)); and

- In the court's discretion, employee benefits or self-employment benefits, taking into consideration the benefit to the employee or self-employed person, any corresponding reduction in living expenses, and other relevant facts (Fam C §4058(a)(3)). (Note that although a party's inheritance is not income under Fam C §4058(a)(1), a court may consider it as a "corresponding reduction in living expenses" under §4058(a)(3); see *County of Kern v Castle* (1999) 75 CA4th 1442, 89 CR2d 874 (support obligor used inheritance to pay off mortgage and thus reduced living expenses); but see *Marriage of Loh* (2001) 93 CA4th 325, 331, 112 CR2d 893. And an increased, unrealized equity value in obligor spouse's residence is not to be calculated as income in child support modification proceeding. *Marriage of Henry* (2005) 126 CA4th 111, 118, 23 CR3d 707.

List is illustrative, not exclusive. This approach to defining gross income, including the list of items, is based on that in former CC §4721. Note that the list is expressly made illustrative rather than exclusive ("includes, but is not limited to"). Fam C §4058(a); see *County of Contra Costa v Lemon* (1988) 205 CA3d 683, 688, 252 CR 455 (lottery winnings includable in gross income under former CC §4721 although statute did not specifically list them). See *Marriage of Kerr* (1999) 77 CA4th 87, 95, 91 CR2d 374 (trial court properly used unexercised stock options for spousal and child support but erred in awarding percentage amounts beyond marital standard of living or children's needs). See also *Stewart v Gomez* (1996) 47 CA4th 1748, 1754, 1755, 55 CR2d 531 (rental value of payer's rent-free housing; payer's meal allowance); but see *In re Loh* (2001) 93 CA4th 325, 334, 112 CR2d 893 (criticizing *Stewart*'s "anything that reduces living expenses is income" approach as out of step with basic child support statutes and suggesting that such benefits be considered as basis for adjustment under Fam C §4057).

In *Marriage of Rocha* (1998) 68 CA4th 514, 80 CR2d 376, the court of appeal reversed the trial court's inclusion of student loan proceeds not used for books and tuition, noting that the obligation of repayment distinguishes loan proceeds from other Fam C §4058 sources of income. Life insurance death benefits also are not within the scope of gross income as defined by §4058, but income earned on the benefits is. *Marriage of Scheppers* (2001) 86 CA4th 646, 103 CR2d 529. But see *County of Placer v Andrade* (1997) 55 CA4th 1393, 64 CR2d 739 (past bonus and overtime payments may be excluded from income calculation only if payer is unlikely to receive them in future). A lump-sum personal injury award that is not differentiated among the various elements of damages (*i.e.,* medical expenses, pain and suffering, lost wages) is not gross income for purposes of child support calculation. *Marriage of Heiner* (2006) 136 CA4th 1514, 1524, 39 CR3d 730 (decision to include damages in calculation of parent's income is fact-driven determination best left to trial court's discretion). Also not to be treated as gross income is unliquidated, but marketable, stock received by a business owner in connection with the sale of a business, although the court has discretion to attribute a rate of return to non-income producing assets, including unsold stock available for sale. *Marriage of Perlstein* (2006) 137 CA4th 1361, 1375, 40 CR3d 910.

Counsel, particularly when representing the support recipient, must be very careful about investigating and ascertaining the opposing party's gross income. When, for example, the support payer is doing business in a sole proprietorship or a partnership, it is essential to scrutinize Schedule C on his or her income tax return and to inquire about the reasonableness of certain claimed business expenses, *e.g.,* entertainment, travel, outside services, depreciation.

When a support obligor has refused to cooperate with discovery requests or the court believes a party has committed perjury on the income and expense declarations provided, it may rely on other evidence, such as mortgage applications, to determine that party's income. See *Marriage of Calcaterra and Badakhsh* (2005) 132 CA4th 28, 33 CR3d 246; *Marriage of Chakko* (2004) 115 CA4th 104, 8 CR3d 699.

Parent's earning capacity. The court may, in its discretion and consistent with the children's best interests, consider a parent's earning capacity instead of his or her actual income. Fam C §4058(b). This provision is based on one in former CC §4721. See *Marriage of Kepley* (1987) 193 CA3d 946, 953, 238 CR 691 (former CC §4721 required court to consider earning capacity of either parent to extent needs of children did not require parent to remain at home). Note that, when the court does consider earning capacity instead of actual income, it is only actual *earned* income that is *replaced* by earning capacity; the court may consider *both* earning capacity and actual *unearned* income, and add the two items together. *Stewart v Gomez* (1996) 47 CA4th 1748, 1752, 55 CR2d 531 (court properly added earning capacity and disability income in determining payer's gross income under Fam C §4058). See also *Marriage of Cheriton* (2001) 92 CA4th 269, 111 CR2d 755 (court must make express or implied finding that imputing earning capacity to parent is in children's best interest).

In *Marriage of Regnery* (1989) 214 CA3d 1367, 263 CR 243, the court of appeal held that when the supporting party has the ability and the opportunity to earn more than he or she is earning, but is unwilling to do so, the court may apply an earning-capacity standard to deter that party's shirking of family obligations. Compare

Regnery with *Marriage of Everett* (1990) 220 CA3d 846, 269 CR 917, which affirmed a refusal to impute additional income to the support payer, despite evidence of his substantially higher income years before in the same profession, based on the payer's sincere efforts to make a success of his business and pay child support and on concern that a higher order might not be in the children's best interests. See also *State of Oregon v Vargas* (1999) 70 CA4th 1123, 83 CR2d 229 (court must use actual income rather than earning capacity standard when payer lacks opportunity or ability to work; payer's status as prison inmate not inevitable bar to earning capacity). The earning capacity test set forth in *Vargas* applies regardless of the nature of the offense for which the noncustodial parent is incarcerated. *Marriage of Smith* (2001) 90 CA4th 74, 108 CR2d 537.

For other cases discussing the earning capacity standard, see:

- *Marriage of Eggers* (2005) 131 CA4th 695, 32 CR3d 292 (improper to impute income to parent terminated from employment for misconduct without first providing opportunity to present proof of ability or opportunity to work);

- *Marriage of Reynolds* (1998) 63 CA4th 1373, 74 CR2d 636 (68-year-old payer could not be compelled to work after usual retirement age of 65 in order to maintain level of spousal support he was paying while working);

- *Marriage of LaBass & Munsee* (1997) 56 CA4th 1331, 66 CR2d 393 (parent who shows other parent had ability and opportunity to work full-time but was unwilling to do so need not show that other parent would actually secure work if he or she sought it);

- *Marriage of Hinman* (1997) 55 CA4th 988, 64 CR2d 383 (payer's motive for reducing income irrelevant; decision must be based on whether payer has ability and opportunity to work and whether considering earning capacity would be in best interests of children for whom support is sought);

- *Marriage of Paulin* (1996) 46 CA4th 1378, 1383, 54 CR2d 314 (affirmed imputing of income from previous employment when party left employment voluntarily and did not document efforts to find other employment);

- *Marriage of Padilla* (1995) 38 CA4th 1212, 1218, 45 CR2d

555 (payer's motivation for reducing available income irrelevant when ability and opportunity to adequately and reasonably provide for child are present);

- *Marriage of Ilas* (1993) 12 CA4th 1630, 16 CR2d 345 (affirmed refusal to reduce spousal and child support when payer quit job as pharmacist to become full-time medical student and payee was unemployed);

- *Marriage of Meegan* (1992) 11 CA4th 156, 13 CR2d 799 (affirmed reduction of spousal support to zero when payer who quit job to take residence at monastery and prepare for priesthood acted in good faith and payee would suffer only minimal reduction in living standard).

A determination of the supporting party's earning capacity should not be based, however, on an extraordinary work regimen, even if engaged in by the supporting spouse during the marriage. Rather, the determination should be based on an "objectively reasonable work regimen" as it would exist at the time the support determination is made. *Marriage of Simpson* (1992) 4 C4th 225, 234, 14 CR2d 411.

Earning capacity of parent's investment assets. Under Fam C §4058, the trial court may consider the earning capacity of a parent's investment assets when setting support. See *Marriage of Cheriton* (2001) 92 CA4th 269, 111 CR2d 755; *Marriage of Destein* (2001) 91 CA4th 1385, 111 CR2d 487. When computing support, the court can attribute a reasonable rate of return to these investment assets, even if they had previously been non-income-producing (*Destein*), and may consider a parent's wealth (*Cheriton*). See also *Marriage of De Guigne* (2002) 97 CA4th 1353, 1362, 119 CR2d 430 (when nonworking parents financed family's lifestyle in part by liquidating husband's assets, proper to consider all husband's assets, including separate property mansion surrounded by 47 acres of undeveloped land in determining his earning capacity); *Marriage of Dacumos* (1999) 76 CA4th 150, 154, 90 CR2d 159 (income imputed to child support payer from rental property rented at below-market value); *Marriage of Cohn* (1998) 65 CA4th 923, 76 CR2d 866 (income imputable to self-employed party with substantial likelihood of producing income with reasonable effort, but amount imputed must have some tangible evidentiary foundation). But see *Marriage of Henry*

(2005) 126 CA4th 111, 23 CR3d 707 (court declined to count increased, unrealized equity value in obligor spouse's residence as income in determining child support).

§8.11 (2) Deductions from Gross Income

After each parent's gross income is ascertained (see §8.10), his or her net disposable income is calculated by deducting from gross income the actual amounts attributable to the following items:

- **State and federal income taxes.** The deductions must bear an accurate relationship to the parent's tax status (*i.e.*, single, married filing jointly, married filing separately, or head of household) and the number of dependents. Amounts deducted must be taxes actually payable (not necessarily the amounts currently withheld), after considering appropriate filing status and all available exclusions, deductions, and credits. Unless the parties stipulate otherwise, the tax effects of spousal support ordered in the present case must not be considered in determining net disposable income for child support purposes, although they must, consistent with Fam C §§4330–4339 (see §6.10), be considered in determining spousal support. Fam C §4059(a) (former CC §4721(g)(1)). Note that taxes may not be deducted from gross income unless they are actually being paid. See *Marriage of McQuoid* (1991) 9 CA4th 1353, 12 CR2d 737. Note also that Fam C §4057.5, which generally precludes consideration of income of a subsequent spouse or nonmarital partner in the determination of child support (see §8.22), does not prohibit consideration of such income in determining a parent's actual tax liability for purposes of allowable deductions from gross income. *County of Tulare v Campbell* (1996) 50 CA4th 847, 57 CR2d 902.

- Contributions under the Federal Insurance Contributions Act (FICA) (IRC §§3101–3128). A party not subject to FICA may deduct, to the extent of his or her actual contributions to secure retirement or disability benefits, the amount that would be deducted under FICA if he or she were subject to it. Fam C §4059(b).

- Deductions for union dues and retirement benefits, when they are required as a condition of employment. Fam C §4059(c).

- Deductions for health insurance or health plan premiums for the parent, and for any children the parent has an obligation to support, and deductions for state disability insurance premiums. Fam C §4059(d).

- Any child or spousal support actually being paid under a court order to, or for the benefit of, anyone whose support is not a subject of the present case. Child support actually being paid without a court order may also be deducted, to the extent it does not exceed the amount established by the statewide guideline, as long as the support is for a natural or adopted child who does not reside in the paying parent's home, who is not a subject of the order to be established by the court, and for whom the paying parent has a duty of support. The parent claiming the deduction must prove that the support is actually being paid. Fam C §4059(e).

- Job-related expenses, to the extent allowed by the court after consideration of whether the expenses are necessary, the benefit to the employee, and other relevant facts. Fam C §4059(f).

- A deduction for hardship, as defined by Fam C §§4070–4073 and applicable published appellate decisions. Fam C §4059(g).

Under Fam C §§4070–4073, hardship deductions are allowed for:

- Extraordinary health expenses for which the parent is financially responsible. Fam C §4071(a)(1).

- Uninsured catastrophic losses. Fam C §4071(a)(1).

- Minimum basic living expenses of the parent's natural or adopted children from other marriages or relationships who reside with the parent and whom the parent has the obligation to support. Fam C §4071(a)(2). Family Code §§4070–4073 do not provide a hardship deduction for stepchildren. *Haggard v Haggard* (1995) 38 CA4th 1566, 45 CR2d 638. A hardship deduction based on minimum basic living expenses of one or more stepchildren must be allowed, however, when income of the stepparent's subsequent spouse or nonmarital partner is allowed to be considered, under Fam C §4057.5, in determining child support. Fam C §4057.5(d); see §8.22.

Only the expenses specifically enumerated in Fam C §4071 (*i.e.*, extraordinary health expenses, uninsured catastrophic losses, living expenses of children from other marriages or relationships residing with the parent) can be allowed as hardship deductions. *Marriage of Butler & Gill* (1997) 53 CA4th 462, 465, 61 CR2d 781 (support of parent not included).

Granting of a hardship deduction is not automatic. The parent must be "experiencing extreme financial hardship" as a result of justifiable expenses of the kinds specifically allowable as hardship deductions. Whether to grant a hardship deduction, as well as the amount of such a deduction, is discretionary. See *Marriage of Paulin* (1996) 46 CA4th 1378, 54 CR2d 314 (affirmed trial court's setting of hardship deduction for expenses of father's other children at one half of computer-calculated amount).

Family Code §§4070–4073 provide that the maximum hardship deduction for each child from another relationship who resides with the parent may not exceed the support allocated each child for whom support is being established. For purposes of calculating the deduction, the amount of support per child established by the statewide guideline will be the total amount ordered, divided by the number of children, and not the unequal amounts per child established under Fam C §4055(b)(8). Fam C §4071(b).

The legislature has directed the Judicial Council to develop a formula for calculating the maximum hardship deduction and submit it to the legislature for its consideration on or before July 1, 1995. Fam C §4059(g). To date, however, no such formula has been adopted.

If deductions for hardship expenses are allowed, the court must, in writing or on the record, state the reasons supporting the deductions; document the underlying facts and circumstances; specify the amount of deductions allowed; and, whenever possible, specify the period during which any deduction will be in effect. Fam C §4072; *Marriage of Carlsen* (1996) 50 CA4th 212, 57 CR2d 630 (allowance of hardship deduction reversed for prejudicial failure to make required findings). Any hardship deduction is from the income of the parent to whom it applies, not from the amount of child support to be paid. Fam C §4059(g).

§8.12 b. Respective Periods of Primary Physical Responsibility for Children

A factor to be decided before the guideline formula amount may be calculated is the approximate respective periods of time in which each parent has primary physical responsibility for the children. See Fam C §4055(a), (b)(1)(D). Although there is no universal approach in determining the approximate respective periods of primary physical responsibility, it appears that judges often look at the distribution of overnights between the parents. See *Marriage of Whealon* (1997) 53 CA4th 132, 145, 61 CR2d 559 (appropriate to give custodial parent, in effect, credit for time child spends in day care because custodial parent finds, arranges, and advances money for day care, delivers and picks up child, and suffers employment disruptions for, *e.g.,* illness). See also *DaSilva v DaSilva* (2004) 119 CA4th 1030, 15 CR3d 59 (when father was partially responsible for child during school hours, trial court erred in calculating timeshare solely on his awarded hours of physical custody). When the parents have different time-sharing arrangements for different children, the approximate percentage of time with each parent, for purposes of the formula, is the average of the approximate percentages of time the parent spends with the individual children. Fam C §4055(b)(1)(D).

In any default proceeding in which proof is by declaration under Fam C §2336, or in any child support proceeding in which a party fails to appear after valid notice, the portion of time that the noncustodial parent has primary physical responsibility for the children is deemed to be zero when there is no evidence presented that demonstrates the percentage of time that the noncustodial parent has primary physical responsibility. The noncustodial parent's portion of time with primary physical responsibility is not deemed to be zero, however, when the moving party in the default proceeding is the noncustodial parent or the nonappearing but duly noticed party is the custodial parent. A statement by the party not in default regarding the percentage of time the noncustodial parent has primary physical responsibility will be deemed sufficient evidence. Fam C §4055(b)(6).

§8.13   2. Application of Formula

After the net monthly disposable income (see §§8.9–8.11) has been calculated for each parent, the formula in Fam C §4055(a)-(b) is applied. See *Marriage of Whealon* (1997) 53 CA4th 132, 144, 61 CR2d 559 (reversed trial court that ran computation based on erroneous timeshare figures and then estimated result based on correct figures to avoid rerunning computation). As a practical matter, attorneys and courts apply the formula through a variety of tables, computers, and calculators. For Judicial Council standards for computer software used in support determinations, see Cal Rules of Ct 5.275, adopted under Fam C §3830. Nevertheless, it may be helpful for the practitioner to understand conceptually how the formula works. Counsel may thus be able, for example, to argue more effectively for or against the presumption that the formula amount is the correct amount.

The result produced by the formula depends on the parents' disposable incomes (see §§8.9–8.11), the number of children for whom support is being determined, and the parents' respective periods of primary physical responsibility for the children (see §8.12). Basically, the formula assigns a percentage of the parents' net monthly disposable income that is to be allocated for the children's support and then arrives at the child support amount required so that the particular percentage of each parent's income is contributed. Each parent is deemed (1) to be providing the required amount of support directly during the periods when he or she has primary physical responsibility for the children and (2) to owe the required amount of support to the other parent for the remaining periods. The respective amounts owed by each parent to the other are then, in effect, offset against one another, resulting in a single child support amount payable by one parent to the other.

The formula's approach may be illustrated by use of an example:

Assume that the parties have two children, that the noncustodial parent (NCP) has a net monthly disposable income (NDI) of $3000, and that the custodial parent (CP) has a net monthly disposable income of $1000. Thus, the noncustodial parent has 75 percent of the combined net monthly disposable income ($3000 ÷ $4000) and the custodial parent has 25 percent ($1000 ÷ $4000). Assume further that the custodial parent has primary physical responsibility for the children 80 percent of the time and that the noncustodial parent has primary physical responsibility 20 percent of the time.

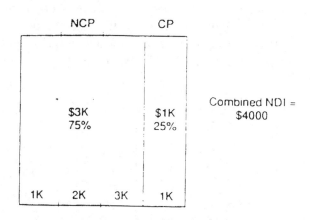

The total support amount to be made available for the children by the parents combined is calculated by taking a particular percentage of the parents' combined disposable income. The applicable percentage depends on (1) the parents' combined disposable income, (2) the respective periods in which each has primary physical responsibility for the children, and (3) the number of children subject to the order. For parents with a combined disposable income of $800 per month or less, the applicable percentage increases as the combined income increases. The percentage is the same for all parents between $801 and $6666 per month. For parents above $6666, the percentage decreases as the combined income increases. The applicable percentage increases as the respective periods of primary physical responsibility become more equal (*i.e.*, as the primary physical responsibility time of the "noncustodial parent" increases) and as the number of children subject to the order increases. To find the percentage to be applied in a given case, first ascertain the percentage applicable for one child (*i.e.*, "K"), given the parents' particular income range and their respective periods of primary physical responsibility, by reference to Fam C §4055(b)(3). Then, if there is more than one child, multiply by the applicable factor by referring to Fam C §4055(b)(4).

In this example, the parents' total net disposable income per month is $4000 and the high earner's approximate percentage of primary physical responsibility time (*i.e.*, 20 percent), expressed as a decimal, is 0.2. Thus K is $(1 + 0.2) \times 0.25$, or 0.3. The applicable factor for two children is 1.6. Therefore, the percentage of each parent's disposable income to be allocated for child support, expressed as a decimal, is 0.3 × 1.6, or 0.48. Because the parents' total disposable income is $4000, the amount to be allocated for child support by the parents combined is 0.48 × $4000, or $1920.

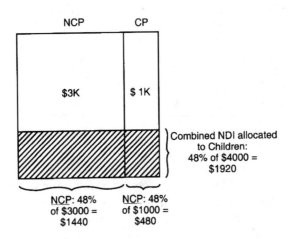

The amount of time in which each parent has primary physical responsibility is then factored in again. As indicated above, each parent is deemed in effect to be providing child support when he or she has primary physical responsibility for the children and pays child support to the other parent for the times that the other parent has primary physical responsibility.

In our example, the custodial parent has primary physical responsibility for the children 80 percent of the time and the noncustodial parent has primary physical responsibility 20 percent of the time. The support amount to be provided by the parents combined during the 80 percent of the time that the custodial parent has primary physical responsibility for the children is 80 percent of $1920, or $1536. The custodial parent is deemed to be providing his or her share directly. The noncustodial parent is to provide his or her share by paying child support. For this 80-percent period, the child support to be paid will be 75 percent (the noncustodial parent's share of the combined income) of $1536 (the total child support to be provided for the period by the parents combined), or $1152.

Continuing with the example, the amount to be provided during the remaining 20 percent of the time, when the noncustodial parent has primary physical responsibility, is 20 percent of $1920, or $384. The noncustodial parent is deemed to be providing his or her share directly, and the custodial parent will pay child support of 25 percent (the custodial parent's share of combined income) of $384 (the total child support for the period), or $96.

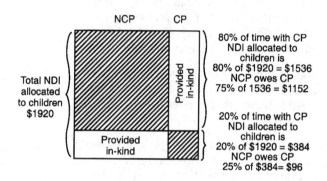

The two child support figures are then, in effect, offset against each other, resulting in a child support payment by the noncustodial parent to the custodial parent in the amount of the difference: $1152 − $96 = $1056. This is the result produced by assuming the figures in this example and either applying the guideline formula or using the appropriate tables, computers, or calculators.

To summarize how the formula is applied, each parent is required to pay the other parent the product of (1) the parent's net monthly disposable income, (2) the applicable percentage of disposable income, expressed as a decimal, to be allocated for child support, and (3) the approximate percentage of time, likewise expressed as a decimal, that the other parent is deemed to have primary physical responsibility for the children. The two amounts are then offset against each other to produce the child support figure.

The following is a worksheet that illustrates the underlying approach and that may be used to apply the formula.

1. Enter the father's net monthly disposable income (see §§8.9–8.13). $_____

2. Enter the mother's net monthly disposable income. $_____

3. Enter the applicable adjustment factor (*i.e.,* "K") from Fam C §4055(b)(3) or, if more than one child, multiply K by the applicable factor from Fam C §4055(b)(4). This is the percentage, expressed as a decimal, of each parent's disposable income to be allocated for child support.   _____

4. Enter the approximate percentage of time, expressed as a decimal (*e.g.,* 0.20), that the father is deemed to have primary physical responsibility for the children.   _____

5. Enter the approximate percentage of time, expressed as a decimal, that the mother is deemed to have primary physical responsibility for the children.   _____

6. Enter the product of line 1 × line 3 × line 5.   _____

7. Enter the product of line 2 × line 3 × line 4.   _____

Do only one of the following,
whichever applies:

8. If the amount on line 6 is larger than that on line 7, subtract line 7 from line 6. This is the formula child support amount, to be paid by the father to the mother.   _____

9. If the amount on line 7 is larger than that on line 6, subtract line 6 from line 7. This is the formula child support amount, to be paid by the mother to the father.   _____

§8.14   B. Low-Income Adjustment

In any case in which the obligor's net monthly disposable income is less than $1000, there is a rebuttable presumption that the obligor is entitled to a low-income adjustment. Fam C §4055(b)(7), as amended effective January 1, 2004, Stats 2003, ch 25, §1. The presumption may be rebutted by evidence showing that it would be unjust and inappropriate to apply the low-income adjustment in the particular case. In ruling whether the presumption is rebutted, the court must consider the principles provided in Fam C §4053 that courts must follow in implementing the statewide uniform guideline and the impact of the contemplated adjustment on the parties' respective net incomes. Fam C §4055(b)(7), as amended effective January 1, 2004, Stats 2003, ch 25, §1. See *City and County of San Francisco v Miller* (1996) 49 CA4th 866, 869, 56 CR2d 887 (no abuse of discretion to reduce father's support to zero when application of formula would have left him with $14 a month for expenses and when he maintained physical responsibility of children for 20 percent of time). The low-income adjustment reduces the child support amount otherwise set under the guideline formula by an amount not to exceed the amount calculated by multiplying the child support amount otherwise set under the formula by a specified fraction. The numerator of the fraction is 1000 minus the obligor's net monthly disposable income and the denominator of the fraction is 1000. Fam C §4055(b)(7). Thus, the maximum reduction is the percentage by which the obligor's net monthly income is less than $1000. When, for example, the obligor has a net monthly disposable income of $900 (*i.e.,* 10 percent less than $1000), the greatest possible reduction in the child support amount otherwise set under the guideline formula (CS) will be one-tenth of that support amount: CS × ((1000 − 900) ÷ 1000).

If the court uses a computer to calculate the child support order, the computer program may not automatically detect whether a low-income adjustment is to be applied and, if the adjustment is applied, the program may not provide the amount of the adjustment. Rather, the user must be asked whether or not to apply the adjustment and, if the user answers affirmatively, the program must provide only the range of the adjustment permitted under Fam C §4055(b)(7). Fam C §4055(c). In the example above, the range of the permitted adjustment would be from zero to one-tenth of the support amount otherwise determined under the guideline formula.

§8.15   C. Rebuttable Presumption That Formula Amount Is Correct Amount

There is a rebuttable presumption affecting the burden of proof that the amount of child support determined by applying the statewide guideline formula (see §§8.8-8.13) is the correct child support amount to be ordered. Fam C §4057(a).

On factors on which rebuttal may be based, see §§8.16-8.21.

§8.16 D. Factors on Which Rebuttal May Be Based

Under the statewide guidelines, the presumption that the amount of child support determined by application of the guideline formula (see §§8.8-8.13) is the correct amount (see §8.15) may be rebutted by admissible evidence showing that application of the formula would be unjust or inappropriate in the particular case. Rebuttal requires that one or more of the factors specified in Fam C §4057(b)(1)-(5) (see §§8.17-8.21) be found, by a preponderance of the evidence, applicable. Fam C §4057(b); *Marriage of Carter* (1994) 26 CA4th 1024, 1026, 33 CR2d 1. Rebuttal also requires that the court state, in writing or on the record, the amount of support that would have been ordered under the guideline formula, the reasons the amount of support ordered differs from the guideline formula amount, and the reasons the amount of support ordered is consistent with the children's best interests. Fam C §§4056(a), 4057(b); see *Marriage of Hall* (2000) 81 CA4th 313, 319, 96 CR2d 772 (trial court must state in writing or on record reasons for child support order deviating from guideline providing for a monthly amount plus percentage of payer's income); *Marriage of Gigliotti* (1995) 33 CA4th 518, 526, 39 CR2d 367 (trial court's reduction of guideline amount without providing explanatory statements required by Fam C §4056(a) mandates reversal). Before appealing on the basis of the court's failure to provide the required information, however, counsel should bring the missing information to the court's attention and give the court an opportunity to supply it. *Rojas v Mitchell* (1996) 50 CA4th 1445, 1451, 58 CR2d 354.

§8.17 1. Parties' Stipulation

The presumption that the amount of child support determined by application of the guideline formula is the correct amount may be rebutted by the parties' stipulation to a different amount, subject to court approval. Fam C §§4057(b)(1), 4065(a). When the agreement is for an amount below that established by the statewide uniform guidelines, however, the court may not approve it unless the parties declare the following:

- They are fully informed of their rights concerning child support (Fam C §4065(a)(1));

- The order is agreed to without coercion or duress (Fam C §4065(a)(2));

- The agreement is in the best interests of the children involved (Fam C §4065(a)(3));

- The children's needs will be adequately met by the stipulated amount (Fam C §4065(a)(4)); and

- The right to support has not been assigned to any county under Welf & I C §11477 and no public assistance application is pending (Fam C §4065(a)(5)).

The parties may, by stipulation, require the child support obligor to designate an account for the purpose of paying the child support obligation by electronic funds transfer under Fam C §4508 (see §20.16). Fam C §4065(b).

In any case in which the local child support agency is providing services under Fam C §17400 (former Welf & I C §11475.1), a stipulated agreement is valid only if the local child support agency has signed it. The local child support agency may not stipulate to a child support amount below that established by the statewide guidelines, however, if (1) the children are receiving assistance under the CalWORKs program (formerly Aid to Families with Dependent Children), (2) an application for public assistance is pending, or (3) the parent receiving support has not consented to the amount. Fam C §4065(c).

Even when stipulations meet the requirements expressly listed in Fam C §4065(a), (c), they are still subject to court approval. Fam C §4065(a). This is consistent with case law. Under such law, parties cannot bind the court by their agreement on child support. See *Elkind v Byck* (1968) 68 C2d 453, 457, 67 CR 404; *County of Shasta v Caruthers* (1995) 31 CA4th 1838, 38 CR2d 18. See also *Marriage of Jackson* (2006) 136 CA4th 980, 991, 39 CR3d 365; *Kristine M. v David P.* (2006) 135 CA4th 783, 792, 37 CR3d 748. Thus, a court may reject an agreement that does not adequately provide support for the parties' children. *Marriage of Ayo* (1987) 190 CA3d 442, 448, 235 CR 458.

When the parents agree to a child support amount that is below that established by the statewide uniform guidelines, no change of circumstances need be demonstrated to obtain a modification of the order to the applicable guideline level or above. Fam C §4065(d).

§8.18   2. Rental Value of Family Residence Subject to Deferred Sale Order

The presumption that the amount of child support as calculated under the guideline formula is the correct amount may be rebutted by admissible evidence showing that sale of the family residence is deferred under Fam C §3800–3810 (see §5.90) and that the rental value of the residence exceeds the combined cost for mortgage payments, homeowner's insurance, and property taxes. The amount of any adjustment to the child support must not be greater than the excess amount. Fam C §4057(b)(2). Beyond that, however, the amount is within the court's discretion and is not required to be the excess amount or any other particular amount. *Marriage of Braud* (1996) 45 CA4th 797, 818, 53 CR2d 179.

One published decision suggested that, when the rental value of the family residence in such deferred-sale situations exceeds the residence-related payments, it would appear equitable to offset support by half the difference between the rental value and the payments. *Marriage of Horowitz* (1984) 159 CA3d 368, 373 n5, 205 CR 874. In a later case, however, the same court criticized the offset approach, finding it too mechanical and potentially unfair to the support recipient. Rather, the court called for a more flexible approach that focused on the support recipient's needs. When lower housing expense results from a deferred-sale order, the support recipient's needs are reduced accordingly, making a lower support order appropriate. *Marriage of Stallworth* (1987) 192 CA3d 742, 750, 237 CR 829.

§8.19   3. Payer's Extraordinarily High Income

The presumption that the amount of child support under the guideline formula is the correct amount may be rebutted by admissible evidence showing that the payer has an extraordinarily high income and the amount determined by application of the guideline formula would exceed the children's needs. Fam C §4057(b)(3). As indicated in §8.13, for parents whose combined disposable income exceeds $6666 per month, the percentage of their respective incomes to be allocated for child support decreases as their combined income increases. At the highest income levels, the percentage approaches 12 percent for one child, 19.2 percent for two children, 24 percent for three children, and so forth. See Fam C §4055(b)(3)-(4). Despite the decreasing percentages, Fam C §4057(b)(3) apparently reflects a concern that, at the highest income levels, the percentages may be inappropriately high. This may be particularly true when the child is very young, *e.g.,* the support amount determined for a high-income payer by application of the guideline formula may actually exceed the reasonable monthly needs of an infant.

In *Marriage of Chandler* (1997) 60 CA4th 124, 70 CR2d 109, the trial court attempted to customize child support guideline for a high-income payer by making a child support order of $3000 monthly and establishing a child-support trust funded with $4000 monthly payments for additional, future child-related expenses. The court of appeal held that the use of a trust for this purpose was not justifiable under Fam C §4062 (additional child support for specified expenses) and ordered child support in the total amount of $7000 monthly. Use of a trust to make "affluence participation" more palatable to the payer in this case, who was concerned about the custodial parent benefiting from the wealth, was inappropriate given the statutory directive of Fam C §4053(f) that children share their parents' standard of living and that a child support order may improve the custodial parent's standard of living if it improves the children's lives. 60 CA4th at 130.

It has been held that, despite the statewide uniform guidelines, when a child support payer who is an extraordinarily high earner stipulates that he or she can and will pay any reasonable amount of child support, the court need not calculate the support amount under the guideline formula. *Estevez v Superior Court* (1994) 22 CA4th 423, 27 CR2d 470. The court in *Estevez* indicated, however, that when a high-earner payer resists detailed discovery of his or her financial affairs, the trial court may make such assumptions concerning his or her gross and net disposable incomes as are least beneficial to the payer, and thereby satisfy the requirements of Fam C §4056 (court statements required when varying from guideline amount) (see §8.16). 22 CA4th at 431. A subsequent case noted that the dispute in *Estevez* was not over the amount of child support, but rather the manner in which it was dispensed, and suggested that the rule in *Estevez* might not apply when the amount is in dispute. *McGinley v Herman* (1996) 50 CA4th 936, 944, 57 CR2d

921. The *McGinley* court went on to hold that in high-earner cases in which the amount of support is in dispute, and the court deviates from the guideline amount, the court must at least approximate the point at which the support amount calculated under the formula would exceed the child's needs, and therefore at what point the payer's income becomes extraordinarily high. 50 CA4th at 945. This, in turn, requires at least an approximation of the payer's net disposable monthly income to ensure that he or she in fact qualifies for treatment as an extraordinarily high earner under Fam C §4057(b)(3). 50 CA4th at 945. When children of a high earner are involved, it may not be appropriate to define the children's needs by their expenses. See *Marriage of Cheriton* (2001) 92 CA4th 269, 111 CR2d 755.

In *Johnson v Superior Court* (1998) 66 CA4th 68, 77 CR2d 624, the court of appeal held that when the child support payee lacks sufficient information to enable the trial court to make reasonable assumptions about the payer's income that are least beneficial to the payer, as permitted under *Estevez* when detailed discovery is resisted, the court should permit the limited amount of discovery, if any, required to allow such information to be developed. The court must base the least beneficial income assumptions on reliable factual information, but must also protect the high earner's "legitimate privacy concerns regarding his finances." See *Marriage of Hubner* (2001) 94 CA4th 175, 187, 114 CR2d 646 (case remanded when trial court based child support on "fictional gross income assumptions"; court must make Fam C §4056 findings if it departs from guidelines).

§8.20   4. Parent Not Contributing at Level Commensurate With Custodial Time

The presumption that the amount of child support under the guideline formula is the correct amount may be rebutted by admissible evidence showing that a parent is not contributing to meeting the children's needs at a level commensurate with his or her custodial time. Fam C §4057(b)(4).

§8.21   5. Application of Formula Amount Would Be Unjust or Inappropriate Due to Special Circumstances

The presumption that the amount of child support under the guideline formula is the correct amount may be rebutted by admissible evidence showing that that amount would be unjust or inappropriate because of special circumstances in the particular case. Fam C §4057(b)(5). Such circumstances expressly include, but are not limited to, the following:

- The parents have different time-sharing arrangements for different children (Fam C §4057(b)(5)(A));

- The parents have substantially equal time-sharing for the children and one parent has a much lower or higher percentage of income used for housing than the other (Fam C §4057(b)(5)(B)); and

- The children have special medical or other needs that could require more child support than that calculated under the guideline formula (Fam C §4057(b)(5)(C)).

The list of special circumstances in §4057 is not exhaustive. For example, in the appropriate case, especially when there is evidence of interference with visitation rights by the custodial parent, it may be appropriate for the trier of fact to deduct travel expenses from the guideline support amount in order to allow the noncustodial parent to establish a travel fund. *Wilson v Shea* (2001) 87 CA4th 887, 898, 104 CR2d 880.

In *County of Lake v Antoni* (1993) 18 CA4th 1102, 22 CR2d 804, the court of appeal affirmed a $200 reduction in the presumptive child support amount under former CC §4721(e)(6), predecessor of Fam C §4057(b)(5), based on the payer's providing support for a stepchild who resided with him and the payer's "extraordinarily high amount of monthly debt service, on account of debt seemingly incurred for living needs." 18 CA4th at 1104. The trial court also noted the payer's support for a child who resided with him, but the payer would have been entitled to a hardship deduction (see §8.11) for that child in any event. In rejecting the county's argument that the trial court's approach "would give an obligor parent carte blanche to overspend on optional, nonessential items for himself and others as to whom he has no legal duty of support," the court of appeal noted that the payer's debt burden "already was in place" before the modification was sought. 18 CA4th at 1106.

In *City & County of San Francisco v Funches* (1999) 75 CA4th 243, 247, 89 CR2d 49, the court of appeal affirmed an order significantly reducing arrearages against a father on behalf of a child who had been living in a publicly funded group home because the county had delayed seeking reimbursement and the obligation to make arrearage payments long after the child reached majority would negatively impact his ability to reunify with and care for the child.

In *City & County of San Francisco v Miller* (1996) 49 CA4th 866, 56 CR2d 887, the court of appeal affirmed an order that applied Fam C §4057(b)(5) to reduce a child support obligation to zero. After application of the statewide uniform guideline formula, and allowance of the maximum low-income adjustment under Fam C §4055(b)(7) (see §8.14), the presumptive child support amount was $248 per month. The court noted that, after payment of his monthly rent of $450 and the presumptive support amount, the payer would have had only $14 per month for his remaining expenses.

In *Marriage of Butler & Gill* (1997) 53 CA4th 462, 61 CR2d 781, on the other hand, the court of appeal reversed an order that allowed a reduction in child support based on the payer's support of his elderly mother, finding that the support did not justify application of the special circumstances exception of Fam C §4057(b)(5). The court noted that the fact that the payer's elderly mother looked to him for financial support was not so unusual or extraordinary as to diminish his obligation to his children, and that there was no showing that the payer would have any acute difficulty in providing both the guideline support to his children and support for his mother. 53 CA4th at 468.

In *Marriage of Denise & Kevin C.* (1997) 57 CA4th 1100, 67 CR2d 508, the court of appeal reversed an order that allowed a reduction from the guideline figure of $1121 per month to $816 per month. The trial court had stated that the guideline amount would reduce the payer's standard of living while providing the payee and children with a substantial surplus over their needs. The court of appeal rejected the trial court's factual conclusions regarding the impact on the respective parties of the guideline result and noted that, in any event, protecting the parents' standard of living is not an objective of any of the relevant statutes; some reduction in the payer's discretionary spending is pretty much the rule.

Special circumstances may also justify an award *exceeding* guideline amounts, as long as the court specifically articulates the reasons for deviating from the guideline and how the deviation serves the children's best interests; it is not necessary in all cases that each dollar above guideline be earmarked for a specific purpose. *Marriage of De Guigne* (2002) 97 CA4th 1353, 1362, 119 CR2d 430 (when during marriage husband had chosen to support family by selling assets, not abuse of discretion for court to mitigate children's overall decline in standard of living after dissolution by considering husband's available assets (including separate property mansion on 47 undeveloped acres) and making child support order exceeding guidelines). Deviation from the guideline amount is also appropriate under Fam C §4057 when nontaxable benefits increase a parent's available income for child support. *Marriage of Loh* (2001) 93 CA4th 325, 333, 112 CR2d 893. Thus, for example, a trial court may include the rent received by a parent who subleased a portion of his principal residence when calculating his income. This represents a special circumstance that a court may properly consider, particularly when the parents have limited resources available to provide financially for the child. *County of Orange v Smith* (2005) 132 CA4th 1434, 1448, 34 CR3d 383.

When Fam C §4057.5 prohibits consideration of income of a parent's subsequent spouse or nonmarital partner, that prohibition may not be avoided by treating such income as a special circumstance in the particular case that renders the amount of child support under the statewide guideline formula unjust or inappropriate under Fam C §4057(b)(5). *Marriage of Wood* (1995) 37 CA4th 1059, 1069, 44 CR2d 236.

§8.22 E. Consideration of Income of Subsequent Spouse or Nonmarital Partner

Income of a parent's subsequent spouse or nonmarital partner may not be considered in child support determinations, except in an extraordinary case, *e.g.*, a parent's voluntarily or intentionally quitting work or reducing income, or intentionally remaining unemployed or underemployed and relying on a subsequent spouse's income, in which excluding that income would lead to extreme and severe hardship to a child subject to the child support order. Fam C §4057.5(a)–(b); *Marriage of Wood* (1995) 37 CA4th 1059, 1067, 44 CR2d 236. In that event, however, the court must also consider whether including the income would lead to extreme and severe hardship to any child supported by the parent or the parent's subsequent spouse or nonmarital partner. Fam C §4057.5(a)–(b).

Note that Fam C §4057.5 speaks specifically of "income." Contrast this rule with Fam C §4058(b) (see §8.10), which provides that in determining gross income the court may consider a party's "earning capacity." This limitation in Fam C §4057.5 is consistent with preexisting case law, which has not considered a new spouse's or partner's ability to earn, as distinguished from his or her actual income. *Marriage of Williams* (1984) 155 CA3d 57, 64, 202 CR 10.

Although the statute does not specify what a court is to do with the income of a parent's subsequent spouse or nonmarital partner after it has determined that the income will be considered, the likelihood is that most courts will add some portion of that income to the parent's income in applying the statewide uniform guideline formula. The result will generally be a higher child support award when the parent is the support payer and a lower award when the parent is the support recipient.

When income of a parent's subsequent spouse or nonmarital partner is allowed to be considered, discovery to determine income must be based on W-2 and 1099 income tax forms, except when the court determines that application of this rule would be unjust or inappropriate. Fam C §4057.5(c). On when a court might determine that limiting discovery in such instances to W-2 and 1099 forms would be unjust or inappropriate, see, *e.g., Schnabel v Superior Court* (1993) 5 C4th 704, 21 CR2d 200 (when one spouse in marital action seeks discovery from third party, court must balance spouse's need for discovery against third party's privacy interests; corporation required to produce business records, corporate tax returns, and payroll tax returns regarding other spouse, but not payroll tax information identifying third persons).

When income of a parent's subsequent spouse or nonmarital partner is allowed to be considered, the court must allow a hardship deduction (see §8.11) based on the minimum living expenses for one or more stepchildren of the parent. Fam C §4057.5(d). Family Code §4057.5(d) was amended, effective January 1, 1995, to specify that, in allowing a hardship deduction, the court must comply with Fam C §§4070, 4071, 4072, and 4073, sections that address the hardship deduction.

The establishment of Fam C §4057.5 constitutes cause to seek modification of a child support order entered before January 1, 1994. Fam C §4057.5(e). Although it is not clear from the wording of Fam C §4057.5(e), it appears that the establishment of §4057.5 should provide cause to seek modification only when income of a parent's subsequent spouse or nonmarital partner was considered in making the order whose modification is sought.

In an uncodified section of 1994 legislation, the legislature expressed its intent that the restrictions of Fam C §4057.5 on the use of a subsequent spouse's or nonmarital partner's income not be subject to court standardization, but rather be subject to judgment on a case-by-case basis, and that §4057.5 prohibit the establishment or use of any formula or local court guideline devised to determine when consideration of a subsequent spouse's or nonmarital partner's income is appropriate. Stats 1994, ch 1140, §3.

When Fam C §4057.5 prohibits consideration of income of a parent's subsequent spouse or nonmarital partner, that prohibition may not be avoided by treating such income as a special circumstance in the particular case that renders the amount of child support under the statewide guideline formula unjust or inappropriate under Fam C §4057(b)(5) (see §8.21). *Marriage of Wood* (1995) 37 CA4th 1059, 1069, 44 CR2d 236.

Family Code §4057.5 may not be applied retroactively. 37 CA4th at 1070.

Note that Fam C §4057.5 does not prohibit consideration of income of a subsequent spouse or nonmarital partner in determining a parent's actual tax liability for purposes of allowable deductions from gross income (see §8.11). *County of Tulare v Campbell* (1996) 50 CA4th 847, 57 CR2d 902.

§8.23   F. Addition of Amounts for Related Expenses

Depending on the circumstances, the court may be required or permitted to order the parents to bear certain expenses related to child support. These expenses are in addition to, and are determined after, the amounts of child support allocated to the parents under the guideline formula, as modified based on any applicable rebuttal factors. Fam C §§4061–4062; see §§8.24–8.25. Any such amounts are considered additional child support. Fam C §4061.

Any additional child support must be ordered to be paid by the parents equally, unless either parent requests a different apportionment and presents documentation showing that a different apportionment would be more appropriate. Fam C §4061(a). See *Marriage of De Guigne* (2002) 97 CA4th 1353, 1368, 119 CR2d 430. The trial court may allocate add-on expenses based on the parents' income as of the time that the expenses were incurred. *Marriage of Lusby* (1998) 64 CA4th 459, 474, 75 CR2d 263 (not error to allocate add-on expenses to payer at the reduced percentage that he had been paying for child support when the expenses were incurred due to his unemployment at the time, even though he subsequently obtained employment and had a higher income at the time of the add-on hearing). If a different apportionment is requested and the court decides it is appropriate to grant the request, the apportionment must be in proportion to the parents' respective adjusted net disposable incomes, determined in accordance with Fam C §4061(b)–(d) as follows (Fam C §4061(b)):

- If spousal support is or has been ordered to be paid by one parent to the other, the amount of spousal support paid and received is deducted from the *gross* income of the payer and added to the recipient's *gross* income for as long as the order remains in effect and is paid. Fam C §4061(c). The respective net incomes are then recalculated based on the new gross incomes. The effect of this recalculation is to consider the tax effects of any spousal support ordered in the present case in determining the parents' adjusted net disposable incomes for purposes of the apportionment of the additional expenses. Note that, unless the parents stipulate otherwise, the tax effects of such a spousal support order are *not* considered in determining net disposable incomes for purposes of calculating the guideline formula amount. See §8.11.

After the net incomes are recalculated, the amount of child support to be paid by the child support payer to the support recipient, as determined under the guideline formula and as modified based on any applicable rebuttal factors, is deducted from the payer's net, but is *not* added to the recipient's net. Fam C §4061(d). The resulting net incomes are those in proportion to which the respective amounts of additional child support must be ordered to be paid.

- If spousal support is not required to be paid by one parent to the other, the net disposable income of the child support payer determined for purposes of applying the guideline formula is reduced by the amount of child support to be paid, as determined under that formula and as modified based on any applicable rebuttal factors. The resulting net income and that of the support recipient, which is not adjusted, are those in proportion to which the respective amounts of additional child support must be ordered to be paid.

§8.24 1. Mandatory Additions

Family Code §4062(a) provides that the court "shall" order the following costs to be paid as additional child support:

- Child care costs related either to employment or to reasonably necessary education or training for employment skills. Fam C §4062(a)(1).

- Reasonable uninsured health care costs for the children. Fam C §4062(a)(2). Except as provided in Fam C §4063(e) (discussed below), there is a rebuttable presumption that amounts actually paid for the children's uninsured health care needs are reasonable. Fam C §4063(d).

Note, with respect to child care costs, that there does not appear to be any requirement that the costs be reasonable, as opposed to actual. *Marriage of Gigliotti* (1995) 33 CA4th 518, 525 n2, 39 CR2d 367. Note also that in *Marriage of Fini* (1994) 26 CA4th 1033, 31 CR2d 749, the trial court declined to make any order regarding employment-related child care costs and was affirmed on appeal. The court of appeal interpreted the order to be that each party bear his or her own work-related child care expenses and held that such an order was, at least when the parties' incomes were not disparate, within the court's discretion.

The legislature has enacted extensive provisions regarding court orders for payment, as additional child support, of uninsured health care costs for children under Fam C §4062(a)(2). Fam C §4063. When making such an order, the court must advise each parent, in writing or on the record, of his or her rights and liabilities, including financial responsibilities (see the Notice of Rights and Responsibilities (Judicial Council Form FL-192), available in California Judicial Council Forms Manual §3 (Cal CEB 1981)), and must include in the order the time period for a parent to reimburse the other parent for the reimbursing parent's share of the uninsured health care costs. Fam C §4063(a). Unless child support rights have been assigned under Welf & I C §11477 (*i.e.,* to receive benefits under the California Work Opportunity and Responsibility to Kids Act (CalWORKs) program (formerly AFDC)), a parent accruing or paying costs under the order must, within a reasonable time not to exceed 30 days, provide the other parent with an itemized statement of the costs, proof of any payment made, and a request for reimbursement or payment of the other parent's share. Fam C §4063(b)(1)-(2). The other parent must make the reimbursement or payment within the time period specified by the court or, if none, within a reasonable time not to exceed 30 days after notification, or according to a payment schedule set up by the health care provider (subject to a written agreement of the parties or a court order for a different schedule). Fam C §4063(b)(3). A reimbursing parent who disputes a request for payment must pay the requested amount and may thereafter seek judicial relief under Fam C §§4063 and 290 (methods of enforcement of Family Code judgments and orders). If the reimbursing parent fails to pay as required, the other parent may seek judicial relief under those sections. Fam C §4063(b)(4). Either party may file a noticed motion to enforce an order under Fam C §4063, in which event the court may award reasonable attorney fees and filing costs if it finds that either party acted without reasonable cause regarding his or her obligations for the children's uninsured health care costs. Fam C §4063(c). The motion will be prepared and processed in the same manner as a noticed motion for temporary orders. For discussion of, and forms for, motions for temporary orders, see §§11.16-11.63.

Normally, the following rules apply regarding health care insurance coverage:

- The coverage provided by a parent in accordance with a court order must be used at all times unless the other parent can show that the coverage is inadequate to meet the child's needs (Fam C §4063(e)(1));

- A parent who obtains coverage in addition to that provided under court order must bear the sole financial responsibility for its costs and for the costs of any care obtained under that coverage in excess of the costs that would have been incurred under the coverage provided for in the court order (Fam C §4063(e)(2));

- If the coverage provided by a parent in accordance with a court order designates a preferred health care provider, that provider must be used at all times, consistent with the coverage (Fam C §4063(f)(1)); and

- If either parent, inconsistent with the coverage provided in accordance with a court order, uses a provider other than the preferred provider, that parent must bear sole responsibility for any nonreimbursable costs in excess of the costs that would have been incurred under the coverage provided for in the court order had the preferred provider been used (Fam C §4063(f)(2)).

When ruling on a motion under Fam C §4063, however, in order to ensure that the child's health care needs are met, the court must consider all relevant facts, including, but not limited to:

- The geographic access and reasonable availability of necessary health care that complies with the terms of the coverage paid for by either parent under a court order (Fam C §4063(g)(1));

- The need for emergency treatment that may have precluded use of the coverage, or use of the preferred provider required under the coverage, provided by either parent in accordance with a court order (Fam C §4063(g)(2));

- The child's special medical needs (Fam C §4063(g)(3)); and

- A parent's reasonable inability to pay the full reimbursement amount within 30 days and the resulting necessity for a court-ordered payment schedule (Fam C §4063(g)(4)).

For further discussion of health insurance coverage for children, see §8.34.

§8.25 2. Discretionary Additions

Family Code §4062(b) provides that the court "may" order the following costs to be paid as additional child support:

- Costs related to the educational or other special needs of the children (Fam C §4062(b)(1)); and

- Travel expenses for visitation (Fam C §4062(b)(2)).

It appears that, under the terms of Fam C §4062(b), travel expenses for visitation may be awarded only as additional child support to the child support payee, and may not be used to reduce the child support otherwise ordered to be paid by the payer. *Marriage of Gi-*

gliotti (1995) 33 CA4th 518, 527, 39 CR2d 367. For a contrary view, however, see *Wilson v Shea* (2001) 87 CA4th 887, 898, 104 CR2d 880; *Marriage of Fini* (1994) 26 CA4th 1033, 1039 n5, 31 CR2d 749.

In the absence of statutory authorization, the trial court has no discretion to fashion its own additions to child support. *Marriage of De Guigne* (2002) 97 CA4th 1353, 1367, 119 CR2d 430 (rental deposit/furniture payment not authorized child support).

§8.26   G. Adjustment to Accommodate Seasonal or Fluctuating Income

The court may adjust the child support order as appropriate to accommodate seasonal or fluctuating income of either parent. Fam C §4064. See, *e.g., Riddle v Riddle* (2005) 125 CA4th 1075, 23 CR3d 273 (trial court abused discretion by using only two months' payroll records to compute husband's income instead of basing award on 12-month representative sample); *Marriage of Hall* (2000) 81 CA4th 313, 318, 96 CR2d 772 (child support order for a monthly amount plus percentage of payer's income to accommodate fluctuations in bonus, dividend, and interest income); *Marriage of Ostler & Smith* (1990) 223 CA3d 33, 272 CR 560 (payer ordered to pay 10 percent of annual gross cash bonus when received as additional child support for each child).

§8.27   H. Family Support

Orders and stipulations otherwise in compliance with the statewide uniform guideline may designate as "family support" an unallocated total sum for support of the other party and any children without specifically labeling all or any portion as "child support," as long as the amount is adjusted to reflect the effect of the additional deductibility and to maximize the tax benefits for both parents. Fam C §4066.

Under Fam C §3586, the court may order family support when the parties agree to it. It would appear that Fam C §4066 provides broader authority, allowing the court to order family support even without the parties' agreement. Note the reference in §4066 to "[o]rders and stipulations."

Attorneys contemplating an agreement for family support, or faced with the prospect of a court's ordering it even without an agreement, should carefully review the current rules on deductibility of such payments and the potential pitfalls to be avoided when drafting such orders. See §6.35.

§8.28   I. Required Findings

At the request of any party, the court must state, in writing or on the record, the following information used in determining the guideline amount (Fam C §4056(b)):

- The net monthly disposable income of each parent (Fam C §4056(b)(1));

- The actual federal income tax filing status of each parent (*i.e.,* single, married filing jointly, married filing separately, or head of household) and number of exemptions (Fam C §4056(b)(2));

- Each parent's deductions from gross income (Fam C §4056(b)(3)); and

- The approximate percentage of time each parent has primary physical responsibility for the children (Fam C §4056(b)(4)).

On court statements required under Fam C §4056(a) by rebuttal of the presumption that the amount of child support under the guideline formula is the correct amount, see §8.16.

On findings required under Fam C §4072 when deductions for hardship expenses are allowed, see §8.11.

On findings required when a low-income adjustment is allowed, see §8.14.

Note also that, at the request of either party, the court must make "appropriate findings" with respect to the circumstances on which a child support order is based. Fam C §4005. As a practical matter, many of these "findings" can be found on the printout of the child support calculation software used by the court or provided by counsel attached to the Findings and Order After Hearing.

§8.29   V. NOTIFICATION REGARDING EMPLOYMENT

Any order for child support, whether an initial order or a modification, must include a provision requiring the obligor and the obligee to notify the other, or to notify the Department of Child Support Services if the order requires payment through that agency, of his or her current employer's name and address. Fam C §4014(a).

§8.30   VI. REQUIRED ATTENDANCE AT JOB TRAINING AND PLACEMENT PROGRAMS

When child support or family support is at issue, the court may require either parent to attend job training, job placement, vocational rehabilitation, and work programs, as designated by the court, at regular intervals and times and to provide documentation of participation in a format acceptable to the court. The court will specify the durations of attendance. The required attendance is to enable the court to make a finding that good faith attempts at job training and placement have been undertaken by the parent. Fam C §3558.

VII. MODIFICATION

§8.31   A. Standard Orders

Child support awards may be modified at any time before termination of the payer's duty of support. Fam C §3651. On termination, see §8.33. Unlike spousal support (see §6.22), child support cannot be made nonmodifiable by agreement of the parties. Fam C §3651 (former CC §4811(a)); *Armstrong v Armstrong* (1976) 15 C3d 942, 947, 126 CR 805. Also unlike spousal support (see §6.21), child support may be ordered and modified by the court in subsequent proceedings even when the original judgment contains no provision for child support. *Krog v Krog* (1948) 32 C2d 812, 816, 198 P2d 510.

A modification may be retroactive at most, however, to the date of service of the notice of motion or order to show cause. Fam C §3653(a); 42 USC §666(a)(9). There are neither equitable nor statutory grounds to modify child support before the date of filing of the motion, and the court may not forgive accrued child support arrearages on the basis of a motion to modify. *County of Santa Clara v Wilson* (2003) 111 CA4th 1324, 4 CR3d 653 (trial court violated Fam C §3651(c) by reducing accrued child support arrearages of incarcerated father in response to his motion for modification).

When the modification is entered because of the unemployment of either party, it must be made retroactive to the later of the date of service or the date of unemployment, unless the court finds good cause not to make the order retroactive and states its reasons on the record. Fam C §3653(b). A determination of good cause requires the court to make a good-faith finding that nonretroactivity is justified by real circumstances, substantial reasons, and objective conditions, and to give due consideration to the statutory principles concerning child support. *Marriage of Leonard* (2004) 119 CA4th 546, 14 CR3d 482. The court balances the needs of the children against the interests of the supporting parent not to be faced with an unjust and unreasonable financial burden resulting from a nonretroactive order. This latter inquiry examines the supporting parent's then-existing financial resources and ability to pay for the support of the children during the period of potential retroactivity being considered. Because the needs of the children are of paramount concern, when retroactivity would result in demonstrable hardship to them, good cause may exist to deny a retroactive support reduction or termination when the supporting parent has the ability to bear that financial burden. 119 CA4th at 560, 561. If the order is entered retroactively, the support obligor may be entitled to, and the support obligee may be ordered to repay, according to the terms specified in the order, any amounts previously paid under the prior order that are in excess of the amounts due under the retroactive order. Fam C §3653(c). See *Marriage of Dandona & Araluce* (2001) 91 CA4th 1120, 1124, 111 CR2d 390 (reimbursement under Fam C §3653 retroactive; court has discretion to order repayment). The court may order that the repayment by the support obligee be made over any period and in any manner (including, but not limited to, an offset against future support payments or a future wage assignment) that the court deems just and reasonable. Fam C §3653(c). In determining whether to order a repayment, and in establishing the terms of repayment, the court must consider all the following factors (Fam C §3653(c)):

- The amount to be repaid;

- The duration of the support order before modification or termination;

- The financial impact on the support obligee of any particular method of repayment, *e.g.*, an offset against future support payments or a future wage assignment; and

- Any other facts or circumstances that the court deems relevant.

Determination of child support awards in modification proceedings, as in initial proceedings, is governed by the statewide uniform guideline (see §§8.7–8.28).

The general rule is that to obtain a modification there must be a showing of a material change of circumstances since the most recent order. *Philbin v Philbin* (1971) 19 CA3d 115, 119, 96 CR 408. Note, however, that the establishment of the statewide uniform guideline constitutes a change of circumstances. Fam C §4069; *Marriage of Gigliotti* (1995) 33 CA4th 518, 527, 39 CR2d 367. It is not clear what is meant by "establishment," but Fam C §4069 arguably provides the requisite change of circumstances whenever an intervening amendment to the statewide uniform guideline would result in an order different from the one the moving party seeks to modify. Note further that, when a court makes a child support order on or after July 1, 1992, that is based on the parents' agreement to an amount below that established by the statewide uniform guidelines, no change of circumstances need be demonstrated to obtain a subsequent modification of the order to or above the applicable amount. Fam C §§4051, 4065(d). Finally, the establishment of Fam C §4057.5, limiting consideration of the income of a parent's subsequent spouse or nonmarital partner in child support determinations (see §8.22), constitutes cause to seek modification of a child support order entered before January 1, 1994. Fam C §4057.5(e). Although it is not clear from the wording of Fam C §4057.5(e), it appears that the establishment of §4057.5 should provide cause to seek modification only when income of a parent's subsequent spouse or nonmarital partner was considered in making the order whose modification is sought.

When the parties stipulate to a child support order for less than the guideline amount, no change of circumstances is required to obtain a modification that increases the amount to guideline or above. Fam C §4065(d). Changed circumstances must be shown, however, if the modification seeks to *reduce* the amount of the stipulated award to the guideline level or below. *Marriage of Laudeman* (2001) 92 CA4th 1009, 112 CR2d 378. For preguideline cases, see, *e.g., Marriage of Thomas* (1981) 120 CA3d 33, 35, 173 CR 844; *Singer v Singer* (1970) 7 CA3d 807, 87 CR 42.

Unlike spousal support orders (see §6.25), child support orders may be modified largely, and perhaps entirely, on the basis of the supporting party's increased ability to pay. See *Marriage of Hubner* (1988) 205 CA3d 660, 252 CR 428; *Marriage of Catalano* (1988) 204 CA3d 543, 251 CR 370.

On modification generally, see chap 21.

8.31A   B. Military Servicemembers

Members of the armed forces who are activated to United States military duty or National Guard service and are deployed out of state are afforded special consideration regarding support, custody, and visitation orders. With respect to child, family, or spousal support, a servicemember may request modification of a support order by filing a notice of activation of military service indicating a date of deployment, in lieu of a conventional order to show cause or notice of motion. Fam C §3651. For further discussion and the mandatory form (Judicial Council Form FL-398), see §§21.32–21.33.

§8.32   C. Two-Step Phase-In Orders

When a court is requested to modify a child support order issued before July 1, 1992, for the purpose of conforming to the statewide guideline, it may, in its discretion, order a two-step phase-in of the new support amount in order to provide the obligor with time for transition to the new amount. A two-step phase-in may be ordered only when the court does not use its discretionary authority under Fam C §4057(b)(3)–(5) (see §§8.19–8.21) to depart from the guideline formula amount and the amount to be ordered is the formula amount under Fam C §4055 (see §§8.8–8.13). Fam C §4076(a). Further, all the following must be true:

- The phase-in period is carefully limited to the time necessary for the obligor to rearrange his or her financial obligations to meet the new support amount (Fam C §4076(a)(1));

- The obligor is immediately being ordered to pay child support in an amount that includes the prior support amount plus at least 30 percent of the increase (Fam C §4076(a)(2)); and

- The obligor has not unreasonably increased his or her financial obligations following notice of the motion for modification, has no arrearages owing, and has a history of good faith compliance with prior support orders (Fam C §4076(a)(3)).

When the court orders a phase-in, it must state in writing:

- The specific reasons that (1) the immediate imposition of the full formula amount would place an extraordinary hardship on the obligor and (2) the hardship would outweigh the hardship caused the supported children by the phase-in (Fam C §4076(b)(1)); and

- The full guideline amount of support, the date and amount of each phase-in, and the date the obligor must begin paying the full amount (Fam C §4076(b)(2)).

In no event may the date the obligor begins paying the full support amount be later than 1 year after the filing of the motion for modification. Fam C §4076(b)(2).

If the obligor violates the phase-in schedule or intentionally lowers the income available for payment of child support during the phase-in period, the court may order the immediate payment of the full guideline amount, retroactive to the effective date of the initial modification order, in addition to any other penalties provided for by law. Fam C §4076(c).

§8.33 VIII. TERMINATION

A child support order normally terminates on the first of the following occurrences, regardless of whether the order itself expressly provides for such termination:

- The child attains age 18 (except that child support for a full-time high school student who is not self-supporting continues until the child graduates or attains age 19, whichever occurs first) (Fam C §§4001, 6500, 3901(a));

- The child dies; or

- The child becomes "emancipated," as defined by the Emancipation of Minors Law (Fam C §§7000–7143), *i.e.,* enters into a valid marriage, is on active duty with the armed forces, or receives a declaration of emancipation under the Act (Fam C §§7002, 7050(a)).

There is no requirement that a supported child demonstrate a good-faith effort to graduate from high school as soon as possible, nor is a parent's duty of support conditioned on "the child's participation only in those classes that propel her or him toward graduation at the earliest possible date." *Marriage of Hubner* (2001) 94 CA4th 175, 189, 114 CR2d 646.

Note that emancipation as established under case law will not terminate the payer's support obligation unless the court order specifies that support will terminate in that event. When the order does not specify termination, the support payer will have to seek modification of the order to avoid continuing liability even though the child has become emancipated. *Marriage of Lehrer, supra.*

There are two circumstances under which child support may continue beyond the normal termination date: (1) by agreement of the parties (Fam C §3587) and (2) in the case of an incapacitated and needy child (Fam C §3910; see §8.2).

A child support obligation fixed by a court order or agreement of the parents does not terminate at the payer's death. Rather, it survives as a charge against his or her estate in the amount required to pay the support until the obligation would have terminated. The payer may, however, discharge that obligation by appropriate testamentary disposition or designation of life insurance beneficiaries, as long as the disposition or designation is *intended* to discharge the obligation. *Taylor v George* (1949) 34 C2d 552, 212 P2d 505. Note that the rule is the same in the case of support for an adult child for whom support is authorized under Fam C §3910 (adult child who is incapacitated from earning living and without sufficient means) (see §8.2). *Marriage of Drake* (1997) 53 CA4th 1139, 1163, 62 CR2d 466. Note also that the child support obligation may be enforced against the deceased payer's living trust just as it could be enforced against his or her estate. *Marriage of Perry* (1997) 58 CA4th 1104, 68 CR2d 445. The D.C. Circuit Court of Appeals has also held that an obligation, based on a settlement agreement, to pay child support even after the child reaches majority, is not dischargeable in bankruptcy, even though the child in question had reached age 18. *Richardson v Edwards* (DC Cir 1997) 127 F3d 97.

Likewise, a child support order does not terminate at the payee's death, even when the payer assumes custody. Rather, the payer must seek judicial termination of the order. *Marriage of McCann* (1994) 27 CA4th 102, 107, 32 CR2d 639.

§8.33A   IX. SET ASIDE

Under the set-aside provisions of Fam C §§3690–3693, a court may, on any terms that may be just, relieve a party from all or any parts of a support order after the 6-month time limit of CCP §473 (see §§18.24–18.35) has run. Fam C §3690(a). For mandatory Judicial Council forms, see §§8.33F–8.33H.

One appellate court has also determined that the 6-month time limit of CCP §473 may be extended when required by public policy, as stated in the Child Support Enforcement Fairness Act of 2000 (Stats 1999, ch 653, §1). *County of Los Angeles v Navarro* (2004) 120 CA4th 246, 14 CR3d 905. In that case, a default judgment wrongly established paternity, and county officials were made aware of the mistake. The court held that the county was obligated to correct the mistake, even though the time for setting aside the judgment under CCP §473 had long passed.

However, at least one court of appeal declined to authorize a restitution remedy to a nonbiological father from the biological father for child support paid in the past for a child not biologically related to him on a cause of action alleging unjust enrichment, citing public policy grounds. *McBride v Boughton* (2004) 123 CA4th 379, 392, 20 CR3d 115.

§8.33B   A. Requisite Findings for Granting of Relief

Before granting relief, the court must find that the facts alleged as the grounds for relief materially affected the original order and that the moving party would materially benefit from the granting of the relief. Fam C §3690(b).

§8.33C   B. Relief Available

The court may set aside only those provisions materially affected by the circumstances leading to the court's decision to grant relief, except that the court has discretion to set aside the entire order, if necessary, for equitable considerations. Fam C §3693.

§8.33D   C. Grounds and Time Limits

The grounds and respective time limits for an action or motion to set aside all or any parts of a support order are as follows:

Actual fraud. The moving party must have been fraudulently prevented from fully participating in the proceeding either by being kept in ignorance or in some other manner but not as a result of his or her own lack of care or attention. Actions or motions based on fraud must be brought within 6 months after the moving party discovered, or reasonably should have discovered, the fraud. Fam C §3691(a).

Perjury. Actions or motions based on perjury must be brought within 6 months after the moving party discovered, or reasonably should have discovered, the perjury. Fam C §3691(b).

Lack of notice. When service of a summons has not resulted in notice to a party in time to defend the action for support and a default or default judgment has been entered against him or her, the party may serve and file a notice of motion to set aside the default and for leave to defend the action. The notice of motion must be served and filed within a reasonable time and within 6 months after the party obtains, or reasonably should have obtained, notice (1) of the support order or (2) that the party's income and assets are subject to attachment under the order. Fam C §3691(c)(1). A notice of motion to set aside a support order for lack of notice must be accompanied by an affidavit showing, under oath, that the party's lack of notice in time to defend the action was not caused by his or her avoidance of service or inexcusable neglect. The party must serve and file with the notice a copy of the answer, motion, or other pleading proposed to be filed in the action. Fam C §3691(c)(2). The court may not set aside or otherwise relieve a party from a support order for lack of notice if service of the summons was accomplished in accordance with existing requirements of law regarding service of process. Fam C §3691(c)(3).

Notwithstanding any other provision of Fam C §§3690–3693, or any other law, a support order may not be set aside simply because the court finds that it was inequitable when made or simply because subsequent circumstances caused it to become excessive or inadequate. Fam C §3692. See form, §8.33F.

§8.33E   D. No Effect on Specified Family Code Sections

Nothing in Fam C §§3690–3693 may limit or modify the provisions of Fam C §17432 or §17433. Fam C §3690(c).

§8.33F   E. Form: Request for Hearing and Application to Set Aside Support Order Under Fam C §3691 (Judicial Council Form FL-360)

FL-360

ATTORNEY OR PARTY WITHOUT ATTORNEY OR GOVERNMENTAL AGENCY *(Name, State Bar number, and address):*	FOR COURT USE ONLY

TELEPHONE NO.:   FAX NO. *(Optional):*

E-MAIL ADDRESS *(Optional):*

ATTORNEY FOR *(Name):*

SUPERIOR COURT OF CALIFORNIA, COUNTY OF

STREET ADDRESS:

MAILING ADDRESS:

CITY AND ZIP CODE:

BRANCH NAME:

PETITIONER/PLAINTIFF:

RESPONDENT/DEFENDANT:

OTHER PARENT:

REQUEST FOR HEARING AND APPLICATION TO SET ASIDE SUPPORT ORDER UNDER FAMILY CODE SECTION 3691	CASE NUMBER:

1. To ☐ petitioner *(specify name):*   ☐ respondent *(specify name):*

     ☐ local child support agency   ☐ other parent *(specify name):*

     ☐ other *(specify):*

A hearing on this application will be held as follows:

a. Date: Time: Dept.:   Div.:   Room:

b. The address of the court where the hearing will be held is ☐ same as above ☐ other *(specify):*

2. An order was entered in this case on *(date):*   requiring ☐ petitioner *(specify name):*

   ☐ respondent *(specify name):*   ☐ other parent *(specify name):*

   to pay support. I request that the order be set aside.

3. Grounds for this request are *(check all that apply):*
   a. ☐ Fraud
   b. ☐ Perjury
   c. ☐ Lack of notice

4. ☐ I have complied with the time limits for filing this request to set aside the order *(check one):*
   a. ☐ Request brought within six months after the date I discovered or reasonably should have discovered the fraud.
   b. ☐ Request brought within six months after the date I discovered or reasonably should have discovered the perjury.
   c. ☐ Request brought within six months after the date:
     (1) ☐ I obtained or reasonably should have obtained notice of the support order **or**
     (2) ☐ my income and assets were subject to attachment under the support order.

Page 1 of 2

FL-360

PETITIONER/PLAINTIFF:	CASE NUMBER:
RESPONDENT/DEFENDANT:	
OTHER PARENT:	

5. ☐ FACTS IN SUPPORT of relief requested are *(specify):*

☐ Contained in the attached declaration.

I declare under penalty of perjury under the laws of the State of California that the foregoing is true and correct.

Date:

_____   ▶   _____
(TYPE OR PRINT NAME)   (SIGNATURE OF DECLARANT)

NOTICE FOR CASES INVOLVING A LOCAL CHILD SUPPORT AGENCY

This case may be referred to a court commissioner for hearing. By law, court commissioners do not have the authority to issue final orders and judgments in contested cases unless they are acting as temporary judges. The court commissioner in your case will act as a temporary judge unless, *before the hearing,* you or any other party objects to the commissioner acting as a temporary judge. The court commissioner may still hear your case to make findings and a recommended order. If you do not like the recommended order, you must object to it within 10 court days; otherwise, the recommended order will become a final order of the court. If you object to the recommended order, a judge will make a temporary order and set a new hearing.

Request for Accommodations
Assistive listening systems, computer-assisted real-time captioning, or sign language interpreter services are available if you ask at least five days before the proceeding. Contact the clerk's office or go to *www.courtinfo.ca.gov/forms* for *Request for Accommodations by Persons With Disabilities and Response* (form MC-410). (Civil Code, § 54.8)

FL-360 [Rev. January 1, 2007]

**REQUEST FOR HEARING AND APPLICATION
TO SET ASIDE SUPPORT ORDER
(Family Law—Governmental)**

Page 2 of 2

§8.33G **F. Form: Responsive Declaration to Application to Set Aside Support Order (Judicial Council Form FL-365)**

FL-365

GOVERNMENTAL AGENCY (under Fam. Code, §§ 17400, 17406) or ATTORNEY OR PARTY WITHOUT ATTORNEY (Name, state bar number, and address):	FOR COURT USE ONLY

TELEPHONE NO.: FAX NO. (Optional):

E-MAIL ADDRESS (Optional):

ATTORNEY FOR (Name):

SUPERIOR COURT OF CALIFORNIA, COUNTY OF

STREET ADDRESS:

MAILING ADDRESS:

CITY AND ZIP CODE:

BRANCH NAME:

PETITIONER/PLAINTIFF:

RESPONDENT/DEFENDANT:

OTHER PARENT:

RESPONSIVE DECLARATION TO APPLICATION TO SET ASIDE SUPPORT ORDER

HEARING DATE: TIME: DEPT., ROOM, OR DIVISION: CASE NUMBER:

1. ☐ I consent to the set aside of the support order.

2. ☐ I do not consent to the set aside of the support order.

3. ☐ SUPPORTING INFORMATION (specify):
   ☐ Contained in the attached declaration.

I declare under penalty of perjury under the laws of the State of California that the foregoing is true and correct.

Date:

▶

_____ _____
(TYPE OR PRINT NAME) (SIGNATURE OF DECLARANT)

Page 1 of 1

Form Adopted for Mandatory Use
Judicial Council of California
FL-365 [Rev. January 1, 2003]

RESPONSIVE DECLARATION TO APPLICATION TO SET ASIDE SUPPORT ORDER

Family Code, §§ 3690–3693
www.courtinfo.ca.gov

§8.33H   G. Form: Order After Hearing on Motion to Set Aside Support Order (Judicial Council Form FL-367)

FL-367

GOVERNMENTAL AGENCY (under Fam. Code, §§ 17400, 17406) or ATTORNEY OR PARTY WITHOUT ATTORNEY (Name, state bar number, and address):	FOR COURT USE ONLY

TELEPHONE NO.:   FAX NO. (Optional):

E-MAIL ADDRESS (Optional):

ATTORNEY FOR (Name):

SUPERIOR COURT OF CALIFORNIA, COUNTY OF

STREET ADDRESS:

MAILING ADDRESS:

CITY AND ZIP CODE:

BRANCH NAME:

PETITIONER/PLAINTIFF:

RESPONDENT/DEFENDANT:

OTHER PARENT:

ORDER AFTER HEARING ON MOTION TO SET ASIDE SUPPORT ORDER	CASE NUMBER:

1. This proceeding was heard
   on (date):   at (time):   in Dept: Room:
   by Judge (name):   ☐ Temporary Judge

2. a. ☐ Petitioner/plaintiff present   ☐ Attorney present (name):
   b. ☐ Respondent/defendant present   ☐ Attorney present (name):
   c. ☐ Other parent present   ☐ Attorney present (name):
   d. ☐ Governmental agency   ☐ By (name):

3. The support order filed (date):   ordering (name):
   to pay support to (name):
   a. ☐ is not set aside
   b. ☐ is set aside on the following grounds (specify):

4. Other (specify):

Date:

_____
JUDICIAL OFFICER

Approved as conforming to court order:

▶

_____   SIGNATURE OF ATTORNEY FOR   ☐ PETITIONER/PLAINTIFF
(TYPE OR PRINT NAME)   ☐ RESPONDENT/DEFENDANT
                                                                                                       ☐ OTHER PARENT

Page 1 of 1

Form Adopted for Mandatory Use Judicial Council of California FL-367 [Rev. January 1, 2003]	ORDER AFTER HEARING ON MOTION TO SET ASIDE SUPPORT ORDER	Family Code, §§ 3690–3693 www.courtinfo.ca.gov

§8.34   X. HEALTH INSURANCE

In any child support proceeding, the court must consider the parties' health insurance coverage, if any. Fam C §4006. In any case in which an amount is set for current child support, any parent who has health insurance (including dental-care and vision-care coverage) available for a supported child at no cost or at a reasonable cost must be ordered to maintain the insurance. Fam C §§3750, 3751(a)(2). Any cost of maintaining the insurance will be in addition to the child support amount ordered under the statewide uniform guideline (Fam C §§4050–4076; see §§8.7–8.28). Allowance for the cost of health insurance actually obtained must be given due consideration under Fam C §4059(d) (statewide uniform guideline deduction from gross income for health insurance premiums; see §8.11). Fam C §3753. If health insurance for the children is not available without cost or at a reasonable cost, the court must order that each parent obtain it if it becomes available on such terms in the future. Fam C §3751(b). Health insurance coverage will be rebuttably presumed to be reasonable in cost if it is employment-related group health insurance or other group health insurance, regardless of the service delivery mechanism. The actual cost of the health insurance to the parent must be considered in determining whether the cost of insurance is reasonable. If the court determines that the cost of health insurance coverage is not reasonable, it must state its reasons on the record. Fam C §3751(a)(2). On enforcement through a health insurance coverage assignment, see §§20.66–20.72.

Federal law requires group health plans to provide benefits in accordance with the requirements of any "qualified medical child support order." 29 USC §1169(a)(1). An order in a marital action that provides for coverage under a group health plan is "qualified" if it specifies the name and last known mailing address of the plan participant and each child covered by the order (except that, to the extent provided in the order, the name and address of a government official may be substituted for one or more of these), a reasonable description of the type of coverage to be provided or the manner in which the type of coverage is to be determined, the plan and period to which the order applies, and if it does not require the plan to provide any benefit that it does not otherwise provide. 29 USC §1169(a)(2)–(4).

When health insurance coverage is provided for a child under a court or administrative order, California law requires that the insurer provide any information (including, but not limited to, the child's health insurance membership card) that is provided to the covered parent to the noncovered custodial parent or any other custodial person, and allow such parent or custodial person to submit claims without the covered parent's approval and to receive payment on them. See Fam C §3751.5(c). The noncovered or custodial parent may contact the insurer for information that is specific to the child's health insurance coverage and the insurer must provide the requested information. See Fam C §3751.5(i).

On notice requirements regarding coverage, see Fam C §§3751(a)(1), 3751.5(g)–(h) (under certain circumstances, insurer must notify covered and noncovered custodial parent of health insurance termination), 3752(a) (health insurance orders must require child support obligor to keep the local child support agency informed of whether obligor has coverage at reasonable cost and, if so, of policy information), 3752.5 (child support orders must require parents to keep each other informed of whether each has group health insurance and, if so, of policy information).

For further discussion of health insurance coverage for children, see §8.24.

§8.35 XI. RELATIONSHIP BETWEEN CHILD SUPPORT AND VISITATION

The existence or enforcement of a noncustodial parent's duty of support is not affected by "a failure or refusal by the custodial parent to implement any rights as to custody or visitation granted by a court to the noncustodial parent." Fam C §3556 (former CC §4382). In *Marriage of Damico* (1994) 7 C4th 673, 29 CR2d 787, however, the California Supreme Court held that when a custodial parent not merely interferes with the noncustodial parent's custody or visitation rights, but actively conceals himself or herself and the child from the noncustodial parent until the child reaches the age of majority, despite reasonably diligent efforts by the noncustodial parent to locate them, the custodial parent is estopped from later collecting child support arrearages for the period of concealment. 7 C4th at 685. But see *Cooper v O'Rourke* (1995) 32 CA4th 243, 247, 38 CR2d 444 (custodial parent's failure to give notice of move from California to Florida and failure to provide any information about child's whereabouts for 3 months after move constituted only interference, not concealment).

The California Supreme Court subsequently held that the *Damico* rule of estoppel based on concealment does not apply (1) when the concealment ends while the child is still a minor, or (2) against a public entity when the custodial parent has obtained public assistance payments and assigned his or her child support rights to the public entity. *Marriage of Comer* (1996) 14 C4th 504, 59 CR2d 155. See *Marriage of Vroenen* (2001) 94 CA4th 1176, 114 CR2d 860 (no estoppel defense when concealment ended while children were minors, even though motion to collect arrearages was not filed until after they had reached majority). In *Marriage of Walters* (1997) 59 CA4th 998, 1006, 70 CR2d 354, the court of appeal held that the mother's concealment of the child from the father for ten years did not estop either the county or the mother from collecting child support arrearages. Even though the father's request of the child support office for the mother's address at the time the child disappeared was refused by a clerk, the court reasoned he could have pursued his request with the DA; estopping the county from collecting reimbursement would undermine the strong public policy of protecting public funds by collecting AFDC (now CalWORKs) reimbursement. Because the child support order directed that payments should have been made to the court trustee, the mother's concealment of the child did not prevent him from meeting his child support obligation; the father was therefore also liable for nonwelfare support arrearages. For the opposite result, see *County of Orange v Carl D.* (1999) 76 CA4th 429, 434, 90 CR2d 440 (county estopped from collecting AFDC reimbursements in child concealment case). In *Carl D.*, the county had made affirmative statements to the juvenile court about its inability to locate Carl, during which time his children were living in foster care pending dependency proceedings; at that same time, the DA had located Carl's address and was pursuing AFDC reimbursement. The pending dependency proceedings imposed on the county a "due process obligation" to notify Carl that did not exist in *Comer*.

§8.36   XII. TAX ASPECTS

Child support payments are neither includable in the support payee's gross income nor deductible by the support payer. IRC §§71(c), 215. Each parent is entitled, however, to medical expense deductions for amounts paid by him or her for the child's medical care. IRC §§213(a), (d)(5); Rev & T C §17201.

9

Attorney Fees and Costs

§9.1   I. SCOPE OF CHAPTER

This chapter covers attorney fees and costs in a marital action. The focus is on the bases for court orders for fees and costs: (1) the relative circumstances of the parties, (2) conduct of a party or an attorney that frustrates the policy of the law to promote settlement and encourage cooperation, and (3) bad faith actions or tactics. With respect to court orders, the chapter also discusses the authority for such orders, the parties who may be payors or payees, and tax aspects.

The use of a real property lien to secure payment of attorney fees is also addressed.

NOTE➤ As indicated in this chapter, the court may order any party, except a governmental entity, to pay the amount reasonably necessary for attorney fees and costs in dissolution of marriage, nullity of marriage, or legal separation proceedings. Fam C §2030(a). The legislature has enacted similar provisions that would apply to actions for the exclusive custody of a child and specified child custody and visitation proceedings (*i.e.*, in nonmarital actions), and that are based on an assessment of income and needs. These provisions also permit a party who lacks the financial ability to hire an attorney to request the court to order the other party to pay a reasonable amount to allow the unrepresented party to retain an attorney in a timely manner. Fam C §7605, operative January 1, 2005.

§9.2   II. AUTHORITY

Any award of attorney fees or costs in a marital action must be based on (1) a determination of ability to pay and (2) consideration of the parties' respective incomes and needs in order to ensure each party's access to legal representation to preserve all of his or her rights. Fam C §2030(a).

Most awards of attorney fees and costs in marital actions are made under Fam C §2032 and are based on the parties' relative circumstances (see §9.3). The scope of the costs recoverable is broader in such actions than in civil actions generally. Family Code §2030(a) allows the court to award "the amount reasonably necessary for attorney's fees and for the cost of maintaining or defending the proceeding." As a practical matter, courts routinely consider applications for cost awards for such items as accountant, actuary, and appraiser fees, none of which is recoverable in civil actions generally (see CCP §1033.5(b)(1)).

Awards of attorney fees and costs under Fam C §2032 may be made at any time "during the pendency" of any marital action. Fam C §§2030(a), 2032(a). The awards may be made for services rendered and costs incurred before, as well as after, commencement of the proceeding. Fam C §2030(b). At any time before entry of judgment, including after any appeal has been concluded, the court may augment or modify an original award as may be reasonably necessary to maintain or defend the proceeding or any related proceeding. Fam C §2030(a), (c). *Marriage of Hobdy* (2004) 123 CA4th 360, 20 CR3d 104 (request by one spouse for attorney fees under Fam C §2030 after being denied them at earlier hearing is not motion for reconsideration under CCP §1008). On determining whether a non-marital proceeding is "related," see *Askew v Askew* (1994) 22 CA4th 942, 28 CR2d 284 (consolidation with marital action not required; fraud proceeding related to marital action because issues should have been litigated in marital action); *Marriage of Green* (1992) 6 CA4th 584, 7 CR2d 872 (malicious prosecution and other separate proceedings related to marital action because brought for improper motive and intended to produce result in marital action); *Marriage of Seaman & Menjou* (1991) 1 CA4th 1489, 2 CR2d 690 (juvenile court dependency proceeding ordinarily not related to marital action). With respect to services rendered and costs incurred *after* entry of judgment, the court may award such attorney fees and costs as may be reasonably necessary to maintain or defend any subsequent proceeding and may augment or modify any such award. Fam C §2030(c). It appears that awards under Fam C §271 (see §9.4) and under CCP §128.5 or §128.7 (see §9.5), like those under Fam C §2032, are available at any time that an action is pending, including when post-judgment matters are before the court. However, if ordering a party to pay attorney fees or costs, the court must first determine that the party has or is reasonably likely to have the ability to pay. Fam C §270. Note that the court's authority to award attorney fees and costs in nullity proceedings is limited by Fam C §2255, providing that the court may award attorney fees and costs in an action based on a voidable marriage (see Fam C §2210; §§3.10–3.15) only to a party found to be innocent of fraud or wrongdoing in inducing or entering into the marriage and free from knowledge of the existence of a prior marriage or other impediment to the contracting of the present marriage.

Note that attorney fees may be awarded to legal services organizations that provide services to their clients free of charge. *Marriage of Ward* (1992) 3 CA4th 618, 623, 4 CR2d 365.

A request for attorney fees and costs should generally be supported by submission of an Income and Expense Declaration and attachments (see §§11.25 (discussion), 11.26–11.29 (forms)) or a Financial Statement (Simplified) (see §§11.30 (discussion), 11.31 (form)). Cal Rules of Ct 5.128.

III. TYPES OF AWARDS

§9.3   A. Based on Relative Circumstances of Parties

The court may award attorney fees and costs when the making of the award and the amount awarded are "just and reasonable under the relative circumstances of the respective parties." Fam C §2032(a). In determining what is just and reasonable under the parties' relative circumstances, the court must evaluate the need for the award in order for each party, to the extent practical, to have sufficient financial resources to adequately present his or her case, taking into consideration, to the extent relevant, the parties' circumstances as described in Fam C §4320 (mandatory considerations in awarding long-term spousal support; see §6.10). Fam C §2032(b).

That the party requesting the award has the resources to pay his or her own attorney fees and costs is not in itself a bar to ordering the other party to pay part or all of the fees and costs requested. Financial resources are only one factor the court considers in apportioning the litigation costs equitably between the parties under their relative circumstances. Fam C §2032(b); *Marriage of O'Connor* (1997) 59 CA4th 877, 884, 69 CR2d 480 (husband's net worth of $2 million did not bar attorney fees based on "need" because wife's ability to pursue the litigation was very high given her net worth of $40 million; husband's ability to secure sufficient representation to protect his rights would be impaired if he had to pay all his own attorney fees and costs).

At any time before trial, either party may seek to have the court direct the implementation of a case-management plan designed to allocate attorney fees, court costs, and expert and consultant fees equitably between the parties. Fam C §2032(d). The party files a noticed motion requesting the court to (1) make a finding that the case involves complex or substantial issues of fact or law related to property rights, visitation, custody, or support and (2) direct implementation of a case management plan. On making the requested finding, the court may in its discretion direct implementation of the plan, which must focus on specific, designated issues. The plan may provide for the allocation of separate or community assets, security against such assets, and payments from income or anticipated income of either party to achieve the desired equitable allocation and for the benefit of one or both parties. Payments may be authorized only on the parties' agreement or court order. The court may order that a referee be appointed under CCP §639 to oversee the case management plan. Fam C §2032(d). A motion under §2032(d) is prepared and processed in the same manner as a noticed motion for temporary orders. For discussion of, and forms for, motions for temporary orders, see §§11.16–11.63.

Provisions in the Family Code addressing attorney fees not explicitly discussed below include:

- Reasonable attorney fees incurred in enforcing the right of reimbursement for payment of a debt incurred by the spouse (Fam C §916(b));

- Attorney fees and court costs incurred in an action for breach of fiduciary duty by a spouse (Fam C §1101 (g));

- Attorney fees during a period of continuance for reconciliation (Fam C §2334;

- Attorney fees in a proceeding to recover monetary sanctions for a false accusation of child abuse or neglect (Fam C §3027; see §7.55);

- Attorney fees in a proceeding to recover compensation for a party's failure to assume his or her caretaker responsibility or for thwarting the other parent's visitation or custody rights (Fam C §3028);

- Appointment of counsel to represent a child in a custody or visitation proceeding (Fam C §§3114, 3150–3153, 3184);

- A court must ensure that each party has access to legal representation to preserve each party's rights by ordering one party to pay to the other party or that party's attorney whatever amount is reasonably necessary for attorney fees and for the cost of maintaining or defending the proceeding in an independent action for the exclusive custody of the children of the marriage (Fam C §§3120, 3121);

- Attorney fees when a custody or visitation proceeding is commenced in a clearly inappropriate forum (Fam C §3407);

- Attorney fees if jurisdiction is declined by reason of conduct of a parent who wrongfully removed children (Fam C §3408);

- Attorney fees for the enforcement of a sister-state custody order (Fam C §3416);

- Attorney fees in a proceeding to modify or terminate a child support order (Fam C §3652);

- Attorney fees for agency enforcement of child, spousal, or parent's right to support (Fam C §§4002, 4303, 4403;

- Attorney fees and costs in a proceeding under the Uniform Interstate Family Support Act (Fam C §4927);

- Earnings assignment order (Fam C §5283(d));

- Attorney fees in a proceeding under the Domestic Violence Prevention Act (Fam C §§6344, 6386);

- Contract for attorney fees for services in litigation for a minor (Fam C §6602);

- Counsel fees and costs under Uniform Parentage Act (Fam C §7640);

- Appointment of counsel in proceeding to declare child free from parental custody and control (Fam C §§7827, 7860–7864, 7895);

- Independent adoption (Fam C §8800).

§9.4   B. As Sanction for Frustrating Policy of Law to Promote Settlement and Encourage Cooperation

Notwithstanding any other Family Code provision, the court may base an award of attorney fees and costs on the extent to which each party's or attorney's conduct furthers or frustrates the policy of the law to promote settlement and to reduce the cost of litigation by encouraging cooperation between the parties and attorneys. Fam C §271(a).

An award of attorney fees and costs under Fam C §271 is in the nature of a sanction. In making such an award, the court must take into consideration all evidence concerning the parties' incomes, assets, and abilities. The court may not order a sanction under Fam C §271 that imposes an unreasonable financial burden on the party against whom it is imposed. To obtain such an award, the requesting party need not demonstrate any financial need. Fam C §271(a).

An award under Fam C §271 may be imposed only after the

party against whom the sanction is requested has received notice and been provided an opportunity to be heard. Fam C §271(b).

The statute contemplates assessing a sanction at the end of the lawsuit, when the extent and severity of the improper conduct can be judged, and the amount is not limited to costs incurred by the innocent party as a result of the improper conduct. *Marriage of Quay* (1993) 18 CA4th 961, 970, 22 CR2d 537 (upheld award of $100,000 in attorney fees under former CC §4370.6, predecessor of Fam C §271). On the other hand, the amount assessed need not compensate the innocent party for all fees and costs expended. *Marriage of Battenburg* (1994) 28 CA4th 1338, 1345, 33 CR2d 871, disapproved on other grounds in *Marriage of Whealon* (1997) 53 CA4th 132, 140, 61 CR2d 559.

Sanctions under the statute may be assessed only against a party; they may not be assessed against an attorney, even when the attorney is solely responsible for the conduct on which the sanctions are based and the client is blameless. If sanctions against an attorney are desired, they must be sought under CCP §128.5 or §128.7 (see §9.5). *Marriage of Daniels* (1993) 19 CA4th 1102, 1110, 23 CR2d 865. Note, however, that the burden of proof under CCP §128.5 or §128.7 is greater than under Fam C §271. For sanctions against an attorney who has knowingly made a false accusation of child abuse or neglect during a custody proceeding, see §7.55.

An award of sanctions under Fam C §271 may be conditional. *Marriage of Hargrave* (1995) 36 CA4th 1313, 1323, 43 CR2d 474 (court of appeal upheld award of sanctions conditional on sanctioned party's failure to comply with court order for payment of taxes to IRS). An overreaching settlement demand may be the basis of Fam C §271 sanctions. *Marriage of Abrams* (2003) 105 CA4th 979, 992, 130 CR2d 16 (settlement offer so onerous it will not seriously be considered by opposing party held not designed to promote settlement, but to antagonize or to gain unfair advantage).

The attorney should keep an ongoing record of conduct by the opposing party or attorney that might support an award of fees and costs under Fam C §271.

§9.5　C. As Sanction for Bad Faith Actions or Tactics

In actions filed before January 1, 1995, the court may order a party, the party's attorney, or both to pay reasonable expenses, including attorney fees, incurred by another party as the result of "bad-faith actions or tactics that are frivolous or solely intended to cause unnecessary delay." CCP §128.5(a). Unfortunately, the appellate courts have reached conflicting conclusions on the meaning of the quoted language. Compare *Javor v Dellinger* (1992) 2 CA4th 1258, 3 CR2d 662 (Second Dist., Div. Four) (actions or tactics subject to sanctions under CCP §128.5 if in bad faith *and* either frivolous or solely intended to cause unnecessary delay), which appears to be the better reasoned interpretation, with *On v Cow Hollow Prop.* (1990) 222 CA3d 1568, 1575, 272 CR 535 (First Dist., Div. One) (conduct subject to sanctions under §128.5 if it constitutes bad faith action *or* tactics that are frivolous or solely intended to cause unnecessary delay). "Frivolous" means totally and completely without merit or for the sole purpose of harassing an opposing party. CCP §128.5(b)(2). This award may not be ordered except after notice and an opportunity to be heard. CCP §128.5(c). See also *Marriage of Reese & Guy* (1999) 73 CA4th 1214, 1221, 87 CR2d 339 (trial court error to impose CCP §128.5 sanctions against wife and her attorney when husband had sought only CCP §128.7 sanctions). In *Reese,* the court reasoned that the motion for §128.7 sanctions had not put the wife on notice that she might be personally liable for sanctions and did not provide opportunity for the wife and her attorney to prepare a defense against allegations of bad faith or frivolous tactics. 73 CA4th at 1221. See *Laborde v Aronson* (2001) 92 CA4th 459, 112 CR2d 119 (clarifying that although §128.7(b)(2) sanction at issue in *Marriage of Reese & Guy* could not be imposed on represented party, §128.7(b)(1) and (b)(3)-(4) sanctions can be imposed on represented party).

The attorney should keep an ongoing record of conduct by the opposing party or attorney that might support an award of expenses under CCP §128.5.

For actions filed on or after January 1, 1995, CCP §128.5 is superseded by CCP §128.7. CCP §128.7(i). Under §128.7, every pleading, petition, written notice of motion, or other similar paper must be signed by at least one attorney of record in the attorney's individual name, or by the party if he or she is unrepresented, and state the signer's address and telephone number, if any. An unsigned paper must be stricken unless the omission is corrected promptly after being called to the attention of the attorney or party. CCP §128.7(a).

By presenting any such document to the court, an attorney or unrepresented party is certifying that, to the best of his or her knowledge, information, and belief, formed after an inquiry reasonable under the circumstances, all the following conditions are met:

- The document is not being presented primarily for an improper purpose, *e.g.,* to harass or to cause unnecessary delay or needless increase in litigation costs (CCP §128.7(b)(1));

- The document's claims, defenses, and other legal contentions are warranted by existing law or by a nonfrivolous argument for the extension, modification, or reversal of existing law or the establishment of new law (CCP §128.7(b)(2));

- The allegations and other factual contentions have evidentiary support or, if specifically so identified, are likely to have evidentiary support after a reasonable opportunity for further investigation or discovery (CCP §128.7(b)(3)); and

- Any denials of factual contentions are warranted on the evidence or, if specifically so identified, are reasonably based on a lack of information or belief (CCP §128.7(b)(4)).

If any of these conditions is not met, a motion for sanctions describing the specific underlying conduct may be served as provided in CCP §1010 (service of notices), but the motion may not be filed if the challenged document is withdrawn or appropriately corrected within 21 days after service or within another time period prescribed by the court. CCP §128.7(c)(1). See *Hart v Avetoom* (2002) 95 CA4th 410, 115 CR2d 511 (abuse of discretion to grant sanctions motion that was filed after case dismissed and that was different from motion served). A court may also issue an order to show cause on its own motion. CCP §128.7(c)(2). In either event, if the court subsequently finds, after considering whether the party seeking sanctions has exercised due diligence, that the condition has not been met, it may impose an appropriate sanction on the attorneys, law firms, or parties that violated the requirements or are responsible for the violation. CCP §128.7(c). Sanctions must be limited to what is sufficient to deter repetition of the conduct or comparable conduct by others similarly situated. They may be monetary (except those against a represented party for a violation of §128.7(b)(2)) or nonmonetary and may include an order for payment of some or all of the reasonable attorney fees and other expenses incurred as a direct result of the violation. CCP §128.7(d). The court may also award to the prevailing party the reasonable expenses and attorney fees incurred in presenting or opposing the motion. CCP §128.7(c)(1).

Code of Civil Procedure §128.7 does not apply to disclosures or to discovery requests, responses, objections, or motions. CCP §128.7(g).

Note that whether CCP §128.5 or CCP §128.7 applies depends on when the action was filed, not, *e.g.*, when a particular motion was filed. *Marriage of Drake* (1997) 53 CA4th 1139, 1169, 62 CR2d 466.

§9.6   D. In Support Enforcement Proceedings

Despite any other provision of law, and without good cause to the contrary, the court must award reasonable attorney fees to the support payee in any child or spousal support enforcement proceeding, as long as the court (1) makes a determination of ability to pay and (2) considers the parties' respective incomes and needs in order to ensure each party's access to legal representation to preserve all of his or her rights. Fam C §3557. Family Code §3557 expressly includes any action to enforce a child support penalty incurred under Fam C §§4720-4733 (see §§20.94-20.96). Fam C §3557(a)(1)(B). The section may not be construed to allow an award of attorney fees to or against a governmental entity. Fam C §3557(b).

§9.7   E. As Sanction for Attempted Murder of Spouse

When a spouse is convicted of attempting to murder the other spouse as punishable under Pen C §664(a), whether or not physical injury occurred, the victim spouse will be entitled to an award of reasonable attorney fees and costs as a sanction. Fam C §§274(a), 4324. The award may be imposed only after the party to be sanctioned has notice and an opportunity to be heard. Fam C §274(b). The party requesting the award need not demonstrate any financial need for the award, which is payable only from the property or income of the sanctioned party, including that party's share of the community property. Fam C §274(c).

§9.8 IV. AWARD PAYER

Awards of attorney fees and costs in marital actions are almost always made against the petitioner or respondent whose marriage is the subject of the proceeding. Note, however, that the court in a marital action may not order a party to pay attorney fees to his or her own attorney. *Wong v Superior Court* (1966) 246 CA2d 541, 54 CR 782. Under Fam C §2030, awards of attorney fees and costs may be made against a properly joined nongovernmental party other than the petitioner or respondent, but they must be limited to an amount reasonably necessary to maintain or defend the action on the issues relating to that party. See *Marriage of Perry* (1998) 61 CA4th 295, 310, 71 CR2d 499 (grandmother ordered to pay attorney fees incurred by father of her grandchild as a result of custody claims she made); *Marriage of Jovel* (1996) 49 CA4th 575, 56 CR2d 740 (third party may be ordered to pay all of attorney fees and costs incurred by spouse parties when issue or issues heard affect both third party and spouse parties). See also *Nicholson v Fazeli* (2003) 113 CA4th 1091, 6 CR3d 881 (Fam C §§271 and 2030 attorney fee award against third party cross-complainant did not bar wife from suing third party for malicious prosecution; primary rights and duties of family law attorney fee awards (right to adequately litigate dissolution) differ from those of malicious prosecution (right to be free from malicious and unmeritorious litigation)).

Family Code §2030 may not be applied, however, to allow an award of attorney fees against a retirement plan. *AT&T Management Pension Plan v Tucker* (CD Cal 1995) 902 F Supp 1168. On joinder generally, see chap 12. Attorney fees may be awarded against a governmental agency only when sanctions are appropriate under CCP §128.5 (see §9.5) or Fam C §271 (see §9.4). Fam C §273; see Fam C §2030(a). Presumably, attorney fees could likewise be awarded against a governmental agency, in an action filed on or after January 1, 1995, when sanctions are appropriate under CCP §128.7 (see §9.5). Although Fam C §273 does not so expressly provide, the omission appears to be inadvertent.

It appears that Fam C §§2030, 2032, and 271 provide no authority for a court to order any part of a party's attorney fees and costs to be paid by the other party's *attorney*. The sections provide for the making of such an award only against a "party," and an attorney is not a party (*Marriage of Tushinsky* (1988) 203 CA3d 136, 249 CR 611). One court did express the view that when it was not a party, but the party's attorney, who was responsible for the inappropriate handling of a case that justified sanctions under former CC §4370.5(b)(2), which provided the same basis for sanctions as current Fam C §271(a), the court could allocate to the attorney the responsibility to pay all or a portion of the fees assessed. *Marriage of Melone* (1987) 193 CA3d 757, 766 n9, 238 CR 510. Nevertheless, the conclusion of the *Melone* court, although probably an equitable one, appears to be an erroneous interpretation of the statute. Under CCP §128.5 or §128.7 (see §9.5), on the other hand, the court may order a party, the party's attorney, or both to pay the amounts assessed.

§9.9   V. AWARD PAYEE

When the court orders a party to pay attorney fees and costs for the benefit of another party, it may order them payable to the other party or to the other party's attorney. Fam C §272(a). Although an order made payable to the attorney may be enforced directly by the attorney in his or her own name (Fam C §272(b)), any fees paid to the attorney by another party under a court order must be credited to the amount payable by the client under the fee agreement with the attorney, unless the agreement expressly provides otherwise. *Mahoney v Sharff* (1961) 191 CA2d 191, 196, 12 CR 515.

An attorney fee award may be made to an attorney who has already been discharged if that attorney's former client has expressly or impliedly sanctioned a motion for fees. This motion is commonly called a *"Borson* motion." *Marriage of Borson* (1974) 37 CA3d 632, 112 CR 432. The court will retain jurisdiction to make such an award, even if a substitution of attorney form has been filed, when the motion for fees was filed while the attorney was still of record. *Marriage of Erickson & Simpson* (2006) 141 CA4th 707, 714, 46 CR3d 253.

VI. ATTORNEY'S REAL PROPERTY LIEN

§9.10   A. Discussion

To retain or maintain legal counsel in a marital action, either party may encumber his or her interest in community real property to secure payment of reasonable attorney fees. Known as a "family law attorney's real property lien," the encumbrance attaches only to the encumbering party's interest in the property. Fam C §2033(a).

The attorney to whom the lien is granted must comply with Cal Rules of Prof Cond 3-300 ("Avoiding Interests Adverse to a Client"). Fam C §2033(e); *Fletcher v Davis* (2004) 33 C4th 61, 69, 14 CR3d 58 (charging lien is adverse interest within meaning of rule 3-300 and thus requires client's informed written consent).

Notice of the lien, including a declaration under penalty of perjury containing specified information, must be served either personally or on the other party's attorney of record at least 15 days before the encumbrance is recorded. Fam C §2033(b). The other party may file an ex parte objection to the lien. The objection, which also includes a declaration under penalty of perjury containing specified information, must request a stay of the recordation until further notice of the court and must contain a copy of the notice received. Fam C §2033(c). Except as otherwise provided by Fam C §2033, existing procedural rules on ex parte motions will apply. Fam C §2033(d).

On application, the court may deny the lien if it finds that it would likely result in an unequal division of property by impairing the encumbering party's ability to meet his or her fair share of the community obligations or would otherwise be unjust under the circumstances of the case. The court may also limit the amount of the lien for good cause, but such a limitation may not be construed as a determination of reasonable attorney fees. Fam C §2034(a).

On receiving an objection to establishment of a lien, the court may, on its own motion, determine whether to direct implementation of a case management plan in accordance with Fam C §2032(d). Fam C §2034(b). For discussion of Fam C §2032(d), see §9.3.

The court has jurisdiction to resolve any dispute arising from the existence of a family law attorney's real property lien. Fam C §2034(c).

A party opposing a family law attorney's real property lien would presumably file a noticed motion to deny the lien under Fam C §2034(a) that includes an ex parte motion for a stay of recordation under Fam C §2033(c). The motion to deny the lien will be prepared and processed in the same manner as a noticed motion for temporary orders. For discussion of, and forms for, motions for temporary orders, see §§11.16-11.63. On ex parte motions generally, see §11.15.

§9.11 B. Form: Notice of Family Law Attorney's Real Property Lien

_ _[Attorney name]_ _
_ _[State Bar number]_ _
_ _[Address]_ _
_ _[Telephone number]_ _

Attorney for _ _[name]_ _

SUPERIOR COURT OF CALIFORNIA
COUNTY OF _ _ _ _ _ _

Marriage of	)	No. _ _ _ _ _ _
	)	
Petitioner: _ _ _ _ _ _	)	**NOTICE OF FAMILY LAW**
	)	**ATTORNEY'S REAL**
Respondent: _ _ _ _ _ _	)	**PROPERTY LIEN**
	)	
_____	)	

NOTICE IS HEREBY GIVEN that _ _[name]_ _, _ _[petitioner/respondent]_ _, intends to grant a family law attorney's real property lien encumbering _ _[his/her]_ _ interest in the community real property located at _ _[address]_ _ to secure payment of reasonable attorney fees to _ _[name of attorney]_ _.

DECLARATION OF _ _[NAME]_ _

I, _ _[name]_ _, declare as follows:

1. The legal description of the community real property to be encumbered is as follows:

[Provide legal description of property]

2. In my opinion, the fair market value of the property is $_ _ _ _ _ _. This opinion is based on _ _[e.g., the appraisal of _ _[name and title of appraiser]_ _, of _ _[date]_]_ _.

3. As of the date of this declaration, the encumbrances on the property are as follows:

[List]

4. As of the date of this declaration, the community assets and liabilities and their estimated values are as follows:

[List]

5. The amount of the family law attorney's real property lien is $_ _ _ _ _ _.

I declare under penalty of perjury under the laws of the State of California that the foregoing is true and correct.

Date: _____   __*[Signature]*__
_ _*[Typed name]*_ _

Copies: Original (file with court clerk); copy for service on other party; office copies.

§9.12   VII. TAX ASPECTS

Legal fees relating to marital actions are generally not deductible. Reg §1.262–1(b)(7). Rather, such expenses are generally treated as nondeductible personal expenses arising from the marriage relationship. See, *e.g., U.S. v Gilmore* (1963) 372 US 39, 51, 9 L Ed 2d 570, 578, 83 S Ct 623, 630; *U.S. v Patrick* (1963) 372 US 53, 56, 9 L Ed 2d 580, 583, 83 S Ct 618, 620. See also *Justin R. Melat,* TC Memo 1993-247 (legal fees incurred in valuation of law partnership interest for purposes of property division constituted nondeductible personal expenses). However, two exceptions are recognized: Fees incurred for obtaining or enforcing a spousal support order in connection with a marital action are deductible under IRC §212(1) as ordinary and necessary expenses for the production or collection of income. Reg §1.262–1(b)(7). Likewise, fees incurred for tax counsel in connection with such an action are deductible under IRC §212(3) as ordinary and necessary expenses in connection with the determination, collection, or refund of any tax. Reg §1.212–1(*l*).

Even when legal fees are deductible, however, they may be deducted only by a party who actually incurs and pays them. *U.S. v Davis* (1962) 370 US 65, 74, 8 L Ed 2d 335, 343, 82 S Ct 1190, 1195. Therefore, if one party pays otherwise deductible legal fees incurred by the other party, even when paid under a court order, neither party may deduct the fees unless they file a joint return.

When keeping time records, the attorney should indicate by some code whenever the fees charged are in connection with securing spousal support or for tax advice. It will then be a simple matter to provide the client with an accounting at the end of the year as to what fees, if any, are potentially deductible. When providing the accounting, the attorney should recommend that the client review the matter with his or her accountant.

10

Petition, Response, and Related Matters

§10.1   I. SCOPE OF CHAPTER

This chapter covers initial steps by the parties, except those relating to temporary orders (see chap 11). Emphasis for the petitioner is on the petition and supplemental papers and on service of process. Emphasis for the respondent is on the response and supplemental papers and on available motions.

Also covered are motions available to the petitioner after the response is filed, amended and supplemental pleadings, and proceeding in forma pauperis.

II. INITIATING THE ACTION

A. Petition and Supplemental Papers

1. Petition

§10.2   a. Discussion

A party who seeks a judicial determination altering his or her marital status under the Family Code, *i.e.,* a judgment of dissolution, legal separation, or nullity, must commence the proceeding by filing a petition. See Cal Rules of Ct 5.108. The petition must not contain any matter not specifically required by the Judicial Council petition form. See Judicial Council Form FL-100 (Petition (Family Law)); see §10.12.

The discussion in §§10.3–10.11 is keyed to the Judicial Council form (see §10.12).

NOTE➤ On and after January 1, 2005, a separate form of petition must be used in judicial proceedings for dissolution, legal separation, or nullity of a registered domestic partnership. See §10.12A. This form (Judicial Council Form FL-103) closely parallels the form of petition used in the context of marital dissolution proceedings. In limited circumstances (similar to those for summary dissolution of marriage), a domestic partnership may be terminated through the office of the Secretary of State by an administrative notice procedure. See Fam C §299. For a full discussion of actions to terminate registered domestic partnerships, see California Domestic Partnerships (Cal CEB 2005).

§10.3 (1) Court

On ascertaining in what county or counties the petition may properly be filed, see §4.8. To ascertain any limitations on the branch court in which the petition may properly be filed in counties with more than one superior court branch, consult local rules and practice. See, *e.g.,* Los Angeles Ct R 2.0(c) (action may be filed in district where petitioner or respondent resides).

§10.4 (2) Parties

In almost every instance, the petitioner and the respondent will be the two spouses or domestic partners (see Cal Rules of Ct 5.102(a), (b)), with the spouse or domestic partner who files the action being the petitioner (Cal Rules of Ct 5.100, 5.102). In the case of a married couple, generally the only persons permitted to be parties in a dissolution, legal separation, or nullity of marriage proceeding are the spouses, and, similarly, in the case of registered domestic partners, the only persons permitted to be parties to a dissolution, separation, or nullity of partnership proceeding are the domestic partners—except as provided in Cal Rules of Ct 5.102(c) or in Rules 5.150–5.160. Cal Rules of Ct 5.102(a), (b).

In some actions for a judgment of nullity, however, a third party (*e.g.,* a parent of a minor married without the required parental and court consents) may be the one who files the action. Fam C §2211(a)–(c). In that event, the third party is the petitioner, and both spouses, in the case of a nullity of marriage, are respondents. See Cal Rules of Ct 5.102(c) (referring both to spouses and domestic partners regarding nullity proceedings brought by third parties). The caption in a nullity of marriage proceeding might be modified as follows:

Petitioner: JOHN SMITH
Marriage of
Respondent: PAULA JONES
Respondent: MICHAEL JONES

Parties may be identified by the names by which they are known, *e.g.*, the wife may be identified by her birth name. *Weathers v Superior Court* (1976) 54 CA3d 286, 289, 126 CR 547. Although the specific forms in which the names are listed will not be significant in most cases, some attention should be given to the matter because there may be exceptions. When, for example, the petitioner will record a lis pendens (see §§10.23–10.24), care should be taken to identify the respondent on the petition by the name in which he or she holds title to the real property at issue so that the lis pendens will give constructive notice of the pendency of the action. Likewise, if an effort is subsequently made to enforce an order against the respondent by recording an Abstract of Judgment (Judicial Council Form EJ-001) (see form in §20.35) or an Abstract of Support Judgment (Judicial Council Form FL-480) (see form in §20.34), the abstract will call for the respondent's "full name as it appears in [the judgment]" (*i.e.*, the document containing the order). If the respondent owns property to which title was taken in a name different from that listed on the document (*e.g.*, "Edward Smith" rather than "Teddy Smith"), the abstract may not succeed in creating a lien against the property.

When a party is appearing through a guardian, conservator, or guardian ad litem, the caption should indicate that fact, as in the following example:

Marriage of
Petitioner: JOHN JONES, a Conservatee, by MARY SMITH, his
Guardian Ad Litem
Respondent: JANE JONES

When an incompetent person or one for whom a conservator has been appointed is a party, he or she must appear by a guardian ad litem or conservator of the estate. CCP §372; *Marriage of Caballero* (1994) 27 CA4th 1139, 1148, 33 CR2d 46. Appointment need not be made before the summons is issued; rather, it should be made whenever the need is brought to the court's attention. 27 CA4th at 1149. When the petitioner is incompetent or has a conservator, his or her counsel should arrange for the party to appear by a guardian ad litem or conservator of the estate and attempt to ensure that that person is a conscientious and capable individual who does not have a conflict of interest with the petitioner. When the incompetent or conservatee is the client's spouse, counsel should ensure that the same steps are taken in order to prevent a subsequent attack on any temporary orders or judgment. Any party to an action may apply to have a guardian ad litem appointed for another party. CCP §373(c).

A minor will not need to appear by a guardian or guardian ad litem in a dissolution or legal separation action, because entry into a valid marriage results in the minor's becoming "emancipated" (Fam C §7002(a)), and he or she is then considered an adult for purposes of litigation (Fam C §7050(e)(4)-(5)). Likewise, a guardian or guardian ad litem will not be required for a minor petitioner seeking a judgment of nullity based on a voidable marriage (see §§3.10-3.15), because a voidable marriage is valid unless and until it is judicially declared a nullity (*McDonald v McDonald* (1936) 6 C2d 457, 461, 58 P2d 163). But a guardian or guardian ad litem will be required for a minor petitioner seeking a judgment of nullity based on a *void* marriage (see §§3.8-3.9) because a void marriage is invalid from the beginning (Fam C §§2200 (incestuous marriages), 2201 (bigamous marriages)).

On guardians ad litem generally, including forms of petition and order for appointment of a guardian ad litem, see California Civil Procedure Before Trial, chap 9 (4th ed Cal CEB 2004).

On joinder of an employee benefit plan, see §§12.7-12.25. On joinder of a party other than an employee benefit plan, see §§12.26-12.45.

§10.5   (3) Nature of Action

The nature of the action is indicated by checking the appropriate box in the caption. On choosing the form of action, see §§3.35-3.37.

Note that the petition may seek alternative relief, *e.g.,* judgment of dissolution *or* nullity when proof of grounds for nullity may be difficult (see §3.36). Cal Rules of Ct 5.114. On indicating that the relief sought is in the alternative when more than one box is checked, see §10.11.

§10.6   (4) Residence (Item 1)

Before a petition for dissolution may be filed, at least one of the parties must have been a resident of the county in which the petition is filed for at least three months, and of California for at least six months, immediately preceding the filing of the petition. Fam C §2320; see CCP §395. On the meaning of "resident" for purposes of §2320, see §4.3. There is no statutory residency requirement, however, for a petition for legal separation or nullity. On filing a petition for legal separation when the dissolution residency requirement has not been met and then amending it, after the requirement is met, to a petition for dissolution, see §3.3.

§10.7 (5) Statistical Facts (Item 2)

The date of separation can have significant consequences, because property acquired by either spouse after separation is ordinarily separate property. Fam C §771(a). The separation date is not necessarily the date the spouses began living in separate residences. Although the date of separation listed in the petition is not binding on the petitioner, it may be considered as evidence on the issue. See *Marriage of Umphrey* (1990) 218 CA3d 647, 657, 267 CR 218. Consequently, counsel should inquire about relevant facts and not merely ask the client for the date of separation.

Technically, spouses who separate and then reconcile may have more than one period during their marriage for which the property acquired is separate property. *Patillo v Norris* (1976) 65 CA3d 209, 135 CR 210. Consequently, when the facts suggest it, the attorney should consider the possibility that there may have been more than one period of separation.

On the date of separation generally, see §5.12.

§10.8 (6) Minor Children (Item 3)

The form calls for listing minor children of the parties' relationship born before or during the marriage or adopted during the marriage. With respect to children born before the marriage, a paternity determination under the Uniform Parentage Act (Fam C §§7600–7630) may be made in the marital action. Fam C §2330.1. See Item 7.d.

When custody, visitation, or child support is requested, however, with respect to another child (*e.g.,* child support under Fam C §3901(a) for an 18-year-old child who is an unmarried full-time high school student who is not self-supporting), that fact should be clearly indicated, probably at Item 7.j (see §10.11), to provide the respondent with notice of the request. See *Marriage of Lippel* (1990) 51 C3d 1160, 1167, 276 CR 290 (in default proceeding, petitioner may not be granted relief that was not requested in petition unless respondent so stipulates); see §14.9. Otherwise, note that preprinted paragraph 8 on child support makes reference to the court ordering support on request and submission of financial forms by the requesting party. If a party is requesting visitation orders pursuant to Fam C §3101 pertaining to a stepchild (*i.e.*, a biological child of the other party who has not been adopted by the party completing the form), the child should be listed along with the children of the marriage.

Note that if there are minor children of the petitioner and respondent listed on the petition, a declaration under the Uniform Child Custody Jurisdiction and Enforcement Act (UCCJEA) (Fam C §§3400–3465) must be attached (see §10.17), regardless of whether a dispute over custody jurisdiction exists. See Fam C §3429(a).

If there is a dispute between states about which court has authority to make custody and visitation orders, the courts will look to the UCCJEA to determine where jurisdiction properly lies. See Fam C §3421.

§10.9 (7) Separate Assets and Obligations (Item 4)

The items the petitioner wishes to have confirmed as the separate assets and obligations of either party should be listed at Item 4 or in an attachment to the petition. When the items will be listed in an attachment, the Judicial Council property declaration forms (see §§10.19–10.21) may be used for that purpose. On determining whether particular assets and obligations are community or separate, see §§5.9–5.40, 5.77–5.81, 5.83–5.84. On listing assets with both community- and separate-property components, and on the degree of detail to use in identifying assets and obligations, see §10.10.

§10.10 (8) Community and Quasi-Community Assets and Obligations (Item 5)

When community or quasi-community assets or obligations have not been disposed of by written agreement, they should be listed at Item 5 or in an attachment to the petition. When the items will be listed in an attachment, the Judicial Council property declaration forms (Judicial Council Forms FL-160–FL-161; see §§10.19–10.21) may be used for that purpose. On determining whether particular assets and obligations are community or separate, see §§5.9–5.40, 5.77–5.81, 5.83–5.84. On the definition of quasi-community property, see §5.4. When assets have both community- and separate-property components, it will probably be best to list each component (*e.g.,* "Community property interest in ABC Retirement System, account number 123–456–7890") under the applicable item.

It is generally not necessary to identify the particular assets and obligations in great detail as long as they are sufficiently identified to avoid any uncertainty over the items being referred to. For example, "1995 Toyota Corolla automobile" should be a sufficient identification, assuming that the parties have only one such automobile, without including the license number or other identifying information. Counsel should take care, however, to make the list as complete as possible to avoid the necessity for subsequently amending the petition (see §10.68) to list omitted items. Although some attorneys routinely include a provision indicating that there are other items of community property presently unknown to the petitioner and that the petitioner will seek leave to amend the petition to add them when they are discovered, the inclusion of such a provision does not appear to have any legal effect.

In drafting the list of community or quasi-community assets and obligations, counsel should be aware that, in a default proceeding, the petitioner may not be granted relief that was not requested in the petition unless the respondent so stipulates. *Marriage of Lippel* (1990) 51 C3d 1160, 1167, 276 CR 290. For a good illustration of the relationship between the list of assets and obligations at Item 5 on the petition and the relief available in a default proceeding, see *Marriage of Andresen* (1994) 28 CA4th 873, 34 CR2d 147. In *Andresen,* the trial court divided the community assets and liabilities identified in the petition between the parties and ordered the respondent to make an equalizing payment to the petitioner. 28 CA4th at 877. On appeal, the respondent contended that the orders were void because the petition did not allege values for the property items, identify all community assets ultimately awarded to the petitioner, or request an equalizing payment. 28 CA4th at 877. The court of appeal held that the petition was sufficient to support the judgment because the petitioner had properly completed the Judicial Council petition form, checking the box in Item 7 requesting that property rights be determined and listing the assets and obligations in an attached Judicial Council property declaration form. As the court noted, the property declaration form expressly provides that, when it is attached to a petition or response, values and proposals for division need not be completed. 28 CA4th at 879. However, a provision in an earlier judgment that required the respondent to execute a $50,000 note payable to the petitioner as reimbursement for separate money she had contributed to the marriage was void because it was not requested in the petition.

Specificity also is paramount when a party wishes to file a lis pendens on real property. See *Gale v Superior Court* (2004) 122 CA4th 1388, 19 CR3d 554.

§10.11 (9) Relief Requested (Items 6–7)

The nature of the judgment sought (*i.e.*, dissolution, legal separation, nullity) is indicated at Item 6, along with the grounds. When alternative relief (*e.g.*, judgment of dissolution or nullity) is sought (see §10.5), the words "in the alternative" may be added after the words "Petitioner requests." Dissolutions and legal separations are almost invariably sought on the grounds of irreconcilable differences and the existence of the grounds is rarely an issue in such proceedings. See §3.2. On the grounds for a judgment of nullity, which will in some instances be more difficult to establish, see §§3.7–3.15.

The specific relief requested is indicated at Item 7. Note that in a default proceeding the petitioner may not be granted relief that was not requested in the petition unless the respondent so stipulates. *Marriage of Lippel* (1990) 51 C3d 1160, 1167, 276 CR 290, 293; see §14.9. Compare *Lippel* with *Marriage of Liss* (1992) 10 CA4th 1426, 13 CR2d 397 (affirmed reservation of jurisdiction over spousal support for each party in nondefault case despite respondent's failure to request spousal support in his response, noting petitioner's presence and opportunity to object). Clearly the prudent approach is to request *all* the relief that might subsequently be desired in the proceeding. Certainly, unreasonable requests should be avoided; but it is usually better practice to include a reasonable request about which the petitioner is uncertain than to omit it and risk being required to seek leave to amend (see §10.68) if the client subsequently insists on making the request.

An exception to the requirement that the relief sought in a default proceeding must have been requested in the petition is a request for restoration of a party's former name, which may be set forth at Item 7(i). Fam C §2080.

Item 7.j ("other" orders) should not be overlooked. There are some orders that are not covered by Items 7.a-7.i. Examples include protective orders and custody, visitation, and child support orders concerning adult children or children of a party's prior relationship in those limited circumstances (see §§7.3, 8.2) in which such orders may be made. In response to *Marriage of Lippel, supra,* in which it was held that a petitioner who did not check the box indicating that child support was requested could not be awarded child support in a default judgment, the Judicial Council eliminated child support from the specific preprinted requests in Item 7 and added Item 8, providing notice that child support orders will be made for minor children of the marriage and a wage assignment issued, without further notice to either party, and that any party required to pay support must pay interest on overdue amounts at the "legal" rate (currently 10 percent). Nevertheless, there seems to be no reason not to request such support expressly, when applicable, at Item 7.j.

When the parties have an agreement or understanding regarding custody or temporary custody, a copy of the agreement or a declaration regarding the understanding must be attached to a petition or motion. As promptly as possible after the filing, the court must, except in exceptional circumstances, enter an order granting temporary custody in accordance with the agreement or understanding. Fam C §3061.

§10.12   b. Form: Petition—Marriage (Judicial Council Form FL-100)

FL-100

ATTORNEY OR PARTY WITHOUT ATTORNEY *(Name, State Bar number, and address):*	FOR COURT USE ONLY
TELEPHONE NO.: FAX NO. *(Optional):* E-MAIL ADDRESS *(Optional):* ATTORNEY FOR *(Name):*	

SUPERIOR COURT OF CALIFORNIA, COUNTY OF
STREET ADDRESS:
MAILING ADDRESS:
CITY AND ZIP CODE:
BRANCH NAME:

MARRIAGE OF
PETITIONER:

RESPONDENT:

PETITION FOR	CASE NUMBER:
☐ **Dissolution of Marriage** ☐ **Legal Separation** ☐ **Nullity of Marriage** ☐ **AMENDED**	

1. RESIDENCE (Dissolution only) ☐ Petitioner ☐ Respondent   has been a resident of this state for at least six months and of this county for at least three months immediately preceding the filing of this *Petition for Dissolution of Marriage.*

2. STATISTICAL FACTS
    a. Date of marriage:
    b. Date of separation:
        c. Time from date of marriage to date of separation *(specify):*
            Years: Months:

3. DECLARATION REGARDING MINOR CHILDREN *(include children of this relationship born prior to or during the marriage or adopted during the marriage):*
    a. ☐ There are no minor children.
    b. ☐ The minor children are:

Child's name	Birthdate	Age	Sex

☐ Continued on Attachment 3b.
    c. If there are minor children of the Petitioner and Respondent, a completed *Declaration Under Uniform Child Custody Jurisdiction and Enforcement Act (UCCJEA)* (form FL-105) must be attached.
    d. ☐ A completed voluntary declaration of paternity regarding minor children born to the Petitioner and Respondent prior to the marriage is attached.

4. SEPARATE PROPERTY
    Petitioner requests that the assets and debts listed ☐ in *Property Declaration* (form FL-160) ☐ in Attachment 4
    ☐ below   be confirmed as separate property.
    Item   Confirm to

NOTICE: You may redact (black out) social security numbers from any written material filed with the court in this case other than a form used to collect child or spousal support.

Page 1 of 2

PETITION—MARRIAGE
(Family Law) Family Code, §§ 2330, 3409;
www.courtinfo.ca.gov

MARRIAGE OF *(last name, first name of parties)*:

CASE NUMBER:

---

5. DECLARATION REGARDING COMMUNITY AND QUASI-COMMUNITY ASSETS AND DEBTS AS CURRENTLY KNOWN
   a. ☐ There are no such assets or debts subject to disposition by the court in this proceeding.
   b. ☐ All such assets and debts are listed ☐ in *Property Declaration* (form FL-160) ☐ in Attachment 5b.
      ☐ below *(specify)*:

6. **Petitioner requests**
   a. ☐ dissolution of the marriage based on
      (1) ☐ irreconcilable differences. (Fam. Code, § 2310(a).)
      (2) ☐ incurable insanity. (Fam. Code, § 2310(b).)
   b. ☐ legal separation of the parties based on
      (1) ☐ irreconcilable differences. (Fam. Code, § 2310(a).)
      (2) ☐ incurable insanity. (Fam. Code, § 2310(b).)
   c. ☐ nullity of void marriage based on
      (1) ☐ incestuous marriage. (Fam. Code, § 2200.)
      (2) ☐ bigamous marriage. (Fam. Code, § 2201.)
   d. ☐ nullity of voidable marriage based on
      (1) ☐ petitioner's age at time of marriage. (Fam. Code, § 2210(a).)
      (2) ☐ prior existing marriage. (Fam. Code, § 2210(b).)
      (3) ☐ unsound mind. (Fam. Code, § 2210(c).)
      (4) ☐ fraud. (Fam. Code, § 2210(d).)
      (5) ☐ force. (Fam. Code, § 2210(e).)
      (6) ☐ physical incapacity. (Fam. Code, § 2210(f).)

7. **Petitioner requests** that the court grant the above relief and make injunctive (including restraining) and other orders as follows:

	Petitioner	Respondent	Joint	Other
a. Legal custody of children to	☐	☐	☐	☐
b. Physical custody of children to	☐	☐	☐	☐
c. Child visitation be granted to	☐			☐

As requested in form: ☐ FL-311 ☐ FL-312 ☐ FL-341(C) ☐ FL-341(D) ☐ FL-341(E) ☐ Attachment 7c.
   d. ☐ Determination of parentage of any children born to the Petitioner and Respondent prior to the marriage.
   e. Attorney fees and costs payable by .... ☐ ☐
   f. Spousal support payable to (earnings assignment will be issued) .... ☐ ☐
   g. ☐ Terminate the court's jurisdiction (ability) to award spousal support to Respondent.
   h. ☐ Property rights be determined.
   i. ☐ Petitioner's former name be restored to *(specify)*:
   j. ☐ Other *(specify)*:

   ☐ Continued on Attachment 7j.

8. **Child support**–If there are minor children born to or adopted by the Petitioner and Respondent before or during this marriage, the court will make orders for the support of the children upon request and submission of financial forms by the requesting party. An earnings assignment may be issued without further notice. Any party required to pay support must pay interest on overdue amounts at the "legal" rate, which is currently 10 percent.

9. **I HAVE READ THE RESTRAINING ORDERS ON THE BACK OF THE SUMMONS, AND I UNDERSTAND THAT THEY APPLY TO ME WHEN THIS PETITION IS FILED.**

I declare under penalty of perjury under the laws of the State of California that the foregoing is true and correct.

Date:

▶

_____
(TYPE OR PRINT NAME)

_____
(SIGNATURE OF PETITIONER)

Date:

▶

_____
(TYPE OR PRINT NAME)

_____
(SIGNATURE OF ATTORNEY FOR PETITIONER)

NOTICE: Dissolution or legal separation may automatically cancel the rights of a spouse under the other spouse's will, trust, retirement plan, power of attorney, pay on death bank account, survivorship rights to any property owned in joint tenancy, and any other similar thing. It does not automatically cancel the right of a spouse as beneficiary of the other spouse's life insurance policy. You should review these matters, as well as any credit cards, other credit accounts, insurance polices, retirement plans, and credit reports to determine whether they should be changed or whether you should take any other actions. However, some changes may require the agreement of your spouse or a court order (see Family Code sections 231–235).

FL-100 [Rev. January 1, 2005]

PETITION—MARRIAGE
(Family Law)

Page 2 of 2

Copies: Original (file with court clerk); copies for service (see §10.30); office copies.

§10.12A c. Form: Petition—Domestic Partnership (Judicial Council Form FL-103)

FL-103

ATTORNEY OR PARTY WITHOUT ATTORNEY *(Name, State Bar number, and address):*	FOR COURT USE ONLY
TELEPHONE NO. : FAX NO. *(Optional):* E-MAIL ADDRESS *(Optional):* ATTORNEY FOR *(Name):*	

SUPERIOR COURT OF CALIFORNIA, COUNTY OF
   STREET ADDRESS:
   MAILING ADDRESS:
   CITY AND ZIP CODE:
   BRANCH NAME:

DOMESTIC PARTNERSHIP OF
   PETITIONER:

   RESPONDENT:

PETITION FOR	CASE NUMBER:
☐ **Dissolution of Domestic Partnership** ☐ **Legal Separation of Domestic Partnership** ☐ **Nullity of Domestic Partnership** ☐ **AMENDED**	

1. STATISTICAL FACTS
   a. Date of registration of domestic partnership or equivalent:
   b. Date of separation:
   c. Time from date of registration of domestic partnership to date of separation *(specify):*   Years   Months

2. RESIDENCE (Partnerships established out of state only)
   a. ☐ Our domestic partnership was established in another state *(specify state):*
   b. ☐ Petitioner ☐ Respondent has been a resident of this state of California for at least six months and of this county for at least three months immediately preceding the filing of this *Petition for Dissolution of Domestic Partnership.*

3. DECLARATION REGARDING MINOR CHILDREN *(include children of this relationship born prior to or during this domestic partnership or adopted during this domestic partnership):*
   a. ☐ There are no minor children.
   b. ☐ The minor children are:

Child's name	Birthdate	Age	Sex

   ☐ Continued on Attachment 3b.
   c. If there are minor children of the petitioner and respondent, a completed *Declaration Under Uniform Child Custody Jurisdiction and Enforcement Act (UCCJEA)* (form FL-105) must be attached.

4. SEPARATE PROPERTY
   Petitioner requests that the assets and debts listed ☐ in *Property Declaration* (form FL-160) ☐ in Attachment 4
   ☐ below   be confirmed as separate property.
   Item   Confirm to

NOTICE: You may redact (black out) social security numbers from any written material filed with the court in this case other than a form used to collect child or partner support.

Form Adopted for Mandatory Use
 Judicial Council of California
 FL-103 [New January 1, 2005]

PETITION—DOMESTIC PARTNERSHIP
(Family Law)

Family Code, §§ 299, 2330;
 Cal. Rules of Court, rule 5.28 <br> www.courtinfo.ca.gov

DOMESTIC PARTNERSHIP OF *(Last name, first name of each party)*:	CASE NUMBER:

5. DECLARATION REGARDING COMMUNITY AND QUASI-COMMUNITY ASSETS AND DEBTS AS CURRENTLY KNOWN
   - a. ☐ There are no such assets or debts subject to disposition by the court in this proceeding.
   - b. ☐ All such assets and debts are listed ☐ in *Property Declaration* (form FL-160) ☐ in Attachment 5b.
     - ☐ below *(specify)*:

6. **Petitioner requests**
   - a. ☐ dissolution of the domestic partnership based on
     - (1) ☐ irreconcilable differences. (Fam. Code, § 2310(a).)
     - (2) ☐ incurable insanity. (Fam. Code, § 2310(b).)
   - b. ☐ legal separation of the domestic partnership based on
     - (1) ☐ irreconcilable differences. (Fam. Code, § 2310(a).)
     - (2) ☐ incurable insanity. (Fam. Code, § 2310(b).)
   - c. ☐ nullity of void domestic partnership based on
     - (1) ☐ incest. (Fam. Code, § 2200.)
     - (2) ☐ bigamy. (Fam. Code, § 2201.)
   - d. ☐ nullity of voidable domestic partnership based on
     - (1) ☐ petitioner's age at time of registration of domestic partnership. (Fam. Code, § 2210(a)
     - (2) ☐ prior existing marriage or domestic partnership. (Fam. Code, § 2210(b).)
     - (3) ☐ unsound mind. (Fam. Code, § 2210(c).)
     - (4) ☐ fraud. (Fam. Code, § 2210(d).)
     - (5) ☐ force. (Fam. Code, § 2210(e).)
     - (6) ☐ physical incapacity. (Fam. Code, § 2210(f).)

7. **Petitioner requests** that the court grant the above relief and make injunctive (including restraining) and other orders as follows:

	Petitioner	Respondent	Joint	Other
a. Legal custody of children to	☐	☐	☐	☐
b. Physical custody of children to	☐	☐	☐	☐
c. Child visitation granted to	☐	☐	☐	☐

   As requested in form: ☐ FL-311 ☐ FL-312 ☐ FL-341(C) ☐ FL-341(D) ☐ FL-341(E) ☐ Attachment 7c
   - d. ☐ Determination of parentage of any children born to the Petitioner and Respondent prior to the domestic partnership.
   - e. Attorney fees and costs payable by .... ☐ ☐
   - f. Partner support payable to .... ☐ ☐
   - g. ☐ Terminate court's jurisdiction (ability) to award partner support to respondent.
   - h. ☐ Property rights be determined.
   - i. ☐ Petitioner's former name be restored to *(specify)*:
   - j. ☐ Other *(specify)*:

     ☐ Continued on Attachment 7j.

8. **Child support**–If there are minor children who were born to or adopted by the petitioner and respondent before or during this domestic partnership, the court will make orders for the support of the children upon request and submission of financial forms by the requesting party. An earnings assignment may be issued without further notice. Any party required to pay support must pay interest on overdue amounts at the "legal" rate, which is currently 10 percent.

9. **I HAVE READ THE RESTRAINING ORDERS ON THE BACK OF THE SUMMONS, AND I UNDERSTAND THAT THEY APPLY TO ME WHEN THIS PETITION IS FILED.**

I declare under penalty of perjury under the laws of the State of California that the foregoing is true and correct.

Date:

_____   ▶ _____
(TYPE OR PRINT NAME)   (SIGNATURE OF PETITIONER)

Date:

_____   ▶ _____
(TYPE OR PRINT NAME)   (SIGNATURE OF ATTORNEY FOR PETITIONER)

NOTICE: Dissolution or legal separation may automatically cancel the rights of a domestic partner under the other domestic partner's will, trust, retirement plan, power of attorney, pay-on-death bank account, survivorship rights to any property owned in joint tenancy, and any other similar thing. It does not automatically cancel the right of a domestic partner as beneficiary of the other partner's life insurance policy. You should review these matters, as well as any credit cards, other credit accounts, insurance polices, retirement plans, and credit reports, to determine whether they should be changed or whether you should take any other actions. However, some changes may require the agreement of your partner or a court order (see Fam. Code, §§ 231–235).

PETITION—DOMESTIC PARTNERSHIP   Page 2 of 2
                                        (Family Law)

2. Summons

§10.13   **a. Discussion**

The front side of the family law summons form (Judicial Council Form FL-110), except for the "Notice to the Person Served" at the bottom, should be completed before it is submitted to the court clerk for issuance. Item 1 or 2 of the "Notice to the Person Served" on the respondent's copy should be completed at or before the time of service. See §10.30 on what persons may be served on behalf of the respondent.

The procedure for issuance of the family law summons form is the same as that in civil actions generally. Cal Rules of Ct 5.110(a). The summons is normally presented to the clerk for issuance when the petition is filed and the required filing fees are paid or an Order on Application for Waiver of Court Fees and Costs (In Forma Pauperis) (Judicial Council Form 982(a)(18)) is filed. See CCP §412.10. On proceeding in forma pauperis, see §§10.69–10.71.

The statute governing procedure in the case of a lost summons was amended, effective January 1, 2006, to provide that the clerk keep each original summons in the court records and provide a copy of each summons issued to the plaintiff who requested issuance of the summons. CCP §412.10.

§10.14   b. Form: Summons (Judicial Council Form FL-110)

FL-110

SUMMONS (Family Law)

CITACIÓN (Derecho familiar)

NOTICE TO RESPONDENT *(Name):*

AVISO AL DEMANDADO (Nombre):

FOR COURT USE ONLY
(SÓLO PARA USO DE LA CORTE)

> **You are being sued.** *Lo están demandando.*

Petitioner's name is:

Nombre del demandante:

CASE NUMBER *(NÚMERO DE CASO):*

You have **30 calendar days** after this *Summons* and *Petition* are served on you to file a *Response* (form FL-120 or FL-123) at the court and have a copy served on the petitioner. A letter or phone call will not protect you.

If you do not file your *Response* on time, the court may make orders affecting your marriage or domestic partnership, your property, and custody of your children. You may be ordered to pay support and attorney fees and costs. If you cannot pay the filing fee, ask the clerk for a fee waiver form.

If you want legal advice, contact a lawyer immediately. You can get information about finding lawyers at the California Courts Online Self-Help Center (www.courtinfo.ca.gov/selfhelp), at the California Legal Services Web site (www.lawhelpcalifornia.org), or by contacting your local county bar association.

Tiene 30 días corridos después de haber recibido la entrega legal de esta Citación y Petición para presentar una Respuesta (formulario FL-120 ó FL-123) ante la corte y efectuar la entrega legal de una copia al demandante. Una carta o llamada telefónica no basta para protegerlo.

Si no presenta su Respuesta a tiempo, la corte puede dar órdenes que afecten su matrimonio o pareja de hecho, sus bienes y la custodia de sus hijos. La corte también le puede ordenar que pague manutención, y honorarios y costos legales. Si no puede pagar la cuota de presentación, pida al secretario un formulario de exención de cuotas.

Si desea obtener asesoramiento legal, póngase en contacto de inmediato con un abogado. Puede obtener información para encontrar a un abogado en el Centro de Ayuda de las Cortes de California (www.sucorte.ca.gov), en el sitio Web de los Servicios Legales de California (www.lawhelpcalifornia.org) o poniéndose en contacto con el colegio de abogados de su condado.

NOTICE: The restraining orders on page 2 are effective against both spouses or domestic partners until the petition is dismissed, a judgment is entered, or the court makes further orders. These orders are enforceable anywhere in California by any law enforcement officer who has received or seen a copy of them.

AVISO: Las órdenes de restricción que figuran en la página 2 valen para ambos cónyuges o pareja de hecho hasta que se despida la petición, se emita un fallo o la corte dé otras órdenes. Cualquier autoridad de la ley que haya recibido o visto una copia de estas órdenes puede hacerlas acatar en cualquier lugar de California.

1. The name and address of the court are *(El nombre y dirección de la corte son):*

2. The name, address, and telephone number of the petitioner's attorney, or the petitioner without an attorney, are:
   (El nombre, dirección y número de teléfono del abogado del demandante, o del demandante si no tiene abogado, son):

Date *(Fecha):*   Clerk, by *(Secretario, por)* _____, Deputy *(Asistente)*

[SEAL]

NOTICE TO THE PERSON SERVED: You are served

AVISO A LA PERSONA QUE RECIBIÓ LA ENTREGA: Esta entrega se realiza

a. ☐ as an individual. *(a usted como individuo.)*

b. ☐ on behalf of respondent who is a *(en nombre de un demandado que es):*

   (1) ☐ minor *(menor de edad)*

   (2) ☐ ward or conservatee *(dependiente de la corte o pupilo)*

   (3) ☐ other *(specify) (otro – especifique):*

(Read the reverse for important information.)
(Lea importante información al dorso.)

Page 1 of 2

Form Adopted for Mandatory Use
Judicial Council of California
FL-110 [Rev. January 1, 2006]

SUMMONS
(Family Law)

Family Code §§ 232, 233, 2040, 7700;
Code of Civil Procedure, §§ 412.20, 416.60–416.90
www.courtinfo.ca.gov

FL-110

WARNING—IMPORTANT INFORMATION

WARNING: California law provides that, for purposes of division of property upon dissolution of a marriage or domestic partnership or upon legal separation, property acquired by the parties during marriage or domestic partnership in joint form is presumed to be community property. If either party to this action should die before the jointly held community property is divided, the language in the deed that characterizes how title is held (i.e., joint tenancy, tenants in common, or community property) will be controlling, and not the community property presumption. You should consult your attorney if you want the community property presumption to be written into the recorded title to the property.

STANDARD FAMILY LAW RESTRAINING ORDERS

Starting immediately, you and your spouse or domestic partner are restrained from

1. removing the minor child or children of the parties, if any, from the state without the prior written consent of the other party or an order of the court;

2. cashing, borrowing against, canceling, transferring, disposing of, or changing the beneficiaries of any insurance or other coverage, including life, health, automobile, and disability, held for the benefit of the parties and their minor child or children;

3. transferring, encumbering, hypothecating, concealing, or in any way disposing of any property, real or personal, whether community, quasi-community, or separate, without the written consent of the other party or an order of the court, except in the usual course of business or for the necessities of life; and

4. creating a nonprobate transfer or modifying a nonprobate transfer in a manner that affects the disposition of property subject to the transfer, without the written consent of the other party or an order of the court. Before revocation of a nonprobate transfer can take effect or a right of survivorship to property can be eliminated, notice of the change must be filed and served on the other party.

You must notify each other of any proposed extraordinary expenditures at least five business days prior to incurring these extraordinary expenditures and account to the court for all extraordinary expenditures made after these restraining orders are effective. However, you may use community property, quasi-community property, or your own separate property to pay an attorney to help you or to pay court costs.

ADVERTENCIA – INFORMACIÓN IMPORTANTE

ADVERTENCIA: De acuerdo a la ley de California, las propiedades adquiridas por las partes durante su matrimonio o pareja de hecho en forma conjunta se consideran propiedad comunitaria para los fines de la división de bienes que ocurre cuando se produce una disolución o separación legal del matrimonio o pareja de hecho. Si cualquiera de las partes de este caso llega a fallecer antes de que se divida la propiedad comunitaria de tenencia conjunta, el destino de la misma quedará determinado por las cláusulas de la escritura correspondiente que describen su tenencia (por ej., tenencia conjunta, tenencia en común o propiedad comunitaria) y no por la presunción de propiedad comunitaria. Si quiere que la presunción comunitaria quede registrada en la escritura de la propiedad, debería consultar con un abogado.

ÓRDENES DE RESTRICCIÓN NORMALES DE DERECHO FAMILIAR

En forma inmediata, usted y su cónyuge o pareja de hecho tienen prohibido:

1. Llevarse del estado de California a los hijos menores de las partes, si los hubiera, sin el consentimiento previo por escrito de la otra parte o una orden de la corte;

2. Cobrar, pedir prestado, cancelar, transferir, deshacerse o cambiar de los beneficiarios de los beneficiarios de cualquier seguro u otro tipo de cobertura, tal como de vida, salud, vehículo y discapacidad, que tenga como beneficiario(s) a las partes y su(s) hijo(s) menor(es);

3. Transferir, gravar, hipotecar, ocultar o deshacerse de cualquier manera de cualquier propiedad, inmueble o personal, ya sea comunitaria, cuasicomunitaria o separada, sin el consentimiento escrito de la otra parte o una orden de la corte, con excepción las operaciones realizadas en el curso normal de actividades o para satisfacer las necesidades de la vida; y

4. Crear o modificar una transferencia no testamentaria de manera que afecte el destino de una propiedad sujeta a transferencia, sin el consentimiento por escrito de la otra parte o una orden de la corte. Antes de que se pueda eliminar la revocación de una transferencia no testamentaria, se debe presentar ante la corte un aviso del cambio y hacer una entrega legal de dicho aviso a la otra parte.

Cada parte tiene que notificar a la otra sobre cualquier gasto extraordinario propuesto, por lo menos cinco días laborales antes de realizarlo, y rendir cuenta a la corte de todos los gastos extraordinarios realizados después de que estas órdenes de restricción hayan entrado en vigencia. No obstante, puede usar propiedad comunitaria, cuasicomunitaria o suya separada para pagar a un abogado o para ayudarle a pagar los costos de la corte.

FL-110 [Rev. January 1, 2006]   **SUMMONS** (Family Law)   Page 2 of 2

Copies: Original (submit to court clerk for issuance and return); copies for service (see §10.30); office copies.

3. Confidential Counseling Statement

§10.15   **a. Discussion**

Effective January 1, 2001, former Cal Rules of Ct 1224 and 1284 (confidential counseling statement must be submitted with petition or response in counties having conciliation court) were repealed.

§10.16   **b. Form: Confidential Counseling Statement (Marriage) (Judicial Council Form 1284) [Deleted]**

Effective January 1, 2001, Judicial Council Form 1287 was revoked.

4. Declaration Under Uniform Child Custody Jurisdiction Act

§10.17   **a. Discussion**

The Declaration Under Uniform Child Custody Jurisdiction and Enforcement Act (see Fam C §§3400–3465) (Judicial Council Form FL-105) is designed to inform the court of other proceedings, in California or elsewhere, concerning children who are subject to the present action so that the court may be aware of any facts that may affect its jurisdiction over custody and visitation issues. As indicated on the petition form (Judicial Council Form FL-100; see form in §10.12) at Item 3.c, a completed Declaration Under Uniform Child Custody Jurisdiction and Enforcement Act must be attached to the petition if there are minor children of the petitioner and respondent.

When there are allegations of domestic violence or child abuse, any addresses of the party alleging violence or abuse and of the child that are unknown to the other party will be confidential and are not to be disclosed on the Declaration Under Uniform Child Custody Jurisdiction and Enforcement Act. Fam C §3429(a).

§10.18 b. Form: Declaration Under Uniform Child Custody Jurisdiction and Enforcement Act (Judicial Council Form FL-105/ GC-120)

FL-105/GC-120

ATTORNEY OR PARTY WITHOUT ATTORNEY *(Name, State Bar number, and address):*	FOR COURT USE ONLY
TELEPHONE NO.: FAX NO. *(Optional):* E-MAIL ADDRESS *(Optional):* ATTORNEY FOR *(Name):*	

SUPERIOR COURT OF CALIFORNIA, COUNTY OF

STREET ADDRESS:

MAILING ADDRESS:

CITY AND ZIP CODE:

BRANCH NAME:

PETITIONER:

RESPONDENT:

DECLARATION UNDER UNIFORM CHILD CUSTODY JURISDICTION AND ENFORCEMENT ACT (UCCJEA)	CASE NUMBER:

1. **I am a party** to this proceeding to determine custody of a child.

2. ☐ My present address is not disclosed. It is confidential under Family Code section 3429. I have listed the address of the children presently residing with me as confidential.

3. *(Number):* _____ minor children are subject to this proceeding as follows:

   (Insert the information requested below. The residence information must be given for the last FIVE years.)

a. Child's name		Place of birth	Date of birth	Sex
Period of residence	**Address**	**Person child lived with** *(name and present address)*		**Relationship**
to present	☐ Confidential			
to				
to				
to				

b. Child's name		Place of birth	Date of birth	Sex
☐ Residence information is the same as given above for child a. *(If NOT the same, provide the information below.)*				
Period of residence	**Address**	**Person child lived with** *(name and present address)*		**Relationship**
to present	☐ Confidential			
to				
to				

c. ☐ Additional children are listed on Attachment 3c. *(Provide all requested information for additional children.)*

Page 1 of 2

DECLARATION UNDER UNIFORM CHILD CUSTODY JURISDICTION AND ENFORCEMENT ACT (UCCJEA)

CEB

Family Code, § 3400 et seq.
 Probate Code, §§ 1510(f), 1512 <br> www.courtinfo.ca.gov

SHORT TITLE:	CASE NUMBER:

4. Have you participated as a party or a witness or in some other capacity in another litigation or custody proceeding, in California or elsewhere, concerning custody of a child subject to this proceeding?

    ☐ No ☐ Yes *(If yes, provide the following information)*:

    a. Name of each child:

    b. I was a: ☐ party ☐ witness ☐ other *(specify)*:

    c. Court *(specify name, state, location)*:

    d. Court order or judgment *(date)*:

5. Do you have information about a custody proceeding pending in a California court or any other court concerning a child in this case, other than that stated in item 4?

    ☐ No ☐ Yes *(If yes, provide the following information)*:

    a. Name of each child:

    b. Nature of proceeding: ☐ dissolution or divorce ☐ guardianship ☐ adoption ☐ other *(specify)*:

    c. Court *(specify name, state, location)*:

    d. Status of proceeding:

6. ☐ One or more domestic violence restraining /protective orders are now in effect. (Attach a copy of the orders if you have one.)
    The orders are from the following court or courts *(specify county and state)*:

    a. ☐ Criminal: County/state: _____   c. ☐ Juvenile: County/state: _____
      Case No. *(if known)*: _____   Case No. *(if known)*: _____

    b. ☐ Family: County/state: _____   d. ☐ Other: County/state: _____
      Case No. *(if known)*: _____   Case No. *(if known)*: _____

7. Do you know of any person who is not a party to this proceeding who has physical custody or claims to have custody of or visitation rights with any child in this case?

    ☐ No ☐ Yes *(If yes, provide the following information)*:

a. Name and address of person	b. Name and address of person	c. Name and address of person
☐ Has physical custody ☐ Claims custody rights ☐ Claims visitation rights	☐ Has physical custody ☐ Claims custody rights ☐ Claims visitation rights	☐ Has physical custody ☐ Claims custody rights ☐ Claims visitation rights
Name of each child	Name of each child	Name of each child

I declare under penalty of perjury under the laws of the State of California that the foregoing is true and correct.

Date:

▶

_____   _____
      (TYPE OR PRINT NAME)   (SIGNATURE OF DECLARANT)

8. ☐ Number of pages attached after this page: _____

> **NOTICE TO DECLARANT:** You have a continuing duty to inform this court if you obtain any information about a custody proceeding in a California court or any other court concerning a child subject to this proceeding.

FL-105/GC-120 [Rev. January 1, 2007]   **DECLARATION UNDER UNIFORM CHILD CUSTODY JURISDICTION AND ENFORCEMENT ACT (UCCJEA)**   CEB   Page 2 of 2

Copies: Original (file with court clerk); copies for service (same as for summons and petition); office copies.

5. Property Declaration

§10.19   a. Discussion

As an alternative to listing assets and obligations on the petition form itself (Judicial Council Form FL-100; see form in §10.12), these items may be listed on property declaration forms (Judicial Council Forms FL-160, 161) and attached to the petition. When the forms are used in this manner, only the identifying descriptions are required; values and a proposed division need not be indicated. *Marriage of Andresen* (1994) 28 CA4th 873, 879, 34 CR2d 147.

Community (including quasi-community) property and separate property must not be listed on the same form. Quasi-community property (see §5.4 for definition) must be identified as such.

For further discussion of listing assets and obligations, see §§10.9–10.10.

§10.20   b. Form: Property Declaration (Judicial Council Form FL-160)

FL-160

ATTORNEY OR PARTY WITHOUT ATTORNEY *(Name, State Bar number, and address)*:	FOR COURT USE ONLY
TELEPHONE NO.: FAX NO. *(Optional)*: E-MAIL ADDRESS *(Optional)*: ATTORNEY FOR *(Name)*:	

SUPERIOR COURT OF CALIFORNIA, COUNTY OF
  STREET ADDRESS:
  MAILING ADDRESS:
  CITY AND ZIP CODE:
  BRANCH NAME:

PETITIONER:

RESPONDENT:

☐ PETITIONER'S ☐ RESPONDENT'S
    ☐ COMMUNITY AND QUASI-COMMUNITY PROPERTY DECLARATION
    ☐ SEPARATE PROPERTY DECLARATION
	CASE NUMBER:

INSTRUCTIONS

When this form is attached to the *Petition* or *Response*, values and your proposal regarding division need not be completed. Do not list community, including quasi-community, property with separate property on the same form. Quasi-community property must be so identified. For additional space, use *Continuation of Property Declaration* (form FL-161).

ITEM NO. BRIEF DESCRIPTION	GROSS FAIR MARKET VALUE	AMOUNT OF DEBT	NET FAIR MARKET VALUE	PROPOSAL FOR DIVISION Award to:	
				PETITIONER	RESPONDENT
1. REAL ESTATE	$	$	$	$	$
2. HOUSEHOLD FURNITURE, FURNISHINGS, APPLIANCES					
3. JEWELRY, ANTIQUES, ART, COIN COLLECTIONS, etc.					
4. VEHICLES, BOATS, TRAILERS					

Page 1 of 2

FL-160

ITEM NO. BRIEF DESCRIPTION	GROSS FAIR MARKET VALUE	AMOUNT OF DEBT	NET FAIR MARKET VALUE	PROPOSAL FOR DIVISION Award to: PETITIONER	RESPONDENT
5. SAVINGS, CHECKING, CREDIT UNION, CASH	$	$	$	$	$
6. LIFE INSURANCE (CASH VALUE)					
7. EQUIPMENT, MACHINERY, LIVESTOCK					
8. STOCKS, BONDS, SECURED NOTES					
9. RETIREMENT, PENSION, PROFIT-SHARING, ANNUITIES					
10. ACCOUNTS RECEIVABLE, UNSECURED NOTES, TAX REFUNDS					
11. PARTNERSHIPS, OTHER BUSINESS INTERESTS					
12. OTHER ASSETS AND DEBTS					
13. TOTAL FROM CONTINUATION SHEET					
14. TOTALS					

15. ☐ A *Continuation of Property Declaration* (form FL-161) is attached and incorporated by reference.

I declare under penalty of perjury under the laws of the State of California that, to the best of my knowledge, the foregoing is a true and correct listing of assets and obligations and the amounts shown are correct.

Date:

▶

_____
(TYPE OR PRINT NAME)

_____
(SIGNATURE)

FL-160 [Rev. January 1, 2007]   **PROPERTY DECLARATION**
(Family Law)

CEB   Page 2 of 2

Copies: Original (file with court clerk); copies for service (same as for summons and petition); office copies.

§10.21   c. Form: Continuation of Property Declaration (Judicial Council Form FL-161)

FL-161

MARRIAGE OF (Last name—first names of parties)				CASE NUMBER		

☐ PETITIONER'S   ☐ RESPONDENT'S

☐ COMMUNITY AND QUASI-COMMUNITY PROPERTY DECLARATION

☐ SEPARATE PROPERTY DECLARATION

ITEM NO.	BRIEF DESCRIPTION	GROSS FAIR MARKET VALUE	AMOUNT OF DEBT	NET FAIR MARKET VALUE	PROPOSAL FOR DIVISION AWARD TO	
					PETITIONER	RESPONDENT
		$	$	$	$	$

Page 1 of 2

Form Adopted for Mandatory Use
Judicial Council of California
FL-161 [Rev. January 1, 2003]

CONTINUATION OF PROPERTY DECLARATION
(FAMILY LAW)

Family Code, §§ 2500–2600
www.courtinfo.ca.gov

ITEM NO.	BRIEF DESCRIPTION	GROSS FAIR MARKET VALUE	AMOUNT OF DEBT	NET FAIR MARKET VALUE	PROPOSAL FOR DIVISION AWARD TO	
					PETITIONER	RESPONDENT
		$	$	$	$	$

FL-161 [Rev. January 1, 2003]

CONTINUATION OF PROPERTY DECLARATION
(FAMILY LAW)

Page 2 of 2

Copies: Original (file with court clerk); copies for service (same as for summons and petition); office copies.

§10.22 6. Order to Show Cause for Temporary Orders

When temporary orders are sought at the outset of the case, the order to show cause and accompanying documents (see §§11.16–11.33) may be processed along with the petition. On temporary orders generally, see chap 11.

7. Lis Pendens

§10.23 a. Discussion

A petitioner who asserts any real property claim in a marital action may wish to record a lis pendens, as provided in CCP §405.20, particularly if he or she claims a community interest in real property held in the respondent's name alone. Recording a lis pendens prevents the respondent from conveying or encumbering the petitioner's interest. If the filing of a lis pendens is contemplated, it is important to list the real property at issue as a community asset on the petition. *Gale v Superior Court* (2004) 122 CA4th 1388, 1396, 19 CR3d 554 (wife's merely checking item 5c of petition form without specifying property on which claim is made clearly not sufficient for purposes of lis pendens statute).

A lis pendens is a notice of the pendency of the action, and its recordation gives subsequent purchasers and creditors constructive notice of the pendency of the action as it relates to the property and to the parties designated in the notice. CCP §405.24. Before recordation, a copy of the lis pendens must be mailed, by registered or certified mail, return receipt requested, to all known addresses of the parties to whom the real property claim is adverse and to all owners of record of the property affected by the property claim as shown by the latest county assessment roll, and a copy must be filed in the action. CCP §405.22. A proof of service must be recorded with the notice. CCP §405.23. When an address is unknown, a declaration under penalty of perjury to that effect may be recorded instead of a proof of service as to that individual. CCP §405.22.

§10.24 b. Form: Lis Pendens

After recording, return to:

_ _[Attorney name]_ _
_ _[State Bar number]_ _
_ _[Address]_ _
_ _[Telephone number]_ _

**SUPERIOR COURT OF CALIFORNIA
COUNTY OF _ _ _ _ _ _**

Marriage of	)	**No.** _ _ _ _ _ _
	)	
Petitioner: _ _ _ _ _ _	)	**NOTICE OF PENDING**
	)	**ACTION (CCP §405.20)**
Respondent: _ _ _ _ _ _	)	
	)	
_____	)	

NOTICE IS HEREBY GIVEN that this proceeding was commenced on _ _[date]_ _, by _ _[name]_ _, petitioner, against _ _[name]_ _, respondent, and is now pending in the Court named above.

In this action, petitioner asserts a claim relating to real property located in _ _ _ _ _ _ County, California, commonly known as _ _[street address or other common designation]_ _, and described as follows:

[Give legal description of property]

Date: _____

__[Signature]__
_ _[Typed name]_ _
Attorney for Petitioner

Copies: Original (submit, with proof of service, to county recorder for recording); copy for filing with court clerk; copies for service on respondent, any other parties to whom the real property claim is adverse, and any other owners of record; office copies.

Comment: The lis pendens should always be acknowledged before a notary public to ensure that it may be recorded.

§10.25 8. Local Requirements

Some courts require that the petition be accompanied by special local forms (*e.g.,* "fast-track" forms providing initial case information or forms designating venue among a court's various branches). See, *e.g.,* Sacramento Ct. R 14.26 (requiring counsel for petitioner to provide client "Notice Regarding Mediation" and discuss with client possibility of mediated resolution of legal issues prior to filing petition or moving papers and requiring responding party(ies) and counsel to review and discuss them). Additionally, some courts have special format requirements. Counsel should consult local rules and practice.

§10.26 B. Service of Process

Proper service of process is one of three basic jurisdictional requirements; the others are subject matter jurisdiction (see §4.2) and personal jurisdiction (see §§4.4–4.5). For special rules concerning obtaining personal jurisdiction over a member of the armed forces, see §2.4. The discussion in §§10.27–10.42 assumes that the person over whom jurisdiction is sought is the respondent spouse. For a complete discussion of service of process, see California Civil Procedure Before Trial, chap 17 (4th ed Cal CEB 2004).

§10.27 1. Papers to Be Served

Papers to be served include (1) a copy of the summons (see §10.14) and (2) a copy of the petition (see §10.12), including any attachments (see §§10.18, 10.20–10.21). Cal Rules of Ct 5.110. When temporary orders are sought at the outset of the case, the order to show cause and accompanying documents (see §§11.16–11.33) may be served with the summons and petition. On temporary orders generally, see chap 11.

§10.28 2. Effect of Failure to Make Proper Service

If service is not properly made, the resulting jurisdictional defect may be raised by (1) moving to quash service of summons under CCP §418.10 (see §10.61), (2) moving to vacate any resulting default or default judgment for lack of jurisdiction, (3) bringing an independent action in equity to set aside the judgment, or (4) asserting the judgment's invalidity as a defense to enforcement.

When actual notice of the litigation has been received, however, courts have gone to some lengths to uphold jurisdiction even when service was technically deficient. The legislature intended that CCP §§413.10–417.40 be "liberally construed to effectuate service and uphold the jurisdiction of the court if actual notice has been received by the defendant, and in the last analysis the question of service should be resolved by considering each situation from a practical standpoint." Report of the Judicial Council's Special Committee on Jurisdiction, 14–15 (1968), quoted with approval in *Pasadena Medi-Center Assoc. v Superior Court* (1973) 9 C3d 773, 778, 108 CR 828. See also CCP §§4, 187; *Hammer Collections Co. v Ironsides Computer Corp.* (1985) 172 CA3d 899, 218 CR 627. Nevertheless, the attorney should not be careless in complying with statutory requirements for service of process. Courts cannot necessarily be relied on to construe the provisions liberally and accept defects in service. Rather, strict compliance should always be a priority.

§10.29   3. Who May Serve

A summons may be served by anyone who is at least age 18 and is not a party to the action. CCP §414.10. It should be noted that anyone named as a person to be protected under restraining orders issued in an action will be deemed a "party" under CCP §414.10 and thereby precluded from serving the summons. See *Caldwell v Coppola* (1990) 219 CA3d 859, 268 CR 453. Service may be made by a marshal or sheriff (Govt C §26665); by a professional process server; or even by the petitioner's attorney or other agent (*Sheehan v All Persons* (1926) 80 CA 393, 398, 252 P 337). As a rule, professional process servers are the best choice to make personal service (see §10.31), or substituted service (see §10.32) if personal service cannot be made, because they generally serve the papers more quickly than a sheriff and have a disinterested status that the petitioner's attorney lacks.

§10.30   4. Persons on Whom Summons May Be Served

A summons may be served on a respondent by delivering a copy of the summons and petition to the respondent or to someone authorized by him or her to receive service of process. CCP §416.90. Whether a person has been authorized by a respondent to receive service of process under CCP §416.90 is determined by common-law agency principles of actual and ostensible authority and of ratification. See generally 2 Witkin, Summary of California Law, Agency and Employment §§75–98 (9th ed 1987). An attorney is not necessarily considered an agent for service of process on behalf of a client simply because of present or prior representation of the client related to the subject matter of the litigation. See *Wilson v Eddy* (1969) 2 CA3d 613, 82 CR 826. Service by delivery to an attorney is valid, however, when the facts establish the necessary authority or ratification. See *Warner Bros. Records v Golden W. Music Sales* (1974) 36 CA3d 1012, 1017, 112 CR 71 (specific appointment not required when nature of relationship makes it highly probable defendant will receive actual notice). Nevertheless, the safer course is to deliver the documents directly to the respondent whenever possible.

Under CCP §416.60, a summons may be served on a minor respondent by delivering a copy of the summons and petition (1) to the minor's parent or to his or her guardian or similar fiduciary, or (2) if no such person can be found with reasonable diligence, to any person having the care or control of the minor or with whom the minor resides or by whom the minor is employed. A minor is someone under age 18. Fam C §6500. If the minor is at least age 12, a copy of the summons and petition must also be delivered to him or her. CCP §416.60.

It may be that CCP §416.60 does not apply to a minor who has entered into a valid marriage. Such a minor is an emancipated minor. Fam C §7002(a). An emancipated minor is considered an adult for specified purposes, including that of the capacity to sue or be sued in his or her own name. Fam C §7050(e)(4). But because the Emancipation of Minors Law (Fam C §§7000–7143) does not specifically mention service of process, the safer approach will be to comply with CCP §416.60 when serving a respondent who is a minor, even if the minor has entered into a valid marriage.

Under CCP §416.70, a summons may be served on an adult respondent for whom a conservator or similar fiduciary has been appointed by delivering a copy of the summons and petition to both the conservator or similar fiduciary and the individual. When good cause is shown (*e.g.,* when the individual is unable to comprehend the nature of the documents being served or would suffer severe mental harm from the service), the court may dispense with the requirement that delivery be made to him or her. CCP §416.70.

5. Manner of Service

a. Within California

§10.31   (1) Personal Service

A summons may be served by personal delivery of a copy of the summons and petition to the respondent (or other person to be served; see §10.30). Service made in this manner is deemed complete at the time of delivery. CCP §415.10. The process server is not required to identify himself or herself to the person being served or disclose the nature of the documents being delivered (*Sorrell v Superior Court* (1946) 73 CA2d 194, 201, 166 P2d 80), but it is better practice to do so.

"Personal delivery" as used in CCP §415.10 usually requires actual physical delivery of the summons and petition by the process server to the person served while in each other's presence. *Sternbeck v Buck* (1957) 148 CA2d 829, 832, 307 P2d 970. Actual delivery is not necessary, however, when the person to be served is in physical proximity to the process server but refuses to accept delivery. After the process server reasonably attempts to make actual delivery, the papers should be left in as close proximity to the person as is feasible under the circumstances and he or she should be made aware of their location. The process server should also attempt to inform the person served of the nature of the documents. For examples of valid service under such circumstances, see, *e.g., Trujillo v Trujillo* (1945) 71 CA2d 257, 259, 162 P2d 640 (process server attempted to inform defendant of nature of documents through window of defendant's car and placed papers under windshield wiper); *In re Ball* (1934) 2 CA2d 578, 38 P2d 411 (process server, who had previously served defendant at same location, approached within 12 feet of defendant and stated "I have here another one of those things for you," then tossed papers toward defendant as defendant walked away).

Sometimes a respondent conceals himself or herself from the process server (*e.g.,* separated by a door that the respondent refuses to open), perhaps making it difficult to prove his or her identity if the papers are left nearby. In that event, as in any event in which the respondent cannot be personally served with reasonable diligence, substituted service (see §10.32) should be considered.

§10.32   (2) Substituted Service

A method for making "substituted service" of a summons and petition (*i.e.,* a substitute for personal delivery under CCP §415.10; see §10.31) is set forth in CCP §415.20(b). The respondent (or other person to be served; see §10.30) may be served in this manner only after the petitioner has, "with reasonable diligence," first attempted to effect personal service. CCP §415.20(b).

Substituted service under CCP §415.20(b) is made by:

- Leaving a copy of the summons and petition at the dwelling, usual place of abode, usual place of business, or usual mailing address (other than a United States Postal Service post office box) of the person to be served, in the presence of a person at least age 18 who is either a competent member of the household or a person apparently in charge of the office, place of business, or mailing address, and informing the person of the contents; and

- Mailing a copy of the summons and petition (by first-class mail, postage prepaid), addressed to the person to be served at the place where a copy of the summons and petition was left.

On determining whether a particular individual is a competent member of a household or a person apparently in charge of an office, place of business, or mailing address, see *Bein v Brechtel-Jochim Group, Inc.* (1992) 6 CA4th 1387, 8 CR2d 351 (residential gate guard must be considered competent member of household and person apparently in charge when guard's relationship with parties made it more likely than not that he would deliver process to them). See also *Ellard v Conway* (2001) 94 CA4th 540, 114 CR2d 399 (service on Postal Service Manager at private, commercial post office box (as opposed to U.S. Postal Service) was authorized substituted service under CCP §415.20(b)).

Section 415.20(b) requires that the person with whom the copy of the summons and petition is left "be informed of the contents." If the process server states that the documents are a summons and petition in a court case involving the respondent, this statement should be sufficient.

As with personal service (see §10.31), actual delivery is not necessary when the person with whom the papers are to be left is in physical proximity to the process server but refuses to accept delivery. *Khourie, Crew & Jaeger v Sabek, Inc.* (1990) 220 CA3d 1009, 1013, 269 CR 687.

Properly effected substituted service is considered to be complete on the tenth day after the date of mailing. CCP §415.20(b).

If a respondent challenges substituted service, the burden is on the petitioner to show that reasonable attempts to effect personal service were made; each case must be judged on its own facts. *Evartt v Superior Court* (1979) 89 CA3d 795, 801, 152 CR 836. Compare *Espindola v Nunez* (1988) 199 CA3d 1389, 245 CR 596 (substituted service permitted when, after three unsuccessful attempts to serve defendant at his residence shortly after plaintiff learned where defendant lived, process server left papers at residence with defendant's wife), with *Evartt v Superior Court, supra* (substituted service rejected when plaintiff waited until three days before expiration of three-year period under former CCP §581a (substance continued in CCP §583.210(a)) to attempt service and, finding defendant away on vacation, left papers with defendant's house sitter).

(3) Service by Mail and Acknowledgment of Receipt

§10.33 (a) Discussion

Code of Civil Procedure §415.30 sets forth how a petitioner may effect service by mailing a copy of the summons and petition to the respondent (or other person to be served; see §10.30). This method should not be confused with service by mail and return receipt under CCP §415.40 (see §10.40), which is available only when the respondent is outside California. Service under §415.30 is made by:

- Mailing (by first-class mail, postage prepaid) a copy of the summons and petition, two copies of the notice and acknowledgment of receipt (Judicial Council Form FL-117) (see CCP §415.30), and a self-addressed stamped envelope to the respondent; and

- Having the respondent complete and sign one copy of the acknowledgment of receipt and return it to the sender.

If the respondent completes and signs the acknowledgment of receipt and returns it to the sender, service is considered to be complete on the date of signing. CCP §415.30(c).

In many instances, it is sound to initially attempt service by mail and acknowledgment of receipt because this approach may save costs and may facilitate some degree of cooperation between the parties. This approach may not be advisable, however, when (1) prompt service is essential (*e.g.,* when an order to show cause and accompanying papers are also being served) or (2) the respondent is unaware of the filing of the action and is likely to make service difficult after being informed of the action.

It should be noted that the execution and return of an acknowledgment of receipt merely acknowledges receipt of the documents and should not be viewed as constituting a general appearance (see CCP §1014). A respondent does not consent to the court's personal jurisdiction (see §§4.4–4.5) over him or her by merely executing and returning the acknowledgment of receipt. *Marriage of Merideth* (1982) 129 CA3d 356, 361, 180 CR 909.

When the respondent does not execute and return the acknowledgment of receipt, the petitioner must resort to another means of service. When the respondent does not complete, sign, and return the acknowledgment to the sender within 20 days after mailing, however, the respondent is liable to the petitioner for the reasonable expenses of serving or attempting to serve the summons and petition in any other permissible manner. Except for good cause shown, such expenses are recoverable on a motion, with or without notice and whether or not the petitioner is otherwise entitled to recover costs in the action. CCP §415.30(d).

On service by mail and notice and acknowledgement of receipt in a joinder procedure on an employee benefit plan, see §12.20.

§10.34 (b) Form: Notice and Acknowledgment of Receipt (Judicial Council Form FL-117)

FL-117

ATTORNEY OR PARTY WITHOUT ATTORNEY (Name, State Bar number, and address):	FOR COURT USE ONLY

TELEPHONE NO.:   FAX NO. (Optional):

E-MAIL ADDRESS (Optional):

ATTORNEY FOR (Name):

SUPERIOR COURT OF CALIFORNIA, COUNTY OF

STREET ADDRESS:

MAILING ADDRESS:

CITY AND ZIP CODE:

BRANCH NAME:

PETITIONER:

RESPONDENT:

OTHER:

NOTICE AND ACKNOWLEDGMENT OF RECEIPT	CASE NUMBER:

To (name of individual being served): _____

NOTICE

The documents identified below are being served on you by mail with this acknowledgment form. You must personally sign, or a person authorized by you must sign, this form to acknowledge receipt of the documents.

If the documents described below include a summons and you fail to complete and return this acknowledgment form to the sender within 20 days of the date of mailing, you will be liable for the reasonable expenses incurred after that date in serving you or attempting to serve you with these documents by any other methods permitted by law. If you return this form to the sender, service of a summons is deemed complete on the date you sign the acknowledgment of receipt below. This is **not** an answer to the action. If you do not agree with what is being requested, you must submit a completed *Response* form to the court within 30 calendar days.

Date of mailing: _____

▶

_____   _____
(TYPE OR PRINT NAME)   (SIGNATURE OF SENDER—MUST NOT BE A PARTY IN THIS CASE AND MUST BE 18 OR OLDER)

ACKNOWLEDGMENT OF RECEIPT
(To be completed by sender before mailing)

I agree I received the following:

a. ☐ Family Law: *Petition* (form FL-100), *Summons* (form FL-110), and blank *Response* (form FL-120)

b. ☐ Family Law—Domestic Partnership: *Petition—Domestic Partnership* (form FL-103), *Summons* (form FL-110), and blank *Response—Domestic Partnership* (form FL-123)

c. ☐ Uniform Parentage: *Petition to Establish Parental Relationship* (form FL-200), *Summons* (form FL-210), and blank *Response to Petition to Establish Parental Relationship* (form FL-220)

d. ☐ Custody and Support: *Petition for Custody and Support of Minor Children* (form FL-260), *Summons* (form FL-210), and blank *Response to Petition for Custody and Support of Minor Children* (form FL-270)

e. ☐ (1) ☐ Completed and blank *Declaration Under Uniform Child Custody Jurisdiction and Enforcement Act (UCCJEA)* (form FL-105)

   (2) ☐ Completed and blank *Declaration of Disclosure* (form FL-140)

   (3) ☐ Completed and blank *Schedule of Assets and Debts* (form FL-142)

   (4) ☐ Completed and blank *Income and Expense Declaration* (form FL-150)

   (5) ☐ Completed and blank *Financial Statement (Simplified)* (form FL-155)

   (6) ☐ *Order to Show Cause* (form FL-300), *Application for Order and Supporting Declaration* (form FL-310), and blank *Responsive Declaration to Order to Show Cause or Notice of Motion* (form FL-320)

   (7) ☐ Other (specify):

(To be completed by recipient)
Date this acknowledgment is signed: _____

▶

_____   _____
(TYPE OR PRINT NAME)   (SIGNATURE OF PERSON ACKNOWLEDGING RECEIPT)

Page 1 of 1

Form Approved for Optional Use Judicial Council of California FL-117 [Rev. January 1, 2005]	**NOTICE AND ACKNOWLEDGMENT OF RECEIPT** (Family Law)	Code of Civil Procedure, §§ 415.30, 417.10 www.courtinfo.ca.gov

American LegalNet, Inc.
www.USCourtForms.com

Copies: Original and one copy (mail to party to be served); office copies.

Comment: The entire form should be completed before mailing, except for the portion at the bottom labeled "To be completed by recipient."

(4) Service by Publication

§10.35 (a) Discussion

A petitioner may effect service by publication when the court is satisfied that the respondent (or other person to be served; see §10.30) cannot with reasonable diligence be served by another method specified in CCP §§415.10–415.50. CCP §415.50. See *Transamerica Title Ins. Co. v Hendrix* (1995) 34 CA4th 740, 746, 40 CR2d 614 (when party knew opposing party's post office address and that his mail was being picked up from that box, failure to attempt service by mail under CCP §415.30 invalidated party's application for service by publication). Reasonable diligence requires an effort such as a reasonable person who truly desired to give notice would have made under the circumstances. *Donel, Inc. v Badalian* (1978) 87 CA3d 327, 333, 150 CR 855. As a condition of establishing that the party cannot reasonably be served in another manner, the court may not require that a search of databases be made, *e.g.*, voter registration rolls, which a registered process server is prohibited from accessing. CCP §415.50(e).

In addition to the reasonable diligence requirement, the court must find either of the following:

- That a cause of action exists against the party to be served or that the party is a necessary or proper party to the action (CCP §415.50(a)(1)); or

- That the party has or claims an interest in real or personal property in California which is subject to the court's jurisdiction or that the relief demanded would exclude the party from any interest in such property (CCP §415.50(a)(2)).

A petitioner seeking an order permitting service by publication should prepare an ex parte application for an order for publication of summons, a declaration in support of the application, and an order for publication of summons. The declaration must set forth the facts establishing both reasonable diligence and compliance with CCP §415.50(a). *Harris v Cavasso* (1977) 68 CA3d 723, 137 CR 410 (affidavit for order for publication of summons insufficient for failure to show that cause of action exists).

The statute requires that a court allowing service by publication order the summons to be published in a named California newspaper, or, if the party resides out of state, in a named newspaper outside the state, that is most likely to give notice to the party to be served. CCP §415.50(b), as amended by Stats 2003, ch 449, §8, effective January 1, 2004. As a practical matter, notice is usually published in a local legal newspaper. However, it is possible the court may not find that a local legal newspaper is the most likely to give notice to the party to be served, *e.g.*, if the party does not speak English and has a history of residing in a neighborhood serviced by a newspaper published in his or her first language. Counsel might suggest to the court that the local legal newspaper is not likely to give notice to the responding party and request authorization to publish the service in a neighborhood newspaper that may be published in the responding party's language. The court must also direct that a copy of the summons, the petition, and the order for publication be mailed forthwith to the party if his or her address is learned before the end of the publication period. CCP §415.50(b). On the meaning of "forthwith," see *Anderson v Goff* (1887) 72 C 65, 73, 13 P 73.

The summons is normally published once a week for four successive weeks. CCP §415.50(b); Govt C §6064. The publication notice period starts with the first day of publication and consists of 28 consecutive days, including the first day of publication. Govt C §6064. Service is considered to be complete on the 28th day. CCP §415.50(c). Note that the date on which service is deemed complete will usually *not* be the date of the last publication.

If it becomes possible to serve the party by another method specified in CCP §§415.10–415.50, the petitioner may do so and the service will supersede any published summons. CCP §415.50(d).

§10.36   (b) Form: Application for Order for Publication of Summons

_ _[Attorney name]_ _
_ _[State Bar number]_ _
_ _[Address]_ _
_ _[Telephone number]_ _

Attorney for _ _[name]_ _

SUPERIOR COURT OF CALIFORNIA
COUNTY OF _ _ _ _ _ _

Marriage of	)	**No.** _ _ _ _ _ _
	)	
Petitioner: _ _ _ _ _ _	)	**APPLICATION FOR ORDER**
	)	**FOR PUBLICATION OF**
Respondent: _ _ _ _ _ _	)	**SUMMONS (CCP §415.50;**
	)	**GOVT C §6064)**
_____	)	

_ _[Name]_ _, **petitioner, hereby applies for an order for service of summons on** _ _[name]_ _, **respondent, by publication and alleges as follows:**

1. The petition for _ _[dissolution of marriage/legal separation/nullity of marriage]_ _ **in this action was filed, and the summons was issued, on** _ _[date]_ _.

2. As shown by the declaration of _ _[name]_ _, **submitted in support of this application, respondent cannot with reasonable diligence be served in another manner specified by Code of Civil Procedure sections 415.10–415.50.**

3. As shown by the verified petition on file in this action, a cause of action for _ _[dissolution of marriage/legal separation/nullity of marriage]_ _ **exists against respondent.**

4. The _ _[name of newspaper]_ _ **is the newspaper of general circulation published in this state that is most likely to give actual notice to respondent.**

WHEREFORE, petitioner prays for an order for service of summons on respondent by publication in the _ _[name of *newspaper]_ _* **under Code of Civil Procedure section 415.50 and Government Code section 6064.**

Date: _____   __*[Signature]*__
                                    _ _*[Typed name]_ _*
                                    Attorney for Petitioner

Copies: Original (submit to court clerk for presentation to judge); office copies.

§10.37   (c) Form: Declaration in Support of Application for Order for Publication of Summons

_ _*[Attorney name]_ _*
_ _*[State Bar number]_ _*
_ _*[Address]_ _*
_ _*[Telephone number]_ _*

Attorney for _ _*[name]_ _*

**SUPERIOR COURT OF CALIFORNIA
COUNTY OF _ _ _ _ _ _**

Marriage of	)	**No. _ _ _ _ _ _**
	)	
Petitioner: _ _ _ _ _ _	)	**DECLARATION IN SUPPORT**
	)	**OF APPLICATION FOR**
Respondent: _ _ _ _ _ _	)	**ORDER FOR PUBLICATION**
	)	**OF SUMMONS**
_____	)	

I, _ _*[name]_ _*, declare as follows:

[Set forth in numbered paragraphs facts establishing that respondent cannot with reasonable diligence be served in another manner specified by CCP §§415.10–415.50, e.g., facts known regarding respondent's possible whereabouts, efforts to locate respondent, and results of those efforts]

I declare under penalty of perjury under the laws of the State of California that the foregoing is true and correct.

Date: _____   __*[Signature]*__
                                    _ _*[Typed name]_ _*

Copies: Original (submit to court clerk for presentation to judge); office copies.

Comment: The declarant is usually the petitioner, but might, when someone else has made the inquiries, be that person, *e.g.,* the petitioner's attorney or a private investigator.

§10.38   (d) Form: Order for Publication of Summons

_ _[Attorney name]_ _
_ _[State Bar number]_ _
_ _[Address]_ _
_ _[Telephone number]_ _

Attorney for _ _[name]_ _

**SUPERIOR COURT OF CALIFORNIA
COUNTY OF _ _ _ _ _ _**

Marriage of	)	**No.** _ _ _ _ _ _
	)	
Petitioner: _ _ _ _ _ _	)	**ORDER FOR PUBLICATION**
	)	**OF SUMMONS**
Respondent: _ _ _ _ _ _	)	
	)	
_____	)	

   The Court has considered the application and supporting declaration for an order for publication of summons, and it appears that respondent cannot with reasonable diligence be served in another manner specified by Code of Civil Procedure sections 415.10–415.50 and that a cause of action for _ _[dissolution of marriage/legal separation/nullity of marriage]_ _ exists against respondent.

   THEREFORE, IT IS ORDERED that service of summons on respondent in this action be made by publication in _ _[name of newspaper]_ _, a newspaper of general circulation hereby designated as the newspaper most likely to give notice to respondent, and that the publication be made at least once a week for four weeks. If respondent's address is ascertained before expiration of the time prescribed for publication of the summons, petitioner will mail a copy of the summons, the petition, and this order to respondent forthwith.

[continue]

Date: _____

_____

Judge of the Superior Court

Copies: Original (submit to court clerk for presentation to judge); copy for newspaper; office copies.

b. Outside California

§10.39 (1) Within United States

Service of a summons and petition in connection with a California action may be made outside California but within the United States (CCP §413.10(b)):

- In any manner provided by CCP §§415.10–415.50, including personal service (see §10.31), substituted service (see §10.32), service by mail and acknowledgment of receipt (see §§10.33–10.34), service by mail and return receipt (see §10.40), and service by publication (see §§10.35–10.38); or

- As prescribed by the law of the place where the service of the respondent (or other person to be served; see §10.30) occurs (see §10.41).

§10.40 (a) Service by Mail and Return Receipt

Code of Civil Procedure §415.40 sets forth how a petitioner may effect service outside California by mail and return receipt. This method should not be confused with service by mail and acknowledgment of receipt under CCP §415.30 (see §§10.33–10.34), which is available whether the respondent (or other person to be served; see §10.30) is within or outside California. Service under CCP §415.40 is attempted by sending a copy of the summons and petition to the respondent by first-class mail requiring a return receipt.

If the return receipt is returned with no signature because the mail was not accepted, service under CCP §415.40 will not have been made. *Stamps v Superior Court* (1971) 14 CA3d 108, 92 CR 151. When the return receipt is signed, however, service may, in limited circumstances, be found to have been made even though the signer was not the respondent. See *Marriage of Tusinger* (1985) 170 CA3d 80, 215 CR 838 (service proper when respondent's mother signed return receipt and respondent's attorney indicated in letter to petitioner's attorney that respondent had received papers); *Neadeau v Foster* (1982) 129 CA3d 234, 180 CR 806 (service proper when return receipt was signed by office manager of party to be served, who was authorized to sign for and accept mail addressed to party).

Service, if made, is considered to be complete on the tenth day after the date of mailing. CCP §415.40.

§10.41   (b) Service as Prescribed by Local Law

Under CCP §413.10(b), service may be made outside California but within the United States in accordance with the law of the place where service occurs. In some instances, service in another state may be easier to achieve under the law of that state than under California law. In some states, for example, a petitioner may effect substituted service on a respondent (or other person to be served; see §10.30) without first attempting personal service with reasonable diligence, as is required under CCP §415.20(b), discussed in §10.32. Consequently, when service is to be made in another state, counsel should check, and consider using, the law of that state.

§10.42   (2) Outside United States

Under CCP §413.10(c), a petitioner effecting service of process outside the United States in a California action may proceed as follows:

- In any manner provided by CCP §§415.10–415.50, including personal service (see §10.31), substituted service (see §10.32), service by mail and acknowledgment of receipt (see §§10.33–10.34), service by mail and return receipt (see §10.40), and service by publication (see §§10.35–10.38);

- As directed by the court in which the action is pending; or

- If the court before or after service finds that the service is reasonably calculated to give actual notice, as prescribed by the law of the place where the service of the respondent (or other person to be served; see §10.30) occurs or as directed by the foreign authority in response to a letter rogatory.

The flexibility of these procedures is important when service is made outside the United States because a number of foreign jurisdictions refuse to recognize a foreign judgment unless service has been made in accordance with their own laws. See Comment to CCP

§413.10. Note, however, that §413.10(c) is expressly subject to the Hague Service Convention on Service Abroad of Judicial and Extrajudicial Documents in Civil or Commercial Matters (20 UST 361, TIAS 6638). The Convention governs service of process abroad for the signatory nations. (The United States, Japan, and most Western European countries are signatories.) See, *e.g., Dr. Ing H.C. F. Porsche A.G. v Superior Court* (1981) 123 CA3d 755, 177 CR 155 (California court had no jurisdiction over German automobile manufacturer when Hague Convention service requirements not observed). A copy of the Convention may be found following Fed R Civ P 4 in Title 28 of the United States Code Annotated.

C. Return of Service

§10.43   1. Discussion

After service of process is made, proof of service of the summons must be filed as required by CCP §417.10 (service in California) or CCP §417.20 (service outside California), unless the respondent has made a general appearance. CCP §417.30. Proof of service should be made on the Judicial Council form for Proof of Service of Summons (Judicial Council Form FL-115). See CCP §417.10(f). When service is made by a professional process server or a sheriff, he or she will usually prepare a proof of service form and provide it to the person who requested the service. When service is made by a private individual, however, the petitioner's attorney should provide the form for the individual to execute.

A return of service in proper form is prima facie evidence that service of process has been made, but the presumption may be overcome by other evidence. See *City of Los Angeles v Morgan* (1951) 105 CA2d 726, 731, 234 P2d 319. If service itself was proper, however, the fact that the return is defective (*e.g.,* because of a defect in the proof of service) need not divest the court of jurisdiction thus acquired. See *Morrissey v Gray* (1911) 160 C 390, 117 P 438; *Willen v Boggs* (1971) 21 CA3d 520, 97 CR 917. In such circumstances, the return of service may usually be amended. See 21 CA3d at 524.

Note that the statute governing procedure in the case of a lost summons was amended, effective January 1, 2006, to provide that the clerk must keep each original summons in the court records and provide a copy of each summons issued to the plaintiff who requested issuance of the summons. CCP §412.10.

§10.44   2. Form: Proof of Service of Summons (Judicial Council Form FL-115)

FL-115

ATTORNEY OR PARTY WITHOUT ATTORNEY *(Name, State Bar number, and address):*	FOR COURT USE ONLY

TELEPHONE NO.:   FAX NO. *(Optional):*
E-MAIL ADDRESS *(Optional):*
ATTORNEY FOR *(Name):*

SUPERIOR COURT OF CALIFORNIA, COUNTY OF
  STREET ADDRESS:
  MAILING ADDRESS:
  CITY AND ZIP CODE:
  BRANCH NAME:

PETITIONER:

RESPONDENT:

PROOF OF SERVICE OF SUMMONS	CASE NUMBER:

1. At the time of service I was at least 18 years of age and not a party to this action. **I served the respondent with copies of:**
   a. ☐ Family Law: *Petition* (form FL-100), *Summons* (form FL-110), and blank *Response* (form FL-120)
   —or—
   b. ☐ Family Law—Domestic Partnership: *Petition—Domestic Partnership* (form FL-103), *Summons* (form FL-110), and blank *Response—Domestic Partnership* (form FL-123)
   —or—
   c. ☐ Uniform Parentage: *Petition to Establish Parental Relationship* (form FL-200), *Summons* (form FL-210), and blank *Response to Petition to Establish Parental Relationship* (form FL-220)
   —or—
   d. ☐ Custody and Support: *Petition for Custody and Support of Minor Children* (form FL-260), *Summons* (form FL-210), and blank *Response to Petition for Custody and Support of Minor Children* (form FL-270)

   and

   e. ☐ (1) ☐ Completed and blank *Declaration Under Uniform Child Custody Jurisdiction and Enforcement Act* (form FL-105)
       (2) ☐ Completed and blank *Declaration of Disclosure* (form FL-140)
       (3) ☐ Completed and blank *Schedule of Assets and Debts* (form FL-142)
       (4) ☐ Completed and blank *Income and Expense Declaration* (form FL-150)

       (5) ☐ Completed and blank *Financial Statement (Simplified)* (form FL-155)
       (6) ☐ Completed and blank *Property Declaration* (form FL-160)
       (7) ☐ *Order to Show Cause* (form FL-300), *Application for Order and Supporting Declaration* (form FL-310), and blank *Responsive Declaration to Order to Show Cause or Notice of Motion* (form FL-320)
       (8) ☐ Other *(specify):*

2. Address where respondent was served:

3. I served the respondent by the following means *(check proper box):*
   a. ☐ **Personal service.** I personally delivered the copies to the respondent (Code Civ. Proc., § 415.10)
   on *(date):*   at *(time):*
   b. ☐ **Substituted service.** I left the copies with or in the presence of *(name):*
   who is *(specify title or relationship to respondent):*
       (1) ☐ **(Business)** a person at least 18 years of age who was apparently in charge at the office or usual place of business of the respondent. I informed him or her of the general nature of the papers
       (2) ☐ **(Home)** a competent member of the household (at least 18 years of age) at the home of the respondent. I informed him or her of the general nature of the papers

Page 1 of 2

Form Approved for Optional Use Judicial Council of California FL-115 [Rev. January 1, 2005]	**PROOF OF SERVICE OF SUMMONS** **(Family Law—Uniform Parentage—Custody and Support)**	Code of Civil Procedure, § 417.10 www.courtinfo.ca.gov

PETITIONER:	CASE NUMBER:
RESPONDENT:	

3. b. *(cont.)* on *(date):*   at *(time):*

I thereafter mailed additional copies (by first class, postage prepaid) to the respondent at the place where the copies were left (Code Civ. Proc., § 415.20b) on *(date):*

A **declaration of diligence** is attached, stating the actions taken to first attempt personal service.

c. ☐ **Mail and acknowledgment service.** I mailed the copies to the respondent, addressed as shown in item 2, by first-class mail, postage prepaid, on *(date):*   from *(city):*

(1) ☐ with two copies of the *Notice and Acknowledgment of Receipt (Family Law)* (form FL-117) and a postage-paid return envelope addressed to me. **(Attach completed *Notice and Acknowledgment of Receipt (Family Law)* (form FL-117).)** (Code Civ. Proc., § 415.30.)

(2) ☐ to an address outside California (by registered or certified mail with return receipt requested). **(Attach signed return receipt or other evidence of actual delivery to the respondent.)** (Code Civ. Proc., § 415.40.)

d. ☐ **Other** *(specify code section):*

☐ Continued on Attachment 3d.

4. The "NOTICE TO THE PERSON SERVED" on the *Summons* was completed as follows (Code Civ. Proc., §§ 412.30, 415.10, 474):

a. ☐ As an individual   **or**

b. ☐ On behalf of respondent who is a

(1) ☐ minor. (Code Civ. Proc., § 416.60.)

(2) ☐ ward or conservatee. (Code Civ. Proc., § 416.70.)

(3) ☐ other *(specify):*

5. **Person who served papers**

Name:

Address:

Telephone number:

This person is

a. ☐ exempt from registration under Business and Professions Code section 22350(b).

b. ☐ not a registered California process server.

c. ☐ a registered California process server: ☐ an employee or ☐ an independent contractor

(1) Registration no.:

(2) County:

d. **The fee** for service was *(specify):* $

6. ☐ **I declare** under penalty of perjury under the laws of the State of California that the foregoing is true and correct.

—or—

7. ☐ **I am a California sheriff, marshal, or constable,** and I certify that the foregoing is true and correct.

Date:

▶

_____   _____
(NAME OF PERSON WHO SERVED PAPERS)   (SIGNATURE OF PERSON WHO SERVED PAPERS)

PROOF OF SERVICE OF SUMMONS
(Family Law—Uniform Parentage—Custody and Support)

Copies: Original (attach to original of summons and file with court clerk); office copies.

III. RESPONDING TO PETITION

A. Response and Supplemental Papers

1. Response

§10.45　　a. Discussion

The respondent sets forth his or her position in answer to the petition by filing a response (Judicial Council Form FL-120). Cal Rules of Ct 5.108, 5.120, unless he or she files a motion to quash service of summons or to stay or dismiss the action pursuant to CCP §418.10 (see §§10.60–10.64). The response must not contain any matter not specifically required by the Judicial Council response form (Judicial Council Form FL-120; see §10.52).

Ordinarily, the response should be filed and a copy served within 30 days after the respondent is served with a copy of the summons and petition. See Fam C §2020. The 30-day time limit will be extended, however, when there is (1) an extension of time to respond by stipulation or court order (see CCP §1054; Cal Rules of Ct 5.15), (2) a notice of motion to quash service of summons for lack of personal jurisdiction (see §10.61), (3) a notice of motion to quash the proceeding (see §10.62), (4) a notice of motion for change of venue on the ground of improper court (see §10.63), or (5) a notice of motion to stay or dismiss the action on the ground of inconvenient forum (see §10.64). On a respondent's ability to serve and file a response after the time to respond has run, see §14.8.

A copy of the response, including any attachments, must be served on the petitioner's attorney (or the petitioner if he or she is not represented). CCP §465; Cal Rules of Ct 5.10(b). The copy of the response may be served personally or by mail. CCP §§1011–1012. The original of the response is filed, with the original of the proof of service attached. CCP §465. When temporary orders are sought at the time the response is filed, the notice of motion or order to show cause and accompanying documents (see §§11.16–11.33) may be served with the response. On temporary orders generally, see chap 11.

The discussion in §§10.46–10.51 is keyed to the Judicial Council form (see §10.52).

NOTE➤ On and after January 1, 2005, a separate form of response must be used in proceedings for dissolution, legal separation, or nullity of a registered domestic partnership. See §10.52A.

This form (Judicial Council Form FL-123) closely parallels the form of response used in the context of marital dissolution proceedings. In limited circumstances (similar to those for summary dissolution of marriage), a domestic partnership may be terminated through the office of the Secretary of State by an administrative notice procedure. See Fam C §299. For a full discussion of actions to terminate registered domestic partnerships, see California Domestic Partnerships (Cal CEB 2005).

§10.46   (1) Nature of Action

The part of the caption immediately below the names of the parties need be completed only when the respondent seeks relief that is different from that sought by the petitioner in the petition, in which event the box preceding the words "and REQUEST FOR" and the box preceding the relief sought should be checked. On choosing the form of action, see §§3.35–3.37.

Note that the response may seek alternative relief, *e.g.,* judgment of dissolution *or* nullity when proof of grounds for nullity may be difficult (see §3.36). Cal Rules of Ct 5.114. On indicating that the relief sought is in the alternative when more than one box is checked, see §10.51.

§10.47   (2) Statistical Facts (Item 2)

The considerations in determining the date of separation (Item 2) are the same as for the corresponding portions of the petition. §10.7 On the date of separation generally, see §5.12.

§10.48   (3) Minor Children, Separate Assets and Obligations, and Community and Quasi-Community Assets and Obligations (Items 3–5)

The considerations in completing the portions of the response addressing minor children, separate assets and obligations, and community and quasi-community assets and obligations (Items 3-5, respectively) are the same as for the corresponding portions of the petition. For discussion, see §§10.8–10.10, respectively.

NOTE➤ If respondent is the stepparent of one or more of the petitioner's children, respondent may wish to list these stepchildren in the "children of the marriage" section of the response form in order to raise the issue of visitation in the proceeding (see Fam C §3101), including addressing that issue in child custody mediation.

§10.49   (4) Reconciliation (Item 6)

The box at Item 6 should be checked if the respondent contends that there is a reasonable possibility of reconciliation. See §3.2.

§10.50   (5) Denial of Grounds Set Forth in Petition (Item 7)

The box at Item 7 should be checked if the respondent denies the grounds set forth by the petitioner in Item 6 of the petition. See §10.11.

§10.51   (6) Relief Requested (Items 8–9)

Item 8 is completed only when the respondent seeks relief that is different from that sought by the petitioner in Item 6 of the petition, in which event the part of the caption immediately below the names of the parties will have been completed (see §10.46). When alternative relief (*e.g.,* judgment of dissolution or nullity) is sought (see §10.46), the words "in the alternative" may be added following the words "Respondent requests." On opposing a petitioner's request for a legal separation, see §3.4.

The considerations in completing Item 9 regarding the specific relief requested are the same as for the corresponding portion (*i.e.,* Item 7) of the petition. For discussion, see §10.11.

§10.52 b. Form: Response—Marriage (Judicial Council Form FL-120)

FL-120

ATTORNEY OR PARTY WITHOUT ATTORNEY *(Name, State Bar number, and address):*	FOR COURT USE ONLY

TELEPHONE NO.:   FAX NO. *(Optional):*

E-MAIL ADDRESS *(Optional):*

ATTORNEY FOR *(Name):*

SUPERIOR COURT OF CALIFORNIA, COUNTY OF

    STREET ADDRESS:

    MAILING ADDRESS:

    CITY AND ZIP CODE:

    BRANCH NAME:

MARRIAGE OF

    PETITIONER:

    RESPONDENT:

RESPONSE ☐ **and REQUEST FOR**

    ☐ **Dissolution of Marriage**

    ☐ **Legal Separation**

    ☐ **Nullity of Marriage**   ☐ AMENDED

CASE NUMBER:

1. RESIDENCE (Dissolution only) ☐ Petitioner ☐ Respondent   has been a resident of this state for at least six months and of this county for at least three months immediately preceding the filing of the *Petition for Dissolution of Marriage.*

2. STATISTICAL FACTS
    a. Date of marriage: c. Time from date of marriage to date of separation *(specify):*
    b. Date of separation: Years: Months:

3. DECLARATION REGARDING MINOR CHILDREN *(include children of this relationship born prior to or during the marriage or adopted during the marriage):*
    a. ☐   There are no minor children.
    b. ☐   The minor children are:

Child's name	Birthdate	Age	Sex

    ☐ Continued on Attachment 3b.

    c. If there are minor children of the Petitioner and Respondent, a completed *Declaration Under Uniform Child Custody Jurisdiction and Enforcement Act (UCCJEA)* (form FL-105) must be attached.

    d. ☐   A completed voluntary declaration of paternity regarding minor children born to the Petitioner and Respondent prior to the marriage is attached.

4. SEPARATE PROPERTY
    Respondent requests that the assets and debts listed ☐ in *Property Declaration* (form FL-160) ☐ in Attachment 4 ☐ below   be confirmed as separate property.

    Item   Confirm to

NOTICE: You may redact (black out) social security numbers from any written material filed with the court in this case other than a form used to collect child or spousal support.

Page i of 2

Form Adopted for Mandatory Use
Judicial Council of California
FL-120 [Rev. January 1, 2005]

RESPONSE—MARRIAGE
(Family Law)

Family Code, § 2020
www.courtinfo.ca.gov.

MARRIAGE OF *(last name, first name of parties):*	CASE NUMBER:

5. DECLARATION REGARDING COMMUNITY AND QUASI-COMMUNITY ASSETS AND DEBTS AS CURRENTLY KNOWN

     a. ☐   There are no such assets or debts subject to disposition by the court in this proceeding.

     b. ☐   All such assets and debts are listed ☐ in *Property Declaration* (form FL-160) ☐ in Attachment 5b.

            ☐   below *(specify):*

6. ☐   **Respondent contends** that the parties were never legally married.

7. ☐   **Respondent denies** the grounds set forth in item 6 of the petition.

8. **Respondent requests**

     a. ☐   dissolution of the marriage based on   d. ☐   nullity of voidable marriage based on

         (1) ☐   irreconcilable differences. (Fam. Code, § 2310(a).)   (1) ☐   respondent's age at time of marriage.

         (2) ☐   incurable insanity. (Fam. Code, § 2310(b).)   (Fam. Code, § 2210(a).)

     b. ☐   legal separation of the parties based on   (2) ☐   prior existing marriage.

         (1) ☐   irreconcilable differences. (Fam. Code, § 2310(a).)   (Fam. Code, § 2210(b).)

         (2) ☐   incurable insanity. (Fam. Code, § 2310(b).)   (3) ☐   unsound mind. (Fam. Code, § 2210(c).)

     c. ☐   nullity of void marriage based on   (4) ☐   fraud. (Fam. Code, § 2210(d).)

         (1) ☐   incestuous marriage. (Fam. Code, § 2200.)   (5) ☐   force. (Fam. Code, § 2210(e).)

         (2) ☐   bigamous marriage. (Fam. Code, § 2201.)   (6) ☐   physical incapacity. (Fam. Code, § 2210(f).)

9. **Respondent requests** that the court grant the above relief and make injunctive (including restraining) and other orders as follows:

	Petitioner	Respondent	Joint	Other
a. Legal custody of children to	☐	☐	☐	☐
b. Physical custody of children to	☐	☐	☐	☐
c. Child visitation be granted to	☐	☐	☐	☐

         As requested in form: ☐ FL-311 ☐ FL-312 ☐ FL-341(C) ☐ FL-341(D) ☐ FL-341(E) ☐ Attachment 9c.

     d. ☐   Determination of parentage of any children born to the Petitioner and Respondent prior to the marriage.

     e. Attorney fees and costs payable by ....

     f. Spousal support payable to (wage assignment will be issued) ....

     g. ☐   Terminate the court's jurisdiction (ability) to award spousal support to Petitioner.

     h. ☐   Property rights be determined.

     i. ☐   Respondent's former name be restored to *(specify):*

     j. ☐   Other *(specify):*

         ☐   Continued on Attachment 9j.

10. **Child support–** If there are minor children born to or adopted by the Petitioner and Respondent before or during this marriage, the court will make orders for the support of the children upon request and submission of financial forms by the requesting party. An earnings assignment may be issued without further notice. Any party required to pay support must pay interest on overdue amounts at the "legal" rate, which is currently 10 percent.

I declare under penalty of perjury under the laws of the State of California that the foregoing is true and correct.

Date:

▶

_____   _____
(TYPE OR PRINT NAME)   (SIGNATURE OF RESPONDENT)

Date:

▶

_____   _____
(TYPE OR PRINT NAME)   (SIGNATURE OF ATTORNEY FOR RESPONDENT)

The original response must be filed in the court with proof of service of a copy on Petitioner.

FL-120 [Rev. January 1, 2005]   **RESPONSE—MARRIAGE**   Page 2 of 2
(Family Law)

Copies: Original (file with court clerk); copy for service on petitioner; office copies.

§10.52A c. Form: Response—Domestic Partnership (Judicial Council Form FL-123)

FL-123

ATTORNEY OR PARTY WITHOUT ATTORNEY *(Name, State Bar number, and address):*	FOR COURT USE ONLY

TELEPHONE NO.:   FAX NO. *(Optional):*

E-MAIL ADDRESS *(Optional):*

ATTORNEY FOR *(Name):*

SUPERIOR COURT OF CALIFORNIA, COUNTY OF

STREET ADDRESS:

MAILING ADDRESS:

CITY AND ZIP CODE:

BRANCH NAME:

DOMESTIC PARTNERSHIP OF

PETITIONER:

RESPONDENT:

RESPONSE ☐ **and REQUEST FOR**	CASE NUMBER:

☐ **Dissolution of Domestic Partnership**

☐ **Legal Separation of Domestic Partnership**

☐ **Nullity of Domestic Partnership**   ☐ **AMENDED**

1. STATISTICAL FACTS
   a. Date of registration of domestic partnership:
   b. Date of separation:
   c. Time from date of registration of domestic partnership to date of separation *(specify):*   Years   Months

2. RESIDENCE (Partnerships established out of state only)
   a. ☐ Our domestic partnership was established in another state *(specify state):*
   b. ☐ Petitioner ☐ Respondent has been a resident of this state of California for at least six months and of this county for at least three months immediately preceding the filing of this *Petition for Dissolution of Domestic Partnership.*

3. DECLARATION REGARDING MINOR CHILDREN *(include children of this relationship born prior to or during this domestic partnership or adopted during this domestic partnership):*
   a. ☐ There are no minor children.
   b. ☐ The minor children are:

Child's name	Birthdate	Age	Sex

   ☐ Continued on Attachment 3b.
   c. If there are minor children of the petitioner and the respondent, a completed *Declaration Under Uniform Child Custody Jurisdiction and Enforcement Act (UCCJEA)* (form FL-105) must be attached.

4. SEPARATE PROPERTY
   Respondent requests that the assets and debts listed ☐ in *Property Declaration* (form FL-160) ☐ in Attachment 4 ☐ below be confirmed as separate property.

Item	Confirm to

NOTICE: You may redact (black out) social security numbers from any written material filed with the court in this case other than a form used to collect child or partner support.

Page 1 of 2

Form Adopted for Mandatory Use
Judicial Council of California
FL-123 [New January 1, 2005]

RESPONSE—DOMESTIC PARTNERSHIP
(Family Law)

Family Code, §§ 299, 2020
www.courtinfo.ca.gov

DOMESTIC PARTNERSHIP OF (Last name, first name of each party):	CASE NUMBER:

5. DECLARATION REGARDING COMMUNITY AND QUASI-COMMUNITY ASSETS AND DEBTS AS CURRENTLY KNOWN
   a. ☐ There are no such assets or debts subject to disposition by the court in this proceeding.
   b. ☐ All such assets and debts are listed ☐ in *Property Declaration* (form FL-160) ☐ in Attachment 5b.
   ☐ below *(specify)*:

6. ☐ **Respondent contends** that there is not a valid domestic partnership or equivalent.

7. ☐ **Respondent denies** the grounds set forth in item 6 of the petition.

8. **Respondent requests**
   a. ☐ dissolution of the domestic partnership based on
      (1) ☐ irreconcilable differences. (Fam. Code, § 2310(a).)
      (2) ☐ incurable insanity. (Fam. Code, § 2310(b).)
   b. ☐ legal separation of the domestic partners based on
      (1) ☐ irreconcilable differences. (Fam. Code, § 2310(a).)
      (2) ☐ incurable insanity. (Fam. Code, § 2310(b).)
   c. ☐ nullity of void domestic partnership based on
      (1) ☐ incest. (Fam. Code, § 2200.)
      (2) ☐ bigamy. (Fam. Code, § 2201.)
   d. ☐ nullity of voidable domestic partnership based on
      (1) ☐ respondent's age at time of domestic partnership. (Fam. Code, § 2210(a).)
      (2) ☐ prior existing marriage or domestic partnership. (Fam. Code, § 2210(b).)
      (3) ☐ unsound mind. (Fam. Code, § 2210(c).)
      (4) ☐ fraud. (Fam. Code, § 2210(d).)
      (5) ☐ force. (Fam. Code, § 2210(e).)
      (6) ☐ physical incapacity. (Fam. Code, § 2210(f))

9. **Respondent requests** that the court grant the above relief and make injunctive (including restraining) and other orders as follows:

	Petitioner	Respondent	Joint	Other
a. Legal custody of children to	☐	☐	☐	☐
b. Physical custody of children to	☐	☐	☐	☐
c. Child visitation granted to	☐	☐		☐

   As requested in form: ☐ FL-311 ☐ FL-312 ☐ FL-341(C) ☐ FL-341(D) ☐ FL-341(E) ☐ Attachment 9c.
   d. ☐ Determination of parentage of any children born to the petitioner and respondent prior to the domestic partnership.

| e. Attorney fees and costs payable by | ☐ | ☐ | | |
| f. Partner support payable to | ☐ | ☐ | | |

   g. ☐ Terminate court's jurisdiction (ability) to award partner support to the petitioner.
   h. ☐ Property rights be determined.
   i. ☐ Respondent's former name be restored to *(specify)*:
   j. ☐ Other *(specify)*:

   ☐ Continued on Attachment 9j.

10. **Child support** –If there are minor children who were born to or adopted by the petitioner and the respondent before or during this domestic partnership, the court will make orders for the support of the children upon request and submission of financial forms by the requesting party. An earnings assignment may be issued without further notice. Any party required to pay support must pay interest on overdue amounts at the "legal" rate, which is currently 10 percent.

I declare under penalty of perjury under the laws of the State of California that the foregoing is true and correct.

Date:

_____   ▶ _____
(TYPE OR PRINT NAME)   (SIGNATURE OF RESPONDENT)

Date:

_____   ▶ _____
(TYPE OR PRINT NAME)   (SIGNATURE OF ATTORNEY FOR RESPONDENT)

The original response must be filed in the court with proof of service of a copy on petitioner.

§10.53 2. Confidential Counseling Statement

Effective January 1, 2001, former Cal Rules of Ct 1224 and 1284 (confidential counseling statement must be submitted with petition or response in counties having conciliation court) were repealed.

§10.54 3. Declaration Under Uniform Child Custody Jurisdiction Act

The considerations in completing the Declaration Under Uniform Child Custody Jurisdiction Act (see Fam C §3429) (the Act is now called the Uniform Child Custody Jurisdiction and Enforcement Act (see Fam C §§3400–3465)) are the same as for the corresponding portions of the petition. For discussion, see §10.17.

For the UCCJA declaration form, see §10.18.

§10.55 4. Property Declaration

As an alternative to listing assets and obligations on the response form itself (see §10.52), these items may be listed on property declaration forms (Judicial Council Forms FL-160-FL-161) and attached to the response. For discussion, see §10.19. For the property declaration forms, see §§10.20–10.21.

§10.56 5. Notice of Motion or Order to Show Cause for Temporary Orders

When temporary orders are sought at the time the response is filed, the notice of motion or order to show cause and accompanying documents (see §§11.16–11.33) may be processed along with the response. On temporary orders generally, see chap 11.

§10.57 6. Other Motions

In some instances, a motion to quash the proceeding (see §10.62), a motion for a change of venue (see §10.63), a motion to stay or dismiss the action on the ground of inconvenient forum (see §10.64), or a motion to strike (see §10.65) will be filed at the same time as the response.

§10.58 7. Lis Pendens

A respondent who asserts any real property claim in a marital action may wish to record a lis pendens, as provided in CCP §405.20, particularly when he or she claims a community interest in real property held in the petitioner's name alone. Recording a lis pendens will prevent the petitioner from conveying or encumbering the respondent's interest. See §§10.23 (discussion), 10.24 (form).

§10.59   8. Local Requirements

Some courts have special format requirements and special rules concerning child custody mediation. Counsel should consult local rules and practice.

§10.60   B. Motions Available to Respondent

Depending on the particular circumstances, several motions are potentially available to a respondent who has been served with a petition in a marital action, including motions (1) to quash service of summons (see §10.61), (2) to quash the proceeding (see §10.62), (3) for a change of venue (see §10.63), (4) to stay or dismiss the action on the ground of inconvenient forum (see §10.64), and (5) to strike (see §10.65). Special attention must be paid to any time limitations on filing the motion and to whether the motion constitutes a general appearance. Also, the motions must be considered in conjunction with the response (see §§10.45–10.52). The respondent may move to quash the summons, stay or dismiss the action on the grounds of inconvenient forum, or dismiss for delay in prosecution, and, *at the same time*, answer, demur, or move to strike the petition without being deemed to have made a general appearance, unless the court denies the motion, in which case the respondent is deemed to have generally appeared on entry of the order denying the motion. CCP §418.10(e). If the respondent moves to quash the summons, stay or dismiss the action on the grounds of inconvenient forum, or dismiss for delay in prosecution in lieu of filing the answer, the respondent is not deemed to have made a general appearance, and the time to answer is extended. CCP §418.10(a)–(c). See Cal Rules of Ct 5.120(a), as amended effective January 1, 2006. If respondent answers, files a demurrer, or moves to strike without filing a motion to quash service of summons, however, he or she will be deemed to have waived any objections to jurisdiction, thereby precluding consideration of the motion to quash. See §10.61.

NOTE➤ Cal Rules of Ct 5.121 sets out the procedures and time limits for making a motion to quash a proceeding (or a request for affirmative relief in a response). See §10.62. Rule 5.121 is silent about whether the motion to quash constitutes a general appearance, but because the motion has been removed from the Rule 5.120 list of methods by which a respondent or defendant appears in a family code proceeding, making a motion to quash apparently does *not* constitute a general appearance. See Cal Rules of Ct 5.120(a).

All the motions discussed in §§10.61-10.65 are prepared and processed in the same manner as a notice of motion for temporary orders. For discussion of, and forms for, motions for temporary orders, see §§11.16-11.63. The respondent prepares the Judicial Council forms for Notice of Motion (see §11.20) and Application for Order and Supporting Declaration (see §11.22). In the caption of the Notice of Motion form, the box labeled "Other (specify)" is checked and the subject matter of the motion, *e.g.,* "Quash Service of Summons," is indicated. The relief requested is more specifically indicated at Item 9 on the Application for Order and Supporting Declaration.

The box at Item 3.e of the Notice of Motion form is checked if a memorandum of points and authorities is attached. Note that a memorandum need not be filed unless the court requires it. Cal Rules of Ct 5.118(a). Even when the court does not require a memorandum of points and authorities, however, one should probably be submitted for most motions seeking relief other than that specifically listed on the application form, including those covered in §§10.61-10.65. In some instances, *e.g.,* a motion to quash the proceeding on the ground that there is a prior judgment or another action pending between the same parties for the same cause, a very brief memorandum might be appropriate. In other instances, *e.g.,* a motion to quash service of summons on the ground that the court lacks personal jurisdiction over the respondent, a more substantial memorandum might be required.

The box at Item 3.f of the Notice of Motion form is checked if there are any additional supporting attachments. The most common additional attachment is a supporting declaration. Facts in support of the relief requested may be provided either at Item 10 of the application form or in an attached declaration.

§10.61   1. Motion to Quash Service of Summons

A respondent who contends that the court in which the action is pending does not have jurisdiction over him or her may file a noticed motion to quash service of summons. CCP §418.10(a)(1). The asserted ground may be either lack of personal jurisdiction (see §§4.4–4.5) or failure to properly effect service of process (see §§10.26–10.42). The motion must be filed within the respondent's time to plead. CCP §418.10(a)(1).

A respondent who files a motion to quash is not considered to have made a general appearance. CCP §418.10(d). Service and filing of the notice of motion extends the respondent's time to plead until 15 days after service on him or her of a written notice of entry of an order denying the motion or for up to 20 days beyond that if extended by the court for good cause shown. CCP §418.10(b).

A challenging respondent may, simultaneously with the motion to quash, file an answer, demurrer, or motion to strike the petition, without being deemed to have made a general appearance and to have waived objections to jurisdiction, unless the court enters an order denying the motion. CCP §418.10(e). If the motion to quash is denied and respondent petitions for a writ of mandate, he or she is not deemed to have generally appeared until the writ proceedings are concluded. CCP §418.10(e)(2). The respondent's failure to move to quash when filing a demurrer or motion to strike is a waiver of the issues of lack of personal jurisdiction, inadequacy of process, inadequacy of service, inconvenient forum, and delay in prosecution. CCP §418.10(e)(3). A challenging respondent who appears, however, only in opposition to a request for temporary orders while a motion to quash service of summons is pending will *not* be deemed to have made a general appearance. Fam C §2012; *Marriage of Fitzgerald & King* (1995) 39 CA4th 1419, 1429, 46 CR2d 558 (party who appeared in opposition to requested temporary orders while motion to quash was pending not deemed to have made general appearance simply because she asked that stay away orders and restraints on personal conduct be made mutual and be construed to include harassing facsimiles).

For a complete discussion of challenging jurisdiction over the person, see California Civil Procedure Before Trial, chap 19 (4th ed Cal CEB 2004).

§10.62   2. Motion to Quash Proceeding

Under Cal Rules of Ct 5.121 (adopted effective January 1, 2004), a respondent may move to quash the proceeding (or a petitioner may move to quash a request for affirmative relief in the response; see §10.66), in whole or in part, on any of the following grounds:

- The lack of legal capacity to sue (Cal Rules of Ct 5.121(a)(1));

- The existence of a prior judgment or pending action between the same parties for the same cause (Cal Rules of Ct 5.121(a)(2));

- The failure to meet the residence requirement of Fam C §2320 (see §§4.3, 4.8) (Cal Rules of Ct 5.121(a)(3)); or

- The proceeding is one for a judgment of nullity and is barred by the statute of limitations in Fam C §2211 (see §§3.10-3.15) (Cal Rules of Ct 5.121(a)(4)).

The hearing on the motion to quash must be scheduled not more than 20 days from the date the notice of motion is filed (Cal Rules of Ct 5.121(b). If the court grants a motion to quash ((Cal Rules of Ct 5.121(e)):

- It may also grant leave to amend the petition and set a date for filing the amended pleadings;

- It may dismiss the proceeding without leave to amend; or

- It may grant leave to amend and dismiss the proceeding or request for affirmative relief if the amendment is not made within the time set by the court.

A party who does not file a timely motion to quash is deemed to waive the right to attack the proceedings on any of the grounds enumerated in Cal Rules of Ct 5.121(a). Cal Rules of Ct 5.121(d). See *Zaragoza v Superior Court* (1996) 49 CA4th 720, 57 CR2d 1 (just as party may waive defective service by making general appearance, so party may waive right to plead existence of divorce judgment by failing to raise it).

NOTE➤ In the absence of a specific rule or statute, the court may adopt any suitable process that "is consistent with the spirit of the Family Code." Cal Rules of Ct 5.140 (former Cal Rules of Ct 1249). Although the "motion to quash a proceeding" is the family law equivalent of a demurrer in civil actions generally, under Cal Rules of Ct 5.108(a) (former Cal Rules of Ct 1215) demurrers as such must not be used in family law proceedings. For a complete discussion of demurrers, see California Civil Procedure Before Trial, chap 23 (4th ed Cal CEB 2004).

When a respondent makes a motion to quash a petition, in whole or in part (Cal Rules of Ct 5.121(a)–(b)):

- The respondent must make the motion within the time for filing a response to the petition;

- No default may be entered against the respondent;

- The respondent's time to file a response is extended until 15 days after service of the court's order on the motion.

§10.63   3. Motion for Change of Venue

A respondent may move for a change of venue on any of the following grounds:

- The court in which the action is pending is not one in which the petition may properly be filed. CCP §397(a). On ascertaining where a petition may properly be filed, see §4.8.

- There is reason to believe that an impartial trial cannot be had in the present venue. CCP §397(b).

- The convenience of witnesses and the ends of justice would be promoted by the change. CCP §397(c). Generally, only convenience of nonparty, nonexpert witnesses is considered, not that of parties or of expert witnesses with no personal knowledge of the facts. *Wrin v Ohlandt* (1931) 213 C 158, 1 P2d 991. Under limited circumstances, however, the court may consider the convenience of a party, *e.g.,* one whose physical condition prevents travel to trial in the other county and whose testimony is material. *Lieberman v Superior Court* (1987) 194 CA3d 396, 401, 239 CR 450. The convenience of the parties' counsel is not a permissible basis for a change of venue. *Lieppman v Lieber* (1986) 180 CA3d 914, 920, 225 CR 845.

- There is no judge in the present venue qualified to act. CCP §397(d). As a practical matter, this ground is rarely used. When no judge in the county is qualified to act, the Judicial Council chair may assign an outside judge to hear the matter. CCP §170.8.

- The action is one for a marital dissolution and the ends of justice would be promoted by a change of venue from the county of the petitioner's residence to the county of the respondent's residence. CCP §397(e). See, *e.g., Silva v Superior Court* (1981) 119 CA3d 301, 173 CR 832 (trial court abused discretion in denying change of venue when economic, educational, and financial disruption of family unit would result if venue were not changed).

A motion for a change of venue on the ground that the court in which the action is pending is not one in which the petition may properly be filed (CCP §397(a)) must be made at the time the respondent files a response, a motion to quash the proceedings (the family law equivalent of a demurrer in civil actions generally, see §10.62), or a motion to strike or, without filing any of these, within the time that the respondent has to respond to the petition. CCP §396b(a). No time limit is prescribed by statute when the motion is made on other grounds, but case law suggests that such motions (1) may not be made before the filing of the response, because the court will not be able to determine what matters are at issue and what testimony will be material (see *Johnson v Superior Court* (1965) 232 CA2d 212, 214, 42 CR 645), but (2) must be made within a "reasonable" time after the filing of the response (see *Pascoe v Baker* (1910) 158 C 232, 233, 110 P 815).

NOTE➤ On a court's authority to make temporary orders concerning child custody, visitation, and support, spousal support, and attorney fees and costs before ruling on a motion to change venue, see CCP §396b(c).

By filing a motion for a change of venue (except as provided in CCP §418.10), a respondent makes a general appearance. Cal Rules of Ct 5.120(a)(1)(3). When a motion made under CCP §396b (improper court) is denied, the court must allow the respondent time to plead if he or she has not previously filed a response. CCP §396b(e). If the motion is granted, the respondent's time to file a response is extended to 30 days after the mailing of notice of the filing and case number by the clerk of the court to which the action is transferred. CCP §586(a)(6)(B).

Before determining a motion for a change of venue, the court may consider and determine motions for temporary spousal support, child support, attorney fees, and costs, and make all necessary and proper orders in connection with such motions. CCP §397(e); *Thompson v Thames* (1997) 57 CA4th 1296, 67 CR2d 695.

For a complete discussion of motions to change venue, see California Civil Procedure Before Trial, chap 20 (4th ed Cal CEB 2004).

§10.64 4. Motion to Stay or Dismiss Action on Ground of Inconvenient Forum

A respondent may move to stay or dismiss the action on the ground of inconvenient forum (also called forum non conveniens). The motion may be made at any time. CCP §410.30. If it is made within the respondent's time to respond to the petition, the motion constitutes a special appearance and the respondent's time to file a response is extended until 15 days after service on him or her of a written notice of entry of an order denying the motion or for up to 20 days beyond that if extended by the court for good cause shown. CCP §418.10(a)–(b). Likewise, a respondent who appears only in opposition to a request for temporary orders while a motion to stay or dismiss the action on the ground of inconvenient forum is pending will not be deemed to have made a general appearance. Fam C §2012.

If the respondent moves to stay or dismiss on the grounds of inconvenient forum at the same time as respondent responds to the petition, and the court denies the motion, the respondent is considered to have made a general appearance on entry of the order denying the motion. CCP §418.10(e)(1). If the motion is denied and the respondent petitions for a writ of mandate, the respondent is not deemed to have generally appeared until the final completion of the writ proceedings. CCP §418.10(e)(2). The failure to make a motion under CCP §418.10 at the time of filing a motion to strike (or, apparently, at the time of moving to quash under Cal Rules of Ct 5.121) waives the issues of lack of personal jurisdiction, inadequacy of process or service of process, or inconvenient forum. See CCP §418.10(e)(3).

Note that a motion to stay or dismiss on the grounds of inconvenient forum is not limited to the respondent; the petitioner may also file such a motion. *Marriage of Taschen* (2005) 134 CA4th 681, 688, 36 CR3d 286.

For a complete discussion of motions to dismiss or stay on grounds of inconvenient forum, see California Civil Procedure Before Trial, chap 21 (4th ed Cal CEB 2004). Note that Fam C §3427, part of the Uniform Child Custody Jurisdiction and Enforcement Act (Fam C §§3400–3465), governs inconvenient forum motions in child custody matters. See §§7.12, 7.15.

§10.65   5. Motion to Strike

The respondent may file a noticed motion to strike matter that should not be in the petition. See CCP §435(b)(1); see also Cal Rules of Ct 5.120(a)(2). A motion to strike must be filed within the time allowed for the filing of the response (CCP §435(b)(1)), and the motion constitutes a general appearance (Cal Rules of Ct 5.120(a)(2)). As a practical matter, a motion to strike is unlikely to be worth the time and expense and is rarely used. The court will likely disregard the prohibited matter in any event.

For a complete discussion of motions to strike, see California Civil Procedure Before Trial, chap 24 (4th ed Cal CEB 2004).

IV. MOTIONS AVAILABLE TO PETITIONER

§10.66   A. Motion to Quash Respondent's Request for Affirmative Relief

A petitioner may move to quash, in whole or in part, any request for affirmative relief in the response. Cal Rules of Ct 5.121. Such a motion allows a petitioner to attack the response in much the same way that a respondent may attack the petition by a motion to quash the proceeding (see §10.62), and the available grounds are the same:

- The respondent lacks the legal capacity to sue (see Cal Rules of Ct 5.121(a)(1));

- There is a prior judgment, or another action is pending, between the same parties for the same cause (Cal Rules of Ct 5.121(a)(2));

- The residence requirement of Fam C §2320 (see §§4.3, 4.8) has not been met (Cal Rules of Ct 5.121(a)(3)); or

- The proceeding is one for a judgment of nullity and is barred by the applicable statute of limitations in Fam C §2211 (see §§3.10–3.15) (Cal Rules of Ct 5.121(a)(4)).

The petitioner's motion to quash any request for affirmative relief must be made within 15 days after the filing of the response to the petition. Cal Rules of Ct 5.121(c). The motion to quash must be served in compliance with CCP §1005(b). Cal Rules of Ct 5.121(b). Like the respondent's motion to quash the proceeding, the hearing on the petitioner's motion to quash must be scheduled not more than 20 days from the date the notice of motion is filed (Cal Rules of Ct 5.121(b). If the court grants a motion to quash ((Cal Rules of Ct 5.121(e)):

- It may also grant leave to amend the petition and set a date for filing the amended pleadings;

- It may dismiss the proceeding without leave to amend; or

- It may grant leave to amend and dismiss the proceeding or request for affirmative relief if the amendment is not made within the time set by the court.

A party who does not file a timely motion to quash is deemed to waive the right to attack the proceedings on any of the grounds enumerated in Cal Rules of Ct 5.121(a). Cal Rules of Ct 5.121(d). See §10.62. A petitioner's motion to quash is prepared and processed in the same manner as the respondent's motions covered in §§10.61–10.65 (see §10.60).

The petitioner is not required to file a reply if the respondent has filed a response. Cal Rules of Ct 5.108(b).

§10.67   B. Motion to Strike

The petitioner may also file a noticed motion to strike matter in the response just as a respondent may do in response to the petition (see §10.65). A motion to strike must be filed within the time allowed to respond to a pleading (CCP §435(b)(1)), and the motion to quash is the only other way a petitioner may respond to the response.

A petitioner's motion to strike is prepared and processed in the same manner as the respondent's motions covered in §§10.61–10.65 (see §10.60).

The petitioner is not required to file a reply if the respondent has filed a response. Cal Rules of Ct 5.108(b).

§10.68   V. AMENDED AND SUPPLEMENTAL PLEADINGS

Amended pleadings and amendments to pleadings may be served and filed in conformity with the provisions applicable in civil actions generally. If both parties have filed pleadings, no default may be entered on an amended pleading of either party. Cal Rules of Ct 5.108(b). Whereas an amended pleading is an entire new document, an amendment to a pleading is an additional document that specifies the changes to the pleading being amended and must be read in conjunction with it. An amended pleading is usually the preferable approach because it allows all the contents of the pleading to be set forth in familiar order in a single document. The Judicial Council form for petition (see §10.12) or response (see §10.52) is used, and the box next to the word "AMENDED" is checked.

The petition may be amended once "of course," *i.e.*, without court order, before the response is filed by filing the amended petition and serving a copy on the respondent. Because the court's jurisdiction over a respondent who has been properly served with summons continues throughout subsequent proceedings in the action (CCP §410.50), the petitioner need not obtain an additional summons to serve with an amended petition. When the respondent has not filed a response or otherwise made a general appearance, however, the amended petition must be served in the same manner as a summons. The respondent's time to respond begins running anew from the time of service of the amended petition. CCP §472.

A response may also be amended once of course. CCP §472; California Civil Procedure Before Trial §25.73 (4th ed Cal CEB 2004). This amended response must apparently be filed within the same period allowed for a motion to quash the respondent's request for affirmative relief (see §10.66). In a general civil action, a defendant may amend the answer without court order within the time during which the plaintiff may demur to the answer. CCP §472; *Bank of America v Goldstein* (1938) 25 CA2d 37, 45, 76 P2d 545. The motion to quash is the comparable action in a marital action, in which demurrers are not permitted (see Cal Rules of Ct 5.108(a)).

When a party may no longer amend his or her pleading of course, the required court approval may be granted only after a noticed motion, except that leave to amend by adding or striking the name of any party or correcting a mistake in the name of any party or otherwise may be granted without notice. CCP §473(a)(1). The noticed motion requirement may be avoided, however, by a stipulation of the parties to the amendment. It is unclear whether a court could deny permission to file an amendment to which the parties agree, but it is good practice to submit a written order permitting the amendment for the court to sign and file.

Either party may be allowed, on motion, to file a supplemental petition or response to allege material facts occurring after the petition or response was filed. CCP §464(a); Cal Rules of Ct 5.108(b) (former Cal Rules of Ct 1215(d)). Code of Civil Procedure §464(a) does not specify whether the motion must be noticed, but the party seeking to file the supplemental document should proceed by noticed motion. A supplemental request regarding paternity or support of an additional child of the parties (presumably one born after the filing of the petition) may be filed, either before or after judgment, without leave of court. CCP §464(b); Fam C §2330.1; see Fam C §3651(b).

When required, a motion for an order granting leave to amend or supplement a pleading is prepared and processed in the same manner as the respondent's motions covered in §§10.61–10.65 (see §10.60).

On amended and supplemental pleadings in civil actions generally, see Civ Proc Before Trial, chap 16 (complaints), chap 25 (answers).

VI. PROCEEDING IN FORMA PAUPERIS

§10.69   A. Discussion

A petitioner or respondent for whom payment of the court fee for filing his or her initial pleading poses a financial hardship may apply, on the application for waiver of court fees and costs (Judicial Council Form 982(a)(17)), for an order waiving the fee. Waiver must be granted if (Govt C §68511.3; Cal Rules of Ct 985):

- The applicant is receiving benefits under the Supplemental Security Income (SSI) and State Supplemental Payments (SSP) programs, the California Work Opportunity and Responsibility to Kids Act (CalWORKs) program (formerly AFDC), the Food Stamp program, or County Relief, General Relief (GR), or General Assistance (GA) (see Item 4 on application form);

- The applicant's gross monthly income is less than that shown on the Judicial Council Information Sheet on Waiver of Court Fees and Costs (Judicial Council Form 982(a)(17)(A)), which is tied to the current monthly poverty line established annually by the Secretary of Health and Human Services (see Item 6 on application form); or

- The court determines that a waiver is appropriate because the applicant cannot proceed without using money that is necessary to provide for the common necessaries of life of the applicant or his or her family (see Items 7–12 on application form).

Also waived if the application is approved is any sheriff's fee for service of process. Govt C §26721; Cal Rules of Ct 985(i)(6). Further, at least in dissolution actions, if service by publication (see §§10.35–10.38) would ordinarily be required, an indigent petitioner is entitled to an order providing instead for service by mail and posting at the respondent's last known address. *Cohen v Board of Supervisors* (1971) 20 CA3d 236, 97 CR 550.

If there is good reason to doubt the factual allegations of the application, or if the information provided is incomplete, the litigant may be asked to comply with a request for additional documentation so that his or her financial condition can be verified. See Cal Rules of Court 985(b).

§10.70   B. Form: Application for Waiver of Court Fees and Costs (Judicial Council Form FW-001)

— *THIS FORM MUST BE KEPT CONFIDENTIAL* —   **FW-001**

ATTORNEY OR PARTY WITHOUT ATTORNEY *(Name, state bar number, and address)*:	FOR COURT USE ONLY

TELEPHONE NO.:   FAX NO. *(Optional)*:
E-MAIL ADDRESS *(Optional)*:
ATTORNEY FOR *(Name)*:

NAME OF COURT:
STREET ADDRESS:
MAILING ADDRESS:
CITY AND ZIP CODE:
BRANCH NAME:

PLAINTIFF/ PETITIONER:
DEFENDANT/ RESPONDENT:

APPLICATION FOR **WAIVER OF COURT FEES AND COSTS**	CASE NUMBER

I request a court order so that I do not have to pay court fees and costs.

1. a. ☐ I am *not* able to pay any of the court fees and costs.
   b. ☐ I am able to pay *only* the following court fees and costs *(specify)*:

2. My current street or mailing address is *(if applicable, include city or town, apartment no., if any, and zip code)*:

3. a. My occupation, employer, and employees address are *(specify)*:

   b. My spouse's occupation, employer, and employees address are *(specify)*:

4. ☐ I am receiving financial assistance under one or more of the following programs:
   a. ☐ **SSI and SSP:** Supplemental Security Income and State Supplemental Payments Programs
   b. ☐ **CalWORKs:** California Work Opportunity and Responsibility to Kids Act, implementing TANF, Temporary Assistance for Needy Families (formerly AFDC)
   c. ☐ **Food Stamps:** The Food Stamp Program
   d. ☐ **County Relief, General Relief (G.R.), or General Assistance (G.A.)**

5. *If you checked box 4, you must check and complete **one of the three boxes below**, unless you are a defendant in an unlawful detainer action. Do not check more than one box.*
   a. ☐ *(Optional)* My Medi-Cal number is *(specify)*:
   b. ☐ *(Optional)* My social security number is *(specify)*:
      ☐☐☐ - ☐☐ - ☐☐☐☐   and my date of birth is *(specify)*:
      [Federal law does not require that you give your social security number. However, if you don't give your social security number, you must check box c and attach documents to verify the benefits checked in item 4.]
   c. ☐ I am attaching documents to verify receipt of the benefits checked in item 4, if requested by the court.
      [See Form FW-001-INFO, Information Sheet on Waiver of Court Fees and Costs, available from the clerk's office, for a list of acceptable documents.]

[If you checked box 4 above, skip items 6 and 7, and sign at the bottom of this side.]
6. ☐ My total gross monthly household income is less than the amount shown on the *Information Sheet on Waiver of Court Fees and Costs* available from the clerk's office.

[if you checked box 6 above, skip item 7, complete items 8, 9a, 9d, 9f, and 9g on the back of this form, and sign at the bottom of this side.]
7. ☐ My income is not enough to pay for the common necessaries of life for me and the people in my family whom I support and also pay court fees and costs. *[If you check this box, you must complete the back of this form.]*

WARNING: You must immediately tell the court if you become able to pay court fees or costs during this action. You may be ordered to appear in court and answer questions about your ability to pay court fees or costs.

I declare under penalty of perjury under the laws of the State of California that the information on both sides of this form and all attachments are true and correct.

Date:

▶

_____   _____
(TYPE OR PRINT NAME)   (Financial information on reverse)   (SIGNATURE)   Page 1 of 2

Form Adopted for Mandatory Use   **APPLICATION FOR WAIVER OF COURT FEES AND COSTS**   Government Code,
Judicial Council of California   (Fee Waiver)   **CEB**   § 68511.3
FW-001 [Rev. January 1, 2007]   www.courtinfo.ca.gov

FW-001

PLAINTIFF/PETITIONER:	CASE NUMBER:
DEFENDANT/RESPONDENT:	

FINANCIAL INFORMATION

8. ☐ My pay changes considerably from month to month. *[If you check this box, each of the amounts reported in item 9 should be your average for the past 12 months.]*

9. **MY MONTHLY INCOME**
   a. My gross monthly pay is: . . . . $ _____
   b. **My payroll** deductions are *(specify purpose and amount):*
      (1) _____ $ _____
      (2) _____ $ _____
      (3) _____ $ _____
      (4) _____ $ _____
      My TOTAL payroll deduction amount is: $ _____
   c. My monthly take-home pay is
      (a. minus b.): . . . . $ _____
   d. Other money I get each month is *(specify source and amount; include spousal support, child support, parental support, support from outside the home, scholarships, retirement or pensions, social security, disability, unemployment, military basic allowance for quarters (BAQ), veterans payments, dividends, interest or royalty, trust income, annuities, net business income, net rental income, reimbursement of job-related expenses, and net gambling or lottery winnings):*
      (1) _____ $ _____
      (2) _____ $ _____
      (3) _____ $ _____
      (4) _____ $ _____
      The TOTAL amount of other money is: $ _____
      (If more space is needed, attach page labeled Attachment 9d.)
   e. **MY TOTAL MONTHLY INCOME IS**
      (c. plus d.): . . . . $ _____
   f. Number of persons living in my home: _____
      Below list all the persons living in your home, including your spouse, who depend in whole or in part on you for support, or on whom you depend in whole or in part for support:

Name	Age	Relationship	Gross Monthly Income
(1) _____	___	_____	$ _____
(2) _____	___	_____	$ _____
(3) _____	___	_____	$ _____
(4) _____	___	_____	$ _____
(5) _____	___	_____	$ _____

   The TOTAL amount of other money is: $ _____
   (If more space is needed, attach page labeled Attachment 9f.)
   g. **MY TOTAL MONTHLY HOUSEHOLD INCOME IS**
      (a. plus d. plus f): . . . . $ _____

10. I own or have an interest in the following property:
    a. Cash . . . . $ _____
    b. Checking, savings, and credit union accounts *(list banks):*
       (1) _____ $ _____
       (2) _____ $ _____
       (3) _____ $ _____
       (4) _____ $ _____

10. c. Cars, other vehicles, and boats *(list make, year, fair market value (FMV), and loan balance of each):*

Property	FMV	Loan Balance
(1) _____	$ _____	$ _____
(2) _____	$ _____	$ _____
(3) _____	$ _____	$ _____

   d. Real estate *(list address, estimated fair market value (FMV), and loan balance of each property):*

Property	FMV	Loan Balance
(1) _____	$ _____	$ _____
(2) _____	$ _____	$ _____
(3) _____	$ _____	$ _____

   e. Other personal property — jewelry, furniture, furs, stocks, bonds, etc. *(list separately):*
   _____ $ _____

11. My monthly expenses not already listed in item 9b above are the following:
    a. Rent or house payment & maintenance $ _____
    b. Food and household supplies . . . . $ _____
    c. Utilities and telephone . . . . $ _____
    d. Clothing . . . . $ _____
    e. Laundry and cleaning . . . . $ _____
    f. Medical and dental payments . . . . $ _____
    g. Insurance (life, health, accident, etc.) $ _____
    h. School, child care . . . . $ _____
    i. Child, spousal support (prior marriage) $ _____
    j. Transportation and auto expenses (insurance, gas, repair) . . . . $ _____
    k. Installment payments *(specify purpose and amount):*
       (1) _____ $ _____
       (2) _____ $ _____
       (3) _____ $ _____
       The TOTAL amount of monthly installment payments is: . . . . $ _____
    l. Amounts deducted due to wage assignments and earnings withholding orders: $ _____
    m. Other expenses *(specify):*
       (1) _____ $ _____
       (2) _____ $ _____
       (3) _____ $ _____
       (4) _____ $ _____
       (5) _____ $ _____
       The TOTAL amount of other monthly expenses is: . . . . $ _____
    n. **MY TOTAL MONTHLY EXPENSES ARE** *(add a. through m.):* . . . . $ _____

12. Other facts that support this application are *(describe unusual medical needs, expenses for recent family emergencies, or other unusual circumstances or expenses to help the court understand your budget; if more space is needed, attach page labeled Attachment 12):*

WARNING: You must immediately tell the court if you become able to pay court fees or costs during this action. You may be ordered to appear in court and answer questions about your ability to pay court fees or costs.

FW-001 [Rev. January 1, 2007]   **APPLICATION FOR WAIVER OF COURT FEES AND COSTS**   CEB   Page 2 of 2
(Fee Waiver)

Copies: Original (submit to court clerk); office copies.

§10.71   C. Form: Order on Application for Waiver of Court Fees and Costs (Judicial Council Form FW-003)

<table>
<tr><td colspan="2" align="right">FW-003</td></tr>
<tr>
<td>ATTORNEY OR PARTY WITHOUT ATTORNEY (Name, state bar number, and address):</td>
<td>FOR COURT USE ONLY</td>
</tr>
</table>

TELEPHONE NO: FAX NO :

E-MAIL ADDRESS (Optional):

ATTORNEY FOR (Name):

SUPERIOR COURT OF CALIFORNIA, COUNTY OF

STREET ADDRESS:

MAILING ADDRESS:

CITY AND ZIP CODE:

BRANCH NAME:

PLAINTIFF/ PETITIONER:

DEFENDANT/ RESPONDENT: CASE NUMBER:

ORDER ON APPLICATION FOR WAIVER OF COURT FEES AND COSTS

1. The application was filed on (date):   ☐ A previous order was issued on (date):

2. The application was filed by (name):

3. ☐ IT IS ORDERED that the application is **granted** ☐ in whole ☐ in part (complete item 4 below).

    a. ☐ **No payments.** Payment of all the fees and costs listed in California Rules of Court, rule 3.61, **is waived.**

    b. ☐ The applicant shall pay all the fees and costs listed in California Rules of Court, rule 3.61, EXCEPT the following:

        (1) ☐ Filing papers.   (6) ☐ Sheriff and marshal fees.

        (2) ☐ Certification and copying.   (7) ☐ Reporter's fees* (valid for 60 days).

        (3) ☐ Issuing process and certification.   (8) ☐ Telephone appearance (Gov. Code, § 68070.1 (c))

        (4) ☐ Transmittal of papers.   (9) ☐ Other (specify code section):

        (5) ☐ Court-appointed interpreter.

        Reporter's fees are per diem pursuant to Code Civ. Proc., §§ 269, 274c, and Gov. Code, §§ 69947, 69948, and 72195.

    c. **Method of payment.** The applicant shall pay all the fees and costs when charged, EXCEPT as follows:

        (1) ☐ Pay (specify):   percent. (2) ☐ Pay: $ per month or more until the balance is paid.

    d. The clerk of the court, county financial officer, or appropriate county officer is authorized to require the applicant to appear before and be examined by the court no sooner than four months from the date of this order, and not more than once in any four-month period. ☐ The applicant is ordered to appear in this court as follows for review of his or her financial status:

Date:	Time:	Dept.:	Div.:	Room:

    e. ☐ The clerk is directed to mail a copy of this order only to the applicant's attorney or to the applicant if not represented.

    f. All unpaid fees and costs shall be deemed to be taxable costs if the applicant is entitled to costs and shall be a lien on any judgment recovered by the applicant and shall be paid directly to the clerk by the judgment debtor upon such recovery.

4. ☐ IT IS ORDERED that the application is **denied** ☐ in whole ☐ in part for the following reasons (see Cal. Rules of Court, rules 3.50–3.63):

    a. ☐ Monthly household income exceeds guidelines (Gov. Code, § 68511.3(a)(6)(B); form FW-001-INFO).

    b. ☐ Other (Complete line 4b on page 2).

    c. The applicant shall pay any fees and costs due in this action within 10 days from the date of service of this order or any paper filed by the applicant with the clerk will be of no effect.

    d. The clerk is directed to mail a copy of this order to all parties who have appeared in this action.

5. ☐ IT IS ORDERED that a **hearing** be held.

    a. The substantial evidentiary conflict to be resolved by the hearing is (specify):

    b. The applicant should appear in this court at the following hearing to help resolve the conflict:

Date:	Time:	Dept.:	Div.:	Room:

    c. The address of the court is (specify):

        ☐ Same as above

    d. The clerk is directed to mail a copy of this order only to the applicant's attorney or to the applicant if not represented.

NOTICE: If item 3d or item 5b is filled in and the applicant does not attend the hearing, the court may revoke or change the order or deny the application without considering information the applicant wants the court to consider.

WARNING: The applicant must immediately tell the court if he or she becomes able to pay court fees or costs during this action. The applicant may be ordered to appear in court and answer questions about his or her ability to pay fees or costs.

Date:

☐ _____   ☐ Clerk, by _____ , Deputy

    JUDICIAL OFFICER   (Clerk may GRANT in full a nondiscretionary fee waiver; see Cal. Rules of Court, rule 3.55.)

Form Adopted for Mandatory Use
Judicial Council of California
FW-003 [Rev. January 1, 2007]

ORDER ON APPLICATION FOR WAIVER OF COURT FEES AND COSTS (Fee Waiver)

CEB

Government Code, § 68511.3;
Cal. Rules of Court, rules 3.50–3.63
www.courtinfo.ca.gov

Page 1 of 2

PLAINTIFF/PETITIONER (Name):	FW-003
	CASE NUMBER
DEFENDANT/RESPONDENT (Name):	

4b ☐ Application is denied in whole or in part (specify reasons):

CLERK'S CERTIFICATE OF MAILING

I certify that I am not a party to this cause and that a true copy of the foregoing was mailed first class, postage prepaid, in a sealed envelope addressed as shown below, and that the mailing of the foregoing and execution of this certificate occurred at (place):   , California, on (date):

Clerk, by _____ , Deputy

(SEAL)

CLERK'S CERTIFICATE

I certify that the foregoing is a true and correct copy of the original on file in my office.

Date:

Clerk, by _____ , Deputy

Copies: Original (submit to court clerk); office copies.

VII. RIGHT TO REQUEST SEALING OF PLEADINGS CONTAINING FINANCIAL INFORMATION

§10.72　　A. Discussion

Family C §2024.6 requires a court, on request by a party to a petition for marital dissolution, legal separation, or annulment, to order the sealing of any pleading that lists the parties' financial assets and liabilities and provides the location or identifying information about those assets and liabilities. The statute permits the request to be made by ex parte application Fam C §2024.6(a). However, one court of appeal has held the statute to be unconstitutional and review of the case by the California Supreme Court was denied. *Burkle v Burkle* (2006) 135 CA4th 1045, 1063, 37 CR 3d 805. The appellate court reasoned that the statute was "not narrowly tailored to serve the privacy interests it is intended to protect, and less restrictive means of protecting the privacy interests are available," using the standard established in *NBC Subsidiary (KNBC-TV), Inc. v Superior Court* (1999) 20 C4th 1178, 86 CR2d 778. 135 CA4th at 1063. Family C §2024.6 has not been repealed, but in light of *Burkle*, counsel should not rely on it.

CAUTION➤ Although the Judicial Council form created in compliance with Family C §2024.6 (Judicial Council Form FL-316) no longer appears valid in light of *Burkle*, it has not been revoked. Pending any action taken to amend the statute or the form, counsel and clients must fall back on their ability to redact truly confidential information, such as Social Security and financial account numbers, from documents concerning assets to be filed with the court. On authority to seal court documents in family law cases, see *Marriage of Lechowick* (1998) 65 CA4th 1406, 77 CR2d 395.

§10.73　　C. Form: Ex Parte Application and Order to Seal Financial Forms (Judicial Council Form FL-316) [Deleted]

This section has been deleted because Fam C §2024.6, on which the form was based, was found unconstitutional (see §10.72).

11

Temporary Orders

§11.1   I. SCOPE OF CHAPTER

This chapter addresses all aspects of temporary orders, with emphasis on procedures for both moving and responding parties with respect to noticed motions.

II. AVAILABLE ORDERS

§11.2   A. Child Custody and Visitation

While any marital action is pending, the court may make orders, either ex parte or on noticed motion, deciding the temporary custody of any minor children of the marriage and visitation rights regarding the children. Fam C §§6323, 6340(a); see Items 1–2 on Application for Order and Supporting Declaration (Judicial Council Form FL-310) in §11.22. The legal guidelines are the same as those for long-term custody and visitation awards. On child custody and visitation generally, see chap 7.

Counsel must be sensitive to the importance of the initial custody and visitation orders. They should not be treated lightly, with the expectation that an unsatisfactory order will be corrected later, whether by mediation, evaluation, or litigation. Custody and visitation patterns established early on tend to be difficult to change. Arguments for maintaining an arrangement the children have become used to can be hard to overcome. Thus, for example, a parent who hopes to have substantial contact in the future with a child who is now an infant may need to seek a significant measure of contact with the child now; otherwise, when the request for substantial contact is made, the other parent may argue that contact should not be increased significantly, because the child is not used to being with the requesting parent.

When the parties have an agreement or understanding regarding custody or temporary custody, a copy of the agreement or a declaration regarding the understanding must be attached to a petition or motion. As promptly as possible after the filing, the court must, except in exceptional circumstances, enter an order granting temporary custody in accordance with the agreement or understanding. Fam C §3061.

The court may not grant or modify a custody order *on an ex parte basis* unless a showing has been made of (1) immediate harm to the child or (2) immediate risk that the child will be removed from California. "Immediate harm to the child" includes having a parent who has committed acts of domestic violence (for definition, see Fam C §6211), when the court finds that those acts were committed recently or are part of a demonstrated and continuing pattern. Fam C §3064.

When the court *does* grant or modify a custody order on an ex parte basis, it must make an order restraining the person receiving custody from removing the child from California, pending notice and a hearing on the temporary custody motion. Fam C §3063. When counsel is aware of any facts that might indicate there is a risk of abduction by a parent, appropriate relief under Fam C §3048(b)(2)(A)-(K) should be requested.

An ex parte order for custody or visitation must specify the time, day, place, and manner of transfer of the child in order to limit the child's exposure to potential domestic conflict or violence and to ensure the safety of all family members. When the court finds that a party is staying in a shelter or other confidential location, the order must be designed to prevent disclosure of the location. Fam C §6323(c). Further, the court must consider whether the child's best interests, based on the circumstances of the case, require that any custody or visitation arrangement be limited to situations in which a third party specified by the court is present, or that custody or visitation be suspended or denied. Fam C §6323(d).

Note that an automatic order is issued on the commencement of every marital action that restrains both parties from removing any minor child of the parties from California without the other party's prior written consent or a court order. Fam C §2040(a)(1); see Item 1 on the back of the family law summons form (Judicial Council Form FL-110) in §10.14. For further discussion of automatic orders, see §11.11.

§11.3   B. Child Support

While any marital action is pending, the court may order either party to pay child support for any minor child of the marriage or for any adult child of the marriage for whom support is authorized under Fam C §3901 (unmarried 18-year-old child who is full-time high school student and not self-supporting) or Fam C §3910 (incapacitated and needy adult child). Fam C §3600; see Item 3 on Application for Order and Supporting Declaration (Judicial Council Form FL-310) in §11.22. The legal guidelines are the same as those for long-term child support awards. On child support generally, see chap 8.

An original order for child support may be made retroactive to the date of filing the petition, complaint, or other initial pleading. If, however, the parent ordered to pay support was not served with the petition, complaint, or other initial pleading within 90 days after filing and the court finds that the parent was not intentionally evading service, the child support must be effective no earlier than the date of service. Fam C §4009. A procedure by which an "expedited support order" may be obtained ex parte is set forth in Fam C §§3620–3634. It is questionable, however, whether such an order will truly provide support in a more timely fashion than an order sought under the standard procedures. An expedited order is not effective until 30 days after service on the obligated parent of the proposed order and accompanying papers (Fam C §3624); that date will be stayed pending a noticed hearing if the obligated parent contests the order by timely filing a response and an Income and Expense Declaration (Fam C §§3625(c), 3626–3627). At a noticed hearing, however, the court's award may be made retroactive to the date the application was filed. Fam C §3632. For expedited support order forms (Judicial Council Forms FL-380, 382), see California Judicial Council Forms Manual §3 (Cal CEB 1981).

§11.4 C. Spousal Support

While a dissolution or legal separation action is pending, the court may order either party to pay spousal support to the other, consistent with Fam C §§4320 (i), (m), and 4325. Fam C §3600; see Item 4 on Application for Order and Supporting Declaration (Judicial Council Form FL-310) in §11.22. The same is true in a nullity action, as long as the party for whose benefit the order is made is found to be a putative spouse. Fam C §2254. On qualifying as a putative spouse, see §3.19. On legal guidelines for determining the amount of temporary, as distinguished from long-term, spousal support, see §§6.3–6.4.

It had long been assumed that the earliest date to which an order for temporary spousal support may be made retroactive is the date of filing of the notice of motion or order to show cause. See, *e.g.*, *Marriage of Economou* (1990) 224 CA3d 1466, 1476, 274 CR 473. In *Marriage of Dick* (1993) 15 CA4th 144, 165, 18 CR2d 743, however, the court held that a temporary spousal support order could be made retroactive to the date of filing of a petition requesting spousal support. For further discussion of this issue, see §6.2.

PRACTICE TIP➤ Ex parte requests for spousal support are disfavored and rarely, if ever, granted despite the technical statutory authority courts have to award support during the "pendency" of dissolution-related proceedings. See Fam C §3600. Courts much prefer to wait until a conventionally noticed hearing, at which time the court could also potentially consider a request for a *retroactive* award under the principles discussed above. A possible alternative approach is to request an order shortening time for hearing on the issue of granting temporary support. See CCP §1005(b). In addition, a court may be receptive to making an ex parte order requiring a party to pay certain debts of the parties, and this is provided for in the "property control" portions of the Judicial Council forms that are used to apply for and recite temporary orders (see §§11.22, 11.24). On spousal support generally, see chap 6.

§11.5   D. Attorney Fees and Costs

While any marital action is pending, and in any proceeding after a related judgment, the court may order either party (except a governmental entity) to pay any amount reasonably necessary for the other party's attorney fees and costs of maintaining or defending the proceeding. Fam C §2030(a); see Item 5 on Application for Order and Supporting Declaration (Judicial Council Form FL-310) in §11.22. In a nullity action based on a voidable marriage (see Fam C §2210), however, attorney fees and costs may be awarded only to a party found to be innocent of fraud or wrongdoing in inducing or entering into the marriage and free from knowledge of the existence of any prior marriage or other impediment to contracting the present marriage. Fam C §2255. On attorney fees and costs generally, see chap 9. For additional provisions on attorney fees and costs, see Fam C §§2031, 3121, 6340, 6341, 6344, and 7605.

An application for a temporary order for attorney fees or costs must be made by a Notice of Motion or an Order to Show Cause, except that it may be made without notice by an oral motion in open court (1) at the hearing of the cause on its merits or (2) at any time before entry of judgment against a party whose default has been entered. The court must rule on any such motion (see Fam C §2031(b)) within 15 days and before the entry of any judgment.

§11.6   E. Protective Orders

While any marital action is pending, the court may make a variety of orders restraining the conduct of one party to protect the peace and safety of the other party and, in some instances, of specified third parties. The most common protective orders are set forth below. When considering whether to make any ex parte orders under Fam C §§6320–6327, the court must consider whether failure to make them may jeopardize the safety of the petitioner and the children for whom custody and visitation orders are sought. Fam C §6340(a).

A person subject to one of these orders must not own, possess, purchase, receive, or attempt to purchase or receive a firearm while the protective order is in effect; a person who does so is punishable under Pen C §12021(g). Fam C §6389(a). On related criminal provisions, see Pen C §136.2.

Restraint on personal conduct. The court may order, either ex parte or on noticed motion, that one party not harass, attack, strike, threaten, assault (sexually or otherwise), hit, follow, stalk, molest, destroy personal property of, disturb the peace of, keep under surveillance, or block movements of the other party. On a showing of good cause, the court may extend the order to protect other named family and household members. Fam C §§6320, 6340(a); see Item 3 on Request for Order (Judicial Council Form DV-100) in §11.31B.

The court may not issue *mutual* restraining orders under Fam C §6320 unless (a) both parties personally appear and each party presents written evidence of abuse or domestic violence, and (b) the court makes detailed findings of fact indicating that both parties acted primarily as aggressors and that neither party acted primarily in self-defense. Fam C §6305. See also *Kobey v Morton* (1991) 228 CA3d 1055, 1059, 278 CR 530 (in action for injunction prohibiting harassment under CCP §527.6, court held that mutual orders restraining personal conduct may not be issued after a hearing unless both parties have filed papers requesting them). On orders to restrain a party from seeking the address or location of a protected party, see Fam C §§6252.5, 6322.7.

Stay-away orders. The court may order, either ex parte or on noticed motion, that one party stay at least a specified distance (*e.g.,* 100 yards) from the other party and from specified places relating to the other party (*e.g.,* residence, place of work, school). On a showing of good cause, the court may extend the order to other named family and household members and to places relating to them. Fam C §§6320, 6322, 6340(a); see Item 3 on Request for Order in §11.31B. The limitations on mutual restraining orders noted above with respect to restraints on personal conduct also apply to stay-away orders.

Residence exclusion order. The court may order, either ex parte or on noticed motion, that one party move out of the family dwelling, the dwelling of the other party, the common dwelling of both parties, or the dwelling of the person who has custody of a child to be protected from domestic violence, regardless of which party holds legal or equitable title or is the lessee. Fam C §§6321(a), 6340(a); see Item 8 on Request for Order in §11.31B. Before such an order may be made ex parte, there must be a showing that (1) the party who will stay in the dwelling has a right under color of law to possession of the premises, and (2) the party to be excluded has assaulted or threatens to assault, and that physical or emotional harm would otherwise result to, (a) the other party; (b) any person under the care, custody, and control of the other party; or (c) any minor child of the parties or of the other party. Fam C §6321(b). After notice and a hearing, on the other hand, it must only be shown that physical or emotional harm would otherwise result to such a person; a showing of assault or threatened assault is not required. Fam C §6340(b).

Before hearing on protective order. Before a hearing on any protective order, the court must ensure that a search of all readily available and reasonably accessible records and databases is or has been made to determine if the subject of the proposed order has any prior criminal conviction for a violent or serious felony (Pen C §§667.5, 1192.7); misdemeanor conviction involving domestic or other violence; outstanding warrants; prior restraining order or restraining order violation; or is on parole or probation. Fam C §6306(a).

Before deciding whether to issue a protective order or when determining appropriate temporary custody and visitation orders, the court must consider any conviction revealed by the search. After issuing its ruling, the court must advise the parties that they can request the information relied on and must release the information, on a party's request, to the parties (or a party's attorney, if requested). Fam C §6306(c). All information must be maintained in a confidential file, to be disclosed to the court-appointed mediator or child custody evaluator. Fam C §6306(d).

If there are outstanding warrants or the subject of the order is on probation or parole, the clerk of the court must notify appropriate law enforcement officials. Fam C §6306(e)-(f). If a protective order may be granted without the information from the database search, the court must issue it and then ensure that the search is conducted before the hearing. Fam C §6306(g).

There is no filing fee for an application seeking a protective order under the Domestic Violence Prevention Act (Fam C §§6200-6409). There also is no fee for a responsive pleading, or an order to show cause that seeks to obtain, modify, or enforce a protective order or other order authorized by the DVPA when the request for the other order is necessary to obtain or give effect to a protective order. Likewise, there is no fee for a subpoena filed in connection with that application, responsive pleading, or order to show cause. Fam C §6222. See CCP §527.6.

NOTE➤ In addition to protective orders that counsel may seek on behalf of an individual, police authorities are authorized to seek emergency protective orders in certain circumstances. See generally Fam C §§6240-6275.

§11.7   F. Property Restraints

While any marital action is pending, the court may make a variety of orders, either ex parte or on noticed motion, that restrain conduct with respect to property, including the following:

- An order prohibiting the transferring, encumbering, hypothecating, concealing, or disposing of any real or personal property (whether community, quasi-community, or separate), except in the usual course of business or for the necessities of life. The order often includes a provision that the other party be notified of any proposed extraordinary expenditures and that an accounting of them be made to the court. Fam C §2045(a); see Items 6.a and b on Application for Order and Supporting Declaration (Judicial Council Form FL-310) in §11.22. An automatic order including both provisions is issued on the commencement of every marital action and restrains both parties absent the other party's written consent or a court order. Fam C §2040(a)(2); see Item 3 and admonition following item 4 on the back of the family law summons form (Judicial Council Form FL-110) in §10.14. Severance of a joint tenancy with right of survivorship by recording a declaration of severance is not considered a transfer or disposition of property and does not violate an automatic TRO, but notice of the change must be filed and served on the other party. *Estate of Mitchell* (1999) 76 CA4th 1378, 1389, 91 CR2d 192; Fam C §2040(b)(3). For further discussion of automatic orders, see §11.11.

- An order prohibiting the cashing, borrowing against, canceling, transferring, disposing of, or changing the beneficiaries of any insurance or other coverage, including life, health, automobile, and disability, held for the benefit of the parties or their minor children. Fam C §2045(a); see Item 6.b on Application for Order and Supporting Declaration (Judicial Council Form FL-310) in §11.22. An automatic order to this effect is issued against both parties on the commencement of every marital action. Fam C §2040(a)(3); see Item 2 on the back of the family law summons form (Judicial Council Form FL-110) in §10.14. For further discussion of automatic orders, see §11.11. To protect against the other party's taking any action in violation of restraining orders with respect to insurance coverage, the attorney may take advantage of Fam C §§2050–2053. Under these provisions, a notice may be sent to a health, life, or disability insurance carrier or plan, requiring it to maintain named beneficiaries or covered dependents, unless policy terms or provisions of law require otherwise, until termination as specified in a court order or receipt of a court order or an agreement of the parties providing other instructions. Fam C §§2050–2051. The notice may be sent at any time during the proceeding (Fam C §§2050–2051) and may require that the coverage be administered according to an accompanying court order or judgment (Fam C §2051).

- An order prohibiting the incurring of any liabilities for which the other party may be held responsible, other than in the ordinary course of business or for the necessities of life. Fam C §2045(a); see Item 6.c on Application for Order and Supporting Declaration (Judicial Council Form FL-310) in §11.22.

Note that property restraints under Fam C §2045(a), unlike protective orders under Fam C §§6320–6322 and 6340 (see §11.6), may be directed to nonparties. *Schnabel v Superior Court* (1993) 21 CA4th 548, 552, 26 CR2d 169; see Cal Rules of Ct 5.106. Note, too, that Prob C §5600 will cause nonprobate transfers, other than insurance beneficiary designations, to fail if the beneficiary is not a surviving spouse at the time of decedent's death, as would be the case if marital status had been bifurcated with remaining property issues reserved. For a discussion of protecting the client in a bifurcation, see §14.61.

§11.8   G. Property Control

While any marital action is pending, the court may make an order, either ex parte or on noticed motion, determining the temporary use, possession, and control of the parties' real or personal property. Fam C §§6324, 6340(a); see Item 7.a on Application for Order and Supporting Declaration (Judicial Council Form FL-310) in §11.22.

§11.9   H. Payment of Debts

While any marital action is pending, the court may make an order, either ex parte or on noticed motion, determining who will pay liens or encumbrances as they come due. Fam C §§6324, 6340(a); see Item 7.b on Application for Order and Supporting Declaration (Judicial Council Form FL-310) in §11.22.

§11.10   I. Other Relief

There are a variety of orders other than those addressed in §§11.2–11.9 that the court may make while a marital action is pending. See Item 9 on Application for Order and Supporting Declaration (Judicial Council Form FL-310) in §11.22. A common example is an order for an examination by a vocational training consultant under Fam C §4331 when spousal support is at issue. Less common examples include a pendente lite sale of property (see *Lee v Superior Court* (1976) 63 CA3d 705, 711, 134 CR 43) and appointment of a receiver (see *Quaglino v Quaglino* (1979) 88 CA3d 542, 546, 152 CR 47).

Regarding the pendente lite sale of property, the holding of *Lee v Superior Court, supra*, is codified in Fam C §2108. That section provides that, on a party's motion and a showing of good cause, the court may order the liquidation of community or quasi-community assets in order to avoid unreasonable market or investment risks, given the relative nature, scope, and extent of the community estate. No such motion may be granted, however, unless the moving party has served any declaration of disclosure required by Fam C §§2100–2113. On declarations of disclosure, see §§13.44–13.49.

III. METHODS OF OBTAINING ORDERS

§11.11   A. Automatic Orders on Commencement of Action

On the commencement of every marital action, orders automatically go into effect that restrain both parties from:

- Removing any minor child of the parties from California without the other party's prior written consent or a court order. Fam C §2040(a)(1).

- Cashing, borrowing against, canceling, transferring, disposing of, or changing the beneficiaries of any insurance or other coverage, including life, health, automobile, and disability, held for the benefit of the parties or their minor children. Fam C §2040(a)(3). On notice to the carrier or the plan to protect against violation of the order, see §11.7. The orders are set forth on the back of the family law summons form (Judicial Council Form FL-110) in §10.14.

• Transferring, encumbering, hypothecating, concealing, disposing of, or changing the beneficiaries of any real or personal property (whether community, quasi-community, or separate) without a court order or the other party's written consent, except in the usual course of business or for the necessities of life.

• Creating or modifying a nonprobate transfer in a manner that affects the disposition of property subject to the transfer, without the other party's written consent or a court order. Fam C §2040(a)(4). A nonprobate transfer is an instrument other than a will that makes a transfer of property on death, including a revocable trust, pay on death account, Totten trust, or transfer on death registration of personal property, or other instrument of a type described in Prob C §5000; it is *not* an insurance policy provision subject to Fam C §2040(a)(3) that is held for the benefit of the parties and their children. Fam C §2040(d)(1)-(2). Section 2040(a)(4) does not apply to creating, modifying, or revoking a will; revoking a nonprobate transfer, including a revocable trust. or eliminating a right of survivorship to property, provided that notice of the change is filed and served on the other party before the change takes effect; creating an unfunded revocable or irrevocable trust; or executing and filing a disclaimer under Part 8 of Division 2 of the Probate Code. Fam C §2040(b)(1)-(5).

Severance of a joint tenancy with right of survivorship by recording a declaration of severance is not considered a transfer or disposition of property and does not violate an automatic TRO, but notice of the change must be filed and served on the other party. *Estate of Mitchell* (1999) 76 CA4th 1378, 1389, 91 CR2d 192; Fam C §2040(b)(3). Each party must also notify the other party of any proposed extraordinary expenditures at least 5 business days before incurring them and account to the court for all such expenditures.

The parties are specifically not precluded from using community property, quasi-community property, or their own separate property to pay reasonable attorney fees and costs to retain legal counsel in the marital action. A party who uses community or quasi-community property or property subsequently determined to be the other party's separate property to pay his or her attorney's retainer, however, must account for the use of the property. Fam C §2040(a)(2).

The automatic restraining orders are effective against the respondent when he or she is personally served (or waives and accepts service). Fam C §233(a). It is not clear when the orders are effective against the petitioner. Fam C §233(a) indicates that they are effective against the petitioner, as is true of the respondent, when the respondent is served. But Item 9 on the Judicial Council petition form (see form in §10.12) states that the orders are effective against the petitioner when the petition is filed. Clearly, the safer course for the petitioner's attorney is to assume that the orders are effective against his or her client when the petition is filed and to ensure that the client is so informed.

The attorney must be sure, when filing on behalf of the petitioner or when the respondent, having been served, brings in the papers received, to explain to the client what kinds of acts may be covered by the automatic restraining orders. For example, a client may believe that it is permissible to take money from a bank account to pay income taxes because such a transfer is "in the usual course of business or for the necessities of life" (Fam C §2040(a)(2)), but it is safer to obtain an agreement from the opposing attorney before doing so. What constitutes "in the usual course of business" may vary depending on the circumstances of the parties. *Marriage of McTiernan & Dubrow* (2005) 133 CA4th 1090, 1102, 35 CR3d 287 (court rejected husband's arguments that community obligations "ipso facto" were necessities of life and that sale of stock constituted "usual course of business" because he always managed community property); *Gale v Superior Court* (2004) 122 CA4th 1388, 1392, 19 CR3d 554 (automatic restraining orders in summons did not preclude sale of property by husband's management company in "usual course of business").

The orders remain in effect against both parties until the judgment is entered, the petition is dismissed, or the court makes further orders. Fam C §233(a). Either party may apply for further temporary orders or for modification or revocation of automatic orders. Fam C §235.

§11.12   B. Stipulation

Temporary orders may be obtained by stipulation of the parties. The negotiations should be conducted with reference to the moving party's Application for Order and Supporting Declaration (Judicial Council Form FL-310; see form in §11.22) to ensure that all the issues raised will be addressed.

Although stipulations are commonly entered into in court at the time of the hearing itself, they tend to be underused in advance of the hearing date. Attorneys who resolve temporary order issues by stipulation before the hearing date may save their clients the time, expense, and stress of a court appearance. Resolving the issues before the hearing date may also allow for more thoughtful consideration and drafting of the particular provisions than would otherwise be possible. When a stipulation is negotiated before the hearing date, it should be drafted on pleading paper or an appropriate Judicial Council Form and submitted to the court for approval and filing. For a sample form, see §11.13. When an agreement is reached in court at the time of the hearing, steps should be taken to ensure that it may be reduced to a written order with a minimum of difficulty. Some courts have forms for agreements on temporary orders that are recommended or even required for the parties' use. If such a form is not used, the stipulation will probably be read into the record. Although stipulations may be read into the record from rough notes, it is preferable to write out the entire stipulation, with copies for the court and each attorney or unrepresented party. This procedure will facilitate the subsequent drafting of an order that will be approved by the other attorney and the court clerk as conforming to the court order. Stipulations are often written on blank sheets, but it may be helpful to use the applicable Judicial Council forms for orders after hearing (see forms in §§11.54–11.61). Even when drafting the stipulation on blank sheets, however, the attorneys may wish to refer to the Judicial Council forms for ideas on the wording of individual provisions.

When child support is the subject of a stipulation, a Stipulation to Establish or Modify Child Support and Order (Judicial Council Form FL-350; see §11.14) is required. One important function this form performs is to enable the court, on any subsequent motion for modification, to ascertain whether the amount agreed to was below that established by the statewide uniform guidelines. If the amount was below the established amount, no change of circumstances will be required to obtain a modification of the award to or above the applicable amount. Fam C §4065(d).

Any time an order concerning child support is entered, Judicial Council Form FL-192 (Notice of Rights and Responsibilities: Health-Care Costs and Reimbursement Procedures and Information Sheet on Changing a Child Support Order) must be submitted with the order. Fam C §§4063(a)(1), (2), 4010. Each time an initial court order for child support or family support or a modification of a court order for child support is filed with the court, a Child Support Case Registry Form (Judicial Council Form FL-191) must be completed by both parties and filed with the court. The form is not filed in the court file but is stored in a nonpublic area until it is forwarded to the California Department of Social Services. Cal Rules of Ct 5.330(f). Local rules and practice should also be consulted. When the parties have an agreement or understanding regarding custody or temporary custody, a copy of the agreement or a declaration regarding the understanding must be attached to a petition or motion. As promptly as possible after the filing, the court must, except in exceptional circumstances, enter an order granting temporary custody in accordance with the agreement or understanding. Fam C §3061.

§11.13   1. Form: Stipulation and Order

_ _[Attorney name]_ _
_ _[State Bar number]_ _
_ _[Address]_ _
_ _[Telephone number]_ _

Attorney for _ _[name]_ _

SUPERIOR COURT OF CALIFORNIA
COUNTY OF _ _ _ _ _ _

Marriage of	)	**No.** _ _ _ _ _ _
	)	
Petitioner: _ _ _ _ _ _ _ _	)	**STIPULATION AND ORDER**
	)	
Respondent: _ _ _ _ _ _ _	)	
	)	
_____	)	

_ _[Name]_ _, **petitioner, and** _ _[name]_ _, **respondent, hereby stipulate that the Court may enter the following orders, pending trial or until further order in this action:**

[Set forth orders]

The foregoing is agreed to by:

Date: _____   __[Signature]__
                                     _ _[Typed name]_ _
                                     Petitioner

Date: _____   __[Signature]__
                                     _ _[Typed name]_ _
                                     Respondent

Approved as conforming to the agreement of the parties:

Date: _____   __[Signature]__
                                     _ _[Typed name]_ _
                                     Attorney for Petitioner

Date: _____   __[Signature]__
                                     _ _[Typed name]_ _
                                     Attorney for Respondent

ORDER

Good cause appearing, the stipulation of the parties set forth above is hereby approved and made an order of the Court and the parties are ordered to comply with its terms.

Date: _____   _____
                                     Judge of the Superior Court

Copies: Original (submit to court clerk); copy for other attorney or party; office copies.

Comment: This form of stipulation and order is used only when the agreement on temporary orders is reached before the hearing date. When the agreement has been reached in court at the time of the hearing, it should be prepared on the applicable Judicial Council forms for orders after hearing (see forms in §§11.54–11.61). Note that Judicial Council Form FL-350 must be used to file a stipulation concerning child support.

§11.14   2. Form: Stipulation to Establish or Modify Child Support and Order (Judicial Council Form FL-350)

FL-350

ATTORNEY OR PARTY WITHOUT ATTORNEY (Name and Address):	TELEPHONE NO.:	FOR COURT USE ONLY

ATTORNEY FOR (Name):

SUPERIOR COURT OF CALIFORNIA, COUNTY OF
STREET ADDRESS:
MAILING ADDRESS:
CITY AND ZIP CODE:
BRANCH NAME:

PETITIONER/PLAINTIFF:

RESPONDENT/DEFENDANT:

STIPULATION TO ESTABLISH OR MODIFY CHILD SUPPORT AND ORDER	CASE NUMBER:

1. a. ☐ Mother's net monthly disposable income: $
   Father's net monthly disposable income: $
   —OR—
   b. ☐ A printout of a computer calculation of the parents' financial circumstances is attached.
2. ☐ Percentage of time each parent has primary responsibility for the children: Mother   %   Father   %
3. a. ☐ A hardship is being experienced by the mother for: $ per month because of (specify):

   The hardship will last until (date):
   b. ☐ A hardship is being experienced by the father for: $ per month because of (specify):

   The hardship will last until (date):
4. The amount of child support payable by (name):   , referred to as the "obligor" below,
   as calculated under the guideline is: $ per month.
5. ☐ We agree to guideline support.
6. ☐ The guideline amount should be rebutted because of the following:
   a. ☐ We agree to child support in the amount of: $ per month; the agreement is in the best interest of
      the children; the needs of the children will be adequately met by the agreed amount; and application of the guideline
      would be unjust or inappropriate in this case.
   b. ☐ Other rebutting factors (specify):
7. Obligor must pay child support as follows beginning (date):
   a. BASIC CHILD SUPPORT

Child's name	Monthly amount	Payable to (name)

   Total: $ payable ☐ on the first of the month   ☐ other (specify):
   b. ☐ In addition obligor must pay the following:
      ☐ $ per month for child care costs to (name):   on (date):
      ☐ $ per month for health care costs not deducted from gross income
         to (name):   on (date):
      ☐ $ per month for special educational or other needs of the children
         to (name):   on (date):
      ☐ other (specify):

   c. **Total monthly child support** payable by obligor will be: $
      payable ☐ on the first of the month   ☐ other (specify):

Form Adopted for Mandatory Use
Judicial Council of California
FL-350 [Rev. July 1, 2003]

**STIPULATION TO ESTABLISH OR MODIFY
CHILD SUPPORT AND ORDER**

Family Code, § 4065
www.courtinfo.ca.gov

| PETITIONER/PLAINTIFF: | CASE NUMBER: |
| RESPONDENT/DEFENDANT: | |

8. a. Health insurance will be maintained by *(specify name):*

    b. ☐ A health insurance coverage assignment will issue if available through employment or other group plan or otherwise available at reasonable cost. Both parents are ordered to cooperate in the presentation, collection, and reimbursement of any medical claims.

    c. Any health expenses not paid by insurance will be shared: Mother   %   Father   %

9. a. An Order/Notice to Withhold Child Support (form FL-195) will be issued.

    b. ☐ We agree that service of the earnings assignment be stayed because we have made the following alternative arrangements to ensure payment *(specify):*

10. ☐ Travel expenses for visitation will be shared: Mother   %   Father   %

11. ☐ We agree that we will promptly inform each other of any change of residence or employment, including the employer's name, address, and telephone number.

12. ☐ Other *(specify):*

13. We agree that we are fully informed of our rights under the California child support guidelines.

14. We make this agreement freely without coercion or duress.

15. The right to support

    a. ☐ has not been assigned to any county and no application for public assistance is pending.

    b. ☐ has been assigned or an application for public assistance is pending in *(county name):*

    If you checked b., an attorney for the local child support agency must sign below, joining in this agreement.

Date:

              (TYPE OR PRINT NAME)   ▶   (SIGNATURE OF ATTORNEY FOR LOCAL CHILD SUPPORT AGENCY)

Notice: If the amount agreed to is less than the guideline amount, no change of circumstances need be shown to obtain a change in the support order to a higher amount. If the order is above the guideline, a change of circumstances will be required to modify this order. This form must be signed by the court to be effective.

Date:

                  ▶   (SIGNATURE OF PETITIONER)

Date: (TYPE OR PRINT NAME)

                  ▶   (SIGNATURE OF RESPONDENT)

Date: (TYPE OR PRINT NAME)

                  ▶   (SIGNATURE OF ATTORNEY FOR PETITIONER)

Date: (TYPE OR PRINT NAME)

                  ▶   (SIGNATURE OF ATTORNEY FOR RESPONDENT)

               (TYPE OR PRINT NAME)

THE COURT ORDERS

16. a. ☐ The guideline child support amount in item 4 is rebutted by the factors stated in item 6.

    b. Items 7 through 12 are ordered. All child support payments must continue until further order of the court, or until the child marries, dies, is emancipated, or reaches age 18. The duty of support continues as to an unmarried child who has attained the age of 18 years, is a full-time high school student, and resides with a parent, until the time the child completes the 12th grade or attains the age of 19 years, whichever first occurs. Except as modified by this stipulation, all provisions of any previous orders made in this action will remain in effect.

Date:

                          JUDGE OF THE SUPERIOR COURT

NOTICE: Any party required to pay child support must pay interest on overdue amounts at the "legal" rate, which is currently 10 percent per year. This can be a large added amount.

FL-350 [Rev. July 1, 2003]   **STIPULATION TO ESTABLISH OR MODIFY**   Page 2 of 2
                        CHILD SUPPORT AND ORDER

Copies: Original (submit to court clerk); copy for other attorney or party; office copies.

Comment: On additional forms to include along with the above form, see §11.12.

§11.15   C. Ex Parte Motion

An ex parte motion is one that is made without following the general procedures for setting a noticed hearing, but may require at least minimal telephonic or similar notice, depending on local practice. See §§11.2–11.9 on specific types of temporary orders to ascertain which may be sought on an ex parte basis.

Although ex parte motions do not require the formal notice required for noticed motions (see §11.34), *some* form of notice may, depending on the circumstances, be required. Protective orders (see §11.6) may be issued "with or without notice." Fam C §6300. Other temporary restraining orders, however, may not be granted without notice unless it appears from facts shown in the application or supporting declaration that "great or irreparable injury" would otherwise result to the applicant before the matter can be heard on notice. Fam C §241.

In addition to these statutory guidelines, local rules and practice often provide more detailed guidance on notice requirements for ex parte motions, as well as procedures on submitting opposing papers and appearances to argue the motions, and counsel who is unfamiliar with local rules and practice should inquire about them in every instance. In Santa Clara County, for example, the standard procedure is that notice to the other party precedes submission of the application. Santa Clara Fam. Ct R 5.E.(3). The other party then has 24 hours after submission in which to submit any objections in writing. Santa Clara Fam. Ct R 5.E.(6). The rules expressly provide exceptions to the notice requirement, however, when (1) there is an agreement, (2) it is impossible to give notice, or (3) notice would result in irreparable injury. Santa Clara Fam. Ct R 5.E.(3). Notice may also be excused when the requests are for orders (1) directing the parties to orientation and mediation at Family Court Services, (2) restraining both parties from removing minor children of the parties from the Greater Bay Area if the children are in the Greater Bay Area at the time of the request, (3) directing the parties to exchange state and federal tax returns and payroll stubs at least 5 court days before the hearing of any motion for support or attorney fees and costs, or (4) directing any party who incurs postseparation expenses in the ordinary course of business or for the necessaries of life to pay them from separate property income before using community assets. Santa Clara Fam. Ct R 5.E.(7)(a)–(d).

A party applying for ex parte orders in a marital action normally makes the application by preparing and submitting the following forms:

If orders other than protective orders (see §11.6) are sought

- Order to Show Cause (Judicial Council Form FL-300);

- Application for Order and Supporting Declaration (Judicial Council Form FL-310), on which the orders requested ex parte are indicated by checking, for each such order requested, the box labeled "To be ordered pending the hearing"; and

- Temporary Restraining Orders (Judicial Council Form FL-305), containing the proposed ex parte orders.

If protective orders are sought

- Request for Order (Judicial Council Form DV-100 and attachments, as required, DV-101, 105, 108); and

- Temporary Restraining Order and Notice of Hearing (CLETS) (Judicial Council Form DV-110).

When required by local rules

- Declaration Regarding Notice.

For discussion and forms, see §§11.17–11.18, 11.21–11.24, 11.31A–11.31D, 11.33. The only order among those discussed in §§11.2–11.9 and available ex parte that is sought by using other forms is the expedited child support order. See §11.3.

Applications for ex parte orders must be granted or denied on the day the application is submitted, unless the application is submitted too late in the day to permit effective review, in which case the application must be granted or denied on the next day of judicial business, in sufficient time for any order granted to be filed that day with the court clerk. Fam C §246.

Ex parte orders must be made returnable for a hearing on an Order to Show Cause within 20 days or, for good cause, 25 days. Fam C §242(a).

If an ex parte restraining order is issued with notice to the responding party pending the hearing, the applicant must serve the Request for Order and Temporary Restraining Order and Notice of Hearing, and any supporting documents, on the respondent at least 15 (not 16) days before the hearing. Fam C §243(c).

D. Noticed Motion

1. Moving Party's Papers

§11.16   **a. Choosing Order to Show Cause or Notice of Motion**

A party seeking temporary orders other than protective orders (see §11.6) in a marital action proceeds either by an Order to Show Cause (see §§11.17-11.18) or by a Notice of Motion (see §§11.19-11.20). The Order to Show Cause should routinely be used in two circumstances:

- When the petitioner seeks temporary orders at the outset of the case, before the respondent has filed a response or otherwise made a general appearance. See 6 Witkin, California Procedure, *Proceedings Without Trial* §§55, 56 (4th ed 1997).

- When the moving party, whether the petitioner or the respondent, seeks ex parte orders (see §11.15). See Fam C §242(a). Note that the Order to Show Cause (Judicial Council Form FL-300; see §11.18) specifically refers to attached temporary orders at Item 3.c; the Notice of Motion (Judicial Council Form FL-301; see §11.20) contains no such reference.

In other circumstances, either the Order to Show Cause or the Notice of Motion may be used. See *Donald J. v Evna M.* (1978) 81 CA3d 929, 933, 147 CR 15 (Order to Show Cause is, in effect, a Notice of Motion). When either approach may be used, the Notice of Motion is usually selected. The Notice of Motion offers the advantage that it may be issued by the attorney, whereas the Order to Show Cause must be submitted to the court for issuance.

A party seeking temporary *protective* orders must proceed by a Request for Order and Temporary Restraining Order and Notice of Hearing (CLETS) (see §§11.31C-11.31D), and attachments, DV-101, 105, 108, as required, if orders for child custody and visitation and support are also sought.

b. Preparation

(1) Order to Show Cause

§11.17   (a) Discussion

When the party seeking temporary orders proceeds by an Order to Show Cause, use of Judicial Council Form FL-300 is mandatory, and the form must be submitted for the judge's signature before it may be filed or served. The usual procedure is to deliver by hand the Order to Show Cause and accompanying papers to the judge's department and then return to that department to pick up the papers and obtain a hearing date from the clerk.

The boxes checked in the caption should correspond to the relief requested in the Application for Order and Supporting Declaration (Judicial Council Form FL-310; see §11.22). The name in Item 1 is that of the opposing party, not his or her attorney.

When documents listed in Item 3.a(1)–(5) are being submitted, the corresponding boxes should be checked and copies of the documents should be served along with the Order to Show Cause, the Application for Order and Supporting Declaration, and a blank Responsive Declaration (Judicial Council Form FL-320; see §11.36). When any other documents, *e.g.,* a declaration on notice when ex parte relief is sought, are being submitted, the box at Item 3(5) should be checked, the documents specified, and copies served.

When an order shortening time is sought, the requested order should be indicated at Item 3.b. When temporary restraining orders are requested, the box at Item 3.c should be checked and a copy of the Temporary Restraining Orders (Judicial Council Form FL-305; see §11.24) should be served.

Any additional orders sought should be indicated at Item 3.d. An example that can be quite helpful, particularly when the time to the hearing is so short that formal discovery is impracticable, and that many judges will grant when applicable to the relief requested, is an order requiring the production of financial documents such as recent wage stubs and tax returns. The order might require, for example, that the documents be brought to the hearing or be provided to the moving party's attorney by a specified date before the hearing.

When the parties have an agreement or understanding regarding custody or temporary custody, a copy of the agreement or a declaration regarding the understanding must be attached to a petition or motion. As promptly as possible after the filing, the court must, except in exceptional circumstances, enter an order granting temporary custody in accordance with the agreement or understanding. Fam C §3061.

Note that a party seeking temporary *protective* orders must proceed by a Request for Order and Temporary Restraining Order and Notice of Hearing (CLETS) (see §§11.31C–11.31D), and attachments, DV-101, 105, 108, as required, if orders concerning child custody and visitation and support are also sought.

§11.18   (b) Form: Order to Show Cause (Judicial Council Form FL-300)

FL-300

ATTORNEY OR PARTY WITHOUT ATTORNEY *(Name, State Bar number, and address)*	FOR COURT USE ONLY

TELEPHONE NO.:   FAX NO. *(Optional)*:

E-MAIL ADDRESS *(Optional)*:

ATTORNEY FOR *(Name)*:

SUPERIOR COURT OF CALIFORNIA, COUNTY OF

STREET ADDRESS:

MAILING ADDRESS:

CITY AND ZIP CODE:

BRANCH NAME:

PETITIONER/PLAINTIFF:

RESPONDENT/DEFENDANT:

ORDER TO SHOW CAUSE
- [ ] Child Custody
- [ ] Child Support
- [ ] Attorney Fees and Costs

- [ ] **MODIFICATION**
- [ ] Visitation
- [ ] Spousal Support

- [ ] Injunctive Order
- [ ] Other *(specify)*:

CASE NUMBER:

1. TO *(name)*:

2. YOU ARE ORDERED TO APPEAR IN THIS COURT AS FOLLOWS TO GIVE ANY LEGAL REASON WHY THE RELIEF SOUGHT IN THE ATTACHED APPLICATION SHOULD NOT BE GRANTED. **If child custody or visitation is an issue in this proceeding, Family Code section 3170 requires mediation before or concurrently with the hearing listed below.**

  a. Date: Time: [ ] Dept.:   [ ] Room:

  b. The address of the court is [ ] same as noted above [ ] other *(specify)*:

  c. [ ] The parties are ordered to attend custody mediation services as follows:

3. THE COURT FURTHER ORDERS that a completed *Application for Order and Supporting Declaration* (form FL-310), a **blank** *Responsive Declaration* (form FL-320), and the following documents be served with this order:

  a. (1) [ ] Completed *Income and Expense Declaration* (form FL-150) and a **blank** *Income and Expense Declaration*
    (2) [ ] Completed *Financial Statement (Simplified)* (form FL-155) and a **blank** *Financial Statement (Simplified)*
    (3) [ ] Completed *Property Declaration* (form FL-160) and a **blank** *Property Declaration*
    (4) [ ] Points and authorities
    (5) [ ] Other *(specify)*:

  b. [ ] Time for [ ] service [ ] hearing is shortened. Service must be on or before *(date)*:
    Any responsive declaration must be served on or before *(date)*:
  c. [ ] You are ordered to comply with the temporary orders attached.
  d. [ ] Other *(specify)*:

Date: _____

JUDICIAL OFFICER

NOTICE: If you have children from this relationship, the court is required to order payment of child support based on the incomes of both parents. The amount of child support can be large. It normally continues until the child is 18. You should supply the court with information about your finances. Otherwise, the child support order will be based on the information supplied by the other parent.

You do not have to pay any fee to file declarations in response to this order to show cause (including a completed Income and Expense Declaration (form FL-150) or Financial Statement *(Simplified)* (form FL-155) that will show your finances). In the absence of an order shortening time, the original of the responsive declaration must be filed with the court and a copy served on the other party at least nine court days before the hearing date. Add five calendar days if you serve by mail within California. (See Code of Civil Procedure 1005 for other situations.) To determine court and calendar days, go to *www.courtinfo.ca.gov/selfhelp/courtcalendars/.*

Requests for Accommodations
Assistive listening systems, computer-assisted real-time captioning, or sign language interpreter services are available if you ask at least five days before the proceeding. Contact the clerk's office or go to *www.courtinfo.ca.gov/forms* for *Request for Accommodations by Persons With Disabilities and Response* (Form MC-410). (Civil Code, § 54.8.)

Page 1 of 1

Form Adopted for Mandatory Use
Judicial Council of California
FL-300 [Rev. January 1, 2007]

ORDER TO SHOW CAUSE

CEB   Family Code, §§ 215, 270 et seq., 3000 et seq., 3500 et seq., 4300
www.courtinfo.ca.gov

Copies: Original (submit to court clerk); copy for service; office copies.

(2) Notice of Motion

§11.19   (a) Discussion

When the party seeking temporary orders proceeds by Notice of Motion, use of Judicial Council Form FL-301 is mandatory. Unlike the Order to Show Cause (see §11.17), the form need not be submitted for the judge's signature before it may be filed or served, unless an order shortening time is requested. The usual procedure is to obtain a hearing date from the clerk by telephone before service and filing of the Notice of Motion, though this practice will vary by county.

The boxes checked in the caption should correspond to the relief requested in the Application for Order and Supporting Declaration (Judicial Council Form FL-310; see form in §11.22). The name in Item 1 is that of the opposing party, not his or her attorney.

When documents listed in Item 3.b-3.e are being submitted, the corresponding boxes should be checked and copies of the documents should be served along with the Notice of Motion, the Application for Order and Supporting Declaration, and a blank Responsive Declaration (Judicial Council Form FL-320; see §11.36). When any other documents are being submitted, the box at Item 3.f should be checked, the documents specified, and copies served. When an order shortening time is sought, the requested order should be indicated at Item 4.

When the parties have an agreement or understanding regarding custody or temporary custody, a copy of the agreement or a declaration regarding the understanding must be attached to a petition or motion. As promptly as possible after the filing, the court must, except in exceptional circumstances, enter an order granting temporary custody in accordance with the agreement or understanding. Fam C §3061.

Note that a party seeking temporary *protective* orders must proceed by a Request for Order and Temporary Restraining Order and Notice of Hearing (CLETS) (see §§11.31C–11.31D), and attachments, DV-101, 105, 108, as required, if orders for child custody and visitation and support are also sought.

§11.20   (b) Form: Notice of Motion (Judicial Council Form FL-301)

FL-301

ATTORNEY OR PARTY WITHOUT ATTORNEY *(Name, State Bar number, and address)*	FOR COURT USE ONLY

TELEPHONE NO.:   FAX NO. *(Optional)*

E-MAIL ADDRESS *(Optional)*

ATTORNEY FOR *(Name)*:

SUPERIOR COURT OF CALIFORNIA, COUNTY OF

STREET ADDRESS:

MAILING ADDRESS:

CITY AND ZIP CODE:

BRANCH NAME:

PETITIONER/PLAINTIFF:

RESPONDENT/DEFENDANT:

NOTICE OF MOTION		CASE NUMBER:
☐ Child Custody ☐ MODIFICATION ☐ Injunctive Order		
☐ Child Support ☐ Visitation ☐ Other *(specify)*:		
☐ Attorney Fees and Costs ☐ Spousal Support		

1. TO *(name)*:

2. A hearing on this motion for the relief requested in the attached application will be held as follows:

a. Date: Time: ☐ Dept.:   ☐ Rm.:

b. Address of court ☐ same as noted above ☐ other *(specify)*:

3. Supporting attachments:

a. Completed *Application for Order and Supporting Declaration* (form FL-310) and a **blank** *Responsive Declaration* (form FL-320)

b. ☐ Completed *Income and Expense Declaration* (form FL-150) and a **blank** *Income and Expense Declaration*

c. ☐ Completed *Financial Statement (Simplified)* (form FL-155) and a **blank** *Financial Statement (Simplified)*

d. ☐ Completed *Property Declaration* (form FL-160) and a **blank** *Property Declaration*

e. ☐ Points and authorities

f. ☐ Other *(specify)*:

Date:

_____   ▶   _____
(TYPE OR PRINT NAME)   (SIGNATURE)

ORDER

4. ☐ Time for ☐ service ☐ hearing is shortened. Service must be on or before *(date)*:

5. Any responsive declaration must be served on or before *(date)*:

6. If child custody or visitation is an issue in this proceeding, Family Code section 3170 requires mediation before or concurrently with the hearing listed above. The parties are ordered to attend orientation and mandatory custody services as follows:

Date:

_____
JUDICIAL OFFICER

NOTICE: If you have children from this relationship, the court is required to order payment of child support based on the incomes of both parents. The amount of child support can be large. It normally continues until the child is 18. You should supply the court with information about your finances. Otherwise, the child support order will be based on the information supplied by the other parent.

You do not have to pay any fee to file declarations in response to this *Notice of Motion* (including a completed Income and Expense Declaration (form FL-150) or Financial Statement *(Simplified)* (form FL-155) that will show your finances). In the absence of an order shortening time, the original of the responsive declaration must be filed with the court and a copy served on the other party at least nine court days before the hearing date. Add five calendar days if you serve by mail within California. (See Code of Civil Procedure 1005 for other situations.) To determine court and calendar days, go to *www.courtinfo.ca.gov/selfhelp/courtcalendars/*.

FL-301

PETITIONER/PLAINTIFF:	CASE NUMBER:
RESPONDENT/DEFENDANT:	

7. PROOF OF SERVICE BY MAIL

  a. I am at least age 18, **not a party to this action,** and am a resident or employed in the county where the mailing took place. My residence or business address is:

  b. I served copies of the following documents by enclosing them in a sealed envelope with postage fully prepaid, depositing them in the United States mail as follows:

    (1) Papers served:

      (a) *Notice of Motion* and a completed *Application for Order and Supporting Declaration* (form FL-310) **and** a blank *Responsive Declaration* (form FL-320)

      (b) ☐ Completed *Income and Expense Declaration* (form FL-150) **and** a blank *Income and Expense Declaration*

      (c) ☐ Completed *Financial Statement (Simplified)* (form FL-155) **and** a blank *Financial Statement (Simplified)*

      (d) ☐ Completed *Property Declaration* (form FL-160) **and** a blank *Property Declaration*

      (e) ☐ Points and authorities

      (f) Other *(specify):*

    (2) Manner of service:

      (a) Date of deposit:

      (b) Place of deposit *(city and state):*

      (c) Addressed as follows:

  c. I declare under penalty of perjury under the laws of the State of California that the foregoing is true and correct.

Date:

      [TYPE OR PRINT NAME] ▶ (SIGNATURE OF DECLARANT)

Requests for Accommodations
Assistive listening systems, computer-assisted real-time captioning, or sign language interpreter services are available if you ask at least five days before the proceeding. Contact the clerk's office or go to *www.courtinfo.ca.gov/forms* for *Request for Accommodations by Persons With Disabilities and Response* (Form MC-410). (Civil Code, § 54.8.)

FL-301 [Rev. January 1, 2007]   **NOTICE OF MOTION**   ℂEB   Page 2 of 2

Copies: Original (file with court clerk); copy for service; office copies.

(3) Application for Order and Supporting Declaration

§11.21 (a) Discussion

The Application for Order and Supporting Declaration (Judicial Council Form FL-310) indicates what orders are being requested and provides facts supporting the requests. Whenever child custody or visitation orders, or orders with respect to property restraints, property control, or payment of debts, are desired *pending the hearing,* this is indicated by checking the appropriate box for the particular orders.

When a child custody order is sought, the applicant should indicate at Item 1 what order is requested on physical custody and what order is requested on legal custody.

In requests for child support, spousal support, and attorney fees and costs (Items 3–5), it is probably best to simply state "Reasonable" for the amounts requested. When the moving party indicates a specific figure, the court may be inclined to limit him or her to that amount, particularly if the other party does not appear. See *Marriage of Lippel* (1990) 51 C3d 1160, 1166, 276 CR 290 (party served with lawsuit has right, in view of relief sought, to decide not to appear and defend). Alternatively, although the amount requested should not be clearly unreasonable, it is better to err on the high side than the low. This discussion applies to child support requests notwithstanding the form's call for a monthly amount only "if not by guideline" (Item 3.b). If the quoted phrase refers to the statewide uniform guideline (see §§8.7–8.28), it makes no sense because the court is required to apply the guideline. If the phrase refers to the amount calculated under the guideline formula (see §§8.8–8.13) without consideration of allowable adjustments, the applicant probably has nothing to gain by leaving Item 3.b blank and possibly being limited to that amount.

A matter that perhaps tends to receive less attention than it should in proceedings for temporary orders is that of responsibility for payment of debts. The same is true for the related issue of reimbursement for such payments. A party intending to seek reimbursement for payment of community debts should get the issue out in the open early on by requesting an order providing for such reimbursement at the hearing on temporary orders. See *Marriage of Hebbring* (1989) 207 CA3d 1260, 1272, 255 CR 488 (temporary orders that specify responsibility for payments of community debts and that specify which payments are, and are not, to be reimbursed encourage payment, thereby avoiding problems with creditors; settle reimbursement issue; and assist parties in settling other issues before trial). Although Item 7.b refers to payments on "liens and encumbrances," payment of other debts may also be addressed. Orders on reimbursement issues may be requested either at Item 7.b or Item 9 (other relief). On reimbursement generally when a party uses separate property to pay community debts after separation, see §5.99.

When a party requests an Order Shortening Time for service of the Order to Show Cause or the Notice of Motion and accompanying papers (Item 8), facts supporting the request must be set forth in an attached declaration. Orders shortening time are most commonly granted when the need for an early hearing precludes service as far in advance of the court date as would normally be required under CCP §1005(a)(13)–(b) (see §11.34).

Facts in support of the relief requested (Item 10) must be prepared with care. Note that, with respect to its rulings at the hearing as well as its rulings on ex parte requests, the court can grant or deny relief solely on the basis of the documents filed. See Cal Rules of Ct 3.1306; see §11.51. Consequently, supporting facts should be provided for every item of relief requested. With respect, for example, to attorney fees and costs, a declaration by counsel, itemizing both anticipated expenses and those already incurred, will be of greater assistance to the court in evaluating a request than a mere statement of an amount.

When the relief requested is financial (*e.g.*, child support, spousal support, payment of attorney fees) a completed Income and Expense Declaration (FL-150) must be filed and served with the moving papers, and a blank Income and Expense Declaration served on the opposing party along with a blank Responsive Declaration (FL-320). See §11.25, 11.37. On use of a Financial Statement (Simplified) (Judicial Council Form FL-155), see §11.30.

Some additional points to remember in preparing supporting declarations:

- The client's supporting declaration is not an opportunity for him or her to spin a long tale of woe. Judges are very busy and court time is short. To be effective, a declaration should be reasonably brief. It is a good idea to provide a numbered or bulleted summary of the orders requested at the beginning of the declaration.

- The attorney should resist putting words in the client's mouth. It is the client's declaration and the client must feel comfortable with it.

- The declarations, especially longer ones, should be well organized. Headings, *e.g.*, dividing the statements into subparts by the particular issues addressed, can assist the court in following the declaration and finding specific material during the hearing.

Note that a party seeking temporary *protective* orders must use a Request for Order ((Judicial Council Form DV-100); see §§11.31A–11.31B), and attachments, DV-101, 105, 108, as required, if orders concerning child custody and visitation and support are also sought.

§11.22 (b) Form: Application for Order and Supporting Declaration (Judicial Council Form FL-310)

FL-310

PETITIONER:	CASE NUMBER:
RESPONDENT:	

APPLICATION FOR ORDER AND SUPPORTING DECLARATION
—THIS IS NOT AN ORDER—

☐ Petitioner ☐ Respondent ☐ Claimant requests the following orders:

1. ☐ CHILD CUSTODY ☐ To be ordered pending the hearing

   a. <u>Child</u> *(name, age)*   b. <u>Legal custody to</u>   c. <u>Physical custody to</u>
                       (person who makes decisions   (person with whom child lives.)
                       about health, education, etc.) *(name)*   *(name)*

☐ Modify existing order
   (1) filed on *(date):*
   (2) ordering *(specify):*

☐ As requested in form ☐ FL-311 ☐ FL-312 ☐ FL-341(C) ☐ FL-341(D) ☐ FL-341(E)

2. ☐ CHILD VISITATION ☐ To be ordered pending the hearing

   a. As requested in: (1) ☐ Attachment 2a (2) ☐ Form FL-311 (3) ☐ Other *(specify):*

   b. ☐ Modify existing order
      (1) filed on *(date):*
      (2) ordering *(specify):*

   c. ☐ One or more domestic violence restraining/protective orders are now in effect. *(Attach a copy of the orders if you have one.)* The orders are from the following court or courts *(specify county and state):*

     (1) ☐ Criminal: County/state: _____   (3) ☐ Juvenile: County/state: _____
                Case No. *(if known):* _____   Case No. *(if known):* _____
     (2) ☐ Family: County/state: _____   (4) ☐ Other: County/state: _____
                Case No. *(if known):* _____   Case No. *(if known):* _____

3. ☐ CHILD SUPPORT *(An earnings assignment order may be issued.)*

   a. <u>Child</u> *(name, age)*   b. <u>Monthly amount</u> (if not by guideline)
                                $

   c. ☐ Modify existing order
      (1) filed on *(date):*
      (2) ordering *(specify):*

4. ☐ SPOUSAL OR PARTNER SUPPORT *(An earnings assignment order may be issued.)*
   a. ☐ Amount requested *(monthly):* $ c. ☐ Modify existing order
   b. ☐ Terminate existing order   (1) filed on *(date):*
      (1) filed on *(date):*   (2) ordering *(specify):*
      (2) ordering *(specify):*

5. ☐ ATTORNEY FEES AND COSTS   a. ☐ Fees: $ b. ☐ Costs: $

NOTE: To obtain domestic violence restraining orders, you must use the forms *Request for Order (Domestic Violence Prevention)* (form DV-100) and *Temporary Restraining Order and Notice of Hearing (Domestic Violence Prevention)* (form DV-110).

Form Adopted for Mandatory Use
Judicial Council of California
FL-310 [Rev. January 1, 2007]

APPLICATION FOR ORDER AND SUPPORTING DECLARATION

Page 1 of 2

Family Code, §§ 2045, 6224, 6226,
6320–6326, 6380–6383
www.courtinfo.ca.gov

FL-310

PETITIONER:	CASE NUMBER:
RESPONDENT:	

6. ☐ PROPERTY RESTRAINT　　☐ **To be ordered pending the hearing**

　　a. The ☐ petitioner ☐ respondent ☐ claimant　is restrained from transferring, encumbering, hypothecating, concealing, or in any way disposing of any property, real or personal, whether community, quasi-community, or separate, except in the usual course of business or for the necessities of life.

　　　　☐ The applicant will be notified at least five business days before any proposed extraordinary expenditures, and an accounting of such will be made to the court.

　　b. ☐ Both parties are restrained and enjoined from cashing, borrowing against, canceling, transferring, disposing of, or changing the beneficiaries of any insurance or other coverage, including life, health, automobile, and disability, held for the benefit of the parties or their minor children.

　　c. ☐ Neither party may incur any debts or liabilities for which the other may be held responsible, other than in the ordinary course of business or for the necessities of life.

7. ☐ PROPERTY CONTROL　　☐ **To be ordered pending the hearing**

　　a. ☐ The petitioner ☐ respondent　is given the exclusive temporary use, possession, and control of the following property that we own or are buying (specify):

　　b. ☐ The petitioner ☐ respondent　is ordered to make the following payments on liens and encumbrances coming due while the order is in effect:

Debt	Amount of payment	Pay to

8. ☐ **I request** that time for service of the *Order to Show Cause* and accompanying papers be shortened so that these documents may be served no less than (specify number):　　days before the time set for the hearing. I need to have the order shortening time because of the facts specified in the attached declaration.

9. ☐ OTHER RELIEF (specify):

10. ☐ FACTS IN SUPPORT of relief requested and change of circumstances for any modification are (specify):
　　☐ contained in the attached declaration.

I declare under penalty of perjury under the laws of the State of California that the foregoing is true and correct.

Date:

▶

_____　　　　_____
(TYPE OR PRINT NAME)　　　　　　　　　　　　(SIGNATURE OF APPLICANT)

FL-310 [Rev. January 1, 2007]　　**APPLICATION FOR ORDER AND SUPPORTING DECLARATION**　　Page 2 of 2

Copies: Original (submit to court clerk); copy for service; office copies.

(4) Temporary Restraining Orders

§11.23 (a) Discussion

Restraining orders sought pending the hearing on temporary orders are set forth in Judicial Council Form FL-305 (Temporary Orders).

Note that a party seeking temporary *protective* orders must use a Request for Order (Judicial Council Form DV-100) and a Temporary Restraining Order and Notice of Hearing (Judicial Council Form DV-110) (see §§11.31A–11.31D) and attachments, DV-101, 105, 108, as required, if orders concerning child custody and visitation and support are also sought.

§11.24   (b) Form: Temporary Orders (Judicial Council Form FL-305)

FL-305

PETITIONER/PLAINTIFF:	CASE NUMBER:
RESPONDENT/DEFENDANT:	

TEMPORARY ORDERS
Attachment to Order to Show Cause (FL-300)

1. ☐ PROPERTY RESTRAINT

    a. ☐ Petitioner ☐ Respondent is restrained from transferring, encumbering, hypothecating, concealing, or in any way disposing of any property, real or personal, whether community, quasi-community, or separate, except in the usual course of business or for the necessities of life.

        ☐ The other party is to be notified of any proposed extraordinary expenditures and an accounting of such is to be made to the court.

    b. ☐ Both parties are restrained and enjoined from cashing, borrowing against, canceling, transferring, disposing of, or changing the beneficiaries of any insurance or other coverage including life, health, automobile, and disability held for the benefit of the parties or their minor child or children.

    c. ☐ Neither party may incur any debts or liabilities for which the other may be held responsible, other than in the ordinary course of business or for the necessities of life.

2. ☐ PROPERTY CONTROL

    a. ☐ Petitioner ☐ Respondent is given the exclusive temporary use, possession, and control of the following property the parties own or are buying (specify):

    b. ☐ Petitioner ☐ Respondent is ordered to make the following payments on liens and encumbrances coming due while the order is in effect:

Debt	Amount of payment	Pay to

3. ☐ MINOR CHILDREN

    a. ☐ Petitioner ☐ Respondent will have the temporary physical custody, care, and control of the minor children of the parties, ☐ subject to the other party's rights of visitation as follows:

    b. ☐ Petitioner ☐ Respondent must not remove the minor child or children of the parties

      (1) ☐ from the State of California.

      (2) ☐ from the following counties (specify):

      (3) ☐ other (specify):

    c. ☐ Child abduction prevention orders are attached (see form FL-341(B)).

    d. (1) Jurisdiction: This court has jurisdiction to make child custody orders in this case under the Uniform Child Custody Jurisdiction and Enforcement Act (part 3 of the California Family Code, commencing with § 3400).

      (2) Notice and opportunity to be heard: The responding party was given notice and an opportunity to be heard as provided by the laws of the State of California.

      (3) Country of habitual residence: The country of habitual residence of the child or children is ☐ the United States of America ☐ other (specify):

      (4) Penalties for violating this order: If you violate this order you may be subject to civil or criminal penalties, or both.

4. ☐ OTHER ORDERS (specify):

Date: _____

_____
JUDGE OF THE SUPERIOR COURT

5. **The date of the court hearing is** (insert date when known):

CLERK'S CERTIFICATE

[SEAL]   I certify that the foregoing is a true and correct copy of the original on file in my office.

    Date: _____   Clerk, by _____, Deputy

Page 1 of 1

Form Adopted for Mandatory Use	TEMPORARY ORDERS	Family Code, §§ 2045, 6224, 6226, 6302
Judicial Council of California		6320–6326, 6380–6383
FL-305 [Rev. July 1, 2003]		www.courtinfo.ca.gov

Copies: Original (submit to court clerk); copy for service; office copies.

(5) Income and Expense Declaration

§11.25   (a) Discussion

The Income and Expense Declaration (Judicial Council Form FL-150) will often be among the most important documents filed in the action. It has a great bearing on the determination of financial issues. Indeed, the document, even standing alone without oral testimony, is a sufficient basis for an order. *Marriage of McQuoid* (1991) 9 CA4th 1353, 1359, 12 CR2d 737. When successfully challenged, it can be devastating to the court's perception of the client's credibility. It may also be the focus of attention years later in modification proceedings. For all these reasons, the Income and Expense Declaration must be prepared with great care. The following discussion is keyed to the Judicial Council forms.

NOTE➤ The Income and Expense Declaration is a four-page form that includes the former Income, Expense, and Child Support Information forms. See Judicial Council Form FL-150, pages 1–4, in §11.26.

As indicated by its title, the Income and Expense Declaration was primarily designed to provide the court with information on the incomes and expenses of the parties. As will be shown, however, this matter is seldom a simple one, and considerable care must be taken if the forms are to provide the court with the information it needs to resolve financial issues. With respect to income, the Income Information page takes two approaches, requesting (1) figures for the preceding month alone and (2) average figures for the preceding 12 months. As a practical matter, what the court needs to find is the figure for net monthly disposable income that best represents the projected income for the party over future months. See Fam C §4060 (after dividing annual net disposable income by 12 to obtain monthly net disposable income, court may adjust resulting figure to reflect actual or prospective earnings at time support determination is made). Sometimes, *e.g.,* when the party changed employment a few months before the filing and his or her income varies from month to month, it may be wise to provide an additional set of figures in line 9 (change in income) or on an attachment that projects the likely average monthly figures over future months, along with an explanation of how the figures were calculated and why they should be accepted by the court.

When the client is uncertain about expenses, it might be appropriate to indicate on the Expense Information page that some of the figures provided, or all of them, are merely estimates. It may be helpful for the client if the attorney explains what kinds of expenses fit under each category listed on the form, so that the client will not overlook expenses and underestimate needs. The client may also benefit from reviewing check records covering the previous six months to a year before preparing the Expense Information form and then organizing the expenditures into the categories listed there.

Note that the Income Information page requires that the party attach a copy of his or her pay stubs for the last two months and proof of any other income. In addition, some courts require other specific financial documents to be attached to the Income and Expense Declaration. See, *e.g.,* San Diego Ct R 5.6.3 (attachments to Income and Expense Declarations).

NOTE► Many counties have local rules defining a "current" Income and Expense Declaration and specify a maximum number of days that may elapse between the execution of the declaration and the hearing date. See, *e.g.,* San Diego Ct R 5.6.2. See also *Marriage of Tydlaska* (2003) 114 CA4th 572, 7 CR3d 594 (trial court properly denied husband's request to modify support order, because of his noncompliance with local rule stating declaration must be executed within 60 days of hearing).

Note that, under specified circumstances, a party may use a simplified financial statement (Judicial Council Form FL-155; see §11.31) in place of the Income and Expense Declaration and its accompanying pages. For discussion, see §11.30.

§11.26 (b) Form: Income and Expense Declaration (Judicial Council Form FL-150)

FL-150

ATTORNEY OR PARTY WITHOUT ATTORNEY (Name, State Bar number, and address):	FOR COURT USE ONLY
TELEPHONE NO.: E-MAIL ADDRESS (Optional): ATTORNEY FOR (Name):	

SUPERIOR COURT OF CALIFORNIA, COUNTY OF
STREET ADDRESS:
MAILING ADDRESS:
CITY AND ZIP CODE:
BRANCH NAME:

PETITIONER/PLAINTIFF:
RESPONDENT/DEFENDANT:
OTHER PARENT/CLAIMANT:

INCOME AND EXPENSE DECLARATION	CASE NUMBER:

1. **Employment** (Give information on your current job or, if you're unemployed, your most recent job.)

Attach copies of your pay stubs for last two months (black out social security numbers).

  a. Employer:
  b. Employer's address:
  c. Employer's phone number:
  d. Occupation:
  e. Date job started:
  f. If unemployed, date job ended:
  g. I work about   hours per week.
  h. I get paid $ gross (before taxes) ☐ per month ☐ per week ☐ per hour.

(If you have more than one job, attach an 8½-by-11-inch sheet of paper and list the same information as above for your other jobs. Write "Question 1—Other Jobs" at the top.)

2. **Age and education**
  a. My age is (specify):
  b. I have completed high school or the equivalent: ☐ Yes ☐ No   If no, highest grade completed (specify):
  c. Number of years of college completed (specify): ☐ Degree(s) obtained (specify):
  d. Number of years of graduate school completed (specify): ☐ Degree(s) obtained (specify):
  e. I have: ☐ professional/occupational license(s) (specify):
       ☐ vocational training (specify):

3. **Tax information**
  a. ☐ I last filed taxes for tax year (specify year):
  b. My tax filing status is ☐ single ☐ head of household ☐ married, filing separately
      ☐ married, filing jointly with (specify name):
  c. I file state tax returns in ☐ California ☐ other (specify state):
  d. I claim the following number of exemptions (including myself) on my taxes (specify):

4. **Other party's income.** I estimate the gross monthly income (before taxes) of the other party in this case at (specify): $
This estimate is based on (explain):

(If you need more space to answer any questions on this form, attach an 8½-by-11-inch sheet of paper and write the question number before your answer.) Number of pages attached: _____

I declare under penalty of perjury under the laws of the State of California that the information contained on all pages of this form and any attachments is true and correct.

Date:

_____ ▶ _____
(TYPE OR PRINT NAME)   (SIGNATURE OF DECLARANT)

Form Adopted for Mandatory Use
Judicial Council of California
FL-150 [Rev. January 1, 2007]

INCOME AND EXPENSE DECLARATION

Page 1 of 4
Family Code, §§ 2030–2032,
2100–2113, 3552, 3620–3634,
4050–4078, 4300–4339
www.courtinfo.ca.gov

FL-150

PETITIONER/PLAINTIFF:	CASE NUMBER:
RESPONDENT/DEFENDANT:	
OTHER PARENT/CLAIMANT:	

Attach copies of your pay stubs for the last two months and proof of any other income. Take a copy of your latest federal tax return to the court hearing. (Black out your social security number on the pay stub and tax return.)

5. **Income** *(For average monthly, add up all the income you received in each category in the last 12 months and divide the total by 12.)*   Last month   Average monthly

   a. Salary or wages (gross, before taxes). . . . . $_____ _____

   b. Overtime (gross, before taxes) . . . . $_____ _____

   c. Commissions or bonuses. . . . . $_____ _____

   d. Public assistance (for example: TANF, SSI, GA/GR) ☐ currently receiving . . . . $_____ _____

   e. Spousal support ☐ from this marriage ☐ from a different marriage . . . . $_____ _____

   f. Partner support ☐ from this domestic partnership ☐ from a different domestic partnership $_____ _____

   g. Pension/retirement fund payments. . . . . $_____ _____

   h. Social security retirement (not SSI) . . . . $_____ _____

   i. Disability: ☐ Social security (not SSI) ☐ State disability (SDI) ☐ Private insurance . $_____ _____

   j. Unemployment compensation . . . . $_____ _____

   k. Workers' compensation . . . . $_____ _____

   l. Other (military BAQ, royalty payments, etc.) *(specify):* . . . . $_____ _____

6. **Investment income** *(Attach a schedule showing gross receipts less cash expenses for each piece of property.)*

   a. Dividends/interest. . . . . $_____ _____

   b. Rental property income . . . . $_____ _____

   c. Trust income. . . . . $_____ _____

   d. Other *(specify):* . . . . $_____ _____

7. **Income from self-employment, after business expenses for all businesses.** . . . . $_____ _____

   I am the ☐ owner/sole proprietor ☐ business partner ☐ other *(specify):*

   Number of years in this business *(specify):*

   Name of business *(specify):*

   Type of business *(specify):*

   Attach a profit and loss statement for the last two years or a Schedule C from your last federal tax return. Black out your social security number. If you have more than one business, provide the information above for each of your businesses.

8. ☐ **Additional income.** I received one-time money (lottery winnings, inheritance, etc.) in the last 12 months *(specify source and amount):*

9. ☐ **Change in income.** My financial situation has changed significantly over the last 12 months because *(specify):*

10. **Deductions**   Last month

   a. Required union dues . . . . $_____

   b. Required retirement payments (not social security, FICA, 401(k), or IRA). . . . . $_____

   c. Medical, hospital, dental, and other health insurance premiums *(total monthly amount)*. . . . . $_____

   d. Child support that I pay for children from other relationships . . . . $_____

   e. Spousal support that I pay by court order from a different marriage. . . . . $_____

   f. Partner support that I pay by court order from a different domestic partnership . . . . $_____

   g. Necessary job-related expenses not reimbursed by my employer *(attach explanation labeled "Question 10g")* . . . . . $_____

11. **Assets**   Total

   a. Cash and checking accounts, savings, credit union, money market, and other deposit accounts . . . . $_____

   b. Stocks, bonds, and other assets I could easily sell . . . . $_____

   c. All other property, ☐ real and ☐ personal *(estimate fair market value minus the debts you owe)* . . . . $_____

FL-150

PETITIONER/PLAINTIFF: RESPONDENT/DEFENDANT: OTHER PARENT/CLAIMANT:	CASE NUMBER:

12. **The following people live with me:**

Name	Age	How the person is related to me? *(ex: son)*	That person's gross monthly income	Pays some of the household expenses?
a.				☐ Yes ☐ No
b.				☐ Yes ☐ No
c.				☐ Yes ☐ No
d.				☐ Yes ☐ No
e.				☐ Yes ☐ No

13. **Average monthly expenses**   ☐ Estimated expenses   ☐ Actual expenses   ☐ Proposed needs

   a. Home:

      (1) ☐ Rent or ☐ mortgage... $ _____

      If mortgage:

         (a) average principal: $ _____
         (b) average interest: $ _____

      (2) Real property taxes . . . . $ _____

      (3) Homeowner's or renter's insurance
         (if not included above) . . . . $ _____

      (4) Maintenance and repair . . . . $ _____

   b. Health-care costs not paid by insurance. . . $ _____

   c. Child care . . . . $ _____

   d. Groceries and household supplies. . . . . . $ _____

   e. Eating out. . . . . $ _____

   f. Utilities (gas, electric, water, trash) . . . . . $ _____

   g. Telephone, cell phone, and e-mail . . . . . . $ _____

   h. Laundry and cleaning . . . . $ _____

   i. Clothes . . . . $ _____

   j. Education . . . . $ _____

   k. Entertainment, gifts, and vacation. . . . . . . $ _____

   l. Auto expenses and transportation
     (insurance, gas, repairs, bus, etc.) . . . . . . $ _____

   m. Insurance (life, accident, etc.; do not
     include auto, home, or health insurance). . . $ _____

   n. Savings and investments. . . . . $ _____

   o. Charitable contributions. . . . . $ _____

   p. Monthly payments listed in item 14
     (itemize below in 14 and insert total here). . $ _____

   q. Other *(specify):* . . . . $ _____

   r. **TOTAL EXPENSES** (a–q) *(do not add in
     the amounts in a(1)(a) and (b))* $ _____

   s. **Amount of expenses paid by others** $ _____

14. **Installment payments and debts not listed above**

Paid to	For	Amount	Balance	Date of last payment
		$	$	
		$	$	
		$	$	
		$	$	
		$	$	
		$	$	

15. **Attorney fees** *(This is required if either party is requesting attorney fees.):*

   a. To date, I have paid my attorney this amount for fees and costs *(specify):* $
   b. The source of this money was *(specify):*
   c. I still owe the following fees and costs to my attorney *(specify total owed):* $
   d. My attorney's hourly rate is *(specify):* $

I confirm this fee arrangement.

Date:

▶

_____
(TYPE OR PRINT NAME OF ATTORNEY)

_____
(SIGNATURE OF ATTORNEY)

INCOME AND EXPENSE DECLARATION

FL-150

PETITIONER/PLAINTIFF:	CASE NUMBER:
RESPONDENT/DEFENDANT:	
OTHER PARENT/CLAIMANT:	

CHILD SUPPORT INFORMATION
(NOTE: Fill out this page only if your case involves child support.)

16. **Number of children**
    a. I have *(specify number):*   children under the age of 18 with the other parent in this case.
    b. The children spend   percent of their time with me and   percent of their time with the other parent.
       (If you're not sure about percentage or it has not been agreed on, please describe your parenting schedule here.)

17. **Children's health-care expenses**
    a. ☐ I do   ☐ I do not   have health insurance available to me for the children through my job.
    b. Name of insurance company:
    c. Address of insurance company:

    d. The monthly cost for the **children's** health insurance is or would be *(specify):* $
       (Do not include the amount your employer pays.)

18. **Additional expenses for the children in this case**   Amount per month
    a. Child care so I can work or get job training. . . . . $ _____
    b. Children's health care not covered by insurance . . . . $ _____
    c. Travel expenses for visitation . . . . $ _____
    d. Children's educational or other special needs *(specify below):* . . . . $ _____

19. **Special hardships.** I ask the court to consider the following special financial circumstances
    (attach documentation of any item listed here, including court orders):   Amount per month   For how many months?
    a. Extraordinary health expenses not included in 18b. . . . . $ _____   _____
    b. Major losses not covered by insurance (examples: fire, theft, other
        insured loss) . . . . $ _____   _____
    c. (1) Expenses for my minor children who are from other relationships and
           are living with me . . . . $ _____   _____
        (2) Names and ages of those children *(specify):*

        (3) Child support I receive for those children. . . . . $ _____

    The expenses listed in a, b, and c create an extreme financial hardship because *(explain):*

20. **Other information I want the court to know concerning support in my case** *(specify):*

Copies: Original (file with court clerk); copy for service; office copies.

§11.27 (c) Income Information [Deleted]

The Income Information form is now page 2 of Judicial Council Form FL-150; see §11.26.

§11.28 (d) Expense Information [Deleted]

The Expense Information form is now page 3 of Judicial Council Form FL-150; see §11.26.

§11.29 (e) Child Support Information [Deleted]

The Child Support Information form is now page 4 of Judicial Council Form FL-150; see §11.26.

(6) Simplified Financial Statement

§11.30 (a) Discussion

Under specified circumstances, parties may use a simplified financial statement (Judicial Council Form FL-155) in place of the Income and Expense Declaration and its accompanying pages (Judicial Council Form FL-150; see §11.26). As set forth in the form instructions, a party is eligible to use the form only if:

- Neither party is requesting spousal support or a modification of spousal support;
- Neither party is requesting an award of attorney fees;
- The filing party receives no income from any source other than welfare, salary or wages, disability, unemployment, interest, worker's compensation, social security, or retirement; and
- The filing party is not self-employed.

Instructions for completing the simplified financial statement and providing required documentation are provided on the form itself. The filing party must attach copies of his or her pay stubs for the last two months, and pay stubs received with any other income, to the form and must bring to the hearing a copy of his or her latest federal income tax return. Copies of the pay stubs, other payment stubs, and tax return must be attached to the copy of the form served on the other party.

Note that even if a party is eligible to use the simplified financial statement, he or she may choose instead to use the Income and Expense Declaration and attachments.

§11.31   (b) Form: Financial Statement (Simplified) (Judicial Council Form FL-155)

FL-155

Your name and address or attorney's name and address:	TELEPHONE NO.:	FOR COURT USE ONLY

ATTORNEY FOR *(Name)*:

SUPERIOR COURT OF CALIFORNIA, COUNTY OF

STREET ADDRESS:

MAILING ADDRESS:

CITY AND ZIP CODE:

BRANCH NAME:

PETITIONER/PLAINTIFF:

RESPONDENT/DEFENDANT:

OTHER PARENT:

FINANCIAL STATEMENT (SIMPLIFIED)	CASE NUMBER:

NOTICE: Read page 2 to find out if you qualify to use this form and how to use it.

1. a. ☐ My only source of income is TANF, SSI, or GA/GR.
   b. ☐ I have applied for TANF, SSI, or GA/GR.
2. I am the parent of the following number of natural or adopted children from this relationship .... ____
3. a. The children from this relationship are with me this amount of time .... ____ %
   b. The children from this relationship are with the other parent this amount of time .... ____ %
   c. Our arrangement for custody and visitation is *(specify, using extra sheet if necessary)*:

4. My tax filing status is: ☐ single ☐ married filing jointly ☐ head of household ☐ married filing separately.
5. My current gross income *(before taxes)* per month is .... $_____

   Attach 1 copy of pay stubs for last 2 months here (cross out social security numbers)
   This income comes from the following:
   ☐ Salary/wages: Amount before taxes per month.................................... $_____
   ☐ Retirement: Amount before taxes per month.. $_____
   ☐ Unemployment compensation: Amount per month.................................. $_____
   ☐ Workers' compensation: Amount per month .... $_____
   ☐ Social security: ☐ SSI ☐ Other   Amount per month .... $_____
   ☐ Disability: Amount per month .... $_____
   ☐ Interest income (from bank accounts or other): Amount per month .... $_____
   I have no income other than as stated in this paragraph.

6. I pay the following monthly expenses for the children in this case:
   a. ☐ Day care or preschool to allow me to work or go to school .... $_____
   b. ☐ Health care not paid for by insurance .... $_____
   c. ☐ School, education, tuition, or other special needs of the child .... $_____
   d. ☐ Travel expenses for visitation .... $_____
7. ☐ There are *(specify number)* _____ other minor children of mine living with me. Their monthly expenses
   that I pay are .... $_____
8. I spend the following average monthly amounts *(please attach proof)*:
   a. ☐ Job-related expenses that are not paid by my employer *(specify reasons for expenses on separate sheet)* $_____
   b. ☐ Required union dues .... $_____
   c. ☐ Required retirement payments (not social security, FICA, 401k or IRA) .... $_____
   d. ☐ Health insurance costs .... $_____
   e. ☐ Child support I am paying for other minor children of mine who are not living with me ... $_____
   f. ☐ Spousal support I am paying because of a court order for another relationship.......... $_____
   g. ☐ Monthly housing costs: ☐ rent or ☐ mortgage .... $_____
   If mortgage: interest payments $_____ real property taxes $_____
9. Information concerning ☐ my current employment ☐ my most recent employment:
   Employer:
   Address:
   Telephone number:
   My occupation:
   Date work started:
   Date work stopped *(if applicable)*:   What was your gross income *(before taxes)* before work stopped?:

Page 1 of 2

Form Approved for Optional Use
Judicial Council of California
FL-155 [Rev. January 1, 2004]

FINANCIAL STATEMENT (SIMPLIFIED)   CEB

Family Code, § 4068(b)
www.courtinfo.ca.gov

PETITIONER/PLAINTIFF:	CASE NUMBER:
RESPONDENT/DEFENDANT:	
OTHER PARENT:	

10. My estimate of the other party's gross monthly income *(before taxes)* is .... $ _____

11. My current spouse's monthly income *(before taxes)* is .... $ _____

12. Other information I want the court to know concerning child support in my case *(attach extra sheet with the information)*.

13. ☐ I am attaching a copy of page 3 of form FL-150, *Income and Expense Declaration* showing my expenses.

I declare under penalty of perjury under the laws of the State of California that the information contained on all pages of this form and any attachments is true and correct.

Date:

▶

_____
(TYPE OR PRINT NAME)

_____
(SIGNATURE OF DECLARANT)

☐ PETITIONER/PLAINTIFF   ☐ RESPONDENT/DEFENDANT

INSTRUCTIONS

Step 1: Are you eligible to use this form? *If your answer is YES to any of the following questions, you may NOT use this form:*

- Are you asking for spousal support (alimony) or a change in spousal support?
- Is your spouse or former spouse asking for spousal support (alimony) or a change in spousal support?
- Are you asking the other party to pay your attorney fees?
- Is the other party asking you to pay his or her attorney fees?
- Do you receive money (income) from any source other than the following?

  - Welfare (such as TANF, GR, or GA)
  - Salary or wages
  - Disability
  - Unemployment
  - Interest
  - Workers' compensation
  - Social security
  - Retirement

- Are you self-employed?

If you are eligible to use this form and choose to do so, you do not need to complete the *Income and Expense Declaration* (form FL-150). Even if you are eligible to use this form, you may choose instead to use the *Income and Expense Declaration* (form FL-150).

Step 2: Make 2 copies of each of your pay stubs for the last two months. If you received money from other than wages or salary, include copies of the pay stub received with that money.

Privacy notice: If you wish, you may cross out your social security number if it appears on the pay stub, other payment notice or your tax return

Step 3: Make 2 copies of your most recent federal income tax form.

Step 4: Complete this form with the required information. Type the form if possible or complete it neatly and clearly in black ink. If you need additional room, please use plain or lined paper, 8½-by-11", and staple to this form.

Step 5: Make 2 copies of each side of this completed form and any attached pages.

Step 6: Serve a copy on the other party. Have someone other than yourself mail to the attorney for the other party, the other party, and the local child support agency, if they are handling the case, 1 copy of this form, 1 copy of each of your stubs for the last two months, and 1 copy of your most recent federal income tax return.

Step 7: File the original with the court. Staple this form with 1 copy of each of your pay stubs for the last two months. Take this document and give it to the clerk of the court. Check with your local court about how to submit your return.

Step 8: Keep the remaining copies of the documents for your file.

Step 9: Take the copy of your latest federal income tax return to the court hearing.

It is very important that you attend the hearings scheduled for this case. If you do not attend a hearing, the court may make an order without considering the information you want the court to consider.

FL-155 [Rev. January 1, 2004]   **FINANCIAL STATEMENT (SIMPLIFIED)**   ⚫EB   Page 2 of 2

Copies: Original (file with court clerk); copy for service; office copies.

(7) Request for Order

§11.31A   (a) Discussion

Whenever temporary *protective* orders (see §11.6) are sought, the moving party must use a Request for Order (Judicial Council Form DV-100) and Child Custody, Visitation, and Support Request (DV-105) if orders concerning child custody and visitation and support are also sought. With respect to Personal Conduct Orders (Item 6) and Stay-Away Orders (Item 7), note that the court may not issue *mutual* restraining orders unless (a) both parties personally appear and each party presents written evidence of abuse or domestic violence, and (b) the court makes detailed findings of fact indicating that both parties acted primarily as aggressors and that neither party acted primarily in self-defense. See Fam C §6305. See also *Kobey v Morton* (1991) 228 CA3d 1055, 1059, 278 CR 530 (in action for injunction prohibiting harassment under CCP §527.6, court held that mutual orders restraining personal conduct may not be issued after a hearing unless both parties have filed papers requesting them).

§11.31B   (b) Form: Request for Order (Domestic Violence Prevention) (Judicial Council Form DV-100)

DV-100   **Request for Order**

Clerk stamps date here when form is filed.

(1) Your name (person asking for protection):

_____

Your address *(skip this if you have a lawyer):* *(If you want your address to be private, give a mailing address instead):*

_____

City: _____ State: _____ Zip: _____

Your telephone number *(optional):* _____

Your lawyer *(if you have one):* *(Name, address, telephone number, and State Bar number):*

_____

_____

_____

Fill in court name and street address:

Superior Court of California, County of

(2) Name of person you want protection from:

_____

Description of that person: Sex: ☐ M ☐ F Height: _____
Weight: _____ Race: _____ Hair Color: _____
Eye Color: _____ Age: _____ Date of Birth: _____

Clerk fills in case number when form is filed.

Case Number:

(3) Besides you, who needs protection? *(Family or household members):*

Full Name	Age	Lives with you?	How are they related to you?
_____	_____	☐ Yes ☐ No	_____
_____	_____	☐ Yes ☐ No	_____
_____	_____	☐ Yes ☐ No	_____
_____	_____	☐ Yes ☐ No	_____

☐ *Check here if you need more space. Attach Form MC-020 and write "DV-100, Item 3—Protected People" by your statement. NOTE: In any item that asks for Form MC-020, you can use an 8 1/2 x 11-inch sheet of paper instead.*

(4) What is your relationship to the person in **(2)**? *(Check all that apply):*

a. ☐ We are now married or registered domestic partners.
b. ☐ We used to be married or registered domestic partners.
c. ☐ We live together.
d. ☐ We used to live together.
e. ☐ We are relatives, in-laws, or related by adoption *(specify relationship):* _____
f. ☐ We are dating or used to date.
g. ☐ We are engaged to be married or were engaged to be married.
h. ☐ We are the parents together of a child or children under 18:
   Child's Name: _____ Date of Birth: _____
   Child's Name: _____ Date of Birth: _____
   Child's Name: _____ Date of Birth: _____
   ☐ *Check here if you need more space. Attach Form MC-020 and write "DV-100, Item 4h" by your statement.*
i. ☐ We have signed a Voluntary Declaration of Paternity for our child or children. *(Attach a copy if you have one.)*

This is not a Court Order.

Judicial Council of California, www.courtinfo.ca.gov
Revised July 1, 2006, Mandatory Form
Family Code, § 6200 et seq.

Request for Order
(Domestic Violence Prevention)

DV-100, Page 1 of 4
→

Case Number:

Your name: _____

(5) Other Court Cases

  a. Have you and the person in ② been involved in another court case?   ☐ No ☐ Yes
      If yes, where? County: _____ State: _____
      What are the case numbers? *(If you know):* _____
      What kind of case? *(Check all that apply):*
      ☐ Registered Domestic Partnership   ☐ Divorce/Dissolution   ☐ Parentage/Paternity   ☐ Legal Separation
      ☐ Domestic Violence   ☐ Criminal   ☐ Juvenile   ☐ Child Support   ☐ Nullity   ☐ Civil Harassment
      ☐ Other *(specify):* _____

  b. Are there any domestic violence restraining/protective orders now (criminal, juvenile, family)?
      ☐ No ☐ Yes *If yes, attach a copy if you have one.*

What orders do you want? Check the boxes that apply to your case. ☑

(6) ☐ Personal Conduct Orders

  I ask the court to order the person in ② not to do the following things to me or any of the people listed in ③:

  a. ☐ Harass, attack, strike, threaten, assault (sexually or otherwise), hit, follow, stalk, molest, destroy
         personal property, disturb the peace, keep under surveillance, or block movements
  b. ☐ Contact (either directly or indirectly), or telephone, or send messages or mail or e-mail
  *The person in ② will be ordered not to take any action to get the addresses or locations of any protected
  person, their family members, caretakers, or guardians unless the court finds good cause not to make the order.*

(7) ☐ Stay-Away Order

  I ask the court to order the person in ② to stay at least _____ yards away from *(check all that apply):*

  a. ☐ Me   e. ☐ The children's school or child care
  b. ☐ The people listed in ③   f. ☐ My vehicle
  c. ☐ My home   g. ☐ Other *(specify):* _____
  d. ☐ My job or workplace

  If the person listed in ② is ordered to stay away from all the places listed above, will he or she still be able
  to get to his or her home, school, job, or place of worship? ☐ Yes ☐ No *(If no, explain):* _____

(8) ☐ Move-Out Order

  I ask the court to order the person in ② to move out from and not return to *(address):*

  _____

  I have the right to live at the above address because *(explain):* _____

(9) ☐ Child Custody, Visitation, and Child Support

  I ask the court to order child custody, visitation, and/or child support. *You must fill out and attach
  Form DV-105.*

(10) ☐ Spousal Support

  *You can make this request only if you are married to, or are a registered domestic partner of, the person in ②
  and no spousal support order exists. To ask for spousal support, you must fill out, file, and serve Form FL-150
  before your hearing.*

This is not a Court Order.

	Case Number:

Your name: _____

What orders do you want? Check the boxes that apply to your case. ☑

(11) ☐ **Record Unlawful Communications**

I ask for the right to record communications made to me by the person in ② that violate the judge's orders.

(12) ☐ **Property Control**

I ask the court to give *only* me temporary use, possession, and control of the property listed here:

_____

(13) ☐ **Debt Payment**

I ask the court to order the person in ② to make these payments while the order is in effect:

☐ *Check here if you need more space. Attach Form MC-020 and write "DV-100, Item 13—Debt Payment" by your statement.*

Pay to: _____ For: _____ Amount: $ _____ Due date: _____

Pay to: _____ For: _____ Amount: $ _____ Due date: _____

Pay to: _____ For: _____ Amount: $ _____ Due date: _____

(14) ☐ **Property Restraint**

I am married to or have a registered domestic partnership with the person in ②. I ask the judge to order that the person in ② not borrow against, sell, hide, or get rid of or destroy any possessions or property, except in the usual course of business or for necessities of life. I also ask the judge to order the person in ② to notify me of any new or big expenses and to explain them to the court.

(15) ☐ **Attorney Fees and Costs**

I ask that the person in ② pay some or all of my attorney fees and costs.

You must complete and file Form FL-150, Income and Expense Declaration.

(16) ☐ **Payments for Costs and Services**

I ask that the person in ② pay the following:

You can ask for lost earnings or your costs for services caused directly by the person in ② (damaged property, medical care, counseling, temporary housing, etc.). You must bring proof of these expenses to your hearing.

Pay to: _____ For: _____ Amount: $ _____

Pay to: _____ For: _____ Amount: $ _____

Pay to: _____ For: _____ Amount: $ _____

(17) ☐ **Batterer Intervention Program**

I ask the court to order the person listed in ② to go to a 52-week batterer intervention program and show proof of completion to the court.

(18) **No Fee to Serve (Notify) Restrained Person**

If you want the sheriff or marshal to serve (notify) the restrained person about the orders for free, ask the court clerk if you need to file more forms. You may need Form CH-101/DV-290 and Form 982(a)(17).

This is not a Court Order.

Case Number:

Your name: _____

What orders do you want? Check the boxes that apply to your case. ☑

(19) ☐ **More Time for Notice**

I need extra time to notify the person in ② about these papers. Because of the facts explained on this form, I want the papers served up to _____ days before the date of the hearing. *For help, read Form DV-210-INFO.*

If necessary, add additional facts: _____

_____

(20) ☐ **Other Orders**

What other orders are you asking for? _____

_____

☐ *Check here if you need more space. Attach Form MC-020 and write "DV-100, Item 20—Other Orders" by your statement.*

(21) **Guns or Other Firearms**

I believe the person in ② owns or possesses guns or firearms. ☐ Yes ☐ No ☐ I don't know

If the judge approves the order, the person in ② will be required to sell to a gun dealer or turn in to police any guns or firearms that he or she owns or possesses.

(22) Describe the most recent abuse.

  a. Date of most recent abuse: _____

  b. Who was there? _____

  c. What did the person in ② do or say that made you afraid?

_____

_____

_____

_____

_____

  d. Describe any use or threatened use of guns or other weapons: _____

_____

  e. Describe any injuries: _____

_____

  f. Did the police come? ☐ No ☐ Yes

    If yes, did they give you an Emergency Protective Order? ☐ Yes ☐ No ☐ I don't know

    Attach a copy if you have one.

    ☐ *Check here if you need more space. Use Form MC-020 and write "DV-100, Item 22—Recent Abuse" by your statement.*

    ☐ *Check here if the person in ② has abused you (or your children) other times. Use Form DV-101 or Form MC-020 to describe any previous abuse.*

I declare under penalty of perjury under the laws of the State of California that the information above is true and correct.

Date: _____

▶

_____   _____

Type or print your name   *Sign your name*

This is not a Court Order.

Copies: Original (file with court clerk); copy for service; office copies.

Comment: On additional forms that must accompany the above form, see §11.31A.

(8) Temporary Restraining Order and Notice of Hearing (CLETS)

§11.31C   (a) Discussion

Whenever temporary *protective* orders (see §11.6) are sought, the moving party must use a Temporary Restraining Order and Notice of Hearing (CLETS) form and Child Custody, Visitation, and Support Request in addition to using an Application for Order and Supporting Declaration (see §§11.16–11.20, 11.23–11.24) if orders concerning child custody and visitation and support are also sought.

§11.31D   (b) Form: Temporary Restraining Order and Notice of Hearing (CLETS) (Domestic Violence Prevention) (Judicial Council Form DV-110)

| **DV-110** | **Temporary Restraining Order and Notice of Hearing** | Clerk stamps date here when form is filed. |

(1) Name of person asking for protection (protected person):

Protected person's address *(skip this if you have a lawyer): (If you want your address to be private, give a mailing address instead):*

City: _____ State: _____ Zip: _____
Telephone number: _____
Protected person's lawyer *(if any): (Name, address, telephone number, and State Bar number):*

Fill in court name and street address:
Superior Court of California, County of

(2) Restrained person's name:

Description of that person: Sex: ☐ M ☐ F Height: _____
Weight: _____ Race: _____ Hair Color: _____
Eye Color: _____ Age: ____ Date of Birth: _____

Fill in case number:
Case Number:

(3) List the full names of all family or household members protected by this order: _____

(4) **Court Hearing Date *(Fecha de la Audiencia)***
Clerk will fill out section below.

Name and address of court if different from above:

Hearing Date → Date: _____ Time: _____ _____
Dept.: _____ Rm.: _____ _____

To the person in (2) : At the hearing, the judge can make restraining orders that last for up to 5 years. The judge can also make other orders about your children, child support, spousal support, money, and property. File an answer on Form DV-120 before the hearing. At the hearing, you can tell the judge that you do not want the orders against you. Even if you do not attend the hearing, you *must* obey the orders.

Para la persona nombrada en (2) : En esta audiencia el juez puede hacer que la orden de restricción sea válida hasta un máximo de 5 años. El juez puede también hacer otras órdenes acerca de niños, manutención, dinero y propiedad. Presente una respuesta en el formulario DV-120 antes de la audiencia. Si Usted se opone a estas órdenes, vaya a la audiencia y dígaselo al juez. Aunque no vaya a la audiencia, tiene que obedecer estas órdenes.

To the person in (1): At the hearing, the judge will consider whether denial of any orders will jeopardize your safety and the safety of children for whom you are requesting custody, visitation, and child support. Safety concerns related to the financial needs of you and your children will also be considered.

(5) **Temporary Orders (Ordenes Temporales)**
Any orders made in this form end at the time of the court hearing in (4), unless a judge extends them.
Read this form carefully. All checked boxes ☑ and items 10 and 11 are court orders.

Todas las órdenes hechas en esta formulario terminarán en la fecha y hora de la audiencia en (4), al menos que un juez las extienda. Lea este formulario con cuidado. Todas las casillas marcadas ☑ y los artículos 10 y 11 son órdenes de la corte.

This is a Court Order.

Judicial Council of California, www.courtinfo.ca.gov
Revised July 1, 2006, Mandatory Form
Family Code, § 6200 et seq. Approved by DOJ

Temporary Restraining Order and Notice of Hearing (CLETS—TRO)
(Domestic Violence Prevention)

DV-110, Page 1 of 5
→

Case Number: _____

Your name: _____

(6) ☐ **Personal Conduct Orders**

The person in ② must *not* do the following things to the protected people listed in ① and ③ :

a. ☐ Harass, attack, strike, threaten, assault (sexually or otherwise), hit, follow, stalk, molest, destroy personal property, disturb the peace, keep under surveillance, or block movements

b. ☐ Contact (either directly or indirectly), or telephone, or send messages or mail or e-mail

☐ Except for brief and peaceful contact as required for court-ordered visitation of children unless a criminal protective order says otherwise

c. ☐ Take any action, directly or through others, to get the addresses or locations of any protected persons or of their family members, caretakers, or guardians. *(If item c is not checked, the court has found good cause not to make this order.)*

Peaceful written contact through a lawyer or through a process server or another person in order to serve legal papers is allowed and does not violate this order.

☐ A criminal protective order on Form CR-160 is in effect. Case Number: _____

County *(if known):* _____ Expiration Date: _____ *(If more orders, list them in item* ⑯)

(7) ☐ **Stay-Away Order**

The person in ② must stay at least_____ yards away from:

a. ☐ The person listed in ①

b. ☐ The people listed in ③

c. ☐ Home ☐ Job ☐ Vehicle of person in ①

d. ☐ The children's school or child care

e. ☐ Other *(specify):* _____

(8) ☐ **Move-Out Order**

The person in ② must take only personal clothing and belongings needed until the hearing and move out immediately from *(address):* _____

(9) ☐ **Child Custody and Visitation Order**

a. ☐ You and the other parent must make an appointment for court mediation *(address and phone number):*

_____

b. ☐ Follow the orders listed in Form DV-140, which is attached.

(10) **No Guns or Other Firearms**

The person in ② cannot own, possess, have, buy or try to buy, receive or try to receive, or in any other way get a gun or firearm.

(11) **Turn in or sell guns or firearms.**

The person in ②:

• Must sell to a licensed gun dealer or turn in to police any guns or firearms that he or she has or controls. This must be done within 24 hours of receiving this order.

• Must bring a receipt to the court within 72 hours of receiving this order, to prove that guns and firearms have been turned in or sold.

(12) ☐ **Property Control**

Until the hearing, *only* the person in ① can use, control, and possess the following property and things:

_____

_____

This is a Court Order.

**Temporary Restraining Order
and Notice of Hearing (CLETS—TRO)**
(Domestic Violence Prevention)

Your name: _____

Case Number:

(13) ☐ **Property Restraint**

If the people in ① and ② are married to each other or are registered domestic partners, they must not transfer, borrow against, sell, hide, or get rid of or destroy any property, except in the usual course of business or for necessities of life. In addition, each person must notify the other of any new or big expenses and explain them to the court. *(The person in ② cannot contact the person in ① if the court has made a "no contact" order.)*

(14) ☐ **Unlawful communications may be recorded.**

The person in ① can record communications made by the person in ② that violate the judge's orders.

(15) **No Fee to Notify (Serve) Restrained Person**

If the sheriff serves this order, he or she will do it for free.

(16) ☐ **Other Orders** *(specify):* _____

_____

_____

(17) If the judge makes a restraining order at the hearing, which has the same orders as in this form, the person in ② will get a copy of that order by mail at his or her last known address. *(Write restrained person's address here):*

_____

If this address is not correct, or to know if the orders were made permanent, contact the court.

(18) ☐ **Time for Service**

Ⓐ **To: Person Asking for Order**	**Ⓑ** **To: Person Served With Order**
Someone 18 or over—**not you or the other protected people**—must personally "serve" a copy of this order to the restrained person at least _____ days before the hearing.	If you want to respond in writing, someone 18 or over—**not you**—must "serve" Form DV-120 on the person in ①, then file it with the court at least _____ days before the hearing.

For help with Service or answering, read Form DV-210-INFO or DV-540-INFO.

Date: _____   ▶ _____
                                                    Judge (or Judicial Officer)

Certificate of Compliance With VAWA

This temporary protective order meets all Full Faith and Credit requirements of the Violence Against Women Act, 18 U.S.C. § 2265 (1994) (VAWA) upon notice of the restrained person. This court has jurisdiction over the parties and the subject matter; the restrained person has been or will be afforded notice and a timely opportunity to be heard as provided by the laws of this jurisdiction. **This order is valid and entitled to enforcement in each jurisdiction throughout the 50 United States, the District of Columbia, all tribal lands, and all U.S. territories, commonwealths, and possessions and shall be enforced as if it were an order of that jurisdiction.**

This is a Court Order.

Your name: _____

Case Number: _____

Warnings and Notices to the Restrained Person in ❷

(19) **If you do not obey this order, you can be arrested and charged with a crime.**

- It is a felony to take or hide a child in violation of this order. You can go to prison and/or pay a fine.
- If you travel to another state or to tribal lands or make the protected person do so, with the intention of disobeying this order, you can be charged with a federal crime.
- If you do not obey this order, you can go to prison and/or pay a fine.

(20) **You cannot have guns or firearms.**

You cannot own, have, possess, buy or try to buy, receive or try to receive, or otherwise get a gun while the order is in effect. If you do, you can go to jail and pay a $1,000 fine. You must sell to a gun dealer or turn in to police any guns or firearms that you have or control. The judge will ask you for proof that you did so. If you do not obey this order, you can be charged with a crime. Federal law says you cannot have guns or ammunition if you are subject to a restraining order made after a noticed hearing.

(21) **After You Have Been Served With a Restraining Order**

- Obey all the orders.
- If you want to respond, fill out Form DV-120. Take it to the court clerk with the forms listed in item (22).
- File DV-120 and have all papers served on the protected person by the date listed in item (18) of this form.
- At the hearing, tell the judge if you agree or disagree with the orders requested.
- Even if you do not attend the hearing, the judge can make the restraining orders last for 5 years.

(22) **Child Custody, Visitation, and Support**

- Child Custody and Visitation: If you do not go to the hearing, the judge can make custody and visitation orders for your children without hearing your side.
- Child Support: The judge can order child support based on the income of both parents. The judge can also have that support taken directly from your paycheck. Child support can be a lot of money, and usually you have to pay until the child is 18. File and serve a *Financial Statement* (Form FL-155) or an *Income and Expense Declaration* (Form FL-150) so the judge will have information about your finances. Otherwise, the court may make support orders without hearing your side.
- Spousal Support: File and serve a *Financial Statement* (Form FL-155) or an *Income and Expense Declaration* (Form FL-150) so the judge will have information about your finances. Otherwise, the court may make support orders without hearing your side.

(23) **Requests for Accommodations**

Assistive listening systems, computer-assisted real-time captioning, or sign language interpreter services are available if you ask at least five days before the proceeding. Contact the clerk's office or go to *www.courtinfo.ca.gov/forms* for *Request for Accommodations by Persons With Disabilities and Order* (Form MC-410). (Civil Code, § 54.8.)

This is a Court Order.

Case Number: _____

Your name: _____

Instructions for Law Enforcement

(24) Start Date and End Date of Orders

The start date is the date next to the judge's signature on page 3. The orders end on the hearing date on page 1 or the hearing date on Form DV-125, if attached.

(25) Arrest Required If Order Is Violated

If an officer has probable cause to believe that the restrained person had notice of the order and has disobeyed the order, the officer must arrest the restrained person. (Penal Code, §§ 836(c)(1), 13701(b).) A violation of the order may be a violation of Penal Code section 166 or 273.6.

(26) Notice/Proof of Service

Law enforcement must first determine if the restrained person had notice of the orders. If notice cannot be verified, the restrained person must be advised of the terms of the orders. If the restrained person then fails to obey the orders, the officer must enforce them. (Family Code, § 6383.)

Consider the restrained person "served" (noticed) if:

- The officer sees a copy of the *Proof of Service* or confirms that the *Proof of Service* is on file; *or*
- The restrained person was at the restraining order hearing or was informed of the order by an officer. (Fam. Code, § 6383; Pen. Code, § 836(c)(2).) An officer can obtain information about the contents of the order in the Domestic Violence Restraining Orders System (DVROS). (Fam. Code, § 6381(b)(c).)

(27) If the Protected Person Contacts the Restrained Person

Even if the protected person invites or consents to contact with the restrained person, the orders remain in effect and must be enforced. The protected person cannot be arrested for inviting or consenting to contact with the restrained person. The orders can be changed only by another court order. (Pen. Code, § 13710(b).)

(28) Child Custody and Visitation

- Custody and visitation orders are on Form DV-140, items ③ and ④. They are sometimes also written on additional pages or referenced in DV-140 or other orders that are not part of the restraining order.
- **Forms DV-100 and DV-105 are not orders. Do not enforce them.**

(29) Enforcing the Restraining Order in California

Any law enforcement officer in California who receives, sees, or verifies the orders on a paper copy, or on the California Law Enforcement Telecommunications System (CLETS), or in an NCIC Protection Order File must enforce the orders.

(30) Conflicting Orders

A protective order issued in a criminal case on Form CR-160 takes precedence in enforcement over any conflicting civil court order. (Pen. Code, § 136.2(e)(2).) Any nonconflicting terms of the civil restraining order remain in full force. An emergency protective order (Form EPO-001) that is in effect between the same parties and is more restrictive than other restraining orders takes precedence over all other restraining orders.

Clerk's Certificate

[seal]

I certify that this Temporary Restraining Order is a true and correct copy of the original on file in the court.

Date: _____ Clerk, by _____ , Deputy

This is a Court Order.

Temporary Restraining Order and Notice of Hearing (CLETS—TRO) (Domestic Violence Prevention)

Copies: Original (submit to court clerk); copy for service; copies for police; office copies.

§11.32 (9) Memorandum of Points and Authorities

A memorandum of points and authorities need not be filed unless required by the court on a case-by-case basis (Cal Rules of Ct 5.118(a)), and it is unlikely that the court will require one in connection with a motion for temporary orders. Even when the court does not require a memorandum of points and authorities, however, submitting one should be considered when seeking relief other than that specifically listed on the Application for Order and Supporting Declaration (Judicial Council Form FL-310; see §11.22), particularly if the relief requested is unusual, *e.g.,* pendente lite sale of property (see Fam C §2108; *Lee v Superior Court* (1976) 63 CA3d 705, 711, 134 CR 43) or appointment of a receiver (see *Quaglino v Quaglino* (1979) 88 CA3d 542, 546, 152 CR 47). The court may grant or deny the requested relief solely on the basis of the written materials, including any accompanying memorandum of points and authorities. Cal Rules of Ct 5.118(f).

On the memorandum of points and authorities generally, see California Civil Procedure Before Trial §§12.30–12.42 (4th ed Cal CEB 2004).

§11.33 (10) Declaration Regarding Notice When Ex Parte Relief Sought

When notice is required in regard to a request for ex parte relief absent a showing that justifies the granting of the requested orders without it (see §11.15), a declaration should be submitted along with the application, showing either that notice has been given or the reason it has not been given. The declaration should be very specific, *e.g.,* the method of giving notice, to whom it was given, when it was given, and the response. For an example of a declaration, see §10.37 (Declaration in Support of Application for Order for Publication of Summons). Some courts have their own forms for the declaration.

§11.34 c. Service and Filing

Any Order to Show Cause or Notice of Motion, along with all supporting papers, must be served and filed at least 16 court days before the date set for hearing. CCP §1005(a)(13)–(b). Note that, in addition to the completed moving papers that must be served, the moving party must also serve *blank* copies of any applicable Responsive Declaration (see forms in §§11.36–11.36A) and, when a completed copy is required of the moving party, the Income and Expense Declaration and accompanying pages (see form in §11.26) or Financial Statement (Simplified) (see form in §11.31). Cal Rules of Ct 5.118(c)–(e). When service is by mail, the 16-court-day period is increased by 5 calendar days if the place of mailing and the place of address are in California, by 10 calendar days if either the place of mailing or the place of address is outside California but in the United States, and by 20 calendar days if either place is outside the United States. When service is by facsimile transmission, Express Mail, or another method of overnight delivery, the 16-court-day period is increased by 2 calendar days. CCP §1005(a)(13)–(b).

The court may prescribe a shorter time for service than that normally required. CCP §1005(a)(13)–(b). On preparation of forms when applying for an Order Shortening Time, see §§11.17 (Order to Show Cause), 11.19 (Notice of Motion), 11.21 (Application for Order and Supporting Declaration). See also forms in §§11.31B (Item 18) and 11.31D (Item 12) (applications for protective orders).

When the petitioner seeks temporary orders at the outset of the case, before the respondent has filed a response or otherwise made a general appearance, or when the moving party obtains ex parte orders (see §11.15), any Order to Show Cause and supplemental papers should be served on the respondent in the same manner as a summons. Under CCP §17(b)(6), an Order to Show Cause is "process" and, under CCP §1016, the provisions of CCP §§1010–1015 (service of notices and other papers) do not apply to service of process. On service of summons, see §§10.26–10.42. As a practical matter, personal service (see §10.31) should be used whenever possible to ensure that service is made within the time permitted and, for ex parte orders, that the party against whom the orders were made has the requisite knowledge of the orders to permit their being enforced, if necessary, by contempt (see §20.40). If an ex parte restraining order is issued with notice to the responding party pending the hearing, the applicant must serve the application and order to show cause, and any supporting documents, on the respondent at least 15 (not 16) days before the hearing. Fam C §243(c).

When the party to be served has appeared, any Order to Show Cause or Notice of Motion and the supplemental papers are served on the attorney (or on the party if he or she is appearing in pro per). CCP §1015. Service is made in the manner prescribed for service of notices and other papers under CCP §§1010–1020. Service is typically by mail (CCP §1012), although personal service and substituted service may also be used (CCP §1011). On service of notices and other papers generally, see California Civil Procedure Before Trial, §§12.69–12.73 (4th ed Cal CEB 2004). When the moving party has obtained ex parte orders, however, the Order to Show Cause and supplemental papers should be personally served on the other party, in addition to service on the attorney as described above, to ensure that the orders will be enforceable by contempt.

A Proof of Service should be completed and filed with the court. When any Order to Show Cause and accompanying papers are personally served on the respondent at the outset of the case along with the Summons and Petition, all the documents may be listed on the Proof of Service of Summons form (see form in §10.44). The Proof of Service should then be attached to the Summons form (see form in §10.14). When any Order to Show Cause or Notice of Motion and accompanying papers are served on the petitioner, or on the respondent but not together with the Summons and Petition, a different Proof of Service form should be used; see, *e.g.*, the form in §11.63. For other Judicial Council proof of service forms that may be used, see Proof of Personal Service (Judicial Council Form FL-330) and Proof of Service by Mail (Judicial Council Form FL-335).

When the court has made orders that may require police enforcement (*i.e.*, child custody, protective orders, property control), copies of any Order to Show Cause (see forms in §§11.18 and 11.31D) and any separate Temporary Restraining Orders (see form in §11.24), along with a copy of the Proof of Service, should be delivered or mailed to the police department in each jurisdiction where it is reasonably likely that enforcement will be required. See Fam C §6381(b).

Some courts require that the moving papers be filed with the clerk in the department in which the matter is pending, rather than in the county clerk's office. Whether required or not, whenever the papers are filed close to the hearing date, they should be filed with, or endorsed-filed copies should be delivered by hand to, the clerk in the department where the hearing will be held to ensure that the court will have them at the hearing.

On choosing between the Order to Show Cause and the Notice of Motion, see §11.16.

2. Responding Party's Papers

a. Preparation

(1) Responsive Declarations

§11.35 (a) Discussion

The Responsive Declaration (Judicial Council Form FL-320), used to respond to a request for temporary orders in an Application for Order and Supporting Declaration (see §§11.21–11.22) (*i.e.,* orders other than protective orders), provides fewer options on issues affecting children than on other issues. With respect to the moving party's requests for custody, visitation, and child support orders (Items 1–3), the form seems to require that the responding party either consent to the order requested or propose an alternative order. Because contested custody issues are required to be addressed in mediation, anything other than consent to the order requested will trigger the parties' obligation to attend child custody mediation. Fam C §2170. With respect to the remaining requests (Items 4–8), the form allows the responding party to simply indicate a refusal to consent to the order requested without having to propose an alternative.

Note that the Responsive Declaration may seek affirmative relief as an alternative to that requested by the moving party *on the same issues raised by the moving party.* Fam C §213; *Brody v Kroll* (1996) 45 CA4th 1732, 53 CR2d 280. Thus, *e.g.,* when the moving party has requested custody and child support but not spousal support, the responding party may request custody and child support in the Responsive Declaration, but could request spousal support only by filing and serving a separate Order to Show Cause or Notice of Motion and supporting documents.

Supporting information (Item 9) must be prepared with care. Note that the court can grant or deny relief solely on the basis of the documents filed. See Cal Rules of Ct 5.118(f); 3.1306(a) (evidence at law and motion hearing must be by declaration, or request for judicial notice unless the court orders otherwise); see §11.51. Consequently, supporting facts should be provided for every position taken by the responding party.

A party responding to a request for temporary protective orders in a Request for Order (see §§11.31A–11.31B) must use an Answer to Temporary Restraining Order (Judicial Council Form DV-120) (see §11.36A). In the latter event, it would appear that, to the extent that the two responsive declarations cover the same issues, the responding party could respond in the broader responsive declaration alone, without repeating those responses in the responsive declaration to the request for protective orders.

§11.36   (b) Form: Responsive Declaration to Order to Show Cause or Notice of Motion (Judicial Council Form FL-320)

FL-320

ATTORNEY OR PARTY WITHOUT ATTORNEY *(Name, state bar number, and address)*:	FOR COURT USE ONLY

TELEPHONE NO.:   FAX NO.:

ATTORNEY FOR *(Name)*:

SUPERIOR COURT OF CALIFORNIA, COUNTY OF

STREET ADDRESS:

MAILING ADDRESS:

CITY AND ZIP CODE:

BRANCH NAME:

PETITIONER/PLAINTIFF:

RESPONDENT/DEFENDANT:

RESPONSIVE DECLARATION TO ORDER TO SHOW CAUSE OR NOTICE OF MOTION	CASE NUMBER:

HEARING DATE: TIME: DEPARTMENT OR ROOM:

1. ☐ CHILD CUSTODY
     a. ☐ I consent to the order requested.
     b. ☐ I do not consent to the order requested but I consent to the following order:

2. ☐ CHILD VISITATION
     a. ☐ I consent to the order requested.
     b. ☐ I do not consent to the order requested but I consent to the following order:

3. ☐ CHILD SUPPORT
     a. ☐ I consent to the order requested.
     b. ☐ I consent to guideline support.
     c. ☐ I do not consent to the order requested, but I consent to the following order:
          (1) ☐ Guideline
          (2) ☐ Other *(specify):*

4. ☐ SPOUSAL SUPPORT
     a. ☐ I consent to the order requested.
     b. ☐ I do not consent to the order requested.
     c. ☐ I consent to the following order:

5. ☐ ATTORNEY FEES AND COSTS
     a. ☐ I consent to the order requested.
     b. ☐ I do not consent to the order requested.
     c. ☐ I consent to the following order:

Form Adopted for Mandatory Use
Judicial Council of California
FL-320 [Rev. January 1, 2003]   **RESPONSIVE DECLARATION TO ORDER TO SHOW CAUSE OR NOTICE OF MOTION**

PETITIONER/PLAINTIFF:	CASE NUMBER:
RESPONDENT/DEFENDANT:	

6. ☐ PROPERTY RESTRAINT
    a. ☐ I consent to the order requested.
    b. ☐ I do not consent to the order requested.
    c. ☐ I consent to the following order:

7. ☐ PROPERTY CONTROL
    a. ☐ I consent to the order requested.
    b. ☐ I do not consent to the order requested.
    c. ☐ I consent to the following order:

8. ☐ OTHER RELIEF
    a. ☐ I consent to the order requested.
    b. ☐ I do not consent to the order requested.
    c. ☐ I consent to the following order:

9. ☐ SUPPORTING INFORMATION
    ☐ contained in the attached declaration.

NOTE: To respond to a request for domestic violence restraining orders requested in the *Request for Order (Domestic Violence Prevention)* (form DV-100) you must use the *Answer to Temporary Restraining Order (Domestic Violence Prevention)* (form DV-120).

I declare under penalty of perjury under the laws of the State of California that the foregoing is true and correct.

Date:

▶

_____
(TYPE OR PRINT NAME)

_____
(SIGNATURE OF DECLARANT)

FL-320 [Rev. January 1, 2003]   **RESPONSIVE DECLARATION TO ORDER TO SHOW CAUSE OR NOTICE OF MOTION**   Page 2 of 2

Copies: Original (file with court clerk); copy for service; office copies.

§11.36A (c) Form: Answer to Temporary Restraining Order (Judicial Council Form DV-120)

DV-120   **Answer to Temporary Restraining Order**

Clerk stamps date here when form is filed.

(1) Name of person who asked for the order (protected person):

_____

(2) Your name: _____

Your address *(skip this if you have a lawyer): (If you want your address to be private, give a mailing address instead):*

_____

City: _____ State: _____ Zip: _____

Fill in court name and street address:

Superior Court of California, County of

Your telephone *(optional):* _____

Your lawyer *(if you have one): (Name, address, telephone number, and State Bar number):*

_____
_____
_____

Clerk fills in case number:

Case Number:

Give the judge your answers to DV-100:

(3) ☐ **Personal Conduct Orders**
   I ☐ do ☐ do not   agree to the order requested.

(4) ☐ **Stay-Away Order**
   I ☐ do ☐ do not   agree to the order requested.

The judge can consider your Answer at the hearing. Write your hearing date and time here:

Hearing Date → Date: _____ Time: _____
Dept.: _____ Room: _____

(5) ☐ **Move-Out Order**
   I ☐ do ☐ do not   agree to the order requested.

(6) ☐ **Child Custody**
   a. I ☐ do ☐ do not   agree to the custody order requested.
   b. ☐ I am not the parent of the child listed in DV-105.
   c. ☐ I ask for the following custody order *(specify):*

You must obey the orders until the hearing. If you do not come to this hearing, the judge can make the orders last for 3 years or longer.

   _____

   d. I ☐ do ☐ do not   agree to the orders requested to prevent child abduction.

(7) ☐ **Visitation**
   a. I ☐ do ☐ do not   agree to the visitation order requested.
   b. ☐ I ask for the following visitation order *(specify):* _____

   _____

(8) ☐ **Child Support**
   a. I ☐ do ☐ do not   agree to the order requested.
   b. ☐ I agree to pay guideline child support.
   You must fill out, serve, and file Form FL-150 or FL-155.

(9) ☐ **Spousal Support**
   I ☐ do ☐ do not   agree to the order requested.
   Whether or not you agree, you must fill out, serve, and file Form FL-150.

Judicial Council of California, www.courtinfo.ca.gov
Revised January 1, 2006, Mandatory Form
Family Code, § 6200 et seq.

Answer to Temporary Restraining Order
(Domestic Violence Prevention)

DV-120, Page 1 of 2 →

Your name: _____

Case Number:

(10) ☐ **Property Control**
   I ☐ do ☐ do not   agree to the order requested.
   If you have other requests, list them in **(19)** *below.*

(11) ☐ **Debt Payment**
   I ☐ do ☐ do not   agree to the order requested.
   If you have other requests, list them in **(19)** *below.*

(12) ☐ **Property Restraint**
   I ☐ do ☐ do not   agree to the order requested.
   If you have other requests, list them in **(19)** *below.*

(13) ☐ **Attorney Fees and Costs**
   I ☐ do ☐ do not   agree to the order requested.

(14) ☐ **Payments for Costs and Services**
   I ☐ do ☐ do not   agree to the order requested.

(15) ☐ **Batterer Intervention Program**
   I ☐ do ☐ do not   agree to the order requested.

(16) ☐ **Other Orders** *(see item 20 on Form DV-100)*
   I ☐ do ☐ do not   agree to the orders requested.

(17) ☐ **Turn in guns or other firearms.**
   a. ☐ I do not own or have any guns or firearms.
   b. ☐ I ☐ have ☐ have not turned in my guns and firearms to the police or a licensed gun dealer.
   c. ☐ A copy of the receipt ☐ is attached. ☐ has already been filed with the court.
   You must file a receipt with the court within 72 hours after receiving Form DV-110.

(18) ☐ **I ask the court to order payment of my**
   a. ☐ Attorney fees
   b. ☐ Out-of-pocket expenses because the temporary restraining order was issued without
      enough supporting facts. The expenses are:
   Item: _____ Amount: $ _____ Item: _____ Amount: $ _____
   You must fill out, serve, and file Form FL-150.

(19) ☐ **My Answer to the Statements in DV-100 and Other Requests**
   Please attach your statement. Write "DV-120, Item 19—More Information" at the top. Be specific.

(20) I declare under penalty of perjury under the laws of the State of California that the information above is true and
   correct.

   Date: _____

_____   ▶   _____
Type or print your name   *Sign your name*

§11.37   (2) Income and Expense Declaration

When financial issues (*i.e.,* child support, spousal support, attorney fees and costs) are at issue, the responding party must submit an Income and Expense Declaration (see §11.26). For discussion of preparation of the form, see §11.25.

§11.38   b. Service and Filing

The responsive declaration or declarations (see §11.35) and any accompanying documents, usually the Income and Expense Declaration (see form in §11.26), must be served and filed at least 9 court days before the hearing. CCP §1005(a)(13)–(b). They must be served by personal delivery, facsimile transmission, express mail, or other means consistent with CCP §§1010, 1011, 1012, and 1013 that are reasonably calculated to ensure delivery not later than the close of the next business day after the time they are filed. CCP §1005(c). The papers are served on the attorney, rather than the party, unless the party is appearing in pro per. CCP §1015. A Proof of Service should be completed and filed with the court; see, *e.g.,* the form in §11.63. For other Judicial Council proof of service forms that may be used, see Proof of Personal Service (Judicial Council Form FL-330) and Proof of Service by Mail (Judicial Council Form FL-335). On service of notices and other papers generally, see California Civil Procedure Before Trial §§12.69–12.73 (4th ed Cal CEB 2004).

Many courts require that the responsive papers be filed with the clerk in the department in which the matter is pending, rather than in the county clerk's office. Whether required or not, whenever the papers are filed close to the hearing date, they should be filed with, or endorsed-filed copies should be delivered by hand to, the clerk in the department where the hearing will be held to ensure that the court will have them at the time of the hearing. No filing or subpoena fee is required for the responsive declaration or declarations. See Govt C §26826(b)(2); Fam C §6222.

When the attorney is first contacted by the client so close to the hearing date that the 10-day service and filing requirement cannot be met, the attorney should try to ascertain the practice of the particular court or judge with respect to late filing of responsive papers. See, *e.g.,* Alameda Ct R 11.0(3)(J) (court, in its discretion, may refuse to consider responsive pleadings not timely filed). Depending on that practice, it may be necessary to seek a stipulation from the opposing attorney waiving the 10-day rule. For form of stipulation waiving any service and filing requirement, see §11.39. Alternatively, perhaps opposing counsel will stipulate to a continuance of the hearing date. See form in §11.43.

If a stipulation cannot be obtained from the opposing attorney, counsel might apply to the court for an Order Shortening Time. For a form of application for Order Shortening Time and order, see §11.40. Alternatively, counsel might apply to the court for a continuance. Continuances should always be sought as far in advance of the hearing as possible. See, *e.g.,* Alameda Ct R 11.0(3)(G) (request for continuance must be made by noon 2 court days prior to the hearing and will be viewed with disfavor (and the court may impose a $100 sanction) if made at time of hearing unless good cause shown). For a form of application for continuance and order, see §11.44.

When the responding party requests affirmative relief on issues not raised by the moving party, an Order to Show Cause or Notice of Motion will be required. See §11.35. In that event, the responding party may wish to set the hearing on his or her requests for the same time as that on the moving party's requests, but the responding party's motion will be subject to the 16-court-day notice requirement of CCP §1005(a)(13)–(b). See §11.34. Consequently, when the attorney wishes to set the hearing on the responding party's requests at the same time as that on the moving party's requests, the hearing date for the latter might not allow for the requisite notice. In that event, depending on local practice, the attorney might seek a stipulation from the opposing attorney either waiving the 16-court-day requirement (for a form of stipulation waiving any service and filing requirement, see §11.39) or continuing the hearing date (see form in §11.43) and, failing that, apply to the court for an Order Shortening Time (see Item 8 on Application for Order and Supporting Declaration in §11.22; Item 18 on Request for Order in §11.31B; Item 3.b on Order to Show Cause in §11.18; Item 4 on Notice of Motion in §11.20; Item 18 on Temporary Restraining Order and Notice of Hearing (CLETS) in §11.31D) or a continuance (see form in §11.44). On the importance of local practice, see, *e.g.,* Santa Clara Fam. Ct R 5.I.(7) (anything other than continuances may be obtained only on application, for good cause).

§11.39   (1) Form: Stipulation Acknowledging Service of Papers and Waiving Service and Filing Requirement

_ _[Attorney name]_ _
_ _[State Bar number]_ _
_ _[Address]_ _
_ _[Telephone number]_ _

Attorney for _ _[name]_ _

SUPERIOR COURT OF CALIFORNIA
COUNTY OF _ _ _ _ _ _ _ _

Marriage of	) **No.** _ _ _ _ _
	)
Petitioner: _ _ _ _ _ _ _ _	) **STIPULATION**
	) **ACKNOWLEDGING**
Respondent: _ _ _ _ _ _ _	) **SERVICE OF PAPERS AND**
	) **WAIVING SERVICE AND**
	) **FILING REQUIREMENT**
_____	)

_ _[Name]_ _, **petitioner, and** _ _[name]_ _, **respondent, hereby stipulate that the** _ _[responsive papers to/moving papers on]_ _ _ _[petitioner's/respondent's]_ _ _ _[specify, e.g., Order to Show Cause]_ _ **filed on** _ _[date]_ _ **have been received by** _ _[petitioner's/respondent's]_ _ **attorney and that any requirement that the papers be served and filed a specified number of days before the hearing is hereby waived.**

Date: _____   _ _[Signature]_ _
                             _ _[Typed name]_ _
                             Attorney for Petitioner

Date: _____   _ _[Signature]_ _
                             _ _[Typed name]_ _
                             Attorney for Respondent

Copies: Original (file with court clerk); copy for other attorney or party; office copies.

§11.40 (2) Form: Application for Order Shortening Time and Order

_ _[Attorney name]_ _
_ _[State Bar number]_ _
_ _[Address]_ _
_ _[Telephone number]_ _

Attorney for _ _[name]_ _

SUPERIOR COURT OF CALIFORNIA
COUNTY OF _ _ _ _ _ _ _ _ _

Marriage of	)	**No.** _ _ _ _ _ _
	)	
Petitioner: _ _ _ _ _ _ _ _	)	**APPLICATION FOR ORDER**
	)	**SHORTENING TIME AND**
Respondent: _ _ _ _ _ _ _	)	**ORDER**
	)	
_____	)	

I, _ _[name]_ _, **declare as follows:**

1. I am the attorney for _ _[name]_ _, _ _[petitioner/respondent]_ _ **in this action.**

2. It is necessary that time for service and filing of the responsive papers to _ _[respondent's/petitioner's]_ _ _ _[specify, e.g., Order to Show Cause]_ _ **filed on** _ _[date]_ _ **be shortened so that service and filing be on or before** _ _[date]_ _.

3. _ _[Indicate necessity for order, e.g., respondent, who had difficulty retaining counsel, did not contact me until three days before the date set for hearing, which left insufficient time to prepare and submit responsive papers at least 9 court days before the hearing, as required by statute and local rule, and opposing counsel would not stipulate to waiving the time requirements]_ _.

[Add if notice required by local rules]

4. _ _[Indicate manner in which notice has been given or reason it has not been given]_ _.

[Continue]

I declare under penalty of perjury under the laws of the State of California that the foregoing is true and correct.

Date: _____

__[Signature]__
_ _[Typed name]_ _
Attorney for
_ _[Petitioner/Respondent]_ _

ORDER

Good cause appearing, it is ordered that time for service and filing of the responsive papers to _ _[petitioner's/respondent's]_ _ _ _[specify, e.g., Order to Show Cause]_ _ filed on _ _[date]_ _ be shortened so that service and filing be on or before _ _[date]_ _.

Date: _____ _____
Judge of the Superior Court

Copies: Original (submit to court clerk); copy for other attorney or party; office copies.

§11.41 3. Moving Party's Reply Papers

There should rarely be any need for the moving party to file reply papers in response to the responding party's opposition papers, except perhaps when the responding party has used those papers to request affirmative relief as allowed under Fam C §213 (see §11.35). Any reply papers must be filed and served at least 5 court days before the hearing. CCP §1005(a)(13)–(b). They must further be served by personal delivery, facsimile transmission, express mail, or other means consistent with CCP §§1010, 1011, 1012, and 1013 that are reasonably calculated to ensure delivery not later than the close of the next business day after the time they are filed. CCP §1005(c).

When the responsive papers request affirmative relief that the moving party's attorney believes requires reply papers, but the responsive papers are served and filed too late to allow a timely reply, counsel should consider seeking a stipulation waiving the 5-court-day requirement or an order shortening time.

The moving party's reply papers may respond only to the responding party's opposition papers. To the extent that the reply papers present new factual or legal issues, they are in substance moving papers and must be served and filed in accordance with the requirement of CCP §1005(a)(13)-(b) for moving papers (see §11.34) unless an Order Shortening Time is obtained. Otherwise, if the time of service does not allow the responding party an adequate opportunity to contest the new claims, the court must either grant a continuance or refuse to consider the new issues. *Marriage of Hoffmeister* (1984) 161 CA3d 1163, 1169, 208 CR 345.

4. Hearing

§11.42   a. Continuances

The responding party to an Order to Show Cause or Notice of Motion rarely receives much more than the minimum 16-court-day notice required by CCP §1005(a)(13)-(b) and may, on an Order Shortening Time, receive considerably less. When the papers are served at the outset of the case and the responding party decides only after being served to retain an attorney, there may be insufficient time for the attorney to prepare adequately for the hearing, particularly when complex issues are involved. Consequently, it is not uncommon under such circumstances for the responding party to seek a continuance of the hearing. An attorney seeking a continuance must do so, however, at the earliest possible time. See, *e.g.,* Alameda Ct R 11.0(3)(G) (request for continuance must be made by 2 court days prior to the hearing and will be viewed with disfavor if made at hearing unless good cause shown).

The logical first step is to approach the opposing attorney and request a stipulation to the continuance. Written stipulations to a first continuance are rarely denied when local court rules are followed. See, *e.g.,* Santa Clara Fam. Ct R 5.I. (7)(a) (before first hearing date, one continuance may be obtained by telephone call to calendar secretary and confirmed by letter if parties stipulate to continuance and new date). Often, however, the opposing attorney will require, as a condition of the stipulation, that any orders granted by the court pending the hearing remain in effect until the new hearing date. For a form of stipulation for continuance, see §11.43.

If the opposing attorney will not stipulate to a continuance, an application will have to be made to the court. There is no policy of liberality in favor of parties seeking continuances. Rather, continuances should be granted grudgingly and only on a showing of good cause. *Marriage of Hoffmeister* (1984) 161 CA3d 1163, 1168, 208 CR 345, 348. Consequently, requests for continuances must, as indicated above, always be made at the earliest possible time, and the requesting attorney should be prepared to proceed if the request is denied. For a form of application for continuance and order, see §11.44.

§11.43   (1) Form: Stipulation for Continuance

_ _[Attorney name]_ _
_ _[State Bar number]_ _
_ _[Address]_ _
_ _[Telephone number]_ _

Attorney for _ _[name]_ _

**SUPERIOR COURT OF CALIFORNIA
COUNTY OF** _ _ _ _ _ _ _ _ _

Marriage of	)	**No.** _ _ _ _ _
	)	
Petitioner: _ _ _ _ _ _ _ _	)	**STIPULATION FOR**
	)	**CONTINUANCE**
Respondent: _ _ _ _ _ _ _	)	_ _[AND ORDER]_ _
	)	
_____	)	

_ _[Name]_ _, **petitioner, and** _ _[name]_ _, **respondent, hereby stipulate that the hearing set for** _ _[date]_ _ **on** _ _[petitioner's/respondent's]_ _ _ _[specify, e.g., Order to Show Cause]_ _ **be continued to** _ _[date]_ _ **and** _ _[time]_ _ **in Department** _ _ _ _ _ _.

[Add if applicable]

All temporary restraining orders granted by the Court on _ _[date]_ _ **will remain in effect until the new hearing date.**

[Continue]

Date: _____   _ _[Signature]_ _
                            _ _[Typed name]_ _
                            Attorney for Petitioner

Date: _____   __*[Signature]*__
                        _ _*[Typed name]*_ _
                        Attorney for Respondent

*[Add if local rules require court approval of continuance
before calendaring new date]*

ORDER

The hearing set for _ _*[date]*_ _ **on** _ _*[petitioner's/respon-*
*dent's]*_ _ _*[specify, e.g., Order to Show Cause]*_ _ **is continued
to** _ _*[date]*_ _ **and** _ _*[time]*_ _ **in Department** _ _ _ _ _ _.

[Add if applicable]

All temporary restraining orders granted by this Court on
_ _*[date]*_ _ **will remain in effect until the new hearing date.**

[Continue]

Date: _____   _____
                        Judge of the Superior Court

Copies: Original (submit to court clerk); copy for other attorney
or party; office copies.

§11.44   (2) Form: Application for Continuance and Order

_ _[Attorney name]_ _
_ _[State Bar number]_ _
_ _[Address]_ _
_ _[Telephone number]_ _

Attorney for _ _[name]_ _

**SUPERIOR COURT OF CALIFORNIA
COUNTY OF _ _ _ _ _ _ _ _ _**

Marriage of	)	**No.** _ _ _ _ _
	)	
Petitioner: _ _ _ _ _ _ _ _	)	**APPLICATION FOR**
	)	**CONTINUANCE AND**
Respondent: _ _ _ _ _ _ _	)	**ORDER**
	)	
_____	)	

I, _ _[name]_ _, **declare as follows:**

1. I am the attorney for _ _[name]_ _, _ _[petitioner/respondent]_ _ **in this action.**

2. It is necessary that the hearing on _ _[petitioner's/respondent's]_ _ _ _[specify, e.g., Order to Show Cause]_ _ **filed on** _ _[date]_ _ **be continued to** _ _[date]_ _.

3. _ _[Indicate necessity for order, e.g., respondent, who had difficulty retaining counsel, did not contact me until three days before the date set for hearing, which left insufficient time to prepare adequately for the hearing because determination of the opposing party's business income for purposes of support issues requires the taking of his deposition and the obtaining and review of voluminous records, and opposing counsel would not stipulate to a continuance]_ _.

[Add if applicable]

4. All temporary restraining orders granted by the Court on _ _[date]_ _ **may remain in effect until the new hearing date.**

[Add if notice required by local rules]

[5]. _ _*[Indicate manner in which notice has been given or reason it has not been given.]* _ _

[Continue]

I declare under penalty of perjury under the laws of the State of California that the foregoing is true and correct.

Date: _____   __*[Signature]*__
                             _ _*[Typed name]* _ _
                             Attorney for _ _*[Petitioner/ Respondent]* _ _

ORDER

Good cause appearing, it is ordered that the hearing on _ _*[petitioner's/respondent's]* _ _ _ _*[specify, e.g., Order to Show Cause]* _ _ **filed on** _ _*[date]* _ _ **be continued to** _ _*[date]* _ _ **and** _ _*[time]* _ _ **in Department** _ _ _ _ _ _ .

[Add if applicable]

All temporary restraining orders granted by this Court on _ _*[date]* _ _ **will remain in effect until the new hearing date.**

[Continue]

Date: _____   __*[Signature]*__
                             _ _*[Typed name]* _ _
                             Attorney for _ _*[Petitioner/ Respondent]* _ _

Date: _____   _____
                             Judge of the Superior Court

Copies: Original (submit to court clerk); copy for other attorney or party; office copies.

§11.45   b. "Meet and Confer" Requirements; Production of Financial Documents

Some courts have adopted local rules requiring the attorneys to "meet and confer" before the hearing. The purpose and content of such rules are well illustrated by Alameda Ct R 11.0(3)(A). The Alameda County rule requires attorneys and parties to meet before their matter is heard to review the pending issues, inspect documents, and exchange information so that issues may be resolved, facts stipulated to, and the remaining issues clearly delineated and presented to the court at the hearing. The court may, in its discretion, refuse to admit in evidence documents and information not exchanged before the hearing. When the hearing is called, the attorneys must advise the court on which issues have been resolved and which are still contested. On stipulations regarding temporary orders, see §§11.12 (discussion), 11.13 (form).

Another requirement sometimes found in local rules is for the production of financial documents (*e.g.,* wage stubs, tax returns), either before or on the date of the hearing when there are requests for support, attorney fees, or other financial relief. See, *e.g.,* Contra Costa Ct R 12.4.F.3 (when support at issue, income documents to be furnished to other party at least 7 calendar days before hearing).

c. Peremptory Challenge of Hearing Judge

§11.46 (1) Discussion

Any party or attorney may prevent any judge, court commissioner, or referee from presiding at a hearing on temporary orders by making a timely challenge under CCP §170.6. The challenge is an oral or written motion, supported by an affidavit, a declaration under penalty of perjury, or an oral statement under oath that the judicial officer before whom the matter is pending or to whom it is assigned is prejudiced against a party or attorney, or against a party's or attorney's interest, so that the challenging party or attorney cannot, or believes he or she cannot, have a fair and impartial hearing before the officer. CCP §170.6(a)(2). Challenges under §170.6 are known as "peremptory" challenges because the section allows for automatic disqualification without specific allegations or proof of grounds. CCP §170.6(a)(3). Only one peremptory challenge is allowed a party or an attorney in any one action. CCP §170.6(a)(3).

Judicial officers may also be challenged for cause under CCP §170.1, but, because specific allegations and proof are required, peremptory challenges under §170.6 are much more common. A challenge for cause might be based, for example, on such matters as personal knowledge of disputed evidentiary facts, related service as an attorney, financial interest, relationship to a party or attorney, prospective employment or service as a dispute resolution neutral, or direction of the parties to participation in an alternative dispute resolution process in which the neutral has a previous relationship with the judicial officer. Code of Civil Procedure §170.6(a)(2) provides that the motion may not be made after the hearing commences and sets out several specific deadlines for making the motion:

- When the judicial officer, except for a judge assigned to the case for all purposes, is known at least ten days before the hearing date, the motion must be made at least five days before that date (the "ten-day/five-day" rule);

- When there is a master calendar, the motion must be made to the judge supervising the master calendar no later than when the cause is assigned for hearing;

- When the case has been assigned to a judge for all purposes, the motion must be made to the assigned judge or to the presiding judge within ten days after notice of the all-purpose assignment or, when the moving party has not yet appeared, within ten days after his or her appearance; and

- When the court has only one judge, the motion must be made within 30 days after the appearance of the party who is making the motion or whose attorney is making the motion.

For purposes of the ten-day/five-day rule, the judicial officer is "known" when there is "reasonable assurance" that the officer assigned to preside at the hearing will in fact do so. *People v Superior Court* (Lavi) (1993) 4 C4th 1164, 1183, 17 CR2d 815.

For the master calendar rule to apply, there must be a true master calendar assignment of a ready case to a ready courtroom. 4 C4th at 1177. A "ready" courtroom is one that is available or reasonably expected to become available shortly so that the hearing may commence. 4 C4th at 1177 n8.

The all-purpose assignment rule applies when (1) the method of assigning cases instantly pinpoints the judicial officer whom the parties can expect to ultimately preside at trial, and (2) that same judicial officer will be expected to process the case in its totality from the time of the assignment. 4 C4th at 1180. An assignment to a department by number, rather than to a judicial officer by name, can be an all-purpose assignment if (1) a particular judicial officer, whose identity is either known to the litigant or discoverable on reasonable inquiry, regularly presides in that department, and (2) there is reasonable certainty that that judicial officer will ultimately preside at the hearing. 4 C4th at 1180 n11. For purposes of the 10-day time limit following notice of the all-purpose assignment, service of the notice by mail extends the period for filing a peremptory challenge by 5 days. *California Bus. Council v Superior Court* (1997) 52 CA4th 1100, 62 CR2d 7. When a judge is replaced after a party has appeared, the parties have 15 days from the assignment to file a peremptory challenge to the successor judge. *Cybermedia, Inc. v Superior Court* (Brown) (1999) 72 CA4th 910, 82 CR2d 126. For purposes of the 10-day time limit following a party's appearance, the appearance referred to is a general appearance. A special appearance, *e.g.,* a motion to quash service, does not start the time limit running. *La Seigneurie U.S. Holdings, Inc. v Superior Court* (1994) 29 CA4th 1500, 35 CR2d 175.

Note that a peremptory challenge under CCP §170.6 need not be used to disqualify a commissioner, referee, or attorney sitting as a temporary judge. Rather, the party may simply refuse to stipulate to the temporary judge. Counsel should be aware, however, that the stipulation may be oral, written, express, or implied. See §11.49.

§11.47 (2) Form: Peremptory Challenge

_ _[Attorney name]_ _
_ _[State Bar number]_ _
_ _[Address]_ _
_ _[Telephone number]_ _

Attorney for _ _[name]_ _

SUPERIOR COURT OF CALIFORNIA
COUNTY OF _ _ _ _ _ _ _ _ _

Marriage of	)	No. _ _ _ _ _
	)	
Petitioner: _ _ _ _ _ _ _ _	)	**PEREMPTORY CHALLENGE**
	)	
Respondent: _ _ _ _ _ _ _	)	
	)	
_____	)	

I, _ _[name]_ _, **declare as follows:**

1. I am the _ _[petitioner/respondent/petitioner's attorney/respondent's attorney]_ _ **in this action.**

2. The Honorable _ _[name]_ _, **the** _ _[judge/court commissioner/referee]_ _ _ _[before whom a hearing in this action is pending/to whom a hearing in this action is assigned]_ _ **is prejudiced against**

[Either]

_ _[my client/me]_ _.

[Or]

_ _[my client's interest/my interest]_ _.

[Continue]

3. I cannot, or believe that I cannot, have a fair and impartial hearing before the _ _[judge/court commissioner/referee]_ _.

WHEREFORE, I request that the Honorable _ _[name]_ _ **be disqualified under Code of Civil Procedure section 170.6 from hearing any matter in this action.**

I declare under penalty of perjury under the laws of the State of California that the foregoing is true and correct.

Date: _____   _ _[Signature]_ _
                              _ _[Typed name]_ _
                              _ _[Petitioner/Respondent/
                              Attorney for Petitioner/Attorney
                              for Respondent]_ _

Copies: Original (file with court clerk); copy for other attorney or party; office copies.

Comment: Any affidavit, declaration under penalty of perjury, or oral statement under oath supporting a peremptory challenge must be in substantially the form provided in CCP §170.6(a)(5). CCP §170.6(a)(5)–(6). Printed forms for making challenges under CCP §170.6 are available in some courts and should be used when available. Otherwise, the form provided here may be used. When a printed form is not available and a written challenge has not been prepared, an oral challenge may be made. In that event, counsel should advise the court: "There will be a challenge under CCP §170.6, Your Honor. May I please be sworn?" The form provided here may be used for oral, as well as written, challenges. For oral challenges, the form should be modified by eliminating the first and last sentences and the paragraph numbers.

§11.48   d. Presence of "Support Person" When Protective Orders Sought

When protective orders under Fam C §§6320–6322 (see §11.6) are being sought, a "support person" must be permitted to accompany either party to the hearing. Fam C §6303(b). The party may select any individual to act as the support person; no certification, training, or other special qualification is required. Fam C §6303(a). When the party is not represented by an attorney, the support person may sit with the party at the table that is generally reserved for the party and his or her attorney. Fam C §6303(b). The support person's role is to provide moral and emotional support for the party, not to act as a legal adviser or to give legal advice. Fam C §6303(a). The court may remove the support person if it would be in the interest of justice to do so or if the court believes that he or she is prompting, swaying, or influencing the party. Fam C §6303(e).

e. Conduct of Hearing

§11.49   (1) Temporary Judge as Hearing Officer

Many counties use temporary judges (commissioners, referees, and attorneys) to preside over hearings on temporary orders. A temporary judge may act only on stipulation of the "parties litigant." Cal Const art VI, §21. In this regard, "parties litigant" refers only to parties appearing at the hearing. Thus, when one party does not appear, the appearing party's agreement to the temporary judge is sufficient. *Sarracino v Superior Court* (1974) 13 C3d 1, 10, 118 CR 21.

In the case of a court commissioner, the stipulation need not be in writing. Indeed, it may even be implied by the parties' conduct. An appearance before a commissioner and submission of the matter to him or her for consideration constitute a "de facto stipulation" sufficient to empower the commissioner to act as a temporary judge. *E.N.W. v Michael W.* (1983) 149 CA3d 896, 899, 198 CR 355. If a party refuses to stipulate to a commissioner as a temporary judge, the Presiding Judge can appoint the commissioner to preside as a fact finding referee and report the findings to the court. CCP §259. Such a reference must be limited to the determination of specific factual issues and may not include legal issues. See *Settlemire v Superior Court* (2003) 105 CA4th 666, 129 CR2d 560 (broad order for reference improperly delegated judicial duties).

For anyone other than a court commissioner (or, in a small claims case, a temporary judge under Cal Rules of Ct 2.816) to act as a temporary judge, Cal Rules of Ct 2.831 prescribes certain requirements for the stipulation, including that it be in writing and submitted for approval to the presiding judge (or the supervising judge of a branch court). But the California Supreme Court has held that these requirements are not mandatory, but merely directory, and has approved the view that, for referees as well as for commissioners, a party's consent may be oral, written, express, or implied. *In re Richard S.* (1991) 54 C3d 857, 865, 2 CR2d 2.

§11.50   (2) Time Allotted

Because of their case loads, most courts have stated time limits, *e.g.,* 15 or 20 minutes, for hearings on Orders to Show Cause and Notices of Motion. When a longer hearing will be necessary, counsel should inform the court, ideally at the time the hearing is set. Some courts have special setting calendars or procedures for longer hearings. When a matter set for the standard hearing calendar appears to require extended time, the court may allow it to remain on the calendar or require that other arrangements be made. See, *e.g.,* Marin Ct R 6.15(D) (when both parties believe that matter cannot be completed in 20 minutes, they must so inform court when matter called; judge may set matter on another date or, if calendar permits, order matter to proceed as set).

§11.51   (3) Procedure

Family law courts have considerable discretion to limit the presentation of evidence at hearings. Indeed, except for contempt proceedings, courts may exercise that discretion to exclude oral testimony entirely. *Reifler v Superior Court* (1974) 39 CA3d 479, 485, 114 CR 356. Consequently, counsel must prepare moving or opposition papers with the understanding that the court has the authority to decide the matter solely on the basis of those papers. See Cal Rules of Ct 3.1306(a) (evidence received at law and motion hearing must be by declaration, or request for judicial notice without testimony or cross-examination, unless the court orders otherwise for good cause shown). See also Cal Rules of Ct 5.118(f) (court may grant or deny relief solely on basis of application, responses, and any points and authorities memorandum). Under Cal Rules of Ct 3.1306(b) a party seeking to introduce oral testimony must file a written request no later than 3 court days before the hearing. Note that some counties require advance notice when a party wants the judge to read the file before the hearing. San Diego Ct R 5.5.11 (J), upheld in *Lammers v Superior Court* (2000) 83 CA4th 1309, 100 CR2d 455.

Because of their case loads, most courts have developed hearing procedures designed to significantly limit the time consumed by the individual cases on their hearing calendars. The standard approach is to emphasize reliance on the moving and opposing declarations and to strongly discourage oral testimony. See, *e.g.,* San Diego Ct R 5.5.11(H) (court policy to consider only filed papers; oral testimony will generally not be received). In *Marriage of Stevenot* (1984) 154 CA3d 1051, 1059 n3, 202 CR 116, the appellate court endorsed the trial court's approach in reviewing the moving and responding papers before hearing, allowing counsel to make offers of proof of matters not in the declarations, making inquiries of the parties and attorneys as necessary to gain information needed to make its decision, and permitting counsel to argue their positions. Even under abbreviated procedures, however, evidence must be presented in declarations under penalty of perjury, by offers of proof, or through oral testimony to support the court's decision. *County of Alameda v Moore* (1995) 33 CA4th 1422, 1424, 40 CR2d 18 (trial court decision reversed because based on unsworn statements of counsel).

The time pressure inherent in hearings on temporary orders places a premium on effective preparation, organization, and presentation. This task will be made easier if the attorney is familiar with the approach of the particular court and judge. New attorneys will benefit from consulting experienced ones in that regard and even, if practical, from observing temporary order proceedings before the particular judge prior to the hearing date. The client should always be informed in advance about the realities of the court calendar and the procedures likely to be followed.

It may be helpful for the attorney to have a concise list of the relief requested by the parties. This will enable him or her to argue in an orderly fashion and, when the judge announces the rulings, to check them off against the list to ensure that the judge rules on all the requested items.

5. Order After Hearing

§11.52   a. Statement of Decision; Findings

Parties are generally not entitled to a statement of decision under CCP §632 or otherwise to written findings after a hearing on temporary orders (see *Maria P. v Riles* (1987) 43 C3d 1281, 1294, 240 CR 872, 880), but there are exceptions. For example, Fam C §4056(b) requires the court to make several specific findings on child support issues on a party's request. The findings are listed in §8.28. Also on a party's request, findings are required in custody proceedings (*Michael U. v Jamie B.* (1985) 39 C3d 787, 792, 218 CR 39, 42), and a statement of "reasons" is required whenever a request for joint custody is granted or denied (Fam C §3082).

§11.53   b. Form of Order

The Judicial Council has adopted a Restraining Order After Hearing form to be used whenever protective orders (see §11.6) are made. The Council has also adopted a Findings and Order After Hearing form (Judicial Council Form FL-340) to be used whenever any orders *other than* protective orders are made. Finally, the Council has adopted seven attachment forms to be used, depending on the particular orders made, in conjunction with these forms:

- Child Custody and Visitation Order Attachment (Judicial Council Form FL-341);

- Supervised Visitation Order (Judicial Council Form FL-341(A));

- Child Support Information and Order Attachment (Judicial Council Form FL-342);

- Non-Guideline Child Support Findings Attachment (Judicial Council Form FL-342(A));

- Spousal, Partner, or Family Support Order Attachment (Judicial Council Form FL-343);

- Property Order Attachment to Findings and Order After Hearing (Judicial Council Form FL-344); and

- Other Orders (Domestic Violence Prevention) (Judicial Council Form DV-170).

When orders are made that address issues that are not specifically provided for on the forms (*e.g.,* examination by vocational training consultant, pendente lite sale of property, or appointment of receiver), they should be set forth on an attachment to the Findings and Order After Hearing form and referred to at Item 8 on that form.

§11.54 (1) Form: Restraining Order After Hearing (CLETS) (Judicial Council Form DV-130)

DV-130

Restraining Order After Hearing (Order of Protection)

Clerk stamps date here when form is filed.

(1) Protected person's name:

_____

(*first*)   (*middle*)   (*last*)

Protected person's address *(skip this if you have a lawyer)*: *(If you want your address to be private, give a mailing address instead):*

City: _____ State: _____ Zip: _____
Telephone number *(optional)*: _____

Lawyer *(if any)*: *(Name, address, telephone number, and State Bar number)*: _____

Fill in court name and street address:

Superior Court of California, County of

(2) List the full names of all family or household members protected by this order: _____

_____

_____

Fill in case number:

Case Number:

(3) Restrained person's name:

_____

(*first*)   (*middle*)   (*last*)

Description of that person: Sex: ☐ M ☐ F Height: _____ Weight: _____ Race: _____
Hair Color: _____ Eye Color: _____ Age: _____ Date of Birth: _____
Relationship to protected person: _____

(4) **The court orders are on pages 2 and 3 and attachment pages *(if any).***

The hearing was on *(date)*: _____ with *(name of judicial officer)*: _____

The orders end on *(date)*: [_____] at *(time)*: [_____]
- *If no end date is written, the restraining order ends 3 years after the date of the hearing.*
- *If no time is written, the restraining order ends at midnight on the end date.*
- *Note: Custody, visitation, child support, and spousal support orders have different end dates. Custody, visitation, and child support orders usually end when the child is 18.*

(5) ☐ The people in (1) and (3) must return to court/department _____ on *(date)*: _____
     at *(time)*: _____ ☐ a.m. ☐ p.m. to review *(specify issues)*: _____

Certificate of Compliance With VAWA

This protective order meets all Full Faith and Credit requirements of the Violence Against Women Act, 18 U.S.C. § 2265 (1994) (VAWA). This court has jurisdiction over the parties and the subject matter; the restrained person has been afforded reasonable notice and an opportunity to be heard as provided by the laws of this jurisdiction. **This order is valid and entitled to enforcement in each jurisdiction throughout the 50 United States, the District of Columbia, all tribal lands, and all U.S. territories, commonwealths, and possessions and shall be enforced as if it were an order of that jurisdiction.**

This is a Court Order.

Judicial Council of California, www.courtinfo.ca.gov
Revised July 1, 2006, Mandatory Form
Family Code, § 6200 et seq. Approved by DOJ

Restraining Order After Hearing (CLETS—OAH)
(Order of Protection)
(Domestic Violence Prevention)

DV-130, Page 1 of 5 →

Case Number: _____

Your name: _____

(6) ☐ **Personal Conduct Orders**

The person in ③ must **not** do the following things to the protected people listed in ① and ②:

 a. ☐ Harass, attack, strike, threaten, assault (sexually or otherwise), hit, follow, stalk, molest, destroy personal property, disturb the peace, keep under surveillance, or block movements

 b. ☐ Contact (either directly or indirectly), telephone, or send messages or mail or e-mail

   ☐ Except for brief and peaceful contact as required for court-ordered visitation of children unless a criminal protective order says otherwise

 c. ☐ Take any action, directly or through others, to get the addresses or locations of any protected persons or of their family members, caretakers, or guardians. *(If item c is not checked, the court has found good cause not to make this order.)*

Peaceful written contact through a lawyer or through a process server or another person in order to serve legal papers is allowed and does not violate this order.

 ☐ A criminal protective order on Form CR-160 is in effect. Case Number: _____

 County *(if known):* _____ Expiration Date: _____ *(If more orders, list them in item* ⑰*))*

(7) ☐ **Stay-Away Order**

The person in ③ must stay at least _____ yards away from:

 a. ☐ The person listed in ①   d. ☐ The children's school or child care

 b. ☐ The people listed in ②   e. ☐ Other *(specify):* _____

 c. ☐ Home ☐ Job ☐ Vehicle of person in ①   _____

(8) ☐ **Move-Out Order**

The person in ③ must move out immediately from *(address):* _____

(9) ☐ **Child Custody and Visitation**

Child custody and visitation are ordered on the attached Form DV-140 or *(specify other form):* _____

(10) ☐ **Child Support**

Child support is ordered on the attached Form DV-160 or *(specify other form):* _____

(11) ☐ **Spousal Support**

Spousal support is ordered on the attached Form FL-343 or *(specify other form):* _____

(12) **No Guns or Other Firearms**

The person in ③ **cannot own, possess, have, buy or try to buy, receive or try to receive, or in any other way get a gun or firearm.**

(13) **Turn in or sell guns and firearms.**

The person in ③:

• Must sell to a licensed gun dealer or turn in to police any guns or firearms that he or she has or controls. This must be done within 24 hours of receiving this order.

• Must bring a receipt to the court within 72 hours of receiving this order, to prove that guns and firearms have been turned in or sold.

This is a Court Order.

Revised July 1, 2006   **Restraining Order After Hearing (CLETS—OAH)**   DV-130, Page 2 of 5
        (Order of Protection)   ➜
        (Domestic Violence Prevention)

	Case Number:
Your name: _____	

(14) ☐ Record Unlawful Communications

The person in ①has the right to record communications made by the person in ③ that violate the judge's orders.

(15) ☐ Batterer Intervention Program

The person in ③ must go to and pay for a 52-week batterer intervention program and show written proof of completion to the court. This program must be approved by the probation department.

(16) No Fee to Notify (Serve) Restrained Person

If the sheriff or marshal serves this order, he or she will do it for free.

(17) ☐ Other Orders

Other orders relating to property control, debt payment, attorney fees, restitution, and/or other issues are in attached Form DV-170 or *(specify other form):* _____

(18) Service

a. ☐ The people in ① and ③ were at the hearing or agreed in writing to this order. No other proof of service is needed.

b. ☐ The person in ① was at the hearing. The person in ③ was not.

    (1) ☐ Proof of service of Form DV-110 was presented to the court. The judge's orders in this form are the same as in Form DV-110 except for the end date. The person in ③ must be served. This order can be served by mail.

    (2) ☐ Proof of service of Form DV-110 was presented to the court. The judge's orders in this form are different from the orders in Form DV-110. Someone—not the people in ① or ②—must personally "serve" a copy of this order to the person in ③.

(19) Attached pages are orders.

- Number of pages attached to this 5-page form: _____
- All of the attached pages are part of this order.
- Attachments include *(check all that apply):*

    ☐ DV-140 ☐ DV-145 ☐ DV-150 ☐ DV-160 ☐ DV-170 ☐ FL-343
    ☐ Other *(specify):* _____

Date: _____

▶ _____

Judge (or Judicial Officer)

This is a Court Order.

Case Number: _____

Your name: _____

Instructions for Law Enforcement

(20) Start Date and End Date of Orders

The orders *start* on the earlier of the following dates:
- The hearing date on page 1 *or*
- The date next to the judge's signature on page 3.

The orders *end* on the end date in item 4 on page 1. If no end date is listed, they end 3 years from the hearing date.

(21) Arrest Required If Order Is Violated

If an officer has probable cause to believe that the restrained person had notice of the order and has disobeyed the order, the officer must arrest the restrained person. (Penal Code, §§ 836(c)(1), 13701(b).) A violation of the order may be a violation of Penal Code section 166 or 273.6.

(22) Notice/Proof of Service

Law enforcement must first determine if the restrained person had notice of the orders. If notice cannot be verified, the restrained person must be advised of the terms of the orders. If the restrained person then fails to obey the orders, the officer must enforce them. (Family Code, § 6383.)

Consider the restrained person "served" (noticed) if:
- The officer sees a copy of the *Proof of Service* or confirms that the *Proof of Service* is on file; *or*
- The restrained person was at the restraining order hearing or was informed of the order by an officer. (Fam. Code, § 6383; Pen. Code, § 836(c)(2).) An officer can obtain information about the contents of the order in the Domestic Violence Restraining Orders System (DVROS). (Fam. Code, § 6381(b)(c).)

(23) If the Protected Person Contacts the Restrained Person

Even if the protected person invites or consents to contact with the restrained person, the orders remain in effect and must be enforced. The protected person cannot be arrested for inviting or consenting to contact with the restrained person. The orders can be changed only by another court order. (Pen. Code, § 13710(b).)

(24) Child Custody and Visitation
- The custody and visitation orders are on Form DV-140, items (3) and (4). They are sometimes also written on additional pages or referenced in DV-140 or other orders that are not part of the restraining order.
- **Forms DV-100 and DV-105 are not orders. Do not enforce them.**

(25) Enforcing the Restraining Order in California

Any law enforcement officer in California who receives, sees, or verifies the orders on a paper copy, the California Law Enforcement Telecommunications System (CLETS), or in an NCIC Protection Order File must enforce the orders.

(26) Conflicting Orders

A protective order issued in a criminal case on Form CR-160 takes precedence in enforcement over any conflicting civil court order. (Pen. Code, § 136.2(e)(2).) Any nonconflicting terms of the civil restraining order remain in full force. An emergency protective order (Form EPO-001) that is in effect between the same parties and is more restrictive than other restraining orders takes precedence over all other restraining orders. (Pen. Code, § 136.2.)

This is a Court Order.

Your name: _____

Case Number: _____

Warnings and Notices to the Restrained Person in ❸

(27) **If you do not obey this order, you can be arrested and charged with a crime.**
- It is a felony to take or hide a child against this order. You can go to prison and/or pay a fine.
- If you travel to another state or to tribal lands or make the protected person do so, with the intention of disobeying this order, you can be charged with a federal crime.
- If you do not obey this order, you can go to prison and/or pay a fine.

(28) **You cannot have guns or firearms.**

You cannot own, have, possess, buy or try to buy, receive or try to receive, or otherwise get a gun or firearm while the order is in effect. If you do, you can go to jail and pay a $1,000 fine. You must sell to a licensed gun dealer or turn in to police any guns or firearms that you have or control. The judge will ask you for proof that you did so. If you do not obey this order, you can be charged with a crime. Federal law says you cannot have guns or ammunition while the order is in effect.

(Clerk will fill out this part)
—Clerk's Certificate—

[seal]

I certify that this *Restraining Order After Hearing (Order of Protection)* is a true and correct copy of the original on file in the court.

Date: _____   Clerk, by _____, Deputy

This is a Court Order.

Copies: Original (submit to court clerk); copy for other attorney or party; office copies.

§11.55   (2) Form: Findings and Order After Hearing (Judicial Council Form FL-340)

FL-340

ATTORNEY OR PARTY WITHOUT ATTORNEY *(Name and address)*	FOR COURT USE ONLY

FAX NO. *(optional):*

TELEPHONE NO.:

ATTORNEY FOR *(Name):*

SUPERIOR COURT OF CALIFORNIA, COUNTY OF

STREET ADDRESS:

MAILING ADDRESS:

CITY AND ZIP CODE:

BRANCH NAME:

PETITIONER/PLAINTIFF:

RESPONDENT/DEFENDANT:

OTHER:

	CASE NUMBER:
FINDINGS AND ORDER AFTER HEARING	

1. This proceeding was heard
   on *(date):*   at *(time):*   in Dept.:   Room:
   by Judge *(name):*   ☐ Temporary Judge

   ☐ Petitioner/plaintiff present   ☐ Attorney present *(name):*
   ☐ Respondent/defendant present   ☐ Attorney present *(name):*
   ☐ Other present   ☐ Attorney present *(name):*
   On the order to show cause or motion filed *(date):*   by *(name):*

2. **THE COURT ORDERS**

3. Custody and visitation: ☐ As attached on form FL-341   ☐ Not applicable

4. Child support: ☐ As attached on form FL-342   ☐ Not applicable

5. Spousal or family support: ☐ As attached on form FL-343   ☐ Not applicable

6. Property orders: ☐ As attached on form FL-344   ☐ Not applicable

7. Other orders: ☐ As attached   ☐ Not applicable

8. ☐ Attorney fees *(specify amount):* $
   Payable to *(name and address):*

   Payable   ☐ forthwith   ☐ other *(specify):*

9. All other issues are reserved until further order of court.

Date: _____

▶ _____
JUDICIAL OFFICER

Approved as conforming to court order.

▶ _____

SIGNATURE OF ATTORNEY FOR ☐ PETITIONER / PLAINTIFF ☐ RESPONDENT / DEFENDANT

Page 1 of ___

Form Adopted for Mandatory Use Judicial Council of California FL-340 [Rev. July 1, 2003]	**FINDINGS AND ORDER AFTER HEARING** (Family Law—Custody and Support—Uniform Parentage)	www.courtinfo.ca.gov

Copies: Original (submit to court clerk); copy for other attorney or party; office copies.

§11.56 (3) Form: Child Custody and Visitation Order Attachment (Judicial Council Form FL-341)

FL-341

PETITIONER/PLAINTIFF:	CASE NUMBER:
RESPONDENT/DEFENDANT:	

CHILD CUSTODY AND VISITATION ORDER ATTACHMENT

TO ☐ *Findings and Order After Hearing* ☐ *Judgment*

☐ *Stipulation and Order for Custody and/or Visitation of Children*

☐ *Other (specify):*

1. ☐ **Custody.** Custody of the minor children of the parties is awarded as follows:

Child's name	Date of birth	Legal custody to (person who makes decisions about health, education, etc.)	Physical custody to (person with whom the child lives)

2. ☐ **Visitation**

a. ☐ Reasonable right of visitation to the party without physical custody (**not appropriate in cases involving domestic violence**)

b. ☐ See the attached _____-page document dated *(specify date):*

c. ☐ The parties will go to mediation at *(specify location):*

d. ☐ No visitation

e. ☐ Visitation for the ☐ petitioner ☐ respondent will be as follows:

  (1) ☐ **Weekends starting** *(date):*

    (The first weekend of the month is the first weekend with a Saturday.)

    ☐ 1st ☐ 2nd ☐ 3rd ☐ 4th ☐ 5th weekend of the month

    from _____ at _____ ☐ a.m. ☐ p.m.
       (day of week)   *(time)*

    to _____ at _____ ☐ a.m. ☐ p.m.
      (day of week)   *(time)*

    (a) ☐ The parents will alternate the fifth weekends, with the ☐ petitioner ☐ respondent having the initial fifth weekend, which starts *(date):*

    (b) ☐ The petitioner will have fifth weekends in ☐ odd ☐ even months.

  (2) ☐ **Alternate weekends starting** *(date):*

    The ☐ petitioner ☐ respondent will have the children with him or her during the period

    from _____ at _____ ☐ a.m. ☐ p.m.
       (day of week)   *(time)*

    to _____ at _____ ☐ a.m. ☐ p.m.
      (day of week)   *(time)*

  (3) ☐ **Weekdays starting** *(date):*

    The ☐ petitioner ☐ respondent will have the children with him or her during the period

    from _____ at _____ ☐ a.m. ☐ p.m.
       (day of week)   *(time)*

    to _____ at _____ ☐ a.m. ☐ p.m.
      (day of week)   *(time)*

  (4) ☐ **Other** *(specify days and times as well as any additional restrictions):*

☐ See Attachment 2e(4).

Page 1 of 2

Form Approved for Optional Use
Judicial Council of California
FL-341 [Rev. July 1, 2006]

CHILD CUSTODY AND VISITATION ORDER ATTACHMENT

Family Code, §§ 3020, 3022, 3025, 3040–3043, 3048, 3100, 6340, 7604
www.courtinfo.ca.gov

FL-341

PETITIONER/PLAINTIFF:	CASE NUMBER:
RESPONDENT/DEFENDANT:	

3. ☐ **The court acknowledges** that criminal protective orders in case number (specify):
In (specify court): relating to the parties in this case are in effect
under Penal Code section 136.2, are current, and have priority of enforcement.

4. ☐ **Supervised visitation.** Until ☐ further order of the court ☐ other (specify):
the ☐ petitioner ☐ respondent will have supervised visitation with the minor children according to the schedule
set forth on page 1. **(You must attach form FL-341(A).)**

5. ☐ **Transportation for visitation**

a. ☐ Transportation to the visits will be provided by the ☐ petitioner ☐ respondent
☐ other (specify):

b. ☐ Transportation from the visits will be provided by the ☐ petitioner ☐ respondent
☐ other (specify):

c. ☐ Drop-off of the children will be at (address):
d. ☐ Pick-up of the children will be at (address):
e. ☐ The children will be driven only by a licensed and insured driver. The car or truck must have legal child restraint
devices.
f. ☐ During the exchanges, the parent driving the children will wait in the car and the other parent will wait in his or
her home while the children go between the car and the home.
g. ☐ Other (specify):

6. ☐ **Travel with children.** The ☐ petitioner ☐ respondent ☐ other (name):
must have written permission from the other parent or a court order to take the children out of
a. ☐ the state of California.
b. ☐ the following counties (specify):
c. ☐ other places (specify):

7. ☐ **Child abduction prevention.** There is a risk that one of the parents will take the children out of California without the other
parent's permission. Form FL-341(B) is attached and must be obeyed.

8. ☐ **Holiday schedule.** The children will spend holiday time as listed in the attached ☐ form FL-341(C)
☐ other (specify): ♦

9. ☐ **Additional custody provisions.** The parents will follow the additional custody provisions listed in the attached
☐ form FL-341(D) ☐ other (specify):

10. ☐ **Joint legal custody.** The parents will share joint legal custody as listed in the attached ☐ form FL-341(E)
☐ other (specify):

11. ☐ **Other** (specify):

12. **Jurisdiction.** This court has jurisdiction to make child custody orders in this case under the Uniform Child Custody Jurisdiction and
Enforcement Act (part 3 of the California Family Code, commencing with section 3400).

13. **Notice and opportunity to be heard.** The responding party was given notice and an opportunity to be heard, as provided by the
laws of the State of California.

14. **Country of habitual residence.** The country of habitual residence of the child or children in this case is
☐ the United States ☐ other (specify):

15. **Penalties for violating this order.** If you violate this order, you may be subject to civil or criminal penalties, or both.

FL-341 [Rev. July 1, 2006] **CHILD CUSTODY AND VISITATION ORDER ATTACHMENT** Page 2 of 2

Copies: Original (submit to court clerk); copy for other attorney
or party; office copies.

§11.57 (4) Form: Supervised Visitation Order (Judicial Council Form FL-341(A))

FL-341(A)

PETITIONER / PLAINTIFF:	CASE NUMBER:
RESPONDENT / DEFENDANT:	

SUPERVISED VISITATION ORDER
Attachment to Child Custody and Visitation Order Attachment (form FL-341)

1. Evidence has been presented in support of a request that the contact of ☐ Petitioner ☐ Respondent with the child(ren) be supervised based upon allegations of
   ☐ abduction of child(ren) ☐ physical abuse ☐ drug abuse ☐ neglect
   ☐ sexual abuse ☐ domestic violence ☐ alcohol abuse ☐ other *(specify)*:

   ☐ Petitioner ☐ Respondent disputes these allegations and the court reserves the findings on these issues pending further investigation and hearing or trial.

2. The court finds, under Family Code section 3100, that the best interest of the child(ren) requires that visitation by
   ☐ Petitioner ☐ Respondent must, until further order of the court, be limited to contact supervised by the person(s) set forth in item 6 below pending further investigation and hearing or trial.

THE COURT MAKES THE FOLLOWING ORDERS

3. **CHILD(REN) TO BE SUPERVISED**

Child's name	Birth date	Age	Sex

4. **TYPE**
   a. ☐ Supervised visitation   b. ☐ Supervised exchange only   c. ☐ Therapeutic visitation

5. **SUPERVISED VISITATION PROVIDER**
   a. ☐ Professional (individual provider or supervised visitation center)   b. ☐ Nonprofessional

6. **AUTHORIZED PROVIDER**

Name	Address	Telephone

   ☐ Any other mutually agreed-upon third party as arranged.

7. **DURATION AND FREQUENCY OF VISITS** *(see form FL-341 for specifics of visitation)*:

8. **PAYMENT RESPONSIBILITY**   Petitioner: _____%   Respondent: _____%

9. ☐ Petitioner will contact professional provider or supervised visitation center no later than *(date)*:
   ☐ Respondent will contact professional provider or supervised visitation center no later than *(date)*:

10. **THE COURT FURTHER ORDERS**

Date: _____

_____
JUDICIAL OFFICER

Page 1 of 1

Form Adopted for Mandatory Use
Judicial Council of California
FL-341(A) [Rev. January 1, 2003]

SUPERVISED VISITATION ORDER

Family Code, §§ 3100, 3031
www.courtinfo.ca.gov

§11.58   (5) Form: Child Support Information and Order Attachment (Judicial Council Form FL-342)

FL-342

PETITIONER/PLAINTIFF:	CASE NUMBER:
RESPONDENT/DEFENDANT:	
OTHER PARENT:	

CHILD SUPPORT INFORMATION AND ORDER ATTACHMENT

Attachment to ☐ Findings and Order After Hearing ☐ Restraining Order After Hearing (CLETS)
☐ Judgment ☐ Other

THE COURT USED THE FOLLOWING INFORMATION IN DETERMINING THE AMOUNT OF CHILD SUPPORT:

1. ☐ A printout of a computer calculation and findings is attached and incorporated in this order for all required items not filled out below.

2. ☐ **Income**

	Gross monthly income	Net monthly income	Receiving TANF/CalWORKS
a. Each parent's monthly income is as follows:			
petitioner/plaintiff:	$	$	☐
respondent/defendant:	$	$	☐
other parent:	$	$	☐

   b. Imputation of income. The court finds that the ☐ petitioner/plaintiff ☐ respondent/defendant ☐ other parent has the capacity to earn:
   $_____ per:_____ and has based the support order upon this imputed income.

3. ☐ **Children of This Relationship**
   a. Number of children who are the subjects of the support order (specify):
   b. Approximate percentage of time spent with: petitioner/plaintiff ____%
   respondent/defendant ____%
   other parent ____%

4. ☐ **Hardships**
   Hardships for the following have been allowed in calculating child support:

	petitioner/ plaintiff	respondent/ defendant	other parent	Approximate ending time for the hardship
a. ☐ Other minor children:	$	$	$	
b. ☐ Extraordinary medical expenses:	$	$	$	
c. ☐ Catastrophic losses:	$	$	$	

THE COURT ORDERS

5. ☐ **Low-Income Adjustment**
   a. ☐ The low-income adjustment applies.
   b. ☐ The low-income adjustment does not apply because (specify reasons):

6. ☐ **Child Support**
   a. **Base child support**
   ☐ Petitioner/plaintiff ☐ Respondent/defendant ☐ Other parent must pay child support beginning (date):_____ and continuing until further order of the court, or until the child marries, dies, is emancipated, reaches age 19, or reaches age 18 and is not a full-time high school student, whichever occurs first, as follows:

Child's name	Date of birth	Monthly amount	Payable to (name)

   Payable ☐ on the 1st of the month ☐ one-half on the 1st and one-half on the 15th of the month
   ☐ other (specify):

   b. ☐ **Mandatory additional child support**
   (1) ☐ Child-care costs related to employment or reasonably necessary job training.
   ☐ Petitioner/plaintiff must pay: ____% of total or ☐ $____ per month child-care costs.
   ☐ Respondent/defendant must pay: ____% of total or ☐ $____ per month child-care costs.
   ☐ Other parent must pay: ____% of total or ☐ $____ per month child-care costs.
   ☐ Costs to be paid as follows (specify):

THIS IS A COURT ORDER.   Page 1 of 2

PETITIONER/PLAINTIFF:	CASE NUMBER:
RESPONDENT/DEFENDANT:	
OTHER PARENT:	

THE COURT FURTHER ORDERS

6. b. **Mandatory additional child support** *(continued)*

    (2) ☐ Reasonable uninsured health-care costs for the children

        ☐ Petitioner/plaintiff must pay: ____ % of total or ☐ $ ____ per month.
        ☐ Respondent/defendant must pay: ____ % of total or ☐ $ ____ per month.
        ☐ Other parent must pay: ____ % of total or ☐ $ ____ per month.
        ☐ Costs to be paid as follows *(specify):*

  c. ☐ **Additional child support**

    (1) ☐ Costs related to the educational or other special needs of the children

        ☐ Petitioner/plaintiff must pay: ____ % of total or ☐ $ ____ per month.
        ☐ Respondent/defendant must pay: ____ % of total or ☐ $ ____ per month.
        ☐ Other parent must pay: ____ % of total or ☐ $ ____ per month.
        ☐ Costs to be paid as follows *(specify):*

    (2) ☐ Travel expenses for visitation

        ☐ Petitioner/plaintiff must pay: ____ % of total or ☐ $ ____ per month.
        ☐ Respondent/defendant must pay: ____ % of total or ☐ $ ____ per month.
        ☐ Other parent must pay: ____ % of total or ☐ $ ____ per month.
        ☐ Costs to be paid as follows *(specify):*

Total child support per month: $

7. **Health-Care Expenses**

  a. Health insurance coverage for the minor children of the parties must be maintained by the
    ☐ petitioner/plaintiff ☐ respondent/defendant ☐ other parent if available at no or reasonable cost through their respective places of employment or self-employment. Both parties are ordered to cooperate in the presentation, collection, and reimbursement of any health-care claims.

  b. ☐ Health insurance is not available to the ☐ petitioner/plaintiff ☐ respondent/defendant ☐ other parent at a reasonable cost at this time.

  c. ☐ The party providing coverage must assign the right of reimbursement to the other party.

8. **Earnings Assignment**

An *Order/Notice to Withhold Income for Child Support* (form FL-195) must issue. **Note:** The payor of child support is responsible for the payment of support directly to the recipient until support payments are deducted from the payor's wages, and for any support not paid by the assignment.

9. ☐ **Non-Guideline Order**

This order does not meet the child support guideline set forth in Family Code section 4055. A *Non-Guideline Child Support Findings Attachment* (form FL-342(A)) is attached.

10. ☐ **Employment Search Order (Family Code, § 4505)**

  ☐ Petitioner/plaintiff ☐ Respondent/defendant ☐ Other parent is ordered to seek employment with the following terms and conditions:

11. **Other Orders** *(specify):*

12. **Required Attachments**

A *Notice of Rights and Responsibilities—Health Care Costs and Reimbursement Procedures* and *Information Sheet on Changing a Child Support Order* (form FL-192) must be attached and is incorporated into this order.

13. **Child Support Case Registry Form**

Both parties must complete and file with the court a *Child Support Case Registry Form* (form FL-191) within 10 days of the date of this order. Thereafter, the parties must notify the court of any change in the information submitted within 10 days of the change by filing an updated form.

NOTICE: Any party required to pay child support must pay interest on overdue amounts at the legal rate, which is currently 10 percent per year.

THIS IS A COURT ORDER.

Copies: Original (submit to court clerk); copy for other attorney or party; office copies.

§11.58A   (6) Form: Non-Guideline Child Support Findings Attachment (Judicial Council Form FL-342(A))

FL-342(A)

PETITIONER/PLAINTIFF:	CASE NUMBER:
RESPONDENT/DEFENDANT:	

NON-GUIDELINE CHILD SUPPORT FINDINGS ATTACHMENT

Attachment to ☐ Child Support Information and Order Attachment (form FL-342)
☐ Judgment (Family Law) (form FL-180)   ☐ Other (specify):

The court makes the following findings required by Family Code sections 4056, 4057, and 4065:

1. **STIPULATION TO NON-GUIDELINE ORDER**
   ☐ The child support agreed to by the parties is ☐ below or ☐ above the statewide child support guidelines. The amount of support that would have been ordered under the guideline formula is: $_____ per month. The parties have been fully informed of their rights concerning child support. Neither party is acting out of duress or coercion. Neither party is receiving public assistance and no application for public assistance is pending. The needs of the children will be adequately met by this agreed-upon amount of child support. If the order is below the guideline, no change of circumstances will be required to modify this order. If the order is above the guideline, a change of circumstances will be required to modify this order.

OTHER REBUTTAL FACTORS
2. ☐ **Support calculation**
   a. The guideline amount of child support calculated is: $_____ per month **payable** by ☐ mother ☐ father

   b. The court finds by a preponderance of the evidence that rebuttal factors exist. The rebuttal factors result in an ☐ increase ☐ decrease in child support. The revised amount of support is: $_____ per month.

   c. The court finds the child support amount revised by these factors to be in the best interest of the child and that application of the formula would be unjust or inappropriate in this case.
      These changes remain in effect ☐ until (date):
                                   ☐ until further order

   d. **The factors are:**
      (1) ☐ The sale of the family residence is deferred under Family Code section 3800, and the rental value of the family residence in which the children reside exceeds the mortgage payments, homeowners insurance, and property taxes by: $_____ per month. (Fam. Code, § 4057(b)(2).)

      (2) ☐ The parent paying support has extraordinarily high income, and the amount determined under the guideline would exceed the needs of the child. (Fam. Code, § 4057(b)(3).)

      (3) ☐ The ☐ mother ☐ father is not contributing to the needs of the children at a level commensurate with that party's custodial time. (Fam. Code, § 4057(b)(4).)

      (4) ☐ Special circumstances exist in this case. The special circumstances are:
         (i) ☐ The parents have different timesharing arrangements for different children. (Fam. Code, § 4057(b)(5)(A).)
         (ii) ☐ The parents have substantially equal custody of the children and one parent has a much lower or higher percentage of income used for housing than the other parent. (Fam. Code, § 4057(b)(5)(B).)
         (iii) ☐ The child has special medical or other needs that require support greater than the formula amount. These needs are (Fam. Code, § 4057(b)(5)(C)) (specify):

         (iv) ☐ Other (Fam. Code, § 4057(b)(5)) (specify):

Form Adopted for Mandatory Use
Judicial Council of California
FL-342(A) [Rev. January 1, 2003]

NON-GUIDELINE CHILD SUPPORT FINDINGS ATTACHMENT

Family Code, § 4056
www.courtinfo.ca.gov

§11.59   (7) Form: Spousal, Partner, or Family Support Order Attachment (Judicial Council Form FL-343)

FL-343

PETITIONER/PLAINTIFF:	CASE NUMBER:
RESPONDENT/DEFENDANT:	
OTHER PARENT:	

SPOUSAL, PARTNER, OR FAMILY SUPPORT ORDER ATTACHMENT

TO ☐ *Findings and Order After Hearing*   ☐ *Judgment*   ☐ Other *(specify):*

THE COURT FINDS

1. A printout of a computer calculation of the parties' financial circumstances is attached for all required items not filled out below.

2. **Net income.** The parties' monthly income and deductions are as follows *(complete a, b, or both):*

	Total gross monthly income	Total monthly deductions	Total hardship deductions	Net monthly disposable income
a. Petitioner: ☐ receiving TANF/CalWORKS				
b. Respondent: ☐ receiving TANF/CalWORKS				

3. **Other factors regarding spousal or partner support**
   a. ☐ The parties were married for *(specify numbers):* _____ years _____ months.
   b. ☐ The parties were registered as domestic partners or the equivalent on *(date):*
   c. ☐ The Family Code section 4320 factors were considered, as listed in Attachment 3c.
   d. ☐ The marital standard of living was *(describe):*

     ☐ See Attachment 3d.

   e. ☐ Other *(specify):*

THE COURT ORDERS

4. a. The ☐ petitioner ☐ respondent   must pay to the ☐ petitioner ☐ respondent
   as ☐ temporary ☐ spousal support ☐ family support ☐ partner support
   $ _____ per month, beginning *(date):* _____ , payable through *(specify end date):*

   ☐ payable on the *(specify):* _____ day of each month.
   ☐ Other *(specify):*

   b. ☐ Support must be paid by check, money order, or cash. The support payor's obligation to pay support will terminate on the death, remarriage, or registration of a new domestic partnership of the support payee.

   c. ☐ An earnings assignment for the foregoing support will issue. **(Note:** The payor of spousal, family, or partner support is responsible for the payment of support directly to the recipient until support payments are deducted from the payor's earnings, and for any support not paid by the assignment.)

   d. ☐ Service of the earnings assignment is stayed provided the payor is not more than *(specify number):* _____ days late in the payment of spousal, family, or partner support.

Page 1 of 2

PETITIONER/PLAINTIFF:	CASE NUMBER:
RESPONDENT/DEFENDANT:	
OTHER PARENT:	

5. ☐ The parties must promptly inform each other of any change of employment, including the employer's name, address, and telephone number.

6. ☐ **NOTICE:** It is the goal of this state that each party must make reasonable good faith efforts to become self-supporting as provided for in Family Code section 4320. The failure to make reasonable good faith efforts may be one of the factors considered by the court as a basis for modifying or terminating support.

7. ☐ This order is for family support. Both parties must complete and file with the court a *Child Support Case Registry Form* (form FL-191) within 10 days of the date of this order. The parents must notify the court of any change of information submitted within 10 days of the change by filing an updated form. Form FL-192, *Notice of Rights and Responsibilities* and *Information Sheet on Changing a Child Support Order*, is attached.

8. ☐ The issue of spousal or partner support for the ☐ petitioner ☐ respondent is reserved for a later determination.

9. ☐ The court terminates jurisdiction over the issue of spousal or partner support for the ☐ petitioner ☐ respondent.

10. ☐ Other *(specify):*

NOTICE: Any party required to pay support must pay interest on overdue amounts at the "legal" rate, which is currently 10 percent.

THIS IS A COURT ORDER

| FL-343 [Rev. January 1, 2005] | **SPOUSAL, PARTNER, OR FAMILY SUPPORT ORDER ATTACHMENT**
(Family Law) | Page 2 of 2 |

Copies: Original (submit to court clerk); copy for other attorney or party; office copies.

§11.60 (8) Form: Property Order Attachment to Findings and Order After Hearing (Judicial Council Form FL-344)

FL-344

PETITIONER :	CASE NUMBER:
RESPONDENT:	

PROPERTY ORDER ATTACHMENT
TO FINDINGS AND ORDER AFTER HEARING

THE COURT ORDERS

1. ☐ **Property restraining orders**

   a. The ☐ petitioner ☐ respondent ☐ claimant is restrained from transferring, encumbering, hypothecating, concealing, or in any way disposing of any property, real or personal, whether community, quasi-community, or separate, except in the usual course of business or for the necessities of life.

   b. The ☐ petitioner ☐ respondent must notify the other party of any proposed extraordinary expenses at least five business days before incurring such expenses, and make an accounting of such to the court.

   c. The ☐ petitioner ☐ respondent is restrained from cashing, borrowing against, cancelling, transferring, disposing of, or changing the beneficiaries of any insurance or other coverage, including life, health, automobile, and disability, held for the benefit of the parties or their minor child or children.

   d. The ☐ petitioner ☐ respondent must not incur any debts or liabilities for which the other may be held responsible, other than in the ordinary course of business or for the necessities of life.

2. ☐ **Possession of property.** The exclusive use, possession, and control of the following property that the parties own or are buying is given as specified:

   Property   Given to

   ☐ See Attachment 2.

3. ☐ **Payment of debts.** Payments on the following debts that come due while this order is in effect must be paid as follows:

Total debt	Amount of payments	Pay to	Paid by
$	$		
$	$		
$	$		
$	$		

   ☐ See Attachment 3.

4. ☐ These are temporary orders only. The court will make final orders at the time of judgment.

5. ☐ Other (specify):

Form Adopted for Mandatory Use
Judicial Council of California
FL-344 [Rev. January 1, 2007]

PROPERTY ORDER ATTACHMENT
TO FINDINGS AND ORDER AFTER HEARING
(Family Law)

CEB

Page 1 of 1
Family Code, §§ 2045, 6324
www.courtinfo.ca.gov

Copies: Original (submit to court clerk); copy for other attorney or party; office copies.

§11.61   (9) Form: Other Orders (Domestic Violence Prevention) (Judicial Council Form DV-170)

DV-170 Other Orders	Case Number:

☑ This form is attached to Form DV-130, Restraining Order After Hearing *(Order of Protection).*

(1) Protected person's name: _____

(2) Restrained person's name: _____

(3) ☐ **Property Control**

Only the person in ① can use, possess, and control the following property: _____

_____

(4) ☐ **Debt Payment**

The person in ② must make these payments until this order ends:

☐ *Check here if you need more space. Attach Form MC-020 or a sheet of paper and write "DV-170, Item 4—Debt Payment" at the top.*

Pay to: _____ for: _____ Amount: $_____ Due date: _____

Pay to: _____ for: _____ Amount: $_____ Due date: _____

Pay to: _____ for: _____ Amount: $_____ Due date: _____

(5) ☐ **Property Restraint**

The people in ① and ② must not transfer, borrow against, sell, hide, or get rid of any property, except in the usual course of business or for the necessities of life. In addition, each person must notify the other of any new or big expenses and explain them to the court. *(The person in ② cannot contact the person in ① if the court has made a "no contact" order.)*

(6) ☐ **Attorney Fees and Costs**

The person in ② must pay the following lawyer fees and costs:

Pay to: _____ for: _____ Amount: $_____ Due date: _____

Pay to: _____ for: _____ Amount: $_____ Due date: _____

(7) ☐ **Payments for Costs and Services**

The person in ② must pay the following:

Pay to: _____ for: _____ Amount: $_____ Due date: _____

Pay to: _____ for: _____ Amount: $_____ Due date: _____

Pay to: _____ for: _____ Amount: $_____ Due date: _____

(8)   **Other Orders**   ,

_____

_____

_____

_____

_____

This is a Court Order.

Judicial Council of California, www.courtinfo.ca.gov
Revised July 1, 2006, Mandatory Form
Family Code, §§ 6324, 6340-6344   **Other Orders**
(Domestic Violence Prevention)   DV-170, Page 1 of 1

Copies: Original (submit to court clerk); copy for other attorney or party; office copies.

§11.62   c. Filing and Service

When both parties were represented at the hearing, the applicable Judicial Council forms for the orders after hearing (see forms in §§11.54–11.61) should be submitted to the opposing attorney for approval as conforming to the court's orders before submission to the court for the judge's signature and filing. The cover letter should inform opposing counsel that you expect to receive the signed forms within a specified period, *e.g.,* 10 days. If no response is forthcoming within that period, the orders should be submitted to the court without the attorney's signature, along with a cover letter informing the court of the situation and a copy of the letter (with a proof of service) to the opposing attorney. Assuming that the court approves the orders, the originals will be filed and the submitted copies returned to the attorney. A copy of the orders should be sent to opposing counsel.

The importance of drafting and filing the Findings and Order After Hearing cannot be stressed enough. Minute orders, often issued on thin paper or NCR forms, can be hard to read, even when they are created with an electronic printer, and when they are in the judge's handwriting it can be impossible for someone who did not attend the hearing (such as law enforcement personnel) to decipher.

When the opposing party was not present in court, or when the court did not announce its decision from the bench, it is advisable to have the orders personally served on the party or to have him or her execute and return a Notice and Acknowledgment of Receipt (see form in §10.34). These procedures become particularly important if later efforts are required to enforce the orders by contempt, because it will be necessary to show that the party had the requisite knowledge of the orders to permit such enforcement (see §20.40).

A Proof of Service should be completed and filed with the court; see, *e.g.,* form in §11.63. For other Judicial Council proof of service forms that may be used, see Proof of Personal Service (Judicial Council Form FL-330) and Proof of Service by Mail (Judicial Council Form FL-335). When the court has made orders that may require police enforcement (*i.e.,* child custody, protective orders, property control), a copy of the orders, along with a copy of a Proof of Service unless the other party was present in court when the orders were made, should be delivered or mailed to the police department in each jurisdiction where it is reasonably likely that enforcement will be required. See Fam C §6381(b).

§11.63   **d. Forms: Proof of Service (In Person) (CLETS) (Domestic Violence Prevention) (Judicial Council Form DV-200); Proof of Service by Mail (CLETS) (Judicial Council Form DV-250); Proof of Personal Service (Judicial Council Form FL-330); Proof of Service by Mail (Judicial Council Form FL-335)**

| **DV-200**   **Proof of Service (In Person)** | *Clerk stamps below when form is filed.* |

1 Protected person's name:

2 Restrained person's name:

3 **Notice to Server**
You must:
- Be 18 or over.
- Not be listed on the restraining order.
- Give a copy of all documents checked in **4** to the restrained person in **2**. (You cannot send them by mail.) Then sign this form and give or mail it to the protected person.

Court name and street address:
Superior Court of California, County of

Case Number:

4 I gave the person in **2** a copy of all documents checked below:
- a. ☐ DV-110 with DV-100 and a blank DV-120 (Temporary Restraining Order and Notice of Hearing; Request for Order; blank Answer to Temporary Restraining Order)
- b. ☐ DV-105 and DV-140 (Child Custody, Visitation, and Support Request; Child Custody and Visitation Order)
- c. ☐ FL-150 with a blank FL-150 (Income and Expense Declaration)
- d. ☐ FL-155 with a blank FL-155 (Simplified Financial Statement)
- e. ☐ DV-125 (Reissue Temporary Restraining Order)
- f. ☐ DV-130 (Restraining Order After Hearing)
- g. ☐ Other *(specify):* _____

5 I gave copies of the documents checked above to the person in **2** on:
- a. Date: _____   b. Time: _____ ☐ a.m. ☐ p.m.
- c. At this address: _____

6 **Server's Information**
Name: _____
Address: _____
Telephone: _____
(If you are a process server):
County of registration: _____ Registration number: _____

7 I declare under penalty of perjury under the laws of the State of California that the information above is true and correct.
Date: _____

➤

_____   _____
Type or print server's name   *Server to sign here*

Judicial Council of California, www.courtinfo.ca.gov   **Proof of Service (In Person) (CLETS)**   DV-200, Page 1 of 1
Rev. January 1, 2003, Optional Form   (Domestic Violence Prevention)
Family Code, §§ 6324, 6340–6344

DV-250   Proof of Service by Mail

Clerk stamps below when form is filed.

1 Protected person's name:

2 Restrained person's name:

3 **Notice to Server**
You must:
- Be 18 or over.
- Not be listed on the restraining order.
- Mail a copy of all documents checked in ❹ to the person in ❺.

Court name and street address:
Superior Court of California, County of

4 I mailed to the person in ❺ a copy of all documents checked below:
- a. ☐ DV-120 (Answer to Temporary Restraining Order)
- b. ☐ FL-150 (Income and Expense Declaration)
- c. ☐ FL-155 (Simplified Financial Statement)
- d. ☐ DV-130 (Restraining Order After Hearing)
- e. ☐ Other *(specify):* _____

Case Number:

Remember: You cannot serve DV-100, DV-105, DV-110, or DV-125 by mail.

5 I placed copies of the documents checked above in a sealed envelope and mailed them as listed below:
- a. Date: _____   b. Mailed from *(city):* _____ *(state):* _____
- c. Mailed to *(write name):* _____
- d. At this address: _____

6 **Server's Information**
Name: _____
Address: _____
Telephone: _____
(If you are a process server):
County of registration: _____ Registration number: _____

7 I declare under penalty of perjury under the laws of the State of California that the information above is true and correct.

Date: _____

➤

_____   _____
Type or print server's name   *Server to sign here*

Judicial Council of California, www.courtinfo.ca.gov
Rev. July 1, 2003, Optional Form
Family Code, §§ 6324, 6340-6344

Proof of Service by Mail (CLETS)
(Domestic Violence Prevention)

DV-250, Page 1 of 1

FL-330

ATTORNEY OR PARTY WITHOUT ATTORNEY OR GOVERNMENTAL AGENCY (under Family Code, §§ 17400, 17406) *(Name, state bar number, and address):*	FOR COURT USE ONLY

TELEPHONE NO.:   FAX NO.:

ATTORNEY FOR *(Name):*

SUPERIOR COURT OF CALIFORNIA, COUNTY OF

   STREET ADDRESS:

   MAILING ADDRESS:

   CITY AND ZIP CODE:

   BRANCH NAME:

PETITIONER/PLAINTIFF:

RESPONDENT/DEFENDANT:

OTHER PARENT:

PROOF OF PERSONAL SERVICE	CASE NUMBER:

1. I am at least 18 years old, not a party to this action, and not a protected person listed in any of the orders.

2. Person served *(name):*

3. I served copies of the following documents *(specify):*

4. By personally delivering copies to the person served, as follows:
   a. Date: b. Time:
   c. Address:

5. I am
   a. ☐ not a registered California process server.
   b. ☐ a registered California process server.
   c. ☐ an employee or independent contractor of a registered California process server.
   d. ☐ exempt from registration under Bus. & Prof. Code section 22350(b).
   e. ☐ a California sheriff or marshal.

6. My name, address, and telephone number, and, if applicable, county of registration and number *(specify):*

7. ☐ I declare under penalty of perjury under the laws of the State of California that the foregoing is true and correct.

8. ☐ I am a California sheriff or marshal and I certify that the foregoing is true and correct.

Date:

▶

_____   _____
(TYPE OR PRINT NAME OF PERSON WHO SERVED THE PAPERS)   (SIGNATURE OF PERSON WHO SERVED THE PAPERS)

Page 1 of 2

INFORMATION SHEET FOR PROOF OF PERSONAL SERVICE

Use these instructions to complete the *Proof of Personal Service* (form FL-330).

A person at least 18 years of age or older must serve the documents. There are two ways to serve documents: (1) personal delivery and (2) by mail. See the *Proof of Service by Mail* (form FL-335) if the documents are being served by mail. The person who serves the documents must complete a proof of service form for the documents being served. **You cannot serve documents if you are a party to the action.**

INSTRUCTIONS FOR THE PERSON WHO SERVES THE DOCUMENTS (TYPE OR PRINT IN BLACK INK)

You must complete a proof of service for each package of documents you serve. For example, if you serve the Respondent and the Other Parent, you must complete two proofs of service, one for the Respondent and one for the Other Parent.

Complete the top section of the proof of service forms as follows:
<u>First box, left side</u>: In this box print the name, address, and phone number of the person for whom you are serving the documents.
<u>Second box, left side</u>: Print the name of the county in which the legal action is filed and the court's address in this box. Use the same address for the court that is on the documents you are serving.
<u>Third box, left side</u>: Print the names of the Petitioner/Plaintiff, Respondent/Defendant, and Other Parent in this box. Use the same names listed on the documents you are serving.
<u>First box, top of form, right side</u>: Leave this box blank for the court's use.
<u>Second box, right side</u>: Print the case number in this box. This number is also stated on the documents you are serving.

1. You are stating that you are over the age of 18 and that you are neither a party of this action nor a protected person listed in any of the orders.
2. Print the name of the party to whom you handed the documents.
3. List the name of each document that you delivered to the party.
4. a. Write in the date that you delivered the documents to the party.
   b. Write in the time of day that you delivered the documents to the party.
   c. Print the address where you delivered the documents.
5. Check the box that applies to you. If you are a private person serving the documents for a party, check box "a."
6. Print your name, address, and telephone number. If applicable, include the county in which you are registered as a process server and your registration number.
7. You must check this box if you are not a California sheriff or marshal. You are stating under penalty of perjury that the information you have provided is true and correct.
8. Do not check this box unless you are a California sheriff or marshal.

Print your name, fill in the date, and sign the form.

If you need additional assistance with this form, contact the Family Law Facilitator in your county.

FL-335

ATTORNEY OR PARTY WITHOUT ATTORNEY OR GOVERNMENTAL AGENCY (under Family Code, §§ 17400, 17406) (Name, state bar number, and address):	FOR COURT USE ONLY
TELEPHONE NO.: FAX NO.:	
ATTORNEY FOR (Name):	

SUPERIOR COURT OF CALIFORNIA, COUNTY OF

STREET ADDRESS:

MAILING ADDRESS:

CITY AND ZIP CODE:

BRANCH NAME:

PETITIONER/PLAINTIFF:

RESPONDENT/DEFENDANT:

OTHER PARENT:

PROOF OF SERVICE BY MAIL	CASE NUMBER:

NOTICE: To serve temporary restraining orders you must use personal service (see form FL-330).

1. I am at least 18 years of age, not a party to this action, and I am a resident of or employed in the county where the mailing took place.

2. My residence or business address is:

3. I served a copy of the following documents (specify):

by enclosing them in an envelope AND

a. ☐ **depositing** the sealed envelope with the United States Postal Service with the postage fully prepaid.

b. ☐ **placing** the envelope for collection and mailing on the date and at the place shown in item 4 following our ordinary business practices. I am readily familiar with this business's practice for collecting and processing correspondence for mailing. On the same day that correspondence is placed for collection and mailing, it is deposited in the ordinary course of business with the United States Postal Service in a sealed envelope with postage fully prepaid.

4. The envelope was addressed and mailed as follows:
   a. Name of person served:
   b. Address:

   c. Date mailed:
   d. Place of mailing (city and state):

5. I declare under penalty of perjury under the laws of the State of California that the foregoing is true and correct.

Date:

▶

_____   _____
(TYPE OR PRINT NAME)   (SIGNATURE OF PERSON COMPLETING THIS FORM)

Page 1 of 2

Form Approved for Optional Use Judicial Council of California FL-335 [Rev. January 1, 2003]	**PROOF OF SERVICE BY MAIL**	Code of Civil Procedure, §§ 1013, 1013a www.courtinfo.ca.gov

INFORMATION SHEET FOR PROOF OF SERVICE BY MAIL

Use these instructions to complete the *Proof of Service by Mail* (form FL-335).

A person at least 18 years of age or older must serve the documents. There are two ways to serve documents: (1) personal delivery and (2) by mail. See the *Proof of Personal Service* (form FL-330) if the documents are being personally served. The person who serves the documents must complete a proof of service form for the documents being served. **You cannot serve documents if you are a party to the action.**

INSTRUCTIONS FOR THE PERSON WHO SERVES THE DOCUMENTS (TYPE OR PRINT IN BLACK INK)

You must complete a proof of service for each package of documents you serve. For example, if you serve the Respondent and the Other Parent, you must complete two proofs of service, one for the Respondent and one for the Other Parent.

Complete the top section of the proof of service forms as follows:
First box, left side: In this box print the name, address, and phone number of the person for whom you are serving the documents.
Second box, left side: Print the name of the county in which the legal action is filed and the court's address in this box. Use the same address for the court that is on the documents you are serving.
Third box, left side: Print the names of the Petitioner/Plaintiff, Respondent/Defendant, and Other Parent in this box. Use the same names listed on the documents you are serving.
First box, top of form, right side: Leave this box blank for the court's use.
Second box, right side: Print the case number in this box. This number is also stated on the documents you are serving.

You cannot serve a temporary restraining order by mail. You must serve those documents by personal service.

1. You are stating that you are at least 18 years old and that you are not a party to this action. You are also stating that you either live in or are employed in the county where the mailing took place.
2. Print your home or business address.
3. List the name of each document that you mailed (the exact names are listed on the bottoms of the forms).
   a. Check this box if you put the documents in the regular U.S. mail.
   b. Check this box if you put the documents in the mail at your place of employment.
4. a. Print the name you put on the envelope containing the documents.
   b. Print the address you put on the envelope containing the documents.
   c. Write in the date that you put the envelope containing the documents in the mail.
   d. Write in the city and state you were in when you mailed the envelope containing the documents.
5. You are stating under penalty of perjury that the information you have provided is true and correct.

Print your name, fill in the date, and sign the form.

If you need additional assistance with this form, contact the Family Law Facilitator in your county.

Copies: Original (file with court clerk); office copies.

e. Child Support Case Registry Form

§11.63A   (1) Discussion

To the extent required by federal law, and subject to applicable confidentiality provisions of state or federal law, any order for child support in a case in which the local child support agency is not providing services pursuant to Fam C §17400 must include a provision requiring the obligor and the obligee to file certain information with the court. This requirement is applicable to both initial orders and modifications. The information to be provided includes residential and mailing address; social security number; telephone number; driver's license number; name, address, and telephone number of employer; and any other information prescribed by the Judicial Council. The order must specify that each parent is responsible for providing his or her own information, that the information must be filed with the court within ten days after the court order, and that new or different information must be filed with the court within ten days after any event causing a change in previously provided information. Fam C §4014(b); see Item 12 on Child Support Information and Order Attachment in §11.58 and Item 4.h. on Judgment in §14.56. Once the child support registry described in Welf & I C §16576 is operational, any child support order in a case in which the local child support agency is not providing services pursuant to Fam C §17400 must require this information to be filed and kept updated with the child support registry. Fam C §4014(c).

§11.63B   (2) Form: Child Support Case Registry Form (Judicial Council Form FL-191)

FL-191

ATTORNEY OR PARTY WITHOUT ATTORNEY *(Name, State Bar number, and address)*:	COURT PERSONNEL: *STAMP DATE RECEIVED HERE*
TELEPHONE NO.: FAX NO. *(Optional)*: E-MAIL ADDRESS *(Optional)*: ATTORNEY FOR *(Name)*:	**DO NOT FILE**

SUPERIOR COURT OF CALIFORNIA, COUNTY OF
STREET ADDRESS:
MAILING ADDRESS:
CITY AND ZIP CODE:
BRANCH NAME:

PETITIONER/PLAINTIFF:

RESPONDENT/DEFENDANT:

OTHER PARENT:

CHILD SUPPORT CASE REGISTRY FORM ☐ Mother ☐ First form completed ☐ Father ☐ Change to previous information	CASE NUMBER:

THIS FORM WILL NOT BE PLACED IN THE COURT FILE. IT WILL BE MAINTAINED IN A CONFIDENTIAL FILE WITH THE STATE OF CALIFORNIA.

Notice: Pages 1 and 2 of this form must be completed and delivered to the court along with the court order for support. Pages 3 and 4 are instructional only and do not need to be delivered to the court. If you did not file the court order, you must complete this form and deliver it to the court within 10 days of the date on which you received a copy of the support order. Any later change to the information on this form must be delivered to the court on another form within 10 days of the change. It is important that you keep the court informed in writing of any changes of your address and telephone number.

1. Support order information *(this information is on the court order you are filing or have received)*.
   a. Date order filed:
   b. ☐ Initial child support or family support order   ☐ Modification
   c. Total monthly base current child or family support amount ordered for children listed below, plus any monthly amount ordered payable on past-due support:

Child Support:	Family Support:	Spousal Support:

(1) ☐ Current $
    base child
    support:
    ☐ Reserved order
    ☐ $0 (zero) order
	☐ Current $
	    base family
	    support:
	    ☐ Reserved order
	    ☐ $0 (zero) order
		☐ Current $
		    spousal
		    support:
		    ☐ Reserved order
		    ☐ $0 (zero) order

(2) ☐ Additional $
    monthly
    support:
	☐ Additional $
	    monthly
	    support:	

(3) ☐ Total $
    past-due
    support:
	☐ Total $
	    past-due
	    support:
		☐ Total $
		    past-due
		    support:

(4) ☐ Payment $
    on past-
    due support:
	☐ Payment $
	    on past-
	    due support:
		☐ Payment $
		    on past-
		    due support:

   (5) Wage withholding was ☐ ordered ☐ ordered but stayed until *(date)*:

2. Person required to pay child or family support *(name)*:
   Relationship to child *(specify)*:

3. Person or agency to receive child or family support payments *(name)*:
   Relationship to child *(if applicable)*:

TYPE OR PRINT IN INK

PETITIONER/PLAINTIFF:	CASE NUMBER:
RESPONDENT/DEFENDANT:	
OTHER PARENT:	

4. The child support order is for the following children:

         Child's name   Date of birth   Social security number

    a.

    b.

    c.

    ☐ Additional children are listed on a page attached to this document.

You are required to complete the following information about yourself. You are not required to provide information about the other person, but you are encouraged to provide as much as you can. This form is confidential and will not be filed in the court file. It will be maintained in a confidential file with the State of California.

5. Father's name: 6. Mother's name:

    a. Date of birth: a. Date of birth:

    b. Social security number: b. Social security number:

    c. Street address: c. Street address:

      City, state, zip code: City, state, zip code:

    d. Mailing address: d. Mailing address:

      City, state, zip code: City, state, zip code:

    e. Driver's license number: e. Driver's license number:

      State: State:

    f. Telephone number: f. Telephone number:

    g. ☐ Employed ☐ Not employed ☐ Self-employed   g. ☐ Employed ☐ Not employed ☐ Self-employed

      Employer's name: Employer's name:

      Street address: Street address:

      City, state, zip code: City, state, zip code:

      Telephone number: Telephone number:

7. ☐ A restraining order, protective order, or nondisclosure order due to domestic violence is in effect.

    a. The order protects: ☐ Father ☐ Mother ☐ Children

    b. From: ☐ Father ☐ Mother

    c. The restraining order expires on *(date)*:

I declare under penalty of perjury under the laws of the State of California that the foregoing is true and correct.

Date:

                               ▶

_____   _____

(TYPE OR PRINT NAME)   (SIGNATURE OF PERSON COMPLETING THIS FORM)

INFORMATION SHEET FOR CHILD SUPPORT CASE REGISTRY FORM
(Do NOT deliver this Information Sheet to the court clerk.)

Please follow these instructions to complete the *Child Support Case Registry Form* (form FL-191) if you do not have an attorney to represent you. Your attorney, if you have one, should complete this form.

Both parents must complete a *Child Support Case Registry Form*. The information on this form will be included in a national database that, among other things, is used to locate absent parents. When you file a court order, you must deliver a completed form to the court clerk along with your court order. If you did not file a court order, you must deliver a completed form to the court clerk **WITHIN 10 DAYS** of the date you received a copy of your court order. If any of the information you provide on this form changes, you must complete a new form and deliver it to the court clerk within 10 days of the change. The address of the court clerk is the same as the one shown for the superior court on your order. This form is confidential and will not be filed in the court file. It will be maintained in a confidential file with the State of California.

INSTRUCTIONS FOR COMPLETING THE *CHILD SUPPORT CASE REGISTRY FORM* (TYPE OR PRINT IN INK):

If the top section of the form has already been filled out, skip down to number 1 below. If the top section of the form is blank, you must provide this information.

<u>Page 1, first box, top of form, left side</u>: Print your name, address, telephone number, fax number, and e-mail address, if any, in this box. Attorneys must include their State Bar identification numbers.

<u>Page 1, second box, top of form, left side</u>: Print the name of the county and the court's address in this box. Use the same address for the court that is on the court order you are filing or have received.

<u>Page 1, third box, top of form, left side</u>: Print the names of the petitioner/plaintiff, respondent/defendant, and other parent in this box. Use the same names listed on the court order you are filing or have received.

<u>Page 1, fourth box, top of form, left side</u>: Check the box indicating whether you are the mother or the father. If you are the attorney for the mother, check the box for mother. If you are the attorney for the father, check the box for father. Also, if this is the first time you have filled out this form, check the box by "First form completed." If you have filled out form FL-191 before, and you are changing any of the information, check the box by "Change to previous information."

<u>Page 1, first box, right side</u>: Leave this box blank for the court's use in stamping the date of receipt.

<u>Page 1, second box, right side</u>: Print the court case number in this box. This number is also shown on the court papers.

<u>Instructions for numbered paragraphs:</u>

1. a. Enter the date the court order was filed. This date is shown in the "COURT PERSONNEL: STAMP DATE RECEIVED HERE" box on page 1 at the top of the order on the right side. If the order has not been filed, leave this item blank for the court clerk to fill in.

    b. If the court order you filed or received is the first child or family support order for this case, check the box by "Initial child support or family support order." If this is a change to your order, check the box by "Modification."

    c. Information regarding the amount and type of support ordered and wage withholding is on the court order you are filing or have received.

    (1) If your order provides for any type of current support, check all boxes that describe that support. For example, if your order provides for both child and spousal support, check both of those boxes. If there is an amount, put it in the blank provided. If the order says the amount is reserved, check the "Reserved order" box. If the order says the amount is zero, check the "$0 (zero) order" box. Do not include child care, special needs, uninsured medical expenses, or travel for visitation here These amounts will go in (2). Do NOT complete the Child Support Case Registry form if you receive spousal support only.

    (2) If your order provides for a set monthly amount to be paid as additional support for such needs as child care, special needs, uninsured medical expenses or travel for visitation check the box in Item 2 and enter the monthly amount. For example, if your order provides for base child support and in addition the paying parent is required to pay $300 per month, check the box in item 2 underneath the "Child Support" column and enter $300. Do NOT check this box if your order provides only for a payment of a percentage, such as 50% of the childcare.

(3) If your order determined the amount of past due support, check the box in Item 3 that states the type of past due support and enter the amount. For example, if the court determined that there was $5000 in past due child support and $1000 in past due spousal support, you would check the box in item 3 in the "Child Support" column and enter $5000 and you would also check the box in item 3 in the "Spousal Support" column and enter $1000.

(4) If your order provides for a specific dollar amount to be paid towards any past due support, check the box in Item 4 that states the type of past due support and enter the amount. For example, the court ordered $350 per month to be paid on the past due child support, you would check the box in Item 4 in the "Child Support" column and enter $350.

(5) Check the "ordered" box if wage withholding was ordered with no conditions. Check the box "ordered but stayed until" if wage withholding was ordered but is not to be deducted until a later date. If the court delayed the effective date of the wage withholding, enter the specific date. Check only one box in this item.

2. a. Write the name of the person who is supposed to pay child or family support.
   b. Write the relationship of that person to the child.

3. a. Write the name of the person or agency supposed to receive child or family support payments.
   b. Write the relationship of that person to the child.

4. List the full name, date of birth, and social security number for each child included in the support order. If there are more than five children included in the support order, check the box below item 4e and list the remaining children with dates of birth and social security numbers on another sheet of paper. Attach the other sheet to this form.

The local child support agency is required, under section 466(a)(13) of the Social Security Act, to place in the records pertaining to child support the social security number of any individual who is subject to a divorce decree, support order, or paternity determination or acknowledgment. This information is mandatory and will be kept on file at the local child support agency.

Top of page 2, box on left side: Print the names of the petitioner/plaintiff, respondent/defendant, and other parent in this box. Use the same names listed on page 1.

Top of page 2, box on right side: Print your court case number in this box. Use the same case number as on page 1, second box, right side.

You are required to complete information about yourself. If you know information about the other person, you may also fill in what you know about him or her.

5. If you are the father in this case, list your full name in this space. See instructions for a–g under item 6 below.

6. If you are the mother in this case, list your full name in this space.

   a. List your date of birth.
   b. Write your social security number.
   c. List the street address, city, state, and zip code where you live.
   d. List the street address, city, state, and zip code where you want your mail sent, if different from the address where you live.
   e. Write your driver's license number and the state where it was issued.
   f. List the telephone number where you live.
   g. Indicate whether you are employed, not employed, self-employed, or by checking the appropriate box. If you are employed, write the name, street address, city, state, zip code, and telephone number where you work.

7. If there is a restraining order, protective order, or nondisclosure order, check this box.

   a. Check the box beside each person who is protected by the restraining order.
   b. Check the box beside the parent who is restrained.
   c. Write the date the restraining order expires. See the restraining order, protective order, or nondisclosure order for this date.

If you are in fear of domestic violence, you may want to ask the court for a restraining order, protective order, or nondisclosure order.

You must type or print your name, fill in the date, and sign the *Child Support Case Registry Form* under penalty of perjury. When you sign under penalty of perjury, you are stating that the information you have provided is true and correct.

Copies: Original (deliver to court clerk); office copies.

§11.64 IV. DURATION

Temporary orders typically last until superseded by other temporary orders or the judgment in the action, which under prior law was for a period of up to 3 years, subject to renewal. Operative January 1, 2006, a court has discretion to issue orders for up to 5 years, subject to the preexisting provisions of law for termination or modification. Fam C §§6345(a), 6361(b). These orders may be renewed for up to 5 years, or permanently, without a showing of further abuse since issuance of the original order, subject to modification or termination on stipulation of both parties or on the motion of a party. Fam C §§6345(a), 6361(b). Note, however, that the legislature left unchanged the provision of Fam C §6345(c) that the failure to state an expiration date on the face of the form (containing the order) creates an order having a duration of 3 years from the date of issuance. Consequently, when a party who has obtained protective orders (see §11.6) believes that such protection is still needed, further protective orders should be sought as part of the judgment, even when the expiration date stated in the temporary orders has not arrived.

§11.65 V. ATTACKS ON TEMPORARY ORDERS

Depending on the circumstances, several potential mechanisms are available for attacking temporary orders:

Motion to reconsider or renewed motion. Under CCP §1008(a), a party may, based on new or different facts, circumstances, or law, apply to the judge who made the order to reconsider the matter and modify, amend, or revoke the order. Under CCP §1008(b), a party may, based on new or different facts, circumstances, or law, renew an application that was previously denied, in whole or part, or granted conditionally or on terms. For further discussion of these procedures, see California Civil Procedure Before Trial §§12.113-12.114 (4th ed Cal CEB 2004). A motion for reconsideration or a renewed motion is prepared and processed in the same manner as a noticed motion for temporary orders. For discussion of, and forms for, motions for temporary orders, see §§11.16-11.63.

Motion to set aside under CCP §473. The court may set aside an order taken against a party through his or her "mistake, inadvertence, surprise, or excusable neglect." For discussion, see §§18.24-18.33 (addressing §473 motion in context of attacks on judgments).

Motion to set aside based on extrinsic fraud. The court may set aside an order obtained by extrinsic fraud. *Greene v Superior Court* (1961) 55 C2d 403, 405, 10 CR 817. For discussion, see §§18.36–18.40, 18.44–18.45 (addressing motion to set aside based on extrinsic fraud in context of attacks on judgments).

Motion for new trial; motion to vacate. It is unclear whether temporary orders are subject to a motion for a new trial under CCP §657 or to a motion to vacate a judgment and enter a different one under CCP §663. Compare *Greene v Superior Court* (1961) 55 C2d 403, 405, 10 CR 817 (court may correct judicial error in granting of order on motion for new trial or motion to vacate order and enter different one), and *Marriage of Beilock* (1978) 81 CA3d 713, 719, 146 CR 675 (motion for new trial appropriate after granting of motion to quash writ of execution), with *San Francisco Lathing, Inc. v Superior Court* (1969) 271 CA2d 78, 80, 76 CR 304 (motion for new trial does not lie to secure reexamination of decision on a motion), and *Mann v Superior Court* (1942) 53 CA2d 272, 285, 127 P2d 970, 977 (no new trial may be granted on issue of fact brought forward by motion in case). For discussion of motion for new trial and motion to vacate, see §§18.2–18.23 (addressing motions in context of attacks on judgments).

Appeal; writ. An appeal may be taken from an order granting or dissolving an injunction (*e.g.,* protective order, property restraint) or refusing to grant or dissolve an injunction. CCP §904.1(a)(6). An appeal may also be taken from an order regarding child custody, child support, spousal support, or attorney fees. See *Marriage of Skelley* (1976) 18 C3d 365, 368, 134 CR 197. Absent special circumstances, the right to immediate review by appeal renders review by writ inappropriate. 18 C3d at 369. Depending on the circumstances, however, appeal after a hearing on temporary orders may not be a viable remedy because of the length of time it takes to obtain a decision. For discussion of appeals and writs generally, see chap 19.

12

Joinder

§12.1　　I. SCOPE OF CHAPTER

A third party who claims or controls an interest that is subject to disposition in a marital action may be joined as a party to that action. This chapter discusses the types of issues involving third parties that may be litigated in the action, the parties who may request joinder of a third party, and the factors to consider in deciding whether and when to request joinder. The chapter provides a detailed explanation of the procedural steps for requesting joinder and preparing the required pleading, responding to a request for joinder, and obtaining an order for joinder.

§12.2 II. JOINDER OVERVIEW

Joinder is a procedure whereby a person or entity, other than the spouses, who has or claims an interest in the proceeding may be made a party to a marital action. Fam C §2021; Cal Rules of Ct 5.150. By allowing all interested parties to present their claims in the action, the court may make a single, final determination of all the parties' rights, and multiple legal actions may be avoided.

On the related topics of consolidation of actions (permitting the court to bring together two or more civil actions pending in the same county that involve common issues of law or fact for simultaneous disposition) and coordination of actions (providing for the unified management of actions pending in different counties and sharing common issues of law or fact), see California Civil Procedure Before Trial, chaps 43 ("Consolidation and Severance"), 44 ("Coordination") (4th ed Cal CEB 2004).

§12.3 A. Parties Who May Be Joined

State statutes provide two distinct procedures for effecting joinder in a marital action—one for employee benefit plans (Fam C §§2060-2074; Cal Rules of Ct 5.162; see §§12.7-12.25) and one for all other interested parties (Fam C §2021(a); Cal Rules of Ct 5.150-5.160); see §§12.26-12.45). Parties other than benefit plans who may have an interest in a marital action include, *e.g.*:

- A third party who claims an interest in real or personal property subject to disposition in the marital action (Cal Rules of Ct 5.154(a); see §12.27);

- A third party who has or claims custody of, or visitation rights with, a minor child subject to the action (Cal Rules of Ct 5.154(a)-(b), 5.158(a); see §§12.28-12.30); or

- A third party who is served with a temporary restraining order affecting the use of property or the custody or visitation of minor children subject to the action (Cal Rules of Ct 5.154(c); see §12.31).

Joinder of an interested party may be either mandatory or permissive, as provided by statute and rules of court. Joinder of a benefit plan is mandatory, however, when a party to the proceeding requests it. Fam C §2060(a); see §12.16. The court must also join as a party anyone it "discovers" who has custody of, or claims custody or visitation rights with respect to, a minor child of the marriage. Cal Rules of Ct 5.158(a); see §12.28.

As to all other interested parties, joinder is *permissive, i.e.,* discretionary with the court. If the court finds that (1) it would be appropriate to determine a particular issue in the proceeding and (2) the party to be joined is indispensable to a determination of the issue or necessary to the enforcement of any judgment rendered on that issue, the court may order joinder. Cal Rules of Ct 5.158(b); see §12.32. In deciding whether it is appropriate to determine the particular issue in the proceeding, the court must consider (1) the effect that joinder would have on the marital action, including whether the determination of the issue to be joined would unduly delay the disposition of the proceeding; (2) whether other parties would need to be joined to render an effective judgment between the parties; (3) whether determination of the issue to be joined would confuse other issues in the proceeding; and (4) whether joinder would complicate, delay, or otherwise interfere with the effective disposition of the proceeding. Cal Rules of Ct 5.158(b).

Except as otherwise provided in Cal Rules of Ct 5.150–5.162, all provisions of law relating to the joinder of parties in civil actions generally also apply to joinder in marital actions. Cal Rules of Ct 5.150. Note the apparent conflict between Cal Rules of Ct 5.158(b), which allows the court discretion to join an indispensable party in marital actions, and CCP §389(a), which requires joinder of such a party in civil actions generally. Under Cal Rules of Ct 5.150, the rule of permissive joinder prevails in marital actions.

§12.4   B. Requirement of a Pleading

A person who is joined as a party to a marital action, or who is sought or seeking to be joined, is referred to as a "claimant." Cal Rules of Ct 5.152. Under Cal Rules of Ct 5.156(a), all applications for joinder other than for an employee pension benefit plan must be made by serving and filing a Notice of Motion and Declaration for Joinder (Judicial Council Form FL-371) accompanied by an "appropriate pleading," setting forth the claimant's interest in the proceeding and the relief sought by the applicant. Except as set forth in Cal Rules of Ct 5.150–5.162 or by the court, the law applicable to civil actions in general governs all pleadings, motions, and other matters brought in that portion of the marital action on which the claimant is joined. Cal Rules of Ct 5.160.

When the claimant is an employee benefit plan, the required pleadings are set forth on the Judicial Council form of Pleading on Joinder—Employee Benefit Plan (see form in §12.19). Those who request joinder of any other interested party must prepare a separate complaint or petition stating the cause of action sought to be joined, as though a separate proceeding were being brought by, or against, the claimant. Cal Rules of Ct 5.156(a). For discussion and sample of the required pleading, and examples of causes of action that may be stated, see §§12.38–12.39.

NOTE➤ While Fam C §2060(b) provides that an order or judgment in the family law proceeding is not enforceable against an employee benefit plan unless the plan has been joined as a party, some employee benefit plans cannot or may refuse to be joined, including federal plans and private plans governed by the Employee Retirement Income Security Act of 1974 (ERISA). See §12.6. ERISA, as amended by the Retirement Equity Act of 1984 (REA), provides that an order or judgment dividing the community interest in a pension plan is binding and enforceable against the plan (whether or not the plan is joined as a party) as long as the order or judgment is a "qualified domestic relations order" (QDRO). 29 USC §1056(d)(3)(A). In such cases, the nonemployee spouse may be better protected by service of a notice of adverse interest on the plan (see §12.9), which puts the federal or ERISA plan on notice of the pending dissolution action. A temporary restraining order could also be served on a nonjoined or nonjoinable plan on the basis of Cal Rules of Ct Rule 5.150. On the importance of obtaining a domestic relations order concerning employee retirement benefits before bifurcation of marital status, see §14.60. On other risks associated with dissolution and retirement benefits, see Dividing Pensions and Other Employee Benefits in California Divorces (Cal CEB 2006).

§12.5   C. Jurisdiction and Venue

For a claimant to be joined as a party to a marital action, he or she must be subject to the personal jurisdiction of the court, and the county in which the marital action is located must be the proper venue for the claim sought to be joined. If the proposed claimant is a nonresident, he or she must have sufficient "minimum contacts" with the state for the court to establish personal jurisdiction. When a nonresident is personally served in the forum state, however, the minimum contacts requirement does not apply. *Burnham v Superior Court* (1990) 495 US 604, 109 L Ed 2d 631, 110 S Ct 2105. For a general background on the doctrine of minimum contacts, see *Hanson v Denckla* (1958) 357 US 235, 2 L Ed 2d 1283, 78 S Ct 1228; *McGee v International Life Ins. Co.* (1957) 355 US 220, 2 L Ed 2d 223, 78 S Ct 199; *International Shoe Co. v Washington* (1945) 326 US 310, 90 L Ed 95, 66 S Ct 154. See also *Marriage of Martin* (1989) 207 CA3d 1426, 255 CR 720 (payments by Michigan dental plan to Michigan father for services provided to children in California were insufficient contact to give California courts personal jurisdiction over plan).

The county in which the marital action is filed must also be the proper venue for the claim by or against the person sought to be joined. If, for example, the claim involves a dispute with a third party as to the ownership of real property located in a county other than that in which the action is pending, an attempt to join the third party may not survive a motion for change of venue. See CCP §392(a)(1).

If the court cannot resolve an issue in the marital proceeding because of jurisdiction or venue problems, a request may be made for the court to reserve jurisdiction over the issue until the claim has been separately adjudicated. Cal Rules of Ct 5.106(b). An order reserving jurisdiction should accurately specify the nature of the issue reserved, and counsel should immediately take action to have the reserved issue decided in a separate proceeding. Note, however, that such a reservation of jurisdiction may not protect a nonemployee spouse's interest in an employee benefit plan without joinder of, or, at a minimum, service of a notice of adverse interest on, the plan. See §§12.7–12.13.

On personal jurisdiction in civil actions generally, see California Civil Procedure Before Trial §§6.66–6.88 (4th ed Cal CEB 2004). On venue in civil actions generally, see Civ Proc Before Trial, chap 8.

§12.6　D. Removal to Federal Court

When a claim sought to be joined in a marital action would be removable to federal court if sued on alone, either the claim or the entire action may be removed to federal court, within the discretion of that court. 28 USC §1441(c). Removal to federal court may be sought, *e.g.,* when (1) a federal agency is sought to be joined as a party (see 28 USC §§1441–1442) or (2) a nonresident pension plan is attempted to be joined (compare *Marriage of Pardee* (CD Cal 1976) 408 F Supp 666, in which removal was held to be improper, with *Stone v Stone* (ND Cal 1978) 450 F Supp 919, in which the court, declining to follow *Pardee,* allowed removal in an action to enforce payment of benefits to a nonemployee spouse). See also *Steel v U.S.* (9th Cir 1987) 813 F2d 1545, 1548, in which the division of a community interest in military pension benefits was held not within the "federal question" jurisdiction of the federal court.

Even though the federal court may ultimately decide that the entire proceeding belongs back in the state court, significant disruption and delay may be caused in the marital action by a request for removal. In one case, for example, dissolution proceedings were significantly delayed when an ERISA pension plan that was joined by a husband removed the case to federal court. After a federal magistrate ordered the case remanded to state court, the plan appealed and the Ninth Circuit held there was no federal jurisdiction to order remand because the parties had not clearly and unambiguously consented to jurisdiction of a federal magistrate. Note, however, that on remand to the federal district court, that court found that removal was improper and ordered the plan to pay the parties' considerable attorney fees incurred as a result of the removal. *Nasca v PeopleSoft* (ND Cal 1999) 87 F Supp 2d 967, 975. If counsel for the nonemployee spouse anticipates that a request for joinder of a benefit plan or federal entity may result in an attempted removal to federal court (and if citation to the parties and court of the *PeopleSoft* case is unpersuasive), it may be advisable to consider one or more of the following:

- Use other means to put the plan on notice that the nonemployee spouse claims an interest in the benefits (see §12.9); or

- Delay joinder until temporary orders are obtained (see generally chap 11), a judgment on the bifurcated issue of marital status has been granted (see §§14.59–14.70), or it is known that the client will receive an interest in pension benefits and not in other assets of equal value (see §§5.85–5.87, 5.92).

A temporary QDRO (or corresponding temporary order, in the case of a public entity plan) may, in an appropriate case, be the most effective option pending resolution of all issues and has the advantage of providing protection to the nonemployee party (alternate payee) by the very terms of ERISA or the federally regulated plan. Such a temporary order may secure for the nonemployee spouse the status of "surviving spouse" after the parties' marital status has terminated. See Dividing Pensions and Other Employee Benefits in California Divorces, chaps 2, 6 (Cal CEB 2006).

§12.7 III. JOINDER OF EMPLOYEE BENEFIT PLANS

When there is a community property interest in an employee benefit plan (see §5.30), it may be advisable or even necessary to join the plan as a party to the marital action to protect the nonemployee spouse's interest. For instance, the California State Teachers Retirement System *must* be joined before service of an order dividing plan benefits. Ed C §22656 (CalSTRS). To ascertain whether joinder is indicated, state and federal statutory requirements affecting joinder of benefit plans and the enforceability of marital action orders against benefit plans should be consulted.

§12.8 A. State Law and Federal Preemption

California statutes provide that no order or judgment in a marital action is enforceable against an employee benefit plan unless the plan has been joined as a party to the proceeding (Fam C §2060(b)), and they prescribe a simplified procedure for joining a benefit plan using Judicial Council forms (Fam C §§2060–2074; see §§12.15–12.23). The operation of these statutes has been affected, however, by the Employee Retirement Income Security Act of 1974 (ERISA) (29 USC §§1001–1461), which established a comprehensive federal regulatory program governing all *private* qualified employee pension plans. ERISA does not regulate the public benefit plans of governmental entities or agencies.

ERISA superseded all state laws insofar as they concern private pension plans. 29 USC §1144(a). Nevertheless, it is well established that ERISA does not (1) preempt California community property law in general, (2) prohibit a California court in a marital action from ordering a benefit plan to pay a portion of a participant's benefits to a former spouse, (3) preempt state laws that provide for joinder of a benefit plan, or (4) require joinder of a benefit plan in marital actions. *Marriage of Baker* (1988) 204 CA3d 206, 211, 219, 251 CR 126. Rather, ERISA provides that an order or judgment dividing the community interest in a pension plan is binding and enforceable against the plan (whether or not the plan is joined as a party) as long as the order or judgment is a "qualified domestic relations order" (QDRO). 29 USC §1056(d)(3)(A); 204 CA3d at 217. ERISA further specifies the requirements that a marital action order or judgment must meet in order to be recognized as a QDRO, and it provides for the procedures a plan must follow on receipt of a QDRO. 29 USC §1056(d).

To the extent that Fam C §2060(b) (former CC §4351) and Fam C §§2070-2074 (former CC §4363.2) provide that a private plan, once joined as a party to the action, is bound by a state court order that is not a QDRO, the statutes are preempted by ERISA. 204 CA3d at 218.

For a comprehensive discussion of QDROs, including sample forms, see §§17.68-17.79, and Dividing Pensions and Other Employee Benefits in California Divorces, chap 6 (Cal CEB 2006). On joinder issues in general, and the practical inability to join federal plans to a California dissolution proceeding, see Dividing Pensions, chap 2.

B. Whether to Request Joinder

§12.9   1. Notice of Adverse Interest

Under Fam C §755 (former CC §5106), a notice of adverse interest may be served on a benefit plan in order to give notice that a nonemployee spouse claims an interest in payments to be made under the plan. Such notice may be given to all types of benefit plans, including those governed by the Employee Retirement Income Security Act of 1974 (ERISA) (29 USC §§1001-1461), because ERISA does not preempt the statutory procedure for a notice of adverse interest. *Marriage of Baker* (1988) 204 CA3d 206, 218, 251 CR 126.

CAUTION► Although California's provisions for notice of an adverse interest and joinder (Fam C §§755, 2060-2074) and cases such as *Marriage of Baker* that uphold them have never been addressed by the United States Supreme Court, counsel should be aware that a potential argument may be made that ERISA preempts those provisions, given the Supreme Court's broad view of ERISA preemption of state law. See *Boggs v Boggs* (1997) 520 US 833, 844, 138 L Ed 2d 45, 117 S Ct 1754. The Ninth Circuit has recognized that ERISA assigns to plan administrators the fiduciary duty to ensure that an alternate payee's rights are protected, and that California courts recognize that under ERISA, a plan need not be a party to a state court domestic relations proceeding in order to be bound by a QDRO that issues from that proceeding. *Trustees of Directors Guild v Tise* (9th Cir. 2000) 234 F3d 415, 418 n2 (citing Baker); *Stewart v Thorpe Holding Co. Profit Sharing Plan* (9th Cir 2000) 207 F3d 1143, 1156 (plan participant's former spouse had standing to bring action seeking community property share in participant's interest in pension plan). Counsel should keep in mind that in the event of a conflict between California law and the statutes comprising ERISA, the latter will govern the plan administrator's duty to preserve the parties' interest in benefits, with or without joinder or notice of adverse interest.

If a benefit plan will not be joined as a party at the commencement of a marital action, a notice of adverse interest should be served on the plan to advise the plan of the pending dissolution action and alert it to the need to protect the nonemployee spouse's interest in benefits to be paid under the plan. Note, however, that a notice of adverse interest may be served even before an action is commenced when protection is desired during that period.

If the plan has not received a notice of adverse interest or an order for joinder (see §12.17), the nonemployee spouse may have no recourse against a plan that pays the entire community interest to the employee spouse either (1) before the court determines the parties' respective interests in pension benefits or (2) after the determination if the plan is a private plan that has not been served with an effective QDRO (see §17.68) or a public plan that has not been similarly bound under applicable procedures. However, if a plan receives a notice of adverse interest or an order for joinder, and nonetheless pays the community interest to the employee spouse, it is liable to and must pay the nonemployee spouse that portion of the benefits awarded to him or her by court order. 204 CA3d at 215. On the possible preemption of *Baker* holding by ERISA, see the Caution above.

The notice of adverse interest should clearly identify (1) the benefit plan, (2) the participant, and (3) the party claiming the interest by virtue of his or her marriage to the participant. It should indicate that an interest is being claimed in the plan and cite Fam C §755 as the authority for the notice. The notice should normally be served on the plan sponsor or administrator, and service should be effected in a manner that will facilitate proof of receipt by the sponsor or administrator, *i.e.*, personal service (see §10.31), service by mail and acknowledgment of receipt (see §§10.33–10.34), or service by mail and return receipt (signed by the addressee only) (see §10.40).

On comparison of notice of adverse interest and joinder, see §§12.10–12.12.

§12.10   2. Plans Governed by ERISA

A private pension plan governed by the Employee Retirement Income Security Act of 1974 (ERISA) (29 USC §§1001–1461) does not need to be joined as a party to the marital action in order to be bound by an order dividing a community interest in the plan, as long as the order is a QDRO. See 29 USC §1056(d)(3)(A); *Marriage of Baker* (1988) 204 CA3d 206, 218, 251 CR 126; see §12.8. However, if the plan is actually joined, the plan will at least be on notice of the need to protect the nonemployee spouse's interest in the pension benefits. In addition, joinder possibly may trigger the plan administrator's duty to communicate the plan's QDRO procedures to the parties and their counsel pending issuance of a QDRO. Further, after joinder, an injunctive order, *e.g.*, prohibiting the plan from honoring an election by the employee spouse that would diminish the nonemployee spouse's benefits in the plan (see *Marriage of Baker, supra*), may be enforceable against a plan pursuant to Cal Rules of Ct 5.154(c), indicating a person may be served with an order temporarily restraining the use of property in his or her possession or control.

If counsel chooses not to or is unable to join an ERISA plan at the commencement of the action, or desires to protect the client's interest before the action is commenced, a notice of adverse interest (see §12.9) should be served on the plan to protect the nonemployee spouse until the plan is joined or a QDRO is issued and served.

On the necessity of obtaining a QDRO if the employee spouse is approaching or has already entered "pay status," see Dividing Pensions and Other Employee Benefits in California Divorces, chap 6 (Cal CEB 2006).

§12.11 3. State Pension Plans

State public pension plans should always be joined as a party at the commencement of the marital action.

By statute, the State Teachers' Retirement System (STRS; see Ed C §§22000–24944) must be joined as a party for a judgment or order, awarding a share of the benefits in the STRS Defined Benefit Program to a nonemployee spouse, to be binding on the plan. Ed C §22656. Moreover, the plan must be served with a certified copy of the judgment or order. Ed C §22656. The Defined Benefit Program is the STRS program for public school teachers. The STRS also has a Cash Balance Benefit Program for other persons employed in instructional programs less than half-time by school employers who elect to provide that program. See Ed C §§26000–28101. In 2000, a Defined Benefit Supplement Program was established for members of the Defined Benefit Program in order to provide them supplemental retirement, disability, and final or termination benefits, payable in a lump-sum or annuity, as specified. See Ed C §§25000–25025.

There is no statute requiring joinder of the Public Employees' Retirement System (PERS; see Govt C §§20000–21692). Family Code §2060(b), however, requires joinder of *all* plans for a judgment or order dividing a community interest in benefits to be enforceable against a plan; and ERISA, which provides that a QDRO is enforceable against a private pension plan without joinder (see §12.8), does not apply to public plans. PERS, however, has historically cooperated in the joinder procedure established under Cal Rules of Ct 5.162. For related discussion and required Judicial Council forms, see §§12.15–12.25.

If protection is desired against payment of the benefits to the employee spouse before the action is commenced, a notice of adverse interest (see §12.9) should be served on the plan.

NOTE➤ The legislature added Ed C §§22007.5 and 26002.5, effective January 1, 2005, to Parts 13 and 14 of the Education Code governing STRS, to include California registered domestic partners within the definition of "spouses," with limited exceptions. However, as of January 1, 2006, Ed C §26002.5 provides that, except as excluded in Ed C §26004, 26807.5(d), 269.6.5(d), or 27406, a person who is the registered domestic partner of a member (as established under Fam C §297 or Fam C §299.2) must be treated in the same manner as a "spouse," as defined in Ed C §26140. For comprehensive treatment of the California Domestic Partner Rights and Responsibilities Act of 2003, effective January 1, 2005, see California Domestic Partnerships (Cal CEB 2005).

§12.12   4. Federal Pension Plans

Federal pension benefits are generally divisible as community property in state court marital actions. On current substantive law in this area, see §§5.37–5.38. A federal plan that counsel has tried to join as a party may, however, move to quash service of the summons (see §10.61) or initiate proceedings in federal court to remove the cause of action asserted against it, or even to remove the entire action, from the state court (see §12.6). Fortunately, joinder of a federal plan appears to be unnecessary under statutes that provide for the division of a community interest in federal pension benefits.

The Federal Uniformed Services Former Spouses' Protection Act (FUSFSPA) (10 USC §1408) specifies a detailed procedure that, if followed, renders an order dividing a community interest in military retirement benefits binding on the military service, even though the service is not joined as a party to the action. 10 USC §1408(a)(2), (b). The Railroad Retirement Board is also required by federal statute (overturning *Hisquierdo v Hisquierdo* (1979) 439 US 572, 59 L Ed 2d 1, 99 S Ct 802) to make payments in accordance with an order dividing a community property interest in railroad retirement benefits. 45 USC §231m(b)(2). In addition, the Office of Personnel Management must comply with a court order dividing a community interest in federal civil service pension benefits, whether or not the government is joined as a party, as long as all required documentation is provided. 5 USC §8345(j).

When a nonemployee spouse has an interest in federal pension benefits, a notice of adverse interest (see §12.9) should be served on the plan to notify the plan of the pending dissolution and claim on that interest until an order dividing the benefits can be issued and served on the plan.

§12.13   5. Nonresident Pension Plans

A nonresident pension plan may be joined as a party only if the state court in the marital action can obtain personal jurisdiction over the plan, *i.e.*, the plan has sufficient minimum contacts with California to justify California's exercise of personal jurisdiction over it. See §12.5. Compare *Marriage of Martin* (1989) 207 CA3d 1426, 1435, 255 CR 720 (payment of insurance claims by nonresident insurer to nonresident father for health services provided to children in California is insufficient contact to join insurer), with *Marriage of Bastian* (1979) 94 CA3d 483, 156 CR 524 (nonresident pension plan contributed to by California employers and making payments to California beneficiaries is subject to California jurisdiction). In many cases, nonresident pension plans will satisfy the minimum contacts requirement and be subject to joinder.

A nonresident pension plan may contest joinder by moving to quash service of summons on the ground that the court lacks jurisdiction over it. See CCP §418.10(a)(1). It may also attempt to remove to federal court the cause of action asserted against it, or even the entire marital action. 28 USC §1441. On removal to federal court and considerations that may indicate delaying joinder when removal is threatened see §12.6.

§12.14   6. Enforcement of Support Orders

An employee benefit plan need *not* be joined as a party to the marital action for a child or spousal support order to be enforceable against the plan. An execution lien may be levied against the employee's right to payment of benefits under the plan, whether or not the plan is joined as a party, and the lien will continue until the plan has withheld and paid the full amount of support specified. Fam C §5103. Note, however, that private plans governed by ERISA are bound only by support orders that meet federal requirements as a QDRO. 29 USC §1056(d)(3).

§12.15   C. Procedure for Joinder

The procedure for joinder of an employee benefit plan is relatively quick and simple. All pleadings are prepared on Judicial Council forms (Fam C §2062(a); Cal Rules of Ct 5.162) and, on request, the court clerk enters an order for joinder without a hearing (Fam C §2060(a)).

1. Request and Order for Joinder

§12.16   a. Discussion

In preparing the request for joinder, it is essential to name the plan correctly. The plan is usually a legal entity separate from the employer itself; use of the employer's name, instead of the plan's name, may result in an ineffective joinder of the plan as claimant. The plan's correct name may be ascertained from, *e.g.,* the plan itself, the spouse's employer, or plan documents provided to employees. Alternatively, within 30 days after written request, the employee spouse is required to furnish (as to each plan covering him or her) the name of the plan and the name, title, address, and telephone number of the plan's trustee, administrator, or agent for service of process. Fam C §2062(c). The plan's correct name can then be ascertained by contacting that party.

The request for joinder is signed by the attorney for the applicant. On receiving the request, the clerk must enter an order joining the benefit plan as a party. Fam C §2060(a).

§12.17 **b. Form: Request for Joinder of Employee Benefit Plan and Order (Judicial Council Form FL-372)**

FL-372

ATTORNEY OR PARTY WITHOUT ATTORNEY *(Name, state bar no., and address)*:	FOR COURT USE ONLY

TELEPHONE NO.: FAX NO. *(Optional)*:

E-MAIL ADDRESS *(Optional)*:

ATTORNEY FOR *(Name)*:

SUPERIOR COURT OF CALIFORNIA, COUNTY OF

STREET ADDRESS:

MAILING ADDRESS:

CITY AND ZIP CODE:

BRANCH NAME:

MARRIAGE OF

PETITIONER:

RESPONDENT:

CLAIMANT:

REQUEST FOR JOINDER OF EMPLOYEE BENEFIT PLAN AND ORDER	CASE NUMBER:

TO THE CLERK

1. Please join as a party claimant to this proceeding *(specify name of employee benefit plan)*:

2. The pleading on joinder is submitted with this application for filing.

Dated:

▶ _____

(SIGNATURE OF ☐ ATTORNEY FOR)

☐ PETITIONER ☐ RESPONDENT

_____

(TYPE OR PRINT NAME)

ORDER OF JOINDER

3. IT IS ORDERED
   a. The claimant listed in item 1 is joined as a party claimant to this proceeding.
   b. The pleading on joinder be filed.
   c. Summons be issued.
   d. Claimant be served with a copy of the pleading on joinder, a copy of this request for joinder and order, the summons, and a blank *Notice of Appearance and Response of Employee Benefit Plan* (form FL-374).

Dated: Clerk, By _____, Deputy

Page 1 of 1

Form Adopted for Mandatory Use	**REQUEST FOR JOINDER OF EMPLOYEE**	Family Code, §§ 2010, 2021,
Judicial Council of California	**BENEFIT PLAN AND ORDER**	2060–2065, 2070–2074
FL-372 [Rev. January 1, 2003]		www.courtinfo.ca.gov

Copies: Original (submit to court clerk); copy for service on plan; courtesy copy for other party; office copies.

2. Pleading on Joinder—Employee Benefit Plan

§12.18   a. Discussion

On entry of the order for joinder, the requesting party files the Pleading on Joinder—Employee Benefit Plan. Fam C §2061. See form in §12.19. In practice, the pleading is usually submitted to the clerk at the same time as the request for joinder (see form in §12.17), together with the Summons (see form in §12.21) for issuance by the clerk.

Under most circumstances, Items 7.a-d of the pleading are checked as elements of relief requested by the applicant. Further relief may be specifically requested at Item 7.e, *e.g.,* prohibiting the plan from honoring specified elections by the employee spouse (the nature of which may be ascertained by a careful review of the plan documents). The pleading is signed by the applicant's attorney.

§12.19   b. Form: Pleading on Joinder—Employee Benefit Plan (Judicial Council Form FL-370)

FL-370

ATTORNEY OR PARTY WITHOUT ATTORNEY *(Name, state bar number, and address):*	FOR COURT USE ONLY

TELEPHONE NO.:   FAX NO. *(Optional):*

E-MAIL ADDRESS *(Optional):*

ATTORNEY FOR *(Name):*

SUPERIOR COURT OF CALIFORNIA, COUNTY OF

STREET ADDRESS:

MAILING ADDRESS:

CITY AND ZIP CODE:

BRANCH NAME:

MARRIAGE OF

PETITIONER:

RESPONDENT:

CLAIMANT:

PLEADING ON JOINDER—EMPLOYEE BENEFIT PLAN	CASE NUMBER:

TO THE CLAIMANT: You have been joined as a party claimant in this proceeding because an interest is claimed in the employee benefit plan that is or may be subject to disposition by this court. The party who obtained the order for your joinder declares:

1. Information concerning the employee covered by the plan:
   a. Name:
   b. Employer *(name):*
   c. ☐ Name of labor union representing employee:
   d. ☐ Employee identification number:
   e. Other *(specify):*

2. Petitioner's

   a. ☐ Attorney *(name, address, and telephone number):*

   b. ☐ Address and telephone number, if unrepresented by an attorney:

3. Respondent's

   a. ☐ Attorney *(name, address, and telephone number):*

   b. Address and telephone number, if unrepresented by an attorney:

Form Adopted for Mandatory Use
Judicial Council of California
FL-370 [Rev. January 1, 2003]

PLEADING ON JOINDER—EMPLOYEE BENEFIT PLAN

Family Code, §§ 2060–2065
www.courtinfo.ca.gov

PETITIONER:	CASE NUMBER:
RESPONDENT:	

4. Petition for dissolution ☐ and response states
   a. Date of marriage:
   b. Date of separation:

5. ☐ Response states
   a. Date of marriage:
   b. Date of separation:

6. Judgment
   a. ☐ has not been entered
   b. ☐ was entered on *(date)*:
     (1) ☐ and disposes of each spouse's interest in the employee benefit plan.
     (2) ☐ and does not dispose of each spouse's interest in the employee benefit plan.

7. The following relief is sought:
   a. ☐ An order determining the nature and extent of both employee and nonemployee spouse's interest in employee's benefits under the plan.
   b. ☐ An order restraining claimant from making benefit payments to employee spouse pending the determination and disposition of nonemployee spouse's interest, if any, in employee's benefits under the plan.
   c. ☐ An order directing claimant to notify nonemployee spouse when benefits under the plan first become payable to employee.
   d. ☐ An order directing claimant to make payment to nonemployee spouse of said spouse's interest in employee's benefits under the plan when they become payable to employee.
   e. ☐ Other *(specify)*:

   f. Such other orders as may be appropriate.

Dated: ▶

(SIGNATURE OF ☐ ATTORNEY FOR)

☐ PETITIONER   ☐ RESPONDENT

(TYPE OR PRINT NAME)

Copies: Original (file with court clerk); copy for service on plan; courtesy copy for other party; office copies.

3. Service of Summons and Other Documents

§12.20 **a. Discussion**

After the Order for Joinder has been issued and the Pleading on Joinder has been filed, the documents are served on the benefit plan with the Summons (see form in §12.21). The summons should be presented for issuance by the court clerk when the request for joinder and the pleading are submitted. A blank copy of the Notice of Appearance and Response of Employee Benefit Plan (see form in §12.23) must also be served on the plan with the summons, request and order for joinder, and pleading on joinder. Fam C §2062(a).

Although Fam C §2062(b) states that service is to be "in the same manner as service of papers generally" (*i.e.,* as prescribed by CCP §§1010–1020), the safer course, in order to ensure the court's jurisdiction over the plan, is to serve it in the same manner as service of summons (*i.e.,* as prescribed by CCP §§415.10–415.50; see §§10.31–10.42). As a practical matter, most plan administrators will accept service by signing and returning a notice and acknowledgment of receipt (see §§10.33–10.34) or will agree to file a notice of appearance and response without any formal service of process. Note that to facilitate identification and service the employee spouse is required to furnish (as to each plan covering him or her) the name of the plan and the name, title, address, and telephone number of the plan's trustee, administrator, or agent for service of process within 30 days after written request. Fam C §2062(c).

In completing the summons form for presentation to the court clerk for issuance, the box is checked, and the name of the plan is entered, at Item 2. After issuance but before service, on the copy to be served, the box at 3.c should be checked, the name of the plan entered, and the last of the eight following boxes checked.

§12.21 b. Form: Summons (Joinder) (Judicial Council Form FL-375)

FL-375

ATTORNEY OR PARTY WITHOUT ATTORNEY *(Name, state bar number, and address):*	FOR COURT USE ONLY

TELEPHONE NO. *(Optional):*   FAX NO. *(Optional):*
E–MAIL ADDRESS *(Optional):*
ATTORNEY FOR *(Name):*

SUPERIOR COURT OF CALIFORNIA, COUNTY OF
STREET ADDRESS:
MAILING ADDRESS:
CITY AND ZIP CODE:
BRANCH NAME:

MARRIAGE OF

PETITIONER:

RESPONDENT:

CLAIMANT:

SUMMONS (JOINDER)	CASE NUMBER:

NOTICE! You have been sued. The court may decide against you without your being heard unless you respond within 30 days. Read the information below.

If you wish to seek the advice of an attorney in this matter, you should do so promptly so that your response or pleading, if any, may be filed on time.

¡AVISO! Usted ha sido demandado. El tribunal puede decidir contra Ud. sin audiencia a menos que Ud. responda dentro de 30 días. Lea la información que sigue.

Si Usted desea solicitar el consejo de un abogado en este asunto, debería hacerlo inmediatamente, de esta manera, su respuesta o alegación, si hay alguna, puede ser registrada a tiempo.

1. ☐ TO THE ☐ PETITIONER ☐ RESPONDENT ☐ CLAIMANT
A pleading has been filed under an order joining *(name of claimant):*

as a party in this proceeding. If you fail to file an appropriate pleading within **30** days of the date this summons is served on you, your default may be entered and the court may enter a judgment containing the relief requested in the pleading, court costs, and such other relief as may be granted by the court, which could result in the garnishment of wages, taking of money or property, or other relief.

2. ☐ TO THE CLAIMANT EMPLOYEE BENEFIT PLAN
A pleading on joinder has been filed under the clerk's order joining *(name of employee benefit plan):*

as a party claimant in this proceeding. If the employee benefit plan fails to file an appropriate pleading within **30** days of the date this summons is served on it, a default may be entered and the court may enter a judgment containing the relief requested.

Dated: Clerk, By _____, Deputy

3. NOTICE TO THE PERSON SERVED: You are served

(SEAL)

a. ☐ As an individual.

b. ☐ As (or on behalf of) the person sued under the fictitious name of:

c. ☐ On behalf of:

Under: ☐ CCP 416.10 (Corporation)   ☐ CCP 416.60 (Minor)
☐ CCP 416.20 (Defunct Corporation)   ☐ CCP 416.70 (Incompetent)
☐ CCP 416.40 (Association or Partnership)   ☐ CCP 416.90 (Individual)
☐ Other: ☐ FC 2062 (Employee Benefit Plan)

d. ☐ By personal delivery on *(date):*

Page 1 of 2

Form Adopted for Mandatory Use
Judicial Council of California
FL-375 [Rev. January 1, 2003]

SUMMONS (JOINDER)

www.courtinfo.ca.gov.

PROOF OF SERVICE—SUMMONS (JOINDER)
(Use separate proof of service for each person served)

1. I served the

  a. *Summons and (1)* ☐ *Request for Joinder of Employee Benefit Plan and Order, Pleading on Joinder-Employee Benefit Plan, blank Notice of Appearance and Response of Employee Benefit Plan*

    (2) ☐ *Notice of Motion and Declaration for Joinder*   (3) ☐ *Order re Joinder*

    (4) ☐ *Pleading on Joinder* (specify title):

    (5) ☐ *Other:*

  b. On *(name of party or claimant):*

  c. By serving   (1) ☐ Party or claimant.   (2) ☐ Other *(name and title or relationship to person served):*

  d. ☐ By delivery at ☐ home   ☐ business (1) Date of:

    (2)   Time of: (3) Address:

  e. ☐ By mailing (1) Date of: (2) Place of:

2. Manner of service: *(check proper box)*

  a. ☐ **Personal service.** By personally delivering copies. (CCP 415.10)

  b. ☐ **Substituted service on corporation, unincorporated association (including partnership), or public entity.** By leaving, during usual office hours, copies in the office of the person served with the person who apparently was in charge and thereafter mailing (by first-class mail, postage prepaid) copies to the person served at the place where the copies were left. (CCP 41 5.20(a))

  c. ☐ **Substituted service on natural person, minor, incompetent, or candidate.** By leaving copies at the dwelling house, usual place of abode, or usual place of business of the person served in the presence of a competent member of the household or a person apparently in charge of the office or place of business, at least 18 years of age, who was informed of the general nature of the papers, and thereafter mailing (by first-class mail, postage prepaid) copies to the person served at the place where the copies were left. (CCP 415.20(b)) **(Attach separate declaration or affidavit stating acts relied on to establish reasonable diligence in first attempting personal service.)**

  d. ☐ **Mail and acknowledgment service.** By mailing (by first-class mail or airmail) copies to the person served, together with two copies of the form of notice and acknowledgment and a return envelope, postage prepaid, addressed to the sender. (CCP 415.30) **(Attach completed acknowledgment of receipt.)**

  e. ☐ **Certified or registered mail service.** By mailing to address outside California (by registered or certified airmail with return receipt requested) copies to the person served. (CCP 415.40) **(Attach signed return receipt or other evidence of actual delivery to the person served.)**

  f. ☐ Other *(specify code section):*

    ☐ Additional page is attached.

3. The notice to the person served (item 3 on the copy of the summons served) was completed as follows (CCP 412.30, 415.10, and 474):

  a. ☐ As an individual.

  b. ☐ As the person sued under the fictitious name of:

  c. ☐ On behalf of:

    Under: ☐ CCP 416.10 (Corporation)   ☐ CCP 416.60 (Minor)

          ☐ CCP 416.20 (Defunct Corporation)   ☐ CCP 416.70 (Incompetent)

          ☐ CCP 416.40 (Association or   ☐ CCP 416.90 (Individual)

              partnership)   ☐ FC 2062 (Employee Benefit Plan)

  d. By personal delivery on *(date):*

4. At the time of service I was at least 18 years of age and not a party to this action.

5. Fee for service: $ . . . .

6. Person serving

  a. ☐ Not a registered California process server.

  b. ☐ Registered California process server.

  c. ☐ Exempt from registration under Bus. & Prof. Code 22350(b).

  d. ☐ California sheriff, marshal, or constable.

  e. Name, address, telephone number, and, if applicable, county of registration and number:

I declare under penalty of perjury that the foregoing is true and correct and that this declaration is executed on *(date):* at *(place):* , California.	(For California sheriff, marshal, or constable use only) I certify that the foregoing is true and correct and that this certificate is executed on *(date):* at *(place):* , California.
_____ (Signature)	_____ (Signature)

Copies: Original (submit to court clerk for issuance and return); copy for service on plan; courtesy copy for other party; office copies.

4. Notice of Appearance and Response

§12.22   a. Discussion

After the benefit plan has been served, it has 30 days to file and serve a responsive document on the requesting party. Cal Rules of Ct 5.158(c). The plan may file a notice of appearance and response (see Judicial Council Form FL-374; see §12.23) and do nothing further, in which case joinder is complete; it may file a response on the same form as the notice of appearance; if it contests jurisdiction, it may file a motion to quash service (CCP §418.10; see §10.61); or it may do nothing (see §12.24). If the plan simply files a notice of appearance and does not file a response, all statements of facts and requests for relief in the pleading are deemed controverted. Fam C §2063(b). A notice of appearance must be filed, if at all, within 30 days after service on the plan of a copy of the joinder request and summons. Fam C §2063(a).

§12.23　　b. Form: Notice of Appearance and Response of Employee Benefit Plan (Judicial Council Form FL-374)

FL-374

ATTORNEY OR PARTY WITHOUT ATTORNEY *(Name, state bar number and address):*	FOR COURT USE ONLY

TELEPHONE NO. *(Optional):*　　　　　FAX NO. *(Optional):*
E-MAIL ADDRESS *(Optional):*
ATTORNEY FOR *(Name):*

SUPERIOR COURT OF CALIFORNIA, COUNTY OF
STREET ADDRESS:
MAILING ADDRESS:
CITY AND ZIP CODE:
BRANCH NAME:

MARRIAGE OF
PETITIONER:

RESPONDENT:

CLAIMANT:

CASE NUMBER:

NOTICE OF APPEARANCE ☐ **AND RESPONSE OF EMPLOYEE BENEFIT PLAN**

1. An appearance in this proceeding is entered by claimant employee benefit plan *(name):*

2. Service on claimant may be made as follows

　a. ☐ Attorney for claimant *(name, address, and telephone number):*

　b. ☐ Other *(name, title, address, and telephone number):*

3. ☐ Claimant responds to the pleading on joinder and states that the allegations of the pleadings are

　a. ☐ correct

　b. ☐ incorrect as set forth in ☐ attachment 3b or ☐ as follows *(specify):*

Dated:

_____
(TYPE OR PRINT NAME)

Claimant

By _____
(SIGNATURE)

Page 1 of 1

NOTICE OF APPEARANCE AND RESPONSE OF EMPLOYEE BENEFIT PLAN

Family Code, §§ 80, 2010, 2021, 2060–2065, 2070–2074
www.courtinfo.ca.gov

Copies: Blank copy for service on pension plan.

§12.24   5. Default

If, within 30 days after service, or such further time as may be allowed, the plan does not file a notice of appearance, a notice of motion to quash service, or a notice of filing a petition for writ of mandate after denial of a motion to quash, the court clerk must enter the plan's default on the application of the party requesting joinder. Fam C §2065. On the procedure for, and the effect of, entry of a party's default, see §§14.6–14.16. If a plan allows its default to be entered, it may not thereafter appear in the proceeding but must simply await issuance and service of a court order directing the distribution of the benefits.

§12.25   6. Procedure After Appearance or Default

Prior to trial, either party may notify the plan of a proposed settlement and, if so notified, the plan may stipulate to the settlement or notify the parties that it will contest the settlement. Fam C §2071. As a practical matter, it is advisable to submit any proposed settlement, at least insofar as it relates to benefits, to the plan before submitting it to the court. The plan may have helpful suggestions on the wording of the benefit provisions. Further, many plans will provide counsel with sample judgment provisions before any settlement is reached between the spouses. Drafting provisions in accordance with the plan's specifications facilitates implementation of the agreement; however, a sample domestic relations order provided by a plan should not be approached as a simple fill-in-the-blanks exercise. Counsel may wish to associate-in an attorney who specializes in pension or ERISA matters rather than attempting to draft a (qualified) domestic relations order without adequate knowledge of the complexities involved.

The plan may, but need not, appear as a party at any hearing in the proceeding. Fam C §2072. The provisions of any order entered by stipulation of the parties or entered at or as a result of a hearing not attended by the plan, and that affect the plan or either spouse's interest under the plan, must be stayed until 30 days after the order has been served on the plan. Fam C §2073(a). The plan may waive all or any part of the 30-day period. Fam C §2073(b). If, within the 30-day period, the plan files a motion to set aside or modify the provisions of the order affecting the plan, those provisions will be stayed until the court rules on the motion. Fam C §2073(c). The30-day period must be extended to 60 days if the plan files and serves a request for extension within the 30-day period. Fam C §2073(d). Either spouse may seek an order staying any other provisions of the order or associated orders related to or affected by the provisions to which the plan has objected until the court resolves the motion. Fam C §2073(e). If the provisions affecting the plan are modified by the court, either party may request modification of any other provision of the order or associated orders (*e.g.,* support, division of other property) that is related to or affected by the benefit plan provisions. Fam C §2074(c).

For an argument that ERISA may potentially preempt Fam C §§2072–2074 if these statutes conflict with ERISA or an ERISA-covered plan's written procedures, see §12.9.

IV. JOINDER OF PARTIES OTHER THAN EMPLOYEE BENEFIT PLANS

§12.26　　A. Parties Who May Be Joined

Under Fam C §2021, anyone who claims an interest in a marital action may be joined as a party in accordance with the Family Law Rules of Court. California Rules of Court 5.150, 5.152, and 5.154 describe the specific circumstances under which a person who claims or controls an interest subject to disposition in the marital action may be joined.

§12.27　　1. Interest Claimed in Marital Property

If third persons hold title to or otherwise claim an interest in real or personal property subject to disposition in the proceeding, a request may be made to join such persons as parties to the action. Fam C §2021; Cal Rules of Ct 5.150, 5.154(a). Once jurisdiction has been acquired over the marital "res" (typically, by a claim of community interest in the property), the court has the power to decide the rights of anyone who claims an interest in the res, as long as the due process requirements of notice and an opportunity to be heard are met. These requirements are met by properly joining the interested persons as parties to the action. *Marriage of Davis* (1977) 68 CA3d 294, 301, 137 CR 265. See also *Schnabel v Superior Court*

(1994) 30 CA4th 758, 36 CR2d 677 (held abuse of discretion to refuse to join corporation in which parties owned 30 percent of stock and which had actively taken sides in dissolution proceedings); *Babcock v Superior Court* (1994) 29 CA4th 721, 725, 35 CR2d 462 (affirmed joinder of party's nonmarital partner who allegedly received gifts of community property from that party).

The petitioner or the respondent may request joinder of a party who claims an interest in marital property; the person who claims the interest is not given authority by statute or rule of court to make the request. Fam C §2021; Cal Rules of Ct 5.154(a). However, dicta in *Marriage of Davis, supra* (68 CA3d at 303), quoting *Elms v Elms* (1935) 4 C2d 681, 683, 52 P2d 223, states that "if neither party . . . names as defendants the third parties who claim rights in property alleged to be community, such parties may intervene themselves in the divorce action and establish their rights."

Joinder of a party who claims an interest in marital property is permissive, not mandatory. See Cal Rules of Ct 5.150. See §12.3 for the factors to be weighed by the court in determining permissive joinder. On possible causes of action that may be alleged in a complaint or a petition for joinder when a third party claims an interest in marital property, see §12.38.

§12.28   2. Claim of Custody or Visitation Rights

Although the first order of preference in awarding custody of minor children is to the parents, or either of them, the court may award custody or visitation rights to a third party in the marital action. Fam C §§3040(a), 3100(a), 3103(a). The petitioner, the respondent, or a third party claiming custody or visitation rights may apply for joinder. Cal Rules of Ct 5.154(a)-(b). Further, the court has the affirmative duty to order joinder of any third party it "discovers" has or claims custody, physical control, or visitation rights with respect to the minor children of the marriage. Cal Rules of Ct 5.158(a). On possible causes of action that may be alleged in a complaint or a petition for joinder when custody or visitation rights with respect to a minor child of the marriage are claimed by a third party, see §12.38.

§12.29   a. Stepparent Visitation

A party in a marital action may petition the court for reasonable visitation rights with respect to the minor child of his or her spouse. Fam C §3101(a). Note that joinder is neither required nor applicable, because the stepparent is already a party to the action.

§12.30   b. Grandparent Visitation

In marital actions, the court may award reasonable visitation rights to a grandparent of a minor child of a party to the marriage. Fam C §3103(a). Section 3103(a) does not indicate whether a grandparent seeking visitation rights under it must be joined as a party to the action, but it would seem prudent for him or her to request to be joined. Note that the court will be required to grant the request. Cal Rules of Ct 5.158(a).

WARNING> When advising a grandparent who seeks visitation in a marital action, counsel should ensure the client understands that awards of attorney fees and costs "reasonably necessary to maintain or defend the action on the issues relating to that party" may be made against a properly joined nongovernmental (and nonspousal) party. Fam C §2030(d). See *Marriage of Perry* (1998) 61 CA4th 295, 310, 71 CR2d 499 (grandmother ordered to pay attorney fees incurred by father of her grandchild as result of custody claims she made).

§12.31   3. Person Served With Restraining Order

A person who has been served with a temporary restraining order affecting the custody or visitation of a minor child subject to the action, or the use of property in his or her possession or control or that he or she claims to own, may apply to be joined as a party to the marital action. Cal Rules of Ct 5.154(c). The joinder of such a party is permissive, not mandatory; on factors the court must consider in deciding permissive joinder, see §12.3. A common example of a party who may seek joinder under this rule is a closely held corporation that is partially owned by the community. On ex parte orders that may be sought against a third party in a marital action, see Fam C §2045(a); Cal Rules of Ct 5.106. See §11.7.

A person served with such an order may also contest the restraint at the hearing on the order to show cause without seeking to be joined as a party. See Fam C §§242–243; Cal Rules of Ct 5.118. However, if the TRO involves a substantial right of the restrained person that should be adjudicated only after a full evidentiary hearing, joinder may be necessary to protect that person's rights. Cal Rules of Ct 5.158(b).

§12.32   4. Indispensable or Necessary Party

Under Cal Rules of Ct 5.158(b), the court may order that a person be joined as a party to the action if the court finds that (1) it would be appropriate to determine a particular issue in the proceeding and (2) the party to be joined is indispensable to a determination of the issue or necessary to the enforcement of any judgment rendered on that issue. On factors the court must consider in deciding whether it is appropriate to determine the particular issue in the proceeding, see §12.3. Joinder of such a party is permissive, not mandatory. See Cal Rules of Ct 5.158(b).

For examples of indispensable parties, see *Schnabel v Superior Court* (1994) 30 CA4th 758, 36 CR2d 677 (held abuse of discretion to refuse to join corporation in which parties owned 30 percent of stock and which had actively taken sides in dissolution proceedings); *Marriage of Mena* (1989) 212 CA3d 12, 19, 260 CR 314 (as welfare recipient's assignee, county was indispensable party with regard to subsequent child support proceedings). For an example of a party necessary to enforcement, see *Marriage of Wilson* (1989) 209 CA3d 720, 257 CR 477 (labor union was necessary to enforcement of child support order and could be ordered to provide District Attorney with prompt notification of obligor's being sent to fill employment request).

B. Procedure for Joinder

§12.33   1. When to Request Joinder

It is usually advisable to begin joinder proceedings as early as possible in the action. If pretrial motions or discovery proceedings become necessary with respect to the claimant, early joinder will avoid delay in bringing the case to trial or settlement. If desired, a request for joinder may be filed at the commencement of the marital action and served on the respondent with the summons and petition.

However, joinder may be requested at any time during the proceeding. If joinder of a party is likely to delay or disrupt the action (see §§12.5–12.6), it may be desirable to wait until temporary orders are obtained (see generally chap 11) or a judgment on the bifurcated issue of marital status has been granted (see §§14.59–14.70).

2. Notice of Motion and Declaration for Joinder

§12.34   a. Discussion

A party to a marital action or a third party claimant may apply for joinder (when permitted; see §§12.26–12.32) by completing, serving, and filing the Judicial Council form of Notice of Motion and Declaration for Joinder (Judicial Council Form FL-371; see §12.37), together with an appropriate pleading (Cal Rules of Ct 5.156(a); see sample pleading in §12.39).

§12.35   (1) Notice of Motion

The notice of motion sets the hearing date, time, and place at which the court will decide whether it should issue an order for joinder. Counsel must ascertain from the court clerk the appropriate day, time, and department in which a hearing for joinder may be scheduled and set a hearing date that complies with court rules and statutes. Under Cal Rules of Ct 5.156(a), the hearing date must be less than 30 days after the date the notice of motion was filed.

The California Rules of Court do not specify how many days' notice must be given. Without any other specified notice requirement, counsel should comply with the 16-court-day notice required by CCP §1005(a)(13)–(b). If the notice of motion is served by mail, the 16-court-day notice requirement is extended by an additional 5, 10, or 20 days, depending on where the notice is sent. If the notice is served by facsimile transmission, Express Mail, or another method of overnight delivery, the 16-day notice requirement is extended by 2 days. Because Cal Rules of Ct 5.156(a) requires that the hearing date be set within 30 days after the filing of the notice of motion, it will often be necessary to seek a stipulation shortening the time for service or, alternatively, continuing the hearing date. See California Civil Procedure Before Trial §§12.61, 12.62 (4th ed Cal CEB 2004). If the other side will not stipulate, it will be necessary to request an order shortening time, as permitted under CCP §1005(b), from the court. See Civ Proc Before Trial §12.63. On service of the notice of motion and other documents, see §12.40.

The Notice of Motion is signed by the attorney for the party requesting joinder and must be accompanied by a proof of service when filed. See Cal Rules of Ct 5.10(e).

§12.36 (2) Declaration for Joinder

The applicant should set forth at Item 5 of the declaration for joinder specific facts showing that each person sought or seeking to be joined claims or controls an interest subject to disposition in the proceeding. See Cal Rules of Ct 5.150, 5.154. If the statement of facts demonstrates that the party has physical custody or claims custody or visitation rights with respect to a minor child of the marriage, joinder is mandatory (Cal Rules of Ct 5.158(a)) and, consequently, Items 6 and 7 need not be completed.

In all other cases, the applicant should state facts at Item 6 showing that it would be appropriate for the court to determine the issue underlying the request for joinder in the proceeding. See Cal Rules of Ct 5.158(b). The facts should address the effect of the proposed joinder on the proceeding, including the mandatory considerations in that regard that are set forth in Cal Rules of Ct 5.158(a) (see §12.3).

Likewise, when joinder is not mandatory, facts should be stated at Item 7 showing that the proposed claimant is indispensable to the determination sought or necessary to the enforcement of any judgment rendered (*e.g.,* a judgment awarding real property to either or both spouses is not binding and enforceable against a person who claims ownership of the property unless he or she is joined as a party). See Cal Rules of Ct 5.158(b); see §12.32.

If it is necessary to add continuation pages to complete any of the above items, the Judicial Council form of Additional Page, available in California Judicial Council Forms Manual §11 (Cal CEB 1981) or pleading paper may be used, as permitted by local rules. The declaration must be signed under penalty of perjury by the person applying for joinder, not by the attorney.

§12.37   b. Form: Notice of Motion and Declaration for Joinder (Judicial Council Form FL-371)

FL-371

ATTORNEY OR PARTY WITHOUT ATTORNEY *(Name, state bar number, and address)*:	FOR COURT USE ONLY

TELEPHONE NO.:   FAX NO. *(Optional)*:
E-MAIL ADDRESS *(Optional)*:
ATTORNEY FOR *(Name)*:

SUPERIOR COURT OF CALIFORNIA, COUNTY OF
STREET ADDRESS:
MAILING ADDRESS:
CITY AND ZIP CODE:
BRANCH NAME:

MARRIAGE OF
PETITIONER:

RESPONDENT:

NOTICE OF MOTION AND DECLARATION FOR JOINDER	CASE NUMBER:

NOTICE OF MOTION

1. TO ☐ Petitioner ☐ Respondent

2. A hearing on this motion for joinder will be held as follows:

a. Date: Time: Dept.:   Rm.:

b. The address of court: ☐ is shown above ☐ is:

c. ☐ Petitioner ☐ Respondent ☐ Claimant   will apply to this court for an order joining claimant as a party to this proceeding on the grounds set forth in the Declaration below.

3. The pleading on joinder accompanies this notice of motion.

Dated:

▶

_____   _____
(TYPE OR PRINT NAME)   (SIGNATURE)

DECLARATION FOR JOINDER

4. The name of the person to be joined is:

5. Facts showing that each person sought or seeking to be joined possesses or controls or claims to own any property subject to disposition by this court, or that such person has or claims custody, physical control, or visitation rights with respect to any minor child of the marriage, are *(specify)*:

Form Adopted for Mandatory Use
Judicial Council of California
FL-371 [Rev. January 1, 2003]

NOTICE OF MOTION AND DECLARATION FOR JOINDER

Family Code, § 2021
www.courtinfo.ca.gov

PETITIONER:	CASE NUMBER:
RESPONDENT:	

6. Facts showing that it would be appropriate for this court to determine the particular issue in the proceedings are:

7. Facts showing that each person sought or seeking to be joined is either indispensable to a determination of the particular issue or necessary to the enforcement of any judgment rendered on the issue are:

I declare under penalty of perjury under the laws of the State of California that the foregoing is true and correct.

Date:

▶

_____   _____
(TYPE OR PRINT NAME)   (SIGNATURE OF DECLARANT)

Copies: Original (submit to court clerk); copy for service on each party; copy to be held for service on claimant after joinder has been granted; office copies.

3. Pleading

§12.38   a. Discussion

The applicant for joinder must prepare an "appropriate pleading," setting forth his or her cause of action against, or as, the proposed claimant, as though the pleading were to be filed in a separate action or proceeding. Cal Rules of Ct 5.156(a). A copy of the pleading accompanies the notice of motion and declaration filed with the court and the copies served on those entitled to receive notice (see §12.40). The original pleading is not filed, nor is a copy served on the claimant, until joinder is granted by the court.

Counsel should approach the drafting of the causes of action for joinder as though a separate proceeding were being brought against or by the claimant. Almost any cause of action relating to a claim of interest in real or personal property (see §12.27), or to the custody or visitation of minor children (see §12.28), may be stated in the pleading. The following list of causes of action is not intended to be exhaustive, but only as illustrative of the broad range of possibilities that counsel may consider:

- If joinder is sought on an issue involving real property, a cause of action may be stated for partition, declaratory relief, to quiet title, to establish a constructive or resulting trust, or to set aside a fraudulent conveyance.

- If the issue involves personal property, the pleading may state a cause of action for conversion or for claim and delivery, or to establish a constructive or resulting trust.

- If the issue involves a community interest in a corporation or partnership, and if the applicant seeks to join the business entity as a party to the action, the pleading might request declaratory relief and a division of the parties' interests in the business. See *Marriage of Siller* (1986) 187 CA3d 36, 231 CR 757.

- When the issue involves child custody or visitation, the pleading might be framed as a petition for guardianship, a motion to modify a prior custody or visitation order, an application for a writ of habeas corpus, or a complaint for declaratory relief.

Following the causes of action, the applicant sets forth a prayer for the relief requested. The nature of this relief will depend on the causes of action stated and may also include a prayer for attorney fees and costs (except as against a county in a support action). The possibility of a judgment against the claimant for attorney fees and costs is a powerful tactical consideration in deciding to seek joinder of a party.

§12.39   b. Form: Complaint for Joinder

_ _[Attorney name]_ _
_ _[State Bar number]_ _
_ _[Address]_ _
_ _[Telephone number]_ _

Attorney for _ _[name]_ _

SUPERIOR COURT OF CALIFORNIA
COUNTY OF _ _ _ _ _ _ _ _

_ _ _ _ _ _ _ _ _ _ _,) **Plaintiff**)) **vs.**))) _ _ _ _ _ _ _ _ _ _ _,) **Defendant**)) _____)	**No.** _ _ _ _ _ _ _ _[same as marital action no.]_ _ **COMPLAINT** _ _[CAUSE(S) OF ACTION]_ _

Plaintiff alleges:

[Set forth cause(s) of action as though asserted in a separate action or proceeding (Cal Rules of Ct 5.156(a)); on possible causes of action that may be asserted, see §12.38]

WHEREFORE, plaintiff prays for judgment as follows:

[Set forth applicant's prayer for judgment]

Date: _____   __[Signature]__
                                 _ _[Typed name]_ _
                                 Attorney for _ _[party]_ _

Copies: Original and copy (hold for filing with court clerk and service on claimant after joinder has been granted); copy (for filing with court clerk with motion for joinder); copy for each party; office copies.

Comment: This pleading illustrates the format of a complaint that may be drafted by the petitioner or the respondent as an "appropriate pleading" for joinder of a third party. Cal Rules of Ct 5.156(a). When the applicant for joinder is the claimant, the pleading is captioned "Petition for Joinder." On drafting complaints generally, see California Civil Procedure Before Trial, chap 15 (4th ed Cal CEB 2004).

§12.40   4. Service of Notice of Motion and Other Documents

The notice of motion and declaration (see §§12.34–12.37), together with a copy of the pleading (see §§12.38–12.39), must be filed with the court clerk and served on the opposing party or parties, accompanied by the following:

- Any additional documents that may be necessary or helpful in establishing the applicant's claim for which joinder is sought (*e.g.,* a deed showing title to real property in the proposed claimant's name, a letter from a parent giving custody of the parties' minor child to the proposed claimant);

- A memorandum of points and authorities, if required by the court or otherwise appropriate (see §11.32 for discussion in context of motion for temporary orders); and

- Proof of service of all required documents.

If the person requesting joinder is the petitioner or the respondent, only the opposing party is served; the proposed claimant receives no notice of the joinder proceedings until after joinder has been ordered. If the proposed claimant is requesting joinder, he or she must serve both the petitioner and the respondent.

Service may generally be accomplished in the manner prescribed by CCP §§1010–1020 for service of papers, and the documents are typically served by mail. On time limitations for service, see §12.34. If the petitioner files a request for joinder concurrently with the marital action petition, however, the documents are served on the respondent with the summons and petition, typically by personal service (see §10.31) or by mail and acknowledgment of receipt (see §§10.33–10.34).

5. Responsive Declaration

§12.41   a. Discussion

A party may respond to a notice of motion for joinder by preparing, serving, and filing Judicial Council Form FL-373 (Responsive Declaration to Motion for Joinder; see §12.42). The form allows the responding party to consent to the request for joinder and to an order joining the claimant as a party or, alternatively, to oppose joinder and state the reasons for opposition. The discussion below is keyed to the Judicial Council form.

To consent to joinder, the box marked "Consent Order of Joinder" is checked, as is Item 1.a. Item 2 is left blank, and the responding party signs as declarant. On the reverse side of the form, the consent order is completed by checking the appropriate boxes to indicate which party or parties have consented, by checking boxes 3.c. (unless the proposed claimant is seeking joinder, in which case summons does not issue) and 3.d., and by inserting the date of the hearing to be taken off the calendar. The form is then submitted to the court for the judge's signature on the consent order.

If the responding party opposes joinder, Item 1.b. is checked, as is Item 2, followed by a complete and concise statement of the reasons why the moving party's declaration is incorrect or insufficient. In preparing the statement, reference should be made to the rules governing decisions on joinder motions. See §§12.26–12.31. If it is necessary to add continuation pages to complete the declarant's statement, the Judicial Council form of Additional Page, available in California Judicial Council Forms Manual §11 (Cal CEB 1981), or pleading paper may be used, as permitted by local rules. The declarant executes the form, and the reverse side is left blank.

Other documents that may be appropriate to serve and file in opposition to a request for joinder include documents that may support the declarant's statement under Item 2 and a memorandum of points and authorities, if required by the court or otherwise appropriate.

A proof of service must be completed and filed with the responsive declaration. Service and filing requirements are the same as for a response to a motion for temporary orders. See §11.38.

§12.42 b. Form: Responsive Declaration to Motion for Joinder and Consent Order of Joinder (Judicial Council Form FL-373)

FL-373

ATTORNEY OR PARTY WITHOUT ATTORNEY *(Name, state bar number, and address):*	FOR COURT USE ONLY

TELEPHONE NO. *(Optional):* FAX NO. *(Optional):*
E-MAIL ADDRESS *(Optional):*
ATTORNEY FOR *(Name):*

SUPERIOR COURT OF CALIFORNIA, COUNTY OF
STREET ADDRESS:
MAILING ADDRESS:
CITY AND ZIP CODE:
BRANCH NAME:

MARRIAGE OF
PETITIONER:

RESPONDENT:

CLAIMANT:

RESPONSIVE DECLARATION TO MOTION FOR JOINDER ☐ **CONSENT ORDER OF JOINDER**	CASE NUMBER:

1. ☐ Petitioner ☐ Respondent

  a. ☐ Consents to the requested joinder and stipulates to an order joining claimant as a party to this proceeding.
  b. ☐ Does not consent to the requested joinder of claimant as a party to this proceeding.

2. ☐ The statements contained in the declaration for joinder are incorrect or insufficient as follows *(specify):*

I declare under penalty of perjury under the laws of the State of California that the foregoing is true and correct.

dated:

_____   _____
(TYPE OR PRINT NAME)   (SIGNATURE OF DECLARANT)

Page 1 of 2

Form Adopted for Mandatory Use
Judicial Council of California
FL-373 [Rev. January 1, 2003]

RESPONSIVE DECLARATION TO MOTION FOR JOINDER
CONSENT ORDER OF JOINDER

www.courtinfo.ca.gov

CONSENT ORDER

3. ☐ Petitioner ☐ Respondent having consented and good cause appearing,
IT IS ORDERED that

a. The claimant is joined as a party to this proceeding.

b. The clerk file the original of the submitted pleadings.

c. ☐ *Summons (Joinder)* be issued and claimant be served with a copy of the motion for joinder with pleading attached and a copy of the *Summons (Joinder)*.

d. ☐ The hearing on the motion for joinder is taken off calendar for *(date):*

Dated: _____

_____
JUDICIAL OFFICER

Copies: Original (file with court clerk); copy for other party (and, if claimant is requesting joinder, for claimant); office copies.

§12.43　6. Hearing on Contested Motion

At a contested hearing on joinder, the court may allow testimony by the applicant and any opposing party, or it may make a determination based solely on the declarations and other documents filed in connection with the motion and opposition. The court clerk and local rules should be consulted to ascertain local practice. Even when the court does not allow testimony, the judge may ask questions of counsel, *e.g.*, with respect to the effect joinder would have on the proceeding.

On the circumstances under which joinder is mandatory or permissive, and the factors the court will consider in deciding whether to grant permissive joinder, see §12.3.

§12.44　7. Order After Hearing

An order for joinder made by the court after a contested hearing should be prepared on the Judicial Council form, Findings and Order After Hearing (see form in §11.55) and an attachment on pleading paper. On use of the consent order on the Responsive Declaration (see form in §12.42) when the motion is uncontested, see §12.41.

At Item 8 on the Findings and Order, the box before the words "As attached" should be checked. In drafting the terms of the attached order, reference may be made to the wording of the consent order on the Responsive Declaration, specifically Items 3.a-3.b and, unless the party seeking joinder is the proposed claimant, 3.c (with the addition of the Findings and Order to the documents to be served). If the motion for joinder is denied, the attachment should simply indicate that.

§12.45　8. Service of Summons and Other Documents

When the claimant is ordered joined as a party at the request of the petitioner or the respondent, the court must direct that a summons issue for service on the claimant. Cal Rules of Ct 5.158(c). The Judicial Council form of Summons (Joinder) (see form in §12.21) is used for this purpose and should be prepared by the party who sought joinder.

The summons should be presented for issuance by the court clerk after joinder has been ordered, when the original pleading (see §12.38) is filed. It is thereafter served on the claimant with the

Notice of Motion and Declaration for Joinder (see §§12.34–12.37), complaint for joinder (see §§12.38–12.39), and order for joinder, either in the form of a consent order (see §§12.41–12.42) or of a Findings and Order After Hearing (see §§11.55, 12.44). Service of summons on the claimant is effected in the same way as service of process in civil actions generally, usually by personal service (see §10.31) or by mail and acknowledgment of receipt (see §§10.33–10.34).

After service, the claimant has 30 days in which to file an appropriate response to the complaint. Cal Rules of Ct 5.158(c). If a response is not timely filed, a default judgment may be taken against the claimant. CCP §585. On the procedure for, and the effect of, entry of a party's default, see §§14.6–14.16.

Once the claimant has been ordered joined as a party to the action, all documents filed thereafter in the proceeding must be served on the claimant, as long as the claimant's default has not been entered. See CCP §1010. If a claimant is represented by counsel after being joined as a party, any notice or other paper that would be required to be served on the claimant must be served on his or her attorney of record. Cal Rules of Ct 5.10(b).

13

Discovery and Declarations of Disclosure

§13.1 I. SCOPE OF CHAPTER

"Discovery" refers to the obtaining of information, whether in oral or written form, for use in a legal action or proceeding. This chapter addresses discovery in the context of a marital action, including its uses, the client's role, development of a discovery plan, and implementation of the plan. Emphasis is on providing a general overview of the topic and details specific to actions under the Act. For a more detailed treatment of the subject matter, see California Civil Discovery Practice (3d ed Cal CEB 1998), which is frequently referred to in this chapter. See also Planning and Conducting Family Law Discovery (Cal CEB Action Guide September 2004).

This chapter also addresses the declarations of disclosure required under Fam C §§2100–2113.

NOTE▶ Effective July 1, 2005, the "Civil Discovery Act of 1986"

(CCP §§2016–2036) was repealed and replaced by a new "Civil Discovery Act" (CCP §§2016.010–2036.050). Although the character of the reform was nonsubstantive, all provisions of the 1986 Discovery Act have been renumbered, redundancies eliminated, and improvements made to grammar and clarity. The California Law Revision Commission recommended that long and complex passages of the discovery statute be divided into short sections, each with its own heading, to make provisions easier to locate and use, and to simplify the legislative process for amending the statute in the future. To minimize disruption to courts and practitioners, the new provisions closely track preexisting language and sequencing and retain the same base number as the section from which they were derived, *e.g.,* the section on oral depositions in California (see CCP §2025) becomes Chapter 9, with the subdivisions grouped consecutively under six articles, as separate sections (see CCP §§2025.010–2025.570). See 33 Cal L Rev'n Comm'n Reports 789 (2003).

II. DISCOVERY

A. Uses

§13.2   1. Temporary Orders

Discovery directed toward a hearing on temporary orders typically focuses on financial issues, *e.g.,* child support, spousal support, and attorney fees and costs. There often is a reduced need for formal discovery efforts as a result of the requirement that the parties submit Income and Expense Declarations when relevant to the relief requested (Cal Rules of Ct 5.118(b), 5.128) and additional requirements imposed by local court rules. See, *e.g.,* Contra Costa Ct R 12.4.F.3 (fully completed, current Income and Expense Declaration (or Simplified Financial Statement, when appropriate) to be served on other party at least 7 calendar days before hearing); Orange Ct R 702(c) (pay stubs, state and federal tax returns, W-2 form, and, if self-employed, 1099 forms, profit and loss statement, and balance sheet to be brought to hearing). Nevertheless, discovery directed toward a hearing on temporary orders can be crucial, particularly when either the information desired is not provided by the other party or there is reason to question its completeness or accuracy.

Discovery efforts for hearings on temporary orders are often significantly burdened by an early hearing date. Obviously, the moving party can avoid this problem by setting the hearing date far enough in advance to allow for compliance with the normal requirements for use of the desired discovery methods, but in many instances this is not practical. One reason is that the moving party often cannot wait long for the relief, *e.g.,* child support or spousal support, to which the discovery is relevant. Another reason is that ex parte temporary orders have a maximum duration of 25 days (Fam C §242(a)), and the party will not want them to expire before the hearing. On the other hand, the responding party whose discovery efforts are burdened by an early hearing date can seek a continuance (see §§11.43–11.45), but it may not be granted. Consequently, discovery for hearings on temporary orders will often require a stipulation or order shortening time for the discovery. To cite a common example, a petitioner might file an Order to Show Cause at the same time as the Petition, hoping to take the respondent's deposition as part of the preparation for the hearing on temporary orders. But, without the court's permission, the petitioner cannot serve the Notice of Deposition until at least 20 days after either service of the Summons and Petition or the respondent's appearance (CCP §2025.210) and cannot schedule the deposition itself less than 10 days after service of the Notice (CCP §2025.270(a)). Consequently, if the respondent's deposition is to be effective, the petitioner will often have to obtain a stipulation, or a court order under CCP §2025.210, allowing early service, a reduced notice period, or both.

A party taking the other party's deposition for purposes of a hearing on temporary orders may not want to be limited to that one deposition for the entire action. He or she may desire, for example, to address that particular deposition only to matters relevant to the temporary orders and to depose the other party at a later time on matters relevant to trial. It should be noted, however, that CCP §2025.610(a)–(b) precludes a second deposition of a given deponent absent a stipulation or leave of court. Consequently, when a party taking a deposition for a hearing on temporary orders does not want to be limited to that one deposition, a stipulation should be obtained or local rules and practice should be consulted. See, *e.g.,* Marin Ct R 6.24 (court policy to interpret CCP §2025.610(a)–(b) as permitting bifurcated deposition in family law cases).

When the moving party is proceeding by an Order to Show Cause, it may be possible, as an alternative to formal discovery, to obtain a court order requiring the responding party to produce financial documents such as recent wage stubs and tax returns when their production is not required by local rules. See §11.17.

When financial information is voluminous or complicated, another solution might be to negotiate temporary support and fee awards as part of a stipulated order that these awards are subject to retroactive adjustment when financial discovery has been completed.

On temporary orders generally, see chap 11.

§13.3　　2. Settlement Negotiations

Adequate discovery is essential to settlement negotiations. Simply stated, no settlement should ever be entered into until all reasonably necessary discovery has been completed. Certainly, formal discovery has disadvantages (see §13.18) and is not appropriate in every instance, but a party who enters into a settlement without knowledge of certain relevant facts or whose knowledge is based entirely on the other party's representations proceeds at his or her peril.

It is true that in some instances in which counsel is guilty of inadequate discovery, remedies may be available. For example, Fam C §1100 requires spouses to fully disclose on request all material facts and information on the existence, characterization, and valuation of all actual or possible community assets and debts. The obligation continues until the assets and liabilities have been divided by the spouses or by a court. Fam C §1100(e). Remedies for breach are provided by Fam C §1101. Further, in proceedings commenced on or after January 1, 1993, Fam C §§2100–2113 require declarations of disclosure and provide for setting aside a subsequent judgment when perjury is committed on a declaration of disclosure. Fam C §§2103–2105, 2113. Also, properly drafted warranties can provide protection against nondisclosure and misrepresentations. See, *e.g.*, *Marriage of Lane* (1985) 165 CA3d 1143, 211 CR 262. But, even when remedies may be available, counsel should conduct adequate discovery so that reliance on the remedies is not necessary. It is far better to discover the relevant facts before entering into an agreement than to be required to take remedial action afterwards. On the tension that may exist between the cost of discovery and the need to obtain thorough discovery, see §13.8 and Dissolution Strategies: From Intake to Judgment (Cal CEB Annual).

On the settlement process generally, see California Marital Settlement and Other Family Law Agreements, chap 1 (3d ed Cal CEB 2005).

§13.4   3. Trial

Discovery is, of course, best known in the context of preparation for trial and is most often undertaken for that purpose. Thus, the consequences of inadequate discovery for trial should be obvious.

In some instances of inadequate discovery, remedies may be available. See, *e.g., Marriage of Modnick* (1983) 33 C3d 897, 191 CR 629 (judgment after trial set aside because party failed to disclose existence of community asset); *Marriage of Brewer & Federici* (2001) 93 CA4th 1334, 1341, 113 CR2d 849 (judgment set aside when wife's statement that value of pension plan was "unknown" led to mistake of fact). But, even then, it would be far better to discover the relevant facts before trial than to be required to take remedial action afterwards.

On trial preparation generally, see chap 15.

§13.5   4. Modification

Discovery directed toward a hearing on a motion for modification will typically have much in common with that for a hearing on temporary orders. Consequently, the reader should see the discussion of discovery directed toward a hearing on temporary orders in §13.2. Obviously, the discussion of bifurcated depositions in that section does not apply to motions for modification.

It should be noted that, in some instances, discovery for a postjudgment motion for modification may be considerably more extensive than for a motion for temporary orders. When spousal support modification is at issue, for example, issues such as change of circumstances, employability, and the marital standard of living may require extensive discovery. Likewise, a postjudgment motion to modify child custody may require as much discovery as a trial on that issue.

Counsel should be aware that there is a special discovery method that is exclusively available for possible postjudgment motions for modification, *i.e.,* the Request for Production of an Income and Expense Declaration. See §§13.37–13.38.

On modification generally, see chap 21.

B. Client's Role

1. In Gathering Information

§13.6   **a. Discussion**

Counsel's starting point in gathering information is the client. A client who has been heavily involved with the couple's financial affairs may be able to provide sufficient information to make any acquisition from other sources unnecessary. But even a client with limited involvement will be able to provide some assistance in this regard, if only in ascertaining what might be available and potential sources for obtaining it, and should be encouraged to do so.

Although most clients should be encouraged to provide as much information as possible that appears reasonably likely to be relevant to the case, it is usually helpful for both the attorney and the client if the attorney can refer to a list in requesting information from the client. Of course, the information required depends on the matters that are or may be at issue. On identifying the issues in a particular case, see §13.9.

Although the attorney is likely to benefit most from developing his or her own list based on experience, a good initial source is the Judicial Council form of Form Interrogatories—Family Law and the accompanying Schedule of Assets and Debts (see forms in §§13.27–13.28). Although the forms are designed to be sent to the other party, they may be viewed, for the purpose of developing a list of desired information, as directed to the client, and then modified and expanded as appropriate. In addition, a checklist of documents that may be helpful is provided in §13.7.

The attorney should always obtain as much relevant information as possible from the client and should do so as soon as possible, both for the value of the information itself and to limit the need to obtain it from other sources. When the parties are about to separate, the client should be encouraged to take appropriate steps to obtain all available relevant documents immediately so that the other party cannot make them difficult or impossible to obtain.

§13.7   **b. Checklist of Documents**

The following documents may be helpful, when applicable:

Employment

- Contracts, memorandums, and correspondence regarding employment;

- Job applications and resumes; and

- Wage stubs.

Finances

- Bank statements;

- Canceled checks or bookkeeping software reports;

- Cash receipts and disbursements records;

- Certificates of deposit;

- Check registers or stubs;

- Credit and loan applications;

- Credit reports;

- Documents evidencing any outstanding debts or obligations;

- Monthly statements and charge vouchers for VISA, MasterCard, American Express, Diner's Club, and other credit cards;

- Safe deposit box rental agreements and inventories;

- Savings passbooks; and

- Statements of personal net worth.

Property Generally

- Agreements, monthly statements, and bylaws relating to memberships in social clubs;

- Agreements, plans, employee benefit booklets, beneficiary statements, annual benefit statements, and correspondence relating to pension plans, profit-sharing plans, and stock-option plans;

- Appraisals;

- Automobile insurance policies;

- Bond certificates;

- Contracts, memoranda, and correspondence relating to any change in character of property;

- Disability insurance policies;

- Documents evidencing any interest of either party in any testamentary trust, inter vivos trust, or estate;

- Escrow instructions, deeds, title insurance policies, tax bills, notes, trust deeds, contracts, and correspondence relating to real property owned;

- Homeowners' insurance policies;

- Leases on real property owned or leased;

- Life insurance policies (including, e.g., records and correspondence on loans, changes of beneficiaries);

- Ownership documents, purchase agreements, and registration certificates for automobiles, trucks, boats, and trailers;

- Promissory notes given or received and any related security documents and payment records;

- Stock certificates; and

- Summary sheets, monthly statements, purchase or sale confirmations, and account agreements relating to any stock, commodity, or brokerage account.

Business Interests

- Books of account, payroll, and expense account records reflecting moneys paid to or for the benefit of one of the parties for salary, commissions, bonuses, expenses, loans, advances, and pension or profit-sharing contributions, as well as any accounts receivable;

- Financial statements (including balance sheets and profit and loss statements);

- Fire insurance policies on inventory, premises, or other business-owned property;

- Minute books, stock certificate books, articles of incorporation, and bylaws of closely held and professional corporations; and

- Partnership, limited partnership, and joint venture agreements, buy-sell or other agreements, and modifications limiting the transferability or setting the value of partnership or stock interests.

Taxes

- Corporate tax returns (closely held and professional corporations);

- Gift tax returns;

- IRS Forms W-2, 1099, and K-1 for years for which no tax return has been prepared;

- Individual federal and state income tax returns and all supporting IRS Forms W-2, 1099, and K-1; and

- Partnership tax returns.

Miscellaneous

- Contracts, memorandums, correspondence, bills, and canceled checks relating to employment and compensation of counsel;

- Judgments of dissolution of marriage or nullity with respect to prior marriages;

- Marriage certificates;

- Medical records and reports;

- Pleadings from any pending litigation involving either party;

- Premarital- and postnuptial agreements between the parties;

- School records and reports; and

- Wills and other estate planning documents.

§13.8   2. In Developing the Discovery Plan

The client's involvement in developing a discovery plan is essential. The client is the logical first source for obtaining information, both for what the client can actually provide and for what he or she can suggest about other potential sources. On the client's role in gathering information, see §§13.6–13.7.

The attorney should always take steps to ensure that the client understands and approves any discovery plan before it is implemented. The attorney and client need to agree on a proper balance between the benefits of discovery and its costs.

Obviously, the safest practice would always be to undertake extensive discovery. If the attorney does so, however, without first informing the client of the potential benefits and probable costs and obtaining the client's consent, the attorney has not fulfilled his or her responsibilities to the client, and the attorney-client relationship may be seriously undermined as a result. In some instances, the client may balk at the plan proposed by the attorney, in order to save money or to avoid alienating the other party. When the attorney feels strongly that protection of the client's interests requires more discovery than the client is willing to authorize, the attorney should ask the client to sign a letter memorializing the attorney's advice and the client's restrictions on the attorney's authority to conduct discovery. In extreme cases, *e.g.,* a large-asset case in which the client imposes serious discovery restraints, some attorneys even consider withdrawal. See Cal Rules of Prof Cond 3–700(c)(1)(d) (attorney may request permission to withdraw in pending action, or withdraw in other matters, when client's conduct renders it unreasonably difficult for attorney to carry out employment effectively). Note, however, that in moving to withdraw, the attorney-client privilege still may not be breached.

C. Developing a Plan

§13.9   1. Identify Issues

The first step in developing a discovery plan is to identify the issues. When the discovery is directed toward settlement negotiations (see §13.3) or trial (see §13.4), the logical starting points in identifying the issues are the Petition (see form in §10.12) and the Response (see form in §10.52). Based on Items 4–7 on the Petition and 4–9 on the Response, one can make at least a preliminary determination as to which of the following matters are or may be at issue:

- Confirmation of separate assets and obligations;

- Disposition of community assets and obligations;

- Whether grounds exist to grant a judgment and, if so, what type (*i.e.,* dissolution, legal separation, or nullity);

- Legal custody;

- Physical custody;

- Child visitation;

- Child support (note that there is no box to check on the Petition to request relief on this issue; rather, the respondent is put on notice with respect to a potential child support award by the statement in Item 8);

- Spousal support;

- Attorney fees and costs; and

- Other matters (*e.g.,* protective orders).

The Petition and Response will also indicate whether there is any disagreement over the date of marriage or the date of separation, items that may be significant for some of the matters listed above, notably disposition of property (see §5.12).

The Petition and Response are, however, only a rough guide to the issues in the case, and may be no guide at all if the community and separate property sections are completed in only the most general terms pending disclosure and discovery (*e.g.,* "other assets and debts, the exact nature and extent of which are presently undetermined"). The indications obtained from the Petition and Response can be modified or supplemented initially by impressions gained from the other party or the other attorney, or both, and refined as the case proceeds. When discovery is directed toward a hearing on temporary orders (see §13.2) or on a motion for modification (see §13.5), the logical starting points in identifying the issues are the Application for Order and Supporting Declaration (see form in §11.22) and the Responsive Declaration (see form in §11.36).

§13.10   2. Ascertain Information Required

After the issues have been identified (see §13.9), the next step is to ascertain the information required with respect to each issue. Some of the desired items will overlap, *e.g.,* the financial information required may be much the same with respect to child support, spousal support, and attorney fees and costs.

The particular information that might be sought depends on the issues and circumstances of the particular case and the ingenuity of the attorney and his or her client. As suggested in §13.6 on gathering information from the client, some ideas might be acquired by reference to the Judicial Council form of Form Interrogatories, the accompanying Schedule of Assets and Debts (see forms in §§13.27–13.28), and the checklist of documents in §13.7.

§13.11   3. Identify Potential Sources

After the required information has been determined (see §13.10),potential sources should be identified. Information may be acquired from (1) the other party, (2) third parties, and (3) public records. Among third parties who often possess relevant information in marital actions are banks and other financial institutions, brokerage houses, employers, title companies, accountants, schools, health care providers, government agencies, and friends and acquaintances of the parties. Sources of relevant public records include the offices of county recorders, clerks, and assessors; the Department of Motor Vehicles; the Internal Revenue Service; the Secretary of State; and the Social Security Administration.

§13.12   4. Determine Methods and Sequences

After the required information has been ascertained (see §13.10) and the potential sources identified (see §13.11), a determination is made of the methods to be employed and their sequences.

In some cases, extensive formal discovery is clearly indicated. This will be true when (1) the case is complex; (2) the client has limited knowledge of, and access to, relevant information; and (3) the anticipated costs of discovery are no obstacle. In such instances, determinations about the methods to be employed may be made by simply comparing the available formal discovery methods, primarily in terms of their anticipated effectiveness. For discussion of these methods, see §§13.19-13.38. When any of these three conditions is not present, significant limitations on the nature and extent of formal discovery may be appropriate or necessary. In these cases, it becomes important to seriously consider not only the anticipated effectiveness of the available methods but also the importance of obtaining the information to be sought and the probable cost of obtaining it.

In proceedings commenced on or after January 1, 1993, Fam C §§2100-2113 generally require preliminary and final declarations of disclosure to be provided by each party to the other. Fam C §§2103-2105, 2113. Obviously, this requirement must be considered in determining methods and sequences of discovery from the other party. It may be advisable to hold off discovery until the preliminary declaration of disclosure is received, in order, *e.g.,* to avoid requesting information and materials from the other party that might be provided in any event through the preliminary declaration and to use the preliminary declaration in developing the overall approach to discovery. For discussion of declarations of disclosure, including the Judicial Council form, see §§13.44–13.49.

D. Implementing Plan

§13.13   1. Informal Discovery

"Informal" discovery is that undertaken without using formal discovery methods such as those discussed in §§13.19–13.38. Informal discovery consists simply of requesting specified information and documents and accepting what is offered.

The advantages of informal discovery are significant. Compared with formal discovery, it provides substantial savings in time and money. Informal discovery also encourages cooperation between the parties and tends to minimize the degree of bad feeling between them.

Counsel should note that the disadvantages of informal discovery can be substantial. The requesting party will be limited to what the other party is willing to provide voluntarily, and the procedural benefits of formal discovery (*e.g.,* deposition testimony under oath, matters conclusively established through requests for admission, sanctions for noncompliance) will not be available. There is also a real danger that the attorney may be lulled into complacency by promises that are never fulfilled and then find himself or herself too close to the discovery cutoff before trial (see §13.42) to conduct effective formal discovery. Consequently, when informal discovery is proving to be unsatisfactory, the attorney must be sure to move on to formal discovery methods early enough to avoid problems with the discovery cutoff.

§13.14   a. From Other Party

When there is cooperation between the parties and their attorneys, informal discovery from the other party can be accomplished in several ways. In simple matters, a telephone call between the attorneys may yield the information, or it can be sent from one attorney to the other by an exchange of letters. Counsel wishing to initiate informal discovery might call or write to the other attorney, suggesting a mutual exchange of information and documents and perhaps reminding the other attorney of the benefits of informal discovery (see §13.13). In more complex matters, the parties and attorneys might meet personally to discuss and exchange relevant information. When appropriate, they might arrange for third parties, *e.g.,* bookkeepers and accountants, to meet with them.

The attorney must exercise his or her judgment in deciding what items to request. Although the attorney should certainly endeavor to obtain everything that might reasonably be expected to aid in preparing for settlement or trial, items should not be requested that will simply increase the burden on the other party without providing tangible benefits.

Although informal discovery from the other party has its advantages, the attorney must be aware of the possible dangers of relying on the information provided without any independent inquiry. See §§13.3–13.4.

There are some kinds of discovery, *e.g.,* a demand for production of documents, that cost very little and can provide a valuable backup to informal requests. Even when cooperation seems to be forthcoming, the task of responding to discovery requests can fall to the bottom of a busy attorney's work pile, especially when there is no formal deadline for the response. A cordial letter accompanying a demand for production of documents, explaining that the sender desires to work cooperatively and does not anticipate problems, but believes that a formal request assists by providing a deadline to work against, should ensure a timely response without discouraging a spirit of cooperation.

The declarations of disclosure required under Fam C §§2100–2113 must be considered in approaching discovery from the other party, as in approaching discovery generally. See §13.12.

b. From Third Parties

§13.15   (1) Discussion

Informal discovery from third parties consists of information obtained from, *e.g.,* banks and other financial institutions, brokerage houses, employers, title companies, accountants, schools, health care providers, government agencies, and friends and acquaintances of the parties. Acquiring information from third parties without using formal discovery will often require written authorization from the client, the other party, or both. For a sample authorization form, see §13.16.

§13.16 (2) Form: Authorization and Request for Release of Information and Documents

AUTHORIZATION AND REQUEST FOR RELEASE OF INFORMATION AND DOCUMENTS

TO: _ _ _ _ _ _ _ _ _ _ _ _ _ _

RE: _ _ _ _ _ _ _ _ _ _ _ _ _ _

You are hereby authorized and requested to release and give to _ _[my/my spouse's]_ _ attorney, _ _[name, address, and telephone number]_ _, or to _ _[his/her]_ _ representative, the bearer of this AUTHORIZATION AND REQUEST FOR RELEASE OF INFORMATION AND DOCUMENTS, any information and documents in your possession or under your control relating to _ _[specify, e.g., the financial statement prepared by me in connection with my loan application dated September 2, 1991]_ _.

You are further authorized and requested to allow _ _[my/my spouse's]_ _ attorney or the bearer of this document to review any records relating to me and to furnish copies of such records.

A photocopy of this document will have the same effect as the original.

Any prior authorizations are hereby canceled.

Date: _____

_ _[Signature]_ _
_ _[Typed name of authorizing party]_ _

Comment: Some third parties will have their own authorization forms, in which event they should be used.

§13.17 c. From Public Records

A search of public records can provide valuable information. Possible sources include the following:

- County Recorder's office (recorded documents affecting real property);

- County Clerk's office (court action registers and files and fictitious business name filings);

- County Assessor's office (records relating to real and personal property assessments);

- Department of Motor Vehicles (vehicle registrations);

- Internal Revenue Service (copies of tax returns of requesting party);

- Secretary of State (corporate filings); and

- Social Security Administration (earnings and benefits information of requesting party).

§13.18   2. Formal Discovery

Formal discovery is undertaken using formal methods such as those discussed in §§13.19–13.38. Unlike informal discovery (see §§13.13–13.17), formal discovery may require substantial investments of time and money. It may also discourage cooperation between the two sides and cause or increase the amount of bad feeling between them. It does, however, allow the requesting party to obtain information the other party may not provide voluntarily, and it offers procedural benefits (*e.g.,* deposition testimony under oath, matters conclusively established through requests for admission, sanctions for noncompliance) that are not available with informal discovery.

Particularly when discovery is sought from third parties, considerations of relevance and privacy rights may limit the ability of the party undertaking the discovery to obtain what he or she seeks. See, *e.g., Schnabel v Superior Court* (1993) 5 C4th 704, 21 CR2d 200 (when one spouse in marital action seeks discovery from third party, court must balance spouse's need for discovery against third party's privacy interests; corporation required to produce business records, corporate tax returns, and payroll tax returns regarding other spouse, but not payroll tax information identifying third persons); *City of Los Angeles v Superior Court (Williamson)* (2003) 111 CA4th 883, 3 CR3d 915 (although peace officer's payroll records are personnel records subject to "*Pitchess* motion" under Pen C §832.8, officer's spouse in dissolution can obtain the records without making *Pitchess* motion); *Babcock v Superior Court* (1994) 29 CA4th 721, 35 CR2d 462 (party entitled to discovery from spouse's nonmarital partner, who allegedly received gifts of community property from spouse, but nonmarital partner entitled to in camera presentation of documents and to protective order to limit disclosure). See also *Weingarten v Superior Court* (2002) 102 CA4th 268, 125 CR 2d 371 (defendant's husband must be given notice and opportunity to be heard before court compels disclosure of joint tax returns); Fam C §4057.5(c) (when income of parent's subsequent spouse or nonmarital partner is allowed to be considered in determining child support, discovery for purposes of determining that income must be based on W-2 and 1099 income tax forms, except when court determines that application of rule would be unjust or inappropriate). On limitations on discovery of specific information generally, see §§13.40–13.41.

CAUTION➤ California disclosure requirements are preempted by federal securities laws governing insider trading. *Marriage of Reuling* (1994) 23 CA4th 1428, 1435, 28 CR2d 726.

Note that one court of appeal has held that, despite the statewide uniform guideline, when a child support payor who is an extraordinarily high earner stipulates that he or she can and will pay any reasonable amount of child support, the payee is not entitled to discovery of the payor's net worth and lifestyle. *Estevez v Superior Court* (1994) 22 CA4th 423, 27 CR2d 470. But see *Johnson v Superior Court* (1998) 66 CA4th 68, 77 CR2d 624 (when child support payee lacks sufficient information to enable court to make reasonable assumptions about payor's income that are least beneficial to payor, court should permit limited amount of discovery, if any, required to allow such information to be developed). See also *Marriage of Hubner (II)* (2001) 94 CA4th 175, 187, 114 CR2d 646. See discussion in §8.19.

The declarations of disclosure required under Fam C §§2100–2113 must be considered in approaching formal discovery, as in approaching discovery generally. See §13.12.

It is good practice to make a prominent notation in the case file when a party other than the petitioner and respondent has been joined and has appeared in the action. Otherwise, the third party may be forgotten when formal discovery is undertaken that requires service on all parties who have appeared. See, *e.g.,* CCP §2031.040) (demand for production of documents must be served on party to whom directed and on all other parties who have appeared in the action).

Note that a narrowly drawn protective order for which there is good cause may limit a party's dissemination of information obtained through formal discovery without violating his or her First Amendment right of free speech. *Marriage of Candiotti* (1995) 34 CA4th 718, 40 CR2d 299: US Const amend I.

a. Methods

(1) Oral Deposition

§13.19 (a) Discussion

An oral deposition is an oral examination under oath that is transcribed by a court reporter. An oral deposition may be taken of anyone, including a party (CCP §2025.010), but, without a stipulation or leave of court, only one deposition may be taken of a given deponent (CCP §2025.610(a)–(b)). Without the court's permission, the petitioner cannot serve a deposition notice until at least 20 days after service of the Summons and Petition or the appearance of the respondent (CCP §2025.210(b)), and neither party can schedule the deposition itself sooner than 10 days after service of the notice (CCP §2025.270(a)).

When the deponent is a party, or a party representative (*i.e.,* an officer, director, managing agent, or employee of a party), a Notice of Deposition (see form in §13.20) is used to compel his or her attendance and, if desired, that the deponent bring specified documents or other tangible things. CCP §2025.280(a)). For other deponents, either a Deposition Subpoena for Personal Appearance (see form in §13.21) or a Deposition Subpoena for Personal Appearance and Production of Documents and Things (see form in §13.21A) is used (CCP §2025.280(b)), although a Notice of Deposition, with a copy of the applicable Deposition Subpoena attached, must still be served on each party (CCP §2025.240). A nonparty deponent may appear at his or her deposition by telephone if the court finds there is good cause and no prejudice to any party. CCP §2025.310(b).

A person served with a Notice of Deposition or a Deposition Subpoena, or any other affected person or organization, may promptly move for a protective order as long as the motion is accompanied by a declaration stating facts showing that a reasonable and good faith attempt has first been made to informally resolve each issue presented by the motion. CCP §2025.420(a).

The primary purposes of oral depositions are (1) to learn relevant information about the case; (2) to fix the deponent's position for use, if necessary, to contradict or impeach his or her later testimony in court; and (3) to evaluate the deponent. Usually, an oral deposition is better designed to accomplish these purposes than any other discovery method. Sometimes its effectiveness may be reduced by an evasive deponent or one with limited knowledge of the relevant facts. Also, an oral deposition is probably the most expensive of the discovery methods, except perhaps for a physical, mental, or vocational examination.

Special considerations arise when an oral deposition will be taken for purposes of a hearing on temporary orders. On addressing timing problems caused by an early hearing date and on the possibility of bifurcating the deposition into temporary-order and trial portions, see §13.2.

For a complete discussion of oral depositions, see California Civil Discovery Practice, chaps 4–5 (3d ed Cal CEB 1998).

§13.20 (b) Form: Notice of Deposition

_ _[Attorney name]_ _
_ _[State Bar number]_ _
_ _[Address]_ _
_ _[Telephone number]_ _

Attorney for _ _[name]_ _

SUPERIOR COURT OF CALIFORNIA
COUNTY OF _ _ _ _ _ _

Marriage of	)	**No.** _ _ _ _ _ _
	)	
Petitioner: _ _ _ _ _ _ _ _	)	**NOTICE OF DEPOSITION**
	)	
Respondent: _ _ _ _ _ _ _ _	)	
	)	
—————————————	)	

   NOTICE IS HEREBY GIVEN that on _ _[date]_ _, **at** _ _[time]_ _, **at** _ _[address]_ _, _ _[name of party noticing deposition]_ _ **will take the deposition of** _ _[name and (if not a party) address and telephone number of deponent]_ _.

   [Add if deponent is to bring documents or other tangible things]

   The deponent is required to bring to the deposition the following materials: _ _[Specify with reasonable particularity the materials or categories of materials]_ _.

[Continue]

Date: _____

__*[Signature]*__
_ _*[Typed name]*_ _
Attorney for _ _*[Petitioner/
Respondent]*_ _

Copies: Original (retain, with original proof of service, for filing with court clerk if required in connection with future motion); copies for service on each attorney or party; office copies.

Comment: A Notice of Deposition is used to compel the attendance of, and, when desired, the production of materials by, a deponent who is a party or a party representative (*i.e.,* an officer, director, managing agent, or employee of a party). CCP §2025.280(a). For other deponents, a Deposition Subpoena (see forms in §§13.21-13.21A) is used. CCP §2025.280(b). Note that, when a Deposition Subpoena is used, a Notice of Deposition must be prepared and served, with a copy of the Deposition Subpoena attached, on each party. CCP §2025.220(a)-(b).

If the deposing party intends to record the testimony by audio or video technology, in addition to the stenographic recording by the court reporter, or to record the testimony by the stenographic method through the instant visual display of the testimony, that intention must be indicated in the Notice of Deposition. CCP §2025.220(a)(5). If the deposition will be conducted using instant visual display, a copy of the deposition notice must be given to the deposition officer, and the party requesting the instant visual display or rough draft of transcripts must pay the reasonable costs of those services. CCP §2025.220(a)(5). The notice must also set forth any intention to reserve the right to use at trial a video recording of the deposition testimony of any expert witness, or of a treating or consulting physician, under CCP §2025.620(d). CCP §2025.220(a)(6). If the deponent is not a natural person (*e.g.,* is a corporation), the notice must describe with reasonable specificity the matters the deposition will cover. CCP §2025.230. All the parties or attorneys for parties on whom the notice is served must be listed on the notice itself or on the accompanying proof of service. CCP §2025.240(a).

Service is made on the attorney, unless the party has not yet appeared or is appearing in pro per. CCP §1015. When personal service is used, a Notice of Deposition must be served at least 10 days before the deposition date. CCP §2025.270(a). The notice is usually served by mail, however, unless the deposing party wants to avoid the resulting extension of the normal notice period or unless the other party has not appeared in the action, in which event personal service should be used. When service is by mail, the required notice period is extended by 5 calendar days, assuming that the places of address and of mailing are in California. CCP §2016.050.

§13.21   (c) Form: Deposition Subpoena for Personal Appearance (Judicial Council Form SUBP-015)

SUBP-015

ATTORNEY OR PARTY WITHOUT ATTORNEY *(Name, State Bar number, and address):*	FOR COURT USE ONLY
TELEPHONE NO.: FAX NO. *(Optional):*	
E-MAIL ADDRESS *(Optional):*	
ATTORNEY FOR *(Name):*	

SUPERIOR COURT OF CALIFORNIA, COUNTY OF
STREET ADDRESS:
MAILING ADDRESS:
CITY AND ZIP CODE:
BRANCH NAME:

PLAINTIFF/ PETITIONER:

DEFENDANT/ RESPONDENT:

DEPOSITION SUBPOENA FOR PERSONAL APPEARANCE	CASE NUMBER:

THE PEOPLE OF THE STATE OF CALIFORNIA, TO *(name, address, and telephone number of deponent, if known):*

1. YOU ARE ORDERED TO APPEAR IN PERSON TO TESTIFY AS A WITNESS in this action at the following date, time, and place:

Date: Time: Address:

a. ☐ As a deponent who is not a natural person, you are ordered to designate one or more persons to testify on your behalf as to the matters described in item 2. (Code Civ. Proc., § 2025.220(a)(6).)

b. ☐ This deposition will be recorded stenographically   ☐ through the instant visual display of testimony, and by ☐ audiotape   ☐ videotape.

c. ☐ This videotape deposition is intended for possible use at trial under Code of Civil Procedure section 2025.620(d).

2. ☐ If the witness is a representative of a business or other entity, the matters upon which the witness is to be examined are as follows:

3. *At the deposition, you will be asked questions under oath. Questions and answers are recorded stenographically at the deposition; later they are transcribed for possible use at trial. You may read the written record and change any incorrect answers before you sign the deposition. You are entitled to receive witness fees and mileage actually traveled both ways. The money must be paid, at the option of the party giving notice of the deposition, either with service of this subpoena or at the time of the deposition.*

DISOBEDIENCE OF THIS SUBPOENA MAY BE PUNISHED AS CONTEMPT BY THIS COURT. YOU WILL ALSO BE LIABLE FOR THE SUM OF FIVE HUNDRED DOLLARS AND ALL DAMAGES RESULTING FROM YOUR FAILURE TO OBEY.

Date issued:

_____   ▶ _____
(TYPE OR PRINT NAME)   (SIGNATURE OF PERSON ISSUING SUBPOENA)

_____
(TITLE)

(Proof of service on reverse)   Page 1 of 2

Form Adopted for Mandatory Use Judicial Council of California SUBP-015 [Rev. January 1, 2007]	**DEPOSITION SUBPOENA FOR PERSONAL APPEARANCE**	Code of Civil Procedure, §§ 2020.310, 2025.220, 2025.620 Government Code, § 68097.1 www.courtinfo.ca.gov

SUBP-015

PLAINTIFF/PETITIONER:	CASE NUMBER:
DEFENDANT/RESPONDENT:	

PROOF OF SERVICE OF DEPOSITION SUBPOENA FOR PERSONAL APPEARANCE

1. I served this *Deposition Subpoena for Personal Appearance* by personally delivering a copy to the person served as follows:
   a. Person served *(name)*:

   b. Address where served:

   c. Date of delivery:

   d. Time of delivery:

   e. Witness fees and mileage both ways *(check one)*:
      (1) ☐ were paid. Amount: . . . . $ _____
      (2) ☐ were not paid.
      (3) ☐ were tendered to the witness's
          public entity employer as
          required by Government Code
          section 68097.2. The amount
          tendered was *(specify)*: . . . . $ _____

   f. Fee for service: . . . . $ _____

2. I received this subpoena for service on *(date)*:

3. Person serving:
   a. ☐ Not a registered California process server.
   b. ☐ California sheriff or marshal.
   c. ☐ Registered California process server.
   d. ☐ Employee or independent contractor of a registered California process server.
   e. ☐ Exempt from registration under Business and Professions Code section 22350(b).
   f. ☐ Registered professional photocopier.
   g. ☐ Exempt from registration under Business and Professions Code section 22451.
   h. Name, address, telephone number, and, if applicable, county of registration and number:

I **declare** under penalty of perjury under the laws of the State of California that the foregoing is true and correct.

Date:

► _____
(SIGNATURE)

(For California sheriff or marshal use only)
I **certify** that the foregoing is true and correct.

Date:

► _____
(SIGNATURE)

SUBP-015 [Rev. January 1, 2007]

**PROOF OF SERVICE OF
DEPOSITION SUBPOENA FOR PERSONAL APPEARANCE**

Page 2 of 2

Copies: Original (retain, with original proof of service, for filing with court clerk if required in connection with future motion); copies for service on deponent and on each attorney or party; office copies.

Comment: See comment following form in §13.21A.

§13.21A   (d)   Form: Deposition Subpoena for Personal Appearance and Production of Documents and Things (Judicial Council Form SUBP-020)

SUBP-020

ATTORNEY OR PARTY WITHOUT ATTORNEY *(Name, State Bar number, and address)*:	FOR COURT USE ONLY

TELEPHONE NO.:   FAX NO. *(Optional)*:
E-MAIL ADDRESS *(Optional)*:
ATTORNEY FOR *(Name)*:

SUPERIOR COURT OF CALIFORNIA, COUNTY OF
  STREET ADDRESS:
  MAILING ADDRESS:
  CITY AND ZIP CODE:
  BRANCH NAME:

PETITIONER:

RESPONDENT:

DEPOSITION SUBPOENA FOR PERSONAL APPEARANCE AND PRODUCTION OF DOCUMENTS AND THINGS	CASE NUMBER:

THE PEOPLE OF THE STATE OF CALIFORNIA, TO *(name, address, and telephone number of deponent, if known)*:

1. **YOU ARE ORDERED TO APPEAR IN PERSON TO TESTIFY AS A WITNESS** in this action at the following date, time, and place:

Date: Time: Address:

  a. ☐   As a deponent who is not a natural person, you are ordered to designate one or more persons to testify on your behalf as to the matters described in item 4. (Code Civ. Proc., § 2025.220(a)(6)).
  b. ☐   You are ordered to produce the documents and things described in item 3.
  c. ☐   This deposition will be recorded stenographically   ☐ through the instant visual display of testimony, and by ☐ audiotape ☐ videotape
  d. ☐   This videotape deposition is intended for possible use at trial under Code of Civil Procedure section 2025.620(d).

2. The personal attendance of the custodian or other qualified witness and the production of the original records are required by this subpoena. The procedure authorized by Evidence Code sections 1560(b), 1561, and 1562 will not be deemed sufficient compliance with this subpoena.

3. The documents and things to be produced and any testing or sampling being sought are described as follows:

  ☐   Continued on Attachment 3.

4. If the witness is a representative of a business or other entity, the matters upon which the witness is to be examined are described as follows:

  ☐ Continued on Attachment 4.

5. **IF YOU HAVE BEEN SERVED WITH THIS SUBPOENA AS A CUSTODIAN OF CONSUMER OR EMPLOYEE RECORDS UNDER CODE OF CIVIL PROCEDURE SECTION 1985.3 OR 1985.6 AND A MOTION TO QUASH OR AN OBJECTION HAS BEEN SERVED ON YOU, A COURT ORDER OR AGREEMENT OF THE PARTIES, WITNESSES, *AND* CONSUMER OR EMPLOYEE AFFECTED MUST BE OBTAINED BEFORE YOU ARE REQUIRED TO PRODUCE CONSUMER OR EMPLOYEE RECORDS.**

6. At the deposition, you will be asked questions under oath. Questions and answers are recorded stenographically at the deposition; later they are transcribed for possible use at trial. You may read the written record and change any incorrect answers before you sign the deposition. You are entitled to receive witness fees and mileage actually traveled both ways. The money must be paid, at the option of the party giving notice of the deposition, either with service of this subpoena or at the time of the deposition.

DISOBEDIENCE OF THIS SUBPOENA MAY BE PUNISHED AS CONTEMPT BY THIS COURT. YOU WILL ALSO BE LIABLE FOR THE SUM OF FIVE HUNDRED DOLLARS AND ALL DAMAGES RESULTING FROM YOUR FAILURE TO OBEY.

Date issued:

▶

_____   _____
(TYPE OR PRINT NAME)   (SIGNATURE OF PERSON ISSUING SUBPOENA)

_____
(Proof of service on reverse)   (TITLE)   Page 1 of 2

Form Adopted for Mandatory Use Judicial Council of California SUBP-020 [Rev. January 1, 2007]	**DEPOSITION SUBPOENA FOR PERSONAL APPEARANCE AND PRODUCTION OF DOCUMENTS AND THINGS**	Code of Civil Procedure, §§ 2020.510, 2025.220, 2025.620; Government Code, § 68097.1 www.courtinfo.ca.gov

PLAINTIFF/PETITIONER:	CASE NUMBER:
DEFENDANT/RESPONDENT:	

**PROOF OF SERVICE OF DEPOSITION SUBPOENA FOR PERSONAL APPEARANCE
AND PRODUCTION OF DOCUMENTS AND THINGS**

1. I served this *Deposition Subpoena for Personal Appearance and Production of Documents and Things* by personally delivering a copy to the person served as follows:

   a. Person served *(name)*:

   b. Address where served:

   c. Date of delivery:

   d. Time of delivery:

   e. Witness fees and mileage both ways *(check one)*:
      - (1) ☐ were paid. Amount: .... $ _____
      - (2) ☐ were not paid.
      - (3) ☐ were tendered to the witness's public entity employer as required by Government Code section 68097.2. The amount tendered was *(specify)*: .... $ _____

   f. Fee for service: .... $ _____

2. I received this subpoena for service on *(date)*:

3. Person serving:
   a. ☐ Not a registered California process server.
   b. ☐ California sheriff or marshal.
   c. ☐ Registered California process server.
   d. ☐ Employee or independent contractor of a registered California process server.
   e. ☐ Exempt from registration under Business and Professions Code section 22350(b).
   f. ☐ Registered professional photocopier.
   g. ☐ Exempt from registration under Business and Professions Code section 22451.
   h. Name, address, telephone number, and, if applicable, county of registration and number:

I **declare** under penalty of perjury under the laws of the State of California that the foregoing is true and correct.

Date:

▶ _____
(SIGNATURE)

(For California sheriff or marshal use only)
I **certify** that the foregoing is true and correct.

Date:

▶ _____
(SIGNATURE)

**PROOF OF SERVICE
DEPOSITION SUBPOENA FOR PERSONAL APPEARANCE
AND PRODUCTION OF DOCUMENTS AND THINGS**

Comment: A Deposition Subpoena for Personal Appearance (Judicial Council Form 982(a)(15.3)) (see form in §13.21) is used to compel the attendance of a deponent who is neither a party nor a party's representative (*i.e.,* an officer, director, managing agent, or employee of a party). CCP §2025.280(b). When the production of materials is also sought, a Deposition Subpoena for Personal Appearance and Production of Documents and Things is used. For deponents who are parties or party representatives, a Notice of Deposition (see form in §13.20) is used. CCP §2025.280(a).

If the deponent is not a natural person (*e.g.,* is a corporation), the subpoena must describe with reasonable specificity the matters the deposition will cover. CCP §2025.230.

The subpoena must be personally served on the deponent. CCP §§2020.220(b), 2025.280(b). The applicable statute does not specify a date for service but indicates only that the time of service must provide the deponent with a reasonable amount of time to locate and produce any required materials and to travel to the place of deposition. CCP §2020.220(a). A Notice of Deposition, with a copy of the subpoena attached, must be served on each party (CCP §§2025.220(a)-(b), 2025.240(a)). Common practice is to serve the subpoena on the deponent at the same time that the Notice of Deposition is served on each party. On service of the Notice of Deposition, see §13.20.

When a Deposition Subpoena for Personal Appearance and Production of Documents and Things commands the deponent to produce personal records of a consumer (for definition, see CCP §1985.3(a)(1)-(2)), the deposition must be scheduled at least 20 days after issuance of the subpoena. CCP §2025.270(a). Unless the subpoenaing party is the consumer, and the consumer is the only subject of the subpoenaed records (CCP §1985.3(l)), service of the Deposition Subpoena must be accompanied by a copy of the Proof of Service of the notice to consumer described in CCP §1985.3(e) or by the consumer's written authorization, described in CCP §1985.3(c)(2), to release personal records. CCP §2020.510(c). Presumably, similar steps should be taken when the Deposition Subpoena commands the deponent to produce employment records of an employee (for definition, see CCP §1985.6(a)(1)-(2)) under CCP §1985.6. On the notice to consumer or employee, see §§13.22 (discussion), 13.24 (form).

(2) Deposition for Production of Business Records

§13.22 (a) Discussion

A nonparty may be compelled to produce business records (for definition, see Evid C §1560(a)(1)-(2); CCP §2020.010(a)(3) for inspection and copying by use of a Deposition Subpoena for Production of Business Records (see form in §13.23). The subpoena must be personally served on the deponent. CCP §2020.220(b). Compliance may be required no earlier than 20 days after issuance of the subpoena or 15 days after service, whichever is later. CCP §2020.410(c). A copy of the subpoena must be served on each party. CCP §2025.240(a). The applicable statutes do not appear to specify a date for such service, unlike that on the deponent, but the common practice is to serve the copy on each party at the same time that the subpoena is served on the deponent.

A person served with a Deposition Subpoena for Production of Business Records or any other affected person or organization may promptly move for a protective order as long as the motion is accompanied by a declaration stating facts showing that a reasonable and good faith attempt has first been made to informally resolve each issue presented by the motion. CCP §2025.420(a).

When the Deposition Subpoena commands the production of personal records of a consumer or employee (see CCP §§1985.3(a)(1)-(2), 1985.6(a)(1)-(2) for definitions), service of the subpoena must be accompanied by a copy of the Proof of Service of the notice to consumer or employee described in CCP §1985.3(e) or §1985.6(b), as applicable (see form in §13.24), or by the consumer or employee's written authorization, described in CCP §1985.3(c)(2) or §1985.6(c)(2), as applicable, to release personal records, unless the subpoenaing party is the consumer or employee, and the consumer or employee is the only subject of the subpoenaed records (CCP §§1985.3(l), 1985.6(k)). CCP §2020.410(d). Service of the notice on the consumer or employee must be made at least 5 days before service of the subpoena on the custodian of the records, plus the additional time provided under CCP §1013 if service is by mail. CCP §§1985.3(b)(3), 1985.6(b)(3). A copy of the subpoena (and, in the case of a Deposition Subpoena for Personal Appearance and Production of Documents and Things, the notice of deposition) must be attached. CCP §2025.240(a)-(c).

Unless the parties and, if a consumer or employee's personal records are to be produced, the consumer or employee agree to an earlier date, the custodian of records must not deliver the records before the date and time specified in the Deposition Subpoena. CCP §2020.430(d).

When a deposition is only for the production of business records, the entire process, including preparation and service of the Deposition Subpoena (and, if applicable, the notice to consumer or employee) and obtaining of the records, is routinely handled by attorney services providers. See CCP §2020.420.

For a complete discussion of depositions for production of business records, see California Civil Discovery Practice §§4.52–4.69 (3d ed Cal CEB 1998).

§13.23 (b) Form: Deposition Subpoena for Production of Business Records (Judicial Council Form SUBP-002)

SUBP-002

ATTORNEY OR PARTY WITHOUT ATTORNEY (Name, state bar number, and address):	FOR COURT USE ONLY
TELEPHONE NO.: FAX NO.:	
ATTORNEY FOR (Name):	
NAME OF COURT:	
STREET ADDRESS:	
MAILING ADDRESS:	
CITY AND ZIP CODE:	
BRANCH NAME:	
PLAINTIFF/ PETITIONER:	
DEFENDANT/ RESPONDENT:	
CIVIL SUBPOENA (DUCES TECUM) for Personal Appearance and Production of Documents and Things at Trial or Hearing AND DECLARATION	CASE NUMBER:

THE PEOPLE OF THE STATE OF CALIFORNIA, TO (name, address, and telephone number of witness, if known):

1. YOU ARE ORDERED TO APPEAR AS A WITNESS in this action at the date, time, and place shown in the box below UNLESS your appearance is excused as indicated in box 3b below or you make an agreement with the person named in item 4 below.

   a. Date: Time: ☐ Dept.: ☐ Div.: ☐ Room:
   b. Address:

2. IF YOU HAVE BEEN SERVED WITH THIS SUBPOENA AS A CUSTODIAN OF CONSUMER OR EMPLOYEE RECORDS UNDER CODE OF CIVIL PROCEDURE SECTION 1985.3 OR 1985.6 AND A MOTION TO QUASH OR AN OBJECTION HAS BEEN SERVED ON YOU, A COURT ORDER OR AGREEMENT OF THE PARTIES, WITNESSES, AND CONSUMER OR EMPLOYEE AFFECTED MUST BE OBTAINED BEFORE YOU ARE REQUIRED TO PRODUCE CONSUMER OR EMPLOYEE RECORDS.

3. YOU ARE (item a or b must be checked):

   a. ☐ Ordered to appear in person and to produce the records described in the declaration on page two or the attached declaration or affidavit. The personal attendance of the custodian or other qualified witness and the production of the original records are required by this subpoena. The procedure authorized by Evidence Code sections 1560(b), 1561, and 1562 will not be deemed sufficient compliance with this subpoena.

   b. ☐ Not required to appear in person if you produce (i) the records described in the declaration on page two or the attached declaration or affidavit and (ii) a completed declaration of custodian of records in compliance with Evidence Code sections 1560, 1561, 1562, and 1271. (1) Place a copy of the records in an envelope (or other wrapper). Enclose the original declaration of the custodian with the records. Seal the envelope. (2) Attach a copy of this subpoena to the envelope or write on the envelope the case name and number; your name; and the date, time, and place from item 1 in the box above. (3) Place this first envelope in an outer envelope, seal it, and mail it to the clerk of the court at the address in item 1. (4) Mail a copy of your declaration to the attorney or party listed at the top of this form.

4. IF YOU HAVE ANY QUESTIONS ABOUT THE TIME OR DATE YOU ARE TO APPEAR, OR IF YOU WANT TO BE CERTAIN THAT YOUR PRESENCE IS REQUIRED, CONTACT THE FOLLOWING PERSON BEFORE THE DATE ON WHICH YOU ARE TO APPEAR:

   a. Name of subpoenaing party or attorney: b. Telephone number:

5. **Witness Fees:** You are entitled to witness fees and mileage actually traveled both ways, as provided by law, if you request them at the time of service. You may request them before your scheduled appearance from the person named in item 4.

DISOBEDIENCE OF THIS SUBPOENA MAY BE PUNISHED AS CONTEMPT BY THIS COURT. YOU WILL ALSO BE LIABLE FOR THE SUM OF FIVE HUNDRED DOLLARS AND ALL DAMAGES RESULTING FROM YOUR FAILURE TO OBEY.

Date issued:

_____ ▶ _____
(TYPE OR PRINT NAME) (SIGNATURE OF PERSON ISSUING SUBPOENA)

(Declaration in support of subpoena on reverse) (TITLE)

Form Adopted for Mandatory Use
Judicial Council of California
SUBP-002 [Rev. January 1, 2007]

CIVIL SUBPOENA (DUCES TECUM) FOR PERSONAL APPEARANCE AND PRODUCTION OF DOCUMENTS AND THINGS AT TRIAL OR HEARING AND DECLARATION

Page 1 of 3

CEB Code of Civil Procedure, § 1985 et seq.

SUBP-002

PLAINTIFF/PETITIONER:	CASE NUMBER:
DEFENDANT/RESPONDENT:	

The production of the documents or the other things sought by the subpoena on page one is supported by *(check one)*:
☐ the attached affidavit or declaration ☐ the following declaration:

**DECLARATION IN SUPPORT OF CIVIL SUBPOENA (DUCES TECUM) FOR PERSONAL
APPEARANCE AND PRODUCTION OF DOCUMENTS AND THINGS AT TRIAL OR HEARING
(Code Civ. Proc., §§ 1985, 1987.5)**

1. I, the undersigned, declare I am the ☐ plaintiff ☐ defendant ☐ petitioner ☐ respondent
   ☐ attorney for *(specify)*: ☐ other *(specify)*:
   in the above-entitled action.

2. The witness has possession or control of the following documents or other things and shall produce them at the time and place
   specified in the *Civil Subpoena for Personal Appearance and Production of Documents and Things at Trial or Hearing* on page one
   of this form *(specify the exact documents or other things to be produced)*:

☐ Continued on Attachment 2.

3. Good cause exists for the production of the documents or other things described in paragraph 2 for the following reasons:

☐ Continued on Attachment 3.

4. These documents or other things described in paragraph 2 are material to the issues involved in this case for the following reasons:

☐ Continued on Attachment 4.

I declare under penalty of perjury under the laws of the State of California that the foregoing is true and correct.

Date:

▶

....		
(TYPE OR PRINT NAME)	(SIGNATURE OF ☐ SUBPOENAING PARTY	☐ ATTORNEY FOR SUBPOENAING PARTY)

(Proof of service on page three)

Page 2 of 3

SUBP-002 [Rev. January 1, 2007]   **CIVIL SUBPOENA (DUCES TECUM) FOR PERSONAL APPEARANCE
AND PRODUCTION OF DOCUMENTS AND THINGS
AT TRIAL OR HEARING AND DECLARATION**   CEB

Copies: Original (retain, with original proof of service, for filing with court clerk if required in connection with future motion); copies for service on deponent and on each attorney or party; office copies.

§13.24 (c) Form: Notice to Consumer or Employee and Objection (Judicial Council Form SUBP-025)

SUBP-025

ATTORNEY OR PARTY WITHOUT ATTORNEY *(Name, State Bar number, and address)*:	FOR COURT USE ONLY
TELEPHONE NO.: FAX NO. *(Optional)*: E-MAIL ADDRESS *(Optional)*: ATTORNEY FOR *(Name)*:	

SUPERIOR COURT OF CALIFORNIA, COUNTY OF
   STREET ADDRESS:
   MAILING ADDRESS:
   CITY AND ZIP CODE:
   BRANCH NAME:

PLAINTIFF / PETITIONER:	CASE NUMBER:
DEFENDANT / RESPONDENT:	
NOTICE TO CONSUMER OR EMPLOYEE AND OBJECTION (Code Civ. Proc., §§ 1985.3, 1985.6)	

NOTICE TO CONSUMER OR EMPLOYEE

TO *(name)*:

1. PLEASE TAKE NOTICE THAT **REQUESTING PARTY** *(name)*:
   SEEKS YOUR RECORDS FOR EXAMINATION by the parties to this action on *(specify date)*:
   The records are described in the subpoena directed to **witness** *(specify name and address of person or entity from whom records are sought)*:
   A copy of the subpoena is attached.

2. IF YOU OBJECT to the production of these records, YOU MUST DO ONE OF THE FOLLOWING BEFORE THE DATE SPECIFIED. IN ITEM a. OR b. BELOW:
   a. If you are a party to the above-entitled action, you must file a motion pursuant to Code of Civil Procedure section 1987.1 to quash or modify the subpoena and give notice of that motion to the **witness** and the **deposition officer** named in the subpoena at least five days before the date set for production of the records.
   b. If you are not a party to this action, you must serve on the **requesting party** and on the **witness**, before the date set for production of the records, a written objection that states the specific grounds on which production of such records should be prohibited. You may use the form below to object and state the grounds for your objection. You must complete the Proof of Service on the reverse side indicating whether you personally served or mailed the objection. The objection should **not** be filed with the court. **WARNING: IF YOUR OBJECTION IS NOT RECEIVED BEFORE THE DATE SPECIFIED IN ITEM 1, YOUR RECORDS MAY BE PRODUCED AND MAY BE AVAILABLE TO ALL PARTIES.**

3. YOU OR YOUR ATTORNEY MAY CONTACT THE UNDERSIGNED to determine whether an agreement can be reached in writing to cancel or limit the scope of the subpoena. If no such agreement is reached, and if you are not otherwise represented by an attorney in this action, YOU SHOULD CONSULT AN ATTORNEY TO ADVISE YOU OF YOUR RIGHTS OF PRIVACY.

Date:

_____
(TYPE OR PRINT NAME)

▶ _____
(SIGNATURE OF ☐ REQUESTING PARTY ☐ ATTORNEY)

OBJECTION BY NON-PARTY TO PRODUCTION OF RECORDS

1. ☐ I object to the production of all of my records specified in the subpoena.

2. ☐ I object only to the production of the following specified records:

3. The specific grounds for my objection areas follows:

Date:

_____
(TYPE OR PRINT NAME)

▶ _____
(SIGNATURE)

(Proof of service on reverse)

Form Adopted for Mandatory Use
Judicial Council of California
SUBP-025 [Rev. January 1, 2007]

NOTICE TO CONSUMER OR EMPLOYEE AND OBJECTION

CEB

Page 1 of 2

Code of Civil Procedure,
§§ 1985.3, 1985.6,
2020.010–202.510
www.courtinfo.ca.gov

PLAINTIFF/PETITIONER:	CASE NUMBER:
DEFENDANT/RESPONDENT:	

PROOF OF SERVICE OF NOTICE TO CONSUMER OR EMPLOYEE AND OBJECTION
(Code Civ. Proc., §§ 1985.3, 1985.6)

☐ Personal Service ☐ Mail

1. At the time of service I was at least 18 years of age and **not a party to this legal action.**
2. I served a copy of the *Notice to Consumer or Employee and Objection* as follows *(check either a or b):*
   a. ☐ **Personal service.** I personally delivered the *Notice to Consumer or Employee and Objection* as follows:
      (1) Name of person served: (3) Date served:
      (2) Address where served: (4) Time served:

   b. ☐ **Mail.** I deposited the *Notice to Consumer or Employee and Objection* in the United States mail, in a sealed envelope with postage fully prepaid. The envelope was addressed as follows:
      (1) Name of person served: (3) Date of mailing:
      (2) Address: (4) Place of mailing *(city and state):*

      (5) I am a resident of or employed in the county where the *Notice to Consumer or Employee and Objection* was mailed.
   c. My residence or business address is *(specify):*
   d. My phone number is *(specify):*

I declare under penalty of perjury under the laws of the State of California that the foregoing is true and correct.
Date:

▶

_____   _____
[TYPE OR PRINT NAME OF PERSON WHO SERVED]   (SIGNATURE OF PERSON WHO SERVED)

PROOF OF SERVICE OF OBJECTION TO PRODUCTION OF RECORDS
(Code Civ. Proc., §§ 1985.3, 1985.6)

☐ Personal Service ☐ Mail

1. At the time of service I was at least 18 years of age and **not a party to this legal action.**
2. I served a copy of the *Objection to Production of Records* as follows *(complete either a or b):*
   a. ON THE REQUESTING PARTY
      (1) ☐ **Personal service.** I personally delivered the *Objection to Production of Records* as follows:
         (i) Name of person served: (iii) Date served:
         (ii) Address where served: (iv) Time served:

      (2) ☐ **Mail.** I deposited the *Objection to Production of Records* in the United States mail, in a sealed envelope with postage fully prepaid. The envelope was addressed as follows:
         (i) Name of person served: (iii) Date of mailing:
         (ii) Address: (iv) Place of mailing *(city and state):*

         (v) I am a resident of or employed in the county where the *Objection to Production of Records* was mailed.
   b. ON THE WITNESS
      (1) ☐ **Personal service.** I personally delivered the *Objection to Production of Records* as follows:
         (i) Name of person served: (iii) Date served:
         (ii) Address where served: (iv) Time served:

      (2) ☐ **Mail.** I deposited the *Objection to Production of Records* in the United States mail, in a sealed envelope with postage fully prepaid. The envelope was addressed as follows:
         (i) Name of person served: (iii) Date of mailing:
         (ii) Address: (iv) Place of mailing *(city and state):*

         (v) I am a resident of or employed in the county where the *Objection to Production of Records* was mailed.
3. My residence or business address is *(specify):*
4. My phone number is *(specify):*

I declare under penalty of perjury under the laws of the State of California that the foregoing is true and correct.
Date:

▶

_____   _____
[TYPE OR PRINT NAME OF PERSON WHO SERVED]   (SIGNATURE OF PERSON WHO SERVED)

SUBP-025 [Rev. January 1, 2007]   **NOTICE TO CONSUMER OR EMPLOYEE AND OBJECTION**   CEB   Page 2 of 2

Copies: Original (retain, with original proof of service, for filing with court clerk if required in connection with future motion); copy for service on consumer or employee or his or her attorney; office copies.

(3) Interrogatories

§13.25 (a) Discussion

Interrogatories are written questions to be answered in writing under oath and may be directed only to a party. CCP §§2030.010(a), 2030.250(a)-(c). Without leave of court, the petitioner cannot serve interrogatories until at least 10 days after either service of the summons and petition on the party to whom they are directed or that party's appearance. The respondent may serve interrogatories without leave of court at any time. CCP §2030.020(a)-(c).

A party may propound to another party, in one or more sets, a maximum of 35 specially prepared interrogatories, and any additional number of official form interrogatories from among those approved by the Judicial Council. CCP §§2030.030(a)-(c), 2033.710. The Judicial Council has published a set of approved Form Interrogatories— Family Law (see form in §13.27) and an accompanying Schedule of Assets and Debts (see form in §13.28).

Subject to the responding party's right to seek a protective order under CCP §2030.090(a), the propounding party may propound more than 35 specially prepared interrogatories as long as he or she attaches the declaration required by CCP §2030.050 and the greater number is warranted by (1) the complexity or quantity of the issues, (2) the financial burden of conducting discovery by the oral deposition method, or (3) the expedience of using interrogatories to provide to the responding party the opportunity to resort to files or records for the information sought. CCP §2030.040(a). Subject to specified restrictions, a party may also propound supplemental interrogatories to elicit any later-acquired information bearing on answers that were previously made to interrogatories. CCP §2030.070(a).

The name of the propounding party, the set number of the interrogatories, and the name of the responding party must appear in the first paragraph immediately below the title of the case. Each set of interrogatories must be numbered consecutively. CCP §2030.060(a)-(b). Each interrogatory in a set must be set forth separately, be identified by a number or a letter, and be complete in itself. CCP §2030.060(c)-(d). Any term specially defined in a set of interrogatories must be typed with all letters capitalized whenever the term appears. No specially prepared interrogatory may contain subparts, or a compound, conjunctive, or disjunctive question. CCP §2030.060(e)-(f).

The statute provides that no preface or instruction may be included with a set of interrogatories unless it has been approved under CCP §§2033.710–2033.740. CCP §2030.060(d). This restriction appears to limit prefaces and instructions to those that appear in the Form Interrogatories.

Interrogatories are served on the party to whom they are directed and, unless the court dispenses with the requirement on noticed motion, on all other parties who have appeared in the action. CCP §2030.080. The statute allows the responding party 30 days after service of interrogatories in which to serve the response on the propounding party. CCP §2030.260(a). Interrogatories are typically served, however, by mail, in which event the period for service of the response is extended by 5 calendar days, assuming that the place of address and place of mailing are in California. CCP §2015.050.

A party served with interrogatories or any other party or affected person or organization may promptly move for a protective order as long as the motion is accompanied by a declaration stating facts showing that a reasonable and good faith attempt has first been made to informally resolve each issue presented by the motion. CCP §2030.090(a).

Like oral depositions (see §13.19), interrogatories have as their primary purposes (1) to learn relevant information about the case and (2) to fix the responding party's position for use, if necessary, to contradict or impeach his or her later testimony in court. Although an oral deposition is probably better designed to accomplish these purposes in most instances, interrogatories are usually less expensive than depositions and, unlike depositions, do not permit the responding party to claim ignorance when the requested information (1) is reasonably available to the party or (2) could be obtained from other persons or organizations through a reasonable and good faith effort yet is not equally available to the propounding party (CCP §2030.220(c)).

For a complete discussion of interrogatories, see California Civil Discovery Practice, chap 7 (3d ed Cal CEB 1998).

§13.26 (b) Form: Interrogatories

_ _[Attorney name]_ _
_ _[State Bar number]_ _
_ _[Address]_ _
_ _[Telephone number]_ _

Attorney for _ _[name]_ _

SUPERIOR COURT OF CALIFORNIA
COUNTY OF _ _ _ _ _ _

Marriage of	)	**No.** _ _ _ _ _ _
	)	
Petitioner: _ _ _ _ _ _ _ _	)	**INTERROGATORIES**
	)	
Respondent: _ _ _ _ _ _ _ _	)	
	)	
_____	)	

PROPOUNDING PARTY: _ _[Petitioner/Respondent]_ _,
_ _[name]_ _

SET NO.: _ _ _ _ _ _

RESPONDING PARTY: _ _[Respondent/Petitioner]_ _, _ _[name]_ _

_ _[Petitioner/Respondent]_ _, _ _[name]_ _, **requests that** _ _[re-spondent/petitioner]_ _, _ _[name]_ _, **answer the following interrogatories under oath, under Code of Civil Procedure sections 2030.010–2030.410), within 30 days after the date of service.**

[Add applicable definitions, if desired]

[Set out each interrogatory in separately numbered paragraphs]

Date: _____

          __[Signature]__
          _ _[Typed name]_ _
          Attorney for _ _[Petitioner/Respondent]_ _

Copies: Original (retain, with original proof of service, for possible filing with court clerk); copies for service on each attorney or party; office copies.

§13.27   (c) Form: Form Interrogatories (Family Law) (Judicial Council Form FL-145)

FL-145

ATTORNEY OR PARTY WITHOUT ATTORNEY *(Name, State Bar number, and address):*	TELEPHONE NO.:

ATTORNEY FOR *(Name):*

SUPERIOR COURT OF CALIFORNIA, COUNTY OF

SHORT TITLE:

FORM INTERROGATORIES–FAMILY LAW	CASE NUMBER:
Asking Party:	
Answering Party:	
Set No.:	

Sec. 1. Instructions to Both Parties

The interrogatories on page 2 of this form are intended to provide for the exchange of relevant information without unreasonable expense to the answering party. They do not change existing law relating to interrogatories, nor do they affect the answering party's right to assert any privilege or make any objection. **Privileges must be asserted.**

Sec. 2. Definitions

Words in **boldface** in these interrogatories are defined as follows:

(a) **Person** includes a natural person; a partnership; any kind of business, legal, or public entity; and its agents or employees.

(b) **Document** means all written, recorded, or graphic materials, however stored, produced, or reproduced.

(c) **Asset** or property includes any interest in real estate or personal property. It includes any interest in a pension, profit-sharing, or retirement plan.

(d) **Debt** means any obligation, including debts paid since the date of separation.

(e) **Support** means any benefit or economic contribution to the living expenses of another person, including gifts.

(f) If asked to **identify a person**, give the person's name, last known residence and business addresses, telephone numbers, and company affiliation at the date of the transaction referred to.

(g) If asked to **identify a document**, attach a copy of the document unless you explain why not. If you do not attach the copy, describe the document, including its date and nature, and give the name, address, telephone number, and occupation of the person who has the document.

Sec. 3. Instructions to the Asking Party

Check the box next to each interrogatory you want the answering party to answer.

Sec. 4. Instructions to the Answering Party

You must answer these interrogatories under oath within 30 days, in accordance with Code of Civil Procedure section 2030.260.

You must furnish all information you have or can reasonably find out, including all information (not privileged) from your attorneys or under your control. If you don't know, say so.

If an interrogatory is answered by referring to a document, the document must be attached as an exhibit to the response and referred to in the response. If the document has more than one page, refer to the page and section where the answer can be found.

If a document to be attached to the response may also be attached to the *Schedule of Assets and Debts* (form FL-142), the document should be attached only to the response, and the form should refer to the response.

If an interrogatory cannot be answered completely, answer as much as you can, state the reason you cannot answer the rest, and state any information you have about the unanswered portion.

Sec. 5. Oath

Your answers to these interrogatories must be under oath, dated, and signed. Use the following statement **at the end of your answers:**

I declare under penalty of perjury under the laws of the State of California that the foregoing answers are true and correct.

_____   ▶ _____
(DATE)   (SIGNATURE)

Form Approved for Optional Use
Judicial Council of California
FL-145 [Rev. January 1, 2006]

FORM INTERROGATORIES–FAMILY LAW

Code of Civil Procedure,
§§ 2030.010–2030.410, 2033.710
www.courtinfo.ca.gov

FL-145

1. **Personal history.** State your full name, current residence address and work address, social security number, any other names you have used, and the dates between which you used each name.

2. **Agreements.** Are there any agreements between you and your spouse or domestic partner, made before or during your marriage or domestic partnership or after your separation, that affect the disposition of **assets, debts,** or **support** in this proceeding? If your answer is yes, for each agreement state the date made and whether it was written or oral, and attach a copy of the agreement or describe its contents.

3. **Legal actions.** Are you a party or do you anticipate being a party to any legal or administrative proceeding other than this action? If your answer is yes, state your role and the name, jurisdiction, case number, and a brief description of each proceeding.

4. **Persons sharing residence.** State the name, age, and relationship to you of each **person** at your present address.

5. **Support provided others.** State the name, age, address, and relationship to you of each **person** for whom you have provided **support** during the past 12 months and the amount provided per month for each.

6. **Support received for others.** State the name, age, address, and relationship to you of each **person** for whom you have received **support** during the past 12 months and the amount received per month for each.

7. **Current income.** List all income you received during the past 12 months, its source, the basis for its computation, and the total amount received from each. Attach your last three paycheck stubs.

8. **Other income.** During the past three years, have you received cash or other property from any source not identified in item 7? If so, list the source, the date, and the nature and value of the property.

9. **Tax returns.** Attach copies of all tax returns and tax schedules filed by or for you in any jurisdiction for the past three calendar years.

10. **Schedule of assets and debts.** Complete the *Schedule of Assets and Debts* (form FL-142) served with these interrogatories.

11. **Separate property contentions.** State the facts that support your contention that an asset or debt is separate property.

12. **Property valuations.** During the past 12 months, have you received written offers to purchase or had written appraisals of any of the assets listed on your completed *Schedule of Assets and Debts?* If your answer is yes, **identify the document.**

13. **Property held by others.** Is there any **property** held by any third party in which you have any interest or over which you have any control? If your answer is yes, indicate whether the property is shown on the *Schedule of Assets and Debts* completed by you. If it is not, describe and identify each such asset, state its present value and the basis for your valuation, and **identify the person** holding the asset.

14. **Retirement and other benefits.** Do you have an interest in any disability, retirement, profit-sharing, or deferred compensation plan? If your answer is yes, **identify** each plan and provide the name, address, and telephone number of the administrator and custodian of records.

15. **Claims of reimbursement.** Do you claim the legal right to be reimbursed for any expenditures of your separate or community property? If your answer is yes, state all supporting facts.

16. **Credits.** Have you claimed reimbursement credits for payments of community debts since the date of separation? If your answer is yes, **identify** the source of payment, the creditor, the date paid, and the amount paid. State whether you have added to the debt since the separation.

17. **Insurance.** Identify each health, life, automobile, and disability insurance policy or plan that you now own or that covers you, your children, or your assets. State the policy type, policy number, and name of the company. **Identify** the agent and give the address.

18. **Health.** Is there any physical or emotional condition that limits your ability to work? If your answer is yes, state each fact on which you base your answer.

19. **Children's needs.** Do you contend that any of your children have any special needs? If so, identify the child with the need, the reason for the need, its cost, and its expected duration.

20. **Attorney fees.** State the total amount of attorney fees and costs incurred by you in this proceeding, the amount paid, and the source of the money paid. Describe the billing arrangements.

21. **Gifts.** List any gifts you have made without the consent of your spouse or domestic partner in the past 24 months, their values, and the recipients.

Copies: Original (retain, with original proof of service, for possible filing with court clerk); copies for service on each attorney or party; office copies.

§13.28   (d) Form: Schedule of Assets and Debts (Judicial Council Form FL-142)

THIS FORM SHOULD NOT BE FILED WITH THE COURT   FL-142

ATTORNEY OR PARTY WITHOUT ATTORNEY *(Name and Address)*:	TELEPHONE NO.:

ATTORNEY FOR *(Name)*:

SUPERIOR COURT OF CALIFORNIA, COUNTY OF

PETITIONER:

RESPONDENT:

SCHEDULE OF ASSETS AND DEBTS ☐ Petitioner's ☐ Respondent's	CASE NUMBER:

— INSTRUCTIONS —

List all your known community and separate assets or debts. Include assets even if they are in the possession of another person, including your spouse. If you contend an asset or debt is separate, put P (for Petitioner) or R (for Respondent) in the first column (separate property) to indicate to whom you contend it belongs.

All values should be as of the date of signing the declaration unless you specify a different valuation date with the description. For additional space, use a continuation sheet numbered to show which item is being continued.

ITEM NO.	ASSETS DESCRIPTION	SEP. PROP	DATE ACQUIRED	CURRENT GROSS FAIR MARKET VALUE	AMOUNT OF MONEY OWED OR ENCUMBRANCE
1.	REAL ESTATE *(Give street addresses and attach copies of deeds with legal descriptions and latest lender's statement.)*			$	$
2.	HOUSEHOLD FURNITURE, FURNISHINGS, APPLIANCES *(Identify.)*				
3.	JEWELRY, ANTIQUES, ART, COIN COLLECTIONS, etc. *(Identify.)*				

Form Approved for Optional Use
Judicial Council of California
FL-142 [Rev. January 1, 2005]   **SCHEDULE OF ASSETS AND DEBTS**
(Family Law)   Code of Civil Procedure, §§ 2030(c), 2033.5
www.courtinfo.ca.gov

ITEM NO.	ASSETS DESCRIPTION	SEP. PROP	DATE ACQUIRED	CURRENT GROSS FAIR MARKET VALUE	AMOUNT OF MONEY OWED OR ENCUMBRANCE
				$	$
4.	VEHICLES, BOATS, TRAILERS (Describe and attach copy of title document.)				
5.	SAVINGS ACCOUNTS (Account name, account number, bank, and branch. Attach copy of latest statement.)				
6.	CHECKING ACCOUNTS (Account name and number, bank, and branch. Attach copy of latest statement.)				
7.	CREDIT UNION, OTHER DEPOSIT ACCOUNTS (Account name and number, bank, and branch. Attach copy of latest statement.)				
8.	CASH (Give location.)				
9.	TAX REFUND				
10.	LIFE INSURANCE WITH CASH SURRENDER OR LOAN VALUE (Attach copy of declaration page for each policy.)				

ITEM NO.	ASSETS DESCRIPTION	SEP. PROP	DATE ACQUIRED	CURRENT GROSS FAIR MARKET VALUE	AMOUNT OF MONEY OWED OR ENCUMBRANCE
				$	$
11.	STOCKS, BONDS, SECURED NOTES, MUTUAL FUNDS *(Give certificate number and attach copy of the certificate or copy of latest statement.)*				
12.	RETIREMENT AND PENSIONS *(Attach copy of latest summary plan documents and latest benefit statement.)*				
13.	PROFIT - SHARING, ANNUITIES, IRAS, DEFERRED COMPENSATION *(Attach copy of latest statement.)*				
14.	ACCOUNTS RECEIVABLE AND UNSECURED NOTES *(Attach copy of each.)*				
15.	PARTNERSHIPS AND OTHER BUSINESS INTERESTS *(Attach copy of most current K-1 form and Schedule C.)*				
16.	OTHER ASSETS				
17.	TOTAL ASSETS FROM CONTINUATION SHEET				
18.	TOTAL ASSETS			$	$

ITEM NO.	DEBTS—SHOW TO WHOM OWED	SEP. PROP.	TOTAL OWING	DATE INCURRED
19. STUDENT LOANS *(Give details.)*			$	
20. TAXES *(Give details.)*				
21. SUPPORT ARREARAGES *(Attach copies of orders and statements.)*				
22. LOANS—UNSECURED *(Give bank name and loan number and attach copy of latest statement.)*				
23. CREDIT CARDS *(Give creditor's name and address and the account number. Attach copy of latest statement.)*				
24. OTHER DEBTS *(Specify.):*				
25. TOTAL DEBTS FROM CONTINUATION SHEET				
26. TOTAL DEBTS			$	

27. ☐ *(Specify number):*_____ pages are attached as continuation sheets.

I declare under penalty of perjury under the laws of the State of California that the foregoing is true and correct.

Date:

▶

_____
(TYPE OR PRINT NAME)

_____
(SIGNATURE OF DECLARANT)

FL-142 [Rev. January 1, 2005]   **SCHEDULE OF ASSETS AND DEBTS**
                                        (Family Law)   Page 4 of 4

Copies: Original (retain, with original proof of service, for possible filing with court clerk); copies for service on each attorney or party; office copies.

(4) Requests for Admission

§13.29　　(a) Discussion

Requests for admission ask the responding party to admit the genuineness of specified documents or the truth of specified matters and may be directed only to a party. CCP §2033.010. Without leave of court, the petitioner cannot serve requests for admission until at least 10 days after service of the Summons and Petition on the party to whom they are directed or that party's appearance. The respondent may serve requests for admission without leave of court at any time. CCP §2033.210(a)-(c).

A party may request, in one or more sets, that the responding party admit a maximum of 35 matters that do not relate to the genuineness of documents. CCP §2033.030(a). Subject to the responding party's right to seek a protective order under CCP §2033.080(a), the propounding party may request that the responding party admit more than 35 such matters, as long as the propounding party attaches the declaration required by CCP §2033.050 and the greater number is warranted by the complexity or quantity of the issues. CCP §2033.040(a). The number of requests to admit the genuineness of documents is limited only as justice requires to protect the responding party from unwarranted annoyance, embarrassment, or oppression or undue burden and expense. CCP §2033.030(c).

The name of the requesting party, the set number of the requests for admission, and the name of the responding party must appear in the first paragraph immediately below the title of the case. Each set of requests must be numbered consecutively. CCP §2033.060(a)-(b). Each request in a set must be set forth separately, be identified by a number or letter, and be complete in itself. CCP §2033.060(c)-(d). Any term specially defined in a set of requests for admission must be typed with all letters capitalized whenever the term appears. No request may contain subparts, or a compound, conjunctive, or disjunctive request unless approved under CCP §§2033.710- 2033.740. CCP §2033.060(f). To date, there have been no such approvals.

The statute provides that no preface or instruction may be included with a set of requests unless it has been approved under CCP §§2033.710-2033.740. CCP §2033.060(d). This restriction appears to limit prefaces and instructions to the very brief ones that appear in the Judicial Council form of requests for admission (see form in §13.30).

A party requesting admissions of the genuineness of any document must attach copies of the documents to the requests and make the originals available for inspection on the responding party's demand. CCP §2033.060(g).

Requests for admission may not be combined with any other discovery method (*e.g.,* interrogatories) in a single document. CCP §2033.060(h).

Requests for admission are served on the party to whom they are directed and on all other parties who have appeared in the action. CCP §2033.070. The statute allows the responding party 30 days after service of the requests in which to serve the response on the requesting party. CCP §2033.250. Requests for admission are typically served by mail, however, in which event the period for service of the response is extended by 5 calendar days, assuming that the place of address and place of mailing are in California. CCP §2016.050.

A party served with requests for admission may promptly move for a protective order as long as the motion is accompanied by a declaration stating facts showing that a reasonable and good faith attempt has first been made to informally resolve each issue presented by the motion. CCP §2033.080(a). Any matter admitted in response to a request for admission is conclusively established, for purposes of the pending action, against the party making the admission, unless the court permits withdrawal or amendment of the admission. CCP §2033.410(a).

For a complete discussion of requests for admission, see California Civil Discovery Practice, chap 9 (3d ed Cal CEB 1998).

§13.30   (b) Form: Request for Admissions (Judicial Council Form DISC-020)

DISC-020

ATTORNEY OR PARTY WITHOUT ATTORNEY *(Name, State Bar number, and Address)*	FOR COURT USE ONLY
TELEPHONE NO.: FAX NO. *(Optional)*: E-MAIL ADDRESS *(Optional)*: ATTORNEY FOR *(Name)*:	

SUPERIOR COURT OF CALIFORNIA, COUNTY OF
STREET ADDRESS:
MAILING ADDRESS:
CITY AND ZIP CODE:
BRANCH NAME:

SHORT TITLE:

REQUEST FOR ADMISSIONS ☐ Truth of Facts ☐ Genuineness of Documents Requesting Party: Responding Party: Set No.:	CASE NUMBER:

You are requested to admit within thirty days after service of this *Request for Admissions* that

1. ☐ each of the following facts is true *(number each fact consecutively)*:

☐ Continued on Attachment 1

2. ☐ the original of each of the following documents, copies of which are attached, is genuine *(number each document consecutively)*:

☐ Continued on Attachment 2

▶

_____   _____
(TYPE OR PRINT NAME)   (SIGNATURE OF PARTY OR ATTORNEY)

Page 1 of 1

Form Approved by the
Judicial Council of California   **REQUEST FOR ADMISSIONS**   CEB   Code Civil Procedure,
DISC-020 [Rev. January 1, 2007]   §§ 2033.010–2033.420, 2033.710
                                                                              www.courtinfo.ca.gov

Copies: Original (retain, with original proof of service, for possible filing with court clerk); copies for service on each attorney or party; office copies.

Comment: Use of this Judicial Council form is optional. CCP §2033.740(a).

§13.31   (c) Form: Requests for Admission (Sample Form)

_ _[Attorney name]_ _
_ _[State Bar number]_ _
_ _[Address]_ _
_ _[Telephone number]_ _

Attorney for _ _[name]_ _

**SUPERIOR COURT OF CALIFORNIA
COUNTY OF** _ _ _ _ _ _

Marriage of	)	**No.** _ _ _ _ _ _
	)	
Petitioner: _ _ _ _ _ _ _ _	)	**REQUESTS FOR**
	)	**ADMISSION**
Respondent: _ _ _ _ _ _ _ _	)	
	)	
_____	)	

REQUESTING PARTY: _ _[Petitioner/Respondent]_ _, _ _[name]_ _

SET NO.: _ _ _ _ _ _

RESPONDING PARTY: _ _[Respondent/Petitioner]_ _, _ _[name]_ _

_ _[Petitioner/Respondent]_ _, _ _[name]_ _, **requests that** _ _[respondent/petitioner]_ _, _ _[name]_ _, **admit under oath, under Code of Civil Procedure sections 2033.010–2033.740, within 30 days after the date of service, that:**

A. Each of the following is true:

[*Set out statements in separate paragraphs, numbered consecutively*]

B. The original of each of the following documents, copies of which are attached, is genuine:

[Identify documents in separate paragraphs, numbered consecutively]

Date: _____   __*[Signature]*__
                 _ _*[Typed name]*_ _
                 Attorney for _ _*[Petitioner/*
                 *Respondent]*_ _

Copies: Original (retain, with original proof of service, for possible filing with court clerk); copies for service on each attorney or party; office copies.

Comment: The form may include requests for admission of the truth of matters, the genuineness of documents, or both. When both types of requests are used, each type should have its own individual numbering of paragraphs.

(5) Demand for Production of Documents

§13.32   (a) Discussion

A party may demand the production, for inspection and copying, of documents that are in the responding party's possession, custody, or control. CCP §2031.010(b). The code also addresses inspection of tangible things and of land or other property (CCP §2031.010(c)–(d)), but, because of their limited applicability to marital actions, those subsections are not discussed here.

A demand for production may be directed only to a party. CCP §2031.010(b). Absent leave of court, the petitioner cannot serve a demand for production until at least 10 days after service of the Summons and Petition on the party to whom it is directed or that party's appearance. The respondent may serve a demand for production without leave of court at any time. CCP §2031.020(a)–(b).

The name of the demanding party, the set number of the demand for production, and the name of the responding party must appear in the first paragraph immediately below the title of the case. Each set of demands must be numbered consecutively. Each demand in a set must be set forth separately and identified by number or letter. CCP §2031.030(a)–(c). Each demand must (1) designate the documents to be inspected either by specifically describing each individual item or by reasonably specifying each category of item; (2) specify a reasonable time for the inspection that is, without leave to specify an earlier date, at least 30 days after service of the demand; and (3) specify a reasonable place for the inspection and copying. CCP

§2031.030(c)(1)–(3). Reasonable places for inspection and copying might include, *e.g.,* the office of a certified public accountant retained to assist with the case or the office of a copy service.

Demands for production are served on the party to whom they are directed and on all other parties who have appeared in the action. CCP §2031.040. The statute allows the responding party 30 days after service of the demand in which to serve the response on the requesting party. CCP §2031.260. Demands for production, however, are typically served by mail, in which event the period for service of the response is extended to 35 days, and the usual 30-day minimum period between service of the demand and the time specified for the inspection is likewise extended by 5 calendar days, assuming that the place of address and place of mailing are in California. CCP §1013(a), CCP §2016.050.

A party served with a demand for production or any other party or affected person or organization may promptly move for a protective order as long as the motion is accompanied by a declaration stating facts showing that a reasonable and good faith attempt has first been made to informally resolve each issue presented by the motion. CCP §2031.060(a).

For a complete discussion of demands for production, including inspection of tangible things and of land or other property, see California Civil Discovery Practice, chap 8 (3d ed Cal CEB 1998).

§13.33   (b) Form: Demand for Production of Documents

_ _[Attorney name]_ _
_ _[State Bar number]_ _
_ _[Address]_ _
_ _[Telephone number]_ _

Attorney for _ _[name]_ _

SUPERIOR COURT OF CALIFORNIA
COUNTY OF _ _ _ _ _ _

Marriage of	)	**No.** _ _ _ _ _ _
	)	
Petitioner: _ _ _ _ _ _ _ _	)	**DEMAND FOR**
	)	**PRODUCTION OF**
Respondent: _ _ _ _ _ _ _ _	)	**DOCUMENTS**
	)	
_____	)	

DEMANDING PARTY: _ _[Petitioner/Respondent]_ _, _ _[name]_ _

SET NO.: _ _ _ _ _ _

RESPONDING PARTY: _ _[Respondent/Petitioner]_ _, _ _[name]_ _

 _ _[Petitioner/Respondent]_ _, _ _[name]_ _, **demands, under Code of Civil Procedure sections 2031.010–2031.510, that** _ _[respondent/petitioner]_ _, _ _[name]_ _, **produce the items described below, for inspection and copying by** _ _[name]_ _, _ _[capacity, e.g., petitioner's attorney]_ _, **on** _ _[date]_ _, **at** _ _[time]_ _, **at** _ _[e.g., the office of petitioner's attorney]_ _, **located at** _ _[address]_ _.

The items to be produced are:

[List each item or category of items in separately numbered paragraphs]

Date: _____	__[Signature]__
	_ _[Typed name]_ _
	Attorney for _ _[Petitioner/ Respondent]_ _

Copies: Original (retain, with original proof of service, for filing with court clerk if required in connection with future motion); copies for service on each attorney or party; office copies.

§13.34 (6) Motion for Physical, Mental, or Vocational Examination

Any party may file a noticed motion for a physical or mental examination of another party, or of a child in the custody of a party, as long as the mental or physical condition of the party or child to be examined is in controversy in the action. CCP §§2032.020(a), 2032.310(a). The motion must specify the time, place, manner, conditions, scope, and nature of the examination and the identity and the specialty, if any, of the person or persons who will perform it. CCP §2032.310(b). The parties may arrange and carry out an examination under a written agreement (CCP §2016.030), and any motion must be accompanied by a declaration demonstrating a reasonable and good faith attempt to reach and implement such an agreement (CCP §2032.310(b)).

In any proceeding in which spousal support is at issue, any party may file a noticed motion for an order that another party submit to an examination by a "vocational training counselor." Fam C §4331(a)–(b). The examination must include an assessment of the party's ability to obtain employment based on his or her age, health, education, marketable skills, and employment history, and the current availability of employment opportunities. The focus of the examination must be on an assessment of the party's ability to obtain employment that would allow the party to maintain himself or herself at the marital standard of living. Fam C §4331(a). On marital standard of living, see §6.9.

A "vocational training counselor" is defined as an individual who has "sufficient knowledge, skill, experience, training, or education in interviewing, administering, and interpreting tests for analysis of marketable skills, formulating career goals, planning courses of training and study, and assessing the job market" to qualify as an expert in vocational training under Evid C §720. Fam C §4331(d). The vocational training counselor must possess certain minimum specified qualifications. Fam C §4331(e).

Because the order for a vocational examination must specify the time, place, manner, conditions, and scope of the examination and the person or persons who will perform it (Fam C §4331(b)), the motion should specify these items.

A motion for a physical, mental, or vocational examination is prepared and processed in the same manner as a noticed motion for temporary orders and may be sought in connection with such a motion. For discussion of, and forms for, motions for temporary orders, see §§11.16–11.63. The moving party prepares the Judicial Council forms of (1) Order to Show Cause (see form in §11.18) or Notice of Motion (see form in §11.20) and (2) Application for Order and Supporting Declaration (see form in §11.22). On choosing between the Order to Show Cause and the Notice of Motion, see §11.16. In the caption of the Order to Show Cause or Notice of Motion form, the box labeled "Other (specify)" is checked and the subject matter of the motion, *e.g.,* "Vocational Examination," is indicated. The relief requested is more specifically indicated at Item 13 on the Application form. Facts in support of the relief requested may be provided either at Item 14 of the Application or in an attached declaration. On service and filing of an Order to Show Cause or Notice of Motion, see §11.34.

For a complete discussion of motions for physical and mental examinations, see California Civil Discovery Practice, chap 10 (3d ed Cal CEB 1998).

(7) Demand for Exchange of Expert Trial Witness Information

§13.35   (a) Discussion

After the setting of the initial trial date for the action, any party may demand that all parties simultaneously exchange information concerning their expert trial witnesses. CCP §2034.210(a). Each party must then provide either (1) the name and address of every person (including the party) whose oral or deposition testimony in the form of an expert opinion the party expects to offer in evidence at trial or (2) a statement that the party does not presently intend to offer the testimony of any expert witness. CCP §§2034.210(a), 2034.260(b). If any expert designated is a party or an employee of a party, or has been retained by a party to form and express an opinion in anticipation of litigation or in preparation for trial, the person's designation must include or be accompanied by an expert witness declaration that contains (CCP §§2034.210(b), 2034.260(c)):

• A brief narrative statement of the expert's qualifications;

- A brief narrative statement of the general substance of the testimony the expert is expected to give;

- A representation that the expert has agreed to testify at trial;

- A representation that the expert will be sufficiently familiar with the action to submit to a meaningful oral deposition concerning the specific testimony, including any opinion and its basis, that the expert is expected to give at trial; and

- A statement of the expert's hourly and daily fee for providing deposition testimony and for consulting with the retaining attorney.

The exchange demanded may include production for inspection and copying of all discoverable reports and writings, if any, made by any expert designated, in the course of preparing the expert's opinion. CCP §§2034.210(c), 2034.270.

If any expert designated is a party or an employee of a party, or has been retained by a party to form and express an opinion in anticipation of the litigation or in preparation for trial, the demand must be made no later than 10 days after the initial trial date has been set or 70 days before that trial date, whichever is closer to the trial date. CCP §2034.220. The demand must identify the party making the demand below the title of the case, state the CCP section under which the demand is being made, and specify the date for the exchange of the expert trial witness information. The date must be 50 days before the initial trial date or 20 days after service of the demand, whichever is closer to the trial date, unless the court, on a motion and for good cause shown, orders an earlier or later date. CCP §2034.230(a)-(b). Demands for exchange of expert trial witness information, which must be served on all parties who have appeared in the action CCP §2034.240), are usually served by mail. It is unclear whether service by mail extends the date for exchange by 5 days. CCP §2016.050 provides that CCP §1013, which addresses extensions of time when service is by mail, applies to any discovery method provided for in the Civil Discovery Act (CCP §§2016.010-2036.050), which includes CCP §§2034.210-2034.730. But §2034.260 itself, in discussing the time of exchange of information, refers specifically to the date of exchange "specified in the demand." CCP §2034.260. The safer approach would probably be to allow the responding parties the extra 5 days when service is by mail and to specify the exchange date accordingly.

A party served with a demand for exchange of expert trial witness information may promptly move for a protective order. The motion must be accompanied by a meet and confer declaration stating facts showing that a reasonable and good faith attempt has first been made to informally resolve each issue presented by the motion. CCP §§2016.040, 2034.250(a).

For a complete discussion of demands for exchange of expert trial witness information, see California Civil Discovery Practice, chap 11 (3d ed Cal CEB 1998).

NOTE► The legislature has added a clause to the Civil Discovery Act, indicating that when the last day to complete any act falls on a Saturday, Sunday, or holiday, the time limit is extended until the next day that is not a Saturday, Sunday, or holiday. CCP §2016.060.

§13.36   (b) Form: Demand for Exchange of Expert Trial Witness Information

_ _[Attorney name]_ _
_ _[State Bar number]_ _
_ _[Address]_ _
_ _[Telephone number]_ _

Attorney for _ _[name]_ _

SUPERIOR COURT OF CALIFORNIA
COUNTY OF _ _ _ _ _ _

Marriage of	)	**No.** _ _ _ _ _ _
	)	
Petitioner: _ _ _ _ _ _ _ _	)	**DEMAND FOR EXCHANGE**
	)	**OF EXPERT TRIAL**
Respondent: _ _ _ _ _ _ _ _	)	**WITNESS INFORMATION**
	)	_ _[AND FOR PRODUCTION_
_____	)	OF EXPERT REPORTS AND
		WRITINGS]_ _

DEMANDING PARTY: _ _[Petitioner/Respondent]_ _, _ _[name]_ _

TO: _ _[Respondent/Petitioner]_ _, _ _[name]_ _, **and** _ _[his/her]_ _ **attorney of record:**

_ _[Petitioner/Respondent]_ _, _ _[name]_ _, **hereby demands under Code of Civil Procedure sections 2034.010–2034.730 that, on or before** _ _[date of exchange]_ _, **the parties to this action participate in a mutual and simultaneous exchange of information concerning each party's expert trial witnesses to the following extent:**

1. A list containing the name and address of each natural person, including the party, whose oral or deposition testimony in the form of an expert opinion the party expects to offer in evidence at the trial or, in the alternative, a statement that the party does not presently intend to offer the testimony of any expert witness.

2. If any witness on the list is the party or an employee of the party or has been retained by the party for the purpose of forming and expressing an opinion in anticipation of the litigation or in preparation for the trial of the action, an expert witness declaration signed by the party's attorney (or by the party if appearing without an attorney), containing for each such witness:

(a) A brief narrative statement of the expert's qualifications;

(b) A brief narrative statement of the general substance of the testimony that the expert is expected to give;

(c) A representation that the expert has agreed to testify at the trial;

(d) A representation that the expert will be sufficiently familiar with the pending action to submit to a meaningful oral deposition concerning the specific testimony, including any opinion and its basis, that the expert is expected to give at trial; and

(e) A statement of the expert's hourly and daily fee for providing deposition testimony.

[Add if production of discoverable reports and writings of listed experts is demanded]

3. Production, for inspection and copying, of all discoverable reports and writings, if any, made in the course of preparing an expert opinion by any witness on the list who is the party

or an employee of the party or has been retained by the party for the purpose of forming and expressing an opinion in anticipation of the litigation or in preparation for the trial of the action.

[Continue]

Date: _____

___[Signature]___
_ _[Typed name]_ _
Attorney for _ _[Petitioner/
Respondent]_ _

Copies: Original (retain, with original proof of service, for possible filing with court clerk); copies for service on each attorney or party; office copies.

(8) Postjudgment Request for Production of Income and Expense Declaration

§13.37 (a) Discussion

At any time following a judgment of dissolution or legal separation, or a paternity determination, that provides for payment of child, spousal, or family support, a party paying or receiving such support may, without leave of court, serve on the other party a Request for Production of Income and Expense Declaration After Judgment (Judicial Council Form FL-396; see §13.38). Fam C §3664(a). The Request for Production (along with a blank copy of the Income and Expense Declaration and attachments (see forms in §§11.26–11.29)) must be served by certified mail, postage prepaid, return receipt requested, to the last known address of the party to be served, or by personal service. Fam C §3664(e). The responding party must attach a copy of the prior year's federal and state personal income tax returns to the Income and Expense Declaration. Fam C §3665(a).

The purpose of this discovery device is to permit inexpensive discovery of facts before the institution of proceedings for support modification or termination. Fam C §3660. Other discovery methods may be used after judgment for this purpose only if a motion for modification is pending. Fam C §3662. Without such a pending motion, this method may be used no more than once a year. Fam C §3663.

The request may be enforced in the manner specified in any statute applicable to enforcement of discovery procedures. Fam C §3666.

On the subsequent filing by the requesting party of a motion for modification or termination of the support order, the court may order sanctions against the responding party, in the form of payment of all costs of the motion, on a finding that the income and expense declaration submitted by that party was incomplete, inaccurate, or missing the prior year's federal and state personal income tax returns, or that the declaration was not submitted in good faith. Costs include the filing fee, and the costs of depositions and subpoenas necessary to obtain complete and accurate information. Fam C §3667. By its terms, §3667 applies whether or not the requesting party has used Fam C §3664(b), discussed below, which provides for service on the responding party's employer of a request for information on income and benefits provided to the employee.

If there is no response within 35 days after service of the request, or if the responsive income and expense declaration is incomplete regarding any wage information, including the attachment of pay stubs and income tax returns, the requesting party may serve a request on the other party's employer for information limited to the income and benefits provided to the employee using Judicial Council Form FL-397 (Request for Income and Benefit Information From Employer; see §13.39). The date specified for production of the information must be at least 15 days after issuance of the request. Fam C §3664(b). Service of the request must be by certified mail, postage prepaid, return receipt requested, to the last known address of the employer, or by personal service. Fam C §3664(e).

A copy of the request to the employer must be served on the employee or the employee's attorney before the date specified for the employer's production of the income and benefit information. Fam C §3664(c). The copy must be accompanied by a notice, in a typeface that is intended to call attention to its terms, that indicates that (Fam C §3664(c)(1)–(4)):

- Information limited to the income and benefits provided to the employee by the employer is being sought from the employer;

- The information may be protected by the right of privacy;

- If the employee objects to the production of the information by the employer, the employee must notify the court of the objection in writing before the date specified for the production; and

- If the requesting party does not agree in writing to cancel or narrow the scope of the request, the employee should consult an attorney about the employee's right to privacy and how to protect that right.

Before the date specified for production, the employee may file a motion under CCP §1987.1 to quash or modify the request in the same manner as applies to a subpoena duces tecum. Notice of the motion must be given to the employer before the date specified for production. Fam C §3664(d).

The completed form for income and benefit information provided by the employer may be admissible in a proceeding for modification or termination of an order for child, spousal, or family support if (1) the completed form complies with Evid C §§1561–1562 (admissibility of business records) and (2) a copy of the completed form and notice was served on the employee as provided in Fam C §3664. Evid C §1567.

Note that no employer may be required to produce the requested information, except on court order or on agreement of the parties and the employer. Fam C §3664(d).

§13.38 (b) Form: Request for Production of an Income and Expense Declaration After Judgment (Judicial Council Form FL-396)

FL-396

ATTORNEY OR PARTY WITHOUT ATTORNEY *(Name and Address):*	TELEPHONE NO.:	FOR COURT USE ONLY

ATTORNEY FOR *(Name):*

SUPERIOR COURT OF CALIFORNIA, COUNTY OF
STREET ADDRESS:
MAILING ADDRESS:
CITY AND ZIP CODE:
BRANCH NAME:

PETITIONER/PLAINTIFF:

RESPONDENT/DEFENDANT:

REQUEST FOR PRODUCTION OF AN INCOME AND EXPENSE DECLARATION AFTER JUDGMENT	CASE NUMBER:

(NOTE: This request must be served on the petitioner or respondent and not on an attorney who was or is representing that party.)

To *(name):*

1. a. As permitted by Family Code section 3664(a), declarant requires that you complete and return the attached *Income and Expense Declaration* (form FL-150) within 30 days after the date this request is served on you. Family Code section 3665(a) requires you to attach copies of your most recent state and federal income tax returns (whether individual or joint) to the completed *Income and Expense Declaration* (form FL-150).

   b. The completed *Income and Expense Declaration* (form FL-150) should be mailed to the following person at the following address *(specify):*

2. You may consult an attorney about completion of the *Income and Expense Declaration* (form FL-150) or you may proceed without an attorney. The information provided will be used to determine whether to ask for a modification of child, spousal, or family support at this time.

3. If you wish to do so, you may serve a request for a completed *Income and Expense Declaration* (form FL-150) on me. Each of us may use this procedure once a year after judgment even though no legal matter is pending.

Date:

▶

_____   _____
(TYPE OR PRINT NAME)   (SIGNATURE OF DECLARANT)

WARNING: If a court later finds that the information provided in response to this request is incomplete or inaccurate or missing the prior year's tax returns, or that you did not submit the information in good faith, the court may order you to pay all costs necessary for me to get complete and accurate information. In addition you could be found to be in contempt and receive other penalties.

Form Adopted for Mandatory Use
Judicial Council of California
FL-396 [Rev. January 1, 2003]

**REQUEST FOR PRODUCTION OF AN INCOME
AND EXPENSE DECLARATION AFTER JUDGMENT**

Family Code, §§ 3664,
3665, 3668
www.courtinfo.ca.gov

PETITIONER/PLAINTIFF:	CASE NUMBER:
RESPONDENT/DEFENDANT:	

PROOF OF SERVICE BY MAIL
REQUEST FOR PRODUCTION OF AN INCOME AND EXPENSE DECLARATION AFTER JUDGMENT

1. I am at least 18 years old and **not a party to this cause.** I am a resident of or employed in the county where the mailing took place, and my residence or business address is *(specify):*

2. I served a copy of the following documents:
   a. a completed *Request for Production of an Income and Expense Declaration After Judgment,* and
   b. a **blank** *Income and Expense Declaration* (a four-page form) (form FL-150).

3. I served a copy of the foregoing documents by mailing them in a sealed envelope with postage fully prepaid, certified mail, return receipt requested, as follows:
   a. ☐ I deposited the envelope with the United States Postal Service.
   b. ☐ I placed the envelope for collection and processing for mailing following this business's ordinary practice with which I am readily familiar. On the same day correspondence is placed for collection and mailing, it is deposited in the ordinary course of business with the United States Postal Service.

4. Manner of service
   a. Date of mailing:
   b. Place mailed from:
   c. Addressed as follows:
      Name:

      Street:

   City, state, and zip code:

I declare under penalty of perjury under the laws of the State of California that the foregoing is true and correct.

Date:

_____
(TYPE OR PRINT NAME)

▶ _____
(SIGNATURE OF DECLARANT)

Copies: Original (retain, with original proof of service, for filing with court clerk if required in connection with future motion); copy for service; office copies.

§13.39 (c) Form: Request for Income and Benefit Information from Employer (Judicial Council Form FL-397)

FL-397

ATTORNEY OR PARTY WITHOUT ATTORNEY *(Name, state bar number, and address)*:	FOR COURT USE ONLY
TELEPHONE NO. *(Optional)*: FAX NO. *(Optional)*:	
E-MAIL ADDRESS *(Optional)*:	
ATTORNEY FOR *(Name)*:	

SUPERIOR COURT OF CALIFORNIA, COUNTY OF
STREET ADDRESS:
MAILING ADDRESS:
CITY AND ZIP CODE:
BRANCH NAME:

PETITIONER/PLAINTIFF:

RESPONDENT/DEFENDANT:

REQUEST FOR INCOME AND BENEFIT INFORMATION FROM EMPLOYER	CASE NUMBER:

To *(employer name)*:

1. This notice is served on you, under California Family Code section 3664(b), in regard to your employee *(name)*:

2. I previously served a request for an *Income and Expense Declaration* (form FL-150) after judgment on your employee and:
   a. ☐ There was no response within 35 days
      or
   b. ☐ The response was incomplete as to wage information.

3. I request that the information sought be sent to me on or before *(date)*:   , which is at least 15 days from the date of this request.

4. I request that you, as the employer of the above employee, provide the following information (indicated by checked boxes below). If you wish, you may return a copy of this form with the information filled out or provide the information on a separate form.
   a. ☐ Occupation of employee:
   b. ☐ (1) Presently employed: ☐ Yes ☐ No
      (2) If employed, current employment status: ☐ Full time ☐ Part time
      (3) If not presently employed:
         (a) Date of separation:
         (b) Reasons for separation:
   c. ☐ Starting date of employment:
   d. ☐ Gross salary or wages for the previous month (including commissions, bonuses, and overtime):
   e. ☐ Total salary or wages for the previous 12 months (including commissions, bonuses, and overtime):
   f. ☐ Federal income tax withheld for the previous month:
   g. ☐ State income tax withheld for the previous month:
   h. ☐ Social Security and Medicare Tax ("FICA" and "MEDI") deducted for the previous month:
   i. ☐ Any other deductions from the paycheck for the previous month *(for each deduction state purpose and amount)*:

Form Adopted for Mandatory Use
Judicial Council of California
FL-397 [Rev. January 1, 2003]

REQUEST FOR INCOME AND BENEFIT INFORMATION FROM EMPLOYER

Page 1 of 2
Family Code, § 3664
www.courtinfo.ca.gov

PETITIONER/PLAINTIFF:	CASE NUMBER:
RESPONDENT/DEFENDANT:	

j. ☐ Benefits provided:

(1) ☐ Vision insurance   ☐ Not available   ☐ Not enrolled   ☐ Enrolled *(specify value to employee):*

(2) ☐ Life insurance   ☐ Not available   ☐ Not enrolled   ☐ Enrolled *(specify value to employee):*

(3) ☐ Health insurance   ☐ Not available   ☐ Not enrolled   ☐ Enrolled *(specify value to employee):*

(4) ☐ Contributions toward   ☐ Not available   ☐ Not enrolled   ☐ Enrolled *(specify asset value to*
retirement plan   *employee):*

(5) ☐ Use of company assets *(vehicle, housing, health club facility, etc.)*
☐ Not available   ☐ Not enrolled   ☐ Enrolled *(specify value to employee):*

k. ☐ Attach a copy of the employee's three most recent pay stubs.

5. You are entitled to have me pay the reasonable costs of copying the information in this request.

6. Under Family Code section 3664(f), your compliance with this request is voluntary except upon order of the court or upon agreement of the parties, employers, and employee affected.

Date:

_____   ▶   _____
(TYPE OR PRINT NAME)   (SIGNATURE OF REQUESTING PARTY)

NOTICE TO EMPLOYEE

I have served a copy of the attached *Request for Income and Benefit Information From Employer* on your employer under Family Code section 3664(b).

Under Family Code section 3664(c), you are notified that:

1. The information sought by me is limited to the income and benefits provided to you by your employer.

2. The information may be protected by right of privacy.

3. If you object to the production of this information by the employer to me, you must notify the court, in writing, of this objection prior to the date specified in paragraph 3 of the attached request.

4. If, upon your objection, I do not agree, in writing, to cancel or narrow the scope of my request, you should consult an attorney regarding your right to privacy and how to protect this right.

5. You may have other rights provided by Family Code section 3664 and otherwise.

NOTICE TO REQUESTING PARTY

Under Family Code section 3664(e), service of this request on the employer and of the copy of the request on the employee must be by certified mail, postage prepaid, return receipt requested, to the last known address of the party to be served, or by personal service.

Copies: Original (retain, with original proof of service, for filing with court clerk if required in connection with future motion); copies for service on employee and employer or employer's attorney; office copies.

b. Limitations on Discovery of Specific Information

§13.40 (1) Relevance

The basic relevance requirement for discovery under the Civil Discovery Act (CCP §§2016.010-2036.050) is set forth in CCP §2017.010. That subsection provides that the information sought must be (1) relevant to the subject matter of the action or to the determination of any motion made in the action and (2) either admissible itself or appearing to be reasonably calculated to lead to the discovery of admissible evidence. This requirement is incorporated by reference into the sections regulating oral depositions and depositions for production of business records (see CCP §2025.010), interrogatories (see CCP §2030.010(a)), requests for admission (see CCP §2033.010), and demands for the production of documents (see CCP §2031.010(a)). With respect to physical and mental examinations, discovery is available only when the mental or physical condition of the party to be examined is in controversy in the action (CCP §2032.020(a)) and when good cause is shown (CCP §2032.320(a)). With respect to vocational examinations, the applicable statute requires only that good cause be shown. Fam C §4331(b).

For a complete discussion of relevance as a factor affecting discoverability of specific information, see California Civil Discovery Practice §§2.19-2.47 (3d ed Cal CEB 1998).

For a discussion of the limitations on discovery on a motion to show cause under Fam C §2556, see *Marriage of Hixson* (2003) 111 CA4th 1116, 1122, 4 CR3d 483.

§13.41 (2) Privilege and Work Product

Discovery of relevant material is limited by rules on privilege and work product. Privileged matters are not discoverable through any discovery method. See CCP §2017.010). The primary privileges applicable in a marital action are the following:

- Privilege against self-incrimination (see Evid C §940);

- Lawyer-client privilege (see Evid C §§950-962);

- Physician-patient privilege (see Evid C §§990-1007);

- Psychotherapist-patient privilege (see Evid C §§1010-1027);

- Clergyman-penitent privilege (see Evid C §§1030–1034);

- Sexual assault victim-counselor privilege (see Evid C §§1035–1036.2); and

- Domestic violence victim-counselor privilege (see Evid C §§1037–1037.7).

Privileges apply, even when the information sought is relevant, unless waived or subject to a statutory exception. *Koshman v Superior Court* (1980) 111 CA3d 294, 297, 168 CR 558. Perhaps the most significant statutory exception for marital actions is that the physician-patient and psychotherapist-patient privileges do not apply when the patient tenders the issue of his or her physical or psychological condition (Evid C §§996, 1016). It is unclear, however, under what particular circumstances such a tender might be found. See *Simek v Superior Court* (1981) 117 CA3d 169, 172 CR 564 (patient does not tender his or her condition as an issue, thereby making medical and psychiatric records discoverable, simply by asserting presumptive right of visitation); *Koshman v Superior Court, supra* (mother's medical records not discoverable when father tendered issue by seeking modification of custody order based on assertions of mother's hospitalization for treatment for narcotics overdose). Note, however, that a claim of privilege could not be raised to prevent a court from ordering a physical or mental examination under CCP §2032.310(a) (see §13.34) or from considering the resulting evaluation. *Simek v Superior Court* (1981) 117 CA3d 169, 177, 172 CR 564. On waiver, see Evid C §912.

Under the statutory scheme for mediation in Evid C §§1115–1128, any communications between mediation participants that are materially related to the mediation are confidential, and evidence about the communications is inadmissible unless there is an express waiver. *Eisendrath v Superior Court* (2003) 109 CA4th 351, 134 CR2d 716 (motion to correct spousal support agreement could not rest on confidential mediation communications unless both parties to communications executed express waivers). Even communications that occur outside the mediator's presence are confidential if they are made before the end of mediation and are materially related to the mediation's purpose. 109 CA4th at 364.

It should be noted that the husband-wife privileges normally applicable in other proceedings usually do not apply in marital actions.

These include (1) the privilege not to testify against a spouse; (2) the privilege, when a spouse is a party, not to be called as a witness by an adverse party; and (3) the privilege for confidential marital communications. See Evid C §§972(a), (g), 984(a). The *"Pitchess* motion" procedure that protects the privacy of peace officer personnel records need not be followed by spouse in a dissolution action who seeks the officer spouse's payroll records. *City of Los Angeles v Superior Court (Williamson)* (2003) 111 CA4th 883, 896, 3 CR3d 915 (*Pitchess* procedure in Evid C §§1043, 1045 and Pen C §832.5 not "an absolute evidentiary privilege").

An attorney's work product is not discoverable unless the court determines that denial of discovery will unfairly prejudice the party seeking discovery in preparing that party's case or will result in an injustice. CCP §2018.030(b). Any writing that reflects an attorney's impressions, conclusions, opinions, or legal research or theories is not discoverable under any circumstances. CCP §2018.030(c).

For a complete discussion of privileges, work product, and other sources of protection for confidential information, see California Civil Discovery Practice, chap 3 (3d ed Cal CEB 1998).

§13.42   c. Time Limits for Completion of Discovery

Unless the parties stipulate otherwise or the court, on a party's motion, extends the time in which to complete discovery, or reopens discovery after a new trial date is set, discovery must generally be completed on or before the 30th day before the initial trial date. CCP §2024.020(a). Discovery is considered complete on the day a response is due or a deposition begins. CCP §2024.010. Any discovery motion must be heard on or before the 15th day before the initial trial date. CCP §2024.020(a). A party may complete discovery proceedings pertaining to a witness identified under CCP §§2034.010–2034.730 (demand for exchange of expert trial witness information; see §§13.35–13.36) on or before the 15th day, and have motions concerning that discovery heard on or before the 10th day, before the initial trial date. CCP §2024.030.

§13.43   d. Compelling Discovery; Sanctions

In each statute governing a discovery method, provision is made for compelling that discovery if the responding party fails to respond in a timely fashion or responds only partially, evasively, or with meritless objections.

Code of Civil Procedure §2023.010(a)–(i) provides a nonexclusive list of discovery misuses for which sanctions may be imposed. The five types of sanctions available—monetary, issue, evidence, terminating, and contempt—are defined in CCP §2023.030(a)–(e). The sanctions available for a particular misuse of the discovery process are specified in the section governing the particular discovery method. See CCP §2023.030.

For a complete discussion of sanctions, see California Civil Discovery Practice §§2.93–2.114 (3d ed Cal CEB 1998).

§13.44   III. DECLARATIONS OF DISCLOSURE

Under Fam C §§2100–2113, each party to a marital action must serve on the other party a preliminary declaration of disclosure and a final declaration of disclosure, unless service of the final declaration is waived, and must file a proof of service of each with the court. Fam C §2103. On waivers of the final declaration, see §13.46. Each party has a continuing duty to update and augment the disclosures to the extent that there have been any material changes. Fam C §2100(c). The provisions apply to any proceeding commenced on or after January 1, 1993. Fam C §2113.

Note that the commission of perjury on a declaration of disclosure may be grounds for setting aside the judgment, partially or completely, under Fam C §§2120–2129. Fam C §§2104(a), 2105(a). Counsel should take preparation of the declarations seriously, not only for the same reasons that any papers provided to another party should be addressed with care, but also to discourage motions to set aside.

Counsel should begin preparing the preliminary declaration of disclosure at the beginning of the case, when preparing the petition or response, to avoid potential problems later on, *e.g.,* having default judgment papers rejected for failure to serve a declaration of disclosure.

§13.45   A. Preliminary Declaration of Disclosure

Each party must serve a preliminary declaration of disclosure on the other party after or concurrently with service of the petition. The declaration must be executed under penalty of perjury on Judicial Council Form FL-140 (see §13.49). The commission of perjury on the preliminary declaration of disclosure may be grounds for setting aside the judgment, partially or completely, under Fam C §§2120–2129 (see §§18.47–18.54), in addition to remedies otherwise available under existing law for commission of perjury. Fam C §2104(a). The preliminary declaration is not filed with the court, except on court order, but a proof of service of the declaration must be filed with the court. Fam C §2104(b).

The preliminary declaration of disclosure must identify all assets in which the declarant has or may have an interest, and all liabilities for which the declarant is or may be liable, regardless of the characterization of the asset or liability as community, quasi-community, or separate. The identity of the assets and liabilities must be set forth with sufficient particularity that a person of reasonable and ordinary intelligence can ascertain the items. Fam C §2104(c)(1). The declarant must set forth his or her percentage of ownership in each asset and percentage of obligation for each liability when the asset or liability is not solely that of one or both of the parties to the action. The declarant may set forth his or her characterization of each asset or liability. Fam C §2104(c)(2). Along with the preliminary declaration of disclosure, each party must provide the other with a completed Income and Expense Declaration unless one has already been provided and is current and valid. Fam C §2104(e). A simplified financial statement (see form and discussion in §§11.30–11.31) may be used in place of the Income and Expense Declaration if the requirements for use set forth in the form instructions are met. See Fam C §2101(e). A party may amend his or her preliminary declaration of disclosure without leave of court. Proof of service of any amendment must be filed with the court. Fam C §2104(d).

A preliminary declaration of disclosure by the petitioner is required even in the case of a default judgment, *i.e.,* a judgment taken after entry of the respondent's default and not based on an agreement of the parties. Fam C §§2101(b), 2110. One court has held that although the exchange of preliminary declarations is mandatory and the trial court errs by entering judgment without them, such error is harmless unless the party seeking to set aside the judgment on this basis shows prejudice. *Marriage of McLaughlin* (2000) 82 CA4th 327, 336, 98 CR2d 136. Apparently in response to *McLaughlin*, in 2001 the legislature enacted Fam C §2107(d), which provides that if a court enters a judgment when the parties have failed to comply with all disclosure requirements, the judgment must be set aside; failure to comply is *not* harmless error. See Stats 2001, ch 703. Since the addition of Fam C §2107(d), at least one appellate court has held that to the extent that this provision stands for the proposition that a judgment must be set aside or a new trial granted solely because of a failure to comply with disclosure requirements, it is inconsistent with article VI, §13, of the California Constitution. *Marriage of Steiner* (2004) 117 CA4th 519, 11 CR3d 671 (failure to exchange final declaration of disclosure does not entitle party to new trial, absent showing of miscarriage of justice under Cal Const art VI, §13).

§13.45A   B. Continuing Duty of Disclosure

Family Code §2102 imposes on the parties an ongoing duty of disclosure about activities that affect assets and liabilities of the other party, including investment opportunities, business opportunities, business activity, or other income-producing opportunity of either spouse. The disclosure must be made in writing, giving ample time to the other spouse to make an informed decision regarding his or her participation or to allow sufficient time for the court to resolve any dispute regarding the right of participation. This duty continues from date of separation to the date of distribution of the asset (Fam C §2102(a)) and includes the duty to make an immediate, full, and accurate update or augmentation to the extent there have been any material changes. Fam C §2102(a)(1). See also Fam C §2100 (each party has continuing duty to update and augment disclosures).

In 2001, the legislature provided that each party is subject to the fiduciary duty of Fam C §721: (1) as to all activities affecting the assets or liabilities of the other party from the date that a binding resolution about their disposition is reached until they are actually distributed (Fam C §2102(b)); and (2) as to all issues relating to child or spousal support and attorney fees, from the date of separation until the date of a binding resolution of all issues relating to support and fees. Fam C §2102(c). The 2001 legislation applies to any judgment that becomes final on or after January 1, 2002. Stats 2001, ch 703, §8.

A spouse who fails to disclose information when he or she is in a superior position to obtain information and records from which an asset can be valued, breaches the continuing duty to update and augment information. *Marriage of Brewer & Federici* (2001) 93 CA4th 1334, 1341, 113 CR2d 849 (wife's statement that value of pension plan was "unknown" constituted breach of fiduciary duty leading to mistake of fact justifying set-aside of judgment).

§13.46 C. Final Declaration of Disclosure

Before or when the parties enter into a marital settlement agreement addressing property or support issues or, if the case goes to trial, at least 45 days before the first assigned trial date, each party, or his or her attorney, must serve on the other party a final declaration of disclosure and current income and expense declaration. See Fam C §§2105–2106. The declaration must be executed under penalty of perjury on Judicial Council Form FL-140 (see §13.49). The commission of perjury on the final declaration of disclosure may be grounds for setting aside the judgment, partially or completely, under Fam C §§2120–2129 (see §§18.47–18.54), in addition to other remedies available under existing law for commission of perjury. Fam C §2105(a). The final declaration of disclosure must include all material facts and information on the following:

- The characterization of all assets and liabilities (Fam C §2105(b)(1));

- The valuation of all assets that are contended to be community property, whether partially or entirely (Fam C §2105(b)(2));

- The amounts of all obligations that are contended to be community obligations, whether partially or entirely (Fam C §2105(b)(3)); and

- The earnings, accumulations, and expenses of each party that have been set forth in the Income and Expense Declaration (Fam C §2105(b)(4)).

Each party or his or her attorney must file with the court a declaration regarding service of the final Declaration of Disclosure and Income and Expense Declaration or that service has been waived. Fam C §2106. For form of declaration, see §13.50.

Note that a simplified financial statement (see form and discussion in §§11.30–11.31) may be used in place of the Income and Expense Declaration if the requirements for use set forth in the form instructions are met. See Fam C §2101(e).

The petitioner may waive the final declaration of disclosure requirements in the case of a default judgment, *i.e.,* a judgment taken after entry of the respondent's default and not based on an agreement of the parties. Fam C §§2101(b), 2110. See Item 6.b. on Declaration for Default or Uncontested Dissolution or Legal Separation (see form in §14.24).

The parties may stipulate to a mutual waiver of the final declaration of disclosure by execution of a waiver under penalty of perjury entered into in open court or by separate stipulation. Fam C §2105(d), as amended by Stats 2001, ch 703, §4. Note that the waiver can no longer be part of the marital settlement agreement, and thus that a change may be expected to be made to Item 6.c. on the Declaration for Default or Uncontested Dissolution or Legal Separation (see form in §14.24). The 2001 legislation applies to any judgment that becomes final on or after January 1, 2002. Stats 2001, ch 703, §8.

The waiver must include all of the following representations:

(1) Both parties have complied with Fam C §2104 (preliminary declarations of disclosure; see §13.45) and the preliminary declarations have been completed and exchanged (Fam C §2105(d)(1));

(2) Both parties have completed and exchanged a current income and expense declaration that includes all material facts and circumstances about that party's earnings, accumulations, and expenses (Fam C §2105(d)(2));

(3) Both parties have fully complied with Fam C §2102 (fiduciary relationship) and have fully augmented the preliminary declarations of disclosure, including disclosure of all material facts and information about the characterization of all assets and liabilities, the valuation of all assets that are contended to be community property or in which it is contended the community has an interest, and the amounts of all obligations that are contended to be community obligations or for which it is contended the community has liability (Fam C §2105(d)(3));

(4) The waiver is knowingly, intelligently, and voluntarily entered into by each of the parties (Fam C §2105(d)(4)); and

(5) Each party understands that the waiver does not limit the parties' legal disclosure obligations, but rather is a statement under penalty of perjury that those obligations have been fulfilled. Each party further understands that noncompliance with those obligations will result in the court setting aside the judgment. Fam C §2105(d)(5).

Under Fam C §2105(d)(5), as amended by Stats 2001, ch 703, noncompliance with the legal disclosure obligations "will result in the court setting aside the judgment." For cases decided before the 2001 changes to Fam C §2105, see *Marriage of McLaughlin* (2000) 82 CA4th 327, 98 CR2d 136 (failure to comply with disclosure requirements not fatal unless complaining party can demonstrate miscarriage of justice); *Marriage of Jones* (1998) 60 CA4th 685, 694, 70 CR2d 542 (husband's noncompliance with Fam C §2105 did not require vacation of judgment because wife could not show that she was prejudiced by outcome); *Marriage of Fell* (1997) 55 CA4th 1058, 64 CR2d 522 (parties executed and filed purported "waiver of declarations of disclosure requirement," but neither obtained court order nor made required representations; setting aside of dissolution judgment and marital settlement agreement affirmed). Since the addition of Fam C §2107(d), the Fourth Circuit has held that to the extent that §2107(d) stands for the proposition that a judgment must be set aside or a new trial granted *solely* because of a failure to file a final declaration of disclosure, it is inconsistent with the California Constitution. Noting that *McLaughlin* and *Jones* did not rely exclusively on statutory construction, *Marriage of Steiner* (2004) 117 CA4th 519, 11 CR3d 671, held that the failure of the parties to exchange final declarations of disclosure did not require a new trial, absent a showing of miscarriage of justice pursuant to Cal Const art VI, §13.

C. Effects of Noncompliance

§13.47   1. Entry and Set Aside of Judgment

Except for mutual waiver of the final declaration of disclosure under Fam C §2105(d) or the petitioner's waiver of the final declaration in the case of a default judgment (see §13.46), and absent good cause, no judgment may be entered with respect to the parties' property rights without each party, or each party's attorney, having executed and served the final declaration of disclosure and current income and expense declaration (or, if applicable, simplified financial statement; see Fam C §2101(e)). Fam C §2106. Judgment may not be entered without the service of preliminary declarations (see Fam C §2104) and there appears to be no exception for good cause or waiver. Each party or his or her attorney must file with the court a declaration regarding service of those documents (for form of declaration, see §13.50) or a declaration stating that service has been waived under Fam C §2105(d) or §2110. Fam C §2106. Note that Fam C §2106 applies even to a judgment confirming an arbitration award settling marital property rights. *Elden v Superior Court* (1997) 53 CA4th 1497, 1509, 62 CR2d 322.

A court may set aside a judgment in full for failure to comply with Fam C §2105 (final declaration of disclosure) or limit such a set aside to those portions of the judgment materially affected by the nondisclosure. Fam C §2105(c). Under Fam C §2105(d)(5) (as amended by Stats 2001, ch 703, §4), noncompliance with the disclosure obligations will result in the court setting aside the judgment. The court must set aside a judgment entered when the parties have failed to comply with all disclosure requirements; the failure to comply with the disclosure requirements is not harmless error. Fam C §2107(d), as amended by Stats 2001, ch 703, §6. The 2001 legislation applies to judgments that become final on or after January 1, 2002. See Stats 2001, ch 703, §8.

NOTE➤ Since the addition of Fam C §2107(d), at least one appellate court has held that to the extent that this provision stands for the proposition that a judgment must be set aside or a new trial granted solely because of a failure to comply with disclosure requirements, it is inconsistent with article VI, §13, of the California Constitution. *Marriage of Steiner* (2004) 117 CA4th 519, 11 CR3d 671 (failure to exchange final declaration of disclosure does not entitle party to new trial, absent showing of miscarriage of justice under Cal Const art VI, §13).

§13.48   2. Complying Party's Remedies

If a party fails to serve on the other party either a preliminary or final declaration of disclosure under Fam C §§2104–2105, or fails to provide the information in such a declaration with sufficient particularity, and if the other party has served the particular declaration on the noncomplying party, the complying party may, within a reasonable time, request preparation of the particular declaration or further particularity. Fam C §2107(a). If the other party fails to comply, the complying party may file a motion to compel a further response, a motion for an order preventing the noncomplying party from presenting evidence on issues that should have been covered in the declaration of disclosure, or both. Fam C §2107(b).

If one party complies with Fam C §§2100–2113 and the other party fails to do so, the court must, in addition to any other remedy provided by law, impose sanctions on the noncomplying party in an amount sufficient to deter repetition of the conduct, including reasonable attorney fees, costs incurred, or both, unless the court finds that the noncomplying party acted with substantial justification or that other circumstances make the imposition of the sanction unjust. Fam C §2107(c). The sanctions provision was added by Stats 2001, ch 703.

§13.49 D. Form: Declaration of Disclosure (Judicial Council Form FL-140)

FL-140

ATTORNEY OR PARTY WITHOUT ATTORNEY *(Name and Address):*	TELEPHONE NO.:

ATTORNEY FOR *(Name):*

SUPERIOR COURT OF CALIFORNIA, COUNTY OF
STREET ADDRESS:
MAILING ADDRESS:
CITY AND ZIP CODE:
BRANCH NAME:

PETITIONER:

RESPONDENT:

DECLARATION OF DISCLOSURE	CASE NUMBER:
☐ Petitioner's ☐ Preliminary	
☐ Respondent's ☐ Final	

DO NOT FILE WITH THE COURT

Both the preliminary and the final declaration of disclosure must be served on the other party with certain exceptions. Neither disclosure is filed with the court. A declaration stating service was made of the final declaration of disclosure must be filed with the court (see form FL-141).

A preliminary declaration of disclosure but not a final declaration of disclosure is required in the case of a summary dissolution (see Family Code section 2109) or in a default judgment (see Family Code section 2110) provided the default is not a stipulated judgment or a judgment based upon a marriage settlement agreement.

A declaration of disclosure is required in a nullity or legal separation action as well as in a dissolution action.

Attached are the following:

1. ☐ A completed *Schedule of Assets and Debts* (form FL-142).

2. ☐ A completed *Income and Expense Declaration* (form FL-150 (as applicable)).

3. ☐ A statement of all material facts and information regarding valuation of all assets that are community property or in which the community has an interest *(not a form)*.

4. ☐ A statement of all material facts and information regarding obligations for which the community is liable *(not a form)*.

5. ☐ An accurate and complete written disclosure of any investment opportunity, business opportunity, or other income-producing opportunity presented since the date of separation that results from any investment, significant business, or other income-producing opportunity from the date of marriage to the date of separation *(not a form)*.

I declare under penalty of perjury under the laws of the State of California that the foregoing is true and correct.

Date:

_____   ▶ _____
(TYPE OR PRINT NAME)   (SIGNATURE)

Page 1 of 1

Form Adopted for Mandatory Use Judicial Council of California FL-140 [Rev. January 1, 2003]	**DECLARATION OF DISCLOSURE** (Family Law)	Family Code, §§ 2102, 2104, 2105, 2106, 2112 www.courtinfo.ca.gov

Copies: Preliminary Declaration: Original (retain, with original proof of service, to be filed only on court order); copy for service on other attorney or party; office copies. Final Declaration: Original (retain); copy for service on other attorney or party; office copies.

Comment: With respect to the preliminary declaration, it appears that only Items 1 and 2 on the form are applicable. Those boxes may be checked and the corresponding forms completed and attached. For the form Schedule of Assets and Debts see §13.28. On the forms of Income and Expense Declaration see §§11.25 (discussion), 11.26–11.29 (forms). Note that a simplified financial statement (see form and discussion in §§11.30–11.31) may be used in place of the Income and Expense Declaration if the requirements for use set forth in the form instructions are met. See Fam C §2101(e). When an asset or liability is not solely that of one or both of the parties, the declaration of disclosure must set forth the declarant's percentage of ownership or obligation. Fam C §2104(c)(2). This might be done in an attachment to the Schedule of Assets and Debts.

With respect to the final declaration, it appears that Items 1–4 on the form are applicable. In addition, the declaration must include all material facts and information regarding the characterization of all assets and liabilities (Fam C §2105(b)(1)) and regarding the earnings, accumulations, and expenses that have been set forth in the Income and Expense Declaration (or simplified financial statement) (Fam C §2105(b)(4); see Fam C §2101(e)). These might be set forth in separate statements attached to the Declaration of Disclosure form.

Note that, at least with respect to the preliminary declaration, an Income and Expense Declaration (or, if applicable, simplified financial statement) need not be provided with the Declaration of Disclosure when one has previously been provided and remains current. Fam C §2104(e).

At Item 5, the form calls for disclosure of any investment opportunity presented since the date of separation. This requirement is found in Fam C §2102(a)(2). That subsection does not specify, however, that such disclosures are to be made as part of the declarations of disclosure, and they could presumably be made either separately or as part of a Declaration of Disclosure. Note that a disclosure of an investment opportunity must be made in sufficient time for the other spouse to make an informed decision on whether to participate and for the court to resolve any dispute about the other spouse's right to participate in the opportunity. Fam C §2102(a)(2). In some instances, this may require making the disclosure of investment opportunity separately from a declaration of disclosure.

§13.50   E. Form: Declaration Regarding Service of Declaration of Disclosure and Income and Expense Declaration (Judicial Council Form FL-141)

FL-141

ATTORNEY OR PARTY WITHOUT ATTORNEY *(Name, state bar number, and address):*	FOR COURT USE ONLY

TELEPHONE NO.:   FAX NO.:

ATTORNEY FOR *(Name):*

SUPERIOR COURT OF CALIFORNIA, COUNTY OF
STREET ADDRESS:
MAILING ADDRESS:
CITY AND ZIP CODE:
BRANCH NAME:

PETITIONER:

RESPONDENT:

DECLARATION REGARDING SERVICE OF DECLARATION OF DISCLOSURE AND INCOME AND EXPENSE DECLARATION ☐ Petitioner's ☐ Preliminary ☐ Respondent's ☐ Final	CASE NUMBER:

1. I am the ☐ Attorney for ☐ Petitioner ☐ Respondent in this matter.

2. ☐ Petitioner's ☐ Respondent's *Preliminary Declaration of Disclosure* and *Income and Expense Declaration* was served on:
   ☐ Attorney for ☐ Petitioner ☐ Respondent by: ☐ personal service ☐ mail ☐ other *(specify):*

   on *(date):*

3. ☐ Petitioner's ☐ Respondent's *Final Declaration of Disclosure* and *Income and Expense Declaration* was served on:
   ☐ Attorney for ☐ Petitioner ☐ Respondent by: ☐ personal service ☐ mail ☐ other *(specify):*

   on *(date):*

4. ☐ Service of the *Final Declaration of Disclosure* has been waived under Family Code section 2105, subdivision (d).

I declare under penalty of perjury under the laws of the State of California that the foregoing is true and correct.

Date:

_____   ▶ _____
(TYPE OR PRINT NAME)   (SIGNATURE)

> **Note:**
> **File this document with the court.**
> **Do not file a copy of either the *Preliminary* or *Final Declaration of Disclosure* with this document.**

Form Adopted for Mandatory Use
Judicial Council of California
FL-141 [Rev. January 1, 2003]

DECLARATION REGARDING SERVICE OF DECLARATION OF DISCLOSURE
(Family Law)

Page 1 of 1
Family Code, §§ 2104, 2106, 2112
www.courtinfo.ca.gov

Copies: Original (file with court clerk); office copies.

14

Uncontested Proceedings

§14.1 I. SCOPE OF CHAPTER

A marital action may be resolved by an uncontested proceeding when (1) the respondent fails to file a response or other appropriate document in the time allowed and a default is entered, with or without a written agreement between the parties resolving all the issues in the case; or (2) the respondent appears in the action and the parties reach an agreement. This chapter covers the steps in obtaining an uncontested judgment once the respondent has failed to appear or an agreement has been reached, with emphasis on entry of the respondent's default or joint filing of an Appearance, Stipulations, and Waivers; presenting proof to the court, whether by means of a declaration or at an uncontested hearing; and preparing the judgment itself. The chapter also discusses bifurcation of the issue of marital status.

For a comprehensive treatment of the negotiation and drafting of agreements in marital actions, see California Marital Settlement and

Other Family Law Agreements, chaps 1 ("Developing the Case and Negotiating the Agreement"), 2 ("Mediation"), 3 ("The Agreement in Its Legal Context"), 4 ("Drafting and Implementing the Agreement"), 5–16 (sample marital settlement agreement provisions and commentary), 20 ("QDROs and Other Retirement Benefits Orders"), Apps A-C (complete sample agreements) (3d ed Cal CEB 2005).

II. SPECIAL CONSIDERATIONS FOR COUNSEL IN UNCONTESTED PROCEEDINGS

§14.2 A. Representing Both Parties

Many courts have indicated that it is far preferable for each party in marital actions to be represented by independent counsel. See, e.g., *Gregory v Gregory* (1949) 92 CA2d 343, 349, 206 P2d 1122. An agreement of the parties that is reached without each party's being independently represented is vulnerable to attack for misrepresentation, fraud, and overreaching. *Marriage of Brennan* (1981) 124 CA3d 598, 604, 177 CR 520; *Klemm v Superior Court* (1977) 75 CA3d 893, 901, 142 CR 509.

The Rules of Professional Conduct do not preclude an attorney from representing both parties in a marital action. The rules do provide that an attorney may not represent more than one client in a matter in which their interests potentially or actually conflict without the informed written consent of each. Cal Rules of Prof Cond 3–310(C)(1)–(2). If the conflict of interests is merely potential, and if the parties are not in dispute on any point in litigation, an attorney may represent both parties as long as there is full disclosure to, and informed consent of, both clients. 75 CA3d at 899.

When dual representation of both clients is permitted, the parties' consent must be in writing after full disclosure by the attorney of all facts and circumstances regarding the subject matter of the litigation, including areas of potential conflict and the desirability of seeking independent legal advice. 75 CA3d at 901. An attorney who fails to make the required disclosure to both clients may be civilly liable to a client who thereby suffers a loss. 75 CA3d at 901.

§14.3 B. Dealing With Unrepresented Party

When an attorney for one of the parties must deal directly with a spouse who does not retain his or her own counsel, the attorney has a strict duty to deal with the unrepresented party fairly and objectively. *Gregory v Gregory* (1949) 92 CA2d 343, 349, 206 P2d 1122. Communication with an unrepresented party should include advising that party, preferably in writing, that the interests of the two spouses are adverse, that the attorney represents the interests of his or her client alone, and that the other party is strongly encouraged to seek independent legal advice.

This advice should be repeated before the unrepresented party's signing of a proposed marital settlement agreement or stipulated judgment. If the unrepresented spouse continues to refuse to obtain legal advice before signing the agreement, he or she should be asked to sign an acknowledgment, set forth as a provision of the agreement, stating that the unrepresented party was strongly and repeatedly advised to obtain independent counsel and that the advice was voluntarily and knowingly rejected. For sample language of acknowledgment, see California Marital Settlement and Other Family Law Agreements §16.24 (3d ed Cal CEB 2005). If the unrepresented spouse agrees to attend the uncontested hearing, he or she should also be questioned on the same matters for the court record. It is good practice for the attorney to advise his or her own client, and to memorialize the advice in a *separate* writing, that any agreement reached with the unrepresented spouse may be subject to collateral attack in the future.

§14.4   C. Declarations of Disclosure

Family Code §§2100–2113 generally require preliminary and final declarations of disclosure to be provided by each party to the other in proceedings commenced on or after January 1, 1993. Fam C §§2103–2105, 2113. In the case of a judgment taken after entry of the respondent's default and not based on an agreement of the parties, the petitioner must file a preliminary declaration of disclosure, but may waive the requirement of a final declaration of disclosure. Fam C §§2101(b), 2110. See Item 6.b. on Declaration for Default or Uncontested Dissolution or Legal Separation (see form in §14.24).

The parties may stipulate to a mutual waiver of the final declaration of disclosure by executing a waiver under penalty of perjury entered into in open court or by separate stipulation. Fam C §2105(d). See Item 6.c. on Declaration for Default or Uncontested Dissolution or

Legal Separation (see form in §14.24). For the representations the waiver must include, see §13.46.

Whether execution of a mutual waiver of the final declaration of disclosure will affect either party's right to have the judgment set aside, or the fiduciary obligations of each party to the other, will be decided by a court based on the law and the facts of each particular case. The authority to execute a mutual waiver of the final declaration is not intended, in and of itself, to affect the law regarding the fiduciary obligations owed by the parties, their rights with respect to setting aside a judgment, or any other rights or responsibilities of the parties as provided by law. Fam C §2105(d)(5).

On declarations of disclosure generally, see §§13.44–13.50.

§14.5   III.   CIRCUMSTANCES GIVING RISE TO UNCONTESTED PROCEEDINGS

Only a small percentage of the marital actions filed each year in California are resolved by contested trial, according to unofficial statistics of the Judicial Council. An action for dissolution, legal separation, or nullity may proceed to judgment without a contested trial when (1) the respondent's default has been entered (see §§14.6–14.16) or (2) the respondent has appeared in the action and the parties have reached an agreement resolving all the issues in their case (see §§14.17–14.20).

The respondent's default may be entered after he or she fails to file a response, or any other document specified in Cal Rules of Ct 5.122, in the time permitted. See §§14.6–14.8. Often, the respondent will allow a default to be entered by not participating in the proceeding in any way. In other cases, the petitioner and the respondent will reach an agreement settling all the issues in the action without the respondent's having made an appearance, and the respondent will allow a default to be entered with the understanding that the petitioner will present the agreement to the court and request a judgment in accordance with the terms of the agreement.

If the parties enter into an agreement settling all the issues in their case after the respondent has filed a response or otherwise appeared, the action may proceed as an uncontested matter on the stipulation of both parties. See §§14.17–14.20. As long as the agreement is fair and well drafted, uncontested proceedings are generally preferable to contested trials for many reasons, including the following:

- The financial and emotional costs of a contested trial can be substantial;

- Settlement is more predictable than a judge's decision and allows the parties to agree to options that are unavailable to the court, *e.g.,* an unequal division of community property, or the payment of child support through college;

- A court appearance may be completely avoided in most instances by filing a Declaration for Default or Uncontested Dissolution (see §§14.22–14.24);

- Uncontested proceedings can generally be set on the court calendar much sooner than contested trials; and

- Even when a hearing is required, usually only one party need attend, which saves attorney time and client expense.

On considerations in choosing whether to proceed by default or stipulation when agreement is reached before the respondent appears, see §14.17.

A. Default

§14.6　1. When Available

The petitioner may apply for entry of the respondent's default if, within the time prescribed by law (normally 30 days after service of the summons and petition; see §14.6), the respondent does not do any of the following (Cal Rules of Ct 5.122(a)(1)):

- Make an appearance as set forth in Cal Rules of Ct 5.120 by

  - filing a response or answer, except as provided in CCP §418.10 (see form in §10.52);

  - filing a notice of motion to strike under CCP §435;

  - filing a notice of motion for change of venue under CCP §395 (see §10.63); or

  - filing a written notice of his or her appearance; or

- File a notice of motion to quash service of summons (see §10.61) (Cal Rules of Ct 5.122(a)(2)); or

- File a petition for writ of mandate after denial of a motion to quash service (see CCP §418.10(c); Cal Rules of Ct 5.122(a)(3)).

§14.7   2. Extension of Time to Respond; Advantages

After the summons and petition have been served, one of the parties may suggest that the petitioner extend the time in which the respondent may file a response. The purpose of the extension is often to allow the parties to seek a settlement of the issues before (1) the respondent incurs the expense of filing a response and (2) the proceeding becomes adversarial by virtue of a response being filed.

One advantage to agreeing to an extension under such circumstances is that a first step toward negotiation is taken that may lead to others. If the parties can also agree on temporary orders, if necessary, to be in effect during the negotiation period, an important second step will also have been achieved. On temporary orders generally, see chap 11.

The granting of the extension and its terms should be in writing, either in letter or stipulation form. The extension can last for an indefinite period, usually terminable on a specified written notice (*e.g.,* 10 or 15 days) to the respondent. If the petitioner has the respondent's default entered without giving the requisite notice, the respondent should be able to set aside the default under CCP §473 (see §§18.25–18.33). Alternatively, the extension can be for a fixed period of time, by the end of which the response must be filed.

§14.8   3. When to Request Entry of Default

The petitioner may file a Request to Enter Default (see form in §14.14) at any time after 30 days have elapsed from the date that the summons and petition were served on the respondent, as long as the respondent has not filed a response or any other document specified in Cal Rules of Ct 5.122 (see §14.6) and as long as any extensions of time to respond (see §14.7) have expired. Fam C §2020; Cal Rules of Ct 5.122. Note that the respondent's default may not be entered after a response has been filed, even when the response was filed after expiration of the 30-day period. If service was made by the respondent's executing and returning a Notice and Acknowledgment of Receipt (see form in §10.34), entry of default may not be requested until the 31st day after the form was executed, even though the respondent may have received the form much earlier. See CCP §415.30(c).

Before requesting entry of default, counsel for the petitioner might consider sending a warning letter to the respondent, and to any attorney known to represent the respondent, granting an additional period in which to respond to the action, in an effort to avoid a later motion to set aside the default. Such a letter must be carefully drafted, setting forth the expiration date of the extended time period and the fact that entry of default will be requested thereafter, so that the respondent cannot later claim to have misunderstood the petitioner's intent.

§14.9   4. Scope of Relief on Default

Before requesting entry of the respondent's default, counsel should review the petition carefully to make sure that it requests all the relief that the petitioner may require. Code of Civil Procedure §580 provides that the "relief granted to the plaintiff, if there is no answer, cannot exceed that demanded in the complaint."

In *Marriage of Lippel* (1990) 51 C3d 1160, 276 CR 290, the California Supreme Court disapproved a line of cases that had carved out an exception to CCP §580 and had allowed an award of child or spousal support in default marital judgments even though such relief had not been requested in the petition. See, *e.g., Cohen v Cohen* (1906) 150 C 99, 102, 88 P 267. *Lippel* held that a court, when entering a default judgment in a marital action, may not award child support if it was not requested in the petition. 51 C3d at 1171. The court concluded that a default judgment granting relief not requested in the petition is void for lack of notice to the respondent and therefore subject to collateral attack. 51 C3d at 1163. There is now a preprinted notice on the Petition, however, advising the petitioner concerning child support, as discussed in chap 10.

In *Marriage of Andresen* (1994) 28 CA4th 873, 34 CR2d 147, also a default proceeding, the trial court divided the community assets and liabilities identified in the petition between the parties and ordered the respondent to make an equalizing payment to the petitioner. 28 CA4th at 877. On appeal, the respondent contended that the orders were void because the petition did not allege values for the property items, identify all community assets ultimately awarded to the petitioner, or request an equalizing payment. 28 CA4th at 877. The court of appeal held that the petition was sufficient to support the judgment because the petitioner had properly completed the Judicial Council petition form, checking the box in Item 7 requesting that property rights be determined, and listing the assets and obligations in an attached Judicial Council property declaration form. As the court noted, the property declaration form expressly provides that, when it is attached to a petition or response, values and proposals for division need not be completed. 28 CA4th at 879. However, a provision in an earlier judgment that required the respondent to execute a $50,000 note payable to the petitioner as reimbursement for separate money she had contributed to the marriage was void because it was not requested in the petition.

In *Marriage of Wells* (1988) 206 CA3d 1434, 254 CR 185, however, the trial court's reservation of jurisdiction over spousal support as to both parties in a default judgment was affirmed, even though spousal support was not requested in the petition. The facts that the respondent had received notice of and had attended the default hearing, and that both parties would have the opportunity to be heard before any support was awarded, were important to the court's finding that no due process violation of CCP §580 had occurred. 206 CA3d at 1439. Although *Lippel* was decided later, it did not specifically disapprove *Wells*, leaving the effect of *Wells* unclear.

Nonetheless, *Lippel* and *Andresen* make it clear that counsel should review the petition before requesting entry of default and, if the petition is found lacking in any respect, should consider preparing, filing, and serving an amended petition (see §10.68). Note that the court will not allow the petition to be amended at any time after the default has been entered.

5. Submitting Forms

a. Request to Enter Default

§14.10 (1) Attachments

The Judicial Council Form FL-165 (Request to Enter Default) requires at Item 2 that an Income and Expense Declaration (see forms in §§11.26–11.29) or a Financial Statement (Simplified) (see form in §11.31), and a Property Declaration (see forms in §§10.20–10.21) be attached to the request unless: (1) These documents were previously filed and there have been no changes; (2) there is a written agreement settling all issues subject to disposition in the action; (3) there are no issues of child, partner, or spousal support or attorney fees and costs; (4) the petition does not request money, property, costs, or attorney fees; (5) there are no issues of division of community property; or (6) the action is one to establish a parental relationship (*i.e.*, an action under the Uniform Parentage Act (Fam C §§7600-7730)), rather than a marital action. Local rules should be consulted, however, on whether and when these documents must be submitted with the Request to Enter Default.

§14.11 (2) Declaration of Mailing

No mailing is required when the respondent was served by publication (see §§10.35-10.38) and his or her address remains unknown. In this event, Item 3.a of the request should be checked. In all other cases, Item 3.b should be checked and complied with, and the address that appeared on the envelope should be provided on the form. The court clerk will then mail a copy of the Request to Enter Default to the defaulting spouse. Note that a judgment of dissolution or legal separation, including relief requested in the petition, may not be denied solely because the Request to Enter Default was returned unopened to the court, but that the court clerk must maintain any such document returned by the post office as part of the court file. Fam C §2335.5

§14.12 (3) Memorandum of Costs

The petitioner must specify at Item 4 of the Request to Enter Default whether recovery of costs incurred in the action is sought against the respondent or is waived. If recovery of costs is requested, the petitioner must itemize the amounts spent for filing fees, service of process, and other recoverable expenses, *e.g.*, court transcript costs and reporter's deposition fees. On what costs are recoverable in a marital action, see §9.2. If additional costs are incurred after the Request to Enter Default has been filed, a supplemental memorandum of costs may be filed at a later date or presented at the default hearing.

§14.13 (4) Declaration of Nonmilitary Status

The Request to Enter Default contains a declaration at Item 5 that the respondent is not in the military service and is not entitled to the benefits of the Servicemembers Civil Relief Act (50 USC App §§501–596), which protects persons on active or training duty in any branch of the military service from default judgments (see 50 USC App §§511, 521). Note that the Act does not protect the respondent against entry of a default, as distinguished from a default judgment. *Interinsurance Exch. v Collins* (1994) 30 CA4th 1445, 37 CR2d 126.

In most instances, the petitioner (as distinguished from counsel) will have sufficient personal knowledge of the respondent to knowingly execute the declaration of nonmilitary status. The petitioner's attorney should ascertain whether the petitioner can truthfully declare that the respondent is not in the military service. The penalty for filing a knowingly false declaration is imprisonment not to exceed one year, a fine not to exceed $1000, or both. 50 USC App §521(c).

If the petitioner cannot knowingly declare that the respondent is not in military service, inquiries may be sent to each of the armed forces to ascertain whether the respondent is on active or training duty. The current mailing address of each service branch follows:

ARMY
Commander
U.S. Army Enlisted Records
& Evaluation Center
  Attn: Locator
8899 East 56th Street
Fort Benjamin Harrison, IN
46249-5301
http://www.hrc.army.mil

NAVY
World Wide Locator
Bureau of Naval Personnel
PERS 312F
5720 Integrity Drive
Millington, TN 38055-3120
(901) 874-3388

AIR FORCE
World Wide Locator
HQ AFMPC/RMIQL
550 "C" Street West, Suite 50
Randolf AFB, TX 78150-4752
(210) 652-5775

MARINES
World Wide Locator
Commandant of the Marine
Corps
Headquarters, USMC
Code MMSB-10
Quantico, VA 22134-5030
(703) 640-3942/43

COAST GUARD
United States Coast Guard
Personnel Command Branch
2100 2d Street, S.W.
Washington, DC 20593-0001
  Attn: World Wide Locator
(202) 267-0581
E-mail: Locator@comdt.
uscg.mil

A request should be made for the respondent's military mailing address and I.D. number or, if the respondent is not serving in that branch, for an affidavit to that effect.

If the respondent qualifies for protection under the Servicemembers Civil Relief Act, a default judgment may not be entered unless the court first appoints an attorney to represent the service person in the marital proceeding. 50 USC App §521(b)(2). If a default judgment is taken against a respondent in the military service, the court shall reopen the judgment to allow the servicemember to defend the action if it appears that the servicemember was materially affected by reason of that service in making a defense to the action and had a meritorious or legal defense to the action or some part of it. 50 USC App

§521(g)(1). The servicemember must file an application to vacate or set aside the default judgment under this section not later than 90 days after the date of termination or release from military service. 50 USC App §521(g)(2). The protections of the Act may be waived by a service person, without representation by counsel, by executing an Appearance, Stipulations, and Waivers form (see form in §14.19) on which Item 3 has been checked. No fee is charged to a member of the armed forces to file this form. Govt C §26857.5.

§14.14 (5) Form: Request to Enter Default (Judicial Council Form FL-165)

FL-165

ATTORNEY OR PARTY WITHOUT ATTORNEY *(Name, State Bar number, and address)*:	FOR COURT USE ONLY

TELEPHONE NO.:   FAX NO. *(Optional)*:
E-MAIL ADDRESS *(Optional)*:
ATTORNEY FOR *(Name)*:

SUPERIOR COURT OF CALIFORNIA, COUNTY OF
STREET ADDRESS:
MAILING ADDRESS:
CITY AND ZIP CODE:
BRANCH NAME:

PETITIONER:

RESPONDENT:

REQUEST TO ENTER DEFAULT	CASE NUMBER:

1. **To the clerk:** Please enter the default of the respondent who has failed to respond to the petition.

2. A completed *Income and Expense Declaration* (form FL-150) or *Financial Statement (Simplified)* (form FL-155)
   ☐ is attached ☐ is not attached.
   A completed *Property Declaration* (form FL-160) ☐ is attached ☐ is not attached
   because *(check at least one of the following):*
   (a) ☐ there have been no changes since the previous filing.
   (b) ☐ the issues subject to disposition by the court in this proceeding are the subject of a written agreement.
   (c) ☐ there are no issues of child, spousal, or partner support or attorney fees and costs subject to determination by the court.
   (d) ☐ the petition does not request money, property, costs, or attorney fees. (Fam. Code, § 2330.5.)
   (e) ☐ there are no issues of division of community property.
   (f) ☐ this is an action to establish parental relationship.

Date:

_____ ▶ _____
(TYPE OR PRINT NAME)   (SIGNATURE OF [ATTORNEY FOR] PETITIONER)

3. **Declaration**
   a. ☐ No mailing is required because service was by publication or posting and the address of the respondent remains unknown.
   b. ☐ A copy of this *Request to Enter Default,* including any attachments and an envelope with sufficient postage, was provided to the court clerk, with the envelope addressed as follows *(address of the respondent's attorney or, if none, the respondent's last known address):*

I declare under penalty of perjury under the laws of the State of California that the foregoing is true and correct.

Date:

_____ ▶ _____
(TYPE OR PRINT NAME)   (SIGNATURE OF DECLARANT)

FOR COURT USE ONLY
☐ *Request to Enter Default* mailed to the respondent or the respondent's attorney on *(date):*
☐ Default entered as requested on *(date):*
☐ Default **not** entered. Reason:
Clerk, by _____ , Deputy

Page 1 of 2

Form Adopted for Mandatory Use	**REQUEST TO ENTER DEFAULT**	Code of Civil Procedure, §§ 585, 587;
Judicial Council of California	**(Family Law—Uniform Parentage)**	Family Code, § 2335.5
FL-165 [Rev. January 1, 2005]		www.courtinfo.ca.gov

CASE NAME *(Last name, first name of each party):*	CASE NUMBER:

4. **Memorandum of costs**

   a. ☐ Costs and disbursements are waived.

   b. Costs and disbursements are listed as follows:

     (1) ☐ Clerk's fees .... $.............................

     (2) ☐ Process server's fees .... $.............................

     (3) ☐ Other *(specify):* .... $.............................

       .... $.............................

       .... $.............................

       .... $ ——————

     TOTAL .... $.............................

   c. I am the attorney, agent, or party who claims these costs. To the best of my knowledge and belief, the foregoing items of cost are correct and have been necessarily incurred in this cause or proceeding.

I declare under penalty of perjury under the laws of the State of California that the foregoing is true and correct.

Date:

▶

_____   _____
(TYPE OR PRINT NAME)   (SIGNATURE OF DECLARANT)

5. **Declaration of nonmilitary status.** The respondent is not in the military service of the United States as defined in section 511 et seq. of the Servicemembers Civil Relief Act (50 U.S.C. Appen. § 501 et seq.), and is not entitled to the benefits of such act.

I declare under penalty of perjury under the laws of the State of California that the foregoing is true and correct.

Date:

▶

_____   _____
(TYPE OR PRINT NAME)   (SIGNATURE OF DECLARANT)

Copies: Original (file with court clerk); copy for submission to court clerk; office copies.

§14.15   b. Additional Forms

The additional forms the petitioner will submit in connection with the default proceedings depend on the circumstances, the particular issues of the case, and local rules and practice. When the petitioner proceeds by declaration (see §§14.23–14.24), all documents appropriate to be submitted are usually submitted with the Request to Enter Default. When the petitioner proceeds by hearing (see §§14.25–14.35), the additional forms may be submitted with the Request to Enter Default, at the hearing itself, or at times in between. Additional forms that may be filed include the following:

- Summons (see §§10.13–10.14) and Proof of Service of Summons (see §§10.43–10.44);

- Declaration for Default or Uncontested Dissolution (see §§14.23–14.24);

- Request to set a default or uncontested hearing (see §14.25);

- Income and Expense Declaration (see §11.25);

- Property Declaration (see §§10.19–10.21);

- Stipulation to Establish or Modify Child Support and Order (see form in §11.14);

- Declaration of Disclosure (see §§13.44–13.49, 14.4);

- Declaration Regarding Service of Final Declaration of Disclosure and Income and Expense Declaration (see §§13.44–13.49, 14.4);

- Judgment (see §§14.51–14.56);

- Notice of Entry of Judgment (see §§14.57–14.58), along with two preaddressed stamped envelopes; and

- Child Support Case Registry Form (see §§11.63A–11.63B).

Note that the petitioner must submit to the court clerk, along with the Request to Enter Default, a stamped envelope, bearing sufficient postage, addressed to the defaulting spouse, with the address of the court clerk as the return address. Fam C §2335.5. For further discussion, see §14.11.

Any time an order or Judgment concerning child support is entered, Judicial Council Form FL-192 (Notice of Rights and Responsibilities:

Health-Care Costs and Reimbursement Procedures and Information Sheet on Changing a Child Support Order) must be submitted with the order. Fam C §§4063(a)(1), (2), 4010.

§14.16   6. Entry of Default

The court clerk must enter the respondent's default on filing of the Request to Enter Default (Judicial Council Form FL-165; see §14.14) and any appropriate attachments. "Entry" of the default occurs when the clerk notes it in the court's register of actions. No notice of the entry of default need be given to the respondent, and the respondent cannot thereafter participate in the proceeding, except to move to set the default aside.

Once the default has been entered, the petitioner may apply to the court for the relief sought in the petition. The petitioner may choose to "prove up" the case by filing a Declaration for Default or Uncontested Dissolution (Judicial Council Form FL-170; see §14.24) or by testifying at a default hearing. On considerations and procedures for each method of proving the petitioner's case, see §§14.22–14.35.

§14.17   B. Stipulation

Parties to a marital action who reach an agreement resolving all the issues in the action usually proceed to entry of judgment based on their agreement by executing and filing the Appearance, Stipulations and Waivers form (see §14.19). The respondent thereby makes an appearance, if he or she has not already done so, and agrees with the petitioner that the action may be heard as an uncontested matter.

Parties who settle their case may also proceed to judgment *without* the respondent's making an appearance. In that event, the judgment is obtained by default (see §§14.6–14.16) rather than by stipulation to an uncontested proceeding (see §§14.17–14.20). If the respondent has not yet appeared when a settlement is reached, a decision will have to be made on whether to proceed by default or to file an Appearance, Stipulations and Waivers form.

Proceeding by default enables the respondent to have the agreement presented to the court without paying a filing fee. Govt C §26826(b)(3). If the parties proceed by Appearance, Stipulations and Waivers, however, the respondent, by checking the appropriate items on the form (see §14.19), can ensure that the stipulation to an uncontested proceeding will be binding only if the court approves the parties' agreement. If either party, in relying on this stipulation, does not appear at the uncontested proceeding, and if the court's judgment is inconsistent with the parties' written agreement, the judgment exceeds the court's jurisdiction and is subject to collateral attack. See *Marriage of Nicolaides* (1974) 39 CA3d 192, 198, 114 CR 56. Either party may prepare the Appearance, Stipulations and Waivers form, although both parties, and their respective counsel, if any, must sign it. Once the form is filed with the court, the same procedure is followed as if a default had been entered, *i.e.,* the matter may be submitted to the court by declaration (see §§14.22–14.24) or at an uncontested hearing (see §§14.25–14.35).

PRACTICE TIP➤ The methods of reaching a stipulation are many. They range, for example, from informal telephone conferences and meetings to formal private mediation sessions and mandatory settlement conferences. The relatively recent method of achieving settlement through collaborative practice is yet another vehicle, and one that is now recognized by statute. See Fam C §2013. For related discussion, see chap 3 and Dissolution Strategies: From Intake to Judgment, chap 4 (Cal CEB Annual).

1. Appearance, Stipulations, and Waivers

§14.18   a. Discussion

Use of the Judicial Council Form FL-130 (Appearance, Stipulations, and Waivers) is optional (unless made mandatory by local rules), but its choice of provisions is convenient, and it is routinely used in marital actions. The following discussion is keyed to the Judicial Council form:

Item 1.a: If the respondent has not previously made a general appearance, he or she must do so in order for the waivers or stipulations contained in the form to be effective. By making a general appearance, the respondent admits jurisdiction over his or her person. 2 Witkin, California Procedure, *Jurisdiction* §184 (4th ed 1997).

Item 1.b: This item must be checked if the respondent has already filed a response or otherwise made a general appearance.

Item 1.c: If the respondent qualifies for protection under the Servicemembers Civil Relief Act (50 USC App §§501–596), the action may proceed as an uncontested matter only if the service person is represented by counsel *or* agrees, by checking this item, to waive all rights under the Act. See §14.13.

Item 1.f: This item pertains only to actions under the Uniform Parentage Act (Fam C §§7600–7730) and has no application to marital actions.

Item 2.a: By stipulating that the action may be heard as an uncontested matter, one party alone may thereafter appear in court to request relief. It is therefore critical that Items 2.d. and 2.e. are also checked, to ensure that the court will not make orders contrary to the parties' agreement.

Item 2.b: This waiver may, but need not, be used to expedite the scheduling of the uncontested proceeding and entry of judgment. If the parties wish to waive only a portion of the rights specified, some may be crossed out. On the importance of waiving notice of trial if one party will not appear at the uncontested hearing, see §14.28.

Item 2.c: In some counties, stipulating to a commissioner sitting as a temporary judge may expedite the scheduling of the uncontested hearing.

Item 2.d: This item will be checked when the parties have entered into a written agreement, depending on whether the agreement is in the form of a stipulated judgment (see §14.40) or a marital settlement agreement (see §§14.41–14.45), and on any requirements of local rules or practice.

Item 2.e: This stipulation protects both parties, but especially a party who does not appear at the uncontested trial, from a judgment that varies from the parties' written agreement. It should be checked whenever Item 2.a. is checked.

Item 3: Any additional stipulations or waivers of the parties may be inserted here. For example, if the Appearance, Stipulations, and Waivers applies only to the status of the marriage, this restriction should be inserted here and the words "for status only" added in the caption.

§14.19 b. Form: Appearance, Stipulations, and Waivers (Judicial Council Form FL-130)

FL-130

ATTORNEY OR PARTY WITHOUT ATTORNEY *(Name, State Bar number, and address)*:	FOR COURT USE ONLY

TELEPHONE NO.:   FAX NO. *(Optional)*:

E-MAIL ADDRESS *(Optional)*:

ATTORNEY FOR *(Name)*:

SUPERIOR COURT OF CALIFORNIA, COUNTY OF

STREET ADDRESS:

MAILING ADDRESS:

CITY AND ZIP CODE:

BRANCH NAME:

PETITIONER:

RESPONDENT:

APPEARANCE, STIPULATIONS, AND WAIVERS	CASE NUMBER:

1. **Appearance by respondent** *(you must choose one)*:
   a. ☐ By filing this form, the respondent makes a general appearance.
   b. ☐ The respondent has previously made a general appearance.
   c. ☐ The respondent is a member of the military services of the United States of America and waives all rights under the Servicemembers Civil Relief Act (50 U.S.C. Appen. § 501 et seq.). No appearance fee is required.

2. **Agreements, stipulations, and waivers** *(choose all that apply)*:
   a. ☐ The parties agree that this cause may be decided as an uncontested matter.
   b. ☐ The parties waive their rights to notice of trial, a statement of decision, a motion for new trial, and the right to appeal.
   c. ☐ This matter may be decided by a commissioner sitting as a temporary judge.
   d. ☐ We have a written agreement, or a stipulation for judgment will be submitted to the court.
   e. ☐ None of these agreements or waivers will apply unless the court approves the stipulation for judgment or incorporates the written settlement agreement into the judgment.
   f. ☐ This is a parentage case, and both parties have signed an *Advisement and Waiver of Rights Re: Establishment of Parental Relationship* (form FL-235) or its equivalent.

3. **Other** *(specify)*:

Date:

_____ ▶ _____
(TYPE OR PRINT NAME)   (SIGNATURE OF PETITIONER)

Date:

_____ ▶ _____
(TYPE OR PRINT NAME)   (SIGNATURE OF RESPONDENT)

Date:

_____ ▶ _____
(TYPE OR PRINT NAME)   (SIGNATURE OF ATTORNEY FOR PETITIONER)

Date:

_____ ▶ _____
(TYPE OR PRINT NAME)   (SIGNATURE OF ATTORNEY FOR RESPONDENT)

Page 1 of 1

Form Approved for Optional Use
Judicial Council of California
FL-130 [Rev. January 1, 2006]

APPEARANCE, STIPULATIONS, AND WAIVERS
(Family Law—Uniform Parentage—Custody and Support)

www.courtinfo.ca.gov

Copies: Original (file with court clerk); copy for other party or counsel; office copies.

§14.20　　2. Additional Forms

When the parties proceed by stipulation, the additional forms among those listed in §14.15 to be filed in connection with the uncontested proceedings depend on the circumstances, the particular issues in the case, and local rules and practice. As with the Request to Enter Default (see §14.15), when the party seeking the uncontested judgment proceeds by declaration (see §§14.22-14.24), all appropriate documents are usually submitted with the Appearance, Stipulations and Waivers. When the party proceeds by hearing (see §§14.25-14.35), the additional forms may be submitted with the Appearance, Stipulations and Waivers or at the hearing itself.

§14.21　　C. Other Uncontested Matters

When the respondent has appeared in the proceeding (see Cal Rules of Ct 5.120) or has filed a notice of motion to quash service of summons or a petition for a writ of mandate (see Cal Rules of Ct 5.122(a)(2), (3)), but then fails to appear or respond, the case apparently may be heard as an uncontested matter after proper notice to the respondent. See CCP §594. On uncontested actions, see California Civil Procedure Before Trial §38.10 (4th ed Cal CEB 2004).

§14.22　　IV. METHOD OF PROOF

Regardless of whether the parties are proceeding by default (see §§14.6-14.16) or by stipulation (see §§14.17-14.20), the court must receive proof of the grounds alleged and the facts stated in the petition before it can issue a judgment and grant the relief requested. Fam C §2336(a); Cal Rules of Ct 5.122(b).

In a dissolution or legal separation action, the proof may be provided either by submitting a Declaration for Default or Uncontested Dissolution or Legal Separation (see §§14.23-14.24) or by testifying at an uncontested hearing (see §§14.25-14.35). Fam C §2336(a). When proof is made by declaration, the declarant's personal appearance may be required only when it appears to the court that (1) reconciliation of the parties is reasonably possible; (2) a proposed child custody order is not in the children's best interests; (3) a proposed child support order is less than a noncustodial parent is capable of paying; or (4) a personal appearance of any party or interested person would be in the best interests of justice. Fam C §2336(b).Because Fam C §2336 does not apply to nullity actions (see Fam C §2336(a)), proof in uncontested nullity cases must be by testimony at a hearing.

Providing proof by declaration has become increasingly common; some local court rules even present this method of proof as the standard approach (see, *e.g.,* San Francisco Local R11(34)(A)(1), renumbered 11(15)(A)(1) effective January 1, 2005). Certainly, many clients prefer to avoid the financial expense and emotional strain of appearing in court, even on an uncontested matter. Nonetheless, counsel should determine which procedure—declaration or hearing—will be most advantageous in the particular case to be presented to the court, and not routinely use one procedure or the other.

There seems to be little reason not to proceed by way of declaration in cases, *e.g.,* that involve relatively short marriages without minor children and in which the parties are both self-supporting and have relatively modest community assets and liabilities, a straightforward division of community property, and a solid settlement agreement. At the other end of the spectrum, it may be advisable to schedule an uncontested hearing when there is, *e.g.,* an extremely valuable community property estate, a substantially unequal division of community property, a failure to provide for child support or visitation with a minor child, or issues involving the validity of service in a default proceeding. If counsel is uncertain of the need for a hearing, and if the client prefers not to appear in court, one option may be to submit the proposed judgment to the court by declaration and simply allow the court to order a hearing if it believes one is necessary.

When there is a last-minute, or extremely "shaky," agreement, or when prior agreements have been made and then disavowed, the agreement's chances of surviving any future challenge may benefit from having one or even both clients present at an uncontested hearing. In such cases, all significant provisions of the agreement should be read into the record, and counsel or the court should query each client present about his or her understanding and acceptance of the agreement.

A. Declaration

§14.23   1. Discussion

Judicial Council Form FL-170 (Declaration for Default or Uncontested Dissolution or Legal Separation) sets forth, under penalty of perjury, the statements that would be offered as testimony at an uncontested hearing. When the respondent's default has been entered, the declaration is made by the petitioner. If the parties have stipulated to an uncontested hearing, either party may submit the declaration, although the petitioner usually does so. When the court accepts proof by declaration, neither party need appear or testify in order for a judgment to issue.

The declaration sets forth the jurisdictional facts of residency for dissolution (see Item 19) and the legal grounds for dissolution or legal separation (see Item 20). The specific items of relief requested are indicated by reference to the proposed judgment that is submitted with the declaration. The following discussion is keyed to the Judicial Council form:

Item 4: Note that when proceeding by default (unlike when proceeding by stipulation), the proposed judgment may not include any relief not requested in the petition. For discussion, see §14.9. When the parties stipulate to an uncontested proceeding, their stipulation is usually set forth in the Appearance, Stipulations and Waivers form (see §14.19).

Item 5: If the parties have a settlement agreement, it must be submitted to the court, subject to local rules or practice. If the parties have community (or quasi-community) assets or liabilities and there is no agreement, a completed Property Declaration form (Judicial Council Form FL-160; see §§10.19–10.21) must be submitted (unless a current form is on file) and the proposed judgment must provide for disposition of the property. See, *e.g.,* Alameda Ct R 11.8(1)(H).

Items 9–10: When a support order or attorney fees are requested in the proposed judgment, an Income and Expense Declaration form (see §§11.25–11.26) must be submitted (unless a current form is on file) and must include a "best estimate" of the other party's income. Local rules and practice, however, should be consulted. See, *e.g.,* Alameda Ct R 11.8(1)(F), requiring the filing party to submit an Income and Expense Declaration if (a) support is to be ordered; (b) there are minor children; (c) jurisdiction over spousal support is to be terminated; or (d) the length of marriage is ten years or more, unless both parties have been represented and have otherwise agreed in a marital settlement agreement or stipulation for judgment.

Item 11: Note that when the right to support has been assigned or a public assistance application is pending, no child support order may be made unless the district attorney for the providing county consents or is given the opportunity to be heard. See, *e.g., Marriage of Mena* (1989) 212 CA3d 12, 260 CR 314 (county providing public assistance is indispensable party entitled to notice of child support proceedings). See also Alameda Ct R 11.0(3)(D). When the right to support is assigned, payments must be ordered paid directly to the providing agency. See Item 12.

Item 21: This item is checked only when the issue of marital status has been bifurcated (*i.e.,* severed) from other issues in the action. See §§14.59–14.73.

When additional information is required to answer questions that might arise concerning the nature of relief requested, it should be added to the declaration (*e.g.,* facts justifying the absence of a support award or of a provision for child visitation).

§14.24   2. Form: Declaration for Default or Uncontested Dissolution or Legal Separation (Judicial Council Form FL-170)

FL-170

ATTORNEY OR PARTY WITHOUT ATTORNEY *(Name, State Bar number, and address)*	FOR COURT USE ONLY
TELEPHONE NO.: FAX NO. *(Optional)*: E-MAIL ADDRESS *(Optional)*: ATTORNEY FOR *(Name)*:	

SUPERIOR COURT OF CALIFORNIA, COUNTY OF

STREET ADDRESS:

MAILING ADDRESS:

CITY AND ZIP CODE:

BRANCH NAME:

PETITIONER:

RESPONDENT:

DECLARATION FOR DEFAULT OR UNCONTESTED ☐ DISSOLUTION ☐ LEGAL SEPARATION	CASE NUMBER:

(NOTE: Items 1 through 16 apply to both dissolution and legal separation proceedings.)

1. I declare that if I appeared in court and were sworn, I would testify to the truth of the facts in this declaration.

2. I agree that my case will be proven by this declaration and that I will not appear before the court unless I am ordered by the court to do so.

3. All the information in the ☐ *Petition* ☐ *Response* is true and correct.

4. **Default or uncontested** *(Check a or b.)*
   a. ☐ The default of the respondent was entered or is being requested, and I am not seeking any relief not requested in the petition. **OR**
   b. ☐ The parties have agreed that the matter may proceed as an uncontested matter without notice, and the agreement is attached or is incorporated in the attached settlement agreement or stipulated judgment.

5. **Settlement agreement** *(Check a or b.)*
   a. ☐ The parties have entered into ☐ an agreement ☐ a stipulated judgment regarding their property their marriage or domestic partnership rights, including support, the original of which is or has been submitted to the court. I request that the court approve the agreement. **OR**
   b. ☐ **There is no agreement or stipulated judgment**, and the following statements are true *(check at least one, including item (2) if a community estate exists)*:
      (1) ☐ There are no community or quasi-community assets or community debts to be disposed of by the court.
      (2) ☐ The community and quasi-community assets and debts are listed on the attached **completed** current *Property Declaration* (form FL-160), which includes an estimate of the value of the assets and debts that I propose to be distributed to each party. The division in the proposed *Judgment (Family Law)* (form FL-180) is a fair and equal division of the property and debts, or if there is a negative estate, the debts are assigned fairly and equitably.

6. **Declaration of disclosure** *(Check a, b, or c.)*
   a. ☐ Both the petitioner and respondent have filed, or are filing concurrently, a *Declaration Regarding Service of Declaration of Disclosure* (form FL-141) and an *Income and Expense Declaration* (form FL-150).
   b. ☐ This matter is proceeding by default. I am the petitioner in this action and have filed a proof of service of the preliminary *Declaration of Disclosure* (form FL-140) with the court. I hereby waive receipt of the final *Declaration of Disclosure* (form FL-140) from the respondent.
   c. ☐ This matter is proceeding as an uncontested action. Service of the final *Declaration of Disclosure* (form FL-140) is mutually waived by both parties. A waiver provision executed by both parties under penalty of perjury is contained in the settlement agreement or proposed judgment or another, separate stipulation.

7. ☐ **Child custody** should be ordered as set forth in the proposed *Judgment (Family Law)* (form FL-180).

8. ☐ **Child visitation** should be ordered as set forth in the proposed *Judgment (Family Law)* (form FL-180).

9. **Spousal, partner, and family support** *(If a support order or attorney fees are requested, submit a completed Income and Expense Declaration (form FL-150) unless a current form is on file. Include your best estimate of the other party's income. Check at least one of the following.)*
   a. ☐ I knowingly give up forever any right to receive spousal or partner support.
   b. ☐ I ask the court to reserve jurisdiction to award spousal or partner support in the future to *(name)*:
   c. ☐ Spousal support should be ordered as set forth in the proposed *Judgment (Family Law)* (form FL-180).
   d. ☐ Family support should be ordered as set forth in the proposed *Judgment (Family Law)* (form FL-180).

Form Adopted for Mandatory Use
 Judicial Council of California
 FL-170 [Rev. January 1, 2007]

**DECLARATION FOR DEFAULT OR UNCONTESTED
 DISSOLUTION or LEGAL SEPARATION
 (Family Law)**

Ⓒ EB

Family Code, § 2336 <br> www.courtinfo.ca.gov

FL-170

PETITIONER:	CASE NUMBER:
RESPONDENT:	

10. ☐ **Child support** should be ordered as set forth in the proposed *Judgment (Family Law)* (form FL-180).

11. a. I ☐ am receiving ☐ am not receiving ☐ intend to apply for public assistance for the child or children listed in the proposed order.

  b. To the best of my knowledge, the other party ☐ is ☐ is not receiving public assistance.

12. ☐ The petitioner ☐ respondent is presently receiving public assistance, and all support should be made payable to the local child support agency at the address set forth in the proposed judgment. A representative of the local child support agency has signed the proposed judgment.

13. If there are minor children, check and complete item a and item b or c:

  a. My gross (before taxes) monthly income is *(specify)*: $

  b. ☐ The estimated gross monthly income of the other party is *(specify)*: $

  c. ☐ I have no knowledge of the estimated monthly income of the other party for the following reasons *(specify)*:

  d. ☐ I request that this order be based on the ☐ petitioner's ☐ respondent's earning ability. The facts in support of my estimate of earning ability are *(specify)*:

    ☐ Continued on Attachment 13d.

14. ☐ **Parentage** of the children of the petitioner and respondent born prior to their marriage or domestic partnership should be ordered as set forth in the proposed *Judgment (Family Law)* (form FL-180). A declaration regarding parentage is attached.

15. ☐ **Attorney fees** should be ordered as set forth in the proposed *Judgment (Family Law)* (form FL-180).

16. ☐ The petitioner ☐ respondent requests restoration of his or her former name as set forth in the proposed *Judgment (Family Law)* (form FL-180).

17. There are irreconcilable differences that have led to the irremediable breakdown of the marriage or domestic partnership, and there is no possibility of saving the marriage or domestic partnership through counseling or other means.

18. This declaration may be reviewed by a commissioner sitting as a temporary judge, who may determine whether to grant this request or require my appearance under Family Code section 2336.

STATEMENTS IN THIS BOX APPLY ONLY TO DISSOLUTIONS—Items 19 through 21

19. If this is a dissolution of marriage or of a domestic partnership created in another state, the petitioner and/or the respondent has been a resident of this county for at least three months and of the state of California for at least six months continuously and immediately preceding the date of the filing of the petition for dissolution of marriage or domestic partnership.

20. I ask that the court grant the request for a judgment for dissolution of marriage or domestic partnership based upon irreconcilable differences and that the court make the orders set forth in the proposed *Judgment (Family Law)* (form FL-180) submitted with this declaration.

21. ☐ This declaration is for the termination of **marital or domestic partner status only.** I ask the court to reserve jurisdiction over all issues whose determination is not requested in this declaration.

THIS STATEMENT APPLIES ONLY TO LEGAL SEPARATIONS

22. I ask that the court grant the request for a judgment for legal separation based upon irreconcilable differences and that the court make the orders set forth in the proposed *Judgment (Family Law)* (form FL-180) submitted with this declaration.

  I understand that a judgment of legal separation does not terminate a marriage or domestic partnership and that I am still married or a partner in a domestic partnership.

---

23. ☐ Other *(specify)*:

I declare under penalty of perjury under the laws of the State of California that the foregoing is true and correct.

Date:

▶

_____
(TYPE OR PRINT NAME)

_____
(SIGNATURE OF DECLARANT)

FL-170 [Rev. January 1, 2007]

**DECLARATION FOR DEFAULT OR UNCONTESTED
DISSOLUTION or LEGAL SEPARATION
(Family Law)**

CEB   Page 2 of 2

Copies: Original (file with court clerk); courtesy copy for other counsel in cases of negotiated settlement; office copies.

B. Hearing

§14.25   1. Setting the Hearing

If proof in a marital action is to be made at an uncontested (or "prove up") hearing, a hearing date must be requested from the court clerk. In a default proceeding, the party who requests and will testify at the hearing is always the petitioner. When the parties have stipulated to an uncontested proceeding, either party may request and appear at the hearing, but it is usually the petitioner who does so.

Local practices for calendaring such hearings differ and can be ascertained by referring to local rules and speaking to the court clerk. Courts in many counties provide printed forms for requesting a date for an uncontested hearing. In other counties, it may be possible to request a hearing date from the court clerk orally or by letter. The attorney for the party requesting the hearing date should consult local rules, any required form for the uncontested setting, and the court clerk to learn whether other papers must be submitted with the hearing date request.

§14.26   2. Hearing Officer

The judge who hears uncontested proceedings may, in some counties, be a temporary judge. See §11.49 for discussion, which, although presented in the context of hearings on temporary orders, also applies to uncontested proceedings.

§14.27   3. Proof of Service

In a hearing for a default judgment, the original summons together with a completed proof of service will have already been filed, either with or before the Request to Enter Default. Nonetheless, the court may wish to verify proof of service at the time of the default hearing, and counsel for the petitioner should be certain that the original proof of service is in the court file before the hearing.

When the parties have stipulated to an uncontested proceeding, the Appearance, Stipulations and Waivers form will have been signed by both parties and filed. Either the respondent will have appeared in the action before the filing of the form or the filing will constitute his or her appearance. In either case, it is not necessary to prove that service was made on the respondent.

§14.28   4. Notice of Trial

When a party has previously appeared in a marital action but is not present at the uncontested hearing, CCP §594(a) requires that proof be provided to the court that the absent party received notice of the trial at least 15 days before the hearing. See, *e.g., Au-Yang v Barton* (1999) 21 C4th 958, 966, 90 CR2d 227 (error for trial court that has advanced previous trial date to proceed with trial if one party is not present and did not receive 15-day notice). Note, however, that §594(a) does not apply when the respondent's default has previously been entered.

The notice to the adverse party required by §594(a) must be introduced into evidence by either an affidavit or certificate, or by other competent evidence. CCP §594(b). Failure to enter the notice into evidence in violation of §594(b) is subject to harmless error analysis. Such a violation does not deprive the court of jurisdiction to proceed in a party's absence if the trial court is satisfied that the party received actual, timely notice of the trial, proof of service of notice of trial was on file with the trial court, and proof of service was part of the record on appeal. *Marriage of Goddard* (2004) 33 C4th 49, 14 CR3d 50 (disapproving *Irvine Nat'l Bank v Han* (1982) 130 CA3d 693, 697, 181 CR 864, to the extent inconsistent with this decision). The notice of trial requirement may be waived, however, and parties who stipulate to an uncontested proceeding will typically waive notice by checking Item 5 on the Appearance, Stipulations and Waivers form (see form in §14.19) and filing it. Alternatively, a written request that the court take judicial notice of the court file containing the notice of trial and proof of service may be filed with the court, in compliance with Evid C §453. See *Irvine Nat'l Bank v Han* (1982) 130 CA3d 693, 695, 181 CR 864, overruled on other grounds in *Marriage of Goddard* (2004) 33 C4th 49, 59, 14 CR3d 50 (court of appeal noted not only that notice and proof of service were not introduced into evidence, but also that trial court was not asked to take judicial notice of file containing them).

§14.29   5. Proof of Facts

The party requesting the uncontested judgment must be prepared to provide to the court a factual basis for the judgment of dissolution, legal separation, or nullity and for all orders sought. Fam C

§2336(a);Cal Rules of Ct 5.122(b). Normally, the requesting party will be sworn as a witness at the hearing and his or her attorney will elicit the necessary facts by direct examination. Judges at most uncontested hearings will allow counsel to ask the party leading questions to prove the grounds for dissolution, legal separation, or nullity and provide the basis for the relief requested. In some cases, it may be necessary or advisable to introduce documentary evidence (see §14.35) to show that the requested orders are appropriate.

§14.30   a. Statutory Grounds and Residency Requirement: Dissolution and Legal Separation

Usually, the party who has requested the hearing will be called to the witness stand to establish that the residency requirement (dissolution only) has been met and that there are legal grounds for granting a judgment of dissolution or legal separation. The attorney should prepare his or her client before the hearing to give brief answers to questions such as the following:

Q. Are all the facts stated in your petition (response) true?

A. Yes.

Q. At the time the petition was filed, had you (your spouse) lived in the State of California for the immediately preceding six months and in the County of _ _ _ _ _ _ _ _ for the immediately preceding three months?

A. Yes.

(Note: The residence of either spouse may be used to satisfy the residency requirement for a judgment of dissolution; however, there are no residency requirements for either spouse for a judgment of legal separation, in which case this question should be omitted. If a petition for legal separation was later amended to a petition for dissolution, however, the appearing party should testify to facts establishing residency at the time the petition was amended.)

Q. During the course of your marriage to respondent (petitioner), did irreconcilable differences arise that led to the irremediable breakdown of your marriage?

A. Yes.

(Note: If the ground for dissolution or legal separation is incurable insanity (Fam C §2310(b)), the petitioner's testimony establishing this fact will be required.)

> Q. Do you feel that counseling or any other assistance of the court could save your marriage?

> A. No.

> Q. Do you ask this court for a judgment dissolving your marriage (judgment of legal separation)?

> A. Yes.

§14.31   b. Statutory Grounds and Special Requirements: Nullity

The party requesting a judgment of nullity can expect to be called to the witness stand to provide testimony establishing that the requisite legal grounds exist. On the grounds for a judgment of nullity, see §§3.7–3.15. Courts will not grant a decree of nullity without the production of "clear, satisfactory and convincing evidence," and this requirement applies even to proceedings in which the respondent makes no appearance. *Maduro v Maduro* (1944) 62 CA2d 776, 779, 145 P2d 683. To meet this standard of proof, it may be necessary or advisable to corroborate the petitioner's testimony by introducing the testimony of third parties or, in appropriate circumstances, documentary evidence.

In some instances, courts may also require proof of other requirements applicable to nullity proceedings, *e.g.,* that the petitioner is a California domiciliary (see §4.3); that the applicable statute of limitations was met (see §§3.10–3.15); or, if orders on certain financial or property issues are sought, that the court has personal jurisdiction over the respondent (see §§4.4–4.5) or that the party requesting the orders is a "putative spouse" (see §3.19).

§14.32   c. Family Code §2336 Requirements

To meet the requirements of Fam C §2336(a), the appearing party should testify to the following:

- If there are minor children of the parties, an estimate of the monthly gross income of each party or, if the appearing party has no knowledge of the other party's estimated monthly income, a statement of why he or she has no knowledge; and

- If there is a community estate, an estimate of the value of the assets and the debts the appearing party proposes to be distributed to each party, unless the party has filed, or will file with the declaration, a complete and accurate property declaration (see §§10.19–10.21).

d. Factual Basis for Relief Requested

§14.33   (1) When Parties Have Written Agreement

When the parties have entered into a marital settlement agreement (see §§14.41–14.49) or a stipulated judgment (see §14.40), it is usually unnecessary for the appearing party to testify on specific provisions of the agreement. Nevertheless, counsel should review with the client all relevant terms of the agreement before the hearing so that, if questioned by the court, the party will be able to testify competently.

The court is most likely to inquire into provisions for the custody and support of minor children, because the court has jurisdiction to make its own orders in the children's best interests, regardless of any agreement between the parties (see §§7.38 (custody), 8.17 (child support), 14.50 (power of court to reject agreement)). The court is also likely to inquire into a waiver of spousal support and termination of the court's jurisdiction as to spousal support to verify that the spouse understands that he or she can never return to court to seek an award of support. Regardless of the specific provisions involved, the party should be prepared to testify to the *knowing and voluntary* nature of his or her agreement. A typical examination follows:

> Q. Have you and the respondent (petitioner) entered into a marital settlement agreement (stipulated judgment)?
>
> A. Yes.
>
> Q. Have you had an opportunity to read the entire agreement?
>
> A. Yes.
>
> Q. Have you reviewed the agreement and discussed each of its provisions with your attorney?

A. Yes.

Q. Do you understand each provision of the agreement?

A. Yes.

Q. Did you enter into this agreement voluntarily and without coercion or duress of any kind?

A. Yes.

Counsel may, at this point, ask such questions as may be appropriate to establish the client's understanding of the agreement, *e.g.,* "Do you understand that you are waiving spousal support forever and will never have the right to ask the court to award spousal support to you, no matter how circumstances may change?"

Q. Have you and the respondent (petitioner) signed the agreement?

A. Yes.

At this point, counsel should show the original marital settlement agreement or stipulated judgment to the witness and ask:

Q. Do you recognize this document as the original of the agreement signed by you and the respondent (petitioner)?

A. Yes.

Q. Are the signatures appearing on the last page of this document yours and the respondent's (petitioner's)?

A. Yes.

If the document is a marital settlement agreement and if incorporation and merger into the judgment are requested:

Q. Do you ask this court to approve the agreement as fair and equitable, order the parties to comply with all its executory provisions, merge the provisions for _ _[e.g., child custody and visitation, child support, and spousal support]_ _ into the judgment, and incorporate the remainder of the agreement in the judgment for the sole purpose of identification (incorporate the agreement in the judgment by reference only)?

A. Yes.

(Note: On incorporation, approval, and merger, see §§14.42–14.44.)

If the document is a stipulated judgment:

> Q. Do you ask this court to make your agreement its judgment in this action?

> A. Yes.

§14.34　(2) When No Agreement Exists

When the petitioner is proceeding after entry of the respondent's default and there is no agreement of the parties, the court has a duty to exercise its discretion in issuing orders requested by the petitioner. For example, the court must determine whether a proposal for custody is in the children's best interests, whether a proposed division of community property is equal, whether a proposed child support order complies with the statewide uniform guideline, and whether proposed orders for spousal support or attorney fees are just and reasonable in light of each party's financial circumstances. Fam C §§2032, 2550, 3040, 4052, 4330. See also Cal Rules of Ct 5.122. Although, in practice, default hearings may be somewhat perfunctory, the petitioner should be prepared to testify, clearly and specifically, to the facts relevant to each requested order. Examples of such testimony might include the following:

Child custody. Facts indicating that the proposed order is in the children's best interests, *e.g.,* each parent's strengths and weaknesses, established custody and visitation schedules, children's special needs.

Child support. Facts amplifying information provided in the Income and Expense Declaration (see form in §11.26), *e.g.,* party's ability to earn income; child's special medical or other needs.

Spousal support. Facts relevant to those circumstances set forth in Fam C §4320 that are significant in the particular case.

Property. Facts relevant to characterization (*e.g.,* source of funds, agreements between the parties) or division of property (*e.g.,* child's needs supporting a deferred sale of home under Fam C §§3800–3810; nonemployee's need for, and employee's ability to pay, "cash out" of interest in employee benefit plan).

On the law applicable generally to individual issues, see chaps 5 (property), 6 (spousal support), 7 (child custody and visitation), 8 (child support), and 9 (attorney fees and costs).

§14.35 (3) Documentary Evidence

The court may accept, as all or any part of the proof required at an uncontested hearing, a completed Income and Expense Declaration (see form in §11.26) and Property Declaration (see forms in §§10.20–10.21). Cal Rules of Ct 5.122(b). These documents are often filed before the hearing (see §§14.10, 14.15, 14.20), but it may be possible to update the information by testimony at the hearing or by filing new or supplemental forms before or at the hearing. Local rules and practice should be consulted.

If the court has appointed an evaluator to conduct a custody investigation and ordered the preparation of a report, the custody evaluator must file a *confidential* written report with the court clerk and serve the parties or (if they are represented) their attorneys at least 10 days before a custody hearing. Fam C §3111(b). In addition, by local rule in some counties a court mediator may make written recommendations to the court on custody or visitation matters. Fam C §3183(a). When it is anticipated that either type of report will be presented to the court, counsel should check before the date of the hearing to see if the report is in the court file, and so advise the court. A custody investigation report requires the stipulation of all interested parties to be received in evidence, but the court may "consider" the report even if it is not so received. Fam C §3111; see §7.49. Consistent with local rules, a mediator's recommendation may also be considered by the court. Fam C §3183(a); see §7.46.

If the characterization, valuation, or proposed division of community property, such as real property or a family business, may be questioned by the court, relevant documents (*e.g.,* a deed, appraisal, or accounting) may be introduced through the appearing party's testimony. If counsel believes that third party testimony is necessary, it would appear that such proof may be presented by affidavit, as well as by live testimony. See Fam C §2336; CCP §2002(1). Documentary evidence, third party testimony, or both, may also be appropriate on other than property issues, *e.g.,* wage stubs of the nonappearing party, or testimony of a fellow employee, on support issues.

The attorney for the appearing party should consult local rules and the court clerk to ascertain whether other papers must be submitted at the time of hearing. See §14.15 for additional documents that may be appropriate to present at the hearing.

§14.36 V. UNCONTESTED JUDGMENT

To obtain an uncontested judgment in a proceeding for dissolution, legal separation, or nullity, the party obtaining the judgment must set forth the requested orders on the Judicial Council form of Judgment (see §14.56) and submit it to the court for approval, signature, and filing. The proposed judgment may be submitted (1) with the Declaration for Default or Uncontested Dissolution or Legal Separation (see §14.24), (2) with the request for the uncontested hearing, or (3) before or at the hearing itself.

When the respondent's default has been entered and there is no agreement between the parties, the petitioner typically prepares and submits a proposed judgment that has not been reviewed or approved by the respondent. When the parties do have an agreement resolving all the issues in their case, then, whether they are proceeding by default or by stipulation, the proposed judgment will be presented to the court as a stipulated judgment (see §14.40) or as a judgment based on a marital settlement agreement (see §§14.41-14.49). For sample forms, see California Marital Settlement and Other Family Law Agreements, Apps B (stipulated judgment) and C (proposed judgment based on marital settlement agreement) (3d ed Cal CEB 2005).

§14.37 A. When No Agreement Exists

To obtain a judgment when the respondent's default has been entered and no agreement exists, the petitioner's attorney must prepare and submit to the court the Judicial Council Form FL-180 (Judgment (Family Law) (see §14.56), setting forth all proposed orders, typically by reference to an attachment. The judgment will include, as appropriate, orders for child custody and visitation, child support, spousal support, confirmation of separate property, division of community property, and attorney fees and costs. If the judgment determines the ownership or possession of real or personal property, it may also include a provision limiting the availability of relief under CCP §473 to 90 days, as long as notice of the judgment and such restriction is served on both the respondent and his or her attorney of record, if any. See CCP §473(b); on obtaining relief from a default judgment under §473, see §§18.24-18.35.

Some indication of the format for the proposed judgment may be obtained by reference to the stipulated judgment in California

Marital Settlement and Other Family Law Agreements, App B (3d ed Cal CEB 2005). Note, however, that the stipulated judgment contains some provisions typical of agreements, and the signatures of the parties and attorneys, that would not appear when the proposed judgment is not an agreement.

The proposed judgment is submitted to the court with the Declaration for Default or Uncontested Dissolution or Legal Separation (Judicial Council Form FL-170) or at the default hearing. It will not be possible for the petitioner to know, before submitting the proposed judgment, whether the court will approve all the orders requested. If the court does not approve the proposed judgment in its entirety, it may make the required changes on the judgment itself; or, particularly when the changes are substantial, counsel may have to prepare a revised judgment to reflect the actual orders of the court.

The attorney for the petitioner in a default proceeding should keep in mind that a unilaterally proposed judgment may be more easily set aside than a judgment based on an agreement. Even when the respondent has not otherwise participated in a default proceeding, it may be possible to obtain his or her consent to a judgment. If so, a marital settlement agreement or a stipulated judgment should be prepared for both parties' signatures. A respondent who signs a marital settlement agreement intended for incorporation in a judgment need not pay a "first appearance" filing fee. Govt C §26826(b)(3). A respondent who signs a stipulated judgment, on the other hand, may be required to pay a filing fee and, if so, it may be easier to obtain his or her signature if the petitioner pays the fee.

§14.38   B. When Parties Have an Agreement

When the parties to a marital action resolve all the issues in their case by agreement, the agreement must be reduced to written form as a stipulated judgment (see §14.40) or a marital settlement agreement (see §§14.41–14.45). On choosing between these forms, see §§14.46–14.49. In either case, a proposed judgment will then be presented to the court.

§14.39   1. Making Enforceable Record of Agreement

An agreement that is reached at a judicially supervised settlement conference, or while the parties and attorneys are in court for the trial of the action, should be stated on the record while both attorneys and both parties are present. The parties should be questioned on the record under oath about their understanding of, and willingness to enter into, the agreement as stated. If counsel intends to prepare a complete marital settlement agreement with standard warranties and other standard clauses, that agreement should be recited as well. It is helpful to carry a set of standard language into trial or a settlement conference so that there is no confusion about what constitutes "standard language." If the court reporter is not available to make a record of the agreement, the major points of agreement should be written out by hand, signed by each party and counsel, and initialed on each page.

If an agreement is negotiated during an informal settlement conference where both attorneys and both parties are present, it should be put into a contemporaneous writing that is signed by all conference participants. The document should indicate that the parties intend to execute a formal written agreement, but that they agree to be presently bound by the terms set forth. The document should not be drafted as merely an agreement to agree, which is unenforceable. Counsel must make sure, before settlement is reached, that the client truly understands and can abide by the terms of the proposed agreement. It should also be explained to the client, before the settlement conference begins, that a signed settlement, even though informally made, is a binding agreement.

If a party later refuses to execute a formal written agreement based on a settlement by the parties entered into orally "before the court" or in a writing signed by the parties outside the court's presence, the other party may request the court to enter judgment pursuant to the terms of the recorded settlement. CCP §664.6; *Richardson v Richardson* (1986) 180 CA3d 91, 225 CR 370 (oral stipulation at settlement conference in judge's chambers); *Corkland v Bosco* (1984) 156 CA3d 989, 203 CR 356 (written out-of-court settlement agreement). The statute applies to partial as well as complete settlement agreements. CCP §664.6. The underlying settlement must be entered into by the parties themselves, and not merely by the parties acting through their attorneys. *Levy v Superior Court* (1995) 10 C4th 578, 586, 41 CR2d 878, 883 (agreement signed by attorney but not by party is not enforceable under CCP §664.6); *Johnson v Department of Corrections* (1995) 38 CA4th 1700, 1703, 45 CR2d 740, 741 (same rule for oral agreements); *Williams v Saunders* (1997)

55 CA4th 1158, 64 CR2d 571 (agreement signed by party's codefendant/spouse not enforceable against party under CCP §664.6).

The California Supreme Court addressed the meaning of the phrase "before the court" in *Marriage of Assemi* (1994) 7 C4th 896, 30 CR2d 265, in which an oral settlement was reached at an arbitration proceeding presided over by a retired judge and was transcribed by a certified reporter. Emphasizing that the retired judge was empowered to adjudicate and render a binding determination of the controverted issues submitted to him, the court concluded that the stipulation was made "before the court" and was therefore enforceable under CCP §664.6. For a case in which a stipulation at an alternative dispute resolution proceeding was deemed not to be "before the court," see *Murphy v Padilla* (1996) 42 CA4th 707, 715, 49 CR2d 722, 726 (retired judge's role deemed most analogous to that of mediator in voluntary settlement conference; he was not empowered to make any binding decisions and did not exercise any adjudicative authority).

Oral agreements that are not reached "before the court" cannot be enforced by this method. *Datatronic Sys. Corp. v Speron, Inc.* (1986) 176 CA3d 1168, 222 CR 658 (oral agreement recorded by court reporter after deposition). See also *Marriage of Maricle* (1990) 220 CA3d 55, 269 CR 204 (former CC §4800(a), predecessor of Fam C §2550, requires that agreement dividing community estate of parties to marital action be written or, if oral, made in open court).

2. Choosing Form of Agreement

§14.40   a. Stipulated Judgment

A stipulated judgment is an agreement of the parties that is set forth directly on the Judicial Council form of Judgment (see §14.56). Cal Rules of Ct 5.116(a). It may be entered into by the parties regardless of whether the action is proceeding by default (see §§14.6–14.16) or by the parties' stipulation for an uncontested judgment (see §§14.17–14.20).

The stipulated judgment must contain "the exact terms of any judgment proposed to be entered in the case" and dispose of, or reserve jurisdiction over, all issues subject to the court's jurisdiction for which adjudication is sought. Cal Rules of Ct 5.116(b). Continuation pages setting forth the proposed orders will usually be attached to the printed judgment form and may be prepared on either plain or pleading paper. At the end of the stipulated judgment, the signatures of both parties and their counsel must be set forth after the words, "The foregoing is agreed to by:" immediately above the space reserved for the judge's signature. If the parties are to proceed to judgment by default, the defaulting party's signature must be notarized. Fam C §2338.5(a). For a complete sample stipulated judgment, see California Marital Settlement and Other Family Law Agreements, App B (3d ed Cal CEB 2005).

The Judicial Council form of Judgment is generally not used to prepare a stipulated judgment on reserved issues when a "status-only" judgment has previously been entered in the proceeding. On bifurcation of the issue of marital status, including preparation and entry of a status-only judgment and of a judgment on reserved issues, see §§14.59–14.74.

§14.41 b. Marital Settlement Agreement

A judgment may be based on a marital settlement agreement whether the action is proceeding by default (see §§14.6–14.16) or by the parties' stipulation for an uncontested judgment (see §§14.17–14.20). For a comprehensive treatment of the preparation of marital settlement agreements, see California Marital Settlement and Other Family Law Agreements, chaps 3 ("The Agreement in Its Legal Context"), 4 ("Drafting and Implementing the Agreement"), 5–16 (sample provisions and commentary), Apps A, C (complete sample agreements) (3d ed Cal CEB 2005).

Unlike a stipulated judgment (see §14.40), a marital settlement agreement is a document that exists separately from the Judicial Council form of Judgment (see §14.56). A marital settlement agreement is generally prepared on plain, rather than pleading, paper. The manner in which and even whether the agreement is presented to the court with the judgment depends on the relationship the parties intend between the agreement and the judgment and on local court rules. Many local rules have specific requirements on the incorporation, approval, and merger of marital settlement agreements, or certain provisions of such agreements. Therefore, local rules should always be consulted before submitting a marital settlement agreement to the court with a proposed judgment.

§14.42 (1) Incorporation of Agreement in Judgment

Incorporating a marital settlement agreement in a judgment makes the agreement part of the judgment. Unless local rules and practice provide otherwise, the agreement may be incorporated in the judgment in one of three ways: (1) Provisions of the agreement may be set forth as a part of the judgment itself; (2) the agreement may be referred to in, and physically attached to, the judgment; or (3) the agreement may be referred to and identified in the judgment without being attached to the judgment (often for reasons of privacy; see §14.49). See *Flynn v Flynn* (1954) 42 C2d 55, 59, 265 P2d 865.

Merely incorporating an agreement in a judgment, however, has no legal effect in itself; the legal effect depends on whether incorporation is *intended* to

- identify the agreement and approve it as fair and equitable; or

- merge the agreement, either wholly or partially, in the judgment. 42 C2d at 58.

In many cases, it may be desirable to incorporate the agreement for both purposes. See §§14.43–14.44. Whatever is the intended relationship between the agreement and the judgment, it should be made clear by setting forth the specific purpose of incorporation in both the agreement and the judgment, taking care that the language is consistent in both documents. For sample incorporation language, see California Marital Settlement and Other Family Law Agreements §§16.20–16.21, Apps A, C (3d ed Cal CEB 2005).

§14.43 (2) Approval of Agreement by Court

If a court approves a marital settlement agreement as fair and equitable and incorporates the agreement in the judgment for the purpose of identification, its validity is established as a part of the judgment and may not be relitigated in a subsequent action. *Flynn v Flynn* (1954) 42 C2d 55, 58, 265 P2d 865, 866. There seems to be no reason not to include such a provision in the agreement and the judgment in every instance. For sample approval language, see California Marital Settlement and Other Family Law Agreements §§16.20–16.21, Apps A, C (3d ed Cal CEB 2005).

An agreement that is incorporated only for identification and approval is not enforceable as a judgment but only in a separate action on the contract. *Marriage of Lane* (1985) 165 CA3d 1143, 1147, 211 CR 262. If enforceability as a judgment is desired, the specific provisions for which such enforceability is sought must be merged into the judgment.

§14.44   (3) Merger of Agreement Into Judgment

Merger is the process by which an agreement of the parties becomes a judgment of the court, enforceable by the judgment remedies of contempt, execution, and receivership. See Fam C §290; see *Tripp v Superior Court* (1923) 61 CA 64, 67, 214 P 252, disapproved on other grounds in 48 C2d at 522. If it is intended that the agreement become an *operable* part of the judgment and no longer have an independent existence, the agreement is "merged" into the judgment and is superseded by the judgment. *Marriage of Lane* (1985) 165 CA3d 1143, 1147, 211 CR 262 (listing factors court considered in deciding whether merger was intended).

The effect of a complete merger is to render each provision of the agreement enforceable by judgment remedies only (see Fam C §290) and not by breach of contract remedies. See §14.46. Often, however, the parties wish to retain a contractual right of enforcement as to certain provisions of the agreement. In this case, it is possible to merge into the judgment only those provisions of the agreement desired to be enforced by judgment remedies. Whatever is the intended extent of the merger of agreement provisions into the judgment, it should be made clear by setting it forth in both the agreement and the judgment, taking care that the language is consistent in both documents. For sample merger language, see California Marital Settlement and Other Family Law Agreements §§16.20–16.21, Apps A, C (3d ed Cal CEB 2005).

Some provisions that counsel may wish to include or exclude from merger are these:

Warranties. Provisions for warranty are not enforceable by judgment remedies and should never be merged into the judgment. On the importance of retaining contractual rights for the enforcement of warranty provisions, see *Marriage of Lane, supra.* In *Lane,* the court rejected the husband's argument that the parties' marital settlement agreement had been completely merged into the judgment, affirming the jury's $2,077,000 award to the wife for the husband's breach of a warranty that information he had provided on the value of community property was accurate. If the entire agreement had been merged into the judgment, neither judgment nor contract remedies would have been available to enforce the warranty and it would, in effect, have been extinguished.

Custody, visitation, and support. Provisions for child custody and visitation, child support, and spousal support are best enforced as part of the judgment by means of contempt and execution; they should routinely be merged into the judgment.

Executory provisions for division of property. Whether an executory provision for the division of community property (including both assets and debts) should be merged depends on whether the particular provision will be enforced better by judgment or contract remedies. If enforcement by execution on the judgment or by contempt is desired, the executory provision should be merged into the judgment. Before assuming that an order for payment of money will be enforceable by contempt, however, constitutional limitations on the use of contempt in such situations should be considered. For discussion, see §20.38.

§14.45 (4) Execution

The marital settlement agreement must be signed by both parties. When parties are represented, it may be that a marital settlement agreement can be enforced without having been signed or approved by their attorneys. Compare *Marriage of Hasso* (1991) 229 CA3d 1174, 1185, 280 CR 919 (absent fraud, coercion, and overreaching, and understanding their rights to advice of counsel, parties may choose to negotiate settlement without their attorneys' involvement), with *Marriage of Wickander* (1986) 187 CA3d 1364, 1367, 232 CR 621 (court should not accept marital settlement agreement entered into by represented party unless signed or assented to by party's attorney). Nevertheless, because signatures of the attorneys, indicating their approval of the document as conforming to the agreement of the parties, may be useful to discourage set-aside efforts, and may be required by local rule, it is the better practice to obtain them. In addition to executing the document, it may be advisable to have the parties and their attorneys initial each page to guard against substitution of pages.

The parties' signatures should be notarized. And, if the parties are to proceed to judgment by *default*, the defaulting party's signature *must* be notarized. Fam C §2338.5(a). Notarization is also required in the rare cases in which the agreement is to be recorded.

c. Considerations in Choosing Form of Agreement

§14.46　　(1) Enforcement

A stipulated judgment is an agreement of the parties when entered into and is enforceable as such until signed by the judge. See Cal Rules of Ct 5.116. Once signed by the judge, however, the entire agreement is merged into and superseded by the judgment. *Marriage of Jacobs* (1982) 128 CA3d 273, 283, 180 CR 234. Thereafter, the agreement is enforceable only by judgment remedies, *e.g.*, execution, appointment of a receiver, or contempt (see Fam C §290). See *Marriage of Lane* (1985) 165 CA3d 1143, 1147, 211 CR 262.

A marital settlement agreement, however, to the extent it is not merged into the judgment, retains its nature and enforceability as a contract. By carefully drafting the merger provisions, an attorney can use the marital settlement agreement format to gain the benefit of judgment remedies for provisions that are merged into the judgment (*e.g.*, custody, support), while retaining contract remedies for provisions that are not merged (*e.g.*, warranties). On which provisions are best enforced by each type of remedy, see §14.44.

§14.47　　(2) Expense

A stipulated judgment is usually faster and easier to prepare than a marital settlement agreement and is therefore less expensive for the client. If neither party will need to rely on a contractual remedy to enforce the agreement, a stipulated judgment may be the preferred format for its savings to the client. On the other hand, a defaulted respondent need not pay a filing fee for signing a marital settlement agreement that is submitted for incorporation in a proposed judgment (Govt C §26826(b)(3)), while a filing fee may be required before a stipulated judgment can be filed.

§14.48　　(3) Stage of Proceeding

Often, when a settlement is reached while the parties and their attorneys are in court for a settlement conference or trial, the agreement is stated on the record, constitutes a stipulated judgment, and is drafted as such. If the protections of a complete marital settlement agreement (see §§14.46, 14.49) are desired, it may be possible to continue the settlement conference or trial to a later date to allow for preparation of the agreement. In this event, all important provisions of the agreement should be read into the record to preserve the agreement, pending preparation of the complete document. Generally, when negotiations result in a settlement prior to the settlement conference or trial, a marital settlement agreement, rather than a stipulated judgment, will be prepared.

§14.49   (4) Privacy

In some cases, the parties may not want their settlement to be accessible to the public. With a stipulated judgment, privacy can be achieved by a court order on noticed motion to seal the file. Such an order may be available only in limited circumstances, depending on the court. With a marital settlement agreement, however, it is usually possible to keep at least those provisions not required by local rules to be expressly set out in the judgment from becoming part of the court file. For example, the marital settlement agreement may be incorporated in the judgment by reference only, rather than physically attached to the judgment. See *Flynn v Flynn* (1954) 42 C2d 55, 265 P2d 865. If the parties intend to incorporate the agreement for reference only, that purpose should be clearly indicated by cover letter or at the court hearing. The parties may also agree, as part of the agreement, that they will not divulge its contents to third parties unless required to do so for purposes of litigation.

On the right to request sealing of pleadings containing financial information, see §10.72.

§14.50   3. Judicial Discretion to Reject Agreement

Whether and to what extent a court may reject a settlement agreement in a marital action depends on the type of provision in question. It has traditionally been the law that the court has jurisdiction to make its own orders for child support, regardless of any agreement between the parents. See *Elkind v Byck* (1968) 68 C2d 453, 457, 67 CR 404, 407; *Marriage of Ayo* (1987) 190 CA3d 442, 451, 235 CR 458, 463. The statewide child support guideline expressly provides that stipulated agreements are subject to court approval. Fam C §4065(a).

It is an often-cited and widely held view that the court need not accept an agreement of the parents on child custody. See *Puckett v Puckett* (1943) 21 C2d 833, 839, 136 P2d 1, 4; *Van der Vliet v Van der Vliet* (1927) 200 C 721, 254 P 945. Nonetheless, the parents' agreement for joint legal and joint physical custody creates a presumption that such an arrangement is in the child's best interests. Fam C §§3002, 3080. Further, the court's authority to override the parents' custody agreement has not gone entirely unquestioned. See *Marriage of Wellman* (1980) 104 CA3d 992, 996, 164 CR 148, 151 (suggesting in dicta that court may not have authority to raise and decide custody issue absent dispute between parents). See also *Marriage of Schwartz* (1980) 104 CA3d 92, 163 CR 408 (accepting trial court's authority to reject parents' agreement, but reversing for ruling on basis of "unshakable prejudice" against parents' agreement).

On whether the court may reject the agreement of the parties on spousal support, earlier authority upheld the court's power to do so. See *Adams v Adams* (1947) 29 C2d 621, 624, 177 P2d 265, 267. More recent authority appears to support the opposite result. Under Fam C §3591(c), the parties now have the ability to make spousal support nonmodifiable. This statute suggests that they also have the ability to determine other aspects of the support provision. See *Marriage of Carletti* (1975) 53 CA3d 989, 995, 126 CR 1, 5. For a contrary view, see *Marriage of Benson* (1985) 171 CA3d 907, 912, 217 CR 589, in which the court suggested in dicta that the trial court could have rejected a stipulated judgment that was insufficient to protect the wife's future security.

Property provisions of a marital settlement agreement, in the absence of fraud or other invalidity, are binding on the court. *Adams v Adams, supra*. The requirement that the community estate be equally divided specifically does not apply when the parties agree otherwise. Fam C §2550.

C. Preparing the Judgment

§14.51   1. Discussion

When the respondent's default has been entered and there is no agreement of the parties (see §14.37), the proposed judgment is usually prepared by counsel for the petitioner without review or approval by the respondent. When the parties do have an agreement, the proposed judgment is prepared either as a stipulated judgment (see

§14.40) or in conjunction with a marital settlement agreement (see §§14.41-14.45). The judgment is prepared on the Judicial Council form of Judgment (usually with the form as the first two of several pages; see §14.54). The discussion in §§14.52-14.55 is keyed to the form.

On preparing a judgment on reserved issues after bifurcation of the issue of marital status, see §14.73.

§14.52 a. Marital Status

The box marked "Status only" should be checked when, on motion to the court, the parties' marital status has been bifurcated from all other issues in the marital action and a judgment is to be entered only for the purpose of terminating the parties' marital status. See Fam C §2337(a). After a status-only judgment has been entered, the box marked "Judgment on reserved issues" should be checked to obtain judgment on the issues reserved for later determination. On bifurcation of the issue of marital status, including preparation and entry of a status-only judgment and a judgment on reserved issues, see §§14.59-14.73.

On rare occasions, the parties may wish to have a judgment entered to determine all the issues of their marriage *except* marital status. In this event, the court will be asked to reserve jurisdiction over the date of termination of the marital status (see Fam C §2343), and the appropriate box in the caption of the form should be checked. Possible reasons for such a request include tax advantage, maintaining health insurance coverage, and qualifying for derivative social security benefits. Alternatively, the parties may desire a final resolution of the issues in the action even though they are attempting to reconcile.

The earliest possible date that the parties' marital status may be terminated is six months after service of process or appearance of the respondent, whichever is first. Fam C §2339. When the judgment will precede this date, the date that the marital status ends should be inserted on the form in the space provided and will usually be the earliest possible date. The parties may specify a later date (*e.g.,* for reasons of tax advantage, maintaining health insurance coverage, or qualifying for derivative social security benefits). If the judgment will be granted after the six-month period has elapsed, the date should be left blank for the court to enter unless a specific, later date is requested.

§14.53   b. Restoration of Former Name

A party is entitled to restoration of a former name on request, except in an action for legal separation. Fam C §2080. The requested order is indicated by checking the appropriate box at Item 4.f on the judgment and inserting the former name. A request to restore the former name need not have been included in the petition or response. See Fam C §2080. Even if the party fails to request the order at the time of the judgment, he or she may make an ex parte application after judgment for such an order. See Judicial Council Form FL-395 (Ex Parte Application for Restoration of Former Name After Entry of Judgment and Order), available in California Judicial Council Forms Manual §3 (Cal CEB 1981). Nothing in Fam C §2080 is to be construed to abrogate the common law right of any person to change one's name. Fam C §2082.

§14.54   c. Other Orders

A request for orders not otherwise specified on the Judicial Council form is indicated by checking Item 4.p. The specific provisions should be numbered consecutively and set forth separately. They may start on the Judicial Council form and continue on additional pages, or the words "See attached" may be inserted on the form with the provisions following on continuation pages. The additional pages may be prepared on either plain or pleading paper.

When the respondent's default has been entered and there is no agreement of the parties (see §14.37), the proposed orders are followed by spaces for the date the judgment is granted and the judge's signature. Neither the petitioner nor his or her attorney signs the proposed judgment.

When the parties are proceeding by stipulated judgment (see §14.40), the proposed judgment is executed at the end of all the provisions by both parties and their counsel, following the words "The foregoing is agreed to by:" immediately above the space reserved for the judge's signature. Cal Rules of Ct 5.116(a). For a complete sample stipulated judgment, see California Marital Settlement and Other Family Law Agreements, App B (3d ed Cal CEB 2005).

When the judgment is based on a marital settlement agreement (see §§14.41–14.45), local court rules may require the text of certain provisions to be set forth in the judgment itself. Care should betaken to phrase the judgment in the language of a court order rather than that of an agreement. Counsel may also wish to set forth other provisions not required by court rules, but desired to be merged into the judgment. See *Marriage of Lane* (1985) 165 CA3d 1143, 1148, 211 CR 262, 265 (physical incorporation of provision in body of judgment a factor in determining intent to merge provision into judgment). This should not be necessary, however, as long as the agreement and the judgment clearly indicate what provisions of the agreement are to be merged into the judgment. For sample merger language, see Marital Settlement Agreements §§16.20–16.21, Apps A, C. But note that local rules and practice should be consulted on whether a marital settlement agreement may be referred to in the judgment. In jurisdictions that so permit, language should be included after the substantive provisions, indicating the action the parties wish the court to take with respect to the marital settlement agreement. A typical provision indicates approval of the entire agreement as fair and equitable, orders the parties to comply with all executory provisions of the agreement, provides for merger of specified provisions (*e.g.,* child custody and visitation, child and spousal support) into the judgment, and incorporates the provisions not merged into the judgment for the sole purpose of identification. Care should be taken that the provision is consistent with that of the marital settlement agreement.

Blank lines for the date and the judge's signature follow these provisions. Where permitted, the original of the marital settlement agreement is then attached, unless the agreement is to be incorporated by reference only. For a complete sample judgment based on a marital settlement agreement, see Marital Settlement Agreements, App C.

Any time an order concerning child support is entered, Judicial Council Form FL-192 (Notice of Rights and Responsibilities: Health-Care Costs and Reimbursement Procedures and Information Sheet on Changing a Child Support Order) must be submitted with the order. Fam C §4063(a)(1), (2), 4010. Each time a modification of a court order for child support is filed with the court, a Child Support Case Registry form (Judicial Council Form FL-191) must be completed by one of the parties and filed with the court. The form is not filed in the court file but is stored in a nonpublic area until it is forwarded to the California Department of Social Services. Cal Rules of Ct 5.330(f).

§14.55   d. Judgment of Legal Separation or Nullity

In most respects, a judgment of legal separation or nullity is the same as a judgment of dissolution. The Judicial Council Form FL-180 (Judgment (Family Law)) is used, with the appropriate boxes in the caption and at Item 4.b or 4.c checked.

On the availability of orders other than the decree of legal separation or nullity itself, see §3.6 (legal separation), §§3.19–3.23 (nullity).

§14.56 2. Form: Judgment (Family Law) (Judicial Council Form FL-180)

FL-180

ATTORNEY OR PARTY WITHOUT ATTORNEY *(Name, State Bar number, and address)*:	FOR COURT USE ONLY

TELEPHONE NO.:   FAX NO. *(Optional)*:

E-MAIL ADDRESS *(Optional)*:

ATTORNEY FOR *(Name)*:

SUPERIOR COURT OF CALIFORNIA, COUNTY OF

STREET ADDRESS:

MAILING ADDRESS:

CITY AND ZIP CODE:

BRANCH NAME:

MARRIAGE OF

PETITIONER:

RESPONDENT:

JUDGMENT

☐ DISSOLUTION   ☐ LEGAL SEPARATION   ☐ NULLITY

    ☐ Status only

    ☐ Reserving jurisdiction over termination of marital or domestic partnership status

    ☐ Judgment on reserved issues

Date marital or domestic partnership status ends:

CASE NUMBER:

1. ☐ This judgment ☐ contains personal conduct restraining orders ☐ modifies existing restraining orders. The restraining orders are contained on page(s)   of the attachment. They expire on *(date)*:

2. This proceeding was heard as follows: ☐ Default or uncontested   ☐ By declaration under Family Code section 2336
   ☐ Contested
   a. Date: Dept.:   Room:
   b. Judicial officer *(name)*:   ☐ Temporary judge
   c. ☐ Petitioner present in court   ☐ Attorney present in court *(name)*:
   d. ☐ Respondent present in court   ☐ Attorney present in court *(name)*:
   e. ☐ Claimant present in court *(name)*:   ☐ Attorney present in court *(name)*:
   f. ☐ Other *(specify name)*:

3. The court acquired jurisdiction of the respondent on *(date)*:
   a. ☐ The respondent was served with process.
   b. ☐ The respondent appeared.

THE COURT ORDERS, GOOD CAUSE APPEARING

4. a. ☐ Judgment of dissolution is entered. Marital or domestic partnership status is terminated and the parties are restored to the status of single persons
       (1) ☐ on *(specify date)*:
       (2) ☐ on a date to be determined on noticed motion of either party or on stipulation.
   b. ☐ Judgment of legal separation is entered.
   c. ☐ Judgment of nullity is entered. The parties are declared to be single persons on the ground of *(specify)*:

   d. ☐ This judgment will be entered nunc pro tunc as of *(date)*:
   e. ☐ Judgment on reserved issues.
   f. The ☐ petitioner's ☐ respondent's former name is restored to *(specify)*:
   g. ☐ Jurisdiction is reserved over all other issues, and all present orders remain in effect except as provided below.
   h. ☐ This judgment contains provisions for child support or family support. Each party must complete and file with the court a *Child Support Case Registry Form* (form FL-191) within 10 days of the date of this judgment. The parents must notify the court of any change in the information submitted within 10 days of the change, by filing an updated form. The *Notice of Rights and Responsibilities—Health Care Costs and Reimbursement Procedures and Information Sheet on Changing a Child Support Order* (form FL-192) is attached.

Form Adopted for Mandatory Use
Judicial Council of California
FL-180 [Rev. January 1, 2007]

JUDGMENT
(Family Law)

CEB   Family Code, §§ 2024, 2340, 2343, 2346
www.courtinfo.ca.gov

Page 1 of 2

FL-180

CASE NAME *(Last name, first name of each party):*	CASE NUMBER:

4. *(Cont'd.)*

  i. ☐ A settlement agreement between the parties is attached.

  j. ☐ A written stipulation for judgment between the parties is attached.

  k. ☐ The children of this marriage or domestic partnership.

      (1) ☐ The children of this marriage or domestic partnership are:

         Name   Birthdate

      (2) ☐ Parentage is established for children of this relationship born prior to the marriage or domestic partnership.

  l. ☐ Child custody and visitation are ordered as set forth in the attached

      (1) ☐ settlement agreement, stipulation for judgment, or other written agreement.

      (2) ☐ *Child Custody and Visitation Order Attachment* (form FL-341).

      (3) ☐ *Stipulation and Order for Custody and/or Visitation of Children* (form FL-355).

      (4) ☐ other *(specify):*

  m. ☐ Child support is ordered as set forth in the attached

      (1) ☐ settlement agreement, stipulation for judgment, or other written agreement.

      (2) ☐ *Child Support Information and Order Attachment* (form FL-342).

      (3) ☐ *Stipulation to Establish or Modify Child Support and Order* (form FL-350).

      (4) ☐ other *(specify):*

  n. ☐ Spousal or partner support is ordered as set forth in the attached

      (1) ☐ settlement agreement, stipulation for judgment, or other written agreement.

      (2) ☐ *Spousal, Partner, or Family Support Order Attachment* (form FL-343).

      (3) ☐ other *(specify):*

      NOTICE: It is the goal of this state that each party will make reasonable good faith efforts to become self-supporting as provided for in Family Code section 4320. The failure to make reasonable good faith efforts may be one of the factors considered by the court as a basis for modifying or terminating spousal or partner support.

  o. ☐ Property division is ordered as set forth in the attached

      (1) ☐ settlement agreement, stipulation for judgment, or other written agreement.

      (2) ☐ *Property Order Attachment to Judgment* (form FL-345).

      (3) ☐ other *(specify):*

  p. ☐ Other *(specify):*

Each attachment to this judgment is incorporated into this judgment, and the parties are ordered to comply with each attachment's provisions.

Jurisdiction is reserved to make other orders necessary to carry out this judgment.

Date:

                                 JUDICIAL OFFICER

5. Number of pages attached: _____   ☐ SIGNATURE FOLLOWS LAST ATTACHMENT

NOTICE

Dissolution or legal separation may automatically cancel the rights of a spouse or domestic partner under the other spouse's or domestic partner's will, trust, retirement plan, power of attorney, pay-on-death bank account, transfer-on-death vehicle registration, survivorship rights to any property owned in joint tenancy, and any other similar thing. It does not automatically cancel the rights of a spouse or domestic partner as beneficiary of the other spouse's or domestic partner's life insurance policy. You should review these matters, as well as any credit cards, other credit accounts, insurance policies, retirement plans, and credit reports, to determine whether they should be changed or whether you should take any other actions.

A debt or obligation may be assigned to one party as part of the dissolution of property and debts, but if that party does not pay the debt or obligation, the creditor may be able to collect from the other party.

An earnings assignment may be issued without additional proof if child, family, partner, or spousal support is ordered.

Any party required to pay support must pay interest on overdue amounts at the "legal rate," which is currently 10 percent.

FL-180 [Rev. January 1, 2007]   **JUDGMENT**   ⒸEB   Page 2 of 2
                                    (Family Law)

Copies: Original (submit to court clerk); one or more copies for court (check local practice); copy for other party or counsel; office copies.

D. Notice of Entry of Judgment

§14.57 **1. Discussion**

Judicial Council Form FL-190 (Notice of Entry of Judgment) is submitted to the court with a stamped envelope for each party, addressed in the same manner as on the form. Cal Rules of Ct 5.136. The return address should be the address of the court clerk. See Fam C §2338.5(c). The appropriate box should be marked on the form, indicating the type of judgment to be entered. The date specified, if any, for the termination of marital status should be the same as on the judgment (see §14.52). The parties' names should be listed in care of their respective counsel, or at their own addresses if unrepresented, for the purpose of mailing the notice of entry of judgment. If service was by publication and the respondent's address is still unknown, this information must be stated in place of the respondent's address. Cal Rules of Ct 5.136(c).

§14.58   2. Form: Notice of Entry of Judgment (Judicial Council Form FL-190)

FL-190

ATTORNEY OR PARTY WITHOUT ATTORNEY (Name, State Bar number, and address):	FOR COURT USE ONLY

TELEPHONE NO.:   FAX NO. (Optional):
E-MAIL ADDRESS (Optional):
ATTORNEY FOR (Name):

SUPERIOR COURT OF CALIFORNIA, COUNTY OF

STREET ADDRESS:
MAILING ADDRESS:
CITY AND ZIP CODE:
BRANCH NAME:

PETITIONER:

RESPONDENT:

NOTICE OF ENTRY OF JUDGMENT	CASE NUMBER:

You are notified that the following judgment was entered on (date):

1. ☐ Dissolution
2. ☐ Dissolution—status only
3. ☐ Dissolution—reserving jurisdiction over termination of marital status or domestic partnership
4. ☐ Legal separation
5. ☐ Nullity
6. ☐ Parent-child relationship
7. ☐ Judgment on reserved issues
8. ☐ Other (specify):

Date:

Clerk, by _____, Deputy

—NOTICE TO ATTORNEY OF RECORD OR PARTY WITHOUT ATTORNEY—

Under the provisions of Code of Civil Procedure section 1952, if no appeal is filed the court may order the exhibits destroyed or otherwise disposed of after 60 days from the expiration of the appeal time.

STATEMENT IN THIS BOX APPLIES ONLY TO JUDGMENT OF DISSOLUTION

Effective date of termination of marital or domestic partnership status (specify):

WARNING: Neither party may remarry or enter into a new domestic partnership until the effective date of the termination of marital or domestic partnership status, as shown in this box.

CLERK'S CERTIFICATE OF MAILING

I certify that I am not a party to this cause and that a true copy of the Notice of Entry of Judgment was mailed first class, postage fully prepaid, in a sealed envelope addressed as shown below, and that the notice was mailed at (place): _____, California, on (date):

Date: Clerk, by _____, Deputy

┌─ Name and address of petitioner or petitioner's attorney ─┐   ┌─ Name and address of respondent or respondent's attorney ─┐

Page 1 of 1

Form Adopted for Mandatory Use
Judicial Council of California
FL-190 [Rev. January 1, 2005]

NOTICE OF ENTRY OF JUDGMENT
(Family Law—Uniform Parentage—Custody and Support)

Family Code, §§ 2338, 7636, 7637
www.courtinfo.ca.gov

Copies: Original and two copies (all submitted to court clerk).

§14.59 VI. BIFURCATION OF MARITAL STATUS ISSUE

Under Fam C §2337(a), the court may, on noticed motion, sever ("bifurcate") and grant an early and separate trial on the issue of the dissolution of the parties' marriage, apart from other issues in the action. See *Marriage of Fink* (1976) 54 CA3d 357, 126 CR 626, decision on reserved issues appealed on other grounds in 25 C3d 877. Whether the court should grant the requested bifurcation and issue a status-only judgment terminating the parties' marriage is an issue of law (*Gionis v Superior Court* (1988) 202 CA3d 786, 790, 248 CR 741), the determination of which is within the judicial discretion of the court (*Marriage of Lusk* (1978) 86 CA3d 228, 235, 150 CR 63).

The court also has the power to bifurcate and try separately issues other than marital status, *e.g.,* child custody (Fam C §3023); child support (Fam C §4003); and other issues in marital actions, *e.g.,* the validity of a postnuptial or premarital agreement, the date of separation, whether property is separate or community (Cal Rules of Ct 5.175). On the utility of bifurcating a "pivotal" issue to encourage settlement of the remaining issues, see *Marriage of Wolfe* (1985) 173 CA3d 889, 894, 219 CR 337.

§14.60 A. Reasons for Bifurcation

One party may request bifurcation of the issue of marital status because of, for example, a desire to remarry or obtain a more favorable tax status, if it appears that other issues in the action (*e.g.,* custody of minor children, division of property) will require a lengthy period before settlement or trial. A legislative intent embodied in the former Family Law Act—that the resolution of marital status not be postponed merely because other issues are not ready for resolution—favors bifurcation (*Gionis v Superior Court* (1988) 202 CA3d 786, 788, 248 CR 741), and the requesting party need show only slight evidence to obtain bifurcation and termination of marital status (202 CA3d at 790).

In *Gionis,* a declaration alleging irrevocable failure of the marriage, the need for discovery and a lengthy trial, a desire to simplify the acquisition of property and credit, and the possibility of remarriage (202 CA3d at 787, 789 n1) stated sufficient grounds for granting bifurcation and dissolving the parties' marriage. Additional grounds for bifurcation might include, *e.g.,* the other party's stated intent to prolong the resolution of the marital action, the other party's refusal to cooperate in business or real property transactions, or resolution of the emotional issue of dissolution to facilitate settlement of the other reserved issues.

To successfully counter a request for bifurcation, the opposing party must show compelling reasons why he or she would be prejudiced by an early termination of marital status. 202 CA3d at 789. When it became effective on January 1, 1989, former CC §4515, predecessor of Fam C §2337, made this burden even more difficult to meet than before because it enabled the court to impose conditions on an order of bifurcation to protect the opposing party from prejudice. The enactment of Prob C §5600 (operative January 1, 2002), however, considerably increased the risk of a bifurcation (to terminate marital status) to the nonmoving party with respect to assets subject to nonprobate transfer or transfer by operation of law. See §14.61.

NOTE➤ Given the historic reluctance of judges to deny requests for bifurcation, counsel for a party who opposes it must use every effort to ensure that real protection is put in place for the client and may have the burden of educating the judge on the potentially draconian effects of leaving the party opposing the bifurcation unprotected against severe financial loss in the event of the other party's death before a judgment on the remaining issues. This is of particular concern if retirement or other deferred compensation benefits have not been divided and the nonemployee spouse has not been designated as surviving spouse with regard to these benefits. Counsel should be especially aware of issues concerning bifurcation and military pensions. On conditions that may be imposed by the court in granting bifurcation, see §14.61.

§14.61 B. Conditional Bifurcation

The granting of bifurcation and a status-only judgment may cause the loss of valuable rights associated with marital status (*e.g.,* health insurance coverage, surviving spouse benefits, derivative Social Security benefits, benefits to a military spouse) earlier than if marital status was determined with all other issues. Under Fam C §2337(c), the court may impose various requirements on a party who seeks bifurcation as a condition to severing the issue of marital status. The party requesting bifurcation can also agree to certain conditions as part of the bifurcation request. See Application for Separate Trial (Judicial Council Form FL-315), §14.67. In the event of that party's death, an order imposing such conditions would continue to be binding on his or her estate. Fam C §2337(c). If the party dies after entry of judgment granting a dissolution of marriage, any obligation imposed by Fam C §2337 will be enforceable against any asset, including proceeds from the asset, against which such obligations would have been enforceable before the person's death. Fam C §2337(e).

Conditional orders that may be imposed. The statute (Fam C §2337) provides that any or all of the following orders may be imposed on the party requesting bifurcation:

- Indemnification of the opposing party from tax liability (including taxes, reassessments, interest, and penalties) that may be caused by the termination of marital status occurring before the division of the parties' community property. Fam C §2337(c)(1).

- Maintenance, until judgment is entered and becomes final on all remaining issues, of existing or comparable health and medical insurance coverage for the opposing party and the minor children or, if insurance is not maintained, payment of health and medical expenses that would have been covered by insurance. Fam C §2337(c)(2).

- Indemnification, until judgment is entered and becomes final on all remaining issues, of the opposing party from adverse consequences caused by a termination of that party's rights (1) to a probate homestead in the residence in which the other party resides at the time the bifurcation is granted and (2) to a probate allowance as the surviving spouse of the other party. Fam C §2337(c)(3)-(4).

- Indemnification, until judgment is entered and becomes final on all remaining issues, of the opposing party from adverse consequences caused by loss of that party's rights to pension benefits, elections, or survivors' benefits under the other party's pension or retirement plan, to the extent that the opposing party would have been entitled to such rights as the surviving spouse. Fam C §2337(c)(5).

- Joinder of the requesting party's pension plan as a party to the marital action and, if applicable, entry of an order under Fam C §2610 with reference to the plan pending the ultimate resolution of the distribution of benefits. Fam C §2337(c)(6).

- Indemnification of the opposing party from adverse consequences caused by the loss of that party's rights to social security benefits or elections, to the extent that the opposing party would have been entitled to such rights as the surviving spouse. Fam C §2337(c)(7).

- Any other condition that the court determines is just and equitable. Fam C §2337(c)(8).

Practical limitations of conditional orders and related issues. Counsel should keep in mind that it is not enough merely to recite the words contained in Fam C §2337 into the bifurcation judgment if one is representing a nonmoving party (often the nonemployee spouse). Despite the availability of the Fam C §2337 conditions, if a court grants a bifurcation, these conditions offer the nonmoving party little practical relief if the other spouse dies after a bifurcation that terminates marital status and before a judgment determining property and support issues. In that event, the former spouse must seek relief in Probate Court, where he or she may be competing with secured creditors, child support obligations from a new marriage, or other heirs. In addition, the nonmoving party risks losing the community property share or survivor benefits associated with bank accounts, certificates of deposit, and other assets of which he or she would otherwise have been the beneficiary. This is because:

- Prob C §5600 provides that a nonprobate transfer to the transferor's former spouse will fail, with limited exceptions; and

- Under Prob C §5601, a joint tenancy in any property will be severed if at the time of the transferor's death, the former spouse is not the surviving spouse as a result of a dissolution, unless, among other measures or circumstances provided in §5600, the parties stipulate or the nonmoving spouse can obtain an order before the bifurcation providing that the nonprobate transfer is not subject to revocation by the transferor at the time of his or her death (see Prob C §5600(b)(3)).

There are several ways to protect the nonmoving, surviving party (the soon-to-be former spouse). Ideally, the party moving to bifurcate to terminate marital status will be willing to cooperate in entering into stipulated "side" orders temporarily dividing the assets subject to Prob C §5600. Alternatively, if it is not possible to obtain agreement on a temporary division, or if there is not enough time to obtain the information necessary to draft orders at the time of bifurcation, then counsel should request that the judgment terminating marital status provide, along with the language of Fam C §2337, an order stating that pending a judgment on reserved issues, all current beneficiary designations, nonprobate transfers, and survivor rights are not subject to automatic revocation on dissolution of marital status, and that the order is intended to comply with Prob C §5600(b)(2) and (3).

If a number of orders dividing the assets are included in the judgment bifurcating marital status, it may be necessary for both parties to serve final declarations of disclosure before the clerk will accept the judgment. For this reason, a simpler alternative would be to include these provisions in a "side" stipulation that is entered before, or simultaneously with, the judgment. If "final" declarations of disclosure are served before discovery is completed, counsel should bear in mind the continuing duty each party has to immediately, fully, and accurately update and augment his or her disclosure to the extent that material changes have occurred. Fam C §2100(c).

In the event the moving party objects to the proposed protective stipulations or requested order, then it will be necessary to persuade the judge to (1) defer the bifurcation of status until the division of the assets subject to nonprobate transfer has been negotiated or litigated, or (2) make an order exempting the relevant assets from Prob C §5600 a further condition of the bifurcation.

In the absence of such stipulations or orders, a notice of adverse interest or even a temporary restraining order pursuant to Cal Rules of Ct 5.106 should be served on the administrator of each account or asset before entry of a bifurcated judgment. See Cal Rules of Ct 5.106 (court may grant injunctive or other relief against or for person who is acting as trustee, agent, custodian, or similar fiduciary with respect to any property subject to disposition by court). In addition, if ERISA-governed retirement benefits are involved, counsel should consider obtaining a temporary or provisional QDRO before entry of the bifurcated judgment, even if that order will later need to be revised and refined. For related discussion and a sample form, see Dividing Pensions and Other Employee Benefits in California Divorces, chap 6 (Cal CEB 2006).

If such an order is not in place, the nonemployee (alternate payee) spouse risks not only the loss of the appropriate share of the benefit but also of any available survivor benefits should the employee spouse die or remarry before the reserved issues have been resolved. See *Hopkins v AT&T Global Information Solutions Co.* (4th Cir 1997) 105 F3d 153, 156 (order attempting to give former spouse interest in qualified joint and survivor annuity was not QDRO, because right vested in employee's second spouse and was no longer payable with respect to participant); *Samaroo v Samaroo* (3d Cir 1999) 193 F3d 185 (nunc pro tunc amendment of divorce decree after employee's death to divide qualified preretirement survivor annuity was not valid QDRO). Even though some more recent cases have resulted in posthumous or nunc pro tunc QDROs being recognized as valid, the lack of uniformity among federal circuits and lack of a case on point in the Ninth Circuit mandate that counsel obtain the best protection possible for the nonempoyee spouse.

On the plan joinder (see Fam C §2060) and related discussion of service of notice of an adverse interest (see Fam C §755), see chap 12 and Dividing Pensions and Other Employee Benefits in California Divorces, chap 2 (Cal CEB 2006). On the requirement that an employee spouse furnish to the nonemployee spouse within 30 days after written request the name of the plan and the name, title, address, and telephone number of the plan's trustee, administrator, or agent for service of process for each employee benefit plan covering him or her, see Fam C §2062(c).

§14.62   C. Procedure

When the respondent's default has been entered and there is no agreement of the parties (see §14.37), the petitioner may prepare and file a Declaration for Default or Uncontested Dissolution or Legal Separation (see §§14.23–14.24), requesting entry of a status-only judgment. The declaration is submitted to the court with a proposed status-only judgment (see §14.70) and a notice of entry of judgment (see §§14.57–14.58).

If the respondent has made an appearance, the party who seeks bifurcation must either obtain the other party's consent (see §§14.63–14.64) or set a hearing for the court to make a decision (see

§§14.65–14.69). In view of the likelihood that the court will grant a request for bifurcation, and at the same time impose conditions, if necessary, to eliminate any prejudice that may be caused by the early termination of marital status (Fam C §2337(c); see §14.61), it may be a savings to both parties to stipulate to bifurcation, agreeing to the conditions that are necessary to prevent loss to the other party. If it is not possible to stipulate to bifurcation, the party wishing an early resolution of marital status must bring a motion in the action or proceed on an Order to Show Cause to request bifurcation.

1. Stipulation for Bifurcation

§14.63   a. Discussion

Parties who agree to bifurcate the issue of marital status may enter into a stipulation and order providing for bifurcation and the entry of a status-only judgment. The stipulation and order should also set forth any requirements agreed to be imposed on the party requesting bifurcation as a condition of the order. See §14.61. The stipulation should be submitted to the court with an Appearance, Stipulations and Waivers (see §§14.18–14.19), a Declaration for Default or Uncontested Dissolution or Legal Separation (see §§14.23–14.24) requesting entry of a status-only judgment (see Item 15), the proposed status-only judgment (see §§14.51–14.53, 14.56), and a notice of entry of judgment (see §§14.57–14.58).

§14.64   b. Form: Stipulation for Bifurcation and Order

_ _[Attorney name]_ _
_ _[State Bar number]_ _
_ _[Address]_ _
_ _[Telephone number]_ _

Attorney for _ _[name]_ _

SUPERIOR COURT OF CALIFORNIA
COUNTY OF _ _ _ _ _ _ _ _

Marriage of	)	**No. _ _ _ _ _ _**
	)	
Petitioner: _ _ _ _ _ _ _ _	)	**STIPULATION FOR**
	)	**BIFURCATION OF MARITAL**
Respondent: _ _ _ _ _ _ _ _	)	**STATUS AND ENTRY OF**
	)	**STATUS-ONLY JUDGMENT;**
_____	)	**ORDER (FAM C §2337)**

   _ _[Name]_ _, **petitioner, and** _ _[name]_ _, **respondent, hereby stipulate that the Court may sever the issue of the dissolution of the parties' marriage from other issues in this action; that the Court may impose on** _ _[petitioner/respondent]_ _ **the conditions set forth below on granting a severance of the issue of the dissolution of the marriage; that, in the event of the death of** _ _[petitioner/respondent]_ _, **the following conditions will continue to be binding on** _ _[his/her]_ _ **estate; and that the Court may enter a judgment of dissolution of the parties' marriage in the form agreed to by the parties, a copy of which is attached to this document.**

[Insert conditions of bifurcation (see §14.61)]

   The foregoing is agreed to by:

Date: _____

                                __[Signature]__
                                _ _[Typed name]_ _
                                Petitioner

Date: _____

                                __[Signature]__
                                _ _[Typed name]_ _
                                Respondent

Approved as conforming to the agreement of the parties:

Date: _____   __[Signature]__
                                _ _[Typed name]_ _
                                Attorney for Petitioner

Date: _____   __[Signature]__
                                _ _[Typed name]_ _
                                Attorney for Respondent

ORDER

Good cause appearing, it is ordered that:

1. The issue of the dissolution of the parties' marriage is severed from other issues in this action.

2. The following conditions are imposed on _ _[petitioner/respondent]_ _:

[Insert conditions of bifurcation as set forth in stipulation]

3. In the event of the death of _ _[petitioner/respondent]_ _, the foregoing conditions will continue to be binding on _ _[his/her]_ _ estate.

4. The judgment of dissolution of the parties' marriage will be entered in this action.

Date: _____   _____
                                Judge of the Superior Court

Copies: Original (submit to court clerk); copy for other party or counsel; office copies.

§14.65   2. Motion to Bifurcate

If the parties cannot agree to bifurcate the issue of marital status from the other issues in the action, the party seeking bifurcation may file an Application for Separate Trial and supporting documents with the court to obtain a hearing on the matter. See §14.66 and the comment to §14.67 regarding how it is filed. A preliminary declaration of disclosure (see §§13.45, 13.49) with a completed Schedule of Assets and Debts (see §13.28) must be served on the nonmoving party with the Request for Separate Trial unless the preliminary declaration has been served previously or the parties stipulate in writing to defer its service until a later time. Fam C §2337(b). The motion shall be heard no later than the trial-setting conference. Cal Rules of Ct 5.175(a).

When the motion to bifurcate is granted at the hearing, the issue of marital status is typically then heard as part of the same hearing.

a. Application for Separate Trial

§14.66   (1) Discussion

The party requesting bifurcation completes, files, and serves the Judicial Council Form FL-315 (Application for Separate Trial) as an attachment to an Order to Show Cause or a Notice of Motion, though some court clerks will accept the Application for Separate Trial as a stand-alone form (see the Comment to §14.67). A Preliminary Declaration of Disclosure (see §§13.45, 13.49) with a completed Schedule of Assets and Debts (see §13.28) must be served on the nonmoving party with the Request for Separate Trial unless the preliminary declaration has been served previously or the parties stipulate in writing to defer its service until a later time. Fam C §2337(b). The hearing date is obtained from the court. A declaration from the party should always be submitted with the request form, briefly stating the party's reasons for seeking bifurcation (see §14.60). Submission of a brief memorandum of points and authorities discussing Fam C §2337 and relevant case law is advisable. The request form must be signed by the requesting party under penalty of perjury. See form in §14.67.

On preparing a motion and proceeding on an Order to Show Cause, see §§11.16–11.20.

§14.67 (2) Form: Application for Separate Trial (Judicial Council Form FL-315)

FL-315

PETITIONER:	CASE NUMBER:
RESPONDENT:	
OTHER:	

APPLICATION FOR SEPARATE TRIAL

Attachment to ☐ Order to Show Cause ☐ Notice of Motion
(form FL-300) (form FL-301)

I, *(name):* , request that the court sever (bifurcate) and grant an early and separate trial on the following issue or issues:

1. a. ☐ Dissolution of the status of the marriage (Fam. Code, § 2337).
   I will serve with this application my preliminary *Declaration of Disclosure* and completed *Schedule of Assets and Debts* unless they have been previously served or the parties have stipulated in writing to defer service.

   b. ☐ I request the following conditions be made:
   (1) ☐ That I indemnify and hold the other party harmless from "taxes, reassessments, interest, and penalties" payable in the event that a dissolution prior to the property division results in taxes that would not have been payable if the parties were still married at the time of the division.
   (2) ☐ That I maintain health and medical insurance for the other party and minor children as long as possible, and then must obtain comparable coverage or pay any expenses that would have been covered by insurance.
   (3) ☐ That I hold the other party harmless re probate homestead.
   (4) ☐ That I hold the other party harmless re probate family allowance.
   (5) ☐ That I hold the other party harmless re pension benefits, elections, or survivors' benefits.
   (6) ☐ That I join the pension plan and, if the other party has a private plan covered by ERISA, will cause a Qualified Domestic Relations Order (QDRO) to be served on the plan.
   (7) ☐ That I hold the other party harmless re social security benefits.
   (8) ☐ Any other condition that the court determines is just and equitable.

2. ☐ Permanent custody and visitation of the children of the marriage.

3. ☐ Date of separation of the parties.

4. ☐ Alternate valuation date for property.

5. ☐ Validity of marital settlement agreement entered into prior to or during the marriage.

6. ☐ Other *(specify):*

7. a. ☐ I request that the court conduct this separate trial on the hearing date.
   or
   b. ☐ I will, at the hearing, ask the court to set a date for this separate trial.

8. The reasons in support of this request are *(specify):*
   ☐ Points and authorities attached. ☐ Supporting declarations attached.

I declare under penalty of perjury under the laws of the State of California that the foregoing is true and correct.

Date:

▶

_____ _____
(TYPE OR PRINT NAME) (SIGNATURE OF DECLARANT)

Page 1 of 1

Form Adopted for Mandatory Use	**APPLICATION FOR SEPARATE TRIAL**	Family Code, § 2337
Judicial Council of California	**(Family Law)**	www.courtinfo.ca.gov
FL-315 [Rev. January 1, 2003]		

Copies: Original (file with court clerk); copy for service; office copies.

Comment: This form is designed to be filed as an attachment to Judicial Council Forms FL-300 or FL-301 and that is the customary practice in most courts. Some court clerks, however, will accept this form without an accompanying Order to Show Cause or Notice of Motion cover sheet. If not familiar with local practice, counsel should check with the court clerk before proceeding.

§14.68   b. Response

If the other party does not consent to bifurcation, or requests protective orders as a condition of bifurcation (see §14.61), it appears that he or she must file and serve papers opposing the application as he or she would any notice of motion or Order to Show Cause. See §11.38. The opposition should take the form of a declaration and a memorandum of points and authorities.

The responding party's declaration must show "compelling" reasons to justify a denial of the requested bifurcation. *Gionis v Superior Court* (1988) 202 CA3d 786, 790, 248 CR 741. It may be possible to meet this burden by showing that anticipated prejudice cannot be cured by imposing protective conditions on the requesting party. In most cases, however, protective conditions can eliminate any expected loss, and the declarant should specify all conditions required in his or her declaration. On conditions that may be imposed, see §14.61. The declaration should state why an early termination of marital status will cause prejudice that cannot be cured by the imposition of conditions or, if conditions are requested, why they are necessary to protect the responding party from prejudice. On considerations regarding Prob C §5600, see §14.60.

There would appear to be no reason the responding party could not oppose the motion for bifurcation and, in the alternative, request conditions if the motion is granted.

§14.69   c. Findings and Order After Hearing

The Judicial Council form of Findings and Order After Hearing (see §11.55) is used to set forth the court's order bifurcating marital status in a dissolution proceeding. At Item 8, the box labeled "As attached" is checked. The order itself should be set forth on pleading paper, provide that the motion for bifurcation is granted, and state the terms of any conditions imposed on the party requesting bifurcation.

NOTE► In some counties, only the Judicial Council form of Judgment (see §14.56) is used to reflect the outcome of the bifurcation hearing, as opposed to using both that form and the Findings and Order After Hearing form. If bifurcation has been sought on an issue *other than* termination of marital status, however, such as to determine the validity of a premarital agreement, the Findings and Order After Hearing form would be needed. Counsel should otherwise verify the local practice with respect to using the Findings and Order After Hearing form in marital status-only bifurcations.

§14.70   3. Status-Only Judgment

The Judicial Council form of Judgment (see §14.56) is used to enter the status-only judgment. In the caption of the form, the box for "Status only" will be checked. The date that the marital status ends should be inserted in the caption, and at Item 4.a.(1), and will usually be the earliest possible date, *i.e.,* six months after service of process or appearance of the respondent, whichever is first (Fam C §2339(a)). If the judgment will be granted after the six-month period has elapsed, and if the judgment is submitted based on a stipulation of the parties, the date should be left blank for the court to enter. If the judgment is submitted after a hearing, the hearing date should be inserted as the date the marital status ends, unless the hearing is before the six-month period has elapsed, in which case the six-month date should be inserted. Item 4.g. of the judgment, providing for a reservation of jurisdiction over all other issues in the action, must also be checked. See Fam C §2337(d).

To obtain entry of the judgment, the Judicial Council form of Notice of Entry of Judgment (see §14.58) is submitted to the court, together with the status-only judgment and a stamped envelope for each party, addressed in the same manner as on the form. Cal Rules of Ct 5.136. On obtaining entry of the judgment generally, see §14.57.

The status-only judgment is immediately appealable on certification by the trial court (Fam C §2025; CCP §904.1(a)(10); see *Kinsler v Superior Court* (1981) 121 CA3d 808, 175 CR 564; *Marriage of Fink* (1976) 54 CA3d 357, 360, 126 CR 626, 628, decision on reserved issues appealed on other grounds in 25 C3d 877), as long as the appellant objected to the termination of marital status at the trial of that issue (Fam C §2341(b)).

PRACTICE TIP➤ Counsel should keep track of clients who filed or were served with petitions in the first half of the year and timely inquire about whether a status-only judgment would benefit them. Court processing of status-only judgments can become delayed towards the end of the year, so it is wise to know the court's deadline for submission of such judgments.

§14.71   D. Disposition of Reserved Issues

After entry of the status-only judgment, the court's jurisdiction continues over all issues other than marital status until judgment is rendered on the reserved issues. The death of a party after a status-only judgment does not abate an action; the court retains jurisdiction to dispose of the remaining issues. *Kinsler v Superior Court* (1981) 121 CA3d 808, 175 CR 564.

§14.72   1. Dismissal of Action

Under CCP §§583.310 and 583.360, civil actions generally (including marital actions; see Cal Rules of Ct 5.21) must be dismissed, on the court's own motion or on that of the defendant or respondent, if not brought to trial within five years after the action was commenced. Note, however, that an action for dissolution of marriage or legal separation may not be dismissed when:

- An order for child support has been issued and has not been terminated by the court or by operation of law (CCP §583.161(a));

- An order for spousal support has been issued and has not been terminated by the court (CCP §583.161(b)); or

- The action is for dissolution and a separate trial has been held on the issue of the status of the marriage (CCP §583.161(c)).

Thus, when a child support order has not been terminated by the court or by operation of law or a spousal support order has not been terminated by the court, the five-year statute is tolled as to *all* reserved issues. See *Lakkees v Superior Court* (1990) 222 CA3d 531, 539, 271 CR 845. Further, if, at the time the statute resumes running, less than six months remains to bring an action to trial, the petitioner has six months to bring the case to trial before it may be dismissed. CCP §583.350; see *Lakkees v Superior Court, supra.*

The separate "trial" on the issue of the status of the marriage that is required under CCP §583.161(c) to preclude dismissal may be either contested or uncontested. *Marriage of Dunmore* (1996) 45 CA4th 1372, 1375, 53 CR2d 450.

§14.73   2. Judgment on Reserved Issues

Once marital status has been terminated, the remaining issues may be resolved by agreement or brought to trial. In either case, the reserved issues are resolved by a judgment on reserved issues that is prepared on the Judicial Council form of Judgment (see §14.56).

If a marital settlement agreement will be attached and incorporated in the judgment, then the judgment (like any judgment incorporating a marital settlement agreement) must (1) expressly set forth those provisions required by local rules or practice to be set forth in full in the judgment and (2) indicate the court action being taken with respect to the agreement. On provisions to include in the judgment, see §14.54; on incorporation, approval, and merger of marital settlement agreements, see §§14.42–14.44.

Any time an order concerning child support is entered, including a judgment on reserved issues, Judicial Council Form FL-192 (Notice of Rights and Responsibilities: Health-Care Costs and Reimbursement Procedures and Information Sheet on Changing a Child Support Order) must be submitted with the order. Fam C §4063(a)(1), (2), 4010. Each time an initial court order for child support or family support or a modification of a court order for child support is filed with the court, a Child Support Case Registry form (Judicial Council Form FL-191) must be completed by one of the parties and filed with the court.

15

Pretrial Procedures and Trial Preparation

§15.1   I. SCOPE OF CHAPTER

This chapter addresses pretrial procedures and trial preparation in marital actions. The sections on pretrial procedures cover case management plans, at-issue memoranda, trial-setting conferences, settlement conferences, and trial continuances. The sections on trial preparation provide a general overview, with an emphasis on aspects peculiar to marital actions. No attempt is made to discuss in depth the principles of trial preparation, which are the same in trials of marital actions as in other civil trials. For further discussion, see California Trial Practice: Civil Procedure During Trial (3d ed Cal CEB 1995); Effective Introduction of Evidence in California (2d ed Cal CEB 2000); Effective Direct & Cross-Examination (Cal CEB 1986).

§15.2   II. PRETRIAL PROCEDURES

Because there are no California Rules of Court that specifically address pretrial procedures in marital actions, the general provisions in the rules apply. See Cal Rules of Ct 5.21. In addition, counties typically adopt local rules governing pretrial procedures, some applicable to civil actions generally and others (see, *e.g.,* Alameda Ct R 11.0–11.4, 5) specifically applicable to family law actions. See CCP §575.1. It is imperative that counsel become familiar with applicable local rules in every instance.

Traditionally, most California courts have followed a "master calendar" system, in which cases are kept in a pool, assigned (usually by the presiding judge) for different types of proceedings (*e.g.,* law and motion arguments, discovery disputes) to various judicial officers, and then, when ready for trial, assigned to the first available trial judge. Courts typically have family law departments that hear pendente lite and postjudgment proceedings, but most of them maintain the master calendar system for trials. The pretrial procedures discussed in §§15.4–15.7 are traditional master calendar procedures for bringing cases to trial.

Some courts (*e.g.,* Alameda, Contra Costa, Los Angeles Central District) have adopted an "individual calendar" system (also known as "direct calendaring") for family law cases, in which a case is assigned at the time of filing to one department for all purposes, including trial. Such courts often have local rules on bringing family law cases to trial, which differ significantly from the traditional master calendar procedures discussed in §§15.4–15.7. Effective July 1, 1997, all dissolution actions, to the greatest extent possible, must be assigned to the same superior court department for all purposes, in order that all decisions in a case through judgment will be made by the same judicial officer. Fam C §2330.3.

Note that family law cases are exempt from the "fast-track" program under the Trial Court Delay Reduction Act (Govt C §§68600–68620). Govt C §68608(a).

On pretrial procedures in civil actions generally, see California Civil Procedure Before Trial, chaps 12–13, 32–34, 40–50 (4th ed Cal CEB 2004).

§15.3 A. Case Management Plan

The legislature has provided for ordering of a case management plan. Fam C §§2450–2452. The purpose of case management is to provide judicial assistance and management to the parties in dissolution actions in order to expedite the processing of the case, reduce litigation expense, and focus on early resolution by settlement. Fam C §2450(a).

On the motion of a party, or the court's own motion, the court must hold a preliminary status conference to consider whether case management will be undertaken and a case management plan ordered. A party's motion would presumably be prepared and processed in the same manner as a notice of motion for temporary orders. For discussion of, and forms for, motions for temporary orders, see §§11.16–11.63. The moving party prepares the Judicial Council forms of Notice of Motion (see §11.20) and Application for Order and Supporting Declaration (see §11.22). A case management plan requires the parties' stipulation and may be terminated at any time on the parties' stipulation or court order. Fam C §2450(b). By contrast, under Fam C §2032(d), after a court makes a requested finding that a case involves complex or substantial issues (involving property, visitation, custody, or support), the court may order a case management plan to allocate various fees and costs between the parties—potentially over a party's objection. The court may also order that a referee be appointed pursuant to CCP §639 to oversee the case management plan.

A case management plan may include, *e.g.*, early neutral case evaluation, alternative dispute resolution, limitations on discovery, use of telephone conference calls, modification or waiver of requirements of procedural statutes, jointly selected or court-appointed expert witnesses, and bifurcation of issues for trial. Fam C §2451.

§15.4 B. Case Management Conference

To substitute a contemporary case management approach for the

older "at issue" approach to trial setting, former Cal Rules of Ct
209 (Civil Cases at Issue) was repealed effective July 1, 2002, and
replaced by new Cal Rules of Ct 209, which requires courts to adopt
local rules to differentiate between types of cases and the time required for their disposition. See Notes, Cal Rules of Ct 3.110. The
approach of the new and amended Rules of Court that became effective July 1, 2002, requires, in most cases, a case management conference attended by the parties' counsel at which the court issues orders
to control the subsequent course of the case. Cal Rules of Ct
212(b)(1), (i). No later than 30 calendar days before the conference,
the parties must meet and confer about matters to be discussed at
the conference (*e.g.,* a discovery schedule) (Cal Rules of Ct 212(f)),
and they must file a written case review conference statement 15
calendar days before the conference. Cal Rules of Ct 212(g). On
the parties' stipulation or the court's own motion, the court may
order that the case is a short cause case exempted from case management and set it for trial. Cal Rules of Ct 3.735.

For the most part, family law cases are *excluded* from the coverage
of the new rules. See Cal Rules of Ct 3.110(a) (new rules for service
of pleadings do not apply in Family Code proceedings); 3.712(a)-(b)
(civil trial court management rules in Cal Rules of Ct Title III, Div
7, chap 2 apply to all civil cases *except* family law cases and certain
others). Counsel should check local rules carefully; it is possible
that local rules may require case management in family law cases.
Under Fam C §2450(b), a party may by motion request a case management plan.

See generally California Civil Procedure Before Trial, chap 40
(4th ed Cal CEB 2004).

§15.5   C. Trial-Setting Conference

Effective July 1, 2002, the former calendar management and trial-
setting rules were repealed and their main features incorporated in
new civil trial court case management rules, many of which do not
apply to family law cases. See Cal Rules of Ct 3.712(a)-(b) (in Cal
Rules of Ct Title III, Div 7, chap 2 (*i.e.,* Cal Rules of Ct 3.700-3.735,
10.900-10.901(4); "general civil case" means all civil cases except
family law cases, among others). The trial-setting rules in former
Cal Rules of Ct 215-221 have been repealed. On case management
conferences under new Cal Rules of Ct 3.720-3.730, see §15.4.

It appears that family law cases are subject to Cal Rules of Ct 3.1380, which states that the court may set a mandatory settlement conference on the court's own motion or at a party's request. Cal Rules of Ct 3.1380(a). On mandatory settlement conferences, see §15.6.

On case management in civil actions generally, see California Civil Procedure Before Trial, chap 40 (4th ed Cal CEB 2004).

§15.6   D. Settlement Conference

Judicially-conducted settlement conferences are usually mandatory. Mandatory settlement conferences may be held on the court's own motion or at the request of any party. Cal Rules of Ct 3.1380(a). Settlement conferences may also occur by virtue of local court rules, rather than by specific orders in individual cases. See, *e.g.,* Alameda Ct R 11.05 (mandatory settlement conference in all contested family law cases, whether long or short cause).

Any party may ask the court to order that a settlement conference be held. Cal Rules of Ct 3.1380(a). A formal noticed motion does not seem to be required, but it is appropriate to notify the opposition that the request will be made to allow them time to submit reasons that such a conference should not be ordered.

Counsel must prepare and submit settlement conference statements no later than 5 court days before the date set for the settlement conference. Cal Rules of Ct 3.1380(c). Often, local rules prescribe the contents of the settlement conference statements in substantial detail. Typically, the statement must describe the case; list the contested issues; set forth the party's contentions on those issues, including supporting authorities; and set forth a proposal for settlement. This statement should be prepared with great care, because it is likely to influence the court's and opposing counsel's impressions of the case. Note that, in some courts, the parties are required to meet and attempt in good faith to prepare and submit a joint statement of agreed and contested issues. Only when they cannot agree on a joint statement may they file separate settlement conference statements. See, *e.g.,* Alameda Ct R 11.0(5)(F)(4).

Mandatory settlement conferences require the presence of both parties and the lawyers who will try the case, unless excused by the court for good cause. Cal Rules of Ct 3.1380(b). Although the parties and attorneys often come to settlement conferences having already attempted but failed to settle the case, most cases do settle as a result of the conference. There are probably two primary reasons for this. One is that the approaching trial date is a powerful inducement to settle, and the other is the presence of the settlement conference judge. The judge may indicate what results are likely if the case goes to trial. Particularly in counties in which the settlement conference judge will also be the trial judge, the judge's indication of the likely outcome at trial provides a significant impetus toward settlement.

The attorney should prepare the client for the settlement conference. The procedure used by the particular settlement conference judge (*e.g.,* meetings with attorneys outside of clients' presence) should be explained so that the client will not be surprised or unduly disturbed by it. The settlement posture of the case should be discussed with the client to prepare him or her for settlement decisions that are reasonably likely to arise.

At the settlement conference, the attorney should bring a document against which to check off the issues covered by any settlement that is reached, to ensure that no issue is missed on which an order is desired. Ideally, the document should be a list specifically prepared for this purpose, but the settlement conference statement might suffice.

If a settlement is reached, its terms should be stated on the record before the attorneys or parties leave the courtroom. In addition, the parties should be questioned on the record under oath, either by counsel or the court, about their understanding of, and willingness to enter into, the agreement as stated. If one party subsequently attempts to disavow the agreement, the judgment may be entered, in accordance with the agreement as announced on the record, on the other party's motion under CCP §664.6. If there is concern that putting the agreement on the record immediately will not allow sufficient time and reflection for a satisfactory and comprehensive settlement, it might be possible to continue the settlement conference so that a complete agreement can be prepared and executed. In such instances, the terms agreed on might be stated on the record, with an indication that a more complete agreement is anticipated, but that the terms stated are binding.

If an entire case is settled or otherwise disposed of, the petitioner must immediately file written notice of the settlement or other disposition with the court and file written notice on any arbitrator or other court-connected ADR neutral involved in the case and give oral notice if a hearing, conference, or trial is imminent. Cal Rules of Ct 3.1385(a).

On settlement conferences in civil actions generally, see California Civil Procedure Before Trial, chap 40 (4th ed Cal CEB 2004).

§15.7   E. Trial Continuances

Many courts, especially those in metropolitan counties, have adopted strong policies against continuances to aid in relieving backlogs of untried civil cases, including marital actions. Support for these policies is found in Cal Rules of Ct 3.1332, which provides that continuances are "disfavored," the date set for trial must be "firm," and a continuance cannot be granted without a showing of good cause. Note that while Cal Rules of Ct 3.1332 can probably be cited regarding general policy on civil trial continuances, technically it does not apply to family law trials. See Cal Rules of Ct 3.1100–3.1103(a). In the absence of clear authority, however, family law courts may look to other sources of guidance that are consistent with the spirit of the Family Code and the Rules of Court. Cal Rules of Ct 5.140. Former Cal Rules of Ct Appendix Div I §9, which was repealed January 1, 2004, contained many of the same policies as Cal Rules of Ct 3.1332 and was probably a stronger authority than Cal Rules of Ct 3.1332 because applied to family law trials. For a case relying on Cal Rules of Ct Appendix Div I §9 in addressing good cause for a continuance, see *County of San Bernardino v Doria Mining & Eng'g Corp.* (1977) 72 CA3d 776, 140 CR 383.

Unless local court rules provide otherwise, as discussed below, a party seeking a continuance of a trial date must make the request by a noticed motion or an ex parte application under Cal Rules of Ct 3.1200–3.1207 as soon as reasonably practical once the need for the continuance is discovered. The motion or ex parte application is necessary, even if the request is uncontested or stipulated to by the parties. Cal Rules of Ct 3.1332(b). Continuances of trials are disfavored, and the court may grant a continuance only upon an affirmative showing of good cause. Examples of circumstances that may indicate good cause include the unavailability of counsel, an essential witness, or a party because of death, illness, or other excusable circumstances; the substitution of counsel when such substitution is required in the interests of justice; or a party's excused inability to obtain essential testimony documents or other material evidence despite diligent efforts. Cal Rules of Ct 3.1332(c). In ruling on a motion or application for continuance, the court must consider all the facts and circumstances that are relevant to the determination. Cal Rules of Ct 3.1332(d).

Local courts, however, vary in the degree to which any statewide policies on continuances are followed. Consequently, counsel must consult local rules of court to learn the specifics of court practices in a particular county. See, *e.g.,* San Francisco Ct R §11.7.D.7; Solano Ct R §5.15.c.

Note that under CCP §595.2, the court is authorized to postpone a trial for a period not exceeding 30 days when all attorneys of record for parties who have appeared agree in writing to a postponement. Case law explains that despite the apparently mandatory language of the statute ("the court shall postpone"), §595.2 is only directory. *Pham v Nguyen* (1997) 54 CA4th 11, 15, 62 CR2d 422; *County of San Bernardino v Doria Mining & Eng'g Corp.* (1977) 72 CA3d 776, 784, 140 CR 383, 388, citing *Lorraine v McComb* (1934) 220 C 753, 32 P2d 960 (construing same language in former CCP §595).

For sample forms of notice of motion and declaration, see California Civil Procedure Before Trial §§42.31–42.32 (4th ed Cal CEB 2004).

On trial continuances in civil actions generally, see Civ Proc Before Trial, chap 42.

III. TRIAL PREPARATION

§15.8   A. Timing and Importance

To represent a client in a marital action is to engage in a continuous process of preparation, leading either to settlement or to trial. The process begins with the initial contact between the attorney and the client and concludes only when the case is settled or the trial begins.

Although many factors contribute to obtaining a positive result, including the attorney's courtroom skill, the weight and credibility of the evidence, the demeanor of the witnesses, and the court's attitude about the issues, the cornerstone of a successful result at trial (or, for that matter, in settlement negotiations) is preparation. Sufficient preparation is necessary even when a settlement appears likely. For one thing, the lawyer cannot competently achieve a settlement for the client without undertaking a certain level of preparation to develop and assert the client's position on the various issues. In addition, the other side may be less inclined to settle if it believes the attorney is not adequately prepared for trial. For a comprehensive discussion of the settlement process, see California Marital Settlement and Other Family Law Agreements, chap 1 (3d ed Cal CEB 2005).

B. Preliminary Considerations

§15.9   1. Impact of Emotion

Marital actions involve a much greater degree of emotion, interacting with economic and other practical considerations, than most other actions. A typical business litigation client, for example, readily acknowledges litigation costs as a factor to consider in relation to potential results. Marital action clients, however, are often too distraught to be practical and consequently must be counseled about economic realities.

In terms only of the result obtained, it may not be possible to overprepare a case. One can, however, overprepare a case in terms of the cost relative to that result. In preparing for trial in a marital action, the attorney must attempt to prepare adequately while avoiding a degree of preparation that is unreasonable in light of the particular circumstances and issues in the case and the range of likely outcomes. Clients have been known, for example, to incur more in attorney fees and costs litigating property issues than the value of the property involved. Obviously, there are limits to the validity of cost-benefit analysis and the extent to which various outcomes in a marital action can be valued in purely economic terms. But the attorney who ignores such considerations completely does the client a disservice and significantly increases the likelihood that the client will be dissatisfied with the outcome.

Another result of the emotion inherent in marital actions is the need for the attorney to accommodate the client's legitimate goals and directives without giving in to those that seem designed solely to harm others. When, *e.g.,* the client seeks to assert a position without probable cause and for the purpose of harassing or maliciously injuring another person, the attorney should advise the client in writing that the Rules of Professional Conduct do not permit an attorney to assert such a position and, if the client persists, the attorney must withdraw. See Cal Rules of Prof Cond 3-700(b)(1).

§15.10 2. Multiplicity of Issues

Litigation in marital actions is unique in the variety of issues that may arise in even a relatively simple case. See §16.7. As a result, the attorney must bear in mind the kinds of cost-benefit concerns discussed in §15.9, not only in determining the amount of preparation on the case as a whole but also on specific issues. It generally makes little sense, for example, to spend substantially more on expert valuations of a particular property item than the difference in the parties' respective positions on its value.

C. Mechanics of Preparation

§15.11 1. Identify Issues

The first step in trial preparation is to identify the issues. The logical starting points are the Petition (see form in §10.12) and the Response (see form in §10.52). Based on Items 4–7 on the Petition and 4–9 on the Response, one can make a preliminary determination on which of the following matters may be at issue:

- Confirmation of separate assets and obligations;

- Disposition of community assets and obligations;

- Whether grounds exist for the granting of a judgment and, if so, what type (*i.e.*, dissolution, legal separation, or nullity);

- Legal custody;

- Physical custody;

- Child visitation;

- Child support (note that there is no box to check on the Petition to request relief on this issue; rather, the respondent is put on notice with respect to a potential child support award by the statement in Item 8);

- Spousal support;

- Attorney fees and costs; and

- Other matters (*e.g.*, protective orders).

The Petition and Response will also provide a preliminary indication of whether any disagreement exists over the date of marriage or the date of separation, items that may be significant for some of the matters listed above, particularly disposition of property (see §5.12).

The indications obtained from the Petition and Response should be modified on the basis of information and impressions gained as the case proceeds from, *e.g.,* discovery, settlement negotiations, and stipulations. Often, the best and most up-to-date indication of issues for trial will come from an analysis of the opponent's settlement conference statement (see §15.6), but trial preparation should be initiated long before the statement is available.

2. Proceed Issue by Issue

§15.12 a. Ascertain What Is to Be Proved and Prepare Presentation of Evidence

Once the issues are identified (see §15.11), the attorney should proceed, issue by issue, to ascertain what is to be proved and to prepare the presentation of the evidence. Legal research will enable the attorney to ascertain what is to be proved. Evidence will typically be presented through the testimony of witnesses (*i.e.,* the parties, other lay witnesses, and expert witnesses) and through documentary and demonstrative evidence.

Assume, for example, that an issue exists on characterizing stock options granted to the employee-spouse before the date of separation but not exercisable until after separation, *i.e.,* "intermediate" options. On characterization of stock options generally, see §5.31. The facts that may, depending on the circumstances, have to be proved include:

- The date of marriage;

- The date of separation;

- The date of commencement of employment;

- The date the options were granted;

- The number of shares subject to the options;

- The employer's intent in granting the options;

- The date the options were or will be exercisable; and

- The date on which the stock was or will be vested and no longer subject to divestment.

Again, depending on the circumstances, the evidence on the issue may be presented through the following:

- Lay testimony by such persons as the parties, acquaintances of the parties, and the employer or representatives of the employer;

- Expert testimony by persons particularly knowledgeable about stock options and similar employee-benefit practices (*e.g.,* employee-benefit specialists, executive-search consultants); and

- Documents obtained from the employer, the parties, or both.

For a comprehensive discussion, see California Trial Practice: Civil Procedure During Trial, chaps 3 (organizing trial materials), 5 (preparing witnesses for trial), 13 (trial exhibits) (3d ed Cal CEB 1995); California Expert Witness Guide (2d ed Cal CEB 1991).

§15.13 b. Anticipate and Prepare to Meet Opponent's Evidence

In addition to preparing one's own evidence on the issues to be contested (see §15.12), the attorney should attempt to anticipate and prepare to meet the opponent's evidence. Assume, for example, as in §15.12, that an issue exists over characterizing stock options granted to the employee-spouse before the date of separation but not exercisable until after separation. On characterization of stock options generally, see §5.31. Assume further that the parties agree on all relevant dates and numbers but disagree on the employer's intent in granting the options. The attorney should attempt to anticipate what evidence the opponent will present on that issue and prepare to meet it. If the opposition will present documents it claims support its position on the employer's intent, the attorney might prepare to show, *e.g.,* that the views shown in the documents are not those of the persons who ultimately made the decision to grant the options or that the views shown were later changed before the options were granted. If the opposition will present testimony, whether lay or expert, the attorney should prepare for cross-examination. See generally Effective Direct & Cross-Examination (Cal CEB 1986).

§15.14 3. Organize Materials

Organizing trial materials in a marital action is complicated considerably by the multiplicity of issues. The attorney cannot be certain whether one party will present his or her evidence on all issues and the other party will then do likewise or the court will proceed issue by issue. In the latter event, the attorney cannot be certain in what order the issues will be taken up. On order of proof, see §16.15. Consequently, it is perhaps even more important in marital actions than in civil actions generally that trial materials be organized so that any particular item is readily obtainable. Although there are many ways of organizing trial materials, the heart of the organization is typically a list showing, issue by issue, the specific materials to be used (*e.g.,* questions for witnesses, documentary and demonstrative evidence) and their location.

On organizing trial materials generally, see California Trial Practice: Civil Procedure During Trial, chap 3 (3d ed Cal CEB 1995).

§15.15 4. Secure Attendance of Witnesses and Production of Documents

An essential step in preparing for trial is securing the attendance of witnesses and the production of documents. Most friendly witnesses appear voluntarily without the necessity of a subpoena. Most neutral witnesses and all unfriendly witnesses, however, should be subpoenaed (see CCP §1985) to secure their presence at trial. When documents are desired, either with or without the personal appearance of a witness, the same principles apply. See CCP §1985; Evid C §1560.

On compelling attendance and production of evidence generally, see California Trial Practice: Civil Procedure During Trial, chap 4 (3d ed Cal CEB 1995).

16
Trial

§16.1   I. SCOPE OF CHAPTER

This chapter discusses the trial of a marital action, with emphasis on the aspects peculiar to such cases. Discussion is limited to trial of contested cases; uncontested proceedings are covered in chap 14.

No attempt is made to discuss in depth general trial procedures or the rules of evidence, which are generally the same in trials of marital actions as in other civil trials. For a comprehensive discussion of these topics, see California Trial Practice: Civil Procedure During Trial (3d ed Cal CEB 1995), which is frequently referred to in this chapter; Effective Introduction of Evidence in California (2d ed Cal CEB 2000); Effective Direct & Cross-Examination (Cal CEB 1986).

CAUTION➤ As this release was going to press, a petition for review remained pending in *Elkins v Superior Court (Elkins)* (review granted Feb. 1, 2006, S139073). Elkins involves a challenge to a local court rule (Contra Costa County Superior Court Local Rule 12.5(b)(3)) and a trial scheduling order from the same county that limits the form of testimony and the presentation of evidence at trial in a family law proceeding. Its resolution may affect other, similar, local rules. This chapter will be updated with the outcome in a forthcoming release.

§16.2   II. PEREMPTORY CHALLENGE OF JUDGE

Any party or attorney may prevent any judge, court commissioner, or referee from presiding at the trial of a marital action, as in civil actions generally, by making a timely challenge under CCP §170.6. These challenges are known as "peremptory" challenges because §170.6 allows automatic disqualification without any specific allegations or proof of grounds. CCP §170.6(3). Special attention must be paid to deadlines for bringing peremptory challenges, particularly in counties that assign marital actions to a specific department for all purposes. For further coverage of peremptory challenges, see §§11.46 (discussion), 11.47 (form).

Judicial officers may also be challenged for cause under CCP

§170.1, but, because specific allegations and proof are required, peremptory challenges under §170.6 are much more common. A challenge for cause might raise such matters as personal knowledge of disputed evidentiary facts, related service as an attorney, financial interest, relationship to a party or attorney, prospective employment or service as a dispute resolution neutral, or direction of the parties to participation in an alternative dispute resolution process in which the neutral has a previous relationship with the judicial officer.

Note that a peremptory challenge under CCP §170.6 need not be used to disqualify a commissioner, referee, or attorney sitting as a temporary judge. Rather, the party may simply refuse to stipulate to the temporary judge. Counsel should be aware, however, that the stipulation may be oral, written, express, or implied. See §11.49 for further discussion, which, although presented in the context of hearings on temporary orders, also applies to trials.

§16.3   III. NATURE OF FAMILY LAW TRIALS

Because marital actions are civil actions, trials of marital actions are governed by the same rules that apply to trials of civil actions generally. See Cal Rules of Ct 5.21. There are, nevertheless, significant differences between them.

A. Similarity to Civil Trials Generally

§16.4   1. Elements of Proof

As in all civil actions, a party advancing a particular legal contention at trial in a marital action must prove the elements required to establish that contention. A party contending, for example, that property acquired by the parties in joint form during marriage is his or her separate property must prove that there was a clear statement in the deed or other documentary evidence of title by which the property was acquired that it was separate property or that there was a written agreement between the parties to that effect. See §5.20. The proof must in turn be made by the introduction of competent evidence or reliance on applicable presumptions.

§16.5   2. Rules of Evidence

The same rules of evidence apply at trial in a marital action as in civil actions generally. Thus, facts must be established by admissible evidence, and objections must be properly stated and based on the Evidence Code or other applicable statutes or court rules. Experts must be properly qualified, documents properly marked and offered, and questions to witnesses properly stated. See generally California Trial Practice: Civil Procedure During Trial, chaps 11, 13 (3d ed Cal CEB 1995).

A litigant has a right to present evidence at trial and, although the court can exclude otherwise admissible evidence because it is unduly time-consuming, prejudicial, confusing, or misleading, outright denial of the right to present evidence is error. See Evid C §§352, 354. The court's discretion to exclude oral testimony entirely (discussed in §11.51 in the context of hearings for temporary orders) does not apply to trials. See *Reifler v Superior Court* (1974) 39 CA3d 479, 483, 114 CR 356, 358.

Despite the applicability of rules of evidence to trials of marital actions, counsel should be aware that some judges do place special restrictions on the presentation of evidence in such trials. See §16.10.

In cases involving novel or groundbreaking legal theories, complex facts, or any other elements that create a likelihood that a client may wish to appeal the trial court's ruling, it could be a wise precaution to associate an appellate specialist early in the case to assist counsel in ensuring a clear record is made of all testimony and objections.

§16.6   3. Applicability of Rules of Court

California Rules of Court 5.10–5.500 apply specifically to marital actions. These rules are, in effect, procedural statutes and are binding on the court and counsel. Fam C §211; *Marriage of McKim* (1972) 6 C3d 673, 678 n4, 100 CR 140.

B. Differences From Civil Trials Generally

§16.7   1. Multiplicity of Issues

A trial in a marital action is unique in that it typically encompasses a wide spectrum of issues and subissues, each one distinct in itself and potentially difficult to resolve. For example, the complex substantive law on commingling and tracing (see §5.23) and on other property issues bears no relationship to the law of spousal support or to that of child custody and visitation, although the issues may coexist in a particular case. Moreover, determining the amount of spousal support is distinct from determining the duration of spousal support, even though both are subissues of the same basic subject.

§16.8   2. Relative Informality

Judges often conduct trials in marital actions in a somewhat informal manner. Examples of such informality include (1) frequent use of in-chambers conferences, *e.g.*, in efforts to speed the trial, resolve issues, or settle the entire matter; (2) proposals for stipulations, or indications of likely rulings, on particular issues; and (3) relaxation of rules of evidence. Although the attorney may accept, and even appreciate, this informality, the attorney must not become lulled into relaxing his or her standard of performance. Such a mistake can be costly, *e.g.*, if it becomes necessary to prosecute or defend an appeal.

In addition, the relative informality of family court does not mean that counsel may disregard time limitations that are set for trial, given the trial court's extensive authority to control the proceedings. See generally Evid C §352. On the other hand, a trial judge may not act arbitrarily and unreasonably in prescribing a time for trial. See *Blumenthal v Superior Court* (2006) 137 CA4th 672, 682, 40 CR3d 509 (trial court abused discretion in declaring mistrial after parties failed to complete trial within arbitrary deadline imposed by judge).

§16.9   3. Emotional Aspects

The trial of a marital action is typically notable for the strong emotions and, often, outright hostility that can result from a failed marriage. The court is called on to decide a matter involving parties, and possibly children and other relatives, who have experienced a close personal relationship with each other. The precise nature of the emotional conflict may vary widely, but its presence is always felt. The attorney must be careful not to be drawn into the parties' emotional combat zone or to allow their animosity to extend to his or her relationship with opposing counsel or the court. Witnesses may also be affected in this manner and, consequently, should be advised against argumentative or hostile behavior toward any party or attorney or toward the court.

§16.10   4. Judicial Attitude

Traditionally, trial judges have often regarded trials in marital actions as somehow less important than other civil litigation. This attitude has been both recognized and strongly criticized by appellate courts. See, *e.g., Marriage of Brantner* (1977) 67 CA3d 416, 422, 136 CR 635, 638, quoted with approval in *Marriage of Morrison* (1978) 20 C3d 437, 450, 143 CR 139, 148:

While the speedy disposition of cases is desirable, speed is not always compatible with justice. Actually, in its use of courtroom time the present judicial process seems to have its priorities confused. Domestic relations litigation, one of the most important and sensitive tasks a judge faces, too often is given the low-man-on-the-totem-pole treatment, quite often being fobbed off on a commissioner. One of the paradoxes of our present legal system is that it is accepted practice to tie up a court for days while a gaggle of professional medical witnesses expound to a jury on just how devastating or just how trivial a personal injury may be, all to the personal enrichment of the trial lawyers involved, yet at the same time we begrudge the judicial resources necessary for careful and reasoned judgments in this most delicate field—the breakup of a marriage with its resulting trauma and troublesome fiscal aftermath. The courts should not begrudge the time necessary to carefully go over the wreckage of a marriage in order to effect substantial justice to all parties involved.

Although there are now many judges who bring great sensitivity to marital action trials, the attitude described above still persists and the attorney must be prepared to deal with it, *e.g.,* in deciding on order of proof (see §16.15).

§16.11   5. No Right to Jury Trial

Unlike most civil litigants, those in marital actions do not have an inherent right to a jury trial. See CCP §592; *Sharon v Sharon* (1885) 67 C 185, 193, 7 P 456, 460. Although the court has discretion under §592 to order factual issues to be tried by a jury, it rarely does so, perhaps in part because the jury's verdict would be merely advisory (*Cutter Labs. v R.W. Ogle & Co.* (1957) 151 CA2d 410, 418, 311 P2d 627, 633).

§16.12   C. Closure of Proceedings; Exclusion of Witnesses

The court may, in the interests of justice and the persons involved, direct that the trial of a marital action, or any of its issues, be held in private. The court may exclude everyone but court officers and the parties, their witnesses, and the attorneys. Fam C §214. The parties can stipulate to a closed trial, and the court will sometimes arrange a closed trial informally. The better practice, however, is to make a formal motion, preferably at the pretrial in-chambers conference immediately before trial (see §16.17). Such motions are frequently made and granted in custody cases. See *Whitney v Whitney* (1958) 164 CA2d 577, 582, 330 P2d 947, 951.

As in other trials, the court has discretion to exclude any nonparty witness from the courtroom while the witness is not giving testimony, so that the witness cannot hear the testimony of other witnesses. Evid C §777. For discussion, see California Trial Practice: Civil Procedure During Trial §§6.105–6.108 (3d ed Cal CEB 1995).

§16.13   IV. PRETRIAL CHAMBERS CONFERENCE

In marital actions, as in civil actions generally, the trial judge commonly invites counsel into chambers before the trial commences to discuss the case. Discussions typically cover what issues must be tried, order of proof, and any stipulations that might facilitate an efficient trial. Counsel may wish to make various motions in limine, *e.g.,* to preclude or permit introduction of evidence. The conference in chambers may also provide what may be the final opportunity to reach a settlement.

When trial briefs are prepared, the trial judge will usually want to review them before the chambers conference. Counsel should check with the clerk well before the trial date to ascertain whether the trial brief should be given to the clerk for presentation to the judge on arriving for the conference or whether submission is required prior to the trial date.

If for any reason an attorney will refuse to participate in a pretrial chambers conference (*e.g.,* client objects to conference in his or her absence), the refusal should be brought to the judge's attention as early as practicable. If the judge indicates that any action will be taken in response that is prejudicial to the client, the attorney should request an opportunity to state on the record the reasons for refusing to participate.

§16.14   A. Identification of Issues

A typical trial in a marital action involves many legal and factual issues relating, *e.g.,* to property characterization, valuation, and division; spousal support; child custody and visitation; child support; and attorney fees and costs. The issues are usually identified by the court and counsel in chambers before trial and discussed along with related evidentiary problems.

Identification of trial issues at the chambers conference helps to provide for an orderly, well-tried case. This is counsel's first opportunity to attempt to ensure that the court will address and rule on all the issues the client wants to have heard. In courts in which a settlement conference is presided over shortly before trial by the same judge who will preside at trial, identification of issues should be much less demanding.

For further discussion, see §15.11.

§16.15   B. Order of Proof

The judge usually discusses the order of proof with counsel in chambers before trial. Order of proof can be particularly important in marital actions because of the variety and complexity of the issues. In some instances, the judge will proceed, as in civil trials generally, by having one party present his or her evidence on all the issues and then having the other party do the same. In other instances, the judge will take the case up issue by issue. The latter approach is particularly appropriate when the resolution of individual issues may avoid the hearing of others. This occurs when the resolution of one issue may allow settlement of others, *e.g.,* resolution of custody issue allows parties to settle child support. It also occurs when a party must prevail on one issue to be able to litigate another, *e.g.,* determination by court of the date of separation eliminates the need to litigate division of property acquired thereafter. Considerable time, irritation, and expense can be saved by making intelligent decisions on order of proof.

In civil cases generally, the plaintiff typically has the burden of proof and is heard first at trial. Although it may be pure chance in a marital action trial that one party is the petitioner and not the other, traditionally the petitioner proceeds first just by virtue of being the petitioner. In some circumstances, however, it may be better for the respondent to proceed first, at least on issues for which that order facilitates proper allocation of the burden of proof. If the respondent is, for example, asserting that property acquired during marriage and before separation is his or her separate property, it may be appropriate for the respondent to proceed first because the respondent has the burden of proof on that issue. The petitioner should not be in the position of trying to prove that the property is community property, lest the court forget that the law presumes the property to be community property and that the burden is on the respondent to prove otherwise.

In considering the order of proof, the attorney must take into account the court's attitude toward marital action trials and, in particular, whether the court will permit sufficient time for the matter to be tried properly. When the attorney believes that insufficient time may be allowed, an order of proof should be sought that will allow the issues most important to the client to be taken up early in the trial.

§16.16   C. Stipulations

Stipulations on matters at issue are potentially important to the orderly and efficient trial of almost every marital action. A binding stipulation, when accepted by the court, eliminates the need to produce evidence on the stipulated facts. *Leonard v City of Los Angeles* (1973) 31 CA3d 473, 476, 107 CR 378. Offered evidence that is contrary to the stipulation is inadmissible. *Clejan v Reisman* (1970) 5 CA3d 224, 241, 84 CR 897.

Stipulations on factual matters are binding on the court unless they are contrary to law or public policy. Stipulations on questions of law, including legal conclusions to be drawn from admitted or stipulated facts, are not binding on the court. *Leonard v City of Los Angeles, supra.*

To be binding, a written stipulation must be filed and an oral stipulation must be entered on the court minutes. CCP §283(1); *Harrold v Harrold* (1950) 100 CA2d 601, 605, 224 P2d 66. Stipulations reached in chambers should always be transcribed by the court reporter in the proceedings. For lengthy or complex stipulations, it is good practice to order the original reporter's transcript and file it with the court clerk as part of the record.

PRACTICE TIP► Some courts do not routinely provide court reporters, and it is up to the parties and their counsel to arrange to have one available at trial. Other courts are using newer technology, such as electronic recording to CDs, which may result in unanticipated technological problems. If it is important to make a record, then it may be worth hiring a court reporter.

The validity of a stipulation on substantive issues (*e.g.,* termination of spousal support, division of community property) depends on the client's knowledge and consent to the stipulation. See *Marriage of Lionberger* (1979) 97 CA3d 56, 61, 158 CR 535.

In addition to factual matters and substantive issues, another common subject for stipulations at the pretrial chambers conference is the admissibility of documentary and demonstrative evidence, thereby eliminating the need for foundational testimony at trial.

The court can relieve a party from the effect of a stipulation in the interests of fairness. *Kerr Chems. v Crown Cork & Seal Co.* (1971) 21 CA3d 1010, 1017, 99 CR 162.

§16.17   D. Motions in Limine

Various motions relating to the conduct of the trial, *e.g.,* to preclude or permit introduction of evidence, may be made during the chambers conference. Proceedings on such matters should always be transcribed by the court reporter. Counsel should be aware that many motions, *e.g.,* for alternate valuation date, should be made as early before trial as practicable. Even motions that typically should be made before trial will sometimes have to be made at trial because facts on which they are based were not previously known.

§16.18   E. Settlement

Although the widespread use of mandatory settlement conferences held shortly before trial has reduced the frequency of settlements reached at trial itself, such settlements are not uncommon. Except in counties where the settlement conference judge is also the trial judge, the trial judge's "suggestions" for settlement, because they tend to indicate what the court's rulings will be if settlement is not reached, provide an impetus toward settlement that was previously missing.

To prevent claims of coercion, the trial judge, except when he or she was also the settlement conference judge, will usually not entertain settlement discussions if a party or an attorney objects. See, *e.g.,* Los Angeles Ct R 8.21 (judge urged not to engage in settlement discussions unless all counsel and parties agree on record to discussions with judge and to waiver of any right to assert disqualification based on judge's participation).

A settlement reached at trial should be stated on the record before the attorneys or parties leave the courtroom. In addition, the parties should be questioned on the record under oath, either by counsel or the court, about their understanding of, and willingness to enter into, the agreement as stated. If one party subsequently attempts to disavow the agreement, judgment may be entered, in accordance with the agreement as announced on the record, on the other party's motion under CCP §664.6. If there is concern that putting the agreement on the record immediately will not allow sufficient time and reflection for a satisfactory and comprehensive settlement, it might be possible to continue the trial so that a complete agreement can be prepared and executed. In such instances, the terms agreed on might be stated on the record, with an indication that a more complete agreement is anticipated, but that the terms stated are binding.

V. PRESENTING CASE AT TRIAL

A. Stylistic Considerations

§16.19   1. Decorum

The unusual emotional aspects of many trials in marital actions (see §16.9) do not justify a departure from the attorney's customary duty to maintain a high standard of courtroom decorum. Indeed, those aspects may make it even more important than in civil cases generally that attorneys act in ways that exemplify and encourage civility. Family law judges do not usually appreciate, *e.g.,* argumentative or intimidating questioning of witnesses; unnecessarily disparaging argument, particularly when unsupported by the record; or gratuitous criticism of the opposing party or attorney.

§16.20   2. Effect of Overtrying Case

Although overpreparing a case may raise costs unjustifiably, it will probably not have a negative effect on the outcome. There is, after all, no substitute for good preparation. Unlike overpreparing a case, however, overtrying one can be disastrous. Basically, a case is overtried when the attorney presents more evidence to the court than is reasonably necessary to establish the client's position on the issues. Thus, the attorney should limit the quantity of evidence presented, *e.g.*, by avoiding that which is merely cumulative, as distinguished from the quality of evidence presented.

The effect of overtrying a case will vary. Simply presenting an additional witness whose testimony is cumulative on one issue generally has no adverse effect on the outcome of the trial. However, a lawyer who is inclined to overtry a case often displays that tendency on all issues. Possible results are witnesses who contradict each other, reports that conflict with one another, and unwitting exposure of the weakest witness to cross-examination by the opposing attorney. If, for example, three witnesses testify to the same facts or circumstances, the weakest of the three may be pursued on cross-examination, with the result that damage done to that witness has a similar effect on the others' testimony. In addition, cumulative evidence or witnesses have the effect of diluting the impact of the evidence in the judge's mind. To these effects must be added the risk of annoying the judge.

Overtrying the case is not limited to the presentation of one's own evidence; it can extend to cross-examination. Inexperienced attorneys frequently cross-examine a witness at length, only to find that they have magnified and enhanced the witness's testimony. In many instances, the answers to questions on cross-examination actually make the case that the opposing attorney failed to make on direct examination. It is well to remember that the purpose of cross-examination is to elicit contradictory and hence favorable responses from the witness. Lengthy cross-examination can be dangerous. In some instances, the best strategy is not to cross-examine at all.

PRACTICE TIP➤ To balance the weight and impact of the testimony already given with the necessity of eliciting further confirming or contradictory evidence, it is important to keep a running assessment, preferably making brief notes when practical, of what factual information needs to be presented to the judge in order for counsel's theory of the case to be proven. Remember that a reviewing court will be limited to the facts in the record and must otherwise assume the trial court's findings were reasonable.

§16.21   B. Issues to Be Decided

The issues to be decided in a marital action vary, depending on the particular facts and circumstances and the extent to which the parties have been able to reach an agreement. On identifying the issues, see §15.11.

C. Evidence

§16.22   1. Witnesses

Typical witnesses in a marital action include the parties, other lay witnesses, and expert witnesses. On examining witnesses generally, see California Trial Practice: Civil Procedure During Trial, chap 11 (3d ed Cal CEB 1995).

§16.23   2. Documentary and Demonstrative Evidence

As in civil trials generally, documentary evidence plays a significant role in trials of marital actions. Examples include letters, records, and reports. Documentary evidence is usually, although not necessarily, created during the course of the marriage itself, rather than for the purposes of the legal proceeding.

Potentially of equal value but often overlooked is demonstrative evidence. Examples include charts, schedules, and photographs. Demonstrative evidence is usually created for purposes of the legal proceeding, rather than during the course of the marriage itself. Such evidence can cost from a few dollars to several thousand dollars to prepare and may be used with great effect to illustrate complex matters. For example, color bars or graphs can be used to show increases or decreases in the value of a separately owned business resulting from one spouse's efforts during the periods between (1) marriage and separation and (2) separation and trial (see discussion of substantive law in §§5.16–5.17).

Note that demonstrative evidence, like documentary evidence, may not be considered by the court unless it is admitted into evidence. This can sometimes be done by stipulation between counsel at the pretrial chambers conference, which obviates the need to call witnesses whose only function is to provide foundational testimony. Otherwise, the item should be marked for identification and a proper foundation laid for its use, and it should be offered into evidence at an appropriate time.

On trial exhibits generally, see California Trial Practice: Civil Procedure During Trial, chap 13 (3d ed Cal CEB 1995).

§16.24 3. Use of Pretrial Discovery

Information obtained during pretrial discovery may be used at trial for many purposes, including:

- To impeach an adverse party or witness by showing a prior inconsistent statement (see CCP §2025.620(a)); Evid C §§770, 1235);

- To refresh the memory of a party or witness (see Evid C §771);

- To rehabilitate a witness whose credibility has been attacked on cross-examination, by showing the existence of prior statements consistent with the offered testimony (see Evid C §791); and

- To substitute for testimony of a witness who is unavailable as specifically defined or when exceptional circumstances make it desirable in the interests of justice (see CCP §2025.620(c)(1)–(3); Evid C §240).

In addition, the deposition of a party, a person for whose immediate benefit the proceeding is prosecuted or defended, or an officer, director, agent, or employee of a party may be used by the adverse party for any purpose. CCP §2025.620(b)).

On use of discovery materials generally, see California Trial Practice: Civil Procedure During Trial, chap 12 (3d ed Cal CEB 1995). On discovery in marital actions generally, see chap 13.

§16.25 D. Oral Argument

In a nonjury trial, unlike a trial by jury, there is no absolute right to oral argument. *Gillette v Gillette* (1960) 180 CA2d 777, 781, 4 CR 700. See also CCP §§631.7, 607. Nevertheless, the court should permit oral argument in most instances. *Center v Kelton* (1912) 20 CA 611, 615, 129 P 960. Some courts tend to discourage argument or minimize the time allowed for it, whereas others encourage it or request it on one or more particular issues. Regardless of judicial attitude, the attorney should always consider asking to present argument at the conclusion of the trial. Experienced trial lawyers attest to the positive effect on the court's decision of an articulate, well-reasoned argument.

The court will often allow a recess after all the evidence has been received to permit the attorneys to gather and organize notes, documents, and exhibits for purposes of preparing closing arguments. In lengthy trials, the court will often hear argument on the day after the close of evidence to give the attorneys an opportunity to prepare overnight. Even in shorter matters, the court may entertain a request to adjourn for purposes of argument preparation. But the court is under no obligation to grant an adjournment or recess and, consequently, the attorney must strive during trial to keep all exhibits marked and organized and to maintain a well-organized set of trial notes capable of being outlined quickly for argument.

In a trial of a marital action, the petitioner is treated for argument purposes in the same fashion as the plaintiff in civil actions generally. Consequently, in closing argument, the petitioner has the right to proceed first and, after the respondent's argument, to make the concluding presentation. CCP §§631.7, 607. Either party may waive argument.

Argument should be organized on an issue-by-issue basis. In deciding which issues to argue first, consideration should be given to their relative importance to the client and to the attorney's anticipated ability to affect the judge's view of the issues through oral argument.

Charts, schedules, and other demonstrative evidence can have a strong effect on the judge. Frequently, such items are admitted into evidence without testimony by any witness on their pertinent facts or the conclusions they invite. Even when specific facts have been presented or opinions given in oral testimony, their impact can often be diminished in complex litigation by the passage of time during trial or by the magnitude and extent of other evidence. The attorney should use the time for argument to highlight for the court the importance of the demonstrative evidence, the facts shown, and the conclusions that can be drawn from them.

§16.26   VI. REQUEST FOR STATEMENT OF DECISION

Counsel must remember that for trials concluded within 1 day, or in less than 8 hours over more than 1 day, the request for a statement of decision must be made before the matter is submitted for decision. CCP §632. At the time the request is made, counsel must be prepared to articulate the principal controverted issues on which a statement is desired. Failure to make a timely request for the statement of decision will result in a waiver. It is advisable to request a statement of decision before submitting the matter for decision even if counsel believes a multi-day trial took longer than 8 hours to be concluded. See *Marriage of Gray* (2002) 103 CA4th 974, 978, 127 CR2d 271 (although trial took place over multiple days during year and wife argued it was "inconceivable" that trial lasted less than one day, she failed to show that trial court's finding that trial lasted less than eight hours was in error).

In trials lasting 8 hours or more over more than 1 day, the request for a statement of decision must be made within 10 days after the court announces its tentative decision. CCP §632. On tentative decisions, see §16.27.

The time requirements governing requests for a statement of decision also apply to bifurcated trials. Cal Rules of Ct 3.1591. Thus, when a bifurcated trial is concluded within 1 day, or in less than 8 hours over more than 1 day, a request for a statement of decision on the bifurcated issue or issues must be made before the issues are submitted.

For a complete discussion of statements of decision, see §§17.5–17.31. On the request in particular, see §§17.18–17.24.

§16.27   VII. TENTATIVE DECISION

In any trial of fact lasting longer than one day, the court must announce its tentative decision. Cal Rules of Ct 3.1590(a), (h). It may be rendered by an oral statement entered in the minutes or by a written statement filed with the court clerk. Cal Rules of Ct 3.1590(a). The tentative decision sets forth the court's decision and the reasons for it, including the authorities relied on. The tentative decision is not a judgment and is not binding on the court. Cal Rules of Ct 3.1590(a).

When the court announces its tentative decision from the bench at the conclusion of the trial, counsel should have some document available against which to check off the issues covered by the court, in order to ensure that the court does not fail to rule on any issue on which a ruling is desired. Ideally, the document should be a list specially prepared for this purpose, but a settlement conference statement or trial brief might suffice. If the court neglects an issue, counsel can call the omission to the court's attention immediately and avoid any subsequent action.

When the trial is "completed within one day," no tentative decision need be made by the court. Cal Rules of Ct 3.1590(h). Because of the language of CCP §632, it seems likely that a tentative decision is not required when the trial is completed in less than eight hours over more than one day.

For further discussion of tentative decisions, see §§17.2–17.4.

17

Judgment After Trial

§17.1   I. SCOPE OF CHAPTER

After a contested trial of a marital action, the court's decision must be rendered in the form of a judgment. If the trial lasted longer than 1 day, the judge must first announce a tentative decision. Regardless of the length of the trial, a party may request that a statement of decision be rendered, setting forth the factual and legal basis for the court's decision. Based on the court's decision, a proposed judgment is prepared that, after signature by the court and filing, becomes the final decision on the issues in the action. This chapter describes the strategic considerations and procedures leading to preparation of the judgment, provides a complete explanation of the substantive and procedural requirements for preparing and obtaining a judgment after trial, and discusses special types of judgments and withdrawal of the attorney after judgment.

§17.2　　II. TENTATIVE DECISION

In any trial of fact lasting longer than 1 day, the court must announce its tentative decision. Cal Rules of Ct 3.1590(a), (h). If, on the other hand, the trial "was completed within one day," the court need not make a tentative decision. Cal Rules of Ct 3.1590 (h). A tentative decision is probably not required when the trial was completed in less than 8 hours over more than 1 day. See CCP §632, on statements of decision, in which reference is made to trials concluded "within one calendar day or in less than eight hours over more than one day." It is advisable to request a statement of decision before submitting the matter for decision even if counsel believes a multiday trial took longer than 8 hours to be concluded. See *Marriage of Gray* (2002) 103 CA4th 974, 978, 127 CR2d 271 (although trial took place over multiple days during year and wife argued it was "inconceivable" that trial lasted less than 1 day, she failed to show that trial court's finding that trial lasted less than 8 hours was in error).

The tentative decision is not a judgment. Sometimes referred to as an "intended decision," a "memorandum decision," or a "memorandum of intended decision," the tentative decision is neither binding on the court nor appealable. Cal Rules of Ct 3.1590(a); see *Marriage of Hafferkamp* (1998) 61 CA4th 789, 793, 71 CR2d 761 (wife could not appeal from order purporting to grant new trial on spousal support, child support, and other matters because underlying ruling by trial court was not a statement of decision or a judgment, but rather a "tentative decision"); *Burgess v Board of Educ.* (1974) 41 CA3d

571, 582, 116 CR 183. On modification of a tentative decision, see §17.4.

§17.3   A. Nature and Effect

The tentative decision may be rendered by an oral statement entered in the minutes or by a written statement filed with the court clerk. Cal Rules of Ct 3.1590(a). It sets forth the court's decision and the reasons for it, including the authorities relied on. The tentative decision may also provide that (1) a designated party, or the court, will prepare a statement of decision, if requested; and (2) the tentative decision will be the statement of decision unless, within 10 days, either party specifies controverted issues or makes proposals not covered in the tentative decision. Cal Rules of Ct 3.1590(a). In trials lasting 8 hours or more over more than 1 day, the announcement of the tentative decision begins a ten-day time period within which a request for a statement of decision, if any, must be made. CCP §632.

No time limit is prescribed by statute or rules of court within which the tentative decision must be announced. However, a trial judge's salary will be held back if any cause "remains pending and undetermined for 90 days after it has been submitted for decision." Cal Const art VI, §19. In practice, this condition is satisfied when the tentative decision is announced. Unless the decision is announced in open court in the presence of all parties who appeared at the trial, the clerk must forthwith mail to all parties who appeared at the trial a copy of the minute entry or written tentative decision. Cal Rules of Ct 3.1590(a).

§17.4   B. Modification

Because the tentative decision is not a judgment and is not binding on the court (Cal Rules of Ct 3.1590(a)), the court may modify its announced tentative decision at any time before signing the judgment. See §17.5. In this event, the clerk must mail a copy of the modification to all parties who appeared at the trial. Cal Rules of Ct 3.1590(a). Although it is not required, some judges may hold an informal conference at the request of a party to discuss questions or problems regarding the tentative decision. Further, if counsel believes that the tentative decision misstates the facts or the law of the case, a request for a statement of decision (see §§17.18–17.23) should be considered.

When a tentative decision is issued and a substantial change in the facts of the case occurs after the trial but before judgment is entered, counsel should request the court to reopen the case for additional evidence and to modify the tentative decision. See CCP §662; *Marriage of Zaentz* (1990) 218 CA3d 154, 164, 267 CR 31, 37 (trial reopened to allow evidence of posttrial profits of movie *Amadeus* attributable to preseparation efforts). For example:

- When a community asset has substantially increased or decreased in value after trial due to a sale or forfeiture, the trial court may reopen the case for revaluation if judgment has not yet been entered. See §5.43.

- When it is impossible or impracticable to present evidence on the tax consequences of the division of property until the intended award is announced, and when the tentative decision does not reserve jurisdiction to take the tax consequences into account, counsel should move to reopen the trial to present expert testimony on the issue.

On motion for new trial based on newly discovered evidence, see §§18.2–18.15.

§17.5   III. STATEMENT OF DECISION

Regardless of the length of trial, and on the request of any party appearing at trial, the court must issue a statement of decision explaining the legal and factual basis for its decision on each of the principal controverted issues. Fam C §2338(a); CCP §632; Cal Rules of Ct 3.1590. Effective January 1, 1982, the provision for statements of decision superseded the previous requirement that findings of fact and conclusions of law be made on request.

In trials lasting longer than 1 day, the procedure for requesting and proposing a statement of decision (see §§17.17–17.31) allows counsel to argue for or against the court's tentative decision. The "prevailing" party may seek to preserve the tentative decision by requesting and proposing a statement providing ample factual and legal bases for upholding the decision on appeal. See Cal Rules of Ct 3.1590(b)–(c). The "losing" party, on the other hand, may seek to modify the tentative decision by requesting its own statement of decision (see §§17.18-17.22); by making proposals as to content (see §17.25); or by filing objections to the proposed statement (see §17.28), showing that the facts and the law do not support the court's tentative decision. See Cal Rules of Ct 3.1590(b)-(d). If the court declines to change its tentative decision, the "losing" party can later attack the judgment in the trial court (see chap 18) or on appeal (see chap 19). On form of statement of decision in trials lasting longer than 1 day, see §17.30.

Although a statement of decision is also required on request in a trial completed within 1 day (see Fam C §2338(a); CCP §632), the procedure for requesting and proposing a statement of decision set forth in Cal Rules of Ct 3.1590 does not apply to such trials. Cal Rules of Ct 3.1590(h). On requesting a statement of decision in trials completed within 1 day, see §§17.17-17.19; on form of statement of decision in such trials, see §17.30. Likewise, Cal Rules of Ct 3.1590 probably does not apply to trials completed in less than 8 hours over more than 1 day. See CCP §632, in which reference is made to trials concluded "within one calendar day or in less than 8 hours over more than one day."

A. Nature

§17.6   1. Legal and Factual Basis

A statement of decision must contain, as an essential element, an explanation of the legal and factual bases for the court's decision. *Marriage of Buser* (1987) 190 CA3d 639, 642, 235 CR 785; *Miramar Hotel Corp. v Frank B. Hall & Co.* (1985) 163 CA3d 1126, 1129, 210 CR 114. The trial court is required only to state the ultimate facts necessary to support its findings. *Wolfe v Lipsy* (1985) 163 CA3d 633, 643, 209 CR 801. A detailed analysis of evidentiary facts is not required. *People v Casa Blanca Convalescent Homes, Inc.* (1984) 159 CA3d 509, 524, 206 CR 164.

An example of an ultimate fact would be: "There was no agreement or understanding that the Tahoe vacation cabin would be other than community property." It would be improper and surplusage to include evidentiary facts in the statement of decision, such as: "The meeting alleged by husband to have occurred at the family home on April 5, 1989, to discuss the nature of title to the Tahoe vacation cabin did not occur, as shown by the fact that wife was in London on that date." See *Denbo v Senness* (1953) 120 CA2d 863, 869, 262 P2d 31.

Nevertheless, the statement of decision must be more than merely conclusory. See *Miramar Hotel Corp. v Frank B. Hall & Co., supra*. See also *Marriage of Hargrave* (1985) 163 CA3d 346, 353, 209 CR 764 (valuation of business remanded for further hearing because statement of decision offered no evidentiary basis for trial court's valuation).

§17.7 2. Principal Controverted Issues

The statement of decision must cover each of the principal controverted issues at trial, as specified by the party making the request (see §17.21) and by any other party making proposals on the content of the statement (see §17.25). CCP §632. The purpose of this requirement is to narrow the issues required to be addressed in the statement to those in dispute at the trial. Counsel must give careful consideration to the language used to state the controverted issues. If an issue is not properly addressed, a statement of decision will be waived on that issue. *Marriage of Aninger* (1990) 220 CA3d 230, 238, 269 CR 388; see §17.23.

§17.8 3. Rulings on Motions

A statement of decision under CCP §632 is generally not required to be made by the court, even if requested, after a ruling on a motion. *Marriage of Baltins* (1989) 212 CA3d 66, 79, 260 CR 403. However, the trial court may issue a statement of decision after a hearing on a motion if it chooses to do so. *Khan v Superior Court* (1988) 204 CA3d 1168, 1173 n4, 251 CR 815.

Statutory and case law have created several exceptions to the general rule, requiring the court to issue a statement of decision or other "findings" on making certain orders regarding child custody, child support, and spousal support, whether after a hearing on a motion or after trial. See §§17.12–17.15.

Another exception to the general rule occurs when an order on a motion determines a sufficiently important issue, such as custody of a minor child. In such cases, a statement of decision may be required if appellate review cannot effectively be accomplished in its absence. *Marriage of Wood* (1983) 141 CA3d 671, 679, 190 CR 469, 475. See also *Marriage of S.* (1985) 171 CA3d 738, 217 CR 561 (order modifying custody reversed for lack of a statement of decision, even without a finding that appellate review was impaired).

§17.9   B. Importance

Statements of decision are generally underused in marital actions. Counsel often fail to realize that a statement of decision may be the critical factor in preserving a party's right to appeal or in establishing the foundation for a subsequent change of circumstances for modification of a custody or support order. On the other hand, if the right of appeal and the possibility of a future modification of orders are not important factors, a statement of decision may in some cases reduce the court's flexibility in arriving at an equitable result (*e.g.,* as to an overall division of community property) by requiring a detailed explanation of the factual and legal bases for the decision.

§17.10   1. Appellate Review

A party who fails to request a statement of decision may be severely handicapped in attacking the trial court's determination of issues. In the absence of a statement of decision, a judgment or order of a lower court is presumed correct on appeal, and the appellate court will imply "every essential fact" necessary to sustain the trial court's order ("doctrine of implied findings"). *Marriage of Jones* (1990) 222 CA3d 505, 515, 271 CR 761, 768; *Marriage of Aninger* (1990) 220 CA3d 230, 238, 269 CR 388, 392. The appellate court's task in such cases is limited to searching the record for "any substantial evidence" that will support the judgment. *Marriage of Jones, supra.* It must accept as true all evidence favorable to the prevailing party and discard all contrary evidence as unaccepted by the trier of fact. *Marriage of Aninger, supra.*

The only way to avoid implied findings in favor of the judgment is to request a statement of decision (see §17.23) and to object to the proposed statement, if necessary, in the manner provided by CCP §§632 and 634 (see §17.28). If omissions or ambiguities in the statement of decision are timely brought to the trial court's attention, the appellate court will not imply findings in favor of the prevailing party. CCP §634; see *Marriage of Arceneaux* (1990) 51 C3d 1130, 1133, 275 CR 797. For further discussion of the need to object to a proposed statement of decision to avoid implied findings in favor of the trial court's decision and to preserve an issue for appeal, see §17.28.

Although it is often a practical necessity, a statement of decision is not an absolute prerequisite to the appeal of an order. If the transcript of the proceeding adequately sets forth the basis of the trial court's ruling, the appellate court may review the court's decision in the absence of a statement of decision. *Marriage of Powers* (1990) 218 CA3d 626, 634 n5, 267 CR 350. See also *Marriage of Tallman* (1994) 22 CA4th 1697, 1699, 28 CR2d 323 (record, although sparse and somewhat confusing, provided sufficient basis to determine single legal issue in appeal that presented no factual disputes).

§17.11 2. Modification of Custody or Support

When orders for child custody, child support, or spousal support are sought to be modified based on an alleged change of circumstances (see §§6.24 (spousal support), 7.60 (child custody), 8.31 (child support)), the court must be able to identify the facts underlying the initial order before it can decide whether a change has occurred that allows a modification. When no statement of decision is issued, it may not be possible, on a future motion for modification, to ascertain what the underlying circumstances were at the time of the order. See *Marriage of Reilley* (1987) 196 CA3d 1119, 1126, 242 CR 302.

Note, however, that in many instances the lack of a statement of decision will not create a problem for future modification proceedings. Common alternatives to a statement of decision in establishing the circumstances underlying an order are "findings" (see §§17.12–17.15) and the filing of Income and Expense Declarations (see §§11.25–11.26). Also, no change of circumstances is required to modify a child support order when (1) the order was entered in accordance with an agreement of the parties and without any adjudication based on evidence presented to the court (*Singer v Singer* (1970) 7 CA3d 807, 87 CR 42); (2) there is no evidence of the circumstances under which the order was made (*Marriage of Thomas* (1981) 120 CA3d 33, 35, 173 CR 844); or (3) if the parties' stipulated agreement calls for child support below the guideline. Fam C §4065(d). Note that a change of circumstances *is* required to obtain a *downward* modification of child support order to the guideline level or below. *Marriage of Laudeman* (2001) 92 CA4th 1009, 1015, 112 CR2d 378.

The findings sought by each party in a statement of decision may be quite different from the facts each sought to prove at trial. Depending on whether counsel wishes to facilitate or discourage future modification of support and custody orders, findings may be proposed that either maximize or minimize a change of circumstances that might occur in the future. For example, it is in the payor's best interest at trial to prove the lowest level of income possible when support is being set; but after the tentative decision is made, the payor may prefer a finding of a higher level of income to minimize the change caused by a future increase in his or her earnings. On the other hand, the payee will try to establish a higher level of income for the payor at trial and, after the tentative decision, may favor findings of a lower level of income to maximize the change caused by a future increase in the payor's earnings.

§17.12 C. Required "Findings" Distinguished

Whether or not a statement of decision is requested under CCP §632, the court may be required, under the Family Code or by case law, to make certain findings on custody of minor children (see §17.13), child support (see §17.14), spousal support (see §17.15), or property division (see §17.16).

§17.13 1. Child Custody Orders

On the request of any party, the court must state in its decision the reasons for granting or denying a request for joint custody. Fam C §3082. Similarly, if the court modifies or terminates an existing order for joint custody over the objection of either parent, the court's decision must include the reasons for the modification or termination. Fam C §3087. The request for a statement of reasons must be made within a "reasonable" time, *i.e.,* within the same period of time as a request for a statement of decision (see §§17.19–17.20). *Marriage of Buser* (1987) 190 CA3d 639, 642, 235 CR 785.

The statement of reasons required by Fam C §3082 is different in both substance and purpose from the statement of decision required by CCP §632. Instead of providing a basis for appellate review, the statement of reasons is intended to provide parents with the reasons, in plain English, for the court's granting or denying a request for joint custody. *Marriage of Buser, supra.* A statement that joint physical custody is, or is not, in the child's best interests is not sufficient to meet the requirement. Fam C §3082.

§17.14 2. Child Support Orders

The statewide uniform child support guideline requires a number of findings at the request of any party. See Fam C §4056(b); §8.28. On court statements required by rebuttal of the presumption that the amount of child support under the guideline formula is the correct amount, see Fam C §4056(a); *Marriage of Hall* (2000) 81 CA4th 313, 319, 96 CR2d 772 (trial court must state in writing or on record reasons for child support order deviating from guideline providing for monthly amount plus percentage of payor's income); §8.16.

On findings required when deductions for hardship expenses are allowed, see Fam C §4072; §8.11.

On findings required in connection with health insurance coverage for children, see Fam C §§3751(a)(2), 3761(a), 3762(b).

At the request of either party, an order modifying, terminating, or setting aside an existing child support order must include a "statement of decision." Fam C §3654.

§17.15 3. Spousal Support Orders

Family Code §4330 provides that in any judgment of dissolution or legal separation the court may order spousal support, based on the standard of living established during the marriage and taking into consideration specified circumstances. The court must make "specific factual findings" on the standard of living, whether or not requested, and, if requested, "appropriate factual determinations" with respect to other circumstances. Fam C §4332. There is no statutory authority, however, for requesting findings on the issuance of temporary orders for spousal support.

At the request of either party, an order modifying, terminating, or setting aside an existing spousal support order must include a "statement of decision." Fam C §3654. See *Marriage of Sellers* (2003) 110 CA4th 1007, 2 CR3d 293 (when one party requested statement of decision about modification order, reversible error for court not to issue it).

§17.16 4. Orders Dividing Property

Under Fam C §2550, and subject to limited exceptions, the court must divide the community estate of the parties equally. See §5.70. To ensure an equal division, the trial court must make findings of fact on the nature and value of the specific items of community property. *Marriage of Tammen* (1976) 63 CA3d 927, 930, 134 CR 161.

§17.17   D. Procedure

A statement of decision is issued only on a party's request and only for those controverted issues specified in the request. See §17.7. California Rules of Ct 3.1590 sets forth the procedure for requesting and obtaining a statement of decision in trials lasting longer than 1 day. After a request is made, any party may make proposals on the content of the statement. Cal Rules of Ct 3.1590(b); see §17.25. The party designated to prepare the statement, or the court, prepares a proposed statement of decision (Cal Rules of Ct 3.1590(c); see §§17.26–17.27), and any objections to the statement must then be filed with the court (Cal Rules of Ct 3.1590(d); see §17.28). The court may grant a hearing to settle the statement of decision if it wishes (Cal Rules of Ct 3.1590(f); see §17.29), and a final statement is then issued (see §17.30).

Rule 3.1590 does not apply to statements of decision in trials that are completed within 1 day. Cal Rules of Ct 3.1590(h); see §17.19. Any questions of procedure on these trials that are not provided for in CCP §632 either are governed by local court rule or are within the court's discretion. See §§17.19, 17.30.

§17.18   1. Request

A court has no duty to issue a statement of decision unless a request is timely made under CCP §632. The trial court has no duty to advise a party of the right to request a statement of decision. *Marriage of Johnson* (1982) 134 CA3d 148, 163, 184 CR 444.

a. When to Request

§17.19   (1) Trials of 1 Day or Less

For trials concluded within 1 day, or in less than 8 hours over more than 1 day, the request for a statement of decision must be made before the matter is submitted for decision. CCP §632. A trial that occurs over several days but takes less than 8 hours as determined by court records comes within CCP §632. *Marriage of Gray* (2002) 103 CA4th 974, 127 CR2d 271. A case is considered submitted on the first of the following to occur: (1) the date the court orders the matter submitted, or (2) the date the final paper is required to be filed or the date argument is heard, whichever is later. Cal Rules of Ct 825(a). At the time of submission, counsel must be prepared to articulate the principal controverted issues on which a statement is desired. See *Marriage of Katz* (1991) 234 CA3d 1711, 1717, 286 CR 495 (statement of decision on specific controverted issue waived when request not timely made).

Failure to make a timely request normally results in a waiver of the right to a statement, but exceptions may be granted in exceptional cases. See *Marriage of Ramer* (1986) 187 CA3d 263, 271, 231 CR 647; *Gordon v Wolfe* (1986) 179 CA3d 162, 224 CR 481. On waiver of the right to a statement of decision, see §17.23. To avoid the consequences of an untimely request, counsel should consider filing a written request for a statement of decision at the outset of a trial, or even a few days before the trial. In any event, it is wise to prepare the request before the commencement of trial. On content and form of the request, see §§17.21–17.22.

§17.20 (2) Trials of More Than 1 Day

In trials lasting 8 hours or more over more than 1 day, the request for a statement of decision must be made within 10 days after the court announces its tentative decision. CCP §632. See *Staten v Heale* (1997) 57 CA4th 1084, 68 CR2d 35 (request for statement of decision deemed made when received by court, not when mailed). If the tentative decision is announced orally in open court, the 10-day period begins to run from the date of that announcement. If a written tentative decision is mailed to the parties, the period for requesting a statement of decision begins to run from the date of mailing (*Hutchins v Glanda* (1990) 216 CA3d 1529, 265 CR 596) and is extended as provided in CCP §1013(a), *e.g.*, by 5 calendar days if mailed to an address in California from an address in California. See *Marriage of McDole* (1985) 176 CA3d 214, 219, 221 CR 734, disapproved on other grounds in *Marriage of Fabian* (1986), 41 C3d 440, 451, 224 CR 333.

Under CCP §632, a request for a statement of decision in a trial lasting 8 hours or more over more than 1 day must be made after the court announces its tentative decision. Nonetheless, a request made just before the court's announcement of its intended decision was found to be effective in at least one case, when the request was confined to a single issue. *Marriage of Ananeh-Firempong* (1990) 219 CA3d 272, 284, 268 CR 83. On content and form of the request, see §§17.21–17.22.

b. Content and Form

§17.21 (1) Discussion

The request for a statement of decision must specify the principal controverted issues on which a statement of decision is requested. CCP §632; see §17.7. The request must be specific on the findings requested; a general request that a statement of decision be made is probably insufficient. See *Marriage of Warren* (1972) 28 CA3d 777, 784, 104 CR 860 (failure to request specific finding on expenditure of community assets on wife's separate property constituted waiver of finding on that issue). See also *Marriage of Katz* (1991) 234 CA3d 1711, 1717, 286 CR 495.

It has been held that the request, regardless of the length of trial, may be made orally or in writing. *Marriage of Ananeh-Firempong* (1990) 219 CA3d 272, 284, 268 CR 83. But see *Martinez v County of Tulare* (1987) 190 CA3d 1430, 1434, 235 CR 851 (criticized in *Ananeh-Firempong*), requiring a written request in trials lasting longer than 1 day, unless the parties otherwise agree. The safer approach would appear to be to make the request in writing. If the request is made orally, counsel should make sure that it is made part of the court record.

See §17.22 for a hypothetical example, for illustrative purposes only, of a written request for a statement of decision on certain limited issues.

§17.22 (2) Form: Request for Statement of Decision (Sample Form)

Barbara Smith
State Bar No. 65432
567 Main St.
Mayfair, CA 91234
Telephone: (787) 711–2000

Attorney for Respondent LINDA ROSE

SUPERIOR COURT OF CALIFORNIA
COUNTY OF LAS PALMAS

Marriage of	)	No. 67890
	)	
Petitioner: EDWARD ROSE	)	REQUEST FOR STATEMENT
	)	OF DECISION
Respondent: LINDA ROSE	)	(CCP §632)
	)	
_____	)	

NOTICE IS HEREBY GIVEN that respondent, LINDA ROSE, requests that the Court issue a Statement of Decision setting forth the factual and legal basis for its Tentative Decision, announced in open court on September 18, 2005, on the following principal controverted issues:

1. The date of separation of the parties;

2. The value of the family residence located at 1519 Eldridge Way, Mayfair, California, and the method of determining that value;

3. The value of the community property interest in the retirement benefits earned through petitioner's employment with West Utility Corp. and the method of determining that value; and

4. The standard of living of the parties during marriage and the circumstances on which the award of spousal support to respondent is based.

Date: September 24, 2005

_____
Barbara Smith
Attorney for Respondent

Copies: Original (submit to court clerk); copy for other attorney or party; office copies.

§17.23   c. Waiver

A statement of decision may be waived by express consent, by the failure to timely request it, by the failure to timely prepare it, or by the failure to specify a particular controverted issue in a timely manner. *Marriage of Hebbring* (1989) 207 CA3d 1260, 1274, 255 CR 488. A statement of decision may also be waived by failing to object to a trial court's alternative procedure, even when the procedure does not meet the statutory requirements and when a timely request is later made. *Whittington v McKinney* (1991) 234 CA3d 123, 285 CR 586. A party who waives a statement of decision may be unable to attack the trial court's determination of issues. On appeal, the judgment or order of the trial court will be presumed correct, and "every essential fact" necessary to sustain the lower court's order will be implied (the "doctrine of implied findings"). See *Marriage of Jones* (1990) 222 CA3d 505, 515, 271 CR 761; *Marriage of Aninger* (1990) 220 CA3d 230, 238, 269 CR 388. On the effect of a waiver on appeal, see §17.10.

If a statement of decision has not been requested, the trial court's tentative decision cannot be reviewed on appeal to determine the basis of the decision. The tentative decision is not binding on the trial court, it is not part of the record on appeal, and it will not avoid the application of the doctrine of implied findings. *Marriage of Ditto* (1988) 206 CA3d 643, 253 CR 770. On tentative decisions generally, see §§17.2–17.4. In contrast, a settled statement may provide the appellate court with a sufficient basis for review and thus avoid the presumption of all facts necessary to support the judgment, if it sets forth all the testimony at a hearing, the decision of the court, and the reasons for the decision. *Marriage of Fingert* (1990) 221 CA3d 1575, 1580, 271 CR 389.

§17.24 d. Failure to Render When Requested

When a statement of decision is timely requested under CCP §632, it is reversible error for the trial court to fail to issue the statement. *Marriage of Ananeh-Firempong* (1990) 219 CA3d 272, 284, 268 CR 83 (judgment on valuation of medical practice reversed for failure to render statement of decision on issue of calculations used to determine value); *Marriage of McDole* (1985) 176 CA3d 214, 221 CR 734, disapproved on other grounds in *Marriage of Fabian* (1986), 41 C3d 440, 451, 224 CR 333. Under former CCP §632, a judgment rendered without requested findings of fact was void. See, *e.g., Marriage of McNaughton* (1983) 145 CA3d 845, 849, 194 CR 176.

These cases must be distinguished from those in which the court renders a requested statement of decision but fails to address all issues requested. In the latter event, the failure is reversible error only if the omission was timely brought to the court's attention.

In *Marriage of Arceneaux* (1990) 51 C3d 1130, 275 CR 797, the court required, when a statement of decision fails to resolve a controverted issue, that a two-step procedure be followed to avoid application of the doctrine of implied findings (see §17.10). First, the issue must be specified in the request for a statement of decision; and second, the party claiming a deficiency in the statement must bring the defect to the trial court's attention, either before entry of judgment or in conjunction with a motion for new trial or a motion to vacate and enter a different judgment. CCP §634; 51 C3d at 1133. On objections to proposed statement of decision generally, see §17.28.

If, on modifying an award of custody or support, a trial court fails to issue a requested statement of decision or statutory finding (see §§17.12-17.15), the modification may be reversed unless the appellate court can ascertain from the record the criteria used by the trial court in reaching its decision. *Marriage of Wood* (1983) 141 CA3d 671, 190 CR 469 (order modifying custody affirmed because transcript record and statutory guidelines permitted meaningful review even without express findings; order modifying support reversed because impossible to determine basis of trial court's decision from record).

§17.25 2. Proposals on Content

After a request has been made for a statement of decision, any party may submit proposals on the content of the statement. CCP §632. If the trial lasted longer than 1 day, proposals on content must be made within 10 days after the date the statement of decision is requested. Cal Rules of Ct 3.1590(b), (h).

California Rules of Ct 3.1590 does not state whether a party may make proposals on content that go beyond the scope of the issues set forth in the request for a statement of decision. Before its amendment in 1981, former Cal Rules of Ct 232(d) permitted a party to request "further or specific findings" after an initial request for findings was made. However, findings were formerly required, if requested, on all issues of fact material to the judgment (former Cal Rules of Ct 232(e)), not just those "principal controverted issues" specified by the party requesting a statement of decision (CCP §632;

see §17.7). A party wishing a statement of decision on certain issues should therefore make an initial request within the time permitted. See §§17.18–17.20.

Rule 3.1590 does not apply to trials completed within 1 day. Cal Rules of Ct 3.1590(h). Counsel should consult local rules for the procedure and time period for submitting proposals in such cases or ask the trial court for direction. On trials completed in less than 8 hours over more than 1 day, see §17.5.

3. Proposed Statement of Decision

§17.26   a. Discussion

A tentative decision may provide that it will become the statement of decision if the parties fail, within 10 days after its announcement, to specify controverted issues or to make proposals not covered in the tentative decision. Cal Rules of Ct 3.1590(a). On when a tentative decision is required, see §17.2.

The tentative decision may also designate a party to prepare the statement of decision, if one is requested. Cal Rules of Ct 3.1590(a). If the tentative decision does not make such a designation, the court has (1) 5 days after a statement of decision is requested to notify a party to prepare a proposed statement of decision and proposed judgment or (2) 15 days after expiration of the time for proposals on the statement's content to prepare and mail the documents itself. Cal Rules of Ct 3.1590(c). On tentative decisions generally, see §§17.2–17.4. Usually, the judge will delegate the responsibility for preparing the statement to the "prevailing party."

A party who has been designated or notified to prepare the statement of decision must serve and submit to the court a proposed statement of decision and a proposed judgment within 15 days after the time to submit proposals has expired (see Cal Rules of Ct 3.1590(c); §16.25) or within 15 days after notice, whichever is later. If the designated party fails to serve and submit the proposed statement and the proposed judgment within the time allowed, any other party who appeared at trial may either serve and submit a proposed statement of decision and judgment or may file a motion for an order that the statement of decision be deemed waived. Cal Rules of Ct 3.1590(c).

Rule 3.1590 does not apply to trials completed within 1 day. Cal Rules of Ct 3.1590(h). Counsel should consult local rules on preparing, filing, and serving the proposed statement of decision in such cases or ask the trial court for direction. Regarding trials completed in less than 8 hours over more than 1 day, see §17.5.

See §17.27 for a hypothetical example, for illustrative purposes only, of a proposed statement of decision, based on the sample request for statement of decision in §17.22.

§17.27　b. Form: Proposed Statement of Decision (Sample Form)

Robert Jones
State Bar No. 76543
345 Broadway
Mayfair, CA 91234
Telephone: (787) 711-4500

Attorney for Petitioner EDWARD ROSE

SUPERIOR COURT OF CALIFORNIA
COUNTY OF LAS PALMAS

Marriage of　　　　　　　　　)	No. 67890
)	
Petitioner: EDWARD ROSE　)	PROPOSED STATEMENT
)	OF DECISION
Respondent: LINDA ROSE　)	(CAL RULES OF CT
)	3.1590(c))
_____)	

This matter came on regularly for trial on August 21–22 and September 18, 2005, in Department IV of the court shown above, the Honorable Carol F. Stone presiding. Petitioner was present and was represented by his attorney, Robert Jones. Respondent was present and was represented by her attorney, Barbara Smith. Oral and documentary evidence was received, arguments were made on behalf of both parties, and the matter was submitted for decision on September 18, 2005. The Court, having orally announced its Tentative Decision in open court on September 18, 2005, in the presence of both parties and counsel, and a Request for Statement of Decision having been timely filed by respondent on September 24, 2005, now makes this written Statement of Decision. The following paragraph numbers correspond to those in respondent's Request for Statement of Decision.

1. The date of separation of the parties was August 3, 2004. Although the parties lived apart for brief periods of time before the date of separation, these periods were temporary in nature and for economic or social reasons only. Not until August 3, 2004, was there a "complete and final break in the marital relationship" in which petitioner and respondent had a "parting of the ways with no present intention of resuming marital relations." *Marriage of Marsden* (1982) 130 CA3d 426, 434, 181 CR 910, 914; *Marriage of Imperato* (1975) 45 CA3d 432, 435, 119 CR 590, 592.

2. The value of the family residence located at 1519 Eldridge Way, Mayfair, California, was $275,000 on the date of trial. The debt owed on that residence at the time of trial was $104,200, leaving a net equity of $170,800. The determination of value is based on information on comparable sales and replacement cost in the appraisal offered and accepted into evidence, and the testimony at trial, of petitioner's expert witness, Alice Crane. Ms. Crane is a certified appraiser and real estate agent with 25 years' experience in the community where the family residence is located. The testimony of respondent's witness, Alan Simon, on the value of the residence was not persuasive in that Mr. Simon had less experience as a real estate agent and his experience was primarily in commercial, not residential, real property.

3. The value, on the date of trial, of the community property interest in the retirement benefits earned through petitioner's employment with Western Utility Corp. was $47,078. The determination of that value is based on the formula for establishing the value of such an interest as set forth in *Marriage of Bergman* (1985) 168 CA3d 742, 748 n4, 214 CR 661, 664 n4.

The Western Utility Corp. Retirement Fund is a defined contribution plan to which petitioner and his employer, Western Utility Corp., made contributions during the continuous 15-year period of petitioner's employment, beginning 1 year before the parties' marriage and continuing to the date of trial. In *Marriage of Bergman, supra*, the court defined the value of the community interest in a defined contribution plan at dissolution as "the amount of contributions made between the marriage and separation, plus accruals thereon, and all accruals thereon between the date of separation and trial of the issue." *Marriage of Bergman* (1985) 168 CA3d 742, 748 n4, 214 CR 661, 664 n4.

Applying this formula, the contributions made to the retirement plan from the date of marriage, July 19, 1987, to the date of separation, August 3, 2004, were $36,973 (hereafter, "contributions during marriage"); accruals on the contributions during marriage from the date of marriage to the date of separation were $8,659; and accruals on the contributions during marriage from the date of separation to the date of trial were $1,446. These amounts were established through the uncontroverted testimony of petitioner's witness, Margaret Cohen, Secretary of Personnel in the Office of the Plan Administrator of the Western Utility Corp. Retirement Fund.

The sum of these amounts, *i.e.,* $47,078, is the value, as of the date of trial, of the community property interest of petitioner and respondent in Western Utility Corp. Retirement Fund.

4. The court finds the following facts with respect to the parties' standard of living during marriage: At the date of separation, the parties enjoyed a comfortable lifestyle, as evidenced by (1) their family residence, a ranch-style three-bedroom home located in a new, well-maintained, and attractive residential development known as Woodhaven, a suburb of Mayfair; (2) their practice, over the past several years, of taking at least one vacation abroad each year; (3) their ownership of a one-third interest in a vacation condominium at Aspen, Colorado, where they vacation two or three times each year; and (4) their ownership of a 2005 Volvo sedan, and a 2003 Toyota Solara convertible.

The court finds the following facts with respect to the circumstances on which the award of spousal support to respondent is based: Petitioner, age 38, is in good health and has been employed for 15 years by Western Utility Corp., presently as regional sales manager earning an annual salary of $95,000. Respondent, age 36, is also in good health and is employed outside the home on a part-time basis as a teacher's aide at Laurel Glen Elementary School, earning an annual salary of $18,000. Respondent is needed in the home on a part-time basis to care for the parties' minor son, David, age 8. Both parties have actual earnings at or close to their earning capacities at the present time.

Date: _ _ _ _ _ _   _____
                                     Judge of the Superior Court

Copies: Original (submit to court clerk); copy for other attorney or party; office copies.

§17.28   4. Objections

Under Cal Rules of Ct 3.1590(d), any party affected by the judgment may serve and file objections to the proposed statement of decision within 15 days after the proposed statement and the proposed judgment have been served. The objection should clearly set forth that portion of the proposed statement of decision to which objection is made, the reason for the objection, and the preferred statement of facts or law. Rule 3.1590 does not apply to trials completed within 1 day. Cal Rules of Ct 3.1590(h). Counsel should consult local rules regarding objections to proposed statements of decision in such cases or ask the trial court for direction. Regarding trials completed in less than 8 hours over more than 1 day, see §17.5.

If the proposed statement of decision does not resolve a controverted issue, or if it is ambiguous, CCP §634 provides that the omission or ambiguity must be brought to the trial court's attention before appeal. If it is not, the objection is waived and all findings necessary to support the trial court's decision will be implied on appeal ("doctrine of implied findings"; see §17.10). The defect may be brought to the court's attention before judgment (presumably by filing an objection under Cal Rules of Ct 3.1590(d)) or in conjunction with either a motion for new trial (CCP §657) or a motion to vacate and enter a different judgment (CCP §663). CCP §634.

The fact that the omitted or ambiguous issue was specified in the request for statement of decision is not sufficient to avoid the doctrine of implied findings. Rather, both stages of a two-step process must be taken: First, a statement of decision must be requested on the specific issue; second, the statement's omission or ambiguity on the specified issue must be brought to the trial court's attention before appeal. *Marriage of Arceneaux* (1990) 51 C3d 1130, 1133, 275 CR 797, 798. The two-step requirement described in *Arceneaux* appears to apply regardless of the length of the trial.

§17.29   5. Hearing

The trial court has discretion to order a hearing on proposals or objections to the proposed statement of decision. Cal Rules of Ct 3.1590(f). Under former law, the court had discretion to grant a hearing on findings of fact on its own motion or on the motion of a party. *Kanner v Globe Bottling Co.* (1969) 273 CA2d 559, 78 CR 25. However, Cal Rules of Ct 3.1590(f) does not specifically provide that a hearing may be requested by a party.

§17.30　6. Final Statement of Decision

When the trial is concluded within 1 day, or in less than 8 hours over more than 1 day, the statement of decision may be made orally on the record, in the parties' presence. CCP §632; *Marriage of Katz* (1991) 234 CA3d 1711, 1717, 286 CR 495. Should it choose to do so, the court also has the discretion to issue a statement in writing after such a trial. *Khan v Superior Court* (1988) 204 CA3d 1168, 1173 n4, 251 CR 815.

In trials lasting 8 hours or more over more than 1 day, the statement must be in writing unless the parties appearing at trial agree otherwise. CCP §632. No particular form is required for the statement of decision, as long as it adequately sets forth the factual and legal basis of the court's decision and complies with CCP §632. *Wolfe v Lipsy* (1985) 163 CA3d 633, 643, 209 CR 801. The final statement may be the tentative decision (see §17.3); the proposed statement of decision prepared by a party or by the court (see §17.26); or a revision of the proposed statement, prepared by a party or by the court, based on proposals as to content, objections, or hearing (see §§17.25, 17.28–17.29).

Court rules do not specify a time period within which a final statement of decision must be rendered. Presumably, it may not be issued before expiration of the 15-day period for filing objections to the proposed statement (Cal Rules of Ct 3.1590(d); see §17.28) but may be issued immediately thereafter. Former Cal Rules of Ct 232(g), requiring the court to sign and file its findings within 10 days after expiration of the time for filing objections, or after a hearing on objections, was deleted when the rules were amended, effective January 1, 1982, to provide for statements of decision.

§17.31　7. Extension of Time Limits

On a showing of good cause at any time before entry of judgment, the court on written order may excuse noncompliance with and extend any of the time limits set by Cal Rules of Ct 3.1590. Cal Rules of Ct 3.1590(g). When the time requirements have not been followed but neither party has objected, the record should be protected by obtaining a written order excusing whatever noncompliance has occurred. Note, however, that Rule 3.1590(g) does not provide for extending the time for requesting a statement of decision, the time limits for which are prescribed by CCP §632. Failure to make a timely request will result in a waiver of the right to a statement although, in exceptional cases, relief may be granted from a waiver caused by a slight delay. See *Marriage of Ramer* (1986) 187 CA3d 263, 271, 231 CR 647; *Gordon v Wolfe* (1986) 179 CA3d 162, 224 CR 481.

§17.32 IV. JUDGMENT

The judgment is "the final determination of the rights of the parties in an action or proceeding" (CCP §577), although in a marital action, that determination may be subject to postjudgment modification (see chap 21). The judgment must be prepared on the Judicial Council form of Judgment (see form in §14.56) unless the issue of marital status has already been (or will be) decided separately (see §17.66). The discussion in §§17.33–17.58 is limited to judgments after contested trials. On judgments in uncontested proceedings, see §§14.36–14.58.

§17.33 A. Single Judgment

Before July 1, 1984, California had a two-step procedure for entering a judgment of dissolution of marriage. First, the parties obtained an interlocutory judgment, which determined all issues in the action except for the actual termination of marital status. Once the interlocutory judgment was entered, and after six months had elapsed from the date the court acquired jurisdiction over the respondent, either party could apply for entry of a final judgment, legally dissolving the marriage. On obtaining a final judgment in a pending action when an interlocutory judgment was entered before July 1, 1984, see §§17.84–17.86.

Actions for legal separation and nullity have always been single-judgment actions. Effective July 1, 1984, dissolution actions likewise became single-judgment actions with the abolition of the interlocutory judgment. Family Code §2338 now provides that if the court determines that a dissolution should be granted "a judgment" will be entered. This single judgment incorporates all functions of the previous interlocutory and final judgments, *i.e.,* it adjudicates all issues in the action, including the status of marriage. Note, however, that in bifurcated proceedings there may be more than one judgment, each adjudicating separate issues. See §§14.59–14.74, 17.65–17.66.

§17.34　　B. Finality and Modifiability of Judgment

Unless certain issues have been bifurcated or reserved for separate trial (see §§14.59–14.74, 17.65), the judgment is a final, binding adjudication of all issues to be determined in the action, including marital status, division of property, child custody and support, spousal support, attorney fees and costs, and injunctive orders. Once the judgment becomes final (see §§17.40, 17.47), the doctrine of res judicata prevents relitigation of any issues. However, child custody and child support orders contained in the judgment are modifiable, based on postjudgment circumstances, and in most cases the same is true of spousal support orders. On modification generally, see chap 21.

§17.35　　1. Marital Status

A judgment terminating the status of marriage necessarily determines that the marriage ended was valid, and the judgment is res judicata on that issue as between the former spouses and those in privity with them. The judgment does not, however, establish the validity of the marriage as against third persons who were not and had no right to be heard in the action. As between strangers, or strangers and parties, the judgment is res judicata only on the subsequent unmarried status of the parties. *Rediker v Rediker* (1950) 35 C2d 796, 801, 221 P2d 1. See also 11 Witkin, Summary of California Law, Husband and Wife §§167–168 (9th ed 1990).

2. Division of Property

§17.36　　a. Not Modifiable

Judgment provisions regarding property rights are not modifiable. *Leupe v Leupe* (1942) 21 C2d 145, 148, 130 P2d 697; *Esserman v Esserman* (1982) 136 CA3d 572, 186 CR 329.

§17.37　　b. Effective Date of Division

The question may arise whether a division of community property is immediately effective on entry of the judgment, or whether its effect is delayed until the judgment becomes final. On finality of judgment, see §§17.40, 17.47. This problem may occur when there is a significant delay between entry and finality of the judgment, because either (1) the trial or settlement of the action precedes expiration of the six-month waiting period (see §17.47) or (2) the filing of a motion for new trial or a notice of appeal delays the finality of the judgment (see §17.40). For the effect of a reconciliation on an entered, but not final, judgment, see §17.41.

Earlier cases discouraged or prohibited an immediately effective disposition of property. *Gudelj v Gudelj* (1953) 41 C2d 202, 214, 259 P2d 656; *Leupe v Leupe* (1942) 21 C2d 145, 149, 130 P2d 697. But the present rule allows a judgment to make an immediate and conclusive disposition of property, unless (1) the judgment is challenged by appeal or (2) jurisdiction is reserved to divide the property at a later date. *Marriage of Brown* (1976) 15 C3d 838, 851 n13, 126 CR 633; *Decker v Occidental Life Ins. Co.* (1969) 70 C2d 842, 848, 76 CR 470 (note Justice Mosk's concurring opinion, 70 C2d at 848, arguing for an explicit overruling of *Gudelj*). Although these cases were decided before interlocutory judgments were abolished, the underlying reasoning should apply to the present single judgment.

§17.38   3. Child Custody and Support

The court has continuing jurisdiction under the Family Code, during the pendency of the proceeding and at any time after judgment, to hear and decide all matters that concern the welfare of the parties' minor children. By statute, the custody and support of a minor child remain modifiable after judgment during the minority of the child, even if the judgment attempts to preclude modifiability. Fam C §§3022, 3651; *Marriage of Goodarzirad* (1986) 185 CA3d 1020, 230 CR 203. On modification generally, see §§7.59–7.60 (custody), 8.31 (child support).

§17.39   4. Spousal Support

The right to a long-term or "permanent" (as opposed to temporary) award of spousal support is properly in issue when the case is tried and determined and any temporary award of support is terminated by the judgment. See *Wilson v Superior Court* (1948) 31 C2d 458,

462, 189 P2d 266. By statute, an order for spousal support is modifiable and terminable after judgment unless the parties agree otherwise. Fam C §3651. When the judgment neither awards spousal support nor reserves jurisdiction to do so, however, it may not subsequently be modified to provide for spousal support. *McClure v McClure* (1935) 4 C2d 356, 359, 49 P2d 584. On modification and termination of spousal support generally, see §§6.20–6.27.

5. Provisions and Events Affecting Finality

§17.40　　a. Time for Filing Notice of Intention to Move for New Trial or Notice of Appeal

If a motion for a new trial is made (see §§18.2–18.15) or if an appeal is taken (see chap 19), the judgment will not become final until the motion or appeal is finally disposed of; nor will it become final even then if the motion is granted or the judgment is reversed. Fam C §2341(a). Despite the filing of a notice of intention to move for a new trial or a notice of appeal, that portion of the judgment restoring the parties to the status of unmarried persons will become final on the date specified in the judgment unless (1) the moving or appealing party objects to the termination of marital status in the notice of intention or notice of appeal and (2) the objection was also made at the time of trial. Fam C §2341(b).

Even if no notice of intention to move for a new trial or notice of appeal is filed, the period allowed by statute for the filing of the notice of intention (see §18.7) or notice of appeal (see §19.47) effectively delays the finality of the judgment (except for that portion restoring the parties to unmarried status). When the six-month waiting period has passed and neither party contemplates moving for a new trial or taking an appeal, the parties can ensure the immediate finality of the judgment by agreeing to waive the right to move for a new trial or to appeal. Any agreement of this nature should either be in the form of a written stipulation, signed by the parties and attorneys and filed with the court, or be stated in open court and made a part of the record.

§17.41　　b. Reconciliation

After the judgment is entered and before it becomes final (see

§17.47), neither party may dismiss the action without the other party's consent. Fam C §2338(c). If the parties reconcile during this period, they may together dismiss the action and resume their marital relationship. All orders previously entered in the proceeding will be canceled on dismissal of the action. On voluntary dismissals generally, see California Civil Procedure Before Trial, chap 39 (4th ed Cal CEB 2004).

Before interlocutory judgments were abolished, if the parties reconciled during the period between entry of the interlocutory and final judgments, all orders in the interlocutory judgment were canceled and the parties had restored to them all the rights and obligations arising from the marital relationship. *People v Howard* (1984) 36 C3d 852, 857, 206 CR 124. The reconciliation destroyed the parties' right to a final judgment and required the court to set aside the interlocutory judgment and dismiss the action. *Marriage of Modnick* (1983) 33 C3d 897, 911, 191 CR 629. If the reconciliation failed, the canceled judgment was not revived (36 C3d 852, 858 n10), but the parties could bring a subsequent action based on irreconcilable differences arising after the reconciliation (33 C3d 897, 911). Although the reasoning in *Modnick* and *Howard* appears to yield a similar result under the current single-judgment procedure, no decision has yet held that a reconciliation after entry of the single judgment, but before termination of marital status, results in dismissal of the action and a cancellation of orders in the judgment. However, once marital status is terminated and the judgment is final, a reconciliation will not restore the parties' marital status or cancel the orders.

By statute, although temporary orders for child support are not enforceable during a period of reconciliation (Fam C §3602), they remain in effect until terminated by the court or by operation of law (Fam C §3601(a)). Thus, temporary child support orders are clearly protected if a reconciliation occurs, and then fails, before a judgment is entered. Once entered, however, a judgment's orders supersede and revoke all temporary orders. If the approach of *People v Howard, supra,* applies under the single-judgment procedure, a reconciliation that occurs after judgment is entered but before marital status ends could effectively cancel orders for child support, regardless of Fam C §3601(a).

The burden of proving a reconciliation rests with the party seeking to establish it. That party must show that the intention to reconcile is "unconditional and contemplate[s] a complete restoration of all marital rights." *Marriage of Modnick, supra*. In *Modnick*, the parties cohabited, traveled, celebrated holidays, and entertained together after entry of an interlocutory judgment. However, the court did not find that they "mutually intended to permanently reunite," because they filed separate tax returns as single persons, treated new acquisitions as separate property, and continued to pay and receive spousal support. 33 C3d at 912.

§17.42   c. Death of Party

Under Fam C §310(a), a marriage is dissolved by the death of one of the parties. In this event, except in bifurcated proceedings as discussed below, any dissolution action abates and the court loses jurisdiction to make any further determinations in the action. Nonetheless, the court can enter judgment in conformity with matters already adjudicated before the death. *Marriage of Mallory* (1997) 55 CA4th 1165, 64 CR2d 667; *Estate of Blair* (1988) 199 CA3d 161, 167, 244 CR 627, 630; *Marriage of Shayman* (1973) 35 CA3d 648, 651, 111 CR 11, 13. The court in *Shayman* had filed its Findings of Fact and Conclusions of Law, setting forth the decision of the court, when one party died. The trial court's entry of judgment based on its findings was upheld. Unlike a dissolution action, a nullity action survives the death of a party, even before any adjudication has occurred, and the decedent's estate is properly substituted as a party in the decedent's place. *Marriage of Goldberg* (1994) 22 CA4th 265, 27 CR2d 298.

If a party dies after judgment of dissolution is entered but before the date specified for termination of marital status, it is unclear what effect, if any, the death has on the date the judgment becomes final and the marital status terminates. Family Code §2344(a) provides that the party's death will not impair the court's power to enter final judgment. Clearly, then, the marital status will terminate on the date specified in the judgment, if not before. But Fam C §2344(a) does not preclude an argument that marital status terminates automatically on the date of death (see Fam C §310(a)) or that the court may terminate the marital status as of a date between the date of death and the date specified in the judgment.

In a bifurcated dissolution action (see §§14.59-14.74, 17.65-17.66), when a judgment terminating marital status and reserving jurisdiction over all other issues has been entered, and a party dies before the reserved issues are decided, the court retains jurisdiction to dispose of the remaining issues. The decedent's estate is properly substituted as a party to the action in place of the deceased spouse. *Kinsler v Superior Court* (1981) 121 CA3d 808, 175 CR 564. See *Marriage of Hilke* (1992) 4 C4th 215, 221, 14 CR2d 371, 375 (former CC §4800.1, predecessor of Fam C §2581, applies to division of property held in joint tenancy form if former spouse dies after entry of bifurcated judgment dissolving parties' marital status and reserving property issues for later adjudication). On potential dangers to the surviving divorced spouse if the other spouse dies before a judgment on reserved issues, see §14.61.

§17.43   C. Preparing the Judgment

After a contested trial, a proposed judgment must be prepared and submitted to the court in conformity with the decision rendered. CCP §664. Use of the Judicial Council form of Judgment (see form in §14.56) is mandatory for adjudicating marital status in all dissolution, legal separation, and nullity proceedings. On judgments in bifurcated proceedings, see §§17.65–17.66. On judgments in uncontested marital proceedings, see §§14.36–14.58.

§17.44   1. Who Prepares; When Submitted

For trials lasting longer than 1 day, Cal Rules of Ct 3.1590 governs the procedure for preparing the proposed judgment. See Cal Rules of Ct 3.1590(h). When a statement of decision is not requested or is otherwise waived (see §17.23), the court must, within 10 days after expiration of the time for requesting the statement or after the waiver, prepare and mail a proposed judgment to all parties who appeared at trial. Alternatively (and typically), the court may notify a party to prepare, serve, and submit a proposed judgment within 10 days after notification. Any party affected by the judgment may serve and file objections within 10 days after service of the proposed judgment. Cal Rules of Ct 3.1590(e). The court may order a hearing if objections are filed. Cal Rules of Ct 3.1590(f). Within 10 days after expiration of the time for filing objections or, if a hearing is held, within 10 days after the hearing, the court must sign and file its judgment. Cal Rules of Ct 3.1590(e).

When a statement of decision is requested for a trial lasting longer than 1 day, the court must, within 15 days after expiration of the period (see Cal Rules of Ct 3.1590(b)) for submitting proposals on the content of the statement of decision, prepare and mail a proposed judgment (together with a proposed statement of decision) to all parties who appeared at trial. Alternatively (and typically), the court may, in its tentative decision or within 5 days after a request for a statement of decision, designate a party to prepare a proposed statement of decision. A party so designated must submit a proposed judgment (together with a proposed statement of decision) within 15 days after expiration of the period for submitting proposals on the content of the statement of decision or after notice, whichever is later. Cal Rules of Ct 3.1590(c).

Rule 3.1590 does not apply to trials completed within 1 day. Cal Rules of Ct 3.1590(h). Counsel should consult local rules on preparation of the proposed judgment in such cases or ask the trial court for direction. Regarding trials completed in less than 8 hours over more than 1 day, see §17.5.

§17.45   2. Discussion

The discussion in §§17.46–17.55 is keyed to the Judicial Council form of Judgment (see form in §14.56).

§17.46   a. Type of Proceeding

The Judicial Council form of Judgment is used in all marital actions, *i.e.,* actions for dissolution, legal separation, and nullity. The type of judgment is indicated by marking the appropriate box in the caption. On completing Item 4, see §17.50.

§17.47   b. Marital Status

If the court determines that a judgment of dissolution should be granted, a judgment is entered. Fam C §2338(c). The judgment cannot be final for the purpose of terminating the marriage, however, until at least six months have elapsed from the date of service on, or appearance by, the respondent, whichever occurred first. Fam C §2339(a). For good cause shown, the court may extend the six-month waiting period for termination of the marriage. Fam C §2339(b). The court has no authority, however, to shorten the six-month waiting period. Fam C §2339(a). The date on which the judgment becomes final for the purpose of terminating the marriage must be specified in the judgment (Fam C §2340) unless the court reserves jurisdiction over the issue for later determination (Fam C §2343).

When the judgment will be entered before the earliest possible date for termination of the marital status, the specific date on which the marriage will end is inserted in the caption and at Item 4.a.(1) of the judgment, unless the court reserves jurisdiction over the termination date.

If the judgment will be entered after the earliest possible date for termination, marital status will usually end on the date of entry of the judgment, in which case the date should be left blank for the court clerk to complete at that time. Alternatively, the court may have reserved jurisdiction over the termination date (in which case the date is left blank) or ordered a later date (in which case that date is inserted). Fam C §2343.

Whenever the court reserves jurisdiction, the appropriate box in the caption and the box at Item 4.a.(2) are checked.

§17.48   c. Hearing

Specific information on the trial is provided at Item 2 of the judgment. When the judgment is made after a contested trial, the box marked "contested" is checked; each date on which the trial was heard, or partially heard, is inserted; and the department and room number, if applicable, is given. The name of the trial judge is specified and, if he or she was only temporarily appointed to hear the trial as a commissioner or otherwise, the box marked "temporary judge" is checked. See Cal Const art VI, §21; *E.N.W. v Michael W.* (1983) 149 CA3d 896, 198 CR 355. Each party and attorney present at trial is indicated.

§17.49   d. Jurisdiction Over Respondent

The date on which the court acquired jurisdiction over the respondent is specified at Item 3 of the form and the appropriate box marked to indicate whether the respondent was served with process or made an appearance on that date. When six months have elapsed since service, but not since the appearance of the respondent, proof of service should be filed with the court.

§17.50   e. Type of Judgment

When a judgment of dissolution is granted, Item 4.a. is checked.

On insertion of the proper date for termination of marital status, see §17.47. When a judgment of legal separation is granted, Item 4.b. is checked. When a judgment of nullity is granted, Item 4.c. is checked and the specific ground (see §§3.8–3.15) stated.

§17.51　　f. Restoration of Former Name

In an action for dissolution or nullity of marriage, a party is entitled to restoration of a former name on request, whether or not a request was included in his or her petition or response. Fam C §2080. The order is indicated by checking the appropriate box at Item 4.f. and inserting the former name. For further discussion, see §14.53.

§17.52　　g. Entry of Judgment Nunc Pro Tunc

When, through mistake, negligence, or inadvertence, a judgment of dissolution was not entered, or was not entered as soon as it could have been, the court may order that it be deemed entered as of the date that it originally could have been entered. Fam C §2346(a), (c). In no event, however, may a judgment obtained by a contested trial be deemed entered as of a date before the trial. Fam C §2346(d). When the judgment will be entered nunc pro tunc, Item 4.d. is checked and the nunc pro tunc date indicated. On nunc pro tunc judgments generally, see §§17.59–17.64.

§17.53　　h. Reservation of Jurisdiction

When the contested trial addresses only certain bifurcated issues, with the court reserving jurisdiction over the remainder, the box at Item 4.g. is checked.

§17.54　　i. Other Orders

All court orders not otherwise specified on the judgment form are set forth at Item 4.o. Counsel should take particular care to use clear and precise language. The specific provisions should be numbered consecutively and set forth separately. They may start on the form and continue on additional pages, or the words "See attached" may be inserted on the form with the provisions following on continuation pages. The additional pages may be prepared on either plain or pleading paper.

§17.55   D. Signature and Filing

In trials lasting longer than 1 day, Cal Rules of Ct 3.1590(e) requires that the court sign and file its judgment within 10 days after expiration of the time for filing objections to the proposed judgment or, if a hearing is held on the objections, within 10 days after the hearing.

Rule 3.1590 does not apply to trials completed within 1 day. Cal Rules of Ct 3.1590(h). Note, however, that a trial judge's salary will be held back if any cause "remains pending and undetermined for 90 days after it has been submitted for decision." Cal Const art VI, §19. If a determination of the case has not otherwise been made as a tentative decision, as a statement of decision, or in the minutes of the court, the judgment must be signed and filed within the prescribed time limit. Regarding trials completed in less than 8 hours over more than 1 day, see §17.5.

If the trial judge becomes unavailable before signing the judgment, CCP §635 allows the presiding judge, or a judge designated by the presiding judge, to sign the judgment if the "decision of the court" was entered in the minutes. However, if a statement of decision was requested, the trial judge must have provided the statement before becoming unavailable; the presiding judge cannot sign a judgment based only on the trial court's tentative decision. *Armstrong v Picquelle* (1984) 157 CA3d 122, 127, 203 CR 552. Nevertheless, a presiding judge's entry of judgment based on a deceased trial judge's "Intended Decision" was upheld when there was no indication that the trial judge would have modified his decision, the intended decision was "in reality" a proposed statement of decision, and the proposed decision afforded an adequate basis for appellate review. *Leiserson v City of San Diego* (1986) 184 CA3d 41, 48, 229 CR 22. These cases were decided before the amendment to CCP §635, effective January 1, 1993, that allows not only the presiding judge, but also a judge designated by the presiding judge, to sign the judgment under the circumstances in which §635 applies. Presumably the holdings of these cases would now apply to such designated judges as well as presiding judges.

§17.56   E. Entry of Judgment

A judgment must be entered by the court clerk in conformity with the decision rendered by the court immediately on the filing of the decision. The judgment is not effective for any purpose until it is entered. CCP §664. Even if the six-month waiting period (see §17.47) has elapsed at the time the judgment is submitted, at least a week should be allowed (longer, if there is a possibility of appeal from the judgment as to status of marriage; see §17.40), and actual entry of the judgment should be verified before a party remarries. A marriage that occurs before entry of a judgment dissolving a previous marriage is bigamous and void. Fam C §2201; *Vickers v State Bar* (1948) 32 C2d 247, 255, 196 P2d 10. See *Marriage of Campbell* (2006) 136 CA4th 502, 507, 38 CR3d 908 (attempt to remarry before entry of judgment dissolving current marriage does not trigger cessation of spousal support under Fam C §4337).

§17.57   1. Procedure

To obtain entry of the judgment, an original and two copies of the Judicial Council form of Notice of Entry of Judgment see form in §14.58) are submitted to the court, together with the proposed judgment and two stamped envelopes, addressed in the same manner as on the form. On preparing the form, see §14.57. Failure to properly complete the form or submit the envelopes can result in the court's refusal to sign the judgment. Cal Rules of Ct 5.136(d). The court clerk, not a party, mails out the notice of entry after the judgment has been signed by the court, filed, and entered.

§17.58   2. Service on Opposing Party

Although a judgment is not required to be served on opposing counsel, it is customary for the party who has prepared the judgment to send a conformed copy of the filed and entered judgment to him or her. On service on the other party, see §11.62. Although that discussion is presented in the context of temporary orders, it is equally applicable to judgments.

V. SPECIAL TYPES OF JUDGMENTS

§17.59   A. Judgment Nunc Pro Tunc

When a judgment of dissolution ought to have been or was granted but, by mistake, inadvertence, or negligence, the judgment either was not entered or was not entered as early as it could have been entered, the court may cause the judgment to be signed, filed, and entered as of the earliest date it could have been entered. Fam C §2346(a), (c). On the necessary showing of "mistake," "inadvertence," or "negligence," see *Berry v Berry* (1956) 140 CA2d 50, 59, 294 P2d 757. In no event, however, may a judgment be entered as of a date before submission of the matter to the court by way of trial, uncontested hearing, or declaration. Fam C §2346(d). But see *Tamraz v Tamraz* (1994) 24 CA4th 1740, 1748, 30 CR2d 233 (when marital settlement agreement obligated husband to proceed to default hearing and he failed to do so, wife was entitled to judgment entered nunc pro tunc as of effective date of agreement even though matter was never submitted to court by trial, uncontested hearing, or declaration). Before granting a nunc pro tunc judgment, the court must also be satisfied that no appeal will be taken or motion made for a new trial or to set aside the judgment. Fam C §2346(a).

§17.60   1. Who May Apply

The court may grant nunc pro tunc entry of a judgment on its own motion or on that of a party to the action. Fam C §2346(b). In addition, anyone "whose rights are threatened by a delay which is not his fault" may apply for relief under the court's authority to grant the remedy on its own motion. *Hurst v Hurst* (1964) 227 CA2d 859, 867, 39 CR 162. This right has been extended to the putative spouse of one whose previous marriage was not finally terminated at the time of the subsequent marriage (*Hamrick v Hamrick* (1953) 119 CA2d 839, 845, 260 P2d 188; *Armstrong v Armstrong* (1948) 85 CA2d 482, 193 P2d 495); a child seeking to establish his or her legitimacy (*Hurst v Hurst* (1964) 227 CA2d 859, 867, 39 CR 162); and the personal representative of a deceased party (*Marriage of Mallory* (1997) 55 CA4th 1165, 64 CR2d 667; *Waller v Waller* (1970) 3 CA3d 456, 83 CR 533). See also *Marriage of Shayman* (1973) 35 CA3d 648, 111 CR 11 (after party's death, attorney allowed to file motion for nunc pro tunc entry of interlocutory judgment despite failure to substitute personal representative).

§17.61   2. When Applicable

Nunc pro tunc entry of judgment may be requested in a variety of contexts, but it is perhaps most often used to validate a subsequent marriage entered into by a party who mistakenly believed a previous marriage was finally dissolved. See *Marriage of Frapwell* (1975) 53 CA3d 479, 483, 125 CR 878.

§17.62 a. Invalid Subsequent Marriage

Before July 1, 1984, dissolution of marriage required a two-step procedure: (1) The entry of an interlocutory judgment resolving all issues of the marriage other than marital status, and (2) the subsequent entry of a final judgment terminating the marriage. Parties were not free to remarry until the final judgment was entered, and the final judgment was not entered until it was affirmatively requested. Occasionally, however, a party, believing that the judgment "automatically" became final after entry of the interlocutory judgment, would enter into a subsequent (bigamous and void) marriage before his or her marital status was terminated in the previous marriage. See Fam C §2201. To validate the subsequent marriage, a final judgment dissolving the previous marriage could be entered nunc pro tunc as of the earliest possible date. *Marriage of Frapwell* (1975) 53 CA3d 479, 483, 125 CR 878. Although interlocutory judgments have now been abolished, a party may still discover that a subsequent marriage is void for an inadvertent failure to enter a final judgment when an interlocutory judgment was entered before July 1, 1984. On entry of final judgment after an interlocutory judgment has been entered, see §§17.84–17.86.

When a subsequent marriage occurs before a previous marriage is dissolved, and an interlocutory judgment was not entered before July 1, 1984, a nunc pro tunc judgment may be used to validate the subsequent marriage only if that marriage occurred after the action for dissolution of the previous marriage was submitted to the court by way of trial, uncontested hearing, or declaration. Fam C §2346(d).

§17.63 b. Death of Party Before Judgment Is Final

When a party dies after the court has rendered a decision in the action but before the judgment becomes final, the court may enter judgment nunc pro tunc to the date of its decision. See CCP §669; *Marriage of Mallory* (1997) 55 CA4th 1165, 64 CR2d 667; *Marriage of Shayman* (1973) 35 CA3d 648, 111 CR 11; *Hamrick v Hamrick* (1953) 119 CA2d 839, 260 P2d 188. Entry of a judgment nunc pro tunc may be requested by the decedent's putative spouse in order to legitimize his or her status as surviving spouse, when the "marriage" to the decedent occurred after the previous judgment of dissolution could have been entered but before it was actually entered. *Hamrick v Hamrick, supra.* See also *Estate of Hughes* (1947) 80 CA2d 550, 554, 182 P2d 253.

A judgment may be entered nunc pro tunc to a date prior to the death of a party even though (1) no subsequent marriage is involved and (2) a surviving spouse will be divested of rights by such entry of judgment. *Waller v Waller* (1970) 3 CA3d 456, 466, 83 CR 533. A nunc pro tunc entry of judgment is not proper, however, when it is sought solely to defeat the rights of the surviving spouse and will not preserve any significant rights to the decedent's estate. *Marriage of Frapwell* (1975) 53 CA3d 479, 485, 125 CR 878.

§17.64   3. Procedure

When a stipulation to nunc pro tunc entry of a judgment cannot be obtained, a motion may be prepared and processed in the same manner as a noticed motion for temporary orders. For discussion of, and forms for, motions for temporary orders, see §§11.16–11.63. Local rules and practice may be consulted to ascertain whether, and under what circumstances, the motion may be made ex parte. See Fam C §2346(b), requiring notice only in "contested cases." It would appear to be the safer practice, however, to proceed by noticed motion in all cases.

The applicant should prepare, serve, and submit the following documents:

- A Notice of Motion (see form in §11.20) or an Order To Show Cause (see form in §11.18). In the caption, the box labeled "Other (specify)" should be checked and "Nunc Pro Tunc Entry of Judgment" or similar wording inserted.

- An Application for Order and Supporting Declaration (see form in §11.22). The specific relief requested should be indicated at Item 13. Facts in support of the relief requested may be provided at Item 14, or in an attached declaration, and should include (1) facts showing the grounds of mistake, inadvertence, or negligence in failing to enter the judgment when it could have been entered; and (2) the reasons for requesting entry of the judgment nunc pro tunc to the date it could have been entered.

- A memorandum of points and authorities (see §11.32).

- A Request and Declaration for Final Judgment of Dissolution of Marriage (see discussion in §17.85 and form in §17.86) when a pre-July 1, 1984, interlocutory judgment was previously entered.

- A Judgment (see form in §14.56), indicating in the caption, and at Items 4.a.(1) and 4.d., the date requested for nunc pro tunc termination of marital status and entry of judgment. Item 2 should be completed with reference to the hearing on the motion for nunc pro tunc entry, not to a previous proceeding resulting in a judgment. Items 3 and 4 are completed as in any judgment. If judgment was not previously entered in the action, all orders made by the court must be set forth on the form. When judgment was previously entered, the new judgment form should indicate, at Item 4.o., that the previously entered judgment, which should be identified by date, remains in effect and is unchanged, except for the date of termination of the parties' marital status.

- Notice of Entry of Judgment with stamped envelopes addressed to the parties. See §§14.57 (discussion), 14.58 (form).

§17.65　　B. Bifurcated Judgment

On noticed motion, the court may sever ("bifurcate") and grant an early and separate trial on the issue of the dissolution of the parties' marriage, apart from other issues in the action. Fam C§2337(a); *Marriage of Fink* (1976) 54 CA3d 357, 126 CR 626, decision on reserved issues appealed on other grounds in 25 C3d 877. See §§14.59–14.74. Once the parties' marital status has been terminated, the remaining (*i.e.,* "reserved") issues may be resolved by agreement or brought to trial. The court also has the power to bifurcate and try separately issues other than marital status (see §14.59), leaving the remaining issues (including marital status) to be resolved subsequently by agreement or trial.

Each judge who tries a separate issue or issues in a case must, depending on the length of the trial (see §17.2), announce a separate tentative decision, and issue a statement of decision if requested. A judge may proceed with the trial of subsequent issues before a statement of decision is rendered on previously tried issues. A proposed judgment is not prepared until all issues are tried, except when "a separate judgment may otherwise be properly entered" on the issues tried. The judge who tries the final issue prepares the proposed judgment. Cal Rules of Ct 3.1591.

§17.66   1. Preparation of Judgment

When the court grants a status-only judgment, terminating the parties' marriage and reserving jurisdiction over the remaining issues, the status-only judgment is prepared on the Judicial Council form of Judgment (see form in §14.56). On preparation of the judgment, see §14.70. On preparation of the subsequent judgment on reserved issues, see §§14.73–14.74.

When the court bifurcates issues other than marital status and tries them separately, a separate judgment is usually prepared on pleading paper, with the remaining issues (including marital status) resolved later, resulting in a judgment on the Judicial Council form. Local court rules and practice should, however, be consulted. The judgment on pleading paper may be captioned "Judgment on Bifurcated Issues of [specify issues]." Its preliminary provisions should recite (1) the date and contents of the court order bifurcating the issues determined in the judgment; (2) the date and department of the trial on the bifurcated issues; and (3) the judge presiding, appearances by counsel, and parties present at the trial. Following these preliminary matters, the substantive court orders are set forth as in any other judgment after contested trial, followed by the date and the judge's signature.

§17.67   2. Motion for New Trial and Appeal

A motion for a new trial may be made in a bifurcated trial only after all the issues have been tried. If different issues were tried by different judges, each judge must hear and decide the motion for new trial on the issues tried by that judge. Cal Rules of Ct 3.1591.

When the issue of marital status is bifurcated, an immediate and separate appeal may be filed from the judgment dissolving the marriage and from the subsequent judgment on reserved issues. *Marriage of Fink* (1976) 54 CA3d 357, 366, 126 CR 626, decision on reserved issues appealed on other grounds in 25 C3d 877. Issues other than marital status that have been bifurcated and determined in an early, separate trial may be accepted for review by an appellate court if the superior court that heard the issues certifies that the appeal is appropriate. Fam C §2025; Cal Rules of Ct 5.175-5.180. For further discussion of appeal in bifurcated proceedings, see §19.6.

§17.68   C. Qualified Domestic Relations Order (QDRO)

The Employee Retirement Income Security Act of 1974 (ERISA) (29 USC §§1001-1461) established a comprehensive federal regulatory program governing private employee pension plans. ERISA does not regulate the public pension plans of governmental entities or agencies, *e.g.*, federal military and civil service plans, Public Employees' Retirement System, or State Teachers' Retirement System (see §§17.80-17.83).

Provisions of ERISA, as amended by the Retirement Equity Act of 1984 (REA) (Pub L 98-397, 98 Stat 1426) and other subsequent legislation, provide that benefits payable under covered plans may not be assigned or alienated to persons other than a plan participant, unless the assignment or alienation is created under a qualified domestic relations order ("QDRO"). 29 USC §§1056(d)(3)(A), 1144(b)(7). To the extent that state statutes provide otherwise, *e.g.*, that a private pension plan, if joined as a party to the marital action, is bound by a non-QDRO judgment (see Fam C §§2060(b), 2070-2074, they are preempted by ERISA and REA. *Marriage of Baker* (1988) 204 CA3d 206, 218, 251 CR 126. Thus, a state court judgment may order a private pension plan to pay part of a participant's benefits to an "alternate payee" (typically, the nonemployee spouse), but only if the judgment qualifies as a QDRO (see §§17.69-17.77). This rule does not apply to public benefit plans (see §§17.80-17.83). On protecting the alternate payee spouse when the employee spouse is requesting a bifurcation of marital status from other issues, see §14.61.

For a comprehensive discussion of QDROs, including sample clauses and a complete sample agreements, see California Marital Settlement and Other Family Law Agreements, chap 20 (3d ed Cal CEB 2005) and Dividing Pensions and Other Employee Benefits in California Divorces, chap 6 (Cal CEB 2006).

§17.69   1. Statutory Requirements

A QDRO is a judgment, decree, or order that is made under a state domestic relations law and that (1) relates to the provision of child support, spousal support, or marital property rights to an "alternate payee" (*i.e.,* a spouse, former spouse, child, or other dependent of a participant in an ERISA-regulated plan); (2) creates, acknowledges, or assigns to an alternate payee a right to receive benefits under the plan; and (3) meets certain statutory requirements (see §§17.70–17.72). 29 USC §1056(d)(3)(B)(ii). See *Branco v UFCW-N. Cal. Employers Joint Pension Plan* (9th Cir 2002) 279 F3d 1154 (when wife died, surviving participant husband was entitled to full pension amount despite stipulated court order granting wife share in husband's pension benefits; order not a QDRO because deceased wife cannot be "qualifying recipient" and her estate and heirs cannot be "beneficiary" or "alternate payee"); *Marriage of Marshall* (1995) 36 CA4th 1170, 1174, 43 CR2d 38 (party not entitled to QDRO to enforce order assigning tax liability to other party, because order does not relate to "marital property rights"). For a detailed discussion of the statutes governing QDROs, see Dividing Pensions and Other Employee Benefits in California Divorces, chap 6 (Cal CEB 2006).

§17.70   a. Mandatory Provisions

A QDRO must contain the following information (29 USC §1056(d)(3)(C)):

- The name and last known mailing address of the participant and each alternate payee covered by the order.

- The amount or percentage of the participant's benefits to be paid to each alternate payee, or the method of determining such amount or percentage. (The benefits to be paid to the participant and each alternate payee may also be segregated into separate accounts, as in an order dividing certain state public pension plan benefits (see §§17.82–17.83). IRS Letter Rulings 8334088, 8330119.)

- The number of payments or the period to which the order applies.

- Each plan to which the order applies.

§17.71   b. Prohibited Provisions

A judgment will not qualify as a QDRO if it contains any of the following provisions (29 USC §1056(d)(3)(D)-(E)):

- An award of any type or form of benefit, or any option, not otherwise provided under the plan, except that:

  - (1) Payments may be made to an alternate payee before the participant actually retires but after the participant reaches "the earliest retirement age" (similar to a "*Gillmore* order"; see §5.93);

  - (2) Payments may be made to an alternate payee "as if the participant had retired on the date on which such payment is to begin" (limited, however, to the present actuarial value of the total benefits actually accrued on the "early retirement" date and excluding any employer subsidy that might be paid if the participant actually took early retirement); and

  - (3) Payments may be made to an alternate payee in any form that may be (but not necessarily is being) paid under the plan to the participant (except that a joint and survivor annuity may not be paid to the alternate payee and his or her subsequent spouse).

- An award with an actuarial present value in excess of the total value of benefits available to the participant.

- An award of benefits to an alternate payee when, under a previous QDRO, the same benefits were ordered to be paid to a different alternate payee (see §17.76).

§17.72   c. Surviving Spouse Provisions

A QDRO is permitted by statute, but not required, to provide that a former nonemployee spouse, if married to a plan participant for at least 1 year, be treated as a surviving spouse for the purpose of receiving survivor annuity benefits. See 29 USC §§1055(a), 1056(d)(3)(F). To the extent that a former spouse is treated as a current spouse under the terms of a QDRO, an actual current spouse will not share in survivor benefits. The QDRO may altogether exclude a current spouse from sharing in survivor benefits, or it may provide for a sharing of benefits between former spouses or between a former and a current spouse. For example, the former spouse's survivor benefits may be limited to those accrued before dissolution. Reg §1.401(a)-13(g)(4).

Waiver or revocation of benefits. The plan participant may not waive or revoke surviving spouse benefits, select another beneficiary, or use the accrued benefits as security for a loan without the written consent of the spouse or former spouse who is entitled to receive the benefits. 29 USC §1055(c). The nonemployee spouse's written consent to a waiver of benefits need not be in a QDRO. See *Fox Valley & Vicinity Constr. Workers Pension Fund v Brown* (7th Cir 1990) 897 F2d 275 (spouse's waiver of benefits in non-QDRO property settlement is effective even though she remains named as beneficiary at time of participant's death). If the nonemployee spouse dies, ERISA-governed pension plans must restore full benefits to the survivor employee-spouse. *Marriage of Rich* (1999) 73 CA4th 419, 423, 86 CR2d 452.

Bifurcation of marital status. When the issue of marital status is bifurcated and a status-only judgment is entered before other issues are resolved, the nonemployee spouse must take special precautions to ensure that his or her survivor benefits are not lost if the participant retires or dies before issuance of a QDRO. The bifurcation may be conditioned on the joinder of the plan as a party to the action, on the completion of a QDRO, on the participant's indemnification of the nonemployee spouse from loss resulting from the bifurcation, or more than one of these. See Fam Code §2337; §14.61.

For a case involving survivor benefits and bifurcation of marital status—but decided before the enactment of §2337 and in which no similar bifurcation conditions were imposed—see *Marriage of Allison* (1987) 189 CA3d 849, 854, 234 CR 671 (nonemployee wife entitled either to actuarial value of survivor benefits or to QDRO converting employee husband's life annuity—which he elected intending to defeat wife's right to survivor benefits—to joint and survivor annuity; court remanded with directions to issue QDRO). To avoid placing a nonemployee spouse in such a dangerous position, counsel should consider the need for imposing conditions such as those referred to above (see Fam C §2337) when a bifurcated judgment is proposed that only terminates the parties' marital status.

§17.73   2. Nonstatutory Protections

In addition to statutory requirements, the QDRO may include the following protections for the alternate payee:

- A statement binding "successor plans," in addition to current and predecessor plans, if the existing plan is merged or if its assets and liabilities are transferred;

- A penalty provision if benefit payments do not start on the anticipated date; and

- Protection against the possible reduction of benefits caused by underfunding of the plan, changes in administration of the plan, termination of the plan, or actions of the plan participant.

§17.74   3. Determination of QDRO Status

On receipt of a domestic relations order, the plan administrator must "promptly" notify the plan participant and each alternate payee of the receipt of the order and the plan's procedures for determining whether the order qualifies as a QDRO. Within a reasonable period after receipt of the order, the administrator must determine whether the order qualifies as a QDRO. 29 USC §1056(d)(3)(G)(i). If the administrator determines that the order does not qualify as a QDRO, counsel may serve the plan administrator with an order to show cause asking the trial court to determine that the order is a QDRO and to direct the plan to qualify and implement the order. *Marriage of Oddino* (1997) 16 C4th 67, 65 CR2d 566; *Marriage of Levingston* (1993) 12 CA4th 1303, 16 CR2d 100. See also *Board of Trustees of Laborers Pension Trust Fund v Levingston* (ND Cal 1993) 816 F Supp 1496 (federal court in litigation involving same parties as *Marriage of Levingston* defers to California court of appeal's determination, agreeing that federal and state courts have concurrent jurisdiction to review plan administrator's decision that particular order is not a QDRO). Presumably, if the administrator fails to make a timely determination of QDRO status, counsel could proceed in the same manner. Counsel should not hesitate to protect the client's interest by seeking such directives to the plan administrator when the administrator appears to be acting in ways that frustrate implementation of orders dividing retirement benefits.

During the period in which the qualification of the order is being determined, the administrator must "separately account for" the benefits that would have been payable to the alternate payee during that period if the order had already been found to be a QDRO. If the order is determined to be a QDRO within 18 months after the date that payments are to commence under the order, the alternate payee's benefits accrued during the period of determination (and any interest on the benefits) must be paid to the alternate payee. 29 USC §1056(d)(3)(H)(i)-(ii).

If the determination that the order is a QDRO occurs after the 18-month period, or if it is determined that the order does not qualify as a QDRO, the benefits that would otherwise have been paid to the alternate payee for the determination period (and accrued interest) will be paid to the plan participant. If the order is found to be a QDRO after the 18-month period, only prospective benefits will be paid to the alternate payee in accordance with the order. 29 USC §1056(d)(3)(H)(iii)-(iv). If an order is not qualified as a QDRO until after the 18-month period because of an unreasonable delay by the plan administrator, an alternate payee who loses the benefits accrued during that period may have a cause of action against the administrator for breach of fiduciary duty.

If a plan administrator determines that an order does not qualify as a QDRO, he or she may nonetheless delay the payment of benefits to the plan participant on receiving notice that the parties are attempting to cure the defects in the order. Moreover, the administrator must honor a restraining order prohibiting disposition of a participant's benefits pending resolution of a dispute with respect to a QDRO. Senate Rep No. 313, 99th Cong, 2d Sess 1105 (1986), reprinted in BNA Tax Mgmt Portfolios, The Tax Reform Act of 1986, vol 1, Legislative History, at 670. For discussion of issues relating to standing to sue when dissolution order does not qualify as QDRO, see *Stewart v Thorpe Holding Co. Profit Sharing Plan* (9th Cir 2000) 207 F3d 1143, 1158 (wife's interest in community property gave her "right to obtain a valid QDRO" in context of trustees' failure to ensure that she received her court-ordered benefits).

§17.75   a. Pre-1985 Orders

If, under court order, a plan was paying benefits to someone other than a plan participant on January 1, 1985 (the effective date of the Retirement Equity Act of 1984 (REA)), the plan must treat the order as a QDRO, even if the requirements for a QDRO are not met. REA §303(d)(1). An order entered before the effective date of the REA but on which a plan was not paying benefits may be treated as a QDRO in the discretion of the plan, even if it does not meet all the requirements of a QDRO. REA §303(d)(2); *Cum-*

mings v Briggs & Stratton Retirement Plan (7th Cir 1986) 797 F2d 383, 388. But see *Horton v Ford Motor Co.* (C D Ohio 2005) 427 F3d 382, 385 (when husband retired effective June 1, 1983, and did not work or receive paid leave on or after August 23, 1984, wife was not protected by spousal consent provision of REA).

§17.76   b. First in Time

Benefits may not be paid to an alternate payee when a previous QDRO orders the same benefits to be paid to a different alternate payee. 29 USC §1056(d)(3)(D)–(E). The first of two or more conflicting orders that is determined to be a QDRO by the plan administrator will be the only one given effect by the plan. For this reason, and because benefits that accrue during the determination period are forfeited if the order is not determined to be a QDRO within 18 months, the QDRO should be submitted to the plan administrator for comments and approval before it is issued by the court. See §17.78. Similarly, a request for determination of QDRO status should be made as to any pre-1985 order previously served on the plan if benefits are not yet being paid under the order. See §17.75.

§17.77   c. Amendment of Plan or Law

Under the Retirement Equity Act of 1984, an order may not qualify as a QDRO if it provides for any form of benefit not otherwise provided under the plan. 29 USC §1056(d)(3)(D)(i). Nonetheless, a QDRO will not lose its status as a QDRO if the form of a benefit provided under the order is no longer permitted under the plan because of a plan amendment or a change in the law. If a change in the form of benefits is due to a plan amendment, the alternate payee remains entitled to receive the form of benefit specified in the QDRO unless he or she elects to receive a different form of benefit that does not affect the amount received. If the change in form of benefit is due to a change in the law that makes the form specified in the QDRO impermissible, the plan must permit the alternate payee to select an alternative form of benefit that does not affect the amount received. Senate Rep No. 313, 99th Cong, 2d Sess 1105 (1986), reprinted in BNA Tax Mgmt Portfolios, The Tax Reform Act of 1986, vol 1, Legislative History, at 670.

4. Preparing the QDRO

§17.78   a. Discussion

The QDRO may be prepared either as part of the judgment or as a separate order. The advantages of preparing the QDRO as a separate order include:

Clarity. Orders concerning division of pension plan benefits may more easily qualify as a QDRO and be more readily enforced by the plan administrator if set forth separately;

Privacy. The parties may not wish the plan administrator to be aware of other provisions, *e.g.,* custody, support, or division of other community property; and

Immediate enforceability of other orders. The time required for approval of a QDRO by the plan administrator may delay issuance and enforcement of the judgment on the remaining issues unless the QDRO is prepared as a separate document.

If the order dividing pension benefits is determined to be a QDRO more than 18 months after benefits are to commence under the order, the alternate payee will lose those benefits that accrue during the 18-month period. See §17.74. To preserve these benefits and to ensure that the order is first in time (see §17.76), the proposed QDRO may be submitted to the plan administrator (and to opposing counsel) for a preliminary determination of its status as a QDRO before submission to the court. After any required modifications are made, the order should first be submitted to the plan administrator for execution and acknowledgment that it qualifies as a QDRO before it is signed by the court.

Some plans have their own form of QDRO that, if agreed to by counsel, make acceptance by the plan much easier. If the plan's QDRO does not impair any significant rights or benefits of the client, counsel should consider agreeing to its use.

Federal statutes do not provide for the manner in which the QDRO is to be submitted to the pension plan. However, after the order is signed by the court and filed, a certified copy should be served on the plan administrator in a manner that creates a record of receipt by the plan, *e.g.,* by certified or registered mail, return receipt requested. Once the plan receives the proposed QDRO, it must promptly notify the participant and each alternate payee of its receipt of the order and the plan's procedures for determining its qualification as a QDRO. 29 USC §1056(d)(3)(G). On determination of the order's status as a QDRO, see §§17.74–17.77.

For a comprehensive discussion of QDROs, including sample clauses and a complete sample agreements, see California Marital Settlement and Other Family Law Agreements, chap 20 (3d ed Cal CEB 2005) and Dividing Pensions and Other Employee Benefits in California Divorces, chap 6 (Cal CEB 2006).

For the Judicial Council forms of Qualified Domestic Relations Order for Support and Attachment, see §§17.79A–17.79B.

§17.79   b. Form: Qualified Domestic Relations Order

_ _[Attorney name]_ _
_ _[State Bar number]_ _
_ _[Address]_ _
_ _[Telephone number]_ _

Attorney for _ _[name]_ _

SUPERIOR COURT OF CALIFORNIA
COUNTY OF _ _ _ _ _ _

Marriage of	)	**No.** _ _ _ _ _ _
	)	
Petitioner: _ _ _ _ _ _ _ _	)	**QUALIFIED DOMESTIC**
	)	**RELATIONS ORDER**
Respondent: _ _ _ _ _ _ _ _	)	
	)	
_____	)	

WHEREAS, petitioner and respondent were married to each other on _ _[date]_ _ **and separated on** _ _[date]_ _;

This Court entered a judgment _ _[dissolving the marriage of/granting a legal separation to/nullifying the marriage of]_ _ **petitioner and respondent in this action on** _ _[date]_ _ **and ordering a certain disposition of the community property interest of petitioner and respondent in benefits accrued under** _ _[name(s) of plan(s)]_ _;

It is the intent of this Court that this Order be a Qualified Domestic Relations Order (hereafter "QDRO"), as that term is used in the Retirement Equity Act of 1984 (hereafter "REA"), as codified in 29 USC section 1056(d)(3), and in the Internal Revenue Code (hereafter "IRC"), as codified in IRC section

414(p), to effect the disposition of benefits provided for in the judgment; and

This Court has, and will retain, personal jurisdiction over petitioner and respondent and jurisdiction over the subject matter of this Order and this action for _ _[dissolution of marriage/legal separation/nullity of marriage]_ _;

IT IS HEREBY ORDERED:

1. As used in this Order, the following terms will have the meanings stated:

a. "Participant" means the _ _[petitioner/respondent]_ _, _ _[name]_ _, whose Social Security number will be provided by separate correspondence, and whose last known mailing address is _ _[address]_ _.

b. "Alternate Payee" means the _ _[respondent/petitioner]_ _, _ _[name]_ _, whose Social Security number will be provided by separate correspondence, and whose last known mailing address is _ _[address]_ _. The Alternate Payee is the _ _[spouse/ former spouse]_ _ of the Participant.

c. "Plan" means the following: _ _[Insert names of all plans affected by the order]_ _; the "Trustee" of the Plan is _ _[insert name and last-known address of trustee]_ _; the assets of the Plan are currently held by the Trustee.

d. "Plan Administrator" means _ _[name of administrator]_ _, whose last known mailing address is _ _[address]_ _.

2. This Order is issued under the California Family Code and relates to the division of the community property interest of the Participant and the Alternate Payee in benefits under the Plan and the payment to the Alternate Payee of _ _[his/her]_ _ share of that interest.

3. This Order creates, recognizes as to the Plan, and assigns to the Alternate Payee the right to receive benefits under the Plan

[Add if a defined contribution plan]

in an amount equal to half of all the contributions made to the Plan, by or on behalf of the Participant, between the date of marriage, _ _[date]_ _, and the date of separation, _ _[date]_ _, together with the accumulated interest, appreciation, and yield realized on those contributions to the date of this Order. A schedule and valuation of all assets currently held by the Plan that are attributable to the Participant's account is attached to this Order as Exhibit "A." The appropriate division of these assets, and the value assigned to each party, is set forth in Exhibit "B," which is attached to this Order.

[Add if a defined benefit plan]

in an amount equal to half of the community's interest in the Plan. The community's interest is calculated as a fraction of the Participant's total benefits under the Plan, the numerator of that fraction being the number of months of the Participant's service between the date of marriage, _ _[date]_ _, and the date of separation, _ _[date]_ _, and the denominator being the number of months of the Participant's total service.

[Continue]

4. From and after the date of this Order, the Alternate Payee will have the following exclusive rights with respect to _ _[his/her]_ _ interest in the Plan:

a. To designate a beneficiary in the event of _ _[his/her]_ _ death, without regard to any beneficiary designated by the Participant with respect to the Participant's interest in the Plan. Except as otherwise provided in this Order, the beneficiary may exercise, after the Alternate Payee's death, any rights the Alternative Payee could have exercised under this Order during _ _[his/her]_ _ lifetime.

b. To withdraw all or part of _ _[his/her]_ _ interest from the Plan at any time on or after the earliest retirement age of the Participant, as defined in 29 USC section 1056(d)(3)(E)(ii), subject to Paragraph 6 of this Order.

c. To transfer or roll over _ _[his/her]_ _ interest in the Plan to an Individual Retirement Account established for _ _[his/her]_ _ benefit, within 60 days after the receipt of such interest and in accordance with IRC section 402(e)(1)(B). **This right is personal to the Alternate Payee and may not be exercised by _ _[his/her]_ _ beneficiary.**

   d. **To be paid benefits in any form permitted by the Plan that is selected by the Alternate Payee, as long as the form selected does not adversely affect the selection by the Participant of a form of benefit payment (including the Participant's right to designate a survivor beneficiary other than, or in addition to, the Alternate Payee).**

[Other rights that may be included under Paragraph 4, depending on the type of plan, the agreement of the Plan Administrator, or both, are:]

[Add if defined contribution plan]

To direct and manage the investment of _ _[his/her]_ _ interest in the Plan, over which the Participant will have no control.

[Add if defined contribution plan; noncash assets]

To direct the Plan Administrator to convey legal and equitable title to the assets listed in Exhibit "B" of this Order to the Alternate Payee, or to the Alternate Payee's agent or representative.

[Add if defined benefit plan]

To be paid _ _[his/her]_ _ share of the benefits directly by the Plan when the Participant is receiving retirement benefits at any time during which payment is due the Alternate Payee. To be paid _ _[his/her]_ _ share of the benefits by the Participant on the _ _[specify]_ _ day of each month when:

(1) Because of the Participant's actions (for any reason except the Participant's refusal to take retirement at the earliest retirement age), the Participant is not receiving retirement benefits at any time during which payment is due the Alternate Payee; or

(2) For any other reason, benefits are not paid to the Alternate Payee by the Plan at any time during which payment is due _ _[him/her]_ _.

[Add if defined benefit plan]

To be paid _ _*[his/her]*_ _ share of benefits directly by the Plan commencing on the Participant's earliest retirement age, when the Participant does not take retirement at the earliest retirement age. If such right of payment does not exist under the Plan, to be paid _ _*[his/her]*_ _ share of benefits directly by the Participant commencing on the Participant's earliest retirement age.

[Add if defined benefit or defined contribution plan]

To withdraw all or a portion of _ _*[his/her]*_ _ interest from the Plan at any time on or after the date of this Order. To provide for such withdrawal, the Plan shall be amended, if necessary, by adding the following provision:

"Despite any provision in this Plan to the contrary, payments under a QDRO made to an alternate payee under IRC section 414(p), as amended, or any successor statute, may be made at any time."

[Continue]

5. If the Participant dies before payment to the Alternate Payee of all amounts due _ _*[him/her]*_ _ under this Order, the Alternate Payee will be treated as the surviving spouse of the Participant for purposes of IRC sections 401(a)(11) and 417 and 29 USC sections 1055(a) and 1056(d)(3)(F), with respect to all amounts held for the Alternate Payee in the Plan, and all such amounts will be paid to _ _*[him/her]*_ _ as a survivor death benefit, in addition to and regardless of any other survivor benefits that may be payable to any other beneficiary or to the Participant under the Participant's written election, the terms of the Plan, or federal law.

6. The Alternate Payee will be responsible for and will include all amounts received under this Order in _ _*[his/her]*_ _ gross taxable income. The Alternate Payee will be treated as the distributee under IRC sections 72 and 402, as amended, as to any payment or distribution that is made to the Alternate Payee under the Participant's assignment of benefits herein.

7. Nothing in this Order may be construed to require the Plan or Plan Administrator:

a. To provide to the Alternate Payee any type or form of benefit or any option not otherwise available to the Participant under the Plan;

b. To provide to the Alternate Payee increased benefits (determined on the basis of actuarial value) not available to the Participant; or

c. To pay any benefits to the Alternate Payee that are required to be paid to another alternate payee under another order determined to be a QDRO before this Order is determined to be a QDRO.

8. Copies of this Order will be mailed by counsel for the Alternate Payee to the Plan Administrator who will, on receipt of the Order, and under 29 USC section 1056(d)(3)(G):

a. Promptly notify the Participant, the Alternate Payee, and any other alternate payees, of (1) the receipt of a copy of this Order by the Plan Administrator and (2) the Plan's procedure for determining the qualified status of domestic relations orders;

b. Within a reasonable period of time after receipt of a copy of this Order, determine whether this Order is a QDRO and notify the Court, the Participant, the Alternate Payee, and any other alternate payees, of such determination; and

c. Pending the determination of whether or not this Order is a QDRO, segregate in a separate account in the Plan (the "Alternate Payee's account"), and administer as a separate account under the terms of the Plan, the amounts that would have been payable to the Alternate Payee during the period of determination had this Order already been determined to be a QDRO under 29 USC section 1056(d)(3)(H)(i).

9. Pending the determination of whether this Order is a QDRO, the Participant will honor any written directions and instructions _ _[she/he]_ _ may receive from the Alternate Payee with respect to the rights set forth in Paragraphs 4.a. through 4._ _. of this Order, and the Participant will execute and deliver to the Plan Administrator, or other appropriate official of the Plan, written instructions to implement the Alternate Payee's written instructions with respect to such rights.

10. This Order is issued for the purpose of creating, recognizing as to the Plan, and assigning to the Alternate Payee an interest in benefits under the Plan in conformity with the requirements of the REA and the IRC, and its provisions will be administered and interpreted in conformity with these statutes. It is the intent of this Court that this Order presently constitutes, and will continue in the future to constitute, a QDRO. Therefore, if the REA, the IRC, or any other law affecting QDROs is amended, modified, enacted, or repealed, the parties to this Order, or their successors, will immediately take such steps as are necessary to amend this QDRO to comply with any such change in the law or, if permissible under any such change in the law, the Plan Administrator will continue to treat this Order as a QDRO.

11. This Court hereby retains jurisdiction to amend this Order and, if necessary, to amend the Judgment of _ _[Dissolution of Marriage/Legal Separation/Nullity of Marriage]_ _ in this action, to establish or maintain the qualification of this Order as a QDRO.

12. Execution of this Order by the Plan Administrator acknowledges the following: (a) that this Order is determined by the Plan Administrator to qualify as a QDRO and (b) that after this Order, in the form executed by the Plan Administrator, is executed by the Court and filed in this action, the Plan, on receipt of a certified copy of the Order, will provide for the payment of benefits to the Alternate Payee in accordance with the terms and conditions of this Order under 29 USC section 1056(d)(3)(A).

Date: _ _ _ _ _ _   _____
                                   Judge of the Superior Court

Approved as a Qualified Domestic Relations Order:

Date: _ _ _ _ _ _   _____
                                   _ _[Typed name]_ _,
                                   Plan Administrator

Copies: Original (submit to court clerk); copies for pension plan and other attorney or party; office copies.

§17.79A   c. Form: Qualified Domestic Relations Order for Support (Judicial Council Form FL-460)

FL-460

ATTORNEY OR PARTY WITHOUT ATTORNEY OR GOVERNMENTAL AGENCY (under Fam. Code, §§ 17400, 17406) *(Name, state bar number, and address):*	FOR COURT USE ONLY

TELEPHONE NO.:   FAX NO.:

ATTORNEY FOR *(Name):*

SUPERIOR COURT OF CALIFORNIA, COUNTY OF

STREET ADDRESS:

MAILING ADDRESS:

CITY AND ZIP CODE:

BRANCH NAME:

PETITIONER/PLAINTIFF:

RESPONDENT/DEFENDANT:

OTHER PARENT:

QUALIFIED DOMESTIC RELATIONS ORDER FOR SUPPORT (EARNINGS ASSIGNMENT ORDER FOR SUPPORT) ☐ Modification ☐ Child Support ☐ Spousal or Family Support	CASE NUMBER:

TO THE PAYOR/PLAN: This is an earnings assignment order for support governed by Chapter 8 of the Family Code and is intended to be a qualified domestic relations order (QDRO) under applicable federal law. This order applies to the following named plan:

Name:

Address:

This order requires you to withhold a portion of the benefits payable under the Plan with respect to *(specify Obligor/Participant's full legal name and, if known, mailing address, date of birth, and employee identification number):*

Name: DOB: ID#:

Address:

and pay as directed below.

Note: A separate *Attachment to Qualified Domestic Relations Order for Support* (form FL-461) that sets forth the social security number of any participant named above must be completed and served on the Plan with a copy of this order. The Plan will require this information for tax reporting purposes. **Do not file a copy of form FL-461 with the court.**

THE COURT ORDERS THE FOLLOWING:

1. **WITHHOLDING OF PERIODIC BENEFIT PAYMENTS**

   a. If Participant has commenced receiving benefits under the Plan in the form of monthly or other periodic payments or has applied to receive monthly or other periodic payments *(if benefits are not in pay status and have not been applied for, see item 5; if benefits are payable in a lump sum, see item 3),* withhold the following amounts from the monthly benefits otherwise payable to the Participant:

   (1) ☐ $____ per month current **child support**   (4) ☐ $____ per month **child support arrearages**

   (2) ☐ $____ per month current **spousal support**   (5) ☐ $____ per month **spousal support arrearages**

   (3) ☐ $____ per month current **family support**   (6) ☐ $____ per month **family support arrearages**

   b. **Total monthly support obligation of** (sum of item 1a(1) through (6)): $____

   c. If the total monthly support obligation **exceeds 50 percent** of Participant's periodic benefits, withhold the greater of 50 percent or the percentage, if any, set forth in item 12.

   d. If Participant's benefits are payable on a periodic basis other than monthly (e.g., quarterly, semiannually, or annually), multiply each of the amounts in items 1a and 1b by the number of months included in the payment period, and withhold the adjusted amounts (subject to the limitations in item 1c, taking into account the adjustment of the amount in item 1b) from each benefit payment.

   e. If the amount withheld is less than the total monthly support obligation, prorate the amount first to current child support, then to current family support, and then to current spousal support. Apply any remainder in the same order of priority to support arrearages.

Page 1 of 4

Form Approved for Optional Use
Judicial Council of California
FL-460 [Rev. January 1, 2003]

QUALIFIED DOMESTIC RELATIONS ORDER FOR SUPPORT
(EARNINGS ASSIGNMENT ORDER FOR SUPPORT)

Family Code, § 5206; Code of
Civil Procedure, § 706.052;
26 U.S.C. § 414(p); 29 U.S.C. § 1056(d)
www.courtinfo.ca.gov

PETITIONER/PLAINTIFF: RESPONDENT/DEFENDANT: OTHER PARENT:	CASE NUMBER:

2. **ARREARAGES:** For purposes of this order, the total arrearages are set as follows (interest that has not been calculated or included is not waived):

                       <u>Amount</u>   <u>As of (date)</u>

    a. ☐ Child support: $
    b. ☐ Spousal support: $
    c. ☐ Family support: $

3. **WITHHOLDING FROM LUMP SUM DISTRIBUTIONS:** Withhold from any lump sum distributions currently payable to Participant under the Plan as follows:

    a. An amount equal to the total of the support arrearages, if any, set forth in item 2.

    b. To the extent the amounts withheld under item 3a are for child support arrearages, withhold from the lump sum distribution and pay over to the appropriate taxing authorities an additional amount sufficient to satisfy the Plan's mandatory federal and state income tax withholding obligations with respect to those arrearages and with respect to all additional amounts withheld under this item 3b. Any amounts withheld under this item 3b may not be applied to reduce the amount of the child support arrearages.

    c. To the extent the amounts withheld under item 3a are for support arrearages other than child support, withhold from those amounts and pay over to the appropriate taxing authorities an additional amount sufficient to satisfy the Plan's mandatory federal and state income tax withholding obligations with respect to those arrearages. Any amounts withheld under this item 3c must be applied proportionally to reduce the amount of the family support arrearages and spousal support arrearages.

    d. If the amounts withheld under item 3a are less than the total of the support arrearages, if any, set forth in item 2, prorate the amounts first to child support arrearages, then to family support arrearages, and then to spousal support arrearages.

    e. If the amounts to be withheld under items 3a and 3b would exceed the total amount of the lump sum distribution currently payable, withhold the entire amount of the lump sum distribution, allocate from it an amount sufficient to satisfy the Plan's mandatory federal and state income tax withholding obligations with respect to the amount of such distribution, and allocate the balance to satisfaction of the child support arrearages. Any income tax withheld under this item 3e may not be applied to reduce the amount of the child support arrearages.

    f. The limitations on withholding set forth in items 1 and 12 do not apply to the withholding provisions of this item 3.

4. **DISTRIBUTE AMOUNTS WITHHELD OR ALLOCATED AS FOLLOWS:**

    a. **Child Support:** All amounts withheld or payable for child support under this order are for the benefit of *(specify name of each Alternate Payee, with date of birth, if available)*:

         <u>Name of each child</u>   <u>Date of birth of each child</u>

    b. Amounts withheld for child support must be paid to *(specify name, capacity, and mailing address of agent to receive payments— hereinafter "Agent")*:

       Name: Capacity:

       Address:

    c. **Spousal or Family Support**

       (1) All amounts withheld or payable for spousal/family support under this order are for the benefit of *(specify name of Spousal or Family Alternate Payee, with date of birth, if available)*:

       Name: DOB:

       Note: A separate *Attachment to Qualified Domestic Relations Order for Support* (form FL-461) that sets forth the social security number of any Spousal or Family Alternate Payee named in item 4c(1) must be completed and served on the Plan with a copy of this order. The Plan will require this information for tax reporting purposes. Do not file a copy of form FL-461 with the court.

       (2) Amounts withheld for spousal or family support must be paid to *(check one)*:

          (a) ☐ Spousal or Family Alternate Payee at the following address *(specify mailing address of Alternate Payee)*:
                Address:

          (b) ☐ Spousal or Family Alternate Payee's Agent *(specify name, mailing address, and capacity of agent to receive payments)*:
                Name: Capacity:
                Address:

QUALIFIED DOMESTIC RELATIONS ORDER FOR SUPPORT
(EARNINGS ASSIGNMENT ORDER FOR SUPPORT)

PETITIONER/PLAINTIFF: RESPONDENT/DEFENDANT: OTHER PARENT:	CASE NUMBER:

5. **IF BENEFITS ARE NOT CURRENTLY IN PAY STATUS:**

    a. If Participant applies for benefits (including a lump sum distribution) within 90 days after the Plan receives this order or while the temporary restraining order in item 13 remains in effect, the withholding provisions of this order must take effect once such benefits become payable.

    b. If Participant has not commenced receiving benefits under the Plan (other than by reason of the temporary restraining order in item 13), and does not apply to receive benefits by the end of the period specified in item 5a, the Plan has no obligation under this order to withhold payments from Participant's benefits, provided the Plan sends prompt written notice to Alternate Payee(s) stating that no benefits are currently available for distribution under this order and specifying the earliest date on which Participant could begin receiving benefits under the Plan if Participant terminated employment.

6. Any notices required or permitted under this order to any Alternate Payee must be sent by first-class mail, postage prepaid, to the Alternate Payee or to the Alternate Payee's Agent, if one is designated, at the address set forth in item 4, or such other address as the Alternate Payee/Agent may specify by written notice to the Plan.

7. This order upon approval as a QDRO *(check appropriate box, if either is applicable):*

    (a) ☐ amends/replaces any existing QDRO with respect to support for any Alternate Payee's named herein.

    (b) ☐ supplements but does not amend or replace any existing payment obligations under a previous QDRO issued with respect to any Alternate Payee named herein.

8. This order must not be interpreted to require payment of benefits in any form not permitted by the Plan or in an amount greater than the actuarial value of Participant's benefits, less any benefits otherwise payable to another alternate payee under another order previously determined to be a QDRO.

9. Upon approval of this order as a QDRO, the Plan must send to Alternate Payee(s) any forms or notices that the Plan may require in order to effectuate the distribution of benefits as specified herein. This requirement does not apply if item 5b applies.

10. This order affects all benefits of Participant payable beginning as soon as possible but not later than 10 days after you receive it, including any retroactive benefit payments, whether those payments relate to a period before or after the date you receive this order. You must withhold from retroactive benefit payments according to the provisions of item 1 as if the payments had been made when due. The payments ordered herein will continue until further court order or notarized written notice from the Alternate Payee(s).

11. The Plan must give the Obligor/Participant a copy of this order and the accompanying blank *Request for Hearing Regarding Earnings Assignment* (form FL-450) within 10 days.

12. ☐ **MAXIMUM WITHHOLDING PERCENTAGE GREATER THAN 50%** *(If a maximum withholding percentage greater than 50% has been authorized by court order, check the box to the left and complete the following.)*
By order entered on *(date):* _____ , by stipulation or following noticed motion and appropriate proceedings, the court has determined, following Code of Civil Procedure section 706.052, that because support arrearages exist and/or when Participant's disposable earnings from all sources are taken into account, the maximum percentage of Participant's benefits under the Plan that are subject to withholding pursuant to item 1 of this order is *(check one):*

    (a) ☐ **100%**

    (b) ☐ _____ % *(If this box is checked, fill in the maximum percentage specified in the order.)*

13. **TEMPORARY RESTRAINING ORDER:** During any period in which the status of this order as a QDRO is being determined (by the Plan, a court of competent jurisdiction, or otherwise) and such further period as may be ordered by the court, the Plan is hereby **TEMPORARILY RESTRAINED** from making any distribution to Participant or Participant's beneficiary (other than a beneficiary under another QDRO) of any amount that would have been payable during such period to any Alternate Payee named herein if this order had been determined to be a QDRO. In no event may this temporary restraining order remain in effect for a period of more than 18 months after the date of this order.

14. **OTHER PROVISIONS**

    (a) ☐ The Plan must provide to the Alternate Payee, or to the Alternate Payee's agent, a copy of the Summary Plan Description; any subsequent summaries of material modifications with respect to the Plan; and the Plan's QDRO procedures, if any.

    (b) ☐ Other *(specify):*

Date: _____

                            _____
                                   JUDICIAL OFFICER

QUALIFIED DOMESTIC RELATIONS ORDER FOR SUPPORT
(EARNINGS ASSIGNMENT ORDER FOR SUPPORT)

PETITIONER/PLAINTIFF:	CASE NUMBER:
RESPONDENT/DEFENDANT:	
OTHER PARENT:	

INSTRUCTIONS FOR QUALIFIED DOMESTIC RELATIONS ORDER
(EARNINGS ASSIGNMENT ORDER FOR SUPPORT)

1. DEFINITIONS OF IMPORTANT WORDS IN THE ORDER

(a) **Alternate payee:** any spouse, former spouse, child, or other dependent of the Participant.

(b) **Participant/Obligor:** any person ordered by a court to pay child support, spousal support, or family support who has an accrued benefit or account balance (whether or not vested) under a Plan.

(c) **Agent:** any person, including the district attorney or other governmental agency, to whom the support is to be paid on behalf of an alternate payee.

(d) **Payor/Plan:** any employee benefit plan described in Family Code section 80 that is not a governmental plan as defined in 29 U.S.C. § 1002(32). The term includes plans benefiting self-employed individuals such as partners and sole proprietors. If an entity other than the Plan pays benefits to participants under the Plan, the term Payor/Plan also includes that entity.

(e) **QDRO:** an order that has been approved by the administrator of the Plan (or by a court of competent jurisdiction) as meeting the requirements for a qualified domestic relations order under 29 U.S.C. § 1056(d) or 26 U.S.C. § 414(p).

(f) **Annuity:** a form of benefit in which periodic payments (usually monthly) are made for the life of the recipient and/or the recipient's survivor. This order applies to annuities and to any other form of benefit payment or distribution allowable under the Plan (e.g., single sum, installments, and other periodic payments).

2. TAX INFORMATION FOR PAYORS

Generally speaking, for federal income tax purposes, the Participant will be taxed on any child support paid from a Plan based on this order. Amounts paid by the Plan for spousal or family support generally will be taxable to the Alternate Payee for whose benefit those amounts are paid.

2. TAX INFORMATION FOR PAYORS *(continued)*

You should consult with your professional tax advisor on the specific tax treatment and reporting requirements applicable to distributions under this order.

3. OTHER INFORMATION FOR PAYORS

This order, which is an earnings assignment order, and you as the Payor are governed by Chapter 8, beginning with section 5200, of the Family Code and related provisions of that code and the Code of Civil Procedure. Your attention is directed particularly to the provisions of Chapter 8 that set forth your obligations as a Payor (referred to therein as the "Employer").

When benefits under the Plan are currently payable to the Participant, withholding under this order should commence as soon as possible but no later than 10 days after you receive the *Qualified Domestic Relations Order for Support.* If benefits are not currently payable but Participant has applied to receive benefits, or applies within 90 days after you receive this order or while the temporary restraining order contained in item 13 of this order is in effect, this order (including the temporary restraining order) applies to the benefits Participant has applied for and becomes entitled to receive under the terms of the Plan.

Once this order has been approved as a QDRO, all benefits withheld pursuant to the temporary restraining order must be disbursed in accordance with the terms of this order or, to the extent those benefits are not affected by this order, to the person or persons entitled to them under the terms of the Plan.

If you have any questions about this order, please contact the office that sent this form to you, as shown in the upper left-hand corner.

4. INFORMATION FOR ALL PARTICIPANTS: You should have received a *Request for Hearing Regarding Earnings Assignment* (form FL-450) with the *Qualified Domestic Relations Order for Support.* If not, you may get one from either the court clerk or the local child support agency. If you want the court to stop or modify the assignment of your benefits under the Plan, you must file (hand-deliver or mail) an original copy of form FL-450 with the court clerk within 10 days of the date you received this order. Keep a copy of the form for your records.

If you think your support order is wrong, you can ask for a modification of the order, or in some cases you can have the order set aside and a new order issued. You can talk to any attorney or visit the family law facilitator if you need more help.

QUALIFIED DOMESTIC RELATIONS ORDER FOR SUPPORT
(EARNINGS ASSIGNMENT ORDER FOR SUPPORT)

Copies: Original (submit to court clerk); copies for pension plan and other attorney or party; office copies.

§17.79B   d. Form: Attachment to Qualified Domestic Relations Order for Support (Judicial Council Form FL-461)

PETITIONER/PLAINTIFF:	CASE NUMBER:
RESPONDENT/DEFENDANT:	
OTHER PARENT:	

ATTACHMENT TO
QUALIFIED DOMESTIC RELATIONS ORDER FOR SUPPORT (form FL-460)

STATEMENT OF CONFIDENTIAL INFORMATION

DO NOT FILE WITH COURT

This separate statement of confidential information sets forth the social security number of the Employee and any alternate participant for whose benefit **spousal or family support** is being withheld under the *Qualified Domestic Relations Order for Support* (form FL-460). The Plan will require this information for tax reporting purposes. Do not include social security numbers for persons receiving child support or for a child alternate payee. **This form must be completed and served on the Plan with a copy of the order.**

1. EMPLOYEE INFORMATION

    a. Employee name:

    b. Employee social security number:

2. SPOUSAL OR FAMILY ALTERNATE PAYEE INFORMATION *(for spousal or family support only):*

    a. Spousal or family alternate payee's name:

    b. Spousal or family alternate payee's social security number:

Form Approved for Optional Use
Judicial Council of California
FL-461 [Rev. January 1, 2003]

**ATTACHMENT TO QUALIFIED DOMESTIC RELATIONS ORDER
FOR SUPPORT (EARNINGS ASSIGNMENT ORDER FOR SUPPORT)**

Family Code, § 5208; 42 U.S.C. § 405
www.courtinfo.ca.gov

Copies: Original (for service on pension plan); office copies.

§17.80   D. Orders Dividing Public Pension Benefits

Under Fam C §2610, the court must make whatever orders are necessary or appropriate to ensure that each party receives his or her full community property share in any retirement plan, public or private. See, *e.g., Marriage of Schofield* (1998) 62 CA4th 131, 139, 73 CR2d 1 (trial court could make postjudgment order that increased wife's share of husband's federal civil service pension to include payment of arrearages after husband had made efforts to prevent wife from receiving benefits from the account allocated to her by combining two retirement accounts that had been divided between the parties at the time of the dissolution judgment). Each public pension system is governed by its own applicable law, which must be consulted to learn permitted methods of division and procedural requirements.

Unless otherwise required by the plan, an order dividing an interest in public pension benefits may be set forth either as a provision of the judgment in the action or as a separate document submitted for signature by the judge and filing with the court. The advantages of preparing the order as a separate document are the same as for a QDRO. See §17.78.

As with private pension plans (see §17.78), public plans should be contacted, before submission of the order to the court, on any requirements or suggestions they may have.

§17.81   1. Federal Pension Plans

A state court judgment that divides a community interest in federal pension benefits may be required to meet certain requirements in order to be binding on the plan.

Military. The Federal Uniformed Services Former Spouses' Protection Act (FUSFSPA) (10 USC §1408) specifies a detailed procedure that, if satisfied, renders an order dividing a community interest in military retirement benefits binding on the military service. 10 USC §1408(a)(2), (b).

Civil service. The Office of Personnel Management (OPM) must comply with a court order dividing a community interest in federal civil service pension benefits, as long as all required documentation is provided. 5 USC §8345(j). For a case discussing OPM regulations concerning the definition of a "first order dividing marital property," see *Rafferty v Office of Personnel Management* (5th Cir 2005) 407 F3d 1317 (construing 5 CFR §838.1004(e)(4)(ii)(B); regulations specifically exclude any court order issued under reserved jurisdiction or any other court orders issued subsequent to the original written order that divide any marital property regardless of the effective date of the court order)."

Railroad Retirement benefits. The Railroad Retirement Board is also required to make payments in accordance with an order dividing a community property interest in Railroad Retirement benefits. 45 USC §231m(b)(2).

Importance of consulting with plan. When a party intends to ask the trial court to order a federal pension plan to pay a portion of pension benefits to a nonemployee spouse, counsel should consult the plan to learn any substantive or procedural regulations governing the enforcement of such an order before submitting the issue to the court.

2. State Pension Plans

§17.82   ### a. Public Employees' Retirement System (PERS)

Family Code §2610(a)(3)(A) authorizes the court to divide a community property interest in the Public Employees' Retirement System (PERS) as provided in Govt C §§21290–21298 (former Govt C §§21215–21215.8). If orders affecting the community interest are to be made under Fam C §2610(a)(3)(A), the accumulated contributions and service credit attributable to employment during marriage will be divided into two separate and distinct accounts for the member and nonmember spouses. Govt C §21290(b). The nonmember spouse becomes entitled to receive the retirement benefits in his or her account (other than by refund; see Govt C §21292) on written application to PERS and satisfaction of the following two conditions: The member must have sufficient credit service to retire on the date marital status ends, and both the member and the nonmember must have attained the minimum retirement age applicable to the member. Govt C §21295.

The judgment or order served on PERS must include the date of separation of the member and nonmember spouses. Govt C §21290(a). In addition, the court must address the following rights of the nonmember spouse and the disposition of these rights should be set forth in the order: (1) The right to a retirement allowance; (2 the right to a refund of accumulated contributions; (3) the right to redeposit accumulated contributions; (4) the right to purchase service credits; (5) the right to designate a beneficiary; and (6) a limited right to elect coverage in the second tier. Govt C §21290(c). Any service credit or accumulated contributions that are not explicitly awarded in the judgment will thereafter be the exclusive property of the member spouse. Govt C §21290(b).

Note that, by its own terms, Fam C §2610(a)(3) is applicable only with the consent of the nonemployee spouse. When a PERS pension is involved, counsel should ascertain, probably with an actuary's assistance, whether the client will fare better under the code sections whose use is authorized by Fam C §2610(a)(3)(A) or under another approach. Division of the benefits into separate accounts in accordance with §2610(a)(3)(A) generally works to the disadvantage of the nonemployee spouse.

§17.83 b. State Teachers' Retirement System (STRS)

Family Code §2610(a)(3)(B) authorizes the court to divide a community interest in the State Teachers' Retirement System (STRS) Defined Benefit Program as provided in Ed C §§22650–22666, provisions that are similar to those for PERS (see §17.82). If orders affecting the community interest are to be made under Fam C §2610(a)(3)(B), the retirement benefits of the member and nonmember spouses are divided into two separate accounts (Ed C §22652(b)), as are PERS benefits, and the accounts are administered separately (Ed C §22658). Eligibility of the nonmember to receive benefits from his or her separate account requires satisfaction of the following conditions: The member must have performed at least 5 years of credited service during marriage, with certain restrictions; the nonmember must have at least two and one-half years of credited service in his or her separate account; and the nonmember must be at least 55 years of age. Ed C §22664(a).

The judgment or order must set forth the date of separation and address all the same rights as in a division of PERS benefits (see §17.82), and any service credit or accumulated contributions not explicitly awarded in the judgment are thereafter the exclusive property of the member spouse, as under PERS. Ed C §22652. In addition,

STRS must be joined as a party to the action (see §12.11) and must be served with a certified copy of the order or judgment. Ed C §22656.

Note that, by its own terms, Fam C §2610(a)(3) is applicable only with the consent of the nonemployee spouse. When an STRS Defined Benefit Program pension is involved, counsel should ascertain, probably with an actuary's assistance, whether the client will fare better under the code sections whose use is authorized by Fam C §2610(a)(3)(B) or under another approach. Division of the benefits into separate accounts in accordance with §2610(a)(3)(B) generally works to the disadvantage of the nonemployee spouse.

The Defined Benefit Program is the STRS program for public school teachers. The STRS also has a Cash Balance Benefit Program for other persons employed in instructional programs less than half-time by school employers who elect to provide that program. See Ed C §§26000–28101; Fam C §2610(a)(3)(E).

NOTE▶ The legislature added Ed C §22007.5 and 26002.5, operative January 1, 2005, to Parts 13 and 14 of the Education Code governing STRS, to include California registered domestic partners within the definition of "spouses," with certain exceptions. However, as of January 1, 2006, Ed C §26002.5 provides that except as excluded in Ed C §26004, 26807.5(d), 26906.5(d), or 27406, a person who is the registered domestic partner of a member (under Fam C §297 or Fam C §299.2), must be treated in the same manner as a "spouse," as defined in Ed C §26140. For comprehensive treatment of the California Domestic Partner Rights and Responsibilities Act of 2003, effective January 1, 2005, see California Domestic Partnerships (Cal CEB 2005).

§17.84   E. Final Judgment After Interlocutory

Before July 1, 1984, entry of a judgment for dissolution of marriage required a two-step procedure: (1) The entry of an interlocutory judgment resolving all issues of the marriage other than marital status, and (2) the subsequent entry of a final judgment terminating the marriage. The final judgment was not entered until it was affirmatively requested. If an interlocutory judgment was entered before July 1, 1984, but a final judgment was never entered, a request may be made for a final judgment by submitting:

- The Judicial Council form of Request and Declaration for Final Judgment of Dissolution of Marriage (Judicial Council Form FL-970).

- The Judicial Council form of Judgment (see form in §14.56). The form should indicate, at Item 4.o., that the previously entered interlocutory judgment, which should be identified by date, remains in effect and that this judgment serves only to terminate the parties' marital status.

- The Judicial Council form of Notice of Entry of Judgment with stamped envelopes addressed to the parties. See §§14.57 (discussion), 14.58 (form).

After an interlocutory judgment has been entered, a final judgment must be granted on request if (1) no reconciliation or dismissal has occurred and (2) there is no pending appeal or motion seeking to abrogate the interlocutory decree. If the court refuses to enter the final decree when these requirements are met, mandamus will lie. *Marriage of Sanabia* (1979) 95 CA3d 483, 157 CR 56.

On entry of a judgment, including a final judgment after an interlocutory, nunc pro tunc, see §§17.59–17.64. The discussion in §17.85 is keyed to the Judicial Council form of Request and Declaration for Final Judgment of Dissolution of Marriage.

§17.85   1. Discussion

On the request and declaration for final judgment, the date on which the court acquired jurisdiction over the respondent, by service or by his or her appearance, is inserted at Item 1. The date on which the interlocutory judgment was entered is inserted at Item 2. If entry of the judgment is requested nunc pro tunc as of an earlier date, Item 4.b should be checked, inserting the date on which entry of the judgment is requested to be effective at (1) and the reason for the request at (2). On entry of judgment nunc pro tunc, see §§17.59–17.64.

If other relief in addition to termination of the marital status is requested, *e.g.,* restoration of former name, Item 5 should be checked and the nature of the relief specified.

§17.86 **2. Form: Request and Declaration for Final Judgment of Dissolution of Marriage (Judicial Council Form FL-970)**

FL-970

ATTORNEY OR PARTY WITHOUT ATTORNEY (NAME AND ADDRESS)	TELEPHONE NO.:	FOR COURT USE ONLY

ATTORNEY FOR (NAME):

SUPERIOR COURT OF CALIFORNIA, COUNTY OF
STREET ADDRESS:
MAILING ADDRESS:
CITY AND ZIP CODE:
BRANCH NAME:

MARRIAGE OF
PETITIONER:

RESPONDENT:

REQUEST AND DECLARATION FOR FINAL JUDGMENT OF DISSOLUTION OF MARRIAGE	CASE NUMBER:

1. The court acquired jurisdiction of the respondent on (date):

2. An Interlocutory Judgment of Dissolution of Marriage was entered on (date):

3. Since entry of the Interlocutory Judgment the parties have not become reconciled and have not agreed to dismiss this proceeding. No motion or other proceeding to set aside or annul, and no appeal from that part of the interlocutory judgment granting dissolution of the marriage, is pending and undetermined, and that part of the judgment has become final.

4. I request that final judgment of dissolution of marriage be entered.

   a. ☐ Endorsed copies of a Joint Petition for Summary Dissolution and a Notice of Revocation are attached and I request entry of final judgment pursuant to Family Code sections 2339-2344.

   b. ☐ I request judgment be entered effective (nunc pro tunc)
     (1) As of (date):
     (2) For the following reason:

5. ☐ Other request (specify):

6. I declare under penalty of perjury under the laws of the State of California that the foregoing is true and correct.

Date:

_____   _____
(Type or print name)   (Signature of declarant)

_____   _____
(Type or print name)   (Signature of attorney for declarant)

Page 1 of 1

Form Adopted for Mandatory Use Judicial Council of California FL-970 [Rev. January 1, 2003]	**REQUEST AND DECLARATION FOR FINAL JUDGMENT OF DISSOLUTION OF MARRIAGE** (Family Law)	Family Code, §§ 2339-2344 www.courtinfo.ca.gov

Copies: Original (submit to court clerk); courtesy copy for other attorney or party; office copies.

VI. WITHDRAWAL OF ATTORNEY AFTER JUDGMENT

§17.87 A. Discussion

An attorney of record in any marital action may withdraw at any time after the judgment becomes final, and before service on him or her of any subsequent pleadings or motion papers, by filing a notice of withdrawal. CCP §285.1. It appears that in the usual case, in which there is a single judgment (*i.e.,* no bifurcation) and no appeal from the judgment or motion for a new trial, the judgment of dissolution of marriage becomes "final," for purposes of CCP §285.1, on the date the marital status is terminated. See Fam C §§2337(a), 2340-2341. Code of Civil Procedure §285.1 does not allow withdrawal in this manner after a *status-only* judgment. See Judicial Council form of Notice of Withdrawal of Attorney of Record in §17.88. Use of the Judicial Council form is mandatory.

A copy of the notice must be mailed to the party at his or her last known address and be served on the other party. CCP §285.1. As long as the other party has appeared, service on that party is typically made by mail, to the party's attorney of record, if any, or to the party if he or she is unrepresented. See CCP §§1012, 1015.

After entry of the judgment in a marital action, no subsequent orders in the action, including orders modifying the judgment, will be valid unless any required advance notice is served on the other party himself or herself. Service on the party's attorney of record will not be sufficient. Fam C §215. Consequently, even when an attorney of record has not filed a notice of withdrawal under CCP §285.1, notice of subsequent proceedings in the action must normally be served on the client, not on the attorney. *Albrecht v Superior Court* (1982) 132 CA3d 612, 183 CR 417. Nevertheless, in most instances, it is probably better to file a notice of withdrawal than to rely entirely on Fam C §215, which may require some affirmative steps by the attorney if he or she is served with postjudgment papers. 132 CA3d 612, 617 n5 (despite former CC §4809, counsel remains attorney of record in marital action unless he or she withdraws under CCP §285.1).

Depending on the circumstances, it may be appropriate to send the client a cover letter, along with the notice of withdrawal, explaining the reason for the notice and assuring the client, if such is the case, that the attorney remains available for subsequent consultation and representation in the marital action if the need arises.

For discussion of withdrawing as attorney from a limited representation of a client, see §§3.38–3.40.

§17.88   B. Form: Notice of Withdrawal of Attorney of Record (Judicial Council Form FL-960)

FL-960

ATTORNEY OR PARTY WITHOUT ATTORNEY *(Name, state bar number, and address)*:	FOR COURT USE ONLY

TELEPHONE NO.:   FAX NO.:

ATTORNEY FOR *(Name)*:

SUPERIOR COURT OF CALIFORNIA, COUNTY OF

STREET ADDRESS:

MAILING ADDRESS:

CITY AND ZIP CODE:

BRANCH NAME:

PETITIONER/PLAINTIFF:

RESPONDENT/DEFENDANT:

	CASE NUMBER:
NOTICE OF WITHDRAWAL OF ATTORNEY OF RECORD	

1. In accordance with the provisions of section 285.1 of the Code of Civil Procedure, I withdraw as Attorney of Record for:
   ☐ Petitioner   ☐ Respondent

2. The final judgment of dissolution, legal separation, nullity, parentage, or postjudgment order was entered on *(specify date)*: and no motions or other proceedings are pending at this time.

3. The last known address for the   ☐ Petitioner   ☐ Respondent   is:

4. The last known telephone number for the   ☐ Petitioner   ☐ Respondent   is:

5. I mailed a copy of this *Notice of Withdrawal* to   ☐ Petitioner   ☐ Respondent   at the address set forth in item 3.

I declare under penalty of perjury under the laws of the State of California that the foregoing is true and correct.

Date:

▶

_____   _____
(TYPE OR PRINT NAME)   (SIGNATURE)

WARNING
This form may not be used after a status-only judgment.

Form Adopted for Mandatory Use
Judicial Council of California
FL-960 [Rev. January 1, 2003]   **NOTICE OF WITHDRAWAL OF ATTORNEY OF RECORD**   Code of Civil Procedure, § 285.1
www.courtinfo.ca.gov

| PETITIONER/PLAINTIFF: | CASE NUMBER: |
| RESPONDENT/DEFENDANT: | |

PROOF OF SERVICE BY ☐ **PERSONAL SERVICE** ☐ **MAIL**

1. At the time of service I was at least 18 years of age and **not a party to this legal action.**

2. I served a copy of the *Notice of Withdrawal of Attorney of Record* as follows *(check either a. or b. below):*
   a. ☐ **Personal service.** I personally delivered the *Notice of Withdrawal of Attorney of Record* as follows:
      (1) Name of person served:
      (2) Address where served:

      (3) Date served:
      (4) Time served:

   b. ☐ **Mail.** I deposited the *Notice of Withdrawal of Attorney of Record* in the United States mail, in a sealed envelope with postage fully prepaid. The envelope was addressed and mailed as follows:
      (1) Name of person served:
      (2) Address:

      (3) Date of mailing:
      (4) Place of mailing *(city and state):*
      (5) I am a resident of or employed in the county where the *Notice* was mailed.

   c. My residence or business address is *(specify):*

   d. My phone number is *(specify):*

I declare under penalty of perjury under the laws of the State of California that the foregoing is true and correct.

Date:

▶

_____   _____
(TYPE OR PRINT NAME)   (SIGNATURE OF PERSON SERVING NOTICE)

Copies: Original (file with court clerk); copies for service on parties; office copies.

18

Attack on Judgment in the Trial Court

§18.1   I. SCOPE OF CHAPTER

After a judgment has been entered in a marital action, both statutory law and principles of equity provide various procedures for attacking the judgment at the trial court level. In many cases, relief is available whether the judgment was entered in an uncontested proceeding or after a contested trial. This chapter discusses the legal or equitable bases for relief and the procedural requirements for each of the various methods. Counsel should pay particular attention to the time period during which relief is available under each procedure, because failure to comply with deadlines is one of the most common reasons for denying relief. Seeking relief from a judgment by means of appeal or writ is discussed in chap 19.

§18.2   II. MOTION FOR NEW TRIAL

When a party believes that his or her substantial rights have been materially affected at trial, for causes defined in CCP §§657–657.1 (see §18.3), a new trial may be requested. Code of Civil Procedure §656 defines a new trial as "a re-examination of an issue of fact in the same court after a trial and decision." It is now well settled that issues of law, as well as fact, may be the subject of a motion for new trial. See CCP §657; *Marriage of Beilock* (1978) 81 CA3d 713, 720, 146 CR 675. The request for a new trial must be brought before the same judge who presided at the original trial, unless he or she is unable to hear the matter (see §18.12). Strict time requirements apply to all filings in the motion for new trial procedure; if the requirements are not met, the right to request a new trial is lost. See §18.5.

For a comprehensive discussion of motions for new trial, see California Trial Practice: Civil Procedure During Trial §§25.22–25.71 (3d ed Cal CEB 1995). For the effect of a motion for new trial on the finality of a marital action judgment, see §17.40; for its effect on the time for filing a notice of appeal, see §18.14.

A. When Motion Is Available

§18.3 **1. Statutory Grounds**

The only grounds for granting a new trial are those listed in CCP §§657–657.1. *Fomco, Inc. v Joe Maggio, Inc.* (1961) 55 C2d 162, 166, 10 CR 462. Those statutory grounds that are pertinent to a marital action include the following:

- Irregularity in the proceedings of the court or the adverse party, or any order of the court or abuse of discretion that prevented either party from having a fair trial. CCP §657(1).

- Accident or surprise, which ordinary prudence could not have guarded against. CCP §657(3).

- Newly discovered evidence, material for the moving party, which could not, with reasonable diligence, have been discovered and produced at the trial. CCP §657(4). On reopening a case to introduce evidence of events occurring after trial, see §17.4.

- Insufficiency of the evidence to justify the court's decision, or the decision is against law. CCP §657(6).

- Error in law, occurring at the trial and excepted to by the moving party. CCP §657(7).

- Inability to obtain a transcript because of the death or disability of the court stenographer or because of the loss or destruction of the reporter's notes. CCP §§657.1, 914.

Before a new trial will be granted, the party applying for relief, in addition to proving one or more of the statutory grounds, must show that (1) the error was promptly called to the trial court's attention at the earliest possible moment (*People ex rel Dep't of Pub. Works v Hunt* (1969) 2 CA3d 158, 168, 82 CR 546) and (2) substantial rights of the moving party were materially affected (CCP §657).

§18.4   2. Proceedings to Which Applicable

In most cases, a motion for new trial (as well as a motion to vacate and enter a different judgment; see §§18.16–18.23) is appropriate only after a trial, *i.e.,* "the examination before a competent tribunal, according to the law of the land, of questions of fact or of law put in issue by pleadings, for the purpose of determining the rights of the parties." *Marriage of Beilock* (1978) 81 CA3d 713, 721, 146 CR 675. In some instances, a motion for new trial may be available after a motion. See §11.65 for discussion in context of attacks on temporary orders.

A new trial may also be granted after a judgment of dismissal (see 81 CA3d 713, 720) and after a judgment entered in accordance with an appellate court's direction to vacate the original judgment and enter a different judgment (see *Woodcock v Fontana Scaffolding & Equip. Co.* (1968) 69 C2d 452, 459, 72 CR 217). The availability of a motion for new trial after a default judgment depends on whether the ground for the motion is one that a defaulting party is permitted to assert. *Don v Cruz* (1982) 131 CA3d 695, 704, 182 CR 581.

§18.5   B. Procedure

To request a new trial, a notice of intention to move for a new trial must be filed within the statutory time period after entry of the judgment. See §18.7. The trial court must rule on the motion within a 60-day period; otherwise, the motion will be deemed denied. See §18.13. There are additional time requirements for filing points and authorities (see §18.9) and affidavits (see §18.10), hearing the motion (see §18.12), filing a notice of appeal after a motion for new trial is denied (see §18.14), and filing a notice of appeal and a cross-appeal from an order granting a new trial (see §18.15). The right to request a new trial and the right to an appeal may be lost by failing to comply with any of these time requirements; it is therefore essential that counsel carefully calendar each procedural step of a motion for new trial.

§18.6   1. Notice of Intention

Only a "party aggrieved" may request a new trial; the court is without jurisdiction to grant a new trial on its own motion. CCP §657; *Smith v Superior Court* (1976) 64 CA3d 434, 436, 134 CR 531. A party intending to move for a new trial must file with the clerk and serve on each adverse party a notice of intention to move for a new trial. CCP §659. The notice does not set a date for a hearing on the motion; the court itself must give notice of the hearing. See §18.12.

The notice of intention is deemed by statute to be a motion for a new trial on the grounds stated in the notice. The notice must designate *all* the grounds on which the motion will be made (see §18.3) and whether the motion will be based on affidavits, the minutes of the court, or both. CCP §659. When the application is made on the ground of irregularity in the proceedings, accident or surprise, or newly discovered evidence, the motion must be made on affidavits. CCP §658; see §18.10. A motion made on any other ground must be made on the minutes of the court. CCP §658.

§18.7 a. Time for Filing

The notice of intention to move for a new trial must be filed either before the entry of judgment or by the earlier of (1) 15 days after the clerk mails, or the moving party serves, the notice of entry of judgment or (2) 180 days after the entry of judgment. CCP §659. Although the statute permits the filing of a notice of intention before the entry of judgment, the notice must be filed after a decision is rendered (and after all the issues are decided in a bifurcated trial; see §17.65); otherwise, it is a nullity. See *Tabor v Superior Court* (1946) 28 C2d 505, 507, 170 P2d 667 (motion for new trial is a nullity if there remains "something more for the court to do before judgment could be entered"); *Marriage of Hafferkamp* (1998) 61 CA4th 789, 793, 71 CR2d 761 (wife could not appeal from order purporting to grant new trial on spousal support, child support, and other matters because underlying ruling by trial court was a "tentative decision"; document was not entitled "judgment" and was not signed by the court); *Ehrler v Ehrler* (1981) 126 CA3d 147, 152, 178 CR 642 (notice of intention filed after tentative decision but before signing and filing of findings of fact, conclusions of law, and judgment, held to be premature and void).

If a party files a notice of intention to seek a new trial only as to some issues, any other party who wants a new trial as to other issues has 15 days after service of the first notice of intention to also file and serve a notice of intention. CCP §659. The times specified in the statute are jurisdictional and may not be extended by court order, stipulation of the parties, or under CCP §1013 for service by mail. CCP §659; see *Marriage of Beilock* (1978) 81 CA3d 713, 721, 146 CR 675.

§18.8   b. Statement of Grounds

A new trial may be granted only on the grounds stated in the notice of intention to move for a new trial. *Malkasian v Irwin* (1964) 61 C2d 738, 744, 40 CR 78. If a ground is omitted from the notice of intention, it may be supplied by an amended notice or by a declaration filed within the period for filing the original notice (see §18.7). *Galindo v Partenreederei M.S. Parma* (1974) 43 CA3d 294, 301, 117 CR 638. The omitted ground may not be supplied by points and authorities or other documents filed after the filing period for the notice of intention. *Wagner v Singleton* (1982) 133 CA3d 69, 73, 183 CR 631. Because a second motion for new trial may not be brought after a first motion is denied (see §18.14), it is good practice for counsel to set out all the arguably applicable statutory grounds for granting a motion for new trial in the original notice of intention. See CCP §657 and §18.3.

§18.9   c. Points and Authorities

The moving party must serve and file a memorandum of points and authorities within ten days after the notice of intention is filed; otherwise, the court has discretion to deny the motion without a hearing on the merits. Within ten days after the memorandum is served and filed, the adverse party may serve and file points and authorities in reply. Cal Rules of Ct 3.1600. The careful preparation of points and authorities may assist the court in drafting its statement of grounds and specification of reasons if the motion for new trial is granted (see §18.15).

On the memorandum of points and authorities generally, see California Civil Procedure Before Trial §§12.30-12.42 (4th ed Cal CEB 2004).

§18.10   d. Supporting Affidavits

When an application for new trial is made on the grounds of an irregularity in the proceedings, accident or surprise, or newly discovered evidence, affidavits (or declarations; see CCP §2015.5) must be submitted in support of the motion. CCP §658. The moving party must serve and file any affidavits intended to be used in the motion within ten days after serving the notice of intention to move for new trial. CCP §659a. Counsel should therefore confirm the availability of any required affidavits before filing the notice of intention. The other party has ten days after service of the affidavits to file and serve counteraffidavits on the moving party. CCP §659a.

The time period for filing affidavits and counteraffidavits may, for good cause, be extended by court order for an additional period, not to exceed 20 days. CCP §659a. However, in requesting an extension, counsel must be aware that the 60-day period for ruling on a motion for new trial is jurisdictional and cannot be extended (see §18.13); any order made beyond that time is void. *Siegal v Superior Court* (1968) 68 C2d 97, 101, 65 CR 311.

For an example of a declaration, see §10.37 (Declaration in Support of Application for Order for Publication of Summons).

§18.11   e. Format

A motion for new trial may be prepared on the Judicial Council form of Notice of Motion (see form in §11.20) or as a separate pleading, as in civil actions generally. Counsel should check local court rules and the court clerk to ascertain the appropriate format in a particular county.

If the Judicial Council form is used, the moving party prepares the Notice of Motion and an Application for Order and Supporting Declaration (see form in §11.22). In the caption of the Notice of Motion form, the box labeled "Other (specify)" is checked and language such as "For New Trial" is inserted. The date of the hearing is *not* inserted in the Notice of Motion; the court itself must give notice of the hearing date. See §18.12. Item 13 of the application should be checked and language inserted, on the form or in an attachment, requesting a new trial, stating the grounds for the request (see §18.8) and whether the motion will be based on affidavits or the court's minutes (see §18.6). If affidavits will be submitted, Item 14 and the accompanying box, indicating that affidavits will be attached, should also be checked.

If a separate pleading is used, see California Trial Practice: Civil Procedure During Trial §25.93 (3d ed Cal CEB 1995) for a sample Notice of Intention to Move for New Trial.

§18.12   2. Hearing on Motion

When the time to file counteraffidavits expires (see §18.10), the clerk must "forthwith" call the motion to the attention of the judge who presided at the trial (CCP §661) and a determination on the motion must be made "at the earliest possible moment" (CCP §660). If the trial judge is out of the county or is otherwise unable to hear the motion, another judge of the same court may hear and determine it. CCP §661. If a judge other than the trial judge is hearing the motion, the motion must be argued, or submitted without argument as the judge directs, no later than ten days before the court's power to act on the motion expires (see §18.13). CCP §661.

The parties are entitled to a hearing on the motion, and to notice of the hearing, unless waived. *Avery v Associated Seed Growers, Inc.* (1963) 211 CA2d 613, 626, 27 CR 625. The court sets the hearing date, and the clerk must give the parties 5 days' notice by mail of the time for oral argument, if any. CCP §661; see *Jones v Evans* (1970) 4 CA3d 115, 118, 84 CR 6. Although the parties have the right to a hearing, the court is apparently not required to hear oral argument (see *Kimmel v Keefe* (1970) 9 CA3d 402, 408, 88 CR 47); nonetheless, it is usually allowed.

In all cases, reference may be had at the hearing to the pleadings and orders of the court on file; when the motion is made on the court minutes (see §18.6), reference may also be had to any depositions and documentary evidence offered at the trial and to the court reporter's record of the proceedings or transcript. CCP §660. Oral testimony is not permitted at the hearing, although certain grounds for the motion require the presentation of affidavits. *Linhart v Nelson* (1976) 18 C3d 641, 644, 134 CR 813; see CCP §658 and §18.10.

§18.13   3. Ruling on Motion

The court's power to rule on a motion for new trial expires 60 days after the clerk mails under CCP §664.5, or any party serves the moving party with, a notice of entry of judgment, whichever is earlier. If a notice of intention to move for a new trial is filed before notice of entry of judgment is given, the court's power to rule on that motion expires 60 days after the notice of intention to move for a new trial is filed. CCP §660; *Marriage of Liu* (1987) 197 CA3d 143, 242 CR 649. Except when a prevailing party in a contested action is not represented, for the clerk's mailing to start the 60 days running, the clerk's notice must affirmatively state that it was given "upon order by the court" or "under section 664.5," and a certificate of mailing the notice must be executed and placed in the file. *Van Beurden Ins. Servs., Inc. v Customized Worldwide Weather Ins. Agency, Inc.* (1997) 15 C4th 51, 61 CR2d 166. An order that purports to rule on a motion for new trial after expiration of the 60 days is in excess of the court's jurisdiction and is void. *Siegal v Superior Court* (1968) 68 C2d 97, 101, 65 CR 311. If the court fails to rule on a motion within the 60 days, or within any extension of that period, the motion is deemed denied by operation of law. CCP §660. In ruling on a motion for new trial, the court is not limited to granting or denying the request. The court may, on such terms as may be just (CCP §662):

- Grant a new trial on all or part of the issues;

- Change or add to the statement of decision;

- Modify the judgment, in whole or in part;

- Vacate the judgment, in whole or in part; or

- Vacate and set aside the statement of decision and judgment and reopen the case for further proceedings and the introduction of additional evidence.

A judgment that is entered after any of the foregoing orders is subject to a subsequent motion for new trial. CCP §662.

§18.14 a. Order Denying New Trial

If the court denies a motion for new trial, no reasons for the denial are required. The effect of the denial is to terminate the trial court's jurisdiction over the action, except to provide relief under CCP §473. See §§18.24–18.35. The order denying relief is not appealable, nor does the court have jurisdiction to hear a subsequent motion for new trial. The moving party's only remedy is to seek reversal of the judgment itself on appeal. *Wenzoski v Central Banking Sys.* (1987) 43 C3d 539, 237 CR 167.

If a party wishes to appeal a judgment after denial of a motion for new trial, a notice of appeal must be filed within 30 days after the superior court clerk mails, or a party serves, an order denying the motion or a notice of entry of that order, or within 30 days after denial of the motion by operation of law, but in no event later than 180 days after judgment was entered. Cal Rules of Ct 8.108(a). However, if the motion for new trial was denied because the notice of intention was invalid (*e.g.,* for failure to meet the statutory time requirements; see §18.7), the extension to appeal the judgment under Cal Rules of Ct 8.108(a) may not apply, and the usual period to file an appeal may already have expired. See Cal Rules of Ct 8.104; *Marriage of Eben-King & King* (2000) 80 CA4th 92, 95 CR2d 113 (time limits for filing appeal from dissolution judgment are not extended by Fam C §2122's longer set-aside limits). Therefore, if the validity of the notice of intention is in any doubt, counsel should file a notice of appeal within the normal 60-day time period after judgment (Cal Rules of Ct 8.104; see §19.47), in addition to moving for a new trial. The trial court will still retain jurisdiction to hear and decide the motion for new trial, which, if granted, will vacate the judgment (see §18.15) and render the appeal ineffective. See *Neff v Ernst* (1957) 48 C2d 628, 634, 311 P2d 849. On appeals generally, see chap 19.

§18.15   b. Order Granting New Trial

An order granting a new trial vacates the court's decision and returns the case to its exact state before the trial. *Barbaria v Independent Elevator Co.* (1955) 133 CA2d 657, 285 P2d 91. When granting such a motion, whether on some or all of the issues, the court must state in the order the grounds relied on and the reasons for granting the new trial as to each stated ground. See *Mercer v Perez* (1968) 68 C2d 104, 65 CR 315. If the order does not contain a statement of grounds and reasons, a separate statement may be filed, but only within 10 days after the original order. The court may not direct a party's attorney to prepare the order or the statement of grounds and reasons; however, an attorney may call a deficiency in the order to the court's attention within the 10-day period for filing the statement, so that the court may correct the order within the jurisdictional period. CCP §657; see *La Manna v Stewart* (1975) 13 C3d 413, 424, 118 CR 761.

An order granting a new trial is appealable (unlike an order denying a motion for new trial; see §18.14) within the usual time for filing a notice of appeal (Cal Rules of Ct 8.104; see §19.47). However, an order granting a new trial will not be disturbed on appeal unless a "manifest and unmistakable abuse of discretion clearly appears." *Jiminez v Sears, Roebuck & Co.* (1971) 4 C3d 379, 387, 93 CR 769. The order must be affirmed if it should have been granted on *any* ground stated in the notice of intention to move for a new trial, whether or not that ground was included in the order or in the statement of grounds and reasons. CCP §657. In fact, the appellate court has the duty to review the entire record to ascertain whether any grounds exist on which the order can be upheld. *Marriage of Beilock* (1978) 81 CA3d 713, 728, 146 CR 675. An exception to this rule applies when the ground for granting a new trial is insufficiency of the evidence to justify the decision (or excessive or inadequate damages), in which case the ground must be stated in the order, unless it was the only ground specified in the motion. *La Manna v Stewart* (1975) 13 C3d 413, 418, 118 CR 761.

If the order granting a new trial is reversed on appeal, the judgment is automatically reinstated. 13 C3d at 425. To protect against reinstatement, the party who requested and was granted the new trial may, within 20 days after the clerk's mailing of the notice of appeal from the new trial order, file a cross-appeal from the judgment. See Cal Rules of Ct 8.108 (e); on cross-appeals generally, see §19.53.

§18.16 III. MOTION TO VACATE AND ENTER DIFFERENT JUDGMENT

When the facts of a case were correctly determined and support the court's decision, but the judgment does not conform to the facts found at the trial or to the statement of decision, a motion to vacate the judgment and enter a different judgment is appropriate. See *County of Alameda v Carleson* (1971) 5 C3d 730, 738, 97 CR 385. The motion to vacate, if granted, substitutes the judgment that should have been given as a matter of law, based on the facts found at trial, for a judgment already given that is an incorrect conclusion from the facts. The court cannot, on a motion to vacate and enter a different judgment, change any of the facts found at the trial. *Dahlberg v Girsch* (1910) 157 C 324, 327, 107 P 616.

A motion for new trial (see §§18.2–18.5), on the other hand, is typically requested when a party believes that the facts or the law of the case were not correctly determined. That motion attacks the decision itself and requests a reexamination of the facts or the law applied. The errors for which relief may be sought by a motion to vacate and enter a different judgment or by a motion for new trial may be characterized as "judicial errors" (as distinguished from "clerical mistakes," from which relief may be sought under CCP §473). See §18.35.

For the effect of a motion to vacate and enter a different judgment on the finality of a marital action judgment, see §17.40; for its effect on the time for filing a notice of appeal, see §18.22.

§18.17 A. Statutory Basis

Code of Civil Procedure §663 provides that a judgment may, on motion of an "aggrieved party," be set aside and vacated by the same court, and another and different judgment entered, when an incorrect or erroneous legal basis for the decision is inconsistent with, or not supported by, the facts. Anyone who is legally aggrieved by the judgment may move to vacate and enter a different judgment, even one who was not an original party to the action. See *County of Alameda v Carleson* (1971) 5 C3d 730, 736, 97 CR 385. This remedy is available only when the error in the judgment materially affects the substantial rights of the party. When the motion is granted, the statement of decision must also be amended and corrected. CCP §663.

In some instances, a motion to vacate and enter a different judgment may be available after a motion. See §11.65 for discussion in context of attacks on temporary orders.

B. Procedure

§18.18 1. Notice of Intention

A motion to vacate the judgment and enter a different judgment is brought by filing a notice of intention with the clerk and serving it on the adverse party. The notice must designate the grounds on which the motion will be made and specify the particulars in which the legal basis for the decision is not consistent with, or supported by, the facts. CCP §663a. Although not specifically required by court rules, a memorandum of points and authorities should be filed and served with the notice of intention.

On the memorandum of points and authorities generally, see California Civil Procedure Before Trial §§12.30–12.42 (4th ed Cal CEB 2004).

§18.19 a. Time for Filing

The notice of intention must be filed either before the entry of judgment or by the earlier of (1) 15 days after the clerk mails, or the moving party serves, the notice of entry of judgment or (2) 180 days after the entry of judgment. CCP §663a. Although the statute permits the filing of a notice of intention before the entry of judgment, it is likely that the notice must be filed after the judgment sought to be vacated has been rendered, as in a motion for new trial (see §18.7). The time periods specified in the statute are not extended by CCP §1013 for service by mail. CCP §663a.

§18.20 b. Format

A motion to vacate and enter a different judgment may be prepared on the Judicial Council form of Notice of Motion (see form in §11.20) or as a separate pleading, as in civil actions generally. Counsel should check local court rules and the court clerk to ascertain the appropriate format in a particular county. The notice of motion must be filed at least 16 court days before the hearing; the time for service depends on the method used. CCP §1005(a)(13)–(b).

If the Judicial Council form is used, the moving party prepares the Notice of Motion and an Application for Order and Supporting Declaration (see form in §11.22). In the caption of the Notice of Motion form, the box labeled "Other (specify)" is checked and language such as "To Vacate Judgment and Enter Different Judgment" is inserted. The hearing date must be specified in the notice, as for most motions. Item 13 of the application should be checked and language inserted, on the form or in an attachment, requesting that the judgment be vacated and a new judgment entered, and stating the grounds for the request and the particulars in which the legal basis for the decision is not consistent with or supported by the facts. If an affidavit will be submitted, Item 14 and the accompanying box, indicating that an affidavit will be attached, should also be checked.

If a separate pleading is used, see California Trial Practice: Civil Procedure During Trial §25.96 (3d ed Cal CEB 1995) for a sample Notice of Motion to Vacate Judgment and Enter Different Judgment.

§18.21 2. Hearing and Ruling on Motion

The motion to vacate and enter a different judgment must be

heard and determined by the judge who presided at the trial. However, in the event of the judge's inability, death, or absence from the county at the time of the hearing, the motion may be heard and determined by another judge of the same court. Cal Rules of Ct 3.1602. There is no period of time designated by court rule or statute, as there is for a motion for new trial (see §18.13), after which the court's power to rule on the motion expires.

§18.22   a. Order Denying Motion to Vacate

An order denying a motion to vacate and enter a different judgment may be directly appealed (*Socol v King* (1949) 34 C2d 292, 296, 209 P2d 577), or the original judgment itself may be appealed after denial of the motion. To appeal from the judgment, counsel must file a notice of appeal within the earliest of (1) 30 days after the court clerk mails, or a party serves, an order denying the motion or a notice of entry of that order; (2) 90 days after filing the first notice of intention to move to vacate and enter a different judgment; or (3) 180 days after entry of the judgment. Cal Rules of Ct 8.108(b).

However, if the motion to vacate and enter a different judgment was denied because the notice of intention was invalid (*e.g.,* for failure to meet the statutory time requirements; see §18.19), the extension to appeal the judgment under Cal Rules of Ct 8.108(b) may not apply, and the usual period to file an appeal may already have expired. See Cal Rules of Ct 2. Therefore, if the validity of the notice of intention is in any doubt, counsel should file a notice of appeal from the original judgment within the normal 60-day period after judgment (Cal Rules of Ct 2; see §19.47), in addition to moving to vacate and enter a different judgment. It is neither inconsistent nor improper to file both a notice of appeal and a motion for new trial (see *Neff v Ernst* (1957) 48 C2d 628, 634, 311 P2d 849); this reasoning would seem to apply equally to a motion to vacate and enter a different judgment. If a notice of appeal is filed within the normal 60-day period after entry of judgment (Cal Rules of Ct 8.104(a)), then the appeal is timely, even if filed more than 90 days after giving notice of intent to move to vacate the judgment, *i.e.,* Rule 8.108(b) time limits for the motion to vacate do not shorten the Rule 8.104(a) time limits for filing a notice of appeal. See, *e.g.,* *Maides v Ralph's Grocery Co.* (2000) 77 CA4th 1363, 1367, 92 CR2d 542 (plaintiffs moved to vacate before entry of judgment;

appeal filed within 60 days after entry of judgment but more than 90 days after the notice of intention to move to vacate judgment was timely).

§18.23   b. Order Granting Motion to Vacate

If the motion to vacate and enter a different judgment is granted, the order must not only set aside the incorrect judgment but also enter a different judgment. An order that sets aside the original judgment but leaves the case undecided is void. *Dolan v Superior Court* (1920) 47 CA 235, 241, 190 P 469.

An order granting a motion to vacate and enter a different judgment is appealable. CCP §663a. If successful, the appeal may have the effect of automatically reinstating the original judgment. See *La Manna v Stewart* (1975) 13 C3d 413, 425, 118 CR 761. To protect against reinstatement, the party who requested the order vacating the original judgment may, within 20 days after the clerk's mailing of the notice of appeal from the order, file a cross-appeal from the original judgment. See Cal Rules of Ct 8.108(e); on cross-appeals generally, see §19.53.

§18.24   IV. RELIEF FROM JUDGMENT UNDER CCP §473

A party may seek relief under CCP §473 from a judgment, dismissal, order, or other proceeding entered as a result of his or her mistake, inadvertence, surprise, or excusable neglect. The granting of relief is discretionary with the court. See §18.33. However, relief sought from a default or default judgment on the basis of an attorney's mistake, inadvertence, surprise, or (not necessarily excusable) neglect must be granted if the default was in fact caused by the attorney's error. See §18.33. The application for relief under §473 must be made within a reasonable time, not to exceed 6 months after entry of default (see §18.30), and must be accompanied by a copy of the responsive pleading sought to be filed in the case (see §18.31).

Code of Civil Procedure §473 also permits, without any showing of mistake, surprise, inadvertence, or neglect, the setting aside of a void judgment (see §18.34) and the correction of clerical error in a judgment (see §18.35).

A. Setting Aside Judgment for Mistake, Inadvertence, Surprise, or Neglect

§18.25   1. Proceedings to Which Applicable

Relief requested under CCP §473 is usually from the entry of a default or default judgment because of mistake, inadvertence, surprise, or excusable neglect. However, the statute also permits relief from other "procedural steps." *Pollock v Standard Oil Co.* (1967) 256 CA2d 307, 310, 64 CR 66. The proceedings to which the statute has been applied, in addition to defaults and default judgments, include a judgment based on a stipulation of the parties (*Marriage of Jacobs* (1982) 128 CA3d 273, 180 CR 234) or on a marital settlement agreement (*Marriage of Testa* (1983) 149 CA3d 319, 321, 196 CR 780); dismissal of an action (*Bergloff v Reynolds* (1960) 181 CA2d 349, 5 CR 461); an order denying a motion for new trial (*Pollock v Standard Oil Co.* (1967) 256 CA2d 307, 64 CR 66); failure to file a memorandum of costs (*Soda v Marriott* (1933) 130 CA 589, 20 P2d 758) or to take required procedural steps in perfecting an appeal (*Paramore v Colby* (1918) 37 CA 648, 174 P 677); an order made by a subsequently disqualified judge (*Estate of Grivel* (1929) 208 C 77, 280 P 122); and an order granting a change of venue (*Badella v Miller* (1955) 44 C2d 81, 279 P2d 729). However, when relief is sought on the basis of an attorney's mistake, inadvertence, surprise, or neglect, it is limited to the set aside of a default and default judgment. See §18.27.

When the judgment from which relief is sought under CCP §473 is based on the parties' stipulated judgment (see §14.40), the vacation of the judgment necessarily sets aside the underlying stipulation. This is because, once signed by the judge, the parties' stipulation is merged into and superseded by the judgment. *Marriage of Jacobs* (1982) 128 CA3d 273, 283, 180 CR 234. On whether the setting aside of a judgment based on a marital settlement agreement (see §§14.41–14.45) will also set aside the underlying agreement, one case expressed the view that a marital settlement agreement could not be set aside under CCP §473. *Marriage of Testa* (1983) 149 CA3d 319, 322, 196 CR 780. Later cases, however, appear to reject this view. See *Marriage of Jones* (1987) 195 CA3d 1097, 1103, 241 CR 231 (vacation of judgment will set aside marital settlement agreement to extent that agreement is merged into judgment (see §14.44), as long as moving party specifically requests that relief);

Marriage of Stevenot (1984) 154 CA3d 1051, 1072, 202 CR 116 (motion to set aside judgment based on marital settlement agreement must include motion to set aside agreement).

On the importance, when relief is sought from a default judgment, of requesting relief from the default as well, see §18.29.

2. Statutory Basis for Relief

§18.26　　a. Error of Party

Relief may be granted under CCP §473 on the basis of a party's mistake, inadvertence, surprise, or excusable neglect. A mistake of fact as well as a mistake of law will justify relief. A mistake of fact exists when a person believes the facts to be other than they really are. See *Marriage of Brewer and Federici* (2001) 93 CA4th 1334, 1345, 113 CR2d 849 (judgment set aside based on mistake of fact after wife disclosed one pension plan with total value of $168,561, when there were two pension plans, with total value exceeding $500,000); *Salazar v Steelman* (1937) 22 CA2d 402, 409, 71 P2d 79 (plaintiff dismissed action on promissory note, intending to foreclose on trust deed, then discovered prior trust deed had been foreclosed, leaving note unsecured). A mistake of law occurs when a party misunderstands the legal consequences of known facts. See *Marriage of Jacobs* (1982) 128 CA3d 273, 286, 180 CR 234 (parties' stipulation for judgment based on misunderstanding of legal effect of "gift" to minor children). A mistake of law must be distinguished, however, from ignorance of the law, which, when coupled with negligence in ascertaining the law, will justify the denial of relief. *A & S Air Conditioning v Moore Co.* (1960) 184 CA2d 617, 620, 7 CR 592.

Relief may be granted on the grounds of surprise, inadvertence, or excusable neglect, as long as the party seeking relief has exercised the reasonable diligence that a person of ordinary prudence usually bestows on important business. *Luz v Lopes* (1960) 55 C2d 54, 62, 10 CR 161. Surprise and inadvertence may result when a party is unexpectedly placed in a situation to his or her detriment, through no fault of his or her own. See *Miller v Lee* (1942) 52 CA2d 10, 16, 125 P2d 627. A postjudgment change in value is not a basis for setting aside a stipulated judgment, however. See *Marriage of Heggie* (2002) 99 CA4th 28, 120 CR2d 707 (no set-aside when imbalance in community property division attributable to postjudgment change in market values; no "windfall theory" for set-asides). Disability is often a basis for granting relief on the ground of excusable neglect. See *Marriage of Kerry* (1984) 158 CA3d 456, 204 CR 660 (mental confusion); *Buck v Buck* (1954) 126 CA2d 137, 271 P2d 628 (inability to speak or understand English); *Fink & Schindler Co. v Gavros* (1925) 72 CA 688, 237 P 1083 (illness); *Stone v McWilliams* (1919) 43 CA 490, 185 P 478 (age, blindness, illiteracy).

Although CCP §473 does not specifically refer to fraud as an independent basis for relief, the court may nonetheless grant relief under the statute on grounds of fraud, whether extrinsic (see §18.38) or intrinsic (see §18.39). *Rice v Rice* (1949) 93 CA2d 646, 651, 209 P2d 662.

On sanctions that may be imposed when relief is granted for a party's mistake, inadvertence, surprise, or excusable neglect, see §18.33.

On moving to set aside or vacate a judgment establishing paternity under Fam C §§7557–7649.5, see §8.4.

§18.27   b. Error of Attorney

When an application under CCP §473 for relief from a default or default judgment is (1) filed within 6 months after entry of judgment, (2) in proper form, and (3) accompanied by an attorney's sworn affidavit (or declaration; see CCP §2015.5) attesting to his or her mistake, inadvertence, surprise, or neglect, the court must vacate any resulting default or default judgment entered against the client unless the court finds that the default was not in fact caused by the attorney's mistake, inadvertence, surprise, or neglect. CCP §473(b). When all these requirements are satisfied, the court is without discretion and may not consider the presence or absence of a satisfactory excuse for the attorney's mistake, etc. See *Marriage of Hock and Gordon-Hock* (2000) 80 CA4th 1438, 1444, 96 CR2d 546 (attorney's failure to appear at trial was procedural equivalent of default); *Billings v Health Plan of Am.* (1990) 225 CA3d 250, 256, 275 CR 80. When, on the other hand, the default was not caused by the attorney's mistake, inadvertence, surprise, or neglect, it may not be vacated. See *Todd v Thrifty Corp.* (1995) 34 CA4th 986, 40 CR2d 727. Note that the *default* must have been caused by the attorney's mistake, etc.; it is not sufficient that a default judgment was so caused. *Cisneros v Vueve* (1995) 37 CA4th 906,44 CR2d 682. Note also that some courts interpret §473(b) strictly. See *English v Ikon Bus. Solutions, Inc.* (2001) 94 CA4th 130, 114 CR2d 93 (not sufficient that judgment be "in the nature of a default"; relief denied when judgment entered against plaintiff on motion for summary judgment that her attorney failed to oppose).

On sanctions that must be imposed against the attorney when relief is granted on his or her affidavit of fault, see §18.33.

§18.28   c. No Relief From Judicial Error

A judgment that is based on judicial error, *i.e.*, error in the exercise of the court's judgment, may not be set aside or corrected under CCP §473. Such error may be corrected only by a motion for new trial, a motion to vacate judgment, an appeal, or, in some circumstances, an equitable proceeding. See *Stevens v Superior Court* (1936) 7 C2d 110, 112, 59 P2d 988; 7 Witkin, California Procedure, *Judgment* §67 (4th ed 1997). See §18.35 for comparison of judicial and clerical error.

3. Procedure

§18.29   a. Notice of Motion

A request for relief under CCP §473 may be made by a party or his or her legal representative by serving and filing a noticed motion in the underlying action. The motion must be accompanied by a copy of the Judicial Council form of Response (see form in §10.52) or other pleading proposed to be filed in the action. CCP §473(b).

If relief is sought from a default judgment, the motion should request that the entry of default also be set aside. If only the judgment is set aside, the default remains of record and prevents the defaulted party from filing any pleadings in the action, and the court may immediately render another default judgment. *Howard Greer Custom Originals v Capritti* (1950) 35 C2d 886, 221 P2d 937; *Rutan v Summit Sports, Inc.* (1985) 173 CA3d 965, 970, 219 CR 381. See, however, *Airline Transp. Carriers, Inc. v Batchelor* (1951) 102 CA2d 241, 227 P2d 480 (holding that the court *intended* to vacate the default as well as the default judgment).

If the motion is made after entry of a judgment, notice of the motion must be served on the party; service on the party's attorney of record is not sufficient. Fam C §215. An order rendered after improper notice is void on its face and subject to collateral attack at any time. *Marriage of Kreiss* (1990) 224 CA3d 1033, 1039, 274 CR 226.

§18.30 (1) Time for Filing

Application for relief under CCP §473 must be made "within a reasonable time, in no case exceeding 6 months, after the judgment, dismissal, order or proceeding was taken." CCP §473(b). When relief is sought from a default and default judgment, the general rule is that the 6-month period runs from the entry of default, not from the entry of judgment. *Rutan v Summit Sports, Inc.* (1985) 173 CA3d 965, 970, 219 CR 381. When the default was the result of attorney error (see §18.27), however, the 6-month period runs from the entry of judgment. *Sugasawara v Newland* (1994) 27 CA4th 294, 32 CR2d 484. On the importance of setting aside both the default and the default judgment, see §18.29.

The 6-month period may be shortened to 90 days when (1) the judgment or order determines the ownership or right of possession of real or personal property, (2) a written notice is personally served in California on the party against whom the judgment or order was taken and on his or her attorney of record, and (3) the notice provides that any right to apply for relief under §473 expires 90 days after service of the notice. CCP §473(b).

A motion may be denied if the court finds that there was an unreasonable or unexplained delay, or a lack of diligence, in filing the motion, even when it was filed within the 6-month period. *Ludka v Memory Magnetics Int'l* (1972) 25 CA3d 316, 321, 101 CR 615 (motion denied for unexplained three-month delay following knowledge of default). Whether the motion was filed within a "reasonable time" is a question of fact for the trial court to determine, unless the circumstances demonstrate an unreasonable delay as a matter of law. *Outdoor Imports, Inc. v Stanoff* (1970) 7 CA3d 518, 523, 86 CR 593.

At least one appellate court has determined that the 6-month time limit of CCP §473 may be extended when required by the public policy set forth in the Child Support Enforcement Fairness Act of 2000 (Stats 1999, ch 653, §1). *County of Los Angeles v Navarro*

(2004) 120 CA4th 246, 14 CR3d 905. A default judgment of paternity was later shown to be wrong. The judgment was set aside on appeal because enforcement of child support under these circumstances would be unjust.

§18.31   (2) Accompanying Documents

The motion is accompanied by the following documents:

Responsive pleading. A copy of the Judicial Council form of Response (see form in §10.52), or other pleading proposed to be filed in the action, must accompany the motion (CCP §473(b)); relief will be denied in its absence (*Bailiff v Hildebrandt* (1920) 47 CA 564, 567, 191 P 42). On whether the responsive pleading may be filed after expiration of the statutory period for filing the application for relief from default but before the hearing on the application, compare *Puryear v Stanley* (1985) 172 CA3d 291, 295, 218 CR 196 (declined to extend concept of "substantial compliance" to embrace such circumstances), with *County of Stanislaus v Johnson* (1996) 43 CA4th 832, 51 CR2d 73, and *Job v Farrington* (1989) 209 CA3d 338, 257 CR 210 (held that late filing of proposed pleading, in "substantial compliance" with statute, is sufficient).

Affidavit. When relief is requested based on a party's mistake, inadvertence, surprise, or excusable neglect, a declaration should be filed showing the nature of and the reason for the error, why the error should be excused, and that the party diligently sought relief. Although the declaration is not required by statute, it may be the party's only opportunity to be heard, because the court has discretion to refuse oral testimony (*Marriage of Jacobs* (1982) 128 CA3d 273, 287, 180 CR 234). The moving party need not show facts establishing that his or her underlying case is meritorious, as was previously required. When mandatory relief from a default judgment is sought because of an attorney's error (see §18.27), the attorney's sworn affidavit must be filed, showing that the judgment was caused by his or her own mistake, inadvertence, surprise, or neglect. CCP §473(b).

For an example of a declaration, see §10.37 (Declaration in Support of Application for Order for Publication of Summons).

§18.32   (3) Format

A motion for relief under CCP §473 may be prepared on the

Judicial Council form of Notice of Motion (see form in §11.20) or as a separate pleading, as in civil actions generally. Counsel should check local court rules and the court clerk to ascertain the appropriate format in a particular county. The notice of motion must be filed at least 16 court days before the hearing; the time for service depends on the method used. CCP §1005(a)(13)–(b).

If the Judicial Council form is used, the moving party prepares the Notice of Motion and an Application for Order and Supporting Declaration (see form in §11.22). In the caption of the Notice of Motion form, the box labeled "Other (specify)" is checked and language such as "To Set Aside Default and Default Judgment" is inserted. Item 9 of the application should be checked and language inserted, on the form or in an attachment, requesting that the default and the default judgment be set aside and stating the grounds for the motion (see §§18.26–18.27). Item 10 and the accompanying box, indicating that a declaration (see §18.31) will be attached, should also be checked.

If a separate pleading is used, see California Civil Procedure Before Trial §38.92 (4th ed Cal CEB 2004) for a sample Notice of Motion to Set Aside Default and Default Judgment.

§18.33   b. Ruling on Motion

When relief from a default or default judgment is requested on an attorney's sworn affidavit of mistake, inadvertence, surprise, or neglect (see §18.27), and the court finds that the default in fact resulted from the attorney's error, the motion *must* be granted. The court is required in such cases to order the attorney to pay reasonable compensatory legal fees and costs to the opposing counsel or parties. CCP §473(b). When relief is requested on the basis of a party's mistake, inadvertence, surprise, or excusable neglect, the granting of relief is within the court's discretion. Its determination, particularly when the result is to compel a hearing on the merits, will not be disturbed on appeal unless there is a clear showing of abuse of discretion. *Marriage of Jacobs* (1982) 128 CA3d 273, 280, 180 CR 234.

When ruling on a motion that is within its discretion, the court must balance the policy favoring the finality of judgments with the policy favoring the hearing of controversies on their merits. *Lynch v Betts* (1962) 198 CA2d 755, 758, 18 CR 345. Any doubt that may exist should be resolved in favor of a hearing on the merits. *Beckley v Reclamation Bd.* (1957) 48 C2d 710, 717, 312 P2d 1098. See also *Airline Transp. Carriers, Inc. v Batchelor* (1951) 102 CA2d 241, 227 P2d 480.

Whenever the court grants a motion under CCP §473, it may do so on "any terms as may be just." These terms may include an order that the moving party pay the attorney fees and costs incurred by the other party as a result of the error, as long as such condition is "just." *Marriage of Kerry* (1984) 158 CA3d 456, 463, 204 CR 660 (order for payment of attorney fees was abuse of discretion when moving party could not pay). When the court grants relief from a default or default judgment under any of the provisions of §473, it may order an offending attorney or defaulting party to pay a penalty up to $1000, order an offending attorney to pay up to $1000 to the State Bar Client Security Fund, or grant other relief as is appropriate. CCP §473(c)(1). When the court grants relief from a default or default judgment, however, based on an attorney's affidavit regarding his or her mistake, inadvertence, surprise, or neglect, the relief may not be made conditional on the attorney's payment of compensatory legal fees or costs or monetary penalties imposed by the court or on compliance with other sanctions ordered by the court. CCP §473(c)(2).

An order granting or denying a motion to set aside a judgment under CCP §473 is immediately appealable. If an appeal is not timely filed after the order is issued, the right to appeal will be lost. See §19.9.

§18.34　　B. Setting Aside Void Judgment

On motion of either party and after notice to the other party, the court may set aside any void judgment or order. CCP §473(d). A judgment is void when the court that rendered it lacked personal or subject matter jurisdiction. *Marriage of Goodarzirad* (1986) 185 CA3d 1020, 1030, 230 CR 203; *Sternbeck v Buck* (1957) 148 CA2d 829, 832, 307 P2d 970. On jurisdiction, see §§4.2 (subject matter), 4.4–4.5 (personal).

A judgment that is void on its face, *i.e.*, requires only an inspection of the judgment roll or record to show its invalidity, is subject to attack under CCP §473 at any time. *Hayashi v Lorenz* (1954) 42 C2d 848, 851, 271 P2d 18; *Thorson v Western Dev. Corp.* (1967)

251 CA2d 206, 210, 59 CR 299. When a judgment is void but its invalidity does not appear on its face, a request to set aside the judgment under CCP §473 must be made within a reasonable time after discovery of the default and within the earlier of 2 years after entry of the judgment or 180 days after service of a written notice of entry of the default or default judgment. *Schenkel v Resnik* (1994) 27 CA4th Supp 1, 33 CR2d 60.

On moving to set aside a judgment on noticed motion under CCP §473, see §§18.29–18.32.

§18.35   C. Correcting Clerical Error

When, as a result of clerical error, a signed judgment does not reflect the court's express judicial intention, the judgment may be corrected under CCP §473. *Marriage of Kaufman* (1980) 101 CA3d 147, 151, 161 CR 538, 540. Clerical error may be corrected on the injured party's motion or on the court's own motion. CCP §473(d). The general rule is that the motion may be made at any time, without notice to the other side, regardless of whether the error appears on the face of the record. *Estate of Costa* (1951) 37 C2d 154, 157, 231 P2d 17, 18; *Estate of Goldberg* (1938) 10 C2d 709, 717, 76 P2d 508, 513 (order corrected after 35 years). Under some authority, however, a motion to correct a clerical error must be noticed and brought within the 6-month time requirement of §473 when the error does not appear on the face of the record. 7 Witkin, California Procedure, *Judgment* §77 (4th ed 1997).

Common clerical errors include a mistake in or omission of a party's name, a mistaken term or phrase, an error in a property description, or a mistake in the amount or items included in a judgment. 7 Witkin, Procedure, *Judgment* §70. The error may have been made by the clerk, counsel, or the court and must have been inadvertent, *i.e.,* the judgment signed is not what was intended to be signed. See *Pettigrew v Grand Rent-A-Car* (1984) 154 CA3d 204, 211, 201 CR 125.

Clerical error, which is inadvertent, should not be confused with judicial error, which is advertent, *i.e.,* the court knowingly made a decision without realizing that it was legally erroneous. *Bowden v Green* (1982) 128 CA3d 65, 71, 180 CR 90, 93. See also *Stevens v Superior Court* (1936) 7 C2d 110, 112, 59 P2d 988, 990 (court misunderstood scope of waiver of new trial); *Hunydee v Superior*

Court (1961) 198 CA2d 430, 17 CR 856 (court's setting aside of new trial order, which was based on misunderstanding of law, was improper). A judicial error can be corrected only by a motion for new trial, a motion to vacate judgment, an appeal, or, in some circumstances, an equitable proceeding. 7 Witkin, Procedure, *Judgment* §67.

§18.36   V. EQUITABLE RELIEF FROM JUDGMENT ENTERED BEFORE JANUARY 1, 1993

With respect to judgments entered before January 1, 1993, the court has inherent, equitable power, even after the time for requesting relief under CCP §473 (see §18.30) has expired, to set aside a judgment obtained by extrinsic fraud, mistake, or duress. See *Marriage of Baltins* (1989) 212 CA3d 66, 80, 260 CR 403. In each case, circumstances external to the hearing must have deprived a party of the opportunity to present his or her case to the court and prevented a fair adversary trial at law. 212 CA3d at 87; *Marriage of Stevenot* (1984) 154 CA3d 1051, 1068, 202 CR 116. Equitable relief may be requested by bringing a motion in the marital action or by commencing an independent action in equity. On considerations in choosing between a motion and an independent action, and the procedures for each, see §§18.43–18.46.

In determining whether to grant equitable relief, the court must balance competing public policies, one favoring a fair adversary trial on the merits and the other favoring the finality of judgments. *Marriage of Baltins* (1989) 212 CA3d 66, 81, 260 CR 403. The policy favoring a fair trial predominates during the period that relief is available under CCP §473. Once that period has passed, the policy favoring the finality of judgments predominates, and a judgment will be set aside for equitable reasons only when "exceptional circumstances" require that the consequences of res judicata be denied. See *Marriage of Stevenot* (1984) 154 CA3d 1051, 1070, 202 CR 116.

When the judgment is based on a marital settlement agreement, vacation of the judgment will set aside the marital settlement agreement to the extent that it is merged into the judgment (see §14.44), as long as the moving party specifically requests that relief. *Marriage of Jones* (1987) 195 CA3d 1097, 1103, 241 CR 231.

On setting aside judgments entered on or after January 1, 1993, see §§18.47–18.54.

On availability of a separate tort action for concealment of community assets, see *Dale v Dale* (1998) 66 CA4th 1172, 78 CR2d 513. *Dale* held that such an action could be brought, as an alternative to a motion in the dissolution action to set aside the judgment, at least when no dissolution action was still pending in which property and support rights remained to be determined. 66 CA4th at 1187, 78 CR2d at 522.

A. When Relief Is Available

§18.37   1. Time for Filing

There is no statutory time period within which an equitable proceeding to set aside a judgment entered before January 1, 1993, must be brought. However, the party seeking relief has the burden of showing reasonable diligence in both discovering the grounds for relief and, after discovery, seeking relief. Prejudice caused to the other party by delay is a factor the court may consider in determining whether the party seeking relief has exercised reasonable diligence. The greater the prejudice, the more timely must relief be sought. *Marriage of Baltins* (1989) 212 CA3d 66, 92, 260 CR 403, 419. See also *Marriage of Stevenot* (1984) 154 CA3d 1051, 1071, 202 CR 116, 130.

The court in *Marriage of Baltins, supra,* held that the doctrine of laches is technically inappropriate in such proceedings because the burden should not be on the defending party to prove unreasonable delay, but on the moving party to prove reasonable diligence. 212 CA3d at 92, 260 CR at 419. Other cases, however, have cited the defense of laches as applicable when there is an unreasonable delay in seeking relief and either acquiescence by the moving party in the act complained of or prejudice caused to the other party by the delay. See *Marriage of Nicolaides* (1974) 39 CA3d 192, 203, 114 CR 56.

2. Grounds for Relief

§18.38   a. Extrinsic Fraud

Equitable relief from a judgment entered before January 1, 1993, may be granted when one party is the victim of extrinsic fraud, *i.e.,* is fraudulently prevented from fully participating in the proceeding, other than by his or her own conduct, and is thus deprived of the opportunity to present his or her claim or defense to the court. See *Marriage of Stevenot* (1984) 154 CA3d 1051, 1068, 202 CR 116. A finding of extrinsic fraud does not require actual fraud. Rather, it may be based on constructive fraud, which occurs when conduct, although not actually fraudulent, should be treated as such. *Marriage of Baltins* (1989) 212 CA3d 66, 87, 260 CR 403. Some examples of conduct that supports a finding of extrinsic fraud are these:

- One party and counsel persuade the other party not to obtain counsel (*Marriage of Brennan* (1981) 124 CA3d 598, 177 CR 520) or an unrepresented party to enter into an inequitable agreement (*Marriage of Adkins* (1982) 137 CA3d 68, 186 CR 818).

- One party conceals the existence of community property assets (*Marriage of Modnick* (1983) 33 C3d 897, 191 CR 629; see §18.40); on statutory duty of disclosure, see §18.57.

- One party prevents the other from participating in the proceeding, *e.g.*, by failing to give notice of the action or by failing to disclose to the court the other party's inability to participate (see *Marriage of Park* (1980) 27 C3d 337, 165 CR 792; *Marriage of Stevenot* (1984) 154 CA3d 1051, 1069, 202 CR 116).

- One party obtains a judgment while "reconciled" with, and without the knowledge of, the other party (*Marriage of Grissom* (1994) 30 CA4th 40, 35 CR2d 530) or after representing to the other party that the action would not proceed without further notice (*Marriage of Jones* (1987) 195 CA3d 1097, 241 CR 231).

§18.39 (1) Intrinsic Fraud Distinguished

Fraud is intrinsic and not a basis for equitable relief from a judgment entered before January 1, 1993, when a party has the opportunity to present his or her case to the court and to protect against any mistake or fraud but unreasonably neglects to do so. If the claim of fraud goes to the merits of the action, and if the moving party contributes to the fraud, is negligent in failing to prevent the fraud, or fails to use discovery procedures to investigate, the fraud is intrinsic. *Kulchar v Kulchar* (1969) 1 C3d 467, 472, 82 CR 489; *Marriage of Stevenot* (1984) 154 CA3d 1051, 1069, 202 CR 116. The same is true for a claim of mistake (see §18.41).

Fraud has been found to be intrinsic when a wife and her attorney failed to investigate the nature of assets claimed by her husband to be separate property (*Jorgensen v Jorgensen* (1948) 32 C2d 13, 193 P2d 728), when a husband failed to investigate his tax liability before agreeing to hold his wife harmless from taxes (*Kulchar v Kulchar, supra*), and when a wife failed to seek counsel until all payments due under a marital settlement agreement had been made (*Marriage of Stevenot, supra*). In most cases that have denied equitable relief, the moving party was represented by counsel, dealt with the other party at arm's length, and had ample opportunity to investigate the other party's representations. *Marriage of Baltins* (1989) 212 CA3d 66, 89, 260 CR 403.

§18.40 (2) Concealment of Assets

Courts have uniformly held that a deliberate concealment of assets by one spouse constitutes extrinsic fraud for which equitable relief will be granted. See *Marriage of Umphrey* (1990) 218 CA3d 647, 655, 267 CR 218. Under the court's equitable powers, the entire judgment may be set aside. *Resnik v Superior Court* (1986) 185 CA3d 634, 637, 230 CR 1. Such broad relief may be appropriate, *e.g.*, when the concealed assets are not readily divisible and their value requires a redistribution of all community property to achieve an equal division, or when support issues should be reevaluated in light of discovery of the concealed assets.

In many cases, however, statutory relief may be speedier and more economical. Under Fam C §2556, the court may award community assets or debts omitted from a judgment on a party's postjudgment motion in the marital action. See discussion in §18.56. Family Code §1101 provides other specific remedies (*e.g.*, accounting of assets and obligations, providing access to property, revising title to property, awarding half (or all, when exemplary damages are appropriate) of an undisclosed or transferred asset plus attorney fees and costs) to a spouse whose interest in the community estate is impaired by a breach of fiduciary duty by the other spouse. See Fam C §§721(b), 1100(b), 1101, and discussion in §18.57.

Counsel may also wish to consider a tort action for fraud and conversion against a spouse who conceals community assets. Such an action was held not barred after judgment by the doctrine of res judicata in *Worton v Worton* (1991) 234 CA3d 1638, 286 CR 410.

§18.41   b. Extrinsic Mistake

When the ground for relief is not so much the other spouse's fraud or misconduct as the excusable neglect of the moving party to appear and present his or her case and such neglect results in an unjust judgment without a fair adversary hearing, "extrinsic mistake" may be a basis for relief. *Kulchar v Kulchar* (1969) 1 C3d 467, 471, 82 CR 489; *Marriage of Baltins* (1989) 212 CA3d 66, 83, 260 CR 403. A mistake is not a sufficient basis for granting equitable relief when the party has received notice of the action and has had the opportunity to present his or her case to the court and protect against mistake (*i.e.,* intrinsic mistake). *Marriage of Dorris* (1984) 160 CA3d 1208, 1213, 207 CR 160 (ambiguity in marital settlement agreement prepared by moving party's attorney not extrinsic mistake). Moreover, a mutual mistake that might be sufficient to set aside a contract is not sufficient to set aside a judgment. "A rule which would permit the re-opening of cases previously decided because of error or ignorance during the progress of the trial would in a large measure vitiate the effects of the rules of res judicata." *Kulchar v Kulchar* (1969) 1 C3d 467, 472, 82 CR 489.

Some examples of extrinsic mistake that prevented a fair adversary hearing, and for which relief was granted, include reliance on an attorney who became incapacitated (*Jeffords v Young* (1929) 98 CA 400, 277 P 163), a mistaken belief of one party that prevented proper notice of the action (*Aldabe v Aldabe* (1962) 209 CA2d 453, 26 CR 208), disability of a moving party at the time judgment was entered (*Watson v Watson* (1958) 161 CA2d 35, 325 P2d 1011), and an attorney's negligence in not filing an answer (*Hallett v Slaughter* (1943) 22 C2d 552, 140 P2d 3). See *Kulchar v Kulchar, supra,* for an examination of cases distinguishing extrinsic from intrinsic mistake.

§18.42   c. Duress

In setting aside a judgment, courts have often characterized duress as extrinsic fraud; nonetheless, duress may be an independent ground for equitable relief. *Marriage of Baltins* (1989) 212 CA3d 66, 83, 260 CR 403. Duress occurs when a party intentionally uses threats or pressure to induce action or inaction by the other party to the latter's detriment and the coerced party has no alternative but to succumb. 212 CA3d at 84. There are no arbitrary standards for what constitutes duress; the ultimate fact in issue is whether the victim was bereft of the free exercise of his or her will power. In making that determination, the court may look to the means used to exercise coercion and the age, sex, state of health, and mental characteristics of the injured party. *Marriage of Gonzalez* (1976) 57 CA3d 736, 744, 129 CR 566. Like extrinsic fraud or mistake, duress must have the effect of depriving the victim of a fair adversary hearing. *Marriage of Baltins* (1989) 212 CA3d 66, 87, 260 CR 403.

Duress has been found when a wife waived spousal support soon after her husband severely beat her and threatened to kill her, burn the house down, and take her children away from her (*McIntosh v McIntosh* (1962) 209 CA2d 371, 26 CR 26); when a wife signed a marital settlement agreement after her husband threatened to take their children to a foreign country and have her "exterminated" (*Marriage of Gonzalez, supra*); and when a wife consented to a "grossly unfair" agreement after being effectively deprived of counsel, psychologically undermined, and threatened with bankruptcy by her physician husband (*Marriage of Baltins, supra*).

Note, however, that not all courts may recognize duress as a separate ground for equitable relief. In *Marriage of Alexander* (1989) 212 CA3d 677, 261 CR 9, the trial court set aside a judgment incorporating a marital settlement agreement in which a wife had waived substantial property and spousal support rights. The wife had alleged severe emotional distress and reliance on her husband's statements that she did not need an attorney. The appellate court reversed, holding that "the *only* ground for relief was extrinsic fraud" and citing the trial court's finding that no extrinsic fraud had occurred. 212 CA3d at 681, 261 CR at 11.

B. Procedure

§18.43   1. Motion or Independent Action

Equitable relief from a judgment entered before January 1, 1993, may be sought by bringing a motion within the existing marital action or by commencing a separate action in equity. The two procedures have important substantive and procedural differences, however, that must be considered in choosing whether to proceed by motion or by independent action:

Applicability of Family Code. When a judgment entered before January 1, 1993, is requested to be set aside by a motion in the existing action, the proceeding continues under the Family Code, despite the court's equitable powers in ruling on the motion. Thus, *e.g.,* when relief is sought in the existing action, the court is bound by the requirement of Fam C §2552 (former CC §4800(a)) that property be valued as near as practicable to the time of adjudication. In an independent equitable action, the court is not governed by the Code and may value the property in any manner it deems equitable. *Brink v Brink* (1984) 155 CA3d 218, 222, 202 CR 57.

Testimony of witnesses. In an independent action, the plaintiff may present oral testimony, subpoena unfriendly witnesses, and take depositions; the court can observe the witnesses' demeanor, and there is an opportunity for cross-examination. These procedures are available only at the court's discretion in motion proceedings. See *Estudillo v Security Loan & Trust Co.* (1906) 149 C 556, 564, 87 P 19. See also *Skouland v Skouland* (1962) 201 CA2d 677, 20 CR 185 (court properly declined to hear oral testimony on motion to set aside divorce judgment).

Statement of decision. The court is not required to issue a statement of decision after hearing a motion to set aside a judgment entered before January 1, 1993; as a result, all conflicts in evidence are resolved in favor of the prevailing party on appeal (see §17.10). However, the court must issue a statement of decision, on request, after the trial of an independent action. CCP §632; Cal Rules of Ct 3.1590; *Marriage of Baltins* (1989) 212 CA3d 66, 80, 260 CR 403. On statements of decision generally, see §§17.5–17.31.

Speed and expense of resolution. A motion in an existing action is likely to be resolved by the court within a significantly shorter time period, and at substantially less cost, than an independent action.

Legal versus factual issues. Because of the greater availability of discovery, testimony, and findings in an independent action, this method may be preferable when factual issues predominate; a motion is usually preferable when the issues are legal in nature.

§18.44   2. Judgment Based on Agreement

Equitable relief from a judgment entered before January 1, 1993, that is based on a marital settlement agreement, as from any other judgment, may be requested by bringing either a motion or an independent action. See *Marriage of Testa* (1983) 149 CA3d 319, 322, 196 CR 780. In both cases, care must be taken to request that the agreement and the judgment both be set aside. *Marriage of Stevenot* (1984) 154 CA3d 1051, 1072, 202 CR 116.

When the marital settlement agreement has been merged into the judgment and a request is made to vacate both the agreement and the judgment, the agreement must be set aside if the judgment is set aside. *Marriage of Jones* (1987) 195 CA3d 1097, 1104, 241 CR 231. If the agreement has not been merged into the judgment, it may be attacked in accordance with the procedure for rescission of a contract (see CC §§1689, 1691), as well as by equitable motion or action. Because the principles of res judicata do not apply to such an agreement, it should be less difficult to set aside than one that has been merged into a judgment. See *Kulchar v Kulchar* (1969) 1 C3d 467, 472, 82 CR 489; *Marriage of Carletti* (1975) 53 CA3d 989, 993, 126 CR 1. On merger generally, see §14.44.

§18.45   3. Preparation of Motion

An equitable motion to set aside a judgment is similar in format to a motion to set aside under CCP §473. The motion may be prepared on the Judicial Council form of Notice of Motion (see form in §11.20) or as a separate pleading, as in civil actions generally. Counsel should check local court rules and the court clerk to determine the appropriate format in a particular county. The notice of motion must be filed at least 16 court days before the hearing; the time for service depends on the method used. CCP §1005(a)(13)–(b).

If the Judicial Council form is used, the moving party prepares the Notice of Motion and an Application for Order and Supporting Declaration (see form in §11.22). In the caption of the Notice of Motion form, the box labeled "Other (specify)" is checked and language such as "To Set Aside Judgment" or, when applicable, "To Set Aside Judgment and Marital Termination Agreement" is inserted. Item 9 of the application should be checked and language inserted on the form or in an attachment, requesting that the judgment (and, when applicable, the agreement) be set aside and stating the grounds for the motion (see §§18.38–18.42). If affidavits will be submitted, Item 10 and the accompanying box, indicating that affidavits will be attached, should also be checked.

§18.46   4. Preparation of Independent Action

The procedures for filing an independent action in equity are similar to those for filing any other civil action. On the nature of an equitable action to set aside a judgment generally, see 8 Witkin, California Procedure, *Attack on Judgment in Trial Court* §§214–218 (4th ed 1997). For general procedures in preparing civil complaints, see California Civil Procedure Before Trial, chaps 14 (Ascertaining, Joining, and Naming Parties), 15 (Drafting Complaints), 17 (Service of Summons) (4th ed Cal CEB 2004).

§18.47 VI. RELIEF UNDER FAM C §§2120–2129 FROM JUDGMENT ENTERED ON OR AFTER JANUARY 1, 1993

After the 6-month time limit of CCP §473 has run, Fam C §§2120–2129 govern the setting aside, whether partially or completely, of judgments adjudicating property division or support. Fam C §2121(a). The section applies, however, only to judgments entered on or after January 1, 1993. Fam C §2129. On the law applicable to the setting aside of judgments entered before January 1, 1993, see §§18.36–18.46. On relief from judgments under CCP §473, see §§18.24–18.35.

Family Code §§2120–2129 do not prevent a party from seeking division, under Fam C §2556, of property omitted from a judgment. Fam C §2128(a). On division under Fam C §2556, see §18.56.

On availability of a separate tort action for concealment of community assets, see *Dale v Dale* (1998) 66 CA4th 1172, 78 CR2d 513. *Dale* held that such an action could be brought, as an alternative to a motion in the dissolution action to set aside the judgment, at least when no dissolution action was still pending in which property and support rights remained to be determined. 66 CA4th at 1187. Note, however, that the court did not address the possible impact of Fam C §§2120–2129 when the judgment was entered on or after January 1, 1993. 66 CA4th at 1179 n5. But see *Rubenstein v Rubenstein* (2000) 81 CA4th 1131, 1146, 97 CR2d 707 (*Dale* was "major departure from existing law" and, in any event, is no longer operative).

A. When Relief Is Available

§18.48 1. Requisite Findings for Granting of Relief

Before a court may grant relief under Fam C §§2120–2129, it must find that the facts alleged as the grounds for relief materially affected the original outcome and that the moving party would materially benefit from the relief. Fam C §2121(b).

§18.49 2. Grounds and Time Limits for Action or Motion to Set Aside Judgment

The grounds and respective time limits for an action or a motion to set aside a judgment, whether partially or completely, are described in Fam C §2122 as follows:

Fraud. The moving party must have been fraudulently prevented from fully participating in the proceeding either by being kept in ignorance or in some other manner but not as a result of his or her own lack of care or attention. Actions or motions based on fraud must be brought within 1 year after the moving party discovered, or should have discovered, the fraud. Fam C §2122(a); *Rubenstein v Rubenstein* (2000) 81 CA4th 1131, 1145, 97 CR2d 707. The statute of limitations accrues when a party discovered or should have discovered the facts constituting fraud or perjury, not when the party merely suspected them. Thus, for example, when a husband lied about his interests in property rights, his wife was not able to obtain evidence from his federal case asserting those interests until that litigation commenced. *Rubenstein v Rubenstein* (2000) 81 CA4th 1131, 1145, 97 CR2d 707.

NOTE▶ Though a moving *party* may not be entitled to relief requested once the 1-year statute has run, the court retains the equitable power to set a judgment aside when it is based on a fraud perpetrated on the court. *Marriage of Deffner* (2006) 143 CA4th 662, 684, 49 CR3d 424 (when court papers ostensibly prepared by attorney for one party were really prepared by attorney for other party). **Caution:** Case recently depublished.

Perjury. The perjury must have occurred in the preliminary or final declaration of disclosure, the waiver of the final declaration of disclosure, or in the current Income and Expense Declaration, required under Fam C §§2100–2113. Actions or motions based on perjury must be brought within 1 year after the moving party discovered, or should have discovered, the perjury. Fam C §2122(b); *Rubenstein v Rubenstein* (2000) 81 CA4th 1131, 1145, 97 CR2d 707. On declarations of disclosure under Fam C §§2100–2113, see §§13.44–13.49.

Duress. Actions or motions based on duress must be brought within 2 years after entry of judgment. Fam C §2122(c). See *Mar-*

riage of Rosevear (1998) 65 CA4th 673, 685, 76 CR2d 691 (duress claim rejected when no hint of duress in settlement conference voir dire transcript and party signed stipulated judgment 3 months later).

Mental incapacity. Actions or motions based on mental incapacity must be brought within 2 years after entry of judgment. Fam C §2122(d).

Mistake. This ground applies to stipulated judgments or parts of judgments and to uncontested judgments. The mistake may be either mutual or unilateral and may be either mistake of law or mistake of fact. See *Marriage of Rosevear, supra* (mistake claim rejected when opposing party provided substantial documentation, settlement conference voir dire transcript indicated party claiming mistake understood settlement terms, and party signed stipulated judgment 3 months later); *Marriage of Varner* (1997) 55 CA4th 128, 144, 63 CR2d 894 (failure to disclose existence or value of community asset constitutes basis for setting aside judgment on ground of mistake under Fam C §2122). Actions or motions based on mistake must be brought within one year after entry of judgment. Fam C §2122(e).

Noncompliance with disclosure requirements. A judgment may be set aside for failure to comply with the disclosure requirements of Fam C §§2100–2113. An action or motion based on this ground must be brought within 1 year after the date on which the complaining party either discovered, or should have discovered, the failure to comply. Fam C §2122(f).

Effect of inequitable judgment. A judgment may not be set aside simply because the court finds that it was inequitable when made or simply because subsequent circumstances caused the division of assets or liabilities to become inequitable or the support to become inadequate. Fam C §2123.

Evidence derived from mediation. A judgment cannot be corrected based on evidence about communications between the parties to a mediation unless the parties have executed suitable express waivers. *Eisendrath v Superior Court* (2003) 109 CA4th 351, 134 CR2d 716 (motion to correct spousal support agreement could not rest on confidential mediation communications without express waivers under Evid C §§1115–1128; case remanded to determine which mediation participants, including mediator, would expressly waive their confidentiality rights). See *Marriage of Kieturakis* (2006) 138 CA4th 56, 87, 41 CR3d 119 (judgment not set aside under Fam C §2122;

presumption of undue influence from one spouse obtaining advantage over other does not apply to marital settlement agreement achieved through mediation).

§18.50 3. Effect of Attorney's Negligence

The negligence of an attorney may not be imputed to his or her client to bar an order setting aside a judgment unless the court finds that the client knew or should have known of the attorney's negligence and unreasonably failed to protect himself or herself. Fam C §2124. Attorney negligence, however, is not grounds for setting aside a judgment; one of the five exclusive statutory bases in Fam C §2122 (see §18.49) must be established. *Marriage of Rosevear* (1998) 65 CA4th 673, 686, 76 CR2d 691.

§18.51 B. Procedures

Notice of a motion to set aside a judgment under Fam C §§2120–2129 will typically be prepared on the Judicial Council form of Notice of Motion (see form in §11.20). In the rare event in which the opposing party has not appeared in the proceeding, however, the Judicial Council form of Order to Show Cause (see form in §11.18) will be used. Either way, an Application for Order and Supporting Declaration (see form in §11.22) will also be prepared.

In the caption of the Notice of Motion or Order to Show Cause, the box labeled "Other (specify)" is checked and language such as "To Set Aside Judgment" or, when applicable, "To Set Aside Judgment and Marital Termination (or Settlement) Agreement" (see §18.52) is inserted. Item 9 of the application should be checked and language inserted on the form or in an attachment, requesting that the judgment (and, when applicable, the agreement) be set aside and stating the grounds for the motion (see §18.49). Facts in support of the motion are set forth at Item 10, usually in an attached declaration.

In some instances, a memorandum of points and authorities may be appropriate. See §11.32.

A motion to set aside a judgment will be prepared and processed in much the same manner as a noticed motion for temporary orders. For discussion of, and forms for, motions for temporary orders, see §§11.16–11.63. Note, however, that service of the moving papers must be made *on the party*; service on his or her attorney is not sufficient. Fam C §215.

A party seeking to set aside a judgment may also proceed by a separate action. On considerations in choosing which approach to use, see §18.43, which is presented in the context of attacking judgments entered before January 1, 1993, but also applies to attacks on judgments entered on or after that date.

§18.52 C. Extent of Relief

In addressing the granting of a motion to set aside a judgment, Fam C §2125 provides that a court must set aside only those provisions materially affected by the circumstances leading to the decision to grant relief. However, the section also provides that the court has discretion to set aside the entire judgment, if necessary, for equitable considerations. Thus, when a set-aside motion is granted, §2125 appears to establish a preference for, but not to require, a partial, rather than complete, set aside. But see *Marriage of Varner* (1997) 55 CA4th 128, 144, 63 CR2d 894 (failure to disclose existence or value of community asset constitutes basis for setting aside judgment on ground of mistake under Fam C §2122).

When a marital settlement agreement has been merged into the judgment and a request is made to set aside both the agreement and the judgment, the agreement must be set aside if the judgment is set aside. *Marriage of Jones* (1987) 195 CA3d 1097, 1104, 241 CR 231. When a motion is made to set aside a judgment based on a marital settlement agreement, care should be taken to request that the agreement and the judgment both be set aside. *Marriage of Stevenot* (1984) 154 CA3d 1051, 1072, 202 CR 116.

§18.53 D. When Statement of Decision Required

If a timely request is made, the court must render a statement of decision when it has resolved disputed factual issues. Fam C §2127. On statements of decision generally, see §§17.5–17.31.

§18.54 E. Rules for Subsequent Division of Assets or Liabilities

For purposes of subsequent division of assets or liabilities on which a judgment or part of a judgment has been set aside, the date of valuation will be subject to equitable considerations. The court must divide each such asset or liability equally unless it finds, on a showing of good cause, that the interests of justice require an unequal division. Fam C §2126.

VII. OTHER STATUTORY RELIEF FROM JUDGMENT

§18.55 A. Setting Aside Default When No Actual Notice

When a summons has been properly served but does not result in actual notice to the respondent in time to defend the action, a noticed motion may be brought under CCP §473.5 to set aside a resulting default or default judgment. The failure to receive actual notice must not be caused by the respondent's avoidance of service or inexcusable neglect. CCP §473.5(a)-(b). Forms of service that may fail to provide actual notice include substituted service (CCP §415.20), service outside California by mail and return receipt (CCP §415.40), and service by publication (CCP §415.50).

The notice of motion must be served and filed within a "reasonable time," not to exceed 2 years after entry of the default judgment or 180 days after the moving party is served with written notice of the default or default judgment, whichever is earlier. CCP §473.5(a). The notice of motion must be accompanied by (1) an affidavit (or declaration; see CCP §2015.5) showing that the lack of actual notice in time to defend the action was not caused by the respondent's avoidance of service or inexcusable neglect and (2) a copy of the Response (see form in §10.52) or other pleading proposed to be filed in the action. CCP §473.5(b). Other procedures to follow in requesting relief from a default and a default judgment under CCP §473.5 are the same as for requesting relief under CCP §473 (see §§18.29–18.32). If the court finds that the motion was timely brought and that the respondent's lack of notice was not caused by avoidance of service or inexcusable neglect, it may set aside the default or default judgment on "whatever terms may be just" and allow the respondent to defend the action. CCP §473.5(c).

§18.56 B. Division of Property Omitted From Judgment

If community assets or debts were not adjudicated in the judgment, the parties continue to own the property as tenants in common. *Mar-*

riage of Dorris (1984) 160 CA3d 1208, 1215, 207 CR 160. The court has continuing jurisdiction under Fam C §2556 to order the division of such property on a postjudgment motion or order to show cause in the original proceeding. Note that the property need not have been undiscovered at the time of trial, merely unadjudicated. The statute gives the court jurisdiction over the omitted property even when jurisdiction was not reserved in the judgment and without regard, apparently, to whether the property was previously mentioned in pleadings filed in the original action. For a particularly broad interpretation of what constitutes property unadjudicated in the judgment, see *Marriage of Melton* (1994) 28 CA4th 931, 33 CR2d 761 (when pension payments turn out to be far greater than amounts stated in judgment, excess may be treated as omitted asset). But see *Marriage of Simundza* (2004) 121 CA4th 1513, 18 CR3d 377 (distinguishing *Melton* and determining there was no omitted asset).

Before the enactment of former CC §4353, predecessor of Fam C §2556, effective January 1, 1990, it was necessary to bring an independent *"Henn* action" to partition former community property omitted from the judgment. See *Henn v Henn* (1980) 26 C3d 323,330, 161 CR 502. The statute applies retroactively to pending cases (*Marriage of Umphrey* (1990) 218 CA3d 647, 659, 267 CR 218), and *Henn* actions are no longer necessary to address such property.

On a motion brought under Fam C §2556, the court is required to divide the unadjudicated community assets and debts equally unless it finds, on good cause shown, that the interests of justice require an unequal division. If a party knew that property was omitted from the judgment but failed to timely assert his or her rights, a court could conceivably find that an unequal division of the asset or debt is warranted in the "interests of justice." See *Lakkees v Superior Court* (1990) 222 CA3d 531, 540 n5, 271 CR 845 (court allowed to make "equitable adjustments" in dividing an asset under former CC §4353). However, the doctrine of laches is not available as a defense to a Fam C §2556 action. 222 CA3d 531.

Discovery in a motion under Fam C §2556 is treated the same as discovery in any other family law proceeding; thus, a party may seek to limit or even prevent discovery on such a motion. *Marriage of Hixson* (2003) 111 CA4th 1116, 1122, 4 CR3d 483 (not abuse of discretion for court to rely on prior record until moving party either showed that existing record did not resolve claim or made some showing that undermined record).

If the unadjudicated asset was concealed by one party before judgment, the other party may also have grounds for a motion to set aside the judgment under Fam C §§2120–2129 (judgments entered on or after January 1, 1993; see §§18.47–18.54), an equitable proceeding on the basis of extrinsic fraud (judgments entered before January 1, 1993; see §18.40), a statutory proceeding under Fam C §1101 for breach of the good faith duty to disclose assets (see §18.57), or even a tort action against the concealing spouse (*Worton v Worton* (1991) 234 CA3d 1638, 286 CR 410). A proceeding under Fam C §§2120–2129 or in equity can, in appropriate circumstances, afford the broadest relief by setting aside the entire judgment; it may be preferable to a Fam C §2556 hearing when the concealed assets are not readily divisible and their value requires a redistribution of all community property to achieve an equal division or when support issues should be reevaluated in light of the unadjudicated property. However, when the moving party requires nothing more than an equal division of the concealed assets, a motion under §2556 will limit the issues before the court to the relief requested, thereby likely providing for a speedier and more economical remedy.

Note that Fam C §2556 also governs the division of any gain resulting from an undisclosed investment opportunity whose disclosure was required. Fam C §2102(b). From the date of separation to the date of distribution of the community estate, each party must disclose in writing any investment opportunity that presents itself after the date of separation but that results directly from any activity, involvement, or investment of either spouse from the date of marriage through the date of separation. The written disclosure must be made in sufficient time for the other spouse to make an informed decision on whether to participate in the investment opportunity. Fam C §2102(b).

§18.57 C. Breach of Fiduciary Responsibility in Management of Community Property

Family Code §1100 (former CC §5125) imposes on each spouse a duty to act in accordance with the general rules governing fiduciary relationships in the management and control of community property until such time as the assets and liabilities are divided by the parties or a court. Fam C §1100(e). This duty includes the obligations (1) to make full disclosure to the other spouse, on request, of all material facts and information on the existence, characterization, and valuation of assets in which the community has, or may have, an interest and debts for which the community is or may be liable plus equal access to all information, records, and books that pertain to the value and character of those assets and debts (Fam C §1100(e)), and (2) to act with fiduciary responsibility in all transactions regarding management and control of community property. Fam Code §§721, 1100. See, *e.g.*, *In re Marriage of Hokanson* (1998) 68 CA4th 987, 80 CR2d 699 (delaying tactics in sale of house constituted breach of fiduciary duty triggering mandatory attorney fees award per Fam C §1101(g)). If findings are made pursuant to §1101(g) (breach of fiduciary duty), the value of the asset shall be determined to be its highest value at the date of the breach of the fiduciary duty, the date of the sale or disposition of the asset, or the date of the award by the court.

The statute extends the duty of good faith beyond the separation of the parties, and even beyond the dissolution of the marriage, as long as the property remains undivided by the parties or a court. Fam C §1100(e). Family Code §1100 also prohibits a spouse from making a gift of community personal property, or disposing of such property for less than fair and reasonable value, without the other spouse's written consent. Fam C §1100(b). The duties imposed on each spouse, however, do not impose a fiduciary duty of care to the other spouse with respect to the management of community investments. There is no "prudent investor" rule applicable to a marriage relationship. *Marriage of Duffy* (2001) 91 CA4th 923, 940, 111 CR2d 160. See 2002 Note, Fam C §721, Stats 2002, ch 310, §2.

The standard of care that must be exercised by each spouse continues to be redefined by legislation and case law, in response to the changing roles of husband and wife in the management and control of community property. The current standard of care is based on "the public policy of the state that marriage is an equal partnership and that spouses occupy a confidential and fiduciary relationship with each other." Stats 1991, ch 1026, §1. This confidential and fiduciary relationship imposes on each spouse a duty of the highest good faith and fair dealing toward the other, which is the same as the duty that exists between nonmarital business partners, and includes the following obligations: (1) to provide access to records of transactions; (2) to give full and true information on request about any transactions concerning community property; and (3) to account to and hold as trustee for the other spouse any benefit or profit from a transaction concerning community property entered into without the other's consent. Fam C §721(b).

When a spouse breaches the fiduciary duty imposed by statute, and when that breach results in the impairment of the other spouse's present undivided half interest in community property, the injured spouse has a statutory claim against the other spouse under Fam C §1101. The court may provide a variety of remedies to compensate the injured spouse: It may order an accounting; determine the rights of ownership in, the beneficial enjoyment of, or the access to, community property; determine the classification of all property of the parties; order changes in the title to property (with some exceptions); dispense, under certain circumstances, with the requirement of a spouse's consent to transactions affecting community property; award to the injured spouse half of any asset undisclosed or transferred in breach of the fiduciary duty, plus attorney fees and costs; and, when the imposition of exemplary damages is justified under CC §3294, award to the injured spouse all of any asset undisclosed or transferred in breach of the fiduciary duty. Fam C §1101(a)-(c), (e), (g)-(h). Once fraud is established pursuant to §1101(h), there is a mandatory award of the entire asset to the defrauded spouse where that asset has been fraudulently concealed. *Marriage of Rossi* (2001) 90 CA4th 34, 108 CR2d 270 (deliberate concealment of lottery winnings).

An action for relief under Fam C §1101 may be made "in conjunction with" a marital action, in a separate action, or on the death of a spouse. Fam C §1101(f). If the action is brought in conjunction with a marital action or on the death of a spouse, it may be commenced at any time; otherwise, it must be brought within three years after the date that a petitioning spouse has actual knowledge of the event or transaction from which relief is sought. Fam C §1101(d)(1)-(2). If the action is not timely brought, the defense of laches may bar the action. Fam C §1101(d)(3).

Note that the standard of care, the disclosure requirements, and the remedies now provided in Fam C §§721 and 1100-1101 were enacted by 1991 legislation, effective January 1, 1992. The legislation may not be applied retroactively. *Marriage of Reuling* (1994) 23 CA4th 1428, 1439, 28 CR2d 726, 733. Consequently, the possible applicability of statutes and case law in effect before January 1,

1992, must still be considered. See, *e.g., Marriage of Alexander* (1989) 212 CA3d 677, 261 CR 9; *Marriage of Baltins* (1989) 212 CA3d 66, 260 CR 403; *Marriage of Stevenot* (1984) 154 CA3d 1051, 202 CR 116.

In addition to the remedies provided in Fam C §1101, a spouse's conduct may, in some instances, allow setting aside of the judgment, either under Fam C §§2120–2129 (judgments entered on or after January 1, 1993; see §§18.47–18.54) or on the basis of extrinsic fraud (judgments entered before January 1, 1993; see §§18.38–18.40). See also §18.56 (division of property omitted from judgment). Counsel may even wish to consider filing a tort action for fraud and conversion against a spouse who fails to disclose community assets. See *Worton v Worton* (1991) 234 CA3d 1638, 286 CR 410.

On declarations of disclosure required in proceedings commenced on or after January 1, 1993, see §§13.44–13.49.

§18.58　　D. Discharge of Judgment Obligations in Bankruptcy

Historical distinction between support and property obligations. It has long been the case that a discharge in bankruptcy does not free the debtor from an obligation under a judgment to pay spousal support or child support. 11 USC §523(a)(5). In 1994, Congress added 11 USC §523(a)(15), which provided that a discharge in bankruptcy likewise does not free the debtor from a judgment obligation that relates to marital property rights unless:

- The debtor is unable to pay the debt from income or property not reasonably necessary to support the debtor or his or her dependents or, if applicable, to continue the debtor's business; or

- Discharge would result in a benefit to the debtor that outweighs the resulting detriment to a spouse, former spouse, or child of the debtor.

See *Seixas v Booth (In re Seixas)* (Bankr 9th Cir 1999) 239 BR 398, 406 (obligation to pay half of children's college expenses was nondischargeable debt in nature of support under 11 USC §523(a)(5)). See *Dunn v Dunn (In re Dunn)* (Bankr SD Ohio 1998) 225 BR 393 (benefit of dischargeability to debtor with high standard of living in spite of chronic disabling illness did not outweigh detriment to nondebtor former spouse). On the balancing of detriments, the court said, "[If] the debtor's standard of living would be greater than or approximately equal to the ex-spouse's/creditor's if the debt is not discharged, then the debt should be nondischargeable under 523(a)(15)(b)." 225 BR at 402. See also *Hill v Hill (In re Hill)* (Bankr ND Ill 1995) 184 BR 750 (debtor met burden of demonstrating circumstances meriting dischargeability); *Comisky v Comisky (In re Comisky)* (Bankr ND Cal 1995) 183 BR 883 (court found 11 USC §523(a)(15) to allow *partial* dischargeability); *Fitzsimonds v Haines (In re Haines)* (Bankr SD Cal 1997) 210 BR 586 (11 USC §523(a)(15) does *not* allow partial dischargeability); AFDC (now CalWORKs) (obligations are not dischargeable); 11 USC §523(18) (debt owed to state or municipality in the nature of support and enforceable under Part D, Title IV of the Social Security Act (42 USC §601-619) is not dischargeable). See, *e.g., Leibowitz v County of Orange (In re Leibowitz)* (9th Cir BAP 1999) 230 BR 392, aff'd (9th Cir 2000) 217 F3d 799.

With respect to bankruptcy actions commenced before October 22, 1994, if a judgment under the Family Code ordered a spouse to pay certain debts to a third party or to the other spouse, or to hold the other spouse harmless from joint debts, the debtor spouse could discharge these obligations in bankruptcy without meeting the requirements of 11 USC §523(a)(15).

Current law. As of October 17, 2005, when the Bankruptcy Abuse Prevention and Consumer Protection Act of 2005 (BAPCPA) became effective, both support and property obligations in an order or judgment regarding dissolution are included in the definition of "Domestic Support Obligations." 11 USC §1328(a). Domestic Support Obligations are ahead of all but administration expenses in order of priority of payment (11 USC §507(a)(1)), thus eliminating the court's discretion to weigh whether discharging the debt would create a benefit to the debtor outweighing detrimental consequences to the debtor's spouse, former spouse, or child.

Interest accruing on nondischargeable child and spousal support obligations after filing of a bankruptcy petition is also nondischargeable. See *County of Sacramento v Foross (In re Foross)* 9th Cir BAP 1999) 242 BR 692.

A discharge in bankruptcy does not free the debtor from a judgment obligation to pay attorney fees if the obligation is deemed to be "in the nature of" spousal or child support. 11 USC §523(a)(5); *Gionis v Wayne (In re Gionis)* (Bankr 9th Cir 1994) 170 BR 675,

681, aff'd without published opinion (9th Cir 1996) 92 F3d 1192. However, an attorney-creditor who seeks to obtain a state court order characterizing the fees as "in the nature of" support and thus nondischargeable must petition the bankruptcy court for relief from the automatic stay *before* seeking the state court order; a state court order rendered during the pendency of the 11 USC §362(a) automatic stay will be void. *Marriage of Sprague* (2003) 105 CA4th 215, 129 CR2d 261. On how to petition for relief from the automatic stay in bankruptcy court, see Moving for Relief from Automatic Stay in Bankruptcy (Cal CEB Action Guide 2003). Attorney fees incurred in connection with support awards are generally deemed to be nondischargeable. *Konicki v Kelly (In re Konicki)* (Bankr MD Fla 1997) 208 BR 572. Most courts agree that an award of attorney fees that is in the nature of support is nondischargeable even if payable directly to an attorney. See, *e.g., In re Gionis, supra.*

The BAPCPA language now excepts from discharge any debt "to a spouse, former spouse, or child of the debtor and not of the kind described in paragraph (5) [domestic support obligation] that is incurred by the debtor in the course of a divorce or separation or in connection with a separation agreement, divorce decree or other order of a court of record, or a determination made in accordance with State or territorial law by a governmental unit." 11 USC §523(a)(15). Therefore, it appears that it may not be necessary for an attorney fee award to be explicitly characterized as "in the nature of support" to be nondischargeable in bankruptcy.

In rare cases, a discharge in bankruptcy will not free the debtor from a judgment obligation, because the obligation is deemed to be for willful and malicious injury caused by the debtor to another or another's property. 11 USC §523(a)(6). See, *e.g., Grynevich v Grynevich (In re Grynevich)* (Bankr ND Ill 1994) 172 BR 888 (judgment for failure to make court-ordered mortgage and maintenance payments on family home). Also in rare cases, a bankruptcy petition may be dismissed altogether "for cause." 11 USC §707(a). See, *e.g., Huckfeldt v Huckfeldt (In re Huckfeldt)* (8th Cir 1994) 39 F3d 829 (party assigned debts in divorce judgment filed bankruptcy petition to frustrate that judgment and push ex-spouse, subsequently pursued by creditors on those debts, into bankruptcy).

Note that under the current law (*i.e.*, as revised by the BAPCPA), a Chapter 13 petition will be dismissed if the debtor is falls behind in postpetition domestic support obligations. 11 USC §1307(c)(11).

If a spouse does discharge marital property obligations in a federal court bankruptcy proceeding, any action by a state court that nullifies the discharge, whether directly or indirectly, violates the federal supremacy clause (art VI, cl 2) of the United States Constitution. *Marriage of Cohen* (1980) 105 CA3d 836, 843, 164 CR 672. Thus, a state court may not reassign discharged debts to the bankrupt spouse, order him or her to reimburse the other spouse for payments made on such debts (see Comment to Fam C §916; 105 CA3d at 840), or allow a compensating offset against payments owed to the bankrupt spouse by the other spouse who pays the indebtedness (*Marriage of Williams* (1984) 157 CA3d 1215, 1220, 203 CR 909). However, a state court may order a modification of spousal support when there is a material change in the parties' economic circumstances resulting from a discharge in bankruptcy, assuming that there is an existing order subject to modification or a reservation of jurisdiction to make such an order. Fam C §3592; *Marriage of Clements* (1982) 134 CA3d 737, 746, 184 CR 756. Under prior law, the discharge in bankruptcy of an equalizing payment owed to the supported spouse could be considered in a motion to modify support, but all the Fam C §4320 factors must be considered as well. *Marriage of Lynn* (2002) 101 CA4th 120, 123 CR2d 611; arguably since the passage of BAPCPA discharge of an equalizing payment will no longer be permitted.

§18.59 E. Violation of Servicemembers Civil Relief Act

The Servicemembers Civil Relief Act (50 USC App §§501–596) protects persons on active or training duty in any branch of the military service from default judgments. See 50 USC App §§511, 521. If the respondent qualifies for protection under the Act, a default judgment may not be entered against him or her unless the court first appoints an attorney to represent the service person in the marital proceeding. 50 USC App §521(b)(2). The respondent, without representation by counsel, may waive the protections of the Act by filing a written waiver in the proceeding. See §14.18. If a default judgment is taken against a respondent in the military service he or she may apply to set aside the judgment at any time up to 90 days after termination of military service. 50 USC App §521(g).

§18.60 F. Assumption of Jurisdiction by Court Over Attorney's Practice

When an attorney dies, resigns, becomes an inactive member, is disbarred or suspended from active practice, or becomes incapable of attending to his or her practice, the superior court may assume jurisdiction over the attorney's law practice. See Bus & P C §§6180, 6190. When such jurisdiction has been assumed, a court may relieve a client of the attorney from a judgment, order, or other proceeding taken against him or her, including a dismissal of an action, if the order was made after application was filed for the court to assume jurisdiction over the attorney's practice. CCP §473.1; Bus & P C §6190.1.

The client must apply for relief under CCP §473.1 within a reasonable period of time, not to exceed 6 months, after the court assumes jurisdiction over the attorney's practice. The 6-month period may be shortened, however, to 90 days when (1) the judgment or order determines the ownership or right of possession of real or personal property, (2) a written notice is personally served in California on the party against whom the judgment or order was taken and on the attorney appointed to act under the court's direction, and (3) the notice provides that any right to apply for relief under §473.1 expires 90 days after service of the notice. CCP §473.1.

§18.61 G. Fraudulent Transfer

The California Supreme Court has held that judgments of dissolution and settlements that result in transfers of property between spouses are subject to the Uniform Fraudulent Transfer Act (UFTA) (CC §§3439–3439.12). *Mejia v Reed* (2003) 31 C4th 657, 3 CR3d 390; *Filip v Bucurenciu* (2005) 129 CA4th 825, 838, 28 CR3d 884. A spouse's creditor can thus attack a marital settlement agreement between husband and wife and seek to set aside the transfers of property between them. Spouses drafting settlement agreements must be aware that they do not have "a one-time-only opportunity to defraud creditors by including the fraudulent transfer in an MSA." 31 C4th at 668.

In *Mejia*, the plaintiff mother of the husband's out-of-wedlock child to whom child support was owed alleged that the property division between the spouses was motivated by the intent to put assets out of her reach and was fraudulent under UFTA. The supreme court held that plaintiff did not have a constructive fraud action under CC §3439.05 because the husband was neither insolvent when the property was transferred, nor did the transfer make him insolvent; his future support obligations were not a debt under UFTA. 31 C4th at 672. The court remanded for determination of plaintiff's UFTA action for actual fraud, however.

19

Appeals and Writs

§19.1   I. SCOPE OF CHAPTER

In a marital action, the trial court may issue a number of rulings before or after judgment is entered in the action. In some cases, marital status or other issues normally addressed in the judgment may be bifurcated for separate determination. Counsel must be alert to the appealability of each ruling made by the trial court, whether or not it is part of the judgment. If an appeal is not immediately taken from an appealable determination, the right to review on that determination may be lost.

This chapter summarizes the substantive and procedural law governing review by appeal and by extraordinary writ. In addition to reviewing the law, the practitioner should consult, as necessary, a comprehensive appellate reference text. See California Civil Appellate Practice (3d ed Cal CEB 1996) and California Civil Writ Practice (3d ed Cal CEB 1996), which are frequently referred to in this chapter. See also 9 Witkin, California Procedure, *Appeal* (4th ed 1997); 8 Witkin, Procedure, *Writs*.

II. PRINCIPLES OF APPELLATE REVIEW

§19.2   A. Governing Law

The substantive and procedural principles that govern appellate review in civil actions generally also govern the review of judgments and orders in marital actions. See Cal Rules of Ct 5.21. An attorney faced with the possible review of a judgment or order, by appeal or by writ, should become familiar with the framework for appellate review found in the constitution, statutes, and rules of court.

California Constitution, art VI

Judicial power; courts of record	§1
Structure of courts	§§2–4
Original jurisdiction	§10
Appellate jurisdiction	§§11–12
Overturning erroneous judgments	§13

Code of Civil Procedure

Powers of appellate court	§43
Error affecting substantial rights	§475
Judgment roll	§670
Appeals in general	§§901–914
Stay of enforcement	§§916–936.1

Family Code

Appeals of bifurcated issues	§2025

California Rules of Court

Filing appeal	Rules 8.100–8.108
Record on appeal	Rules 8.130–8.160
Briefs	Rules 8.200-8.224
Hearing and determination	Rules 8.240-8.276 and 8.500-8.552

General provisions	Rules 1.5, 8.1, 8.4, 8.6, 8.13, 8.16, 8.18, 8.23, 8.25, 8.29, 8.32, 8.36, 8.49, 8.54, 8.57, 8.63, 8.66, 8.112, 8.116, 8.163, 10.1, 10.1000(a), 10.1000(b), and 10.1008
Rules on original proceedings	Rules 8.380–8.384, 8.490–8.498
Rules for publication	Rules 8.1105–8.1125
Appeals of bifurcated issues	Rule 5.180

Local Rules of the Courts of Appeal

Each appellate district, and some divisions within the districts, have their own supplemental rules, which are available from the court clerk.

For general rule information, see the judicial branch website at http://www.courtinfo.ca.gov.

§19.3　　B. Appealable Judgments and Orders

In California, the right to appeal is wholly governed by statute; the appellate courts have no jurisdiction to entertain an appeal other than as provided by the legislature. *Marriage of Loya* (1987) 189 CA3d 1636, 1638, 235 CR 198. The appealability of orders and judgments issued in marital actions is the same as in civil actions generally, and is set forth in CCP §904.1.

Unless provided otherwise by statute, an appeal lies only from a judgment that terminates the proceeding in the lower court by disposing of all issues of law and fact, as far as the court has the power to do so. This principle is known as the "one final judgment" rule and is based on the theory that piecemeal disposition and multiple appeals in a single action would be oppressive and costly, and that a review of intermediate rulings should await final disposition of the case. *Marriage of Van Sickle* (1977) 68 CA3d 728, 735, 137 CR 568.

Despite the one final judgment rule, an appeal may be taken from a matter that is collateral to the main controversy and severable from the general subject of the litigation, if a decision on that matter finally determines the rights of the parties with respect to that matter. This exception is based on the theory that such a determination is substantially the same as a final judgment in an independent proceeding. *Marriage of Skelley* (1976) 18 C3d 365, 368, 134 CR 197; *Marriage of Van Sickle, supra.*

§19.4   1. Appeal From Order in Pending Action

The one final judgment rule and its corollary addressing collateral matters (see §19.3) should be considered whenever the question arises whether an appeal should be taken from a trial court ruling before a final judgment is rendered. If review of an appealable order or judgment is not timely sought, it is waived. See §19.26. The question of whether an appeal should be taken before final judgment may arise in connection with temporary orders (see §19.5) and orders made in bifurcated proceedings (see §19.6).

§19.5   a. Appeal From Temporary Order

California courts have long held that temporary orders granting or denying an award of spousal support, child support, or attorney fees satisfy the criteria for appealable collateral matters (see §19.3). The rationale is that an order making such an award is in the nature of a final judgment, *i.e.,* it is immediately enforceable without further court action; it is severable from the relief requested by, and the outcome of, the underlying action; and it finally determines the questions adjudicated in it. *Marriage of Skelley* (1976) 18 C3d 365, 368, 134 CR 197.

A temporary order awarding custody of a minor child is probably equally appealable; however, because of the length of the appellate process, a writ is more often used to review temporary custody orders. See *In re Frost* (1955) 134 CA2d 619, 621, 286 P2d 378 (order issued in postjudgment modification proceeding). On use of writs in custody proceedings, see §19.99.

On temporary orders generally, see chap 11.

§19.6 b. Appeal in Bifurcated Proceeding

There are two types of bifurcated proceedings: (1) When the issue of the status of the parties' marriage is determined in an early and separate trial under Fam C §2337; and (2) when one or more issues are bifurcated and tried separately, before other issues are tried, under Cal Rules of Ct 5.175. When the issue of marital status is bifurcated for separate trial, an immediate and separate appeal may be filed from the judgment dissolving the marriage and from the subsequent judgment on reserved issues. *Marriage of Fink* (1976) 54 CA3d 357, 366, 126 CR 626, 632, decision on reserved issues appealed on other grounds in 25 C3d 877. The time for filing each appeal runs separately from the date each judgment is entered. On bifurcation of the issue of marital status generally, see §§14.59–14.74.

When the trial court orders the bifurcation of one or more issues (other than marital status) for early, separate trial, the "one final judgment" rule (see §19.3) normally prevents an immediate appeal from the ruling on such issues. *Marriage of Loya* (1987) 189 CA3d 1636, 235 CR 198. In conformity with this rule, the court's decision to bifurcate an issue for separate trial is itself an interim ruling and not immediately appealable. *Marriage of Fink* (1976) 54 CA3d 357, 360, 126 CR 626, 628, decision on reserved issues appealed on other grounds in 25 C3d 877. However, an exception to the general rule allows an appeal to be taken from a determination of a bifurcated issue if (1) the trial court, in its discretion, certifies that the appeal is appropriate; and (2) the appellate court, in its discretion, accepts the issue for immediate review. Fam C §2025; Cal Rules of Ct 5.180; see *Marriage of Stevenson* (1993) 20 CA4th 250, 24 CR2d 411 (interlocutory appeal granted); *Marriage of Griffin* (1993) 15 CA4th 685, 19 CR2d 94 (interlocutory appeal dismissed because in derogation of former CC §4365 and former Cal Rules of Ct 1269–1269.5; appeal may be brought following entry of judgment). On the procedure for certification and appeal of a decision on a bifurcated issue, see §§19.88–19.90; on bifurcation of issues, see Cal Rules of Ct 5.175 and §14.59.

§19.7 2. Appeal From Judgment

Under CCP §904.1(a)(1), an appeal may be taken from "a judgment" of the superior court. A tentative decision (see §16.27) is not a judgment and is not appealable. *Jordan v Malone* (1992) 5

CA4th 18, 6 CR2d 454. The judgment contemplated by CCP §904.1 is the "one final judgment in an action ... which in effect ends the suit in the court in which it was entered, and finally determines the rights of the parties in relation to the matter in controversy." *Bank of America v Superior Court* (1942) 20 C2d 697, 701, 128 P2d 357. In determining whether a judgment is final, it is not the form of the decree, but the substance and effect of the adjudication that is determinative. When no issue is left for future consideration except compliance with the decree, the decree is final and appealable. If any further judicial action is essential to a final determination of the parties' rights, the decree is interim and not appealable. *Lyon v Goss* (1942) 19 C2d 659, 670, 123 P2d 11. This principle is known as the "one final judgment" rule. See §19.3.

An appeal may be taken from a judgment as a whole, from a judgment dissolving the parties' marital status (see §19.6), or from a portion of a judgment that decides with finality a severable, collateral matter. *Marriage of Van Sickle* (1977) 68 CA3d 728, 736, 137 CR 568. On appealable collateral matters, see §19.3. Under the doctrine of "divisible appeal," an appeal from one portion of a judgment that contains truly severable portions will bring up for review only that portion. *Marriage of Fink* (1976) 54 CA3d 357, 362, 126 CR 626, 629, decision on reserved issues appealed on other grounds in 25 C3d 877. The appellate court will not have jurisdiction to review other portions of the judgment not included in the appeal. Consequently, any order of reversal, even when stated in general terms, will be construed to apply only to that portion of the judgment reviewed by the court. *G. Ganahl Lumber Co. v Weinsveig* (1914) 168 C 664, 667, 143 P 1025. All other portions of the judgment not appealed from become res judicata when the period for taking an appeal expires. See *Whalen v Smith* (1912) 163 C 360, 362, 125 P 904, 905.

§19.8   3. Appeal From Order After Judgment

Code of Civil Procedure §904.1(a)(2) provides for the appeal of an order made after an appealable judgment. The order sought to be reviewed must, however, satisfy three criteria: (1) The order must affect the judgment in some manner or bear some relation to its enforcement or stay, (2) the appeal from the order must present different questions from those presented in the appeal from the judgment itself, and (3) the order must follow a final judgment. *Marriage of Schultz* (1980) 105 CA3d 846, 852, 164 CR 653. An order does not affect the judgment or relate to its enforcement if it is more accurately understood as being preliminary to a later judgment, at which time it will become ripe for appeal. *Lakin v Watkins Assoc. Indus.* (1993) 6 C4th 644, 652, 25 CR2d 109; *Marriage of Levine* (1994) 28 CA4th 585, 589, 33 CR2d 559 (preliminary orders on OSC re enforcement of judgment provision). If the order appealed from raises the same issues that would have been raised had the judgment itself been appealed from, the appeal will not lie. See *Sharpe v Sharpe* (1942) 55 CA2d 262, 265, 130 P2d 462. A postjudgment order made to enforce a judgment satisfies these criteria and is appealable. *Marriage of Tibbett* (1990) 218 CA3d 1249, 1250 n3, 267 CR 642. A postjudgment order made to modify a judgment (*e.g.,* child or spousal support) is also appealable. *Marriage of Acosta* (1977) 67 CA3d 899, 137 CR 33. On enforcement of judgments generally, see chap 20; on modification of judgments generally, see chap 21.

§19.9   4. Other Appealable Orders

The following orders that may arise in a marital action are specifically appealable under CCP §904.1. It is important to remember that, if a timely appeal is not taken from an appealable order, the right to appellate review of that order is waived. See §19.26.

- Order granting a motion to quash service of summons (see §10.61), or granting a motion to stay the action on the ground of inconvenient forum, or from a written order of dismissal under CCP §581d following an order granting a motion to dismiss the action on the ground of inconvenient forum (see §10.64). CCP §904.1(a)(3). An order denying either motion may be challenged on a writ (see §19.97) or appealed from the final judgment.

- Order granting a motion for a new trial (see §§18.2–18.15). CCP §904.1(a)(4). An order denying a motion for a new trial can be reviewed only on appeal from the judgment (*Wenzoski v Central Banking Sys.* (1987) 43 C3d 539, 237 CR 167), except when a new trial has been requested under CCP §914 for unavailability of the transcript and denied (*Conlin v Coyne* (1936) 15 CA2d 569, 59 P2d 884).

- Order granting or dissolving, or refusing to grant or dissolve, an injunction. CCP §904.1(a)(6). This rule has been applied to injunctions, including temporary restraining orders, issued at any stage of the proceeding. See *McLellan v McLellan* (1972) 23 CA3d 343, 357, 100 CR 258.

- Order appointing a receiver (see §20.91). CCP §904.1(a)(7).

- Order made appealable under the Family Code. CCP §904.1(a)(10). Under the authority of this statute, Fam C §2025 and Cal Rules of Ct 5.175–5.180 permit the immediate appeal, on certification by the trial court and acceptance for review by the appellate court, of a decision on a bifurcated issue. See §§19.88–19.90.

- Order assessing monetary sanctions of more than $5000 against a party or party's attorney. CCP §904.1(a)(11)–(12). Lesser sanctions may be appealed after final judgment or, in the appellate court's discretion, by extraordinary writ. CCP §904.1(b). An order denying sanctions is not appealable. *Wells Prop. v Popkin* (1992) 9 CA4th 1053, 1055, 11 CR2d 845. The appealability of orders assessing monetary sanctions of more than $5000 applies to *discovery* sanctions. *Rail-Transport Employees Ass'n v Union Pac. Motor Freight* (1996) 46 CA4th 469, 54 CR2d 713.

The following orders on motions to vacate a judgment are also made appealable by case law or statute:

- Order granting or denying a statutory motion to vacate an appealable judgment and enter a different judgment under CCP §663 (see §§18.16–18.23). CCP §663(a) (order granting motion); *Socol v King* (1949) 34 C2d 292, 296, 209 P2d 577 (order denying motion).

- Order granting or denying a statutory motion to vacate an appealable judgment under CCP §473 (see §§18.24–18.34). *Stegge v Wilkerson* (1961) 189 CA2d 1, 4, 10 CR 867 (order granting motion).

§19.10   C. Standing to Appeal

An appeal may be pursued only by an "aggrieved party." CCP §902. The term "party" has been construed to mean anyone who is a party of record at the time the appeal is taken. *Rose v Rose* (1952) 110 CA2d 812, 243 P2d 578. A party is considered aggrieved when he or she has an immediate, pecuniary, and substantial interest that is injured by the order or judgment. *County of Alameda v Carleson* (1971) 5 C3d 730, 737, 97 CR 385. As a general rule, a party may not be considered aggrieved by a favorable judgment (*Forkner v Forkner* (1950) 96 CA2d 363, 369, 215 P2d 482); however, a party may appeal from portions of a judgment by which he or she is legally aggrieved, even if the judgment, taken as a whole, is favorable to that party (*Zarrahy v Zarrahy* (1988) 205 CA3d 1, 4, 252 CR 20).

§19.11   1. Standing of Nonparty

A person who is aggrieved by the ruling, but who is not a party to the action, may become a party by moving to intervene under CCP §387 (*Mallick v Superior Court* (1979) 89 CA3d 434, 437, 152 CR 503) or by moving to vacate the judgment under CCP §663 (*County of Alameda v Carleson* (1971) 5 C3d 730, 736, 97 CR 385). In exceptional circumstances, an appeal may be allowed by a "real party in interest," even if the aggrieved person is not a party to the action. See *Marriage of Utigard* (1981) 126 CA3d 133, 141, 178 CR 546 (adult child may be real party in interest as to claim for unpaid child support). If the right to appear is established, the right to appeal should follow. *Guardianship of Pankey* (1974) 38 CA3d 919, 927, 113 CR 858 (grandmother who had filed objections in guardianship proceeding had standing on appeal to assert best interests of children).

§19.12   2. No Standing as Attorney of Record

An attorney of record is not a party to the action and does not have standing to appeal an adverse ruling on the issue of attorney fees. Even though the attorney may have filed a notice of lien in the action, he or she does not thereby become a party. The right to attorney fees belongs to the client alone and accrues to the attorney only indirectly, regardless of whether the award is payable directly to the attorney. The attorney's sole remedy is in an independent action against the client. *Marriage of Tushinsky* (1988) 203 CA3d 136, 249 CR 611.

§19.13   D. Evaluating Prospects for Appeal

Assuming the appealability of a judgment or order from which relief is desired (see §§19.3-19.9), and assuming that the client has standing to appeal (see §§19.10-19.12), counsel should begin evaluating the prospects for an appeal immediately on entry of the judgment or order. An initial evaluation must be completed within the statutory time period to file a notice of appeal (see §§19.47-19.54). Although this analysis should be as complete as time will allow, a more exhaustive evaluation will be possible when the full record is available and more time can be devoted to research. If, at that time, the evaluation reveals that the prospects for appeal are weaker than originally thought, counsel should discuss with the client the possibility of abandoning the appeal. An early abandonment may save the client considerable expense in attorney fees, and may protect both the client and the attorney from later sanctions that may be imposed if the appellate court finds the appeal to be frivolous (see §§19.30, 19.84).

The following issues provide a framework for making an initial decision on whether to file an appeal. The conclusions of the initial analysis may later be refined and expanded to evaluate the possibility of success if an appeal is pursued.

- Did an error occur in the trial court? See §19.14.

- Did the error result in a miscarriage of justice? See §19.15.

- Does the existing record provide an adequate basis for review? See §19.16.

- What standard of review will the appellate court apply to the trial court's ruling? See §§19.17-19.20.

- Was there a waiver of the right to appeal? See §§19.21-19.28.

- Is an appeal in the best interests of the client from a practical point of view? See §19.29.

- Could the appeal be deemed frivolous? See §19.30.

§19.14   1. Errors of Law and Fact

An appeal is simply a method by which litigants may rectify errors, legal or factual, that may have occurred in the trial court. The characterization of an error as one of law or of fact is an important threshold issue, because it determines, in part, the standard under which the appellate court will review the ruling (see §§19.17–19.20), the extent to which new issues may be raised on appeal (see §19.22), and the type of relief available on appeal (see §19.82).

A question of law is presented when the facts of a case are undisputed and the issue can be resolved by determining the appropriate statutory or case law and applying that law to the facts. On review of questions of law, see §19.18.

An issue of fact exists when the trial court is required to evaluate the evidence by weighing the strength of one party's proof against that of the other, *e.g.,* by determining the credibility of witnesses whose testimony contradicts one another's. The trial court's decision on questions of fact can be reviewed on appeal only by attacking the sufficiency of the evidence to support the ruling; such determinations are rarely disturbed on appeal. On review of questions of fact, see §19.19.

§19.15 2. Reversible Error

The mere occurrence of an error in the trial court does not provide a basis for reversal of the trial court's decision. To constitute reversible error, the appellate court must find that the error complained of resulted in a miscarriage of justice. Cal Const art VI, §13. The record must demonstrate that, because of the error, the appellant sustained and suffered substantial injury and that a different result would have been probable if the error had not occurred. Any error that does not affect the substantial rights of the parties must be disregarded on appeal. See CCP §475; *Marriage of Smith* (1978) 79 CA3d 725, 751, 145 CR 205. The appellant thus bears the burden of proving that (1) an error occurred and (2) the error was prejudicial. See *Tupman v Haberkern* (1929) 208 C 256, 263, 280 P 970. Whether a particular error constitutes reversible error depends on the circumstances of the case, the state of the record on appeal, and the appellate court's evaluation of the trial court proceedings.

On factors to look for in evaluating prejudice, see California Civil Appellate Practice §§5.34–5.39 (3d ed Cal CEB 1996). On the reversibility of particular types of errors, see 9 Witkin, California Procedure, *Appeal* §§408–452 (4th ed 1997).

§19.16 3. Record on Appeal

The record on appeal is the only "evidence" on which an appellant may rely to demonstrate to the appellate court that a reversible error occurred at trial. On reversible error generally, see §19.15. In trying to determine whether an error occurred, and whether the error appears in the record, it may be difficult for the trial attorney to step back from his or her personal impressions of what occurred at the trial to objectively view the case from the appellate court's limited perspective. A detailed review of the reporter's transcript may be extremely helpful in determining whether an error was properly preserved in the record for appellate review. Although the reporter's transcript is not necessarily required as part of the record on appeal (see §19.57), the best strategy (when economics allow) may be to file a notice of appeal and obtain the transcript as soon as possible. It will often be helpful to have another attorney review the transcript, or critical portions of it, for a second opinion on whether the record of error may be subject to conflicting interpretations.

In almost all cases, the record itself consists of the trial court's file (*i.e.*, the clerk's transcript or an "appendix" instead of the transcript) and the reporter's transcript. In rare instances, one or both transcripts may be replaced by the judgment roll, an "agreed" statement, or a "settled" statement. On designation of the record on appeal, see §§19.57–19.71.

§19.17 4. Appellate Standards of Review

To evaluate the possible outcome of an appeal, counsel must review the trial court's ruling from the perspective of the appellate court, considering only the evidence that the appellate court will consider (see §19.16) and applying the same standard of review that the court will use. There are three appellate standards of review, each granting a different degree of deference to a particular type of trial court ruling. Issues presenting a question of law are reviewed de novo by the appellate court; challenges to the sufficiency of the evidence to support a ruling are reviewed under the substantial evidence test; and a discretionary trial court ruling will be reviewed for abuse of discretion.

§19.18 a. Question of Law

A question of law is an issue that can be resolved by examining relevant cases and statutes and applying the rules of law extracted from those sources to an established set of facts. The facts essential to deciding a legal question may not be in conflict, and their undisputed nature must be shown as a matter of record. See *Wagner v Chambers* (1965) 232 CA2d 14, 20, 42 CR 334. When a true question of law is presented for review, the appellate court may make its own independent determination of the appropriate legal principles to be applied to the facts. See *Estate of Coate* (1979) 98 CA3d 982, 986, 159 CR 794.

To identify possible errors of law, the trial court proceeding may be analyzed chronologically, listing each action that required the consideration of constitutional, statutory, decisional, or other authority. Some examples of questions of law are (1) whether a statute is applicable to a given set of facts (*Uniroyal Chem. Co. v American Vanguard Corp.* (1988) 203 CA3d 285, 292, 249 CR 787); (2) the interpretation of a statute (see *Olson v Cory* (1983) 35 C3d 390, 402, 197 CR 843); and (3) the interpretation of a written instrument, when no conflicting extrinsic evidence has been admitted in the trial court (*Aviointeriors SpA v World Airways, Inc.* (1986) 181 CA3d 908, 915, 226 CR 527).

§19.19   b. Substantial Evidence Rule

When an appeal is based on the insufficiency of the evidence to support the trial court's ruling on an issue of fact (see §19.14), the appellate court's authority "begins and ends with a determination as to whether there is *any* substantial evidence" to support the ruling. *Overton v Vita-Food Corp.* (1949) 94 CA2d 367, 370, 210 P2d 757. Conflicting evidence must be viewed in the light most favorable to the prevailing party; all reasonable inferences must be indulged to uphold the decision; and all conflicts must be resolved in support of the judgment. *Nestle v City of Santa Monica* (1972) 6 C3d 920, 925, 101 CR 568. Although the trial court's determination is rarely overturned for lack of substantial evidence to support it, the evidence must be credible, reasonable in nature, and of solid value. *Estate of Teed* (1952) 112 CA2d 638, 644, 247 P2d 54. See discussion of substantial evidence rule in 9 Witkin, California Procedure, *Appeal* §§363–368 (4th ed 1997).

If a statement of decision was timely requested in the trial court, the statement will set forth the court's ultimate factual determinations (see §17.6). The sufficiency of the evidence to support each determination can then be analyzed by compiling the evidence that appears in the record in support of each determination. In the absence of a statement of decision, the appellate court will imply every essential fact necessary to sustain the trial court's ruling that is supported by the record, and appellate review will be difficult or, in many cases, impossible. *Marriage of Jones* (1990) 222 CA3d 505, 515, 271 CR 761. On the importance, for purposes of appeal, of requesting a statement of decision, see §17.10.

§19.20   c. Abuse of Discretion

The determination of most issues common to marital actions, *e.g.,* attorney fees, child custody, even the valuation and division of property (as long as the result is an equal division), is within the trial court's discretion. See Fam C §§2032, 3040(b); *Marriage of Gillmore* (1981) 29 C3d 418, 423, 174 CR 493. When an appeal attacks the exercise of discretion by a trial court, it must show that the means by which the lower court resolved an issue were legally improper. The appellate court will not reverse a discretionary ruling merely because the trial court could have made a better choice. See *Marriage of Gonzalez* (1976) 57 CA3d 736, 749, 129 CR 566.

Unless counsel can find a case directly on point, there is no ready answer to the question of whether an abuse of discretion occurred in a given case. However, the following rules define some circumstances under which an abuse of discretion may be found:

- Statutory or case law may prescribe the procedure and standards for a particular exercise of discretion. See, *e.g., Marriage of Lopez* (1974) 38 CA3d 93, 117, 113 CR 58, 73, disapproved on other grounds in 20 C3d at 453 (abuse of discretion for failure to adequately consider essential circumstances to be evaluated in awarding spousal support).

- An exercise of discretion will be reversed when the trial court makes an "arbitrary, capricious or patently absurd determination" (*Adoption of D.S.C.* (1979) 93 CA3d 14, 25, 155 CR 406) or when no other judge would reasonably make the same order in the same circumstances (*Marriage of Lopez* (1974) 38 CA3d 93, 114, 113 CR 58, 72, disapproved on other grounds in 20 C3d at 453).

The appellate court will examine a trial court's discretionary ruling with particular care when it is shown to violate a competing judicial or public policy. See *Marriage of Fingert* (1990) 221 CA3d 1575, 1581, 271 CR 389, 392 (abuse of discretion to award custody on basis of parties' relative economic positions; order compelling custodial mother to move to county of father's residence a violation of constitutional right to travel).

§19.21　　5. Waiver of Right to Appeal

Even when a reversible error (see §19.15) occurred in the trial court, an appellant may waive the right to appeal by his or her actions during or after trial. The right to appeal may be lost by failing to raise an issue at trial (see §19.22), by failing to make a timely objection to an error (see §19.23), or by an express or implied waiver of error or invited error (see §19.24). In addition, it may be lost by stipulation or by consent to entry of an order or judgment (see §19.25), by failure to take the appeal at the proper time (see §19.26), if the appellant is in contempt of court (see §19.27), or by accepting benefits under a judgment (see §19.28).

§19.22　　a. Failure to Raise Issue at Trial

As a general rule, an issue must be raised in the trial court to be argued on appeal. *Marriage of Williams* (1972) 29 CA3d 368, 381, 105 CR 406. Nonetheless, there are exceptional circumstances that allow an issue to be raised for the first time on appeal, such as important public policy considerations or recent changes in the law that could not have been raised at trial. See, *e.g., Marriage of Hinds* (1988) 205 CA3d 1398, 1403, 253 CR 170 (whether pending action containing child support order could be dismissed under CCP §583.320); *Marriage of Higinbotham* (1988) 203 CA3d 322, 334, 249 CR 798 (right to survivor benefits under former CC §4800.8). Generally, the issues that may be raised on appeal for the first time involve pure questions of law; new issues involving controverted facts will not be considered on appeal. *Bogacki v Board of Supervisors* (1971) 5 C3d 771, 780, 97 CR 657. Counsel may not, however, raise for the first time on appeal a question of law that changes the "theory of trial" under which the case was tried. *Planned Protective Servs. v Gorton* (1988) 200 CA3d 1, 12, 245 CR 790, disapproved on other grounds in *Martin v Seto* (2004) 32 C4th 445, 451, 9 CR3d 687.

§19.23 b. Failure to Object to Error

As a general rule, error will be waived and cannot be reviewed on appeal if counsel does not make a proper and timely objection to an error during trial. *Sabella v Southern Pac. Co.* (1969) 70 C2d 311, 318, 74 CR 534. See also Evid C §353(a), which precludes an appeal based on evidentiary errors unless an objection is properly raised in the trial court. The requirements for registering an objection vary, depending on the type of error. Generally, counsel must state the ground for the objection and the court must make a ruling, unless it will be apparent from the record that the ruling would necessarily have been adverse. See *Vannier v Superior Court* (1982) 32 C3d 163, 175, 185 CR 427. To properly object to some errors, counsel must undertake a specific procedure, *e.g.,* a motion to strike or a motion for new trial. On requirements for objecting to specific types of errors, see California Trial Objections (10th ed Cal CEB 2004) (new edition forthcoming). Some errors, however, may be raised on appeal even if not objected to in the trial court, *e.g.,* issues of jurisdiction, failure to state a cause of action, or errors reserved without exception under CCP §647.

§19.24 c. Express and Implied Waiver; Invited Error

Counsel may expressly waive an error as a basis for appeal by stipulation (see *Japan Food Corp. v County of Sacramento* (1976) 58 CA3d 891, 897, 130 CR 392) or by expressly withdrawing an objection to error (*Buchanan v Nye* (1954) 128 CA2d 582, 586, 275 P2d 767, 770). Implied waiver, or abandonment, of an error may result from failing to furnish the court with argument or authority on an issue that is raised in the notice of appeal. *Marriage of Laursen & Fogarty* (1988) 197 CA3d 1082, 1084 n1, 243 CR 398.

An appellant may also be prevented from taking an appeal when his or her own actions invited error, *e.g.,* by making statements at trial that contained the same facts as the allegedly prejudicial statements of the adverse party (see *Zarafonitis v Yellow Cab Co.* (1932) 127 CA 607, 609, 16 P2d 141), by preventing proof of an element of the opposing party's case by erroneous objection to evidence (*Watenpaugh v State Teachers' Retirement Sys.* (1959) 51 C2d 675, 680, 336 P2d 165), or by failing to raise a question of law at trial (*Planned Protective Servs. v Gorton* (1988) 200 CA3d 1, 13, 245 CR 790,

796, disapproved on other grounds in *Martin v Seto* (2004) 32 C4th 445, 451, 9 CR3d 687).

§19.25 d. Waiver by Consent

The parties may expressly stipulate to a waiver of the right to appeal, rendering the judgment immediately enforceable without waiting for the appeal period to expire. See Item 5 on Judicial Council form of Appearance, Stipulations and Waivers (see form in §14.19). Further, a party may waive the right to appeal by stipulating to the entry of an order or judgment. *Marriage of Sheldon* (1981) 124 CA3d 371, 384, 177 CR 380. However, if the voluntary nature of the stipulation is in question, any doubts about the appellant's intent to consent will likely be resolved in favor of the right to appeal. See *Wuest v Wuest* (1942) 53 CA2d 339, 345, 127 P2d 934. For a contrary result, however, see *Marriage of Lionberger* (1979) 97 CA3d 56, 61, 158 CR 535 (silence of party and attorney on recitation of order in open court held a waiver of right to contend that order was not under stipulation). To attack a stipulated order, relief must first be sought from the trial court. *Reed v Murphy* (1925) 196 C 395, 238 P 78. On methods of attacking judgment in trial court, see chap 18.

§19.26 e. Failure to Take Timely Appeal

If a matter is immediately appealable, but no appeal is timely filed, the right to appeal that matter is waived. Thus, if an appeal is not taken from an appealable order in a pending action, the order may not later be reviewed on appeal from the judgment. See *McLellan v McLellan* (1972) 23 CA3d 343, 357, 100 CR 258 (dwelling exclusion order made pendente lite not reviewable on appeal from judgment). On appealability of orders in pending actions, see §§19.4–19.6.

If a partial appeal is taken from portions of a judgment, those portions not appealed from become res judicata on expiration of the appeal period, and the right to appeal such portions is waived. On partial appeals generally, see §§19.7, 19.55.

§19.27 f. Waiver by Contempt

An appellant may lose the right to appeal if he or she is in contempt of court, either in the proceeding on appeal (*Kotteman v Kotteman* (1957) 150 CA2d 483, 487, 310 P2d 49) or in an unrelated proceeding

(*Estate of Scott* (1957) 150 CA2d 590, 592, 310 P2d 46). The court may choose to stay the appeal or order a conditional dismissal until the appellant cures the contempt. See *Krog v Krog* (1948) 32 C2d 812, 818, 198 P2d 510. However, the court may also choose to proceed with the appeal if important rights of others are at stake. See *Smith v Smith* (1955) 135 CA2d 100, 107, 286 P2d 1009 (dissolution involving custody of minor children).

§19.28   g. Acceptance of Benefits Under Judgment

A party who accepts benefits under a judgment may thereby waive the right to appeal. *Lee v Brown* (1976) 18 C3d 110, 114, 132 CR 649. To constitute a waiver, however, the acceptance of benefits must be "unconditional, voluntary and absolute," and the benefits accepted must be those to which the appellant would not be entitled in the event of reversal. Thus, if the benefits are from a severable portion of the judgment, *i.e.,* a portion that would not be affected by a reversal on appeal, acceptance of the benefits will not cause the appellant to lose the right to appeal from other portions of the judgment. *Marriage of Fonstein* (1976) 17 C3d 738, 744, 131 CR 873 (spouse's occupancy of family home, acceptance of spousal and child support, and receipt of shares of stock did not bar appeal from award of community property). On appealing unfavorable, severable portion of generally favorable judgment, see §19.10.

§19.29   6. Practical Considerations

It is not uncommon, at the conclusion of a trial in a marital action, for a party to feel that he or she was treated unfairly by the judicial system. In deciding whether to file an appeal, it is important that counsel assist the client in distinguishing emotional issues from the issues of law and fact that will govern the chances for success on appeal. The client must understand that the appellate court will not reweigh conflicting evidence (see §19.19) or reverse discretionary rulings except in the most egregious circumstances (see §19.20). In some cases, it may be prudent to recommend that the client seek a second opinion from an attorney experienced in appellate practice or to suggest therapeutic intervention.

On the other hand, an appeal can enhance an appellant's position with the possibility of reversing an adverse order or judgment. Taking an appeal may encourage settlement on terms more favorable to the appellant than those obtained in the ruling. The respondent, as well as the appellant, faces substantial costs in defending an appeal, and the respondent risks having the ruling reversed. Moreover, the respondent may wish to avoid a delay of up to two years or more (and considerably longer if a retrial is ordered, and a second appeal taken) in reaching a resolution of the case through the appellate process. Neither party should undertake an appeal, or choose to defend an appeal rather than settle, without considering the direct and indirect costs of doing so. The following questions may be helpful in evaluating these costs:

- What will the appeal itself cost? Some factors to consider are the additional attorney fees generated by an appeal, the fee for filing a notice of appeal (see §19.56), the cost of a transcript of the trial proceedings (see §19.59), the cost of posting a bond or an undertaking to stay enforcement of the order or judgment pending appeal (see §19.34), the cost of reproducing or printing briefs (see §19.80), and the potential liability for payment of the other party's attorney fees and costs (see §19.84).

- Will the order or judgment be enforced pending the appeal? See, *e.g.,* §§19.35 (payment of money, including support), 19.36–19.37 (transfer of property), 19.39 (child custody), 19.43–19.45 (stays by reviewing court).

- Will the trial court make further orders pending the appeal? See §§19.41–19.42. Will a successful appeal afford the relief desired in view of what may transpire in the interim?

- If the appeal is successful, what will be the cost if a retrial is ordered (and if the outcome of the second trial is appealed)?

- Will the opposing party cross-appeal an issue on which the trial court erred favorably to the benefit of the appellant? See §19.53.

- What is the likelihood that the appellate court will find the appeal frivolous, or brought solely for delay, and impose sanctions? See §§19.30, 19.84.

If the decision is made to pursue an appeal, trial counsel should consider whether to refer the case to, or associate with, an appellate specialist. The trial attorney is already familiar with the case and may be able to handle an appeal with greater speed and economy;

the specialist may be more familiar with the appellate process and with recent cases decided in marital actions. Especially important, a specialist may be able to bring a fresh point of view to the case, conceiving of arguments and strategies unnoticed by trial counsel, and may be better able to evaluate the case from the bare record, as will the appellate court. On association of attorneys generally, see California Civil Procedure Before Trial §§4.15–4.18 (4th ed Cal CEB 2004).

§19.30   7. Frivolous Appeals

Under CCP §907 and Cal Rules of Ct 8.276(e)(1)(A), monetary sanctions may be imposed against an attorney of record, as well as against the appellant, for bringing an appeal that is frivolous in nature or solely for the purpose of delay. In considering whether to file an appeal, counsel must be alert to what may be a fine line between the vigorous representation of one's client and the professional obligation not to pursue a frivolous or dilatory appeal. Especially in family law, where statutory and case law can change rapidly, vigorous representation may require an attorney to appeal an issue when the underlying law is unclear or in flux. The appeal of a questionable area of law will not be deemed frivolous unless it is prosecuted for an improper motive (*i.e.,* to harass the respondent or delay the effect of an adverse judgment) or when it "indisputably has no merit" (when any reasonable attorney would agree that the appeal is completely without merit). *Marriage of Flaherty* (1982) 31 C3d 637, 650, 183 CR 508.

Even when an appeal has substantive merit, sanctions may be imposed if it is shown to have been brought solely to delay. *Marriage of Stich* (1985) 169 CA3d 64, 77, 214 CR 919. In this case, however, the court may require that an intent to delay be shown by clear and convincing evidence. The fact that the appellate panel cannot reach a unanimous conclusion may demonstrate that the evidence showing intent to delay is not clear and convincing. *San Bernardino Community Hosp. v Meeks* (1986) 187 CA3d 457, 470, 231 CR 673. On sanctions that may be imposed for frivolous or dilatory appeals, see §19.84.

§19.31   III. STAYS AND ORDERS PENDING APPEAL

An appeal may last one to two years or longer, and in marital

actions, questions of enforcement and modification of orders, particularly orders for support (see §§19.35, 19.42), custody and visitation
(see §§19.39, 19.42), and transfer of property (see §§19.36–19.37)
will often arise during the appeal period. Any party aggrieved by
an appealable order or judgment may request the trial court to immediately and temporarily stay its enforcement, pending posttrial motions and an evaluation of whether to appeal. See §19.32. The trial
court may not, however, make any order, pending appeal, that would
lessen the effectiveness of the appellate court's opinion. *Marriage
of Varner* (1998) 68 CA4th 932, 936, 80 CR2d 628 (trial court precluded from terminating spousal support jurisdiction pending appeal).
Depending on the type of judgment or order in question, its enforcement pending appeal (1) may be automatically stayed (see §19.33);
(2) may be stayed on the posting of security with the trial court
(see §§19.34–19.37); (3) may be stayed in the discretion of, and
on noticed motion to, the trial court, with or without security (see
§§19.38–19.40); (4) may be stayed by the reviewing court (see
§§19.43–19.45); or (5) may not be stayed (see §19.41).

§19.32   A. Immediate Temporary Stays

An immediate temporary stay, until expiration of the time to appeal, may be obtained from the trial court by oral motion on announcement of the judgment or order in open court, by stipulation,
or by ex parte application to the trial judge. See CCP §918(a), (c).
Although a temporary stay is discretionary, it is usually granted.
For a sample form of ex parte application and order, see California
Civil Appellate Practice §6.17 (3d ed Cal CEB 1996). If security
would be required to stay enforcement of the judgment or order
on appeal, the stay may extend without security no longer than 10
days after the last day to file a notice of appeal. CCP §918(b).

§19.33   B. Automatic Stays

Code of Civil Procedure §916(a) states that "the perfecting of
an appeal stays proceedings in the trial court." In practice, a stay
that is automatically perfected on the filing of an appeal is the exception rather than the rule. In most cases, statutory exceptions require
the posting of security (see §19.34), or an order of court on noticed
motion (see §19.38), before a stay may be obtained. Also excluded

from an automatic stay are those matters "not affected by the judgment or order" from which the appeal is taken (see §19.41).

Orders and judgments for which enforcement is automatically stayed by the filing of a notice of appeal include (1) a mandatory injunction (*Byington v Superior Court* (1939) 14 C2d 68, 92 P2d 896); (2) provisions allowing or eliminating restrictions against removal of a minor child from the state (stayed, under CCP §917.7, for 30 days after entry of judgment or order other than by juvenile court in dependency hearing); (3) a judgment for costs alone (*Estate of Neilson* (1960) 181 CA2d 769, 772, 5 CR 542); (4) issuance of a writ of mandamus (*Johnston v Jones* (1925) 74 CA 272, 239 P 862); (5) a judgment requiring the sale of real property not in the appellant's possession (*Keeling Collection Agency v McKeever* (1930) 209 C 625, 289 P 617); and (6) a judgment against a public entity or officer (CCP §995.220). Note, however, that the automatic stay under CCP §917.7 does not apply to orders that are made in proceedings under the Uniform Child Custody Jurisdiction and Enforcement Act (Fam C §§3400-3465) and certain other acts. CCP §917.7.

Even when enforcement of a judgment or order would otherwise be automatically stayed under CCP §916(a), a trial court has discretion to require that security be posted to stay enforcement. CCP §917.9; see §19.34.

§19.34   C. Stays Effective on Posting of Security

By statute, or within the court's discretion, enforcement of many types of judgments and orders can be stayed only if the appellant furnishes security in the form of an undertaking, a bond, or a deposit with the court. CCP §§917.1-917.2, 917.4-917.5, 917.65, 917.9. For a definition of each type of security, and on the interchangeability of types of security, see CCP §§995.140, 995.190, 995.210. Judgments and orders for which the posting of security is required by statute before enforcement may be stayed are those that impose a right-to-attach order (CCP §917.65) or that direct (1) the payment of money (CCP §917.1; see §19.35); (2) the assignment, delivery, or sale of personal property (CCP §917.2; see §19.36); (3) the sale, conveyance, or delivery of real property (CCP §917.4; see §19.37); or (4) the appointment of a receiver (CCP §917.5).

Even when enforcement of a judgment or order would otherwise be automatically stayed under CCP §916(a) (see §19.33), the respondent may move the superior court for an order requiring that security be posted in a particular amount. The motion should explain why security is required under the circumstances of the case and should establish all potential damages for which security should be given. Damages are limited by statute to "reasonable compensation for the loss of use of the money or property." The granting of such a motion is in the court's discretion. CCP §917.9.

The motion may be prepared on the Judicial Council form of Notice of Motion (see form in §11.20) or as a separate pleading, as in civil actions generally. If a separate pleading is used, see California Civil Appellate Practice §6.37 (3d ed Cal CEB 1996) for a sample notice of motion for an order requiring security.

When the posting of security is required by statute or by court order, the amount of security must be fixed by order of the trial court on noticed motion, or by stipulation, unless the amount required is provided by statute. The amount of security will vary, depending on the type of order the enforcement of which is to be stayed. Alternatively, the appellant may be able to obtain a waiver of security from the respondent. On procedure for fixing the amount of security, and for sample motion and waiver, see Civ App Prac §§6.39–6.43. On obtaining and filing the security with the court, see CCP §§995.310–995.730; Civ App Prac §§6.44–6.50. If the respondent is not satisfied with the type or amount of security posted, he or she may timely file a motion objecting to the sufficiency of the security. On procedure and for sample motion, see CCP §§995.910–995.960; Civ App Prac §§6.53–6.62.

§19.35   1. Judgment or Order for Payment of Money, Including Payment of Support

Security must be given to stay enforcement of a judgment or order for the payment of money. CCP §917.1(a). The security is given to ensure that the amount of the judgment or order, all interest accruing during the appeal period, and costs awarded on appeal will be paid if the judgment is affirmed or the appeal is withdrawn or dismissed. The amount of security must be for twice the amount of the order or judgment unless it is given by an admitted surety insurer, in which event it must be for one and one-half times the ordered amount. CCP §917.1(b).

An award of child or spousal support is an order or judgment for the payment of money within the meaning of CCP §917.1(a), and its enforcement may be stayed only on the posting of security. *Smith v Smith* (1927) 201 C 217, 256 P 419. If enforcement is not stayed, all support payments must be made as ordered, pending the appeal. Because the amount of support that will become due pending an appeal is not readily ascertainable, the appellant must apply to the trial court for an order fixing the amount of security. *McClintock v Powley* (1930) 210 C 333, 337, 291 P 833, 835; see §19.34. Once the appellant has posted the required security, the order for support may not be enforced by any means. However, the supported party may request a temporary order for support during the appeal period, from which an appeal may also be taken; and the original order may be modified by the trial court while the appeal is pending. See §19.42.

Note that, when a supported spouse appeals a support award, he or she may be prevented from enforcing the order even when no stay has been obtained. See *Marriage of Horowitz* (1984) 159 CA3d 377, 387, 205 CR 880; *Fontana v Superior Court* (1977) 72 CA3d 159, 162, 139 CR 851.

§19.36   2. Judgment or Order for Transfer of Personal Property

Security must be posted to stay enforcement of a judgment or order to assign or deliver personal property, including documents, or to sell personal property on foreclosure of a mortgage or lien. The security ensures that, if the ruling is affirmed on appeal or the appeal is withdrawn or dismissed, the party obligated by the judgment or order (1) will assign or deliver the property as ordered, (2) will not allow damage to the property, (3) will pay for any damage to the property, and (4) will pay for the value of the use of the property during the appeal period. The appellant may request permission to deposit the property at issue with the court clerk; this fact must be considered by the court in fixing the amount of security. CCP §917.2.

§19.37   3. Judgment or Order for Transfer of Real Property

Enforcement of a judgment or order directing the sale, conveyance, or delivery of possession of real property can be stayed only on the posting of security. Note, however, that when the appellant does not have possession of the real property, enforcement of the judgment or order is automatically stayed. See §19.33. The amount of security must be fixed by the court on the appellant's request. See §19.34. The security must be adequate, in the event the judgment or order is affirmed on appeal or the appeal is withdrawn or dismissed, to ensure against the commission of any waste on the property, and to pay for any damage caused by the waste, and for the value of the use and occupancy of the property from the time of taking the appeal until delivery of possession of the property. If the property is directed to be sold for payment of a deficiency, the security must include the amount of the deficiency. CCP §917.4.

§19.38   D. Discretionary Stays

Under CCP §918, the trial court may stay the enforcement of any judgment or order, whether or not an appeal has been filed. CCP §918(a), (c). Under this authority, the court may stay the enforcement of judgments and orders that are not automatically stayed on filing an appeal (see §19.33) and may stay, without requiring security, the enforcement of judgments and orders for which security must otherwise be posted to stay enforcement (see §§19.34–19.37). However, when the posting of security is required by statute, the court may not grant a stay under §918 that would extend longer than 10 days beyond the last day to appeal. CCP §918(b). On the court's discretion to require security when enforcement of a judgment or order would otherwise be automatically stayed under CCP §916, see §19.34.

When the appellant seeks to stay enforcement of a judgment or order not otherwise stayed by filing an appeal, or seeks to stay, without posting security, enforcement of a judgment or order for which security is otherwise required to stay enforcement, he or she must file a noticed motion in the trial court. The motion should specify the statute authorizing the stay and explain why a stay pending the appeal is necessary. A memorandum of points and authorities and a declaration in support of the motion should accompany the motion.

The motion may be prepared on the Judicial Council form of Notice of Motion (see form in §11.20) or as a separate pleading, as in civil actions generally. Counsel should check local court rules and the court clerk to ascertain the appropriate format in a particular county. If the Judicial Council form is used, the moving party prepares the Notice of Motion and an Application for Order and Supporting Declaration (see form in §11.22). If a separate pleading is used, see California Civil Appellate Practice §6.67 (3d ed Cal CEB 1996) for a sample notice of motion for a stay of enforcement.

§19.39   1. Child Custody; Temporary Dwelling Exclusion

Enforcement of a judgment or order that (1) awards, changes, or otherwise affects the custody, including the right of visitation, of a minor child, or (2) temporarily excludes a party from a dwelling, as provided in the Family Code, is not stayed on the filing of an appeal unless the trial court, in its discretion, so orders. CCP §917.7. The court must decide whether to stay enforcement of a judgment or order affecting custody by deciding whether the best interests of the child will be served by an immediate change or by a continuation of existing custody. *Sanchez v Sanchez* (1960) 178 CA2d 810, 813, 3 CR 501. If the trial court refuses to stay enforcement of the judgment or order affecting custody, the appellate court may order a stay. See §§19.43–19.45. Note, however, that §917.7 provides for an automatic 30-day stay on enforcement of any judgment or order, other than by a juvenile court in a dependency hearing, allowing removal of a minor child from the state. The automatic stay does not apply to orders that are made in proceedings under the Uniform Child Custody Jurisdiction and Enforcement Act (Fam C §§3400–3465) and certain other acts, however. CCP §917.7. On modification of a judgment or order for custody pending appeal, see §19.42.

§19.40   2. Appeal From Bifurcated Issue

A court may, in certain circumstances, bifurcate one or more issues, other than marital status, for an early, separate trial. See §14.59. The decision on a bifurcated issue may be appealed if the trial court certifies that the appeal is appropriate and the appellate court accepts the issue for immediate review. See §§19.88–19.90. If the trial court certifies the issue for appeal, trial of the remaining issues may be stayed. If a stay is granted, further discovery is also stayed, unless otherwise ordered. These stays terminate when the time for filing an appeal expires (if no appeal is filed), when the court of appeal denies all motions for appeal, or when the court of appeal's decision becomes final. Cal Rules of Ct 5.180(c)(2).

E. Power of Trial Court to Make Orders Pending Appeal

§19.41　　1. Matters Not Affected by a Stay

When, under CCP §916, further proceedings are stayed on appeal, the trial court may nonetheless proceed on "any other matter embraced in the action and not affected by the judgment or order." CCP §916(a). The trial court may thus conduct further proceedings on separately appealable judgments or orders, issues that are severable from the judgment or order appealed from, and matters for which enforcement is specifically provided by statute.

Separately appealable judgments and orders. The trial court may enforce a separately appealable postjudgment order, even though enforcement of the original judgment is stayed. See *Kruly v Superior Court* (1963) 216 CA2d 589, 31 CR 122 (trial court may enforce temporary support order notwithstanding stay pending appeal on judgment); see §19.42. Similarly, the stay of a postjudgment order does not stay enforcement of the original judgment. See 9 Witkin, California Procedure, *Appeal* §285 (4th ed 1997).

Severable issues. Under the doctrine of divisible appeal, an appeal from a severable portion of a judgment or order will bring up for review only that portion, leaving all other portions of the judgment or order in full force and effect. *Marriage of Fink* (1976) 54 CA3d 357, 362, 126 CR 626, 629, decision on reserved issues appealed on other grounds in 25 C3d 877; see §19.7. The trial court retains jurisdiction to entertain further proceedings on other portions of the judgment, even when a stay has been ordered pending the appeal.

Status of marriage. The effect of a judgment on the parties' marital status is not stayed by the filing of an appeal from the judgment, unless an objection to the termination of marital status is specified in the notice of appeal. No party may make this objection unless it was also made at the trial. Fam C §2341(b).

Execution of instrument; inspection of records. A judgment or order directing the execution of an instrument may be enforced by the trial court despite the filing of an appeal. However, the appellant may deposit the executed instrument with the court clerk until the reviewing court makes a decision. CCP §917.3. The trial court may also enforce a judgment or order allowing the inspection or copying of corporate documents by a director, stockholder, or member of the corporation while an appeal is pending. CCP §917.8(b).

§19.42   2. Discretionary Orders

The trial court has discretion to make further orders with respect to the following issues in marital actions while an appeal is pending:

Temporary support. The trial court may order temporary support while an appeal is pending, whether or not enforcement of a judgment or order for support has been stayed by the posting of security (see §19.35). Fam C §3600; see *Bain v Superior Court* (1974) 36 CA3d 804, 807, 111 CR 848. See also *Marriage of Askmo* (2000) 85 CA4th 1032, 102 CR2d 662 (temporary support order appropriate during pendency of appeal from default set-aside). The temporary order may be for a different amount, and even for a longer time, than the award from which the appeal is taken. *Bain v Superior Court, supra.* If the temporary award is paid as ordered, the supporting party is entitled to a credit against the judgment for payments made under the award. *Farrar v Farrar* (1920) 45 CA 584, 188 P 289. The supporting spouse may also appeal from the temporary order and seek a stay of that order pending its appeal. *Kruly v Superior Court* (1963) 216 CA2d 589, 591, 31 CR 122.

Modification of support. When an appeal is taken from an order for child or spousal support, the trial court retains jurisdiction to modify that award. See *Marriage of Varner* (1998) 68 CA4th 932, 936, 80 CR2d 628 (trial court precluded from terminating spousal support jurisdiction pending appeal); *Marriage of Horowitz* (1984) 159 CA3d 377, 385, 205 CR 880, 886 (spousal support reduced, pending appeal, to reservation of jurisdiction).

Modification of custody. Whether or not the trial court has stayed enforcement of a custody order (see §19.39), it retains jurisdiction to modify the terms of the order (as well as the terms of the stay, if one was granted) while the appeal is pending. See *Mancini v Superior Court* (1964) 230 CA2d 547, 556, 41 CR 213, 218.

Attorney fees and costs. Under Fam C §2030, the trial court has discretion in a marital action to award attorney fees and costs that are reasonably necessary to maintain or defend the proceeding. The perfecting of an appeal does not deprive the trial court of jurisdiction to award attorney fees and costs necessary for an appeal. *Marriage of Stachon* (1978) 77 CA3d 506, 143 CR 599.

§19.43 F. Power of Reviewing Court to Stay Proceedings

During the pendency of an appeal, a reviewing court may (1) stay proceedings; (2) issue a writ of supersedeas; (3) suspend or modify an injunction; or (4) make any order appropriate to preserve the status quo or the effectiveness of the judgment to be entered on appeal, or otherwise to aid in its jurisdiction. CCP §923. A writ of supersedeas stays the enforcement of a judgment or order pending appeal. *Sacramento Newspaper Guild v Sacramento County Bd. of Supervisors* (1967) 255 CA2d 51, 62 CR 819. A stay order under CCP §923 may have a broader effect, and the request to the appellate court for relief (see §19.45) should be framed to include both types of orders.

§19.44 1. When Stay Is Appropriate

To obtain a stay, the appellant must usually convince the court that a stay is necessary to preserve the issues on appeal, that the respondent will not be unduly prejudiced by a stay, and that the appellant will suffer irreparable harm without a stay. See CCP §923; *Nuckolls v Bank of Cal.* (1936) 7 C2d 574, 61 P2d 927; *Mills v County of Trinity* (1979) 98 CA3d 859, 159 CR 679. The granting of a stay is normally within the appellate court's discretion. *Estate of Murphy* (1971) 16 CA3d 564, 94 CR 141. However, if the stay is requested because the trial court refuses to recognize a stay authorized by statute or perfected by posting security, the appellate court must grant the request. See *Estate of Dabney* (1951) 37 C2d 402, 408, 232 P2d 481. When the trial court has discretion to order a stay, the appellant must request the stay from the lower court before seeking relief from the appellate court. *Nuckolls v Bank of Cal., supra.*

§19.45 2. Procedure

The procedure for obtaining a writ of supersedeas is set forth in Cal Rules of Ct 8.112–8.116; other stay orders permitted under CCP §923 are presumably requested by the same procedure. The appellant must serve and file a verified petition in the appellate court, stating the necessity for the stay and providing supporting points and authorities. If the record on appeal has not yet been filed in the appellate court, the petition must contain a copy of the judgment or order, showing the date of entry; the fact and date of filing of the notice of appeal; and a statement of the case, including a summary of the material facts. Cal Rules of Ct 8112(a). On the form and contents of the petition and filing requirements, see California Civil Appellate Practice §§6.75-6.82 (3d ed Cal CEB 1996).

A request for an immediate temporary stay, pending a decision on the petition, may be included with the petition or made separately. Cal Rules of Ct 8.112(c), 8.116(a). The words "Stay Requested" should be conspicuously noted on the cover of a petition for writ of supersedeas or temporary stay. Cal Rules of Ct 8.116(a)(1). Requirements for the format of a temporary stay petition are described in Cal Rules of Ct 8.116. Except when the custody of a minor is involved, the request for a temporary stay need not be served on the respondent. Cal Rules of Ct 8.112(c)(2).

If the respondent opposes a stay, he or she may file points and authorities, and a statement of any material facts in opposition, within15 days after the petition is filed. Cal Rules of Ct 8.112(b)(1)(2). A hearing must be held if the petition requests the stay of an order awarding or changing the custody of a minor (Cal Rules of Ct 8.112(d)(2)); in other cases, a hearing will normally not be held (see *Mills v County of Trinity* (1979) 98 CA3d 859, 861, 159 CR 679). A stay may be granted on any conditions the appellate court deems just. Cal Rules of Ct 8.112(d)(1). In most cases, the court will require security as a condition for issuing the stay, unless the writ is requested to enforce the appellant's right to a statutory stay without security. See 9 Witkin, California Procedure, *Appeal* §§312-314 (4th ed 1997). The appellate court's denial of a stay is effective immediately; the granting of a stay is final 30 days after filing. Cal Rules of Ct 8.264(b). If the stay is granted, either party may file a petition for rehearing or seek supreme court review of the order. Cal Rules of Ct 8.268, 8.500.

IV. STANDARD PROCEDURE ON APPEAL

§19.46   A. Notice of Appeal

An appeal is initiated by the timely filing of a notice of appeal.

Cal Rules of Ct 8.100(a), 8.104. The filing of an appeal is not merely procedural; it vests jurisdiction in the appellate court and terminates the jurisdiction of the trial court (*Hollister Convalescent Hosp. v Rico* (1975) 15 C3d 660, 666, 125 CR 757), except on matters over which the trial court has continuing jurisdiction (see §§19.41–19.42). The parties cannot confer jurisdiction on the appellate court by consent or stipulation (15 C3d at 666), nor can the lack of appellate jurisdiction be waived by a party (*Marriage of Adams* (1987) 188 CA3d 683, 689, 233 CR 534.

§19.47　　　1. Time for Filing

Unless an extension is provided by law (see §§19.49–19.54), a notice of appeal must be filed on or before the earliest of the following dates (Cal Rules of Ct 8.104(a)):

- 60 days after the date the superior court clerk mails a document entitled "Notice of Entry" of judgment or a file-stamped copy of the judgment, showing the date either was mailed;

- 60 days after the appellant serves or is served with a document entitled "Notice of Entry" of judgment or a file-stamped copy of the judgment, accompanied by proof of service; or

- 180 days after the date of entry of the judgment.

The term "judgment" includes an appealable order. Cal Rules of Ct 8.104(f).

In a marital action, the court clerk prepares and mails notice of entry of judgment to the attorney for each party and to any unrepresented parties. Cal Rules of Ct 5.134. If the clerk delays giving notice and counsel wishes to shorten the time for appeal, counsel may prepare and serve a notice of entry of judgment by mail on the adverse party. Notice of an appealable order should be given by the prevailing party. Service of a file-stamped copy of the judgment or appealable order accompanied by proof of service, in lieu of a separate notice of entry, is sufficient. Cal Rules of Ct 8.104(a)(2). Service by mail does *not* extend the 60-day period for filing an appeal. CCP §1013(a).

§19.48　　　a. Entry of Judgment or Order

If neither the clerk nor the prevailing party provides written notice of entry (see §19.47), the appellant has 180 days after entry of the judgment or appealable order in which to file a notice of appeal. The date on which a judgment is entered depends on the method used by the county to enter judgments. If the county uses a judgment book, the date of entry is the date the judgment is entered in the judgment book. If a county follows the procedure in CCP §668.5 in lieu of maintaining a judgment book, the date of entry is the date the judgment is filed with the clerk.

The date of entry of an appealable order is when it is entered in the court's permanent minutes, unless the minute order expressly directs that a written order be prepared, signed, and filed. In the latter event, or if the order is not entered in the court minutes, the date of entry is the date on which the signed order is filed in the court. Cal Rules of Ct 8.104(d). The preparation and filing of a written order, when not specifically required in the minute order, does not commence the period for filing a notice of appeal. *Marriage of Adams* (1987) 188 CA3d 683, 689, 233 CR 534.

If a notice of appeal is prematurely filed before the judgment or order is entered, but after it is rendered, it is valid and will be deemed to have been filed immediately after entry. A notice of appeal that is filed before a judgment or order is rendered, but after a tentative decision, may be treated as filed immediately after entry of the judgment or order, in the discretion of the appellate court for good cause. Cal Rules of Ct 8.104(e).

§19.49   b. Extension of Time to File

Under Cal Rules of Ct 8.104(a) and 8.308(a), the time for filing a notice of appeal "shall not be extended" by the appellate court. This provision overrides the court's general authority, under Cal Rules of Ct 8.63, to extend, for good cause shown, the time periods provided by the rules of court. However, in certain circumstances, an extension to file a notice of appeal is allowed as a matter of law. See §§19.50–19.54.

§19.50   (1) Motion for Reconsideration

Under Cal Rules of Ct 8.108(d), as repealed and adopted effective January 1, 2002, the filing of a valid motion for reconsideration of an appealable order (see CCP §1008(a); see also §11.65) will extend the time for filing a notice of appeal from that order until the earliest of:

- 30 days after the superior court clerk mails, or a party serves, an order denying the motion or a notice of entry of that order;

- 90 days after the first motion to reconsider is filed; or

- 180 days after the entry of the appealable order.

When prejudgment motions for reconsideration are deemed to extend the time for appeal, only a valid motion (*e.g.*, timely filed) will do so. *Ten Eyck v Industrial Forklifts* (1989) 216 CA3d 540, 545, 265 CR 29. Note that a motion for reconsideration of an order does not survive a subsequent judgment for purposes of extending the time for filing a notice of appeal. *Nave v Taggart* (1995) 34 CA4th 1173, 40 CR2d 714.

With respect to motions for reconsideration of a judgment, the law remains unclear. In *Passavanti v Williams* (1990) 225 CA3d 1602, 1607, 275 CR 887, the court held that a motion to reconsider a judgment is improper and, therefore, cannot extend the time for filing a notice of appeal. On cases that have held to the contrary, see 225 CA3d at 1607 n5. One of those cases (*Miller v United Servs. Auto. Ass'n* (1989) 213 CA3d 222, 227, 261 CR 515) held that, if a motion for reconsideration is not determined within 60 days after service of a notice of entry of judgment, the notice of appeal must be filed within 90 days after service of the notice of entry of judgment, a view that *Passavanti v Williams, supra,* also rejected.

§19.51　　　(2) Motion for New Trial

A notice of appeal may be filed before, at the same time as, or after the filing of a notice of intention to move for a new trial. See *Neff v Ernst* (1957) 48 C2d 628, 634, 311 P2d 849. The trial court retains jurisdiction to determine the motion for new trial while an appeal is pending. *Neff v Ernst, supra.*

When a motion for new trial is denied, the time for filing a notice of appeal is extended until the earlier of (a) 30 days after the superior court clerk mails, or a party serves, an order denying the motion or a notice of entry of that order; (b) 30 days after denial of the motion by operation of law; or (c) 180 days after entry of judgment. Cal Rules of Ct 8.108(a). The notice of intention to move for new trial must be valid (*i.e.,* timely filed, grounds for motion sufficiently designated, timely served on adverse party) for denial of the motion to effectively extend the time for appeal. *Marriage of Patscheck* (1986) 180 CA3d 800, 225 CR 787. The order denying relief is not appealable. See §18.14.

When a motion for a new trial is granted, an immediate appeal may be taken from the order on the motion. CCP §904.1(a)(4); see §18.15. When an appeal is taken from the order granting a new trial, a protective cross-appeal should be filed. See §19.53.

On motions for new trial generally, see §§18.2–18.15.

§19.52   (3) Motion to Vacate Judgment

When a motion to vacate judgment, or, in the case of a motion to vacate and enter a different judgment, a notice of intention to move, is timely served and filed, the time for filing a notice of appeal from the judgment is extended until the earliest of (a) 30 days after the superior court clerk mails, or a party serves, an order denying the motion or a notice of entry of that order; (b) 90 days after the first notice of intention to move or motion to vacate is filed; or (c) 180 days after the entry of judgment. Cal Rules of Ct 8.108(b). Note that the intention of Rule 8.108(b) appears to be to extend, not shorten, the time limit for filing a notice of appeal. See *Maides v Ralph's Grocery Co.* (2000) 77 CA4th 1363, 1367, 92 CR2d 542 (appeal timely when filed within 60 days after entry of judgment but more than 90 days after notice of intention to move to vacate judgment). See also §18.22.

The notice of intention to vacate must be valid under CCP §663a to effectively extend the time to appeal. Unlike a motion for new trial, the trial court is divested of jurisdiction to hear a motion to vacate once a notice of appeal has been filed. *Copley v Copley* (1981) 126 CA3d 248, 298, 178 CR 842. Counsel must therefore wait until the motion to vacate is determined before filing an appeal and must carefully monitor the time for appeal to avoid waiving the right of review. Alternatively, the party attacking the judgment may take an appeal from the order denying the motion to vacate. *Socol v King* (1949) 34 C2d 292, 296, 209 P2d 577; 9 Witkin, California Procedure, *Appeal* §154 (4th ed 1997).

If the motion to vacate is granted, the party who opposed the motion may take an appeal from the order granting the motion or from a new judgment entered subsequently. CCP §§663a, 904.1; *Socol v King, supra*. When an appeal is taken from the order granting a motion to vacate, a protective cross-appeal should be filed. See §19.53.

On motions to vacate generally, see §§18.16–18.23.

§19.53   (4) Cross-Appeal

When a timely notice of appeal is filed from a judgment or appealable order, the time for any other party to appeal from that judgment or order is extended until 20 days after the superior court clerk mails notification of the first appeal. Cal Rules of Ct 8.108(e)(1). A judgment or an order may contain errors that are favorable to each party; the filing of a cross-appeal assures that *all* errors may be considered by the reviewing court and may thus facilitate settlement.

A protective cross-appeal may be taken from a judgment when an appeal is timely filed from an order granting (1) a motion for a new trial; (2) within 150 days after entry of judgment, a motion to vacate the judgment; or (3) a judgment notwithstanding the verdict. Cal Rules of Ct 8.108(e)(2). If the order granting a new trial or vacating the judgment is overturned on appeal, the effect may be to reinstate the original judgment. A protective cross-appeal will preserve the right to take an appeal from the original judgment in this event. The cross-appeal must be filed within 20 days after the court clerk mails notification of the first appeal. See Cal Rules of Ct 8.108(e)(2).

§19.54   (5) Amended Judgment

When the trial court amends a judgment before the appeal period has expired, *e.g.,* on a motion for new trial or on a motion to vacate judgment (see §§18.2–18.23), a new appeal period begins to run from the notice of entry of the amended judgment. *Marriage of Micalizio* (1988) 199 CA3d 662, 670, 245 CR 673. If the amended judgment is subsequently held void and the original judgment is reinstated, a new appeal period begins to run from the date the amended judgment was declared void. 199 CA3d at 672.

§19.55   2. Form and Contents

A notice of appeal must be in writing, must be signed by the appellant or counsel, and must state in substance that the appellant appeals from a specified judgment or appealable order. The notice need not specify the appellate court; it will be deemed to be an appeal to the court of appeal for the district. Cal Rules of Ct 8.104(a)(2).

Most nonappealable pretrial orders are merged into a judgment, and a notice of appeal from "the judgment" will preserve the appellant's right to raise all errors that occurred both at the trial and in pretrial proceedings. See CCP §906. If the appeal seeks review of more than one appealable order, or of one or more appealable orders and the judgment, the notice of appeal should specify each order and the judgment separately. For form of notice of appeal, see California Civil Appellate Practice §7.14 (3d ed Cal CEB 1996).

A partial appeal may be taken from certain specified, severable portions of a judgment, rather than from the judgment as a whole. Care must be taken in drafting the notice of a partial appeal, because the appellate court will limit its review to the matters specified in the notice. *Marriage of Fink* (1976) 54 CA3d 357, 362, 126 CR 626, 629, decision on reserved issues appealed on other grounds in 25 C3d 877. On expiration of the period for filing an appeal, severable portions of the judgment or order not designated in the notice of appeal will become final and res judicata, *i.e.,* the right to appeal those issues will be waived (see §19.26).

If the appellant wishes to object to the termination of marital status, the notice of appeal must so specify; otherwise, the right to appeal this issue will be waived and the parties will be restored to the status of unmarried persons, despite the filing of an appeal. To raise the issue on appeal, the appellant must have objected to the termination of marital status at the trial. Fam C §2341(b); see §19.41.

It is good practice, although not required, to designate the record in the notice of appeal. Cal Rules of Ct 8.120(a). If not filed with the notice of appeal, a notice designating the record must be filed within 10 days thereafter. See §19.57. On designation of the record generally, see §§19.57–19.71.

§19.56   3. Filing and Service Requirements

The original, signed notice of appeal must be filed with the clerk in the court that rendered the judgment or order. Cal Rules of Ct

8.100(a). The notice should be filed well within the appropriate time limit (see §§19.47–19.54) by personal delivery to the clerk, and a file-stamped copy should be obtained for the attorney's files. If mailed, the notice must be received by the clerk within the time allowed by Cal Rules of Ct 8.104(a) (see §19.47). *Thompson, Curtis, Lawson & Parrish v Thorne* (1971) 21 CA3d 797, 801, 98 CR 753 (notice mailed four days before deadline, received and filed one day late; appeal dismissed). On waiver of appeal by failure to timely file notice, see §19.26.

The appellant is required to serve the notice of appeal on other parties to the action. Failure to serve the notice will not prevent its filing and will not affect the appeal's validity, but on reasonable notice the appellant may be required to remedy the failure. Cal Rules of Ct 8.100(a)(3).

The clerk is required to mail notification of the filing of the notice of appeal to the attorney for each represented party, to unrepresented parties, and to the clerk of the reviewing court. Cal Rules of Ct 8.100(d). The clerk's failure to give notice, however, does not affect the validity of the appeal. Cal Rules of Ct 8.100(a)(3).

A $655 filing fee ($485 for the notice of appeal and an additional $170 fee) must be delivered to the superior court clerk with the notice of appeal. See Govt C §§68926–68926.1; Cal Rules of Ct 8.100(b)(1). The fee may be paid in cash or by check or money order made payable to "Clerk, Court of Appeal." Govt C §68926; Cal Rules of Ct 8.100(b)(1). The clerk transmits the filing fee and the notice of appeal to the court of appeal. Cal Rules of Ct 8.100(d)(1), (5). An indigent party may be excused by the trial court from paying the filing fee (Govt C §68511.3(a)(3); Cal Rules of Ct 8.100(b)(1)); waiver of the fee for good cause may also be granted by the appellate court (Cal Rules of Ct 8.100(c)(1)). The trial court must accept the notice of appeal for filing even if the fee is not paid and no fee waiver has been obtained (Cal Rules of Ct 8.100(b)(3)), but the reviewing court may dismiss the appeal if the fee remains unpaid and unexcused 15 days after notice of dismissal is mailed by the reviewing court to the appellant (Cal Rules of Ct 8.100(c)).

A $100 deposit for preparation of the clerk's transcript, payable to the clerk of the superior court, generally must be paid when the notice of appeal is filed unless the superior court waives the deposit under Rule 985. Govt C §68926.1; Cal Rules of Ct 8.100(b)(2).

§19.57   B. Record on Appeal

The scope of an appeal is defined by the notice of appeal and by the judgment or order appealed from, but the issues that can actually be reviewed by the appellate court are effectively limited by the record that is designated on appeal. The appellant's attorney has the primary responsibility for choosing the type of record that will be prepared and submitted to the appellate court. He or she makes the initial designation of record by filing a notice or notices, concurrently with or within 10 days after the filing of the notice of appeal, stating the type of record desired.

In almost all cases, the record will consist of the reporter's transcript (see §19.58), or portions of it, and the clerk's transcript (see §19.61) or an appendix in lieu of the clerk's transcript (see §19.63). This is the only type of record that will allow the appellant to present a complete and sympathetic statement of facts to the appellate court. In rare cases, when the only issues are questions of law or when economics are determinative, the clerk's transcript (and even the clerk's *and* the reporter's transcript) may be replaced by the judgment roll (see §19.65), an agreed statement (see §19.66), or a settled statement (see §19.67). However, these forms of record present an abbreviated and sterile record on appeal and are seldom used.

The time period allowed for designation of the record is often overlooked by the appellant's attorney. Once the period has expired, an appeal may be salvaged only by filing and prevailing on a motion for relief from default in the appellate court. See §19.71. The risk of default can be avoided by combining the notice designating the record with the notice of appeal. In addition to assuring a timely designation of the record, this practice requires counsel, at an early stage in the appellate proceeding, to review the errors made at trial in the context of the issues, evidence, and arguments presented in the record.

§19.58   1. Reporter's Transcript

The reporter's transcript consists of the testimony, evidentiary objections by counsel, rulings by the judge, such portions of depositions as have been read into the record at trial, and other colloquy on the record. Cal Rules of Ct 8.130(a), (e). The reporter's transcript does not include pretrial or posttrial proceedings, opening statements, closing arguments, proceedings on a motion for new trial, depositions lodged with the court but not read into the record at trial, or oral proceedings that are not reported. See Cal Rules of Ct 8.130(a)(4). However, either party may specifically designate an item not required by court rule (Cal Rules of Ct 8.130(a)(2), 8.155(a)(1)(B)) or may move to correct (Cal Rules of Ct 8.155(c)(1)) or augment the record (Cal Rules of Ct 8.155(a), (b); see §19.69).

§19.59   a. Preparation of Reporter's Transcript

Within 10 days after filing the notice of appeal, the appellant must file a notice either designating the reporter's transcript, stating the date the notice of appeal was filed, and identifying the proceedings to be included by specifying the dates of the proceedings to be included (Cal Rules of Ct 8.130(a)(1), (4)), or stating the intention to proceed without a reporter's transcript, unless the appellant proceeds by agreed or settled statement. Cal Rules of Ct 8.130(a)(1). With the designation, the appellant must deposit with the superior court clerk the approximate cost of the transcript or substitute a certified transcript of the designated proceedings. Cal Rules of Ct 8.130(b)(1), (3). The notice designating the reporter's transcript may be combined, or filed concurrently, with the notice designating the clerk's transcript and the notice of appeal. See §19.57. On preparation and form of notice to prepare reporter's transcript, see California Civil Appellate Practice §§9.18-9.20 (3d ed Cal CEB 1996).

The respondent may counter designate additional proceedings by filing a notice within 10 days after service of the appellant's notice of designation. Cal Rules of Ct 8.130(a)(2). On preparation and form of the respondent's notice, see Civ App Prac §§9.21-9.22. The respondent may not designate the reporter's transcript when the appellant fails to do so, but he or she may request the appellate court to augment the record to prevent a miscarriage of justice. Cal Rules of Ct 8.120(a)(3); see §19.69.

If the appellant's deposit appears to the reporter to be inadequate, the reporter may, within fifteen days after the clerk mails the notice of designation, file with the clerk and mail to the appellant an estimate or revised estimate of the transcript's total cost, showing the additional deposit required. Cal Rules of Ct 8.130(b)(2). The additional amount must be deposited within 10 days after the reporter mails the estimate. Cal Rules of Ct 8.130(b)(2). The reporter must prepare, certify, and file the transcript within 30 days after the notice of designation from the clerk is received or mailed. Cal Rules of Ct 8.130(f)(1). In practice, preparing a cost estimate and the transcript often takes considerably longer than the time limits in the rules of court allow. The appellant must diligently seek to procure the filing of the record; otherwise, the appeal may be dismissed. Cal Rules of Ct 8.140 (former Cal Rules of Ct 10(c)); see *Myers v Johnson* (1949) 89 CA2d 800, 803, 201 P2d 884 (discussing former rule). If the reporter fails to transcribe the oral proceedings, a procedure is available for preparing a settled statement of those portions of the proceeding not transcribed. See Cal Rules of Ct 8.130(g).

§19.60 b. Partial Transcript

Under revised Cal Rules of Ct 8.130(a)(4), every notice designating a reporter's transcript must state the date the notice of appeal was filed and identify which proceedings are to be included; an appellant who wants to exclude a portion of the proceedings may do so by describing the portion that should not be transcribed. A partial transcript may be more quickly and economically prepared and will result in a more focused record than a complete transcript, but many appellate attorneys believe that the benefits do not outweigh the risks. To designate a partial transcript, counsel must specify the issues to be raised on appeal. Cal Rules of Ct 8.130(a)(5). The appeal is then limited to those issues (absent special permission of the appellate court), preventing appellate counsel from raising any new issues and precluding any argument based on changes in the law pending appeal. Cal Rules of Ct 8.130(a)(5).

§19.61 2. Clerk's Transcript

The clerk's transcript contains papers or records on file or lodged with the superior court clerk, including trial exhibits admitted into evidence, refused, or lodged. Exhibits will not be copied into the transcript, however, unless specifically designated. Cal Rules of Ct 5(a)(5). The following documents must be included in the clerk's transcript, even if not specifically designated by notice of either party: notice of appeal; judgment or order appealed from and notice of its entry; any notice of intention to move for a new trial, or motion to vacate the judgment, for judgment notwithstanding the verdict, or for reconsideration of an appealed order, and any order on such motion and notice of its entry; notice or stipulation designating the record or to proceed by settled statement; and the register of actions, if any (see §19.65). Cal Rules of Ct 8.120(b)(1). Any additional documents specified in Cal Rules of Ct 8.120(b)(3) may also be specifically designated. Although counsel may specify extremely important exhibits to be included in the transcript, most exhibits are transmitted separately to the appellate court after a hearing has been set. See §19.68.

§19.62 a. Preparation of Clerk's Transcript

The appellant must serve and file a notice designating the clerk's transcript within 10 days after filing the notice of appeal. Cal Rules of Ct 8.120(a)(1). The notice designating the clerk's transcript may be combined with, or filed concurrently with, the notice designating the reporter's transcript and the notice of appeal. Cal Rules of Ct 8.120(a)(2). See §19.57. On preparation and form of notice to prepare clerk's transcript, see California Civil Appellate Practice §§9.41–9.43 (3d ed Cal CEB 1996). The respondent may counter designate additional papers or records to be included in the clerk's transcript by filing a notice within 10 days after service of the appellant's notice of designation. Cal Rules of Ct 8.120(a)(3). On preparation and form of the respondent's notice, see Civ App Prac §§9.44–9.45.

Within 30 days after the respondent's counter designation is filed or due, the superior court clerk must send a notice of the estimated cost of preparing the transcript that shows the date it was sent. Cal Rules of Ct 8.120(c)(1). The estimated cost must be deposited with the clerk within 10 days after notification (Cal Rules of Ct 8.120(c)(3)); the clerk then has 30 days to complete and file the transcript (Cal Rules of Ct 8.120(d)). Problems of delay often occur in the preparation of the clerk's transcript; see §19.59 on the appellant's duty to procure the record or face possible dismissal of the appeal. On preparation of alternatives to the clerk's transcript, see §§19.63–19.65.

b. Alternatives to Clerk's Transcript

§19.63 (1) Appendix

The appellant, or the parties jointly, may create their own appendix in lieu of the clerk's transcript. Cal Rules of Ct 8.124. The appendix, like the transcript, contains photocopies of all pleadings and documents designated by the parties, is continuously paginated, and has alphabetical and chronological indexes. On appendix contents, see Cal Rules of Ct 8.124(b). Using an appendix will save most of the considerable time, and some of the expense, of preparing the clerk's transcript. Rule 8.124 should be studied carefully, however, so that counsel can make an informed decision on whether to commit legal staff to the preparation of this substantial and exacting compilation of documents.

Within 10 days after the notice of appeal is filed, either party may file a notice of election to proceed under Cal Rules of Ct 8.124. The notice must state the date the notice of appeal was filed. Cal Rules of Ct 8.124(a)(1). The superior court clerk must promptly send a copy of the notice of election to the reviewing court. Cal Rules of Ct 8.124(a)(3)(A). For form of notice of election, see California Civil Appellate Practice §9.73 (3d ed Cal CEB 1996).

The parties are encouraged to reach an agreement on a joint appendix. Cal Rules of Ct 8.124(a)(4). If successful, they may file a stipulation designating its contents. For form of stipulation, see Civ App Prac §9.74. If the parties cannot reach an agreement, the appellant must file his or her own appendix, and the respondent may file a "respondent's appendix" containing any documents that could have been included in the appellant's or a joint appendix. Cal Rules of Ct 8.124(b)(6). On obtaining exhibits not in the possession of the party preparing the appendix, see Cal Rules of Ct 8.124(c). On the period for filing each document, the format required, payment of costs, and sanctions for filing nonconforming copies or an inadequate appendix, see Cal Rules of Ct 8.124(d)–(g).

§19.64   (2) Superior Court File

If local appellate court rules so provide, the parties may stipulate to the use of the original superior court file in lieu of a clerk's transcript. In practice, the superior court usually creates an index of documents, copies of which must then be made and correlated to the documents in counsel's file. This practice may result in a cumbersome and time-consuming procedure; an appendix is generally the preferred alternative. The following districts currently permit use of the court file by stipulation: Third and Fifth Districts, and Division Three of the Fourth District; counsel should check with the appellate court clerk.

The stipulation must be filed within 10 days after the notice of appeal is filed (Cal Rules of Ct 8.128(a)); within 10 days thereafter, the superior court must provide the appellant with an estimate of the cost to prepare the file. Cal Rules of Ct 8.128(b)(1). The appellant has 10 days after the clerk mails the estimate to deposit the estimate of costs with the court clerk; the superior court then has 10 additional days to prepare the file; when it is prepared, copies are sent to counsel and unrepresented parties. Cal Rules of Ct 8.128(b)(1)-(3). If no reporter's transcript has been requested, the file is transmitted to the appellate court immediately; otherwise, it is transmitted to the appellate court with the reporter's transcript when the latter is complete and certified. Cal Rules of Ct 8.128(b)(4).

§19.65   (3) Judgment Roll

The judgment roll consists of portions of the clerk's transcript as specified in CCP §670. When an appellant designates only a clerk's transcript, and does not give notice to prepare the reporter's transcript, the respondent may not counter designate any addition to the reporter's transcript. See Cal Rules of Ct 8.130(a)(3).

In contrast, when the appellant designates part or all of the clerk's transcript, and does not give notice to prepare the reporter's transcript, the respondent is permitted to counter designate additional documents that may properly be included in the clerk's transcript. See Cal Rules of Ct 8.120(a)(3)-(5); see also §19.62. In either event, the record may be augmented by the reviewing court to prevent a miscarriage of justice. Cal Rules of Ct 8.130(a)(3); see §19.69.

§19.66   3. Agreed Statement

An appeal may be presented on a record consisting, in whole or in part, of a statement agreed on by both parties. The agreed statement must explain the nature of the action, the basis of the reviewing court's jurisdiction, and how the superior court decided the points to be raised on appeal. However, the statement should include only those facts necessary to a determination of the questions on appeal. Cal Rules of Ct 8.134(a)(1). If the agreed statement replaces the clerk's transcript, it must also contain those documents in the clerk's file specified in Cal Rules of Ct 8.120(b)(1), (2). Cal Rules of Ct 8.134(a)(2).

Concurrent with filing the notice of appeal, or within 10 days thereafter, the appellant must file either an agreed statement or a stipulation that the parties are attempting to agree on a statement. Cal Rules of Ct 8.134(b)(1). The stipulation extends the time for designating any other form of record until 50 days after the date the notice of appeal was filed. Cal Rules of Ct 8.134(b)(3). The agreed statement must be filed with the trial court within 40 days after the notice of appeal was filed. Cal Rules of Ct 8.134(b)(2). If the parties cannot reach an agreement on a statement, the appellant may designate another form of record within the required period. For forms of a preliminary stipulation and an agreed statement, see California Civil Appellate Practice §9.86 (3d ed Cal CEB 1996).

Although costs on appeal may be minimized by proceeding on an agreed statement, any statement agreed to by both parties is likely to present a sterile record on appeal. The statement may exclude evidence crucial to the appellant's case or omit facts necessary to aid the reviewing court in understanding the appellant's point of view. For these reasons, an agreed statement is rarely used as a record on appeal.

§19.67   4. Settled Statement

A settled statement is a condensed statement, in narrative form, of all or such portions of the oral proceedings as are material to the determination of the points on appeal. Cal Rules of Ct 8.137(b). Within 10 days after filing the notice of appeal, an appellant who wants to use a settled statement in lieu of a reporter's transcript (or both a reporter's and a clerk's transcript) must file a motion in superior court supported by a showing that (1) a substantial cost saving will result and the statement can be settled without significantly burdening the parties or the court; (2) the designated oral proceedings were not reported or cannot be transcribed; or (3) the appellant is unable to pay for a reporter's transcript. Cal Rules of Ct 8.137(a)(1)-(2). If the motion is denied, appellant must file the other notices provided for in the rules. If the motion is granted, within 30 days the appellant must follow the detailed procedure in Cal Rules of Ct 8.137(b)-(c).

For forms of the appellant's proposed settled statement and proposed amendments by the respondent, see California Civil Appellate Practice §§9.98-9.99 (3d ed Cal CEB 1996).

Although costs on appeal may be minimized by proceeding on

a settled statement, the problems presented by a limited record when an agreed statement is used (see §19.66) apply to a settled statement as well. In addition, the procedure for obtaining a settled statement is adversarial, and, if the appellant fails to obtain a favorable statement, the appeal may be lost. See, *e.g., Williams v Goldberg* (1944) 66 CA2d 40, 151 P2d 853. For these reasons, a settled statement is rarely used as a record on appeal.

§19.68   5. Transmission of Exhibits

In most cases, counsel specifies the exhibits that will be sent to the appellate court when notification is received that an appeal has been set for hearing. Each party may file with the superior court clerk a notice specifying those original exhibits, either admitted, refused, or lodged at trial, to be transmitted to the reviewing court. In addition, the appellate court may at any time specify original exhibits to be transmitted to it by the superior court clerk. Original exhibits are returned to the superior court when remittitur is issued (see §19.82). Cal Rules of Ct 8.224(d).

In addition, the appellant may request, in the notice to prepare the clerk's transcript (see §19.62), that copies of specified exhibits be included in the transcript. Cal Rules of Ct 8.120(a)(4). Usually, this method is reserved for documents that are an integral part of the testimony at trial, *e.g.,* an income and expense declaration. The respondent may counter designate additional exhibits to be copied at his or her own cost. Cal Rules of Ct 8.120(a)(3), (c). Exhibits may be included in the clerk's transcript regardless of whether they were admitted or refused at trial. Cal Rules of Ct 8.120(a)(5).

6. Power of Reviewing Court to Affect Record

§19.69   a. Augmentation or Correction

On the motion of any party, or on the appellate court's own motion, a judge of the reviewing court may order that the record be augmented or corrected. Cal Rules of Ct 8.155(a)–(c). The record may be *augmented* by any document on file or lodged with the trial court or by a certified transcript or agreed or settled statement of oral proceedings not designated under Cal Rules of Ct 8.130. Cal Rules of Ct 8.155(a)(1). Once transmitted, the augmented material becomes part of the record on appeal. The appellate court may order the *correction* or certification of any part of the record and may order the superior court to settle disputes about the record. Cal Rules of Ct 8.155(c).

If a clerk or reporter *omits* a required or designated portion of the record, a party may serve and file a notice in superior court requesting that the portion be prepared, certified, and sent to the reviewing court. Cal Rules of Ct 8.155(b). If the clerk or reporter fails to timely comply, the party may serve and file a motion to augment under Rule 8.155(a).

For a form of motion to augment or correct the record, see California Civil Appellate Practice §11.66 (3d ed Cal CEB 1996).

§19.70   b. Factual Determinations

In extremely limited circumstances, the appellate court may take evidence concerning facts occurring at any time before the decision on appeal and may make factual determinations contrary to or in addition to those of the trial court. This authority is given to the appellate court so that causes may be finally disposed of by a single appeal and without further trial court proceedings, unless in the interests of justice a new trial is required. CCP §909; Cal Rules of Ct 8.252. Although the appellate court rarely exercises this authority, it may order evidence produced before it on noticed application of any party (Cal Rules of Ct 8.252(c), 8.54(a)(2); see *Jackson v Wallace* (1976) 59 CA3d 784, 788, 131 CR 218) or on the court's own motion (*Bassett v Johnson* (1949) 94 CA2d 807, 811, 211 P2d 939).

On the limited circumstances under which this authority may be exercised, and for forms of motions for factual determinations and for production of additional evidence on appeal, see California Civil Appellate Practice §§11.76–11.85 (3d ed Cal CEB 1996).

§19.71   c. Remedies for Failure to Produce Record

The appellant may seek relief from any default caused by a failure to comply with the rules of court, except for the failure to give timely notice of appeal, by bringing a motion under Cal Rules of Ct 8.60(e). For form of motion for relief from default in the appellate court, see California Civil Appellate Practice §11.62 (3d ed Cal CEB 1996). On the motion of the respondent, or on its own motion, the appellate court may dismiss an appeal for failure by the appellant to procure the filing of the record on appeal. Cal Rules of Ct 8.140.

For form of motion to dismiss for this reason and of supporting declaration, see Civ App Prac §§11.46–11.47.

§19.72   C. Prehearing Conference and Settlement

California Rules of Court 8.248(a)(2) provides that a prehearing conference may be held, at any time after the notice of appeal is filed, to consider the simplification of the issues on appeal, the possibility of settlement, and any other relevant issues. In connection with the conference, the reviewing court may require one or more of the parties to file and serve a short statement of the nature of the case and the issues on appeal. Cal Rules of Ct 8.248(a)(1). Most appellate districts have enacted rules to implement the settlement conference procedure. The rules of each district vary in important respects, are subject to change, and should be consulted for each appeal.

If the case is settled after a notice of appeal has been filed, either as a whole or as to any party, the appellant who has settled must immediately serve and file a notice of settlement. Cal Rules of Ct 8.244(a)(1). If the case settles after the appellant receives notice setting oral argument or a prehearing conference, the appellant must also immediately notify the reviewing court written notice by telephone or other expeditious method. Cal Rules of Ct 8.244(a)(2).

Within 45 days after filing a notice of settlement—unless the court has ordered a longer time period on a showing of good cause—the appellant who filed the notice of settlement must file either an abandonment under Cal Rules of Ct. 8.244(b), if the record has not yet been filed in the court of appeal or a request to dismiss under Cal Rules of Ct. 8.244(c), if the record has already been filed in the court of appeal. Cal Rules of Ct 8.244(a)(3).

If the appellant does not file an abandonment, a request to dismiss, or a letter stating good cause why the appeal should not be dismissed within the time period specified under Rule 8.244(a)(3), the court may dismiss the appeal as to that appellant and order each side to bear its own costs on appeal. Cal Rules of Ct 8.244(a)(4).

California Rules of Court 8.244(a) does not apply to settlements requiring findings to be made by the court of appeal under CCP §128(a)(8). Cal Rules of Ct 8.244(a)(5).

§19.73   D. Appellate Briefs

The briefs filed by each party on appeal present the appellate court with a conceptual framework in which to understand and review the record. As a rule, the appellant files an opening brief, the respondent files a response brief, and the appellant files a final reply brief. Coherent and persuasive writing is of primary importance in preparing an effective brief; however, appellate counsel must also have a firm command of the facts in the record and the applicable legal principles. Access to both the record and the law should be simplified through the preparation of digests, summaries, and indexes before work is begun on the brief.

§19.74   1. Time for Filing

The time for filing briefs depends on the type of record designated. On designation of record, see §§19.57–19.71. The appellant's opening brief must be served and filed within 30 days after the record, or the reporter's transcript after a Rule 8.124 election, is filed in the reviewing court. Cal Rules of Ct 8.212(a)(1)(A). If a reporter's transcript was not requested, the opening brief is due 70 days after filing the notice of election to proceed under Rule 8.124. Cal Rules of Ct 8.212(a)(1)(B). In all cases, the respondent's brief must be filed within 30 days after the appellant's opening brief is filed. Cal Rules of Ct 8.212(a)(2). The appellant's reply brief, if any, must be filed within 20 days after the respondent's brief is filed. Cal Rules of Ct 8.212(a)(3).

The parties may, by stipulation filed before the filing period expires, extend the time for filing each brief up to 60 days. Cal Rules of Ct 8.212(b)(1). For form of stipulation, see California Civil Appellate Practice §12.62 (3d ed Cal CEB 1996). If a stipulation cannot be obtained, or if an extension is sought beyond 60 days, an application for extension may be made to the reviewing court on a showing of good cause. Cal Rules of Ct 8.212(b)(2), 8.50(b). The showing should include documentation of any attempt to obtain a stipulated extension of time. Cal Rules of Ct 8.212(b)(2)(a).

If the appellant's opening brief is not filed when due, the appellate court clerk notifies the parties by mail that, if the brief is not filed within 15 days, the appeal will be dismissed unless good cause is shown for relief. Cal Rules of Ct 8.220(a)(1). If the respondent's brief is not filed when due, the clerk notifies the parties that the case will be submitted for decision on the record and on the appellant's opening brief, unless the brief is filed within 15 days or good cause is shown for relief. Cal Rules of Ct 8.220(a)(2).

§19.75　　2. Form and Contents

California Rules of Court 8.208 specifies requirements that must be followed in preparing a brief. Every brief must begin with a table of contents and a table of authorities, separately listing statutes, court rules, constitutional provisions, and other authorities. Each point in the brief must appear separately under an appropriate, descriptive heading. The statement of any matter in the record must be supported by an appropriate reference to the volume and page number of the record where the matter appears. If any part of the record is submitted in an electronic format, citations to that part must identify, with the same specificity required for the printed record, the place in the record where the matter appears. Cal Rules of Ct 8.208(a). The rule further sets out detailed specifications for production of the brief (Cal Rules of Ct 8.208(b)–(d)) and establishes its permitted length (Cal Rules of Ct 8.208(c)).

§19.76　　a. Appellant's Opening Brief

The importance of the appellant's opening brief cannot be overstated; if this document does not make a significant impact, the prospects of success on appeal are slight. The opening brief generally consists of four basic parts, although the length and complexity of each part will vary considerably, depending on the nature of the case:

- The *preliminary sections*, including a topical index and a table of authorities, a statement explaining why the judgment or order appealed from is immediately appealable, a brief recital of procedural facts, and, in complex cases, a short summary of the argument.

- A *statement of the case*, setting forth the basic facts of the appeal, often separated into procedural and substantive sections. In complex cases, each section may be organized under headings arranged chronologically or substantively. Every recital of fact should be supported by an accurate cite to the record by page and line number.

- A *legal argument*, addressing the prejudicial nature of each error and the authority for granting reversal or modification on the basis of each error. The argument should be organized under separate sections for each issue, with the sections progressing in a logical, persuasive sequence. Each section should be identified with a precisely descriptive, yet argumentative, heading, so that when extracted from the text, the headings create an informative and persuasive table of contents.

- A brief *conclusion*, summing up the argument if the issues are complex, and specifying the relief requested.

On preparation and for sample text of appellant's opening brief, see California Civil Appellate Practice §§12.10–12.52 (3d ed Cal CEB 1996).

§19.77   b. Respondent's Brief

In the normal briefing process, the respondent has only one opportunity to present an argument for affirming the trial court's decision: the respondent's brief. This document should not merely respond to the appellant's opening brief; it should present the respondent's issues within a conceptually independent framework, so that the appellate court can be persuaded of the respondent's position without referring to the appellant's brief. The respondent's brief follows the same general format as the opening brief (see §19.76), with the preliminary sections, a statement of the case, a legal argument, and the conclusion. The respondent should review and argue to advantage the principles of reversible error (see §19.15) and the applicable standard of review (see §§19.17–19.20) to maximize his or her position as the prevailing party in the trial court.

The respondent's brief may also request the court to decide whether the appellant was prejudiced by the error or errors relied on for reversal or modification of the judgment. A cross-appeal is not necessary in order to make this request. CCP §§43, 906.

§19.78   c. Reply Brief

An appellant's reply brief is not required by the rules of court, but it can usually be put to effective use and should be filed in most cases. Any issues that were not raised in the opening brief may not be raised in the reply brief (see, *e.g., Estate of Wallace* (1977) 74 CA3d 196, 204, 141 CR 426), but the reply brief may provide more thorough argument on issues treated summarily in the opening brief. The reply brief is also an excellent forum for discussing decisions that have been rendered or have come to counsel's attention since the time the opening brief was filed.

§19.79   d. Cross-Appeals

If a cross-appeal was taken (see §19.53), a party that is both an appellant and a respondent must combine its respondent's brief with either its appellant's opening or reply brief. Cal Rules of Ct 8.216(b)(1). Whenever any party is both an appellant and a respondent, within 20 days after the second notice of appeal is filed the parties must submit a proposed briefing sequence to the reviewing court which will order a briefing sequence in accordance with Rule 8.212(a). Cal Rules of Ct 8.216(a)(2).

§19.80   3. Filing and Service Requirements

An original and four copies of each brief must be filed with the clerk of the appellate court, along with proof of delivery of four copies to the supreme court. Cal Rules of Ct 8.212(c), 8.40(b)(2)(A). See Cal Rules of Ct 8.40(b)–(c) for manner of duplication and color of cover. The brief must be served on all other parties to the appeal; service may be made in any manner permitted in civil litigation generally. Cal Rules of Ct 8.24(a)(1); for permitted methods of service, see CCP §§1010–1020. It is good practice to serve at least two copies of the brief on each counsel. On the number of copies of supporting documents, see Cal Rules of Ct 8.40(b)(3).

E. Hearing and Determination on Appeal

§19.81   1. Oral Argument

Under Cal Const art VI, §§2–3, oral argument is accorded as a matter of right on appeal from a judgment or order. *Moles v Regents of Univ. of Cal.* (1982) 32 C3d 867, 871, 187 CR 557. The clerk of the reviewing court gives notice to the parties of the time and place set for hearing. Cal Rules of Ct 8.256(b). Although the clerk's notice may encourage waiver of oral argument, in most cases the appellant should not agree to waive argument except for the most compelling reasons. By court rule, counsel for each party is allowed 30 minutes for oral argument, unless otherwise ordered (Cal Rules of Ct 8.256(c)); in practice, however, the time allowed is frequently less.

Perhaps the most important purpose of oral argument is to persuade the court to accept counsel's view as to which facts are the most critical in the case. It is the facts that evoke the principles of law that are dispositive of the case. Counsel should have a thorough familiarity with, and the ability to readily access, the entire record and the key authorities governing each issue in the appeal. If counsel intends to rely on decisions rendered after the briefs were filed, the court and opposing counsel should be notified in writing before oral argument. If matters are raised by the court during oral argument that were not adequately addressed in the briefs, counsel should ask permission to file a supplemental letter briefing. Without court permission, briefs may not be submitted after oral argument. See *Marriage of Green* (1989) 213 CA3d 14, 28 n10, 261 CR 294.

The cause is submitted when the court has heard oral argument, or has approved a waiver of oral argument, and the time has passed for the filing of all briefs and papers, including any supplementary brief allowed by the court. Cal Rules of Ct 8.256(d)(1).

§19.82   2. Decision and Remittitur

The court of appeal is a three-judge court, and the concurrence of two judges present at the argument is necessary for a judgment. Cal Const art VI, §3. After signature by the requisite majority of judges, the opinion is filed with the appellate court clerk and, on filing, the judgment is "rendered." 9 Witkin, California Procedure, *Appeal* §722 (4th ed 1997).

The judgment of the appellate court may affirm, reverse, or modify the judgment or order appealed from; it may direct the proper judgment or order to be entered; or it may order a new trial or further proceedings. CCP §906. A successful appeal seldom results in the reviewing court's ordering entry of a new judgment; such an order may be made, if at all, when the error is one of law and does not require the reexamination of conflicting evidence. See *Pacific Home v County of Los Angeles* (1953) 41 C2d 844, 854, 264 P2d 539. More often, the appellate court reverses the judgment with or without directions and returns it to the trial court.

An appellate court decision usually becomes final 30 days after it is filed. See Cal Rules of Ct 8.264(b). After the decision is final, the appellate court clerk prepares and certifies the remittitur (a form stating the court's decision) and sends it to the trial court with a certified copy of the decision. Cal Rules of Ct 8.264(b). When the remittitur is issued, the appellate court loses jurisdiction (*Riley v Superior Court* (1957) 49 C2d 305, 310, 316 P2d 956) and the trial court is reinvested with jurisdiction, although the remittitur may define and limit the trial court's jurisdiction (*Hampton v Superior Court* (1952) 38 C2d 652, 655, 242 P2d 1). In specified circumstances, the appellate court may stay or recall the remittitur, or may order its immediate issuance. Cal Rules of Ct 8.264(c).

§19.83   3. Recovery of Costs

The "prevailing party" is generally entitled to recover costs on appeal. CCP §1034; Cal Rules of Ct 8.276(a)(1). The appellant is the prevailing party when the judgment or order is reversed in its entirety. Cal Rules of Ct 8.276(a)(2), (3). The respondent is the prevailing party when the judgment or order is affirmed or when the appeal is dismissed. Cal Rules of Ct 8.276(a)(2). Alternatively, the appellate court may award or apportion costs as it deems proper, regardless of who the prevailing party is, when "the interests of justice" so require. Cal Rules of Ct 8.276(a)(4). Costs may also be withheld or imposed as a sanction (see §19.84). Cal Rules of Ct 8.276(e).

When the appellate court specifically awards or denies costs, the clerk must enter on the record and insert in the remittitur a judgment for costs. Cal Rules of Ct 8.276(b)(1). Absent a direction by the court, the clerk must enter a judgment for costs to the prevailing party. Cal Rules of Ct 8.276(b)(1). If the clerk fails to enter judgment as required, the appellate court may recall the remittitur for correction, on motion made no later than 30 days after issuance of the remittitur or on its own motion. Cal Rules of Ct 8.276(b)(2). On remittiturs generally, see §19.82.

The party who is awarded costs must serve on the adverse party and file with the trial court a verified memorandum of costs within 40 days after notice of the remittitur is mailed to the party awarded costs. Cal Rules of Ct 8.276(d)(1). Costs actually incurred for the following items are recoverable: preparation of the record on appeal; reasonable costs for duplication of briefs; production of additional evidence; filing and notary fees and the expense of service, transmission, and filing of documents; the cost to secure a surety bond, including the premium and the cost to secure a letter of credit as collateral, unless the trial court finds that the bond was unnecessary. Cal Rules of Ct 8.276(c)(1)(A)-(E). Typing costs in preparing briefs for photocopying may be recovered as a reasonable duplication cost. *Lubetzky v Friedman* (1988) 199 CA3d 1350, 1356, 245 CR 589.

A party dissatisfied with the costs claimed may, within 15 days after service of the cost memorandum, serve and file a notice of motion to strike or tax costs in the trial court. Cal Rules of Ct 8.276(d)(2). After the costs have been taxed, or after the time for taxing costs has expired, the award of costs may be enforced in the same manner as a money judgment. Cal Rules of Ct 8.276(d)(3), 870(b)(4).

§19.84   4. Attorney Fees and Sanctions

In marital actions, the recovery of attorney fees is authorized under Fam C §2030, and it is well settled that this statute authorizes the recovery of attorney fees incurred on appeal. *Marriage of Stachon* (1978) 77 CA3d 506, 508, 143 CR 599. Although the appellate court may award attorney fees, it will usually remand to the trial court a determination of the amount of the award. See, *e.g., Marriage of Joseph* (1990) 217 CA3d 1277, 1291, 266 CR 548. Although attorney fees awarded on appeal, like those for proceedings in the trial court, are usually based on the relative circumstances of the parties (Fam C §2032; see §9.3), they may be ordered as a sanction for frustrating the policy of the law to promote settlement and encourage cooperation (Fam C §271; see §9.4). *Marriage of Green* (1989) 213 CA3d 14, 29, 261 CR 294. On attorney fees generally, see chap 9.

In general, a respondent who incurs attorney fees as a result of the appeal is more likely to receive an award than the appellant. One possible strategy on behalf of a respondent who is dependent on an attorney fee award to defend the appeal is the following: Before the opening brief is filed, a motion for attorney fees may be made in the trial court to allow the respondent to file a responsive brief. If the award is granted but the attorney fees are not paid, a motion may be made in the appellate court to stay the appeal on the ground that the respondent cannot afford an attorney. If the appeal is stayed and the attorney fees are still not paid, a motion may be brought in the appellate court to dismiss the appeal. See *Krog v Krog* (1948) 32 C2d 812, 818, 198 P2d 510; §18.27.

Sanctions on appeal may also include other penalties, including the withholding or imposing of costs. Cal Rules of Ct 8.276(e)(1). The reviewing court may impose sanctions against an attorney or a party when (1) the appeal is frivolous, (2) the appeal is taken solely for delay, (3) a party has required the inclusion in the record of a matter not reasonably material to the determination of the appeal, or (4) a party has been guilty of any other unreasonable infraction of the rules on appeals. CCP §907; Cal Rules of Ct 8.276(e)(1)(A)–(C). On determining whether an appeal is frivolous or taken solely for delay, see §19.30.

Before sanctions may be imposed, the due process requirements of a fair warning and a hearing must be observed. See *Marriage of Flaherty* (1982) 31 C3d 637, 654, 183 CR 508. On the procedure for requesting sanctions, see Cal Rules of Ct 8.276(e).

§19.85   5. Rehearing

The court of appeal may grant a rehearing in any case that is not final in that court on filing. Cal Rules of Ct 8.268(a)(1). Although a petition for rehearing is rarely granted (and, even when granted, seldom changes the result on appeal), it may be a required first step before seeking a supreme court review (see §19.121). See Cal Rules of Ct 8.500(c)(2).

A petition for rehearing must be filed and served within 15 days after (Cal Rules of Ct 8.268(b)(1)(A)–(D)):

- The court of appeal files its decision;

- A publication order restarts the finality period under Cal Rules of Ct 8.264(b)(5), if the party has not already filed a petition for rehearing;

- A modification order changes the appellate judgment under Cal Rules of Ct 8.264(c)(2);

- A consent is filed under Cal Rules of Ct 8.264(d).

The answer to the petition must be filed within 8 days after the petition is filed. Cal Rules of Ct 8.268(b)(2). If the petition is not acted on before the decision becomes final (*i.e.,* 30 days after decision is filed), it is deemed denied. Cal Rules of Ct 8.268(c). The petition and answer should conform to the requirements for the form of briefs, as far as practicable. Cal Rules of Ct 8.208, 8.268(b)(3).

§19.86   6. Publication

The court of appeal makes the initial determination of whether a decision or a part of a decision will be published in the Official Reports. If the court does not certify the opinion before it becomes final, it loses jurisdiction to do so. See Cal Rules of Ct 8.264(b)(5), 8.1105(b), 8.1110(a). To be considered for publication, a court of appeal opinion must establish a new rule of law, apply an existing rule to facts significantly different from those in other published opinions, modify or criticize an existing rule, resolve or create an apparent conflict in the law, involve a legal issue of continuing public interest, or make a significant contribution by reviewing the development of a common-law rule, constitutional provision, statute, or other written law. Cal Rules of Ct 8.1105(c).

Despite its certification for publication by the court of appeal, an opinion will *not* be published if (1) the supreme court so orders (Cal Rules of Ct 8.1105(d)(2)); (2) the opinion is superseded by a grant of review, rehearing, or other action, unless otherwise ordered by the supreme court (Cal Rules of Ct 8.1105); or (3) a request for depublication is granted (Cal Rules of Ct 8.1105).

Conversely, an opinion that has not been certified for publication by the appellate court *will* be published if the supreme court so orders (Cal Rules of Ct 8.1105(d)(2)) or if a request for publication is granted (Cal Rules of Ct 8.1120). Before requesting publication of a court of appeal opinion, counsel for the prevailing party should consider the possibility that publication may increase the likelihood of review by the supreme court.

§19.87   F. Supreme Court Review

Review of a court of appeal decision may be granted by the California Supreme Court on a party's petition for review or on the supreme court's own motion. Cal Rules of Ct 8.500(a)-(b). A petition for review must be served and filed within 10 days after the court of appeal decision becomes final as to that court. Cal Rules of Ct 8.500(e)(1). The petition must convince the supreme court that the case presents a question of sufficient importance to merit review. A party opposed to review may file an answer to the petition within 20 days after the petition is filed (Cal Rules of Ct 8.500(e)(4)), showing why the case is inappropriate for review and requesting, if desired, the determination of additional issues if it is accepted for review. If the answer presents additional issues for review, the petitioning party may reply to the answer. Cal Rules of Ct 8.500(e)(5).

The petition, answer, and reply must comply in their form, as far as practicable, with the requirements in Cal Rules of Ct 8.208. Additional requirements on form, content, length, and permitted attachments are in Cal Rules of Ct 8.504. For discussion and forms of petition and answer, see California Civil Appellate Practice §§22.24–22.44 (3d ed Cal CEB 1996). On filing and service requirements, see Cal Rules of Ct 8.500(e)–(f), 8.40(a)–(d). The fee for filing a petition is $420. Govt C §68927.

The supreme court may order review (1) to secure uniformity of decision or settle important questions of law, (2) when the court of appeal was without jurisdiction, or (3) when the court of appeal decision lacked the concurrence of the required majority of qualified judges. Cal Rules of Ct 8.500(b)(1)–(3). When review is sought by petition, the supreme court will normally not consider (1) any issue that could have been but was not timely raised in the briefs filed in the court of appeal, or (2) any issue or material fact that was omitted or misstated in the court of appeal's decision, unless such defect was raised in a petition for rehearing. Cal Rules of Ct 8.500(c)(1)–(2).

Whereas a grant of review must be by order and signed by at least four justices (Cal Rules of Ct 8.512(d)(1)), the supreme court may deny review either by order or by inaction. If the court does not rule on the petition within 60 days after the last petition for review is filed, the petition is deemed denied. Cal Rules of Ct 8.512(b)(2). Before the 60-day period or any extension expires, the court may order one or more extensions to a date not later than 90 days after the last petition is filed. Cal Rules of Ct 8.512(b)(1). On or after granting review, the court may order action in the matter deferred pending decision in another case or further order of the court. Cal Rules of Ct 8.512(d)(2). The court may also specify the issues to be briefed and argued. Cal Rules of Ct 8.516(a). Both parties must file briefs with the supreme court; they may use the briefs filed in the court of appeal or they may file new briefs on the merits. Cal Rules of Ct 8.520(a)(1)–(3). See Cal Rules of Ct 8.520 for requirements on time for filing, form, and contents of briefs. Cause will be placed on the calendar for oral argument. The cause is submitted after the court has heard oral argument or approved its waiver, and the time to file all briefs and papers has expired. Cal Rules of Ct 8.524(h).

After review, the court usually affirms, reverses, or modifies the judgment of the court of appeal. Cal Rules of Ct 8.528(a). However, the court may also dismiss review; remand the cause to a court of appeal for decision; transfer the cause to a court of appeal without decision, but with instructions on how to proceed; or, after transferring a cause to itself, retransfer the cause to a court of appeal without decision. Cal Rules of Ct 8.528(b)–(e). The supreme court's decision becomes final 30 days after it is filed unless the court specifies a different time. Cal Rules of Ct 8.532(b)(1)(A), (B). The supreme court may (but rarely does) grant a rehearing, either on its own motion or on the motion of a party made within 15 days after the decision is filed. Cal Rules of Ct 8.258(b), 8.536. When the decision becomes final, the supreme court clerk issues a remittitur and sends it to the court of appeal from which the appeal was taken. Cal Rules of Ct 8.540(b). In specified circumstances, the supreme court may stay or recall the remittitur, or may order its immediate issuance. Cal Rules of Ct 8.540(c). All supreme court opinions are published in the Official Reports. Cal Rules of Ct 8.1105(a).

§19.88 V. PROCEDURE ON APPEAL OF BIFURCATED ISSUE

In certain circumstances, a trial court in a marital action may bifurcate one or more issues, other than marital status, for determination in an early, separate trial. Cal Rules of Ct 5.175; see §14.59. Although the "one final judgment" rule normally prevents an immediate appeal from interim rulings (see §19.3), an appeal may be taken from the decision on a bifurcated issue if the trial court certifies that the appeal is appropriate, and the court of appeal accepts the issue for immediate review. Fam C §2025; Cal Rules of Ct 5.180; see *Marriage of Stevenson* (1993) 20 CA4th 250, 24 CR2d 411 (interlocutory appeal granted); *Marriage of Griffin* (1993) 15 CA4th 685, 19 CR2d 94 (interlocutory appeal dismissed because in derogation of former CC §4365 and Cal Rules of Ct 5.175–5.180; appeal may be brought following entry of judgment). The decision to bifurcate the issue for separate trial is not immediately appealable. See §19.6.

§19.89 A. Certification by Trial Court

In the trial judge's discretion, the order on the bifurcated issue may include a certification that there is probable cause for immediate appellate review of the issue. If no certification is given, a party may notice a motion requesting certification within 10 days after the clerk mails the decision on the bifurcated issue. The motion must be heard within 30 days after the order deciding the bifurcated issue was mailed. If it is not ruled on within 40 days after the order on the bifurcated issue was mailed, the motion is deemed granted. Cal Rules of Ct 5.180(b).

Certification for appeal of a bifurcated issue is within the trial judge's discretion; it is appropriate when the resolution of one issue, e.g., (1) is likely to lead to settlement of the entire case, (2) will simplify the remaining issues, (3) will conserve the courts' resources, or (4) will benefit the well-being of the parties' child or the parties. Cal Rules of Ct 5.180(b)–(c). If certification is granted, trial of the remaining issues and discovery may be stayed while the motion for appeal and the appeal itself (if accepted by the court of appeal; see §19.90) are pending. Cal Rules of Ct 5.180(c)(2). If the trial court denies certification for appeal, the decision on the bifurcated issue may still be reviewed by extraordinary writ or on appeal from the final judgment in the proceeding. Cal Rules of Ct 5.180(g)–(h).

§19.90   B. Acceptance and Determination by Court of Appeal

Within 15 days after the order granting certification is mailed, the moving party must serve and file in the court of appeal a motion to appeal the decision on the bifurcated issue. The appellate court may grant an extension of up to 20 additional days to file the motion. A copy of the motion must be served on the adverse party and the trial court. The motion must state the facts briefly, the issue, and why an immediate appeal is desirable. The motion must include the decision on the bifurcated issue, any statement of decision, the certification of the appeal, and a partial record sufficient to enable the court of appeal to rule on the motion. The motion must be accompanied by a filing fee of $200 and a transcript deposit of $50. Cal Rules of Ct 5.180(d).

An adverse party may file and serve an opposition to the motion for appeal within 10 days after service of the motion. No oral argument is permitted unless specifically ordered by the appellate court. If the appellate court does not deny the motion within 30 days after the filing of the opposition (or the last document requested by the court, whichever is later), the motion for appeal is deemed granted. Cal Rules of Ct 5.180(e).

Once the appeal is accepted, the moving party is deemed an appellant. Thereafter, all rules governing civil appeals generally apply, except as otherwise provided by Cal Rules of Ct 5.180. The appeal is decided on the basis of the partial record filed with the motion, which may be augmented on the request of a party, and on briefs filed under a schedule set by the appellate court. Cal Rules of Ct 5.180(f).

§19.91   VI. REVIEW BY EXTRAORDINARY WRIT

When an appeal is provided for by statute, it must be heard by the reviewing court as a matter of right. A writ, on the other hand, is an extraordinary remedy that the reviewing court may decline to hear on the merits. See *Babb v Superior Court* (1971) 3 C3d 841, 851, 92 CR 179. Approximately 90 percent of all writ petitions filed in the California courts of appeal are summarily denied. See 1986 Judicial Council Report to the Governor and the Legislature, pp 197–205.

A writ will generally be granted only when an appeal is not available or cannot provide adequate relief. See §19.96. The most common use of writs is to review interim rulings that are not immediately appealable. On appealability of interim rulings, see §§19.4–19.6. The advantage of a writ is that it may be requested at any time in a proceeding and, if review is granted, a ruling may be obtained immediately without waiting for final judgment or a lengthy appeal. If the petitioner is unsure whether a ruling is appealable, or whether an appeal would provide an adequate remedy, he or she may file both a notice of appeal and a writ petition. If the writ petition is granted, the appeal will become moot and may be dismissed. If the writ petition is denied, the appeal will proceed as usual.

§19.92   A. Types of Writs

Writs of mandate (also known as mandamus) (see §19.93) and writs of prohibition (see §19.94) are the most common types of extraordinary writs and have broad application in marital actions. Each writ may be issued either as an alternative writ, similar to an order to show cause (see §19.113), or as a peremptory writ, in the nature of a final ruling (see §19.112). Writs of certiorari (see §19.95), also known as writs of review, are most often used to review contempt orders (see §19.102).

§19.93   1. Mandate

The primary purpose of a writ of mandate is to enforce a plain, nondiscretionary legal duty to act, either before, during, or after trial. In marital actions, the writ is usually directed to the trial court, to force the court to perform a duty when it has failed or refused to act. The duties to be enforced by a writ of mandate may include:

- The duty to perform a ministerial act required by statute, *e.g.,* to grant a change of venue on statutory grounds (*Stauffer Chem. Co. v Superior Court* (1968) 265 CA2d 1, 71 CR 202);

- The duty to exercise discretion, *e.g.,* to hear and determine an order to show cause regarding temporary support (*Weber v Superior Court* (1960) 53 C2d 403, 406, 2 CR 9); however, mandate may not be used to direct a court to exercise its discretion in a particular manner (see *Lindell Co. v Board of Permit Appeals* (1943) 23 C2d 303, 315, 144 P2d 4); and

- The duty, in exercising discretion, not to abuse that discretion, by, *e.g.,* denying a continuance (*Whalen v Superior Court* (1960) 184 CA2d 598, 7 CR 610).

It may not always be clear whether relief should be sought by a writ of mandate or by a writ of prohibition (see §19.94). Both writs are issued by the appellate court, if at all, when immediate intervention is required to force the trial court to rule correctly. Mandate is appropriate when the court has ruled incorrectly or has not ruled at all; prohibition is proper when the trial court threatens to rule outside its jurisdiction. The petition for writ (see §19.104) is often phrased in the alternative, to request whichever writ the appellate court deems appropriate.

§19.94   2. Prohibition

A writ of prohibition may be sought to restrain judicial action that is threatened, but not completed, and is without or is in excess of the court's jurisdiction. CCP §1102. Prohibition is not available to prevent an incorrect determination of a question that is properly before the court. The "jurisdictional error" that may be prevented by a writ of prohibition is any act that exceeds the power or competency of the court. A court may act in excess of its power, and a writ of prohibition may therefore issue, even though the court has jurisdiction over the subject matter and the parties. *Abelleira v District Court of Appeal* (1941) 17 C2d 280, 288, 109 P2d 942.

In marital actions, a writ of prohibition is usually directed to the trial court, but it may also issue to restrain a lower appellate court from reviewing a matter outside its jurisdiction. 17 C2d at 287.

If counsel is unsure whether relief should be sought by a writ of prohibition or by a writ of mandate (see §19.93), the petition for writ (see §19.104) may request relief in the alternative.

§19.95   3. Certiorari

The purpose of a writ of certiorari is to review completed judicial action taken without or in excess of jurisdiction when there is no appeal or other adequate remedy. CCP §1068. The person seeking the writ of certiorari must have a beneficial interest in the outcome of the proceedings. CCP §1069. Certiorari is similar to prohibition (see §19.94) in that it lies only to review a jurisdictional defect.

Unlike prohibition, certiorari is available only when there is no right of appeal. Because most jurisdictional defects are eventually reviewable on appeal, certiorari is limited in application to the review of contempt orders (which are not appealable; see CCP §§904.1(a)(1)(B), 1222) and other nonappealable determinations. On the possibility of using certiorari to review a nonappealable interim ruling when a subsequent final judgment may be appealed, see *Howard v Superior Court* (1944) 25 C2d 784, 787, 154 P2d 849.

B. Availability of Writs

§19.96   1. No Adequate Remedy at Law

By statute, an extraordinary writ will not issue if the petitioner has a plain, speedy, and adequate remedy at law. CCP §§1068, 1086, 1103. In most cases, relief by writ will be denied because the appeal process provides an adequate remedy. Other remedies may also provide adequate relief and preclude issuance of a writ.

Whether the right to an immediate appeal precludes review by writ depends on the type of writ requested and on the facts of the case. By statute, a writ of certiorari is not available at all when an immediate appeal can be taken. CCP §1068. Writs of mandate and prohibition will be granted on an appealable matter only if the petitioner can demonstrate that, in the circumstances of the case, an appeal is an inadequate remedy.

Some of the circumstances that may, alone or in combination, justify the issuance of an extraordinary writ, depending on the specific facts of the case, are the following:

- Issues of widespread interest or of significant constitutional import are presented by the writ petition;

- The trial court's order deprives the petitioner of an opportunity to present a substantial portion of the cause of action;

- Conflicting trial court interpretations require a resolution;

- The trial court's order is both clearly erroneous and substantially prejudicial to the petitioner's case;

- The party seeking the writ lacks adequate means, such as a direct appeal, by which to attain relief; and

- The petitioner will suffer harm or prejudice that cannot be corrected on appeal.

Omaha Indem. Co. v Superior Court (1989) 209 CA3d 1266, 1273, 258 CR 66.

§19.97   2. Authorization by Statute

A number of statutes specifically authorize a request for relief by writ. Although such authorization may earn the writ petition more favorable consideration by the court, it is no guaranty that the court will review the writ on its merits. See *Laible v Superior Court* (1984) 157 CA3d 44, 46 n1, 203 CR 513. Courts retain absolute discretion to summarily deny a writ petition, regardless of statutory authorization.

Of those orders for which a request for writ review is authorized by statute, the ones most likely to arise in marital actions are (1) an order denying a motion to quash service of summons, or a motion to stay or dismiss the action for inconvenient forum (see §§10.61, 10.64) (CCP §418.10(c)); (2) an order granting or denying a motion for change of venue (see §10.63) (CCP §400); (3) an order granting or denying expungement of a lis pendens (CCP §405.39); (4) an order concerning coordination of previously unrelated actions (CCP §404.6); and (5) a ruling concerning challenges for cause under CCP §§170.1-170.8 (CCP §170.3(d)). A challenge for cause is *only* reviewable by writ and is therefore more likely to be heard on its merits. Each statute provides for the period of time within which the writ petition must be filed.

§19.98   3. Application in Marital Actions

Marital actions often involve interim rulings that require prompt resolution by the courts and have widespread legal significance to the family law bar. Therefore, although writ petitions are rarely considered on their merits (see §§19.91, 19.96), counsel in marital actions should be aware that a writ petition may, in some cases, provide appropriate and very effective relief.

§19.99   a. Custody and Visitation

Issues of custody and visitation are perhaps the most frequent subject of writ petitions in marital actions. Often, the petition will raise issues of jurisdiction under the Uniform Child Custody Jurisdiction and Enforcement Act (Fam C §§3400-3465) and the Parental Kidnapping Prevention Act of 1980 (Pub L 96-611, §§6-10, 94 Stat 3568; the relevant provisions of the Act are codified in 28 USC §1738A). For discussion, see §§7.4-7.15. The petition may also seek a writ of supersedeas or other stay pending appeal (see §§19.43-19.45), or it may request an immediate, urgent review of a trial court order. Writs have been issued to prevent forum-shopping for a more favorable custody order (*Dover v Dover* (1971) 15 CA3d 675, 93 CR 384); to restrain visitation by a stepparent (*Perry v Superior Court* (1980) 108 CA3d 480, 166 CR 583); and to restrain a trial court from requiring mediation of a custody dispute when local court rules preclude cross-examination of the court mediator (*McLaughlin v Superior Court* (1983) 140 CA3d 473, 189 CR 479).

§19.100   b. Jurisdiction

An extraordinary writ may issue in a marital action to restrain a trial court from exercising in personam jurisdiction, or to order it to do so. Under CCP §418.10(c), a writ of mandate may issue to require a trial court to quash service of summons, or to stay or dismiss the action for inconvenient forum, when the trial court has denied a party's motion for such relief. For example, a trial court that has improperly exercised personal jurisdiction over a party who lacks sufficient minimum contacts with the state may be ordered to quash service of summons and dismiss the proceedings. See *Kumar v Superior Court* (1982) 32 C3d 689, 703, 186 CR 772.

A writ of prohibition may issue to compel a trial court to vacate its order and stay further proceedings when the court has improperly exercised subject matter jurisdiction. *Perry v Superior Court* (1980) 108 CA3d 480, 166 CR 583 (prohibition issued to restrain visitation by stepparent for lack of jurisdiction); *Palm v Superior Court* (1979) 97 CA3d 456, 469, 158 CR 786 (prohibition issued to stay proceedings under former Uniform Child Custody Jurisdiction Act (former Fam C §§3400–3425) when action pending in other state).

§19.101 c. Discovery

Discovery orders are reviewable on appeal from the final judgment, but when the order involves the scope of a privilege, or a matter of general interest that is likely to recur, review may be granted by writ. See *Pacific Tel. & Tel. Co. v Superior Court* (1970) 2 C3d 161, 169, 84 CR 718. A writ is more likely to issue when discovery has been ordered, and should have been denied, than when it has been denied and should have been granted. A writ of prohibition will issue to prevent improperly ordered discovery, and a writ of mandate will issue to order improperly denied discovery.

§19.102 d. Contempt

An order of contempt is not appealable under CCP §904.1 and is therefore reviewable only by writ. Most often, review is sought by certiorari (see §19.95), but a writ of habeas corpus (*In re Jones* (1975) 47 CA3d 879, 120 CR 914) or a writ of prohibition (*Miller v Superior Court* (1937) 9 C2d 733, 72 P2d 868) may also be proper. A writ may issue to nullify a judgment of contempt (*In re Jones, supra*), to nullify an order refusing to adjudge a party in contempt (*Tilghman v Superior Court* (1974) 40 CA3d 599, 115 CR 195), or to restrain further prosecution of a contempt proceeding (*Miller v Superior Court, supra*).

§19.103   e. Other Family Law Issues

An extraordinary writ may issue to remedy a variety of errors in trial court proceedings in marital actions, including (1) the failure to grant an ex parte request for wage assignment (*Lang v Superior Court* (1984) 153 CA3d 510, 200 CR 526); (2) a refusal to vacate a dissolution decree after proof of extrinsic fraud (*Resnik v Superior Court* (1986) 185 CA3d 634, 230 CR 1); (3) an order for sale of property pendente lite without appropriate safeguards (*Lee v Superior Court* (1976) 63 CA3d 705, 134 CR 43); and (4) the failure to permit testimony after ruling, as a matter of law, that a lesbian mother was unfit for custody (*Nadler v Superior Court* (1967) 255 CA2d 523, 63 CR 352). In each of the foregoing cases, a writ of mandate issued.

C. Procedure

§19.104   1. Petition for Writ

The form and contents of a writ petition are generally the same whether the petition seeks a writ of mandate, prohibition, or certiorari, and more than one of these writs may be requested in the same petition. See Cal Rules of Ct 8.490(a), 8.384. A petition for mandate or prohibition may ask for issuance of an alternative writ (in the nature of an order to show cause; see §19.113) or a peremptory writ in the first instance (in the nature of a final judgment; see §19.112). CCP §§1087-1088, 1104. The writ petition may also include an application for a writ of supersedeas or other stay order (see discussion in §§19.43-19.45).

The petition must identify all parties to the writ proceeding, including the petitioner, the respondent, and the real party in interest. In marital actions, these parties will typically be the spouse who seeks the writ, the superior court of the county in which the proceeding is pending, and the other spouse, respectively. The petition should contain an introduction, similar to the preliminary sections in an appellant's opening brief (see §19.76), stating in narrative prose what the case is about, why other remedies are inadequate, and why relief by writ should be granted. The petition must be verified and should include points and authorities, setting forth the exact relief desired, and the legal grounds for granting it. See CCP §§1068, 1086, 1103. For complete requirements of form and content, see Cal Rules of

Ct 8.490(a)-(e); on drafting the writ petition and for sample forms, see California Civil Writ Practice, chap 7, §§10.41–10.77, App B, Forms B-1, B-3 (3d ed Cal CEB 1996).

§19.105 a. Time for Filing

When review by writ is provided by statute (see §19.97), the statute usually specifies the time within which the petition for the writ must be filed. In other instances, however, appellate courts generally expect the petition for an extraordinary writ to be filed as soon as possible, but no later than the 60-calendar-day period that applies to the filing of appeals. See *Popelka, Allard, McCowan & Jones v Superior Court* (1980) 107 CA3d 496, 499, 165 CR 748. But see *Peterson v Superior Court* (1982) 31 C3d 147, 164, 181 CR 784 (prejudice must be shown to deny petition solely because it is untimely). An answer to the writ petition may raise the equitable doctrine of laches, even when statutory deadlines are met. See *People v Department of Hous. & Community Dev.* (1975) 45 CA3d 185, 194, 119 CR 266, 272. When applicable, statutes of limitation may also be raised in a writ proceeding. CCP §1109; *Dillon v Board of Pension Comm'rs* (1941) 18 C2d 427, 430, 116 P2d 37, 39.

§19.106 b. Supporting Documents

The writ petition must be accompanied by a memorandum of points and authorities (Cal Rules of Ct 8.490(b)(5)) and proof of service on the respondent and the real party in interest (Cal Rules of Ct 8.490(f); see §19.104), and the record must include a copy of the ruling from which relief is sought, copies of all documents and exhibits submitted to the trial court supporting and opposing the petitioner's position, copies of any other documents or portions of documents submitted to the trial court that are necessary for a complete understanding of the case and the ruling under review, and a reporter's transcript of the oral proceedings that resulted in the ruling under review (Cal Rules of Ct 8.490(c)(1)). In urgent circumstances, a petition may be filed without these documents if it is accompanied by counsel's declaration explaining the nature of the urgency, the unavailability of the documents, and a summary of their substance. Cal Rules of Ct 8.490(c)(4). If a transcript is unavailable, counsel may substitute an explanation of its unavailability and a summary of the proceedings, or a declaration explaining when the transcript will become available. Cal Rules of Ct 8.490(c)(2)(A), (B). On required format for supporting documents, see Cal Rules of Ct 8.490(d).

§19.107 c. Filing and Service Requirements

An original and four copies of the writ petition are filed in the court of appeal. Cal Rules of Ct 8.40(b)(2)(A). The fee for filing a petition in the court of appeal is $485. Govt C §68926. The petition and one set of supporting documents must be served on the respondent and any real party in interest, unless the respondent is the superior court or a judge of that court, in which case only the petition must be served on the respondent. Cal Rules of Ct 8.490(f)(1), (2). Because the writ petition commences a new proceeding, it may be wise to serve the parties as well as their attorneys. A petition that seeks an immediate stay should be served by personal delivery on counsel. Service on the respondent court is usually made by service on the court clerk; a courtesy copy should be delivered to the trial judge.

The court in its discretion may allow the petition to be filed without service. CCP §1107; Cal Rules of Ct 8.490(f)(6). However, if a writ of mandate or prohibition is allowed without notice to the adverse party, an alternative writ (see §19.113) must first issue. A peremptory writ (see §19.112) may not issue in the first instance until the adverse parties receive notice, from the petitioner or from the court, that issuance of a peremptory writ is being sought or considered. *Palma v U.S. Indus. Fasteners, Inc.* (1984) 36 C3d 171, 180, 203 CR 626, 631. See discussion in §19.112. A writ of certiorari, however, may be granted without notice to the adverse party. CCP §1069.

§19.108 2. Preliminary Opposition

If an alternative writ of mandate or prohibition is sought (see §19.113), the respondent and any real party in interest, within 5 calendar days after the petition is served and filed, may serve and file a preliminary opposition to issuance of the writ. Unless requested by the court, a preliminary opposition is not required to be filed, and the court may grant an alternative writ or a writ of certiorari without waiting for its filing. If the real party in interest wishes to oppose a stay order that has been requested, or argue that a writ should not issue because other adequate remedies exist, a preliminary opposition should be filed immediately. Once an alternative writ issues, it constitutes a determination that there is no other adequate remedy. *Langford v Superior Court* (1987) 43 C3d 21, 27, 233 CR 387. On form and contents of a preliminary opposition, see Cal Rules of Ct 8.490(g).

In deciding whether to file a preliminary opposition, counsel must consider local appellate court practices and procedures. In particular, counsel should ascertain the frequency with which the court, instead of issuing an alternative writ, will either summarily deny the writ petition (see §19.110) or issue a *"Palma* letter," giving notice that it may issue a peremptory writ in the first instance (see §19.112). Where this approach is common, a respondent may have only one opportunity to file an opposition before the court makes a decision on the merits. In these circumstances, it may be better not to file a preliminary opposition but to wait for the appellate court to give notice that a peremptory writ may issue and, if it does so, to then file a complete return. See §19.114. See *Palma v U.S. Indus. Fasteners, Inc.* (1984) 36 C3d 171, 180, 203 CR 626, and Cal Rules of Ct 8.490(h).

§19.109 3. Action on Petition by Reviewing Court

In response to a petition for an extraordinary writ, the reviewing court may (1) summarily deny the petition, (2) issue a temporary stay order, (3) give notice that the court may issue a peremptory writ in the first instance, or (4) grant a hearing on the merits by issuing an alternative writ or a writ of certiorari. There is no hearing at this stage of the proceedings; although a conference may be held to consider the points and authorities submitted by the parties, no attorneys would be present.

§19.110 a. Summary Denial

Approximately 90 percent of all writ petitions filed in the California courts of appeal are summarily denied. See 1986 Judicial Council Report to the Governor and the Legislature, pp 197–205. The denial is made by order and, in most cases, no written statement of reasons is given. The summary denial is final immediately on the clerk's filing of the order. Cal Rules of Ct 8.264(b). The sole avenue for further review is by petitioning for review in the California Supreme

Court (see §19.121); such a petition must be filed within 10 days after the summary denial order becomes final. Although petitions for review are rarely granted, the supreme court may order the matter transferred back to the court of appeal with instructions for further proceedings.

Note that a summary denial of a pretrial writ petition does not establish law of the case precluding reconsideration of the issue on appeal following judgment. *Kowis v Howard* (1992) 3 C4th 888, 891, 12 CR2d 728, 729.

§19.111   b. Temporary Stay

The reviewing court may issue a temporary stay order without first issuing an alternative writ or an order to show cause. The stay order will usually issue when the reviewing court is considering issuance of a peremptory writ in the first instance, or when an immediate stay is required so that the case does not become moot before the court decides whether to rule on the merits of the petition. A temporary stay generally remains in effect until the petition is decided on the merits, or until further order of the court.

§19.112   c. Notice That Peremptory Writ May Issue

The court of appeal may give notice (known as *Palma* notice) that the court may issue a peremptory writ in the first instance, *i.e.,* without first issuing an alternative writ. See CCP §§1087–1088, 1104, 1107; *Palma v U.S. Indus. Fasteners, Inc.* (1984) 36 C3d 171, 178, 203 CR 626. The California Supreme Court has indicated, however, that this accelerated procedure is the exception and should not become routine. Generally, it should be adopted only when the petitioner's entitlement to relief is obvious or when there is an unusual urgency requiring acceleration of the normal process. *Alexander v Superior Court* (1993) 5 C4th 1218, 1223, 23 CR2d 397, disapproved on other grounds in *Hassan v Mercy Am. River Hosp.* (2003) 31 C4th 709, 724 n4, 3 CR3d 623. If *Palma* notice is given, the adverse parties must receive at least 10 calendar days' notice before the peremptory writ is granted. CCP §1088; 36 C3d at 178, 203 CR at 630. After giving *Palma* notice, the court may still summarily deny the petition, it may decide to hold oral argument, or it may issue an opinion and order directing that a peremptory writ issue. On filing an opposition when *Palma* notice is given, see §19.114.

§19.113　　d. Issuance of Alternative Writ or Writ of Certiorari

An alternative writ is an order issued by the reviewing court, instructing the respondent trial court to comply with the directions in the alternative writ or to show cause why it should not be ordered to do so. CCP §§1087–1088 (mandate); 1104 (prohibition); *Palma v U.S. Indus. Fasteners, Inc.* (1984) 36 C3d 171, 177, 203 CR 626. The granting of the alternative writ constitutes a determination that there is no other adequate remedy at law. *Langford v Superior Court* (1987) 43 C3d 21, 27, 233 CR 387. An alternative writ is not, however, a determination of the petition on the merits. If the trial court does not comply with the alternative writ, the real party in interest must file a "return" (see §19.114), showing cause why the trial court's order is proper. The reviewing court must then decide whether to issue a peremptory writ on the merits, usually after oral argument (see §19.116). See *Krueger v Superior Court* (1979) 89 CA3d 934, 939, 152 CR 870.

There is no alternative writ of certiorari. The court may grant a writ of certiorari without notice, require that notice be given to the adverse party, or grant an order to show cause why the writ should not be allowed. CCP §1069. If the court grants the writ, it usually gives a deadline within which the respondent court must provide the record (see §19.114), and a subsequent hearing is held (see §19.117).

§19.114　　4. Return on Writ

When the reviewing court decides that it will rule on the merits of a writ petition, the respondent or the real party in interest may file a "return." Cal Rules of Ct 56(h). The return is the opportunity of the adverse parties to respond to the petition on the merits. Traditionally, it consists of a verified answer, a demurrer, or a combined answer and demurrer, together with points and authorities and any exhibits and declarations necessary to counter the allegations made in the petition. If the return is by demurrer alone and the demurrer is overruled, a peremptory writ may issue without leave to answer. Cal Rules of Ct 8.490(h)(4). For sample return, see California Civil Writ Practice, App B, Form B-6 (3d ed Cal CEB 1996); for sample demurrer, see Civ Writ Prac, App B, Form B-2. In some districts, a formal return is rarely filed; instead, the respondent files points and authorities in response to the writ petition after receiving notice that the court will consider the petition on its merits.

When an alternative writ has issued (see §19.113), or when the parties have been given *Palma* notice that a peremptory writ may issue (see §19.112), the return must be filed within 30 days after the court issues the alternative writ or order to show cause or notifies the parties that it is considering issuing a peremptory writ in the first instance. Cal Rules of Ct 8.490(h)(2). Unless the court orders otherwise, the petitioner may serve and file a reply within 15 days after the return or opposition is filed. Cal Rules of Ct 8.490(h)(3). When the petition requests the issuance of a peremptory writ in the first instance, the return is due 30 days after service of the petition or, if a record of the proceeding has been requested, 30 days after receipt of a copy of the record. CCP §§1089.5, 1105. If a writ of certiorari has issued, the return must be filed by the respondent trial court and consists of the record, which is usually the transcript of the proceedings in that court. The adverse parties may also file an answering pleading, raising legal issues in opposition to the writ of certiorari. Responsive pleadings are usually served by mail on the petitioner and other parties.

§19.115   5. Reply

California Rules of Court 8.490 specifically allows the petitioner to file a reply unless the court orders otherwise. Cal Rules of Ct 8.490(h)(3). Local rules and practice on continuances should be consulted. The reply should respond only to points raised in the opposition and should not raise new issues.

6. Hearing and Determination on Merits

§19.116   a. Mandate and Prohibition

An application for a writ of mandate or prohibition must be heard by the court whether the adverse party appears or not. CCP §§1088, 1105. However, the case may be "heard" on the papers of the applicant (CCP §1094), which is the usual practice when the court considers the petition on its merits (see §19.112) without first issuing an alternative writ (see §19.113). When an alternative writ does issue, oral argument is normally scheduled and will be specified in the alternative writ or in a separate document sent by the court. If the court does not set oral argument, counsel may request that it do so; whether the request is granted is a matter of discretion with the court.

The matter is deemed submitted to the court after oral argument is held or waived and all papers have been filed, or the time for filing has elapsed. Cal Rules of Ct 8.256(d). The court's opinion should be issued within 90 calendar days after the submission date. Cal Const art VI, §19; Govt C §68210. When the court rules in the petitioner's favor and grants prohibition or mandate, the opinion will direct the issuance of a peremptory writ. In some districts, the court may simply file the opinion and transmit a certified copy of the opinion to the lower court. In other districts, the court may direct the petitioner to prepare the peremptory writ. Local rules and the court clerk should be checked to ascertain local practice.

A decision of the court of appeal becomes final regarding that court 30 days after the opinion is filed. Cal Rules of Ct 8.264(b). However, the court of appeal may order earlier finality to prevent mootness or to prevent frustration of the relief granted (Cal Rules of Ct 8.264(b)(3)).

§19.117   b. Certiorari

When a full return has been made on a writ of certiorari (see §19.114), the court must hear oral argument of the parties and make its determination. CCP §1075. The hearing date will be set in the writ or in a separate document sent by the court. The court may affirm, annul, or modify the proceedings in the trial court, but the scope of its judgment cannot exceed a determination of whether the trial court acted within its jurisdiction. CCP §§1074–1075. On finality of the decision, see §19.116.

§19.118   7. Rehearing; Remittitur

Within 15 calendar days after the decision is filed, a petition for rehearing may be served and filed in the court of appeal. Cal Rules of Ct 8.268(b). An answer to the petition for rehearing may be served and filed within 23 calendar days (meaning 8 days after the petition for rehearing is served and filed in court of appeal) from when the decision is filed. Cal Rules of Ct 8.268(b)(2). The petition for rehearing and the answer must conform, as far as practicable, to the format requirements of Cal Rules of Ct 8.240. If no order is made before the decision becomes final (see §19.116), the petition for rehearing is deemed denied by operation of law. Cal Rules of Ct 8.268(c).

After the decision on the writ petition becomes final, the clerk of the reviewing court issues a remittitur and mails notice to the parties that the remittitur has issued. Cal Rules of Ct 8.272(d). On remittiturs generally, see §19.82. For practical purposes, transmission of the remittitur to the trial court is usually sufficient notice to compel obedience to the reviewing court's ruling and, in most cases, it is unnecessary to issue the writ itself. If a writ does issue, it should be served in the same manner as a summons in a civil action, unless the court expressly directs otherwise. CCP §1096. On enforcing compliance with the writ, see California Civil Writ Practice, chap 11 (3d ed Cal CEB 1996).

8. Review by California Supreme Court

§19.119   a. Petition for Original Writ

The filing of original writ petitions in the California Supreme Court is discouraged; writ petitions should normally be filed in the lowest court capable of granting relief. However, an original writ petition may be filed in the supreme court if (1) relief is sought against a court of appeal; (2) the relief requested is of extraordinary public importance or of an urgent or emergency nature; (3) the petition raises questions similar to those raised in a case pending before the supreme court; or (4) review by the supreme court is specifically provided by statute, *e.g.,* review of actions by the State Bar Court (Bus & P C §6082). The procedures for filing an original writ in the supreme court are basically the same as those for filing in a court of appeal (see Cal Rules of Ct 8.490); however, the original of the petition for writ that is filed in the supreme court must be accompanied by 13 copies (Cal Rules of Ct 8.40(b)(1)(A)). The only exception is a petition for review to exhaust state remedies under rule 8.360, which requires an original and 8 copies. Cal Rules of Ct 8.40(b)(1)(D).

§19.120   b. Transfer of Pending Cause

On its own motion, or on the petition of a party, the supreme court may transfer to itself a cause pending in a court of appeal.

Cal Rules of Ct 8.552(a). Transfer will be ordered only if the cause presents issues of "great public importance that the Supreme Court must promptly resolve." Cal Rules of Ct 8.552(c). On form and procedure for transfer, see Cal Rules of Ct 8.552(d).

§19.121 c. Review of Court of Appeal Decision

A party may petition the California Supreme Court for review of a decision of a court of appeal after summary denial (see §19.110), after issuance of an opinion on the merits (see §§19.116–19.117), or after denial of a petition for rehearing (see §19.118). Although the supreme court rarely grants review, it may transfer the cause back to the appellate court with instructions for further proceedings when the petition seeks review of a court of appeal's summary denial of a writ petition.

The petition must be served and filed within 10 days after the court of appeal decision becomes final (see §19.116). The opposing party may file an answer to the petition for review and the petitioner may file a reply. Cal Rules of Ct 8.500(a)(2)–(3) (permitting petitioner to file reply, even if answer does not raise additional issues for review). On form of pleadings for review, see Cal Rules of Ct 8.504. If no petition for review is filed, the supreme court may also, on its own motion, order review of the appellate court decision. See Cal Rules of Ct 8.512(c).

Once a petition for review is filed, the supreme court has 60 calendar days, which may be extended to a total of 90 calendar days, within which to decide whether to grant review. Cal Rules of Ct 8.512(b)(1). If no order is made within the period for granting review, the petition is deemed denied. Cal Rules of Ct 8.512(b)(2). If the petition for review is granted, briefs are filed by both parties, the cause is placed on calendar for oral argument, or the court approves waiver of oral argument. See Cal Rules of Ct 8.516, 8.524. Following oral argument, the supreme court usually issues a written opinion that affirms, reverses, or modifies the appellate court's judgment. See Cal Rules of Ct 8.528(a).

A party who is dissatisfied with the judgment may petition for rehearing (Cal Rules of Ct 8.536); however, rehearings are rarely granted. After the judgment becomes final, a remittitur will issue. Cal Rules of Ct 8.540. On remittiturs generally, see §19.82. The supreme court decision becomes final 30 calendar days after it is filed, unless the court makes an order shortening or extending this period. Cal Rules of Ct 8.532(b)(1)(A), (B).

Rather than ruling on a matter after a petition for review is granted, the supreme court may dismiss review (Cal Rules of Ct 8.528(b)); transfer the matter to the court of appeal with instructions for further proceedings (Cal Rules of Ct 8.528(d)); or, if it had transferred the cause to itself, retransfer it to a court of appeal. Cal Rules of Ct 8.528(e).

20

Enforcement

§20.1 I. SCOPE OF CHAPTER

When a party does not voluntarily comply with court orders, the other party may find it necessary to undertake efforts to enforce the orders. This chapter surveys the methods available to a party seeking to enforce orders obtained in a marital action.

Although a judgment of dissolution may order a party to pay an obligation directly to a creditor, the parties, not the creditor, have the right to enforce the judgment. Fam C §2023; *Pinson v Cole* (2003) 106 CA4th 494, 131 CR2d 113 (ex-wife's creditor could not enforce order that husband pay creditor). On when a creditor can seek to set aside a property transfer for violation of the Uniform Fraudulent Transfer Act (CC §§3439–3439.12), see §18.61.

NOTE➤ Practitioners should be aware that there are federal criminal implications associated with failure to pay certain child support obligations for a child who lives in another state. See the Child Support Recovery Act of 1992 (CSRA) (18 USC §228), a portion of which imposes sanctions on any person who "willfully fails to pay a support obligation with respect to a child who resides in another State, if such obligation has remained unpaid for a period of longer than 1 year, or is greater than $5,000." 18 USCS §228(a)(1). See also *U.S. v Kerley* (2d Cir 2005) 416 F3d 176; *U.S. v Venturella* (2d Cir 2004) 391 F3d 120 (discussing CRSA, as amended by Deadbeat Parents Punishment Act of 1998); *U.S. v Stephens* (9th Cir 2004) 374 F3d 867.

II. METHODS OF ENFORCEMENT

§20.2 A. Earnings Assignment Order for Support

An earnings assignment order for support, also referred to in the statutes as an "assignment order" and commonly referred to as a "wage assignment," is available for enforcement of orders for child, spousal, partner, and family support (see Fam C §§150, 297.5, 5202,

5208; Comment to Fam C §5208) and is probably the most effective and commonly used enforcement method. It has traditionally been prepared on a Judicial Council form regardless of whether child, spousal, or family support orders were being enforced. Effective January 1, 2000, however, all earnings assignment orders for support in any action in which child or family support is ordered must be issued on a form of Order/Notice to Withhold Income for Child Support mandated by 42 USC §666 (see in particular 42 USC §666(b)(6)(A)(ii)). Fam C §5208(b). For form, see §20.5. The Judicial Council form has been revised, effective January 1, 2000, to limit its use to enforcement of spousal support. For form, see §20.5A.

Note that an earnings assignment order for support issued by a court or administrative agency of another state is binding on an employer of the obligee to the same extent as an earnings assignment order made by a California court. Fam C §5230.1.

When an earnings assignment order for support is to be directed at a private employee pension plan, the attorney should use the Judicial Council forms of Qualified Domestic Relations Order for Support and Attachment, provided in §§17.79A–17.79B.

1. Assignment Order; Stay of Service

§20.3   **a. When Support Order Made on or After July 1, 1990**

Effective July 1, 1990, any order for child, spousal, or family support must include an earnings assignment order for support. This requirement applies both to initial orders and to orders modifying existing orders, regardless of when any earlier orders may have been made. The assignment order must be in an amount sufficient to pay the current support order and, when there is any existing arrearage, must include an amount to be paid toward its liquidation. Fam C §5230.

On a finding of good cause, the court may order that service of the assignment order be stayed. Fam C §5260(a). For this purpose, however, a finding of "good cause" requires that all the following conditions exist:

- The court provides a written explanation of why the stay would be in the child's best interests. Fam C §5260(b)(1)(A).

- The obligor has a history of uninterrupted, full, and timely payment, other than through an assignment order or other mandatory process, of previously ordered support during the preceding 12 months. Fam C §5260(b)(1)(B). A "timely" payment is one that is received within 5 days after the due date. Fam C §5220.

- The obligor does not owe any arrearage for prior support. Fam C §5260(b)(1)(C).

- The obligor establishes, by clear and convincing evidence, that service of the assignment order would cause him or her extraordinary hardship. Whenever possible, the court must specify a date on which any stay ordered for this reason will automatically terminate. Fam C §5260(b)(1)(D).

Alternatively, the court may order that service of the assignment order be stayed if the parties provide by written agreement for an arrangement, other than immediate service of the assignment order, to ensure payment as ordered. Fam C §5260(a), (b)(2). Such an agreement may not preclude the obligee from seeking a termination of the stay, as provided in Fam C §5261 and discussed below, if the agreement is violated. The local child support agency must concur with the agreement if support is ordered to be paid through a designated county officer. Fam C §5260(b)(2).

When service of an assignment order has been ordered stayed, the stay will terminate (Fam C §5261(a)-(b)):

- On the filing of a declaration by the obligee under penalty of perjury that the obligor is in arrears in payment of any portion of the support;

- On the request of the local child support agency or the obligor; or

- On the request of the obligee if he or she can establish that good cause to stay service, as defined by Fam C §5260 and discussed above, no longer exists.

An application for a stay of service of an assignment order, or for termination of a stay, is prepared on the Judicial Council form of Stay of Service of Wage Assignment Order and Order (see form in §20.6).

When it is necessary to file an application for an assignment order, an ex parte application may be prepared on the Judicial Council form of Ex Parte Application for Earnings Assignment Order (see form in §20.7).

§20.4 b. When Support Order Made Before July 1, 1990

When a current support order, whether an initial order or a modification, was issued before July 1, 1990, and the court that issued the order did not issue an earnings assignment order for support, the obligee may file an application for an assignment order under Fam C §§5250–5253. The application is made on the Judicial Council form of Ex Parte Application for Earnings Assignment Order (see form in §20.7). An assignment order may be issued under Fam C §§5250–5253, however, only if one of three requirements is met (Fam C §5252(a)):

- The application, signed by the obligee under penalty of perjury, states that the obligor is in default in support payments in a sum equal to the amount of support payable for 1 month;

- The obligee's application states under penalty of perjury that the obligor is in default as a result of some other occurrence specified in the support order; or

- The assignment order is requested by the local child support agency or the obligor.

Likewise, before an assignment order may be issued under Fam C §§5250–5253, the application must state that the obligee has given the obligor written notice of his or her intent to seek an assignment order in the event of a default in support payments and that the notice was transmitted by first-class mail, postage prepaid, or was personally served, at least 15 days before the application was filed. The notice may be given at any time, including the time of filing a petition in which support is requested or any time thereafter. The obligor may waive the requirement of written notice at any time. Fam C §5252(b).

It may be that the obligor was served with a Judicial Council form containing a warning that an assignment order would be issued in the event of a default in specified support payments. For example, before it was revised, effective January 1, 1993, the Judicial Council form of Judgment contained the following warning: "If you fail to pay any court-ordered child support, an assignment of your wages will be obtained without further notice to you." Some commentators have taken the position that such warnings constitute the requisite notice for issuance of an assignment order based on a support order made before July 1, 1990. But until there is case-law support for that position, the safer course is to provide a notice specifically intended to comply with Fam C §5252(b). For a sample form of notice, see §20.8.

On receipt of the application, the court must issue the assignment order. The amount ordered to be assigned must be sufficient to pay both the monthly amount due for current support and an amount to be applied toward any arrearage. Fam C §5253. There is no provision for a court to order that service of an assignment order under Fam C §§5250–5253, unlike one under Fam C §5230 (see §20.3), be stayed.

§20.5   c. Form: Order/Notice to Withhold Income for Child Support (Judicial Council Form FL-195/ OMB 0970-0154) and Instructions with Sample Order/ Notice (FL-196/ OMB 0970-0154)

Form begins on next page.

FL-195
OMB Control No.: 0970-0154

☐ ORDER/NOTICE TO WITHHOLD INCOME FOR CHILD SUPPORT
☐ NOTICE OF AN ORDER TO WITHHOLD INCOME FOR CHILD SUPPORT

☐ Original　　☐ Amended　☐ Termination　Date:_____
　State/Tribe/Territory_____
　City/Co./Dist./Reservation_____
☐ Non-governmental entity or individual _____
　Case Number_____

RE :

Employer's/Withholder's Name	Employee's/Obligor's Name (Last, First, MI)
Employer's/Withholder's Address	Employee's/Obligor's Social Security Number
	Employee's/Obligor's Case Identifier
Employer's/Withholder's Federal EIN Number (if known)	Obligee's Name (Last, First, MI)

ORDER INFORMATION: This document is based on the support or withholding order from _____.
You are required by law to deduct these amounts from the employee's/obligor's income until further notice.
$_____ Per _____ current child support
$_____ Per _____ past-due child support - Arrears greater than12 weeks? ☐ yes ☐ no
$_____ Per _____ current cash medical support
$_____ Per _____ past-due cash medical support
$_____ Per _____ spousal support
$_____ Per _____ past-due spousal support
$_____ Per _____ other (specify) _____
for a total of $_____ per _____ to be forwarded to the payee below.
You do not have to vary your pay cycle to be in compliance with the support order. If your pay cycle does not match the ordered payment cycle, withhold one of the following amounts:
$_____per weekly pay period.　　　　$_____per semimonthly pay period (twice a month).
$_____per biweekly pay period (every two weeks).$_____per monthly pay period.

REMITTANCE INFORMATION: When remitting payment, provide the pay date/date of withholding and the case identifier. If the employee's/obligor's principal place of employment is _____, begin withholding no later than the first pay period occurring_____ days after the date of _____. Send payment within_____working days of the pay date/date of withholding. The total withheld amount, including your fee, may not exceed_____% of the employee's/obligor's aggregate disposable weekly earnings.

If the employee's/obligor's principal place of employment is not _____, for limitations on withholding, applicable time requirements, and any allowable employer fees, follow the laws and procedures of the employee's/obligor's principal place of employment (see #3 and #9, ADDITIONAL INFORMATION TO EMPLOYERS AND OTHER WITHHOLDERS).

Make check payable to: (Payee and Case identifier) _____ Send check to: _____. If remitting payment by EFT/EDI, call _____before first submission. Use this FIPS code:_____:
Bank routing number: _____ Bank account number:_____.

If this is an Order/Notice to Withhold:　　　　**If this is a Notice of an Order to Withhold:**
Print Name _____　　　　　　　　Print Name_____
Title of Issuing Official_____　　　　Title (if appropriate)_____
Signature and Date _____　　　　　　Signature and Date_____
☐ IV-D Agency ☐ Court　　　　　☐ Attorney ☐ Individual ☐ Private Entity
☐ Attorney with authority under state law to issue order/notice.

NOTE: Non-IV-D Attorneys, individuals, and non-governmental entities must submit a Notice of an Order to Withhold and include a copy of the income withholding order unless, under a state's law, an attorney in that state may issue an income withholding order. In that case, the attorney may submit an Order/Notice to Withhold and include a copy of the state law

IMPORTANT: The person completing this form is advised that the information on this form may be shared with the obligor authorizing the attorney to issue an income withholding order/notice.

OMB 0970-0154

FL-195 Page 1 of 2

FL-195 / OMB Control No.: 0970-0154

ADDITIONAL INFORMATION TO EMPLOYERS AND OTHER WITHHOLDERS

☐ If checked, you are required to provide a copy of this form to your employee/obligor. If your employee works in a state that is different from the state that issued this order, a copy must be provided to your employee/obligor even if the box is not checked.

1. **Priority:** Withholding under this Order or Notice has priority over any other legal process under state law (or tribal law, if applicable) against the same income. If there are federal tax levies in effect, please notify the contact person listed below. (See 10 below.)

2. **Combining Payments:** You may combine withheld amounts from more than one employee's/obligor's income in a single payment to each agency/party requesting withholding. You must, however, separately identify the portion of the single payment that is attributable to each employee/obligor.

3. **Reporting the Paydate/Date of Withholding:** You must report the paydate/date of withholding when sending the payment. The paydate/date of withholding is the date on which the amount was withheld from the employee's wages. You must comply with the law of the state of employee's/obligor's principal place of employment with respect to the time periods within which you must implement the withholding and forward the support payments.

4. **Employee/Obligor with Multiple Support Withholdings:** If there is more than one Order or Notice against this employee/obligor and you are unable to honor all support Orders or Notices due to withholding limits, you must follow the state or tribal law/procedure of the employee's/obligor's principal place of employment. You must honor all Orders or Notices to the greatest extent possible. (See 9 below.)

5. **Termination Notification:** You must promptly notify the Child Support Enforcement (IV-D) Agency and/or the contact person listed below when the employee/obligor no longer works for you. Please provide the information requested and return a complete copy of this Order or Notice to the Child Support Enforcement (IV-D) Agency and/or the contact person listed below. (See 10 below.)

   THE EMPLOYEE/OBLIGOR NO LONGER WORKS FOR:_____
   EMPLOYEE'S/OBLIGOR'S NAME: _____ CASE IDENTIFIER: _____
   DATE OF SEPARATION FROM EMPLOYMENT: _____
   LAST KNOWN HOME ADDRESS: _____
   NEW EMPLOYER/ADDRESS: _____

6. **Lump Sum Payments:** You may be required to report and withhold from lump sum payments such as bonuses, commissions, or severance pay. If you have any questions about lump sum payments, contact the Child Support Enforcement (IV-D) Agency.

7. **Liability :** If you have any doubts about the validity of the Order or Notice, contact the agency or person listed below under 10. If you fail to withhold income as the Order or Notice directs, you are liable for both the accumulated amount you should have withheld from the employee's/obligor's income and any other penalties set by state or tribal law/procedure.

8. **Anti-discrimination:** You are subject to a fine determined under state or tribal law for discharging an employee/obligor from employment, refusing to employ, or taking disciplinary action against any employee/obligor because of a child support withholding.

9. **Withholding Limits:** For state orders, you may not withhold more than the lesser of: 1) the amounts allowed by the Federal Consumer Credit Protection Act (15 U.S.C. § 1673(b)); or 2) the amounts allowed by the state of the employee's/obligor's principal place of employment. The federal limit applies to the aggregate disposable weekly earnings (ADWE). ADWE is the net income left after making mandatory deductions such as: state, federal, local taxes, Social Security taxes, statutory pension contributions, and Medicare taxes. The Federal CCPA limit is 50% of the ADWE for child support and alimony, which is increased by 1) 10% if the employee does not support a second family; and/or 2) 5% if arrears greater than 12 weeks.
   For tribal orders, you may not withhold more than the amounts allowed under the law of the issuing tribe. For tribal employers who receive a state order, you may not withhold more than the amounts allowed under the law of the state that issued the order.

   Child(ren)'s Names and Additional Information:_____

10. If you or your employee/obligor have any questions, contact_____ by telephone at
    _____ by Fax at _____ or by internet at_____.

FL-195 Page 2 of 2

FL-196
OMB Control No.: 0970-0154

*Instructions to complete the Order/Notice to Withhold Income for Child Support
or Notice of an Order to Withhold Income for Child Support*

The Order/Notice to Withhold Income for Child Support (Order/Notice) or Notice of an Order to
Withhold Income for Child Support (Notice) is a standardized form used for income withholding in
tribal, intrastate, interstate, and intergovernmental cases. Please note that information provided on
this form may be shared with the obligor. When completing the form, please include the following
information.

**The following information 1a – 1g refers to the government agency, non-government entity, or
individual completing and sending this form to the employer.**

1a.   Check whether this is an Order/Notice to Withhold Income for Child Support or a Notice of an
Order to Withhold Income for Child Support. Attorneys, individuals, and non-governmental
entities must submit a Notice of an Order to Withhold and include a copy of the income
withholding order unless, under a state's law, an attorney in that state may issue an income
withholding order/notice. In that case, the attorney may submit an Order/Notice to Withhold
and include a copy of the state law authorizing the attorney to issue an income withholding
order/notice.

1b.   Check the appropriate status of the Order or Notice.

1c.   Date this form is completed and/or signed.

1d.   Name of the state, tribe or territory sending this form. This must be a governmental entity.

1e.   Name of the county, city, district, or reservation sending this Order or Notice, if appropriate.
This must be a governmental entity.

1f.   Check and indicate the non-governmental entity or individual sending this Order or Notice.
Complete this item only if a non-governmental entity or individual is submitting this Order or
Notice.

1g.   Identifying case number used by the entity or individual sending this Order or Notice. In a IV-D
case, this must be the IV-D case number.

**The following information in 2 and 3 refers to the obligor, obligor's employer, and case
identification.**

2a.   Employer's/Withholder's name.

2b-c.   Employer's/Withholder's mailing address, city, and state. (This may differ from the
Employee's/Obligor's work site.)

2d.   Employer's/Withholder's nine-digit federal employer identification number (if available). Include
three-digit location code.

1

OMB 0970-0154

FL-196 / OMB Control No.: 0970-0154

3a. Employee's/Obligor's last name, first name, and middle initial.

3b. Employee's/Obligor's Social Security Number (if known).

3c. The case identifier used by the order issuing state or tribe for recording payments. (Should be the same as #21.) In a IV-D case, this must be the IV-D case number.

3d. Custodial Parent's last name, first name, and middle initial (if known).

ORDER INFORMATION - **The following information in 4 -14e refers to the dollar amounts taken directly from the child support order.**

4. Name of the state or tribe that issued the support order.

5a-b. Dollar amount to be withheld for payment of current child support, time period that corresponds to the amount in #6a (such as month, week, etc.).

6a-b. Dollar amount to be withheld for payment of past-due child support, time period that corresponds to the amount in #6a (such as month, week, etc.).

7a-b. Dollar amount to be withheld for payment of current cash medical support, as appropriate, based on the underlying order, time period that corresponds to the amount in #7a (such as month, week, etc.).

8a-b. Dollar amount to be withheld for payment of past-due cash medical support, if appropriate, based on the underlying order and the time period that corresponds to the amount in #8a (such as month, week, etc.).

9a-b. Dollar amount to be withheld for payment of spousal support (alimony), if appropriate, based on the underlying order, time period that corresponds to the amount in #9a (such as month, week, etc.).

10a-b. Dollar amount to be withheld for payment of past-due spousal support (alimony), if appropriate, based on the underlying order, time period that corresponds to the amount in #10a (such as month, week, etc.).

11a-c. Dollar amount to be withheld for payment of miscellaneous obligations, if appropriate, based on the underlying order, time period that corresponds to the amount in #11a (e.g., month, week, etc.), and description of the miscellaneous obligation.

12a. Total of #5a, #6a, #7a, #8a, #9a, #10a, and # 11a.

12b. Time period that corresponds to the amount in #12a (e.g., month).

13. Check this box if arrears greater than 12 weeks.

14a. Amount an employer should withhold if the employee is paid weekly.

2

FL-196 / OMB Control No.: 0970-0154

14b. Amount an employer should withhold if the employee is paid every two weeks.

14c. Amount an employer should withhold if the employee is paid twice a month.

14d. Amount an employer should withhold if the employee is paid once a month.

REMITTANCE INFORMATION

15. The state, tribe, or territory from which this Order/Notice or Notice of an Order is sent.

16. Number of days in which the withholding must begin pursuant to the issuing state's or tribe's laws/procedures.

17. The effective date of the income withholding.

18. Number of working days within which an employer or other withholder of income must remit amounts withheld pursuant to the issuing state's law.

19. The percentage of income that may be withheld from the employee's/obligor's income. For state orders, you may not withhold more than the lesser of: 1) the amounts allowed by the Federal Consumer Credit Protection Act (15 U.S.C. § 1673(b)); or 2) the amounts allowed by the state of the employee's/obligor's principal place of employment. The federal limit applies to the aggregate disposable weekly earnings (ADWE). ADWE is the net income left after making mandatory deductions such as: state, federal, local taxes, Social Security taxes, statutory pension contributions, and Medicare taxes.

For tribal orders, you may not withhold more than the amounts allowed under the law of the issuing tribe. For tribal employers who receive a state order, you may not withhold more than the amounts allowed under the law of the state that issued the order.

20. The state, tribe, or territory from which the Order or Notice is sent.

21. Name of the State Disbursement Unit, individual, tribunal/court, or tribal child support enforcement agency specified in the underlying income withholding order to which payments are required to be sent. This form may not indicate a location other than that specified by an entity authorized under state or tribal law to issue an income withholding order. Please include the case identifier used to record payment (should be the same as 3c). In a IV-D case, this must be the IV-D case number.

22. Address of the State Disbursement Unit, tribunal/court, tribal child support enforcement agency, or individual identified in #21. This information is shared with the obligor. Be sure to safeguard confidential addresses.

Complete only for EFT/EDI transmission.

23a. Telephone number of contact to provide EFT/EDI instructions.

3

OMB 0970-0154

FL-196 / OMB Control No.: 0970-0154

23b. Federal Information Process Standard (FIPS) code for transmitting payments through EFT/EDI. The FIPS code is five characters that identify the state, county or tribe. It is seven characters when it identifies the state, county, and a location within the county. It is necessary for centralized collections.

23c. Receiving agency's bank routing number.

23d. Receiving agency's bank account number.

IV-D agencies, courts, and attorneys (with authority to issue an income withholding order/notice) sending an Order/Notice to Withhold Income for Child Support must complete 24a-e.

24a. Print name of the government official authorizing this Order or Notice to Withhold.

24b. Print title of the government official authorizing this Order or Notice to Withhold.

24c. Signature of Government Official authorizing this Order/Notice to Withhold and date of signature. This line may be optional only if the Withholding Order/Notice includes the name and title of a government official (line 24a, 24b) and a signature of the official (line 24c) is not required by state or tribal law. Provide a signature if required by state or tribal law.

24d. Check the appropriate box to indicate whether a child support enforcement agency (IV-D) or court is authorizing this Order or Notice for withholding.

24e. Check the box if you are an attorney with authority to issue an order or notice under state law.

Attorneys, individuals, and private entities sending a Notice of an Order to Withhold Income for Child Support complete 25a-d.

25a. Print name of the individual or entity sending this Notice.

25b. Print title of the individual sending this Notice, if appropriate

25c. Signature of the individual sending this Notice and date of signature.

25d. Please check the appropriate box to indicate whether you are an attorney, individual, or private entity sending this Notice of an Order.

4

OMB 0970-0154

FL-196 / OMB Control No.: 0970-0154

The following information refers to federal, state, or tribal laws that apply to issuing an income withholding order/notice or notice of an order to the employer. Any state or tribal specific information may be included in space provided.

26. Check the box if the state or tribal law requires the employer to provide a copy of the Order or Notice to the employee.

27. Use this space to provide additional information on the penalty and/or citation for an employer who fails to comply with the Order or Notice. The law of the obligor's principal place of employment governs the penalty.

28. Use this space to provide additional information on the penalty and/or citation for an employer, who discharges, refuses to employ, or disciplines an employee/obligor as a result of the Order or Notice. The law of the obligor's principal place of employment governs the penalty.

29. Use this space to provide the child(ren)'s names listed in the support order and/or additional information regarding this income withholding Order or Notice of an Order.

Please provide the following contact information to the employer. Employers may need additional information to process the Order or Notice.

30a. Name of the contact person sending the Order or Notice of an Order that an employer and/or employee/obligor may call for information regarding the Order or Notice of an Order.

30b. Telephone number for the contact person whose name appears in #30a.

30c. Fax number for the person whose name appears in #30a.

30d. Internet address for the person whose name appears in #30a.

If the employer is a Federal Government agency, the following instructions apply.

- Serve the Order or Notice of an Order upon the governmental agent listed in 5 CFR part 581, appendix A.

- Sufficient identifying information must be provided in order for the obligor to be identified. It is, therefore, recommended that the following information, if known and if applicable, be provided:

  - (1) full name of the obligor; (2) date of birth; (3) employment number, Department of Veterans Affairs claim number, or civil service retirement claim number; (4) component of the government entity for which the obligor works, and the official duty station or worksite; and (5) status of the obligor, e.g., employee, former employee, or annuitant.

- You may withhold from a variety of incomes and forms of payment, including voluntary separation incentive payments (buy-out payments), incentive pay, and cash awards. For a

5

OMB 0970-0154

FL-196 / OMB Control No.: 0970-0154

more complete list see 5 CFR 581.103.

****

The Paperwork Reduction Act of 1995

This information collection is conducted in accordance with 45 CFR 303.100 of the child support enforcement program. Standard forms are designed to provide uniformity and standardization for interstate case processing. Public reporting burden for this collection of information is estimated to average one hour per response. The responses to this collection are mandatory in accordance with 45 CFR 303.7. This information is subject to State and Federal confidentiality requirements; however, the information will be filed with the tribunal and/or agency in the responding State and may, depending on State law, be disclosed to other parties. An agency may not conduct or sponsor, and a person is not required to respond to, a collection of information unless it displays a currently valid OMB control number.

FL-196 / OMB Control No.: 0970-0154

1a ☐ ORDER/NOTICE TO WITHHOLD INCOME FOR CHILD SUPPORT
☐ NOTICE OF AN ORDER TO WITHHOLD INCOME FOR CHILD SUPPORT

☐Original ☐Amended ☐Termination **#1b** Date: **#1c**
☐State/Tribe/Territory_____ **#1d**
City/Co./Dist./Reservation_____ **#1e**
☐Non-governmental entity or Individual ___ **#1f**
Case Number_____ **#1g**

#2a	RE:	**#3a**
Employer's/Withholder's Name		Employee's/Obligor's Name (Last, First, MI)
#2b		**#3b**
Employer's/Withholder's Address		Employee's/Obligor's Social Security Number
#2c		**#3c**
		Employee's/Obligor's Case Identifier
		#3d
#2d		Obligee's Name (Last, First, MI)
Employer's/Withholder's Federal EIN Number (if known)		

ORDER INFORMATION: This document is based on the support or withholding order from _____ **#4** .
You are required by law to deduct these amounts from the employee's/obligor's income until further notice.
$___**# 5a**_____ Per ____**# 5b** current child support   **#13**
$___**# 6a**_____ Per ____**# 6b** past-due child support - Arrears greater than 12 weeks? ☐yes ☐no
$___**# 7a**_____ Per ____**# 7b** current cash medical support
$___**# 8a**_____ Per ____**# 8b** past-due cash medical support
$___**# 9a**_____ Per ____**# 9b** spousal support
$___**#10a**_____ Per ____**#10b** past-due spousal support
$___**#11a**_____ Per ____**#11b** other (specify)   **#11c** _____
for a total of $_____**#12a**_____ per _____**#12b**_____ to be forwarded to the payee below.
You do not have to vary your pay cycle to be in compliance with the support order. If your pay cycle does not match the
ordered payment cycle, withhold one of the following amounts:
$__**#14a** per weekly pay period. $_**#14c** per semimonthly pay period (twice a month).
$_**#14b** per biweekly pay period (every two weeks).$_ **#14d**___ per monthly pay period.

REMITTANCE INFORMATION: When remitting payment, provide the pay date/date of withholding and the case identifier. If
the employee's/obligor's principal place of employment is ___**#15**___, begin withholding no later than the first pay period
occurring **#16** days after the date of __**#17**__. Send payment within **#18** working days of the pay date/date of withholding.
The total withheld amount, including your fee, may not exceed **#19** % of the employee's/obligor's aggregate disposable
weekly earnings.

If the employee's/obligor's principal place of employment is not _____**#20**_____, for limitations on
withholding, applicable time requirements, and any allowable employer fees, follow the laws and procedures of the
employee's/obligor's principal place of employment (see #3 and #9, ADDITIONAL INFORMATION TO EMPLOYERS AND
OTHER WITHHOLDERS).

Make check payable to:_____**#21**(Payee and Case Identifier)____ Send check to:_____**#22**_____.
If remitting payment by EFT/EDI, call __**#23a**____before first submission. Use this FIPS code: **#23b**__:
Bank routing number: _____**#23c**_____ Bank account number: **#23d**_____.

If this is an Order/Notice to Withhold:	**If this is a Notice of an Order to Withhold:**
24a Print Name _____	25a Print Name_____
24b Title of Issuing Official_____	25b Title (if appropriate)_____
24c Signature and Date__(if required by state or tribal law)__	25c Signature and Date_____
24d ☐ IV-D Agency ☐Court	25d ☐ Attorney ☐Individual ☐Private Entity

24e ☐ Attorney with authority under state law to issue order/notice.
NOTE: Non-IV-D Attorneys, individuals, and non-governmental entities must submit a Notice of an Order to Withhold and
include a copy of the income withholding order unless, under a state's law, an attorney in that state may issue an income
withholding order. In that case, the attorney may submit an Order/Notice to Withhold and include a copy of the state law

IMPORTANT: The person completing this form is advised that the information on this form may be shared with the obligor.
OMB 0970-0154

FL-196 / OMB Control No.: 0970-0154

authorizing the attorney to issue an income withholding order/notice.

ADDITIONAL INFORMATION TO EMPLOYERS AND OTHER WITHHOLDERS

#26 ☐ If checked, you are required to provide a copy of this form to your employee/obligor. If your employee works in a state that is different from the state that issued this order, a copy must be provided to your employee/obligor even if the box is not checked.

1. **Priority:** Withholding under this Order or Notice has priority over any other legal process under state law (or tribal law, if applicable) against the same income. If there are federal tax levies in effect, please notify the contact person listed below. (See 10 below.)

2. **Combining Payments:** You may combine withheld amounts from more than one employee's/obligor's income in a single payment to each agency/party requesting withholding. You must, however, separately identify the portion of the single payment that is attributable to each employee/obligor.

3. **Reporting the Paydate/Date of Withholding:** You must report the paydate/date of withholding when sending the payment. The paydate/date of withholding is the date on which the amount was withheld from the employee's wages. You must comply with the law of the state of employee's/obligor's principal place of employment with respect to the time periods within which you must implement the withholding and forward the support payments.

4. **Employee/Obligor with Multiple Support Withholdings:** If there is more than one Order or Notice against this employee/obligor and you are unable to honor all support Orders or Notices due to federal, state, or tribal withholding limits, you must follow the state or tribal law/procedure of the employee's/obligor's principal place of employment. You must honor all Orders or Notices to the greatest extent possible. (See 9 below.)

5. **Termination Notification:** You must promptly notify the Child Support Enforcement (IV-D) Agency and/or the contact person listed below when the employee/obligor no longer works for you. Please provide the information requested and return a complete copy of this Order or Notice to the Child Support Enforcement (IV-D) Agency and/or the contact person listed below. (See 10 below.)

THE EMPLOYEE/OBLIGOR NO LONGER WORKS FOR:_____
EMPLOYEE'S/OBLIGOR'S NAME:_____ CASE IDENTIFIER:_____
DATE OF SEPARATION FROM EMPLOYMENT:_____
LAST KNOWN HOME ADDRESS:_____
NEW EMPLOYER/ADDRESS:_____

6. **Lump Sum Payments:** You may be required to report and withhold from lump sum payments such as bonuses, commissions, or severance pay. If you have any questions about lump sum payments, contact the Child Support Enforcement (IV-D) Agency.

7. **Liability:** If you have any doubts about the validity of the Order or Notice, contact the agency or person listed below under 10. If you fail to withhold income as the Order or Notice directs, you are liable for both the accumulated amount you should have withheld from the employee's/obligor's income and any other penalties set by state or tribal law/procedure.
#27_____

8. **Anti-discrimination:** You are subject to a fine determined under state or tribal law for discharging an employee/obligor from employment, refusing to employ, or taking disciplinary action against any employee/obligor because of a child support withholding.
#28_____

9. **Withholding Limits:** For state orders, you may not withhold more than the lesser of: 1) the amounts allowed by the Federal Consumer Credit Protection Act (15 U.S.C. § 1673(b)); or 2) the amounts allowed by the state of the employee's/obligor's principal place of employment. The federal limit applies to the aggregate disposable weekly earnings (ADWE). ADWE is the net income left after making mandatory deductions such as: state, federal, local taxes, Social Security taxes, statutory pension contributions, and Medicare taxes. The Federal CCPA limit is 50% of the ADWE for child support and alimony, which is increased by 1) 10% if the employee does not support a second family; and/or 2) 5% if arrears greater than 12 weeks.
For tribal orders, you may not withhold more than the amounts allowed under the law of the issuing tribe. For tribal employers who receive a state order, you may not withhold more than the amounts allowed under the law of the state that issued the order.

Child(ren)'s Names and Additional Information:___#29_____

10. If you or your employee/obligor have any questions, contact____#30a_____ by telephone at
____#30b_____by Fax at_____#30c___or by internet at_____#30d_____.

FL-196 Page 8 of 8

Comment: All earnings assignment orders for support in any action in which child or family support is ordered must be issued on this form, as mandated by 42 USC §666 (see in particular 42 USC §666(b)(6)(A)(ii)). Fam C §5208(b).

§20.5A   d. Form: Earnings Assignment Order for Spousal or Partner Support (Judicial Council Form FL-435)

FL-435

ATTORNEY OR PARTY WITHOUT ATTORNEY *(Name, State Bar number, and address):*	FOR COURT USE ONLY

TELEPHONE NO.:   FAX NO. *(Optional):*
E-MAIL ADDRESS *(Optional):*
ATTORNEY FOR *(Name):*

SUPERIOR COURT OF CALIFORNIA, COUNTY OF
STREET ADDRESS:
MAILING ADDRESS:
CITY AND ZIP CODE:
BRANCH NAME:

PETITIONER/PLAINTIFF:

RESPONDENT/DEFENDANT:

OTHER PARENT:

EARNINGS ASSIGNMENT ORDER FOR SPOUSAL OR PARTNER SUPPORT ☐ Modification	CASE NUMBER:

TO THE PAYOR: This is a court order. You must withhold a portion of the earnings of *(specify obligor's name and birthdate):*

and pay as directed below. *(An explanation of this order is printed on page 2 of this form.)*

THE COURT ORDERS

1. You must pay part of the earnings of the employee or other person who has been ordered to pay support, as follows:
   a. ☐ $ per month current **spousal or partner support**
   b. ☐ $ per month **spousal or partner support arrearages**
   c. **Total deductions per month:** $

2. ☐ The payments ordered under item 1a must be paid to *(name, address):*

3. ☐ The payments ordered under item 1b must be paid to *(name, address):*

4. The payments ordered under item 1 must continue until further written notice from the payee or the court.

5. ☐ This order modifies an existing order. **The amount you must withhold may have changed.** The existing order continues in effect until this modification is effective.

6. This order affects all earnings that are payable beginning as soon as possible but not later than 10 days after you receive it.

7. You must give the obligor a copy of this order and the blank *Request for Hearing Regarding Earnings Assignment* (form FL-450) within 10 days.

8. ☐ Other *(specify):*

9. For the purposes of this order, spousal or partner support arrearages are set at: $ as of *(date):*

Date: _____

_____
JUDICIAL OFFICER

Page 1 of 2

INSTRUCTIONS FOR EARNINGS ASSIGNMENT ORDER

1. **DEFINITION OF IMPORTANT WORDS IN THE EARNINGS ASSIGNMENT ORDER**

   a. **Earnings:**

      (1) Wages, salary, bonuses, vacation pay, retirement pay, and commissions paid by an employer;

      (2) Payments for services of independent contractors;

      (3) Dividends, interest, rents, royalties, and residuals;

      (4) Patent rights and mineral or other natural resource rights;

      (5) Any payments due as a result of written or oral contracts for services or sales, regardless of title;

      (6) Payments due for workers' compensation temporary benefits, or payments from a disability or health insurance policy or program; and

      (7) Any other payments or credits due, regardless of source.

   b. **Earnings assignment order:** a court order issued in every court case in which one person is ordered to pay for the support of another person. This order has priority over any other orders such as garnishments or earnings withholding orders.

      Earnings should not be withheld for any other order until the amounts necessary to satisfy this order have been withheld in full. However, an *Order/Notice to Withhold Income for Child Support* for child support or family support has priority over this order for spousal or partner support.

   c. **Obligor:** any person ordered by a court to pay support. The obligor is named before item 1 in the order.

   d. **Obligee:** the person or governmental agency to whom the support is to be paid.

   e. **Payor:** the person or entity, including an employer, that pays earnings to an obligor.

2. **INFORMATION FOR ALL PAYORS.** Withhold money from the earnings payable to the obligor as soon as possible but no later than 10 days after you receive the *Earnings Assignment Order for Spousal or Partner Support.* Send the withheld money to the payee(s) named in items 2 and 3 of the order within 10 days of the pay date. You may deduct $1 from the obligor's earnings for each payment you make.

   When sending the withheld earnings to the payee, state the date on which the earnings were withheld. You may combine amounts withheld for two or more obligors in a single payment to each payee, and identify what portion of that payment is for each obligor.

   You will be liable for any amount you fail to withhold and can be cited for contempt of court.

3. **SPECIAL INSTRUCTIONS FOR PAYORS WHO ARE EMPLOYERS**

   a. State and federal laws limit the amount you can withhold and pay as directed by this order. This limitation applies only to earnings defined above in item 1a(1) and are usually half the obligor's disposable earnings.

      Disposable earnings are different from gross pay or take-home pay. Disposable earnings are earnings left after subtracting the money that state or federal law requires an employer to withhold. Generally these required deductions are (1) federal income tax, (2) social security, (3) state income tax, (4) state disability insurance, and (5) payments to public employees' retirement systems.

      After the obligor's disposable earnings are known, withhold the amount required by the order, **but never withhold more than 50 percent of the disposable earnings unless the court order specifies a higher percentage.** Federal law prohibits withholding more than 65 percent of disposable earnings of an employee in any case.

      If the obligor has more than one assignment for support, add together the amounts of support due for all the assignments. If 50 percent of the obligor's net disposable earnings will not pay in full all of the assignments for support, prorate it first among all of the current support assignments in the same proportion that each assignment bears to the total current support owed. Apply any remainder to the assignments for arrearage support in the same proportion that each assignment bears to the total arrearage owed. If you have any questions, please contact the office or person who sent this form to you. This office or person's name appears in the upper left-hand corner of the order.

   b. If the employee's pay period differs from the period specified in the order, prorate the amount ordered withheld so that part of it is withheld from each of the obligor's paychecks.

   c. If the obligor stops working for you, notify the office that sent you this form of that, no later than the date of the next payment, by first-class mail. Give the obligor's last known address and, if known, the name and address of any new employer.

   d. California law prohibits you from firing, refusing to hire, or taking any disciplinary action against any employee ordered to pay support through an earnings assignment. Such action can lead to a $500 civil penalty per employee.

4. **INFORMATION FOR ALL OBLIGORS.** You should have received a *Request for Hearing Regarding Earnings Assignment* (form FL-450) with this *Earnings Assignment Order for Spousal or Partner Support.* If not, you may get one from either the court clerk or the family law facilitator. If you want the court to stop or modify your earnings assignment, you must file (by hand delivery or mail) an original copy of the form with the court clerk within 10 days of the date you received this order. Keep a copy of the form for your records.

   If you think your support order is wrong, you can ask for a modification of the order or, in some cases, you can have the order set aside and have a new order issued. You can talk to an attorney or get information from the family law facilitator about this.

5. **SPECIAL INFORMATION FOR THE OBLIGOR WHO IS AN EMPLOYEE.** State law requires you to notify the payees named in items 2 and 3 of the order if you change your employment. You must provide the name and address of your new employer.

EARNINGS ASSIGNMENT ORDER FOR SPOUSAL OR PARTNER SUPPORT
(Family Law)

Copies: Original (submit to court clerk); copy for service on obligor's employer; office copies.

Comment: Use this form only for enforcement of *spousal or part-*

ner support orders. All earnings assignment orders for support in any action in which child or family support is ordered must be issued on an Order/Notice to Withhold Income for Child Support, as mandated by 42 USC §666 (see in particular 42 USC §666(b)(6)(A)(ii)). Fam C §5208(b). For form, see §20.5.

§20.6   e. Form: Stay of Service of Earnings Assignment Order and Order (Judicial Council Form FL-455)

FL-455

ATTORNEY OR PARTY WITHOUT ATTORNEY *(Name and address)*:	FOR COURT USE ONLY
TELEPHONE NO.:	
ATTORNEY FOR *(Name)*:	

SUPERIOR COURT OF CALIFORNIA, COUNTY OF
STREET ADDRESS:
MAILING ADDRESS:
CITY AND ZIP CODE:
BRANCH NAME:

PETITIONER/PLAINTIFF:

RESPONDENT/DEFENDANT:

OTHER PARENT:

☐ STAY ☐ TERMINATION OF STAY

OF SERVICE OF EARNINGS ASSIGNMENT ORDER

CASE NUMBER:

APPLICATION FOR STAY

(NOTICE: If this application is made separately from a hearing on support, you must get a hearing date from the clerk and give notice. See below.)

I request that the court stay the service of the earnings assignment order in this case because *(check one or more applicable reasons)*:

1. ☐ I have paid fully and on time the previously ordered support for the last 12 months, and I do not owe any back support (arrearages).

2. ☐ I have not been subject to a support order for the last 12 months, but I have posted ☐ cash ☐ a cash bond with the clerk of the court in the amount of $ _____ , which is equal to three months' support, and I do not owe any back support (arrearages).

3. ☐ Service of the earnings assignment would cause extraordinary hardship on me as follows *(state reasons)*:
   (Note: You must prove these reasons at any hearing on this application by clear and convincing evidence.)

4. ☐ I have a written agreement with the party receiving support that provides a stay of service of the earnings assignment order. A copy of the agreement is attached. *(Note: This agreement must be signed by the local child support agency if support is payable to a county officer designated for that purpose.)*

5. ☐ My employer or the local child support agency has been unable to deliver the support payments to the recipient for at least six months because the recipient has not notified my employer or the local child support agency of a change of address. *(Attach a statement made under oath by employer or local child support agency.)*

I declare under penalty of perjury under the laws of the State of California that the foregoing is true and correct.

Date:

▶

_____
(TYPE OR PRINT NAME)

_____
(SIGNATURE OF APPLICANT)

NOTICE OF HEARING

A hearing on this application will be held as follows:

a. Date:	Time:	Dept.:	Room:

b. The address of the court ☐ is shown above ☐ is:

Page 1 of 2

Form Adopted for Mandatory Use
Judicial Council of California
FL-455 [Rev. January 1, 2003]

STAY OF SERVICE OF EARNINGS ASSIGNMENT ORDER

Family Code, §§ 5260, 5261
www.courtinfo.ca.gov

PETITIONER/PLAINTIFF:	CASE NUMBER:
RESPONDENT/DEFENDANT:	
OTHER PARENT:	

APPLICATION FOR TERMINATION OF STAY

I request that the court terminate the stay of service of the earnings assignment previously issued in this case
on *(date):*   because *(check one or more applicable reasons):*

1. ☐   The person required to make payments has missed at least one payment of support, which continues unpaid. *(Note: A false
statement about missed payments is punishable as contempt.)*

2. ☐ I am ☐ the person required to make the payments ☐ the local child support agency,
and I wish the stay terminated.

3. ☐ The reasons for granting the stay no longer exist. *(A hearing is required. See page 1 for notice of hearing.)*
(State facts showing that the previous reasons for granting the stay no longer exist.)

I declare under penalty of perjury under the laws of the State of California that the foregoing is true and correct.
Date:

_____   ▶   _____
(TYPE OR PRINT NAME)   (SIGNATURE OF APPLICANT)

PROOF OF SERVICE BY MAIL

1. I am at least 18 years of age and **not a party to this cause.** I am a resident of or employed in the county where the mailing took
place, and my residence or business address is *(specify):*

2. I served a copy of this *Stay of Service of Earnings Assignment Order* by enclosing it in a sealed envelope with first-class postage
fully prepaid and depositing it in the United States Postal Service as follows:

a. Date of deposit:
b. Place of deposit *(city, state):*
c. Addressed as follows:

I declare under penalty of perjury under the laws of the State of California that the foregoing is true and correct.

Date:

_____   ▶   _____
(TYPE OR PRINT NAME)   (SIGNATURE OF DECLARANT)

ORDER

GOOD CAUSE APPEARING:
1. ☐   Service of the earnings assignment order issued in this action is stayed.
2. ☐   The stay of service granted above will terminate without further order on *(date):*
3. ☐   The previous stay of service of the earnings assignment order made on *(date):*   is terminated,
and the earnings assignment order previously issued in this case may be served.

Date: _____
                                                           (JUDICIAL OFFICER)

FL-455 [Rev. January 1, 2003]   **STAY OF SERVICE OF EARNINGS ASSIGNMENT ORDER**   Page 2 of 2

Copies: Original (submit to court clerk); copy for service; office copies.

§20.7   f. Form: Ex Parte Application for Earnings Assignment Order (Judicial Council Form FL-430)

FL-430

ATTORNEY OR PARTY WITHOUT ATTORNEY OR GOVERNMENTAL AGENCY (under Fam. Code, §§ 17400, 17406) (Name, state bar number, and address):	FOR COURT USE ONLY

TELEPHONE NO.:   FAX NO.:

ATTORNEY FOR (Name):

SUPERIOR COURT OF CALIFORNIA, COUNTY OF
STREET ADDRESS:
MAILING ADDRESS:
CITY AND ZIP CODE:
BRANCH NAME:

PETITIONER/PLAINTIFF:

RESPONDENT/DEFENDANT:

OTHER PARENT:

EX PARTE APPLICATION FOR EARNINGS ASSIGNMENT ORDER ☐ **MODIFICATION**	CASE NUMBER:

APPLICANT DECLARES

1. ☐ **Child support** was ordered as follows:
   a. Date of order:
   b. Payable by ☐ petitioner ☐ respondent ☐ other parent
   c. Payable to ☐ petitioner ☐ respondent ☐ other (specify):
   d. Total amount unpaid is at least: $ as of (date):

2. ☐ **Spousal support** ☐ **family support** was ordered as follows:

   a. Date of order:
   b. Payable by ☐ petitioner ☐ respondent ☐ other parent
   c. Payable to ☐ petitioner ☐ respondent ☐ other (specify):
   d. Total amount unpaid is at least: $ as of (date):

3. ☐ **(Complete for support ordered before July 1, 1990, only)**
   Payment of ☐ child support ☐ spousal support is overdue in the sum of at least one month's payment.
   Written notice of my intent to seek an earnings assignment was
   a. ☐ given at least 15 days before the date of filing this application
      (1) ☐ by first class mail.
      (2) ☐ by personal service.
      (3) ☐ contained in the support order described in item 1 or 2.
      (4) ☐ other (specify):

   b. ☐ waived (explain):

4. ☐ An earnings assignment order has not been issued for support ordered after July 1, 1990.

5. a. The amount of arrears stated in items 1d and 2d ☐ does ☐ does not include interest at the legal rate. (If interest is not included, it is not waived.)

   b. The amount of arrears stated in items 1d and 2d ☐ does ☐ does not include penalties at the legal rate. (If penalties are not included, they are not waived.)

Form Adopted for Mandatory Use Judicial Council of California FL-430 [Rev. January 1, 2003]	**EX PARTE APPLICATION FOR EARNINGS ASSIGNMENT ORDER**	Family Code, §§ 5230, 5252 www.courtinfo.ca.gov

PETITIONER/PLAINTIFF:	CASE NUMBER:
RESPONDENT/DEFENDANT:	
OTHER PARENT:	

6. ☐ Modification of the existing earnings assignment order is requested because

    a. ☐ the following children are emancipated (support is no longer required by law) as of the following dates *(name each and give date):*

    b. ☐ custody of the following children has changed *(specify):*

    c. ☐ the support arrears in this case are paid in full.

    d. ☐ the earnings assignment order must be conformed to the most recent support order as follows *(specify):*

    e. ☐ the local child support agency is no longer enforcing the current support obligation in this case but is required to collect and enforce any arrears owing.

    f. ☐ the earnings assignment order should be terminated as to spousal support because
        (1) ☐ the supported spouse remarried on *(date):*
        (2) ☐ the supported spouse died on *(date):*
        (3) ☐ by terms of the current order, spousal support was to terminate on *(date):*

    g. ☐ other *(specify):*

7. I request an earnings assignment order issue for the following monthly deductions:
    a. ☐ $ _____ per month current **child support.**
    b. ☐ $ _____ per month current **spousal support.**
    c. ☐ $ _____ per month current **family support.**
    d. ☐ $ _____ per month **child support arrears.**
    e. ☐ $ _____ per month **spousal support arrears.**
    f. ☐ $ _____ per month **family support arrears.**
    g. **Total deductions per month: $**

I declare under penalty of perjury under the laws of the State of California that the foregoing is true and correct.

Date:

▶

_____
(TYPE OR PRINT NAME)

_____
(SIGNATURE OF APPLICANT)

Copies: Original (submit to court clerk); office copies.

§20.8　　g. Form: Notice of Intent to Seek Earnings Assignment Order for Support

_ _[Attorney name]_ _
_ _[State Bar number]_ _
_ _[Address]_ _
_ _[Telephone number]_ _

Attorney for _ _[name]_ _

SUPERIOR COURT OF CALIFORNIA
COUNTY OF _ _ _ _ _ _

Marriage of	)	**No.** _ _ _ _ _ _
	)	
Petitioner: _ _ _ _ _ _ _ _	)	**NOTICE OF INTENT TO**
	)	**SEEK EARNINGS**
Respondent: _ _ _ _ _ _ _ _	)	**ASSIGNMENT ORDER FOR**
	)	**SUPPORT**
_____	)	

NOTICE IS HEREBY GIVEN that _ _[name of obligee]_ _ **will seek an earnings assignment order for support, commonly known as a "wage assignment," without further notice to you if you are in default in the** _ _[child/spousal/child or spousal/family]_ _ **support payments ordered by the Court.**

Date: _____　　　　　　_ _[Signature]_ _
　　　　　　　　　　　　　　_ _[Typed name]_ _
　　　　　　　　　　　　　Attorney for _ _[Petitioner/
　　　　　　　　　　　　　Respondent]_ _

Copies: Original (retain, with original proof of service, for filing with application for wage assignment); copy for service; office copies.

§20.9　　2. Service; Employer's Responsibilities

An earnings assignment order for support may be served on the employer by first-class mail as prescribed by CCP §1013. Fam C §5232. The obligee must provide for service, in addition to a copy of the assignment order itself, of a written statement of the obligor's rights to seek to quash, modify, or stay service of the assignment order, a blank form that the obligor can file with the court to request a hearing to quash, modify, or stay service of the assignment order, and instructions on how to file the form and obtain a hearing date. Fam C §§5232, 5234.

Unless the assignment order states a later date, withholding under it, from all earnings payable to the employee, must begin as soon as possible after service of the order on the employer, and in no event later than 10 days after service. Fam C §5233. The employer must forward the withheld amounts to the obligee within the time-frame specified in federal law and must report to the obligee the date on which the amount was withheld from the obligor's wages. Fam C §5235(c). Once the State Disbursement Unit (formerly Child Support Centralized Collection and Distribution Unit) required under Fam C §17309 is operational, the employer must send all withheld earnings to the collection and distribution unit instead of to the obligee. Fam C §5235(e). An employer may not be subject to any civil liability for any amount withheld and paid to the obligee, the local child support agency, or the collection and distribution unit under an assignment order. Fam C §5247. An employer who willfully fails to withhold and forward support following service of a valid assignment order is liable to the obligee for the amount of support not forwarded, including interest, and is subject to being held in contempt. Fam C §5241(a), (c). In addition, if the employer willfully fails to comply with the assignment order on separate occasions within a 12-month period, the court can impose a civil penalty of up to 50 percent of the support amount not paid to the obligee and order electronic transfer from the employer's bank account. Fam C §5241(d). When an employer withholds support as required by an assignment order, the employee may not be held in contempt or subject to criminal prosecution for nonpayment of such withheld support not received by the obligee. Fam C §§5235(a), 5241(b). Note, however, that when an employer fails to pay withheld funds to the obligee, the employee (along with the employer) remains liable to the obligee for the payments. *County of Shasta v Smith* (1995) 38 CA4th 329, 45 CR2d 52.

Within 10 days after service of the assignment order, the employer must deliver a copy of the assignment order, and copies of the other documents required to be served on the employer, to the support obligor. Fam C §5234.

§20.10   3. Priorities

When one or more earnings assignment orders for support served on an employer with respect to a single employee include both current support and payments toward liquidation of arrearages, priority must be given in the following order: (1) Current child support, (2) current spousal support, (3) child support arrearages, and (4) spousal support arrearages. Fam C §5238(a). When there are multiple assignment orders for the same employee, the employer must prorate the withheld payments. Fam C §5238(b). If the obligor has more than one assignment for support, the employer must add together the amounts of support due. Fam C §5238(b)(1). If 50 percent of the obligor's net disposable earnings will not pay in full all of the assignments for support, the employer must prorate the 50 percent among all of the current support assignments in the same proportion that each bears to the total current support owed. Fam C §5238(b)(2). Any remainder must be applied to the assignments for arrearage support in the same proportion that each assignment bears to the total arrearage owed. Fam C §5238(b)(3). An assignment order has priority over any attachment, execution, or other assignment, including an earnings withholding order (see §§20.23, 20.26–20.27). Fam C §5243; CCP §706.031.

§20.11   4. Motion to Quash

The obligor may move to quash an earnings assignment order for support on the grounds that (1) the assignment order does not correctly state the amount of current or overdue support ordered, (2) the alleged obligor is not the obligor from whom support is due, or (3) the amount to be withheld exceeds that allowable under federal law as provided in 15 USC §1673(b) (i.e., from 50 to 65 percent of "disposable earnings," as defined in 15 USC §1672(b), depending on what persons the obligor is supporting and when the arrearage accrued). Fam C §5270(a), (c). When the assignment order is sought under Fam C §§5250–5253 to enforce orders made before July 1, 1990, the obligor may also move to quash service of the order for any of the grounds that would constitute good cause to stay service of an assignment order under Fam C §5260 (see §20.3). Fam C §5270(b). A motion to quash may also be granted on other grounds under the court's authority to fashion an appropriate remedy through the exercise of its inherent equitable and supervisory powers. *Marriage of Johnson-*

Wilkes & Wilkes (1996) 48 CA4th 1569, 56 CR2d 323 (service of earnings assignment order for support on exempt income).

The motion to quash must be filed with the court that issued the assignment order within 10 days after service on the obligor by the employer of notice of the order. Fam C §5271(a). The clerk must set the motion to be heard between 15 and 20 days after receipt of the notice of motion. Fam C §5271(b). Under Fam C §5271(c), the obligor must serve the moving papers on the obligee, personally or by first-class mail with postage prepaid, at least 10 days before the hearing. It appears that the notice must be served at least 15 days in advance when service is by mail. CCP §1013.

Except for these special time requirements, the motion is prepared and processed in the same manner as a notice of motion for temporary orders. For discussion of, and forms for, motions for temporary orders, see §§11.16–11.63. The obligor prepares the Judicial Council forms of Notice of Motion (see form in §11.20) and Application for Order and Supporting Declaration (see form in §11.22).

A finding of error in the amount of the current support or arrearage, or that the amount exceeds federal or state limits, is not grounds to vacate the assignment order. Rather, the remedy is to modify the order to reflect the correct or allowable amount. Nor will the obligor's subsequent payment of arrearages relieve the court of its duty to issue the order. Fam C §5272.

The fact that an assignment order that was issued and served on a prior employer of the obligor is subsequently served on a new employer does not entitle the obligor to move to quash the order on any grounds previously raised when the order was served on the prior employer or on any grounds that the obligor could have raised, but failed to raise, at the time of the earlier service. Fam C §5270(d).

§20.12   5. Obligor's Change of Employment

Earnings assignment orders for support must require that the obligor notify the obligee of any change of employment, and of the name and address of the new employer, within 10 days after obtaining new employment. Fam C §5281.

After the obligor has left his or her employment, the former employer must notify the obligee of that fact, by first-class mail, postage prepaid, to the obligee's last known address, at the time the next payment is due on the assignment order. Fam C §5282.

An assignment order is binding on any employer of the obligor on whom it is served, regardless of whether the obligor was employed by that employer when the order was issued and regardless of whether the order lacks identifying information about the employer or includes incorrect information about the employer. Fam C §5231.

§20.13   6. Obligee's Change of Address

The obligee must notify the obligor's employer, by first-class mail, postage prepaid, of any change of address within a reasonable time after the change. Fam C §5237(a). To avoid any interruption in the receipt of payments, the obligee's attorney should advise his or her client, when the earnings assignment order for support is first obtained, to inform the obligor's employer immediately by mail of any change of address. When the obligee is receiving payments through a court-designated county officer, typically the local child support agency's office, the required notice must go to the county officer. Fam C §5237(b). If the obligee is receiving payments from the State Disbursement Unit (formerly Child Support Centralized Collection and Distribution Unit) required under Fam C §17309, the required notice must go to the collection and distribution unit. Fam C §5237(c).

When the employer, designated county officer, or Child Support Centralized Collection and Distribution Unit is unable to deliver payments for 6 months because of the obligee's failure to provide notification of a change of address, no further payments are to be made and all undeliverable payments are to be returned to the obligor. Fam C §5237(d). In cases where payments are directed to the State Disbursement Unit pursuant to Fam C 5235(d) and the case is not otherwise receiving Title IV-D services, if the State Disbursement Unit is unable to deliver payment under the assignment order for a period of 45 days because of the obligee's failure to provide notification of a change of address, the Title IV-D agency shall immediately return the payments to the obligor if the obligee cannot be located, and notify the employer to suspend withholding pursuant to the wage assignment until the employer or Title IV-D agency is notified of the obligee's whereabouts. Fam C 5237(d)(2).

§20.14   7. Modification

Modification of an earnings assignment order for support may be sought ex parte by filing the Judicial Council form of Ex Parte Application for Earnings Assignment Order (Judicial Council Form FL-430; see §20.7). Modification is specifically requested at Item 6. The proposed modified assignment order should be submitted with the application.

§20.15　8. Termination of Service

After the filing and service of a noticed motion by the obligor, the court must terminate service of an earnings assignment order for support if past-due support has been paid in full, including any interest due, and at least one of the following conditions exists:

- The order is for spousal support and the obligee has died or remarried (Fam C §5240(a));

- The order is for child support and the child has died or become emancipated (Fam C §5240(b));

- There has been only one application for an assignment order and the court finds good cause, as defined in Fam C §5260, to terminate the order (Fam C §5240(c));

- There is a written agreement for an alternative arrangement that meets the requirements of Fam C §5260(b)(2) and an assignment order has not been previously terminated and subsequently initiated (Fam C §5240(d));

- There is no longer a current order for support (Fam C §5240(e));

- An assignment order stay was improperly terminated under Fam C §5261 and termination was based on the obligor's failure to make timely payments as described in Fam C §5261(b) (Fam C §5240(f)); or

- The employer, the designated county officer, or the State Disbursement Unit (formerly Child Support Centralized Collection and Distribution Unit) is unable to deliver payment for 6 months because of the obligee's failure to provide notification of a change of address (Fam C §5240(g)).

§20.16　B. Electronic Funds Transfer for Payment of Child Support

As long as a child support obligor is not subject to an earnings assignment order (see §§20.2–20.15), any child support order may require the obligor to designate an account for the purpose of paying the child support obligation by electronic funds transfer. The order may require the obligor to deposit funds in an interest-bearing account with a state or federally chartered commercial bank, in such an account with a savings and loan association, or in shares of a federally insured credit union doing business in California, and must require the obligor to maintain sufficient funds in the account to pay the monthly child support obligation.

The court may order that each payment be electronically transferred to the support obligee's or the district attorney's account. The obligor must be required to notify the obligee if the depository institution or the account number is changed. Fam C §4508.

No interest will accrue on any amount subject to electronic funds transfer as long as funds sufficient to pay the monthly child support obligation are kept in the account. Fam C §4508.

§20.17   C. Writ of Execution

A writ of execution (see form in §20.22) is an order to a county's levying officer (*i.e.,* its sheriff or marshal), or to a registered process server, to obtain satisfaction of a judgment for a judgment creditor. CCP §§699.510–699.520, 680.260. On a registered process server's authority to enforce a writ, see CCP §§699.080, 715.040. A registered process server may levy more than once under the same writ if the writ is still valid. CCP §699.080(g). The writ may be executed by (1) seizing funds of the judgment debtor and delivering them to the judgment creditor, (2) seizing and delivering real or tangible personal property, or (3) seizing and selling real or tangible personal property and delivering the proceeds.

For a complete discussion of writs of execution, see Debt Collection Practice in California, chap 9 (2d ed Cal CEB 1999).

§20.18   1. Uses

A writ of execution may be used to enforce a wide variety of family law orders calling for the payment of money or the transfer of property. It is probably most commonly used to enforce orders for attorney fees and support. A writ of execution is typically the most effective way to enforce an order for attorney fees because an earnings assignment order for support (see §§20.2–20.15) is available only to enforce support orders (see Fam C §§5200–5295). It appears that an assignment order may include payment of attorney fees, but only to the extent that they are incurred to obtain the assignment order itself. See Item 6 on form of application for wage assignment in §20.7. An assignment order may not be issued to enforce a previously made award for attorney fees.

With respect to enforcement of support orders, an earnings assignment order for support is clearly the best method in most instances. Use of a writ of execution to enforce a support order is usually limited to situations in which either (1) the support order has terminated and only arrearages are owed or (2) a substantial amount of arrearages is owed and the judgment creditor chooses to try to collect them before seeking an assignment order to collect current support. A court may not reduce the balance due on support arrearages. *Marriage of Perez* (1995) 35 CA4th 77, 80, 41 CR2d 377.

§20.19   2. Property Subject to Execution

Generally, all of a judgment debtor's property is subject to execution. See CCP §§695.010, 699.710. There are, however, some exceptions, including the following:

- Property listed in CCP §699.720(a) (*e.g.,* partnership interest; cause of action in pending litigation; debt, other than earnings, owed by public entity) is not subject to execution, although it may be subject to another method of enforcement (CCP §699.720(b));

- Property listed in CCP §§704.010–704.210 (*e.g.,* motor vehicles; household items, clothing, and personal effects; personal property used to earn livelihood; paid earnings) is exempt, but the exemptions are often subject to specific requirements or monetary limits; and

- A homestead is exempt to the extent of $50,000, $75,000, or $150,000 of equity, depending on the circumstances of the residents (CCP §704.730).

On restrictions on execution against the judgment debtor's unpaid earnings, see §20.20.

§20.20   3. Restrictions on Execution Against Unpaid Earnings

When a writ of execution is directed against a judgment debtor's unpaid earnings, a process commonly known as a "wage garnishment," there are a number of restrictions on the amount of the earnings that may be taken. The specific details depend on whether the writ was issued to collect support arrearages or for some other purpose.

When a writ is issued to collect support arrearages, 50 percent of the judgment debtor's "disposable earnings," as defined by 15 USC §1672, plus any amount withheld under any earnings assignment order for support (see §§20.2–20.15), is exempt. CCP §706.052(a). "Disposable earnings" are defined by 15 USC §1672(b) as earnings remaining after deduction of any amounts required by law to be withheld. Absent a motion under CCP §706.052(b), the remaining amount (*i.e.*, the *non*exempt earnings) will be the amount withheld and paid to the judgment creditor.

On the motion of any interested party, however, the court must (1) equitably divide the judgment debtor's earnings, taking into account the needs of all the persons the judgment debtor is obligated to support, and (2) effectuate the division by determining the amount to be withheld under the wage garnishment. CCP §706.052(b). It is true, at least in theory, that the judgment creditor might file such a motion, seeking to increase the amount to be withheld. In that event, the maximum amount that the court could order withheld would be from 50 to 65 percent of disposable earnings, after withholding for any assignment order; the specific percentage would depend on what persons the judgment debtor is supporting and when the arrearage accrued. CCP §§706.031(d), 706.052(c); 15 USC §1673(b)(2). Because the practical reality, however, is that courts are unlikely to increase the withholding above 50 percent of disposable earnings, motions under CCP §706.052(b) are filed almost exclusively by judgment debtors.

When the writ is issued to collect amounts other than support arrearages (*e.g.*, attorney fees), 75 percent of the judgment debtor's disposable earnings, plus any amount withheld under any assignment order, are exempt and not to be withheld by the employer. CCP §§706.031(d), 706.050; 15 USC §1673(a). As a practical matter, there will be cases in which an assignment order takes more than 25 percent of the judgment debtor's disposable earnings, leaving nothing to be taken under the wage garnishment. Beyond this, the wages of a judgment debtor subject to a wage garnishment for other than support arrearages are typically exempt to the extent they are necessary for the support of the judgment debtor or of family members who are supported, in whole or in part, by the judgment debtor. CCP §706.051(b). Entitlement to the latter exemption is asserted by the judgment debtor's filing of Judicial Council Form 982.5(5) (Claim of Exemption) and Judicial Council Form 982.5(5.5) (Financial Statement) both available in California Judicial Council Forms Manual §2 (Cal CEB 1981). See CCP §706.105.

4. Preparation

§20.21   a. Discussion

A writ of execution is sought in the action in which the orders to be enforced were made. For form of writ, see §20.22. Items 1–20 are completed to the extent applicable. The writ is directed (see Item 1) to the sheriff or marshal in the county where the funds or property to be seized is located.

Because the form was developed with an ordinary civil judgment in mind, it is often unclear, when enforcing family law judgments or orders, what figure should be entered at Item 11 ("Total judgment"). When the judgment or order is for a specific amount, *e.g.,* an attorney fee award, that amount should be entered at Item 11 and the following figures determined accordingly. When a support order is being enforced, the figure entered at Item 11 might be the total amount of support that has accrued to date, with the amount paid to date listed at Item 14 ("Credits"). Alternatively, the amount of arrearages might be listed at Item 11, in which event the amount at Item 14 would be zero.

Interest (see Item 16) should not be overlooked, especially when a significant amount has accrued. Interest accrues at the rate of 10 percent per year for any period of delinquency after 1982 and 7 percent per year for any period of delinquency before or during 1982. *Hersch v Citizens Sav. & Loan Ass'n* (1985) 173 CA3d 373, 218 CR 646. For installment payments, *e.g.,* child, spousal, or family support, each installment is treated as a distinct debt in calculating interest. A court may not waive interest due. *Marriage of Perez* (1995) 35 CA4th 77, 81, 41 CR2d 377. See also *Marriage of Cordero* (2002) 95 CA4th 653, 115 CR2d 787 (court calls on legislature to permit trial courts to modify or relieve interest in the interests of justice). A separate declaration should be prepared and filed, setting forth the calculation of the interest claimed. CCP §685.050(a)(2).

§20.22   b. Form: Writ of Execution (Judicial Council Form EJ-130)

EJ-130

ATTORNEY OR PARTY WITHOUT ATTORNEY *(Name, State Bar number and address)*:	FOR COURT USE ONLY

TELEPHONE NO.:   FAX NO. *(Optional)*:

E-MAIL ADDRESS *(Optional)*:

ATTORNEY FOR *(Name)*:

☐ ATTORNEY FOR   ☐ JUDGMENT CREDITOR   ☐ ASSIGNEE OF RECORD

SUPERIOR COURT OF CALIFORNIA, COUNTY OF

STREET ADDRESS:

MAILING ADDRESS:

CITY AND ZIP CODE:

BRANCH NAME:

PLAINTIFF:

DEFENDANT:

	CASE NUMBER:

WRIT OF
☐ EXECUTION (Money Judgment)
☐ POSSESSION OF   ☐ **Personal Property**   ☐ **Real Property**
☐ SALE

1. **To the Sheriff or Marshal of the County of:**

   You are directed to enforce the judgment described below with daily interest and your costs as provided by law.

2. **To any registered process server:** You are authorized to serve this writ only in accord with CCP 699.080 or CCP 715.040.

3. *(Name):*

   is the ☐ judgment creditor ☐ assignee of record   whose address is shown on this form above the court's name.

4. **Judgment debtor** *(name and last known address):*

   ☐ Additional judgment debtors on next page

5. **Judgment entered on** *(date):*

6. ☐ **Judgment renewed on** *(dates):*

7. **Notice of sale** under this writ
   a. ☐ has not been requested.
   b. ☐ has been requested *(see next page).*
8. ☐ Joint debtor information on next page.

[SEAL]

9. ☐ See next page for information on real or personal property to be delivered under a writ of possession or sold under a writ of sale.
10. ☐ This writ is issued on a sister-state judgment.
11. Total judgment .... $
12. Costs after judgment (per filed order or memo CCP 685.090) .... $
13. Subtotal *(add 11 and 12)* .... $
14. Credits .... $
15. Subtotal *(subtract 14 from 13)* ...... $
16. Interest after judgment (per filed affidavit CCP 685.050) (not on GC 6103.5 fees)... $
17. Fee for issuance of writ .... $
18. **Total** *(add 15, 16, and 17)* .... $
19. Levying officer:
    (a) Add daily interest from date of writ *(at the legal rate on 15)* (not on GC 6103.5 fees) of. . . . . . $
    (b) Pay directly to court costs included in 11 and 17 (GC 6103.5, 68511.3; CCP 699.520(i)) . . . . $
20. ☐ The amounts called for in items 11–19 are different for each debtor. These amounts are stated for each debtor on Attachment 20.

Issued on *(date):*	Clerk, by _____, Deputy

NOTICE TO PERSON SERVED: SEE NEXT PAGE FOR IMPORTANT INFORMATION.

Page 1 of 2

Form Approved for Optional Use
Judicial Council of California
EJ-130 [Rev. January 1, 2006]

WRIT OF EXECUTION

Code of Civil Procedure, §§ 699.520, 712.010,
Government Code, § 6103.5.
www.courtinfo.ca.gov

EJ-130

PLAINTIFF:	CASE NUMBER:
DEFENDANT:	

— Items continued from page 1—

21. ☐ **Additional judgment debtor** *(name and last known address):*

22. ☐ **Notice of sale** has been requested by *(name and address):*

23. ☐ **Joint debtor** was declared bound by the judgment (CCP 989–994)
   a. on *(date):*   a. on *(date):*
   b. name and address of joint debtor: b. name and address of joint debtor:

   c. ☐ additional costs against certain joint debtors *(itemize):*

24. ☐ *(Writ of Possession or Writ of Sale)* **Judgment** was entered for the following:
   a. ☐ Possession of real property: The complaint was filed on *(date):*
      (Check (1) or (2)):
      (1) ☐ The Prejudgment Claim of Right to Possession was served in compliance with CCP 415.46.
           The judgment includes all tenants, subtenants, named claimants, and other occupants of the premises.
      (2) ☐ The Prejudgment Claim of Right to Possession was NOT served in compliance with CCP 415.46.
           (a) $ was the daily rental value on the date the complaint was filed.
           (b) The court will hear objections to enforcement of the judgment under CCP 1174.3 on the following
               dates *(specify):*
   b. ☐ Possession of personal property.
      ☐ If delivery cannot be had, then for the value *(itemize in 9e)* specified in the judgment or supplemental order.
   c. ☐ Sale of personal property.
   d. ☐ Sale of real property.
   e. Description of property:

NOTICE TO PERSON SERVED

WRIT OF EXECUTION OR SALE. Your rights and duties are indicated on the accompanying *Notice of Levy* (Form EJ-150).
WRIT OF POSSESSION OF PERSONAL PROPERTY. If the levying officer is not able to take custody of the property, the levying
officer will make a demand upon you for the property. If custody is not obtained following demand, the judgment may be enforced
as a money judgment for the value of the property specified in the judgment or in a supplemental order.
WRIT OF POSSESSION OF REAL PROPERTY. If the premises are not vacated within five days after the date of service on the
occupant or, if service is by posting, within five days after service on you, the levying officer will remove the occupants from the real
property and place the judgment creditor in possession of the property. Except for a mobile home, personal property remaining on
the premises will be sold or otherwise disposed of in accordance with CCP 1174 unless you or the owner of the property pays the
judgment creditor the reasonable cost of storage and takes possession of the personal property not later than 15 days after the
time the judgment creditor takes possession of the premises.
► *A Claim of Right to Possession form accompanies this writ (unless the Summons was served in compliance with CCP 415.46).*

EJ-130 [Rev. January 1, 2006]   **WRIT OF EXECUTION**   Page 2 of 2

Copies: Original (submit to court clerk); copies for levying officer or process server; office copies.

5. Submission

§20.23　　a. Discussion

The writ, accompanied by the applicable fee, is submitted ex parte to the court clerk for issuance. For form of writ, see §20.22. Depending on the particular circumstances and local practice, it may be necessary to obtain a court order directing the clerk to issue the writ. See *Marriage of Farner* (1989) 216 CA3d 1370, 265 CR 531. Further, because the writ form was developed with an ordinary civil judgment in mind, most courts require a separate application or declaration, for which some of them have their own forms, when a family law judgment or order is being enforced. For a sample form of declaration, see §20.24. Note that a separate declaration is routinely required when the writ is sought to enforce a support order (see Fam C §5104) and when postjudgment interest is claimed (see §20.21).

Once issued, the writ, accompanied by the applicable fee, is typically submitted for enforcement to the sheriff or marshal in the county where the property to be seized is located. In some instances, the writ may be enforced by a registered process server, who may levy more than once under the same writ of execution, if it remains valid. See CCP §§699.080, 715.040. Depending on the particular circumstances, papers in addition to the original and copies of the writ may be required. The office to which the writ will be submitted should be contacted to ascertain precisely what papers and fees must be submitted.

Probably the most common target of a writ of execution is the judgment debtor's earnings. When the writ will be enforced in this manner, a process commonly referred to as a "wage garnishment," additional forms are required. The judgment creditor prepares an Application for Earnings Withholding Order (see form in §20.25). Depending on local procedure, either the judgment creditor or the levying officer prepares either an Earnings Withholding Order (see form in §20.26) or an Earnings Withholding Order for Support (see form in §20.27). The latter is used only when the writ of execution was issued to collect delinquent amounts payable for child, spousal, or family support. See CCP §706.030(a).

When the writ will be enforced against property other than the judgment debtor's earnings (*e.g.,* against a bank account), a letter of instructions, specifically describing the property and its location, is often required.

When an attorney seeks to enforce an award of attorney fees or costs in his or her own name and no longer represents the party for whose benefit the order was made, the attorney must give at least 10 days' written notice to the former client or to the successor attorney. During that ten-day period, the former client may file a motion for partial or total reallocation of fees and costs to cover the cost of the successor attorney, in which event enforcement will be stayed until the motion is resolved. Fam C §272.

§20.24   b. Form: Declaration in Support of Issuance of Writ of Execution

_ _[Attorney name]_ _
_ _[State Bar number]_ _
_ _[Address]_ _
_ _[Telephone number]_ _

Attorney for _ _[name]_ _

**SUPERIOR COURT OF CALIFORNIA
COUNTY OF _ _ _ _ _ _**

Marriage of	)	No. _ _ _ _ _ _
	)	
Petitioner: _ _ _ _ _ _ _ _	)	**DECLARATION IN SUPPORT**
	)	**OF ISSUANCE OF WRIT OF**
Respondent: _ _ _ _ _ _ _ _	)	**EXECUTION**
	)	
_____	)	

I, _ _[name of judgment creditor]_ _, **declare as follows:**

1. I am the _ _[petitioner/respondent]_ _ **in this action.**

2. On _ _[date]_ _, **this Court ordered** _ _[respondent/ petitioner]_ _ **to pay me** _ _[e.g., attorney fees in the amount of $350, payable at the rate of $50 per month, on or before the first day of each month, commencing on _ _[date]_ _, with the entire unpaid balance immediately due and payable if payments are delinquent in any amount for 30 days or more]_ _. **This order may be found**

at _ _[specify location, e.g., by paragraph, page, and line numbers]_ _.

3. _ _[Respondent/Petitioner]_ _ _ _[e.g., has made no payments whatever and more than 30 days have passed since the initial payment was due. Consequently, the entire unpaid balance of $350 is due and payable]_ _.

4. I request that a writ of execution issue in my favor in the amount of _ _[e.g., $350]_ _.

I declare under penalty of perjury under the laws of the State of California that the foregoing is true and correct.

Date: _____

                    __[Signature]__
                    _ _[Typed name]_ _
                    _ _[Petitioner/Respondent]_ _

[Add when court order required]

ORDER

Good cause appearing, it is ordered that a writ of execution issue in favor of _ _[name of judgment creditor]_ _ **in the amount of $**_ _ _ _ _ _ _.

[Continue]

Date: _____

               _____
               Judge of the Superior Court

Copies: Original (submit to court clerk with writ of execution); office copies.

§20.25   **c. Form: Application for Earnings Withholding Order (Wage Garnishment) (Judicial Council Form WG-001)**

WG-001

ATTORNEY OR PARTY WITHOUT ATTORNEY *(Name, State Bar number, and address)*. TELEPHONE NO..	LEVYING OFFICER *(Name and Address)*
ATTORNEY FOR *(Name)*:	
NAME OF COURT, JUDICIAL DISTRICT, OR BRANCH COURT, IF ANY	
PLAINTIFF:	
DEFENDANT:	
APPLICATION FOR EARNINGS WITHHOLDING ORDER **(Wage Garnishment)**	LEVYING OFFICER FILE NO. COURT CASE NO..

TO THE SHERIFF OR ANY MARSHAL OR CONSTABLE OF THE COUNTY OF
OR ANY REGISTERED PROCESS SERVER

1. The judgment creditor *(name)*:

   requests issuance of an Earnings Withholding Order directing the employer to withhold the earnings of the judgment debtor (employee).

   ⌐   Name and address of employer   ⌐   Name and address of employee ⌐

   ⌊   ⌊   ⌊

2. The amounts withheld are to be paid to   Social Security Number *(if known)*:
   a. ☐ The attorney (or party without an attorney)   b. ☐ Other *(name, address, and telephone)*:
   named at the top of this page.

3. a. Judgment was entered on *(date)*:
   b. Collect the amount directed by the Writ of Execution unless a lesser amount is specified here:
   $

4. ☐ The Writ of Execution was issued to collect delinquent amounts payable for the **support** of a child, former spouse, or spouse of the employee.

5. ☐ Special instructions *(specify)*:

6. *(Check a or b)*
   a. ☐ I have not previously obtained an order directing this employer to withhold the earnings of this employee.
   —OR—
   b. ☐ I have previously obtained such an order, but that order *(check one)*:
   ☐ was terminated by a court order, but I am entitled to apply for another Earnings Withholding Order under the provisions of Code of Civil Procedure section 706.105(h).
   ☐ was ineffective.

   ▶

   (TYPE OR PRINT NAME)   *(SIGNATURE OF ATTORNEY OR PARTY WITHOUT ATTORNEY)*

   I declare under penalty of perjury under the laws of the State of California that the foregoing is true and correct.

   Date:

   ▶

   (TYPE OR PRINT NAME)   *(SIGNATURE OF DECLARANT)*

Copies: Original (submit to levying officer or process server); office copies.

§20.26   **d. Form: Earnings Withholding Order (Wage Garnishment) (Judicial Council Form WG-002)**

WG-002

ATTORNEY OR PARTY WITHOUT ATTORNEY *(Name, State Bar number, and address)* TELEPHONE AND FAX NOS.	LEVYING OFFICER *(Name and Address)*

ATTORNEY FOR *(Name):*

NAME OF COURT, JUDICIAL DISTRICT, AND BRANCH COURT, IF ANY:

PLAINTIFF:

DEFENDANT:

EARNINGS WITHHOLDING ORDER (Wage Garnishment)	LEVYING OFFICER FILE NO.:	COURT CASE NO.:

EMPLOYEE: *KEEP YOUR COPY OF THIS LEGAL PAPER.*   **EMPLEADO:** *GUARDE ESTE PAPEL OFICIAL*

EMPLOYER: Enter the following date to assist your record keeping.
     Date this order was received by employer (specify the date of personal delivery by levying officer or registered process server or the date mail receipt was signed):

TO THE EMPLOYER REGARDING YOUR EMPLOYEE:
     Name and address of employer   Name and address of employee

Social Security Number *(if known):*

1. A judgment creditor has obtained this order to collect a court judgment against your employee. You are directed to withhold part of the earnings of the employee *(see instructions on reverse of this form).* Pay the withheld sums to the **levying officer** *(name and address above).*
   If the employee works for you now, you must **give the employee a copy of this order and the *Employee Instructions*** (form WG-003) within 10 days after receiving this order.
   Complete both copies of the form *Employer's Return* (form WG-005) and **mail them to the levying officer** within 15 days after receiving this order, whether or not the employee works for you.

2. The total amount due is: $
   Count 10 calendar days from the date when you received this order. If your employee's pay period ends before the tenth day, *do not* withhold earnings payable for that pay period. *Do* withhold from earnings that are payable for any pay period ending on or after that tenth day.

   Continue withholding for all pay periods until you withhold the amount due. The levying officer will notify you of an assessment you should withhold in addition to the amount due. Do not withhold more than the total of these amounts. Never withhold any earnings payable before the beginning of the earnings withholding period.

3. The judgment was entered in the court on *(date):*
   The judgment creditor *(if different from the plaintiff)* is *(name):*

4. The *EMPLOYER'S INSTRUCTIONS* on the reverse tell you how much of the employee's earnings to withhold each payday and answer other questions you may have.

Date:

_____   ▶
(TYPE OR PRINT NAME)   (SIGNATURE)

☐ LEVYING OFFICER   ☐ REGISTERED PROCESS SERVER
(Employer's Instructions on reverse)   Page 1 of 2

Form Adopted by the Judicial Council of California WG-002 [Rev. January 1, 2007]

EARNINGS WITHHOLDING ORDER (Wage Garnishment)

CEB

Code of Civil Procedure, §§ 706.022, 706.108, 706.125 www.courtinfo.ca.gov

EMPLOYER'S INSTRUCTIONS
EARNINGS WITHHOLDING ORDERS

WG-002

The instructions in paragraph 1 on the reverse of this form describe your early duties to provide information to your employee and the levying officer.

Your other duties are TO WITHHOLD THE CORRECT AMOUNT OF EARNINGS (if any) and PAY IT TO THE LEVYING OFFICER during the *withholding period*.

The withholding period is the period covered by the *Earnings Withholding Order* (this order). The withholding period begins ten (10) calendar days after you receive the order and continues until the total amount due, plus additional amounts for costs and interest (which will be listed in a levying officer's notice), is withheld.

It may end sooner if (1) you receive a written notice signed by the levying officer specifying an earlier termination date, or (2) an order of higher priority (explained on the reverse of the *EMPLOYER'S RETURN* is received.

You are entitled to rely on and must obey all written notices signed by the levying officer.

The *Employer's Return* (form WG-005) describes several situations that could affect the withholding period for this order. If you receive more than one *Earnings Withholding Order* during a withholding period, review that form (*Employer's Return*) for instructions.

If the employee stops working for you, the *Earnings Withholding Order* ends after no amounts are withheld for a continuous 180 day period. If withholding ends because the earnings are subject to an order of higher priority, the *Earnings Withholding Order* ends after a continuous two year period during which no amounts are withheld under the order. **Return the Earnings Withholding Order to the levying officer with a statement of the reason it is being returned.**

WHAT TO DO WITH THE MONEY

The amounts withheld during the withholding period must be paid to the levying officer by the 15th of the next month after each payday. If you wish to pay more frequently than monthly, each payment must be made within ten (10) days after the close of the pay period.

Be sure to mark each check with the case number, *the levying officer's file number, if different, and the employee's name so the money will be applied to the correct account.*

WHAT IF YOU STILL HAVE QUESTIONS?

The garnishment law is contained in the Code of Civil Procedure beginning with section 706.010. Sections 706.022, 706.025, and 706.104 explain the employer's duties.

The Federal Wage Garnishment Law and federal rules provide the basic protections on which the California law is based. Inquiries about the federal law will be answered by mail, telephone, or personal interview at any office of the Wage and Hour Division of the U.S. Department of Labor. Offices are listed in the telephone directory under the U.S. Department of Labor in the U.S. Government listing.

THE CHART BELOW AND THESE INSTRUCTIONS DO NOT APPLY TO ORDERS FOR THE SUPPORT OF A SPOUSE, FORMER SPOUSE, OR CHILD.

The chart below shows *HOW MUCH TO WITHHOLD* when the federal minimum wage is $5.15 per hour.
If the *FEDERAL* minimum wage changes in the future, the levying officer will provide a chart showing the new withholding rates.

COMPUTATION INSTRUCTIONS

State and federal law limits the amount of earnings can be withheld. The limitations are based on the employee's disposable earnings, which are different from gross pay or take-home pay.

To determine the CORRECT AMOUNT OF EARNINGS TO BE WITH-HELD (if any), compute the employee's *disposable earnings*.

(A) Earnings include any money (whether called wages, salary, commissions, bonuses, or anything else) that is paid by an employer to an employee for personal services. Vacation or sick pay is subject to withholding as it is received by the employee. Tips are generally not included as earnings since they are not paid by the employer.

(B) *Disposable earnings* are the earnings left after subtracting the part of the earnings a state or federal law requires an employer to withhold. Generally these required deductions are (1) federal income tax, (2) federal social security, (3) state income tax, (4) state disability insurance, and (5) payments to public employee retirement systems. Disposable earnings will change when the required deductions change.

After the employee's *disposable earnings* are known, use the chart below to determine what amount should be withheld. In the column listed under the employee's pay period, find the employee's disposable earnings. The amount shown below that is the amount to be withheld. For example, if the employee is paid disposable earnings of $500 twice a month (semi-monthly), the correct amount to withhold is 25 percent each payday, or $125.

The chart below is based on the minimum wage that was effective September 1, 1997. It will change if the minimum wage changes. Restrictions are based on the minimum wage effective at the time the earnings are payable.

Occasionally, the employee's earnings will also be subject to a *Wage and Earnings Assignment Order*, an order available from family law courts for child, spousal, or family support. The amount required to be withheld for that order should be deducted from the amount to be withheld for this order.

— IMPORTANT WARNINGS —

1. IT IS AGAINST THE LAW TO FIRE THE EMPLOYEE BECAUSE OF *EARNINGS WITHHOLDING ORDERS* FOR THE PAYMENT OF ONLY ONE INDEBTEDNESS. No matter how many orders you receive, so long as they all relate to a single indebtedness (no matter how many debts are represented in that judgment) the employee may not be fired.

2. IT IS ILLEGAL TO AVOID AN *EARNINGS WITHHOLDING ORDER* BY POSTPONING OR ADVANCING THE PAYMENT OF EARNINGS. The employee's pay period must not be changed to prevent the order from taking effect.

3. IT IS ILLEGAL NOT TO PAY AMOUNTS WITHHELD FOR THE *EARNINGS WITHHOLDING ORDER* TO THE LEVYING OFFICER. Your duty is to pay the money to the levying officer who will pay the money in accordance with the law that apply to this case.

IF YOU VIOLATE ANY OF THESE LAWS YOU MAYBE HELD LIABLE TO PAY CIVIL DAMAGES AND YOU MAY BE SUBJECT TO CRIMINAL PROSECUTION!

FEDERAL MINIMUM WAGE: $5.15 per hour   (Beginning April 1, 1991, and continuing indefinitely.)

PAY PERIOD	Daily	Weekly	Every Two Weeks	Twice a Month	Monthly
DISPOSABLE EARNINGS	$0-$154.50	$0-$154.50	$0-$309.00	$0-$334.75	$0-$669.50
WITHHOLD	None	None	None	None	None
DISPOSABLE EARNINGS	$154.51-$206.00	$154.51-$206.00	$309.01-$412.00	$334.76-$446.33	$669.51-$892.67
WITHHOLD	Amount above $154.50	Amount above $154.50	Amount above $309.00	Amount above $334.75	Amount above $669.50
DISPOSABLE EARNINGS	$206.01 or More	$206.01 or More	$412.01 or More	$446.34 or More	$ 892.68 or More
WITHHOLD	Maximum of 25% of Disposable Earnings	Maximum of 25% of Disposable Earnings	Maximum of 25% of Disposable Earnings	Maximum of 25% of Disposable Earnings	Maximum of 25% of Disposable Earnings

WG-002 [Rev. January 1, 2007]

EARNINGS WITHHOLDING ORDER
(Wage Garnishment)   CEB

Page 2 of 2

Copies: Original and copies as required (submit to levying officer or process server); office copies.

Comment: Note that in some counties the form is prepared by the levying officer or process server, rather than being prepared and submitted by the judgment creditor.

§20.27   e. Form: Earnings Withholding Order for Support (Wage Garnishment) (Judicial Council Form WG-004)

WG-004

ATTORNEY OR PARTY WITHOUT ATTORNEY (Name, State Bar number, and address)	TELEPHONE NO.	LEVYING OFFICER (Name and Address):

ATTORNEY FOR (Name):

NAME OF COURT, JUDICIAL DISTRICT, OR BRANCH COURT, IF ANY:

PLAINTIFF:

DEFENDANT:

EARNINGS WITHHOLDING ORDER FOR SUPPORT (Wage Garnishment)	LEVYING OFFICER FILE NO.	COURT CASE NO.

EMPLOYEE: *KEEP YOUR COPY OF THIS LEGAL PAPER.*   ***EMPLEADO:*** *GUARDE ESTE PAPEL OFICIAL.*

EMPLOYER: Enter the following date to assist your record keeping.

Date this order was received by employer (specify the date of personal delivery by levying officer or registered process server or the date mail receipt was signed):

TO THE EMPLOYER REGARDING YOUR EMPLOYEE:

Name and address of employer   Name and address of employee

Social Security Number (if known):

1. A judgment creditor has obtained this order to collect a court judgment against your employee. You are directed to withhold part of the earnings of the employee *(see instructions on reverse of this form)*. Pay the withheld sums to the **levying officer** *(name and address above)*.

   If the employee works for you now, you must **give the employee a copy of this order and the Employee Instructions** within 10 days after receiving this order.

   Complete both copies of the form Employer's Return and mail them to the levying officer within 15 days after receiving this order, whether or not the employee works for you.

2. The total amount due is $

   Count 10 calendar days from the date when you received this order. If your employee's pay period ends before the tenth day, **do not** withhold earnings payable for that pay period. **Do** withhold from earnings that are payable for any pay period ending on or after that tenth day.

   Continue withholding until
   (1) the total amount due has been withheld; or
   (2) you receive a court order or an order from the levying officer telling you to stop the withholding earlier.

3. The judgment was entered in the court shown above. The judgment creditor is *(name):*

4. The EMPLOYER'S INSTRUCTIONS on the reverse tell you how much of the employee's earnings to withhold each payday. Follow those instructions unless you receive a court order or order from the levying officer giving you other instructions.

Date:

....
(TYPE OR PRINT NAME)   ▶_____
                                  (SIGNATURE)
                                  ☐ LEVYING OFFICER   ☐ REGISTERED PROCESS SERVER

The **EMPLOYER'S INSTRUCTIONS** on the reverse contain special rules that apply to Earnings Withholding Order For Support. Read the instructions carefully.
(Employer's Instructions on reverse)   Page 1 of 2

Form Adopted by the Judicial Council of California WG-004 [Rev. January 1, 2007]	**EARNINGS WITHHOLDING ORDER FOR SUPPORT** (Wage Garnishment)	☯EB	Code of Civil Procedure, §§ 706.030, 706.108, 706.052 www.courtinfo.ca.gov

EMPLOYER'S INSTRUCTIONS
(EARNINGS WITHHOLDING ORDERS FOR SUPPORT)

WG-004

These instructions apply *only* to Earnings Withholding Orders for Support. Applicable instructions appear on the reverse of the other types of Earnings Withholding Orders.

The instructions in paragraph 1 on the reverse of this form describe your early duties to provide information to your employee and the levying officer.

Your other duties are TO WITHHOLD THE CORRECT AMOUNT OF EARNINGS (if any) and PAY IT TO THE LEVYING OFFICER during the *withholding period*.

The usual *withholding period* begins ten (10) calendar days after you receive the Earnings Withholding Order. In the case of an Earnings Withholding Order for Support (this Order) the *withholding period continues* until one of two things happens: (1) the total amount specified in the Order, plus any amounts listed in a notice from the levying officer, has been withheld, or (2) you receive a court order or notice signed by the levying officer specifying a termination date.

You are entitled to rely on and should obey all written notices signed by the levying officer.

The form Employer's Return describes several situations that could affect the withholding period for this order. If you receive more than one Earnings Withholding Order during a withholding period, review that form (Employer's Return) for instructions.

Your duty to withhold does not end merely because the employee no longer works for you. Withholding for an Earnings Withholding Order for Support does not automatically terminate until one year after the employment of the employee by the employer ends.

WHAT TO DO WITH THE MONEY

The amounts withheld during the withholding period must be paid to the levying officer by the 15th of the next month after each payday. If you wish to pay more frequently than monthly, each payment must be made within ten (10) days after the close of the pay period.

Be sure to mark each check with the case number, the levying officer's file number, if different, and the employee's name so the money will be applied to the correct account

WHAT IF YOU STILL HAVE QUESTIONS?

The garnishment law is contained in the Code of Civil Procedure beginning with section 706.010. Sections 706.022, 706.025, and 706.104 explain the employer's duties.

The Federal Wage Garnishment Law and federal rules provide the basic protections on which the California law is based.

Inquiries about the federal law will be answered by mail, telephone or personal interview at any office of the Wage and Hour Division of the U.S. Department of Labor. Offices are listed in the telephone directory under the U.S. Department of Labor in the U.S. Government listing.

COMPUTATION INSTRUCTIONS

State and federal law limits the amount of earnings that can be withheld. The limitations are based on the employee's disposable earnings, which are different from gross pay or take-home pay.

To determine the CORRECT AMOUNT OF EARNINGS TO BE WITHHELD (if any), compute the employee's *disposable* earnings.

(A) Earnings include any money, (whether called wages, salary, commissions, bonuses or anything else) that is paid by an employer to an employee for personal services. Vacation or sick pay is subject to withholding as it is received by the employee. Tips are generally not included as earning since they are not paid by the employer.

(B) *Disposable earnings* are the earnings left after subtracting the part of the earnings a state or federal law requires an employer to withhold. Generally these required deductions are (1) federal income tax, (2) federal social security, (3) state income tax, (4) state disability insurance, and (5) payments to public employees' retirement systems. Disposable earnings will change when the required deductions change.

After the employee's disposable earnings are known, WITHHOLD FIFTY (50) PERCENT of the *disposable earnings* for the Withholding Order for Support. For example, if the employee has monthly disposable earnings of $1,432, the sum of $716 would be withheld to pay to the levying officer on account of this order.

Occasionally, the employee's earnings will also be subject to a Wage and Earnings Assignment Order, an order available for child support or spousal support. The amount required to be withheld for that order should be deducted from the amount to be withheld for this order. For example, if the employee is subject to a Wage and Earnings Assignment Order and the employer is required to withhold $300 per month to pay on that order, when the employer receives this Earnings Withholding Order for Support, the employer should deduct the $300 for the Wage and Earnings Assignment Order from the $716 and pay the balance to the levying officer each month for this order.

— IMPORTANT WARNINGS —

1. IT IS AGAINST THE LAW TO FIRE THE EMPLOYEE BECAUSE OF EARNINGS WITHHOLDING ORDERS FOR THE PAYMENT OF ONLY ONE INDEBTEDNESS. No matter how many orders you receive, so long as they all relate to judgment (no matter how many debts are represented in that judgment) the employee may not be fired.

2. IT IS ILLEGAL TO AVOID AN EARNINGS WITHHOLDING ORDER BY POSTPONING OR ADVANCING THE PAYMENT OF EARNINGS. The employee's pay period must not be changed to prevent the order from taking effect.

3. IT IS ILLEGAL NOT TO PAY AMOUNTS WITHHELD FOR THE EARNINGS WITHHOLDING ORDER TO THE LEVYING OFFICER. Your duty is to pay the money to the levying officer who will pay the money in accordance with the laws that apply to this case.

IF YOU VIOLATE ANY OF THESE LAWS, YOU MAY BE HELD LIABLE TO PAY CIVIL DAMAGES AND YOU MAY BE SUBJECT TO CRIMINAL PROSECUTION!

WG-004 [Rev. January 1, 2007] **EARNINGS WITHHOLDING ORDER FOR SUPPORT**   Page 2 of 2
(Wage Garnishment)

Copies: Original and copies as required (submit to levying officer or process server); office copies.

Comment: Note that in some counties the form is prepared by the levying officer or process server, rather than being prepared and submitted by the judgment creditor.

§20.28　　6. Priorities

An earnings assignment order for support (see §§20.2–20.15) must be given priority over any earnings withholding order (*i.e.*, the order enforcing a writ of execution against a judgment debtor's unpaid earnings) directed against the same employee. CCP §706.031(b). Both may be enforced, however, to the extent that the combined withholding does not violate the restrictions on execution against unpaid earnings (see §20.20). CCP §706.031(c)–(d). An earnings withholding order for support has priority over any other earnings withholding order. CCP §706.030(c)(2). Again, both may be enforced to the extent that the combined withholding does not violate the restrictions on execution against unpaid earnings. CCP §706.030(c)(3).

With respect to multiple *nonsupport* earnings withholding orders served on an employer, the first served must be honored. CCP §706.023(a). A nonsupport earnings withholding order is ineffective if served while the employer is required to comply with another such order. CCP §706.023(c).

§20.29　　7. Execution Against Community Property

Community property, most notably the community property interest of a judgment debtor's spouse, is generally subject to execution whenever it would be liable for the underlying debt under the Family Code. See CCP §695.020. On determination of exemptions when the judgment debtor is married, see CCP §§703.110–703.115.

Community property received by a spouse in a property division, however, is not liable for a debt incurred by the other spouse unless the debt is assigned to the nondebtor spouse in the division. Fam C §916(a)(2); *Marriage of Braendle* (1996) 46 CA4th 1037, 1042, 54 CR2d 397. But note that Fam C §916(a)(2) (former CC §5120.160(a)(2)) expressly does not protect property from liability for the satisfaction of a lien against it. See *Lezine v Security Pac. Fin. Servs., Inc.* (1996) 14 C4th 56, 65, 58 CR2d 76. Even when the debt is assigned to the nondebtor spouse, the community property received by that spouse in the division is subject to enforcement of a judgment entered after the division only if he or she is made a party to the judgment for that purpose. Fam C §916(a)(3); *Marriage of Braendle, supra.*

NOTE► The California Supreme Court has held that judgments of dissolution and settlements that result in transfers of property between spouses are subject to the Uniform Fraudulent Transfer Act (UFTA) (CC §§3439–3439.12). *Mejia v Reed* (2003) 31 C4th 657, 3 CR3d 390; *Filip v Bucurenciu* (2005) 129 CA4th 825, 28 CR3d 884. For discussion of when a third party might attack a judgment or settlement agreement as a fraudulent transfer, see §18.61.

§20.30   8. Claim of Exemption

When the property against which the writ of execution is directed is subject to exemption (see CCP §§704.010–704.210), the judgment debtor may contest execution by filing a claim of exemption. The claim of exemption must be filed with the levying officer within 10 days after service on the judgment debtor of the notice of levy. CCP §703.520(a).

When a claim of exemption is filed, the levying officer must promptly serve on the judgment creditor a copy of the claim of exemption and a notice informing the judgment creditor of the requirements for contesting the claim. CCP §703.540. Unless the judgment creditor, within 10 days after service of the claim of exemption by the levying officer, files a notice of opposition and a notice of motion for an order determining the claim, the levying officer must release the property to the extent it is claimed to be exempt. CCP §703.550.

§20.31   9. Motion to Quash

A motion to quash (or recall) a writ of execution is based on the court's inherent power to control its process. See, *e.g., Marriage of Chapman* (1988) 205 CA3d 253, 252 CR 359 (obligation modified by agreement and paid); *Marriage of Peet* (1978) 84 CA3d 974, 149 CR 108 (judgment debtor entitled to credit for earlier overpayments); *Jackson v Jackson* (1975) 51 CA3d 363, 124 CR 101 (during period that child was with support obligor despite custody award to other parent, obligor satisfied support obligation by spending amounts for child in excess of support ordered).

The motion to quash is prepared and processed in the same manner as a noticed motion for temporary orders. For discussion of, and forms for, motions for temporary orders, see §§11.16–11.63. The judgment debtor prepares the Judicial Council forms of (1) Order to Show Cause (see form in §11.18) or Notice of Motion (see form in §11.20) and (2) Application for Order and Supporting Declaration (see form in §11.22). The Order to Show Cause is generally preferable to the Notice of Motion in this context because it allows for an order staying execution pending the hearing.

§20.32   D. Judgment Lien on Real Property

A judgment lien on real property to enforce a money judgment may be created by recordation. CCP §§697.310–697.320. The particular document to be recorded depends on the nature of the money judgment being enforced. When the underlying money judgment is an order for child, spousal, or family support payable in installments, the lien is created by recording an Abstract of Support Judgment (see form in §20.34), an interstate lien form promulgated by the federal Secretary of Health and Human Services (for sister-state judgments or orders), or a certified copy of the order. See CCP §§674(b)–(c), 697.320(a)(1). For any other money judgment, *e.g.,* an order for payment of attorney fees, the lien is created by recording an Abstract of Judgment (see form in §20.35). See CCP §§674(a), 697.310(a).

The judgment lien is a simple and sometimes very effective enforcement method that should not be overlooked. The benefit from the lien is usually realized when the judgment debtor attempts (1) to sell real property in a county in which the document is recorded or (2) to obtain a loan to be secured by real property located in such a county. The prospective purchaser or lender will probably insist that any liens be paid off.

§20.33   1. Procedure

When the underlying money judgment is a support order payable in installments, the judgment creditor may either complete an Abstract of Support Judgment (see form in §20.34) and submit it to the court clerk for issuance or simply obtain a certified copy of the judgment or order containing the support provision to be enforced. The document should then be recorded with the county recorder in every county in which the obligor has or is likely to acquire an interest in real property.

When the underlying money judgment is not a support order, the judgment creditor completes an Abstract of Judgment (see form in §20.35) and submits it first to the court clerk for issuance and then to the appropriate county recorders for recording.

It should be noted that the judgment debtor's driver's license number, social security number, and (for the Abstract of Support Judgment) birthdate must be included on any abstract if known and, if unknown, that fact must be indicated. CCP §674(a)(6); see Items 1.b.-1.d. on the Abstract of Support Judgment form and Items 1.b.-1.c. on the Abstract of Judgment form. When an abstract recorded after January 1, 1979, does not contain a judgment debtor's driver's license number or social security number that was known at the time of recordation, the judgment creditor should record an Amendment to Abstract of Judgment that includes the omitted information. CCP §674(b). Failure to include that information on a recorded abstract when known, unless the failure is corrected by such an amendment, may result in a void lien. See *Keele v Reich* (1985) 169 CA3d 1129, 1131, 215 CR 756 (omission of judgment debtor's social security number when known or immediately accessible to judgment creditor nullifies abstract).

When the underlying judgment is that of a sister-state, it may not be used directly to create a lien against the judgment debtor's real property. Rather, the sister-state judgment must first be reduced to a California judgment, after which an abstract or (if the underlying order is for support) a certified copy of the California judgment may be recorded. *Kahn v Berman* (1988) 198 CA3d 1499, 244 CR 575.

**§20.34   a. Form: Abstract of Support Judgment
(Judicial Council Form FL-480)**

FL-480

ATTORNEY OR PARTY WITHOUT ATTORNEY *(Name and Address)*: ☐ Recording requested by and return to: TELEPHONE NO.: ☐ ATTORNEY FOR ☐ JUDGMENT CREDITOR ☐ ASSIGNEE OF RECORD	FOR RECORDER'S USE ONLY

SUPERIOR COURT OF CALIFORNIA, COUNTY OF
STREET ADDRESS:
MAILING ADDRESS:
CITY AND ZIP CODE:
BRANCH NAME:
PETITIONER/PLAINTIFF:

RESPONDENT/DEFENDANT:

ABSTRACT OF SUPPORT JUDGMENT	CASE NUMBER:

1. The ☐ judgment creditor ☐ assignee of record
applies for an abstract of a support judgment and represents the following:
a. Judgment debtor's
　　　　Name and last known address

    FOR COURT USE ONLY

b. Driver license No. and state:　　　　☐ Unknown
c. Social security number:　　　　　　☐ Unknown
d. Birth date:　　　　　　　　　　　☐ Unknown

Date:

▶

_____　　_____
(TYPE OR PRINT NAME)　　　　　　　　(SIGNATURE OF APPLICANT OR ATTORNEY)

2. I CERTIFY that the judgment entered in this action contains an order for payment of spousal, family, or child support.

3. Judgment creditor *(name)*:

whose address appears on this form above the court's name.

4. ☐ The support is ordered to be paid to the following county officer *(name and address)*:

[SEAL]

This abstract issued on *(date)*:

5. Judgment debtor *(full name as it appears in judgment)*:

6. a. A judgment was entered on *(date)*:
b. Renewal was entered on *(date)*:
c. Renewal was entered on *(date)*:

7. ☐ An execution lien is endorsed on the judgment as follows:
a. Amount: $
b. In favor of *(name and address)*:

8. A stay of enforcement has
a ☐ not been ordered by the court.
b. ☐ been ordered by the court effective until *(date)*
9. ☐ This is an installment judgment.

Clerk, by _____, Deputy

Page 1 of 1

Form Adopted for Mandatory Use
Judicial Council of California
FL-480 [Rev. January 1, 2003]

ABSTRACT OF SUPPORT JUDGMENT

Code of Civil Procedure, §§ 488.480, 674,
697.320, 700.190
www.courtinfo.ca.gov

Copies: Original (submit to court clerk for issuance and then to county recorder for recordation); office copies.

§20.35 b. Form: Abstract of Judgment—Civil and Small Claims (Judicial Council Form EJ-001)

EJ-001

ATTORNEY OR PARTY WITHOUT ATTORNEY (Name, address, State Bar number, and telephone number):

Recording requested by and return to:

☐ ATTORNEY FOR ☐ JUDGMENT CREDITOR ☐ ASSIGNEE OF RECORD

SUPERIOR COURT OF CALIFORNIA, COUNTY OF

STREET ADDRESS:

MAILING ADDRESS:

CITY AND ZIP CODE:

BRANCH NAME:

FOR RECORDER'S USE ONLY

PLAINTIFF:

DEFENDANT:

CASE NUMBER:

ABSTRACT OF JUDGMENT—CIVIL AND SMALL CLAIMS ☐ Amended

FOR COURT USE ONLY

1. The ☐ judgment creditor ☐ assignee of record applies for an abstract of judgment and represents the following:
   a. Judgment debtor's

   Name and last known address

   b. Driver's license No. and state: ☐ Unknown
   c. Social security No.: ☐ Unknown
   d. Summons or notice of entry of sister-state judgment was personally served or mailed to (name and address):

2. ☐ Information on additional judgment debtors is shown on page 2.

3. Judgment creditor (name and address):

4. ☐ Information on additional judgment creditors is shown on page 2.

5. ☐ Original abstract recorded in this county:
   a. Date:
   b. Instrument No.:

Date:

_____
(TYPE OR PRINT NAME)

▶ _____
(SIGNATURE OF APPLICANT OR ATTORNEY)

6. Total amount of judgment as entered or last renewed:
   $

7. All judgment creditors and debtors are listed on this abstract.

8. a. Judgment entered on (date):
   b. Renewal entered on (date):

9. ☐ This judgment is an installment judgment.

[SEAL]

This abstract issued on (date):

10. ☐ An ☐ execution lien ☐ attachment lien is endorsed on the judgment as follows:
    a. Amount: $
    b. In favor of (name and address):

11. A stay of enforcement has
    a. ☐ not been ordered by the court.
    b. ☐ been ordered by the court effective until (date):

12. a. ☐ I certify that this is a true and correct abstract of the judgment entered in this action.
    b. ☐ A certified copy of the judgment is attached.

Clerk, by _____, Deputy

Form Adopted for Mandatory Use
Judicial Council of California
EJ-001 [Rev. January 1, 2006]

ABSTRACT OF JUDGMENT—CIVIL AND SMALL CLAIMS

Page 1 of 2
Code of Civil Procedure, §§ 488.480, 674, 700.190

PLAINTIFF:	CASE NUMBER:
DEFENDANT:	

NAMES AND ADDRESSES OF ADDITIONAL JUDGMENT CREDITORS:

13. Judgment creditor *(name and address):*   14. Judgment creditor *(name and address):*

15. ☐ Continued on Attachment 15.

INFORMATION ON ADDITIONAL JUDGMENT DEBTORS:

16.   Name and last known address   17.   Name and last known address

Driver's license No. & state: ☐ Unknown   Driver's license No. & state: ☐ Unknown
Social security No.:   ☐ Unknown   Social security No.:   ☐ Unknown
Summons was personally served at or mailed to *(address):*   Summons was personally served at or mailed to *(address):*

18.   Name and last known address   19.   Name and last known address

Driver's license No. & state: ☐ Unknown   Driver's license No. & state: ☐ Unknown
Social security No.:   ☐ Unknown   Social security No.:   ☐ Unknown
Summons was personally served at or mailed to *(address):*   Summons was personally served at or mailed to *(address):*

20.   Name and last known address   21.   Name and last known address

Driver's license No. & state: ☐ Unknown   Driver's license No. & state: ☐ Unknown
Social security No.:   ☐ Unknown   Social security No.:   ☐ Unknown
Summons was personally served at or mailed to *(address):*   Summons was personally served at or mailed to *(address):*

22. ☐ Continued on Attachment 22.

EJ-001 [Rev. January 1, 2006]   **ABSTRACT OF JUDGMENT—CIVIL**   Page 2 of 2
                                        AND SMALL CLAIMS

Copies: Original (submit to court clerk for issuance and then to county recorder for recordation); office copies.

§20.36   2. Duration

Unless the money judgment is satisfied or the judgment lien is released, the lien continues for 10 years in the case of a nonsupport judgment and for as long as the judgment remains enforceable in the case of a support judgment. CCP §§697.310(b), 697.320(b). When the underlying judgment or order was issued under the Family Code and is not for support, there appears to be no provision for extending the lien beyond 10 years. Code of Civil Procedure §697.310(b), which applies to such judgments, requires that any extension beyond 10 years be obtained under CCP §683.180. Section 683.180 is expressly inapplicable to judgments issued under the Family Code, unless the Family Code provides otherwise. CCP §683.310. Under Fam C §291, the enforceability and renewal provisions of CCP §§683.010–683.320 apply to judgments or orders under the Family Code for the possession or sale of property. Note that a judgment for child, family, or spousal support, including a judgment for reimbursement or other arrearages, is enforceable until paid in full or otherwise satisfied and is exempt from any renewal requirement, although such a judgment may be renewed under CCP §§683.010–683.320 if desired. Fam C §§291(b)–(c), 4502.

E. Contempt Proceedings

§20.37   1. Nature of Action

Contempt may be either civil or criminal. Civil contempt is governed by CCP §§1209–1222, which provide for a special proceeding intended to implement the inherent power of the court to conduct its business and enforce its orders. The proceeding, although criminal in character, is not construed as a criminal action. *Pacific Tel. & Tel. Co. v Superior Court* (1968) 265 CA2d 370, 371, 72 CR 177. Criminal contempt is contempt in violation of penal statutes. It is considered a crime and is prosecuted and punished as such. See Pen C §166.

In addition to other remedies, when a party fails to comply with a protective order issued under the Domestic Violence Protection Act, that party may be cited for contempt by a district or city attorney. Any attorney fees and costs ordered by the court under CCP §1218(a) against a party who is adjudged guilty of contempt must be paid to the Office of Emergency Services' account established to fund domestic violence shelter service providers. CCP §1218(d).

§20.38　　2. Orders Enforceable; Constitutional Limitations

By statute, contempt proceedings are available to enforce any judgment or order made under the Family Code. Fam C §290. (On the duration of Family Code judgments or orders in general, see §20.36.) If the contempt alleged is for failure to pay child, spousal, or family support, each month for which payment has not been made in full may be alleged and punished as a separate count. CCP §1218.5(a). The limitations period for such a failure is 3 years from the date the payment was due. For enforcement of all other Family Code orders, the limitations period is 2 years from the time the alleged contempt occurred. CCP §1218.5(b).

A court's use of its contempt power is limited by federal and state constitutional provisions that prohibit imprisonment for debt. US Const amend XIII; Cal Const art I, §10. Thus the issue of the availability of contempt may arise whenever a contempt proceeding is brought to enforce an order for payment of money. The specific question is whether the particular order to pay money is an order to pay a debt to a creditor.

Orders to pay spousal support, child support, and attorney fees and costs are not considered orders to pay a debt to a creditor and are clearly enforceable by contempt. *Moss v Superior Court* (1998) 17 C4th 396, 422, 71 CR2d 215; *Miller v Superior Court* (1937) 9 C2d 733, 736, 72 P2d 868 (spousal support); *Bailey v Superior Court* (1932) 215 C 548, 555, 11 P2d 865 (child support); *In re Hendricks* (1970) 5 CA3d 793, 796, 85 CR 220 (attorney fees and costs). Likewise, orders to post security for such payments are enforceable by contempt. *In re Sigesmund* (1961) 193 CA2d 219, 14 CR 221 (security for child support and attorney fees).

The trend has clearly been to take an expansive view of the availability of contempt to enforce family law orders. One approach in allowing the remedy of contempt has been to find that the orders being enforced, although not expressly characterized as support orders, were in the nature of support. See, *e.g., Bushman v Superior Court* (1973) 33 CA3d 177, 181, 108 CR 765 (pendente lite order to make mortgage payments); *In re Hendricks* (1970) 5 CA3d 793, 797, 85 CR 220 (pendente lite order to pay past community debts).

Another approach in allowing the remedy of contempt has been to create an exception to the traditional distinction between orders for support, which could be enforced by contempt, and orders for the division of property, which could not. Thus, contempt has been held available when the orders being enforced, although admittedly property provisions rather than support provisions, were not enforcing payment of a debt owed to a creditor but giving to an owner of an asset his or her interest in the asset. See, *e.g., Verner v Verner* (1978) 77 CA3d 718, 729, 143 CR 826; *Marriage of Fithian* (1977) 74 CA3d 397, 404, 141 CR 506.

It appears, then, that the constitutional prohibition of imprisonment for debt is now limited to the narrow context of an order to pay a sum *from separate funds,* either to the spouse or to a third party, as part of the division of community property. See, *e.g., In re Fontana* (1972) 24 CA3d 1008, 101 CR 465 (contempt unavailable to enforce order to make payments on automobile awarded to spouse); *Martins v Superior Court* (1970) 12 CA3d 870, 90 CR 898 (contempt unavailable to enforce order to pay sum to spouse as part of property division).

When a court orders a party to do an act that does not involve payment of money, the constitutional question does not arise. Thus, contempt is available to enforce orders governing the custody (*Smith v Smith* (1953) 120 CA2d 474, 261 P2d 567), visitation (*Rosin v Superior Court* (1960) 181 CA2d 486, 5 CR 421), or residence (*Olcott v Superior Court* (1945) 68 CA2d 603, 157 P2d 36) of a child; restraining the conduct of one party to protect the peace and safety of the other (*In re Laham* (1956) 145 CA2d 110, 302 P2d 21); and directing one party to convey property to the other (*Sullivan v Superior Court* (1925) 72 CA 531, 237 P 782).

3. Elements

§20.39   a. Valid Order

For contempt to lie, the underlying order must be valid. When the order is void, the citee may not be found in contempt. *Oksner v Superior Court* (1964) 229 CA2d 672, 681, 40 CR 621. An order, for example, changing the terms of a judgment that has become final is beyond the court's jurisdiction and may not be enforced by contempt. *Grant v Superior Court* (1963) 214 CA2d 15, 24, 29 CR 125. The court may presume validity, however, unless the order is void on its face.

The order must also be clear, specific, and unequivocal. *Wilson v Superior Court* (1987) 194 CA3d 1259, 1273, 240 CR 131. Further, it must be in writing, and either signed by the judge and filed with the court, or set forth in a detailed minute order. An indirect contempt finding may not be based upon an oral ruling of the court. *In re Marcus* (2006) 138 CA4th 1009, 41 CR3d 861; *Ketscher v Superior Court* (1970) 9 CA3d 601, 604, 88 CR 357.

§20.40   b. Knowledge of Order

The citee must have knowledge of the order. This requirement is satisfied if the citee was present in court when the order was made or was served with a copy of the order after it was made. *Phillips v Superior Court* (1943) 22 C2d 256, 258, 137 P2d 838. If the citee's attorney has knowledge of the terms of the order, either because the attorney was present in court when it was made or because the attorney was served with a copy of the order, there is a rebuttable presumption that the citee knew of the order. *Mossman v Superior Court* (1972) 22 CA3d 706, 711, 99 CR 638. Nevertheless, when an order enforceable by contempt is made at a time when the party against whom it is made is not present, the safer practice is to have a copy of the order personally served on the party.

§20.41   c. Ability to Comply

The court must find that the citee had the ability to comply with the order. *In re McCausland* (1955) 130 CA2d 708, 279 P2d 820. The ability to comply must be found to have existed, however, only at the time of the act of disobedience, not at the time of imposition of the sentence. *Sorell v Superior Court* (1967) 248 CA2d 157, 161, 56 CR 222. Of course, to order a party jailed until such time as he or she complies with the court order, a *present* ability to comply is required. But that added finding is required only for imposition of the particular penalty and is not a prerequisite to finding the party in contempt. 248 CA2d at 161 n2; see CCP §1219.

Code of Civil Procedure §1209.5 provides that, when the underlying order is for child support, the prima facie case for contempt requires proof only that (1) the order was made and filed, (2) it was served on the obligor or the obligor was present in court when the order was made, and (3) the obligor failed to comply with the order. Code of Civil Procedure §1209.5 applies to family law orders as well as to child support orders. *People v Dilday* (1993) 20 CA4th Supp 1, 25 CR2d 386.

It has long been the law that a contempt order may not be based on the citee's failure to work, as distinguished from his or her actual ability to pay. See *In re Todd* (1897) 119 C 57, 50 P 1071; *In re Jennings* (1982) 133 CA3d 373, 383, 184 CR 53. In a case involving the failure to comply with a child support order, however, the California Supreme Court disapproved *In re Todd* and held that a contempt order resulting in a jail sentence may be based on the child support obligor's failure to seek or obtain work in order to pay the support order. *Moss v Superior Court* (1998) 17 C4th 396, 415, 71 CR2d 215. In *Moss*, the trial court imposed a jail sentence and community service on a father who had been unemployed for at least 4 years. The court dismissed the father's arguments that the contempt order imposed unconstitutional "involuntary servitude" or imprisonment for debt. "There is no 'servitude' since the worker is not bound to any particular employer and has no restrictions on his freedom other than the need to comply with a lawful order to support a child." 17 C4th at 417. The court further reasoned that the father's behavior in failing to make efforts to support his child fell within the fraud exception to the constitutional prohibition of imprisonment for debt that historically was contained in Article I, section 10 of the California Constitution, and is still recognized in case law (*People v Bell* (1996) 45 CA4th 1030, 1043, 53 CR2d 156). In ruling that the father's behavior fell within the fraud exception, the court compared the child support obligation to cases that involved a failure to pay wages when due and relied on *Bradley v Superior Court* (1957) 48 C2d 509, 519, 310 P2d 634 (family support obligations are not ordinary debts subject to the constitutional prohibition of imprisonment for debt).

The supreme court held that in a contempt proceeding, the alleged contemnor bears the burden of proving his or her inability to pay. The court cited approvingly the holding in *In re Feiock* (1989) 215 CA3d 141, 146, 263 CR 437, that ability to pay is not an element of the contempt offense but rather a defense against the contempt charge, but disapproved *Feiock*'s holding that the contemnor bore the burden of proving inability to pay beyond a reasonable doubt. "To prevail on the affirmative defense of inability to comply with the support order, the contemnor must prove such inability by a preponderance of the evidence." 17 C4th at 428. It should be noted that the result in *Moss* leaves open the possibility that *In re Todd* (1897) 119 C 57, 50 P 1071, still applies in a spousal support case.

See also *Lyon v Superior Court* (1968) 68 C2d 446, 450, 67 CR 265 (citee who has the actual ability to partially comply with an order may be found guilty of contempt for failure to do so, despite the fact that he or she lacks the ability to fully comply).

A custodial parent may not be held in contempt for violation of a visitation order based on the failure of an unwilling child to visit unless proof of the parent's ability to compel visitation is shown. *Coursey v Superior Court* (1987) 194 CA3d 147, 154, 239 CR 365.

California courts have held that, when the disobedience of an order to pay money occurs soon after the order is made, ability to pay may be rebuttably presumed because the court ascertained at the time of the order that the party had the ability to pay the amount ordered. When, on the other hand, the alleged contempt occurs years after the court's determination of ability to pay, it is reasonable to require a new finding of ability to pay at the time of the violation. *Sorell v Superior Court, supra.*

§20.42   d. Willful Failure to Comply

To be held in contempt, the accused party must have willfully disobeyed the order. *Coursey v Superior Court* (1987) 194 CA3d 147, 156, 239 CR 365. That the disobedience may have been based on advice of counsel will not justify it, nor will a mistake as to the law excuse it. *City of Vernon v Superior Court* (1952) 38 C2d 509, 518, 241 P2d 243.

A custodial parent may not be held in contempt for violation of a visitation order based on the failure of an unwilling child to visit unless proof is shown that any violation on the parent's part was willful. *Coursey v Superior Court, supra.*

Note that when the underlying order is for child support or family support, willful failure to comply is *not* part of the moving party's prima facie case. CCP §1209.5; *People v Dilday* (1993) 20 CA4th Supp 1, 25 CR2d 386. Consequently, an accused who wishes to defend on the ground that the disobedience was not willful must raise that issue as an affirmative defense. *Moss v Superior Court* (1998) 17 C4th 396, 428, 71 CR2d 215 (addressing inability to pay child support). See §20.41.

4. Order to Show Cause and Attachments

§20.43   a. Discussion

The moving party completes the Judicial Council form of Order to Show Cause and Affidavit for Contempt (see form in §20.44) and any applicable form of Affidavit of Facts Constituting Contempt, *i.e.,* either or both of the forms for violation of financial and injunctive orders (see form in §20.44A) and the form for violation of domestic violence or custody and visitation orders (see form in §20.44B), which will then be attached to the order to show cause form. The court whose order is violated is the proper court to hear a contempt proceeding. *Parker v Superior Court* (1926) 79 CA 618, 620, 250 P 587. Although a contempt proceeding is technically a separate proceeding, the recognized practice is to prosecute the contempt in the case from which it arose. *In re Wales* (1957) 153 CA2d 117, 119, 315 P2d 433. Thus, the caption should have the title and case number of the underlying action. Unless local practice allows the hearing date to be obtained in advance, the date, time, and place on the form should be left blank for the judge or clerk to fill in.

§20.44   b. Form: Order to Show Cause and Affidavit for Contempt (Judicial Council Form FL-410)

FL-410

ATTORNEY OR PARTY WITHOUT ATTORNEY *(Name, state bar number, and address):*	FOR COURT USE ONLY

TELEPHONE NO.:   FAX NO.:

ATTORNEY FOR *(Name)*:

SUPERIOR COURT OF CALIFORNIA, COUNTY OF

STREET ADDRESS:

MAILING ADDRESS:

CITY AND ZIP CODE:

BRANCH NAME:

PETITIONER/PLAINTIFF:

RESPONDENT/DEFENDANT:

OTHER PARENT:

ORDER TO SHOW CAUSE AND AFFIDAVIT FOR CONTEMPT	CASE NUMBER:

NOTICE!	¡AVISO!
A contempt proceeding is criminal in nature. If the court finds you in contempt, the possible penalties include jail sentence, community service, and fine.	Un proceso judicial por desacato es de índole criminal. Si la corte le declara a usted en desacato, las sanciones posibles incluyen penas de prisión y de servicio a la comunidad, y multas.
You are entitled to the services of an attorney, who should be consulted promptly in order to assist you. If you cannot afford an attorney, the court may appoint an attorney to represent you.	Usted tiene derecho a los servicios de un abogado, a quien debe consultar sin demora para obtener ayuda. Si no puede pagar a un abogado, la corte podrá nombrar a un abogado para que le represente.

1. TO CITEE *(name of person you allege has violated the orders):*

2. YOU ARE ORDERED TO APPEAR IN THIS COURT AS FOLLOWS, TO GIVE ANY LEGAL REASON WHY THIS COURT SHOULD NOT FIND YOU GUILTY OF CONTEMPT, PUNISH YOU FOR WILLFULLY DISOBEYING ITS ORDERS AS SET FORTH IN THE AFFIDAVIT BELOW AND ANY ATTACHED *AFFIDAVIT OF FACTS CONSTITUTING CONTEMPT;* AND REQUIRE YOU TO PAY, FOR THE BENEFIT OF THE MOVING PARTY, THE ATTORNEY FEES AND COSTS OF THIS PROCEEDING.

    a. Date: Time: Dept.:   Rm.:

    b. Address of court: ☐ same as noted above   ☐ other *(specify):*

Date:

_____

JUDICIAL OFFICER

AFFIDAVIT SUPPORTING ORDER TO SHOW CAUSE FOR CONTEMPT

3. ☐ An *Affidavit of Facts Constituting Contempt* (form FL-411 or FL-412) is attached.

4. Citee has willfully disobeyed certain orders of this court as set forth in this affidavit and any attached affidavits.

5. a. Citee had knowledge of the order in that
    (1) ☐ citee was present in court at the time the order was made.
    (2) ☐ citee was served with a copy of the order.
    (3) ☐ citee signed a stipulation upon which the order was based.
    (4) ☐ other *(specify):*

        ☐ Continued on Attachment 5a(4).

    b. Citee was able to comply with each order when it was disobeyed.

6. Based on the instances of disobedience described in this affidavit
    a. ☐ I have not previously filed a request with the court that the citee be held in contempt.
    b. ☐ I have previously filed a request with the court that the citee be held in contempt *(specify date filed and results):*

    ☐ Continued on Attachment 6b.

Page 1 of 4

Form Adopted for Mandatory Use Judicial Council of California FL-410 [Rev. January 1, 2003]	ORDER TO SHOW CAUSE AND AFFIDAVIT FOR CONTEMPT	Family Code, § 292; Code of Civil Procedure, §§ 1211.5, 2015.5 www.courtinfo.ca.gov

PETITIONER/PLAINTIFF:	CASE NUMBER:
RESPONDENT/DEFENDANT:	
OTHER PARENT:	

7. ☐ Citee has previously been found in contempt of a court order *(specify case, court, date):*

☐ Continued on Attachment 7.

8. ☐ Each order disobeyed and each instance of disobedience is described as follows:

   a. ☐ Orders for child support, spousal support, family support, attorney fees, and court or other litigation costs (see attached *Affidavit of Facts Constituting Contempt* (form FL-411))

   b. ☐ Domestic violence restraining orders and child custody and visitation orders (see attached *Affidavit of Facts Constituting Contempt* (form FL-412))

   c. ☐ Injunctive or other order *(specify which order was violated, how the order was violated, and when the order was violated):*

   ☐ Continued on Attachment 8c.

   d. ☐ Other material facts, including facts indicating that the violation of the orders was without justification or excuse *(specify):*

   ☐ Continued on Attachment 8d.

   e. ☐ I am requesting that attorney fees and costs be awarded to me for the costs of pursuing this contempt action. (A copy of my *Income and Expense Declaration* (form FL-150) is attached.)

> **WARNING: IF YOU PURSUE THIS CONTEMPT ACTION, IT MAY AFFECT THE ABILITY OF THE DISTRICT ATTORNEY TO PROSECUTE THE CITEE CRIMINALLY FOR THE SAME VIOLATIONS.**

I declare under penalty of perjury under the laws of the State of California that the foregoing is true and correct.

Date:

▶

_____
(TYPE OR PRINT NAME)

_____
(SIGNATURE)

FL-410 [Rev. January 1, 2003]

ORDER TO SHOW CAUSE AND AFFIDAVIT FOR CONTEMPT

Page 2 of 4

INFORMATION SHEET FOR ORDER TO SHOW CAUSE
AND AFFIDAVIT OF FACTS CONSTITUTING CONTEMPT

(Do NOT deliver this Information Sheet to the court clerk.)

Please follow these instructions to complete the *Order to Show Cause and Affidavit for Contempt* (form FL-410) if you do not have an attorney to represent you. Your attorney, if you have one, should complete this form, as well as the *Affidavit of Facts Constituting Contempt* (form FL-411 or form FL-412). You may wish to consult an attorney for assistance. Contempt actions are very difficult to prove. An attorney may be appointed for the citee.

INSTRUCTIONS FOR COMPLETING THE ORDER TO SHOW CAUSE AND AFFIDAVIT OF FACTS CONSTITUTING CONTEMPT (TYPE OR PRINT FORM IN INK):

If the top section of the form has already been filled out, skip down to number 1 below. If the top section of the form is blank, you must provide this information.

Front page, first box, top of form, left side: Print your name, address, telephone number, and fax number, if any, in this box. If you have a restraining order and wish to keep your address confidential, you may use any address where you can receive mail. **You can be legally served court papers at this address.**

Front page, second box, left side: Print the name of the county where the court is located and insert the address and any branch name of the court building where you are seeking to obtain a contempt order. You may get this information from the court clerk. This should be the same court in which the original order was issued.

Front page, third box, left side: Print the names of the Petitioner, Respondent, and Other Parent (if any) in this box. Use the same names as appear on the most recent court order disobeyed.

Front page, first box, top of form, right side: Leave this box blank for the court's use.

Front page, second box, right side: Print the court case number in this box. This number is also shown on the most recent court order disobeyed.

Item 1: Insert the name of the party who disobeyed the order ("the citee").

Item 2: The court clerk will provide the hearing date and location.

Item 3: Either check the box in item 3 and attach an *Affidavit of Facts Constituting Contempt* (form FL-411 for financial orders or form FL-412 for domestic violence, or custody and visitation orders), or leave the box in item 3 blank but check and complete item 8.

Item 5: Check the box that describes how the citee knew about the order that has been disobeyed.

Item 6: a. Check this box if you have not previously applied for a contempt order.

  b. Check this box if you have previously applied for a contempt order and briefly explain when you requested the order and results of your request. If you need more space, check the box that says "continued on Attachment 6b" and attach a separate sheet to this order to show cause.

Item 7: Check this box if the citee has previously been found in contempt by a court of law. Briefly explain when the citee was found in contempt and for what. If there is not enough space to write all the facts, check the box that says "continued on Attachment 7" and attach a separate sheet to this order to show cause.

Item 8: a. Check this box if the citee has disobeyed orders for child support, custody, visitation, spousal support, family support, attorney fees, and court or litigation costs. Refer to item 1a on *Affidavit of Facts Constituting Contempt* (form FL-411).

  b. Check this box if the citee has disobeyed domestic violence orders or child custody and visitation orders. Refer to *Affidavit of Facts Constituting Contempt* (form FL-412).

ORDER TO SHOW CAUSE AND AFFIDAVIT FOR CONTEMPT

Information Sheet *(continued)*

Item 8: c. If you are completing this item, use facts personally known to you or known to the best of your knowledge. State the facts in detail. if there is not enough space to write all the facts, check the box that says "continued on Attachment 8c" and attach a separate sheet to this order to show cause, including facts indicating that the violation of the orders was without justification or excuse.

   d. Use this item to write other facts that are important to this order. If you are completing this item, insert facts personally known to you, or known to the best of your knowledge. State facts in detail. If there is not enough space to write all the facts, check the box that says "Continued on Attachment 8d" and attach a separate sheet to the order to show cause.

   e. If you request attorney fees and/or costs for pursuing this contempt action, check this box. Attach a copy of your *Income and Expense Declaration* (form FL-150).

Type or print and sign your name at the bottom of page 2.

If you checked the boxes in item 3 and item 8a or 8b, complete the appropriate *Affidavit of Facts Constituting Contempt* (form FL-411), following the instructions for the affidavit above.

Make at least three copies of the *Order to Show Cause and Affidavit for Contempt* (form FL-410) and any supporting *Affidavit of Facts Constituting Contempt* (form FL-411 or FL-412) and the *Income and Expense Declaration* (form FL-150) for the court clerk, the citee, and yourself. If the district attorney or local child support agency is involved in your case, you must provide a copy to the district attorney or local child support agency.

Take the completed form(s) to the court clerk's office. The clerk will provide hearing date and location in item 2, obtain the judicial officer's signature, file the originals, and return the copies to you.

Have someone who is at least 18 years of age, who is not a party, serve the order and any attached papers on the disobedient party. For example, a process server or someone you know may serve the papers. **You may not serve the papers yourself. Service must be personal; service by mail is insufficient.** The papers must be served at least 21 calendar days before the court hearing. The person serving papers must complete a *Proof of Personal Service* (form FL-330) and give the original to you. Keep a copy for yourself and file the original *Proof of Personal Service* (form FL-330) with the court.

If you need assistance with these forms, contact an attorney or the Family Law Facilitator in your county.

FL-410 [Rev. January 1, 2003]

ORDER TO SHOW CAUSE AND AFFIDAVIT FOR CONTEMPT

Page 4 of 4

Copies: Original (submit to court clerk); copy for service; office copies.

§20.44A   c. Form: Affidavit of Facts Constituting Contempt—Financial and Injunctive Orders (Judicial Council Form FL-411)

FL-411

PETITIONER/PLAINTIFF:	CASE NUMBER:
RESPONDENT/DEFENDANT:	
OTHER PARENT:	

AFFIDAVIT OF FACTS CONSTITUTING CONTEMPT
Financial and Injunctive Orders
Attachment to *Order to Show Cause and Affidavit for Contempt* (form FL-410)

1. a. Orders for child support, spousal support, family support, attorney fees, and court and litigation costs *(separately itemize each default on installment payments):*

DATE DUE	TYPE OF ORDER AND DATE FILED	PAYABLE TO	AMOUNT ORDERED	AMOUNT PAID	AMOUNT DUE
☐ Continued on Attachment 1a.			TOTAL AMOUNT ORDERED	TOTAL AMOUNT PAID	TOTAL AMOUNT DUE
Summary of contempt counts alleged (including all attachments):					
Child support: Spousal support: Family support: Attorney fees: Court and other costs:					
Total			$	$	$

b. ☐ Other orders *(specify which order was violated, how the order was violated, and when the violation occurred):*

☐ Continued on Attachment 1b.

c. ☐ Other material facts *(specify):*

☐ Continued on Attachment 1c.

I declare under penalty of perjury under the laws of the State of California that the foregoing is true and correct.
Date:

▶

_____   _____
(TYPE OR PRINT NAME)   (SIGNATURE)   Page 1 of 1

| Form Adopted for Mandatory Use Judicial Council of California FL-411 [Rev. January 1, 2003] | **AFFIDAVIT OF FACTS CONSTITUTING CONTEMPT** **Financial and Injunctive Orders** | Family Code, § 292; Code of Civil Procedure, §§ 1209, 1211, 1211.5, 2015.5 www.courtinfo.ca.gov |

Copies: Original (submit to court clerk); copy for service; office copies.

§20.44B   d. Form: Affidavit of Facts Constituting Contempt—Domestic Violence/Custody and Visitation (Judicial Council Form FL-412)

FL-412

PETITIONER/PLAINTIFF:	CASE NUMBER:
RESPONDENT/DEFENDANT:	
OTHER PARENT:	

AFFIDAVIT OF FACTS CONSTITUTING CONTEMPT
Domestic Violence/Custody and Visitation
Attachment to *Order to Show Cause and Affidavit for Contempt* (form FL-410)

1. ☐ The Citee has violated the restraining order issued on *(date):*   by contacting, molesting, harassing, attacking, striking, threatening, sexually assaulting, battering, telephoning, sending any messages to, following, stalking, destroying the personal property of, disturbing the peace of, keeping under surveillance, or blocking movements in public places and thoroughfares of me or any other person protected by the restraining order. *(Specify which order was violated, how the order was violated, and when the violation occurred):*

☐ Continued on Attachment 1.

2. ☐ The Citee has violated the restraining order issued on *(date):*   by not moving from and staying away from the residence as ordered by the court. *(Specify how the order was violated and when the violation occurred):*

☐ Continued on Attachment 2.

3. ☐ The Citee has violated the restraining order issued on *(date):*   by not staying *(specify):*   yards away from me, the other protected persons, my residence, my place of work, the children's school or place of child care, my vehicle, or other *(specify):*
(Specify which order was violated, how the order was violated, and when the violation occurred):

☐ Continued on Attachment 3.

4. ☐ The Citee has violated the restraining order issued on *(date):*   by not relinquishing his or her firearm(s) as ordered by the court. *(Specify which order was violated, how the order was violated, and when the violation occurred):*

☐ Continued on Attachment 4.

5. ☐ The Citee has violated the restraining order issued on *(date):*   by failure to complete court-ordered batterer's treatment/anger management class *(specify how the order was violated):*

☐ Continued on Attachment 5.

6. ☐ The Citee has violated order issued on *(date):*   by violating the following custody or visitation order *(specify which order was violated, how the order was violated, and when the violation occurred):*

☐ Continued on Attachment 6.

7. ☐ The Citee has violated the order issued on *(date):*   by violating other orders *(specify which order was violated and how the order was violated):*

☐ Continued on Attachment 7.

I declare under penalty of perjury under the laws of the State of California that the foregoing is true and correct.
Date:

▶

_____   _____
(TYPE OR PRINT NAME)   (SIGNATURE)

| Form Adopted for Mandatory Use
Judicial Council of California
FL-412 [Rev. January 1, 2003] | **AFFIDAVIT OF FACTS CONSTITUTING CONTEMPT**
Domestic Violence/Custody and Visitation | Page 1 of 1
Family Code, § 292;
Code of Civil Procedure,
§§ 1211.5, 2015.5
www.courtinfo.ca.gov |

Copies: Original (submit to court clerk); copy for service; office copies.

§20.45   e. Filing and Service

The Order to Show Cause must be filed and served at least 21 calendar days before the date set for hearing. CCP §1005(a)(13)–(b).

The form must be submitted for the judge's signature before it may be filed or served. The usual procedure is to hand deliver the Order to Show Cause to the judge's department and then return to that department to pick up the form and obtain a hearing date from the clerk.

Service must be by personal service on the party alleged to be in contempt. CCP §§1015–1016; *Kroneberger v Superior Court* (1961) 196 CA2d 206, 209, 16 CR 339. When, however, the party is concealing himself or herself to avoid service, the court may direct that service be made on his or her attorney of record. 196 CA2d at 210. In that event, however, the moving party must submit a declaration alleging specific facts showing concealment and reasonable efforts to give notice. See *Albrecht v Superior Court* (1982) 132 CA3d 612, 183 CR 417.

5. Citee's Response

§20.46   a. Answer to Charge

The citee may respond to the charge by filing an opposing declaration before the hearing. In most instances, however, the citee will be better served if an opposing declaration is not filed, in order to avoid providing the moving party with advance notice of the basis of the citee's opposition. Although in ordinary family law proceedings on noticed motions the court may decide the matter solely on the basis of the moving and opposing papers (see *Reifler v Superior Court* (1974) 39 CA3d 479, 485, 114 CR 356), that is not the case in contempt proceedings (*Reifler v Superior Court, supra*). Further, the charging declaration is hearsay and therefore inadmissible over an objection. Evid C §1200. Thus, the citee should be able to withhold presentation of his or her opposition until the moving party has established a prima facie case of contempt on the basis of evidence presented at the hearing.

The moving party's Order to Show Cause and Affidavit for Contempt (see form in §20.44) constitutes the complaint, and the opposing declaration, when one is filed, constitutes the answer or plea. Together, when both are filed, these documents serve as the pleadings that frame the issues of fact in the case. *Freeman v Superior Court* (1955) 44 C2d 533, 536, 282 P2d 857; see CCP §1217.

If an opposing declaration is filed, then, like answers generally, it should set forth any denials of allegations in the Order to Show Cause, and any affirmative defenses. Contempt actions are usually defended on the basis of inability to comply (see §20.41). However, note that, when the underlying orders are for child support, inability to comply is not an element of the moving party's prima facie case, but must be raised by the citee as an affirmative defense. See §20.41. Contempt actions may also be defended on the basis that the order was invalid (see §20.39), that the citee lacked knowledge of the order (see §20.40), or that the failure to comply was not willful (see §20.42).

There is no Judicial Council form of declaration in opposition to the Order to Show Cause and Declaration for Contempt. Consequently, if one is to be filed, the declaration should be prepared on pleading paper or on the Judicial Council form of Declaration, available in California Judicial Council Forms Manual §11 (Cal CEB 1981).

§20.47   b. Motion for Discharge

The citee may respond to the charge by moving for a discharge. This motion, which challenges the court's jurisdiction to proceed with a hearing on the contempt charge, serves substantially the same function as a demurrer to the complaint in a civil action. See *Taylor v Superior Court* (1942) 20 C2d 244, 246, 125 P2d 1.

Among the recognized grounds for the motion are the following:

The court lacks jurisdiction to punish for contempt. The only superior court with jurisdiction to punish for contempt is the one whose order was disobeyed. No other court has civil contempt jurisdiction, and the only other court that has criminal contempt jurisdiction is a municipal court. *In re Morris* (1924) 194 C 63, 68, 227 P 914, 915; see Pen C §166.

The order exceeded the court's jurisdiction and is therefore void. A party may not be convicted of contempt for disobeying a void order. *Marr v Superior Court* (1952) 114 CA2d 527, 532,

250 P2d 739; see, *e.g.*, *In re William T.* (1985) 172 CA3d 790, 800, 218 CR 420 (party may not be held in contempt for violating superior court orders that conflict with orders of juvenile court whose jurisdiction is paramount).

The order is uncertain or ambiguous. A party may not be convicted of contempt unless the terms of the underlying order make clear what action is required or prohibited. *Gottlieb v Superior Court* (1959) 168 CA2d 309, 312, 335 P2d 714.

The order is for payment of a debt to a creditor and contempt is thus unavailable to enforce it. See §20.38.

The underlying order has been appealed and enforcement has been stayed pending appeal. A party may not be punished for disobedience of an order whose enforcement has been stayed. *Ex Parte Oxford* (1894) 102 C 656, 658, 36 P 928.

The charging declaration fails to state facts sufficient to establish contempt. Without a sufficient declaration, the court has no power to proceed. *Batchelder v Moore* (1871) 42 C 412; see CCP §1211. But the court may allow the declaration to be amended to correct the defect. CCP §1211.5; *Mossman v Superior Court* (1972) 22 CA3d 706, 710, 99 CR 638.

Prosecution of the charges constitutes double jeopardy. A citee who obtains a discharge *on the merits* may not be placed in jeopardy again for the same charge based on the same facts. See, *e.g.*, *Martin v Superior Court* (1962) 199 CA2d 730, 733, 736, 18 CR 773, (discharge on merits bars recharging on same facts); *In re Toor* (1955) 131 CA2d 75, 76, 280 P2d 79 (discharge on other than merits no bar to recharging).

Enforcement agency lacks standing. The mere registration in California of an out-of-state decree including child support provisions does not give a local child support agency standing to enforce the underlying order. *Codoni v Codoni* (2002) 103 CA4th 18, 126 CR2d 423. One of the Fam C §17400 requirements must be met to allow county enforcement of either an out-of-state or a domestic support order. *Codoni v Codoni, supra.*

6. Conduct of Hearing

§20.48   a. Due Process Considerations

A contempt proceeding brought under CCP §§1209–1222, unlike one prosecuted under Pen C §166, is not, strictly speaking, a criminal proceeding. *Pacific Tel. & Tel. Co. v Superior Court* (1968) 265 CA2d 370, 371, 72 CR 177. The citee has no right to a jury trial, nor does the court have discretion to grant one. 265 CA2d at 375. (In a criminal contempt proceeding, the citee is entitled to a jury trial if he or she is at risk of receiving a sentence of more than 180 days. *In re Kreitman* (1995) 40 CA4th 750, 753, 47 CR2d 595. In most respects, however, the citee in a civil contempt proceeding must receive the same protections as a defendant in a criminal proceeding, including the following:

- The citee must normally appear. The appearance may be in person, by attorney, or by affidavit. A court faced with the nonappearance of the citee may (1) continue the matter, (2) issue a bench warrant to secure the citee's presence, or (3) proceed with trial if it finds that the citee has been properly served and is voluntarily absent with full knowledge of the hearing. *Farace v Superior Court* (1983) 148 CA3d 915, 918, 196 CR 297.

- The court must advise an unrepresented citee of his or her right to counsel. *In re Shelley* (1961) 197 CA2d 199, 202, 16 CR 916. An indigent citee faced with the possibility of imprisonment is entitled to appointed counsel. *County of Santa Clara v Superior Court* (1992) 2 CA4th 1686, 1693, 5 CR2d 7.

- The citee must be given a reasonable opportunity to prepare and present a defense. *In re Shelley, supra.*

- The citee cannot be required to testify against himself or herself. *Ex Parte Gould* (1893) 99 C 360, 33 P 1112. To require the citee to testify would violate the constitutional privilege against self-incrimination. See *People v Barnum* (2003) 29 C4th 1210, 1222, 131 CR2d 499 (privilege against compelled self-incrimination has been viewed as "fundamental"). But the trial court is not required to advise an unrepresented citee of the existence of the privilege against self-incrimination before he or she is called as a witness in the People's case or testifies in his or her own defense. *People v Barnum, supra,* overruling *Killpatrick v Superior Court* (1957) 153 CA2d 146, 149, 314 P2d 164. The filing of a declaration in opposition to the Order to Show Cause (see §20.46) does not in itself constitute a waiver of the citee's right to refuse to testify. *Crittenden v Superior Court* (1964) 225 CA2d 101, 105, 36 CR 903.

- The alleged contempt must be proved beyond a reasonable doubt. *Ross v Superior Court* (1977) 19 C3d 899, 913, 141 CR 133.

§20.49 b. Evidence

Because the citee cannot be compelled to testify (see §20.48), even as an adverse party under Evid C §776, the moving party must be prepared to present evidence without relying on the citee. See *Oliver v Superior Court* (1961) 197 CA2d 237, 240, 17 CR 474. Because the charging declaration is hearsay, however, it is inadmissible over objection. Evid C §1200. The same is true of the citee's opposing declaration.

Either party may present oral testimony. *Reifler v Superior Court* (1974) 39 CA3d 479, 484, 114 CR 356. Further, the record in the underlying proceedings may be offered to support a party's position. See, *e.g., Freeman v Superior Court* (1955) 44 C2d 533, 537, 282 P2d 857 (rebuttable presumption of citee's knowledge of order based on showing from record that citee's attorney was present in court when order made and thereafter served with copy).

§20.50 7. Punishment

A citee who is found in contempt of court for failure to comply with a court order under the Family Code must, at a minimum, be sentenced to the following (CCP §1218(c)):

- On a first finding of contempt, performance of community service of up to 120 hours, or imprisonment of up to 120 hours, for each count. CCP §1218(c)(1).

- On a second finding of contempt, performance of community service of up to 120 hours, and imprisonment of up to 120 hours, for each count. CCP §1218(c)(2).

- On a third or subsequent finding of contempt, imprisonment of up to 240 hours, and performance of community service of up to 240 hours, for each count. CCP §1218(c)(3)(A). If assigned to a community service program, the citee must be ordered to pay an administrative fee not to exceed the actual cost of his or her administration and supervision. CCP §1218(c)(3)(B).

The court must take the parties' employment schedules into consideration when ordering community service, imprisonment, or both. CCP §1218(c)(4).

In all, a citee found guilty of contempt for violation of any civil order or judgment may, for each violation, be imprisoned for up to 5 days, fined up to $1000, payable to the court, or both. CCP §1218(a). When the contempt consists of failing to do an act that the citee still has the ability to perform, the period of incarceration may continue until the citee complies with the order. CCP §1219.

§20.51 8. Attorney Fees and Costs

A person subject to a court order as a party to an action, or any agent of that person, who is adjudged guilty of contempt for violating the court order may be ordered to pay to the party initiating the contempt proceeding the reasonable attorney fees and costs incurred in connection with the proceeding. CCP §1218(a).

§20.52 F. Deposit of Assets to Secure Child Support Payments

When a parent who is subject to a child support order is in arrears in the amount of 60 days or more of payments, and circumstances are such that an earnings assignment order for support (see §§20.2–20.15) would be an impracticable means of securing payment (*e.g.*, the obligor is self-employed or changes employers often), the support obligee may be able to obtain an order, under Fam C §§4600–4641 (former CC §4701.1), that the obligor deposit assets to secure future support payments. Fam C §§4610(a), 4613. The purpose of Fam C §§4600–4641 is to provide an extraordinary remedy for cases of bad faith failure to pay child support obligations. Fam C §4600.

Child support obligees seeking security for the ordered payments are likely to be better served by proceeding under Fam C §§4550–4573 (former CC §4710) (child support security deposit) than under Fam C §§4600–4641. For discussion of Fam C §§4550–4573, referred to by one court as "newer and more liberal" than Fam C §§4600–4641 (*Marriage of Ilas* (1993) 12 CA4th 1630, 1639 n6, 16 CR2d 345), see §§20.58–20.65.

§20.53   1. Obligee's Application

A child support obligee applies for an order for deposit of assets by a noticed motion. Fam C §4610(a). For discussion of, and forms for, motions for temporary orders, see §§11.16–11.63. The motion is prepared and processed in the same manner as a noticed motion for temporary orders. The obligee prepares the Judicial Council forms of (1) Order to Show Cause (see form in §11.18) or Notice of Motion (see form in §11.20) and (2) Application for Order and Supporting Declaration (see form in §11.22).

Whether the Order to Show Cause or the Notice of Motion procedure is used will generally depend on whether the payee seeks ex parte restraining orders pending the hearing. The court may issue an ex parte order restraining any person from transferring, encumbering, hypothecating, concealing, or in any way disposing of any real or personal property, whether community, quasi-community, or separate, except in the usual course of business or for the necessities of life. When the order is directed against a party, the court may require him or her to notify the other party of any proposed extraordinary expenditures and to account to the court for any such expenditure. Fam C §4620(a). When the obligee seeks such orders pending the hearing, the Order to Show Cause must be used. Otherwise, the Notice of Motion is generally used because of its convenience—it need not be submitted to the court for the judge's signature and is typically served by mail rather than personally served. However, note that, after a judgment has been entered, any noticed motion must be served on the opposing party, not on his or her attorney. Fam C §215.

The Application for Order and Supporting Declaration should specify at Item 13 that an order is sought, under Fam C §4610, for deposit of specified assets to secure child support payments. A declaration should be provided at Item 14 that contains facts establishing that (a) the obligor is in arrears in at least the amount of 60 days of payments (see Fam C §4610(a)) and (b) at least one of the conditions set forth in Fam C §4613 (see §20.54) exists. If the property restraint order mentioned above is desired, that request may be set forth at Item 9.a. of the Application and the corresponding order pending hearing may be set forth at Item 4.a. of the Judicial Council form of Temporary Restraining Orders (see form in §11.24), which should, when applicable, be submitted to the court with the other documents.

At the hearing, the court may extend the restraining order for one year, or until deposit of the required assets, whichever occurs first. Fam C §4620(d). When an extended order includes reporting requirements, the court must determine for which property the obligor will be required to report extraordinary expenditures and specify what is deemed an extraordinary expenditure. Fam C §4620(c).

On the obligor's opposition to the application, see §20.56.

§20.54   2. Order for Deposit

Before it may issue the order for deposit of assets, the court must determine that one or more of the following conditions exists:

- The obligor is not receiving a salary or wages subject to an earnings assignment order for support (see §§20.2–20.15), and there is reason to believe that he or she has earned income from some source of employment (Fam C §4613(a));

- An assignment order would not be sufficient to meet the support obligation for reasons other than a change of circumstances that would qualify for a reduction in the amount of child support ordered (Fam C §4613(b)); or

- The obligor's job history shows that an assignment order would be difficult to enforce or would be an impracticable means of securing the payment of the support obligation, because of, *e.g.,* multiple concurrent or consecutive employers (Fam C §4613(c)).

The designation of assets must be based on concern for maximizing liquidity and ready conversion into cash. The assets must include a sum of money or any other assets, personal or real, equal in value to the lesser of one year of support payments or $6000, subject to CCP §703.070 (application of exemptions to judgment for support). Fam C §4614 (former CC §4701.1(c)). The support payments to be compared to $6000 are the total payments for one year for all children, not the payments per child. *Marriage of Ilas* (1993) 12 CA4th 1630, 1639, 16 CR2d 345. The court may permit the obligor, in lieu of depositing cash or other assets, to provide a performance bond secured by any of the obligor's real property or other assets and equal in value to 1 year's payments. Fam C §4615.

The obligor must be directed to deposit the assets with the deposit holder designated by the court. Fam C §4610(a). The order must specify the date of its expiration, which will be after 1 year or on deposit of the specified money or assets, whichever occurs first. Fam C §4620(d).

When the obligor deposits any asset that is not readily convertible into money, the court may, following a hearing on at least 20 days' written notice to the obligor, order that the asset be sold and the proceeds deposited with the deposit holder. Fam C §4616.

§20.55   3. Use or Sale of Deposited Assets

If the obligor fails, within the time specified by the court, to make reasonable efforts to cure the default or to comply with a court-approved payment plan, and if the payments continue in arrears, the deposit holder must proceed, on at least 25 days' written notice served on the obligor by personal service or by mail with return receipt requested, to use the money or to sell or otherwise process the deposited assets to pay the current support and arrearages. Fam C §4630(a). The obligor may file a Notice of Motion to stop the use or sale within 15 days after service of the notice on him or her, in which event the use or sale will be stayed pending the hearing. Fam C §§4630(a), 4631(a). For grounds on which the motion may be based, see §20.56. The obligor must provide at least 20 days' notice of the hearing to the payee. Fam C §4631(b).

§20.56   4. Obligor's Opposition

The obligor may either file a Responsive Declaration to Order to Show Cause or Notice of Motion (see form in §11.36) in opposition to the initial motion (see §20.53), or file his or her own motion to stop the use or sale of assets (see §20.55), on the basis of any of the following grounds (Fam C §4612):

- The absence of arrearages;

- Laches;

- A change in custody of the children;

- A pending motion for a reduction in support because of a reduction in income;

- Illness or disability;

- Unemployment;

- A serious adverse impact on the obligor's immediate family residing with him or her that outweighs the impact on the obligee of denial of the motion or stopping of the sale;

- A serious impairment of the obligor's earning ability; or

- Other emergency conditions.

The obligor must rebut the presumptions that (1) the nonpayment of child support was willful, without good faith, and (2) the obligor had the ability to pay the support. Fam C §4611.

§20.57   5. Return of Assets

The deposit holder must return all assets to the obligor when both of the following events have occurred:

- One year has elapsed since issuance of the order for deposit of assets (Fam C §4640(a)); and

- The obligor has timely made every payment due during that 1-year period (Fam C §4640(b)).

§20.58   G. Child Support Security Deposit

In an order or judgment requiring payment of child support, the court may also require, subject to the restrictions noted in §§20.59–20.60, that the obligor pay up to 1 year's child support, to be known as the "child support security deposit." When the child support obligation will terminate by operation of law in less than a year after the date of the order, the maximum permissible amount of the deposit is reduced accordingly. Fam C §4560(a).

§20.59   1. Notice and Hearing

Before entry of an order for payment of a child support security deposit (see §20.58), the court must give the obligor reasonable notice and an opportunity to file an application to reduce or eliminate the deposit on the ground that the obligor either (1) has provided adequate equivalent security to ensure timely payment of the amount required by Fam C §4560 (apparently 1 year's support unless the obligation will terminate by operation of law before then) or (2) is unable to pay the support deposit required by Fam C §4560 without undue financial hardship. Fam C §4565(a). The application must be supported by all reasonable and necessary financial and other information required by the court to establish the existence of either ground. Fam C §4565(b).

Once the application has been filed and served, the court must provide notice and an opportunity for any parties opposing the application to file responsive financial and other information setting forth factual and legal bases for the opposition. Fam C §4566. After a hearing, the court must enter its order, exercising its discretion under all the facts and circumstances as disclosed in the admissible evidence before it to maximize the payment and deposit of the amount required by Fam C §4560, or an adequate equivalent security for its payment, without causing the obligor undue financial hardship. If necessary to avoid undue financial hardship, the court must reduce the amount to one the obligor can manage without such hardship. Fam C §4567.

For form of order for child support security deposit and evidence of deposit, see §20.64.

§20.60   2. Order for Deposit and Establishment of Account

When making an order for payment of a child support security deposit (see §20.58), the court must direct that the obligor deposit the amount in an interest-bearing account, or in credit union shares, with specified financial institutions and subject to withdrawal only on court authorization. Fam C §4561. The court must order the obligor to supply evidence of the deposit, on the Judicial Council form of Order for Child Support Security Deposit and Evidence of Deposit (Judicial Council Form FL-400), to be served on the obligee and filed with the court within a reasonable time, not to exceed 30 days. Fam C §4562. The deposited amounts must be used exclusively to guarantee the monthly payment of child support. Fam C §4561.

The court may decline to establish such an account when it is expressly waived by the obligee, or when the court finds, *e.g.,* that such an account already exists and is adequately funded or that the obligor has provided adequate equivalent security. Fam C §4560(b).

For form of order for child support security deposit and evidence of deposit, see §20.64.

§20.61   3. Order for Disbursement and Replenishment

On the obligee's application, on Judicial Council Form FL-401 (Application for Disbursement and Order for Disbursement From Child Support Security Deposit), stating that the obligor is ten or more days late in a support payment, the court must immediately order disbursement of funds from an account established under an order for a child support security deposit (see §20.60) to provide the support then in arrears. Fam C §4570(a). The court must also order the obligor to replenish the account in the amount disbursed. Fam C §4570(c). The court must cause a copy of the application for disbursement and order for disbursement to be served on the obligor, who will be subject to contempt of court for failure to comply with the order. Fam C §4571. The court must also cause a copy of its order to be served on the particular financial institution and on the district attorney with jurisdiction over the case. Fam C §4572.

For form of application for disbursement and order for disbursement from child support security deposit, see §20.65. For form of order for child support security deposit and evidence of deposit, including evidence of replenishment, see §20.64.

§20.62   4. Dissolution of Account

An account established under an order for a child support security deposit (see §20.60) must be dissolved and any remaining funds, along with any interest earned, returned to the obligor on the full payment and cessation of the child support obligation as provided by court order or operation of law. Fam C §4563.

§20.63   5. Application of Statute

Except as Fam C §4551 provides, the chapter on child support security deposits (Fam C §§4550–4573):

- Does not apply to temporary support orders (Fam C §4551(a));

- Does apply to applications for modification of child support filed on or after January 1, 1992, but may not constitute the basis for the modification (Fam C §4551(b));

- Applies to applications for modification in any case in which the obligee has previously waived establishment of a child support trust account but now seeks to establish one (Fam C §4551(c)); and

- Applies to any order or judgment entered on or after January 1, 1993, ordering an obligor to pay any child support arrearage that he or she has failed to pay as of the date of that order or judgment, including arrearages incurred before January 1, 1992 (Fam C §4551(d)).

§20.64 6. Form: Order for Child Support Security Deposit and Evidence of Deposit (Judicial Council Form FL-400)

FL-400

ATTORNEY OR PARTY WITHOUT ATTORNEY *(Name and address)*:	TELEPHONE NO.:	FOR COURT USE ONLY

ATTORNEY FOR *(Name)*:

SUPERIOR COURT OF CALIFORNIA, COUNTY OF

STREET ADDRESS:
MAILING ADDRESS:
CITY AND ZIP CODE:
BRANCH NAME:

PETITIONER/PLAINTIFF:

RESPONDENT/DEFENDANT:

ORDER FOR CHILD SUPPORT SECURITY DEPOSIT AND EVIDENCE OF DEPOSIT	CASE NUMBER:

ORDER FOR CHILD SUPPORT SECURITY DEPOSIT

1. Obligor *(name)*: is ordered to deposit the sum of *(specify):* $ as security for the payment of child support. The money must be deposited in an interest-bearing account with a state or federally chartered commercial bank, a trust company authorized to transact trust business in California, or a savings and loan association, or in shares of a federally insured credit union doing business in California and having a trust department. **The money may be withdrawn only upon order of this court.**

2. Evidence of the deposit must be filed with this court by the obligor and served upon the person to whom support is to be paid not later than *(date):*

Date: _____

_____
JUDICIAL OFFICER OF THE SUPERIOR COURT

EVIDENCE OF DEPOSIT

3. ☐ The child support obligor has deposited *(specify):* $ in an interest-bearing account as security for payment of child support on *(date):*

The deposit account is blocked so the sums may be withdrawn only upon presentation of a certified copy of a court order specifying the amount to be withdrawn and the person to whom the money should be paid.

4. ☐ The child support obligor has replenished the child support security deposit by depositing *(specify):* $ on *(date):*

I declare under penalty of perjury under the laws of the State of California that the foregoing is true and correct.

Date: _____

▶

_____
(TYPE OR PRINT NAME)

_____
(SIGNATURE)

Title:
Name of financial institution:
Address:

Telephone No.:
Account No.:

The original signed Evidence of Deposit should be filed with the court and a copy mailed to the person entitled to receive payment.

Page 1 of 1

Form Adopted for Mandatory Use Judicial Council of California FL-400 [Rev. January 1, 2003]	ORDER FOR CHILD SUPPORT SECURITY DEPOSIT AND EVIDENCE OF DEPOSIT	Family Code, §§ 4560-4562 www.courtinfo.ca.gov

Copies: Original (submit to court clerk); copy for service; office copies.

§20.65   **7. Form: Application for Disbursement and Order for Disbursement from Child Support Security Deposit (Judicial Council Form FL-401)**

FL-401

ATTORNEY OR PARTY WITHOUT ATTORNEY *(Name and address):*	TELEPHONE NO.:	FOR COURT USE ONLY

ATTORNEY FOR *(Name):*

SUPERIOR COURT OF CALIFORNIA, COUNTY OF
STREET ADDRESS:
MAILING ADDRESS:
CITY AND ZIP CODE:
BRANCH NAME:

PETITIONER/PLAINTIFF:

RESPONDENT/DEFENDANT:

APPLICATION FOR DISBURSEMENT AND ORDER FOR DISBURSEMENT FROM CHILD SUPPORT SECURITY DEPOSIT	CASE NUMBER:

APPLICATION FOR DISBURSEMENT FROM CHILD SUPPORT SECURITY DEPOSIT

1. The undersigned is entitled to receive child support payments. A deposit has been established to secure payment of the child support. The support is more than 10 days late, as follows:

Amount due as child support	Date due	Amount paid	Amount due

Total amount due:

2. I request that the court order disbursement of the amount due from the child support security deposit.

I declare under penalty of perjury under the laws of the State of California that the foregoing is true and correct.

Date:

▶

_____   _____
(TYPE OR PRINT NAME)   (SIGNATURE)

A copy of this application must be served on the obligor and proof of its service attached to the original that is filed with the court.

ORDER FOR DISBURSEMENT FROM CHILD SUPPORT SECURITY DEPOSIT AND ORDER TO REPLENISH FUNDS

3. The following financial institution *(name):*
must pay the following amount: $ to the following person who is entitled to receive payment of child support *(name):*

4. The obligor *(name):*   must replenish the child support security deposit by depositing the following amount: $ not later than *(date):*
The original evidence of replenishment must be filed with the court. A copy of the evidence of replenishment must be served on the person entitled to receive payment of the child support.

Date:

_____
JUDGE OF THE SUPERIOR COURT

5. I certify that the foregoing order is a copy of the original on file with the court.

Date: Clerk, by _____, Deputy

Page 1 of 1

Form Adopted for Mandatory Use
Judicial Council of California
FL-401 [Rev. January 1, 2003]   **APPLICATION FOR DISBURSEMENT AND ORDER FOR DISBURSEMENT FROM CHILD SUPPORT SECURITY DEPOSIT**   Family Code, §§ 4570–4573
www.courtinfo.ca.gov

Copies: Original (submit to court clerk); copy for service; office copies.

§20.66   H. Health Insurance Coverage Assignment

In any case in which an amount is set for current child support, the court must require that health insurance coverage for supported children of the parties be maintained by either or both parents if it is available at no cost or at a reasonable cost to the parent or parents. Fam C §3751(a)(2); see §8.34. On application by a party or the local child support agency when the court has made such an order, the court must issue a "health insurance coverage assignment," *i.e.,* an order directing the employer or other person providing health insurance to the obligor to enroll the supported children in the plan available to the obligor, unless the court finds good cause not to do so. Fam C §§3760(c), 3761(a). Good cause is limited to grounds that justify quashing the assignment order (see Fam C §3765(a) and §20.71), or terminating it (see Fam C §3770 and §20.72), and the fact that the assignment order would cause extraordinary hardship to the obligor. Fam C §3762.

1. Application and Order

§20.67   a. Discussion

The application is made ex parte on the Judicial Council form of Application and Order for Health Insurance Coverage (see form in §20.68), and the court issues the order on the same form. As indicated at Item 2, written notice of the applicant's intent to seek the order must have been given to the obligor, by first-class mail or personal service, at least 15 days before the filing of the application, unless the obligor has waived such notice. Fam C §3761(b)(1). For a sample form of notice, see §20.69.

It should be noted that the required notice may be given at the time of filing a petition in which child support is requested or any time thereafter. Fam C §3761(b)(1). Consequently, attorneys might consider adding to the petition or the response, or to a motion for temporary orders, a statement that, *e.g.,* "Notice is hereby given that [name] will seek a health insurance coverage assignment without further notice to you if you are in default in instituting coverage on behalf of any child as required by court order in this action."

§20.68   **b. Form: Application and Order for Health Insurance Coverage (Judicial Council Form FL-470)**

ATTORNEY OR PARTY WITHOUT ATTORNEY *(Name, State Bar number, and address)*:

TELEPHONE NO.:   FAX NO. *(Optional)*:
E-MAIL ADDRESS *(Optional)*:
ATTORNEY FOR *(Name)*:

FOR COURT USE ONLY

SUPERIOR COURT OF CALIFORNIA, COUNTY OF
STREET ADDRESS:
MAILING ADDRESS:
CITY AND ZIP CODE:
BRANCH NAME:

MARRIAGE OF
PETITIONER:

RESPONDENT:

APPLICATION AND ORDER FOR HEALTH INSURANCE COVERAGE

CASE NUMBER:

APPLICATION

1. On *(date)*:   , this court ordered obligor *(name)*:
   to provide health insurance coverage for the children named in the order below.

2. a. ☐ On *(date)*:   , which is at least 15 days before the filing of this application,
   I gave written notice to obligor of my intent to seek this order below
   ☐ by first-class mail   ☐ by personal service.
   OR
   b. ☐ Obligor has waived the requirement of written notice.

3. I ask the court to order the employer or other person providing health insurance coverage to enroll or maintain the children in any health insurance coverage available to the obligor.

I declare under penalty of perjury under the laws of the State of California that the foregoing is true and correct.
Date:

_____   ▶   _____
(TYPE OR PRINT NAME)   (SIGNATURE OF APPLICANT)

ORDER FOR HEALTH INSURANCE COVERAGE (ASSIGNMENT)

To employer or other person providing health insurance coverage for obligor (name):
Social security number (if known):

YOU ARE ORDERED TO
1. Begin or maintain health insurance coverage of:
   Name of child   Date of birth   Social security No.

You may deduct any premium or costs from the wages or earnings of obligor.
2. If the obligor works for you or if you provide health insurance coverage to obligor, give him or her a copy of this order within 10 days after you receive it.
3. If no health insurance coverage is available to the obligor, complete and sign the *Declaration of No Health Insurance Coverage* on the reverse and mail this form within 20 days to the attorney or person requesting the assignment.

Date:

_____
(JUDICIAL OFFICER)   **Page 1 of 2**

Form Adopted for Mandatory Use
Judicial Council of California
FL-470 [Rev. January 1, 2007]

APPLICATION AND ORDER FOR
HEALTH INSURANCE COVERAGE

ⓒEB   Family Code, §§ 3780–3772
www.courtinfo.ca.gov

FL-470

MARRIAGE OF *(Last name, first name of each party)*:	CASE NUMBER:

DECLARATION OF NO HEALTH INSURANCE COVERAGE

No health insurance coverage is available to the obligor *(name)*:

because *(state reasons)*:

I declare under penalty of perjury under the laws of the State of California that the foregoing is true and correct.

Date:

▶

_____
(TYPE OR PRINT NAME AND TITLE)

_____
(SIGNATURE OF EMPLOYER OR PERSON PROVIDING HEALTH INSURANCE)

MAIL A COPY OF THIS DECLARATION WITHIN 20 DAYS TO THE ATTORNEY OR PERSON SEEKING THIS ENROLLMENT (SEE INSTRUCTION NO. 5, BELOW).

INSTRUCTIONS
FOR EMPLOYER OR OTHER PERSON PROVIDING HEALTH INSURANCE

These instructions apply only to an *Order for Health Insurance Coverage* issued by a court.

1. If the obligor works for you or is covered by health insurance provided by you, you must give him or her a copy of this order within 10 days after you receive it.

2. Unless you receive a motion to quash the assignment, you must take steps to begin or maintain coverage of the specified children within 30 days after you deliver a copy of this order to the obligor. The coverage should begin at the earliest possible time consistent with group plan enrollment rules.

3. The obligor's existing health coverage will be replaced only if the children are not provided benefits under the existing coverage where they reside.

4. If the obligor is not enrolled in a plan and there is a choice of several plans, you may enroll the children in any plan that will reasonably provide benefits or coverage where they live, unless the court has ordered coverage by a specific plan.

5. If no coverage is available, complete the *Declaration of No Health Insurance Coverage* at the top of this page and mail the declaration by first-class mail to the attorney or person seeking the assignment within 20 days of your receipt of this order. Keep a copy of the form for your records.

6. If coverage is provided, you must supply evidence of coverage to both parents and to any person having custody of the child.

7. Upon request of the parents or person having custody of the child, you must provide all forms and other documentation necessary for submitting claims to the insurance carrier to the extent you provide them to other covered individuals.

8. You must notify the applicant of the effective date of the coverage of the children.

9. You will be liable for any amounts incurred for health care services that otherwise would have been covered under the insurance policy if you willfully fail to comply with this order. You can also be held in contempt of court. California law forbids your firing or taking any disciplinary action against any employee because of this order.

EMPLOYEE INFORMATION

1. This order tells your employer or other person providing health insurance coverage to you to enroll or maintain the named children in a health insurance plan available to you and to deduct the appropriate premium or costs, if any, from your wages or other compensation.

2. You have 15 days after you receive a copy of this order to object to the order. Family Code section 3765 tells you how.

3. Family Code section 3770 tells you how and when to petition the court to end this assignment.

FL-470 [Rev. January 1, 2007]

**APPLICATION AND ORDER FOR
HEALTH INSURANCE COVERAGE**

CEB   Page 2 of 2

Copies: Original (submit to court clerk); copy for service on obligor's employer; office copies.

§20.69   c. Form: Notice of Intent to Seek Health Insurance Coverage Assignment

_ _[Attorney name]_ _
_ _[State Bar number]_ _
_ _[Address]_ _
_ _[Telephone number]_ _

Attorney for _ _[name]_ _

**SUPERIOR COURT OF CALIFORNIA
COUNTY OF _ _ _ _ _ _**

Marriage of	)	**No.** _ _ _ _ _ _
	)	
Petitioner: _ _ _ _ _ _ _ _	)	**NOTICE OF INTENT TO**
	)	**SEEK HEALTH INSURANCE**
Respondent: _ _ _ _ _ _ _ _	)	**COVERAGE ASSIGNMENT**
	)	
_____	)	

    NOTICE IS HEREBY GIVEN that _ _[name]_ _ **will seek a health insurance coverage assignment without further notice to you if you are in default in instituting coverage on behalf of any child as required by Court order in this action.**

Date: _____   __[Signature]__
                                   _ _[Typed name]_ _
                                   Attorney for _ _[Petitioner/
                                   Respondent]_ _

    Copies: Original (retain, with original proof of service, for filing with application for health insurance coverage assignment); copy for service; office copies.

§20.70   2. Service; Employer's Responsibilities

    A health insurance coverage assignment order should be served on the employer (see Fam C §3764(a)) and may be served by mail (Fam C §3764(c)). The party who sought the order must file a certificate of service, showing the method and date of service of the order. Fam C §3761(b)(2). The order normally becomes effective 20 days after service on the employer. Fam C §3764(a). Within 10 days after service, the employer or other person providing health insurance to the obligor must deliver a copy of the order to the obligor. Fam C §3764(b). On its back side, the assignment order contains information for the obligor, as required by §3764(b), of his or her rights, and the relevant procedures, to move to quash the order. For a copy of the assignment order form, see §20.68. Unless he or she has received an order under Fam C §3765 to quash the order (see §20.71), the employer or other person must take steps, consistent with the assignment order, to commence coverage within 30 days after delivery of the copy of the order to the obligor. Fam C §3766(a). An employer or other person providing health insurance to the obligor who willfully fails to comply with a valid assignment order following service is liable to the applicant for the amount incurred for health care services that would otherwise have been covered. Fam C §3768(a).

§20.71   3. Motion to Quash

The obligor may move to quash the assignment order by declaring under penalty of perjury that there is error in that:

- No order to maintain health insurance has been issued under Fam C §§3750–3753 (Fam C §3765(a)(1));

- The amount to be withheld for premiums is greater than that permissible under Fam C §§3750–3753 or greater than the amount otherwise ordered by the court (Fam C §3765(a)(2));

- The amount of the increased premium is unreasonable (Fam C §3765(a)(3));

- The alleged obligor is not the obligor from whom health insurance coverage is due (Fam C §3765(a)(4));

- The child or children are or will be otherwise provided health care coverage (Fam C §3765(a)(5)); or

- The employer's choice of coverage is inappropriate (Fam C §3765(a)(6)).

Presumably, the obligor could also base a motion to quash on the ground that the health insurance coverage assignment would cause him or her extraordinary hardship. See Fam C §3762(b).

The motion to quash must be filed with the court that issued the assignment order within 15 days after service on the obligor by the employer, or other person providing health insurance to the obligor, of notice of the order. The clerk must set the motion to be heard between 15 and 30 days after receipt of the notice of motion. Within 5 days after receipt of the notice of motion, the clerk must deliver a copy of the notice of motion to the district attorney, personally or by first-class mail, and to the applicant and the employer or other person providing health insurance by first-class mail. Fam C §3765(b).

The Judicial Council has promulgated a form effective January 1, 2007, for mandatory use in requesting that an assignment order be quashed. For the Request and Notice of Hearing Regarding Health Insurance Assignment (FL-478) and the Information Sheet and Instructions for Request and Notice of Hearing Regarding Health Insurance Assignment (FL-478 INFO), see §§20.71A–20.71B.

On a finding of error as described above, the court must quash the assignment order. Fam C §3765(c). If the court grants the motion to quash on the ground that the order would cause extraordinary hardship to the obligor, it must specify the nature of that hardship and, whenever possible, a date by which the obligor must obtain health insurance coverage or be subject to a health insurance coverage assignment. Fam C §3762(b).

§20.71A   a. Form: Request and Notice of Hearing Regarding Health Insurance Assignment (FL-478)

FL-478

ATTORNEY OR PARTY WITHOUT ATTORNEY *(Name, State Bar number, and address)*:	FOR COURT USE ONLY
TELEPHONE NO.: FAX NO. *(Optional)*: E-MAIL ADDRESS *(Optional)*: ATTORNEY FOR *(Name)*:	

SUPERIOR COURT OF CALIFORNIA, COUNTY OF

STREET ADDRESS:

MAILING ADDRESS:

CITY AND ZIP CODE:

BRANCH NAME:

PETITIONER/PLAINTIFF:

RESPONDENT/DEFENDANT:

OTHER PARENT:

REQUEST AND NOTICE OF HEARING REGARDING HEALTH INSURANCE ASSIGNMENT	CASE NUMBER:

NOTICE: If you object to the *Application and Order for Health Insurance Coverage* (form FL-470) or *National Medical Support Notice* (form OMB-0970-0222), complete and file this form with the court clerk to request a hearing. This form may not be used to modify your current child support amount. (See "Information Sheet on Changing a Child Support Order" on page 2 of form FL-192.)

1. A hearing on this application will be held as follows *(see instructions for getting a hearing date on form FL-478-INFO)*:

   a. Date: Time: ☐ Dept.:   ☐ Div.:   ☐ Room:

   b. The address of the court is ☐ same as above ☐ other *(specify)*:

2. ☐ I request that service of the *Application and Order for Health Insurance Coverage* (form FL-470) or *National Medical Support Notice* (form OMB-0970-0222) be quashed (set aside) because:

   a. ☐ I am not the obligor named in the *Application and Order for Health Insurance Coverage* or *National Medical Support Notice.*

   b. ☐ Health insurance coverage is not available at a reasonable cost.

   c. ☐ The health insurance premium plus the monthly payment in any earnings assignment order are more than half of my total net income each month from all sources.

   d. ☐ The following children *(name)*:   are emancipated.

   e. ☐ I was not notified at least 15 days before the date of filing of the application that a health insurance coverage assignment was being sought.

   f. ☐ No order to maintain health insurance has been issued.

   g. ☐ Health insurance coverage is or will be provided for the children, but not through a parent's job-related coverage *(explain)*:

   h. ☐ The employer's choice of coverage is inappropriate *(explain)*:

   i. ☐ Other *(specify)*:

I declare under penalty of perjury under the laws of the State of California that the foregoing is true and correct.

Date:

▶

_____   _____
(TYPE OR PRINT NAME OF PERSON REQUESTING HEARING)   (SIGNATURE OF PERSON REQUESTING HEARING)

Page 1 of 2

**REQUEST AND NOTICE OF HEARING REGARDING
 HEALTH INSURANCE ASSIGNMENT
 (Family Law—Governmental—UIFSA)**

Family Code, §§ 3781, 3765, and 3773 <br> www.courtinfo.ca.gov

FL-478

PETITIONER/PLAINTIFF:	CASE NUMBER:
RESPONDENT/DEFENDANT:	
OTHER PARENT:	

NOTICE FOR CASES INVOLVING A LOCAL CHILD SUPPORT AGENCY

This case may be referred to a court commissioner for hearing. By law, court commissioners do not have the authority to issue final orders and judgments in contested cases unless they are acting as temporary judges. The court commissioner in your case will act as a temporary judge unless, *before the hearing,* you or any other party objects to the commissioner acting as a temporary judge. The court commissioner may still hear your case to make findings and a recommended order. If you do not like the recommended order, you must object to it within 10 court days; otherwise, the recommended order will become a final order of the court. If you object to the recommended order, a judge will make a temporary order and set a new hearing.

CLERK'S CERTIFICATE OF MAILING

I certify that I am not a party to this action and that a true copy of the *Request and Notice of Hearing Regarding Health Insurance Assignment* (form FL-478) was mailed, with postage fully prepaid, in a sealed envelope addressed as shown below, and that the request was mailed at *(place):*   on *(date):*

Date:

Clerk, by _____ , Deputy

Request for Accommodations
Assistive listening systems, computer-assisted real-time captioning, or sign language interpreter services are available if you ask at least five days before the proceeding. Contact the clerk's office or go to *www.courtinfo.ca.gov/forms* for *Request for Accommodations by Persons With Disabilities and Response* (form MC-410). (Civil Code, § 54.8)

§20.71B b. Form: Information Sheet and Instructions for Request and Notice of Hearing Regarding Health Insurance Assignment (FL-478 INFO)

INFORMATION SHEET AND INSTRUCTIONS FOR REQUEST AND NOTICE OF HEARING REGARDING HEALTH INSURANCE ASSIGNMENT

(Do *not* deliver this information sheet to the court clerk.)

Please follow these instructions to complete the *Request and Notice of Hearing Regarding Health Insurance Assignment* (form FL-478) if you do not have an attorney representing you. Your attorney, if you have one, should complete this form. You must file the completed *Request and Notice of Hearing* form and its attachments with the court clerk **within 15 days** after the date your employer gave you a copy of *Application and Order for Health Insurance Coverage* (form FL-470) or *National Medical Support Notice* (form OMB-0970-0222). The address of the court clerk is the same as the one shown for the superior court on the health insurance coverage assignment order. If the local child support agency is not involved in your case, you may have to pay a filing fee. If you cannot afford to pay the filing fee, the court may waive it, but you will have to fill out some forms first and ask the court to waive the fees. For more information about the filing fee and waiver of the filing fee, contact the court clerk or the family law facilitator in your county.

THIS FORM MUST BE FILLED OUT IN TYPE OR PRINTED IN INK.

Front page, first box, top of form, left side: Print your name, address, and telephone number in this box if they are not already there.

Item 1. a–b. You should contact the court clerk's office to ask about procedures for getting a hearing date for this motion.

Item 2. Check this box if you want the court to stop the local child support agency or the other parent from collecting a health insurance premium from your wages or earnings. If you check this box, you must check at least one of the boxes beneath it.

   a. Check this box if you are not the person required to pay health insurance premiums in the *Application and Order for Health Insurance Coverage* or *National Medical Support Notice.*

   b. Check this box if you believe that health insurance coverage is not available at a reasonable cost.

   c. Check this box if you believe the health insurance premium plus the monthly payment in any earnings withholding order are more than half of your total net income each month from all sources.

   d. Check this box if you believe the children have reached the legal age of emancipation. Fill in the children's names.

   e. Check this box if you were not notified at least 15 days before the date of filing of the application that a health insurance coverage assignment was being sought.

   f. Check this box if the court has not ordered you to maintain health insurance.

   g. Check this box if you have provided or will provide health insurance for the children, but not through your job-related coverage. This can mean that the other parent or family member is providing, or the child has access to other insurance. Note that governmental medical assistance programs such as MediCal or Healthy Families may not satisfy your obligation to provide health insurance. If you need further information, see your county's family law facilitator or local child support agency.

   h. Check this box if you believe that your employer's choice of coverage is inappropriate and explain why.

   i. Check this box if you have some other reason that this order should not be enforced and explain why.

You must date this *Request and Notice of Hearing Regarding Health Insurance Assignment,* type or print your name, and sign the form under penalty of perjury. When you sign this form, you are stating that the information you have provided is true and correct. You must also complete the certificate of mailing on page 2 of the form by printing the name and address of the other parties or the attorneys for the other parties in brackets and providing the clerk with a stamped envelope addressed to each of the parties or attorneys for parties. Do not date or sign page 2 of the form. The court clerk will explain to you how to get a court date.

You must file your request within 15 days of receiving the *Application and Order for Health Insurance Coverage* or *National Medical Support Notice* from your employer, unless there's been a change of circumstances and you are using the form to change an ongoing health insurance assignment. You may file your request in person at the clerk's office or mail it to the clerk. In either event, it must be received by the clerk within the 15-day period.

If you need additional assistance with this form, contact an attorney or the family law facilitator in your county. The family law facilitator can help you, for free, with any questions you have about the above information. For more information on finding a lawyer or family law facilitator, see the California Courts Online Self-Help Center at www.courtinfo.ca.gov/selfhelp.

NOTICE: Use this form to request a hearing only if you object to the *Application and Order for Health Insurance Coverage* (form FL-470) or *National Medical Support Notice* (form OMB-0970-0222). This form will *not* modify your current support amount. (See "Information Sheet on Changing a Child Support Order" on page 2 of form FL-192.)

Form Approved for Optional Use
Judicial Council of California
FL-478-INFO [New January 1, 2007]

INFORMATION SHEET AND INSTRUCTIONS FOR REQUEST AND NOTICE OF HEARING REGARDING HEALTH INSURANCE ASSIGNMENT
(Family Law—Governmental—UIFSA)

Family Code, §§ 3761, 3765, and 3773
www.courtinfo.ca.gov

§20.72   4. Termination

The obligor may move to terminate a health insurance coverage assignment on the basis of any of the following grounds:

- A new order has been issued under Fam C §§3750–3753 that is inconsistent with the existing assignment (Fam C §3770(a));

- The employer or other person providing health insurance has discontinued the obligor's coverage (Fam C §3770(b));

- There is good cause, consistent with Fam C §3762, to terminate the assignment (Fam C §3770(c)); or

- The child for whom the insurance has been obtained has died or become emancipated (Fam C §3770(d)).

Like a motion to quash (see §20.71), a motion for termination is prepared and processed in the same manner as a notice of motion for temporary orders.

§20.73   I. Collection From State or Local Public Entity Owing Money to Judgment Debtor

When the state or any local public entity (*e.g.,* county, city, district, public authority or agency) owes money to a judgment debtor, a special procedure in CCP §§708.710–708.795 may enable the judgment creditor to have the money paid to him or her to satisfy the judgment. See CCP §§708.710–708.720. The procedure is best known for intercepting state income tax refunds and lottery winnings, but it is not limited to those uses. The procedure is *not* available, however, when the money sought to be applied is earnings of a public officer or employee or when the public entity's obligation is the subject of a pending action or special proceeding. In those instances, other procedures must be employed. CCP §708.720.

1. Enforcing Party's Procedures

§20.74   a. Judgment for Other Than Support

When the underlying judgment or order is for other than child, spousal, or family support, the judgment creditor must file an abstract or a certified copy of the money judgment with the state agency that owes the money to the judgment debtor before the agency presents the judgment debtor's claim to the State Controller for payment.

CCP §§708.730(a), 708.740(a). The abstract or certified copy must be accompanied by an affidavit indicating that the judgment creditor desires the relief provided by CCP §§708.710–708.795 and stating the exact amount required to satisfy the judgment. The affidavit may also state any fact tending to establish the identity of the judgment debtor. CCP §708.730(a). Promptly after filing the abstract or certified copy of the judgment and the affidavit with the public entity, the judgment creditor must serve notice of the filing, either by mail or personal service, on the judgment debtor. CCP §708.730(b).

On the enforcing party's procedures when the underlying judgment or order is for support, see §§20.75–20.78.

b. Judgment for Support

§20.75 (1) Local Child Support Agency Enforcing Obligation

When (1) the underlying judgment or order is for child, spousal, or family support and related costs, (2) the money is owed to the judgment debtor by a state agency (*e.g.*, state income tax refund), and (3) the local child support agency is enforcing the support obligation under Fam C §17400 (former Welf & I C §11475.1), then the local child support agency may file the required affidavit (for details, see §20.74) with the Department of Child Support Services (CSS) without also filing an abstract or certified copy of the judgment. CCP §§708.730(c), (e), 708.740(a). Promptly after the affidavit is filed with the CSS, notice of the filing must be served, by mail or personal service, on the judgment debtor. The CSS may provide the notice. CCP §708.730(b)–(c).

§20.76 (2) Local Child Support Agency Not Enforcing Obligation

If (1) the judgment is for support, (2) the money owed to the judgment debtor is for state *lottery winnings* or a refund of overpayment of state *tax*, penalty, or interest, and (3) the judgment is not being enforced under Fam C §17400 by a local child support agency, the judgment creditor may file an abstract or certified copy of the judgment with the local child support agency in the county where the judgment is entered or registered. CCP §708.740(e). The local child support agency must then file the judgment creditor's claim as provided in CCP §708.730(c) (see §20.75), and on receipt of the funds the agency must discharge any claim of the judgment debtor by forwarding those sums to the court clerk. CCP §708.740(e).

All notices otherwise required of a judgment creditor or the court clerk and any litigation to enforce rights under CCP §708.740(e) are the judgment creditor's responsibility (as if there had been no intervention by the local child support agency). CCP §708.740(e).

It appears, however, that if the funds owed to the debtor by a state public entity *are not* related to lottery winnings or tax refunds, a creditor who seeks to make a claim against them would proceed in the same manner as for judgments unrelated to support, *i.e.*, by filing an abstract or certified copy of the judgment and an affidavit with the state agency or other public entity that owes money to the judgment debtor (see §20.74). CCP §§708.740(a), 708.750.

NOTE➤ If the money owed to a judgment debtor is under $10 and the judgment creditor's claim arises under an affidavit filed under CCP §708.730(c), the State Controller may disregard the creditor's claim and forward the money to the judgment debtor. If there is more than one claimant for a refund, the Franchise Tax Board has discretion in allocating the overpayment among claimants. CCP §§708.740(f).

§20.77 (a) Form: Application for Notice of Support Arrearage (Judicial Council Forms 1297.90 and 1297.91)

The forms in this section were revoked effective January 1, 2003.

§20.78 (b) Form: Notice of Support Arrearage and Notice to Judgment Debtor (Judicial Council Forms 1297.92 and 1297.93)

The forms in this section were revoked effective January 1, 2003.

2. Judgment Debtor's Response

§20.79 a. Local Child Support Agency Processing Claim for Support Through Department of Child Support Services

When the Department of Child Support Services (CSS) has been served with an affidavit from a local child support agency under CCP §708.730(c) and has presented the claim to the State Controller under CCP §708.740(a), the CSS must send a notice of deposit to the judgment debtor, informing him or her with respect to the filing of any requests for relief. CCP §§708.740(a), 708.770(g).The debtor's request for relief under this process must be filed within 15 days after service. CCP §708.770(g). A different time period applies when a judgment creditor's claim is handled under CCP §708.740(e) (see §20.80). CCP §708.770(b), (g).

The judgment debtor may challenge the distribution of the funds on exemption (see CCP §703.520) or other grounds (*e.g.,* satisfied judgment, improper service) and is entitled to a hearing. CCP §708.770(b)-(c). Code of Civil Procedure §703.580(a)-(d) and CCP §§703.590, 703.600 apply to a claim of exemption under CCP §708.770. CCP §708.770(e). A judgment debtor's failure to make a claim of exemption constitutes a waiver of the exemption. CCP §708.770(f).

§20.80 b. Judgment Creditor Processing Claim for Support in Underlying Action

Promptly after a public entity deposits funds claimed by a judgment creditor with the court, the court clerk must serve a notice of deposit on the judgment debtor. CCP §708.770(a).

A judgment debtor who is served by the court clerk with a notice of deposit of the funds with the court has 10 days in which to file a claim of exemption. CCP §708.770(a)-(b). This 10-day period also applies when the judgment creditor's claim is filed under CCP §708.740(e) with respect to state lottery winnings and tax refunds (see §20.76). CCP §708.770(b), (g). In addition, the provisions of CCP §708.770(a)-(f) apply, including those for claiming an exemption (see §20.79). CCP §708.770(g).

§20.81 c. Other Instances

In instances other than those in which the local child support agency is processing a claim for support through the Department of Child Support Services (see §20.79) or the judgment creditor is processing a claim for support in the underlying action (see §20.80), the judgment debtor will be served by the court clerk, either personally or by mail, with a notice of deposit of the funds with the court. CCP §708.770(a). The judgment debtor has 10 days after service in which to file a claim of exemption or otherwise challenge distribution of the funds. CCP §708.770(b).

J. Proceeding Against Military Personnel and Retirees

§20.82　1. Direct Payment of Military Retirement Benefits

With respect to division of property, the Federal Uniformed Services Former Spouses' Protection Act (FUSFSPA) (10 USC §1408) authorizes direct payment to a former spouse of his or her share of military retirement benefits as provided in the court judgment. 10 USC §1408(d)(1). To be eligible for direct payment, however, the former spouse must have been married to the service member for at least ten years, during which the member performed at least ten years of service creditable for retirement purposes. 10 USC §1408(d)(2). That this requirement and a number of others have been met can and should be evidenced by inclusion of appropriate statements in the court judgment dividing the benefits. The copy of the judgment served on the appropriate branch of the service must be certified within 90 days immediately preceding its service. 32 CFR §63.6(c)(2). Service must be by certified or registered mail, return receipt requested, or by personal service. 10 USC §1408(b)(1)(A). In many instances, it will be helpful to contact the appropriate branch of the service, preferably early in the proceedings, to obtain information on its particular requirements, forms, and procedures.

On garnishment of military retirement benefits to enforce support orders, or to enforce division of property other than the retirement benefits themselves, see §20.83.

§20.83　2. Garnishment of Military Pay or Retirement Benefits

The military is required to withhold from a member's pay or retirement benefits to enforce child and spousal support orders in the manner established by state law. 42 USC §659(a) (pay); 10 USC §1408(d)(1) (retirement benefits); see 5 CFR §§581.101-581.501 (implementing regulations). Thus, for example, an earnings assignment order for support (see §§20.2-20.15) could be served on the designated agent for the appropriate branch of the service in the same manner as it may be served on a civilian employer.

Depending on the circumstances, support enforcement may also be possible through the following:

(1) Informal action under the regulations of the particular branch of the service, initiated by contacting the member's commanding officer; or

(2) Involuntary allotment, initiated through the district attorney's office (42 USC §665).

Military retirement benefits may also be garnished to enforce division of property other than the benefits themselves. 10 USC §1408(d)(1), (5). On direct payment of the benefits themselves, see §20.82.

K. Nonissuance of License for Noncompliance With Child Support Order

§20.84   1. Certification of Noncompliance by Local Child Support Agency

The local child support agency must maintain a list of obligors in cases being enforced under Title IV-D of the Social Security Act (42 USC §§651–669b) against whom a support order or judgment has been rendered by, or registered in, a California court and who are not in compliance with that order or judgment. Fam C §17520(b). A party is not in compliance when he or she is more than 30 calendar days in arrears in making payments. Fam C §17520(a)(4). The agency must submit a certified list of the obligors who are not in compliance to the State Department of Social Services and submit an updated certified list monthly. Fam C §17520(b). In practice, each noncomplying obligor will be listed by the local child support agency in the county of venue of the underlying action.

Note that the procedure for nonissuance of licenses under Fam C §17520 is available only in cases being enforced by the local child support agency under Title IV-D. Thus, private attorneys may not use the procedure themselves against noncomplying obligors but must refer the client to the agency for enforcement. Note further that both welfare and nonwelfare cases are enforced by the local child support agency under Title IV-D. The agency may use Fam

C §17520 to enforce spousal support orders only when it is also enforcing a related child support obligation owed to the same parent by the same obligor. Fam C §17520(a)(4).

For purposes of Fam C §17520, "child support" includes "family support." See Fam C §17520(a)(4).

§20.85 2. Notice Procedures

The Department of Child Support Services must consolidate the certified lists of noncomplying obligors received from the local child support agencies (see §20.84) and, within 30 calendar days after receipt, provide a copy of the consolidated list to each state board that is responsible for the regulation of licenses. Fam C §17520(c). Licenses subject to the procedures include membership in the State Bar; business, occupational, and professional licenses; and drivers' licenses. Fam C §17520(a)(5). Before issuance or renewal of a license, each board must ascertain whether the applicant is on the most recent consolidated list provided by the State Department of Social Services (Fam C §17520(e)(1)) and, if so, immediately notify the applicant of the board's intent to withhold issuance or renewal of the license (Fam C §17520(e)(2)). If the applicant is otherwise eligible for a license, the board must issue a temporary license valid for 150 days (Fam C §17520(e)(2)(A)), which may not be extended, except that, in the case of a noncommercial driver's license, the 150-day period must be extended for up to 150 additional days on the local child support agency's request or by court order on a showing of good cause (Fam C §17520(e)(2)(B), (D)).

The notice to the applicant must include the address and telephone number of the local child support agency that submitted the applicant's name and emphasize the need to obtain a release from that agency's office as a condition for the issuance or renewal of the license. Fam C §17520(f). The notice must be accompanied by the form that the applicant must use to request a review by the agency. Fam C §17520(f)(3).

The procedures under Fam C §17520 may also be applied to suspend an existing license of a licensee whose license would not otherwise be eligible for renewal within 6 months after the suspension request by the State Department of Social Services and is not subject to annual renewal or an annual fee, provided that the licensee has been out of compliance with a support judgment or order for more than 4 months. Fam C §17520(e)(3), (f)(2).

The supreme court has adopted Cal Rules of Ct 9.22 authorizing the State Bar to implement Fam C §17520 (former Welf & I C §11350.6) with respect to attorneys delinquent in child or family support payments.

§20.86   3. Obligor's Response; Administrative and Judicial Review

Each local child support agency's office must maintain procedures to allow a support obligor to have the underlying arrearage and any relevant defenses investigated, to provide an obligor information on the process of obtaining a modification of a support order, or to provide an obligor assistance in establishing a payment schedule on arrearages if the circumstances warrant it. Fam C §17520(g).

An applicant who wishes to challenge the submission of his or her name on the certified list must make a timely written request for review on the mandatory form to the local child support agency that certified his or her name. Within 75 days after receipt of the written request, the agency must inform the applicant in writing of its findings on completion of the review. Fam C §17520(h). The agency must immediately send a release to the appropriate board and the applicant if any of the following conditions is met:

- The applicant is found to be in compliance or negotiates an agreement with the agency for a payment schedule on arrearages (Fam C §17520(h)(1));

- The applicant has submitted a timely request for review, but the agency will be unable to complete the review and send notice of its findings to the applicant within 75 days (Fam C §17520(h)(2));

- The applicant has filed and served a timely request for judicial review under Fam C §17520, but a resolution of that review will not be made within 150 days after service of the board's notice to the applicant (see §20.85) (Fam C §17520(h)(3)); or

- The applicant has obtained a judicial finding of compliance (Fam C §17520(h)(4)).

The local child support agency must notify the applicant in writing that the applicant may file an order to show cause or a notice of motion requesting one or more of the following: (1) judicial review of the agency's decision not to issue a release; (2) a judicial determination of compliance; and (3) modification of the support judgment or order. Fam C §17520(j). A request for judicial review must be served on the appropriate local child support agency within 7 calendar days after the application is filed, and the court must hold an evidentiary hearing within 20 calendar days after the filing. If the judicial review results in a finding by the court that the obligor has complied with the support judgment or order, the agency must immediately send a release to the appropriate board and the applicant. The court may also order a conditional release, based on the obligor's needs, and specify the payment terms to be met to maintain the release in effect. Fam C §17520(k).

For Judicial Council forms, see §§20.88 (notice of motion for judicial review of license denial), 20.89 (order after judicial review of license denial).

§20.87   4. Obligor's Other Remedies Preserved

Nothing in Fam C §17520 may be deemed to restrict the obligor's right to file a motion in the underlying action (1) for modification, (2) to fix a payment schedule on arrearages accruing, or (3) for a court finding of compliance with the judgment or order. Fam C §17520(j).

§20.88   5. Form: Notice of Motion for Judicial Review of License Denial (Judicial Council Form FL-670)

ATTORNEY OR PARTY WITHOUT ATTORNEY OR GOVERNMENTAL AGENCY (under Family Code §§ 17400, 17406) *(Name and Address):*	FOR COURT USE ONLY
TELEPHONE NO.: FAX NO.:	
ATTORNEY FOR *(Name):*	

SUPERIOR COURT OF CALIFORNIA, COUNTY OF
STREET ADDRESS:
MAILING ADDRESS:
CITY AND ZIP CODE:
BRANCH NAME:

PETITIONER/PLAINTIFF:
RESPONDENT/DEFENDANT:
OTHER PARENT:

NOTICE OF MOTION FOR JUDICIAL REVIEW OF LICENSE DENIAL	CASE NUMBER:

See reverse for instructions.

1. On *(date):*   the local child support agency of *(specify county):*
   denied a release form that would enable me to obtain the following license *(specify):*

   Name and address of licensing agency:

2. I seek a judicial review of the local child support agency's denial on the following grounds *(check all that apply):*
   a. ☐ There is no order for me to pay child support in this action.

   b. ☐ I am not the person ordered to pay child support in this action.

   c. ☐ I am in compliance with the order to pay child support in this action.

   d. ☐ I am in compliance with payments on the schedule for payment of arrearages or reimbursement.

   e. ☐ Other *(specify):*

   I declare under penalty of perjury under the laws of the State of California that the foregoing is true and correct.

Date:

_____   ▶ _____
(TYPE OR PRINT NAME)   (SIGNATURE OF DECLARANT)

3. A hearing on this motion will be held as follows:

   Date: Time: Room:
   Address:

Form Adopted for Mandatory Use
Judicial Council of California
FL-670 [Rev. January 1, 2003]

**NOTICE OF MOTION FOR
JUDICIAL REVIEW OF LICENSE DENIAL
(Governmental)**

Family Code, § 17520
www.courtinfo.ca.gov

PETITIONER/PLAINTIFF: RESPONDENT/DEFENDANT: OTHER PARENT:	CASE NUMBER:

This motion should be filed with a hearing scheduled *as soon as possible* after your local child support agency review.

INSTRUCTIONS

1. Complete the application on the reverse. Contact the clerk of the court for a hearing date, time, and place. Insert the information in box 3 on the reverse.

2. File the original *Notice of Motion for Judicial Review of License Denial* (form FL-670) with the court and keep two copies, because you will need them later.

3. Serve a copy of this form on the local child support agency which has certified your name for nonpayment of child support not later than seven days after the filing in court. Service of the papers may be made by (a) personal delivery   OR   (b) mailing the papers by first-class mail, postage prepaid, to the last known address of the other party. Anyone at least 18 years of age EXCEPT A PARTY may personally serve or mail the papers. Be sure whoever serves the papers fills out and signs the proof of service below.

PROOF OF SERVICE

4. At the time of service I was at least 18 years of age and not a party to this legal proceeding.

5. I served a copy of the *Notice of Motion for Judicial Review of License Denial* (form FL-670) in the manner shown below.

6. Manner of service on **LOCAL CHILD SUPPORT AGENCY**

   a. ☐ **Personal service.** I personally delivered these papers to the local child support agency as follows:
      (1) Local child support agency *(name):*
      (2) Address where served:

      (3) Date delivered: (4) Time delivered:

   b. ☐ **First-class mail.** I deposited these papers with the United States Postal Service, in a sealed envelope with postage fully prepaid. I am a resident of or employed in the county where the notice was mailed. The envelope was addressed and mailed as follows:
      (1) Local child support agency *(name):*
      (2) Address on envelope:

      (3) Date mailed: (4) Place of mailing *(city, state):*

I declare under penalty of perjury under the laws of the State of California that the foregoing is true and correct.

Date:

▶

_____	_____
(TYPE OR PRINT NAME)	(SIGNATURE OF PERSON WHO SERVED THE NOTICE)

FL-670 [Rev. January 1, 2003]

NOTICE OF MOTION FOR
JUDICIAL REVIEW OF LICENSE DENIAL
(Governmental)

Copies: Original (file with court clerk); copy for service on district attorney; office copies.

§20.89   6. Form: Order After Judicial Review of License Denial (Judicial Council Form FL-675)

FL-675

ATTORNEY OR PARTY WITHOUT ATTORNEY OR GOVERNMENTAL AGENCY (under Family Code §§ 17400, 17406) *(Name, state bar number, and address):*	FOR COURT USE ONLY

TELEPHONE NO.:   FAX NO.:

ATTORNEY FOR *(Name):*

SUPERIOR COURT OF CALIFORNIA, COUNTY OF
STREET ADDRESS:
MAILING ADDRESS:
CITY AND ZIP CODE:
BRANCH NAME:

PETITIONER/PLAINTIFF:

RESPONDENT/DEFENDANT:

OTHER PARENT:

ORDER AFTER JUDICIAL REVIEW OF LICENSE DENIAL	CASE NUMBER:

A hearing was held on:

1. a. Date: ☐ Dept.: ☐ Room:
   b. ☐ Judge *(name):*   ☐ Temporary judge
   c. ☐ License applicant present *(name):*
   d. ☐ Local child support agency attorney present *(name):*

THE COURT FINDS

1. ☐ Declarant obligor is in compliance with the judgment or order for payment of support, arrears, or reimbursement.
2. ☐ The license applicant is not in compliance.
3. ☐ Other *(specify):*

THE COURT ORDERS

4. ☐ The local child support agency must mail a release to the licensing agency and the license applicant.

5. ☐ Other *(specify):*

Date:

_____
JUDICIAL OFFICER

Page 1 of 1

ORDER AFTER JUDICIAL REVIEW OF LICENSE DENIAL
(Governmental)   www.courtinfo.ca.gov

Copies: Original (submit to court clerk); copy for district attorney; office copies.

§20.90   L. Debtor's Examination

A judgment creditor may apply to the proper court for an order requiring the judgment debtor to appear before the court at a specified time and place to furnish information to aid in enforcement of a money judgment. CCP §708.110. Likewise, a judgment creditor may apply to the proper court for a similar order with respect to a third person who has possession or control of property in which the judgment debtor has an interest or is indebted to the judgment debtor in an amount exceeding $250. CCP §708.120. The proper court is usually, but not always, the one in which the money judgment was entered. See CCP §708.160. At a debtor's examination, a spouse is entitled to the supporting spouse's tax returns and information about the supporting spouse's income, but the tax returns must remain confidential. *Marriage of Sachs* (2002) 95 CA4th 1144, 116 CR2d 273. See Fam C §§3552, 3665. Debtors' examinations are governed by CCP §§708.110–708.205.

For a complete discussion of debtors' examinations, see Debt Collection Practice in California §§8.15–8.19 (2d ed Cal CEB 1999).

§20.91   M. Appointment of Receiver

The court may appoint a receiver to enforce any judgment or order. Fam C §290. To support appointment of a receiver, the judgment creditor must show that, considering the interests of both the judgment creditor and the judgment debtor, such an appointment is a reasonable method to obtain the fair and orderly satisfaction of the judgment. CCP §708.620. A receiver may be appointed when a writ of execution would not reach certain property and other remedies appear inadequate. Comment to CCP §708.620. When a receiver is appointed to enforce a judgment, the general receiver provisions of CCP §§564–571 govern the receiver's appointment, qualifications, powers, rights, and duties. CCP §708.610.

Although a receiver may be appointed on the court's own motion (*Venza v Venza* (1949) 94 CA2d 878, 883, 211 P2d 913), the appointment is typically considered on the motion of the party seeking to enforce the judgment or order. The motion is prepared and processed in the same manner as a noticed motion for temporary orders.

For discussion of, and forms for, motions for temporary orders, see §§11.16–11.63. The requesting party prepares the Judicial Council forms of (1) Order to Show Cause (see form in §11.18) or Notice of Motion (see form in §11.20) and (2) Application for Order and Supporting Declaration (see form in §11.22).

Whether the Order to Show Cause or Notice of Motion procedure is used will generally depend on whether the moving party seeks ex parte orders (*e.g.*, appointment of the receiver, property restraints) pending the hearing. If so, the Order to Show Cause must be used. Otherwise, as long as the opposing party has made a general appearance, the Notice of Motion will generally be used for its convenience because it need not be submitted to the court for the judge's signature and is typically served by mail rather than personally served. However, note that, after a judgment has been entered, any noticed motion must be served on the opposing party, not on his or her attorney. Fam C §215.

The Application for Order and Supporting Declaration should, at Item 13, indicate that appointment of a receiver is requested, specify the assets to be subject to the receivership, and identify the judgment provision or order to be enforced. A declaration should be provided at Item 14 that contains facts establishing that the requested appointment is a reasonable method to obtain a fair and orderly satisfaction of the judgment (see CCP §708.620) and that other remedies appear inadequate (see Comment to CCP §708.620). When appointment of a receiver is requested ex parte, the declaration should comply with the requirements of Cal Rules of Ct 3.1175, although the precise applicability of that rule to motions for appointment of a receiver in cases under the Family Code is unclear (see Cal Rules of Ct 3.1103(a)), and the desired order pending hearing may be set forth on the Order to Show Cause form at Item 3c.

Because appointment of a receiver in marital actions is relatively unusual, submission of a memorandum of points and authorities is recommended. On the memorandum of points and authorities generally, see California Civil Procedure Before Trial §§12.30–12.42 (4th ed Cal CEB 2004).

§20.92   N. Charging Order Against Partnership or Limited Liability Company Interest

A judgment debtor's interest in a partnership or a limited liability company may be applied toward the satisfaction of a judgment by an order charging the judgment debtor's interest under former Corp C §15028 (see now Corp C §16504) or Corp C §15673 or Corp C §17302. CCP §708.310.

Service on the judgment debtor, and on the other partners or the partnership, or on the judgment debtor, and on all members of the limited liability company or the limited liability company, of a notice of motion for a charging order creates a lien on the judgment debtor's interest in the partnership or limited liability company. CCP §708.320(a). If the charging order is issued, the lien continues under the terms of the order. If issuance is denied, the lien is extinguished. CCP §708.320(b).

The charging order is directed to the other partners or members of the limited liability company. If they do not obey the order, the court may appoint a receiver and make any additional orders that the circumstances may require. Corp C §§16504(a), 17302. As long as court authorization is obtained and statutory requirements are complied with, a receiver may conduct a sale, which is then subject to court confirmation. CCP §568.5. The partnership or limited liability company may redeem the interest charged. Corp C §§16504(c)(2)-(3), 17302(c)(2)-(3). As a practical matter, such issues are often resolved in this manner.

A motion for a charging order is prepared and processed in the same manner as a noticed motion for temporary orders. For discussion of, and forms for, motions for temporary orders, see §§11.16-11.63. The requesting party prepares the Judicial Council forms of (1) Order to Show Cause (see form in §11.18) or Notice of Motion (see form in §11.20) and (2) Application for Order and Supporting Declaration (see form in §11.22).

Normally, as long as the opposing party has made a general appearance, the Notice of Motion, rather than the Order to Show Cause, will be used because the Notice of Motion need not be submitted to the court for the judge's signature and is typically served by mail rather than personally served. However, note that, after a judgment has been entered, any noticed motion must be served on the opposing party, not on his or her attorney. Fam C §215. The motion should also be served on each other partner or company member. See CCP §708.320(a).

The Application for Order and Supporting Declaration should, at Item 13, indicate that a charging order against the partnership or limited liability company is requested, identify the judgment provision or order to be enforced, and indicate what the partnership is to do under the proposed order. A declaration should be provided at Item 14 that contains facts establishing that the underlying order is not being complied with and that the opposing party has an interest in the particular partnership or limited liability company.

Because a charging order against a partnership or limited liability company in marital actions is relatively unusual, submission of a memorandum of points and authorities is recommended. On the memorandum of points and authorities generally, see California Civil Procedure Before Trial §§12.30–12.42 (4th ed Cal CEB 2004).

For further discussion of charging orders against partnership interests, see Debt Collection Practice in California §§11.7–11.10 (2d ed Cal CEB 1999).

§20.93   O. Assignment Order

On noticed motion by a judgment creditor, the court may order a judgment debtor to assign to the judgment creditor or to a properly appointed receiver all or part of a right to payment due or to become due, including, but not limited to (CCP §708.510(a)):

- Federal government wages that are not subject to an earnings withholding order;

- Rents;

- Commissions;

- Royalties;

- Payments due from a patent or copyright; and

- The loan value on an insurance policy.

In determining whether to order an assignment or the amount of an assignment, the court may take into consideration all relevant factors, including (CCP §708.510(c)):

- The reasonable requirements of a judgment debtor who is a natural person and of persons supported in whole or in part by the judgment debtor;

- Payments the judgment debtor is required to make or that are deducted in satisfaction of other judgments and earnings assignment orders for support;

- The amount remaining due on the money judgment; and

- The amount being or to be received in satisfaction of the right to payment that may be assigned.

The court may issue, either ex parte or on noticed motion, an order restraining the judgment debtor from assigning or otherwise disposing of the right to payment that is sought to be assigned. CCP §708.520. An assignment order itself is subject to exemptions (CCP §§708.510(e)-(f), 708.550) and to a subsequent modification or a set aside on a showing of a material change of circumstances (CCP §708.560).

A motion for an assignment order is prepared and processed in the same manner as a noticed motion for temporary orders. For discussion of, and forms for, motions for temporary orders, see §§11.16-11.63. The requesting party prepares the Judicial Council forms of (1) Order to Show Cause (see form in §11.18) or Notice of Motion (see form in §11.20) and (2) Application for Order and Supporting Declaration (see form in §11.22).

Whether the Order to Show Cause or Notice of Motion procedure is used will generally depend on whether the moving party seeks an ex parte order restraining the judgment debtor from assigning or otherwise disposing of the right to payment that is sought to be assigned. If so, the Order to Show Cause must be used. Otherwise, as long as the opposing party has made a general appearance, the Notice of Motion will generally be used for its convenience because, unlike an Order to Show Cause, it need not be submitted to the court for the judge's signature and may be served by mail rather than personally served (see CCP §§708.510(b), 708.520(d)). Note, however, that after a judgment has been entered, any noticed motion must be served on the opposing party, not on his or her attorney. Fam C §215.

The Application for Order and Supporting Declaration should, at Item 13, indicate that an assignment order is requested, and identify the judgment provision or order to be enforced and the right to payment that is to be assigned. A declaration should be provided at Item 14 that contains facts establishing that the underlying order is not being complied with and demonstrating that the requested order is necessary and appropriate, preferably with specific reference to the factors enumerated in CCP §708.510(c) and above.

Because an assignment order in marital actions is relatively unusual, submission of a memorandum of points and authorities is recommended. On the memorandum of points and authorities generally, see California Civil Procedure Before Trial §§12.30–12.42 (4th ed Cal CEB 2004).

For further discussion of assignment orders, see Debt Collection Practice in California §§11.21–11.32 (2d ed Cal CEB 1999).

§20.94 P. Penalties for Unpaid Child Support

Penalties against support obligor. Statutory interest on unpaid child support payments accrues as a matter of law as to each installment when each becomes due, and accrued arrearages are treated like a money judgment for purposes of assessing statutory interest. CCP §695.221. Therefore, unless otherwise specified in the judgment, interest (currently 10 percent) accrues as to each installment when each installment becomes due and continues to accrue for so long as the arrearage remains unpaid. *Marriage of McClellan* (2005) 130 CA4th 247, 30 CR3d 5. When a father appealed a trial court's ruling that he was still obligated to pay support while his son participated in a high school foreign exchange program, the appellate court's affirmance of that order reinstated the father's obligation to pay child support retroactively, including accrued interest. *Marriage of Hubner (Hubner III)* (2004) 124 CA4th 1082, 22 CR3d 549.

NOTE➤ In any action enforced under Fam C §§17400–17440 (*i.e.*, by local child support agencies) no interest accrues on an obligation for current child, spousal, family, or medical support that is due in a given month until the first day of the following month. Fam C §17433.5.

Family Code §§4720–4733 provide for substantial monetary penalties for unpaid child support. The sections apply to all installments due after December 31, 1991. Fam C §4721(a). The penalties are intended to be applied in "egregious instances of noncompliance with child support orders." Fam C §4721(b). Payments made through wage assignments are not subject to the penalties, regardless of the date of receipt by the support obligee. Fam C §4721(c). The penalties may not be sought by a local child support agency providing support enforcement services under Title IV-D of the Social Security Act (42 USC §§651–669b) (*i.e.,* welfare and nonwelfare support cases handled by the local child support agency). Fam C §4729.

When court-ordered child support payments are more than 30 days in arrears, the support obligee may file and serve a Notice of Delinquency, to be signed under penalty of perjury. Fam C §§4722(a), 4723(a). The notice may be served personally, by certified mail, or in any manner provided for service of summons (*e.g.,* by substituted service; see §10.32). Fam C §4724. Any amount of support specified in the Notice of Delinquency that remains unpaid for more than 30 days after the notice has been filed and served shall incur a penalty of 6 percent of the delinquent amount for each month that it remains unpaid, up to a maximum of 72 percent of the total unpaid amount shown in the notice. Fam C §4722(b).

Under Fam C §4726, no penalties may be imposed if, in the court's discretion, (1) the support obligor files and serves, in a timely fashion after service of the Notice of Delinquency, an Application to Determine Arrearages, attached to a Notice of Motion or Order to Show Cause, and (2) at the hearing, the court finds that the obligor has proved any of the following:

- The payments were not 30 days in arrears as of the date of service of the Notice of Delinquency and are not in arrears as of the date of the hearing (Fam C §4726(b)(1));

- The obligor suffered serious illness, disability, or unemployment that substantially impaired his or her ability to comply fully with the order, and he or she has made every possible effort to comply (Fam C §4726(b)(2));

- The obligor is a public employee and, for reasons relating to fiscal difficulties of the employer, has not received a paycheck for 30 or more days (Fam C §4726(b)(3)); or

- It would not be in the interests of justice to impose a penalty (Fam C §4726(b)(4)).

Section 4726 does not set a specific time limit for the support obligor to file an Application to Determine Arrearages; the trial court has broad discretion to determine what is timely in a particular case. *Marriage of Di Prieto* (2002) 104 CA4th 748, 128 CR2d 380 (17 months reasonable under the circumstances). When ruling on the application, the court has discretion under Fam C §4726 to impose all, part, or none of the penalty. 104 CA4th at 754.

Family Code §§4720-4733 do not indicate the manner of service for the Application to Determine Arrearages (see §20.96) but because it is to be attached to either a Notice of Motion or an Order to Show Cause, it appears that the procedures for filing and service of those two documents should be followed. See §11.34. On preparing and responding to motions and orders to show cause, see §§11.16-11.20, 11.35-11.36A. See also CCP §1005.

If the child support owed or any arrearages, interest, or penalty remains unpaid more than 30 days after service of the Notice of Delinquency, the support obligee may file a motion to obtain a judgment on the amount owed, which will be enforceable in any manner provided for enforcement of judgments generally. Fam C §4725.

A subsequent Notice of Delinquency may be served and filed at any time. Fam C §4731. But when any amounts listed on a subsequent notice have been listed on a previous notice, that fact must be indicated (Fam C §4731), and multiple penalties may not be assessed with respect to the same unpaid installments (Fam C §4727).

Penalties due under Fam C §§4720-4733 may be enforced by issuance of a writ of execution in the same manner as a writ of execution may be issued for unpaid installments of child support, but payment of the penalties may not take priority over payment of current support or support arrearages. Fam C §4728. On enforcement by writ of execution generally, see §§20.17-20.31.

At any hearing to set or modify child support, the court may not consider any penalties imposed under Fam C §§4720-4733 in deciding the amount of current support to be paid. Fam C §4730.

Any penalties collected must be paid to the custodian of the child who is the subject of the underlying order, even when the child is a public assistance recipient. Fam C §4733.

NOTE➤ Federal law imposes sanctions on any person who "willfully fails to pay a support obligation with respect to a child who resides in another State, if such obligation has remained unpaid for a period of longer than 1 year, or is greater than $5,000." 18 USC §228(a)(1). This statute can help enforce a child support obligation when the obligor has left the state. See *U.S. v Venturella* (2d Cir 2004) 391 F3d 120 (court rejected wife-support obligor's argument that "residence" is not same as "domicile" for purposes of CSRA).

Penalties against third parties. In addition to penalties against support obligors, California law holds any person or business entity that knowingly assists a child support obligor to avoid or escape payment of unpaid child support obligations liable for an amount equal to three times the value of the assistance provided (*i.e.*, the fair market value of the obligor's assets that are transferred or hidden). CC §§1714.4, 1714.41.

§20.95   1. Form: Notice of Delinquency (Judicial Council Form FL-485)

FL-485

ATTORNEY OR PARTY WITHOUT ATTORNEY *(Name and Address)*:	TELEPHONE NO.:	*FOR COURT USE ONLY*

ATTORNEY FOR *(Name)*:

SUPERIOR COURT OF CALIFORNIA, COUNTY OF
STREET ADDRESS:
MAILING ADDRESS:
CITY AND ZIP CODE:
BRANCH NAME:

PETITIONER/PLAINTIFF:

RESPONDENT/DEFENDANT:

NOTICE OF DELINQUENCY	CASE NUMBER:

1. NOTICE TO PERSON ORDERED TO PAY CHILD SUPPORT (OBLIGOR)

▶ Obligor's name:

The child support payments listed on this form are more than 30 days in arrears on the date of filing this notice. If they are not paid within 30 days of the date of service of this notice on you, a penalty of 6% per month may be charged on the unpaid balance. The penalty may accumulate to a maximum of 72% of the original amount of the unpaid support.

   California law provides: "Within a timely fashion after service of the Notice of Delinquency the [obligor may file] a motion to determine arrearages" and show the court why the 6% penalty should not be imposed. Forms (FL-490 and FL-301) for filing the motion for a court hearing to establish your possible exemption were served on you with this *Notice of Delinquency*. You should file the motion as soon as possible, before the support obligee obtains a court order or writ of execution.

2. The court ordered payment of child support on *(date)*:

The payments listed below are more than 30 days in arrears on the date of filing this notice:

TOTAL CHILD SUPPORT ORDERED PAID		ACTUALLY PAID			BALANCE DUE		CHECK BOX IF AMOUNT LISTED ON PREVIOUS NOTICE OF DELINQUENCY
DATE DUE	AMOUNT	DATE PAID	ON ORDER	ON ACCRUED INTEREST	ON ORDER	ON ACCRUED INTEREST	
							☐
							☐
							☐
							☐
							☐
							☐
							☐
							☐
							☐

☐ continued on attached page. Total due on order: Total due on interest:

Page 1 of 2

Form Adopted for Mandatory Use
Judicial Council of California
FL-485 [Rev. January 1, 2003]

NOTICE OF DELINQUENCY

Family Code, §§ 4720–4733
www.courtinfo.ca.gov

PETITIONER/PLAINTIFF:	CASE NUMBER:
RESPONDENT/DEFENDANT:	

3. Address of children *(complete a or b):*
   a. ☐ There is a protective order that prohibits the support obligor from knowing the location of the child or children for whom support is payable or that excuses completion of part b.

   —OR—

   b. ☐ The name, current address, and telephone number of children for whom support is due are as follows:
   Name: Address: Phone No.

4. a. ☐ Court papers should be served at the address shown at the top of page 1 of this form.
   b. ☐ The address at which court papers should be served on the support obligee is *(address):*

   I declare under penalty of perjury under the laws of the State of California that the foregoing is true and correct.

Date:

                                        ▶

_____   _____
(TYPE OR PRINT NAME OF SUPPORT OBLIGEE)   (SIGNATURE OF SUPPORT OBLIGEE)

To Support Obligee: Have a completed copy of the *Notice of Delinquency* and a blank *Application to Determine Arrearages* (form FL-490) as well as a blank *Notice of Motion* (form FL-301) served on the support obligor by someone at least age 18 other than yourself. The person serving must complete the proof of service below. The proof of service must be filed with the court before you can collect the penalty.

PROOF OF SERVICE OF NOTICE OF DELINQUENCY

1. At the time of service I was at least 18 years of age and **not a party** to this action. I served the completed *Notice of Delinquency,* blank *Application to Determine Arrearages* (form FL-490), and blank *Notice of Motion* (form FL-301) on *(name):*

   a. ☐ By personal delivery to the person served
      (1) Date served: (3) Address:
      (2) Time served:

   b. ☐ By mailing by certified mail   (1) Date mailed: (2) Place mailed:
      (Attach signed return receipt)

   c. ☐ By mailing (by first-class mail or airmail) copies to the person served, together with two copies of the *Notice and Acknowledgment of Receipt* (form 982(a)(4)) and a return envelope, postage prepaid, addressed to the sender. **(Attach completed Acknowledgment of Receipt)**

   d. ☐ Other *(specify code section):*
      ☐ Additional page is attached.

2. I declare under penalty of perjury under the laws of the State of California that the foregoing is true and correct.

Date:

.

                                        _____
                                        (SIGNATURE OF PERSON SERVING NOTICE)

Name and address of person serving notice:

_____

FL-485 [Rev. January 1, 2003]	**NOTICE OF DELINQUENCY**	Page 2 of 2

Copies: Original (file with court clerk); copy for service on obligor (along with blank Notice of Motion to Determine Arrearages); office copies.

§20.96   2. Form: Application to Determine Arrearages (Judicial Council Form FL-490)

FL-490

PETITIONER: RESPONDENT: OTHER:	CASE NUMBER:

APPLICATION TO DETERMINE ARREARAGES

☐ Child support   ☐ Spousal support   ☐ Family support   ☐ Medical support

☐ Unreimbursed expenses   ☐ Unreimbursed medical expenses
☐ Other *(specify):*

Attachment to ☐ Order to Show Cause (form FL-300)   ☐ Notice of Motion (form FL-301)

1. I ask that arrearages be determined in this case.

2. I have attached *(check all that apply):*
   a. ☐ a *Declaration of Payment History* (FL-420)
   b. ☐ a *Payment History Attachment* (FL-421)
   c. ☐ Other *(specify):*

3. ☐ I ask that the support arrearage be changed as follows:
   a. ☐ I have already paid ☐ some ☐ all of the support ordered. Proof of payment is attached.
   b. ☐ The children for whom support is to be paid were living with me full time for the period from _____
      to _____. I provided all of their support during that period. I am attaching a detailed declaration
      explaining these facts and supporting documentation, including any proof that the children were living with me.
   c. ☐ Other *(specify):*

4. ☐ I have previously asked the other parent for payment and provided the other parent with an itemized statement of the
   unreimbursed ☐ childcare expense ☐ medical expense *(Attach copies of all bills being claimed and proof of any
   payments that you have made on these bills.)*

5. ☐ Attorney fees and costs a. ☐ Fees b. ☐ Costs
   Income and Expense Declaration (form FL-150) is attached.

6. Facts in support of the relief requested are *(specify):*
   ☐ contained in the attached declaration.

I declare under penalty of perjury under the laws of the State of California that the foregoing is true and correct.

Date:

▶

_____   _____
(TYPE OR PRINT NAME)   (SIGNATURE OF DECLARANT)

☐ Petitioner/Plaintiff   ☐ Respondent/Defendant
☐ Attorney   ☐ Other *(specify):*

NOTICE: This form must be attached to an *Order to Show Cause* (FL-300) or a *Notice of Motion* (FL-301).

NOT A COURT ORDER   Page ___ of ___

Form Adopted for Mandatory Use
Judicial Council of California
FL-490 [Rev. July 1, 2003]

APPLICATION TO DETERMINE ARREARAGES

Family Code, §§ 4720–4732
www.courtinfo.ca.gov

Copies: Original (file with court clerk); copy for service on obligee; office copies.

§20.97 Q. Defenses to Enforcement

Partial payment as inadequate defense. Judgments or orders for child, family, or spousal support are enforceable until "paid in full" and are exempt from any requirement that judgments be renewed. Fam C §291(a),(b). See Fam C §4502. The acceptance by the obligee parent of less than the amount of support actually ordered does not support the inference that the obligee agreed to the reduction. *Marriage of Brinkman* (2003) 111 CA4th 1281, 4 CR3d 722, citing *Marriage of Hamer* (2000) 81 CA4th 712, 97 CR2d 195.

Enforceability of pre-1994 judgments. When the support judgment predates the effective date of current law (see a prior version of Fam C §4502, originally operative January 1, 1994, and now superseded in relevant part by Fam C §291, operative January 1, 2007), the issue arises whether the judgment has survived and remains enforceable. See, *e.g., Marriage of Cutler* (2000) 79 CA4th 460, 94 CR2d 156 (under facts of case, 1966 judgment still extant for enforcement in 1997; due diligence no defense); *Marriage of Sweeney* (1999) 76 CA4th 343, 347, 90 CR2d 298 (1963 judgment died in 1973, 10 years after issued).

Laches. Whenever there is a long delay in enforcement of a support judgment, an obligor may attempt to assert a defense of laches. Under Fam C §291(d) and its predecessor—a prior version of Fam C §4502—the defendant in a child, family, or spousal support action may raise the defense of laches only for any part of the judgment owed to the state. The California Supreme Court has resolved a conflict regarding the retroactivity of this provision (see former Fam C §4502(c)), limiting greatly the availability of that defense in private support enforcement actions. *Marriage of Fellows* (2006) 39 C4th 179, 46 CR3d 49. In *Fellows*, a father was ordered by a New York court to pay child support to his child's mother in the amount of $50 per week in 1985. Seventeen years later, the mother registered the order in California, claiming an unpaid support obligation totaling over $26,000. The father was unable to prove that he had paid the support obligation, and asserted a defense of laches. The trial court applied §4502(c) retroactively, holding that the defense was not applicable in a private action to enforce a child support order, and ordered the father to pay arrearages in the amount of $20,800. He appealed, arguing in part that §4502 should not bar his defense, because the statute was enacted after his obligation arose. The court of appeal affirmed the trial court's decision, as did the California Supreme Court.

The California Supreme Court relied on Fam C §4 to support the retroactive application of §4502. It noted that while "nothing in the language or legislative history of section 4502(c) speaks directly to retroactive application," both legislative intent intending to create a unified Family Code and the language of Fam C §4 provided guidance. Fam C §4(c) provides that amendments to the Family Code apply retroactively unless otherwise provided by law. The court also relied on its previous decision in *Rice v Clark* (2002) 28 C4th 89, 120 CR 2d 522, which presented a similar question with respect to a provision in the Probate Code. The court held further that the exceptions to Fam C §4 asserted by the father were inapplicable. See Fam C §4(f)-(g).

Marriage of Fellows resolves a conflict in previous cases that addressed the retroactivity of the laches defense, overruling *Marriage of Garcia* (2003) 111 CA4th 140, 3 CR3d 370, which held that laches was a defense to an action for child support arrearages and that because a 2002 amendment to §4502 changed this law, §4502(c) could not be applied retroactively to bar a laches defense in cases heard before the amendment's effective date. See also *Marriage of Dancy* (2000) 82 CA4th 1142, 98 CR2d 775 (laches can be raised in child support arrearages case, but not available under these facts); *Marriage of Fogarty & Rasbeary* (2000) 78 CA4th 1353, 93 CR2d 653 (notwithstanding Fam C §4502, obligor may claim laches in child support enforcement case); *Marriage of Plescia* (1997) 59 CA4th 252, 261, 69 CR2d 120 (same; spousal support).

NOTE➤ Operative January 1, 2007, the version of Fam C §4502 that was construed in Fellows was repealed and reenacted (Stats 2006, ch 86), and now simply states that Fam C §291 governs the period for enforcement and procedure for renewal a judgment or order for child, family, or spousal support. The provision of Fam C §4502 regarding the applicability of the laches defense only to any portion of the judgment that is owed to the state is now found in Fam C §291(d).

§20.98   R. Private Child Support Collectors

Operative January 1, 2007, the Family Code provides regulations for the practice of child support collection by a "private child support collector": an "individual, corporation, attorney, nonprofit organization, or other nongovernmental entity" who is hired by a support obligee to collect court-ordered child support for a fee or other consideration. Fam C §5610. This includes any private, nongovernmental attorney whose business is substantially comprised of the collection or enforcement of child support. It does not, however, apply to attorneys who are "address[ing] issues of ongoing child support or child support arrearages" in the course of various family law proceedings (*e.g.*, parentage, dissolution, legal separation, nullity, or postjudgment or modification proceedings). Fam C §5610.

The legislation provides for:

- The contents required of any private contract for child support collection (Fam C §5611);

- Disclosures that must be made by the collector in advertising (Fam C §5612);

- Contract cancellation rights (Fam C §5613);

- Disclosure of information by the collector on amounts collected (along with establishing a direct deposit account with the State disbursement unit) (Fam C §5614);

- The right to bring a civil action against the collector for damages for violating the new statutes (Fam C §5615); and

- Inclusion in every court order (including a court-approved agreement) for child support issued on or after January 1, 2010, a separate money judgment owed by the support obligor to pay a fee (not to exceed a certain percentage of support arrearages and not to exceed a certain percentage of a private collector's fee) for collection efforts undertaken by a private collector. That judgment must be in favor of both the collector and the support obligee (Fam C §5616).

21

Modification

§21.1   I. SCOPE OF CHAPTER

Often, orders rendered by a court in a marital action may be modified in subsequent proceedings. The subject matter of the order, and whether it was issued as a temporary order in a pending action or as a long-term order in a judgment, affect its modifiability. This chapter discusses each type of order in terms of its subsequent modifiability, including what change of circumstances, if any, must be shown.

At the outset of any modification proceeding, the attorney must make certain strategic and procedural decisions, based on the particular facts of the case. This chapter addresses the considerations underlying these decisions, and presents the procedures and forms necessary to complete a modification proceeding.

II. MODIFIABILITY OF ORDERS

A. Legal Basis for Modification

§21.2   1. Spousal Support

The court has continuing jurisdiction to modify an order for spousal support in postjudgment proceedings (Fam C §3651(a)) and may modify pendente lite orders as well (Fam C §3603). The court may not, however, modify a spousal support order in these circumstances:

- When the parties have agreed, in writing or orally in open court, that the spousal support order is nonmodifiable (Fam C §3651(d));

- When the judgment did not award spousal support and did not reserve jurisdiction over the issue (*McClure v McClure* (1935) 4 C2d 356, 359, 49 P2d 584); or

- To extend a fixed term of support, unless (1) jurisdiction to do so is expressly retained in the most recent order (Fam C §4335; *Marriage of Segel* (1986) 177 CA3d 1030, 1038, 223 CR 430) or (2) the marriage is of "long duration" (rebuttably presumed in marriages of at least 10 years to the date of separation; Fam C §4336(b)) and the parties have not specifically precluded such modification by written agreement (*Marriage of Jones* (1990) 222 CA3d 505, 514, 271 CR 761).

A court likewise has authority to modify a spousal support agreement, whether entered into before or after judgment, that has not been approved by a court or merged into a judgment or order. Fam C §3591; *Marriage of Maytag* (1994) 26 CA4th 1711, 32 CR2d 334.

An order for modification may have only *prospective* effect; on request, however, it may be made retroactive to the date of filing the notice of motion or the order to show cause. Fam C §§3603, 3651(c). When the modification is entered due to the unemployment of either party, it must be made retroactive to the later of the date of service or the date of unemployment, unless the court finds good cause not to make the order retroactive and states its reasons on the record. Fam C §3653(b). If the order is entered retroactively, the support obligor may be entitled to pay, and the support obligee may be ordered to repay, according to the terms specified in the order, any amounts previously paid under the prior order that are in excess of the amounts due under the retroactive order. Fam C §3653(c). See *Marriage of Dandona & Araluce* (2001) 91 CA4th 1120, 1124, 111 CR2d 390 (reimbursement under Fam C §3653 retroactive; court has discretion to order repayment). The court may order that the repayment by the support obligee be made over any period and in any manner (including, but not limited to, an offset against future support payments or a future wage assignment) that the court deems just and reasonable. Fam C §3653(c). In determining whether to order a repayment, and in establishing the terms of repayment, the court must consider the following factors (Fam C §3653(c)):

- Amount to be repaid;

- Duration of the support order before modification or termination;

- Financial impact on the support obligee of any particular method of repayment, *e.g.,* an offset against future support payments or a future wage assignment; and

- Any other facts or circumstances that the court deems relevant.

See *Marriage of Petropoulos* (2001) 91 CA4th 161, 110 CR2d 111 (giving retroactive effect to 2000 version of §3653(c), permitting reimbursement for spousal support overpayments); *Marriage of Perez* (1995) 35 CA4th 77, 80, 41 CR2d 377 (court's reduction of balance of child support arrearages amounted to impermissible retroactive modification).

On modification of spousal support generally, see §§6.20–6.26. To modify spousal support, the court must have personal jurisdiction over the parties. See §4.4.

§21.3　2. Child Support

An order for child support, whether issued pendente lite or in a judgment, is modifiable at any time. The modification may have a prospective effect only; however, it may normally be made retroactive to the date of service of the notice of motion or the order to show cause, on request (Fam C §3653(a); 42 USC §666(a)(9)). When the modification is entered due to the unemployment of either party, it must be made retroactive to the later of the date of service or the date of unemployment, unless the court finds good cause not to make the order retroactive and states its reasons on the record. Fam C §3653(b); *Marriage of Leonard* (2004) 119 CA4th 546, 14 CR3d 482 (court properly denied retroactive modification to unemployed parent when parent had other financial resources and children's needs made retroactivity unfair). If the order is entered retroactively, the support obligor may be entitled to pay, and the support obligee may be ordered to repay, according to the terms specified in the order, any amounts previously paid under the prior order that are in excess of the amounts due under the retroactive order. Fam C §3653(c). The court may order that the repayment by the support obligee be made over any period and in any manner (including, but not limited to, an offset against future support payments or a future wage assignment) that the court deems just and reasonable. Fam C §3653(c). In determining whether to order a repayment, and in establishing the terms of repayment, the court must consider the following factors (Fam C §3653(c)):

- Amount to be repaid;

- Duration of the support order before modification or termination;

- Financial impact on the support obligee of any particular method of repayment, *e.g.,* an offset against future support payments or a future wage assignment; and

- Any other facts or circumstances that the court deems relevant.

Recall, however, as indicated above, that Fam C §3653 does *not* authorize the court to make a modification retroactive to a date before the date of service of the notice of motion or the order to show cause. See *Marriage of Perez* (1995) 35 CA4th 77, 80, 41 CR2d 377, 378 (court's reduction of balance of child support arrearages amounted to impermissible retroactive modification).

The court's jurisdiction to modify child support is not affected by an agreement between the parties to the contrary. *Elkind v Byck* (1968) 68 C2d 453, 459, 67 CR 404. Even when the original judgment did not provide for child support, the court may enter and subsequently modify an award of child support in postjudgment proceedings. See *Krog v Krog* (1948) 32 C2d 812, 816, 198 P2d 510. On the modification of child support orders generally, see §8.31. To modify child support, the court must have personal jurisdiction over the parties. See §4.4.

To modify child support, the court must have jurisdiction as provided under the Full Faith and Credit for Child Support Orders Act (FFCCSOA) (28 USC §1738B) and California's Uniform Interstate Family Support Act (UIFSA) (Fam C §§4900–5005). See *Kilroy v Superior Court* (1997) 54 CA4th 793, 63 CR2d 390 (upholding constitutionality of FFCCSOA and finding that California had no jurisdiction to modify Georgia child support order when custodial parent and child continued to reside there). Under California's version of UIFSA, which was enacted after FFCCSOA, a California court may modify a child support order of another state only if Fam C §4962 does not apply and, after notice and a hearing, the California court finds either of the following (Fam C §4960(a); see also *Harding v Harding* (2002) 99 CA4th 626, 121 CR2d 450):

- The child, individual obligee, and obligor do not reside in the issuing state; a petitioner who is a nonresident of California seeks modification; and the respondent is subject to the personal jurisdiction of the California tribunal; or

- The child, or a party who is an individual, is subject to the personal jurisdiction of the California tribunal and all of the parties who are individuals have filed written consents in the issuing tribunal for a California tribunal to modify the support order and assume continuing exclusive jurisdiction (with a special exception if the issuing state is a foreign jurisdiction).

It may be permissible for the trial court to set off arrearages against a current support obligation of another state. See *Keith G. v Suzanne H.* (1998) 62 CA4th 853, 859, 72 CR2d 525 (no error to grant the mother a set-off of child support arrearages owed by the father under a previous California order in the father's action to enforce Missouri child support order). According to *Keith G.,* allowing set-off was not an impermissible modification of support because it did not reduce or eliminate the amount of arrearages, but instead affected only the manner of collection.

When California has continuing and exclusive jurisdiction to modify a child support order from another state, California guidelines apply in making the modification. *Marriage of Crosby & Grooms* (2004) 116 CA4th 201, 10 CR3d 146 (trial court did not err in applying California law, despite choice of law provision in marital settlement agreement selecting Idaho).

UIFSA provides a mechanism for determining a "controlling order" in the event that multiple child support orders are entered against a parent. Fam C §4911(b)(2); *Lundahl v Telford* (2004) 116 CA4th 305, 9 CR3d 902. With respect to a spousal support order, however, the court issuing the order retains continuing, exclusive jurisdiction. UIFSA does not provide a mechanism to determine a controlling order when multiple spousal support orders are entered against a spouse, nor does it allow a California court to modify a spousal support order issued by another state. Fam C §4909(f); *Lundahl*, 116 CA4th at 317. For further discussion of foreign judgments, see §21.13.

When a custodial parent seeks postjudgment modification of a child support order but dies before resolution of the matter, the court retains its jurisdiction to resolve the matter and may appoint a successor in interest for the deceased custodial parent. *Marriage of Drake* (1997) 53 CA4th 1139, 1151, 62 CR2d 466.

For child support modification procedures affecting U.S. armed forces servicemembers on active deployment, see §21.32.

§21.4   3. Child Custody and Visitation

Orders for child custody and visitation, whether temporary or long term, may be modified at any time, as long as the child is a minor. See Fam C §§3022, 3087-3088; *Marriage of Jensen* (2003) 114 CA4th 587, 7 CR3d 701. Parents of a minor child cannot, by stipulation, divest the court of jurisdiction to modify custody and visitation. *Marriage of Goodarzirad* (1986) 185 CA3d 1020, 1026, 230 CR 203, 206. On the modification of child custody and visitation orders generally, see §§7.59-7.60.

To modify child custody or visitation, the court must have jurisdiction as provided under the Uniform Child Custody Jurisdiction and Enforcement Act (Fam C §§3400-3465) and the Parental Kidnapping Prevention Act of 1980 (PKPA) (Pub L 96-611, §§6-10, 94 Stat 3568; the relevant provisions of the PKPA are codified in 28 USC

§1738A). For discussion of the jurisdictional requirements for modification under UCCJA and PKPA, see §§7.14–7.15.

When the parties have an agreement or understanding regarding custody or temporary custody, a copy of the agreement or a declaration regarding the understanding must be attached to a petition or motion. As promptly as possible after the filing, the court must, except in exceptional circumstances, enter an order granting temporary custody in accordance with the agreement or understanding. Fam C §3061.

Servicemembers who are activated to United States military duty or National Guard service and are deployed out of state are afforded special consideration regarding child support, custody, and visitation orders. Custody and visitation orders may not be modified based on a servicemember's absence, relocation, or failure to comply with such orders, if the absence, relocation, or failure to comply is a result of the party's activation to military service and deployment out of state. Fam C §3047. For additional discussion and a related form, see §21.32.

§21.5   4. Attorney Fees and Costs

Orders for attorney fees and costs made during the pendency of an action may be augmented or modified before the entry of judgment. Fam C §2030(c). A judgment for attorney fees and costs is res judicata and cannot be modified unless jurisdiction to do so is specifically reserved in the judgment. However, additional fees and costs may be awarded postjudgment on issues not adjudicated in the judgment and to maintain or defend any postjudgment proceeding. Fam C §2030(c).

§21.6   5. Division of Marital Property

Judgment provisions regarding property rights are not modifiable. *Leupe v Leupe* (1942) 21 C2d 145, 148, 130 P2d 697; *Esserman v Esserman* (1982) 136 CA3d 572, 186 CR 329.

§21.7   B. Change of Circumstances Requirement

A party who requests the modification of an order will normally have the burden of proving that there has been a significant change in the circumstances that existed at the time of that order. See discussion in §§21.8–21.9 for required showing on specific types of orders. To evaluate the strength of a client's potential case for modification, the attorney must have a comprehensive understanding of the parties' circumstances at the time of the previous order and at the time of the requested modification.

To establish the circumstances underlying the previous order, counsel should obtain documents relating to the proceeding at which the order was made, *e.g.,* the previous order, any statement of decision, income and expense declarations, property declarations, mediation reports, a transcript of the proceeding, answers to interrogatories, deposition transcripts, business records, tax returns. These documents may be obtained from the client, his or her former attorney, or the court.

On ascertaining the parties' current circumstances, see §§13.6–13.43 (client's role in gathering information; developing and implementing discovery plan).

§21.8   1. Temporary Orders

The usual requirement that a change of circumstances must be shown before modification will be granted does not apply to some types of temporary orders. Case law holds that a temporary spousal support order may be modified without a showing of change of circumstances. See, *e.g., Sande v Sande* (1969) 276 CA2d 324, 329, 80 CR 826. As a practical matter, however, many trial courts will deny modification of temporary spousal support when no change of circumstances is shown. See §6.6.

No change of circumstances need be shown for modification of a temporary order for the custody or visitation of minor children. *Marriage of Lewin* (1986) 186 CA3d 1482, 1487, 231 CR 433. It may be difficult, however, in some cases to discern whether a custody order was intended to be temporary or permanent, particularly in the case of an order by stipulation. See, *e.g., Montenegro v Diaz* (2001) 26 C4th 249, 109 CR2d 575 (stipulated custody order is final judicial custody determination for purposes of changed circumstance rule only if there is clear, affirmative indication parties intended such a result). The showing required to modify a temporary order for child support is the same as for modification of a long-term order for child support (see §21.9).

§21.9   2. Long-Term Orders

A motion for modification of a long-term spousal support order may be granted only when there has been a material change of circumstances since the last order. *Marriage of Gavron* (1988) 203 CA3d 705, 710, 250 CR 148. For discussion, see §6.24.

Generally, a material change of circumstances since the most recent order must be shown to modify an order for child support. *Philbin v Philbin* (1971) 19 CA3d 115, 119, 96 CR 408. No change of circumstances need be shown, however, to modify a child support order in the following situations:

- The establishment of the statewide uniform guidelines has occurred since the order to be modified. Fam C §4069; *Marriage of Gigliotti* (1995) 33 CA4th 518, 527, 39 CR2d 367. It is not clear what is meant by "establishment," but Fam C §4069 arguably provides the requisite change of circumstances whenever an intervening amendment to the statewide uniform guidelines would result in an order different from the one the moving party seeks to modify.

- The order was made on or after July 1, 1992, was based on the parents' agreement to an amount below that established by the statewide uniform guidelines, and is being modified to at least the applicable amount established by the guidelines. Fam C §4065(d).

- The order was made before January 1, 1994 (the effective date of Fam C §4057.5), and income of a parent's subsequent spouse or nonmarital partner was considered in making the order. Fam C §4057.5(e); see §8.22.

- The order was entered in accordance with an agreement of the parties and without any adjudication based on evidence presented to the court. *Singer v Singer* (1970) 7 CA3d 807, 87 CR 42.

- There is no evidence of the circumstances under which the order was made. *Marriage of Thomas* (1981) 120 CA3d 33, 35, 173 CR 844.

A long-term order for child custody generally may be modified only on a showing of a substantial change of circumstances since the order was made. *Marriage of Carney* (1979) 24 C3d 725, 730,

157 CR 383. That one parent has become able to care for the child at home while the custodial parent relies on child care is not an appropriate factor to consider when determining whether a substantial change of circumstances has occurred. *Marriage of Loyd* (2003) 106 CA4th 754, 131 CR2d 80. The requirement of changed circumstances applies to modifications of legal custody as well as to those of physical custody. *Marriage of McLoren* (1988) 202 CA3d 108, 111, 247 CR 897.

However, no change of circumstances need be shown when there is no change in the "label" given the arrangement (*e.g.*, one party retains sole custody, parties retain joint custody), but merely in the specific times the child spends with each parent. *Marriage of Birnbaum* (1989) 211 CA3d 1508, 1513, 260 CR 210 (parties continued to have joint legal and joint physical custody but schedule of times with respective parents was changed); *Enrique M. v Angelina V.* (2004) 121 CA4th 1371, 18 CR3d 306. For further discussion of what constitutes a change of circumstances, see §7.60.

III. PROCEDURE

A. Preliminary Considerations

§21.10   1. Deciding Whether to Seek Modification

A client who consults an attorney about the possible modification of an order rendered in a marital action should be advised on all possible consequences of undertaking a modification proceeding. One common result of filing such a motion is that the other party will file a countermotion for modification. A request for an increase in child support or a reduction in the amount of time the other party spends with a child may result in a motion for a reduction in support or a change of custody. Conversely, a request for a reduction or termination of support may precipitate a countermotion for a support increase and renewed attempts to collect any arrearages owed. Although clients frequently assume that the former spouse will be required to pay the attorney fees and costs incurred in bringing a motion for modification, this result can never be guaranteed.

Even when the opposing party does not counter with a motion of his or her own, voluntary cooperation, such as financial contributions or the sharing of parenting tasks, may end. In sum, the net result of a modification request may be that the client is in a worse position than before the request was made. However, when there has been a significant change in the circumstances of the parties or of the minor children since the previous order, a motion for modification is justified and the chances of success will often outweigh the risks in bringing the motion.

§21.11   2. Substitution of Attorney

If the attorney who represented the moving party in the original marital proceeding did not file a notice of withdrawal under CCP §285.1, and the party will be represented by new counsel in the modification proceeding, a substitution of attorney should be obtained from the former attorney and filed. On substitution of attorneys generally, see California Civil Procedure Before Trial §§4.5–4.12, 4.60 (form) (4th ed Cal CEB 2004).

§21.12   3. Venue

Generally, modification proceedings must be commenced in the same court that rendered the original order. However, when it appears that both parties have moved from the county rendering the order, the court may order that the proceedings be transferred to the county of residence of *either* party when the ends of justice and the convenience of the parties would be promoted by the change. CCP §397.5. Application for a change of venue under §397.5 must be made to the court that rendered the original decree.

§21.13   4. Foreign Judgments

California's jurisdiction to modify child custody, visitation, and support orders that were rendered outside California is governed by statute.

Custody and visitation orders and judgments. Jurisdiction to modify a foreign custody or visitation order is subject to the provisions of the Uniform Child Custody Jurisdiction and Enforcement Act (Fam C §§3400–3465) and the Parental Kidnapping Prevention Act of 1980 (PKPA) (Pub L 96–611, §§6–10, 94 Stat 3568; the relevant provisions of the PKPA are codified in 28 USC §1738A). For discussion of the jurisdictional requirements for modification under UCCJA and PKPA, see §§7.14–7.15.

Support orders and judgments. California's Uniform Interstate

Family Support Act (UIFSA) (Fam C §§4900–5005) governs the procedures for establishing, enforcing, and modifying child support orders when more than one state is involved. Along with the Full Faith and Credit for Child Support Act, 28 USC §1738B, UIFSA (a version of which has been adopted by all states) ensures that only one state exercises jurisdiction over child support at any given time. Under UIFSA, a party may register a foreign support order for enforcement in California. Fam C §4950; *Scheuerman v Hauk* (2004) 116 CA4th 1140, 11 CR3d 125 (UIFSA presupposes existence of current out-of-state order; one state may not validate another state's invalid judgment). Such an order is enforceable in the same manner and is subject to the same procedures as a California order. Fam C §4952(b). See also *Marriage of Crosby & Grooms* (2004) 116 CA4th 201, 10 CR3d 146 (when California assumed jurisdiction over child support order, trial court properly applied California procedural and substantive law, despite choice of law provision in marital settlement agreement selecting Idaho). The nonregistering party is entitled to notice of registration of the order, the date of its pending enforceability, the amount of alleged arrearages owed, and the right to request a hearing within 20 days. Fam C §4954. If that party fails to contest the validity or enforcement of the registered order in a timely manner, the order is confirmed by operation of law, which precludes further contest of the order with respect to any matter that could have been asserted at the time of registration. Fam C §§4955(b), 4957.

General standards for personal and subject matter jurisdiction in UIFSA proceedings are provided in Fam C §§4905–4914. Procedures and special jurisdictional rules to enforce and modify a foreign support order once it is registered in California are provided in Fam C §§4950–4964. A California court may not modify another state's order if the issuing tribunal had jurisdiction. Fam C §4952(c). See *Harding v Harding* (2002) 99 CA4th 626, 121 CR2d 450 (when petitioner was California resident and evidence showed support obligor was Texas resident, no subject matter jurisdiction over petition to modify Texas support decree). Although a California court may modify another state's child support order if all the parties reside in California and the child does not reside in the issuing state (Fam C §4962), residence for UIFSA purposes must mean domicile, "of which there can be only one." *Marriage of Amezquita & Archuleta* (2002) 101 CA4th 1415, 124 CR2d 887. Thus, a spouse stationed in California on military assignment who can show that he or she remains domiciled in the state that issued the support order can deprive California of modification jurisdiction. *Marriage of Amezquita & Archuleta, supra.*

Although the act provides for jurisdiction to modify a foreign child support order (see Fam C §§4960-4963), it does not provide for jurisdiction to modify a foreign spousal support order or provide a mechanism to determine a controlling order when multiple spousal support orders are entered against a spouse. *Lundahl v Telford* (2004) 116 CA4th 305, 9 CR3d 902. But see *Marriage of Newman* (2000) 80 CA4th 846, 851, 95 CR2d 691 (California court did not lose jurisdiction to award spousal support when other state court granted status-only dissolution but made no other orders).

§21.14 5. Mediation of Custody and Visitation Issues

When the custody or visitation of a minor child is at issue in a modification proceeding, the matter must be set for mediation. Fam C §3170. The mediation must be set before, or concurrent with, the setting of the matter for hearing. Fam C §3175. Local rules of court should be consulted to ascertain the procedure for requesting mediation. Some counties require that a modification hearing be set before mediation is allowed; others permit more informal access to mediation on the request of a party or counsel.

If the parties reach an agreement through mediation with respect to custody and visitation issues, a stipulation for modification of the previous order should be prepared, signed by the parties and counsel, and presented to the court for approval and filing. If mediation is unsuccessful, a court hearing on the modification of custody and visitation will be necessary. On mediation of child custody and visitation issues generally, see §§7.39-7.48; on modification of orders by stipulation, see §21.15.

§21.15 6. Stipulation for Modification

Modification of previous orders and judgments may be obtained by stipulation of the parties, with or without filing a notice of motion or order to show cause for modification. When a change in the parties' circumstances is uncontroverted and it appears likely that the court will grant some form of modification, clients may save considerable expense, time, and stress by reaching a stipulated modification.

Clients should be cautioned, however, against agreeing with the other party to informally "waive" compliance with a court order. A party who agrees not to enforce certain terms of an order may be putting the continued effectiveness of that order at risk, while the party who "benefits" from the waiver may risk being held in contempt of court. Any modification reached by stipulation must be reduced to a written order, signed by the judge, and filed with the court, effectively superseding the previous order.

For discussion, and forms, of stipulation, see §§11.12–11.14. Although those sections are presented in the context of temporary orders, they are also generally applicable to modification.

§21.16   7. Discovery

At any time following a judgment of dissolution or legal separation, or a paternity determination, that provides for the payment of child, spousal, or family support, a party paying or receiving such support may, without leave of court, serve on the other party a Request for Production of Income and Expense Declaration After Judgment (see form in §13.38). Fam C §3664(a). The responding party must attach a copy of the prior year's federal and state personal income tax returns to the Income and Expense Declaration. Fam C §3665(a). For discussion of this discovery procedure and form of request, see §§13.37–13.38.

Other discovery methods (*e.g.*, depositions, interrogatories, demands for production of documents) may also be used when a motion for modification has been filed. Fam C §3662. On discovery for purposes of modification proceedings, see §13.5. On discovery in marital actions generally, see chap 13.

B. Motion for Modification

1. Moving Party's Papers

§21.17   a. Order to Show Cause or Notice of Motion

Notice of a motion for modification may be prepared either as an Order to Show Cause (see form in §11.18) or as a Notice of Motion (see form in §11.20). When the opposing party has not appeared in the proceeding, or ex parte orders are sought pending the hearing, the request for modification must be prepared as an Order to Show Cause, which may set forth any ex parte orders (*e.g.,* restraining removal of children) by a check in the box at Item 3.b. and an attachment containing the orders or by a check at Item 3.c., followed by the orders. Otherwise, modification is typically sought by a Notice of Motion. Whether an Order to Show Cause or a Notice of Motion is used, service of the moving papers in a postjudgment proceeding must be made *on the party*; service on his or her attorney is not sufficient. See discussion in §21.22.

Motions for modification are prepared and processed in much the same manner as a noticed motion for temporary orders. For discussion of, and forms for, motions for temporary orders, see §§11.16–11.63. When preparing the notice for a modification proceeding, the caption box indicating "modification" should be checked.

When the parties have an agreement or understanding regarding custody or temporary custody, a copy of the agreement or a declaration regarding the understanding must be attached to a petition or motion. As promptly as possible after the filing, the court must, except in exceptional circumstances, enter an order granting temporary custody in accordance with the agreement or understanding. Fam C §3061.

§21.18   b. Application for Order and Supporting Declaration

An Application for Order and Supporting Declaration (see form in §11.22) must be attached to the Order to Show Cause or the Notice of Motion. Counsel must set forth with care the items of relief requested, because the application in effect constitutes a pleading and limits the moving party to those issues raised.

With respect to the modification of orders for child custody and visitation, child support, or spousal support, the date and contents of the previous order must be specified on the form. See Items 1–4. Facts in support of the relief requested, and a statement of the circumstances that have changed to justify a modification of the previous order, must be set forth at Item 10 of the application. Such facts should be set forth with particularity and should demonstrate how the present circumstances are significantly different from those that existed when the previous order was made. For further discussion of preparing the form, see §11.21. Note, however, that that discussion is presented in the context of temporary orders and that some items of relief that may be requested as temporary orders may not be requested in postjudgment proceedings.

c. Additional Documents

§21.19 (1) Income and Expense Declaration and Attachments

Whenever the financial circumstances of the parties are relevant to the modification requested, a completed Income and Expense Declaration (see form in §11.26) must be filed with the moving papers. Note that a request for attorney fees does put the financial circumstances of the parties in issue and requires the completion of an Income and Expense Declaration. Also, many counties have local rules that define a "current" Income and Expense Declaration and specify a maximum number of days that may elapse between the execution of the declaration and the hearing date. See, *e.g.,* San Diego Ct R §5.6.2. See also *Marriage of Tydlaska* (2003) 114 CA4th 572, 7 CR3d 594 (trial court properly denied husband's request to modify support orders because of his failure to comply with local rule stating declaration is current only if executed within 60 days of hearing). On preparation of the declaration and attachments, see §11.25.

§21.20 (2) Memorandum of Points and Authorities

A memorandum of points and authorities is generally not filed with a request for modification unless the court so requires or the relief requested is unusual. See Cal Rules of Ct 5.118(a). On the memorandum of points and authorities generally, see California Civil Procedure Before Trial §§12.30–12.42 (4th ed Cal CEB 2004).

§21.21 (3) When Custody Is in Issue

When the custody or visitation of minor children is at issue in a modification proceeding, local court rules and practice should be consulted to ascertain whether a Declaration Under Uniform Child Custody Jurisdiction and Enforcement Act (see form in §10.18) must be filed. In the absence of local guidance, the form should probably be filed whenever its filing would be required if the moving party were filing a petition for dissolution (see §10.17). If one of the parents of a child has not appeared in the proceeding, a certified copy of the child's birth certificate may need to be submitted. Fam C §3140.

§21.22   d. Service and Filing

When a motion to modify temporary orders is brought pendente lite, the service and filing requirements are the same as for a motion for temporary orders. For discussion, see §11.34.

When a modification is sought after judgment, the discussion in §11.34 also applies, with this exception: Service must be made directly on the adverse party rather than on opposing counsel. Fam C §215 (former CC §4809). Service on the party may be accomplished in the same manner as for a motion for temporary orders. A modification order that is issued without proper service is void on its face and subject to collateral attack at any time. *Marriage of Kreiss* (1990) 224 CA3d 1033, 1039, 274 CR 226, 230.

In some circumstances, the service requirement of Fam C §215 may be waived when the opposing party has *actual notice* of the hearing in sufficient time to appear and protect his or her interests. Compare *Marriage of Gortner* (1976) 60 CA3d 996, 1001, 131 CR 919, 923 (failure to comply with statute will not invalidate order when party has actual notice), with *Marriage of Kreiss, supra* (failure to give required notice equivalent to failure to serve summons and complaint), and *Marriage of Roden* (1987) 193 CA3d 939, 945, 238 CR 687, 690 (required notice can be waived only by service on opposing counsel *and* voluntary appearance of adverse party). Given the inconsistency of appellate decisions construing a possible waiver of Fam C §215, the safer course is always to serve the opposing party directly. A courtesy copy of the moving papers is normally sent to the attorney of record for the opposing party, unless he or she has filed a notice of withdrawal.

A county that is providing financial assistance on behalf of a minor child is an indispensable party to, and is entitled to notice of, any modification proceeding that requests the suspension or reduction of support for that child. The county will not be bound by any order rendered without the requisite notice. *Marriage of Lugo* (1985) 170 CA3d 427, 217 CR 74.

2. Responding Party's Papers

§21.23 a. Responsive Declaration

A party who opposes a request for modification must file a Responsive Declaration (see form in §11.36) setting forth his or her consent, opposition (if applicable), or proposed order on each item of relief requested by the moving party and facts in support of the responding party's position. For discussion, see §11.35.

§21.24 b. Additional Documents

When appropriate to the issues raised by the moving party and the respondent, the following documents should be filed with the Responsive Declaration:

- Income and Expense Declaration (see discussion and forms in §§11.25–11.26);

- A memorandum of points and authorities (see §21.20); and Declaration Under Uniform Child Custody Jurisdiction and Enforcement Act (see §21.21 and form in §10.18).

§21.25 c. Service and Filing

Service and filing requirements for the Responsive Declaration and any accompanying documents are the same in modification proceedings as on a motion for temporary orders. For discussion, see §§11.38–11.39.

§21.26 3. Moving Party's Reply Papers

The moving party will rarely need to file reply papers to the responding party's opposition to the motion for modification. The considerations and requirements are the same in modification proceedings as on a motion for temporary orders. For discussion, see §11.41.

§21.27 4. Hearing

The procedures and considerations for a hearing on a motion for modification are substantially the same as for a hearing on a motion for temporary orders. See §§11.42–11.51.

§21.28   5. Order After Hearing

On the order after hearing, see the discussion, in the context of temporary orders, in §§11.52–11.63.

Any time an order concerning child support is entered, Judicial Council Form FL-192 (Notice of Rights and Responsibilities: Health-Care Costs and Reimbursement Procedures and Information Sheet on Changing a Child Support Order) must be submitted with the order. Fam C §§4063(a)(1), (2), 4010. Each time an initial court order for child support or family support or a modification of a court order for child support is filed with the court, a Child Support Case Registry form (Judicial Council Form FL-191) must be completed by one of the parties and filed with the court.

6. Attack on Order After Hearing

§21.29   a. Motion for Reconsideration

As long as certain requirements are met, any party affected by an order on a motion for modification may file a motion to reconsider, and the moving party on the motion for modification may file a renewed motion. See §11.65.

§21.30   b. Motion to Set Aside Order

A party may request that an order for modification be set aside on grounds of mistake, inadvertence, surprise, or excusable neglect under CCP §473. For discussion, see §§18.24–18.33 (addressing §473 motion in context of attacks on judgment). If the period within which relief may be granted under CCP §473 has expired, a request may be made to set aside the order on equitable grounds of extrinsic fraud, mistake, or duress. *McClure v McClure* (1935) 4 C2d 356, 361, 49 P2d 584, 587. See discussion in §§18.36–18.42, 18.45 (in context of attacks on judgments).

§21.31   c. Appeal

When a court renders an interlocutory order that is collateral to the main issue, is dispositive of the rights of the parties in relation to the collateral matter, and directs the payment of money or the performance of an act, a direct appeal may be taken from the order. *Marriage of Skelley* (1976) 18 C3d 365, 368, 134 CR 197, 199.

A pendente lite order that modifies a temporary order for support and attorney fees satisfies these criteria and is directly appealable. See *Marriage of Skelley, supra.* In practice, however, an appeal from an order pendente lite may not be a viable remedy because of the length of time it takes to obtain a decision.

An order that follows a final judgment, affects a judgment by enforcing it or staying its execution, and presents different questions on appeal from the judgment itself, is also appealable. *Marriage of Schultz* (1980) 105 CA3d 846, 852, 164 CR 653. An order that modifies a judgment in a marital action satisfies these criteria and is appealable. See CCP §904.1(a)(2); *Marriage of Lugo* (1985) 170 CA3d 427, 432 n7, 217 CR 74 (order for modification affects enforcement of judgment); *Marriage of Acosta* (1977) 67 CA3d 899, 901 n1, 137 CR 33 (order for modification presents different issues from judgment).

On appeals generally, see chap 19.

C. "Simplified" Procedure to Modify Support

§21.31A   1. Discussion

In 1996, the legislature directed the Judicial Council to adopt rules of court and forms for a simplified method to modify support orders, designed to be used by parties who are not represented by counsel. Fam C §3680. In response, the Judicial Council approved four new forms, effective July 1, 1997. For the forms, see §§21.31B–21.31E.

The advantage to unrepresented parties in using these forms appears to be found in the information sheets (see forms in §§21.31C, 21.31E). The forms themselves do not appear to be substantially simpler than the forms used in the standard motion for modification discussed in §§21.17–21.31. Counsel may advise parties who are using these forms and may appear at the hearing on behalf of a party who has previously filed one of these forms.

§21.31B   2. Form: Notice of Motion and Motion for Simplified Modification of Order for Child, Spousal, or Family Support (Judicial Council Form FL-390)

FL-390

ATTORNEY OR PARTY WITHOUT ATTORNEY OR GOVERNMENTAL AGENCY *(pursuant to FC §§ 17400, 17406) (Name, State Bar Number, and Address):* TELEPHONE NO.:	FOR COURT USE ONLY

SUPERIOR COURT OF CALIFORNIA, COUNTY OF
STREET ADDRESS:
MAILING ADDRESS:
CITY AND ZIP CODE:
BRANCH NAME:

PETITIONER/PLAINTIFF:

RESPONDENT/DEFENDANT:

OTHER PARENT:

NOTICE OF MOTION AND MOTION FOR SIMPLIFIED MODIFICATION OF ORDER FOR ☐ CHILD SUPPORT ☐ SPOUSAL SUPPORT ☐ FAMILY SUPPORT	CASE NUMBER:

TO *(name):*

1. A hearing on this motion for the relief requested below will be held as follows:

   a. Date: Time: Dept.:   Room:

   b. Address of court: ☐ same as noted above   ☐ other *(specify):*

2. I am requesting the court to change the amount currently payable by
   ☐ petitioner/plaintiff   ☐ respondent/defendant   ☐ other parent   to the following:
   a. ☐ child support pursuant to the California child support guideline commencing *(date):*
   b. ☐ spousal support of: $ per month beginning *(date):*
   c. ☐ family support of: $ per month beginning *(date):*
   or such other sums as may be appropriate pursuant to applicable guidelines.

3. I am requesting issuance of modified earnings assignment.

4. ☐ I am requesting the court to order the   ☐ petitioner/plaintiff   ☐ respondent/defendant   ☐ other parent
   to provide health insurance coverage for the children as obligated by law, and to issue a Health Insurance Coverage
   Assignment (form FL-470).

5. *(Check whichever statements are true, if any)*
   a. ☐ An application for public assistance (TANF) for the children is pending in *(county name):*   County.
   b. ☐ The children are receiving public assistance from *(county name):*   County.
   c. ☐ This request is made by the governmental agency providing support enforcement services in this action.

6. This request is based on
   a. the attached completed *Financial Statement (Simplified)* (form FL-155) or *Income and Expense Declaration* (form FL-150)
      for the applicant.
   b. ☐ a significant change in the income of   ☐ petitioner/plaintiff   ☐ respondent/defendant   ☐ other parent
   c. ☐ the attached guideline support calculation sheet.
   d. ☐ other *(specify):*

I declare under penalty of perjury under the laws of the State of California that the foregoing is true and correct.

Date:

▶

_____   _____
(TYPE OR PRINT NAME)   (SIGNATURE OF DECLARANT)

Page 1 of 2

PETITIONER/PLAINTIFF:	CASE NUMBER:
RESPONDENT/DEFENDANT:	
OTHER PARENT:	

PROOF OF SERVICE

The *Notice of Motion and Motion* must be served on the other party. If the action was brought by the local child support agency, the local child support agency is enforcing the order, or the children are receiving TANF, the *Notice of Motion and Motion* must also be served on the local child support agency of the county where the action is filed. Service of the motion on the local child support agency and other party may be made by anyone at least 18 years EXCEPT you. Service is made in one of the following ways:

    (1) Personally delivering it to the office of the local child support agency and to the other party.

                OR

    (2) Mailing it, postage prepaid, to the office of the local child support agency, and to the last known address of the other party.

Anyone at least 18 years of age EXCEPT A PARTY in this action may personally serve or mail the motion. Be sure whoever served the motion fills out and signs this proof of service. The *Notice of Motion and Motion* cannot be filed with the court until the local child support agency and the other party (or attorney) are served and this proof of service is properly completed. If this motion is brought after judgment has been entered in the case, service must be made on the party and not the attorney for the party.

1. At the time of service I was at least 18 years of age and not a party to the legal action.

2. I served a copy of the foregoing *Notice of Motion and Motion* as follows (check either a. or b. below for each person served):

    a. ☐ **Personal service.** I personally delivered a copy of the *Notice of Motion and Motion for Simplified Modification of Order for Child, Spousal, or Family Support* and all attachments as follows:

        ☐ (1) Name of party or attorney served: ☐ (2) Name of local child support agency served:

            (a) Address where delivered: (a) Address where delivered:

            (b) Date of delivery: (b) Date of delivery:
            (c) Time of delivery: (c) Time of delivery:

    b. ☐ **Mail.** I deposited a copy of the *Notice of Motion and Motion for Simplified Modification of Order for Child, Spousal, or Family Support* (form FL-390) and all attachments in the United States mail, in a sealed envelope with postage fully prepaid, addressed as follows:

        ☐ (1) Name of party or attorney served: ☐ (2) Name of local child support agency served:

            (a) Address: (a) Address:

            (b) Date of mailing: (b) Date of mailing:
            (c) Time of mailing: (c) Time of mailing:

I declare under penalty of perjury under the laws of the State of California that the foregoing is true and correct.

Date:

▶

_____   _____
(TYPE OR PRINT NAME)   (SIGNATURE OF PERSON WHO SERVED MOTION)

§21.31C   3. Form: Information Sheet—Simplified Way to
           Change Child, Spousal, or Family Support
           (Judicial Council Form FL-391)

FL-391

INFORMATION SHEET
SIMPLIFIED WAY TO CHANGE CHILD, SPOUSAL, OR FAMILY SUPPORT

New laws make it easier for a person to ask the court to raise or lower the amount paid for child, spousal, or family support.

How to Ask for a Change

1. Get copies of these forms:
   • *Notice of Motion and Motion for Simplified Modification of Order for Child, Spousal, or Family Support* ("Notice of Motion") (form FL-390).
   • *Responsive Declaration to Motion for Simplified Modification for Child, Spousal, or Family Support* (form FL-392).
   • *Findings and Order After Hearing* (form FL-340) and *Child Support Information and Order Attachment* (form FL-342).
   • *Financial Statement (Simplified)* (form FL-155) or *Income and Expense Declaration* (form FL-150).
   The court clerk's office, the office of the family law facilitator, or the local child support agency can tell you where to get these forms. You can get them at the Judicial Council website: *www.courtinfo.ca.gov*

2. Fill out and sign the form *Notice of Motion.* **Check with your local court clerk's office or the office of the family law facilitator to see if the forms must be typewritten.**

3. Fill out the form *Financial Statement (Simplified),* if you are allowed to use the form. See the instructions on the back side of the form to see if you qualify; otherwise you must fill out the *Income and Expense Declaration.* You must attach copies of your most recent W-2 form(s) and three most recent paycheck stubs, to the form *Financial Statement (Simplified)* or the form *Income and Expense Declaration.*

4. You must schedule a hearing date with your court clerk's office before filing and serving these papers. You must enter the hearing date in item 1 of the *Notice of Motion.*

5. Make at least three copies of these forms after you have completed them:
   • *Notice of Motion and Motion for Simplified Modification of Order for Child, Spousal, or Family Support* (form FL-390).
   • *Financial Statement (Simplified)* (form FL-155) or *Income and Expense Declaration* (form FL-150).

6. You must have one copy of each of the following papers served on the local child support agency **and on the other party,** if the other party is not the county:
   • Your *Notice of Motion and Motion for Simplified Modification of Order for Child, Spousal, or Family Support* (form FL-390).
   • Your *Financial Statement (Simplified)* (form FL-155) or *Income and Expense Declaration* (form FL-150).
   • A blank *Responsive Declaration to Motion for Simplified Modification of Order for Child, Spousal, or Family Support* (form FL-392).
   • A blank *Financial Statement (Simplified)* (form FL-155) or *Income and Expense Declaration* (form FL-150). *Information Sheet—How to Oppose a Request to Change Child, Spousal, or Family Support* (form FL-393).

   For instructions on how to serve these papers properly, see the information box on the Proof of Service, found on the reverse of the *Notice of Motion* (form FL-390). Whoever serves the papers should fill out and must sign the Proof of Service.

7. Take the original of each of the completed forms to the court clerk's office for filing. If you or your attorney have not filed any other papers in the case, you must do one or more of the following:
   • Pay a first appearance filing fee to the court clerk when you go to file these papers (you can find out what the amount of the fee is from the court clerk's office or the office of the family law facilitator); or
   • Pay a fee to file this motion with the court clerk, even if you or your attorney have already filed papers in this case; or
   • Apply for a fee waiver. For more information on how to request a waiver of the filing fees, get the form *Information Sheet on Waiver of Court Fees and Costs* (form 982(a)(17)(A)).

Using an Attorney

If you use this method to modify support, you may hire an attorney to represent you in court, or you may represent yourself. If you hire an attorney, you will have to pay the cost. The court will not provide you with a free attorney.

If the county is the other party, and if one of the parties is receiving welfare benefits, or if one of the parties has asked the local child support agency to enforce support, a representative from the local child support agency will be present at the hearing.

REMEMBER: The local child support agency does not represent any individual in this lawsuit, including the child, the child's mother, or the child's father.

Agreeing to Support Before the Hearing

A court hearing may not be necessary to modify the current support order, if you are able to reach an agreement with the other party. Note that if an agreement is reached with the other party, you must prepare an order and submit it to the court for the judge's signature and file the order with the court clerk's office. If one of the parties is receiving welfare benefits or the local child support agency is enforcing the support order, the local child support agency must sign the agreement before it is filed with the court.

Hearing

Even if neither the local child support agency nor the other party has filed a response to your *Notice of Motion*, the judge may still require a hearing. Make sure you bring with you a copy of your *Notice of Motion* (form FL-390), *Financial Statement (Simplified)* (form FL-155) or *Income and Expense Declaration* (form FL-150), your most recent federal and state income tax returns and W-2 form(s), and three most recent paycheck stubs. The other party has a right to see your financial information, and you have the right to see the other party's financial information.

Court Order

Once the judge makes a decision, you may be required to prepare the form *Findings and Order After Hearing* (form FL-340) with the *Child Support Information and Order Attachment* (form FL-342). If the support order has changed, you may required to prepare a modified *Order/Notice to Withhold Income for Child Support* (FL-195). You will not have to prepare these documents if the local child support agency is involved. If you have prepared these documents yourself, you must make sure that they are signed by the judge. Check with the court clerk's office or the office of the family law facilitator for the proper procedure. After the *Order/Notice to Withhold Income for Child Support* (FL-195) is signed by the judge and filed, it must be served on the noncustodial parent's employer, on the other party, and on the local child support agency if the local child support agency is involved in the case.

§21.31D   4. Form: Responsive Declaration to Motion for Simplified Modification of Order for Child, Spousal, or Family Support (Judicial Council Form FL-392)

FL-392

ATTORNEY OR PARTY WITHOUT ATTORNEY OR GOVERNMENTAL AGENCY (under Family Code, §§ 17400, 17406) (Name, state bar number, and address):	TELEPHONE AND FAX NOS.:	FOR COURT USE ONLY

SUPERIOR COURT OF CALIFORNIA, COUNTY OF
STREET ADDRESS:
MAILING ADDRESS:
CITY AND ZIP CODE:
BRANCH NAME:

PETITIONER/PLAINTIFF:

RESPONDENT/DEFENDANT:

OTHER PARENT:

RESPONSIVE DECLARATION TO MOTION FOR SIMPLIFIED MODIFICATION OF ORDER FOR CHILD, SPOUSAL, OR FAMILY SUPPORT		CASE NUMBER:
HEARING DATE: TIME: DEPT., ROOM, OR DIVISION:		

1. ☐ I consent to the request contained in the *Notice of Motion and Motion for Simplified Modification of Order for Child, Spousal, or Family Support* (form FL-390).

2. ☐ I object to the request contained in the *Notice of Motion and Motion for Simplified Modification of Order for Child, Spousal, or Family Support* (form FL-390) for the following reasons *(check one or more)*:
   a. ☐ My income is incorrectly stated.
   b. ☐ The other parent's income is incorrectly stated.
   c. ☐ I am entitled to the hardship deductions as shown in my attached *Financial Statement (Simplified)* (form FL-155) or my *Income and Expense Declaration* (form FL-150).
   d. ☐ The other parent is not entitled to hardship deductions as claimed.
   e. ☐ The amount of support is not computed correctly.
   f. ☐ OTHER *(specify)*:

3. I have attached the following:
   a. A completed copy of my *Financial Statement (Simplified)* (form FL-155) or my *Income and Expense Declaration* (form FL-150).
   b. ☐ A guideline support calculation sheet.
   c. ☐ OTHER *(specify)*:

NOTICE TO BOTH PARENTS
You must bring copies of your three most recent pay stubs and your two most recent federal and state tax returns (whether individual or joint) to the hearing.

I declare under penalty of perjury under the laws of the State of California that the foregoing is true and correct.
Date:

▶

_____   _____
(TYPE OR PRINT NAME)   (SIGNATURE OF DECLARANT)

Page 1 of 2

Form Adopted for Mandatory Use Judicial Council of California FL-392 [Rev. January 1, 2003]	RESPONSIVE DECLARATION TO MOTION FOR SIMPLIFIED MODIFICATION OF ORDER FOR CHILD, SPOUSAL, OR FAMILY SUPPORT	Family Code, § 3680 www.courtinfo.ca.gov.

PETITIONER/PLAINTIFF:	CASE NUMBER:
RESPONDENT/DEFENDANT:	
OTHER PARENT:	

PROOF OF SERVICE

This *Responsive Declaration* must be served on the other party. If the action was brought by the local child support agency, the local child support agency is enforcing the order, or the child is receiving TANF, the *Responsive Declaration* must also be served on the local child support agency of the county where the action is filed. Service of the *Responsive Declaration* on the local child support agency and other party may be made by anyone at least 18 years of age EXCEPT you.

Service is made in one of the following ways:
   (1) Personally delivering it to the office of the local child support agency and to the other party.
            OR
   (2) Mailing it, postage prepaid, to the office of the local child support agency and to the other party.
Anyone at least 18 years of age EXCEPT A PARTY to this action may personally serve or mail the *Responsive Declaration*. Be sure whoever served the declaration fills out and signs this proof of service. The *Responsive Declaration* cannot be filed with the court until the local child support agency and the other party are served and this proof of service is properly completed.

1. At the time of service I was at least 18 years of age and not a party to the legal action.

2. I served a copy of the foregoing *Responsive Declaration* as follows *(check either a. or b. below for each person served)*:
   a. ☐ **Personal service.** I personally delivered a copy of the *Responsive Declaration to Motion for Simplified Modification of Order for Child, Spousal, or Family Support* as follows:

      ☐ (1) Name of party or attorney served: ☐ (2) Name of local child support agency served:

        (a) Address where delivered: (a) Address where delivered:

        (b) Date of delivery: (b) Date of delivery:
        (c) Time of delivery: (c) Time of delivery:

   b. ☐ **Mail.** I deposited a copy of the *Responsive Declaration to Motion for Simplified Modification of Order for Child, Spousal, or Family Support* in the United States mail, in a sealed envelope with postage fully prepaid, addressed as follows:

      ☐ (1) Name of party or attorney served: ☐ (2) Name of local child support agency served:

        (a) Address: (a) Address:

        (b) Date of mailing: (b) Date of mailing:
        (c) Time of mailing: (c) Time of mailing:

I declare under penalty of perjury under the laws of the State of California that the foregoing is true and correct.

Date:

▶

_____
(TYPE OR PRINT NAME)

_____
(SIGNATURE OF PERSON WHO SERVED RESPONSIVE DECLARATION)

FL-392 [Rev. January 1, 2003]   **RESPONSIVE DECLARATION TO MOTION FOR SIMPLIFIED MODIFICATION OF ORDER FOR CHILD, SPOUSAL, OR FAMILY SUPPORT**   Page 2 of 2

§21.31E　　5. Form: Information Sheet—How to Oppose a Request to Change Child, Spousal, or Family Support (Judicial Council Form FL-393)

FL-393

INFORMATION SHEET
HOW TO OPPOSE A REQUEST TO CHANGE CHILD, SPOUSAL, OR FAMILY SUPPORT

What to Do

1. If you receive a *Notice of Motion and Motion for Simplified Modification of Order for Child, Spousal, or Family Support* ("*Notice of Motion*") (form FL-390) from the other party or the local child support agency, you have one of two choices:

   * Agree with the proposed changes; or

   * File a response and go to the hearing.

2. You do not need to wait to go to court before modifying the support. If you agree with the changes sought (see item 2 on the front of the *Notice of Motion*), or if you agree that the order should be changed in some way, contact the party that served you so that an agreement should be reached. If an agreement is reached with the other party, an order must be prepared and submitted to the court for the judge's signature and filed with the court clerk's office. If one of the parties is receiving welfare benefits or the local child support agency is enforcing the support order, the local child support agency must sign the agreement before it is filed with the court. If you are able to reach an agreement with the other party and the order is filed with the court clerk's office, you do not need to appear at the hearing. The hearing will simply be taken off calendar.

   NOTICE: Unless you know the hearing has been taken off calendar, you should go to the hearing as scheduled to protect your rights. You might consider calling the court the day before the hearing to see if the hearing is still on calendar.

3. If you do **not** agree with the proposed changes, you must do the following:

   * Complete the *Responsive Declaration to Motion for Simplified Modification of Order for Child, Spousal, or Family Support* ("*Response to Motion*") (form FL-392). If a blank *Response to Motion* was not given to you when you received the *Notice of Motion*, the court clerk's office, the office of the family law facilitator, or the local child support agency can tell you where one can be found. Or you can get one from the Judicial Council's website: *www.courtinfo.ca.gov*. **NOTICE: Check with your local court clerk's office or the office of the family law facilitator to see if the forms must be typewritten. . Make at least three copies of the completed form.**

   * Fill out the form *Financial Statement (Simplified)* (form FL-155), if you are allowed to use the form. See the instructions on the back side of the form to see if you qualify; otherwise, you must fill out the form *Income and Expense Declaration* (form FL-150). You must attach copies of your most recent W-2 form(s) and three most recent paycheck stubs to the form *Financial Statement (Simplified)* (form FL-155) or the form *Income and Expense Declaration* (form FL-150). Make at least three copies of the completed form.

4. You must have one copy of each of the following papers served on the local child support agency **and on the other party**, if the other party is not the local child support agency:

   * Your *Responsive Declaration to Motion* (form FL-392).

   * Your *Financial Statement (Simplified)* (form FL-155) or *Income and Expense Declaration* (form FL-150).

   For instructions on how to serve these papers properly, see the information box on the Proof of Service, found on the reverse of the *Response to Motion* (form FL-392). Whoever serves the papers should fill out and must sign the Proof of Service. **NOTICE: Consult with the office of the family law facilitator or the local court rules to see if there are any other documents you will need to have served on the local child support agency and on the other party.**

Form Approved for Optional Use
Judicial Council of California
FL-393 [Rev. January 1, 2003]

INFORMATION SHEET—HOW TO OPPOSE A REQUEST
TO CHANGE CHILD, SPOUSAL, OR FAMILY SUPPORT

Page 1 of 2
Family Code, § 3680
www.courtinfo.ca.gov.

5. Take the original of each of the completed forms to the court clerk's office for filing. If you or your attorney have not filed any other papers in the case, you must do one of two things:

* Pay a first appearance filing fee to the court clerk when you go to file these papers (you can find out what the amount of the fee is from the court clerk's office or the office of the family law facilitator); or

* Apply for a fee waiver. For more information on how to request a waiver of the filing fees, get the form Information Sheet on Waiver of Court Fees and Costs (form 982(a)(17)(A)).

NOTICE: The existing support order remains in effect and payments must be made according to its terms until any new order is made.

Using an Attorney

If you use this method to modify support, you may hire an attorney to represent you in court, or you may represent yourself. If you hire an attorney, you will have to pay the cost. The court will not provide you with a free attorney.

If the county is the other party, and if one of the parties is receiving welfare benefits, or if one of the parties has asked the local child support agency to enforce support, a representative from the local child support agency will be present at the hearing.

REMEMBER: The local child support agency does not represent any individual in this lawsuit, including the child, the child's mother, and the child's father.

Hearing

Make sure you bring with you a copy of your Response to Motion (form FL-392), Financial Statement (Simplified) (form FL-155) or Income and Expense Declaration (form FL-150), your most recent federal and state income tax returns and W-2 form(s), and three most recent pay check stubs. The other party has a right to see your financial information, and you have the right to see the other party's financial information.

Court Order

Whether you win or lose, once the judge makes a decision, you may be required to prepare the form Findings and Order After Hearing (form FL-340) and Child Support Information and Order Attachment (form FL-342). If the support order has changed, you may also be required to prepare a modified Order/Notice to Withhold Income for Child Support (form FL-195). Usually, the party bringing the motion is supposed to prepare these papers. If that party does not, you must be ready to do it. You will not have to prepare these documents if the local child support agency is involved.

If you have prepared these documents yourself, you must make sure that they are signed by the judge. Check with the court clerk's office or the office of the family law facilitator for the proper procedure. After the Order/Notice to Withhold Income for Child Support (form FL-195) is signed by the judge and filed, it must be served on the noncustodial parent's employer, on the other party, and on the local child support agency if it is involved in the case.

D. Support Modification by Servicemember on Active Deployment

§21.32   1. Discussion

Servicemembers who are activated to United States military duty or National Guard service and are deployed out of state are afforded special consideration regarding child support, custody, and visitation orders:

- A servicemember may request modification of a support order by filing a notice of activation of military service indicating a date of deployment, in lieu of an order to show cause or notice of motion. The court must set a hearing before that date if possible, or stay the proceedings, consistent with federal timelines. Fam C §3651. The court may not hear the matter in the absence of counsel for the servicemember. Fam C §3651(c)(2);

- A servicemember who does not file such a notice and request modification of a support order before deployment is protected from penalties (Fam C §§4720–4733) and interest that would not have accrued had the order been modified before deployment (Fam C §3651(c)(3)–(4)); and

- If an order modifying or terminating a child support order results from a change in income due to deployment of either the obligor or obligee, the order must be made retroactive to the date of service of the notice of activation (or motion or order to show cause), or the date of activation, whichever is later, subject to federal notice requirements and unless the court finds good cause not to make the order retroactive (Fam C §3653(c)).

In addition, the Department of Child Support Services is required to work with the military to make information readily available regarding members' ability to modify support orders based on a change of income, and to develop a form that would permit a member to allow the agency to make a motion to modify a support order in his or her absence. Fam C §17440.

§21.33 ## 2. Form: Notice of Activation of Military Service and Deployment and Request to Modify a Support Order (Judicial Council Form FL-398)

FL-398

ATTORNEY OR PARTY WITHOUT ATTORNEY OR GOVERNMENTAL AGENCY *(under Family Code, §§ 17400 and 17406)* *(Name, State Bar number, and address):*	FOR COURT USE ONLY

TELEPHONE NO.:   FAX NO. *(Optional):*
E-MAIL ADDRESS *(Optional):*
ATTORNEY FOR *(Name):*

SUPERIOR COURT OF CALIFORNIA, COUNTY OF
STREET ADDRESS:
MAILING ADDRESS:
CITY AND ZIP CODE:
BRANCH NAME:

PETITIONER/PLAINTIFF:

RESPONDENT/DEFENDANT:

OTHER PARENT:

NOTICE OF ACTIVATION OF MILITARY SERVICE AND DEPLOYMENT AND REQUEST TO MODIFY A SUPPORT ORDER	CASE NUMBER:

1. TO *(name):*

2. A hearing on this request will be held as follows:

  a. Date: Time: ☐ Dept: ☐ Rm.:

  b. Address of court ☐ same as noted above ☐ other *(specify):*

ORDER SHORTENING TIME

3. ☐ Time for ☐ service ☐ hearing is shortened. Service must be on or before *(date):*

4. Any responsive declaration must be served on or before *(date):*

Date: _____

                            JUDICIAL OFFICER

NOTICE

If you are requesting modification of spousal support or family support, you **MUST** use this form.

If the court grants this *Request,* the new court order will become effective on the date this form was served, or on the date of deployment, whichever is later in time, unless the court determines there is good cause to do otherwise.

The deployed person **MUST** immediately notify the court and all parties when he or she returns from deployment. If the court was not able to hear the modification request before the deployment date, the service member **MUST** ask the court to bring any unresolved modification request to a hearing within 90 days of return or lose the right to change the support order as requested here.

Request for Accommodations
Assistive listening systems, computer-assisted real-time captioning, or sign language interpreter services are available if you ask at least five days before the proceeding. Contact the clerk's office or go to *www.courtinfo.ca.gov/forms* for *Request for Accommodations by Persons With Disabilities and Order* (form MC-410). (Civil Code, § 54.8.)

NOTICE FOR CASES INVOLVING A LOCAL CHILD SUPPORT AGENCY

This case may be referred to a court commissioner for hearing. By law, court commissioners do not have the authority to issue final orders and judgments in contested cases unless they are acting as temporary judges. The court commissioner in your case will act as a temporary judge unless, before the hearing, you or any other party objects to the commissioner acting as a temporary judge. The court commissioner may still hear your case to make findings and a recommended order. If you do not like the recommended order, you must object to it within 10 court days; otherwise, the recommended order will become a final order of the court. If you object to the recommended order, a judge will make a temporary order and set a new hearing.

Form Adopted for Mandatory Use
Judicial Council of California
FL-398 [New December 2, 2005]

NOTICE OF ACTIVATION OF MILITARY SERVICE AND DEPLOYMENT AND REQUEST TO MODIFY A SUPPORT ORDER
(Family Law—Governmental)

Page 1 of 5
Family Code, § 3651
www.courtinfo.ca.gov

FL-398

	CASE NUMBER:
PETITIONER/PLAINTIFF:	
RESPONDENT/DEFENDANT:	
OTHER PARENT:	

5. I am requesting the court to change the existing

   a. ☐ child support   ☐ spousal support   ☐ family support   order made under the case number listed above to an amount based on my income while deployed.

   b. earnings assignment order to state the new support amount if the request in item 5a is granted.

   c. This support is payable by

      ☐ petitioner/plaintiff   ☐ respondent/defendant   ☐ other parent.

6. This request is based on:

   a. ☐ petitioner's/plaintiff's   ☐ respondent's/defendant's   ☐ other parent's   military deployment

   b. completed attached *Financial Statement (Simplified)* (form FL-155) or completed *Income and Expense Declaration* (form FL-150)

   c. ☐ the attached service member's *Notice of Deployment* that has been submitted to the local child support agency *(Attach this form if the local child support agency is involved.)*

7. Additional required information

   a. service member's out-of-state deployment date is *(specify date and attach a copy of the order of deployment)*:

   b. service member's duration of activation is *(specify beginning and end dates)*:

8. A blank *Responsive Declaration to Order to Show Cause or Notice of Motion* (form FL-320) and a **blank** *Financial Statement (Simplified)* (form FL-155) or a **blank** *Income and Expense Declaration* (form FL-150) will be served with the moving papers.

9. Check all that apply *(you must check at least one box)*:

   a. ☐ While the service member is deployed, his or her employer will supplement the military pay *(specify amount per month and attach proof)*: $

   b. ☐ While the service member is deployed, his or her employer will not supplement the military pay, and the service member will only have military pay in the amount stated on the attached *Financial Statement (Simplified)* (form FL-155) or *Income and Expense Declaration* (form FL-150).

   c. ☐ It is unknown whether the service member's employer will supplement the military pay.

   d. ☐ While deployed, the service member will have other income *(specify amount per month, source of income, and attach proof)*: $

10. ☐ The other party and the service member have previously agreed that spousal support cannot be modified or terminated *(attach a copy of the agreement.)*

11. ☐ **The facts in support of this request are** *(specify)*:

   ☐ Contained in an attached declaration.

12. Send notice of the hearing to the service member at *(specify address)*:

13. ☐ I will be deployed out of state at the time of the hearing. I waive appearing in person at the court hearing. I ask the court to go forward with the hearing to decide if the support will be temporarily modified until I can appear in person. This request is not a waiver of my right to a stay or rehearing of the matter under the Servicemembers Civil Relief Act (SCRA). **(This waiver is only valid if the service member signs below.)**

14. Number of pages attached: _____

I declare under penalty of perjury under the laws of the State of California that the foregoing is true and correct.

Date:

            ▶

_____   _____
    (TYPE OR PRINT NAME)   (SIGNATURE)

FL-398

INFORMATION SHEET FOR COMPLETING AND RESPONDING TO NOTICE OF ACTIVATION OF MILITARY SERVICE AND DEPLOYMENT AND REQUEST TO MODIFY A SUPPORT ORDER

If you are the person requesting that the support order be changed:

Please follow these instructions to complete the *Notice of Activation of Military Service and Deployment and Request to Modify a Support Order* if you do not have an attorney to represent you. This form is intended to be used by a service member to ask the court to modify support based on his or her military activation and out-of-state deployment. If you have an attorney, he or she should complete this form. If you would like the local child support agency to assist you, fill out a *Notice of Deployment* and submit it to the local child support agency. They will prepare a request for modification, and you will not need to appear if you are already deployed. The local child support agency must attach the *Notice of Deployment* to form FL-398 to show the court that the service member has authorized the agency to act on his or her behalf. You can obtain a *Notice of Deployment* from any local child support agency. Please note that the child support agency cannot provide services for a modification of spousal support.

You may also ask to appear by telephone. See rule 5.324 of the California Rules of Court, and form FL-679 *Request for Telephone Appearance (Governmental)*. If you are in the military, you may also ask for the assistance of a JAG (Judge Advocate General) officer.

In addition to the modification procedures contained in the *Notice of Activation of Military Service and Deployment and Request to Modify a Support Order*, a service member who has been activated may be eligible for a modification based on a change in circumstances, specifically a change in income due to military activation. To request a modification of support for reasons other than out-of-state deployment, see FL-391 *Information Sheet—Simplified Way to Change Child, Spousal, or Family Support* for what forms to use and instructions. The service member may also have certain protections provided by the Servicemembers Civil Relief Act (SCRA). Please note that a modification of support cannot be effective any earlier than the filing with the court of the request to modify support.

When you have completed this form, file the original and attachments with the court clerk. The address of the court clerk is listed in the telephone directory under "County Government Offices." **Keep two copies of the filed *Notice of Activation of Military Service and Deployment and Request to Modify a Support Order* form and its attachments. Serve one copy as well as a blank *Responsive Declaration to Order to Show Cause or Notice of Motion* (form FL-320) and blank *Income and Expense Declaration* (form FL-150) or *Financial Statement (Simplified)* (form FL-155) on the other party. If the local child support agency is involved, serve it too. Keep another copy for your records.** (See *Information Sheet for Service of Process*, form FL-611, *Proof of Personal Service*, form FL-330, and *Proof of Service by Mail*, form FL-335.)

Request for Accommodations

Assistive listening systems, computer-assisted real-time captioning, or sign language interpreter services are available if you ask at least five days before the proceeding. Contact the clerk's office or go to *www.courtinfo.ca.gov/forms* for *Request for Accommodations by Persons With Disabilities and Order* (form MC-410). (Civil Code, § 54.8.)

INSTRUCTIONS FOR COMPLETING THE *NOTICE OF ACTIVATION OF MILITARY SERVICE AND DEPLOYMENT AND REQUEST TO MODIFY A SUPPORT ORDER* FORM (TYPE OR PRINT FORM IN BLACK INK):

<u>Front page, first box, top of form, left side:</u> Print your name, address, telephone number, and fax number or e-mail address in this box if it is not already there.

<u>Front page, second box, left side:</u> Print your county's name and the court's address in the box. Use the same address for the court that is on your most recent support order or judgment. If you do not have a copy of your most recent support order or judgment, you can get one from either the court clerk or the local child support agency.

<u>Front page, third box, left side:</u> Print the names of the Petitioner/Plaintiff, Respondent/Defendant, and Other Parent in this box. Use the same names listed in your most recent support order or judgment. If no name is listed for the other parent, leave that line blank.

<u>Front page, first box, top of form, right side:</u> Leave this box blank for the court's use.

<u>Front page, second box, right side:</u> Print your case number in this box. Use the same number that is listed on your most recent support order or judgment.

<u>Page 1, items 1 through 4:</u>

1. Insert the name of the person(s) other than you. Include the local child support agency if they are involved in your case.

2. a. You must contact the court clerk's office to get information on obtaining a hearing date for this request. The court clerk will give you the information you need to complete this section. The hearing date must be written on the copies of the pages served on the other party.

    b. Check the first box if the address of the court where the hearing will be held is the same as the one you put at the top of the request. Check the second box if the address of the court where the hearing will be held is different from the one you put at the top of the notice. Print the different court address in the space.

3.–4. If you need to have the court hear your case in less than the statutorily required time, you can ask the court for an order shortening time. If you need assistance, contact the court's family law facilitator in your county or go to *www.courtinfo.ca.gov/selfhelp/*.

Page 2, items 5 through 12:

5. a. Check the box for the type of support order that you are asking to have changed.

  b. If the person who pays support is in the military, and the support order is changed and the court issues a new earnings assignment order to show the new support amount, the new earnings assignment order must be served on one of the following finance centers. If the service member is in the Army, Navy, Air Force or Marines, it must be served on: DFAS Cleveland Center, DFAS-DGI/CL, P.O. Box 998002, Cleveland, OH 44199-8002. If the service member is in the Coast Guard, the new earnings assignment order must be served on: Commanding Officer (LGL), U.S. Coast Guard Pay and Personnel Center, Federal Building, 444 SE Quincy Street, Topeka, KS 66683-3591.

  c. Check the box that correctly describes the person who is paying the support.

6. a. Check the box to show who is being deployed by the military.

  b. Fill out the *Financial Statement (Simplified)* (form FL-155), if you are allowed to use the form. See the instructions on the back side of the form to see if you qualify. If you are not allowed to use the *Financial Statement (Simplified)* (form FL-155), fill out the *Income and Expense Declaration* (form FL-150). You must attach copies of your most recent W-2 forms and paycheck stubs for the last two months to the *Financial Statement (Simplified)* (form FL-155) or *Income and Expense Declaration* (form FL-150). **If you are requesting a modification of spousal support, you must fill out the *Income and Expense Declaration* (form FL-150).**

  A service member must include his or her Basic Pay, Basic Allowance for Subsistence, Basic Allowance for Quarters benefits (BAQ), and any other non-taxable entitlements in the income section of the *Income and Expense Declaration* (form FL-150). Attach a copy of the Leave and Earnings Statement (LES) from the last two months, if available.

  c. Check this box if you are in the military and are asking the local child support agency to seek a modification of support while you are deployed out-of-state. You must attach a completed copy of the *Notice of Deployment* form provided to you by the local child support agency.

7. a. Print the date that the service member was first deployed out of state or the expected date of deployment if he or she has not yet been deployed, and attach a copy of the order of deployment.

  b. Print the dates showing the duration of the service member's activation, listing both the beginning date and the end date.

8. Include a blank *Responsive Declaration to Order to Show Cause or Notice of Motion* (form FL-320) in the papers you serve on the other party. Also include a blank *Financial Statement (Simplified)* (form FL-155) or a blank *Income and Expense Declaration* (form FL-150).

9. Check all boxes that apply.

  a. Check the box if the employer will supplement military pay while the person is deployed; specify monthly amount and attach proof (such as a letter from the employer).

  b. Check the box if the employer will not supplement military pay during the deployment, and the service member will only have military pay in the amount stated on the attached *Financial Statement (Simplified)* (form FL-155) or *Income and Expense Declaration* (form FL-150).

  c. Check the box if it is unknown whether the service member's employer will supplement the military pay.

  d. Check the box if there will be other income (such as rental income); specify the monthly amount and attach proof. You will also need to indicate any investment or other income on the *Income and Expense Declaration* (form FL-150). If you have rental property income you will need to include a schedule showing gross receipts less cash expenses. See form FL-150 for specific instructions on other attachments that may be needed if you have investment or business income.

10. Check the box if you and the other party have previously agreed that spousal support cannot be modified or terminated. Attach a copy of your agreement.

11. Tell the court about any other information that supports your request. If you need additional space, you may attach pages.

12. List the service member's APO address or a local address where the service member will receive timely notice of the court proceedings.

13. If you will be deployed out of state and unavailable to appear at the time of the hearing, you may sign this waiver and ask the court to hold the hearing without you. The court may or may not grant your request. If you check this box, you must sign the bottom of page 2 of the form and make sure that it is fully and accurately completed and has all necessary attachments. You may also have certain protections provided by the Servicemembers Civil Relief Act (SCRA). You may ask for the assistance of a JAG (Judge Advocate General) officer.

14. Put the number of pages attached.

You must date the request, print your name, and sign the form under penalty of perjury. When you sign the form, you are stating that the information you have provided is true and correct.

For instructions on how to complete the *Proof of Service*, see *Information Sheet for Service of Process* (form FL-611). The person who serves the request and its attachments must fill out the *Proof of Service* form. **You cannot serve your own request.**

FL-398 [New December 2, 2005] **INFORMATION SHEET FOR COMPLETING AND RESPONDING TO NOTICE OF**   Page 4 of 5
ACTIVATION OF MILITARY SERVICE AND DEPLOYMENT AND REQUEST
TO MODIFY A SUPPORT ORDER
(Family Law—Governmental)

FL-398

If you are the person receiving the request that the support order be changed:

You will need to file a response and go to the hearing unless a written agreement is reached and signed by the court before the hearing.

- Complete the *Responsive Declaration to Order to Show Cause or Notice of Motion* (form FL-320). If a blank *Responsive Declaration to Order to Show Cause or Notice of Motion* (form FL-320) was not given to you when you received the *Notice of Activation of Military Service and Deployment and Request to Modify a Support Order* (form FL-398), the court clerk's office, the court's Office of the Family Law Facilitator, or the local child support agency can tell you where one can be found. Or you can get one from the California Court's Web site: *www.courtinfo.ca.gov/forms/.*

- Fill out the form *Financial Statement (Simplified)* (form FL-155) if you are allowed to use the form. See the instructions on the back of the form to see if you qualify; otherwise, you must fill out the form *Income and Expense Declaration* (form FL-150). You must attach copies of your most recent W-2 forms and paycheck stubs for the last two months to the *Financial Statement (Simplified)* (form FL-155) or the *Income and Expense Declaration* (form FL-150). Make at least three copies of the completed form and all attachments.

You must have one completed copy of each of the following papers served on the other party. If the local child support agency is involved, serve it to:

- Your *Responsive Declaration to Order to Show Cause or Notice of Motion* (form FL-320).
- Your *Financial Statement (Simplified)* (form FL-155) or *Income and Expense Declaration* (form FL-150).

For instructions on how to serve these papers properly, see *Information Sheet for Service of Process* (form FL-611), *Proof of Personal Service* (form FL- 330) and *Proof of Service by Mail* (form FL-335). Whoever serves the papers should fill out and must sign the *Proof of Service*. If there are reasons to file your own motion for modification, see FL-391 *Information Sheet—Simplified Way to Change Child, Spousal, or Family Support.* **NOTICE: Consult the court's Office of the Family Law Facilitator or the local court rules to see if there are any other documents you will need to have served on the local child support agency and on the other party.**

The local child support agency or the court's family law facilitator's office may be able to provide you with a child support calculation based on both parents' income to determine the amount of guideline support. If you agree with the proposed changes, you may be able to have one of these offices prepare an agreement to change the child support and have it signed by both parents and the court. If you are able to reach an agreement with the other party and the agreement is signed by the court before the hearing, you do not need to appear at the hearing.

NOTICE: Unless you know the hearing has been taken off calendar, you should go to the hearing as scheduled to protect your rights. You might consider calling the court the day before the hearing to see if the hearing is still on the calendar.

If you need additional assistance with this form, contact an attorney or the court's family law facilitator.

Appendix A

FAMILY LAW FORMS

The Family Law and Juvenile Law Advisory Committee recommended and the Judicial Council of California has approved the following new numbering system for family law forms to increase the ability to locate needed forms by arranging them chronologically in the order that forms are likely to be used. Certain clerical and technical changes have also been made to conform to changes in the law and to increase uniformity in the forms. In the table below, an asterisk after a form number signifies that the form is intended for mandatory use. The abbreviation "n/a" signifies that the form was not listed in the prior "1200" numbering series.

— Table current through January 1, 2007 —

Family Law—Dissolutions, Legal Separations, Annulments

Old Number	New Number	Form Name
1281*	FL–100*	Petition—Marriage (Family Law)
n/a	FL–103*	Petition—Domestic Partnership (Family Law)
1282*	FL–120*	Response—Marriage (Family Law)
n/a	FL–123*	Response—Domestic Partnership (Family Law)
1282.50	FL–130	Appearance, Stipulations, and Waivers (Family Law—Uniform Parentage—Custody and Support)
1283*	FL–110*	Summons (Family Law)
1283.5*	FL–115	Proof of Service of Summons (Family Law, Uniform Parentage, Custody and Support)
n/a	FL–117	Notice and Acknowledgment of Receipt (Family Law)

Old Number	New Number	Form Name
1285.50* 1285.50a* 1285.50b* 1285.50c*	FL–150*	Income and Expense Declaration (Family Law) Income Information Expense Information Child Support Information
1285.52	FL–155	Financial Statement (Simplified)
1285.55*	FL–160*	Property Declaration (Family Law)
1285.56*	FL–161*	Continuation of Property Declaration (Family Law)
1285.78 1285.79	FL–192	Notice of Rights and Responsibilities—Health Care Costs and Reimbursement Procedures / Information Sheet on Changing a Child Support Order
1285.92*	FL–191*	Child Support Case Registry Form
1286*	FL–165*	Request to Enter Default (Family Law—Uniform Parentage)
1286.50*	FL–170*	Declaration for Default or Uncontested Dissolution or Legal Separation (Family Law)
1287*	FL–180*	Judgment (Family Law)
1290*	FL–190*	Notice of Entry of Judgment (Family Law—Uniform Parentage—Custody and Support)
n/a	FL–191*	Child Support Case Registry Form
1292*	FL–140*	Declaration of Disclosure (Family Law)
1292.05*	FL–141*	Declaration Regarding Service of Declaration of Disclosure (Family Law)
1292.10	FL–145	Form Interrogatories (Family Law)
1292.11	FL–142	Schedule of Assets and Debts (Family Law)
MC–150	FL–105/GC–120	Declaration Under Uniform Child Custody Jurisdiction and Enforcement Act (UCCJEA)

Old Number	New Number	Form Name
OMB 0970–0154	FL–195/ OMB 0970–0154	Order/Notice to Withhold Income for Child Support or Notice of an Order to Withhold Income for Child Support
OMB 0970–0154	FL–196/ OMB 0970–0154	Instructions to Complete Order/Notice to Withhold Income for Child Support or Notice of an Order to Withhold Income for Child Support

Family Law—Uniform Parentage Actions

Old Number	New Number	Form Name
1296.60	FL–200	Petition to Establish Parental Relationship (Uniform Parentage)
1296.65	FL–220	Response to Petition to Establish Parental Relationship (Uniform Parentage)
1296.70*	FL–230*	Declaration for Default or Uncontested Judgment (Uniform Parentage, Custody and Support)
1296.72	FL–235	Advisement and Waiver of Rights Re: Establishment of Parental Relationship (Uniform Parentage)
1296.74*	FL–240*	Stipulation for Entry of Judgment Re: Establishment of Parental Relationship (Uniform Parentage)
1296.75*	FL–250*	Judgment (Uniform Parentage—Custody and Support)
n/a	FL–272	Notice of Motion to Set Aside Judgment of Paternity (Family Law—Governmental)
n/a	FL–273	Declaration in Support of Motion to Set Aside Judgment of Paternity (Family Law—Governmental)
n/a	FL–274	Information Sheet for Completing Notice of Motion to Set Aside Judgment of Paternity (Family Law—Governmental)
n/a	FL–276	Response to Notice of Motion to Set Aside Judgment of Paternity (Family Law—Governmental)

Old Number	New Number	Form Name
n/a	FL–278	Order After Hearing on Motion to Set Aside Judgment of Paternity (Family Law—Governmental)
1296.77*	FL–280*	Request for Hearing and Application to Set Aside Voluntary Declaration of Paternity
n/a	FL–281	Information Sheet for Completing Request for Hearing and Application to Set Aside Voluntary Declaration of Paternity (Family Law—Governmental)
1296.78*	FL–285*	Responsive Declaration to Application to Set Aside Voluntary Declaration of Paternity
1296.79*	FL–290*	Order After Hearing on Motion to Set Aside Voluntary Declaration of Paternity
1296.80	FL–260	Petition for Custody and Support of Minor Children
1296.81	FL–270	Response to Petition for Custody and Support of Minor Children
1296.605*	FL–210*	Summons (Uniform Parentage—Petition for Custody and Support)

Family Law—Motions

Old Number	New Number	Form Name
1285*	FL–300*	Order to Show Cause
1285.05*	FL–305*	Temporary Orders
1285.10*	FL–301*	Notice of Motion
1285.20*	FL–310*	Application for Order and Supporting Declaration
DV–100A*	FL–311	Child Custody and Visitation Attachment
n/a	FL–312*	Request for Child Abduction Prevention Orders
n/a	FL–325*	Declaration of Court–Connected Child Custody Evaluator Regarding Qualifications
n/a	FL–326*	Declaration of Private Child Custody Evaluator Regarding Qualifications
n/a	FL–327	Order Appointing Child Custody Evaluator

Old Number	New Number	Form Name
1285.27*	FL–350*	Stipulation to Establish or Modify Child Support and Order
1285.30*	FL–390*	Notice of Motion and Motion for Simplified Modification of Order for Child, Spousal, or Family Support
1285.31	FL–391	Information Sheet—Simplified Way to Change Child, Spousal, or Family Support
1285.32*	FL–392*	Responsive Declaration to Motion for Simplified Modification of Order for Child, Spousal, or Family Support
1285.33	FL–393	Information Sheet—How to Oppose a Request to Change Child, Spousal, or Family Support
1285.40*	FL–320*	Responsive Declaration to Order to Show Cause or Notice of Motion
1285.84	FL–330	Proof of Personal Service
1285.85	FL–335	Proof of Service by Mail
1286.75*	FL–315*	Application for Separate Trial (Family Law)
1287.50*	FL–395*	Ex Parte Application for Restoration of Former Name After Entry of Judgment and Order (Family Law)
1291.10*	FL–371*	Notice of Motion and Declaration for Joinder
1291.15*	FL–372*	Request for Joinder of Employee Benefit Plan and Order
1291.20*	FL–373*	Responsive Declaration to Motion for Joinder and Consent Order of Joinder
1291.25*	FL–374*	Notice of Appearance and Response of Employee Benefit Plan
1291.35*	FL–370*	Pleading on Joinder—Employee Benefit Plan
1291.40*	FL–375*	Summons (Joinder)
1292.15*	FL–396*	Request for Production of an Income and Expense Declaration After Judgment
1292.17*	FL–397*	Request for Income and Benefit Information From Employer

Old Number	New Number	Form Name
n/a	FL–398	Notice of Activation of Military Service and Deployment and Request to Modify a Support Order (Family Law—Governmental)
1296.31	FL–340*	Findings and Order After Hearing (Family Law—Custody and Support—Uniform Parentage)
1296.31A*	FL–341*	Child Custody and Visitation Order Attachment
1296.31A(1)*	FL–341(A)*	Supervised Visitation Order
n/a	FL–341(B)*	Child Abduction Prevention Order Attachment
n/a	FL–341(C)	Children's Holiday Schedule Attachment
n/a	FL–341(D)	Additional Provisions—Physical Custody Attachment
n/a	FL–341(E)	Joint Legal Custody Attachment
1296.31B*	FL–342*	Child Support Information and Order Attachment
1296.31B(1)*	FL–342(A)*	Non–Guideline Child Support Findings Attachment
1296.31C	FL–343	Spousal, Partner, or Family Support Order Attachment (Family Law)
1296.31D*	FL–344*	Property Order Attachment to Findings and Order After Hearing (Family Law)
n/a	FL–345	Property Order Attachment to Judgment (Family Law)
1296.87*	FL–360*	Request for Hearing and Application to Set Aside Support Order
1296.88*	FL–365*	Responsive Declaration to Application to Set Aside Support Order
1296.89*	FL–367*	Order After Hearing on Motion to Set Aside Support Order
1297*	FL–380*	Application for Expedited Child Support Order
1297.10*	FL–381*	Response to Application for Expedited Child Support Order and Notice of Hearing
1297.20*	FL–382*	Expedited Child Support Order

Family Law—Enforcement

Old Number	New Number	Form Name
1285.28*	FL–400*	Order for Child Support Security Deposit and Evidence of Deposit
1285.29*	FL–401*	Application for Disbursement and Order for Disbursement From Child Support Security Deposit
1285.60*	FL–410*	Order to Show Cause and Affidavit for Contempt
1285.61A*	FL–411*	Affidavit of Facts Constituting Contempt (Financial and Injunctive Orders)
1285.61B*	FL–412*	Affidavit of Facts Constituting Contempt (Domestic Violence/Custody and Visitation)
1285.62*	FL–420*	Declaration of Payment History (Family Law—Governmental—Uniform Parentage Act)
1285.65*	FL–430*	Ex Parte Application for Earnings Assignment Order
1285.70*	FL–435*	Earnings Assignment Order for Spousal Support (Family Law)
1285.72*	FL–455*	Stay of Service of Earnings Assignment and Order
1285.73	FL–461	Attachment to Qualified Domestic Relations Order for Support (Earnings Assignment Order for Support)
1285.74	FL–460	Qualified Domestic Relations Order for Support (Earnings Assignment Order for Support)
1285.75*	FL–470*	Application and Order for Health Insurance Coverage
1285.76*	FL–475*	Employer's Health Insurance Return
n/a	FL–478*	Request and Notice of Hearing Regarding Health Insurance Assignment
n/a	FL–478–INFO	Information Sheet and Instructions for Request and Notice of Hearing Regarding Health Insurance Assignment
1285.80*	FL–480*	Abstract of Support Judgment

Old Number	New Number	Form Name
1285.82	FL–440	Statement for Registration of California Support Order
1285.625	FL–421	Payment History Attachment (Family Law—Governmental—Uniform Parentage Act)
1296.90*	FL–485*	Notice of Delinquency
1296.91*	FL–490*	Application to Determine Arrearages
1299.28*	FL–450*	Request for Hearing Regarding Earnings Assignment (Family Law—Governmental—UIFSA)

Family Law—Interstate Actions

Old Number	New Number	Form Name
1285.88	FL–570	Notice of Registration of Out–of–State Support Order
1285.89	FL–580	Registration of Out–of–State Custody Decree
1285.90*	FL–575*	Request for Hearing Regarding Registration of Support Order
1298.50*	FL–510*	Summons (UIFSA)
1298.52*	FL–515*	Order to Show Cause (UIFSA)
1298.54*	FL–520*	Response to Uniform Support Petition (UIFSA)
1298.56*	FL–511*	Ex Parte Application for Order for Nondisclosure of Address and Order (UIFSA)
1298.58*	FL–530*	Judgment Regarding Parental Obligations (UIFSA)
1298.60*	FL–560*	Ex Parte Application for Transfer and Order (UIFSA)

Family Law—Governmental Child Support (Selected Forms Only)

Old Number	New Number	Form Name
n/a	FL–643	Declaration of Obligor's Income During Judgment Period–Presumed Income Set–Aside Request
1296.95*	FL–670*	Notice of Motion for Judicial Review of License Denial (Governmental)

Old Number	New Number	Form Name
1296.96*	FL–675*	Order After Judicial Review of License Denial (Governmental)
1298.03*	FL–684*	Request for Order and Supporting Declaration (Governmental)
1298.045*	FL–627*	Order for Genetic (Parentage) Testing
1298.05*	FL–685*	Response to Governmental Notice of Motion or Order to Show Cause (Governmental)
1298.07*	FL–687*	Order After Hearing (Governmental)
1298.06*	FL–690*	Stipulation and Order (Governmental) [for use in actions filed before July 1, 1997]
n/a	FL–692	Minutes and Order or Judgment (Governmental)
1298.085*	FL–697*	Declaration for Default or Uncontested Judgment (Governmental)
1298.09*	FL–680*	Notice of Motion (Governmental)
1298.30*	FL–650*	Statement for Registration of California Support Order (Governmental)
1298.32*	FL–651*	Notice of Registration of California Support Order (Governmental)
1299.01*	FL–600*	Summons and Complaint or Supplemental Complaint Regarding Parental Obligations (Governmental)
1299.04*	FL–610*	Answer to Complaint or Supplemental Complaint Regarding Parental Obligations (Governmental)
1299.05	FL–611	Information Sheet for Service of Process
1299.07*	FL–615*	Stipulation for Judgment or Supplemental Judgment Regarding Parental Obligations and Judgment (Governmental)
1299.10*	FL–620*	Request to Enter Default Judgment (Governmental)
1299.13*	FL–630*	Judgment Regarding Parental Obligations (Governmental)
1299.16*	FL–635*	Notice of Entry of Judgment and Proof of Service by Mail (Governmental)

Old Number	New Number	Form Name
1299.17*	FL–616*	Declaration for Amended Proposed Judgment (Governmental)
1299.19*	FL–640*	Notice and Motion to Cancel (Set Aside) Support Order Based on Presumed Income (Governmental)
1299.22*	FL–625*	Stipulation and Order (Governmental)
1299.40*	FL–676*	Request for Judicial Determination of Support Arrearages (Governmental)
1299.43*	FL–677*	Notice of Opposition and Notice of Motion on Claim of Exemption (Governmental)
1299.46*	FL–678*	Order Determining Claim of Exemption or Third–Party Claim (Governmental)
1299.49*	FL–645*	Notice to Local Child Support Agency of Intent to Take Independent Action to Enforce Support Order (Governmental)
1299.52*	FL–646*	Response of Local Child Support Agency to Notice of Intent to Take Independent Action to Enforce Support Order (Governmental)
1299.55*	FL–632*	Notice Regarding Payment of Support (Governmental)
1299.58*	FL–660*	Ex Parte Motion by Local Child Support Agency and Declaration for Joinder of Other Parent (Governmental)
1299.61	FL–661	Notice of Motion and Declaration for Joinder of Other Parent in Governmental Action (Governmental)
1299.64*	FL–662*	Responsive Declaration to Motion for Joinder of Other Parent—Consent Order of Joinder (Governmental)
1299.67*	FL–663*	Stipulation and Order for Joinder of Other Parent (Governmental)
1299.70*	FL–665*	Findings and Recommendation of Commissioner (Governmental)
1299.72*	FL–666*	Notice of Objection (Governmental)
1299.74*	FL–667*	Review of Commissioner's Findings of Fact and Recommendation (Governmental)

Family Law—Summary Dissolution

Old Number	New Number	Form Name
1295.10*	FL–800*	Joint Petition for Summary Dissolution of Marriage (Family Law—Summary Dissolution)
1295.11*	FL–810*	Summary Dissolution Information—English
1295.12*	FL–812*	Summary Dissolution Information—Spanish
1295.20*	FL–820*	Request for Judgment, Judgment of Dissolution of Marriage, and Notice of Entry of Judgment (Family Law—Summary Dissolution)
1295.30*	FL–830*	Notice of Revocation of Petition for Summary Dissolution (Family Law—Summary Dissolution)

Family Law—Miscellaneous

Old Number	New Number	Form Name
1288*	FL–970*	Request and Declaration for Final Judgment of Dissolution of Marriage (Family Law)
1290.50*	FL–960*	Notice of Withdrawal of Attorney of Record
1294	FL–940	Office of the Family Law Facilitator Disclosure
1294.5	FL–945	Family Law Information Center Disclosure
1299.77	FL–920	Notice of Consolidation

Revoked

1295.11a*	Summary Dissolution Information Insert
1297.90*	Application For Notice of Support Arrearage (Support Arrearage)
1297.91*	Proof of Service of Application (Support Arrearage)
1297.92*	Notice of Support Arrearage (Support Arrearage)
1297.93*	Notice to Judgment Debtor (Support Arrearage)

Appendix B

DISPOSITION OF EXISTING LAW

Note. This table shows the disposition of sections in the Civil Code, Code of Civil Procedure, Evidence Code, and Probate Code, in effect on December 31, 1993, that are repealed in connection with the Family Code legislation. Unless otherwise indicated, all dispositions are to the Family Code, as enacted by 1992 Cal Stat ch 162 (operative Jan. 1, 1994), and amended by 1993 Cal Stat chs 219 and 876. For further detail, see the Comment to the appropriate section in this report, *supra.*

CIVIL CODE

Civil Code	Family Code	Civil Code	Family Code
25	6500	25.9(a) (last snt.)	6924(d)
25.1	6502	25.9(b)	6924(e)
25.5	Omitted	25.9(c)	6924(a)(1)
25.6 (pt.)	7002(a)	25.9(d)	6924(a)(2)
25.6 (pt.)	7050(e)(1)	25.9(e)	6924(a)(3)
25.7 (pt.)	7002(b)	25.9(f)	6924(f)
25.7 (pt.)	7050(e)(1)	26	6500
25.8 (1st pt.)	6903	27	6501
25.8 (2d pt.)	6902	29 (1st pt.)	CC 43.1
25.8 (last pt.)	6901	29 (last pt.)	CCP 340.4
25.8	6910	33	6701
25.9(a) (1st snt., 1st pt.)	6920	34	6700
25.9(a) (1st snt., last pt.)	6924(b)	34.5 (1st ¶, 1st snt., 1st pt.)	6920
25.9(a) (2d snt.)	6921	34.5 (1st ¶, 1st snt., 2d pt.)	6925(a)
25.9(a) (3d snt.)	6920	34.5 (1st ¶, 1st snt., last pt.)	6921
25.9(a) (4th snt.)	6924(c)	34.5 (1st ¶, last snt.)	6920

1129

64(b)(2)	7121(b)	203	7507
64(c) (1st snt.)	7122(b)	204	7505
64(c) (last snt.)	7140	205	3952
64(d)	7123(a)	206 (1st snt., pt.)	3910(a)
64(e)	7123(b)	206 (1st snt., pt.)	4400
64(f)	7122(c)	206 (2d snt.)	4401
65(a)	7132(a)	206 (last snt.)	Omitted
65(b)(1) (1st pt.)	7133(a)	206.5 (1st snt., 1st pt.)	4410
65(b)(1) (last pt.)	7133(c)	206.5 (1st snt., 2d pt.)	4411
65(b)(2)	7133(b)	206.5 (2d–3d snt.)	4412
65(c) (1st snt.)	7130(b)	206.5 (last snt.)	4414(a)
65(c) (2d–last snt.)	7132(b)	206.5 (1st snt., last pt.)	4410
65(d) (1st snt.)	7134		
65(d) (2d–last snt.)	7143	206.5 (last ¶)	4414(b)
65(e)	7135	206.6	4413
66	7141	206.7	Omitted
67	7111	207	3950
68	7142	208	3951
69 (1st ¶, 1st snt.)	7130(a)	208.5	3930
69 (1st ¶, last snt.)	7135	210	7506
69 (last ¶, 1st snt.)	7131	211	7504
69 (last ¶, last snt.)	7133	212	7503
69 (last ¶, last snt.)	7134	213	7501
69 (last ¶, last snt.)	7143	220.10	Omitted
70	7110	220.15	Omitted
196(a)	3900	220.20 (intro.)	8500
196(b)	Omitted	220.20(a)	8503
196a (1st snt.)	3900	220.20(b)	8506
196a (last snt.)	4000	220.20(c)	8509
196.5 (1st ¶, 1st snt.)	3901(a)	220.20(d)	8512
196.5 (1st ¶, last snt.)	4000	220.20(e)	8600
196.5 (last ¶, 1st snt.)	Omitted	220.20(f)	8515
196.5 (last snt.)	3901(b)	220.20(g)	8518
197 (pt.)	3010	220.20(h)	8521
197 (pt.)	7500	220.20(i)	8524
197.5	3102	220.20(j)	8527
201	3902	220.20(k)	8530
202	7502	220.20(l)	8533

220.20(m)	8801(b)	222.13	8701
220.20(n)	Omitted	222.15	8702
220.20(o)	8539	222.18	8703
220.20(p)	8542	222.20	8704
220.20(q)	8545	222.22	8705
220.20(r)	8548	222.26(a)	8706
221.05	8621	222.26(b)	8608
221.07	8622	222.30	8707
221.10	8600	222.35	8708
221.12	8601	222.36	8709
221.13	8602	222.37	8710
221.14	8603	222.38	8711
221.20 (1st ¶, 1st–3d snt.)	8604	222.40	8712
		222.50	8713
221.20 (1st ¶, 4th snt.)	8605	222.70	8714
221.20 (1st ¶, last snt.)	8606	222.71	8714(a)
		222.72	8716
221.20(a)-(c)	8606	222.75	8715
221.30	8607	222.77	8717
221.40	8609	222.78	8718
221.50	8610	222.80	8719
221.60	8611	222.90	8720
221.62	8718	224.10	8800
221.62	8823	224.10(d)	270
221.62	8913	224.20	8801(a)
221.62	9007	224.21	8801.3
221.63(a)	8612(a)	224.24	8801.5
221.63(b)	8612(b)	224.26	8801.7
221.63(c) (1st pt.)	8612(c)	224.30	8802
221.63(c) (last pt.)	8616	224.33	8803
221.65	8613	224.36	8804
221.70	8614	224.37	8805
221.72	8615	224.40	8806
221.74 (1st snt.)	8618	224.42	8807
221.74 (last snt.)	8616	224.44	8808
221.76	8617	224.49	8811
221.80	8619	224.50	Omitted
222.10	8700		

224.61	8813	227.50	9006
224.62	8814	227.60	9007
224.63	8814.5	228.10	9100
224.64	8815	228.13	9101
224.66	8816	228.15	9102
224.70(a)	8817	229.10	9200
224.70(b)	8608	229.20	9201
224.73	8818	229.30	9202
224.76	8819	229.40	9203
224.80	8820	229.50	9204
224.91	8821	229.60	9205
224.93	8822	229.70	9206
224.95	8823	230.10	9300
226.10	8900	230.12	9303
226.11	8901	230.14 (1st snt.)	9304
226.20	8902	230.14 (last snt.)	9305
226.21	8903	230.16	9306
226.23	8904	230.20(a) (1st ¶)	9320
226.25	8905	230.20(a) (last ¶, 1st snt.)	9301
226.27	8906		
226.28	8907	230.20(a) (last ¶, 2d–last snt.)	9302
226.30	8908		
226.40	8910	230.20(b) (1st snt.)	9321(a)
226.50	8911	230.20(b) (2d snt., 1st pt.)	9322
226.52	8912	230.20(b) (2d snt., last pt.)	9324
226.55	8913		
226.57	8914	230.20(b) (3d snt.)	9323
226.59	8915	230.20(b) (last snt.)	9325
226.60	8916	230.20(c) (1st ¶)	9328
226.64	8917	230.20(c) (2d ¶)	9302
226.66	8918	230.20(c) (last ¶)	9328
226.69	8919	230.20(d)	9307
227.10	9000	230.20(e)	9326
227.20	9001	230.20(f)(1)	9321(b)
227.30	9002	230.20(f)(2)	9327
227.40	9003	230.20(g)	9340
227.44	9004	232(a) (intro.)	7820
227.46	9005	232(a) (intro., pt.)	7802

232(a)(1)	7822	235.5	7884
232(a)(2)	7823	236	7883
232(a)(3)	7824	237	7804
232(a)(4)	7825	237.5 (intro.)	7860
232(a)(5)	7826	237.5(a)	7861
232(a)(6)	7827	237.5(b) (1st snt.)	7862
232(a)(7)	7828	237.5(b) (last snt.)	7860
232(a)(8)	7829	237.5(c) (1st snt.)	7860
232(b) (1st snt.)	7890	237.5(c) (2d–last snt.)	7863
232(b) (2d–last ¶)	7892(a)–(b), (d)	237.5(d)	7864
		237.7	7895
232(c)	7821	238	7894
232(c)	7892(c)	239	7893
232(d)	7807	241(a)	Omitted
232(e)	7808	241(b)	3550(a)(2)
232.3(a)–(b)	7870	241(c)	3550(a)(1)
232.3(c)	7871	241(d) (1st pt.)	Omitted
232.5 (1st snt.)	7801	241(d) (last pt.)	3910(a)
232.5 (last snt.)	7890	241(e)	Omitted
232.6 (1st snt.)	7800	242 (pt.)	3900
232.6 (last snt.)	7803	242 (pt.)	3910(a)
232.9	7840	242 (pt.)	4300
233(a) (1st snt., 1st & last pt.)	7841	242 (pt.)	4400
233(a) (1st snt., 2d pt.)	7845	244	3550(b)
		245	200
233(a) (2d snt.)	7806	247 (pt.)	3651
233(a) (3d snt.)	7850	247 (pt.)	4405
233(a) (1st ¶, last snt.–end)	7851	248 (1st snt., pt.)	4000
		248 (pt.)	4002
233(b)	7852	248 (pt.)	4303
233.5 (1st ¶)	7805(a)	248 (pt.)	4403
233.5 (last ¶)	7805(b)	249	3554
233.6	7805(c)	250	3551
234 (1st ¶)	7880	251	4402
234 (2d ¶)	7891	252	Omitted
234(a)–(c)	7891	253	Omitted
235(a)	7881	254	Omitted
235(b)	7882		

264	7900	4205.1	401
265	7901	4205.5	402
266	7902	4206	420(a)
267	7903	4206.5	420(b)
268	7904	4207	421
269	7905	4208(a)	422
270	7906	4208(b)	423
271	7907	4209	424
272	7908	4210	425
273	7909	4212	309
274	7910	4213(a) (1st ¶, 1st snt.)	500
275	7950		
275.1	7951	4213(a) (1st ¶, 2d snt.)	501
275.2	7952		
275.3	7953	4213(a) (1st ¶, 3d snt.)	504
275.4	7954	4213(a) (1st ¶, 4th–6th snt.)	506
4000	Omitted		
4001	211	4213(a) (1st ¶, last snt.)	511(a)
4100	300		
4101(a)	301	4213(a) (2d ¶, 1st snt.)	507
4101(b)	302		
4101(c)	304	4213(a) (2d ¶, last snt.)	508
4102	303		
4103	305	4213(a) (last ¶)	505
4104	308	4213(b) (1st–2d snt.)	503
4200	306	4213(b) (last snt.)	504
4201(a) (1st pt.)	350	4213(c)(1)	530(a)
4201(a) (last pt.)	351	4213(c)(2)	531(a)-(b)
4201(b) (1st snt.)	352	4213(c)(3) (1st snt., 1st pt.)	531(c)
4201(b) (2d snt.)	353		
4201(b) (3d–last snt.)	354	4213(c)(3) (1st snt., last pt.)	536(a)
4201(c)-(d)	355		
4201.5	358	4213(c)(3) (2d snt.)	533
4202	359	4213(c)(3) (3d snt.)	536(b)
4203	360	4213(c)(3) (last snt.)	536(c)
4204 (1st snt.)	356	4213(c)(4)	535(a)
4204 (last ¶)	357	4213(c)(5)	532
4205	400	4213(c)(6)	534
		4213(c)(7)	535(b)

4380	290	4390.5(c) (1st snt.)	5253
4381	2026	4390.5(c) (last snt.)	5208
4382	3556	4390.5(d)–(e)	5252(b)
4383(a) (1st snt.)	5100	4390.6	5280
4383(a) (2d snt.)	5101	4390.7(a)	5281
4383(a) (3d snt.)	5103(a)	4390.7(b)	5282
4383(a) (last snt.)	5103(b)	4390.7(c)	5231
4383(b)	5104	4390.8(a) (1st–2d snt.)	5233
4383(c)	5103(c)		
4384 (1st snt.)	291	4390.8(a) (last snt.)	5232
4384 (last snt.)	5102	4390.8(b)	5234
4384.5 (1st snt.)	4502	4390.9(a)–(c)	5270
4384.5 (last snt.)	CCP 683.130(e)	4390.9(d)	5272
		4390.10(a)	5235
4385	4500	4390.10(b)	5241
4390 (intro.)	5200	4390.10(c)	5242
4390(a)	5202	4390.11	5271
4390(b)	5204	4390.12(a)	5238
4390(c)	5206	4390.12(b)	5243
4390(d)	5210	4390.13	5237
4390(e)	5212	4390.14	5240
4390(f)	5214	4390.15	5295
4390(g)	5216	4390.16(a), (c)	5283
4390(h)	150	4390.16	5236
4390(i)	5220	4390.17	5290
4390.1	5244	4390.18	3555
4390.2	5239	4390.19	5245
4390.3(a) (1st snt.)	5208	4395	3830
4390.3(a)	5230	4400	2200
4390.3(b)	5231	4401	2201
4390.3(c)	5260	4425	2210
4390.4	5261	4426	2211
4390.5(a) (1st ¶, 1st snt.)	5250	4429	2212(a)
		4450	2250
4390.5(a) (1st ¶, last snt.)	5251	4451	2212(b)
		4452 (1st–3d snt.)	2251
4390.5(a) (last ¶)	5252(a)	4452 (last snt.)	2252
4390.5(b)	5252(c)		

4454	2253	4516 (last snt.)	6388
4455	2254	4530(a)	2320
4456	2255	4530(b)	2321
4457(a)	2080	4531	2322
4457(b)	2082	4550	2400
4457(c)	2081	4551	2401
4457(d)	CCP 1279.6	4552	2402
4458 (1st snt.)	6360	4553	2403
4458 (2d snt.)	6361	4554	2404
4458 (3d snt.)	6380	4555	2405
4458 (last snt.)	6388	4556	2406
4501	2300	4600(a) (1st ¶)	3020
4503 (1st snt.)	2330(a)	4600(a) (last ¶, 1st snt.)	3022
4503 (last snt.)	2331		
4506	2310	4600(a) (last ¶, 2d snt.)	3042
4507	2311		
4508(a) (1st snt.)	2333	4600(a) (last snt.)	3043
4508(a) (2d snt.–end)	2334	4600(b)	3040(a)
4508(b) (1st snt.)	2345	4600(c)	3041
4508(b) (last snt.)	2347	4600(d)	3040(b)
4509	2325	4600.1(a)	3060
4510(a)	2312	4600.1(b)	3061
4510(b)	2313	4600.1(c)-(d)	3062
4510(c)-(d)	2332	4600.1(e) (1st snt.)	3063
4511	2336	4600.1(e) (2d snt.–end)	3064
4512	2338		
4513	2346	4600.2	3029
4514(a) (1st snt.)	2339	4600.5(a)	3080
4514(a) (2d snt.)	2340	4600.5(b)	3081
4514(a) (last snt.)	2341(a)	4600.5(c)	3082
4514(b)	2341(b)	4600.5(d)(1)	3002
4514(c)	2342	4600.5(d)(2)	3007
4514(d)	2344	4600.5(d)(3)	3004
4514(e)	2343	4600.5(d)(4)	3006
4515	2337	4600.5(d)(5)	3003
4516 (1st snt.)	6360	4600.5(e)	3083
4516 (2d snt.)	6361	4600.5(f)	3084
4516 (3d snt.)	6380	4600.5(g)	3085

4600.5(h)	3086	4607(e) (4th snt.)	3186
4600.5(i)	3087	4607(e) (5th snt.)	3178(a)
4600.5(j)	3088	4607(e) (6th–7th snt.)	3186
4600.5(k)	3089	4607(e) (last snt.)	3179
4600.5(*l*)	3025	4607(f)	3184
4600.5(m)	3024	4607(g)	3163
4600.6	3023	4607.1	3162
4601	3100(a)	4607.2	3181
4601.5	3100(b)	4608	3011
4602 (1st ¶)	3111	4608.1(a) (1st ¶)	3190
4602 (2d ¶)	3113	4608.1(a) (last ¶)	3191
4602 (3d ¶)	3112	4608.1(b)	3192
4602 (last ¶)	3114	4609	3026
4603	3120	4610	3030
4604(a)	3130	4611	3027
4604(b)	3131	4612	3031
4604(c) (1st snt.)	3132	4700(a) (1st snt.)	4001
4604(c) (2d snt.–end)	3133	4700(a) (2d snt.)	Omitted
4604.5	3140	4700(a) (3d snt.)	4012
4605	3134	4700(a) (4th snt.)	4011
4606(a)–(b)	3150	4700(a) (5th snt.)	3651(a)–(b)
4606(c)–(d)	3151	4700(a) (6th snt.)	4009
4606(e)	3152	4700(a) (last snt.)	3652
4606(f)–(g)	3153	4700(b)	3028, 270
4607(a) (1st snt.)	3170, 3175	4700(c)	4007
4607(a) (2d snt.)	3173	4700(d)	4013
4607(a) (3d snt.)	3161	4700(e)	Omitted
4607(a) (4th snt.)	3180(b)	4700.1(a)	3680
4607(a) (last snt.)	3172	4700.1(b) (1st ¶)	3683(a)
4607(b) (1st snt.)	3160	4700.1(b) (last ¶, 1st snt.)	3683(b)
4607(b) (2d snt.)	3164(a)		
4607(b) (3d snt.)	3160	4700.1(b) (last ¶, 2d snt.)	3683(c)
4607(b) (last snt.)	3164(b)		
4607(c)	3177	4700.1(b) (last ¶, 3d snt.–end)	3684(a)
4607(d) (1st snt.)	3182(a)		
4607(d) (2d snt.)	3180(a)	4700.1(c) (1st snt.)	3685(a)
4607(d) (last snt.)	3181	4700.1(c) (2d snt.)	3685(b)
4607(e) (1st–3d snt.)	3183	4700.1(c) (last snt.)	3693

4701.1(b)	4613
4701.1(c) (1st–2d snt.)	4614
4701.1(c) (last snt.)	4615
4701.1(d)	4620
4701.1(e)	4603
4701.1(f) (intro.)	4640 (intro.)
4701.1(f)(1)-(2)	4640(a)-(b)
4701.1(f) (last ¶)	4641
4701.1(g)	4602
4701.1(h)	4604
4701.1(i)	4600
4701.2	Omitted
4702(a)	4200
4702(b)	4201
4702(c)	4202
4702(d)	4203
4703	4000
4704	Omitted
4704.5 (1st snt.)	3901(a)
4704.5 (1st ¶, last snt.)	4000
4704.5 (2d ¶, 1st snt.)	Omitted
4704.5 (last snt.)	3901(b)
4705	4504
4706	4006
4707	4003
4708	4503
4709	4505
4710 (intro.)	4554
4710(a) (1st & 2d snt.)	4560(a)
4710(a) (3d snt.)	4561
4710(a) (4th snt.)	4562
4710(a) (last snt.)	4561
4710(b) (1st–3d snt.)	4570
4710(b) (4th snt.)	4571
4710(b) (last snt.)	4572
4710(c)	4563
4710(d)	4560(b)
4710(e) (1st & 2d snt.)	4565
4710(e) (3d snt.)	4566
4710(e) (4th snt.)	4567
4710(e) (last snt.)	4573
4710(g)	4551
4720(a)(1) (1st snt.)	4050
4720(a)(1) (2d snt.)	4051
4720(a)(2)	4052
4720(a)(3)	4053
4720(b)-(d)	4054
4721(a)-(b)	4055
4721(c)	4056
4721(d)-(e)	4057
4721(f)	4058
4721(g)	4059
4721(h)	4060
4721(i)	4061
4721(j)	4062
4721(k)	4063
4721(l)	4064
4721(m)-(o)	4065
4721(p)	4066
4721(q)	4067
4721(r)	4068
4721(s)	4069
4722 (intro.)	4070
4722(a)-(b)	4071
4722(c)	4072
4722(d)	4073
4726(a)(1)-(2)	3751(a)(2)-(b)
4726(a)(3)	3750
4726(b)-(c)	3752
4726(d)	3753
4726.1(a)(1) (1st snt.)	3761(a)
4726.1(a)(1) (last snt.)	3760(c)

4726.1(a)(2)	3762	4778	20025
4726.1(b)	3763	4778.5	20026
4726.1(c)	3761(b)	4779	20030
4726.1(d)	3764	4780	20002
4726.1(e)	3765	4781	20031
4726.1(f)	3766	4782	20032
4726.1(g)	3768	4783	20033
4726.1(h)-(i)	3767	4784	20034
4726.1(j)	3766	4785	20035
4726.1(k)	3770	4786	20036
4726.1(l)	3769	4787	20037
4726.1(m)	3760(a)	4788	20038
4726.1(n)	3772	4789	20039
4726.1(o)	3771	4790	20040
4726.1(p)	3760(b)	4791	20041
4731	4074	4792	20042
4732	4075	4793	20043
4750	4700	4800(a) (1st ¶, 1st snt.)	2550
4752(a)-(c)	4701		
4752(d)	Omitted	4800(a) (1st ¶, last snt.)	2552
4760	20000	4800(a) (2d ¶)	2551
4761	20001	4800(a) (last ¶)	63
4762	20002	4800(b) (intro.)	2600
4763	20010	4800(b)(1)	2601
4764	20011	4800(b)(2)	2602
4765	20012	4800(b)(3)	2604
4766	20013	4800(b)(4)	2603
4767	20014	4800(b)(4) (last snt.)	780
4768	20015	4800(b)(5)	2627
4769	20016	4800(c) (intro.)	2620
4770	20017	4800(c)(1)	2621
4771	20018	4800(c)(2)	2622
4772	20019	4800(c)(3)	2623
4773	20020	4800(c)(4)	2624
4774	20021	4800(d)	2625
4775	20022	4800(e)	2626
4776	20023	4800(f)	2553
4777	20024		

4801.9(g)	3692	5102(a) (3d pt.)	6321
4801.9(h)	3693	5102(a) (last pt.)	6340
4801.9(i)	3694	5102(b)	754
4802 (1st pt.)	1620	5103	721
4802 (last pt.)	3580	5104	750
4803	125	5105 (1st snt.)	751
4804 (pt.)	2502	5105 (last snt.)	Omitted
4804 (pt.)	3515	5106	755
4805	4338	5107	770
4806 (1st snt.)	4321	5108	770
4806 (last snt.)	4322	5110 (1st ¶, 1st snt., 1st pt.)	760
4807	4008		
4809	215	5110 (1st ¶, 1st snt., last pt.–end)	803
4810	2555	5110 (2d ¶)	Omitted
4811(a) (1st–2d snt.)	3585	5110 (last ¶)	700
4811(a) (last snt.)	3651(a)-(b), (d)	5110.150	761
4811(b) (1st–2d snt.)	3590	5110.710	850
4811(b) (last snt. pt.)	3591	5110.720	851
4811(b) (last snt. pt.)	3651(a)-(c)	5110.730	852
4811(c) (pt.)	3593	5110.740	853
4811(c) (pt.)	3651(e)	5111	802
4811(d) (1st ¶)	3586	5112	783
4811(d) (1st ¶, last pt.)	92	5113	782
4811(d) (last ¶, 1st snt., 1st pt.)	92	5114	Omitted
		5115	Omitted
4811(d) (last ¶, 1st snt., last pt.)	4501	5118	771
		5119	772
4811(d) (last snt.)	Omitted	5120.010	900
4812	3592	5120.020(a)	760
4813	2011	5120.020(b)	63
5000	2090	5120.030	902
5001	2091	5120.040	903
5002	2092	5120.110(a)	910
5003	3	5120.110(b)	911
5004	2093	5120.110(c)	910
5100	720	5120.120	912
5102(a) (1st pt.)	752	5120.130	913
5102(a) (2d pt.)	753		

5120.140	914	5167	3419
5120.150	915	5168	3420
5120.160	916	5169	3421
5120.210	920	5170	3422
5120.310	930, 931	5171	3423
5120.320	930	5172	3424
5120.330(a)	931	5173	3425
5120.330(b)	Omitted	5174	3400
5122	1000	5180	Omitted
5125	1100	5181	1850(a)-(d)
5125.1	1101	5182	1851
5126	781	5183	1852
5126(a) (last ¶)	Omitted	5200	1500
5127	1102	5201	1501
5128	1103	5202	1502
5131	4302	5203	1503
5132 (1st snt.)	4301	5300	1600
5138	295	5301	3
5150(1)(a)-(h)	3401(a)	5302	1601
5150(1)(i)	3	5310	1610
5150(2)	3401(b)	5311	1611
5151	3402	5312	1612
5152	3403	5313	1613
5153	3404	5314	1614
5154	3405	5315	1615
5155	3406	5316	1616
5156	3407	5317	1617
5157	3408	7000	7600
5158	3409	7001	7601
5159	3410	7002	7602
5160	3411	7003	7610
5161	3412	7004(a)	7611
5162	3413	7004(b)	7611.5
5163	3414	7004(c)	7612
5163.5	3415	7004.5	7604
5164	3416	7005	7613
5165	3417	7006(a)-(c)	7630
5166	3418	7006(d)	7631

7006(e)	7632	7017.2(a)	7667(a)
7006(f)	7633	7017.2(b) (1st snt.)	7667(b)
7006(g)	7634	7017.2(b) (last snt.)	7668(a)
7007(a)	200	7017.2(c)	7668(b)-(d)
7007(b)-(c)	7620	7017.6	7603
7007(d)	7638	7018	13
7008	7635	7020(a)(1)	6320
7010(a)	7636	7020(a)(2)	6321
7010(b)	7639	7020(a)(3)	6322
7010(c)	7637	7020(a)(4)	6323
7010(d)	Omitted	7020(a) (2d snt.)	242(a)
7010(e)	Omitted	7020(a) (last snt.)	243(e)
7011	7640	7020(b) (1st–2d snt.)	6340
7012	7641	7020(b) (3d snt.)	6345
7013	7642	7020(b) (4th–last snt.)	6342
7014	7643	7020(c)	6224
7015	7650	7020(d)	6302
7016	7614	7020(e) (1st snt.)	6380
7017(a)(1)	7660	7020(e) (last snt.)	6382
7017(a)(2)	7661	7020(f)	6305
7017(b)	7662	7020(g)	6383
7017(c)	7663	7020(h)	6388
7017(d)	7664	7021 (1st snt.)	6360
7017(e)	7665	7021 (2d snt.)	6361
7017(f)	7666	7021 (2d snt.)	6380
7017(g)	7669	7021 (last snt.)	6388
7017.1	7670		

Code of Civil Procedure

Code Civ. Proc.	Family Code		
263 (1st–3d ¶)	3111	412.21(a) (6th ¶, 1st snt.)	232
263 (4th ¶)	3115	412.21(a) (6th ¶, 2d & 3d snt.)	233(c)
263 (last ¶)	3116	412.21(a) (7th ¶)	235
412.21(a) (1st snt.), (a)(1)-(3)	2040	412.21(a) (last ¶)	234
412.21(a) (2d snt.)	233(a)	412.21(b) (1st ¶, 1st snt.)	7700
412.21(a) (5th ¶)	233(b)		

550(g)	6384(b)	1691	4842
550(h)	6383	1692	4843
551	6388	1693	4844
552	6224	1694	4845
553	6386	1695	4846
1650	4800	1696	4847
1651	3	1697	4848
1652	4801	1698	4849
1653(a)-(p)	4802	1698.1	4850
1653(k)	155	1698.2	4851
1654	4803	1698.3	4852
1655	4804	1699	4353
1655.5	4805	1699.4	4854
1656	13	1730	1801
1660	4810	1731	1800
1661	4811	1732	12
1670	4820	1733	1802
1671	4821	1740	1810
1672	4822	1741	1811
1672.5	200	1742	1812
1673	4824	1743	1813
1674	4825	1744	1814
1675	4826	1745	1815
1676	4827	1745.5	1816
1677	4828	1746	1817
1678	4829	1747	1818
1679	4830	1748	1819
1680	4831	1749	1820
1681	4832	1760	1830
1682	4833	1761	1831
1683	4834	1762	1832
1684	4835	1763	1833
1685	4836	1764	1834
1686	4837	1765	1835
1687	4838	1766	1836
1688	4839	1767	1837
1689	4840	1768	1838
1690	4841	1769	1839

1770	1840	1771	1841
		1772	1842

Evidence Code

Evid. Code	Family Code	893	7552
621(a)	7540	894	7553
621(b)–(h)	7541	895	7554
890	7550	895.5	7555
891	3	896	7556
892	7551	897	7557

Probate Code

Prob. Code	Family Code
3301 (pt.)	6911
3301 (pt.)	6950
3302	6602

Session Laws

Statute	Family Code
1991 Cal. Stat. ch. 1141, §4	4552
1991 Cal. Stat. ch. 1141, §5	4553

Table of Statutes, Regulations, and Rules

2061: §12.18
2062(a): §§12.15, 12.20
2062(b): §12.20
2062(c): §§12.16, 12.20, 14.61
2063(a): §12.22
2063(b): §12.22
2065: §12.24
2070-2074: §§12.8, 17.68
2071: §12.25
2072: §12.25
2072-2074: §12.25
2073(a): §12.25
2073(b): §12.25
2073(c): §12.25
2073(d): §12.25
2073(e): §12.25
2074(c): §12.25
2080: §§3.6, 3.23, 10.11, 14.53, 17.51
2082: §14.53
2100: §13.45A
2100-2113: §§3.26, 11.10, 13.1, 13.3, 13.12, 13.14, 13.18, 13.44, 13.48, 14.4, 18.49
2100(c): §§13.44, 14.61
2101(b): §§13.45-13.46, 14.4
2101(e): §§13.45-13.47, 13.49
2102: §§13.45A, 13.46
2102(a): §13.45A
2102(a)(1): §13.45A
2102(a)(2): §13.49
2102(b): §§13.45A, 18.56
2102(c): §13.45A
2103: §13.44
2103-2105: §§13.3, 13.12, 14.4
2104: §§13.46-13.47
2104-2105: §§5.28, 13.48
2104(a): §§13.44-13.45
2104(b): §13.45
2104(c)(1): §13.45
2104(c)(2): §§13.45, 13.49
2104(d): §13.45
2104(e): §§13.45, 13.49
2105: §§13.46-13.47
2105-2106: §13.46
2105(a): §§13.44, 13.46
2105(b)(1): §§13.46, 13.49

2105(b)(2): §13.46
2105(b)(3): §13.46
2105(b)(4): §§13.46, 13.49
2105(c): §13.47
2105(d): §§13.46-13.47, 14.4
2105(d)(1): §13.46
2105(d)(2): §13.46
2105(d)(3): §13.46
2105(d)(4): §13.46
2105(d)(5): §§13.46-13.47, 14.4
2106: §§13.46-13.47
2107(a): §13.48
2107(b): §13.48
2107(c): §13.48
2107(d): §§13.45-13.47
2108: §§11.10, 11.32
2109: §3.26
2110: §§13.45-13.47, 14.4
2113: §§3.26, 13.3, 13.12, 13.44, 14.4
2120-2129: §§13.44-13.46, 18.47-18.48, 18.51, 18.56-18.57
2121(a): §18.47
2121(b): §18.48
2122: §§18.14, 18.49-18.50, 18.52
2122(a): §18.49
2122(b): §18.49
2122(c): §18.49
2122(d): §18.49
2122(e): §18.49
2122(f): §18.49
2123: §18.49
2124: §18.50
2125: §18.52
2126: §18.54
2127: §18.53
2128(a): §18.47
2129: §18.47
2170: §11.35
2200: §§3.7-3.8, 10.4
2200-2201: §§3.7, 3.22
2201: §§3.7, 3.9, 10.4, 17.56, 17.62
2210: §§3.7, 3.22, 9.2, 11.5
2210(a): §3.10

6300: §11.15
6303(a): §11.48
6303(b): §11.48
6303(c): §7.45
6303(e): §11.48
6305: §§11.6, 11.31A
6306(a): §11.6
6306(c): §11.6
6306(d): §11.6
6306(e)-(f): §11.6
6306(g): §11.6
6320: §11.6
6320-6322: §§11.7, 11.48
6320-6327: §11.6
6321(a): §11.6
6321(b): §11.6
6322: §11.6
6322.7: §11.6
6323: §§3.23, 11.2
6323(b): §§7.23, 7.25
6323(c): §11.2
6323(d): §11.2
6324: §§11.8-11.9
6340: §§11.5, 11.7
6340(a): §§11.2, 11.6, 11.8-11.9
6340(b): §11.6
6341: §11.5
6344: §§9.3, 11.5
6345(a): §11.64
6345(c): §11.64
6360: §§3.6, 3.23
6361(b): §11.64
6381(b): §§11.34, 11.62
6386: §9.3
6389(a): §11.6
6500: §§8.2, 8.33, 10.30
6602: §9.3
7000-7143: §§8.33, 10.30
7001: §7.61
7002: §§7.61, 8.33
7002(a): §§10.4, 10.30
7050(a): §8.33
7050(b): §7.61
7050(e)(4): §10.30
7050(e)(4)-(5): §10.4
7501: §7.19
7501(a): §7.19

7540: §8.4
7541: §§8.4, 8.6A
7541(b)-(c): §8.4
7550-7557: §§8.4, 8.6, 8.6D-8.6E
7551: §§8.6, 8.6E
7552: §8.6C
7552-7553: §8.6D
7553: §8.6D
7554: §8.6A
7555: §§8.4, 8.6A
7557: §§8.4, 8.6C-8.6D
7557-7649.5: §18.26
7570-7577: §8.4
7600-7630: §10.8
7600-7730: §§8.3, 14.10, 14.18
7605: §§9.1, 11.5
7606: §8.3
7611: §§8.4-8.5, 8.6A
7611(a): §8.5
7611(b): §8.5
7611(c): §8.5
7611(d): §§8.3, 8.5
7611(e): §8.5
7611(f): §8.5
7612: §8.5
7612(a): §8.5
7613: §§8.3-8.4
7620: §8.3
7630: §§8.3-8.4
7633: §8.3
7634: §8.4
7635.5: §8.4
7640: §9.3
7645-7649.5: §8.4
7646(a)(1)-(3): §8.4
7646(a)(3): §8.4
7648.3: §8.4
7648.8: §8.4
7648.9: §8.4
7650: §8.5
7658: §8.4
7822: §§7.24, 7.58
7822(e)(1)-(2): §7.24
7827: §9.3
7860-7864: §9.3
7895: §9.3

Title 32
  63.6(c)(2): §20.82

TREASURY REGULATIONS
  1.212-1(l): §9.12
  1.262-1(b)(7): §9.12
  1.401(a)-13(g)(4): §17.72

TEMPORARY REGULATIONS
  1.71-1T(b) Q&A-5: §6.29
  1.71-1T(b) Q&A-6: §6.30
  1.71-1T(b) Q&A-7: §6.30
  1.71-1T(b) Q&A-9: §6.33
  1.71-1T(b) Q&A-10: §6.34
  1.71-1T(b) Q&A-14: §6.34
  1.71-1T(c) Q&A-18: §6.35
  1.71-1T(e) Q&A-26: §6.28
  1.1041-1T(b) Q&A-7: §5.104
  1.1041-1T(b) Q&A-8: §5.104
  1.1041-1T(c) Q&A-9: §5.104

Court Rules

**FEDERAL RULES OF CIVIL
PROCEDURE**
  4: §10.42

REVENUE RULINGS
  68-609: §5.61
  59-60: §5.62

Rulings

**INTERNAL REVENUE SERVICE
LETTER RULINGS**
  9644053: §5.104
  9348020: §5.104
  9340032: §5.108
  9306015: §5.104
  9251033: §6.35
  8813023: §5.108
  8629030: §5.108
  8334088: §17.70
  8330119: §17.70

SENATE REPORTS
  **313, 99th Cong, 2d Sess 1105
  (1986):** §§17.74, 17.77

Miscellaneous

**Hague Convention on the Civil
Aspects of International
Child Abduction:** §§7.2,
7.4
**Hague Service Convention on
Service Abroad of Judicial
and Extrajudicial Documents
in Civil or Commercial
Matters:** §10.42

Table of Cases

M

S

Table of References

California Civil Appellate Practice. 2 vols (3d ed Cal CEB 1996): §§19.1, 19.15, 19.32, 19.34, 19.38, 19.45, 19.55, 19.59, 19.62–19.63, 19.66–19.67, 19.69–19.71, 19.74, 19.76, 19.87

California Civil Discovery Practice. 2 vols (4th ed Cal CEB 2006): §§13.1, 13.19, 13.22, 13.25, 13.29, 13.32, 13.34–13.35, 13.40–13.41, 13.43

California Civil Procedure Before Trial. 3 vols (4th ed Cal CEB 2004): §§4.4, 4.7, 10.4, 10.26, 10.61–10.65, 10.68, 11.32, 11.34, 11.38, 11.65, 12.2, 12.5, 12.35, 12.39, 14.21, 15.2, 15.4–15.7, 17.41, 18.9, 18.18, 18.32, 18.46, 19.29, 20.91–20.93, 21.11, 21.20

California Civil Writ Practice. 2 vols (3d ed Cal CEB 1996): §§19.1, 19.104, 19.114, 19.118

California Domestic Partnerships (Cal CEB 2005): §§3.1, 5.107, 7.26, 7.63, 8.3, 10.2, 10.45, 12.11, 17.83

California Expert Witness Guide. (2d ed Cal CEB 1991): §15.12

California Judicial Council Forms Manual. 3 vols (Cal CEB 1981): §§3.28–3.30, 8.4, 8.24, 11.3, 12.36, 12.41, 14.53, 20.20, 20.46

California Marital Settlement and Other Family Law Agreements (3d ed Cal CEB 2005): §§5.27–5.28, 5.108, 6.1, 6.12, 6.22–6.23, 6.35, 7.63, 8.2, 13.3, 14.1, 14.3, 14.36–14.37, 14.40–14.44, 14.54, 15.8, 17.68, 17.78

California Trial Objections (10th ed Cal CEB 2004): §19.23

California Trial Practice: Civil Procedure During Trial. 3 vols (3d ed Cal CEB 1995): §§15.1, 15.12, 15.14–15.15, 16.1, 16.5, 16.12, 16.22–16.24, 18.2, 18.11, 18.20

Debt Collection Practice in California (2d ed Cal CEB 1999): §§20.17, 20.90, 20.92–20.93

Dissolution Strategies: From Intake to Judgment (Cal CEB 2005): §§3.43, 13.3, 14.17

Dividing Pensions and Other Employee Benefits in California Divorces (Cal CEB 2006): §§5.31–5.32, 5.38, 5.92, 12.4, 12.6, 12.8, 12.10, 14.61, 17.68–17.69, 17.78

Effective Direct & Cross-Examination (Cal CEB 1986): §§15.1, 15.13, 16.1

Effective Introduction of Evidence in California (2d ed Cal CEB 2000): §§15.1, 16.1

Fee Agreement Forms Manual (Cal CEB 1989): §3.38

Personal and Small Business Bankruptcy Practice in California (Cal CEB 2003): §5.90

Restatement (Second) of Conflict of Laws (1971): §4.3

Witkin, B.E. California Procedure. 10 vols. 4th ed. San Francisco, Bancroft-Whitney, 1997: §§4.8, 11.16, 14.18, 18.28, 18.35, 18.46, 19.1, 19.15, 19.19, 19.41, 19.45, 19.82
————. Summary of California Law. 13 vols. 9th ed. San Francisco, Bancroft-Whitney, 1987: §§10.30, 17.35

Table of Forms

Index

*The symbol "f" after a section number indicates that
a form appears in the section.*